EMPLOYMENT LAW:

Cases and Materials

STEVEN L. WILLBORN
Dean and Richard C. and Catherine Stuart Schmoker
Professor of Law
University of Nebraska-Lincoln

STEWART J. SCHWAB
Allan R. Tessler Dean & Professor of Law
Cornell University

JOHN F. BURTON, JR.
Professor Emeritus, School of Management and Labor Relations
Rutgers, The State University of New Jersey

GILLIAN L. L. LESTER
Professor of Law
University of California at Berkeley

Library of Congress Cataloging-in-Publication Data

Employment law : cases and materials / by Steven L. Willborn, Stewart J. Schwab, John F. Burton, Jr., Gillian L. L. Lester. — 4th ed.

p. cm.

Includes index.

ISBN 0-8205-7089-3 (hard cover)

1. Labor laws and legislation—United States—Cases. I. Willborn, Steven L.

KF3455.A7W55 2007

344.7301—dc22

2006035390

CIP

Editorial Offices
744 Broad Street, Newark, NJ 07102 (973) 820-2000
201 Mission St., San Francisco, CA 94105-1831 (415) 908-3200
701 East Water Street, Charlottesville, VA 22902-7587 (434) 972-7600
www.lexis.com

(Pub. 3044)

To Ted St. Antoine and Clyde Summers,
inspirational leaders in the field of employment law

and

To Mom and Dad,
my first and best teachers
—SLW

To Norma and
Justin, Whitney, Weatherly, Zachary, and Quintin (1st edition)
Soren and Lehman (2nd edition additions)
Harris (3rd edition addition)
and now Juliet (4th edition addition),
may there be many more
—SJS

To Janet
—JFB

To Eric and Grace and Rhys
—GLLL

PREFACE

We are very pleased to join with a new author on this fourth edition, Gillian Lester from the University of California, Berkeley. She assumed primary responsibility for several chapters of the book, but you will see her ideas and constructive influence throughout the volume.

Our primary goal in this edition has been to update and enhance the materials. Much has happened since we last revised the materials in 2002 and it was time to bring the materials up to date. At the same time, however, we used a general presumption against change. We tried to retain as many of the cases and as much of the structure of the book as possible, both to ease the transition for teachers and for substantive reasons. The cases, for the most part, work well as teaching tools and the structure of the book provides flexibility for the many different types of courses professors offer as "employment law."

As with our prior editions, we attempted to edit the materials unobtrusively. We did not indicate when we deleted footnotes and citations to authority, but when we deleted anything other than footnotes or citations, we used ellipses. Citations in cases were often revised without indication (for example, by removing parallel citations). Footnotes that remain have retained their original numbers. For our own citations, except for headings for principal materials, we have followed *The Bluebook: A Uniform System of Citation* (18th ed. 2005).

We offer thanks to all who have helped us with this project. We began working on this book over fifteen years ago, so some of these people may have helped us so long ago that they have forgotten the precise nature of their assistance. While we inevitably will overlook some colleagues, we want to single out for thanks Rick Bales, Bill Corbett, Charles Craver, Ellen Dannin, Rob Denicola, Cynthia Farina, Catherine Fisk, Dan Foote, Marshall Huebner, Alan Hyde, Sam Issacharoff, Pauline Kim, Barbara Lee, William Lyons, Deborah Malamud, Peter Martin, Colleen Medill, Richard Moberly, Alison Morantz, Andrew Morriss, Russell Osgood, Ramona Paetzold, Bob Schopp, Katherine Stone, Kent Syverud, John True, Rip Verkerke, Charles Wolfram, and Bob Works. Research assistants who have helped us include Melissa Barber, Florence Blum, Katherine Cheng, Chad Doornink, Ann Juliano, So-hyun Kim, Andrea Loux, Joshua Mahoney, Joshua Mayes, Katherine McMahon, Audra Mitchell, Rafael Morell, Dan Muffly, Michael Nolan, Marc Pilotin, Anne Marie Pisano, Gregory Porter, J. Michael Roebuck, Michael Rosen-Prinz, Deborah Steiner, Leo Tsao, Andrew Verriere, and Elizabeth Yates. Richard E. Fairfax at the Occupational Safety and Health Administration provided helpful suggestions. Librarians who have helped us significantly include Constance Findlay, Mitch Fontenot, Anna Kurtz, Kris Lauber, Eugene McElroy, and Beth McWilliams.

A special thanks to Carolyn Singleton and Kerry Acker who provided us with considerable secretarial assistance on the first and fourth editions, respectively. Finally, thanks to Fran Warren who was our initial contact with the publisher so many years ago and to Pali Chheda who was our principal editor for this edition.

Steven L. Willborn
Lincoln, Nebraska

Stewart J. Schwab
Ithaca, New York

John F. Burton, Jr.
New Brunswick, New Jersey

Gillian L. L. Lester
Berkeley, California

December 2006

SUMMARY TABLE OF CONTENTS

TABLE OF CONTENTS

Part I

INTRODUCTION TO EMPLOYMENT LAW

Chapter 1

THEMES OF EMPLOYMENT LAW

This book considers the role of the law in regulating the complex and crucially important relationship between employer and employee. In modern society, the law plays a role in defining virtually every aspect of that relationship. From the time people are first permitted to enter the workforce under the child labor laws until they leave the workforce under the protection of the age discrimination laws, the law has something to say on nearly every issue arising out of the relationship — wages, hours, fringe benefits, safety, job security, discrimination, employee privacy.

Despite its pervasiveness, however, the law is a secondary force in the relationship. No law requires employers to hire any particular worker or any workers at all, nor are employees required to work. And, on most issues, the law permits a wide range in the terms of employment. On wages, for example, the minimum is currently $5.15 an hour for most employees, but the maximum wage is infinity, which is about what baseball players and CEOs are getting these days. Thus, the law is secondary in structuring the employment relationship: individual employers and employees establish the relationship and most of its terms by agreement.

The law is also secondary to the actions of employers and employees in the aggregate — to the labor market. Relatively few workers, for example, are paid the minimum wage. BUREAU LAB. STATISTICS, U.S. DEP'T LAB., CHARAC-TERISTICS OF MINIMUM WAGE WORKERS: 2004 (2005), *available at* www.bls.gov/cps/minwage2004.htm (1.6% of all wage and salary workers paid at or below minimum wage). The wages of the rest are determined by the labor market, although the precise manner in which that market operates is in many ways still a mystery. Indeed, one way of viewing all of employment law is as a reaction to the outcomes produced by the primary forces of the labor market: employment legislation is enacted when society, or at least some segment of society, is dissatisfied with the level of wages, safety, or job security produced by the labor market. Employment legislation attempts to change those outcomes by influencing the workings of the labor market.

To say, however, that the law is a secondary force is not to say that it is unimportant. Indeed, for the current generation of workers, the law has become an increasingly significant force. In 1960, the only major federal employment law applying to nonunion workers was the Fair Labor Standards Act, which set the minimum wage, required premium pay for overtime work, and restricted child labor. Since then the federal government has enacted several major laws to regulate various aspects of the employment relationship. The Equal Pay Act of 1963 and Title VII of the Civil Rights Act of 1964 were the first of several laws enacted to prohibit discrimination in the workplace. The Occupational Safety and Health Act of 1970 brought the health and safety of workers under the federal aegis. And in 1974, the Employee Retirement

Income Security Act was enacted to protect the interests of workers in their pensions and other employee benefits. This federal legislative activity continues. In the 1990s, for example, the Americans with Disabilities Act and the Family and Medical Leave Act were enacted.

State government also greatly increased its influence on the employment relationship during this time period. Beginning in the mid-1970s, state courts began to examine more closely the employment decisions — and especially termination decisions — of employers. The employment-at-will doctrine, which had operated for more than a century to shield termination decisions from judicial oversight, began to erode, and today all but a few states have limited the doctrine to some degree. State and local legislatures also began to enact laws on a variety of employment-related topics so that today hundreds of state statutes exist on a wide variety of issues. On testing alone, there are statutes regulating drug testing, polygraphs, genetic testing, and even "truth" testing.

A major, although undoubtedly partial, explanation for this surge of governmental interest in the employment relationship was the failure of the National Labor Relations Act, which regulates the relationship between unions and employers:

> The basic assumption of the National Labor Relations Act was that the labor market would be regulated by collective bargaining, not by legislation. Workers would be protected by their union, not by government officials. Workers' rights would be guaranteed by the collective agreement, not by law. Those rights would be defined and enforced through grievance procedures and arbitration, not through administrative agencies and courts. . . .

> Collective bargaining, where established, served its intended purposes. . . . Collective agreements not only established wage rates and benefits, but also defined rights of employees in the workplace and provided, through grievance and arbitration, a system for adjudicating and enforcing those rights. Through their union, employees obtained a voice in many decisions affecting their working lives. . . .

> [The National Labor Relations Act, however,] failed to achieve its purpose. Collective bargaining never became established except in segments of industry. . . . Instead of expanding, collective bargaining began shrinking in relation to total employment in the 1950's. It now covers less than [13% of all workers and its coverage] continues to shrink.

> Why collective bargaining has not been more widely extended is, for present purposes, unimportant. The significant fact is that collective bargaining does not regulate the labor market. . . . The consequence is foreseeable, if not inevitable; if collective bargaining does not protect the individual employee, the law will find another way to protect the weaker party. The law, either through the courts or the legislatures, will become the guardian. Labor law is now in the midst of that changing of the guard. There is current recognition that if the majority of employees are to be protected, it must be by the law prescribing at

least certain rights of employees and minimum terms and conditions of employment.

Clyde W. Summers, *Labor Law as the Century Turns: A Changing of the Guard,* 67 NEB. L. REV. 7, 9-10 (1988). [*]

Understanding this complex and ever-changing area of the law is no easy task. Employment laws, especially statutes, often pursue broad social goals — to eliminate employment discrimination, reduce the number of workplace injuries, or increase the job security of workers. As a result, an understanding of employment law requires one to analyze what those goals are (or should be) and whether the law is (or can be) effective in pursuing them. But employment law, especially case law, is also interested in the individual interactions between particular employers and employees. When employer and employee enter into a relationship, both parties operate with a considerable degree of uncertainty about such things as the precise work the employer needs done, the ability of the worker to perform it, the employer's long-term need for the worker, and other opportunities which may present themselves to the worker. The agreement between employer and employee, either explicitly or by relying on legal presumptions, must deal with these uncertainties. When should explicit agreements between employer and employee be recognized and enforced by the courts? When should they not? What rules should apply when circumstances arise that the parties have not explicitly considered in their agreement?

In addressing these issues, it is useful to distinguish between two types of legal rules: "immutable" rules that the parties cannot change by agreement and "default" rules that state the applicable rules unless the parties agree to alter them. Laws requiring employers to pay a minimum wage are an example of immutable employment laws. An employee cannot legally contract with an employer to work for a wage lower than the minimum wage. Employment-at-will is a default rule; it determines when an employment contract can be terminated, but applies only when the parties do not agree to another rule.

Some argue that immutable rules are presumptively undesirable. Consider, for example, the issue of workplace safety. A worker who is deciding between two jobs, one safe and one dangerous, will choose the safer one if the wages for the two jobs are the same. As a result, to attract workers, the employer offering the more dangerous job must pay a higher wage. If the wage difference between the two jobs is great enough, the worker may prefer to work at the more dangerous job. The employer offering the dangerous job will pay higher wages, however, only to the extent that the cost of the extra wages is less than the cost of making the job safer. Otherwise, the employer would spend the money to make the job safer and offer lower wages.

Viewed in this way, an immutable rule that required the employer offering the dangerous job to make the job safer would be undesirable. From the perspective of a worker who would prefer to work at the more dangerous job for a higher wage, the rule would mean that that job (and its higher wage) would no longer exist. The worker would be required to work at a safer but lower-paying job. From the perspective of the employer offering the dangerous job, the rule requires the employer to expend the money required to make the job safer even though it might be cheaper to pay higher wages instead. The immutable rule requiring safer jobs is undesirable, then, because it frustrates the preferences of both workers and employers. Indeed, some argue that it infringes on an important type of individual liberty — in this case, for example, the freedom of workers to decide for themselves the trade-off they want between wages and workplace safety. Richard A. Epstein, *In Defense of the Contract at Will,* 51 U. Chi. L. Rev. 947, 953-55 (1984).

But consider several possible responses to this claim that immutable rules are presumptively undesirable:

- *Information.* This bargaining process cannot work perfectly because the parties (especially workers) will not have all the information necessary to make the right trade-off between higher wages and danger on the job. Employers have reason to keep job hazards secret and workers will have trouble discovering them for a number of reasons. For example, some hazards take a long time to develop (such as diseases caused by exposure to workplace chemicals) and hazards may change over time as technology improves, so the past may not be a reliable guide for the future. Immutable rules may be a cheaper and better response to these informational problems than engaging in a massive campaign to educate workers.

- *Psychology.* Even if workers had all the relevant information, the bargaining process may not work properly because workers may not be able to process it appropriately. For example, people systematically tend to underestimate the probability that an unlikely event will happen to them. If this is true for job hazards, workers may discount the likelihood of injury and, consequently, ask for too small a wage premium.

- *Public Goods.* If an employer corrects a job hazard for one worker, it may also necessarily correct it for all workers. Removing a dangerous chemical from the workplace, for example, will benefit all workers; the correction provides a "public good" to all workers. But this means that every individual worker would prefer to have another employee complain and absorb the risk that the employer won't like the complaint and retaliate, which means that the employer may never hear the complaint and, hence, never make the change.

- *Third-Party Effects.* The bargaining process will not work perfectly because not all the relevant parties are represented in the bargaining. Because of health insurance and public subsidies of health care for the poor and aged, when workers are injured, they may not pay for all the costs of their health care. Similarly, they may not weigh properly all the costs of their injuries on their friends and relatives.

- *Norms and Preferences.* By establishing an immutable rule, society may want to alter the prevailing norms about workplace injuries. Society may be attempting to make the statement that, at some level, safety is not simply a commodity that can be bought and sold, but a basic societal expectation. Making the rule immutable contributes to the goal of establishing a norm of workplace safety and, conversely, of delegitimizing highly hazardous workplaces.

Regardless of one's opinion on these issues, one's understanding of immutable employment laws can be enhanced by considering the extent to which they infringe on the preferences of employers and workers, the basic concern of those opposed to immutable rules, and the justifications offered for the infringements, such as informational problems, public-goods issues, and third-party effects. In this book, we will regularly encourage you to do both.

Default rules raise a set of related, but distinct, issues. Consider, for example, the employment-at-will rule. One articulation of the rule is that every employment relationship can be terminated by either side, for any reason or no reason at all, unless the parties reach a different agreement. This is a default rather than an immutable rule because the parties can contract around it. The traditional view of appropriate default terms is that they should reflect the arrangement that *most* bargainers would prefer. If most workers and employers prefer the employment-at-will rule, then reading it into employment relationships that are silent on the issue means that most parties will not have to incur the transaction expenses of negotiating and drafting a termination provision at all. Instead they can simply rely on the default term and split the savings on transaction costs between them. *See* Charles J. Goetz & Robert E. Scott, *The Mitigation Principle: Toward a General Theory of Contractual Obligation,* 69 Va. L. Rev. 967 (1983).

Accepting that rationale, the employment-at-will doctrine raises the issue of whether it actually *is* the arrangement that most workers and employers would prefer. In situations where both sides make investments in training (situations that should be increasingly more common as the need for technical skills in the workplace increases), the parties may instead prefer a termination provision that only permits an employer to discharge a worker for good reasons. Consider, for example, the figure on the next page, which illustrates one model of an employee's work life — the implicit life-cycle model. The employee enters the workforce by accepting employment with the employer at age a and retires at age f. The employer pays the employee wage (W). The opportunity wage (OW) curve represents the best wage the employee could earn with another employer and the marginal productivity (MP) curve represents the productivity of the worker in her current job with the employer. At age a, both the worker and the employer are investing in job training. The worker would be able to earn higher wages with another employer (OW is more than W), but prefers to work for this employer because she is receiving valuable job training which will permit her to earn more later in her career (from age d to f). The employer is paying the worker more than she is producing (W is more than MP) because the employer also anticipates a long-term relationship which will permit it to recoup its investment later (from age b to e). A rule that limited the ability to terminate the employment relationship might better reflect the intentions of this employer and worker than the employment-at-will rule. If the increasing need for job training means that the majority of employment relationships fit this implicit life-cycle model, employment at will may not be the appropriate default term.

Figure 1-1
A Life-Cycle Model of Wages

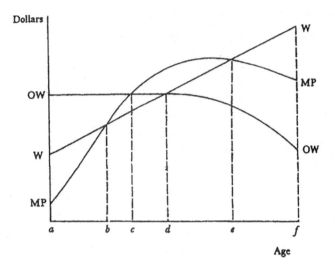

Source: Michael L. Wachter & George M. Cohen, *The Law and Economics of Collective Bargaining: An Introduction and Application to the Problems of Subcontracting, Partial Closure, and Relocation*, 136 U. Pa. L. Rev. 1349, 1362 (1988). Copyright © 1988 by University of Pennsylvania Law Review. Reprinted with permission.

The employment-at-will doctrine also raises questions about the traditional view of how to determine default terms. Under the traditional view, one response to the argument based on the implicit life-cycle model is that, even if true, it does not matter very much because the parties can contract for the termination provision they prefer. To the extent, however, that the parties do *not* contract around the default term, even though it is in their joint interest to do so, the precise setting of the default term is critical.

Consider, then, several factors which may interfere with the ability of the parties to contract around a default rule setting employment at will as the termination provision in an individual employment contract. First, it may be that workers erroneously think that the default rule provides them with protection against discharge. *See, e.g.*, Pauline Kim, *Bargaining with Imperfect Information: A Study of Worker Perceptions of Legal Perception in an At-Will World*, 83 Cornell L. Rev. 105 (1997). If this is the case, workers may not know that they should bargain around the default rule and so it would remain in place even though, had they known their legal situation, they would have bargained for a change.

Second, it may be that the default rule remains in place, even though it is not in the joint interests of the parties, simply because of the high cost of changing the rule. In the employment setting, these transaction costs would include the costs of drafting and bargaining about an alternative rule but, especially for workers, it may include other costs as well. A worker who asks for protection against discharge sends a signal to her employer that she might *need* such protection, which may decrease the employer's willingness to hire her. As a result, the worker may decide not to commence negotiations to revise the employment-at-will default; instead, she may prefer to accept the risk that the employer will breach the implicit lifetime contract at age *e,* rather than the risk that the employer will refuse to hire her if she commences negotiations on the termination clause and sends a signal that she may not be a capable worker. Once again, the default rule would remain in place even though other language on termination may better serve the joint interests of the parties.

Third, default terms may remain in place because, by their very existence, they affect the way the parties value the good. This is a very general phenomenon known as the endowment effect. If you have a ticket to a Nebraska/Notre Dame football game, you may refuse to sell it if offered $250, even though you would never spend $250 to purchase a ticket. You value the ticket differently (and more highly) because you own it. In much the same way, if the default termination rule is set to provide job protection, a worker may not give the rule up even if a good offer is made by the employer (for example, offering to pay a higher hourly wage if the rule is changed to employment at will), even though the worker would be unwilling to spend the same amount to purchase the protection if the default rule is employment at will (for example, by accepting a lower hourly wage).

If default rules are sticky for these types of reasons, setting them appropriately becomes important. There are two general possibilities. One possibility is simply to switch the default rule so that it favors workers and, hence, imposes a burden on employers to seek a change if they do not like it. Whether this is desirable or not would depend on an evaluation of the desirability and stickiness of the new default rule relative to the alternative, employment-at-will default rule. Some of the factors that make an employment-at-will rule sticky may not apply as strongly to a rule which called on employers to act to change the rule. Cass R. Sunstein, *Switching the Default Rule,* 77 N.Y.U. L. Rev. 106 (2002). Another possibility is to set the default not where the parties might want it to be, but at a point where the parties would almost certainly *not* want it to be. Instead of using employment at will as the default, for example, the default termination term might be set as "no termination for any reason during the life of the employee." This type of "penalty" default would force the parties to bargain over the term, and in the process reveal valuable information to each other. Ian Ayres & Robert Gertner, *Majoritarian vs. Minoritarian Defaults,* 51 Stan. L. Rev. 1591 (1999).

This discussion hints at the formidable pedagogical challenges presented by a course on employment law and at the general themes of this book. Employment law is found in hundreds, if not thousands, of separate statutes and cases and covers many substantive areas, including wages, hours, protection from discharge, employee health and safety, and many more. Understanding employment law requires one to consider the causes of and justifications for governmental regulation in all these areas. The broad range of issues covered in employment law poses the risk that the course will turn into "a grab bag of miscellaneous problems which gain no coherence or illumination from each other." Clyde W. Summers, *What We Should Teach in Labor Law: The Need for a Change and a Suggested Direction*, *in* THE PARK CITY PAPERS 193, 195 (1985).

To avoid this grab-bag problem, a textbook on employment law must contain strong unifying themes. This book uses five overlapping themes. First, the book regularly examines the proper roles of economic incentives and legal regulations in achieving desirable outcomes in the workplace. By harnessing the economic incentives of workers and employers where appropriate, society can avoid some of the costs of promulgating and enforcing regulations. When economic incentives produce results that society considers unacceptable, however, legal rules to regulate employer or employee behavior may be necessary. One theme, then, will explore the appropriate blend of economic incentives and legal regulation as methods of achieving desirable outcomes. Although economics in this sense is a principal theme, we want to emphasize that this is not a Law-and-Economics text. Rather, it is a law textbook that uses economics to relate seemingly disparate issues and to explore issues in a rigorous way.

Second, the book pursues a theme focusing on the struggle for authority over the workplace. We encourage students to question the common assumption of overwhelming employer authority over the workplace and to begin to think about the different ways in which employers, employees, and the legislature all exert authority over the workplace and are, conversely, limited in their ability to exert authority.

A third theme focuses on the tension between simple rules and effective rules. A goal of much of employment law is to have rules that are easily and broadly understood, applied, and followed. At the same time, however, employers (and often employees) have many strategies to avoid the intended effect of laws. Employment laws have perhaps an inevitable tendency to become complex in order to counter evasive strategies. As we shall see, much of employment law is complex, and this theme explores the need for and costs of this complexity.

A fourth theme focuses on determining the best level of government to regulate a particular problem. A variety of answers to this question are found in current employment law. The states are the primary regulators on a number of issues (such as job security and employee privacy and loyalty), the federal government has taken control in other areas (such as employee benefits), and various mixes of state and federal authority exist in still other areas (such as employment discrimination and employee safety and health). The text will regularly ask students to consider how authority ought to be allocated between different levels of government.

The fifth theme involves identifying the best enforcement mechanism for a particular regulatory scheme. The mechanisms for enforcing employment laws vary widely and are in considerable flux. Increasingly, private enforcement schemes, such as arbitration, are beginning to challenge public enforcement schemes in importance. Students will regularly be asked to consider both the ability of various mechanisms to further substantive goals and the cost of the mechanisms relative to others that might be used.

We are convinced that these themes satisfy the need for organizing principles in a course on employment law. First, they are general enough to apply
to all of the substantive areas covered. As a result, we use them to tie the
materials together, to provide foci that will be present throughout the volume.
And second, the themes are sufficiently rigorous to provide an intellectually
stimulating framework for the course. Our hope is that these themes will
consolidate the diverse materials of employment law into an understandable
and cohesive package, while simultaneously, and somewhat paradoxically,
expanding the horizons of the course beyond the confines of employment law
to any area of the law where these concerns are present. By the end of the
semester, we are confident that you will share our view that, at the very least,
employment law is a complex and fascinating field well worthy of study and,
for at least some, sufficient to provide a lifetime of interesting work.

Chapter 2

LEGAL BOUNDARIES OF THE EMPLOYMENT RELATIONSHIP

Employment law regulates the employment relationship. An immediate question is what is employment, and how does it differ from other work relationships? Each particular employment law can and usually does define coverage in its own way. Still, some general principles can be found. In this chapter we ask three basic questions: (1) What factors distinguish employees from other workers, particularly independent contractors? (2) Why does a law cover certain employees and not other employees? (3) Why does a law cover certain employers and not others?

A. EMPLOYEES VERSUS INDEPENDENT CONTRACTORS

SECRETARY OF LABOR v. LAURITZEN
United States Court of Appeals, Seventh Circuit
835 F.2d 1529 (1987)

HARLINGTON WOOD, JR., CIRCUIT JUDGE.

This, as unlikely as it may at first seem, is a federal pickle case. The issue is whether the migrant workers who harvest the pickle crop of defendant Lauritzen Farms, in effect defendant Michael Lauritzen, are employees for purposes of the Fair Labor Standards Act of 1938 ("FLSA"), or are instead independent contractors not subject to the requirements of the Act.[2] The Secretary, alleging that the migrant harvesters are employees, not independent contractors, brought this action seeking to enjoin the defendants from violating the minimum wage requirements and to enforce the record-keeping and child labor provisions of the Act. [The district court denied the motion of some migrant workers to intervene to protect their claimed independent contractor status; held that the migrant workers were employees; and] entered final judgment on the issues of record-keeping and child labor violations, enjoining the defendants from further violations of the Act. [Lauritzen appeals.]

I. Factual Background

We must examine the factual background of the case to determine whether the employment status of the migrant workers could be concluded as a matter of law.

---

[2] All the parties refer to the crop to be harvested as the "pickle crop," and so shall we. Perhaps the defendants have developed a remarkable new "pickle" seed. But whether they grow pickles or only potential pickles in the form of cucumbers, the law is the same.

On a yearly basis the defendants plant between 100 to 330 acres of pickles on land they either own or lease. The harvested crop is sold to various processors in the area. The pickles are handpicked, usually from July through September, by migrant families from out of state. Sometimes the children, some under twelve years of age, work in some capacity in the fields alongside their parents. Many of the migrant families return each harvest season by arrangement with the defendants, but, each year, other migrant families often come for the first time from Florida, Texas and elsewhere looking for work. The defendants would inform the families, either orally or sometimes in writing, of the amount of compensation they were to receive. Compensation is set by the defendants at one-half of the proceeds the defendants realize on the sale of the pickles that the migrants harvest on a family basis. Toward the end of the harvest season, when the crop is less abundant and, therefore, less profitable, the defendants offer the migrants a bonus to encourage them to stay to complete the harvest, but some leave anyway. . . .

All matters relating to planting, fertilizing, insecticide spraying, and irrigation of the crop are within the defendants' direction, and performed by workers other than the migrant workers here involved. Occasionally a migrant who has worked for the defendant previously and knows the harvesting will suggest the need for irrigation. In order to conduct their pickle-raising business, the defendants have made a considerable investment in land, buildings, equipment, and supplies. The defendants provide the migrants free housing which the defendants assign, but with regard for any preference the migrant families may have. The defendants also supply migrants with the equipment they need for their work. The migrants need supply only work gloves for themselves.

The harvest area is subdivided into migrant family plots. The defendants make the allocation after the migrant families inform them how much acreage the family can harvest. Much depends on which areas are ready to harvest, and when a particular migrant family may arrive ready to work. The family, not the defendants, determines which family members will pick the pickles. If a family arrives before the harvest begins, the defendants may, nevertheless, provide them with housing. A few may be given some interim duties or be permitted to work temporarily for other farmers. When the pickles are ready to pick, however, the migrant family's attention must be devoted only to their particular pickle plot.

The pickles that are ready to harvest must be picked regularly and completely before they grow too large and lose value when classified. The defendants give the workers pails in which to put the picked pickles. When the pails are filled by the pickers the pails are dumped into the defendants' sacks. At the end of the harvest day a family member will use one of defendants' trucks to haul the day's pick to one of defendants' grading stations or sorting sheds. After the pickles are graded the defendants give the migrant family member a receipt showing pickle grade and weight. The income of the individual families is not always equal. That is due, to some extent, to the ability of the migrant family to judge the pickles' size, color, and freshness so as to achieve pickles of better grade and higher value.

The workers describe their work generally as just "pulling the pickles off." It is not always physically easy, however, because the work involves stooping and kneeling and constant use of the hands, often under a hot sun. Picking pickles requires little or no prior training or experience; a short demonstration will suffice. One migrant worker recalled that when he was ten years old it had taken him about five minutes to learn pickle picking. Pickles continue to grow and develop until picked, but not uniformly, so harvesting is a continuing process. The migrant workers' income depends on the results of the particular family's efforts. The defendants explain that the migrants exercise care for both the plants and the pickles, which results in maximum yields, a benefit to the family as well as to the defendants. Machine harvesting, although advantageous for other crops, is not suitable for pickle harvesting. The defendants leave the when and how to pick to the families under this incentive arrangement. The defendants occasionally visit the fields to check on the families, the crop, and to supervise irrigation. The defendant, Michael Lauritzen, who actually operates the business, is sometimes referred to as the "boss." Some workers expressed the belief that he had the right to fire them. . . .

II. *Standards of Review*

. . . .

It is well recognized that under the FLSA the statutory definitions regarding employment[5] are broad and comprehensive in order to accomplish the remedial purposes of the Act. Courts, therefore, have not considered the common law concepts of "employee" and "independent contractor" to define the limits of the Act's coverage. We are seeking, instead, to determine "economic reality." For purposes of social welfare legislation, such as the FLSA, "employees are those who as a matter of economic reality are dependent upon the business to which they render service." *Mednick v. Albert Enterprises, Inc.,* 508 F.2d 297, 299 (5th Cir. 1975) (quoting *Bartels v. Birmingham,* 332 U.S. 126, 130 (1947)).

In seeking to determine the economic reality of the nature of the working relationship, courts do not look to a particular isolated factor but to all the circumstances of the work activity. Certain criteria have been developed to assist in determining the true nature of the relationship, but no criterion is by itself, or by its absence, dispositive or controlling.

Among the criteria courts have considered are the following six:

1) the nature and degree of the alleged employer's control as to the manner in which the work is to be performed;

2) the alleged employee's opportunity for profit or loss depending upon his managerial skill;

3) the alleged employee's investment in equipment or materials required for his task, or his employment of workers;

4) whether the service rendered requires a special skill;

---

[5] The Act defines an employee simply as "any individual employed by an employer." 29 U.S.C. § 203(e)(1). An "employer" is defined to include "any person acting directly or indirectly in the interest of an employer in relation to an employee." 29 U.S.C. § 203(d). To "[e]mploy includes to suffer or permit to work." 29 U.S.C. § 203(g).

5) the degree of permanency and duration of the working relationship;

6) the extent to which the service rendered is an integral part of the alleged employer's business.

This court previously has held that the determination of workers' status is a legal rather than a factual one, and therefore not subject to the clearly erroneous standard of review. The underlying facts, however, are necessarily subject to that standard. . . .

III. *Analysis*

In a number of agricultural cases, albeit nonpickle cases, courts have applied the six criteria to find an employment, rather than a contractual, relationship. In some other cases involving migrant workers in similar circumstances, an employment relationship was either admitted or assumed, and was therefore not an issue.

In one case, however, *Donovan v. Brandel,* the Sixth Circuit affirmed the district court in classifying migrant workers harvesting pickles, under circumstances similar to those here, as independent contractors, not employees. 736 F.2d 1114 (6th Cir. 1984). . . .

A. *Control*

The *Brandel* court found that the landowner, under a sharecropping arrangement, had effectively relinquished control of harvesting to the migrants. The court considered this to be a factor in its finding that the migrant workers were independent contractors. In view of the pervasive overall control retained by the defendants here, we do not reach the same finding. We view the wage arrangement as no more than a way to effectively motivate employees, and to provide a means of determining their wages.

Brandel, according to the Sixth Circuit, did not retain "the right to dictate the manner in which the details of the harvesting function are executed." *Brandel,* 736 F.2d at 1119. For example, he did not appear in the fields to supervise the workers, or set hours for them to work. In this case, the defendants did occasionally visit the families in the fields. The workers sometimes referred to Michael Lauritzen as the "boss," and some of them expressed a belief that he had the right to fire them. Moreover, unlike the Sixth Circuit, we believe that the defendants' right to control applies to the entire pickle-farming operation, not just the details of harvesting. The defendants exercise pervasive control over the operation as a whole. We therefore agree with the district court that the defendants did not effectively relinquish control of the harvesting to the migrants.

B. *Profit and Loss*

The Sixth Circuit found that the migrant workers had the opportunity to increase their profits through the management of their pickle fields. Although the court found little or no evidence in the record supporting a finding that the workers were exposed to any risk of loss, it found the fact that their

remuneration would increase through their management efforts to be dispositive of the profit and loss analysis. We do not agree. Although the profit
opportunity may depend in part on how good a pickle picker is, there is no
corresponding possibility for migrant worker loss. As the *Gillmor* court held,
a reduction in money earned by the migrants is not a loss sufficient to satisfy
the criteria for independent contractor status. [*Donovan v. Gillmor,* 535 F.
Supp. 154 (N.D. Ohio), *appeal dismissed,* 708 F.2d 723 (6th Cir. 1982)]. The
migrants have invested nothing except for the cost of their work gloves, and
therefore have no investment to lose. Any reduction in earnings due to a poor
pickle crop is a loss of wages, and not of an investment.

C. *Capital Investment*

The capital investment factor is interrelated to the profit and loss consideration. The *Gillmor* court characterized the investment in this context to be
"large expenditures, such as risk capital, capital investments, and not negligi-
ble items or labor itself." The workers here are responsible only for providing
their own gloves. Gloves do not constitute a capital investment. As in *Gillmor,*
"[e]verything else, from farm equipment, land, seed, fertilizer, [and] insecticide
to the living quarters of the migrants is supplied by the defendants." Although
in *Brandel* the migrant furnished the pails, the *Brandel* court minimized this
factor by saying that in pickle harvesting by hand there is no need for heavy
capital investment by the worker, and the overall size of the investment by
the employer relative to that by the worker is irrelevant. To the contrary, we
believe that the migrant workers' disproportionately small stake in the pickle-
farming operation is an indication that their work is not independent of the
defendants.

D. *Degree of Skill Required*

Although a worker must develop some specialized skill in order to recognize
which pickles to pick when, this development of occupational skills is no
different from what any good employee in any line of work must do. Skills
are not the monopoly of independent contractors. The *Brandel* court found
that a high degree of skill is involved in caring for the pickle plants and picking
the pickles. We agree that some skill is required, but we do not find that this
level of skill sets the pickle harvester apart from the harvester of other crops.
The migrants' talent and their physical endurance in the hot sun do not
change the nature of their employment relationship with the defendants.

E. *Permanency*

Another factor in the employment analysis is permanency and duration of
the relationship. The Sixth Circuit in *Brandel* found that the vast majority
of harvesters have only a temporary relationship with the employer which
suggested to the court an independent contractual arrangement. Many
seasonal businesses necessarily hire only seasonal employees, but that fact
alone does not convert seasonal employees into seasonal independent contractors. Many migrant families return year after year. In *Brandel* the returning

migrant families comprised as high a proportion as forty percent to fifty percent of the work force. In this case the district court found that the migrant workers did not have the sort of permanent relationship associated with employment. Nevertheless, when the district court considered its finding in light of the economic reality of the parties' entire work relationship, the court did not consider this one criterion to be dispositive. Although we have serious doubts about this particular district court determination . . . we need not disturb that finding for the purposes of this case. We agree with the *Gillmor* court that however temporary the relationship may be it is permanent and exclusive for the duration of that harvest season. One indication of permanency in this case is the fact that it is not uncommon for the migrant families to return year after year.

F. *Harvesting as an Integral Part of Defendants' Business*

Another factor we consider briefly is the extent to which the service of migrants may be considered an integral part of the pickle-picking business. The district court held that the migrants' work was an integral part of the business, as even the court in *Brandel* conceded. The defendant here takes a contrary view on appeal claiming that the record is insufficient to sustain the district court finding. It does not take much of a record to demonstrate that picking the pickles is a necessary and integral part of the pickle business unless the employer's investment, planting, and cultivating activities are only to serve the purpose of raising ornamental pickle vines. That result would likely disappoint all good pickle lovers.

G. *Dependence of Migrant Workers*

Our final task is to consider the degree to which the migrant families depend on the defendants. Economic dependence is more than just another factor. It is instead the focus of all the other considerations.

> The [other] tests are aids — tools to be used to gauge the degree of dependence of alleged employees on the business with which they are connected. It is *dependence* that indicates employee status. Each test must be applied with that ultimate notion in mind. More importantly, the final and determinative question must be whether the total of the testing establishes the personnel are so dependent upon the business with which they are connected that they come within the protection of the FLSA or are sufficiently independent to lie outside its ambit.

Usery v. Pilgrim Equipment Co., 527 F.2d 1308, 1311-12 (5th Cir.), *cert. denied,* 429 U.S. 826 (1976) (emphasis in original). The district court held that the migrants were economically dependent on the defendants during the harvest season. If the migrant families are pickle pickers, then they need pickles to pick in order to survive economically. The migrants clearly are dependent on the pickle business, and the defendants, for their continued employment and livelihood. That is why many of them return year after year. The defendants contend that skilled migrant families are in demand in the area and do not need the defendants. Were it not for the defendants the migrant families would have to find some other pickle grower who would hire them. Until they found another grower, they would be unemployed. It is not necessary to show that workers are unable to find work with any other employer to find that the workers are employees rather than contractors.

We cannot say that the migrants are not employees, but, instead, are in business for themselves and sufficiently independent to lie beyond the broad reach of the FLSA. They depend on the defendants' land, crops, agricultural expertise, equipment, and marketing skills. They are the defendants' employees.

IV. *Conclusion*

No trial is needed to sort out the material facts in these circumstances in order to come to the conclusion of law that these migrant workers are employees, entitled to the protection of the FLSA. The purpose of the Act is to protect employees from low wages and long hours, and "to free commerce from the interferences arising from the production of goods under conditions that were detrimental to the health and well-being of workers." In this case, for example, some children under twelve years of age are in the fields. Although there is no suggestion in the record that the defendants are abusing the children in any way, the child labor provisions of the Act are intended for their benefit. It may be that the defendants' pickle operation is exemplary and conducted pursuant to standards even higher than those of the FLSA, but that does not allow the defendants to circumvent the Act. Neither does the defendants' gloomy prediction that application of the Act will have a devastating economic impact on the pickle business relieve them from complying with the Act's provisions. In any event, that argument is one for the Congress, not the courts. The basic arrangement between the defendants and the pickle pickers which, according to the defendants, produces the highest economic return for both grower and picker, need not be altered. All that need change is the label which the defendants apply to the arrangement. The defendants need only think of the proceeds paid to the pickle pickers as wages, keep the necessary records, and make sure they abide by the protection that the Act accords to working children.

Affirmed.

EASTERBROOK, CIRCUIT JUDGE, concurring.

Are cucumber pickers "employees" for purposes of the Fair Labor Standards Act? *Donovan v. Brandel,* 736 F.2d 1114 (6th Cir. 1984), says "no" as a matter of law. My colleagues say "yes" as a matter of law. Both opinions march through seven "factors" — each important, none dispositive. As the majority puts it: "Certain criteria have been developed to assist in determining the true nature of the relationship, but no criterion is by itself, or by its absence, dispositive or controlling." Courts must examine "all the circumstances" in search of "economic reality."

It is comforting to know that "economic reality" is the touchstone. One cringes to think that courts might decide these cases on the basis of economic fantasy. But "reality" encompasses millions of facts, and unless we have a legal rule with which to sift the material from the immaterial, we might as well examine the facts through a kaleidoscope. Which facts matter, and why? A legal approach calling on judges to examine all of the facts, and balance them, avoids formulating a rule of decision. The price of avoidance should be committing the decisions to the finders of fact, as our inability to fulfill Justice Holmes's belief that all tort law could be reduced to formulas after some years of experience[1] has meant that juries today decide the most complex products liability cases without substantial guidance from legal principles. Surely Holmes was right in believing that legal propositions ought to be in the form of rules to the extent possible. Why keep cucumber farmers in the dark about the legal consequences of their deeds?

People are entitled to know the legal rules before they act, and only the most compelling reason should lead a court to announce an approach under which no one can know where he stands until litigation has been completed. Litigation is costly and introduces risk into any endeavor; we should struggle to eliminate the risk and help people save the costs. Unless some obstacle such as inexperience with the subject, a dearth of facts, or a vacuum in the statute books intervenes, we should be able to attach legal consequences to recurrent factual patterns. Courts have had plenty of experience with the application of the FLSA to migrant farm workers. Fifty years after the Act's passage is too late to say that we still do not have a legal rule to govern these cases. My colleagues' balancing approach is the prevailing method, which they apply carefully. But it is unsatisfactory both because it offers little guidance for future cases and because any balancing test begs questions about which aspects of "economic reality" matter, and why.

I

Consider the problems with the balancing test. These are not the factors the RESTATEMENT (SECOND) OF AGENCY § 2(3) (1958) suggests for identifying "independent contractors." The RESTATEMENT takes the view that the right to control the physical performance of the job is the central element of status as an independent contractor. My colleagues, joining many other courts, say that this approach is inapplicable because we should "accomplish the remedial purposes of the Act":

> Courts, therefore, have not considered the common law concepts of "employee" and "independent contractor" to define the limits of the Act's coverage. We are seeking, instead, to determine "economic reality."

This implies that the definition of "independent contractor" used in tort cases is inconsistent with "economic reality" but that the seven factors applied in FLSA cases capture that "reality." In which way did "economic reality" elude the American Law Institute and the courts of 50 states? What kind of differences between FLSA and tort cases are justified? A definition under which "in the application of social legislation employees are those who as a matter of economic reality are dependent upon the business to which they render service" does not help to isolate the elements of "reality" that matter.

---

[1] OLIVER WENDELL HOLMES, JR., THE COMMON LAW 111-13, 123-26 (1881).

Consider, too, the seven factors my colleagues distill from the cases. The first is the extent to which the supposed employer possesses a right to control the workers' performance. This is the core of the common law definition. The parties agree that Lauritzen did not prescribe or monitor the migrant workers' methods of work but instead measured output, the weight and kind of cucumbers picked. Lauritzen did not say who could work but instead negotiated only with the head of each migrant family. Lauritzen did not control how long each member of the family worked. This absence of control over who shall work, when, and how, strongly suggests an independent contractor relation at common law.

My colleagues admit that the migrant workers controlled their own working hours and picking methods, but discount these facts on the grounds that what counts is Lauritzen's "right to control . . . the entire pickle-farming operation." If this is so, Pittsburgh Plate Glass must be an "employee" of General Motors because GM controls "the entire automobile manufacturing process" in which windshields from PPG are used. This method of analysis makes everyone an employee.

The second factor is whether the worker has an opportunity to profit (or is exposed to a risk of loss) through the application of managerial skills. My colleagues say that this indicates "employment" here because each worker has "invested nothing except for the cost of . . . work gloves, and therefore [has] no investment to lose." But the opportunity to obtain profit from efficient management is not the same as exposing a stock of capital to a risk of loss. (*That* subject is the third factor, discussed below.) A consultant analyzing the operation of an assembly line also may furnish few tools except for a stopwatch, pencil, and clipboard, but such a person unquestionably is an independent contractor. The "managerial" skill may lie in deploying a work force efficiently. The head of each migrant family decides which family members work, for how long, on what plot of land. That is the same sort of managerial decision customarily made by supervisors in a hierarchical organization.

Third in my colleagues' list is the worker's investment in equipment or materials, that is, physical capital. The record is clear that the migrant workers possess little or no physical capital.[2] This is true of many workers we would call independent contractors. Think of lawyers, many of whom do not even own books. The bar sells human capital rather than physical capital, but this does not imply that lawyers are "employees" of their clients under the FLSA.[3]

The fourth factor, whether the worker possesses a "special skill," would exclude lawyers and others rich in human capital. The migrant workers, by

---

[2] Physical capital is not, however, the same thing as a "disproportionately small stake in the pickle-farming operation." The laborers' share of the farm's gross income exceeds 50%, giving the migrant workers a very large stake indeed in the successful harvest and marketing of the crop. (The migrants receive 50% of Lauritzen's gross, plus housing and end-of-season bonuses.)

[3] A story current among electrical engineers has it that after analyzing a destructive harmonic vibration in one of Edison's new generators, Prof. Steinmetz submitted an invoice for $5,000. An irate Edison demanded itemization. Steinmetz's new bill said:

1. Telling you to remove the third coil from the top $10.00
2. Knowing which coil to remove $4,990.00

Steinmetz, selling only expertise, was the paradigm of an independent contractor.

contrast, are poor in human capital, so this factor augurs for a conclusion of employment.

Fifth in the list is "the degree of permanency and duration of the working relationship." This can be measured, but it is hard to see why it is significant. Lawyers may work for years for a single client but be independent contractors; hamburger-turners at fast-food restaurants may drift from one job to the next yet be employees throughout. The migrant workers who picked Lauritzen's cucumbers labor on many different farms over the course of a year, but work full-time at the pickle operation for more than a month. Surely an engineering consultant who worked full-time on a given job, and frequently worked with a single manufacturer, but did five to ten jobs a year, would be an independent contractor. What matters for the migrant workers: that they have many jobs and float among employers, or that they work full-time for the duration of the harvest? Without a legal theory we cannot tell.

Factor number six, the "extent to which the service rendered is an integral part of the employer's business," is one of those bits of "reality" that has neither significance nor meaning. *Everything* the employer does is "integral" to its business — why else do it? An omission to pick the cucumbers would be fatal to Lauritzen, but then so would an omission to plant the vines or water them. An omission to design a building would be fatal to an effort to build it, but this does not imply that architects are the "employees" of firms that want to erect new buildings. Acquiring tires is integral to the business of Chrysler, but the tires come from independent contractors. Perhaps "integral" in this formulation could mean "part of integrated operation," which would distinguish tires but leave unanswered the question why the difference should have a legal consequence.

Seventh and finally we have "dependence." "Economic dependence is more than just another factor. It is instead the focus of all the other considerations." [Dependence] is the nub of both the district court's opinion and my colleagues' approach. Part of it is factually unsupported. There is no evidence that the migrant families pick only pickles or are "dependent on the pickle business." For all we can tell, these families pick oranges in California, come to Wisconsin to pick cucumbers, and move on to New York to harvest apples. We know they work year-round, and cucumbers are not harvested year-round in the United States. The point of my colleagues' discussion of factors 2-4 is that these migrant workers are not specialized to pickles.

Now the families may be dependent on the pickle business once they arrive at Lauritzen's farm and settle down to work. If a flood carried away the cucumbers, the migrants would be hard pressed to find other work immediately. This, however, is true of anyone, be he employee or independent contractor. A lawyer engaged full-time on a complex case may take a while to find new business if the case unexpectedly settles. Migrant workers are no more dependent on Lauritzen than are sellers of fertilizer, who rely on the trade of the locality and are in the grip of economic forces beyond their control, and the person who fixes Lauritzen's irrigation equipment, a classic independent contractor. The conclusion of dependence in this case is an artifact of looking at the subject *ex post* — that is, after the workers are in the cucumber fields. To determine whether they are dependent on Lauritzen, we have to look at the arrangement *ex ante*.

The usual argument that workers are "dependent" on employers — frequently a euphemism for a concern about monopsony — is that they are immobile. The coal miner in a company town, the weaver who lives next door to one textile mill and 50 miles from the next, may be offered a wage less than the one that would be necessary to induce a new worker to come to town. The employer takes advantage of the family ties and other things that may fracture some labor markets into small regions, each of which may be less than fully competitive. Migrant workers, by definition, have broken the ties that bind them to one locale. They sell their skills in a national market. It is unlikely that they receive less than the competitive wage. That wage may be low — it will be if the skills they possess are common — and the FLSA may have something to say about that wage. It is not possible, however, to get to that conclusion by talking about "dependence." Lauritzen is dependent on migrant labor; he cannot move his farm, or change his crop after planting cucumbers. The workers, by contrast, can and will go elsewhere if Lauritzen offers too little money. The majority's observation when dealing with the fifth "factor" that families come back to Lauritzen year after year, indicates that he offers a satisfactory return on their labor.

So the seven factors are of uncertain import in theory and cut both ways in practice. The list also is curious by its omission. It does not mention the method of compensation. One common feature of an independent contractor relation is compensation by a flat fee (common in the construction business) or a percentage of revenues (the sharecropper and the investment bank). The migrants who picked Lauritzen's crop received more than half of the proceeds of the sales. True, piecework and commission sales are not inconsistent with status as an "employee," but the wrinkle here is that the migrants share the market risk with Lauritzen. Each gets part of the sales price, which may rise or fall with the demand for pickles and the supply of cucumbers each season. If the price collapses, the workers and Lauritzen share the loss; so too they share the gain if the price rises. This is not an ordinary attribute of employment. Employees' "profit sharing" arrangements rarely provide for loss sharing. Why should this be irrelevant to the status of the migrant workers?

If we are to have multiple factors, we also should have a trial. A fact-bound approach calling for the balancing of incommensurables, an approach in which no ascertainable legal rule determines a unique outcome, is one in which the trier of fact plays the principal part. . . .

II

We should abandon these unfocused "factors" and start again. The language of the statute is the place to start. Section 3(g), 29 U.S.C. § 203(g), defines "employ" as including "to suffer or permit to work." This is "the broadest definition '. . . ever included in any one act.'" *United States v. Rosenwasser*, 323 U.S. 360, 363 n.3 (1945), quoting from Sen. Hugo Black, the Act's sponsor, 81 Cong. Rec. 7657 (1937). No wonder the common law definition of "independent contractor" does not govern. The definition, written in the passive, sweeps in almost any work done on the employer's premises, potentially any work done for the employer's benefit or with the employer's acquiescence.

We have been told to construe this statute broadly. *Rutherford Food Corp.*
[v. McComb, 331 U.S. 722 (1947)]; *Tony & Susan Alamo Found. v. Secretary*
of Labor, 471 U.S. 290, 296 (1985). Knowing the end in view does not answer
hard questions, for it does not tell us *how far* to go in pursuit of that end. . . .
To know how far is far enough, we must examine the history and functions
of the statute.

Unfortunately there is no useful discussion in the legislative debates about
the application of the FLSA to agricultural workers. This drives us back to
more general purposes — those of the FLSA in general, and those of the
common law definition of the independent contractor. Section 2 of the FLSA,
29 U.S.C. § 202, supplies part of the need. Courts are "to correct and as rapidly
as practical eliminate," § 2(b), the "labor conditions detrimental to the
maintenance of the minimum standard of living necessary to health, efficiency, and general well-being of workers," § 2(a). We recently summarized
the purposes of the overtime provisions of the FLSA — which turn out to be
the important ones here (in conjunction with the child labor provisions) in light
of the parties' apparent belief that the migrant workers regularly earn more
than the minimum wage. *See Mechmet [v. Four Seasons Hotels, Ltd.,* 825 F.2d
1173, 1176 (7th Cir. 1987)]:

> The first purpose was to prevent workers willing (maybe out of
> desperation . . .) to work abnormally long hours from taking jobs away
> from workers who prefer to work shorter hours. In particular, unions'
> efforts to negotiate for overtime provisions in collective bargaining
> agreements would be undermined if competing, non-union firms were
> free to hire workers willing to work long hours without overtime. The
> second purpose was to spread work and thereby reduce unemploy-
> ment, by requiring the employer to pay a penalty for using fewer
> workers for the same amount of work as would be necessary if each
> worker worked a shorter week. The third purpose was to protect the
> overtime workers from themselves: long hours of work might impair
> their health or lead to more accidents (which might endanger other
> workers as well). This purpose may seem inconsistent with allowing
> overtime work if the employer pays time and a half, but maybe the
> required premium for overtime pay is intended to assure that workers
> will at least be compensated for the increased danger of working when
> tired.

To recite these purposes is not to endorse them; maybe, as Lauritzen says,
the FLSA does more harm than good by foreclosing desirable packages of
incentives (such as payment by reference to results rather than hours) or by
reducing the opportunities for work, and hence the income, of those, such as
migrant farm workers, who cannot readily enter white-collar professions and
make more money while working fewer hours. The system in place on
Lauritzen's farm may be the most efficient yet devised — best for owners,
workers, and consumers alike — but whether it is efficient or not is none of
our business. The judicial function is to implement what Congress did, not
to ask whether Congress did the right thing.[4]

---

[4] Or whether, as seems likely, the parties can cope with a change in the legal rule. If the Act
applies, Lauritzen can maintain a system of incentives tied to the price the cucumbers will fetch.
The farm must keep records and ensure that the total payment exceeds the statutory minimum;
if it does this, the FLSA is indifferent to the device by which the excess is determined.

The purposes Congress identified in § 2 and we amplified in *Mechmet* strongly suggest that the FLSA applies to migrant farm workers. We also observed in *Mechmet* that the statute was designed to protect workers without substantial human capital, who therefore earn the lowest wages. No one doubts that migrant farm workers are short on human capital; an occupation that can be learned quickly does not pay great rewards.

The functions of the FLSA call for coverage. How about the functions of the independent contractor doctrine? This is a branch of tort law, designed to identify who is answerable for a wrong (and therefore, indirectly, to determine who must take care to prevent injuries). To say "X is an independent contractor" is to say that the chain of vicarious liability runs from X's employees to X but stops there. This concentrates on X the full incentive to take care. It is the right allocation when X is in the best position to determine what care is appropriate, to take that care, or to spread the risk of loss. Alan O. Sykes, *The Economics of Vicarious Liability,* 93 YALE L.J. 1231 (1984). This usually follows the right to control the work. Someone who surrenders control of the details of the work — often to take advantage of the expertise (= human capital) of someone else — cannot determine what precautions are appropriate; his ignorance may have been the principal reason for hiring the independent contractor. Such a person or firm specifies the outputs (design the building; paint the fence) rather than the inputs. Imposing liability on the person who does not control the execution of the work might induce pointless monitoring. All the details of the common law independent contractor doctrine having to do with the right to control the work are addressed to identifying the best monitor and precaution-taker.

The reasons for blocking vicarious liability at a particular point have nothing to do with the functions of the FLSA. The independent contractor will have its own employees, who will be covered by the Act. Electricians are "employees" of someone, even though the electrical subcontractor is not the employee of the general contractor. Indeed, the details of independent contractor relations are fundamentally contractual. Firms can structure their dealings as "employment" or "independent contractor" to maximize the efficiency of incentives to work, monitor, and take precautions. Paul H. Rubin, *The Theory of the Firm and the Economics of the Franchise Contract,* 21 J.L. & ECON. 223 (1978). The FLSA is designed to defeat rather than implement contractual arrangements. If employees voluntarily contract to accept $2.00 per hour, the agreement is ineffectual. . . . In this sense "economic reality" rather than contractual form is indeed dispositive.

The migrant workers are selling nothing but their labor. They have no physical capital and little human capital to vend. This does not belittle their skills. Willingness to work hard, dedication to a job, honesty, and good health, are valuable traits and all too scarce. Those who possess these traits will find employment; those who do not cannot work (for long) even at the minimum wage in the private sector. But those to whom the FLSA applies must include workers who possess only dedication, honesty, and good health. So the babysitter is an "employee" even though working but a few hours a week, and the writer of novels is not an "employee" of the publisher even though renting only human capital. The migrant workers labor on the farmer's premises, doing repetitive tasks. Payment on a piecework rate (e.g., 1¢ per pound of cucumbers) would not take these workers out of the Act, any more than payment of the sales staff at a department store on commission avoids the statute. The link of the migrants' compensation to the market price of pickles is not fundamentally different from piecework compensation. Just as the piecework rate may be adjusted in response to the market (e.g., to 1¢ per 1.1 pounds, if the market falls 10%), imposing the market risk on piecework laborers, so the migrants' percentage share may be adjusted in response to the market (e.g., rising to 55% of the gross if the market should fall 10%) in order to relieve them of market risk. Through such adjustments Lauritzen may end up bearing the whole market risk, and in the long run must do so to attract workers.

There are hard cases under the approach I have limned, but this is not one of them. Migrant farm hands are "employees" under the FLSA — without regard to the crop and the contract in each case. We can, and should, do away with ambulatory balancing in cases of this sort. Once they know how the FLSA works, employers, workers, and Congress have their options. The longer we keep these people in the dark, the more chancy both the interpretive and the amending process become.

NOTES

1. *Myriad Definitions of Employee.* The FLSA defines employer and employee curtly but vaguely. Other statutes are more long-winded, in an attempt to be more precise. For an example of a detailed definition, complete with special rules for racing jockeys, see the New York Workers' Compensation Law §§ 2.3-2.4 (in the Statutory Appendix). In 1994, the U.S. Departments of Labor and Commerce released a report prepared by the Commission on the Future of Worker Management Relations (the "Dunlop Commission"), which recommended that all laws adopt "economic realities" as the definition of employee:

> The definition of employee in labor, employment, and tax law should be modernized, simplified, and standardized. Instead of the control test borrowed from the old common law of master and servant, the definition should be based on the economic realities underlying the relationship between the worker and the party benefiting from the worker's services.

Is the Dunlop Commission correct in calling for a single definition of "employee" to replace the various common law and statutory tests? Judge Easterbrook, concurring in *Lauritzen*, suggests otherwise, arguing that whether a worker should be considered an employee depends on the reason for coverage. The policies behind various employment laws differ, suggesting that some workers should be covered employees in one situation but not in another. For example, the FLSA is designed to protect vulnerable workers from employer abuses, such as excessive work hours or low pay. In this case, broad coverage of low-skilled workers would be the desired goal, and the "economic realities" test is appropriate.

By contrast, consider the following language in Justice Souter's opinion for a unanimous Supreme Court in *Nationwide Mutual Insurance Co. v. Darden,*

503 U.S. 318 (1992), which endorsed the use of the common-law test for purposes of the Employee Retirement Income Security Act of 1974 (ERISA):

> While the FLSA, like ERISA, defines an "employee" to include "any individual employed by an employer," it defines the verb "employ" expansively to mean "suffer or permit to work." This latter definition, whose striking breadth we have previously noted, stretches the meaning of "employee" to cover some parties who might not qualify as such under a strict application of traditional agency law principles. ERISA lacks any such provision, however, and the textual asymmetry between the two statutes precludes reliance on FLSA cases when construing ERISA's concept of "employee."

Id. at 326.

2. The IRS and Independent Contractors. The largest day-to-day consequence of the employee/independent contractor label is the differing tax obligations. For employees, the employer must withhold federal and state income taxes, pay the FUTA (unemployment) tax, pay the employer's portion and withhold the employee's portion of FICA taxes (social security and Medicare), and pay state unemployment taxes and workers' compensation premiums. In addition, employers must file various tax forms for employees, such as W-2, W-3, 940, and 941 forms.

The tax rules for independent contractors are simpler. A person in a trade or business must file a Form 1099-MISC to report compensation in excess of $600 paid to a nonemployee. I.R.C. § 6041. The business does not have to pay or withhold any taxes, however, because independent contractors are responsible for making their own estimated income tax payments and paying their own federal income taxes.

The Internal Revenue Code relies on the common law to make the employee/independent contractor distinction. I.R.C. § 3121(d) defines "employee" to mean "any individual who, under the usual common law rules applicable in determining the employer/employee relationship, has the status of an employee." IRS regulations, however, include a 21-factor test for making that determination. Rev. Rul. 87-41, 1987-1 C.B. 296. *See also* 26 C.F.R. §§ 31.3121(d)-1, 31.3306(i)-1, 31.3401(c)-1 (defining employee for purposes of FICA, FUTA, and federal tax withholding, respectively).

3. The Significance of "Control." The common-law "right to control" test, as Judge Easterbrook discusses in his *Lauritzen* opinion, originated within agency law to deal with the issue of who ought to bear responsibility for injuries that occur in the course of work. From the standpoint of efficiency, liability should be placed on the "cheapest cost avoider" of the accident, the party who is in the best position to determine the costs and benefits of steps that might be taken to reduce the risk of accidents. The "right to control" test works well here because the person who controls the details of work is generally in the best position to make the necessary evaluation. *See generally* Alan O. Sykes, *The Economics of Vicarious Liability*, 93 YALE L.J. 1231 (1984).

4. Regulatory Avoidance or Other Motives? *Lauritzen* indicates that the FLSA creates incentives for employers to structure their relationships with workers as principal/independent contractor rather than employer/employee relationships. Other regulatory programs may also influence this decision one way or the other. The desire to limit unionization or to avoid taxes, for example, may push employers towards a principal/independent contractor relationship, while immunity from tort liability under the workers' compensation laws may work the other way.

Independently of incentives created by regulatory programs, however, some parties prefer an employer/employee relationship to a principal/independent contractor relationship, and vice versa. One goal of regulatory law should be to avoid distorting these decisions inadvertently. For example, if employees are more risk averse than employers, an employer/employee relationship may be optimal.

5. *Partners and Employees.* Partners are employers rather than employees, and therefore generally unprotected by employment laws. Thus, as we will see in Chapter 5, an associate (employee) at a law firm may have a claim when fired for reporting unethical conduct by the firm. *See Wieder v. Skala*, 609 N.E.2d 105 (N.Y. 1992). A partner who reports unethical conduct, however, may be unprotected. *See Bohatch v. Butler & Binion*, 977 S.W.2d 543 (Tex. 1988). But is the label "employer" enough to decide all cases? For example, should an associate denied partnership because of her sex have a discrimination claim under Title VII? *See Hishon v. King & Spalding*, 467 U.S. 69 (1984) (holding that Title VII forbids discrimination in promotion of employees to partners, even though it does not cover discrimination on lateral hiring of partners). Is a first-year partner in a 1,000-partner firm functionally more like an owner or an employee?

Recent cases reject per se rules in favor of case-by-case determinations of whether a partner or corporate shareholder-officer should be considered an employee for employment-law purposes. For example, in *Simpson v. Ernst & Young*, 100 F.3d 436 (6th Cir. 1996), the court found a partner at an accounting megafirm could bring an age-discrimination suit as an employee because he could not participate in personnel decisions, vote on the membership of the management committee, or share in firm profits. By contrast, in *Clackamas Gastroenterology Assocs. v. Wells*, 538 U.S. 440 (2003), the Supreme Court suggested that the directors of a professional corporation did not count as employees under Title VII because they shared responsibility for operating the clinic, shared in the profits, and were personally liable for malpractice claims. Both courts endorsed the multi-factored inquiry of the EEOC Compliance Manual § 605:0009 for determining employee status:

- Whether the organization can fire the individual or set the rules and regulations of the individual's work;
- Whether and, if so, to what extent the organization supervises the individual's work;
- Whether the individual reports to someone higher in the organization;
- Whether and, if so, to what extent the individual is able to influence the organization;
- Whether the parties intended that the individual be an employee, as expressed in written agreements or contracts;

- Whether the individual shares in the profits, losses, and liabilities of the organization.

6. *Volunteers.* Volunteers are not employees because they are not compensated for their work. Volunteers therefore are not protected by employment laws. For example, a volunteer intern is not protected against sexual harassment by Title VII. *See O'Connor v. Davis*, 126 F.3d 112 (2d Cir. 1997) ("Where no financial benefit is obtained by the purported employee from the employer, no 'plausible' employment relationship . . . can be said to exist"). But who is a volunteer is not always obvious. *See Tony & Susan Alamo Found. v. Secretary of Labor*, 471 U.S. 290 (1985) (upholding determination that foundation "associates," most of whom were rehabilitating drug addicts, derelicts, and criminals, were employees under FLSA even though they claimed they did not expect compensation, because they worked and were entirely dependent on the Foundation for long periods of time); *Colon v. City of New York*, 359 F.3d 83 (2d Cir. 2004) (participants in city's work experience program, a mandatory welfare work program, would be "employees" for purposes of Title VII if they could prove their allegations that they performed useful work for the city, and received benefits in exchange for their work which included cash, food stamps, transportation, child care expenses, and eligibility for workers' compensation).

7. *Are Independent Contractors an Exploited Group?* Because the FLSA does not protect independent contractors, the *Lauritzen* court wanted to analyze the economic reality and prevent the migrant workers from being termed independent contractors. But are independent contractors an exploited group? According to recent statistics, 79% of all independent contractors are white and 51% are male. In addition, independent contractors are relatively well educated: 37% hold a college degree, compared to only 33% of workers in traditional employment settings. Typical occupations for independent contractors are construction trade workers, salespeople, and miscellaneous managers and administrators. BUREAU OF LABOR STATISTICS, CONTINGENT AND ALTERNATIVE EMPLOYMENT ARRANGEMENTS, FEBRUARY 2005 (July 27, 2005), *available at* www.bls.gov/news.release/pdf/conemp.pdf. Indeed, in the *Lauritzen* case, what did the migrant farmers want? Recall that some of them intervened on Lauritzen's side.

B. COVERED EMPLOYEES

Even if a worker is clearly an employee rather than an independent contractor, he or she may not be subject to the protections of a particular employment law. Employment statutes often exempt part-time workers, home workers, leased workers, or other so-called "contingent" workers. The following case, in addition to wrestling with the consequences of the independent-contractor label, addresses whether an employer can avoid paying benefits to some employees while offering benefits to its core workforce.

WOLF v. COCA-COLA CO.
United States Court of Appeals, Eleventh Circuit
200 F.3d 1337 (2000)

BLACK, CIRCUIT JUDGE:

Appellant Sheila Wolf filed suit against Appellee Coca-Cola Company (Coca-Cola) and a number of individual defendants after being terminated from working at Coca-Cola as a computer programmer and analyst. The district court granted the defendants' motions for summary judgment on all of Appellant's claims. On appeal, Appellant challenges . . . the summary judgment on her claims against Coca-Cola for benefits under the Employee Retirement Income Security Act (ERISA), 29 U.S.C. §§ 1001-1461. . . . We affirm.

I. *Background*

Appellant worked as a computer programmer and analyst at Coca-Cola from February 1988 until she was terminated in March 1994. Appellant obtained this work by answering an ad placed by Access, Inc. (Access), a staffing company independent of Coca-Cola. Appellant's only employment contract was with Access; it provided that Appellant was an "independent contractor" of Access. Appellant performed services at Coca-Cola pursuant to contracts between Access and Coca-Cola. These contracts were one year in length and were renewed annually. The contracts governed the rates of compensation and length of employment for Access workers working at Coca-Cola, including Appellant. Appellant never obtained any written or oral agreement concerning her status at Coca-Cola.

In 1992, Appellant began working on a software project known as the ICS project. Tensions developed, however, with the hardware employees at Coca-Cola, known as the MCS group, over access rights and disk space on the computers. . . . On March 7, 1994, Appellant was terminated when Access was told that Appellant's services were no longer needed at Coca-Cola.

II. *Discussion*

 . . . To assert a claim under ERISA, the plaintiff must be either a "participant" or a "beneficiary" of an ERISA plan. *See* ERISA § 502(a)(1). Appellant asserts she is a participant in Coca-Cola's ERISA plan because she is a former employee who may be entitled to benefits from the plan. A participant is defined as "any *employee* or former *employee* of an employer . . . who is or may become *eligible* to receive a benefit of any type from" the ERISA plan. *Id.* § 3(7) (emphasis added). ERISA thus imposes two requirements for participant status. First, the plaintiff must be an employee. Second, the plaintiff must be "according to the language of the plan itself, eligible to receive a benefit under the plan. An individual who fails on either prong lacks standing to bring a claim for benefits under a plan established pursuant to ERISA." *Clark v. E.I. Dupont De Nemours & Co., Inc.,* 105 F.3d 646 (4th Cir. 1997).

The first prong — whether the plaintiff is an employee — is an independent review by the court of the employment relationship. The Supreme Court held in *Nationwide Mutual Insurance Co. v. Darden*, 503 U.S. 318, 319 (1992), that the term "employee" as used in the ERISA statute refers to the common law analysis, which distinguishes between employees and independent contractors by examining at least 14 factors.[2] Under the common law analysis, how the employment relationship is described by the parties and the employment documents is considered but is not dispositive. For example, in *Daughtrey v. Honeywell, Inc.*, 3 F.3d 1488 (11th Cir. 1993), this Court concluded that the district court had relied too heavily on the parties' contract, which described the ERISA plaintiff as an independent contractor, in determining that the plaintiff was not an employee. Despite the wording of the contract, the plaintiff had introduced sufficient evidence to raise a dispute of material fact over whether she was a common law employee under the full multi-factor *Darden* analysis. Thus, if the plaintiff is a "common law employee" of the company, the first prong is established.

The second prong — whether the plaintiff is eligible for benefits — is an examination of the terms of the company's ERISA plan. The plaintiff must be eligible for benefits under the terms of the plan itself. This requirement is necessary because companies are not required by ERISA to make their ERISA plans available to all common law employees. *See Abraham v. Exxon Corp.*, 85 F.3d 1126 (5th Cir. 1996); *Bronk v. Mountain States Tel. & Tel., Inc.*, 140 F.3d 1335 (10th Cir. 1998). For example, the terms of the ERISA plan in *Abraham* excluded "leased employees" from coverage. The Fifth Circuit concluded that although the leased-employee plaintiffs were common law employees, they were excluded by the plan and therefore had no ERISA claim. Similarly, because the ERISA plan in *Bronk* covered only "regular employees," the Tenth Circuit held that the plaintiffs, who were leased employees, could not prevail, despite their status as common law employees, because the plan specifically excluded them.

Appellant asserts two recent Ninth Circuit cases stand for the proposition that all common law employees are entitled to ERISA benefits. Those cases are distinguishable from this case, however, because of important facts relating to the *second* prong of ERISA standing. In *Vizcaino v. Microsoft Corp.*, 120 F.3d 1006 (9th Cir. 1997) (en banc), the Ninth Circuit held that Microsoft's computer programmer "freelancers" were common law employees, notwithstanding that their contracts specifically described them as independent

---

[2] The common law analysis is a consideration of at least the following factors:

> In determining whether a hired party is an employee under the general common law of agency, we consider the hiring party's right to control the manner and means by which the product is accomplished. Among the other factors relevant to this inquiry are the skill required; the source of the instrumentalities and tools; the location of the work; the duration of the relationship between the parties; whether the hiring party has the right to assign additional projects to the hired party; the extent of the hired party's discretion over when and how long to work; the method of payment; the hired party's role in hiring and paying assistants; whether the work is part of the regular business of the hiring party; whether the hiring party is in business; the provision of employee benefits; and the tax treatment of the hired party.

Darden, 503 U.S. at 323-24 at 1348 (quoting *Community for Creative Non-Violence v. Reid*, 490 U.S. 730, 751-52 (1989)).

contractors without eligibility for benefits. Microsoft's ERISA plan, however, expressly made eligible for benefits any "common law employee . . . who is on the United States payroll." *Id.* at 1010. Thus, once the Ninth Circuit held that the first prong was met, under the terms of Microsoft's plan the freelancers were eligible; the court remanded for a determination whether the freelancers were on the United States payroll. Similarly, in *Burrey v. Pacific Gas & Electric Co.,* 159 F.3d 388 (9th Cir. 1998), the plaintiffs were leased employees. The ERISA plan excluded leased employees *as defined* in I.R.C. [Internal Revenue Code] § 414(n). That section of the I.R.C. defines a leased employee as a person who is not an employee and who meets certain other criteria. The Ninth Circuit held that the I.R.C., like ERISA, refers to the common law definition of employee when it uses the word "employee." The court therefore reasoned that if a person is a common law employee, he or she is not a leased employee under I.R.C. § 414(n). Accordingly, because the employer's plan incorporated the definition of leased employee in I.R.C. § 414(n) for determining who is excluded, the plaintiffs were not excluded as leased employees, under the terms of the plan, if they met the standard for common law employees. Thus, contrary to Appellant's argument, neither *Vizcaino* nor *Burrey* holds that a person meeting the common law employee test must be given ERISA benefits. Rather, *Vizcaino* and *Burrey* simply clarify that if *the plan* makes all common law employees eligible, then meeting the first prong also will satisfy the second prong. When the plan affirmatively excludes certain workers from coverage, however, then meeting the first prong is not sufficient because, as *Abraham* and *Bronk* hold, failing the second prong denies the plaintiff ERISA standing.

In this case, although Appellant may have a legitimate argument that she was a common law employee of Coca-Cola, her claim for ERISA benefits fails the second prong because she is specifically excluded from eligibility by the terms of Coca-Cola's ERISA plan. The plan includes regular employees and excludes temporary and leased employees. The terms of Coca-Cola's ERISA plan include the following language:

> You're eligible for coverage under the plan if you're a regular employee of The Coca-Cola Company or one of its participating subsidiaries. You're not eligible for coverage under the plan if you're a temporary employee or seasonal employee, as defined by your employer. . . .

A "regular employee" is

> An employee . . . who is not classified as a temporary employee and who is normally scheduled to work the number of hours per week and weeks per year that are standard for the division. . . .

Two parts of the plan do not use the "regular employee" definition (excluding "temporary employees"), but these nevertheless exclude from eligibility "leased employees," defined as "individuals who perform services for the Company under an agreement with a leasing organization."

The district court correctly found that Appellant failed to raise a genuine issue of material fact demonstrating that she could be found to be eligible for benefits under these terms. Significantly, Appellant's status at Coca-Cola always was temporary; her only contract was with Access, and Access's contracts with Coca-Cola were only one year in length and were renewed every year. Furthermore, Appellant always was leased by Coca-Cola from Access. Finally, Appellant has not shown any facts suggesting that she could be considered a regular employee. To the contrary, for example, Appellant wore a different color badge than those worn by regular employees, was paid by Access and requested pay raises through Access, was not invited to events for regular Coca-Cola employees such as the Christmas party, and Appellant herself testified in her deposition that she did not consider herself a regular employee of Coca-Cola and had made inquiries about becoming one. Thus, the district court did not err in granting summary judgment to Coca-Cola on Appellant's claim for ERISA benefits because Appellant was not eligible for benefits under the terms of Coca-Cola's ERISA plan. . . .

NOTES

1. *When Is an Employee an "Employee?"* The court does not answer the question of whether Sheila Wolf was a common-law employee. Assuming she was, could Coca-Cola still exclude her from the ERISA plan? The court says yes — because Coca-Cola structured the ERISA plan to exclude temporary and leased employees, and this is permissible under the statute. Often an employment law itself excludes workers who clearly are "employees" from its protection. Many workers' compensation laws, for example, exclude "casual" employees. The Fair Labor Standards Act contains long lists of employees who are not covered by some or all of its provisions, ranging from executive, administrative and professional employees to babysitters and taxicab drivers. 29 U.S.C. § 213. The National Labor Relations Act does not cover agricultural workers or supervisors. 29 U.S.C. § 152(3).

On the other hand, statutes sometimes cover workers who actually are *not* employees. For example, under the Internal Revenue Code, leased workers are considered to be employees of the recipient of their labor if certain criteria are met, even though their employment contracts may be with another party. If the workers perform services for the recipient for a full year on a substantially full-time basis and the services historically have been performed by employees, the worker "shall be treated" as an employee of the recipient for some purposes. I.R.C. § 414(n). Similarly, sometimes protections initially developed to protect employees have been extended to others. *See O'Hare Trucking Serv., Inc. v. City of Northlake*, 518 U.S. 712 (1996) (First Amendment protection generally afforded to public employees also covers independent contractors).

2. *Core and Contingent Workers.* Coca-Cola is typical of modern corporations in employing a permanent core workforce surrounded by contingent workers.

A company's labor force can be comprised of a mix of two general types of workers — core workers and contingent workers. Core workers have a strong affiliation with an employer and are treated by the employer as having a significant stake in the company. Core workers can be thought of as being part of the so-called corporate family. They show long-term attachment to a company and have a real measure of job stability. In the language of economists, core workers have an implicit contract with their employers: if they follow certain rules and norms and meet certain standards, their employers will provide a long-term home of employment and some measure of advancement. In contrast, contingent workers have a weak affiliation with a specific employer and do not have a significant stake in a company. Contingent workers are not considered part of the corporate family. They do not show long-term attachment to a company, and they often do not have a real measure of job stability. Employers generally do not make implicit contracts with contingent workers.

RICHARD S. BELOUS, THE CONTINGENT ECONOMY: THE GROWTH OF THE TEMPORARY, PART-TIME AND SUBCONTRACTED WORKFORCE 5-6 (1989).

Workers often labeled contingent include casual workers, part-time workers, temporary workers, on-call workers, leased workers, independent contractors, subcontractors, flex-time workers, job-sharing workers, self-employed workers, home workers, and workers employed by temporary staffing agencies.

There are several advantages of hiring contingent workers, especially for smaller firms. To take the example of employee leasing, because employee leasing firms tend to be larger and more diverse, they can typically obtain health insurance at cheaper rates than small firms. Furthermore, leasing firms can usually handle compliance with employment laws, such as workers' compensation laws, more efficiently than small firms. Thus, leased employees can receive benefits that they might not get in a traditional employment relationship. Moreover, employers are likely to save money because the costs of complying with employment laws will be less. *See* Steven L. Willborn, *Leased Workers: Vulnerability and the Need for Special Legislation*, 19 COMP. LAB. L. & POL'Y J. 85, 88 (1997) (analogizing leasing companies to union hiring halls).

3. *Reducing the Cost of Firing.* In Part II of the casebook, we will study the circumstances in which job security might legally arise within the employee/employer relationship. Firms may use temporary, leased, or other kinds of contingent workers for the precise reason that they want to avoid such obligations and have the flexibility to terminate a worker's assignment without incurring the costs associated with wrongful-termination liability. In the same vein, a firm might use temporary or leased workers as a relatively low-risk way to screen workers for quality before making a longer-term commitment. For empirical evidence suggesting that firms have used temporary workers as a way to avoid costs associated with wrongful termination liability, see David Autor, *Outsourcing at Will: The Contribution of Unjust Dismissal Doctrine to the Growth of Employment Outsourcing*, 21 J. LAB. ECON. 1 (2003); T.J. Miles, *Common Law Exceptions to Employment At Will and U.S. Labor Markets*, 16 J.L. ECON. & ORG. 74 (2000).

C. COVERED EMPLOYERS

A related issue is whether some firms should be exempted from coverage by an employment law, or whether some firms should be included even though the are not "technically" the employer of the affected employees. The next case examines this issue.

ZHENG v. LIBERTY APPAREL CO.
United States Court of Appeals, Second Circuit
355 F.3d 61 (2003)

JOSE A. CABRANES, CIRCUIT JUDGE.

This case asks us to decide whether garment manufacturers who hired contractors to stitch and finish pieces of clothing were "joint employers" within the meaning of the Fair Labor Standards Act of 1938 ("FLSA") and New York law. Plaintiffs, garment workers in New York City who were directly employed by the contractors, claim that the manufacturers were their joint employers. . . . The manufacturers respond that the contractors . . . were plaintiffs' sole employers. Both plaintiffs and the manufacturers moved for summary judgment on the issue of joint employment.

The United States District Court for the Southern District of New York . . . granted the manufacturers' motion, and held that the manufacturers could not be held liable for violations of the FLSA or its New York statutory analogues.

Background

. . . Plaintiffs-Appellants are 26 non-English-speaking adult garment workers who worked in a factory at 103 Broadway in New York's Chinatown. They brought this action against both (1) their immediate employers, six contractors doing business at 103 Broadway ("Contractor Corporations") and their principals (collectively, "Contractor Defendants"), and (2) Liberty Apparel Company, Inc. ("Liberty") and its principals, Albert Nigri and Hagai Laniado (collectively, "Liberty Defendants"). Because the Contractor Defendants either could not be located or have ceased doing business, plaintiffs have voluntarily dismissed their claims against those defendants with prejudice. Accordingly, plaintiffs now seek damages only from the Liberty Defendants.

Liberty, a "jobber" in the parlance of the garment industry, is a manufacturing company that contracts out the last phase of its production process. That process, in broad terms, worked as follows: First, Liberty employees developed a pattern for a garment, cut a sample from the pattern, and sent the sample to a customer for approval. Once the customer approved the pattern, Liberty purchased the necessary fabric from a vendor, and the vendor delivered the fabric to Liberty's warehouse. There, the fabric was graded and marked, spread out on tables, and, finally, cut by Liberty employees.

After the fabric was cut, Liberty did not complete the production process on its own premises. Instead, Liberty delivered the cut fabric, along with other essential materials, to various contractors for assembly. The assemblers, in turn, employed workers to stitch and finish the pieces, a process that included sewing the fabrics, buttons, and labels into the garments, cuffing and hemming the garments, and, finally, hanging the garments. The workers, including plaintiffs, were paid at a piece rate for their labor.

From March 1997 through April 1999, Liberty entered into agreements with the Contractor Corporations under which the Contractor Corporations would assemble garments to meet Liberty's specifications. During that time period, Liberty utilized as many as thirty to forty assemblers, including the Contractor Corporations. Liberty did not seek out assemblers; instead, assemblers came to Liberty's warehouse looking for assembly work. In order to obtain such work, a prospective assembler was required by Liberty to sign a form agreement.

Plaintiffs claim that approximately 70-75% of their work during the time period at issue was for Liberty. They explain that they knew they were working for Liberty based on both the labels that were sewn into the garments and the specific lot numbers that came with the garments. Liberty's co-owner, Albert Nigri, asserts that the percentage of the Contractor Corporations' work performed for Liberty was closer to 10-15%. He derives that figure from individual plaintiffs' handwritten notes and records.

The parties do not dispute that Liberty employed people to monitor Liberty's garments while they were being assembled. However, the parties dispute the extent to which Liberty oversaw the assembly process. Various plaintiffs presented affidavits to the District Court stating that two Liberty representatives — a man named Ah Sen and "a Taiwanese woman" — visited the factory approximately two to four times a week for up to three hours a day, and exhorted the plaintiffs to work harder and faster. In their affidavits, these plaintiffs claim further that, when they finished working on garments, Liberty representatives — as opposed to employees of the Contractor Corporations — inspected their work and gave instructions directly to the workers if corrections needed to be made. One of the plaintiffs also asserts that she informed the "Taiwanese woman" that the workers were not being paid for their work at the factory.

Albert Nigri, on the other hand, avers that Liberty's quality control person made brief visits to assemblers' factories and was instructed to speak only with Lai Huen Yam, a co-owner of the Contractor Corporations, or with his wife. Furthermore, Nigri asserts in his affidavit that Liberty representatives were expected to spend just thirty minutes at each of the assemblers' work sites. Finally, Nigri states that Liberty did not employ two quality control persons simultaneously; did not employ a quality control person during some of the relevant time period; and did not employ a man as a quality control person. . . .

Discussion

I. FLSA Claims

A. Competing Economic Reality Tests . . .

In the present case, it is undisputed that the Contractor Defendants, who are no longer parties to this suit, employed plaintiffs. The issue is whether the Liberty Defendants also employed them.

In previous cases, we have applied two different tests to determine whether an employment relationship exists in light of the Supreme Court's admonition that "economic reality" govern our application of the FLSA. In *Carter v. Dutchess Community College,* 735 F.2d 8 (2d Cir. 1984), we held that an inmate conducting tutorial classes in a program managed by a community college had raised genuine issues of material fact as to whether the college was an employer under the FLSA, where, among other things, the college sent compensation directly to the inmate and set the inmate's tutoring schedule. To reach that conclusion, we evaluated whether the college

> (1) had the power to hire and fire the employees, (2) supervised and controlled employee work schedules or conditions of employment, (3) determined the rate and method of payment, and (4) maintained employment records.

Four years after deciding *Carter* . . . we decided *Brock v. Superior Care, Inc.,* 840 F.2d 1054 (2d Cir. 1988). There, . . . we applied a different, more expansive test. That test, drawn from cases distinguishing employees from independent contractors, examined

> (1) the degree of control exercised by the employer over the workers, (2) the workers' opportunity for profit or loss and their investment in the business, (3) the degree of skill and independent initiative required to perform the work, (4) the permanence or duration of the working relationship, and (5) the extent to which the work is an integral part of the employer's business.

See Superior Care, 840 F.2d at 1058-59. . . .

B. Need for Remand

We conclude, for the reasons set forth below, that the District Court erred when, based *exclusively* on the four factors mentioned in *Carter,* it determined that the Liberty Defendants were not, as a matter of law, joint employers under the FLSA. . . .

1. The Language of the Statute

As noted above, the relevant provision of the FLSA, 29 U.S.C. § 203(g), defines "employ" as including "to suffer or permit to work." This is " 'the broadest definition [of "employ"] that has ever been included in any one act,' " *United States v. Rosenwasser,* 323 U.S. 360, 363 n. 3 (1937), and it encompasses "working relationships, which prior to [the FLSA], were not deemed to fall within an employer-employee category," *Walling v. Portland Terminal Co.,* 330 U.S. 148 (1947).

Measured against the expansive language of the FLSA, the four-part test employed by the District Court is unduly narrow, as it focuses solely on the formal right to control the physical performance of another's work. . . .

2. Rutherford

Rutherford Food Corp. v. McComb, 331 U.S. 722 (1947), confirmed that the definition of "employ" in the FLSA cannot be reduced to formal control over the physical performance of another's work. In *Rutherford,* the Supreme Court held that a slaughterhouse jointly employed workers who de-boned meat on its premises, despite the fact that a boning supervisor — with whom the slaughterhouse had entered into a contract — directly controlled the terms and conditions of the meat boners' employment. Specifically, the supervisor, *rather than the slaughterhouse,* (i) hired and fired the boners, (ii) set their hours, and, (iii) after being paid a set amount by the slaughterhouse for each one hundred pounds of de-boned meat, paid the boners for their work.

In determining that the meat boners were employees of the slaughterhouse notwithstanding the role played by the boning supervisor, the Court examined the "circumstances of the whole activity," but also isolated specific relevant factors that help distinguish a legitimate contractor from an entity that "suffers or permit[s]" its subcontractor's employees to work. First, the Court noted that the boners "did a specialty job on the production line"; that is, their work was "a part of the integrated unit of production" at the slaughterhouse. The Court noted also that responsibility under the boning contracts passed from one boning supervisor to another "without material changes" in the work performed at the slaughterhouse; that the slaughterhouse's premises and equipment were used for the boners' work; that the group of boners "had no business organization that could or did shift as a unit from one slaughterhouse to another"; and that the managing official of the slaughterhouse, in addition to the boners' purported employer, closely monitored the boners' performance and productivity. Based on its analysis of these factors, the Court imposed FLSA liability on the slaughterhouse.

3. Carter

[The court concludes that *Carter* is consistent with *Rutherford*: the four *Carter* factors are *sufficient* to establish employer status, but are neither necessary, nor exclusive.]

C. Instructions on Remand

1. Factors to be Applied

On remand, the District Court must determine whether the Liberty Defendants should be deemed to have been the plaintiffs' joint employer. This determination is to be based on "the circumstances of the whole activity," *Rutherford,* 331 U.S. at 730, viewed in light of "economic reality," *Goldberg v. Whitaker House Coop., Inc.,* 366 U.S. 28, 33 (1961). We discuss below factors, drawn from *Rutherford,* which we think the court will find illuminating in these circumstances. The court is also free to consider any other factors it deems relevant to its assessment of the economic realities.

The factors we find pertinent in these circumstances, listed in no particular order, are (1) whether Liberty's premises and equipment were used for the plaintiffs' work; (2) whether the Contractor Corporations had a business that could or did shift as a unit from one putative joint employer to another; (3) the extent to which plaintiffs performed a discrete line-job that was integral to Liberty's process of production; (4) whether responsibility under the contracts could pass from one subcontractor to another without material changes; (5) the degree to which the Liberty Defendants or their agents supervised plaintiffs' work; and (6) whether plaintiffs worked exclusively or predominantly for the Liberty Defendants.

These particular factors are relevant because, when they weigh in plaintiffs' favor, they indicate that an entity has functional control over workers even in the absence of the formal control measured by the *Carter* factors. . . .

The first two factors derived from *Rutherford* require minimal discussion. The first factor — namely, whether a putative joint employer's premises and equipment are used by its putative joint employees — is relevant because the shared use of premises and equipment may support the inference that a putative joint employer has functional control over the plaintiffs' work. Similarly, the second factor — namely, whether the putative joint employees are part of a business organization that shifts as a unit from one putative joint employer to another — is relevant because a subcontractor that seeks business from a variety of contractors is less likely to be part of a subterfuge arrangement than a subcontractor that serves a single client. Although neither shared premises nor the absence of a broad client base is anything close to a perfect proxy for joint employment (because they are both perfectly consistent with a legitimate subcontracting relationship), the factfinder can use these readily verifiable facts as a starting point in uncovering the economic realities of a business relationship.

The other factors we have pointed out are less straightforward. *Rutherford* considered the extent to which plaintiffs performed a line-job that is integral to the putative joint employer's process of production. Interpreted broadly, this factor could be said to be implicated in *every* subcontracting relationship, because all subcontractors perform a function that a general contractor deems "integral" to a product or a service. However, we do not interpret the factor quite so broadly. The factor is derived from the *Rutherford* Court's statement that the boners at the slaughterhouse should be considered joint employees because, *inter alia,* "[they] did a specialty job on the production line." Based on this statement in *Rutherford,* along with similar language in decisions interpreting *Rutherford,* . . . we construe *Rutherford* to mean that work on a production line occupies a special status under the FLSA, at least when it lies on "the usual path of an employee."

Rutherford, however, offers no firm guidance as to how to distinguish work that "in its essence, follows the usual path of an employee," from work that can be outsourced without attracting increased scrutiny under the FLSA. In our view, there is no bright-line distinction between these two categories of work. On one end of the spectrum lies the type of work performed by the boners in *Rutherford* — *i.e.,* piecework on a producer's premises that requires minimal training or equipment, and which constitutes an essential step in the producer's integrated manufacturing process. On the other end of the spectrum lies work that is not part of an integrated production unit, that is not performed on a predictable schedule, and that requires specialized skills or expensive technology. In classifying business relationships that fall in between these two poles, we are mindful of the substantial and valuable place that outsourcing, along with the subcontracting relationships that follow from outsourcing, have come to occupy in the American economy. We are also mindful that manufacturers, and especially manufacturers of relatively sophisticated products that require multiple components, may choose to outsource the production of some of those components in order to increase efficiency. Accordingly, we resist the temptation to say that any work on a so-called production line — no matter what product is being manufactured — should attract heightened scrutiny. Instead, in determining the weight and degree of factor (3), we believe that both industry custom and historical practice should be consulted. Industry custom may be relevant because, insofar as the practice of using subcontractors to complete a particular task is widespread, it is unlikely to be a mere subterfuge to avoid complying with labor laws. At the same time, historical practice may also be relevant, because, if plaintiffs can prove that, as a historical matter, a contracting device has developed in response to and as a means to avoid applicable labor laws, the prevalence of that device may, in particular circumstances, be attributable to widespread evasion of labor laws. Ultimately, this factor, like the other factors derived from *Rutherford*, is not independently determinative of a defendant's status, because the mere fact that a manufacturing job is not typically outsourced does not necessarily mean that there is no substantial economic reason to outsource it in a particular case. However, as *Rutherford* indicates, the type of work performed by plaintiffs can bear on the overall determination as to whether a defendant may be held liable for an FLSA violation.

The fourth factor the Court considered in *Rutherford* is whether responsibility under the contracts could pass from one subcontractor to another without material changes. That factor is derived from the *Rutherford* Court's observation that "[t]he responsibility under the boning contracts without material changes passed from one boner to another." *Rutherford*, 331 U.S. at 730. In the quoted passage, the Supreme Court was referring to the fact that, even when the boning supervisor abandoned his position and another supervisor took his place, the *same* employees would continue to do the *same* work in the *same* place. Under *Rutherford*, therefore, this factor weighs in favor of a determination of joint employment when employees are tied to an entity such as the slaughterhouse rather than to an ostensible direct employer such as the boning supervisor. In such circumstances, it is difficult *not* to draw the inference that a subterfuge arrangement exists. Where, on the other hand, employees work for an entity (the purported joint employer) only to the extent that their direct employer is hired by that entity, this factor does not in any way support the determination that a joint employment relationship exists.

The fifth factor listed above — namely, the degree to which the defendants supervise the plaintiffs' work — also requires some comment, as it too can be misinterpreted to encompass run-of-the-mill subcontracting relationships. Although *Rutherford* indicates that a defendant's extensive supervision of a plaintiff's work is indicative of an employment relationship, *Rutherford* indicates also that such extensive supervision weighs in favor of joint employment only if it demonstrates effective control of the terms and conditions of the plaintiff's employment. By contrast, supervision with respect to contractual warranties of quality and time of delivery has no bearing on the joint employment inquiry, as such supervision is perfectly consistent with a typical, legitimate subcontracting arrangement.

Finally, the *Rutherford* Court considered whether the purported joint employees worked exclusively or predominantly for the putative joint employer. In describing that factor, we use the words "exclusively or predominantly" on purpose. As noted in *Lopez v. Silverman,* 14 F. Supp. 2d 405 (S.D.N.Y. 1998), the extent of work performed for a putative joint employer is "not described in any decision . . . as a separate factor for consideration." *Id.* at 417. However, it has "implicitly [been] a factor," *id.,* in cases in which the purported joint employees worked exclusively or predominantly for the purported joint employer. In those situations, the joint employer may *de facto* become responsible, among other things, for the amount workers are paid and for their schedules, which are traditional indicia of employment. On the other hand, where a subcontractor performs merely a majority of its work for a single customer, there is no sound basis on which to infer that the customer has assumed the prerogatives of an employer.

In sum, by looking beyond a defendant's formal control over the physical performance of a plaintiff's work, the "economic reality" test — which has been distilled into a nonexclusive and overlapping set of factors — gives content to the broad "suffer or permit" language in the statute. However, by limiting FLSA liability to cases in which defendants, based on the totality of the circumstances, function as employers of the plaintiffs rather than mere business partners of plaintiffs' direct employer, the test also ensures that the statute is not interpreted to subsume typical outsourcing relationships. The "economic reality" test, therefore, is intended to expose outsourcing relationships that lack a substantial economic purpose, but it is manifestly not intended to bring normal, strategically-oriented contracting schemes within the ambit of the FLSA.

2. Application of the Factors on Remand

We intimate no view as to whether plaintiffs, under a proper application of the economic reality test derived from *Rutherford,* will have presented sufficient evidence to survive a renewed motion for summary judgment on remand. . . .

In order to grant summary judgment for defendants, the District Court would have to conclude that, even where both the historical facts and the relevant factors are interpreted in the light most favorable to plaintiffs, defendants are still entitled to judgment as a matter of law. To reach this conclusion, the Court need not decide that *every* factor weighs against joint employment. . . .

NOTES

1. *Employee Leasing and Evasion of Employment Laws.* Some worry that small firms might use leased employees to evade employment laws. For example, the Family and Medical Leave Act (FMLA) applies only to employers with fifty or more employees. An employer with forty-five "core" employees that needed five additional employees might lease those employees so that the employer could retain its exemption from FMLA. Interestingly, it is the "core" employees who are damaged by this strategy. If the employer had to hire five traditional employees, all of the "core" employees would then be covered by FMLA.

Courts sometimes deal with attempts by firms to evade employment laws by using the joint-employer doctrine. In effect, the courts treat certain employees as having multiple employers. For example, courts may treat both a leasing company and a lessee as employers of leased employees. The leased employees therefore count toward totals for both employers for purposes of small-firm exemptions found in numerous employment statutes. This eliminates the ability of small employers to evade employment laws by leasing rather than hiring employees and makes the decision to lease employees more neutral from an economic standpoint.

2. *Statutory Exemptions for Small Employers.* The coverage of small employers in employment statutes varies greatly. Most statutes define employer coverage by the number of employees, but the number varies statute by statute. The Federal Unemployment Tax Act applies to employers with one or more employees, Title VII and the Americans with Disabilities Act require fifteen employees, the Age Discrimination in Employment Act requires twenty employees, and the Family and Medical Leave Act requires fifty employees. *See* 26 U.S.C. § 3306(a)(FUTA); 42 U.S.C. § 2000e(b) (Title VII); 42 U.S.C. § 12111(5) (ADA); 29 U.S.C. § 630(b) (ADEA); 29 U.S.C. § 2611(4) (FMLA). Occasionally, employer coverage is defined by the dollar volume of the business. Under the Fair Labor Standards Act, for example, "enterprise" coverage generally applies only to employers with $500,000 or more in annual sales. 29 U.S.C. § 203(s). Similarly, the National Labor Relations Board only exerts jurisdiction over employers with a certain amount of sales, for example, $500,000 annually for retail businesses and $250,000 annually for law firms. State employment laws also usually exempt small employers, but typically state laws extend to smaller employers than their federal analogues. For example, most state discrimination statutes extend to employers with fewer than fifteen employees, so they have broader coverage than Title VII, but most also exempt very small employers, for example, employers with fewer than four or five or ten employees. One of the principal purposes of state equivalents of federal statutes is to extend the reach of the policy.

Should small employers be exempt? On the one hand, the procedural or paperwork requirements that accompany these statutes are often particularly burdensome for small employers. On the other hand, an exemption would seem to let small employers violate the policies underlying the act. Or does it? In *Collins v. Rizkana*, 652 N.E.2d 653 (Ohio 1995), an employee in a three-person veterinarian office quit after accusing her employer of sexual harassment. The substance of the employer's actions clearly violated Title VII and the analogous Ohio Human Rights Law, but just as clearly the small employer met neither the fifteen-employee threshold of Title VII nor the four-employee threshold of Ohio law. The Ohio Supreme Court allowed the employee to bring a common-law wrongful-discharge claim in violation of public policy, refusing to find a substantive policy in the four-employee threshold.

> [W]e cannot interpret the [four-employee threshold] as an intent by the General Assembly to grant small businesses in Ohio a license to sexually harass/discriminate against their employees with impunity. Instead, we can only read [the provision] as evidencing an intention to exempt small businesses from [the statute's] burdens, not from its

antidiscrimination policy. [W]e cannot find it to be Ohio's public policy that an employer with three employees may condition their employment upon the performance of sexual favors while an employer with four employees may not.

Id. at 660-61.

3. Counting Employees. Title VII covers employers with "fifteen or more employees for each working day in each of twenty or more calendar weeks in the current or preceding calendar year." 42 U.S.C. § 2000e(b). Suppose an employer has fourteen full-time employees and one part-time employee who does not work on Fridays. Is this employer subject to Title VII? The issue arose in *Walters v. Metropolitan Educational Enterprises, Inc.*, 519 U.S. 202 (1997). The Court of Appeals held that the employer was too small, reasoning that employees should be counted only on days they are actually compensated and determining that the employer did not have fifteen employees "each working day" as required by statute. The Supreme Court reversed, upholding the payroll method of counting employees, which counts all workers as an employee for each working day after they began work until the employment relationship terminates.

4. Exemptions for Public Employers. Many employment laws cover only private employers, exempting government employers. Two conflicting explanations are sometimes given for treating private workplaces differently. On the one hand, government workers have constitutional protections and thus do not need statutory protections. On the other hand, the statutory requirements are sometimes thought to be too burdensome to inflict upon governments.

Title VII, the major federal statute prohibiting sex and race discrimination in employment, illustrates the variation in applying employment laws to government employers. When originally passed as part of the Civil Rights Act of 1964, Title VII applied only to private-sector employers. In 1972, however, Congress extended Title VII's coverage to the public sector. Finally, in 1995 Congress imposed the requirements of Title VII and numerous other employment laws on itself. Congressional Accountability Act, 2 U.S.C. §§ 1301-1438.

In some situations, the Constitution may prohibit Congress from extending employment laws to the states. In *National League of Cities v. Usery*, 426 U.S. 833 (1976), the Supreme Court held that Congress violated the Tenth Amendment (powers not delegated to the United States are reserved to the States or to the people) when it extended the minimum-wage and overtime rules of the Fair Labor Standards Act to state and municipal employees. In 1985, however, the case was overruled by *Garcia v. San Antonio Metropolitan Transit Authority*, 469 U.S. 528.

In *Alden v. Maine*, 527 U.S. 706 (1999), the Supreme Court held that state sovereign immunity, inherent in the constitutional framework, prevented Congress from authorizing a state-court suit for damages by probation officers denied overtime pay by their employer, the state of Maine. That decision was presaged by *Seminole Tribe v. Florida*, 517 U.S. 44 (1996), which held that the Eleventh Amendment prohibited Congress from authorizing private suits for damages against states in federal court. The substantive requirements of the FLSA remain binding on state employers, but damages can only be recovered in suits brought by the Secretary of Labor on behalf of workers. The *Alden* court opined that "the good faith of the States . . . provides an important assurance" that states will obey federal laws like the FLSA. In addition, private suits for injunctive relief remain possible. Importantly, the state sovereignty defense does not apply to municipal employers. *See also Board of Trustees v. Garrett*, 531 U.S. 356 (2001) (holding that state employees cannot sue their employers under the ADEA); *Kimmel v. Florida Bd. of Regents*, 528 U.S. 62 (2000) (holding that state employees cannot sue their employers under the ADA).

Part II

Part II

THE RISE AND FALL OF EMPLOYMENT AT WILL

Chapter 3

HISTORICAL FOUNDATIONS OF EMPLOYMENT AT WILL

STATUTE OF LABOURERS
23 Edw. III (1349)

EDWARD by the grace of God, &c. to the reverend father in Christ, William, by the same grace archbishop of Canterbury, primate of all England, greeting. Because a great part of the people, and especially of workmen and servants, late died of the pestilence, many seeing the necessity of masters, and great scarcity of servants, will not serve unless they may receive excessive wages, (2) and some rather willing to beg in idleness, than by labour to get their living; we, considering the grievous incommodities, which of the lack especially of ploughmen and such labourers may hereafter come, have upon deliberation and treaty with the prelates and the nobles, and learned men assisting us, of their mutual counsel, ordained:

CHAPTER I. Every person able in body under the age of sixty years, not having to live on, being required, shall be bound to serve him that doth require him, or else committed to the gaol, until he find surety to serve.

THAT every man and woman of our realm of *England,* of what condition he be, free or bond, able in body, and within the age of threescore years, not living in merchandize, nor exercising any craft, nor having of his own whereof he may live, nor proper land, about whose tillage he may himself occupy, and not serving any other, if he in convenient service (his Estate considered) be required to serve, he shall be bounden to serve him which so shall him require. And take only the wages, livery, meed, or salary, which were accustomed to be given in the places where he oweth to serve, the xx. year of our reign of *England,* or five or six other common years next before. Provided always, That the lords be preferred before other in their bondmen or their land tenants, so in their service to be retained: so that nevertheless the said lords shall retain no more than be necessary for them. And if any such man or woman, being so required to serve, will not the same do, that proved by two true men before the sheriff or the bailiffs of our sovereign lord the King, or the constables of the town where the same shall happen to be done, he shall anon be taken by them or any of them, and committed to the next gaol, there to remain under strait keeping, till he find surety to serve in the form aforesaid.

CHAPTER II. If a workman or servant depart from service before the time agreed upon, he shall be imprisoned.

ITEM, If any reaper, mower, or other workman or servant, of what estate or condition that he be, retained in any man's service, do depart from the said service without reasonable cause or license, before the term agreed, he shall have pain of imprisonment. And that none under the same pain presume to receive or to retain any such in his service.

47

STATUTE OF ARTIFICERS
5 Eliz., c. 4 (1562)

SECTION 1. ALTHOUGH there remain and stand in force presently a great number of acts and statutes concerning the retaining, departing, wages and orders of apprentices, servants and labourers, as well in husbandry as in divers other arts, mysteries and occupations; (2) yet partly for the imperfection and contrariety that is found, and doth appear in sundry of the said laws, and for the variety and number of them, (3) and chiefly for that the wages and allowances limited and rated in many of the said statutes, are in divers places too small and not answerable to this time, respecting the advancement of prices of all things belonging to the said servants and labourers; (4) the said laws cannot conveniently, without the great grief and burden of the poor labourer and hired man, be put in good and due execution: (5) and as the said several acts and statutes were, at the time of the making of them, thought to be very good and beneficial for the commonwealth of this realm (as divers of them are:) so if the substance of as many of the said laws as are meet to be continued, shall be digested and reduced into one sole law and statute, and in the same an uniform order prescribed and limited concerning the wages and other orders for apprentices, servants and labourers, there is good hope that it will come to pass, that the same law (being duly executed) should banish idleness, advance husbandry, and yield unto the hired person, both in the time of scarcity, and in the time of plenty, a convenient proportion of wages. . . .

SECTION 3. And be it further enacted by the authority aforesaid, That no manner of person or persons, after the aforesaid last day of *September* now next ensuing, shall retain, hire or take into service, or cause to be retained, hired or taken into service, nor any person shall be retained, hired or taken into service, by any means or colour, to work for any less time or term than for one whole year, in any of the sciences, crafts, mysteries or arts of clothiers, woolen cloth weavers, truckers, fullers, clothworkers, sheremen, dyers, hosiers, taylors, shoemakers, tanners, pewterers, bakers, brewers, glovers, cutlers, smiths, farriers, curriers, sadlers, spurriers, turners, cappers, hatmakers or feltmakers, bowyers, fletchers, arrow-head-makers, butchers, cooks or millers.

SECTION 4. [Establishes compulsory service for able-bodied, propertyless adults, along the lines of the Statute of Labourers.]

SECTION 5. And be it further enacted, That no person which shall retain any servant, shall put away his or her said servant, (2) and that no person retained according to this statute, shall depart from his master, mistress or dame, before the end of his or her term; (3) upon the pain hereafter mentioned; (4) unless it be for some reasonable and sufficient cause or matter to be allowed before two justices of peace, or one at the least, within the said county, or before the mayor or other chief officer of the city. . . .

NOTES

1. *The Black Death.* As its preamble suggests, the Statute of Labourers was enacted in response to the labor shortages caused by the "Black Death," a bubonic plague that swept England (and Europe) in 1348, killing perhaps one-third of the total population. Historians often point to this Statute as the beginning of Anglo-American labor legislation. The Statute illustrates the feudal conception of individuals as having fixed positions in society with set rights and duties. In particular, the Statute attempts to compel workers to accept employment at pre-Black Death wages and forbids them to quit before the end of the employment term. The control of labor was a central feature of England's laws in this period. *See* Robert R. Palmer, English Law in the Age of Black Death, 1348-1381 (1993). Economic forces, however, overwhelmed attempts to enforce the feudal status quo. *See* David D. Haddock & Lynne Kiesling, *The Black Death and Property Rights*, 31 J. Legal Stud. S545 (2002) (arguing that the increase in the marginal value of labor due to its new scarcity accelerated the erosion of serfdom and gave workers greater control over their own labor).

As with the Statute of Labourers 200 years earlier, the immediate impetus for the Statute of Artificers in 1562 was an epidemic, this one reducing England's population by five percent. The Statute of Artificers remained in practical force for perhaps 200 years and was not formally repealed until 1875.

2. Symmetry. The Elizabethan statute, unlike the earlier statute, established employer as well as worker duties, suggesting a desire to treat the parties symmetrically. This symmetry rationale reappears often in contemporary employment law arguments. Nevertheless, the penalties were not symmetrical. A worker who quit before the end of the year or who failed to give proper notice could be imprisoned and might lose the year's wages. A master who dismissed a worker prematurely or without notice was subject to a fine of 40 shillings.

3. Modern Issues in Elizabethan Language. Section 1 of the Statute of Artificers complains about the proliferation of laws regulating employment and addresses the problem by enacting another statute. Does not this complaint have a modern ring?

In addition to combating the shortage of labor problem, the Statute of Artificers was designed to shift the burden of caring for the poor from the local parishes to employers. This issue — whether benefits should be provided through the workplace or government programs — remains current nearly half a millennium later.

4. Yearly Contracts and Just-Cause Dismissal. Section 3 of the Statute of Artificers establishes a minimum duration of one year for employment contracts. Does Section 5 require just cause for terminating employment contracts, and specify a procedure for handling wrongful discharge claims? As we shall see at the end of this Part, the Model Employment Termination Act similarly requires good cause for termination and establishes an arbitration procedure to resolve disputes. Are we returning to the Elizabethan model?

1 WILLIAM BLACKSTONE, COMMENTARIES *413 (1765)

If the hiring be general without any particular time limited, the law construes it to be a hiring for a year; upon a principle of natural equity, that the servant shall serve, and the master maintain him, throughout all the revolutions of the respective seasons, as well when there is work to be done, as when there is not: but the contract may be made for any larger or smaller term.

NOTE

Developments in the English Rule. Consider the explanation of Blackstone's rule from Professor Feinman.

> [Blackstone's] rule thus stated expressed a sound principle: injustice would result if, for example, masters could have the benefit of servants' labor during planting and harvest seasons but discharge them to avoid supporting them during the unproductive winter, or if servants who were supported during the hard season could leave their masters' service when their labor was most needed. But the source of the yearly hiring rule was not solely, as might be supposed from Blackstone's statement, in the judges' concern for fairness between master and servant. The rule was also shaped by the requirements of the Statutes of Labourers, which prescribed a duty to work and prohibited leaving an employment or discharging a servant before the end of a term, and by the Poor Laws, which used a test of residence and employment to determine which community was responsible for the support of a person. Thus, despite a concern with the "revolution of the seasons," the rule articulated by Blackstone was not restricted to agricultural and domestic workers. The presumption that an indefinite hiring was a hiring for a year extended to all classes of servants. Because the rule was designed for domestic servants broadly construed, however, those who were clearly not in that group were sometimes excluded. The types of employment now considered usual — where the hours or days of work were limited, or the employment only for a certain job — would sometimes be held not to import a yearly hiring, indicating some sophistication by the law in not extending a concept designed for one purpose beyond its reasonable reach.

> The presumption of a yearly hiring could also be rebutted in specific cases by other means, especially, as the necessity of the rule for settlement cases diminished, when the parties were alleged to have contracted with reference to a custom of the trade for a shorter period of employment. The frequency of periodic payments was a material factor in determining whether the parties intended the contract to be for a shorter period, but periodic payment of wages alone would not ordinarily rebut the presumption. Because the central question in each case was the factual one of the intention of the parties, the court decisions are sometimes apparently in conflict.

> As the law was faced with an increasing variety of employment situations mostly far removed from the domestic relations which had

shaped the earlier law, the importance of the duration of the contract in question diminished and the second issue, the notice required to terminate the contract, moved to the fore. Even when they recognized hirings as yearly ones, the courts refused to consider the contracts as entire and instead developed the rule that, unless specified otherwise, service contracts could be terminated on reasonable notice. This principle was recognized as early as the time of Blackstone, who stated that certain yearly hirings could be terminated on a quarter's notice. What constituted reasonable notice was a question of fact to be decided anew in each case, but certain conventions grew up. Domestic servants, who presumably no longer needed the benefit of the seasons, could be given a month's notice. Other types of employees could also be given a month's notice; three months was another common term, although some special cases required six or even twelve month's notice. Although notice was a separate question in each case, the custom of the trade was often determinative. In the twentieth century the required notice decreased considerably and is now regulated for many employees by the Contracts of Employment Act of 1963, which prescribes periods of required notice from one to eight weeks.

English law thus attempted to adapt to changing conditions and new situations, but more was involved than a simple desire to do justice between the parties. The Master and Servant Act of 1824 made breach of a service contract by an employee a criminal offense, while breach by an employer was still only a civil wrong. Thereafter, workers often sought shorter periods of notice. Among miners, for example, a fortnight's notice was common; in Scotland colliers had achieved "minute contracts" terminable on a minute's notice, allowing the workers to avoid criminal liability for sudden strikes. On the employers' side, the opportunity to hire lower-priced workers and fluctuations in the need for laborers made long notice periods somewhat undesirable, except when organized labor activity was great, in which case the employers desired longer periods of notice to protect themselves from damage from sudden strikes. The involved procedure for obtaining damages from an employee who breached without notice made the requirement of notice nugatory as to the employer, frequently resulting in imprisonment of the employee for debt but no payment to the employer. The real beneficiaries of the notice rule in the nineteenth century may have been the newly enlarged "middle class" employees: newspaper editors, commercial and business agents, etc. The cases suggest that their employers would have preferred to discharge them more easily, but the employees were protected by the notice requirement. Later, however, the shortening of the period of notice reduced the benefits to the employees.

Jay M. Feinman, *The Development of the Employment at Will Rule,* 20 Am. J. Legal Hist. 118, 120-22 (1976).*

HORACE GAY WOOD, MASTER AND SERVANT 272-73 (1877)

With us [in America, unlike in England,] the rule is inflexible, that a general or indefinite hiring is *prima facie* a hiring at will, and if the servant seeks to make it out a yearly hiring, the burden is upon him to establish it by proof. A hiring at so much a day, week, month or year, no time being specified, is an indefinite hiring, and no presumption attaches that it was for a day even, but only at the rate fixed for whatever time the party may serve.[4] It is competent for either party to show what the mutual understanding of the parties was in reference to the matter; but unless their understanding was mutual that the service was to extend for a certain fixed and definite period, it is an indefinite hiring and is determinable at the will of either party, and in this respect there is no distinction between domestic and other servants. But when from the contract itself it is evident that it was the understanding of the parties that the time was to extend for a certain period, their understanding, fairly inferable from the contract, will control. Thus, if A agrees with B to work for him eight months for $104, or $13 a month, this will not only be treated as a contract for eight months' service, but also as an entire contract, performance of which is a condition precedent to a recovery of any portion of the wages, and in *all* cases where a definite term is fixed, the fact that the wages are to be so much a month, and no time is fixed for a payment of the wages, does not make the contract divisible, and full performance is a condition precedent to a recovery of wages. Thus, in one case, the defendant [*sic*] contracted to work for the defendant seven months, at $12 a month, and it was held an entire contract, and that no part of the wages could be recovered until the contract was fully performed, or performance is waived or prevented by the defendant. So where the contract is to work at so much a day for one month or any other period, or at so much a month for six months, no time being fixed for payment, full performance is a condition precedent to a right thereto.

NOTES

1. *Rate-of-Pay Rule.* Most employment contracts state the rate of pay in terms of hourly or weekly wages, or monthly or yearly salaries. Does the fact that a contract calls for a salary of $80,000 per year indicate that the parties intended the employment to last for at least that amount of time? If the employee continues working into the second year, would the yearly presumption continue for the second and subsequent years? Or should the period between actual payments be assumed to be the contract period? Although Wood firmly rejected the rate-of-pay rule, one can find many "yes" answers to these questions in the older cases, and the rule refuses to die completely.

Consider S.D. CODIFIED LAWS ANN. § 60-1-3: "The length of time which an employer and employee adopt for the estimation of wages is relevant to a determination of the term of employment."

---

[4] *De Briar v. Minturn,* 1 Cal. 450 (1851); *The Franklin Mining Co. v. Harris,* 24 Mich. 115 (1871); *Tatterson v. Suffolk Manuf. Co.,* 106 Mass. 56 (1870); *Wilder v. United States,* 5 Ct. Cl. 462 (1869); [citations of 2 English cases omitted].

In *Winograd v. Willis,* 789 S.W.2d 307, 309-10 (Tex. Ct. App. 1990), the letter "outlin[ing] our agreement regarding your employment" called for an annual salary of $52,000. In upholding a jury verdict of wrongful termination, the court said:

> Texas has long adhered to the employment at will doctrine which states that when the term of service is left to the discretion of either employer or employee, either of those parties may terminate the employment relationship at will and without cause. In the absence of special circumstances, however, Texas also follows the general rule practiced in England, which dictates that a hiring at a stated sum per week, month, or year, is a definite employment for the period named and may not be arbitrarily concluded.

The New Jersey Supreme Court rejected the rate-of-pay "feudal custom," allowing summary judgment against an employee fired after eight months who was promised compensation at $80,000 per year. The Court declared that the English view "was appropriate for the agrarian economy of medieval England, where the relationship between masters and servants was governed in part by seasonal and agricultural cycles. With the establishment of a market economy in the United States, there is no longer a need for rules based on feudal custom." *Bernard v. IMI Systems, Inc.,* 618 A.2d 338, 341 (N.J. 1993).

2. *Rejection of Quantum Meruit.* Wood clearly acknowledges that the parties can write a contract of a definite duration. He emphasizes the dangers to employees of such a contract. According to Wood and the cases he cites, an employee who works two months on a yearly contract and then leaves is not entitled to any wages. Wood thus rejects the ability of breaching employees to recover on a quantum meruit theory for the value of services actually performed. Today, state wage laws require frequent payment of wages (monthly, biweekly, or weekly) and payment for actual services.

3. *Sloppy Scholarship.* Horace Wood was a lawyer and prolific treatise writer from Albany, New York. A contemporary review of his Master and Servant treatise declared that "Mr. Wood obtained an excellent reputation as a learned, accurate, and original law author. . . . To bring order, simplicity and symmetry out of [the conflicting common law principles] was the work of a man of genius, and this we have before us." *Book Notice,* 15 ALBANY L.J. 378-79 (1877).

Later reviewers have not been so kind. Professor St. Antoine has described the employment-at-will rule as springing "full-blown in 1877 from [Wood's] busy and perhaps careless pen." Theodore J. St. Antoine, *You're Fired!,* 10 HUM. RTS. Q. 32, 33 (1982). *See also* Clyde Summers, *Individual Protection Against Unjust Dismissal: Time for a Statute,* 62 VA. L. REV. 481, 485 (1976) (the rule has "doubtful antecedents").

4. *Wood's Footnote 4.* In particular, scholars and courts often complain that the four American cases Wood cites in footnote 4 do not support the American rule. Professors Freed and Polsby have defended Wood, however, insisting that the four American cases "do indeed support the principle for which Wood cited them." Mayer G. Freed & Daniel D. Polsby, *The Doubtful Provenance of "Wood's Rule" Revisited,* 22 ARIZ. ST. L.J. 551, 554 (1990).

The problem is that the cases are not direct holdings for the employer's right to fire at any time. *Wilder v. United States* is not an employment case at all. A hauler (analogous to an employee?) contracted with the army to transport supplies for a certain rate of compensation, but for no definite duration. When Indian hostilities greatly increased the cost of transportation, the army agreed to the hauler's demand for a higher price. The army later refused to pay the higher price, but the court upheld the hauler's claim for the full price. In what way does this support an employer's right to fire at any time?

In *Franklin Mining Co.* and *Tatterson,* the appellate courts affirmed jury verdicts for employees with contracts calling for $1,800 per year and $2,000 per year, respectively, finding sufficient evidence for the jury to infer that the employment was for a definite duration. In what way are these cases consistent with Wood's Rule?

In *De Briar,* the case reads in full:

> The defendant was an innkeeper. He employed the plaintiff as a barkeeper, and was to give him three hundred dollars per month for his services, and allow him the privilege of occupying a room so long as he remained in the defendant's employ. The plaintiff was not hired for any definite period, and he was discharged by the defendant. After such discharge, the defendant notified the plaintiff to leave the room which he occupied, at the end of the month. The plaintiff did not comply with the notice, and the defendant put him out of the house by force; and this action is brought to recover damages for being thus ejected. The jury rendered a verdict in favor of the plaintiff for six hundred dollars.

> We do not see how any action can be maintained upon the facts presented. The plaintiff had no right to remain in the defendant's house after being notified to leave, and the defendant had a right to eject him. It does not appear that any more force was used than was necessary, or that the facts would warrant anything more than nominal damages, even if an action could be sustained at all. We think a new trial should be granted.

Is *De Briar* more consistent with Wood's Rule, with the English practice requiring an employer to give reasonable notice, or with a rate-of-pay presumption? The headnote to *De Briar* does state: "Where no definite period of employment is agreed upon between a master and servant, the master has a right to discharge the servant at any time. . . ." Perhaps this is a good illustration for the common warning that lawyers should not rely on headnotes when reading cases.

5. An Inflexible Rule. Horace Wood describes the American at-will rule as "inflexible." In what respect is it inflexible? Consider the following argument:

> The Wood formulation has been characterized as unduly rigid, in that it "force[s]" courts to ignore facts and circumstances indicative of the intention of the parties. But there is nothing "rigid" or inflexible about Wood's formulation. Wood does not suggest that it should be impermissible or even difficult for a plaintiff to prove that the parties intended

that the employment relationship would last for a certain length of time. All it says is that plaintiff has the burden of proving that a contract of employment with no express duration was nevertheless intended by the parties to continue for a fixed duration. Nothing in the rule forecloses a jury from considering all the facts and circumstances from which inferences might be drawn concerning what the contract had been.

Of course, that is the role of a presumption: to decide issues where facts are skimpy or absent; presumptions are not supposed to keep facts from being introduced into evidence, nor are they supposed to decide what "surrounding circumstances" may count as a fact.

Mayer G. Freed & Daniel D. Polsby, *The Doubtful Provenance of "Wood's Rule" Revisited,* 22 ARIZ. ST. L.J. 551, 553 (1990). *

6. *Profound Influence.* Wood's treatise has been credited with the quick spread of the employment-at-will rule throughout the United States. As Professor Feinman says:

Whatever its origin and the inadequacies of its explanation, Wood's rule spread across the nation until it was generally adopted. . . . It is possible, of course, to attribute too much influence to Wood himself. Seldom has one individual been able to shape the law so dramatically through a mere published, ill-supported statement, and this article argues that primary importance must be given to factors external to the law itself. But treatises were important to the bar and bench in this period; a modern, comprehensive treatise stating a clear rule of practical application would almost inevitably attract a wide following and be cited as authority. Wood's treatise alone could not have caused the change to employment at will, but without it, the rule would likely not have developed as quickly and as uniformly as it did.

Jay M. Feinman, *The Development of the Employment at Will Rule,* 20 AM. J. LEGAL HIST. 118, 126-27 (1976).

SANFORD M. JACOBY, THE DURATION OF INDEFINITE EMPLOYMENT CONTRACTS IN THE UNITED STATES AND ENGLAND: AN HISTORICAL ANALYSIS, 5 COMPARATIVE LABOR LAW JOURNAL 85, 116-18 (1982) **

Perhaps the most common explanation for the courts' embrace of the at-will doctrine was the rise of a formalistic approach to contract interpretation. The law focused narrowly on the contract to determine what the parties had intended. According to this logic, if the parties had intended the employment to last for a definite period they would have made that an express term of the contract. The at-will rule was the apotheosis of the laissez-faire conception of a contractual relation: The parties had a limited commitment to each other; they were free to enter or end a relation and define its terms without judicial interference. The period from 1890 to 1910, when the at-will rule became

---

preeminent, marked the zenith of laissez-faire reasoning by the courts. However, the explanation is not entirely convincing, since the at-will doctrine was at variance with the contractarian principle that the courts were supposed to give effect to the parties' manifest intentions.

The rigid presumption of terminability-at-will forced the courts to ignore evidence of the parties' intentions. In cases where the contract specified a rate of payment, a presumption of at-will terminability contradicted the parties' intentions that the relation should last as long as the period of payment. Strict contractarians like Williston argued that by ignoring the payment period, the

> courts had failed to observe that such a construction should, if possible, be put upon the language of the parties who enter into an agreement as will give rise to a legal obligation. [I]t seems a fair presumption that the parties intended the employment to last for at least one such period . . . and should the parties continue their relation after the expiration of the first period, another contract by implication of fact would arise for another similar period.[216]

Also, the at-will doctrine flatly contradicted contractarian logic in cases involving permanent employment contracts. The courts in most jurisdictions after 1890 held that contracts for "permanent" or "lifetime" employment were indefinite as to duration and thus terminable at will. Often the plaintiff had been promised permanent employment in return for dropping an injury claim against his employer. The parties clearly had intended that employment should continue as long as the employee remained able to perform his job. Holding such contracts to be indefinite and terminable at will was a negation of these intentions, an outcome that Williston also found unacceptable. English courts in the late nineteenth century considered these contracts to be perpetual in duration and enforceable, as did some American courts. But most American courts refused to enforce these contracts, which weakens the contractarian explanation for the doctrine.

JAY M. FEINMAN, THE DEVELOPMENT OF THE EMPLOYMENT AT WILL RULE, 20 AMERICAN JOURNAL OF LEGAL HISTORY 118, 131-33 (1976) *

I suggest an alternative explanation for the rise of the employment at will rule: that the rule was an adjunct to the development of advanced capitalism in America. . . .

The participants in the litigation that resulted in the change to Wood's rule were what could loosely be called middle-level employees and their employers. During a period when annual wages in the United States averaged considerably less than $1,000, many of the discharged employees bringing the duration of contract suits received salaries of several thousand dollars. . . . Typical positions held by these employees included corporate secretary, sales agent, attorney, plant superintendent, general manager and cashier, and chief building engineer.

---

[216] S. WILLISTON, [1 THE LAW OF CONTRACTS 62 (1920)].

* Reprinted with permission of American Journal of Legal History.

Of course, there had always been managers, sales agents, and factory superintendents better paid than average workers. But through the first half of the nineteenth century owners and managers of smaller businesses comprised the bulk of the commercial middle class. Enterprises were not usually impersonal; the managers were frequently the owners of the businesses. The primary identifying feature of the old middle group of workers was that most members had an "independent means of livelihood." As the century progressed and the scale of production increased, however, enterprises became larger and more impersonal and many workers became farther removed from ownership. There were still many independent business people, of course, but salaried employees with little control of their employment situation became a larger proportion of the work force and an important segment of the economy. Engineers, foremen, and the new specialists in the management of larger enterprises were an important component of the new economic system, but for the most part they had less control over their positions than many of their predecessors. Thus the many suits brought to establish interests in their jobs were an attempt by a newly-important group in the economy to apply a traditional doctrine to their new situation, but the courts rejected the attempt and instead announced the new principle of employment at will. The reasons for this lie in the class division fundamental to the capitalist system: the distinction between owners and non-owners of capital. The effects of this division are felt in the control of labor and the discharge of employees.

An essential component of a capitalist system is the labor market. The owner of capital — the employer — and the non-owner of capital — the employee — enter into a wage bargain by which the employer becomes entitled to the worker's labor for a certain period and all its fruits in exchange for the payment of wages. The benefit of the bargain to the employer arises essentially because the worker produces more than the wages paid; the benefit to the worker is that wage labor is his sole source of subsistence. A corollary of the wage bargain is that, because the employer has purchased the total effort of the employee for the period, authority over the manner of work and the workplace belongs to the employer, not the employee. In this way the employer can conform the work to the requirements of production, enforcing the most efficient division of labor, for example.

Employment at will is the ultimate guarantor of the capitalist's authority over the worker.[120] The rule transformed long-term and semi-permanent relationships into non-binding agreements terminable at will. If employees could be dismissed on a moment's notice, obviously they could not claim a voice in the determination of the conditions of work or the use of the product of their labor. Indeed, such a fleeting relationship is hardly a contract at all.

The change to Wood's rule takes on added significance when its specific target — middle managers — is considered. This newly-important economic group presented perhaps a greater potential threat to the dominance of the owners of capital than did common laborers. Educated, responsible, and increasingly numerous, the middle level managers and agents of enterprises

---

[120] Of course, the worker need not enter the wage bargain, or may do so only on favorable terms, but in practice most of the advantages in this regard belong to the purchasers, not the suppliers, of labor.

might have been expected to seek a greater share in the profits and direction of enterprises as the owners had to rely more heavily on them with the increasing size of business organizations. But the employment at will rule assured that as long as the employer desired it (and as long as the employee was not irreplaceable, which was seldom the case) the employee's relation to the enterprise would be precarious. An effective way to assert the owners' control and their right to management and profits and a clear division between owners and non-owners of capital was a legal declaration that the employees had no interest in the firm in the form of employment tenure or a right to a long period of notice. So the legal formula conformed to the economic necessities and to the beliefs of the owners in the existence of and the need for an industrial elite of owners of capital with absolute control of their businesses.

NOTE

Spread of the At-Will Rule. In a detailed empirical study of the adoption of the at-will rule by various states in the late nineteenth century, Professor Andrew Morriss attempted to shatter four myths about the rule's creation:

Myth 1: A treatise writer [Horace Wood] made up the employment at-will rule in 1877.

Fact: Employment at-will did not spring from "the busy and perhaps careless pen of an American treatise writer." The at-will rule was adopted by seven states before Horace Wood published his 1877 treatise, was present in the first draft of the proposed New York Civil Code drafted by David Dudley Field in 1862, and was included in the National Currency Act of 1863 for bank officers, as well as in earlier state banking statutes.

Myth 2: The at-will rule was the product of nineteenth century industrialization.

Fact: The pattern of adoption among states strongly suggests, and an empirical analysis confirms, that the at-will rule's spread was not linked to industrialization.

Myth 3: The at-will rule was the result of judicial class prejudice.

Fact: The at-will rule was adopted earlier in states where judicial class prejudice was less (the Midwest) and gained acceptance relatively late in states where judicial class prejudice was greater (New England).

Myth 4: The treatment of employment contracts in the United States was heavily biased against employees by the at-will rule, while European nations provided rules more favorable to employees.

Fact: The European civil law systems did not address the issue of indefinite employment contracts, while the United States' legal system treated employees more favorably than the British legal system in many respects.

Andrew P. Morriss, *Exploding Myths: An Empirical and Economic Reassessment of the Rise of Employment At-Will*, 59 Mo. L. Rev. 679, 681-82 (1994).

Central to Morriss's argument is a detailed empirical study of the timing of adoption of the at-will rule by various states. Maine (1851) and Mississippi (1858) were the first states to adopt the rule through the common law. In general, adoption of employment at will moved from the west to the south and midwest and only after several decades to the more industrialized northeast states. For example, Pennsylvania adopted the rule in 1891 and New York in 1895; those two states accounted for 1/5 to 1/3 of the entire American economy in 1890, depending on the measure used. One interesting finding of Morriss is that, even after controlling for measures of industrialization and political leanings, states whose supreme-court judges were popularly elected were significantly more likely to adopt the at-will rule. Assuming that elected judges are more responsive to middle-class interests than are appointed judges, this finding casts doubt on Feinman's argument that the at-will rule comes from the interests of capitalists in controlling middle managers.

The following run-of-the-mill case shows the severity with which courts applied the employment at will doctrine during its heyday.

SKAGERBERG v. BLANDIN PAPER CO.
Supreme Court of Minnesota
266 N.W. 872 (1936)

JULIUS J. OLSON, JUSTICE.

Defendant's general demurrer to plaintiff's amended complaint was sustained, and he appeals.

. . . .

Plaintiff is a consulting engineer, a specialist in the field of heating, ventilating, and air conditioning. As such he had developed a clientele bringing him a weekly income of approximately $200.

Defendant operates a paper manufacturing plant at Grand Rapids, this state. It had employed plaintiff in his professional capacity in 1926 and again in 1930. He was paid at the rate of $200 per week while so employed. Defendant was planning extensive enlargements of its plant, the estimated expense being about $1,000,000. Ordinarily a consulting engineer's fees for doing the necessary planning and supervision of the contemplated improvements would involve from $35,000 to $50,000. During plaintiff's employment in 1930 there was some discussion between the parties with respect of plaintiff's employment to take this work in hand. At that time, too, he was negotiating with the executive officers of Purdue University relative to taking a position as associate professor in its department of engineering, particularly that branch thereof relating to heating, ventilating, and air conditioning.

The Purdue position carried a salary of $3,300 per year and required only nine months' work in the way of instructions. This would leave plaintiff free to continue his practice as a consulting engineer during a period of three months of each calendar year. He was also privileged, if he entered that position, to continue his practice as a consulting engineer at all times in so far as his professional work at the university permitted him so to do. In addition thereto, he was privileged to contribute to engineering magazines and other publications. All income from such outside engagements was to be his in addition to the stated salary. Plaintiff considered this opportunity as one especially attractive to him. Defendant had full knowledge of all the foregoing facts.

On October 13, 1930, plaintiff, having received a telegram from Purdue University offering him the position and requiring immediate acceptance or rejection thereof, at once called an officer of defendant over the long-distance telephone informing him of the offer and the necessity on his part of making immediate response thereto. Defendant's officer agreed that if plaintiff would reject the Purdue offer and also agree to purchase the home of defendant's power superintendent, it would give plaintiff permanent employment at a salary of $600 per month. Relying thereon, plaintiff rejected the Purdue offer and immediately thereafter moved to Grand Rapids and there entered upon the performance of his duties under this arrangement. He later entered into a contract for the purchase of the superintendent's home. Appropriate to note is the fact that these negotiations were entirely oral and over the long-distance telephone, plaintiff being at Minneapolis and defendant's officer at Grand Rapids. The only writing between the parties is a letter written on October 14, 1930, reading thus:

Blandin Paper Co., Grand Rapids, Minn.

Attention: Mr. C. K. Andrews.

Gentlemen: In accordance with our conversation yesterday when our agreement was settled regarding my position with your company, I have wired Purdue rejecting their offer. Under the circumstances it was impossible for us to get together on a written agreement: I had to wire Purdue at once. However, I am making this move on the assumption that there will be no difficulty in working out our agreement when I get up to Grand Rapids.

Propositions like the one Purdue made are very rare and I am turning it down since I feel that the opportunities with you for applying my past experience are very attractive, the essential consideration being, however, that the job will be a permanent one.

According to the understanding we have, I am to take over Mr. Kull's duties as Power Superintendent and serve also as Mechanical Engineer for your plant, supervising the mechanical construction and maintenance work and other mechanical technical matters. Mr. Kull is to remain for long enough period, about six months, to permit me to get my work organized and get acquainted with the details of his work. If the proposed new construction work is started within that time it may develop that Mr. Kull may remain until that is completed after which he will leave and I take over his duties. As an accommodation to him when he leaves town I am to purchase his house.

My salary is to be six hundred dollars ($600.00) per month and you are to pay my moving expenses to Grand Rapids.

Very truly yours,

RS/m R. Skagerberg.

Plaintiff rendered the services for which he was thus engaged "dutifully, faithfully and to the complete satisfaction of the defendant and was paid the agreed salary, except as to a voluntary reduction, up to September 1, 1932," when, so the complaint alleges, he was "wrongfully, unlawfully and wilfully" discharged from further employment, although "ready, willing and able to perform." By reason of the alleged breach of contract he claims to have suffered general damages in the amount of $25,000, and for this he prays judgment.

From what has been stated it is clear that the issue raised by the demurrer is simply this: Do the allegations set forth in the complaint show anything more than employment of plaintiff by defendant subject to termination at the will of either party?

1. The words "permanent employment" have a well-established meaning in the law. The general rule is well stated in 18 R.C.L. p. 509, § 20: "In case the parties to a contract of service expressly agree that the employment shall be 'permanent' the law implies, not that the engagement shall be continuous or for any definite period, but that the term being indefinite the hiring is merely at will." . . .

2. The difficult question presented is whether the allegations set forth in the complaint bring this case within an exception to the rule stated. We find in 18 R.C.L. p. 510, the following statement: "Under some circumstances, however, 'permanent' employment will be held to contemplate a continuous engagement to endure as long as the employer shall be engaged in business and have work for the employee to do and the latter shall perform the service satisfactorily. This seems to be the established rule in case the employee purchases the employment with a valuable consideration outside the services which he renders from day to day."

Plaintiff cites and relies upon [several cases.] In *Carnig v. Carr,* 46 N.E. 117 (Mass. 1897), plaintiff had been engaged in business for himself as an enameler. Defendant was a business competitor. Being such, and for his own advantage, defendant persuaded plaintiff to give up his business and sell his stock in trade to him. As consideration, in part at least, for entering into this arrangement, defendant agreed to employ plaintiff permanently at a stated salary, his work for defendant being the same as that in which plaintiff had been engaged. It is clear that what defendant sought and accomplished was to get rid of his competitor in business upon a promise on his part to give plaintiff permanent employment. The resulting situation amounted to the same thing in substance and effect as if plaintiff had purchased his job. Under such circumstances there can be no doubt that the exception to the general rule was properly invoked and applied and furnishes an illustration thereof.

In *Pierce v. Tennessee Coal, Iron & Railroad Co.,* 173 U.S. 1 (1899), plaintiff had received an injury while employed by defendant. To settle the difficulty defendant promised employment to plaintiff at certain stated wages and was also to furnish certain supplies as long as his disability to do full work continued by reason of his injury. In consideration for these promises plaintiff released the company from all liability for damages on account of the injuries which caused his disability. Here, too, it is clear that plaintiff purchased from defendant his employment. There are many such cases.

[The court then discusses several other cases.]

3. Plaintiff maintains that four different items of consideration entered into the contract relied upon (in addition to the promised service to be rendered) namely: (1) The rejection of the Purdue offer; (2) the agreement to purchase the superintendent's house; (3) that plaintiff gave up an established business; and (4) that defendant saved the commission that it otherwise would have to pay engineers on new construction work.

Plaintiff obviously could not accept both the Purdue and the defendant's offer. It was for him to take one or the other. He could not possibly serve both masters.

A man capable of earning $600 per month necessarily must be possessed of both learning and experience in his particular line of endeavor. The fact that he was able to command such salary at the time of entering into defendant's service is convincing proof that there must be more than one person or enterprise seeking his talents and services. If plaintiff had elected to go to Purdue and, after having been there employed the same length of time as he was by defendant, was then discharged, does it follow that he could successfully sue Purdue University upon the same theory that he is here making a basis for liability against defendant? We have found no case fitting into plaintiff's claim in this regard.

What has been said in respect of the Purdue opportunity applies with equal force to the third point raised by plaintiff. His capacity as a specialist in his line of endeavor had built up for him a lucrative practice. That practice he could not take with him when he entered defendant's employment. Is not this exactly what every person having any line of employment must do when he seeks and obtains another? If plaintiff had been engaged in the practice of the law and as such had established a clientele bringing the same income and had later taken on a contract to act for a corporate enterprise at a fixed salary of $600 per month upon the same basis as here, do his counsel think, in virtue of the well-established rules of applicable law, that he would have a lifetime job? Would not counsel have insisted upon a more definite agreement than that relied upon here? . . .

With regard to purchase of the superintendent's house, note should be made that in plaintiff's letter written the day following the alleged making of the contract . . . [i]t is difficult to find anything in this language indicating a consideration for, going to, or in any way benefiting defendant to induce it to enter into such contract. Plaintiff's own statement is that "as an accommodation to him [Kull] when he leaves town I am to purchase his house." How this could be of any material interest to or concern of defendant in view of plaintiff's own letter and stipulation is not apparent. Nowhere in the complaint is there any allegation that the purchase of the house from the superintendent in any way benefited defendant or damaged plaintiff. A man in plaintiff's position would necessarily be interested in acquiring a place of abode upon leaving Minneapolis for Grand Rapids. In the very nature of his requirements, he entered into the purchase for his own use and accommodation rather than for any benefit to or advantage of defendant. Nowhere is there any suggestion that defendant was to furnish him with a place of abode or do anything whatever in respect of finding or providing such.

Lastly, we come to plaintiff's claim that he rendered professional services in the construction work worth much more than his stipulated monthly salary. By referring to his letter, it is obvious that that was one of the things he was to take in hand and upon the basis of payment mentioned in the letter. He received that compensation during the time of his employment. He was paid the stipulated price according to his own version of the agreement.

The order sustaining defendant's demurrer is affirmed.

NOTES

1. *The Consideration Requirement.* Professor Clyde Summers insists that the courts misapply the consideration requirement in employment-at-will cases:

> Another spurious contractual doctrine, sometimes used as an exception to the mutuality doctrine and sometimes used independently, was that to overcome the presumption that employment for an indefinite term was employment at will the employee must give some additional consideration. Coming to work, even working for a number of years, was not consideration for a promise of future employment. An employee must give something more. Why something more than faithful service was required was never clearly explained. There seemed to be an assumption that because wages for work performed had been paid, the work could not be consideration for a promise of continued employment. As any first semester law student knows, however, one performance can be consideration to support two or even twenty promises. The work performed could be consideration for both the wages paid and the promise of future employment. The requirement of additional consideration was but a device for converting Wood's presumption into a substantive rule so that even an express promise of permanent employment would not bind the employer.

> The employment at will doctrine is cast in contract language, but it has no basis in contract law. The courts have not asked the basic contract question — what did the parties intend? Both the overloaded presumption and the superimposed spurious doctrines led the courts away from an inquiry into what the parties, as reasonable persons, understood or intended. It led to the anti-contract incantation that in the absence of a specified term the employment was at will, regardless whether that fit the parties' intent in entering and continuing the employment relationship.

Clyde W. Summers, *The Contract of Employment and the Rights of Individual Employees: Fair Representation and Employment at Will*, 52 FORDHAM L. REV. 1082, 1098-99 (1984).*

---

* Reprinted with permission of Fordham Law Review.

2. *Mutuality of Obligation.* Related to the consideration requirement is the notion that contracts must have mutual obligations. Courts sometimes used the mutuality doctrine to defeat employee claims against at-will employment. A typical case is *Meadows v. Radio Industries, Inc.*, 222 F.2d 347, 348-49 (7th Cir. 1955), where the employee had claimed that the employer promised to employ him until the project he was working on was completed. The court, applying Illinois law, refused to enforce the promise, reasoning:

> It is well settled in Illinois that whenever a contract is incapable of being enforced against one party, that party is equally incapable of enforcing it against the other. . . . "Mutuality of obligation means that both parties are bound or neither [is] bound. In other words there must be a valid consideration. Without a valid consideration, a contract cannot be enforced in law or in equity." . . .
>
> In the present case, a careful examination of the record discloses that there was not the slightest bit of evidence that plaintiff ever agreed that he would continue in the employment of defendant for any specified time. In other words, he had a right to terminate his employment at any time and did not promise to perform for any definite length of time. Therefore, the contract could not have been enforced against him and was lacking in mutuality. Consequently, he cannot enforce it against defendant.

3. *Mutuality of Obligation and the Constitution.* During the *Lochner* era, the Supreme Court raised the doctrine of mutuality to constitutional status. In *Adair v. United States,* 208 U.S. 161 (1908), the Supreme Court declared unconstitutional a federal statute prohibiting an employer from discharging a worker for being a union member. The Court, per Justice Harlan, reasoned:

> The right of a person to sell his labor upon such terms as he deems proper is, in its essence, the same as the right of the purchaser of labor to prescribe the conditions upon which he will accept such labor from the person offering to sell it. So the right of the employee to quit the service of the employer, for whatever reason, is the same as the right of the employer, for whatever reason, to dispense with the services of such employee. It was the legal right of the defendant Adair — however unwise such a course might have been — to discharge Coppage because of his being a member of a labor organization, as it was the legal right of Coppage, if he saw fit to do so — however unwise such a course on his part might have been — to quit the service in which he was engaged, because the defendant employed some persons who were not members of a labor organization. In all such particulars the employer and the employee have equality of right, and any legislation that disturbs that equality is an arbitrary interference with the liberty of contract which no government can legally justify in a free land.

208 U.S. at 174-75. The Court acknowledged that "if the parties by contract fix the period of service, and prescribe the conditions upon which the contract may be terminated, such contract would control the rights of the parties as

between themselves, and for any violation of those provisions the party wronged would have his appropriate civil action." *Id.* at 175.

4. *Mutuality of Obligation in Contract Law.* Consider the following:

> The doctrine of mutuality is as spurious contract law as it is misguided constitutional law. Contracts require only exchanged consideration, not mutual obligations. The employee, by coming to work, provides sufficient consideration to make the employer's promise of continued or permanent employment binding. An offer by an employer to employ so long as there is a need and the employee's performance is satisfactory can be viewed as an offer of a unilateral contract, irrevocable after the employee's performance is begun even though there may be no duty of the employee to continue. Mutuality of obligation, particularly in the form of mirrored obligations as required by the courts in these cases, has never been considered essential to make promises binding. The effect of requiring mutuality was to convert the presumption into the substantive rule that unless the employee bound himself to work for a stated term, the employment must be at will. It was impossible for an employee, by accepting employment, to bind the employer to continue the employment so long as the employee was needed and his work was satisfactory.

Clyde W. Summers, *The Contract of Employment and the Rights of Individual Employees: Fair Representation and Employment at Will,* 52 FORDHAM L. REV. 1082, 1098 (1984).

Chapter 4

CONTRACT EROSIONS OF EMPLOYMENT AT WILL

Many employment contracts are informal. The parties often say little about their expectations down the road, limiting themselves to an understanding of the basic terms of pay and the basic job description. The contracts often are not in writing, and employees often respond to an offer of employment, not by words, but by beginning to work.

After the employee is later terminated, courts are asked to fill the gaps in the contract. The presumption of employment at will can be seen as the courts' attempt to fill the gap: unless the parties state otherwise, the employer can discharge the employee for a good reason, bad reason, or no reason at all.

Courts and scholars have developed two basic methods for filling in contractual gaps. First, courts can attempt to determine how the parties would have decided the issue had they focused on the question. This approach is sometimes characterized as "mimicking the market," for it asks whether the employer values the flexibility in dismissal more than employees value job security, and assumes the parties would have contracted for whichever clause is valued more highly.

The second method attempts to create a default rule whereby the parties are encouraged to reveal their true valuations. Consider a job applicant negotiating the terms of the employment contract: if the presumption is at will, the applicant must indicate that he or she prefers job security. Is it likely that the applicant will do this? What kind of adverse signals would an applicant send by asking detailed questions about how the firm gets rid of marginal employees? On the other hand, if the presumption is dismissal for just cause, the employer must get the employee to waive this presumption if it prefers employment at will. Will the employee be likely to waive a just-cause requirement?

In Section A, we examine cases where the parties have (at least arguably) expressly modified the at-will presumption. As cases like *Skagerberg* indicate, in the heyday of employment at will, courts were extremely reluctant to find that the parties had modified the at-will relationship. Courts today seem more willing to do so.

In Section B, we examine actions, rather than words, that may alter the at-will relationship. In Section C, we look at the issues surrounding statements of job security in employee handbooks and the legal effect of an employer's assertion in a manual that the relationship is at will.

A. EXPRESS MODIFICATION OF AT-WILL CONTRACTS, WRITTEN AND ORAL

CHIODO v. GENERAL WATERWORKS CORP.
Supreme Court of Utah
413 P.2d 891 (1966)

CROCKETT, JUSTICE.

The plaintiff, Vincent Chiodo, sued for breach of a contract which employed him for a period of ten years as the manager of the defendant, Bear River Telephone Company, when he was discharged after three years. Defendant seeks to justify its action upon the grounds: (1) that plaintiff was guilty of insubordination and insolence to his superior; (2) that he cheated the company in certain payroll practices; and (3) that he was disloyal. Upon trial to the court it found the issues in favor of the plaintiff and rendered judgment for his salary for the remaining seven years, discounted for payment in cash, in the sum of $81,264.99, plus $6,500 owing on a retirement policy. Defendant appeals.

In 1943, the plaintiff acquired the Bear River Telephone Company, located at Tremonton, Utah, which serves principally Box Elder County in the northwest quadrant of the state. Due to the industrial development attendant upon World War II, particularly because of Thiokol Chemical Corporation, there was a rapid increase in population and business in that area. Under the plaintiff's management the [Bear River Telephone Company] prospered and expanded the number of telephones from about 700 to over 5,000. Because of continued increasing demands and inadequate capital, he decided to sell. After negotiations he accepted an offer from defendant General Waterworks to convey to them for shares of that company upon certain conditions. One of them was that they agreed to employ him as manager of Bear River Telephone Company for ten years at a salary of $12,000 per year. The pertinent language of their letter is thus:

> In accordance with the understanding and agreement, which we have arrived at, *your employment by Bear River is to continue for a period of ten years from the date hereof.* . . . Nothing in this letter agreement, however, shall be held to preclude your continuing employment by Bear River after such ten-year period.

Under a contract of employment for a stated term it is to be assumed that the parties intended that the employee would conform to the usual standards expected of an employee, and that he would render honest, faithful and loyal service in accordance with his ability. If there is a wilful and substantial failure to adhere to those standards it would be justifiable cause for the employer to discharge him. The question of moment here is whether the plaintiff's conduct constituted such justifiable cause for his discharge.

Inasmuch as the contract for plaintiff's employment stated nothing with respect to standards of his conduct, nor of his possible discharge, the trial court properly received evidence relating to the negotiations of the parties which resulted in the contract to determine their intent with respect to these questions. Some of these discussions between plaintiff and defendant (its Vice President, A.W. Sanders) had been recorded and were presented in evidence:

"Mr. Chiodo: I don't want to have this thing [employment contract] come up here with me. I want it tied down so that there's no question about it, *and you decide to fire me, that you're going to pay my $500.00 every two weeks for ten years.*

"Mr. Sanders: My opinion of this is that we can't fire you for ten years. That is what Hansen [defendant's attorney] tells me. . . .

"Mr. Chiodo: Yes, but I can't write myself a check for $500.00 on payday if you refuse to sign the check; then what? I'm fired right?

"Mr. Sanders: No, I'm no attorney, of course, but the attorneys tell me this is all your way. We can't do anything. . . .

"Mr. Sanders: No. As you and I discussed it before, we're going to let you run the property as you see fit."

In an attempt to justify its discharge of the plaintiff the defendant makes these accusations:

Payroll Padding:

(1) That the plaintiff had his adult son, Don Chiodo, on the defendant's payroll while he was working for a construction company in Montana;

(2) That two of plaintiff's sons at various times between July 1961, and December 1962, used other employees of the defendant to do work which the sons had contracted to do for defendant on a fixed-fee-basis, which they received;

(3) That plaintiff improperly had his 14-year-old granddaughter on the payroll and paid her $354.20.

Insubordination:

(1) That the plaintiff refused to obey orders to cancel a policy of insurance on defendant's properties;

(2) That plaintiff told employees of the defendant that certain of defendant's officers were incompetent.

Disloyalty:

That he breached confidence by telling the Public Service Commission of Utah that General Waterworks was trying to sell the company to Mountain States Telephone & Telegraph Company; and that he was himself interested in repurchasing the company.

It is interesting, almost amazing, at times to see how human minds with their own interests to serve see pictures as either black or white and fail to discern and recognize the shadings and the grays. The accusations against plaintiff as stated by the defendant seem impressive, and there appears to be some truth in each, but that does not paint the whole picture as it is filled out by the plaintiff's evidence as to his answers:

Payroll Padding:

(1) The son, Don Chiodo, had worked for defendant during his vacation, had done extensive night work for it on his own time, for which he had not been

paid. In order to make up for this, the plaintiff had kept him on the defendant's payroll during a period of nine days while he was in Montana.

(2) The charge that the defendant's employees were used to perform work on the Don and Gene Chiodo subcontract: Mr. Sanders, the Vice President, who arranged for the work to be done on the contract, knew and agreed that some of defendant's employees would have to be used to perform some of the technical work. The employees who testified stated on cross-examination that they did not know whether the work done by them was included under the Chiodo's sub-contract or not.

(3) Payment to the 14-year-old granddaughter: The plaintiff had for some years followed a policy of determining what the mailing of telephone directories would cost, then permitting employees, including sometimes members of his family, to have the same amount of money for personally delivering them, which work was done by the granddaughter and she was compensated for it.

Insubordination:

(1) Plaintiff admits refusing to follow the directive to cancel a policy of insurance covering properties of the defendant. He had purchased the policy on the basis of bids submitted; under the circumstances felt a moral obligation not to cancel it; thought it was a good policy, necessary for the protection it afforded; and that it was within his prerogative as manager to keep it in force. When he refused to cancel it and so advised the defendant's main office, nothing more was said about the matter until this action was brought over 20 months later.

(2) What he said about the incompetency of certain of defendant's officers was true.

Disloyalty:

In informing the Public Service Commission of pending negotiations for sale, he was keeping faith with the Commission because he had assisted in the transfer of the franchise to defendant by making personal assurances that General Waterworks was not purchasing for purposes of speculation, but with bona fide intention of continuing the operation of the defendant company. He felt that the latter's disregard of the representations made justified his advising the Commission and indicating a willingness to repurchase the company himself.

There were other accusations of less consequence, generally similar to those recited above both in character and in explanation, which we need not detail. For the most part they can be characterized as disagreements between defendant's officers and plaintiff which he insists were provoked by their own mistakes and their continual attempts to interfere with his management.

The decisive answer to defendant's arguments about the matters above recited is that the trial court was persuaded in accordance with the plaintiff's contentions. It is true that some of his remarks in discussing the case could be interpreted as reflecting doubt as to his views on certain of the evidence, and as to the standards of honesty and integrity applied to the plaintiff. But the overall view taken appears to be this: that although the plaintiff's conduct may not have been exemplary in all respects, he had been a good manager as evidenced by the fact that the operation of the company had been profitable under his leadership; and that after friction developed between him and other officers of the company as to various aspects of the management, the latter sought to dredge up accusations of misconduct to justify discharging him. But his explanations of whatever irregularities may have existed were sufficiently reasonable and acceptable under the circumstances that the defendant failed to meet its burden of showing justification for his discharge. . . .

Judgment affirmed.

HENRIOD, C.J., and MCDONOUGH, WADE and CALLISTER, JJ., concur.

NOTES

1. *Firing Employees During Definite-Term Contracts.* This contract was for a specific term — ten years. Do the negotiations between Chiodo and the Telephone Company indicate they thought Chiodo could be fired, even for cause, during the term? Is it reasonable for a court to imply a clause allowing employers to fire employees for cause during a definite-term contract? If so, does a definite-term contract provide any protection for an employee that a just-cause indefinite-term contract would not? Could Chiodo have been terminated if, during a severe recession, the company was losing money?

2. *Moral Hazard.* If an employee is absolutely protected from discharge regardless of his behavior, is he likely to work hard and honestly? He has little incentive to do so. Economists would call this a "moral hazard" problem. When people are fully insured or protected against a bad event (in this case, little work being done), they have little reason to exert effort to see that the bad event does not take place.

Because the employee might shirk if fully protected against discharge for laziness or theft, one would expect that parties who expressly considered the issue would agree that the employee could be fired for cause, even in a definite-term contract. Is this sufficient reason for the law to imply a right to fire for cause when a definite-term contract is silent on the issue? Or should employers be required to obtain an express right-to-fire clause if they agree to hire for a specific term or else suffer the consequences of a shirking employee? This penalty default would encourage employers explicitly to notify employees that they want the right to fire for cause.

3. *Terminations for Business Downturns.* Suppose an employee has a definite-term contract, but the company decides during the term to abolish the position because of adverse business conditions. Does the employee have a breach of contract claim, or does the employer's implied right to terminate for cause include terminations for business downturns? *See Grappone v. City of Miami Beach*, 495 So. 2d 838 (Fla. Ct. App. 1986) (employer bound by its promises); *Helberg v. Community Work & Dev. Ctr. Indus., Inc.*, No. CX-93-958, 1994 WL 1121 (Minn. Ct. App. Jan. 4, 1994) (president who demanded twelve-month contract because of employer's financial hardship is entitled to compensation when discharged after four months).

4. *Statutory Right to Terminate.* The South Dakota legislature has codified the employer's right to terminate for cause during a definite-term contract with the following standard:

> An employment even for a specified term may be terminated at any time by the employer for habitual neglect of duty or continued incapacity to perform or any willful breach of duty by the employee in the course of his employment.

S.D. CODIFIED LAWS ANN. § 60-4-5. *See also* CAL. LAB. CODE § 2924.

5. *Meaning of Just Cause.* Just cause as applied in a particular case is a notoriously slippery concept. A rich body of arbitral decisions has developed determining when employers may fire union workers protected by just cause provisions in collective bargaining agreements. Professors Abrams and Nolan have synthesized these decisions with the following criteria:

A.   Just cause for discipline exists only when an employee has failed to meet his obligations under the fundamental understanding of the employment relationship. The employee's general obligation is to provide satisfactory work. Satisfactory work has four components:

   1.   Regular attendance.

   2.   Obedience to reasonable work rules.

   3.   A reasonable quality and quantity of work.

   4.   Avoidance of conduct, either at or away from work, which would interfere with the employer's ability to carry on the business effectively.

B.   For there to be just cause, the discipline must further one or more of management's three legitimate interests:

   1.   Rehabilitation of a potentially satisfactory employee.

   2.   Deterrence of similar conduct, either by the disciplined employee or by other employees.

   3.   Protection of the employer's ability to operate the business successfully.

C.   The concept of just cause includes certain employee protections that reflect the union's interest in guaranteeing "fairness" in disciplinary situations.

   1.   The employee is entitled to *industrial due process.* This includes:

      a.   actual or constructive notice of expected standards of conduct and penalties for wrongful conduct;

      b.   a decision based on facts, determined after an investigation that provides the employee an opportunity to state his case, with union assistance if he desires it;

      c.   the imposition of discipline in gradually increasing degrees, except in cases involving the most extreme breaches of the fundamental understanding. In particular, discharge may be imposed only when less severe penalties will not protect legitimate management interests, for one of the following reasons: (1) the employee's past record shows that the unsatisfactory conduct will continue, (2) the most stringent form of discipline is needed to protect the system of work rules, or (3) continued employment would inevitably interfere with the successful operation of the business; and

   d.   proof by management that just cause exists.

2.   The employee is entitled to *industrial equal protection*, which requires like treatment of like cases.

3.   The employee is entitled to *individualized treatment*. Distinctive facts in the employee's record or regarding the reason for discipline must be given appropriate weight.

Roger I. Abrams & Dennis R. Nolan, *Toward a Theory of "Just Cause" in Employee Discipline Cases,* 1985 DUKE L.J. 594, 611-12.[*]

6. *Employee Quitting During Term.* Should an employee who quits during a definite-term contract be liable for breach of contract? Or should the court imply that the employee may quit for good cause, just as the employer may fire during the term for good cause? In the principal case, did Chiodo agree to work for ten years?

The issue of employee breach arises with school-teacher contracts, which often are for one year. In *Handicapped Children's Education Board v. Lukaszewski,* 332 N.W.2d 774 (Wis. 1983), a speech therapist signed a contract to teach the following school year in a town forty-five miles from her home. In August, shortly before the school year was to begin, she was offered a teaching job with a twenty percent higher salary in her home town, meaning she no longer had to commute long distances to work. She attempted to resign from her first job, but the School Board sued for breach of contract. The court found her liable for the extra salary the school board paid for a replacement teacher, but indicated she would not have been liable had she resigned for a legitimate medical reason.

In another case, a wholesale broker agreed to work under new management for two years at an annual salary of $68,500, but quit after one year for a better opportunity. *See Equity Insurance Managers v. McNichols,* 755 N.E.2d 75 (Ill. App. Ct. 2001). The court upheld an arbitrator's award for breach of contract, holding the employee liable for the employer's lost profits of $91,000. The arbitrator rejected the employee's claim that the changed conditions of her employment (including increased hours, taking work home, working Sundays, and sexist treatment) created intolerable working conditions amounting to a constructive discharge by the employer.

HETES v. SCHEFMAN & MILLER LAW OFFICE
Court of Appeals of Michigan
393 N.W.2d 577 (1986)

Before Cynar, P.J., and Wahls and E.E. Borradaile, JJ.

Per Curiam.

Plaintiff appeals as of right from a circuit court order granting summary disposition of plaintiff's complaint for breach of an oral employment contract.

Plaintiff was employed as a receptionist for defendant law firm from September, 1983, until May, 1984. Plaintiff did not enter into a written contract. At the time of her hire, the law firm gave plaintiff an office manual which outlined employee duties and responsibilities. The manual did not specify termination procedures. In addition, plaintiff had at least two conversations with representatives of the law firm prior to assuming the receptionist position. Plaintiff testified in her deposition that, in both conversations, she was assured that "I had a job as long as I did a good job."

Plaintiff was discharged from employment on May 9, 1984. The circumstances surrounding her discharge are in dispute. In August, 1984, plaintiff filed a complaint alleging that defendants had breached the employment contract by failing to pay plaintiff's hospitalization benefits and by terminating plaintiff's employment in bad faith and without just cause. . . .

The trial court granted defendants' motion for summary judgment on the basis that plaintiff's deposition testimony established that plaintiff had a "satisfaction" contract and could be terminated at any time without just cause. Plaintiff argues on appeal that the defendants' assurances that she would have a job as long as she "did a good job" constituted an oral promise that she not be discharged except for just cause and that the lower court erred in summarily dismissing her claim. . . .

In *Toussaint v. Blue Cross & Blue Shield of Michigan*, 292 N.W.2d 880, 885 (Mich. 1980), the Supreme Court held that:

> "1) a provision of an employment contract providing that an employee shall not be discharged except for cause is legally enforceable although the contract is not for a definite term — the term is 'indefinite,' and

> "2) such a provision may become part of the contract either by express agreement, oral or written, or as a result of an employee's legitimate expectations grounded in an employer's policy statements."

The oral representations relied upon in *Toussaint* and *Ebling v. Masco Corp.*, its companion case, are almost identical to those given to plaintiff in the present case. Moreover, in both cases, the Court decided that, based on the representations, juries could conclude that the defendant companies had entered into express agreements to discharge Toussaint and Ebling only for cause. We believe that a jury could reach a similar conclusion in the present case.

Here, defendants' representatives orally assured plaintiff that she would remain employed as long as she did a good job. Contrary to the lower court's finding, a jury could reasonably have construed the oral representations as a promise to discharge only for good or just cause. Therefore, the questions of whether plaintiff's contract included a termination for just cause provision and whether she was terminated in breach of the oral contract were for the jury and summary judgment was improperly granted on this basis. . . .

Reversed in part and affirmed in part.

NOTES

1. *Satisfaction, Good Faith, and Just Cause.* An employer's promise that it will provide employment "as long as I am satisfied with your work" is sometimes termed a satisfaction contract. Many courts assume that an employer could never breach such a contract, because the fact of firing shows the employer is no longer satisfied. Is such a contract any different from an at-will contract?

A few courts imply a good-faith obligation on the employer for such a contract, so that the employee might show breach of contract by showing the employer was not "in good faith" dissatisfied with the employee's job performance. In *Hetes*, however, the court interpreted the employer's statement as a promise not to terminate without just cause. The distinction between good faith and just cause is that between a subjective and objective standard.

2. *Casual Words of Encouragement.* Most employees have received encouraging words from a supervisor like "you have a future with this company," or "keep up the good work and we'll look after you." Under the reasoning of *Hetes,* may such employees have their dismissal reviewed by a jury? *See, e.g., Forman v. BRI Corp.,* 532 F. Supp. 49 (E.D. Pa. 1982) (applying Pennsylvania law) (statement in interview that job was good one in which to "stay and grow," and that employer was concerned applicant would take job and "not stay" was sufficient to overcome presumption of employment at will).

3. *Retreat in Michigan.* In *Rowe v. Montgomery Ward & Co.,* 473 N.W.2d 268 (1991), the Michigan Supreme Court reversed a judgment on a jury verdict of $86,500 for an eight-year salesperson fired for being absent from the store for four hours without explanation. When the salesperson had applied for the job, the sales manager told her that "*generally*, as long as *they* generated sales and were honest [commissioned salespersons] had a job at Wards. [A]bout the only way that you could be terminated would be if you failed to make your draw." When hired, the employee signed a "Rules of Personal Conduct" form that enumerated four reasons for immediate discharge.

In finding for the employer, the Court distinguished *Toussaint*, emphasizing that the *Toussaint* employees had applied for singular, executive job positions, had several interviews with top company officials, and had inquired about job security. The Court also emphasized that in *Rowe* the sales manager's words (italicized above) were couched in general terms. The court also emphasized that nothing in the Rules of Personal Conduct suggested that the enumerated conduct was the only basis for dismissal.

After *Rowe*, can low-level employees like Hetes get to a jury in Michigan?

4. *Firing At-Will Employees for Pretextual Reasons.* Suppose an employee concedes she is working under an at-will contract, but claims that the employer's stated reason for firing her (*e.g.,* dishonesty) is false. Must the employer give the employee an opportunity to rebut the charges? *Compare Ferrett v. General Motors Corp.,* 475 N.W.2d 243, 248 (Mich. 1991) (holding that there is "no right arising at common law as a matter of public policy, separate and distinct from any contractual right, to be evaluated or correctly evaluated before being discharged from employment."), *with Prout v. Sears, Roebuck & Co.,* 772 P.2d 288, 292 (Mont. 1989) (holding that the at-will relationship, while giving the employer the right to fire without cause, does "not give the employer the right to fire for a false cause. If the at-will employer who can fire without cause . . . chooses instead to fire an employee for dishonesty, the discharged employee must be given the opportunity to prove the charge of dishonesty false.")

5. *Probationary Periods.* Many employment contracts expressly provide for a short probationary period, during which the employee can be dismissed for any reason. Does such a contract imply that an employee who has survived the probationary period can be dismissed only for cause? Most courts have held that probationary periods are consistent with an implied at-will relationship after probation is over. A few courts have held that a probationary period is evidence that the parties intended greater job protection later. *See, e.g., Washington Welfare Ass'n v. Wheeler,* 496 A.2d 613 (D.C. 1985).

OHANIAN v. AVIS RENT A CAR SYSTEM, INC.
United States Court of Appeals, Second Circuit
779 F.2d 101 (1985)

Before KEARSE and CARDAMONE, CIRCUIT JUDGES, and WYATT, DISTRICT JUDGE.

CARDAMONE, CIRCUIT JUDGE:

Defendant Avis Rent A Car System (Avis) appeals from a judgment entered on a jury verdict in the Eastern District of New York (Weinstein, Ch. J.) awarding $304,693 in damages to plaintiff Robert S. Ohanian for lost wages and pension benefits arising from defendant's breach of a lifetime employment contract made orally to plaintiff. . . . Avis argues that the alleged oral contract is barred by the statute of frauds, is inadmissible under the parol evidence rule and, in any event, that the evidence is insufficient to establish a promise of lifetime employment. [W]e affirm.

Plaintiff Ohanian began working for Avis in Boston in 1967. Later he was appointed District Sales Manager in New York, and subsequently moved to San Francisco. By 1980 he had become Vice President of Sales for Avis's Western Region. Robert Mahmarian, a former Avis general manager, testified that Ohanian's performance in that region was excellent. During what Mahmarian characterized as "a very bad, depressed economic period," Ohanian's Western Region stood out as the one region that was growing and profitable. According to the witness, Ohanian was directly responsible for this success.

In the fall of 1980, Avis's Northeast Region — the region with the most profit potential — was "dying." Mahmarian and then Avis President Calvano decided that the Northeast Region needed new leadership and Ohanian was the logical candidate. They thought plaintiff should return to New York as Vice President of Sales for the Northeast Region. According to Mahmarian, "nobody anticipated how tough it would be to get the guy." Ohanian was happy in the Western Region, and for several reasons did not want to move. First, he had developed a good "team" in the Western Region; second, he and his family liked the San Francisco area; and third, he was secure in his position where he was doing well and did not want to get involved in the politics of the Avis "World Headquarters," which was located in the Northeast Region. Mahmarian and Calvano were determined to bring Ohanian east and so they set out to overcome his reluctance. After several phone calls to him, first from then Vice President of Sales McNamara, then from Calvano, and finally Mahmarian, Ohanian was convinced to accept the job in the Northeast Region. In Mahmarian's words, he changed Ohanian's mind

> On the basis of promise, that a good man is a good man, and he has proven his ability, and if it didn't work out and he had to go back out in the field, or back to California, or whatever else, fine. As far as I was concerned, his future was secure in the company, unless — and I always had to qualify — unless he screwed up badly. Then he is on his own, and even then I indicated that at worst he would get his [severance] because there was some degree of responsibility on the part of management, Calvano and myself, in making this man make this change.

Ohanian's concerns about security were met by Mahmarian's assurance that "[u]nless [he] screwed up badly, there is no way [he was] going to get fired . . . [he would] never get hurt here in this company." Ohanian accepted the offer and began work in the Northeast Region in early February 1981.

In April 1981 Ohanian told Fred Sharp, Vice President of Personnel, that he needed relocation money that had been promised, but not yet received. Sharp subsequently sent two form letters to Ohanian: one from Sharp to Ohanian and the other, prepared by Avis, from Ohanian to Sharp. The second letter was a form with boxes for Ohanian to check to signify his choice of relocation expense plans. Ohanian checked one of the boxes, signed the form, and returned it to Sharp.

The following language appeared on the form that Ohanian signed and returned:

> I also hereby confirm my understanding that nothing contained herein or in connection with the change in my position with Avis shall be deemed to constitute an obligation on the part of Avis to employ me for any period of time, and both the company and I can terminate my employment at will. There are no other agreements or understandings in respect of my change in position with Avis or the moving of my residence except as is set forth or referred to herein, and in your confirmation letter to me dated April 21, 1981, and the agreements and undertakings set forth therein cannot be modified or altered

except by an instrument in writing signed by me and by an executive officer of Avis.

At trial, Ohanian said that he did not believe he read the letter other than to check the relocation plan he desired. He testified that he did not intend this letter to be a contract or to change the terms of his prior agreement with Avis.

Seven months after Ohanian moved to the Northeast Region, he was promoted to National Vice President of Sales and began work at Avis World Headquarters in Garden City, New York. He soon became dissatisfied with this position and in June 1982, pursuant to his request, returned to his former position as Vice President of Sales for the Northeast Region. A month later, on July 27, 1982, at 47 years of age, plaintiff was fired without severance pay. He then instituted this action. Within three months of termination, plaintiff obtained a job as Vice President of Sales for American International Rent A Car. His first year's salary at American International was $50,000 plus a $20,000 bonus. When Ohanian was fired by Avis, his yearly salary was $68,400, and the jury found that he was owed a $17,100 bonus that he had earned before being fired. . . .

The jury returned with a verdict in which it found:

(1)   That Ohanian had proven that Avis agreed to employ him until he retired unless he was terminated for just cause;

(2)   That Avis had not proven that Ohanian was terminated for just cause;

(3)   That Ohanian had proven that he was entitled to lost wages and pension benefits;

(4)   That the present value of Ohanian's lost wages was $245,409;

(5)   That the present value of Ohanian's lost pension benefits was $59,284;

(7)   That Ohanian proved he was entitled to an award representing a $17,100 bonus; and

(8)   That Ohanian proved he was entitled to an award representing incidental relocation expenses of $6,000.

. . . .

Avis does not challenge the jury's finding that it had not proved that plaintiff was terminated for just cause. Neither has it appealed the awards for the bonus and relocation expenses. Both parties agree that New York law applies.

Defendant's principal argument is that the oral contract that the jury found existed is barred under the statute of frauds, § 5-701 (subd. a, para. 1) of the General Obligations Law. Section 5-701 provides in relevant part:

Every agreement, promise or undertaking is void, unless it or some note or memorandum thereof be in writing, and subscribed by the party to be charged therewith, or by his lawful agent, if such agreement, promise or undertaking . . . [b]y its terms is not to be performed within one year from the making thereof or the performance of which is not to be completed before the end of a lifetime.

It has long been held that the purpose of the statute is to raise a barrier to fraud when parties attempt to prove certain legal transactions that are deemed to be particularly susceptible to deception, mistake, and perjury. The provision making void any oral contract "not to be performed within one year" is to prevent injustice that might result either from a faulty memory or the absence of witnesses that have died or moved.

The fact that inconsistent theories have been advanced to explain the statute's enactment perhaps sheds light on modern courts' strict construction of it. Parliament enacted An Act for Prevention of Frauds and Perjuries in 1677 that required certain contracts to be evidenced by a signed writing. One theory for its enactment was that evidence of oral contracts tended to be susceptible to perjury and inherently unreliable. *See, e.g., Burns v. McCormick*, 135 N.E. 273, 274 (N.Y. 1922) (Cardozo, J.) (passage of the statute of frauds was necessary because of the "peril of perjury . . . latent in the spoken promise"). This view is premised on the theory that an interested plaintiff will testify untruthfully about the existence of an oral contract. Another view derives from the fact that in a seventeenth century jury trial the parties and all others interested in the outcome were incompetent to testify as witnesses. T. PLUCKNETT, A CONCISE HISTORY OF THE COMMON LAW 55-56 (2d ed. 1936). To overcome that hurdle, so this theory goes, parties desiring legal protection for their transactions had to embody them in documents whose contents and authenticity were easily ascertainable. *Id.* at 56.

Whatever may be the fact with regard to the history of the statute, and whatever may have been the difficulties arising from proof that all sides agree brought about the enactment of the statute of frauds over 300 years ago, it is an anachronism today. The reasons that prompted its passage no longer exist. And, far from serving as a barrier to fraud — in the case of a genuinely aggrieved plaintiff barred from enforcing an oral contract — the statute may actually shield fraud. Note, *The Statute of Frauds as a Bar to an Action in Tort for Fraud*, 53 FORDHAM L. REV. 1231, 1232-33 (1985).

In fact, New York courts perhaps also believing that strict application of the statute causes more fraud than it prevents, have tended to construe it warily. The one-year provision has been held not to preclude an oral contract unless there is "not . . . the slightest possibility that it can be fully performed within one year." 2 CORBIN ON CONTRACTS § 444, at 535; *Warner v. Texas & Pacific Ry.*, 164 U.S. 418, 434 (1896) ("The question is not what the probable, or expected, or actual performance of the contract was; but whether the contract, according to the reasonable interpretation of its terms, required that it should not be performed within the year."); *D & N Boening, Inc. v. Kirsch Beverages, Inc.*, 472 N.E.2d 992 (N.Y. 1984) ("this court has continued to analyze oral agreements to determine if, according to the parties' terms, there might be any possible means of performance within one year").

It was long ago established that

> [i]t is not the meaning of the statute that the contract must be performed within a year. . . . [I]f the obligation of the contract is not, by its very terms, or necessary construction, to endure for a longer period than one year, it is a valid agreement, although it may be capable of an indefinite continuance.

Trustees of First Baptist Church v. Brooklyn Fire Ins. Co., 19 N.Y. 305, 307 (1859). Therefore, a contract to continue for longer than a year, that is terminable at the will of the party against whom it is being enforced, is not barred by the statute of frauds because it is capable of being performed within one year. *See North Shore Bottling Co. v. C. Schmidt & Sons, Inc.,* 239 N.E.2d 189 (N.Y. 1968). Similarly, it has been held that a contract which provides that either party may rightfully terminate within the year falls outside the statute. *Blake v. Voigt,* 31 N.E. 256 (N.Y. 1892).

When does an oral contract not to be performed within a year fall within the strictures of the statute? A contract is not "to be performed within a year" if it is terminable within that time only upon the breach of one of the parties. *Boening,* 472 N.E.2d 992. That rule derives from logic because "[p]erformance, if it means anything at all, is 'carrying out the contract by doing what it requires or permits' . . . and a breach is the unexcused failure to do so." *Id.* (citing *Blake v. Voigt,* 31 N.E. 256). The distinction is between an oral contract that provides for its own termination at any time on the one hand, and an oral contract that is terminable within a year only upon its breach on the other. The former may be proved by a plaintiff and the latter is barred by the statute.

Avis contends that its oral agreement with Ohanian is barred by the statute of frauds because it was not performable within a year. Avis claims that it could only fire plaintiff if he breached the contract, and breach of a contract is not performance. Defendant further states that an option in plaintiff alone to terminate the contract at will, if there was in fact such an option, also would not remove this agreement from the statute's coverage.

What defendant fails to recognize is that under New York law "just cause" for termination may exist for reasons other than an employee's breach. Thus, for example, in *Weiner v. McGraw-Hill, Inc.,* 443 N.E.2d 441 (N.Y. 1982), the plaintiff was induced to leave his former position to take up employment with defendant McGraw-Hill, in part by an assurance from defendant's representative that "since his company's firm policy was not to terminate employees without 'just cause,' employment by it would, among other things, bring him the advantage of job security." The company handbook describing its dismissal policies stated, " '[t]he company will resort to dismissal for just and sufficient cause only. . . . However, if the welfare of the company indicates that dismissal is necessary, then that decision is arrived at and carried out forthrightly.' " *Id.* The New York Court of Appeals held that the arguably oral contract in question "whether terminable at will or only for just cause, [was] not one which, 'by its terms,' could not be performed within one year and, therefore, [was] not one which [was] barred." *Id.*

Later, in *Boening* the court noted that "the reference in [*Weiner*] . . . to an agreement terminable 'only for just cause' falling outside the Statute of Frauds is not to be construed as including an agreement where 'just cause' can *only* be the other party's breach." (emphasis added). The *Boening* court recognized therefore that some contracts terminable for "just cause" do not require a breach in order to terminate. In *Boening,* the court determined that the supply contract in question required plaintiff to "conduct its subdistributorship satisfactorily, exerting its best efforts and acting in good faith." Defendant was only allowed to terminate the contract for failure to satisfy those requirements. Since the *only possible cause* for termination was plaintiff's breach, the contract was barred by the statute of frauds.

In the instant case, just cause for dismissing Ohanian would plainly include any breach of the contract, such as drinking on the job or refusing to work, since the agreement contemplates plaintiff giving his best efforts. But, as noted, just cause can be broader than breach and here there may be just cause to dismiss without a breach. To illustrate, under the terms of the contract it would be possible that despite plaintiff's best efforts the results achieved might prove poor because of adverse market conditions. From defendant's standpoint that too would force Avis to make a change in its business strategy, perhaps reducing or closing an operation. That is, there would be just cause for plaintiff's dismissal. But if this is what occurred, it would not constitute a breach of the agreement. Best efforts were contemplated by the parties, results were not. Defendant was anxious to have plaintiff relocate because of his past success, but plaintiff made no guarantee to produce certain results. Thus, this oral contract could have been terminated for just cause within one year, without any breach by plaintiff, and is therefore not barred by the statute of frauds.

Defendant's further claim that a contract does not escape the statute if it is terminable at will only by plaintiff is negated by the fact that the contract provided that plaintiff could be terminated for reasons other than the plaintiff's breach. As just stated, defendant could fire the plaintiff on account of conduct that would not constitute breach of contract. Where either party under the contract may rightfully terminate within a year, the contract is outside the statute.

Defendant next urges that any claims based on the oral agreement between Ohanian and Avis are barred by the parol evidence rule. Avis says that the clear and unambiguous letter of April 21, 1981 was signed by plaintiff, and it contradicts plaintiff's assertion that he was promised lifetime employment and severance on termination. It is, of course, a fundamental principle of contract law "that, where parties have reduced their bargain, or any element of it, to writing, the parol evidence rule applies to prevent its variance by parol evidence." *Laskey v. Rubel Corp.,* 100 N.E.2d 140 (N.Y. 1951).

Avis's argument fails for a very basic reason: the jury found that the April 21st letter did not constitute a contract between it and Ohanian. The trial judge had correctly instructed the jury that if it found the letter to be a contract it could not find for plaintiff, and the jury found for plaintiff. Parol evidence is excluded only when used as an attempt to vary or modify the terms of an existing written contract. *See Kirtley v. Abrams,* 299 F.2d 341, 345 (2d Cir. 1962) (the rule does not preclude a party "from attempting to show that there never was any agreement such as the writing purported to be"); *Whipple v. Brown Bros. Co.,* 121 N.E. 748, 750 (N.Y. 1919) ("One cannot be made to stand on a contract he never intended to make.").

This case is quite unlike *Franzek v. Calspan Corp.,* 434 N.Y.S.2d 288 (Fourth Dep't 1980), upon which defendant relies. In *Franzek* the plaintiff, about to embark on a hazardous "white water" raft ride in the Niagara River, was handed and signed a release form. He later claimed he had not read it.

Such failure on his part was held not to raise an issue of fact to relieve plaintiff of its effect when the release was asserted against his claim of injury. But the contrary appears in the present case where there is strong evidence in the record to support the jury's finding that the writing was not intended to be a contract: the letter was on a form; it was sent to Ohanian in response to his request for relocation expenses; and he testified that he did not believe he read the letter other than to check a box indicating the type of relocation reimbursement he wanted. Most significantly, no evidence was presented that suggests that either Ohanian or Sharp, the Avis Vice President who sent the form to plaintiff, intended it to define the terms of Ohanian's employment with Avis.

Avis says that inasmuch as the evidence of an oral promise of lifetime employment was insufficient as a matter of law, that issue should not have gone to the jury. It relies on *Brown v. Safeway Stores, Inc.*, 190 F. Supp. 295 (E.D.N.Y. 1960), as support for this argument. Defendant can draw little solace from *Brown*. In that case the claimed assurances were made in several ways including meetings of a group of employees — the purpose of which was not to discuss length of employment — or during casual conversation. The conversations were not conducted in an atmosphere, as here, of critical one-on-one negotiation regarding the terms of future employment. Further, in *Brown* the district court found as a matter of fact that the alleged promise of lifetime employment was never made. In contrast, in the instant case the evidence was ample to permit the jury to decide whether statements made to Ohanian by defendant were more than casual comments or mere pep talks delivered by management to a group of employees. All of the surrounding circumstances — fully related earlier — were sufficient for the jury in fact to find that there was a promise of lifetime employment to a "star" employee who, it was hoped, would revive a "dying" division of defendant corporation.

Avis argues further that even if a promise of lifetime employment terminable only for just cause is found, evidence of that promise is not sufficiently definite and for that reason cannot be enforced. . . . Yet, promises of lifetime employment have long been enforced if found to be supported by sufficient consideration. *See* 9 WILLISTON ON CONTRACTS § 1017, at 132-35 & nn. 17-19 (3d ed. 1967); 3A CORBIN ON CONTRACTS § 684, at 229 (1960). Defendant does not contend that Ohanian's consideration for the promise of lifetime employment — his relocation from San Francisco to New York — was inadequate. . . .

WYATT, DISTRICT JUDGE, dissenting:

Believing that the oral lifetime employment contract as claimed by plaintiff is void under the New York Statute of Frauds, I am compelled to dissent. . . .

The "oral employment contract," as claimed by Ohanian in this Court — and at all times since the action began — was a "lifetime employment contract," which he could terminate at any time, but which Avis could terminate only for "just cause." The evidence showed that the words "just cause" were never used. The evidence for plaintiff showed, if believed, that Ohanian was guaranteed his job for life "unless he totally screws up," and that Ohanian was told he would not be fired "unless you screwed up badly."

"Just cause" was the legal term selected by counsel for Ohanian as a translation of the words actually used: "totally screws up" and "screwed up badly."
. . .

In the oral contract in suit, Avis had a right to terminate if Ohanian "totally screws up" or "screwed up badly." There is no evidence that these words referred to anything other than a breach by Ohanian of the duties and obligations of an employee, a breach of contract. There is no evidence that the words included a right in Avis to terminate whenever Avis was forced "to make a change in its business strategy" or for reasons other than fault on the part of Ohanian.

The majority opinion recognizes that the promise made by Avis to meet "Ohanian's concerns about security" was: Avis would not fire him unless he "screwed up badly." It then holds, however, that, despite these words, Ohanian could be fired even though he had not done anything in violation of the employment contract. To me, it is inconceivable that Ohanian — demanding *job security* to persuade him to leave California — would agree to leave California for an oral contract which could be terminated by Avis without any breach on his part. To give Avis a right to fire him even though he had not "screwed up badly" or "totally" would deprive Ohanian of the very security on which he was insisting. . . .

The Statute of Frauds does not seem to be an "anachronism" for such cases as that at bar. The oral lifetime employment contract was claimed by Ohanian to have been made in a telephone conversation between him in California and Mahmarian for Avis in New York. The conversation was not recorded; no memoranda were made. The only testimony was, and could only be, that of Ohanian and Mahmarian. Not only was Ohanian a witness hostile to Avis, but, Mahmarian, whose testimony was given by deposition on November 9, 1983, had himself been dismissed by Avis on August 4, 1982, a few days after Ohanian was dismissed, and was presumably hostile to Avis. Thus, Avis was at the mercy of Ohanian and Mahmarian in the sense that no person and no writing was available to confirm or contradict them; they alone had made the claimed oral contract and there was no writing. . . .

NOTES

1. *Irony of Result.* Ohanian wins by convincing the court that the contract gave the employer a right to terminate for adverse market conditions. As a precedent, is this a victory for employees or employers?

2. *Measuring Damages.* The jury in *Ohanian* was instructed to compute lost wages by first multiplying plaintiff's yearly salary by the number of years he would have remained at Avis had he not been fired. The jury was then directed to deduct the amount plaintiff had earned and would earn from other employment. Shouldn't the jury have been instructed to consider that Ohanian might have been dismissed during a later business downturn?

3. *Narrow Reading of Ohanian.* In *Burke v. Bevona*, 866 F.2d 532, 538 (2d Cir. 1989) (applying New York law), the Second Circuit found a supervisor's promise of a job "for as long as you live" to be void under the Statute of Frauds, rejecting an argument that business conditions could have forced the employer to lay off the employee within a year without breaching the contract:

> The New York cases uniformly hold that implied termination terms are not sufficient to take an oral contract out of the statute [of frauds]. The terms must be express. As we read *Ohanian,* it purports to adhere to this established New York rule. . . . To the extent that the *Ohanian* panel may have interpreted the "terms" of the *Ohanian* contract more broadly than other judges would have done, the interpretation was peculiar to the facts of that case.

4. *Statute of Frauds Issues.* A typical statute of frauds declares that oral agreements that cannot be performed within one year are unenforceable. Several recurring patterns in employment contracts trigger this issue, and courts vary in how seriously they take the argument. For example, is a promise of lifetime employment within the statute, given that the worker might die within a year? *Compare Adams v. Greenbrier Oldsmobile/GMC/Volkswagen,* 1999 U.S. App. LEXIS 1140 (4th Cir. 1999) (applying Virginia law) (enforcing oral lifetime contract), *with Burke v. Bevona,* 866 F.2d 532 (2d Cir. 1989) (applying New York law) (refusing to enforce oral lifetime contract). What about a promise of employment until retirement, given that the worker might retire within a year? *Compare Martin v. Fed. Life Ins. Co.,* 440 N.E.2d 998 (Ill. App. Ct. 1982) (enforcing oral contract until retirement), *with Wior v. Anchor Indus.,* 669 N.E.2d 172 (Ind. 1996) (refusing to enforce such a contract). And in direct conflict with *Ohanian's* enforcement of an oral just-cause contract is *Graham v. Central Fidelity Bank,* 428 S.E.2d 916 (Va. 1993), which held that the statute of frauds prevented enforcement of the employer's oral promise not to fire without cause.

5. *Requiring Written Agreements.* Why should courts require a written agreement for a two-year term contract, but not require one in a case like *Ohanian*? Should employees who count on job security be expected to get the agreement in writing? Could Hetes have obtained her assurances in writing?

Because of the importance of job security, parties that have actually focused on the issue might be expected to put their agreement in writing. The Statute of Frauds requirement of a writing perhaps can be justified on grounds of requiring what most parties would have wanted had they focused on the issue. On the other hand, employees might have difficulty getting such promises in writing. Under a penalty-default model, perhaps courts should enforce oral promises of job security, thereby encouraging employers to put disclaimers in writing if they do not want to provide job security.

6. *Parol-Evidence Rule.* The parol-evidence rule prohibits a party from using outside evidence to rebut the meaning of a written contract. This rule is frequently invoked when the employee alleges that oral promises of job security were made at the job interview, but he later signed a contract declaring the job to be at will. The *Ohanian* court recognized this principle, but upheld the jury's determination that the relocation expense reimbursement form declaring at-will status was not a contract, thereby allowing consideration of the prior oral evidence of job security.

Frequently, however, an employer makes oral assurances of job security after the employee signs a written contract specifying at-will status. The parol-evidence rule does not apply here, because the employee is not denying the validity of the written contract but arguing that the later oral agreement modified the written contract. Some courts, however, may question whether the employee has provided independent consideration for the later promise of job security.

7. Right to Lay Off. The basic argument in *Ohanian* is whether Avis had the right to terminate the employee for reasons other than Ohanian's breach of contract. The majority thought the contract allowed Avis to terminate Ohanian if bad conditions at the company required it. Should such a clause be implied in employment contracts like this? What would the parties have wanted? One bit of evidence is that collective-bargaining contracts, which invariably incorporate a just-cause standard, usually allow employers to lay off workers when business conditions are bad.

A puzzle with layoffs for bad business conditions is why workers would not prefer to keep their jobs at reduced pay. One reason why workers might agree to layoffs, but not wage cuts, when business conditions are poor comes from the asymmetry of information between the employer and employees. Employees have difficulty assessing whether business conditions are truly bad when the employer claims they are. Even if conditions were good, the employer has an incentive to claim conditions are bad and cut wages, thereby increasing its profits. If its only permissible response to bad conditions is to lay off workers, however, the employer's claim is self-monitoring. If it falsely claims times are bad and lays off employees, it reduces the output of the firm and lowers its own profits. For a formal model using this argument, see Sanford Grossman & Oliver Hart, *Implicit Contracts, Moral Hazard and Unemployment,* 71 AM. ECON. REV. 301 (1981). Does this self-monitoring argument suggest that courts should imply a contractual right of employers to lay off workers when business conditions are bad, absent specific contractual language to the contrary?

B. RELIANCE AND IMPLIED-IN-FACT CONTRACTS

GROUSE v. GROUP HEALTH PLAN, INC.
Supreme Court of Minnesota
306 N.W.2d 114 (1981)

OTIS, JUSTICE.

Plaintiff John Grouse appeals from a judgment in favor of Group Health Plan, Inc., in this action for damages resulting from repudiation of an employment offer. The narrow issue raised is whether the trial court erred by concluding that Grouse's complaint fails to state a claim upon which relief can be granted. In our view, the doctrine of promissory estoppel entitles Grouse to recover and we, therefore, reverse and remand for a new trial on the issue of damages.

The facts relevant to this appeal are essentially undisputed. Grouse, a 1974 graduate of the University of Minnesota School of Pharmacy, was employed in 1975 as a retail pharmacist at Richter Drug in Minneapolis. He worked approximately 41 hours per week earning $7 per hour. Grouse desired employment in a hospital or clinical setting, however, because of the work environment and the increased compensation and benefits. In the summer of 1975 he was advised by the Health Sciences Placement office at the University that Group Health was seeking a pharmacist.

Grouse called Group Health and was told to come in and fill out an application. He did so in September and was, at that time, interviewed by Cyrus Elliott, Group Health's Chief Pharmacist. Approximately 2 weeks later Elliott contacted Grouse and asked him to come in for an interview with Donald Shoberg, Group Health's General Manager. Shoberg explained company policies and procedures as well as salary and benefits. Following this meeting Grouse again spoke with Elliott who told him to be patient, that it was necessary to interview recent graduates before making an offer.

On December 4, 1975, Elliott telephoned Grouse at Richter Drug and offered him a position as a pharmacist at Group Health's St. Louis Park Clinic. Grouse accepted but informed Elliott that 2 weeks' notice to Richter Drug would be necessary. That afternoon Grouse received an offer from a Veteran's Administration Hospital in Virginia which he declined because of Group Health's offer. Elliott called back to confirm that Grouse had resigned.

Sometime in the next few days Elliott mentioned to Shoberg that he had hired, or was thinking of hiring, Grouse. Shoberg told him that company hiring requirements included a favorable written reference, a background check, and approval of the general manager. Elliott contacted two faculty members at the School of Pharmacy who declined to give references. He also contacted an internship employer and several pharmacies where Grouse had done relief work. Their responses were that they had not had enough exposure to Grouse's work to form a judgment as to his capabilities. Elliott did not contact Richter because Grouse's application requested that he not be contacted. Because Elliott was unable to supply a favorable reference for Grouse, Shoberg hired another person to fill the position.

On December 15, 1975 Grouse called Group Health and reported that he was free to begin work. Elliott informed Grouse that someone else had been hired. Grouse complained to the director of Group Health who apologized but took no other action. Grouse experienced difficulty regaining full time employment and suffered wage loss as a result. He commenced this suit to recover damages; the trial judge found that he had not stated an actionable claim.

In our view the principle of contract law applicable here is promissory estoppel. Its effect is to imply a contract in law where none exists in fact. On these facts no contract exists because due to the bilateral power of termination neither party is committed to performance and the promises are, therefore, illusory. The elements of promissory estoppel are stated in RESTATEMENT OF CONTRACTS § 90 (1932):

> A promise which the promisor should reasonably expect to induce action or forbearance . . . on the part of the promisee and which does induce such action or forbearance is binding if injustice can be avoided only by enforcement of the promise.

Group Health knew that to accept its offer Grouse would have to resign his employment at Richter Drug. Grouse promptly gave notice to Richter Drug and informed Group Health that he had done so when specifically asked by Elliott. Under these circumstances it would be unjust not to hold Group Health to its promise.

The parties focus their arguments on whether an employment contract which is terminable at will can give rise to an action for damages if anticipatorily repudiated. Group Health contends that recognition of a cause of action on these facts would result in the anomalous rule that an employee who is told not to report to work the day before he is scheduled to begin has a remedy while an employee who is discharged after the first day does not. We cannot agree since under appropriate circumstances we believe section 90 would apply even after employment has begun.

When a promise is enforced pursuant to section 90 "[t]he remedy granted for breach may be limited as justice requires." Relief may be limited to damages measured by the promisee's reliance.

The conclusion we reach does not imply that an employer will be liable whenever he discharges an employee whose term of employment is at will. What we do hold is that under the facts of this case the appellant had a right to assume he would be given a good faith opportunity to perform his duties to the satisfaction of respondent once he was on the job. He was not only denied that opportunity but resigned the position he already held in reliance on the firm offer which respondent tendered him. Since, as respondent points out, the prospective employment might have been terminated at any time, the measure of damages is not so much what he would have earned from respondent as what he lost in quitting the job he held and in declining at least one other offer of employment elsewhere.

Reversed and remanded for a new trial on the issue of damages.

VENO v. MEREDITH
Superior Court of Pennsylvania
515 A.2d 571 (1986)

Before CIRILLO, PRESIDENT JUDGE, and CAVANAUGH and TAMILIA, JJ.

CAVANAUGH, JUDGE.

[Veno, the managing editor of The Free Press, was fired by the newspaper's owner for publishing a story criticizing a local judge. Veno filed suit for illegal termination of his employment contract. At the end of Veno's case-in-chief, the trial court issued a nonsuit in favor of the newspaper. Veno appealed.]

Once again, we are asked to decide whether or not an employer had the right to discharge an employee.

In the area of employment relations, Pennsylvania still largely adheres to the "at-will" rule. . . . The essence of the employment-at-will presumption is that the decision to discharge an employee is best left to the managerial prerogative and generally will not be reviewed in a judicial forum. The other side of the rule is that an employee may resign at any time, for any reason, or for no reason at all. Of course, a discharge may be subject to review in a judicial forum if the employer and employee so agree.

The most elementary way that the parties can overcome the at-will presumption is by express contract. For example, a contract may be made for a definite term, or it may forbid discharge in the absence of just cause or without first utilizing an internal dispute resolution mechanism. The presumption may also be overcome by implied contract. That is, all of the surrounding circumstances of the hiring may indicate that the parties did not intend the employment to be "at-will."

Another way that the at-will presumption may be overcome is where the employee gives the employer sufficient consideration in addition to the services for which he was hired. (See our discussion, *infra.*)

In short, if there is a dispute over the discharge of an employee, the threshold inquiry is whether or not the employment was at-will. If it was, then the discharge is not reviewable in a judicial forum. An exception is that the discharge will be reviewable in a judicial forum when there is sufficient evidence to suggest that it was against public policy or made with the specific intent to harm the employee. The latter two causes of action are classified as "wrongful discharge" torts in Pennsylvania. They are limited exceptions to the at-will presumption in this Commonwealth and only rarely occasion relief for the discharged employee. . . .

Moreover, because of its vitality, courts insist that to contract-away the at-will presumption, much clarity is required. The intention to overcome the presumption will not be unheedingly inferred. This court has recently held that the modification of an "at-will" relationship to one that can never be severed without "just cause" is such a substantial modification that a very clear statement of an intention to so modify is required. Absent this clarity, again, the relationship is "at-will" and a discharge is not reviewable in a judicial forum (absent sufficient evidence of "wrongful discharge"). . . .

Turning to the instant case, appellant alleges that he presented sufficient evidence from which a jury could conclude that his employment was not terminable at-will and that therefore the court erred in granting a nonsuit. He alleges the following facts in support of this contention. In April, 1973, when appellant and his wife purchased a home, his employer, Mr. Meredith co-signed both the disclosure statement and demand note in the sum of $5,400.00. Appellant further testified that Mr. Meredith said to him, "We're both the same age, we're both going to retire together, we're not making a lot now, but we'll make it later on. I want you to raise your children here. I want them to go to the school. I want to retire together." Moreover, appellant turned down other job opportunities throughout his employment, including one from his former employer — an offer he made known to Mr. Meredith.

These facts could not support a recovery for appellant. The statements made by the employer are broad, vague, and do not suggest that the parties contemplated a definite duration for the employment. Such statements generally do not overcome the at-will presumption.

Moreover, the statements have an aspirational quality to them. The law does not attach binding significance to comments which merely evince an employer's hope that the employee will remain in his employ until retirement. In the instant case, there was no express contract limiting the employer's ability to discharge; nor was there a reasonable "understanding" to that effect.

Nor do we find the appellant's refusal to take other jobs as significant to his contention. This forebearance was merely a manifestation of his preference to remain with the Free Press and in no way suggests he had the reasonable belief that he could never be fired except for "just cause."

Appellant also contends that he gave his employer sufficient consideration additional to the services for which he was hired and therefore his employment was not at-will. The alleged consideration consists of the following: that appellant gave up a job with a newspaper and moved his family from Newark to Pennsylvania, and that throughout the years he refused other employment opportunities.

We stated in *Darlington v. General Electric Co.,* 504 A.2d at 315:

> [A] court will find "additional consideration" when an employee affords his employer a substantial benefit other than the services which the employee is hired to perform, or when the employee undergoes a substantial hardship other than the services which he is hired to perform. "If the circumstances are such that a termination of the relation by one party will result in great hardship or loss to the other, as they must have known it would when they made the contract, this is a factor of great weight in inducing a holding that the parties agreed upon a specific period." 3 A. CORBIN, CORBIN ON CONTRACTS § 684 (1960).

When sufficient additional consideration is present, an employee should not be subject to discharge without just cause for a reasonable time. The length of time during which it would be unreasonable to terminate, without just cause, an employee who has given additional consideration should be commensurate with the hardship the employee has endured or the benefit he has bestowed.

Appellant has not presented evidence tending to show that he gave his employer sufficient additional consideration. The detriments alleged are commensurate with those incurred by all manner of salaried professionals. We do not believe that appellant's termination by the Free Press some eight years into his employment over a legitimate difference of opinion constitutes the kind of "great hardship or loss" that Professor Corbin referred to, *supra.*

Virtually all terminations result in some hardship and loss to the employee. Instantly, we are not presented with facts to suggest that appellant brought to the employment so substantial a benefit, or incurred so detrimental a hardship in taking the job, that he should be accorded treatment any different from the typical at-will employee.[4]

Order affirmed.

NOTES

1. *Consideration as Interpretation Device.* The *Veno* court suggests that the expenses of moving to a new job could be consideration for an employer's promise of just-cause dismissal. Is there an independent promise of just cause, for which moving is consideration, or does the fact of moving itself create an obligation by the employer to give a reasonable time to recoup the costs of moving?

As the Pennsylvania Superior Court explained in *Darlington v. General Electric Co.,* 504 A.2d 306, 314 (Pa. Super. Ct. 1986):

> The term "consideration" is not used here as it is in the usual contractual context to signify a *validation* device. The term is used, rather, more as an *interpretation* device. When "sufficient additional consideration" is present, courts infer that the parties *intended* that the contract will not be terminable at-will. This inference may be nothing more than a legal fiction because it is possible that in a given case, the parties never truly contemplated how long the employment would last even though additional consideration is present. Even so, the at-will presumption would be overcome. On the other hand, if the parties specifically agreed that the employment would be *at-will,* even though additional consideration were present, we would expect a court to construe the contract according to the parties' stated intention and hold it to be at-will. Thus, we start with the usual at-will presumption which, let us say, has not been overcome by evidence of a contract for a term or for a reasonable length of time. Then, if sufficient additional consideration is present, the law presumes this to be sufficient to rebut the at-will presumption. Such a contract could not be rightfully terminated at-will but would continue for a reasonable length of time.

---

4 . . . Appellant also cites *Lucacher v. Kerson,* 45 A.2d 245 (Pa. Super. Ct. 1946), where an employee was promised "permanent" employment in his new job. In order to take the job, he moved from New York to Philadelphia. Three days into his employment, employee was abruptly discharged. The court allowed recovery and held the contract of "permanent" employment was capable of enforcement due largely to the additional consideration rendered by employee. It is doubtful that the court in *Lucacher* should have enforced the terms of the vague and broad contract which allowed for "permanent" employment. Rather, the court should have ignored the "promise" of permanent employment because of its breadth and vagueness and *inferred* a contract for a reasonable length of time based solely on the sufficient additional consideration. The facts in *Lucacher* are obviously different from those presented instantly. In *Lucacher,* after having moved from New York to Philadelphia in reliance on a promise of a new job, employee was discharged just three days into his employment. Here, in contrast, appellant had been employed for 8 years before he was dismissed. The "reasonable length of time" here has surely passed based on the consideration given.

However, the presumption created by the additional consideration rule could *itself* be rebutted by evidence that the parties specifically contracted for employment at-will.

For an application, see *Cashdollar v. Mercy Hospital,* 595 A.2d 70 (Pa. Super. Ct. 1991) (professional selling house and moving his pregnant wife and child to a different state after quitting secure job paying $82,000 shows "hardships constitut[ing] sufficient additional consideration to rebut the at-will presumption").

2. *Is Reliance Reasonable?* Is it reasonable to incur moving expenses or quit a job in reliance on an offer of at-will employment? Some courts have held no. *See Ferreyra v. E. & J. Gallo Winery,* 41 Cal. Rptr. 819 (Cal. Ct. App. 1964) (Argentinean worker who gave up his job in Argentina and moved his family to United States to become a crew boss of one of Gallo's pruning and irrigation crews did not show sufficient consideration to protect against firing without cause).

Other courts put the issue the other way around. Rather than asking whether an employee should reasonably rely on assurances of an at-will contract, they ask whether an employee who has suffered moving expenses would have done so without some assurances of more than an at-will contract. Thus, in *Miller v. Community Discount Centers,* 228 N.E.2d 113 (Ill. App. Ct. 1967), a job applicant left his family in Toledo, Ohio to move to Chicago after receiving the following letter, which the parties stipulated was the entire agreement between them:

Dear Mr. Miller:

First, let me again extend an official welcome to the Community family; we are certain you have a rewarding and satisfying career ahead of you.

For the record, I should like to confirm the employment arrangements with you. Your beginning salary will be $10,000.00 per year as a Store Management Trainee. Regarding moving expenses, we will pay one-half now and the balance after one year.

Looking forward to seeing you soon.

Sincerely yours,

/s/ Melvin Kent

Director of Personnel

The employee sued when he was dismissed after three months. The court of appeals upheld a trial court judgment for breach of a definite one-year contract, reasoning in part:

Furthermore, we find it inconceivable that a man of plaintiff's age[*] would leave his home to come to Chicago for the mere possibility that he would have a permanent position. It was clearly the intention of the parties, by their words, to have this contract be a contract for at

---

[*] The opinion never reveals the employee's age. What age would make the argument for a definite-term contract most powerful?

least one year and nothing they can say changes that intention of the parties at the time the contract was made.

It was the intention of the parties that this man be hired for a year at least. This is made evident by the reference in the contract in regard to moving expenses. It is clear that if moving expenses are to be paid they are to be paid for coming to Chicago to take a position which would certainly be for a year or more. . . . This, [it] is to be noted, is a construction of language and not the adoption of a new rule. It merely states that when the moving expenses are mentioned, it is to be construed for one year and not at will.

Consider also *Lanier v. Alenco*, 459 F.2d 689, 692-93 (5th Cir. 1972) (applying Louisiana law). Louisiana is one of the few states without a Statute of Frauds, but Louisiana does require that oral contracts with greater than $500 value be proved by corroborating circumstances. The court upheld a finding of a valid oral contract, emphasizing that the employee had given up a secure job:

Lanier, with a wife and four children, left a secure and well-paying position with General Electric, a position that he had held for eleven years, to join Alenco as a branch sales manager. Like the trial judge, we find it unlikely that Lanier would leave that sort of employment without some substantial representation of a secure position at Alenco. Employment at will does not have much security, particularly when there is testimony in the record from former Alenco employees that Alenco had a history of discharges without cause. Furthermore, it does not appear that Lanier was precipitous in his shift of employment to Alenco, for his negotiations with Shelton took longer than one year. . . . We conclude that these factors are not, as a matter of law, insufficient "corroborating circumstances" to overturn the trial court's judgment that Lanier and Shelton agreed upon an oral contract of employment for a fixed term of one year at certain salary and commission levels, including "start up" commissions. Lanier's failure to acquiesce to Alenco's "new offer of reimbursement" at reduced salary and commission levels does not constitute "good cause" for discharge under Louisiana law, for such a substantive change in the terms of a contract requires the consent of both parties.

PUGH v. SEE'S CANDIES, INC.
California Court of Appeal
171 Cal. Rptr. 917 (1981)

GRODIN, ASSOCIATE JUSTICE.

After 32 years of employment with See's Candies, Inc., in which he worked his way up the corporate ladder from dishwasher to vice-president in charge of production and member of the board of directors, Wayne Pugh was fired. Asserting that he had been fired in breach of contract and for reasons which offend public policy he sued his former employer seeking compensatory and punitive damages for wrongful termination, and joined as a defendant a labor organization which, he alleged, had conspired in or induced the wrongful conduct. The case went to trial before a jury, and upon conclusion of the plaintiff's case-in-chief the trial court granted defendants' motions for nonsuit, and this appeal followed. . . .

Pugh began working for See's at its Bay Area plant (then in San Francisco) in January 1941 washing pots and pans. From there he was promoted to candy maker, and held that position until the early part of 1942, when he entered the Air Corps. Upon his discharge in 1946 he returned to See's and his former position. After a year he was promoted to the position of production manager in charge of personnel, ordering raw materials, and supervising the production of candy. When, in 1950, See's moved into a larger plant in San Francisco, Pugh had responsibility for laying out the design of the plant, taking bids, and assisting in the construction. While working at this plant, Pugh sought to increase his value to the company by taking three years of night classes in plant layout, economics, and business law. When See's moved its San Francisco plant to its present location in South San Francisco in 1957, Pugh was given responsibilities for the new location similar to those which he undertook in 1950. By this time See's business and its number of production employees had increased substantially, and a new position of assistant production manager was created under Pugh's supervision.

In 1971 Pugh was again promoted, this time as vice-president in charge of production and was placed upon the board of directors of See's Northern California subsidiary, "in recognition of his accomplishments." In 1972 he received a gold watch from See's "in appreciation of 31 years of loyal service."

In May 1973 Pugh travelled with Charles Huggins, then president of See's, and their respective families to Europe on a business trip to visit candy manufacturers and to inspect new equipment. Mr. Huggins returned in early June to attend a board of director's meeting while Pugh and his family remained in Europe on a planned vacation.

Upon Pugh's return from Europe on Sunday, June 25, 1973, he received a message directing him to fly to Los Angeles the next day and meet with Mr. Huggins. Pugh went to Los Angeles expecting to be told of another promotion. The preceding Christmas season had been the most successful in See's history, the Valentine's Day holiday of 1973 set a new sales record for See's, and the March 1973 edition of See's Newsletter, containing two pictures of Pugh, carried congratulations on the increased production.

Instead, upon Pugh's arrival at Mr. Huggins' office, the latter said, "Wayne, come in and sit down. We might as well get right to the point. I have decided your services are no longer required by See's Candies. Read this and sign it." Huggins handed him a letter confirming his termination and directing him to remove that day "only personal papers and possessions from your office," but "absolutely no records, formulas or other material"; and to turn in and account for "all keys, credit cards, et cetera." The letter advised that Pugh would receive unpaid salary, bonuses and accrued vacation through that date, and the full amount of his profit sharing account, but "No severance pay will be granted." Finally, Pugh was directed "not to visit or contact Production Department employees while they are on the job."

The letter contained no reason for Pugh's termination. When Pugh asked Huggins for a reason, he was told only that he should "look deep within [him]self" to find the answer, that "Things were said by people in the trade that have come back to us." Pugh's termination was subsequently announced to the industry in a letter which, again, stated no reasons.

When Pugh first went to work for See's, Ed Peck, then president and general manager, frequently told him: "if you are loyal to [See's] and do a good job, your future is secure." Laurance See, who became president of the company in 1951 and served in that capacity until his death in 1969, had a practice of not terminating administrative personnel except for good cause, and this practice was carried on by his brother, Charles B. See, who succeeded Laurance as president.

During the entire period of his employment, there had been no formal or written criticism of Pugh's work.[1] No complaints were ever raised at the annual meetings which preceded each holiday season, and he was never denied a raise or bonus. He received no notice that there was a problem which needed correction, nor any warning that any disciplinary action was being contemplated.

Pugh's theory as to why he was terminated relates to a contract which See's at that time had with the defendant union. . . .

In 1968 the supplemental [union] agreement contained a new rate classification which permitted See's to pay its seasonal employees at a lower rate. At a company meeting prior to the 1968 negotiations, Pugh had objected to the proposed new seasonal classification on the grounds that it might make it more difficult to recruit seasonal workers, and create unrest among See's regular seasonal workers who had worked previously for other manufacturers at higher rates. Huggins overruled Pugh's objection and (unknown to Pugh) recommended his termination for "lack of cooperation" as to which Pugh's objection formed "part of the reason." His recommendation was not accepted. . . .

In April [1973], Huggins asked Pugh to be part of the negotiating team for the new union contract. Pugh responded that he would like to, but he was bothered by the possibility that See's had a "sweetheart contract" with the union. In response, someone banged on the table and said, " 'You don't know what the hell you are talking about.' " Pugh said, "Well, I think I know what I am talking about. I don't know whether you have a sweetheart contract, but I am telling you if you do, I don't want to be involved because they are immoral, illegal and not in the best interests of my employees." At the trial, Pugh explained that to him a "sweetheart contract" was "a contract whereby one employer would get an unfair competitive advantage over a competitor by getting a lower wage rate, would be one version of it."

---

[1] Huggins testified that in 1953 there was some personality conflict between Pugh and Huggins' assistant, a Mr. Forrest, on account of which Huggins recommended to Laurance See that Pugh be terminated, but See declined. Huggins again recommended Pugh's termination in 1968, under circumstances to be described in this opinion, and again See declined. It does not appear that Huggins' actions in this regard, or the criticism of Pugh which they implied, were made known to Pugh.

The presumption that an employment contract is intended to be terminable at will is subject, like any presumption, to contrary evidence. This may take the form of an agreement, express or implied, that the relationship will continue for some fixed period of time. Or, and of greater relevance here, it may take the form of an agreement that the employment relationship will continue indefinitely, pending the occurrence of some event such as the employer's dissatisfaction with the employee's services or the existence of some "cause" for termination. Sometimes this latter type of agreement is characterized as a contract for "permanent" employment, but that characterization may be misleading. In one of the earliest California cases on this subject, the Supreme Court interpreted a contract for permanent employment as meaning "that plaintiffs' employment . . . was to continue indefinitely, and until one or the other of the parties wish, for some good reason, to sever the relation." *Lord v. Goldberg*, 22 P. 1126 (Cal. 1889).

A contract which limits the power of the employer with respect to the reasons for termination is no less enforceable because it places no equivalent limits upon the power of the employee to quit his employment. "If the requirement of consideration is met, there is no additional requirement of . . . equivalence in the values exchanged, or 'mutuality of obligation.'" REST. (SECOND) CONTRACTS, § 81 (Tentative Draft No. 2, 1965).

Moreover, while it has sometimes been said that a promise for continued employment subject to limitation upon the employer's power of termination must be supported by some "independent consideration," *i.e.*, consideration other than the services to be rendered, such a rule is contrary to the general contract principle that courts should not inquire into the adequacy of consideration. . . . Thus there is no analytical reason why an employee's promise to render services, or his actual rendition of services over time, may not support an employer's promise both to pay a particular wage (for example) and to refrain from arbitrary dismissal.

The most likely explanation for the "independent consideration" requirement is that it serves an evidentiary function: it is more probable that the parties intended a continuing relationship, with limitations upon the employer's dismissal authority, when the employee has provided some benefit to the employer, or suffers some detriment, beyond the usual rendition of service. . . .

In determining whether there exists an implied-in-fact promise for some form of continued employment courts have considered a variety of factors in addition to the existence of independent consideration. These have included, for example, the personnel policies or practices of the employer, the employee's longevity of service, actions or communications by the employer reflecting assurances of continued employment, and the practices of the industry in which the employee is engaged.

[The court then discusses the implied-in-law covenant of good faith and fair dealing, but says "We need not go that far, however." Results of cases applying that covenant are "equally explicable in traditional contract terms: the employer's conduct gave rise to an implied promise that it would not act arbitrarily in dealing with its employees."]

Here, similarly, there were facts in evidence from which the jury could determine the existence of such an implied promise: the duration of appellant's employment, the commendations and promotions he received, the apparent lack of any direct criticism of his work, the assurances he was given, and the employer's acknowledged policies. While oblique language will not, standing alone, be sufficient to establish agreement, it is appropriate to consider the totality of the parties' relationship: Agreement may be "shown by the acts and conduct of the parties, interpreted in the light of the subject matter and the surrounding circumstances." We therefore conclude that it was error to grant respondents' motions for nonsuit as to See's.

Since this litigation may proceed toward yet uncharted waters, we consider it appropriate to provide some guidance as to the questions which the trial court may confront on remand. We have held that appellant has demonstrated a *prima facie* case of wrongful termination in violation of his contract of employment. The burden of coming forward with evidence as to the reason for appellant's termination now shifts to the employer. Appellant may attack the employer's offered explanation, either on the ground that it is pretextual (and that the real reason is one prohibited by contract or public policy), or on the ground that it is insufficient to meet the employer's obligations under contract or applicable legal principles. Appellant bears, however, the ultimate burden of proving that he was terminated wrongfully. *Cf. McDonnell Douglas Corp. v. Green*, 411 U.S. 792, 802–07 (1973).

By what standard that burden is to be measured will depend, in part, upon what conclusions the jury draws as to the nature of the contract between the parties. The terms "just cause" and "good cause," "as used in a variety of contexts . . . have been found to be difficult to define with precision and to be largely relative in their connotation, depending upon the particular circumstances of each case." Essentially, they connote "a fair and honest cause or reason, regulated by good faith on the part of the party exercising the power." Care must be taken, however, not to interfere with the legitimate exercise of managerial discretion. "Good cause" in this context is quite different from the standard applicable in determining the propriety of an employee's termination under a contract for a specified term. And where, as here, the employee occupies a sensitive managerial or confidential position, the employer must of necessity be allowed substantial scope for the exercise of subjective judgment.

Reversed.

RACANELLI, P. J., and NEWSOM, J., concur.

NOTES

1. *Pugh's Fate on Remand.* While *Pugh* is the leading case establishing implied-in-fact good-cause contracts for long-tenured employees, Pugh himself did not succeed under the standard. At the second trial, See's Candies presented evidence that it had discharged Pugh for good cause. See's employees, former employees, and business associates testified that Pugh was disrespectful to his superiors and subordinates, disloyal to the company, and uncooperative with other administrative staff. Charles Huggins, president and chief executive officer of See's, testified that his complaints about Pugh spanned almost twenty years and that he had recommended Pugh's termination in 1953 and in 1968. The jury found for the defendant in a general verdict, which was upheld on appeal. *Pugh v. See's Candies, Inc.*, 250 Cal. Rptr. 195 (Cal. Ct. App. 1988).

2. *Longevity of Service.* What is the key fact supporting Pugh's claim? Is it the assurances given to him, or is it simply that he has devoted thirty-two years of his life to this company? If the latter, when should the presumption against arbitrary dismissal begin? In *Cleary v. American Airlines,* 168 Cal. Rptr. 722 (Cal. Ct. App. 1980), the court upheld a claim of an employee dismissed without cause after eighteen years of service, holding: "Termination of employment without legal cause after such a period of time offends the implied-in-law covenant of good faith and fair dealing contained in all contracts including employment contracts." In *Foley v. Interactive Data Corp.,* 765 P.2d 373 (Cal. 1988), the California Supreme Court upheld a *Pugh* claim for an employee with six years and nine months of service.

The California Supreme Court later downplayed the significance of longevity of service in *Guz v. Bechtel*, 8 P.3d 1089 (Cal. 2000). Guz had worked for Bechtel for twenty-two years before being dismissed when his work unit was eliminated. In rejecting Guz's implied-contract claim that he could not be dismissed without good cause, the court declared that Guz's longevity, standing alone, could not prove a contractual right to be terminated only for good cause:

> In *Foley*, we identified several factors, apart from express terms, that may bear upon the existence and content of an implied in fact agreement placing limits on the employer's right to discharge an employee. [The court quotes *Foley*'s list of factors, which in turn quoted *Pugh*.] We did not suggest, however, that every vague combination of *Foley* factors, shaken together in a bag, necessarily allows a finding that the employee had a right to be discharged only for good cause, as determined in court. . . .

> [A]n employee's mere passage of time in the employer's service, even where marked with tangible indicia that the employer approves the employee's work, cannot alone form an implied-in-fact contract that the employee is no longer at will. Absent other evidence of the employer's intent, longevity, raises and promotions are their own rewards for the employee's continuing valued service; they do not, in and of themselves, additionally constitute a contractual guarantee of future employment security. A rule granting such contract rights on the basis of successful longevity alone would discourage the retention and promotion of employee.

> On the other hand, long and successful service is not necessarily irrelevant to the existence of such a contract. Over the period of an employee's tenure, the employer can certainly communicate, by its written and unwritten policies and practices, or by informal assurances, that seniority and longevity do create rights against termination at will. The issue is whether the employer's words or conduct, on

which an employee reasonably relied, gave rise to that specific understanding.

Id. at 1101, 1104-05.

3. *Long- and Short-Tenured Employees.* In *Foley v. Community Oil Co.,* 64 F.R.D. 561 (D.N.H. 1974) (applying New Hampshire law), the employee was both long term and a recent mover. Foley had worked for thirty-two years when his company was bought by Community Oil. He continued to work for Community Oil for another five years, when it asked him to move from Maine to New Hampshire. Three years after he sold his house and moved with his wife to New Hampshire, he was fired. The court declared that a forty-year employee's "[l]ongevity of service can also give rise to an implied contract right," explaining that "the employee, in providing long-term employment to a single employer substantially diminishes his economic mobility." In what way is the lack of economic mobility relevant to the employee's claim?

4. *Implied Tenure for Public Employees.* A famous pair of due-process cases illustrates the centrality of long service in finding implied job tenure for public employees. In *Board of Regents v. Roth,* 408 U.S. 564 (1972), a college terminated without reason an assistant professor at his first teaching job upon completion of his one-year contract. The Supreme Court rejected his due-process claim, concluding he had no property interest beyond the one-year job.

In *Perry v. Sindermann,* 408 U.S. 593 (1972), decided the same day, Professor Perry had completed ten one-year contracts in the Texas system and had been a full professor at Odessa Junior College for four years when he was dismissed. The college had no formal tenure system. The Court found he had a property right in his job that could not be taken away without due process. Justice Stewart, writing for the Court, explained that "[a] teacher, like the respondent, who has held his position for a number of years, might be able to show from the circumstances of this service — and from other relevant facts — that he has a legitimate claim of entitlement to job tenure." 408 U.S. at 602.

5. *Defining Good Cause — Good Faith or Just Cause?* When a court finds an implied-in-fact agreement for job security, a remaining issue is how much security to imply. *Pugh* upholds a "good cause" standard, and indicates that it is less stringent than under a definite-term contract. A major question is whether the good-cause standard is closer to subjective good faith or objective just cause.

Suppose, in a *Pugh* situation, the jury finds that the employer had a reasonable belief the employee smoked marijuana on the job in violation of company rules, but the jury also finds that the employee did not, in fact, smoke marijuana. Does the employee win on a claim of breach of the implied-in-fact contract? For a spirited debate on this issue, see *Sanders v. Parker Drilling Co.,* 911 F.2d 191 (9th Cir. 1990), in which the court held that, under Alaska law, the employer must show that the employee actually engaged in prohibited conduct. Judge Kozinski dissented, warning that the majority reaches "a result so preposterous it would be laughable if it were not so scary." *Id.* at 215.

California law apparently differs from Alaskan law on this point, as explored in *Cotran v. Rollins Hudig Hall International, Inc.*, 948 P.2d 412 (Cal. 1998). After two coworkers accused Cotran of sexual harassment, the company conducted twenty-one interviews over two weeks, concluded that the accusations were probably true, and fired him. He filed suit for breach of an implied-in-fact contract not to be fired without good cause. At trial, the court instructed the jury to determine whether Cotran had, in fact, engaged in the alleged sexual harassment. The jury found that Cotran had not and awarded him $1.8 million in compensatory damages. The court of appeals overturned the judgment and the California Supreme Court affirmed, holding that the proper question for the jury was not whether the misconduct had actually occurred, but whether the employer had reasonable grounds for believing it had occurred and acted fairly otherwise.

6. *Good Faith or Just Cause in the Constitution.* The Supreme Court has wrestled with the same issue for public employees with constitutional protection, but has been unable to articulate a clear rule. In *Waters v. Churchill*, 511 U.S. 661 (1994), a supervisor in a public hospital fired a nurse for allegedly making comments that were personal and disruptive. The nurse claimed her comments only criticized the hospital's cross-training policy, which allowed nurses to work in areas without sufficient training. Because the employer was a governmental body subject to the First Amendment, any firing would be subject to the test of *Connick v. Myers*, 461 U.S. 138 (1983), which holds that a governmental employer cannot fire an employee for speaking on a matter of public concern unless the employee's interest in expressing herself is outweighed by any injury the speech could cause to the state's interest in efficient public service by its employees. (*See generally* Chapter 8.) For purposes of the case, the Court assumed that the *Connick* test would forbid the hospital from knowingly firing the nurse for speaking on cross-training, but that the nurse had no claim if she uttered only personal, disruptive comments. The question dividing the Justices was whether the nurse had a claim if she in fact was talking about cross-training but the supervisor thought she was making only comments unprotected by the First Amendment.

Justice O'Connor, writing for four Justices, declared that the *Connick* test should be applied to what the employer thought was said, not to what a fact-finder later determines was actually said. However, the employer must make reasonable efforts to determine the true facts. O'Connor's test could be labeled a reasonable good-faith test.

Justice Scalia, writing for three Justices, rejected any constitutional requirement that the employer must conduct an investigation before firing an employee. He would find that a public employer violated the First Amendment only if the firing was in retaliation for protected speech. His test could be labeled a subjective good-faith test.

Justice Stevens, writing for two Justices, would find the firing impermissible unless a judicial fact-finder determines that the employee in fact made the disparaging remarks. Justice Stevens began his opinion by declaring that "[t]his is a free country," and ended by declaring that freedom of speech requires that "before firing a public employee for her speech, management get its facts straight." His test might be labeled an objective good-cause test.

7. *Enforcing Life-Cycle Contracts.* Many employees spend most of their working life in an internal labor market with a single employer. As with many long-term relationships, an employer and employee have difficulty specifying in advance many of the terms under which they will operate. Of necessity, much of the agreement is implicit rather than explicit. Both the firm and worker make heavy investments in training and recruitment. A problem in such long-term relationships is that neither side can easily terminate it, because of the costs of duplicating these sunk investments. Being locked in can lead to exploitation. The temptation for exploitation is greatly increased when one party has largely completed its investment or promises and the other side has not. A major role for courts might be to enforce the implicit agreements, thereby making them more secure and valuable for both sides.

One common life-cycle model suggests that a firm pays its employees less than they are worth at the beginning of their career with the promise of paying them more than they are worth at the end. This will induce employees to work hard and acquire firm-specific skills, so that both the firm and employees are better off than under an arrangement in which employees are paid their current worth at all times. The danger with this arrangement, however, is that a firm has an incentive to fire workers nearing the end of their life cycle, when they are paid more than they are currently producing. One way to justify the result in *Pugh* is to suggest that the court is enforcing an implicit life-cycle contract. *See* Stewart J. Schwab, *Life-Cycle Justice: Accommodating Just Cause and Employment At Will*, 92 MICH. L. REV. 8 (1993) (excerpted in Chapter 7).

C. EMPLOYMENT MANUALS

WOOLLEY v. HOFFMANN-LA ROCHE, INC.
Supreme Court of New Jersey
491 A.2d 1257, *modified,* 499 A.2d 515 (1985)

WILENTZ, C.J.

I

The issue before us is whether certain terms in a company's employment manual may contractually bind the company. We hold that absent a clear and prominent disclaimer, an implied promise contained in an employment manual that an employee will be fired only for cause may be enforceable against an employer even when the employment is for an indefinite term and would otherwise be terminable at will.

II

Plaintiff, Richard Woolley, was hired by defendant, Hoffmann-La Roche, Inc., in October 1969, as an Engineering Section Head in defendant's Central Engineering Department at Nutley. There was no written employment contract between plaintiff and defendant. Plaintiff began work in mid-November

1969. Some time in December, plaintiff received and read the personnel manual on which his claims are based.

In 1976, plaintiff was promoted, and in January 1977 he was promoted again, this latter time to Group Leader for the Civil Engineering, the Piping Design, the Plant Layout, and the Standards and Systems Sections. In March 1978, plaintiff was directed to write a report to his supervisors about piping problems in one of defendant's buildings in Nutley. This report was written and submitted to plaintiff's immediate supervisor on April 5, 1978. On May 3, 1978, stating that the General Manager of defendant's Corporate Engineering Department had lost confidence in him, plaintiff's supervisors requested his resignation. Following this, by letter dated May 22, 1978, plaintiff was formally asked for his resignation, to be effective July 15, 1978.

Plaintiff refused to resign. Two weeks later defendant again requested plaintiff's resignation, and told him he would be fired if he did not resign. Plaintiff again declined, and he was fired in July.

Plaintiff filed a complaint alleging breach of contract, intentional infliction of emotional distress, and defamation, but subsequently consented to the dismissal of the latter two claims. The gist of plaintiff's breach of contract claim is that the express and implied promises in defendant's employment manual created a contract under which he could not be fired at will, but rather only for cause, and then only after the procedures outlined in the manual were followed.[1] Plaintiff contends that he was not dismissed for good cause, and that his firing was a breach of contract.

Defendant's motion for summary judgment was granted by the trial court, which held that the employment manual was not contractually binding on defendant, thus allowing defendant to terminate plaintiff's employment at will.[2] The Appellate Division affirmed. We granted certification.

---

[1] According to the provisions of the manual, defendant could, and over the years apparently did, unilaterally change these provisions. . . .

[2] . . . It may be of some help to point out some of the manual's general provisions here. It is entitled "Hoffmann-La Roche, Inc. Personnel Policy Manual" and at the bottom of the face page is the notation "issued to: [and then in handwriting] Richard Woolley 12/1/69." The portions of the manual submitted to us consist of eight pages. It describes the employees "covered" by the manual ("all employees of Hoffmann-La Roche"), the manual's purpose ("a practical operating tool in the equitable and efficient administration of our employee relations program"); five of the eight pages are devoted to "termination." In addition to setting forth the purpose and policy of the termination section, it defines "the types of termination" as "layoff," "discharge due to performance," "discharge, disciplinary," "retirement" and "resignation." As one might expect, layoff is a termination caused by lack of work, retirement a termination caused by age, resignation a termination on the initiative of the employee, and discharge due to performance and discharge, disciplinary, are both terminations for cause. There is no category set forth for discharge without cause. The termination section includes "Guidelines for discharge due to performance," consisting of a fairly detailed procedure to be used before an employee may be fired for cause. Preceding these definitions of the five categories of termination is a section on "Policy," the first sentence of which provides: "It is the policy of Hoffmann-La Roche to retain to the extent consistent with company requirements, the services of all employees who perform their duties efficiently and effectively."

III

Hoffmann-La Roche contends that the formation of the type of contract claimed by plaintiff to exist — Hoffmann-La Roche calls it a permanent employment contract for life — is subject to special contractual requirements: the intent of the parties to create such an undertaking must be clear and definite; in addition to an explicit provision setting forth its duration, the agreement must specifically cover the essential terms of employment — the duties, responsibilities, and compensation of the employee, and the proof of these terms must be clear and convincing; the undertaking must be supported by consideration in addition to the employee's continued work. Woolley claims that the requirements for the formation of such a contract have been met here and that they do not extend as far as Hoffmann-La Roche claims. Further, Woolley argues that this is not a "permanent contract for life," but rather an employment contract of indefinite duration that may be terminated only for good cause and in accordance with the procedure set forth in the personnel policy manual. Both parties agree that the employment contract is one of indefinite duration; Hoffmann-La Roche contends that in New Jersey, when an employment contract is of indefinite duration, the inescapable legal conclusion is that it is an employment at will; Woolley claims that even such a contract — of indefinite duration — may contain provisions requiring that termination be only for cause. . . .

We are thus faced with the question of whether this is the kind of employment contract — a "long-range commitment" — that must be construed as one of indefinite duration and therefore at will . . ., or whether ordinary contractual doctrine applies. In either case, the question is whether Hoffmann-La Roche retained the right to fire with or without cause or whether, as Woolley claims, his employment could be terminated only for cause. We believe another question, not explicitly treated below, is involved: should the legal effect of the dissemination of a personnel policy manual by a company with a substantial number of employees be determined solely and strictly by traditional contract doctrine? Is that analysis adequate for the realities of such a workplace? . . .

V

. . . .

We acknowledge that most of the out-of-state cases demonstrate an unwillingness to give contractual force to company policy manuals that purport to enhance job security. These cases, holding that policy manual provisions do not give rise to any contractual obligation, have to some extent confused policy manuals with individual long-term employment contracts and have applied to the manuals rules appropriate only to the individual employment contract. When there was such an individual contract before them (often consisting of oral assurances or a skeletal written agreement) not specifying a duration or term, courts understandably ruled them to be "at-will" contracts. They did so since they feared that by interpreting a contract of indefinite duration to be terminable only for cause, the courts would be saddling an employer with an employee for many years. In order to insure that the employer intended to accept the burdens of such an unusual "lifetime employment," the courts understandably insisted that the contract and the surrounding circumstances demonstrate unmistakably clear signs of the employer's intent to be bound, leading to the requirements of additional independent consideration and convincing specificity. . . .

Whatever their worth in dealing with individual long-term employment contracts, these requirements, over and above those ordinarily found in contract law, have no relevancy when a policy manual is involved. In that case, there is no individual lifetime employment contract involved, but rather, if there is a contract, it is one for a group of employees — sometimes all of them — for an indefinite term, and here, fairly read, one that may not be terminated by the employer without good cause. . . .

What is before us in this case is not a special contract with a particular employee, but a general agreement covering all employees. There is no reason to treat such a document with hostility.

The trial court viewed the manual as an attempt by Hoffmann-La Roche to avoid a collective bargaining agreement.[6] Implicit is the thought that while the employer viewed a collective bargaining agreement as an intrusion on management prerogatives, it recognized, in addition to the advantages of an employment manual to both sides, that unless this kind of company manual were given to the workforce, collective bargaining, and the agreements that result from collective bargaining, would more likely take place.

A policy manual that provides for job security grants an important, fundamental protection for workers. If such a commitment is indeed made, obviously an employer should be required to honor it. When such a document, purporting to give job security, is distributed by the employer to a workforce, substantial injustice may result if that promise is broken.

We do not believe that Hoffmann-La Roche was attempting to renege on its promise when it fired Woolley. On the contrary, the record strongly suggests that even though it believed its manual did not create any contractually binding agreements, Hoffmann-La Roche nevertheless almost invariably honored it. In effect, it gave employees more than it believed the law required. Its position taken before us is one of principle: while contending it treated Woolley fairly, it maintains it had no legal obligation to do so.

VI

Given the facts before us and the common law of contracts interpreted in the light of sound policy applicable to this modern setting, we conclude that the termination clauses of this company's Personnel Policy Manual, including the procedure required before termination occurs, could be found to be contractually enforceable. Furthermore, we conclude that when an employer of a substantial number of employees circulates a manual that, when fairly read, provides that certain benefits are an incident of the employment

---

[6] The trial court, after noting that if Hoffmann-La Roche had been unionized, Woolley would not be litigating the question of whether the employer had to have good cause to fire him, said "[T]here is no question in my mind that Hoffmann-La Roche offered these good benefits to their employees to steer them away from this kind of specific collective bargaining contract. . . ."

(including, especially, job security provisions), the judiciary, instead of "grudgingly" conceding the enforceability of those provisions, should construe them in accordance with the reasonable expectations of the employees.

The employer's contention here is that the distribution of the manual was simply an expression of the company's "philosophy" and therefore free of any possible contractual consequences. The former employee claims it could reasonably be read as an explicit statement of company policies intended to be followed by the company in the same manner as if they were expressed in an agreement signed by both employer and employees. From the analysis that follows we conclude that a jury, properly instructed, could find, in strict contract terms, that the manual constituted an offer; put differently, it could find that this portion of the manual (concerning job security) set forth terms and conditions of employment.

In determining the manual's meaning and effect, we must consider the probable context in which it was disseminated and the environment surrounding its continued existence. The manual, though apparently not distributed to all employees ("in general, distribution will be provided to supervisory personnel . . ."), covers all of them. Its terms are of such importance to all employees that in the absence of contradicting evidence, it would seem clear that it was intended by Hoffmann-La Roche that all employees be advised of the benefits it confers.

We take judicial notice of the fact that Hoffmann-La Roche is a substantial company with many employees in New Jersey. The record permits the conclusion that the policy manual represents the most reliable statement of the terms of their employment. At oral argument counsel conceded that it is rare for any employee, except one on the medical staff, to have a special contract. Without minimizing the importance of its specific provisions, the context of the manual's preparation and distribution is, to us, the most persuasive proof that it would be almost inevitable for an employee to regard it as a binding commitment, legally enforceable, concerning the terms and conditions of his employment. Having been employed, like hundreds of his co-employees, without any individual employment contract, by an employer whose good reputation made it so attractive, the employee is given this one document that purports to set forth the terms and conditions of his employment, a document obviously carefully prepared by the company with all of the appearances of corporate legitimacy that one could imagine. If there were any doubt about it (and there would be none in the mind of most employees), the name of the manual dispels it, for it is nothing short of the official policy of the company, it is the Personnel Policy Manual. As every employee knows, when superiors tell you "it's company policy," they mean business.

The mere fact of the manual's distribution suggests its importance. Its changeability — the uncontroverted ability of management to change its terms — is argued as supporting its non-binding quality, but one might as easily conclude that, given its importance, the employer wanted to keep it up to date, especially to make certain, given this employer's good reputation in labor relations, that the benefits conferred were sufficiently competitive with those available from other employers, including benefits found in collective bargaining agreements. The record suggests that the changes actually made almost always favored the employees.

Given that background, then, unless the language contained in the manual were such that no one could reasonably have thought it was intended to create legally binding obligations, the termination provisions of the policy manual would have to be regarded as an obligation undertaken by the employer. It will not do now for the company to say it did not mean the things it said in its manual to be binding. Our courts will not allow an employer to offer attractive inducements and benefits to the workforce and then withdraw them when it chooses, no matter how sincere its belief that they are not enforceable.

Whatever else the manual may deal with . . . one of its major provisions deals with the single most important objective of the workforce: job security. The reasons for giving such provisions binding force are particularly persuasive. Wages, promotions, conditions of work, hours of work, all of those take second place to job security, for without that all other benefits are vulnerable. . . .

Job security is the assurance that one's livelihood, one's family's future, will not be destroyed arbitrarily; it can be cut off only "for good cause," fairly determined. Hoffmann-La Roche's commitment here was to what working men and women regard as their most basic advance. It was a commitment that gave workers protection against arbitrary termination.

Many of these workers undoubtedly know little about contracts, and many probably would be unable to analyze the language and terms of the manual. Whatever Hoffmann-La Roche may have intended, that which was read by its employees was a promise not to fire them except for cause.

Under all of these circumstances, therefore, it would be most unrealistic to construe this manual and determine its enforceability as if it were the same as a lifetime contract with but one employee designed to induce him to play on the company's baseball team.[8]

VII

Having concluded that a jury could find the Personnel Policy Manual to constitute an offer, we deal with what most cases deem the major obstacle to construction of the terms as constituting a binding agreement, namely, the requirement under contract law that consideration must be given in exchange for the employer's offer in order to convert that offer into a binding agreement. The cases on this subject deal with such issues as whether there was a promise

---

[8] The contract arising from the manual is of indefinite duration. It is not the extraordinary "lifetime" contract. . . . For example, a contract arising from a manual ordinarily may be terminated when the employee's performance is inadequate; when business circumstances require a general reduction in the employment force, the positions eliminated including that of plaintiff; when those same circumstances require the elimination of employees performing a certain function, for instance, for technological reasons, and plaintiff performed such functions; when business conditions require a general reduction in salary, a reduction that brings plaintiff's pay below that which he is willing to accept; or when any change, including the cessation of business, requires the elimination of plaintiff's position, an elimination made in good faith in pursuit of legitimate business objectives: all of these terminations, long before the expiration of "lifetime" employment, are ordinarily contemplated in a contract arising from a manual, although the list does not purport to be exhaustive. The essential difference is that the "lifetime" contract purports to protect the employment against any termination; the contract arising from the manual protects the employment only from arbitrary termination.

in return for the employer's promise (the offer contained in the manual constituting, in effect, a promise), or whether there was some benefit or detriment bargained for and in fact conferred or suffered, sufficient to create a unilateral contract; whether the action or inaction, the benefit or the detriment, was done or not done in reliance on the employer's offer or promise; whether the alleged agreement was so lacking in "mutuality" as to be insufficient for contractual purposes — in other words, whether the fundamental requirements of a contract have been met.

We conclude that these job security provisions contained in a personnel policy manual widely distributed among a large workforce are supported by consideration and may therefore be enforced as a binding commitment of the employer.

In order for an offer in the form of a promise to become enforceable, it must be accepted. Acceptance will depend on what the promisor bargained for: he may have bargained for a return promise that, if given, would result in a bilateral contract, both promises becoming enforceable. Or he may have bargained for some action or nonaction that, if given or withheld, would render his promise enforceable as a unilateral contract. In most of the cases involving an employer's personnel policy manual, the document is prepared without any negotiations and is voluntarily distributed to the workforce by the employer. It seeks no return promise from the employees. It is reasonable to interpret it as seeking continued work from the employees, who, in most cases, are free to quit since they are almost always employees at will, not simply in the sense that the employer can fire them without cause, but in the sense that they can quit without breaching any obligation. Thus analyzed, the manual is an offer that seeks the formation of a unilateral contract — the employees' bargained-for action needed to make the offer binding being their continued work when they have no obligation to continue.

The unilateral contract analysis is perfectly adequate for that employee who was aware of the manual and who continued to work intending that continuation to be the action in exchange for the employer's promise; it is even more helpful in support of that conclusion if, but for the employer's policy manual, the employee would have quit.[9]

Those solutions seem to be technically correct. . . . [I]n *Anthony v. Jersey Cent. Power & Light Co.,* 143 A.2d 762 (N.J. Super. Ct. App. Div. 1958), practically every contractual objection that could be made here was disposed of by the Appellate Division in the context of a claim for pension rights by supervisory personnel based on a company manual (entitled "General Rules"). There, the defendant-employer argued that its severance-pay rule was a mere

---

[9] Third-party-beneficiary doctrines might be used to confer the benefits on all workers; or the employer's offer could be construed as inviting acceptance in the form of continuance of work by merely one worker in order to benefit all.

Similarly, the doctrine of promissory estoppel could be relied on as a rationale for enforcement of an employer's promises in a policy manual or similar document under certain circumstances. . . .

The doctrine of unconscionability of the Uniform Commercial Code is analogous to the employment-at-will rule. The unconscionability doctrine developed to protect the disadvantaged party in a one-sided bargain.

gratuitous promise, not supported by consideration. The court responded, analyzing the promise as an offer of a unilateral contract and the employees' continued services as sufficient acceptance and consideration therefor. To the defendant's argument that there was no evidence of reliance upon its promise, the *Anthony* court responded that reliance was to be presumed under the circumstances. We agree.[10]

VIII

The lack of definiteness concerning the other terms of employment — its duration, wages, precise service to be rendered, hours of work, etc., does not prevent enforcement of a job security provision. The lack of terms (if the complete manual is similarly lacking) can cause problems of interpretation about these other aspects of employment, but not to the point of making the job security term unenforceable. Realistically, the objection has force only when the agreement is regarded as a special one between the employer and an individual employee. There it might be difficult to determine whether there was good cause for termination if one could not determine what it was that the employee was expected to do. That difficulty is one factor that suggests the employer did not intend a lifetime contract with one employee. Here the question of good cause is made considerably easier to deal with in view of the fact that the agreement applies to the entire workforce, and the workforce itself is rather large. Even-handedness and equality of treatment will make the issue in most cases far from complex; the fact that in some cases the "for cause" provision may be difficult to interpret and enforce should not deprive employees in other cases from taking advantage of it. If there is a problem arising from indefiniteness, in any event, it is one caused by the employer. It was the employer who chose to make the termination provisions explicit and clear. If indefiniteness as to other provisions is a problem, it is one of the employer's own making from which it should gain no advantage.

Defendant expresses some concern that our interpretation will encourage lawsuits by disgruntled employees. As we view it, however, if the employer has in fact agreed to provide job security, plaintiffs in lawsuits to enforce that agreement should not be regarded as disgruntled employees, but rather as employees pursuing what is rightfully theirs. The solution is not deprivation of the employees' claim, but enforcement of the employer's agreement. The

---

[10] If reliance is not presumed, a strict contractual analysis might protect the rights of some employees and not others. For example, where an employee is not even aware of the existence of the manual, his or her continued work would not ordinarily be thought of as the bargained-for detriment. Similarly, if it is quite clear that those employees who knew of the offer knew that it sought their continued work, but nevertheless continued without the slightest intention of putting forth that action as consideration for the employer's promise, it might not be sufficient to form a contract. In this case there is no proof that plaintiff, Woolley, relied on the policy manual in continuing his work. Furthermore, as the Appellate Division correctly noted, Woolley did "not bargain for" the employer's promise. The implication of the presumption of reliance is that the manual's job security provisions became binding the moment the manual was distributed. Anyone employed before or after became one of the beneficiaries of those provisions of the manual. And if *Toussaint* [v. *Blue Cross & Blue Shield,* 292 N.W.2d 880 (Mich. 1980)] is followed, employees neither had to read it, know of its existence, or rely on it to benefit from its provisions any more than employees in a plant that is unionized have to read or rely on a collective-bargaining agreement in order to obtain its benefits.

defendant further contends that its future plans and proposed projects are premised on continuance of the at-will employment status of its workforce. We find this argument unpersuasive. There are many companies whose employees have job security who are quite able to plan their future and implement those plans. If, however, the at-will employment status of the workforce was so important, the employer should not have circulated a document so likely to lead employees into believing they had job security. . . .

X

We are aware that problems that do not ordinarily exist when collective bargaining agreements are involved may arise from the enforcement of employment manuals. Policy manuals may not generally be as comprehensive or definite as typical collective bargaining agreements. Further problems may result from the employer's explicitly reserved right unilaterally to change the manual. We have no doubt that, generally, changes in such a manual, including changes in terms and conditions of employment, are permitted. We express no opinion, however, on whether or to what extent they are permitted when they adversely affect a binding job security provision.

XI

Our opinion need not make employers reluctant to prepare and distribute company policy manuals. Such manuals can be very helpful tools in labor relations, helpful both to employer and employees, and we would regret it if the consequence of this decision were that the constructive aspects of these manuals were in any way diminished. We do not believe that they will, or at least we certainly do not believe that that constructive aspect should be diminished as a result of this opinion.

All that this opinion requires of an employer is that it be fair. It would be unfair to allow an employer to distribute a policy manual that makes the workforce believe that certain promises have been made and then to allow the employer to renege on those promises. What is sought here is basic honesty: if the employer, for whatever reason, does not want the manual to be capable of being construed by the court as a binding contract, there are simple ways to attain that goal. All that need be done is the inclusion in a very prominent position of an appropriate statement that there is no promise of any kind by the employer contained in the manual; that regardless of what the manual says or provides, the employer promises nothing and remains free to change wages and all other working conditions without having to consult anyone and without anyone's agreement; and that the employer continues to have the absolute power to fire anyone with or without good cause.

Reversed and remanded for trial.

NOTES

1. *Reliance.* Unlike *Woolley*, many courts require that the employee rely on the manual before its promises can bind the employer. *See, e.g., Weiner*

v. McGraw-Hill, Inc., 443 N.E.2d 441 (N.Y. 1982), where the court sustained a cause of action where the employee rejected other offers of employment in reliance on a manual's promises of job security, which were incorporated by reference in the job application. In many cases, however, the question of what constitutes reliance is more difficult. In *Bulman v. Safeway Inc.,* 27 P.3d 1172 (Wash. 2001), the court overturned a $900,000 judgment based on a jury's finding that the employee justifiably relied on fair-dismissal policies in a manual in staying with the company for 33 years. The majority held, over a vigorous dissent, that it is not enough for an employee to have relied on "an atmosphere of job security and fair treatment" created by "promises of specific treatment in specific situations." Rather, the employee must have been personally aware of, and relied upon, the specific promises themselves. The dissent argued that this standard places unreasonable and impractical burdens on employees.

Should reliance be required, or can the employer be said to have benefited from the manual even if the employee did not rely? If the employer does not benefit from the manual, why did it produce one?

Suppose there are two types of job seekers: (1) cautious types who carefully weigh all parts of the employer's compensation package, including job security and other provisions of the employment manual, before accepting employment; and (2) free riders who assume or hope without inquiring that the employer's compensation package is the best available. If an employer offers job security in its manual, cautious types will be willing to accept a lower wage with the firm than they otherwise would. If the employer must pay all workers similarly, this low-wage, job-security package may be the "market" price.

A rough analogy may be provided by the fraud-on-the-market theory, which the Supreme Court has upheld in securities law. *See Basic Inc. v. Levinson,* 485 U.S. 224 (1988). Suppose an investor sells stock the day before a company merges with another, which drives the price up wildly. He complains that he sold at a depressed price because of a fraudulent statement (*e.g.,* "no merger is planned") by corporate insiders. The investor need not show that he was aware of the fraudulent statement.

2. *Prominent Disclaimers.* At the end of the *Woolley* opinion, the court emphasizes that an employer could disclaim the binding nature of a handbook if it so chose. Some courts refuse, however, to accept the disclaimer unless it is conspicuous and obvious to the employees.

For example, in *McDonald v. Mobil Coal Producing, Inc.,* 789 P.2d 866 (Wyo. 1990), *modified on reh'g,* 820 P.2d 986 (Wyo. 1991), the Wyoming Supreme Court held that Mobil's handbook amendment creating a disclaimer was ineffective. The court emphasized that Mobil's disclaimer was not capitalized, was in the same print as the rest of the handbook, and was contained in the general welcoming section of the handbook. *See also Jones v. Cent. Peninsula Gen. Hosp.,* 779 P.2d 783 (Alaska 1989) (finding one-sentence disclaimer in eighty-five page policy manual to be ineffective, because it did not unambiguously and conspicuously inform employees that the manual was not part of their employment contract).

Other courts have held that a "conspicuous" requirement leads to unnecessary confusion. In *Anderson v. Douglas & Lomason Co.,* 540 N.W.2d 277 (Iowa

1995), the court considered a disclaimer appearing on the last page of a fifty-three page handbook, two inches below the preceding language, that read: "This Employee Handbook is not intended to create any contractual rights in favor of you or the Company. The Company reserves the right to change the terms of this handbook at any time." The court refused to consider arguments that the disclaimer was not displayed prominently enough, declaring that a disclaimer should be considered like any other language in the handbook. The court then enforced the disclaimer as unambiguous.

3. *Usefulness of Meaningless Manuals.* Why would an employer want a manual that is legally meaningless? One possibility is that the manual is primarily addressed to supervisors rather than employees in an attempt to prevent supervisors from making statements inconsistent with basic personnel policy. Another possibility is that the firm is attempting to exploit legally unsophisticated workers by giving the appearance of job security when it knows none really exists.

4. *Dangers of Disclaimers.* Employers sometimes are reluctant to have prominent disclaimers in their handbooks. Most importantly, a prominent disclaimer might erode employee confidence that the employer will treat them fairly, causing morale problems among the current workforce and recruiting problems among applicants. This leads to higher turnover, training costs, and unemployment-compensation costs. In addition, disclaimers might increase the chance of a successful union organizing effort. *See generally* Julius M. Steiner & Allan M. Dabrow, *The Questionable Value of the Inclusion of Language Confirming Employment-At-Will Status in Company Personnel Documents,* 37 LAB. L.J. 63 (1986).

5. *Unions and Employment Law.* If the AFL-CIO were to write an amicus brief in this case, which side should it support? The *Woolley* court suggests that the employer used the employment manual to keep its workforce non-unionized. A legally enforceable manual should provide even greater benefits for workers, giving them even less incentive to unionize. On the other hand, to the extent that the ability to fire at will gives nonunion employers a cost advantage, the *Woolley* holding should reduce the cost disadvantage of unions, perhaps reducing employer opposition to unions. Additionally, of course, can the AFL-CIO publicly support an employer's position against even nonunion workers?

DEMASSE v. ITT CORP.

Supreme Court of Arizona (en banc)
984 P.2d 1138 (1999)

FELDMAN, JUSTICE.

The United States Court of Appeals for the Ninth Circuit certified to us [a question] of Arizona law. . . .

1. Once a policy that an employee will not be laid off ahead of less senior employees becomes part of the employment contract, as a result of the employee's legitimate expectations and reliance on the employer's handbook, may the employer thereafter unilaterally

change the handbook policy so as to permit the employer to layoff employees without regard to seniority? . . .

The [question certified posits] that the layoff seniority provision has become part of the employment contract. Using this assumption, we respond . . . in the negative.

. . . ITT hired Roger Demasse, Maria A. Garcia, Billy W. Jones, Viola Munguia, Greg Palmer, and Socorro Soza (collectively "Demasse employees") as hourly workers at various times between 1960 and 1979. Although it is unclear when ITT first issued an employee handbook, evidently there have been five editions, the most recent in 1989. . . .

The issues presented focus on the 1989 handbook, which included two new provisions. First, a disclaimer added to the first page "Welcome" statement provided that "nothing contained herein shall be construed as a guarantee of continued employment. . . . ITT Cannon does not guarantee continued employment to employees and retains the right to terminate or layoff employees." Second, this Welcome statement included a new modification provision, which read:

> Within the limits allowed by law, ITT Cannon reserves the right to amend, modify or cancel this handbook, as well as any or all of the various policies, rules, procedures and programs outlined in it. Any amendment or modification will be communicated to affected employees, and while the handbook provisions are in effect, will be consistently applied.

. . . When the 1989 handbook was distributed, ITT employees signed an acknowledgment that they had received, understood, and would comply with the revised handbook.

Four years passed before ITT notified its hourly employees that effective April 19, 1993, its layoff guidelines for hourly employees would not be based on seniority but on each employee's "abilities and documentation of performance." Demasse, Soza, and Palmer were laid off ten days after the new policy went into effect, Munguia five days later, and Jones and Garcia almost nine months later. All were laid off before less senior employees but in accordance with the 1993 policy modification.

The Demasse employees brought an action in federal district court alleging they were laid off in breach of an implied-in-fact contract created by the pre-1989 handbook provisions requiring that ITT lay off its employees according to seniority. [The District Court granted summary judgment to the employer. On appeal, the Ninth Circuit certified questions to the Arizona Supreme Court.]

A. *The implied-in-fact contract*

. . . .

Arizona recognizes that implied-in-fact contract terms may create an exception to employment that is completely at will. While employment contracts without express terms are presumptively at will, an employee can overcome this presumption by establishing a contract term that is either expressed or inferred from the words or conduct of the parties. An example of such a term is one that offers the employee job security — one specifying the duration of employment or limiting the reasons for dismissal.

When employment circumstances offer a term of job security to an employee who might otherwise be dischargable at will and the employee acts in response to that promise, the employment relationship is *no longer at will* but is instead governed by the terms of the contract. . . .

When an employer chooses to include a handbook statement that the employer should reasonably have expected the employee to consider as a commitment from the employer, that term becomes an offer to form an implied-in-fact contract and is accepted by the employee's acceptance of employment.

B. *Modification*

ITT argues that it had the legal power to unilaterally modify the contract by simply publishing a new handbook. But as with other contracts, an implied-in-fact contract term cannot be modified unilaterally. Once an employment contract is formed — whether the method of formation was unilateral, bilateral, express, or implied — a party may no longer unilaterally modify the terms of that relationship.

The cases dealing with employment contracts are merely part of the general rule that recognizes no difference in legal effect between an express and an implied contract. Thus an implied-in-fact employment term must be governed by the same traditional contract law that governs express promises and must be modified accordingly. As a result, to effectively modify a contract, whether implied-in-fact or express, there must be: (1) an offer to modify the contract, (2) assent to or acceptance of that offer, and (3) consideration.

The 1989 handbook, published with terms that purportedly modified or permitted modification of pre-existing contractual provisions, was therefore no more than an offer to modify the existing contract. Even if the 1989 handbook constituted a valid offer, questions remain whether the Demasse employees accepted that offer and whether there was consideration for the changes ITT sought to effect.

1. *Continued employment alone does not constitute consideration for modification*

. . . The cases ITT cites hold that continued work alone both manifested the Demasse employees' assent to the modification and constituted consideration for it. We disagree with both contentions and the cases that support them. Separate consideration, beyond continued employment, is necessary to effect a modification. . . . Any other result brings us to an absurdity: the employer's threat to breach its promise of job security provides consideration for its rescission of that promise.

2. *Acceptance*

Continued employment after issuance of a new handbook does not constitute acceptance, otherwise the "illusion (and the irony) is apparent: to preserve their right under the [existing contract] . . . plaintiffs would be forced to quit." *Doyle [v. Holy Cross Hosp.*, 708 N.E.2d 1140, 1145 (Ill. 1999)]. It is "too much to require an employee to preserve his or her rights under the original employment contract by quitting working." *Brodie [v. General Chem. Corp.*,

934 P.2d 1263, 1268 (Wyo. 1997)]. Thus, the employee does not manifest consent to an offer modifying an existing contract without taking affirmative steps, beyond continued performance, to accept. . . .

To manifest consent, the employee must first have legally adequate notice of the modification. Legally adequate notice is more than the employee's awareness of or receipt of the newest handbook. An employee must be informed of any new term, aware of its impact on the pre-existing contract, and affirmatively consent to it to accept the offered modification.

When ITT distributed the 1989 handbook containing the provisions permitting unilateral modification or cancellation, it did not bargain with those pre-1989 employees who had seniority rights under the old handbooks, did not ask for or obtain their assent, and did not provide consideration other than continued employment. The employees signed a receipt for the 1989 handbook stating that they had received the handbook, understood that it was their responsibility to read it, comply with its contents, and contact Personnel if they had any questions concerning the contents. The Demasse employees were not informed that continued employment — showing up for work the next day —would manifest assent, constitute consideration, and permit cancellation of any employment rights to which they were contractually entitled. Thus, even if we were to agree that continued employment could provide consideration for rescission of the job security term, that consideration would not have been bargained for and would not support modification.

C. Arizona courts have not recognized an employer's right to unilaterally modify a pre-existing implied-in-fact employment contract

. . . If a contractual job security provision can be eliminated by unilateral modification, an employer can essentially terminate the employee at any time, thus abrogating any protection provided the employee. For example, an employer could terminate an employee who has a job security provision simply by saying, "I revoke that term and, as of today, you're dismissed" — no different from the full at-will scenario in which the employer only need say, "You're fired." This, of course, makes the original promise illusory.

. . . To those who believe our conclusion will destroy an employer's ability to update and modernize its handbook, we can only reply that the great majority of handbook terms are certainly non-contractual and can be revised, that the existence of contractual terms can be disclaimed in the handbook in effect at the time of hiring and, if not, permission to modify can always be obtained by mutual agreement and for consideration. In all other instances, the contract rule is and has always been that one should keep one's promises. . . .

JONES, VICE CHIEF JUSTICE, concurring in part and dissenting in part:

. . .

The [majority's holding] undermines legitimate employer expectations in a remarkable departure from traditional at-will employment principles. It transforms the conventional employer-employee contract from one that is *unilateral* (performance of an act in exchange for a promise to pay) to one that is *bilateral* (a promise for a promise). . . .

The majority exacts from the certified question the premise that the employment relationship between the Demasse plaintiffs and ITT is "no longer at-will." I disagree. A single contract term in a policy manual may, while it exists, become an enforceable condition of employment, but it does not alter the essential character of the relationship. In my view, ITT, as the party unilaterally responsible for inserting it into the manual may, on reasonable notice, exercise an equal right to remove it.

For purposes of this discussion, it is assumed the reverse-seniority layoff provision became part of the "employment contract" years earlier when ITT initially placed it into the policy manual and that it remained a part of the "contract" as long as it remained a part of the manual. The simple question put to us is whether ITT may unilaterally bring about its removal and thereafter be free of any prospective reverse-seniority obligation in the event of a layoff. That question does not catapult the case beyond the reach of at-will employment principles. . . .

The "at-will" status of the Demasse-ITT contract both before and after the 1989 amendments is confirmed by at least two factors: (1) the contract was always one of indefinite duration, and (2) the Demasse employees had the absolute right to quit at any time. . . .

The right to quit in opposition to changed policies, despite the majority's view, is properly characterized as a right. It is an inherent feature of at-will employment. . . .

In *Wagner* [*v. City of Globe*, 722 P.2d 250, 253 (Ariz. 1986)], this court explained the relationship:

> Employment contracts, particularly those which would be considered at-will, are the best and most typical examples of unilateral contracts. Unlike a bilateral contract, a unilateral contract does not require mutuality of obligation; but there is sufficient consideration in the form of services rendered. This is true despite the fact that the employee may quit at any time.

We thus declared explicitly that employers have authority to modify at-will contracts and are bound by terms added after the employment relationship has begun.

The corollary, however, is also true: just as employers are bound currently by the terms of existing policy manuals, employees must be bound prospectively by amendments to the manual, even though a particular amendment was not bargained for at the point of hire. When ITT modified its policy manual in 1989 by adding the contract disclaimer and the power to amend, and offered continuing employment to employees having received notice and having signed the acknowledgment, the employees effectively gave their acceptance to the amendment by continuing to work. Moreover, in 1993, when ITT revised its layoff policy, the employees had known for four years that such change could occur.

The majority overlooks another point. Just as at-will employees are unilaterally free to quit at any time, employers may be unilaterally forced by economic circumstance to curtail or shut down an operation, something employers have the absolute right to do. When the employer chooses in good faith, in pursuit of legitimate business objectives, to eliminate an employee policy as an alternative to curtailment or total shutdown, there has been forbearance by the employer. Such forbearance constitutes a benefit to the employee in the form of an offer of continuing employment. The employer who provides continuing employment, albeit under newly modified contract terms, also provides consideration to support the amended policy manual.

Such is the nature of the at-will contract; consideration is found in the employer's offer of continuing employment, and the employee accepts the offer by his continued performance. Under the unilateral theory, continuing performance by the employee at a job that the employer continues to offer, subject to modified terms, manifests acceptance of the new terms.

The majority imposes a bilateral principle on the at-will relationship by holding that in order for ITT to eliminate the reverse-seniority layoff policy, some form of new consideration, in addition to an offer of continuing employment, is necessary to support each individual employee's assent to the amended manual. The majority's approach effectively mandates that ITT, in order to free itself of future reverse-seniority obligations, would be required to give a wage increase, a one-time bonus, or some other new benefit to the employees with the explicit understanding that such benefit was given in exchange for the amendment to the policy manual. This becomes artificial because it is foreign to the unilateral at-will relationship and, as a practical matter, it leaves the employer unable, at least in part, to manage its business. I disagree with the proposition that "new" consideration is necessary.

The majority further asserts that ITT's exercise of the unilateral right to amend the handbook renders the employer's original reverse-seniority promise illusory. Once again, I disagree. An illusory promise is one which by its own terms makes performance optional with the promisor whatever may happen, or whatever course of conduct he may pursue. The reverse-seniority promise was not illusory because it was not optional with ITT as long as it remained a part of ITT's handbook policy. During the years of its existence, it was fully enforceable. Moreover, the promise was genuine because it was applicable to all ITT employees, not merely a select few. . . .

The majority opinion produces the net result that the reverse-seniority layoff policy, as a permanent term of the "employment contract" with respect to any employee who at any time worked under it, gains parity with a negotiated collective bargaining agreement having a definite term, usually three years. In fact, the ITT policy would have force and effect even greater than a collective agreement because its existence, as to the Demasse plaintiffs and others similarly situated, becomes perpetual. This result grants preferential treatment to every employee who worked under the policy but denies such treatment to employees hired after its removal. A collective bargaining agreement is bilateral, and to impose a bilateral relationship on simple at-will employment is, in my view, an attempt to place a square peg in a round hole. Inevitably, this will impair essential managerial flexibility in the workplace. It will also cause undue deterioration of traditional at-will principles. . . .

Moreover, failure to include in a first-distributed handbook a provision reserving the power to modify or amend does not alter the analysis.

Other courts have upheld the employer's right to amend by express rejection of strict rules of contract modification. The Michigan Supreme Court adopted this theory, answering a certified question strikingly similar to the question presented here and concluding that an employer must have unilateral ability to amend handbook provisions:

. . . .

The major difficulty [with the idea that a "meeting of the minds" must occur to alter an implied in fact contract] as applied to the question before us is that the contractual obligation which may not be modified without mutual assent . . . could have arisen without mutual assent. . . . Under circumstances where "contractual rights" have arisen outside the operation of normal contract principles, the application of strict rules of contractual modification may not be appropriate.

In re Certified Question (Bankey), 443 N.W.2d 112, 116 (Mich. 1989).

One commentator refers to the *Bankey* approach as an "administrative law model":

The employer, like an agency, is bound by its rules, *but always remains free to change the rules prospectively through proper procedures.* Agencies have wide discretion in amending or revoking their regulations, as long as they meet the requirements set by administrative law for issuing them in the first place. But until modified or revoked, the regulations must be followed by the issuing agency. This is a good model for implied-in-fact contracts of employment security. . . . The general idea is well accepted in other areas of labor and employment law.

HENRY H. PERRITT, JR., EMPLOYEE DISMISSAL LAW & PRACTICE § 4.44 (3d ed. 1992) (citations omitted).

In the case at bar, the majority applies the hypertechnical approach rejected by the *Bankey* court. . . .

Principles of equity and pragmatic reason have also governed the employer's unilateral right to change an implied-in-fact term in a handbook. The federal district court, applying Arizona law in *Bedow*, correctly asserted that the last-distributed handbook controls employment conditions and trumps prior inconsistent handbook terms:

Any other conclusion would create chaos for employers who would have different contracts of employment for different employees depending upon the particular personnel manual in force when the employee was hired. Such a result would effectively discourage employers from either issuing employment manuals or subsequently upgrading or modifying personnel policies.

Bedow v. Valley Nat'l Bank, 5 IER Cases 1678, 1680 (D. Ariz. 1988). . . .

The majority's answer to the certified question will frustrate the legitimate expectations of both employers and employees. . . . We said [in prior cases] that employers should place contract disclaimer language in their handbooks to preserve the at-will relationship. ITT responded by inserting such language. We should leave it at that.

NOTES

1. *Formal and Policy Reasoning.* Judge Jones, in dissent, warns that the majority's approach will limit the flexibility (and ultimately the competitiveness) of employers, discouraging employers from experimenting with greater job protection or other benefits in the first place. The competing policy concern is to protect employees who reasonably rely on company handbooks.

Much of the analysis, of course, is conducted on a formal rather than policy level. The majority emphasizes that the employer never gave any consideration for the manual's modification and the employees never accepted the offered changes. Judge Jones accuses the majority of reaching its pro-employee result by being "hypertechnical" and by incorrectly using bilateral contract theory (a square peg) in a unilateral contract situation (the round hole), itself a technical criticism. In *Woolley*, the hypertechnical criticism went the other way. The *Woolley* court, in holding that employment manuals could be binding against employers, reasoned that the issue should not be "determined solely and strictly by traditional contract doctrine," but should also reflect "the realities of the workplace."

2. *A Middle Ground?* The majority and dissent in *Demasse* stake out polar positions. On the one hand, the majority treats the contract very seriously. Once the employer makes promises accepted by the employees, they can be revoked only if the changes are accepted by employees with independent consideration. To the dissent, on the other hand, the at-will principle means that the employer should always be free to change this kind of promise. The "essential character" of an at-will relationship means that the employee's response to an undesirable change is to quit, not to sue.

One of the majority's strongest arguments, at least rhetorically, is that the job-protection promise is illusory if the employer can simply say one day, "I revoke the promise and now fire you." Some courts finesse this argument by requiring adequate notice. Thus, in *Asmus v. Pacific Bell*, 999 P.2d 71, 71 (Cal. 2000), the court held that employers can terminate job-protection promises of indefinite duration, but only "after a reasonable time, on reasonable notice, and without interfering with the employee's vested benefits." *See also Bankey v. Storer Broadcasting Co.*, 443 N.W.2d 112 (Mich. 1989) (en banc) (holding that right to change with proper notice available even if no express reservation of right to make changes in handbook). This "notice" approach is an attempt to balance the policy concerns of employer flexibility and employee protection but, of course, it will raise significant issues about what notice is reasonable and what rights are vested.

3. *Can an Employer Bind Itself?* From the employer's perspective, the advantage of a binding promise of job security is that employees may have higher morale and productivity and be less likely to unionize. Some employers might calculate that these advantages outweigh the flexibility of changeable promises. But in jurisdictions that adopt the dissent's position in *Demasse* or the "notice" approach of *Asmus* or *Bankey*, can an employer bind itself? In *Asmus*, the employer had promised to maintain its employment-security policy "so long as there is no change that will materially affect [its] business plan achievement." The Court held that this promise was not permanently binding on the employer; the employer could change it with notice. Presumably, as employees learn the ephemeral quality of these promises, the advantages to the employer are reduced. Could an employer seek to regain these advantages and bind itself by saying "the firm will maintain the policy as long as it remains profitable" or "the firm will maintain the policy for at least ten years"?

Chapter 5

TORT EROSIONS OF EMPLOYMENT AT WILL

In this chapter we turn to the inroads on at-will employment made by tort doctrine. Even when the employer and employee clearly agree to at-will employment, so that a discharged employee has no breach-of-contract claim regardless of the reason for discharge, the employee may have a tort claim. One justification for tort law regulation of contractual relationships is to protect third parties. A general goal of this chapter is to see whether employment-law tort cases fit this pattern. In Section A we consider the tort of wrongful discharge in violation of public policy, which also is called the tort of retaliatory discharge or abusive discharge. The third-party rationale fits fairly well. In Section B we examine other torts, particularly intentional infliction of emotional distress. The third-party rationale fares less well, but in some cases the tort is nevertheless compelling.

A. WRONGFUL DISCHARGE IN VIOLATION OF PUBLIC POLICY

NEES v. HOCKS
Supreme Court of Oregon (en banc)
536 P.2d 512 (1975)

DENECKE, JUSTICE.

The principal question is whether the plaintiff alleged and proved conduct of the defendants which amounts to a tort of some nature. . . .

The jury found for plaintiff; therefore, we must consider the facts as established by the evidence most favorable to plaintiff. The plaintiff performed clerical duties for defendants. She started work in 1971. In 1972 she was called for jury duty; however, as she informed defendants, she requested and was granted a 12-month postponement because of her honeymoon. On February 2, 1973, plaintiff was again subpoenaed to serve on the jury. She told defendants and they stated that a month was too long for her "to be gone." Defendants gave her a letter which stated defendants could spare plaintiff "for awhile" but not for a month and asked that she be excused. Plaintiff presented this letter to the court clerk and told the clerk that she had been called before and had to be excused, but she would like to serve on jury duty. The clerk told plaintiff she would not be excused. The plaintiff immediately came back to the office and told defendants that she would have to serve a minimum of two weeks' jury duty. She did not tell defendants she had told the court clerk she really wanted to serve.

Plaintiff started her jury duty on February 26, 1973. On March 1, 1973, she received a termination letter from defendants. The letter stated, in part: "Although we asked you to request an excusal from Jury Duty and wrote a letter confirming the Labls [defendants'] position, it has been brought to our attention you, in fact, requested to be placed on Jury Duty." The letter went on to state the defendants also were not otherwise satisfied with plaintiff's work. Based upon other evidence, however, the jury could have found plaintiff was not terminated because of dissatisfaction with the quality of plaintiff's work.

A representative of the firm that employed plaintiff after she was terminated by defendants testified one of the defendants told him plaintiff was terminated because she went on jury duty.

Plaintiff testified she suffered emotional distress because of her termination. She secured employment commencing one week after she finished jury duty for a higher salary than she had received from defendants. The jury awarded plaintiff compensatory and punitive damages.

Plaintiff has labeled the tort she contends she pleaded and proved, "prima facie tort." This is a label used by some courts, particularly New York. . . . We are of the opinion that the term serves no purpose in Oregon and we will advance the jurisprudence of this state by eliminating it. . . .

This court has not felt unduly restricted by the boundaries of pre-existing common-law remedies. We have not hesitated to create or recognize new torts when confronted with conduct causing injuries which we feel should be compensable. . . .

We recognize, as defendants assert, that, generally, in the absence of a contract or legislation to the contrary, an employer can discharge an employee at any time and for any cause. Conversely, an employee can quit at any time for any cause. Such termination by the employer or employee is not a breach of contract and ordinarily does not create a tortious cause of action. The question to us is, however, are there instances in which the employer's reason or motive for discharging harms or interferes with an important interest of the community and, therefore, justifies compensation to the employee?

Other courts have held that there are such instances. In *Petermann v. International Brotherhood of Teamsters,* 344 P.2d 25 (Cal. Ct. App. 1959), the plaintiff was discharged by his employer for refusing to give perjured testimony before a committee of the legislature. A judgment on the pleadings for the defendant employer was reversed. . . .

In *Frampton v. Central Indiana Gas Co.,* 297 N.E.2d 425 (Ind. 1973), the plaintiff employee alleged he was discharged for filing a workmen's compensation claim. The court reversed the order of the trial court dismissing the complaint for failing to state a cause of action.

The same division of the court that decided the *Petermann* case, cited above, in *Becket v. Welton Becket & Associates,* 114 Cal. Rptr. 531 (Cal. Ct. App. 1974), distinguished *Petermann* and held for the employer. In *Becket* plaintiff was employed by a corporate architectural firm. Plaintiff's father, who owned all of the stock in the firm, died and plaintiff was appointed co-executor of his father's estate. Plaintiff also was the largest legatee. Plaintiff as co-executor brought a suit against the firm and his co-executor alleging breach of fiduciary duties, corporate waste and improper usurpation of corporation control. The defendant firm told plaintiff to drop the litigation or they would discharge him. Plaintiff persisted and he was discharged. The court stated there was no statute evidencing any public policy protecting any right of an employee to sue his employer as a fiduciary or in a stockholder's derivative suit.

Our recent decision in *Campbell v. Ford Industries, Inc.,* 513 P.2d 1153 (Or. 1973), probably falls into the same category as the case just discussed. In both the interest of the employee was purely private and not of general public concern. In *Campbell* the plaintiff alleged he was a minority stockholder and employee of the defendant. He alleged he was discharged because he refused to sell his stock to defendant. We held that while he might be able to recover for any injury to his interest as a shareholder, he could not recover for any injury to his interest as an employee.

We conclude that there can be circumstances in which an employer discharges an employee for such a socially undesirable motive that the employer must respond in damages for any injury done. The next question is, does the evidence in this case permit a finding that such circumstances are present? There is evidence from which the jury could have found that the defendants discharged the plaintiff because, after being subpoenaed, and contrary to the defendants' wishes, plaintiff told the clerk she would like to serve and she did serve on jury duty.[2] Therefore, the immediate question can be stated specifically — is the community's interest in having its citizens serve on jury duty so important that an employer, who interferes with that interest by discharging an employee who served on a jury, should be required to compensate his employee for any damages she suffered?

Art. VII, § 3, of the Oregon Constitution provides that jury trial shall be preserved in civil cases. Art. I, § 11, provides a defendant in a criminal case has a right of trial by jury. Art. VII, § 5, provides: "The Legislative Assembly shall so provide that the most competent of the permanent citizens of the county shall be chosen for jurors."

OR. REV. STAT. § 10.040 provides for certain exemptions from jury duty. OR. REV. STAT. § 10.050 provides for certain excuses from jury duty including health, age and "(c) When serving as a juror would result in extreme hardship to the person including but not limited to unusual and extraordinary financial hardship." OR. REV. STAT. § 10.055 provides for deferment of jury duty "for good cause shown" for not more than one year. OR. REV. STAT. § 10.990 provides that if a juror "without reasonable cause," neglects to attend for jury service the sheriff may impose a fine, not exceeding $20 for each day the juror does not attend.

People v. Vitucci, 199 N.E.2d 78 (Ill. App. Ct. 1964), stated that an employer who discharged an employee who was absent because of jury duty was guilty

---

[2] If the only evidence was that the defendants would have suffered a substantial hardship if plaintiff served this particular month, defendants requested only a postponement of jury service but the plaintiff nevertheless asked to serve this particular month, we probably would regard the discharge as justifiable.

of contempt of court. Massachusetts has a statute making such conduct contemptuous.

These actions by the people, the legislature and the courts clearly indicate that the jury system and jury duty are regarded as high on the scale of American institutions and citizen obligations. If an employer were permitted with impunity to discharge an employee for fulfilling her obligation of jury duty, the jury system would be adversely affected. The will of the community would be thwarted. For these reasons we hold that the defendants are liable for discharging plaintiff because she served on the jury.

[The Court then overturned the award of punitive damages because the cause of action was newly created.]

That part of the judgment awarding $650 compensatory damages is affirmed; that part of the judgment awarding punitive damages in the amount of $3,000 is reversed. The trial court will enter judgment accordingly.

Affirmed in part; reversed in part.

NOTES

1. *Typology of Wrongful Discharge Cases.* *Petermann, Frampton,* and *Nees* illustrate the classic fact patterns where courts have upheld lawsuits for wrongful discharge in violation of public policy:

(1) *Refusing to commit unlawful acts.* The classic example is refusing to commit perjury when the government is investigating the company for wrongdoing. *Petermann v. Int'l Bhd. of Teamsters,* 344 P.2d 25 (Cal. Ct. App. 1959).

(2) *Exercising a statutory right.* The classic example is filing a claim for benefits under the workers' compensation statute. *Frampton v. Central Indiana Gas Co.,* 297 N.E.2d 425 (Ind. 1973).

(3) *Fulfilling a public obligation.* The classic example is serving on jury duty. *Nees v. Hocks,* 536 P.2d 512 (Or. 1975).

A fourth pattern, *whistleblowing,* occurs when an employee reports the company's unlawful conduct to a supervisor or outside authorities. The following lead cases deal with this pattern.

2. *Third-Party Effects.* A classic tort justification for overriding freedom of contract is that the conduct between contracting parties adversely affects third parties. Just as courts will not enforce a contract to murder because enforcement harms a third person, so too the courts should not enforce an at-will contract if the discharge harms third parties. Of the classic categories of wrongful discharge actions, which has the clearest third-party effects? Which is most suspect?

3. *Pigeonholing Fact Patterns.* Can the following cases be put into one of the pigeonholes above? If not, should the claim nevertheless be allowed? When the court rejects a possible public-policy claim, is the asserted interest largely a private one?

(a) A bank manager was fired when he attempted to defend himself after a subordinate physically attacked him. *See McLaughlin v. Barclays Am. Corp.,*

382 S.E.2d 836 (N.C. Ct. App.), *cert. denied,* 385 S.E.2d 498 (N.C. 1989) (rejecting claim that employee was wrongfully fired for engaging in his right to self-defense). *But see Feliciano v. 7-Eleven, Inc.,* 559 S.E.2d 713 (W. Va. 2001) (holding that the termination of employee who successfully fights off and arrests an armed robber violates the public policy in favor of self defense when employee faces imminent danger).

(b) An employee is fired for writing a letter to the editor in the local newspaper criticizing management. *See Schultz v. Indus. Coils, Inc.,* 373 N.W.2d 74 (Wis. Ct. App. 1985) (rejecting claim that state constitutional provision declaring that every person may freely speak, write, and publish his sentiments on all subjects provides public-policy exception).

(c) A gas station attendant is fired for refusing to pump leaded gas into automobile equipped only for unleaded gas, which would violate Federal Clean Air Act. *See Phipps v. Clark Oil & Ref. Corp.,* 396 N.W.2d 588 (Minn. Ct. App. 1986), *aff'd,* 408 N.W.2d 569 (Minn. 1987) (upholding cause of action).

(d) A movie theater employee was fired after he called the police and emptied the theater because he feared there was an intruder in the projection room. *See Girgenti v. Cali-Con, Inc.,* 544 A.2d 655 (Conn. App. Ct. 1988) (claim stated).

(e) An employee is fired for reporting to the company vice president that the FBI is currently investigating the employee's immediate supervisor for embezzlement while at a former employer. *See Foley v. Interactive Data Corp.,* 765 P.2d 373 (Cal. 1988) (rejecting claim of wrongful discharge in violation of public policy because the disclosure of information "serves only the private interest of the employer" and not an independent public interest).

(f) An employee scheduled to work at 3:00 p.m. was in a car accident at 1:00 p.m. and taken by ambulance to a hospital, where he was not released until 5:00 p.m. When he was fired for not reporting for work on time, he filed suit, asserting that "it is the public policy of the State of Illinois for injured persons to receive medical attention, particularly in an emergency situation." *See Thomas v. Zamberletti,* 480 N.E.2d 869 (Ill. App. Ct. 1985) (no claim stated).

(g) An employee was brutally beaten and raped off-work by her estranged husband. To avoid dealing with the situation, the employer fired her. *See Green v. Bryant,* 887 F. Supp. 798 (E.D. Pa. 1995) (applying Pennsylvania law, dismissing wrongful-discharge claim because no public harm occurred).

(h) A bartender was fired for refusing to serve liquor to a visibly intoxicated patron who was going to drive home. *See Woodson v. AMF Leisureland Ctrs., Inc.,* 842 F.2d 699 (3d Cir. 1988) (applying Pennsylvania law, court recognizes cause of action).

(i) An associate in a law firm was fired in retaliation for a letter written by her attorney advising the employer it was unlawfully discriminating against the employee because of her pregnancy. *See Gelini v. Tishgart,* 91 Cal. Rptr. 2d 447 (Cal. Ct. App. 1999) (upholding claim of wrongful discharge in violation of state statute allowing employees to designate bargaining representatives, explaining that "the world of employment today is subject to a vast array of legislative and administrative regulations, at the federal, state, and local levels. Whether this is a good or a bad development, the government as well as the individual employee has a substantial interest in assuring that every worker may seek guidance in penetrating the legal thicket without fear of retaliation.").

(j) A driver of an armored truck delivering money to a bank was discharged for violating company policy against leaving the truck while en route. The driver had left the truck to rescue a bank manager fleeing from a bank robber with a knife. *See Gardner v. Loomis Armored, Inc.*, 913 P.2d 377 (1996) (upholding cause of action because of the policy "of saving persons from life threatening situations").

4. *Finding Public Policy.* Some courts have broadly defined public policy. In *Palmateer v. International Harvester Co.*, 421 N.E.2d 876, 878 (Ill. 1981), the Illinois Supreme Court reversed the dismissal of a complaint alleging an employee was fired for reporting a possible crime to law-enforcement authorities, stating:

> There is no precise definition of the term. In general, it can be said that public policy concerns what is right and just and what affects the citizens of the State collectively. It is to be found in the State's constitution and statutes and, when they are silent, in its judicial decisions.

Accord Pierce v. Ortho Pharmaceutical Corp., 417 A.2d 505, 512 (N.J. 1980) (declaring that "sources of public policy include . . . judicial decisions"; "in certain instances, a professional code of ethics [such as the Hippocratic Oath] may contain an expression of public policy," but an employee's personal morals do not); *Parnar v. Americana Hotels, Inc.*, 652 P.2d 625, 631 (Haw. 1982) ("Courts should inquire whether the employer's conduct contravenes the letter or purpose of a constitutional, statutory, or regulatory provision or scheme. Prior judicial decisions may also establish the relevant public policy"); *Boyle v. Vista Eyewear, Inc.*, 700 S.W.2d 859, 871 (Mo. Ct. App. 1985) (" 'Public policy' is that principle of law which holds that no one can lawfully do that which tends to be injurious to the public or against the public good.").

Other courts, however, have refused to accept such a broad definition of public policy, insisting that an employee point to some specific public policy as articulated in a constitution, statute, or regulation. A leading case following this narrower definition of public policy is *Gantt v. Sentry Ins.*, 824 P.2d 680, 687-88 (Cal. 1992). In upholding a $1.34 million judgment when a manager was terminated in retaliation for testifying truthfully about an employee's sexual-harassment claim in an administrative investigation, the California Supreme Court declared:

> A public policy exception carefully tethered to fundamental policies that are delineated in constitutional or statutory provisions strikes the proper balance among the interests of employers, employees and the public. The employer is bound, at a minimum, to know the fundamental public policies of the state and nation as expressed in their constitutions and statutes; so limited, the public policy exception presents no impediment to employers that operate within the bounds of the law. Employees are protected against employer actions that contravene fundamental state policy. And society's interests are

served through a more stable job market, in which its most important policies are safeguarded.

See also Green v. Ralee Engineering Co., 960 P.2d 1046 (Cal. 1998) (holding that statutorily authorized federal regulations on airline safety were a valid source of public policy, while confirming that judicial decisions alone were not).

5. *Legal Contortions in Finding Statutory Violations.* Courts are understandably nervous about the nebulousness of a general public-policy standard. But a rule that employment terminations only violate public policy if they would violate a specific statute can lead to legal contortions. For example, in *Lucas v. Brown & Root, Inc.*, 736 F.2d 1202 (8th Cir. 1984) (applying Arkansas law), an employee was fired for refusing the sexual advances of her foreman. The court upheld her wrongful-discharge claim, finding that, in effect, she was being asked to violate the anti-prostitution statute. Does this mean that in states where prostitution is lawful, such an employee would have no claim? Does focusing on whether the prostitution statute is violated address the real issues involved, or simply find a pigeonhole in which to afford the employee a remedy?

In *Wagenseller v. Scottsdale Mem'l Hosp.*, 710 P.2d 1025 (Ariz. 1985), a nurse and her supervisor went on an eight-day rafting trip with employees of other hospitals. The nurse refused to join in a parody of "Moon River," where the group mooned the audience. Her refusal led to strained relations with the supervisor and eventually to her being fired. In support of her wrongful-discharge claim, the employee argued that the mooning skit would have violated the indecent-exposure statute, which prohibits exposure of the anus or genitalia if the viewer would be offended or alarmed by the act. The court refused to determine whether mooning would actually violate the statute, finding the policy of the statute to be sufficiently implicated:

> We have little expertise in the techniques of mooning. We cannot say as a matter of law, therefore, whether mooning would always violate the statute by revealing the mooner's anus or genitalia. That question could only be determined, we suppose, by an examination of the facts of each case. We deem such an inquiry unseemly and unnecessary in a civil case. Compelled exposure of the bare buttocks, on pain of termination of employment, is a sufficient violation of the *policy* embodied in the statute to support the action, even if there would have been no technical violation of the statute.

Id. at 1035 n.5.

6. *Federal Law as State Public Policy.* In searching for public policy, courts routinely turn to federal as well as state law, although some cases question whether the search should be so wide-ranging. In *Peterson v. Browning*, 832 P.2d 1280 (Utah 1992), the Utah Supreme Court upheld the claim of a customs officer who claimed he was terminated for refusing to falsify tax documents in violation of federal and Missouri law. The court held that federal or other states' laws could serve as a source of Utah public policy, but warned that not just any violation would suffice: "A plaintiff must establish the connection between the law violated and the public policies of Utah."

Some courts have actually rejected federal law as a source of state public policy. In *Guy v. Travenol Labs.*, 812 F.2d 911 (4th Cir. 1987), the employee claimed retaliatory discharge when he refused to falsify records required by federal food and drug law. The court determined that North Carolina law had no obligation to use its tort system to bolster federal policies. *See also Rachford v. Evergreen Int'l Airlines,* 596 F. Supp. 384 (N.D. Ill. 1984) (declaring that Illinois has general interest in air safety, but no interest in enforcing FAA regulations); *Pratt v. Caterpillar Tractor Co.,* 500 N.E.2d 1001 (Ill. App. Ct. 1986) (holding that refusing to engage in conduct prohibited by Federal Corrupt Practices Act implicates no state policy because no harm to state's citizens alleged). At the other extreme, states may be preempted from bolstering some federal policies through wrongful discharge actions. *See Ingersoll-Rand Co. v. McClendon,* 498 U.S. 133 (1990) (holding that ERISA preempts employee's state-law wrongful-discharge claim that employer fired him to avoid making contributions to his pension fund).

7. *Adequate Legislative Remedies.* A court that allows a claim of wrongful discharge in violation of express statutory policy can be seen as supplementing whatever remedies or penalties the legislature has expressly provided in enacting the statute. The first question is one of legislative preemption. Sometimes Congress or the state legislature explicitly or implicitly preempt common-law claims in favor of the statutory scheme. For example, in *Ingersoll-Rand Co. v. McClendon,* 498 U.S. 133 (1990), the Supreme Court held that Congress preempted state common-law claims of wrongful discharge in violation of public policy when an employee was fired shortly before his pension was to vest. The only remedy was through the federal ERISA statute.

Even if the legislature does not preempt the common-law action, the courts themselves must decide whether, as a matter of common law, they should allow the action in addition to the statutory remedies. For example, consider a jury-service statute that not only imposes criminal penalties on an employer who fires employees for doing jury duty, but also provides that an employee who is fired, demoted, or suspended for taking time off to serve jury duty "shall be entitled to reinstatement and reimbursement for lost wages and work benefits caused by such acts of the employer." Should these remedies be exclusive, or should the courts also recognize a common-law action and remedies? In *Hodges v. S.C. Toof & Co.,* 833 S.W.2d 896 (Tenn. 1992), the Tennessee Supreme Court held that an employee fired for serving jury duty was not limited to the damages laid out in the statute and affirmed an award of $200,000 in compensatory damages. The court vacated a punitive damages award of $375,000, but only to make sure the jury had been instructed on and followed the clear-and-convincing-evidence standard necessary for punitive damages. The court expressly held that punitive damages would be allowed if a jury followed the clear-and-convincing standard. Thus, Tennessee courts will uphold both compensatory and punitive damage awards in jury-duty wrongful-discharge cases, even though the jury-service statute only calls for employee reinstatement and reimbursement for lost wages and benefits.

The trend of courts, however, is to reject wrongful-discharge claims when the legislature has provided an adequate alternative remedy. For example, consider an employee discharged on the basis of race or sex, a matter of the highest public policy. Title VII of the federal Civil Rights Act of 1964 prohibits such discrimination and provides for conciliation by the Equal Employment

Opportunity Commission followed by private lawsuits. Further, section 708 expressly declares that Title VII does not exempt employers from present or future state laws. Nevertheless, most courts will reject a wrongful-discharge claim based on race or sex discrimination. *See, e.g., Clinton v. State ex rel. Logan County Election Bd.*, 29 P.3d 543 (Okla. 2001) (holding that employee may not bring a wrongful-discharge action when discharge violates Oklahoma's clear and compelling public policy against pregnancy discrimination but the employee has an adequate federal statutory remedy).

8. *Arizona Employment Protection Act.* In most states, courts have decided whether to recognize a common-law wrongful-discharge action when adequate statutory remedies exist. In Arizona, however, the legislature acted to permit the cause of action, but limited the remedies to those provided by a statute, if they exist. The Arizona Employment Protection Act of 1996 declares:

> If the statute provides a remedy to an employee for a violation of the statute, the remedies provided to an employee for a violation of the statute are the exclusive remedies for the violation of the statute or the public policy set forth in or arising out of the statute.
>
> . . . .
>
> If the statute does not provide a remedy to an employee for the violation of the statute, the employee shall have the right to bring a tort claim for wrongful termination in violation of the public policy set forth in the statute.

ARIZ. REV. STAT. ANN. § 23-1501(3)(b).

The preamble explains that the legislature enacted the statute in response to *Wagenseller* (noted above). The Arizona Supreme Court upheld the constitutionality of the statute in *Cronin v. Sheldon*, 991 P.2d 231 (Ariz. 1999), but went out of its way to say that cases like *Wagenseller* would not be affected because the statute at issue did not prescribe a separate civil remedy, and therefore the plaintiff "shall have the right to bring a tort claim." *Id.* at 236.

9. *Backbone to Resist a Faustian Bargain.* Consider the following rationale for providing a tort cause of action to at-will employees:

> Imagine in these cases that the employer explained at the initial job interview, "This job pays extra-high wages because it is potentially dangerous. It may require you to be convicted of perjury, or to be held in contempt of court for refusing jury service, or simply to violate your moral beliefs against enabling drunk drivers. But the value to this company of perjury, or constant attendance, or serving customers, outweighs these high wages; that is why we offer the job." The employee then asks: "What happens if I don't agree to this perjury term, or refusing-jury-service term, or must-serve-drunks term?" "If you refuse the term now," the employer replies, "you won't be hired. If you refuse to perform later, you will be fired." If the employee accepts the job with this understanding, presumably it is because the high wages and other aspects of the job are worth the expected criminal/moral penalties from perjury, or refusing jury service, or serving

drunks. Thus, the employer and employee are jointly better off with these conditions than without. But even as valiant a freedom-of-contract buff as Professor Epstein would refuse to enforce such contracts. The rationale is simple. The parties, while furthering their own self-interests, are ignoring the effects of their deal on others. Because the private contract has substantial adverse third-party effects, we refuse to enforce it.

In theory, under this imaginary bargaining story, an employee taking the job agrees to commit perjury, or to refuse jury duty, or to serve drunks. If the employee maintains his end of the bargain, the investigating agency hears perjured testimony, the jury pool lacks a member, and a drunk-driving accident occurs. The employee keeps his job, and no wrongful discharge suit is filed. What the tort of wrongful discharge allows, however, is for the employee to change his mind. He can renege on the Faustian deal without fear of losing the job.

In practice, employers and employees rarely expressly negotiate over job duties that violate the public interest. Even if they did, their agreement rarely would call for civic-minded action by the employee. A public-goods problem exists here. An employee acting in the public interest gets only a small share of the social benefit created. The public-good activity, therefore, will be underproduced unless tort law intervenes. The wrongful discharge tort gives the employee some backbone to look at the overall social interest. The employee deciding whether to testify against his employer or to take time off to perform jury duty knows that, if he is fired, he will be compensated with tort damages. Of course, compensatory damages at best put him in the same position had he not testified or been a juror (and thereby not been fired). If the employee recognizes that he may not win his lawsuit because of the vagaries of trial, or recognizes that he must generally pay attorney fees out of his damage award, he may rationally decide to commit perjury or to reject jury duty. Perhaps an employee's sense of morality is enough to let him take the plunge. Tort law attempts to tip the balance by adding the possibility of punitive damages.

Stewart J. Schwab, *Wrongful Discharge Law and the Search for Third-Party Effects*, 74 TEX. L. REV. 1952-53 (1996).[*]

WRIGHT v. SHRINERS HOSPITAL FOR CRIPPLED CHILDREN
Supreme Judicial Court of Massachusetts
589 N.E.2d 1241 (1992)

Before LIACOS, C.J., and WILKINS, LYNCH, O'CONNOR and GREANEY, JJ.

O'CONNOR, JUSTICE:

In this case, which is here on direct appellate review, we consider the sufficiency of the evidence to warrant a jury's verdict of $100,000 in favor of the plaintiff, Anita Wright against her employer, the defendant Shriners

Hospital for Crippled Children (Shriners Hospital), on Wright's claim that Shriners Hospital wrongfully terminated her at-will employment in violation of public policy. . . . We hold that the evidence was insufficient . . . and that the trial judge should have allowed the defendants' motion for judgment notwithstanding the verdict. . . .

We summarize the evidence in the light most favorable to the plaintiff. Shriners Hospital hired Wright, a registered nurse, in 1976. Subsequently, she became assistant director of nursing, and she held that position until she was discharged in late February of 1987. At all times, she was an employee at will. Wright received excellent evaluations throughout her employment, including an evaluation in December, 1986, two months before her discharge. In June, 1986, a former assistant head nurse wrote a letter to the director of clinical affairs for the Shriners national headquarters detailing her concerns about the medical staff and administration at Shriners Hospital. Shriners Hospital is a separate corporation, but it is one of many Shriners facilities that are affiliated with the national headquarters. As a result of the letter, the national headquarters notified the defendant hospital administrator, Russo, that a survey team would visit Shriners Hospital in November, 1986. Russo was visibly upset. He spoke to the director of nursing about the letter and asked her: "Are you behind this? Is Anita Wright behind this?" The director of nursing denied that she was responsible for the letter. She did not address the question whether Wright was "behind" the letter.

The survey team visited the hospital in November and interviewed Wright and other employees. Wright told the survey team that there were communication problems between the medical and nursing staffs. She detailed problems with the assistant chief of staff and gave specific examples of patient care problems. The survey team reported Wright's comments to the assistant chief of staff.

Two members of the survey team prepared reports. . . . Both reports recommended a follow-up site survey to determine the impact of this conflict on patient care. [One of the reports] stated that during her interview, Wright had made severe criticisms of the medical staff and had expressed concern over a lack of consistent procedures and standards for patient care. Hoard's report stated that Wright discussed the breakdown in communication between the nursing staff and the attending medical staff, which she said was leading to deteriorating morale among nurses.

Upon reading the survey team's reports, Russo again became upset and told the director of nursing that it was the nursing department's fault that the team was making another visit. He also stated at a department managers' meeting in December, 1986, "It seems there are people who spend their time trying to find fault with everything that everyone does, and those kinds of people we don't need here." Russo testified that, when he said that, he "possibly" was referring to statements made to the survey team. After the survey team's November, 1986, visit, Russo stopped speaking to Wright or even acknowledging her presence. The survey team returned on February 18 and 19, 1987, specifically to review the problems between the medical and nursing staffs. On February 26, after consulting with the chairman and several officers of the board of governors of Shriners Hospital and with national corporate counsel, Russo ordered that Wright's employment be terminated for "patient care issues that had arisen as a result of the surveys."

Wright contends, and the defendants dispute, that the jury would have been warranted in finding that Shriners Hospital fired her from her employment at will in retaliation for her having criticized the hospital, specifically in regard to the quality of care rendered to patients, to the Shriners national headquarters survey team. Wright further asserts that such a retaliatory firing violates public policy and is therefore actionable. It is a question of law for the judge to decide whether a retaliatory firing in these circumstances would violate public policy. . . . We hold that a termination of Wright's employment at will in reprisal for her critical remarks to the survey team would not have violated public policy. Therefore, we need not address the disputed matter of the sufficiency of the evidence to warrant a finding that the firing was indeed in retaliation for the criticism.

We begin with the general rule that "[e]mployment at will is terminable by either the employee or the employer without notice, for almost any reason or for no reason at all." We have recognized exceptions to that general rule, however, when employment is terminated contrary to a well-defined public policy. Thus, "[r]edress is available for employees who are terminated for asserting a legally guaranteed right (e.g., filing workers' compensation claim), for doing what the law requires (e.g., serving on a jury), or for refusing to do that which the law forbids (e.g., committing perjury)." We have also held that redress was available to an at-will employee who was discharged in retaliation for his cooperation with a law enforcement investigation concerning his employer. *Flesner v. Technical Communications Corp.*, 575 N.E.2d 1107 (Mass. 1991). Although the employee in *Flesner* was not required by law to cooperate, we reasoned that the Legislature had clearly expressed a policy encouraging cooperation with criminal investigations as indicated by statutes providing for reimbursement of expenses for persons assisting in investigations and immunity for witnesses testifying in grand jury investigation.

The trial judge's view of the law was that public policy was violated if Shriners Hospital fired Wright in reprisal for her having criticized the hospital in interviews with the survey team. As is clear from his instructions to the jury, the judge's view was based in part on "the duty of doctors and nurses, found in their own code of ethics, to report on substantial patient care issues." We would hesitate to declare that the ethical code of a private professional organization can be a source of recognized public policy. We need not consider that question, however, because no code of ethics was introduced in evidence in this case.

It is also clear from his instructions that the judge's view was based in part on "various state laws of the commonwealth, requiring reports on patient abuse." The judge did not identify the State laws he had in mind. General Laws c. 119, § 51A (1990 ed.), requires nurses and others to make a report to the Department of Social Services concerning any child under eighteen years of age who they have reason to believe is suffering from physical or sexual abuse or neglect. Similarly, G.L. c. 19A, § 15(a) (1990 ed.), requires nurses and others who have reasonable cause to believe that an elderly person is suffering from abuse to report it to the Department of Elder Affairs.

Subsection (*d*) of that provision provides that no employer or supervisor may discharge an employee for filing a report. Finally, G.L. c. 111, § 72G (1990 ed.), requires nurses and others to report to the Department of Public Health (department) when they have reason to believe that any patient or resident of a facility licensed by the department is being abused, mistreated, or neglected and provides a remedy of treble damages, costs, and attorney's fees for any employee who is discharged in retaliation for having made such a report. None of these statutes applies to Wright's situation, however, and we are unaware of any statute that does. Also, we are unaware of any statute that clearly expresses a legislative policy to encourage nurses to make the type of internal report involved in this case. In fact, Wright testified that she did not consider the patient care that caused her concern to be abuse, neglect, or mistreatment warranting a report to the department, nor did she feel that there was an issue of physician incompetence warranting a report to the board of registration in medicine as required by G.L. c. 112, § 5F (1990 ed.).

Wright urges us to recognize a regulation promulgated by the Board of Registration in Nursing as a source of public policy sufficient to create an exception to the general rule regarding termination of at-will employment. Title 244 Code Mass. Regs. § 3.02(3)(f) (1986) describes the responsibilities and functions of a registered nurse, including the responsibility to "collaborate, communicate and cooperate as appropriate with other health care providers to ensure quality and continuity of care." Even if that regulation called for Wright to report perceived problems or inadequacies to the survey team, a doubtful proposition, we have never held that a regulation governing a particular profession is a source of well-defined public policy sufficient to modify the general at-will employment rule, and we decline to do so now. Furthermore, as we have noted above, Wright's report was an internal matter, and "[i]nternal matters," we have previously said, "could not be the basis of a public policy exception to the at-will rule." *Smith-Pfeffer v. Superintendent of the Walter E. Fernald State Sch.*, citing *Mello v. Stop & Shop Cos., supra,* 524 N.E.2d 105.

We agree with the dissent that the provision of good medical care by hospitals is in the public interest. It does not follow, however, that all health care employees should be immune from the general at-will employment rule simply because they claim to be reporting on issues that they feel are detrimental to health care. In *Smith-Pfeffer, supra,* we held that there was no violation of a well-established public policy by an employer who discharged an employee for her actions in opposing a management restructuring plan proposed by the defendant acting superintendent as well as the possible appointment of the defendant to the position of permanent superintendent. The employee's opposition to the plan and appointment were based, in part, on her perception that the restructuring would significantly alter the management relationships such that it would "compromise service delivery to the residents" and "constitute[] a threat to the well-being of the institution and its residents". The defendant conceded that the jury could have found that the "plaintiff had performed her duties in a superior manner" and that her "actions were motivated by a sincere commitment to the mentally retarded residents in her unit," and that the defendant terminated her "to get rid of an employee he regarded as a trouble maker, and one with whom he personally did not get along." Although there is no less of a public interest in the provision of good quality care to the residents of a public facility for the retarded than in good care for patients in a hospital, we rejected the plaintiff's argument that the public policy exception to the at-will rule should extend to protect employees who were performing "appropriate, socially desirable duties" from being subject to discharge without cause. We reasoned, "[e]ssentially, the plaintiff's argument would require us to convert the general rule that 'an employment-at-will contract [can] be terminated at any time for any reason or for no reason at all,' into a rule that requires just cause to terminate an at-will employee. The public policy exception to the at-will employment rule is not that broad." We conclude in this case, as we did in *Smith-Pfeffer,* that the evidence did not warrant a verdict for the plaintiff.

. . . .

LIACOS, CHIEF JUSTICE, dissenting:

I disagree with the court's conclusion that a hospital employer violates no public policy when it fires an employee for alerting supervisors to matters detracting from good patient care. The court has construed far too narrowly the public policy exception to the doctrine of employment at will. Moreover, in demanding a statutory basis for public policy, the court has relinquished to the Legislature its role in shaping the common law. I dissent.

. . . .

"[T]he Achilles heel of the [public policy exception] lies in the definition of public policy." *Palmateer v. International Harvester Co.,* 421 N.E.2d 876 (Ill. 1981). It is a proper role of the courts to construe the boundaries of "public policy" and thereby develop common law remedies available to at-will employees who are terminated. I find it disturbing, therefore, that the court would relinquish this role, by requiring a statutory basis for public policy. The court reads *Flesner* too narrowly. In that case, we provided relief because the plaintiff was fired for performing an important public deed, not because the plaintiff was acting in accordance with a legislatively determined public policy. The court also declines to say whether public policy arises from such nonstatutory sources as regulations or the ethical codes of private professional organizations. It thus defers unduly to the Legislature in defining the contours of the public policy exception. This deferral in the realm of common law is inappropriate. The court must determine the boundaries of public policy, by looking not only to statutory law, but also to administrative law, judicial opinions, and even professional codes of conduct (where those codes serve a public interest, not merely the interests of the profession). *See Pierce v. Ortho Pharmaceutical Corp.,* 417 A.2d 505 (N.J. 1980).

. . . .

Given the public interest in good patient care, it must be the public policy of the Commonwealth to protect, if not encourage, hospital employees who perceive and report detriments to patient care. Only when problems are identified can they be adequately addressed; an employee's failure to report perceived detriments to patient care may allow the problems to persist. A hospital employer therefore violates public policy when it fires an employee for trying to improve the quality of patient care. That an employer may deter other employees from reporting problems (for fear of losing their jobs) inhibits the provision of good patient care and offends the public interest.

The plaintiff was terminated for reporting problems affecting patient care to a private, national, supervisory organization. According to her, these problems were causing lowered morale among nurses and conflicts between physicians and nurses, which in turn affected the quality of patient care.[4] As the plaintiff's comments concerned issues affecting patient care, the case does not involve a matter internal to the hospital over which the public has no concern. Furthermore, unlike the situation in *Smith-Pfeffer,* plaintiff raised concerns over employee relationships, not over hospital policy. The plaintiff was not terminated for contributing to the hospital's problems, nor for refusing to accept her supervisor's method of addressing the problems; she was fired for reporting the problems to appropriate accreditation authorities. Such a termination offends the public interest and is actionable.

I dissent.

NOTES

1. *Office Politics versus Ferreting Out Illegality.* Perhaps the major challenge in judicial protection of whistleblowers is the desire to avoid policing internal office politics. Corporations properly have internal debates on how safely to make their product or how to treat customers, for example. Promotions, raises, and terminations often rest on whether the boss appreciates the innovative ideas of subordinates or is irritated by the lack of team play. One of the hallmarks of at-will employment is that courts will not give the losers of these internal debates a second chance in court. On the other hand, whistleblowers serve a valuable public role in uncovering corporate threats to public safety and welfare. Can principled lines be articulated about when courts will intervene? For example, was Wright merely on the losing side of an internal company debate about how best to treat patients, or was she uncovering abuse?

2. *Internal Investigations.* Employees are understandably reluctant to finger supervisors during internal company investigations of wrongdoing, for fear that the supervisor will remain in power and retaliate against defectors. Should employees be able to rely on assurances that "no one will lose their job" for answering questions during an investigation? *See Mueller v. Union Pac. R.R.,* 371 N.W.2d 732 (Neb. 1985) (holding that employees fired after an internal investigation had a valid contract claim, even though public policy was too vague for a wrongful-discharge tort claim).

3. *Internal Versus External Whistleblowers.* Should it matter whether the employee reports the violation internally to a supervisor or externally to the agency regulating the area at issue? If courts are searching for third-party effects from the discharge, should they be more inclined to protect external whistleblowers? If courts draw such a line, will it unduly encourage whistleblowers to go outside the company rather than attempt to resolve the problem internally?

---

[4] The problems did not have to amount to abuse or neglect of patients in order to raise an issue of public concern.

These issues were discussed in *Belline v. K-Mart Corp.*, 940 F.2d 184 (7th Cir. 1991) (applying Illinois law). An employee was fired after reporting to senior K-Mart officials that his manager let a local Rotary Club obtain some merchandise without completing the proper forms. The majority reversed the grant of summary judgment against the employee, rejecting the argument that wrongful-discharge law should not protect internal complaints. "To hold otherwise," the court reasoned, "would be to create perverse incentives by inviting concerned employees to bypass internal channels altogether and immediately summon the police." Judge Easterbrook, in dissent, would have denied the wrongful-discharge claim. He emphasized that theft is an *unconsented* taking, so that Illinois has no interest in the outcome independent of K-Mart's.

Other courts have held that internal whistleblowers have no wrongful-discharge claim. In *Fox v. MCI Communications Corp.*, 931 P.2d 857 (Utah 1997), an employee was fired after reporting to an internal audit committee that other employees were "churning" — making existing customer accounts appear new on the corporate records so they could meet sales quotas and earn higher commissions. The employee alleged the churning was computer-aided fraud in violation of state criminal law. The court rejected her wrongful-discharge claim, emphasizing that the company had not asked her to commit a criminal act and that she had not reported anything to outside authorities:

> [I]f an employee reports a criminal violation to an employer, rather than to public authorities, and is fired for making such reports, that does not, in our view, contravene a clear and substantial public policy. In the instant case, the employer did not require plaintiff to engage in a criminal act or to violate her public duty to disclose criminal conduct. The conduct that plaintiff's co-workers engaged in was dishonest, but it did not cause harm to any of MCIT's customers; no customer was overcharged or defrauded as a result of the dishonest practices of MCIT's employees. The churning and creation of "new" accounts, while clearly intended to produce higher pay for the employees, was a practice defendant knew about and, by tolerating it, acquiesced in. For that reason, the corporation was not defrauded.

> Although employees may have a duty to disclose information concerning the employer's business to their employer, that duty ordinarily serves the private interest of the employer, not the public interest. *Foley v. Interactive Data Corp.*, 765 P.2d 373, 380 (Cal. 1988). Nothing in this case affects the public interest in any significant way. The conduct of plaintiff's co-workers may have resulted in increased costs of the corporation's products and services and thereby adversely affected the corporate shareholders to some minor degree, but that does not violate a clear and substantial public policy. Nor would the effect of the increased costs on the corporation's prices result in a violation of a clear and substantial public policy. There are, no doubt, many instances of avoidable inefficiencies that produce higher costs and affect an employer's profits, but, for the most part, those are matters that involve private policy that is more or less regulated by forces in the marketplace, not matters that rise to a level that implicates a clear and substantial public interest.

Id. at 861. In a later case, the Utah Supreme Court clarified that it would uphold a wrongful-discharge claim by an internal whistleblower if, but only if, the reporting furthered a clear and substantial public policy. *Ryan v. Dan's Food Stores*, 972 P.2d 395 (Utah 1998) (stating pharmacist would have claim if fired for questioning prescriptions irregular on their face, as required by statute).

4. *Wrongful Discipline in Violation of Public Policy?* Should courts entertain claims that an employer violated public policy when it demoted an employee for a questionable reason? Or transfered an employee? Or reduced pay? Or disciplined? Or changed the work schedule? On the one hand, such claims seem doctrinally identical to public-policy discharge claims. This is especially so since these claims often blend into termination claims if the employee quits and alleges the conditions were so intolerable that he was constructively discharged. On the other hand, entertaining all such claims even when the employee does not quit or is not fired might turn courts into super-personnel managers. States differ on their approach to this. *Compare Brigham v. Dillon Cos.*, 935 P.2d 1054 (Kan 1997) (upholding a claim of wrongful demotion), *with White v. State*, 929 P.2d 396 (Wash. 1997) (rejecting claim of a wrongful transfer in violation of public policy).

BALLA v. GAMBRO, INC.
Supreme Court of Illinois
584 N.E.2d 104 (1991)

Justice Clark delivered the opinion of the court:

The issue in this case is whether in-house counsel should be allowed the remedy of an action for retaliatory discharge.

Appellee, Roger Balla, formerly in-house counsel for Gambro, Inc. (Gambro), filed a retaliatory discharge action against Gambro, its affiliate Gambro Dialysatoren, KG (Gambro Germany), its parent company Gambro Lundia, AB (Gambro Sweden), and the president of Gambro in the circuit court of Cook County (Gambro, Gambro Germany and Gambro Sweden collectively referred to as appellants). Appellee alleged that he was fired in contravention of Illinois public policy and sought damages for the discharge. The trial court dismissed the action on appellants' motion for summary judgment. The appellate court reversed. We granted appellant's petition for leave to appeal and allowed amicus curiae briefs from the American Corporate Counsel Association and Illinois Bar Association.

Gambro is a distributor of kidney dialysis equipment manufactured by Gambro Germany. Among the products distributed by Gambro are dialyzers which filter excess fluid and toxic substances from the blood of patients with no or impaired kidney function. The manufacture and sale of dialyzers is regulated by the United States Food and Drug Administration (FDA); the Federal Food, Drug, and Cosmetic Act; FDA regulations; and the Illinois Food, Drug and Cosmetic Act.

Appellee, Roger J. Balla, is and was at all times throughout this controversy an attorney licensed to practice law in the State of Illinois. On March 17, 1980, appellee executed an employment agreement with Gambro which contained the terms of appellee's employment. Generally, the employment agreement provided that appellee would "be responsible for all legal matters within the company and for personnel within the company's sales office." Appellee held the title of director of administration at Gambro. As director of administration, appellee's specific responsibilities included, inter alia: advising, counseling and representing management on legal matters; establishing and administering personnel policies; coordinating and overseeing corporate activities to assure compliance with applicable laws and regulations, and preventing or minimizing legal or administrative proceedings; and coordinating the activities of the manager of regulatory affairs. Regarding this last responsibility, under Gambro's corporate hierarchy, appellee supervised the manager of regulatory affairs, and the manager reported directly to appellee.

In August 1983, the manager of regulatory affairs for Gambro left the company and appellee assumed the manager's specific duties. Although appellee's original employment agreement was not modified to reflect his new position, his annual compensation was increased and Gambro's corporate organizational chart referred to appellee's positions as "Dir. of Admin./Personnel; General Counsel; Mgr. of Regulatory Affairs." The job description for the position described the manager as an individual "responsible for ensuring awareness of and compliance with federal, state and local laws and regulations affecting the company's operations and products." Requirements for the position were a bachelor of science degree and three to five years in the medical device field plus two years' experience in the area of government regulations. The individual in the position prior to appellee was not an attorney.

In July 1985 Gambro Germany informed Gambro in a letter that certain dialyzers it had manufactured, the clearances of which varied from the package insert, were about to be shipped to Gambro. Referring to these dialyzers, Gambro Germany advised Gambro:

> For acute patients risk is that the acute uremic situation will not be improved in spite of the treatment, giving continuous high levels of potassium, phosphate and urea/creatine. The chronic patient may note the effect as a slow progression of the uremic situation and depending on the interval between medical check-ups the medical risk may not be overlooked.

Appellee told the president of Gambro to reject the shipment because the dialyzers did not comply with FDA regulations. The president notified Gambro Germany of its decision to reject the shipment on July 12, 1985.

However, one week later the president informed Gambro Germany that Gambro would accept the dialyzers and "sell [them] to a unit that is not currently our customer but who buys only on price." Appellee contends that he was not informed by the president of the decision to accept the dialyzers but became aware of it through other Gambro employees. Appellee maintains that he spoke with the president in August regarding the company's decision to accept the dialyzers and told the president that he would do whatever necessary to stop the sale of the dialyzers.

On September 4, 1985, appellee was discharged from Gambro's employment by its president. The following day, appellee reported the shipment of the dialyzers to the FDA. The FDA seized the shipment and determined the product to be "adulterated within the meaning of section 501(h) of the [Federal Act]."

On March 19, 1986, appellee filed a four-count complaint in tort for retaliatory discharge seeking $22 million in damages. Counts III and IV for emotional distress were dismissed from the action, as was the president in an order entered by the trial court on November 5, 1986.

On July 28, 1987, Gambro filed a motion for summary judgment[, which the trial court granted].

We agree with the trial court that appellee does not have a cause of action against Gambro for retaliatory discharge under the facts of the case at bar. Generally, this court adheres to the proposition that " 'an employer may discharge an employee-at-will for any reason or for no reason [at all].' " However, in *Kelsay v. Motorola, Inc.,* 384 N.E.2d 353 (Ill. 1978), this court recognized the limited and narrow tort of retaliatory discharge. In *Kelsay,* an at-will employee was fired for filing a worker's compensation claim against her employer. After examining the history and purpose behind the Workers' Compensation Act to determine the public policy behind its enactment, this court held that the employee should have a cause of action for retaliatory discharge. This court stressed that if employers could fire employees for filing workers' compensation claims, the public policy behind the enactment of the Workers' Compensation Act would be frustrated.

Subsequently, in *Palmateer v. International Harvester Co.,* 421 N.E.2d 876 (Ill. 1981), this court again examined the tort of retaliatory discharge. In *Palmateer,* an employee was discharged for informing the police of suspected criminal activities of a co-employee, and because he agreed to provide assistance in any investigation and trial of the matter. Based on the public policy favoring the investigation and prosecution of crime, this court held that the employee had a cause of action for retaliatory discharge. Further, we stated:

> "All that is required [to bring a cause of action for retaliatory discharge] is that the employer discharge the employee in retaliation for the employee's activities, and that the discharge be in contravention of a clearly mandated public policy." (*Palmateer,* 85 Ill. 2d at 134.)

In this case it appears that Gambro discharged appellee, an employee of Gambro, in retaliation for his activities, and this discharge was in contravention of a clearly mandated public policy. Appellee allegedly told the president of Gambro that he would do whatever was necessary to stop the sale of the "misbranded and/or adulterated" dialyzers. In appellee's eyes, the use of these dialyzers could cause death or serious bodily harm to patients. As we have stated before, "there is no public policy more important or more fundamental than the one favoring the effective protection of the lives and property of citizens." (*See Palmateer,* 85 Ill. 2d at 132.) However, in this case, appellee was not just an employee of Gambro, but also general counsel for Gambro.

[I]n *Herbster v. North American Co. for Life & Health Insurance,* 150 Ill. App. 3d 21 (1986), our appellate court held that the plaintiff, an employee and chief legal counsel for the defendant company, did not have a claim for retaliatory discharge against the company due to the presence of the attorney-client relationship. Under the facts of that case, the defendant company allegedly requested the plaintiff to destroy or remove discovery information which had been requested in lawsuits pending against the company. The plaintiff refused arguing that such conduct would constitute fraud and violate several provisions of the Illinois Code of Professional Responsibility. Subsequently, the defendant company discharged the plaintiff.

The appellate court refused to extend the tort of retaliatory discharge to the plaintiff in *Herbster* primarily because of the special relationship between an attorney and client. The court stated:

> "The mutual trust, exchanges of confidence, reliance on judgment, and personal nature of the attorney-client relationship demonstrate the unique position attorneys occupy in our society." (*Herbster,* 150 Ill. App. 3d at 99.)

The appellate court recited a list of factors which make the attorney-client relationship special such as: the attorney-client privilege regarding confidential communications, the fiduciary duty an attorney owes to a client, the right of the client to terminate the relationship with or without cause, and the fact that a client has exclusive control over the subject matter of the litigation and a client may dismiss or settle a cause of action regardless of the attorney's advice. Thus, in *Herbster,* since the plaintiff's duties pertained strictly to legal matters, the appellate court determined that the plaintiff did not have a claim for retaliatory discharge.

We agree with the conclusion reached in *Herbster* that, generally, in-house counsel do not have a claim under the tort of retaliatory discharge. However, we base our decision as much on the nature and purpose of the tort of retaliatory discharge, as on the effect on the attorney-client relationship that extending the tort would have. In addition, at this time, we caution that our holding is confined by the fact that appellee is and was at all times throughout this controversy an attorney licensed to practice law in the State of Illinois. Appellee is and was subject to the Illinois Code of Professional Responsibility (see the Rules of Professional Conduct which replaced the Code of Professional Responsibility, effective August 1, 1990), adopted by this court. The tort of retaliatory discharge is a limited and narrow exception to the general rule of at-will employment. The tort seeks to achieve " 'a proper balance . . . among the employer's interest in operating a business efficiently and profitably, the employee's interest in earning a livelihood, and society's interest in seeing its public policies carried out.' " (*Fellhauer v. City of Geneva,* 568 N.E.2d 870, 875 (Ill. 1991), quoting *Palmateer,* 421 N.E.2d at 878.) Further, as stated in *Palmateer, "the foundation of the tort of retaliatory discharge lies in the protection of public policy. . . ."* (Emphasis added.) *Palmateer,* 421 N.E.2d at 880.

In this case, the public policy to be protected, that of protecting the lives and property of citizens, is adequately safeguarded without extending the tort of retaliatory discharge to in-house counsel. Appellee was required under the Rules of Professional Conduct to report Gambro's intention to sell the "misbranded and/or adulterated" dialyzers. Rule 1.6(b) of the Rules of Professional Conduct reads:

"A lawyer *shall* reveal information about a client to the extent it appears necessary to prevent the client from committing an act that would result in death or serious bodily injury." (Emphasis added.) (134 Ill. 2d R. 1.6(b).)

Appellee alleges, and the FDA's seizure of the dialyzers indicates, that the use of the dialyzers would cause death or serious bodily injury. Thus, under the above-cited rule, appellee was under the mandate of this court to report the sale of these dialyzers.

In his brief to this court, appellee argues that not extending the tort of retaliatory discharge to in-house counsel would present attorneys with a "Hobson's choice." According to appellee, in-house counsel would face two alternatives: either comply with the client/employer's wishes and risk both the loss of a professional license and exposure to criminal sanctions, or decline to comply with client/employer's wishes and risk the loss of a full-time job and the attendant benefits. We disagree. Unlike the employees in *Kelsay* which this court recognized would be left with the difficult decision of choosing between whether to file a workers' compensation claim and risk being fired, or retaining their jobs and losing their right to a remedy (*see Kelsay,* 74 Ill. 2d at 182), in-house counsel plainly are not confronted with such a dilemma. In-house counsel do not have a choice of whether to follow their ethical obligations as attorneys licensed to practice law, or follow the illegal and unethical demands of their clients. In-house counsel must abide by the Rules of Professional Conduct. Appellee had no choice but to report to the FDA Gambro's intention to sell or distribute these dialyzers, and consequently protect the aforementioned public policy.

In addition, we believe that extending the tort of retaliatory discharge to in-house counsel would have an undesirable effect on the attorney-client relationship that exists between these employers and their in-house counsel. Generally, a client may discharge his attorney at any time, with or without cause. This rule applies equally to in-house counsel as it does to outside counsel. Further, this rule "recognizes that the relationship between an attorney and client is based on trust and that the client must have confidence in his attorney in order to ensure that the relationship will function properly." (*Rhoades,* 78 Ill. 2d at 228.) As stated in *Herbster,* "the attorney is placed in the unique position of maintaining a close relationship with a client where the attorney receives secrets, disclosures, and information that otherwise would not be divulged to intimate friends." We believe that if in-house counsel are granted the right to sue their employers for retaliatory discharge, employers might be less willing to be forthright and candid with their in-house counsel. Employers might be hesitant to turn to their in-house counsel for advice regarding potentially questionable corporate conduct knowing that their in-house counsel could use this information in a retaliatory discharge suit.

We recognize that under the Illinois Rules of Professional Conduct, attorneys shall reveal client confidences or secrets in certain situations (*see* 134 Ill. 2d Rules 1.6(a), (b), (c)), and thus one might expect employers/clients to be naturally hesitant to rely on in-house counsel for advice regarding this potentially questionable conduct. However, the danger exists that if in-house counsel are granted a right to sue their employers in tort for retaliatory discharge, employers might further limit their communication with their in-house counsel. As stated in *Upjohn Co. v. United States,* 449 U.S. 383, 389 (1981), regarding the attorney-client privilege:

> "Its purpose is to encourage full and frank communication between attorneys and their clients and thereby promote broader public interests in the observance of law and administration of justice. The privilege recognizes that sound legal advice or advocacy serves public ends and that *such advice or advocacy depends upon the lawyer being fully informed by the client.*" (Emphasis added.)

If extending the tort of retaliatory discharge might have a chilling effect on the communications between the employer/client and the in-house counsel, we believe that it is more wise to refrain from doing so.

Our decision not to extend the tort of retaliatory discharge to in-house counsel also is based on other ethical considerations. Under the Rules of Professional Conduct, appellee was required to withdraw from representing Gambro if continued representation would result in the violation of the Rules of Professional Conduct by which appellee was bound, or if Gambro discharged the appellee. In this case, Gambro did discharge appellee, and according to appellee's claims herein, his continued representation of Gambro would have resulted in a violation of the Rules of Professional Conduct. Appellee argues that such a choice of withdrawal is "simplistic and uncompassionate, and is completely at odds with contemporary realities facing in-house attorneys." These contemporary realities apparently are the economic ramifications of losing his position as in-house counsel. However difficult economically and perhaps emotionally it is for in-house counsel to discontinue representing an employer/client, we refuse to allow in-house counsel to sue their employer/client for damages because they obeyed their ethical obligations. In this case, appellee, in addition to being an employee at Gambro, is first and foremost an attorney bound by the Rules of Professional Conduct. These Rules of Professional Conduct hope to articulate in a concrete fashion certain values and goals such as defending the integrity of the judicial system, promoting the administration of justice and protecting the integrity of the legal profession. An attorney's obligation to follow these Rules of Professional Conduct should not be the foundation for a claim of retaliatory discharge.

We also believe that it would be inappropriate for the employer/client to bear the economic costs and burdens of their in-house counsel's adhering to their ethical obligations under the Rules of Professional Conduct. Presumably, in situations where an in-house counsel obeys his or her ethical obligations and reveals certain information regarding the employer/client, the attorney-client relationship will be irreversibly strained and the client will more than likely discharge its in-house counsel. In this scenario, if we were to grant the in-house counsel the right to sue the client for retaliatory discharge, we would be shifting the burden and costs of obeying the Rules of Professional Conduct from the attorney to the employer/client. The employer/client would be forced to pay damages to its former in-house counsel to essentially mitigate the financial harm the attorney suffered for having to abide by Rules of Professional Conduct. This, we believe, is impermissible for all attorneys know or should know that at certain times in their professional career, they will have to forgo economic gains in order to protect the integrity of the legal profession.

[The Court then reviewed cases from other jurisdictions.]

In light of our decision that in-house counsel generally are not entitled to bring a cause of action for retaliatory discharge against their employer/client, we must consider appellee's argument that he learned of the dialyzers' defect and Gambro's noncompliance with FDA regulations in his role as manager of regulatory affairs at Gambro, and not as corporate counsel. Appellee argues that, if he did learn of Gambro's alleged violation of FDA regulations as manager of regulatory affairs, and acted pursuant to his duties as manager of regulatory affairs, he is merely an "employee" at Gambro and therefore should be entitled to bring a cause of action for retaliatory discharge. The appellate court in this matter agreed with appellee and held that a question of fact exists as to whether "[appellee's] discharge resulted from information he learned as a 'layman' in a nonlegal position."

We disagree. A motion for summary judgment should be granted when the pleadings, depositions, and affidavits reveal that there is no genuine issue as to any material fact and that the moving party is entitled to judgment as a matter of law. In this case, there is no issue of fact as to whether appellee learned of Gambro's violations of FDA regulations as a "layman," as opposed to general counsel for Gambro. After examining the pleadings, exhibits and appellee's deposition testimony, we find that appellee was acting as Gambro's general counsel throughout this ordeal. As noted earlier, at the time of this controversy, appellee not only was acting as general counsel for Gambro, but also was its manager of regulatory affairs. Under the corporate hierarchy at Gambro, the corporate counsel supervised the manager of regulatory affairs. Thus, appellee "supervised" himself in his role as manager of regulatory affairs. More importantly, based on the official job descriptions supplied by Gambro, it is clear that the general counsel and the manager of regulatory affairs performed essentially the same roles with regards to FDA compliance. The job description for the director of administration, which defined the position of general counsel, required appellee to *"coordinate[] and oversee[] corporate activities to assure compliance with applicable laws* and regulations and prevent[] or minimize[] [the] possibility of legal or administrative proceedings."* Along the same vein, the job description for manager of regulatory affairs required appellee to *"establish programs and procedures to ensure compliance with applicable FDA laws and regulations."* Thus, both roles had equivalent duties for assuring compliance with FDA regulations. . . .

Appellee relies on the fact that previous managers of regulatory affairs at Gambro were not attorneys, and the position only required a bachelor of science degree and three to five years' experience in the medical device field as evidence that this position is a nonlegal position. We disagree. Although previous managers evidently were not attorneys, the two roles appellee performed for Gambro were so intertwined and inextricably bound, we fail to see how appellee was not performing his general counsel functions in this matter. As support for our conclusion, we quote from the ABA Formal Opinion No. 328, which addressed the dual role situation appellee confronted:

"If the second occupation is so law-related that the work of the lawyer in such occupation will involve, inseparably, the practice of law, the lawyer is considered to be engaged in the practice of law while conducting that occupation." (ABA Formal Opinion No. 328, at 65 (June 1972).)

In this case, as the trial court explained, appellee investigated certain facts, applied the law to those investigated facts and reached certain conclusions as to whether these dialyzers complied with the FDA regulations. In that sense, appellee inescapably engaged in the practice of law. Consequently, although appellee may have been the manager of regulatory affairs for Gambro, his discharge resulted from information he learned as general counsel, and from conduct he performed as general counsel.

For the foregoing reasons, the decision of the appellate court is reversed, and the decision of the trial court is affirmed.

JUSTICE FREEMAN, dissenting:

I respectfully dissent from the decision of my colleagues. In concluding that the plaintiff attorney, serving as corporate in-house counsel, should not be allowed a claim for retaliatory discharge, the majority first reasons that the public policy implicated in this case, *i.e.*, protecting the lives and property of Illinois citizens, is adequately safeguarded by the lawyer's ethical obligation to reveal information about a client as necessary to prevent acts that would result in death or serious bodily harm. I find this reasoning fatally flawed.

The majority so reasons because, as a matter of law, an attorney cannot even contemplate ignoring his ethical obligations in favor of continuing in his employment. I agree with this conclusion "as a matter of law." However, to say that the categorical nature of ethical obligations is sufficient to ensure that the ethical obligations will be satisfied simply ignores reality. Specifically, it ignores that, as unfortunate for society as it may be, attorneys are no less human than nonattorneys and, thus, no less given to the temptation to either ignore or rationalize away their ethical obligations when complying therewith may render them unable to feed and support their families. . . . I do not believe any useful purpose is served by distinguishing attorneys from ordinary citizens. It is incontrovertible that the law binds all men, kings and paupers alike. An attorney should not be punished simply because he has ethical obligations imposed upon him over and above the general obligation to obey the law which all men have. Nor should a corporate employer be protected simply because the employee it has discharged for "blowing the whistle" happens to be an attorney. . . .

[I]t should be borne in mind that this case involves an attorney discharged from his employment, not one who has voluntarily resigned due to his ethical obligations. I believe the majority's reasoning, in general, and with respect to the question of who should bear the economic burdens of the attorney's loss of job, specifically, would be valid grounds for denying a cause of action to an attorney who voluntarily resigns, rather than is discharged. By focusing upon the immediate economic consequences of the discharge, the majority overlooks the very real possibility that in-house counsel who is discharged, rather than allowed to resign in accordance with his ethical obligations once the employer's persistence in illegal conduct is evident to him, will be stigmatized within the legal profession. That stigma and its apparent consequences, economic and otherwise, in addition to the immediate economic consequences of a discharge, also militate strongly in favor of allowing the attorney a claim for retaliatory discharge. . . .

NOTES

1. *Duty or Discretion to Disclose.* Illinois is one of the few states mandating lawyers to disclose information about future acts of clients that will result in death or serious bodily injury. Most states follow the Model Rules, which state that "a lawyer may reveal information relating to the representation of a client to the extent the lawyer reasonably believes necessary to prevent reasonably certain death or substantial bodily harm." MODEL RULES OF PROFESSIONAL CONDUCT R. 1.6(b)(1). Some codes expand the scope of permissible disclosure to include substantial financial loss as well as serious bodily injury. *See* RESTATEMENT OF THE LAW GOVERNING LAWYERS §§ 66, 67 (2000). Is the *Balla* rationale persuasive in a state with a discretionary disclosure rule?

2. *The California Way.* In *General Dynamics Corp. v. Superior Court*, 876 P.2d 487 (Cal. 1994), an in-house lawyer alleged he was fired for spearheading an investigation into employee drug use, protesting the company's failure to investigate the bugging of the chief of security's office, and advising company officials that the salary policy may violate the federal Fair Labor Standards Act. Expressly rejecting the holding of *Balla*, the California Supreme Court held that an attorney may have a retaliatory-discharge cause of action if the attorney was discharged for adhering to a mandatory ethical obligation prescribed by a professional rule or statute. The Court emphasized that "because their professional work is by definition affected with a public interest, in-house attorneys are even more liable to conflicts between corporate goals and professional norms than their nonattorney colleagues . . . [and] have, if anything, an *even more* powerful claim to judicial protection than their nonprofessional colleagues." *Id.* at 498.

The court went on to recognize another category, where an attorney's conduct is ethically permissible but not required (this category was not at issue in *Balla* because of Illinois's unusual mandatory-disclosure rule). This category revolves around two questions:

> First, whether the employer's conduct is of the kind that would give rise to a retaliatory discharge action by a *non*-attorney; second, the court must determine whether some statute or ethical rule, such as the statutory exceptions to the attorney-client privilege . . . specifically permits the attorney to depart from the usual requirement of confidentiality with respect to the client-employer and engage in the "nonfiduciary" conduct for which he was terminated.

Id. at 503.

3. *The New York Way.* The *Balla* court refused to give tort protection to Illinois attorney whistleblowers, even though Illinois broadly protects a nonattorney in similar situations. *See Palmateer v. International Harvester Co.*,

421 N.E.2d 876 (Ill. 1981). New York courts take the opposite approach, protecting attorneys but not general employees. New York courts do not recognize a general claim of wrongful discharge in violation of public policy for employees. *See Murphy v. American Home Products, infra* Chapter 6. However, they have granted a common-law cause of action to an associate attorney fired for insisting that the firm report professional misconduct of a fellow associate. *See Wieder v. Skala*, 609 N.E.2d 105 (N.Y. 1992) (recognizing cause of action for breach of the implied contract term, so fundamental and essential that it requires no expression, that associate will conduct himself "in accordance with the ethical standards of the profession").

4. *The Independence of In-House Counsel.* The *Balla* court emphasized that lawyers are employed by their clients at will. As the RESTATEMENT OF THE LAW GOVERNING LAWYERS § 44, Comment b (2000), puts it:

> A client may always discharge a lawyer, regardless of whether cause exists for the discharge and regardless of what may have been provided in any contract between them. The client's consent creates the client-lawyer relationship, and withdrawing consent ends it.

Some commentators have argued that the reasons supporting this right do not apply fully to in-house lawyers. In-house lawyers are economically dependent on a single client/employer, who controls their entire compensation, hours, and working conditions. The general concern that unsophisticated clients should not be required to justify their decision to terminate an overreaching outside counsel (even if the contract required just-cause termination) is less relevant for corporations who employ inside counsel.

On the other hand, creating a cause of action may limit desirable flexibility in replacing top corporate officers such as in-house counsel. It is one thing to allow corporate counsel expressly to negotiate a golden parachute or other contract protection against discharge. It is another to say that an at-will lawyer can threaten an implied-in-fact contract claim or a tort claim upon being fired (and what in-house counsel cannot make some claim about disclosing possible corporate fraud?).

Would an acceptable compromise be to create a tort cause of action that is more restrictive for corporate counsel than other employees? Could the tort be limited to health and safety violations? An actual violation, as opposed to counsel's good-faith belief of a violation? Reporting the violation to outsiders, as opposed to internal whistleblowing? Is the *General Dynamics* distinction between mandatory and permissive ethical conduct, discussed in note 2, an effort toward compromise?

5. *Exposing Trivial Violations.* Should an employee be protected from discharge for revealing any violation of law? Consider the hypothetical discussed in *Palmateer v. International Harvester Co.*, 421 N.E.2d 876 (Ill. 1981), of an employee fired for reporting to police that a co-worker had stolen a $2 screwdriver from the company. Is such a firing a wrongful discharge in violation of public policy? The *Palmateer* majority declared the hypothetical would state a cause of action, reasoning that the company's business judgment about how to handle this personnel problem could not override the legislature's determination that the problem was a crime to be resolved by the criminal justice system.

Consider also *Franklin v. Swift Transportation Co.*, 24 IER Cases 1437 (Tenn. Ct. App. 2006). There, a truck driver refused to drive from Mississippi to Texas because the truck was missing its original International Registration Plan registration card, which would have listed all states in which the truck was licensed to operate. His dispatcher told him to take a photocopy, and promised the employer would pay the cost of any citation or fine. The Court recognized that the failure to carry the IRP card appeared to violate a state regulation (but not a criminal or civil code), but rejected the wrongful-discharge claim, declaring that the employee must show more than he was required to perform "illegal activities," but also that the violation would "implicate important public policy concerns as well."

JOHNSTON v. DEL MAR DISTRIBUTING CO.
Court of Appeals of Texas
776 S.W.2d 768 (1989)

Before NYE, C.J., and BENAVIDES and KENNEDY, JJ.

BENAVIDES, JUSTICE.

Nancy Johnston, appellant, brought suit against her employer, Del Mar Distributing Co., Inc., alleging that her employment had been wrongfully terminated. Del Mar filed a motion for summary judgment in the trial court alleging that appellant's pleadings failed to state a cause of action. After a hearing on the motion, the trial court agreed with Del Mar and granted its motion for summary judgment.

On appeal, appellant . . . contends that her pleadings did in fact state a cause of action. We agree. Accordingly, we reverse and remand. . . .

In her petition, appellant alleged that she was employed by Del Mar during the summer of 1987. As a part of her duties, she was required to prepare shipping documents for goods being sent from Del Mar's warehouse located in Corpus Christi, Texas to other cities in Texas. One day, Del Mar instructed appellant to package a semi-automatic weapon (for delivery to a grocery store in Brownsville, Texas) and to label the contents of the package as "fishing gear." Ultimately, the package was to be given to United Parcel Service for shipping. Appellant was required to sign her name to the shipping documents; therefore, she was concerned that her actions might be in violation of some firearm regulation or a regulation of the United Postal Service. Accordingly, she sought the advice of the United States Treasury Department Bureau of Alcohol, Tobacco & Firearms (hereinafter referred to as "the Bureau"). A few days after she contacted the Bureau, appellant was fired. Appellant brought suit for wrongful termination alleging that her employment was terminated solely in retaliation for contacting the Bureau.[3]

In its motion for summary judgment, Del Mar stated that the facts alleged in appellant's petition would be taken as true. Specifically, it acknowledged that it required appellant to package and ship firearms with labels that did

---

[3] Appellant's petition can be construed as alleging that she was fired because (1) she inquired into whether her acts were illegal; and (2) she reported suspected violations to a regulatory agency (commonly referred to as "whistleblowing").

not reflect the package's true contents. It further acknowledged that appellant's employment was terminated when she became concerned about such practices and sought the "advice" of personnel employed by the Bureau.

Del Mar asserted in its motion that, notwithstanding the above described facts, appellant's cause of action was barred by the employment-at-will doctrine. Specifically, Del Mar asserted that since appellant's employment was for an indefinite amount of time, she was an employee-at-will and it had the absolute right to terminate her employment for any reason or no reason at all. . . .

Recently, the Texas Supreme Court, recognizing the need to amend the employment-at-will doctrine, invoked its judicial authority to create a very narrow common law exception to the doctrine. *Sabine Pilot Service, Inc. v. Hauck,* 687 S.W.2d 733, 735 (Tex. 1985). In *Sabine Pilot,* the Texas Supreme Court was faced with a narrow issue for consideration, i.e., whether an allegation by an employee that he or she was discharged for refusing to perform an illegal act stated a cause of action. The Court held that

> public policy, *as expressed in the laws* of this state and the United States which *carry criminal penalties,* requires a very *narrow* exception to the employment-at-will doctrine . . . [t]hat *narrow* exception covers *only* the discharge of an employee for the *sole* reason that the employee refused to perform an *illegal act. Id.* (emphasis ours).

. . . .

On appeal, appellant alleges that her petition did state a cause of action pursuant to the public policy exception announced in *Sabine Pilot.* In her brief, appellant contends that since Texas law currently provides that an employee has a cause of action when she is fired for refusing to perform an illegal act, it necessarily follows that an employee states a cause of action where she alleges that she is fired for simply inquiring into whether or not she is committing illegal acts. To hold otherwise, she argues, would have a chilling effect on the public policy exception announced in *Sabine Pilot.* We agree.

It is implicit that in order to refuse to do an illegal act, an employee must either know or suspect that the requested act is illegal. In some cases it will be patently obvious that the act is illegal (murder, robbery, theft, etc.); however, in other cases it may not be so apparent. Since ignorance of the law is no defense to a criminal prosecution, it is reasonable to expect that if an employee has a good faith belief that a required act might be illegal, she will try to find out whether the act is in fact illegal prior to deciding what course of action to take. If an employer is allowed to terminate the employee at this point, the public policy exception announced in *Sabine Pilot* would have little or no effect. To hold otherwise would force an employee, who suspects that a requested act might be illegal, to: (1) subject herself to possible discharge if she attempts to find out if the act is in fact illegal; or (2) remain ignorant, perform the act and, if it turns out to be illegal, face possible criminal sanctions.

We hold that since the law recognizes that it is against public policy to allow an employer to coerce its employee to commit a criminal act in furtherance of its own interest, then it is necessarily inferred that the same public policy prohibits the discharge of an employee who in good faith attempts to find out if the act is illegal. It is important to note that we are not creating a new exception to the employment-at-will doctrine. Rather, we are merely enforcing the narrow public policy exception which was created in *Sabine Pilot*.

Therefore, we find that the *Sabine Pilot* exception necessarily covers a situation where an employee has a good faith belief that her employer has requested her to perform an act which may subject her to criminal penalties. Public policy demands that she be allowed to investigate into whether such actions are legal so that she can determine what course of action to take (*i.e.*, whether or not to perform the act).

Furthermore, it is the opinion of this Court that the question of whether or not the requested act was in fact illegal is irrelevant to the determination of this case. We hold that where a plaintiff's employment is terminated for attempting to find out from a regulatory agency if a requested act is illegal, it is not necessary to prove that the requested act was in fact illegal. A plaintiff must, however, establish that she had a good faith belief that the requested act might be illegal, and that such belief was reasonable. Accordingly, we sustain appellant's third and fourth points of error.

Del Mar also contends, for the first time on appeal, that this case involves a "whistleblower" fact situation because appellant was fired for reporting suspected illegal activity to a police agency.[4] Del Mar asks this Court not to create a "whistleblower" exception to the employment-at-will doctrine since neither the Legislature nor the Supreme Court has created such an exception. Del Mar cites Tex. R. Civ. Stat. Ann. art. 6252-16a, § 2 (Vernon Supp. 1989) in support of its position.

Article 6252-16a, § 2 provides that a governmental employee cannot be fired because she reports suspected illegal activity to a police agency. Del Mar argues that we must exercise judicial restraint since the Legislature had the opportunity to include employees of the private sector, but declined to do so.

It is well-settled in Texas that a motion for summary judgment shall state with specificity the grounds upon which the movant is relying. Any issues that are not specifically before the trial court at the hearing on the motion may not be considered for the first time on appeal.

Since, in the instant case, Del Mar did not specifically assert this issue in its motion for summary judgment, we will not consider it for the first time on appeal.[5]

The judgment of the trial court is reversed and remanded for trial.

NOTES

1. *Who is a Whistleblower?* A fine line exists between an employee who merely seeks advice on whether she is committing an illegal act and an

---

[4] In its motion for summary judgment, appellee did not make a distinction between an employee who seeks information concerning her own potential criminal activity and an employee who reports the suspected criminal activity of her employer.

[5] Nonetheless, we add that our holdings in the determination of appellant's points of error three and four are not to be construed as creating a whistleblower exception to the employment-at-will doctrine.

employee who reports the company's wrongdoing. Is it defensible to allow a wrongful-discharge claim in the first case but not the second? Are the third-party effects likely to be any different in the two situations? On the other hand, an employee who refuses the boss's order is insubordinate. Is insubordination a more serious offense than merely tattling on others, so that it demands that the employee be correct rather than merely reasonable?

2. *Employees Who Don't Know the Law.* Johnston was right on the facts, but perhaps wrong on the law. She knew what the company had done, but incorrectly thought it was illegal. Other courts are less sympathetic to employees who don't know the law. For example, in *DeSoto v. Yellow Freight Systems, Inc.*, 957 F.2d 655 (9th Cir. 1992), a truck driver refused to drive a trailer because he mistakenly believed the registration papers were invalid, and he was subsequently fired. The Ninth Circuit held that he did not have a wrongful-discharge claim, stating that the employee "was not acting in defense of a public policy of the state of California, but incorrectly asserting his own interpretation of the Law." Additionally, the court noted that operating a trailer without proper registration papers does not implicate fundamental public-policy concerns of safety, health, or crime prevention. The court saw "the failure to carry registration papers simply as one of the '[m]any statutes [that] impose requirements whose fulfillment does not implicate fundamental public policy concerns,'" *quoting Foley v. Interactive Data Corp.*, 765 P.2d 373, 379 (Cal. 1988). Thus, even if the employee was correct, he might not have a wrongful-discharge claim.

Consider also an employee fired for refusing his employer's request to alter the fire alarm system at the Seattle Key Arena (home of the Seattle Supersonics basketball team) without prior approval from the fire department. Should he have a wrongful-discharge claim, even if it turns out that the employer's request was not illegal? *See Ellis v. City of Seattle*, 13 P.3d 1065 (Wash. 2001) (holding that employee presented a genuine issue of material fact justifying trial, because he had an objectively reasonable belief the law may be violated, even if there was no actual violation of law).

3. *Employees Who Don't Know the Facts.* What if the employee is right on the law but wrong on the facts — he thought the company was doing something that would have been illegal, but in fact the company did not do it? Should such an employee get protection? In *Schriner v. Meginnis Ford Co.*, 421 N.W.2d 755 (Neb. 1988), an auto salesman bought a used car with some 48,000 miles from his employer. When the car developed severe engine damage, the salesman checked with the county clerk's office and was "mistakenly" told that records showed the car had over 100,000 miles. When the salesman reported to the Attorney General's office that his employer might be illegally altering odometers, he was fired. Odometer fraud is a felony in Nebraska. The court recognized that a wrongful-discharge action lies "when an at-will employee acts in good faith and upon reasonable cause in reporting his employer's suspected violation of the criminal code." *Id.* at 759. The court upheld summary judgment for the employer, however (two justices dissenting), because the employee had no evidence that the employer had changed the odometer.

4. *Employers Who Don't Know the Facts.* Suppose an employer mistakenly thinks that an employee called the Occupational Safety and Health

Administration or the Department of Labor's Wage and Hour Division to inquire about company violations. The employer fires the employee because of this, although in fact the employee never contacted the agencies. Does the employee have a claim under the anti-retaliation provisions of the statutes or under the common-law tort of wrongful discharge in violation of public policy? *See Saffels v. Rice*, 40 F.3d 1546 (8th Cir. 1994) (yes to both claims).

5. *Mirror Issues.* This debate over reasonable belief versus correctness mirrors the problem explored in the notes following the *Pugh* case in Chapter 4. There, the question was whether the *employer* could fire an employee if it had a reasonable belief of employee wrongdoing, or whether the employer must be correct that the employee engaged in wrongdoing. Here, the focus is whether the *employee* has a tort claim when fired while acting in good faith, or whether the employee must be correct. While there is always an instinct in employment law to treat employer and employee symmetrically, substantive differences in the situations may argue for separate standards.

NOTES ON WHISTLEBLOWER STATUTES

In addition to common-law protection of whistleblowers, both state and federal statutes protect employees who expose wrongdoing by their employers. These statutes raise many similar issues to their common-law counterparts. *See generally* John D. Feerick, *Toward a Model Whistleblowing Law,* 19 FORDHAM URB. L.J. 585 (1992); Richard Moberly, *Sarbanes-Oxley's Structural Model to Encourage Corporate Whistleblowers*, 2006 BYU L. REV. 1107 (forthcoming 2006).

1. *Anti-Retaliation Versus General Whistleblower Statutes.* Specific employment statutes often include an anti-retaliation provision that protects employees who report violations or exercise their rights under the act. For example, section 704 of Title VII of the Civil Rights Act of 1964 (which prohibits discrimination in employment) declares it to be an unlawful employment practice for an employer to discriminate against an employee "because he has opposed any . . . unlawful employment practice, or because he has made a charge, testified, assisted, or participated in any manner in an investigation, proceeding, or hearing under this title." Section 704 has been interpreted to protect even employees who have filed false and malicious charges with the EEOC. *See, e.g.*, *Womack v. Munson*, 619 F.2d 1292 (8th Cir. 1980). The section prohibits such employer reprisal as firing, suspension, demotion, transfers to undesirable positions, filing a retaliatory lawsuit, or withholding reference letters. Many state statutes similarly protect employees from retaliation for fulfilling specific public duties or exercising particular statutory rights. Examples include protecting employees who file workers' compensation charges, who serve on juries, or who vote or hold political office against the wishes of their employers.

In contrast, general whistleblower statutes protect employees who report any of a wide variety of wrongdoing by their employers. The line between anti-retaliation and whistleblower statutes is sometimes indistinct. The key point in practice, however, is to know precisely what types of employee activities are protected by a particular statute.

2. *Scope of the Whistle.* The range of protection for whistleblowers varies greatly among the states. In New Jersey, for example, employees are protected whenever they alert their supervisors or any public body of their reasonable belief of a violation of a law, rule, or regulation. Conscientious Employee Protection Act, N.J. STAT. ANN. § 34:19-3. New Jersey courts have construed the statute liberally and recognize it as "the most far-reaching 'whistleblower statute' in the nation." *Hernandez v. Montville Township Bd. of Educ.*, 808 A.2d 128, 132 (N.J. Super. Ct. App. Div. 2002), *aff'd*, 843 A.2d 1091 (N.J. 2004). In *Hernandez,* an elementary-school custodian was fired after complaining to the principal of clogged and overflowing toilets and a burned-out bulb on an exit sign. The jury returned a verdict of $44,000 for wage loss and $150,000 for emotional distress, but the trial judge granted a motion notwithstanding the verdict, declaring "Talk about trivial. And that's supposed to support a CEPA claim?" The appellate court reversed, reinstating the jury verdict and remanding for a trial on punitive damages.

By contrast, California's whistleblower statute only grants protection after an employee alerts "a government or law enforcement agency" of concerns founded upon recognized state or federal statutes, rules, or regulations. CAL. LAB. CODE § 1102.5. California's statute does not protect employees who report their suspicions directly to their private employers. *See Green v. Ralee Engineering Co.*, 960 P.2d 1046, 1052 (Cal. 1998). New York's statute is even narrower, protecting only disclosures addressing "substantial and specific danger to the public health or safety." N. Y. LAB. LAW § 740. Thus, generally, reporting of white-collar crime is not protected, nor is reporting of activity that threatens the health and safety of only a few individuals. *See Remba v. Federation Employment & Guidance Serv.*, 559 N.E.2d 655 (N.Y. 1990) (employee fired for reporting fraudulent billing practices not protected by New York whistleblower statute); *Kern v. DePaul Mental Health Servs.*, 529 N.Y.S.2d 265 (N.Y. Sup. Ct. 1988), *aff'd*, 544 N.Y.S.2d 252 (N.Y. App. Div. 1989) (whistleblowing on employer's complacency regarding sexual activity between mentally handicapped residents of a state-run facility not protected by statute because threat affected too few individuals).

3. *Public-Policy Discharges Redux.* Whistleblower statutes raise most of the same issues as the tort of wrongful discharge in violation of public policy. For example, the California whistleblower statute has been interpreted to protect only external whistleblowers, while Maine and New Jersey provide protection only if the employee reports internally first. *Hejmadi v. AMFAC, Inc.*, 249 Cal. Rptr. 5 (Cal. Ct. App. 1988) (employee's action dismissed because employee did not report externally); ME. REV. STAT. ANN. tit. 26 § 833 (employee protected only if first brings alleged violation to attention of supervisor); N.J. STAT. ANN. § 34:19-4 (to be protected, employee must give written notice of alleged violation to employer).

Similarly, legislatures in enacting whistleblower statutes (or the courts later) must make decisions about whether to protect mistaken whistleblowers. Most whistleblower statutes make the same decision on this issue as the court in *Johnson v. Del Mar Distributing Co.*, protecting whistleblowers who have a reasonable or good-faith belief that the conduct was illegal. *See, e.g.*, MICH. COMP. LAWS § 15.362 (employee protected unless she "knows that the report is false"); CAL. LAB. CODE § 1102.5 (employee protected if she has "reasonable cause to believe" statute has been violated); ME. REV. STAT. ANN. tit. 26 § 833 ("good faith" employee is protected). *But see Remba v. Federation Employment & Guidance Serv.*, 545 N.Y.S.2d 140 (N.Y. App. Div.), *aff'd*, 559 N.E.2d 655 (N.Y. 1989) (to be protected in New York, employee must show actual violation of law, as opposed to reasonable belief).

4. *Supplanting Common Law.* What is the relationship between whistle-blower statutes and common-law wrongful-discharge actions? Consider, for example, two cases from different states. In Michigan, a court held that the Michigan Whistleblower Protection Act provides the exclusive remedy for employees fired for reporting an employer's violation of the law. Thus, an employee who failed to file suit within the time limitations of the Act was barred from proceeding under a common-law theory of wrongful discharge. *Shuttleworth v. Riverside Osteopathic Hosp.*, 477 N.W.2d 453 (Mich. Ct. App. 1991). In Illinois, in contrast, a court held that a nursing assistant who was fired after reporting that a fellow nurse was sleeping on the job and otherwise endangering patients was protected by the public-policy tort, even though a statute applying specifically to the situation, the Nursing Home Care Reform Act, protected only employees who report abuse externally to the Department of Public Health. The court rejected the employer's argument that the limited anti-retaliation statute showed the legislature was unconcerned with internal reporting of wrongdoing. *Shores v. Senior Manor Nursing Ctr., Inc.*, 518 N.E.2d 471 (Ill. App. Ct. 1988).

New York's whistleblower statute provides a third approach to this issue. The New York statute expressly preserves all available remedies, but provides that "the institution of an action . . . shall be deemed a waiver of the rights and remedies available under any other contract, collective bargaining agreement, law, rule or regulation or under the common law." N.Y. LAB. LAW § 740(7). This issue also arises when there is overlap between federal whisteblower law and the common law. *See English v. General Elec. Co.*, 496 U.S. 72 (1990) (holding that whistleblower provisions of federal Energy Reorganization Act do not preempt a common-law action for intentional infliction of emotional distress).

5. *Procedure and Remedies.* Although many whistleblower statutes allow individual causes of action in the courts, some incorporate administrative procedures. New Hampshire's statute, for example, provides for a hearing before an administrative agency. If the firing is found to violate the statute, the agency may award reinstatement and back pay. Similarly, Section 11(c) of the federal Occupational Safety and Health Act requires employees who believe they have been retaliated against to apply to the Secretary of Labor. Upon investigation, the Secretary may bring a lawsuit on the employee's behalf in federal district court.

Whistleblower statutes may also alter common-law remedies. New York and Connecticut, for example, allow only reinstatement with back pay and attorney fees. Pennsylvania and Michigan allow employees to recover "actual" damages. New Jersey also empowers courts to award punitive damages or a civil fine payable to the state treasury.

6. *Public Versus Private Employers.* Public employees generally have broader whistleblower protections than private employees. For example, the Whistleblower Protection Act of 1989, Pub. L. No. 101-12, 103 Stat. 16 (codified in scattered sections of title 5 U.S.C.), protects federal employees who expose government violations of law, gross waste of funds, or specific danger to public health or safety. The Act creates an independent Office of Special Counsel, to which employees may turn to vindicate their rights under the statute. At the federal level, this protection is backed up by the Federal False Claims Act, a statute originally enacted in 1863 to punish contractors who sold defective supplies to the Union army in the Civil War. Congress amended the statute in 1986 to allow the Government to recover triple damages from contractors defrauding the federal government, and to give individual whistleblowers 15-25% of the government's recovery. 31 U.S.C. § 3729. Some spectacular settlements have occurred under the Act. For example, a former financial officer for United Technologies Corporation received $22.5 million for his share in exposing his company's fraudulent billing practices for military helicopters. This whistleblower statute was part of the plot in John Grisham's best-selling novel, THE PARTNER 163 (1997) (the partner stole from the client's $90 million whistleblower reward of 15% of a $600 million fraud against the government).

At the state level, about half the states have enacted whistleblower statutes to protect public employees. General whistleblower protection for private employees is more limited, but at least eight states, including Michigan, California, Connecticut, and Maine, have enacted such statutes.

SARBANES-OXLEY ACT OF 2002

The financial scandals that engulfed and eventually destroyed Enron, Worldcom, and other high-profile companies created great interest in whistleblower protections for employees who might be able to disclose fraud against shareholders of public companies. As a result, the major legislative response to the scandals, the Sarbanes-Oxley Act of 2002, contains whistleblower protections. Sarbanes-Oxley Act of 2002, §§ 806, 1107, 18 U.S.C. §§ 1514A, 1513(e). This section contains a brief description of the experience of one well-known whistleblower, an analysis of the reasons whistleblowing usually failed to avert the scandals prior to Sarbanes-Oxley, and a description of the new protections.

KATHLEEN F. BRICKEY, FROM ENRON TO WORLDCOM AND BEYOND: LIFE AND CRIME AFTER SARBANES-OXLEY, 81 WASHINGTON UNIVERSITY LAW QUARTERLY 357, 360-68 (2003) *

"I am incredibly nervous that we will implode in a wave of accounting scandals." Thus began Sherron Watkins' odyssey from an obscure corporate whistleblower to one of Time Magazine's Persons of the Year. She voiced her concern about accounting irregularities in an anonymous memo to Enron's Chairman, Ken Lay. The memo followed on the heels of the abrupt and

---

puzzling departure of CEO Jeff Skilling for "personal reasons" after only six months on the job. Wall Street reacted badly to Skilling's resignation, and Enron stock fell more than six percent, continuing a trend that had marked his brief tenure as CEO.

As rumors quickly spread among Enron employees and Wall Street analysts, Mr. Lay invited employees to submit their concerns in a comment box shortly after Skilling resigned. It was in response to these events that Sherron Watkins — an Enron Vice-President who reported to CFO Andy Fastow — warned Ken Lay about "an elaborate accounting hoax." By then Watkins knew that Enron's assets were artificially inflated. She also thought that Skilling knew the accounting problems could not be fixed and that he "would rather abandon ship now than resign in shame in two years."

Shortly after sending the memo, Watkins met with Ken Lay. At that meeting, she provided five new memos that both detailed problems with Enron's off-book partnerships and special purpose entities and suggested a strategy for disclosing the accounting irregularities, restating third quarter earnings, and rebuilding investor confidence. She also encouraged Lay to engage an independent law firm to conduct a preliminary investigation into the accounting problems and urged him not to retain Vinson & Elkins because it had helped structure some of the questionable deals. He agreed to investigate her concerns but gave Vinson & Elkins the nod. The law firm conducted a brief and limited investigation into the allegations and — to no one's surprise — reported that the special purpose entity transactions were not problematic. Ironically, the report came just days before Enron announced its third quarter loss of more than $500 million and its $1 billion write-down in shareholder equity. Three months later, Enron filed for bankruptcy.

Sherron Watkins never brought her concerns to Enron's board or the SEC, but she provided devastating testimony at congressional hearings that probed into Enron's collapse. During a pre-hearing review of subpoenaed Enron documents, she came across a telling e-mail from a Vinson & Elkins lawyer to Enron's Assistant General Counsel. Bearing the subject line "Confidential Employee Matter," the message read in pertinent part:

> Per your request the following are some bullet thoughts on how to manage the case with the employee who made the sensitive report.
>
> . . . .
>
> You . . . asked that I include in this communication a summary of the possible risks associated with discharging (or constructively discharging) employees who report allegations of improper accounting practices:
>
> 1. Texas law does not currently protect corporate whistle-blowers. The Supreme Court has twice declined to create a cause of action for whistle-blowers who are discharged.
>
> . . . .
>
> 4. In addition to the risk of a wrongful discharge claim, there is the risk that the discharged employee will seek to convince some government oversight agency (e.g., IRS, SEC, etc.) that the corporation has

engaged in materially misleading reporting or is otherwise non-compliant. As with wrongful discharge claims, this can create problems even tho [sic] the allegations have no merit whatsoever.

The message was dated just two days after Watkins met with Ken Lay. . . .

Andy Fastow was furious that Watkins had talked to Ken Lay. Upon learning that she had, he told Watkins' direct supervisor that he wanted Watkins "out of here tonight" and seized the laptop computer from her desk. Despite the heated rhetoric, Watkins remained an Enron Vice-President. But she was reassigned from her executive suite to a starkly furnished office 33 floors below and relegated to performing make-work tasks. The environment was so tense that she even sought advice from Enron security personnel. . . .

RICHARD MOBERLY, SARBANES-OXLEY'S STRUCTURAL MODEL TO ENCOURAGE CORPORATE WHISTLEBLOWERS, 2006 BYU L. REV. 1107 (forthcoming 2006) *

Unlike the traditional corporate monitors [such as the Board of Directors or the government] during the recent scandals, some corporate employees successfully identified and reported the corporate fraud, particularly at WorldCom, Kmart, and several mutual funds companies. These whistleblowing employees succeeded for two reasons. First and foremost, they simply spoke out and disclosed their inside knowledge regarding the corporate misconduct. Second, the successful whistleblowers spoke out effectively by disclosing their information directly to traditional corporate monitors rather than to corporate executives.

The most famous example of a successful individual employee whistleblower may be Cynthia Cooper, who was the head of internal auditing at WorldCom. Cooper uncovered a wide variety of illegal accounting practices at WorldCom in 2002 and reported the illegalities directly to WorldCom's Board of Directors. The Board publicly admitted the financial manipulations and fired WorldCom's CFO Scott Sullivan, who allegedly orchestrated the fraud and tried to stop Cooper's investigation. By reporting Sullivan's misconduct directly to the Board, Cooper successfully avoided Sullivan's attempt to block disclosure of the fraud.

Other whistleblowers were similarly effective because they disclosed information directly to the government, another traditional corporate monitor. For example, separate, anonymous whistleblowers brought to light fraud at Symbol Technologies and Kmart when they sent letters to government regulators. More recently, the mutual fund industry paid hundreds of millions of dollars to settle charges arising out of allegations made by employee whistleblowers to government investigators regarding improper practices in the industry.

. . . .

The success of these few individual whistleblowers does not indicate that employee whistleblowing worked effectively. Rather, the small number of successful whistleblowers highlights the overall failure of corporate employees

---

* Reprinted with the permission of Brigham Young University Law Review and the author.

to promptly identify and report the wrongdoing occurring in these companies and others, such as Enron. Employees failed in two respects. First, employees failed to speak out and, second, when they did, they failed to effectively report the misconduct they witnessed.

a. Failing to speak out. Unlike the few successful individual whistleblowers, the vast majority of knowledgeable employees failed to reveal wrongdoing because they were unable or unwilling to speak out. The misconduct at many of the corporations affected by recent scandals occurred over a period of several years. During this time, rank-and-file employees certainly participated, at some level, in the improper practices that led to the fraud. For example, when corporate executives at Enron made outlandish profit predictions, employees knew they must "gin . . . up" earnings and revenues to match the predictions. Thus, executives may have hatched accounting scams, but often their underlings were sent to do the dirty work of executing the plan, despite the underlings' knowledge that such accounting was illegal.

Furthermore, even if employees did not directly participate in the fraud, employees often knew that something in the corporation was amiss. At Enron, for example, knowledge about earnings manipulation was so widespread that employees joked about it at company parties. For months prior to Enron's bankruptcy filing, numerous employees knew that executives' public statements about Enron's financial strength were not true and that the company's business was failing. But despite their lengthy exposure to flawed financial practices and public misrepresentations, few employees came forward to complain. Importantly, this failure to report is not unique to Enron. In fact, studies reveal that the majority of corporate employees who witnessed wrongdoing did not report it. Successful whistleblowers, by definition, overcame this inherent hesitation to speak out.

b. Executive blocking and filtering. A second flow-of-information failure occurred because of executive blocking and filtering of whistleblower reports, so that even if employee spoke out, their disclosures of wrongdoing were ineffective. Many whistleblowers reported information to corporate executives rather than to traditional corporate monitors such as the board of directors. Executives subsequently prevented such information from reaching corporate monitors in order to protect the company from penalties and scandal. Such problems were apparent in many recent cases of corporate fraud; however, the fraud at Enron presents the clearest and most well documented example.

At the core of the Enron scandal were "massive accounting fraud and irregularities, a principal feature of which was the use of structured finance techniques designed to get debt off Enron's balance sheet and inflate Enron's profits." During the course of this fraud, Enron executives successfully blocked many employee complaints regarding improper or illegal business tactics by responding to any complaint with hostility and obfuscation. From the company's earliest days, Enron executives silenced and undermined employees who raised concerns about Enron's accounting and financial practices. This information blocking grew increasingly problematic by the late 1990s, when employees repeatedly complained to Enron's risk assessment group and corporate executives about the off-balance sheet "special purpose entities" that became the center of the Enron scandal. These complaints never made it to the Board of Directors, which, on three separate occasions, waived Enron's Code of Ethics and approved the conflicts of interests these entities created. Enron's Board never substantively investigated the propriety or long-term impact of these entities. Furthermore, in early 2001, as Enron's businesses began to show signs of strain, a few employees reported to corporate executives that large losses were being hidden. Executives disregarded these reports and never completed internal investigations. At least one employee wrote a signed letter to Enron's management and the Secretary of the Board in which she detailed the misrepresentations about Enron's earnings. The letter, however, was never shown to Enron's Board of Directors.

Even if employees avoided management's information blocking, corporate executives often filtered or slanted employee reports before the information reached the monitors. For example, Sherron Watkins, the famed Enron whistleblower, was unsuccessful in stopping Enron's fraud because the information she disclosed about misconduct at Enron was sanitized before it reached the Board of Directors. Watkins' error was that she complained to Enron's CEO, Kenneth Lay, rather than to the full Board of Directors. Lay subsequently hired the law firm of Vinson & Elkins to investigate the allegations — the very same law firm that approved many of the transactions about which Watkins complained. When the Board ultimately learned of Watkins' allegations, the report was whitewashed by Vinson & Elkins' conclusion that the transactions Watkins reported were proper. Thus, by hand-picking his friends at Vinson & Elkins to investigate Watkins' claims, Lay successfully filtered Watkins' full allegations from reaching the Board and the public. Although Watkins certainly deserves credit for her willingness to step forward and report her concerns to Enron's CEO, she ultimately was not effective as a whistleblower because she provided information to Enron's executives rather than directly to Enron's Board.

Finally, any conceivably problematic information that did make it to Enron's traditional monitors often was discounted or ignored based upon the close relationship between the monitors and Enron executives. Enron's Board, although ideally independent on paper, never effectively questioned Enron's management regarding its financial practices. Moreover, "gatekeepers," such as Enron's outside accountants and attorneys who received huge fees from Enron, did not raise red flags to anyone on Enron's Board even though they knew Enron's aggressive accounting techniques were problematic. The close relationships between purportedly independent monitors and Enron execu-tives led to "group think" that prevented them from dispassionately fulfilling their responsibilities and questioning information provided by corporate executives. Unfiltered information from employees, however, might have forced these monitors to fulfill their oversight responsibilities despite their close relationship with Enron management.

NOTES

1. *Civil Protections for Whistleblowers.* The Sarbanes-Oxley Act protects employees of public companies who make specific types of disclosures. Employ-ers cannot discriminate against employees who act reasonably to address mail fraud; fraud by wire, radio, or television; bank fraud; securities fraud; or "any rule or regulation of the Securities and Exchange Commission, or any provision of Federal law relating to fraud against shareholders." Sarbanes-Oxley Act of 2002 § 806, 18 U.S.C. § 1514A. The Act protects employees who "provide information . . . or otherwise assist" in an investigation conducted by a federal agency, a member or committee of Congress, or "a person with supervisory authority over the employee (or such other person working for the employer who has the authority to investigate, discover, or terminate misconduct)" and employees who "file, cause to be filed, testify, participate in, or otherwise assist in a proceeding filed or about to be filed (with any knowledge of the employer) relating to" the specified types of fraud. *Id.*

To receive § 806 protection, an employee must file a complaint with the Secretary of Labor within 90 days of the alleged discrimination. After the Secretary notifies the employer of the complaint, the employer has 20 days to produce clear and convincing evidence that the allegedly discriminatory act against the employee was not performed in response to the employee's protected behavior. If the employer fails to produce such evidence, the Assistant Secretary of Labor will conduct an investigation and issue a reasonable cause finding within 60 days. Either party may then request hearings to review the Secretary's ruling, and may eventually appeal the decision to a federal court of appeals. Sarbanes-Oxley also has a provision that permits employees to remove their case to federal district court if the Secretary of Labor does not issue a final ruling within 180 days of the filing of the complaint, a time deadline that is rarely met. Section 806 provides for "all relief necessary to make the employee whole," including reinstatement, back pay with interest, and special damages "including litigation costs, expert witness fees, and reasonable attorney fees." 18 U.S.C. § 1514A(c). The statute makes no reference to other compensatory or punitive damages.

2. *Required Whistleblowing by Lawyers.* The Sarbanes-Oxley Act also required the Securities and Exchange Commission to adopt rules of professional conduct for attorneys practicing before it who might know of financial improprieties. Sarbanes-Oxley Act of 2002 § 307, 15 U.S.C. § 7245. The SEC subsequently adopted rules requiring attorneys to report "evidence of a material violation" of securities law up the corporate ladder to corporate counsel or the chief executive officer. If the corporation does not respond appropriately, the attorney must report to the corporation's audit committee, another committee of independent directors, or to the full board. In addition, lawyers may reveal confidential information to the SEC to the extent reasonably necessary to prevent a material violation "likely to cause substantial injury to the financial interest or property of the issuer or investors." 17 C.F.R. § 205.3.

3. *Criminal Penalties for Retaliation.* The Sarbanes-Oxley Act also provided criminal penalties for those who retaliate. Section 1107 provided for fines and imprisonment up to ten years for anyone who "knowingly, with the intent to retaliate, takes any action harmful to any person, including interference with lawful employment or livelihood . . . for providing to a law enforcement officer any truthful information relating to the commission or possible commission of any Federal offense. . . ." Sarbanes-Oxley Act of 2002 § 1107, 18 U.S.C. § 1513(e). Unlike § 806, this protection is not limited to specific types of violations and extends far beyond corporate financial improprieties; on the other hand, it is limited to reports made to law-enforcement officers.

B. INTENTIONAL INFLICTION OF EMOTIONAL DISTRESS

While wrongful discharge in violation of public policy is the most important tort claim an employee brings when fired, other torts are alleged in addition or as alternatives. The most common is the claim of intentional infliction of emotional distress.

In *Harless v. First National Bank*, 289 S.E.2d 692 (W. Va. 1982), the court considered the problem of overlapping torts when the employee suffers great upset when fired in violation of public policy. A bank officer was harassed and eventually fired for reporting to the bank's board of directors that his supervisor had illegally overcharged customers who prepaid loans. On his retaliatory-discharge claim, the jury awarded compensatory damages of $20,000 against the bank and $5,000 against the supervisor, and the same amounts in punitive damages. On his intentional infliction of emotional distress claim, the jury awarded compensatory damages of $5,000 against the bank and $20,000 against the supervisor, and the same amounts in punitive damages. Upon review of the retaliatory-discharge claim, the Supreme Court upheld the compensatory damage award but reversed the punitive damages award, holding that punitive damages could only be awarded for "wanton, willful or malicious conduct" not present in this case. The court then turned to the emotional distress award.

> The plaintiff's theory of the tort of outrageous conduct related to the same events that make up the retaliatory discharge claim. . . . The tort of retaliatory discharge differs from the tort of outrageous conduct in several fundamental aspects. First, a retaliatory discharge begins with an employment relationship between the plaintiff and defendant. Second, the discharge is found actionable not because of any outrageous conduct on the part of the employer but because the discharge contravenes a substantial public policy right exercised by the employee.
>
> On the other hand, a degree of congruency exists in the damages recoverable. We permit recovery for emotional distress arising from a retaliatory discharge which is the same type of injury that the tort of outrageous conduct is designed to cover. Courts have also permitted a recovery of punitive damages on a claim for outrageous conduct. As we have earlier pointed out, a claim for punitive damages may also be available in a retaliatory discharge claim if the defendant's conduct is sufficiently aggravated. In substance then the retaliatory discharge cause of action, depending on the facts, is sufficiently accommodating to include outrageous conduct such that there is no need to permit an independent cause of action for outrageous conduct in a retaliatory discharge case.[22]

---

[22] There may be situations where the plaintiff has not been discharged or his termination of employment cannot be fitted into a retaliatory discharge cause of action, yet a cause of action will fall within the tort of outrageous conduct as against his employer.

In the present case, we do not find the conduct of the Bank or Wilson to have reached the level of outrageous conduct that would support a claim for the tort of outrage. Moreover, in this jurisdiction, a claim for the tort of outrageous conduct is duplicitous to a claim for retaliatory discharge. The damages are essentially the same under both claims since we recognize that if the employer's conduct is outrageous punitive damages may be recovered in a retaliatory discharge suit as well as compensatory damages including an award for emotional distress.

Id. at 705.

AGIS v. HOWARD JOHNSON CO.
Supreme Judicial Court of Massachusetts
355 N.E.2d 315 (1976)

Before REARDON, QUIRICO, BRAUCHER and WILKINS, JJ.

QUIRICO, JUSTICE.

This case raises the issue . . . whether a cause of action exists in this Commonwealth for the intentional or reckless infliction of severe emotional distress without resulting bodily injury. Counts 1 and 2 of this action were brought by the plaintiff Debra Agis against the Howard Johnson Company and Roger Dionne, manager of the restaurant in which she was employed, to recover damages for mental anguish and emotional distress allegedly caused by her summary dismissal from such employment. Counts 3 and 4 were brought by her husband, James Agis, against both defendants for loss of the services, love, affection and companionship of his wife. This case is before us on the plaintiffs' appeal from the dismissal of their complaint.

Briefly, the allegations in the plaintiffs' complaint, which we accept as true for purposes of ruling on this motion, are the following. Debra Agis was employed by the Howard Johnson Company as a waitress in a restaurant known as the Ground Round. On or about May 23, 1975, the defendant Dionne notified all waitresses that a meeting would be held at 3 P.M. that day. At the meeting, he informed the waitresses that "there was some stealing going on," but that the identity of the person or persons responsible was not known, and that, until the person or persons responsible were discovered, he would begin firing all the present waitresses in alphabetical order, starting with the letter "A." Dionne then fired Debra Agis.

The complaint alleges that, as a result of this incident, Mrs. Agis became greatly upset, began to cry, sustained emotional distress, mental anguish, and loss of wages and earnings. It further alleges that the actions of the defendants were reckless, extreme, outrageous and intended to cause emotional distress and anguish. In addition, the complaint states that the defendants knew or should have known that their actions would cause such distress. . . .

The most often cited argument for refusing to extend the cause of action for intentional or reckless infliction of emotional distress to cases where there has been no physical injury is the difficulty of proof and the danger of fraudulent or frivolous claims. There has been a concern that "mental anguish, standing alone, is too subtle and speculative to be measured by any known legal standard," that "mental anguish and its consequences are so intangible and peculiar and vary so much with the individual that they cannot reasonably be anticipated," that a wide door might "be opened not only to fictitious claims but to litigation over trivialities and mere bad manners as well," and that there can be no objective measurement of the extent or the existence of emotional distress. There is a fear that "[i]t is easy to assert a claim of mental anguish and very hard to disprove it." *See also* Magruder, *Mental and Emotional Disturbance in the Law of Torts*, 49 HARV. L. REV. 1033 (1936); W. PROSSER, TORTS § 12 (4th ed. 1971).

While we are not unconcerned with these problems, we believe that "the problems presented are not . . . insuperable" and that "administrative difficulties do not justify the denial of relief for serious invasions of mental and emotional tranquility. . . ."

Furthermore, the distinction between the difficulty which juries may encounter in determining liability and assessing damages where no physical injury occurs and their performance of that same task where there has been resulting physical harm may be greatly overstated. "The jury is ordinarily in a better position . . . to determine whether outrageous conduct results in mental distress than whether that distress in turn results in physical injury. From their own experience jurors are aware of the extent and character of the disagreeable emotions that may result from the defendant's conduct, but a difficult medical question is presented when it must be determined if emotional distress resulted in physical injury. . . . Greater proof that mental suffering occurred is found in the defendant's conduct designed to bring it about than in physical injury that may or may not have resulted therefrom." *State Rubbish Collectors Ass'n v. Siliznoff,* 240 P.2d 282, 286 (Cal. 1952). We are thus unwilling to deny the existence of this cause of action merely because there may be difficulties of proof. Instead, we believe "the door to recovery should be opened but narrowly and with due caution." *Barnett v. Collection Serv. Co.,* 242 N.W. 25, 28 (Iowa 1932).

In light of what we have said, we hold that one who, by extreme and outrageous conduct and without privilege, causes severe emotional distress to another is subject to liability for such emotional distress even though no bodily harm may result. However, in order for a plaintiff to prevail in a case for liability under this tort, four elements must be established. It must be shown (1) that the actor intended to inflict emotional distress or that he knew or should have known that emotional distress was the likely result of his conduct, RESTATEMENT (SECOND) OF TORTS sec. 46, comment i (1965); (2) that the conduct was "extreme and outrageous," was "beyond all possible bounds of decency" and was "utterly intolerable in a civilized community," RESTATEMENT (SECOND) OF TORTS sec. 46, comment d (1965); (3) that the actions of the defendant were the cause of the plaintiff's distress; and (4) that the emotional distress sustained by the plaintiff was "severe" and of a nature "that no reasonable man could be expected to endure it." RESTATEMENT (SECOND) OF TORTS sec. 46, comment j (1965). These requirements are "aimed at limiting frivolous suits and avoiding litigation in situations where only bad manners and mere hurt feelings are involved," and we believe they are a "realistic safeguard against false claims. . . ."

Testing the plaintiff Debra Agis's complaint by the rules stated above, we hold that she makes out a cause of action and that her complaint is therefore legally sufficient. While many of her allegations are not particularly well stated, we believe that the "[p]laintiff has alleged facts and circumstances which reasonably could lead the trier of fact to conclude that defendant's conduct was extreme and outrageous, having a severe and traumatic effect upon plaintiff's emotional tranquility." Because reasonable men could differ on these issues, we believe that "it is for the jury, subject to the control of the court," to determine whether there should be liability in this case. While the judge was not in error in dismissing the complaint under the then state of the law, we believe that, in light of what we have said, the judgment must be reversed and the plaintiff Debra Agis must be given an opportunity to prove the allegations which she has made.

[The Court also held that Agis's husband stated a valid claim for loss of consortium as a result of the mental distress and anguish suffered by his wife Debra.]

The judgment entered in the Superior Court dismissing the plaintiffs' complaint is reversed.

NOTES

1. Backdoor Wrongful Discharge Claims. If Howard Johnson could have fired Agis — an at-will employee — for a good reason, bad reason, or no reason, why is her firing improper? Indeed, did not Howard Johnson have a business motivation — deterring theft — for the firing? Could Agis fit her claim into the established pigeonholes of wrongful discharge in violation of public policy? Does the intentional infliction of emotional distress claim address different or larger concerns, or is it simply a backdoor way to bring a wrongful-discharge claim?

2. Manner of Discharge Claims. In some situations, at-will employees concede that they cannot challenge the fact of discharge, but complain about the manner of discharge. Is *Agis* such a case? In *Gwin v. Chesrown Chevrolet, Inc.*, 931 P.2d 466 (Colo. Ct. App. 1996), the court recognized a claim for manner of discharge where the manager stormed into a salesman's meeting shouting expletives and fired the plaintiff in front of his peers. *But see Johnson v. Chesebrough-Pond's USA Co.*, 918 F. Supp. 543, 552-53 (D. Conn. 1996), where the employee was "physically escorted from the building like a criminal," and the court found no extreme and outrageous conduct.

3. Third-Party Effects. Does the infliction of emotional distress hurt anyone besides the plaintiff? If not, the justification for allowing the tort cannot be to regulate third-party effects of contracts. Should the tort nevertheless be allowed? On what theory? Fundamental fairness? Inequality of bargaining power between the parties?

BODEWIG v. K-MART, INC.
Court of Appeals of Oregon
635 P.2d 657 (1981)

Before BUTTLER, P. J., JOSEPH, C. J., and WARREN, J.

BUTTLER, PRESIDING JUDGE.

In this tort action for outrageous conduct, plaintiff seeks damages against her former employer, K-Mart, and a K-Mart customer, Mrs. Golden. Both defendants moved for summary judgment, which the trial court granted. Plaintiff appeals from the resulting final judgments entered. We reverse and remand.

. . . On the evening of March 29, 1979, plaintiff was working as a part-time checker at K-Mart. Defendant Golden entered plaintiff's checkout lane and plaintiff began to ring up Golden's purchases on the cash register. When plaintiff called out the price on a package of curtains, Golden told plaintiff the price was incorrect because the curtains were on sale. Plaintiff called a domestics department clerk for a price check. That clerk told plaintiff the curtains in question were not on sale. Upon hearing this, Golden left her merchandise on plaintiff's counter and returned with the clerk to the domestics department to find the "sale" curtains.

After Golden left, plaintiff moved Golden's merchandise to the service counter, voided the register slip containing the partial listing of Golden's items and began to check out other customers. Three to ten minutes later, Golden returned to plaintiff's checkstand, where another customer was being served. Golden "looked around" that customer and asked what plaintiff had done with her money. When plaintiff replied, "What money?," Golden said that she had left four five-dollar bills on top of the merchandise she was purchasing before she left with the domestics clerk. Plaintiff told Golden she had not seen any money. Golden continued in a loud, abrupt voice to demand her money from plaintiff and caused a general commotion. Customers and store personnel in the area began to look on curiously.

The K-Mart manager, who had been observing the incident from a nearby service desk, walked over to plaintiff's counter. After a short discussion with Golden, he walked up to plaintiff, pulled out her jacket pockets, looked inside and found nothing. Then he, plaintiff and two or three other store employees conducted a general search of the area for the money. When this effort proved fruitless, the manager explained there was nothing more he could do except check out plaintiff's register. Golden said, "Well, do it." The manager and an assistant manager locked plaintiff's register and took the till and the register receipt to the cash cage. While the register was being checked, Golden continued to glare at plaintiff while plaintiff checked out customers at another register. The register balanced perfectly. When the manager so advised Golden, Golden replied that she still believed plaintiff took her money and continued to "cause commotion" and glare at plaintiff. A further general search of the surrounding area was conducted without success. Golden still would not leave; another employee was trying to calm her down.

The manager then told plaintiff to accompany a female assistant manager into the women's public restroom for the purpose of disrobing in order to prove to Golden that she did not have the money. As plaintiff and the assistant manager walked to the restroom, the manager asked Golden if she wanted to watch the search; Golden replied: "You had better believe I do, it is my money." In the restroom, plaintiff took off all her clothes except her underwear while Golden and the assistant manager watched closely. When plaintiff asked Golden if she needed to take off more, Golden replied that it was not necessary because she could see through plaintiff's underwear anyway.

Plaintiff put on her clothes and started to leave the restroom when the assistant manager asked Golden how much money she had in her purse. Golden replied that she did not know the exact amount, but thought she had between five and six hundred dollars. She did not attempt to count it at that time.

Plaintiff then returned to her checkstand. Golden followed plaintiff to the counter and continued to glare at her as she worked. Finally, the manager told Golden nothing more could be done for her, and after more loud protestations, Golden left the store.

Upon arriving home, Golden counted the money in her purse. She had $560. She called plaintiff's mother, whom she knew casually, and related the entire incident to her, stating that she had told K-Mart that plaintiff had taken her money. She described the strip search to plaintiff's mother and stated that when she was asked if she wanted to watch the strip, she responded, "Damn right." The mother expressed concern that plaintiff would lose her job; Golden said she would call the store and ask them not to let her go. Golden did make that call. After the conversation with Golden, plaintiff's mother, father and sister went to K-Mart to see if plaintiff was all right and to take her home.

Plaintiff returned to work the next day and was told that the keys to the cash register were lost and she was to work on a register with another employee. That procedure is known as "piggy-backing," and plaintiff had been told three months earlier that the store would no longer "piggy-back" checkers. Plaintiff believed the store was monitoring her by the "piggy-back" procedure; she quit at the end of her scheduled shift that day. . . .

K-Mart contends that the trial court properly granted its motion, because the facts presented do not constitute outrageous conduct as a matter of law. Its principal argument is that plaintiff consented to the strip search, either expressly as its manager stated, or tacitly by not expressly objecting. Plaintiff stated, variously, that she was told or asked by the manager to disrobe, but, whether asked or told, she did not consider that she had a choice. She thought she would lose her job if she refused, and she needed the job. The issue of lack of consent to that search is an issue of fact, but whether it is an issue of material fact depends upon whether, assuming plaintiff's version to be true, the facts are sufficient to submit the case to the jury on the outrageous conduct theory.

. . . There are at least two versions of the tort [of outrageous conduct]. One is represented by *Turman v. Central Billing Bureau,* 568 P.2d 1382 (Or. 1977), and involves intentional conduct, the very purpose of which is to inflict psychological and emotional distress on the plaintiff. The other is represented by *Rockhill v. Pollard,* 485 P.2d 28 (Or. 1971), where the wrongful purpose was lacking, but "the tortious element can be found in the breach of some obligation, statutory or otherwise, that attaches to defendant's relationship to plaintiff. . . ." *Brewer v. Erwin*, 600 P.2d 398, 411 (Or. 1979). . . .

Neither the Supreme Court nor this court has been presented with the question of whether the employer-employee relationship falls into that special category. This court, however, has treated the landlord-tenant relationship as a "prime consideration" in evaluating the defendant's conduct. We reached that conclusion because landlords were in a position of authority with respect to tenants and could affect the tenants' interest in the quiet enjoyment of their leasehold. An employer has even more authority over an employee, who, by the nature of the relationship, is subject to the direction and control of the employer and may be discharged for any or no reason, absent an agreement restricting that authority. Clearly, that relationship is not an arm's length one between strangers. Accordingly, we conclude that the relationship between plaintiff and K-Mart was a special relationship, based on which liability may be imposed if K-Mart's conduct, though not deliberately aimed at causing emotional distress, was such that a jury might find it to be beyond the limits of social toleration and reckless of the conduct's predictable effects on plaintiff.

We conclude that a jury could find that the K-Mart manager, a 32-year-old male in charge of the entire store, after concluding that plaintiff did not take the customer's money, put her through the degrading and humiliating experience of submitting to a strip search in order to satisfy the customer, who was not only acting unreasonably, but was creating a commotion in the store; that the manager's conduct exceeded the bounds of social toleration and was in reckless disregard of its predictable effects on plaintiff.

Because there was no special relationship between plaintiff and Golden, the evidence must be such that a jury could find Golden's conduct not only socially intolerable, but that it was deliberately aimed at causing plaintiff emotional distress. Golden contends the evidence does not permit those findings, because she was merely trying to get her money back from plaintiff. To sustain that position, it would be necessary to resolve the disputed facts relating to Golden's conduct in her favor. As in the case against K-Mart, those factual issues are material only if, after resolving them in plaintiff's favor, the evidence would permit a jury to find for plaintiff.

We conclude that the facts, viewed most favorably to plaintiff, would permit a jury to find that Golden's entire course of conduct was intended to embarrass and humiliate plaintiff in order to coerce her into giving Golden $20, whether rightfully hers or not; that Golden did not know how much money she had in her purse, variously stated to be between $300 and $600, made no effort to determine if she was, in fact, missing four five dollar bills until she returned home, at which time she found she was mistaken; that Golden's insistence on a check of plaintiff's cash register, her insistence that plaintiff still had her money after the register checked out perfectly, her eager participation in the strip search of plaintiff and her continuing to stare angrily at plaintiff over an extended period, even after all efforts to find her money failed, would permit a jury to find Golden's conduct deliberately calculated to cause plaintiff emotional distress and exceeded the bounds of social toleration.

A jury could also find in Golden's favor, but the mere fact that her stated ultimate objective was to get her money back is not sufficient to defeat plaintiff's claim. . . . There are lawful (socially tolerable) ways to collect money from another, and there are unlawful (socially intolerable) ways to do so.

Common to her claims against both defendants is the requirement that plaintiff prove that she suffered severe emotional distress. If the facts presented are believed, plaintiff suffered shock, humiliation and embarrassment, suffering that was not merely transient. Plaintiff characterized herself as a shy, modest person, and said that she had two or three sleepless nights, cried a lot and still gets nervous and upset when she thinks about the incident. Concededly, this element of the tort has been, and still is, troublesome to courts. K-Mart contends there is no objective evidence of the distress, such as medical, economic or social problems. In *Rockhill v. Pollard, supra,* plaintiff became nervous and suffered from sleeplessness and a loss of appetite over a period of about two years. The court said:

> ". . . Defendant belittles these symptoms, but it is the distress which must be severe, not the physical manifestations. . . ." 485 P.2d 28.

Defendant Golden contends that the purpose of requiring proof of severe emotional distress is to guard against fraudulent or frivolous claims and that some degree of transient and trivial distress is a part of the price of living among people. Here, however, it is not unreasonable to expect that a shy, modest, young woman put in plaintiff's position would suffer the effects she claims to have suffered from the incident, and that her distress was more than that which a person might be reasonably expected to pay as the price of living among people.

We cannot say as a matter of law that plaintiff's evidence of severe emotional distress is insufficient to go to a jury. Because neither defendant was entitled to judgment as a matter of law, neither motion for summary judgment should have been granted.

The judgment for each of the defendants is reversed. The case is remanded for trial.

NOTES

1. *The Special-Relationship Test.* The court in *Bodewig* emphasizes that employers are in a position of authority over employees. Why does this fact support liability for emotional distress that was not purposeful? Is it that employees have less ability to end an abusive relationship with the employer than they would with a stranger who attempts to abuse them? Or is it because the employer is in a better position than are other defendants to know that the employee is particularly vulnerable to harsh conduct? In this case, for example, was the manager in a better position than was the customer to know the employee was shy and modest? In *Rhodes v. Sun Electric Corp.*, 121 L.R.R.M. (BNA) 2203 (N.D. Ill. 1985), a corporate manager of legal affairs was accused of theft and eventually fired. The court refused to dismiss her claim of intentional infliction of emotional distress, emphasizing that the employer had special knowledge that the employee was in a weakened emotional and physical state because she had undergone major surgery and was involved in a contested divorce.

2. *Outrageousness in the Workplace.* Most reported decisions deny employees' claims of intentional infliction of emotional distress. In doing so, courts often follow the RESTATEMENT (SECOND) OF TORTS § 46, comment d, in defining the requisite standard. The defendant's conduct must be

> so outrageous in character, and so extreme in degree, as to go beyond all possible bounds of decency, and to be regarded as atrocious, and utterly intolerable in a civilized community. Generally, the case is one in which the recitation of the facts to an average member of the community would arouse his resentment against the actor, and lead him to exclaim, "Outrageous!"

> The liability clearly does not extend to mere insults, indignities, threats, annoyances, petty oppressions, or other trivialities. The rough edges of our society are still in need of a good deal of filing down, and in the meantime plaintiffs must necessarily be expected and required to be hardened to a certain amount of rough language.

The Restatement would allow recovery for gross insults not amounting to extreme outrage only when there is a special relation between the parties. The Restatement recognizes a special relation between public utilities and their customers, and perhaps between landowners and their business or other invitees.

3. *Special or Harsh Relationship.* Court treatment of workplace claims of intentional infliction of emotional distress can be unpredictable. In *Kentucky Fried Chicken National Management Co. v. Weathersby*, 607 A.2d 8 (Md. 1992), the Maryland Court of Appeals affirmed a judgment notwithstanding the verdict after a jury had ruled for the plaintiff in a suit for intentional infliction of emotional distress. The plaintiff was harassed by her supervisor and suspended in front of customers and employees and told that she was being investigated for missing money, and was later demoted to a position under a person she once supervised at a salary cut of $11,000. The plaintiff was eventually hospitalized and was unable to return to work. The court found that this treatment did not satisfy the level of "outrageous conduct" required for the tort. Judge Bell, in dissent, warned that the decision signaled the end of the tort of emotional distress in the workplace:

> The message that comes through in the case, and, I believe, is intended, is that the tort of intentional infliction of emotional distress does not exist in the employer-employee context; the limitations the majority places on the tort are such that it is virtually inconceivable that any employment case will ever qualify.

The Oklahoma Supreme Court conveyed the same skepticism about emotional-distress employment claims when it declared that "[t]he salon of Madame Pompadour is not to be likened to the rough-and-tumble atmosphere of the American oil refinery." *Eddy v. Brown*, 715 P.2d 74, 77 (Okla. 1986).

A contrasting case is a Fifth Circuit decision upholding a $3.4 million jury award to an employee for intentional infliction of emotional distress and age discrimination. In *Wilson v. Monarch,* 939 F.2d 1138 (5th Cir. 1991) (applying Texas law), a sixty-year-old vice president was demoted to an entry-level warehouse supervisor with menial and demeaning duties, including sweeping up and cleaning the warehouse cafeteria. This treatment eventually caused the plaintiff to be involuntarily hospitalized with a psychotic manic episode. While the Fifth Circuit expressed "real concern about the consequences of applying the cause of action of intentional infliction of emotional distress to the workplace," it found that the defendant's conduct was "so outrageous that civilized society should not tolerate it." The irresistible questions from Professor Alan Hyde are: who swept up and cleaned the cafeteria before Wilson? Was that intentional infliction of emotional distress? Or does this doctrine, too, only protect senior employees at the end of their life cycle who are precipitously demoted — perhaps because their productivity has declined?

4. Is Minor Abuse Justifiable? Professor Regina Austin has criticized the Restatement standard for minimizing the seriousness of the abuse workers — particularly minority or female workers — face in the workplace.

> The approach mandated by Section 46 immediately focuses on whether the employer's or supervisor's coercion was excessive and skips the threshold issue of whether any amount of emotional mistreatment was justified. In this regard, it differs from the 1948 version of the section which required that the defendant show that abuse of the plaintiff was privileged. The legal analysis required by the current version of Section 46 thus allows courts to avoid elaborate explanations for their decisions. Beginning with the assumption that some amount of intentionally inflicted pain is acceptable, they need not and often do not go much beyond quoting the comments to Section 46 and offering several conclusory sentences sprinkled with *Restatement* terminology. . . .

> The gist of the story the courts tell about abuse in the workplace can be summarized as follows: Only the extraordinary, the excessive, and the nearly bizarre in the way of supervisory intimidation and humiliation warrant judicial relief through the tort of intentional infliction of emotional distress. All other forms of supervisory conduct that cause workers to experience emotional harm are more or less "trivial" in the terminology of the *Restatement of Torts.* The very ordinariness of such conduct and the ubiquity of the experience of pain at the hands of supervisors are justification enough for the law's refusal to intervene. . . .

> [The *Restatement's*] solution lies principally in individual workers shrugging off petty insults. Worker self-reliance and stamina are repeatedly touted in the outrage cases. Courts see toughness and strength as such positive attributes that they simply assume that the capacity to tolerate abuse, and the propriety of dishing it out, vary with the nature of the work, the workplace, and the characteristics of the workers. Males and blue-collar workers, for example, may be subjected to harsher supervision than females or white-collar workers because of the acceptability of sex and class distinctions and the implications of group pride that underlie the disparate treatment. . . .

Workers would agree with the law's assessment that supervisory abuse is an ordinary, everyday occurrence in the workplace. They would, however, part company with the courts and commentators when the latter argue that it is so mundane and commonplace that it should escape severe censure. On the contrary, from the workers' perspective, the frequency with which they encounter supervisory mistreatment means that it cannot be warranted or justified in the way the law and the conventional wisdom assert.

Among workers, there is widespread condemnation of close, coercive supervision. It is not acceptable behavior. The hostility to this sort of abusive authority is manifested in the words and actions of workers performing disparate jobs, in disparate workplaces. . . .

[A]buse can be objectionable to workers because it does not reflect objective assessments of their productivity. Whereas the law assumes that abuse is utilized because workers are not contributing to the enterprise as they should be, workers view abuse as a calculated devaluation of themselves and their work. For example, the clerical employees interviewed by Roberta Goldberg for her book ORGANIZING WOMEN OFFICE WORKERS [1983] objected to the close supervision of their work and time away from their desks because it indicated that they were not trusted. They also complained about low pay because it meant that their work was considered trivial and unimportant. They resented the demeaning terms (like "girl" and "honey") others used in referring to them. They especially objected to being asked to do "menial" domestic chores because it meant that their employers did not take them seriously with regard to the tasks they were hired to perform. . . .

Minority and female employees have reason to suspect that the disparagement and mistreatment they receive on the job is motivated by racial prejudice and sexist animosity, not merely by a concern for productivity and profits or by individualized assessments of merit. The young black men investigated by Elijah Anderson for his essay, *Some Observations of Black Youth Employment* [1980], indicated that they were especially oppressed by the distrust and suspicion which pervaded their working environments. Their supervisors and co-workers watched them closely to see if they displayed the inadequacies of the blacks who had preceded them and to prevent them from stealing. Anderson reports that

> it is not uncommon for many black workers to be treated as outsiders . . . even though they have been working on the job for a long time. Among black workers who face such problems on a common job, a standing phrase is the "can I help you?" routine. . . . "When a black arrives at work, some white employee is ready with 'can I help you?'" The blacks interpret this question as a "nice" way of saying "what business do you have here?" . . . It appears to be a device of someone who is very concerned about outsiders committing a crime on the work premises. To be black and young is to be suspect. Black youth understand the nuance here, and they joke about such slights during lunch or breaks. They often gather together on the

job for purposes of social defense, telling "horror stories" and communing in what they see as a hostile social and work environment.

The exclusionary treatment about which these workers complain is, of course, not the sort of overt discriminatory behavior that the tort of outrage reaches.

Regina Austin, *Employer Abuse, Worker Resistance, and the Tort of Intentional Infliction of Emotional Distress,* 41 STAN. L. REV. 1, 7, 18, 21-24 (1988).[*]

Chapter 6

GOOD-FAITH LIMITATIONS ON EMPLOYMENT AT WILL

FORTUNE v. NATIONAL CASH REGISTER CO.
Supreme Judicial Court of Massachusetts
364 N.E.2d 1251 (1977)

Before HENNESSEY, C. J., and KAPLAN, WILKINS, LIACOS and ABRAMS, JJ.

ABRAMS, JUSTICE.

Orville E. Fortune (Fortune), a former salesman of The National Cash Register Company (NCR), brought a suit to recover certain commissions allegedly due as a result of a sale of cash registers to First National Stores Inc. (First National) in 1968. Counts 1 and 2 of Fortune's amended declaration claimed bonus payments under the parties' written contract of employment. The third count sought recovery in quantum meruit for the reasonable value of Fortune's services relating to the same sales transaction. Judgment on a jury verdict for Fortune was reversed by the Appeals Court, and this court granted leave to obtain further appellate review. We affirm the judgment of the Superior Court. We hold, for the reasons stated herein, there was no error in submitting the issue of "bad faith" termination of an employment at will contract to the jury.

The issues before the court are raised by NCR's motion for directed verdicts. Accordingly, we summarize the evidence most favorable to the plaintiff.

Fortune was employed by NCR under a written "salesman's contract" which was terminable at will, without cause, by either party on written notice. The contract provided that Fortune would receive a weekly salary in a fixed amount plus a bonus for sales made within the "territory" (*i.e.*, customer accounts or stores) assigned to him for "coverage or supervision," whether the sale was made by him or someone else.[2] The amount of the bonus was determined on the basis of "bonus credits," which were computed as a percentage of the price of products sold. Fortune would be paid a percentage of the applicable bonus credit as follows: (1) 75% if the territory was assigned to him at the date of the order, (2) 25% if the territory was assigned to him at the date of delivery and installation, or (3) 100% if the territory was assigned to him at both times. The contract further provided that the "bonus interest" would terminate if shipment of the order was not made within eighteen months from the date of the order unless (1) the territory was assigned to him for coverage at the date of delivery and installation, or (2) special engineering was required to fulfill the contract. In addition, NCR

---

[2] Apparently, NCR's use of a "guaranteed territory" was designed to motivate "the salesman to develop good will for the company and also avoided a damaging rivalry among salesmen."

reserved the right to sell products in the salesman's territory without paying a bonus. However, this right could be exercised only on written notice.

In 1968, Fortune's territory included First National. This account had been part of his territory for the preceding six years; he had been successful in obtaining several orders from First National, including a million dollar order in 1963. Sometime in late 1967, or early 1968, NCR introduced a new model cash register, Class 5. Fortune corresponded with First National in an effort to sell the machine. He also helped to arrange for a demonstration of the Class 5 to executives of First National on October 4, 1968. NCR had a team of men also working on this sale.

. . . On November 29, 1968, First National signed an order for 2,008 Class 5 machines to be delivered over a four-year period at a purchase price of approximately $5,000,000. Although Fortune did not participate in the negotiation of the terms of the order, his name appeared on the order form in the space entitled "salesman credited." The amount of the bonus credit as shown on the order was $92,079.99.

On January 6, 1969, the first working day of the new year, Fortune found an envelope on his desk at work. It contained a termination notice addressed to his home dated December 2, 1968. Shortly after receiving the notice, Fortune spoke to the Boston branch manager with whom he was friendly. The manager told him, "You are through," but, after considering some of the details necessary for the smooth operation of the First National order, told him to "stay on," and to "[k]eep on doing what you are doing right now." Fortune remained with the company in a position entitled "sales support." In this capacity, he coordinated and expedited delivery of the machines to First National under the November 29 order as well as servicing other accounts.

Commencing in May or June, Fortune began to receive some bonus commissions on the First National order. Having received only 75% of the applicable bonus due on the machines which had been delivered and installed, Fortune spoke with his manager about receiving the full amount of the commission. Fortune was told "to forget about it." Sixty-one years old at that time, and with a son in college, Fortune concluded that it "was a good idea to forget it for the time being."

NCR did pay a systems and installations person the remaining 25% of the bonus commissions due from the First National order although contrary to its usual policy of paying *only* salesmen a bonus. . . .

Approximately eighteen months after receiving the termination notice, Fortune, who had worked for NCR for almost twenty-five years, was asked to retire. When he refused, he was fired in June of 1970. Fortune did not receive any bonus payments on machines which were delivered to First National after this date.

At the close of the plaintiff's case, the defendant moved for a directed verdict, arguing that there was no evidence of any breach of contract, and adding that the existence of a contract barred recovery under the quantum meruit count. Ruling that Fortune could recover if the termination and firing were in bad faith, the trial judge, without specifying on which count, submitted this issue to the jury. NCR then rested and, by agreement of counsel, the case was sent to the jury for special verdicts on two questions:

1. Did the Defendant act in bad faith . . . when it decided to terminate the Plaintiff's contract as a salesman by letter dated December 2, 1968, delivered on January 6, 1969?

2. Did the Defendant act in bad faith . . . when the Defendant let the Plaintiff go on June 5, 1970?

The jury answered both questions affirmatively, and judgment entered in the sum of $45,649.62.

The central issue on appeal is whether this "bad faith" termination constituted a breach of the employment at will contract. Traditionally, an employment contract which is "at will" may be terminated by either side without reason. . . .

The contract at issue is a classic terminable at will employment contract. It is clear that the contract itself reserved to the parties an explicit power to terminate the contract without cause on written notice. It is also clear that under the express terms of the contract Fortune has received all the bonus commissions to which he is entitled. Thus, NCR claims that it did not breach the contract, and that it has no further liability to Fortune.[7] According to a literal reading of the contract, NCR is correct.

However, Fortune argues that, in spite of the literal wording of the contract, he is entitled to a jury determination on NCR's motives in terminating his services under the contract and in finally discharging him. We agree. We hold that NCR's written contract contains an implied covenant of good faith and fair dealing, and a termination not made in good faith constitutes a breach of the contract.

We do not question the general principles that an employer is entitled to be motivated by and to serve its own legitimate business interests; that an employer must have wide latitude in deciding whom it will employ in the face of the uncertainties of the business world; and that an employer needs flexibility in the face of changing circumstances. We recognize the employer's need for a large amount of control over its work force. However, we believe that where, as here, commissions are to be paid for work performed by the employee, the employer's decision to terminate its at will employee should be made in good faith. NCR's right to make decisions in its own interest is not, in our view, unduly hampered by a requirement of adherence to this standard. On occasion some courts have avoided the rigidity of the "at will" rule by fashioning a remedy in tort.[8] We believe, however, that in this case there is

---

[7] Damages were, by stipulation of the parties, set equal to the unpaid bonus amounts. Thus we need not consider whether other measures of damages might be justified in cases of bad faith termination. Nor do we now decide whether a tort action, with possible punitive damages, might lie in such circumstances. *See, e.g.,* Blades, *Employment at Will vs. Individual Freedom: On Limiting the Abusive Exercise of Employer Power,* 67 COLUM. L. REV. 1404, 1421-1427 (1967).

[8] This theory has generally been utilized in order to protect public policy. *See, e.g., Montalvo v. Zamora,* 86 Cal. Rptr. 401 (Cal. Ct. App. 1970) (employee terminated after having an attorney to negotiate a claim that the employer had violated the minimum wage law); *Petermann v. International Bhd. of Teamsters, Local 396,* 344 P.2d 25 (Cal. Ct. App. 1959) (employee discharged for refusing to commit perjury before government commission); *Frampton v. Central Ind. Gas Co.,* 297 N.E.2d 425 (Ind. 1973) (employee fired for filing a workman's compensation claim); *Nees v. Hocks,* 536 P.2d 512 (Or. 1975) (employee fired for performing jury duty in violation of company policy). *Cf. Geary v. United States Steel Corp.,* 319 A.2d 174 (Pa. 1974) (tort remedy not available where employee fired for not following corporate hierarchy procedure in protesting company policy as to safety of a product).

remedy on the express contract.[9] In so holding we are merely recognizing the general requirement in this Commonwealth that parties to contracts and commercial transactions must act in good faith toward one another. Good faith and fair dealing between parties are pervasive requirements in our law; it can be said fairly, that parties to contracts or commercial transactions are bound by this standard. *See* G.L. c. 106, § 1-203 (good faith in contracts under Uniform Commercial Code); G.L. c. 93B, § 4(3)(c) (good faith in motor vehicle franchise termination). . . .

Recent decisions in other jurisdictions lend support to the proposition that good faith is implied in contracts terminable at will. In a recent employment at will case, *Monge v. Beebe Rubber Co.,* 316 A.2d 549, 552 (N.H. 1974), the plaintiff alleged that her oral contract of employment had been terminated because she refused to date her foreman. The New Hampshire Supreme Court held that "[i]n all employment contracts, whether at will or for a definite term, the employer's interest in running his business as he sees fit must be balanced against the interest of the employee in maintaining his employment, and the public's interest in maintaining a proper balance between the two. . . . We hold that a termination by the employer of a contract of employment at will which is motivated by bad faith or malice . . . constitutes a breach of the employment contract. . . . Such a rule affords the employee a certain stability of employment and does not interfere with the employer's normal exercise of his right to discharge, which is necessary to permit him to operate his business efficiently and profitably."

We believe that the holding in the *Monge* case merely extends to employment contracts the rule that "in *every* contract there is an implied covenant that neither party shall do anything which will have the effect of destroying or injuring the right of the other party to receive the fruits of the contract, which means that in *every* contract there exists an implied covenant of good faith and fair dealing."

In the instant case, we need not pronounce our adherence to so broad a policy nor need we speculate as to whether the good faith requirement is implicit in every contract for employment at will. It is clear, however, that, on the facts before us, a finding is warranted that a breach of the contract occurred. Where the principal seeks to deprive the agent of all compensation by terminating the contractual relationship when the agent is on the brink of successfully completing the sale, the principal has acted in bad faith and the ensuing transaction between the principal and the buyer is to be regarded as having been accomplished by the agent. RESTATEMENT (SECOND) OF AGENCY § 454, and Comment a (1958). The same result obtains where the principal attempts to deprive the agent of any portion of a commission due the agent. Courts have often applied this rule to prevent overreaching by employers and the forfeiture by employees of benefits almost earned by the rendering of substantial services. In our view, the Appeals Court erroneously focused only on literal compliance with payment provisions of the contract and failed to consider the issue of bad faith termination.

NCR argues that there was no evidence of bad faith in this case; therefore, the trial judge was required to direct a verdict in any event. We think that

---

[9] Thus, we do not reach the issues raised by count 3 for quantum meruit recovery.

the evidence and the reasonable inferences to be drawn therefrom support a jury verdict that the termination of Fortune's twenty-five years of employment as a salesman with NCR the next business day after NCR obtained a $5,000,000 order from First National was motivated by a desire to pay Fortune as little of the bonus credit as it could. The fact that Fortune was willing to work under these circumstances does not constitute a waiver or estoppel; it only shows that NCR had him "at their mercy."

NCR also contends that Fortune cannot complain of his firing in June, 1970, as his employment contract clearly indicated that bonus credits would be paid only for an eighteen-month period following the date of the order. As we have said, the jury could have found that Fortune was stripped of his "salesman" designation in order to disqualify him for the remaining 25% of the commissions due on cash registers delivered prior to the date of his first termination. Similarly, the jury could have found that Fortune was fired so that NCR would avoid paying him any commissions on cash registers delivered after June, 1970. . . .

We think that NCR's conduct in June, 1970 permitted the jury to find bad faith. . . .

Judgment of the Superior Court affirmed.

NOTES

1. *NCR's Motivation.* Did NCR have a financial motive in discharging Fortune? On the facts, did denying Fortune his commission increase NCR's profit? Consider Professor Epstein's analysis of the case:

> The decision seems wrong in principle. The contractual provisions concerning commissions represent a rough effort to match payment with performance where the labor of more than one individual was necessary to close the sale. The case is not simply one where a strategically timed firing allowed the company to deprive a dismissed employee of the benefits due him upon completion of performance. Indeed, the firm kept none of the commission at all, so that when the case went to the jury, the only issue was whether the company should be called upon to pay the same commission twice. The court in *Fortune* did not try to understand the commission structure that it was prepared to condemn; instead, it made the chronic mistake of thinking that what it intuited to be an unfortunate business outcome invalidated the entire contractual structure. In its enthusiastic meddling in private contracts, the court nowhere suggested an alternative commission structure that would have better served the joint interests of the parties at the time of contract formation. Here, as in so many cases, an unquestioning adherence to the principle of freedom of contract would have yielded results both simpler and superior to those generated after an extensive but flawed judicial examination of the basic terms.

Richard A. Epstein, *In Defense of the Contract at Will*, 51 U. Chi. L. Rev. 947, 981-82 (1984). *

---

* Reprinted with permission of the University of Chicago Law Review.

2. *The Reach of the Covenant.* Professor Epstein's main argument is that the court in *Fortune* misconstrued the contract and, as a result, misapplied the covenant of good faith and fair dealing. But does he also suggest that courts should *never* imply a covenant of fair dealing in employment contracts? Or is the problem one of drawing lines?

Professor Epstein hints that even he may think the covenant of good faith and fair dealing could play a role in the right case. What if a case, in Professor Epstein's words, is "simply one where a strategically timed firing allowed the company to deprive a dismissed employee of the benefits due him upon completion of performance"? Such cases exist. In *Wakefield v. Northern Telecom, Inc.*, 769 F.2d 109 (2d Cir. 1985), for example, the employment agreement said that an employee who sells a certain amount will receive a commission if he remains with the company until X date. Wakefield sold the specified amount, but the company fired him before X and kept the commission. The court held that this would constitute a violation of the covenant of good faith and fair dealing.

But Professor Esptein worries about all the other variations, such as the one in *Fortune*. In *Tymshare, Inc. v. Covell*, 727 F.2d 1145 (D.C. Cir. 1984), for example, the commission agreement also had a provision that said the employer could change the quota for receiving a commission at any time at its "sole discretion." After Covell made sales above the quota, the employer increased the quota and then fired him, preventing him from meeting the higher quota. Then-judge Scalia held that the covenant of good faith may have been violated because even contract language permitting the quota to be changed at the employer's "sole discretion" was not broad enough to permit a change intended to deprive an employee of the benefit of his bargain.

Some courts have gone even further. In a case representing the high-water mark of the doctrine, the California Supreme Court held that the covenant was violated when an employee was discharged for disclosing within the company that his immediate supervisor was being investigated by the FBI for embezzlement from his prior employer. (The supervisor was later convicted of embezzlement.) *Foley v. Interactive Data Corp.*, 765 P.2d 373 (Cal. 1988). California later stepped back from this, *Guz v. Bechtel National, Inc.*, 8 P.3d 1089 (Cal. 2000), but nevertheless *Foley* nicely illustrates Professor Epstein's concern about the difficulty of limiting the reach of the covenant.

3. *Good Faith and Public Policy.* Footnote 8 of the court's opinion suggests a close relationship between breach of the implied covenant of good faith and fair dealing, and tortious discharge in violation of public policy. Is there a distinction between the cases cited in footnote 8 and *Fortune?* One justification for interfering with private contracts occurs when the parties to the bargain do not consider all the costs of their actions. Arguably, each of the cases in footnote 8 has third-party effects. Are there third-party effects if the court enforces the literal *Fortune* contract? In *Dixon v. Pro Image, Inc.*, 987 P.2d 48, 55 (Utah 1999), the court denied a claim of wrongful discharge in violation of public policy when a corporate president was fired before receiving a $50,000 sale bonus, explaining that "Dixon's claim for wrongful termination does not involve a substantial public policy interest but, rather, concerns only the conduct and rights of Dixon and the corporation for which he worked." Significantly, Utah has not adopted a good-faith exception to employment at will, so that was not an available avenue for Dixon.

4. _Gap-Filling._ Another role of courts in contract cases is to fill the gaps in contracts. A common method for filling a gap is to insert the term that most parties would want, so that most parties can avoid the costs of bargaining for and enforcing the term. _See, e.g._, U.C.C. § 1-203 (implied covenant of good faith in all commercial contracts). The promise of this view of the covenant is that it limits application to situations in which the claim arises out of other provisions of the employment agreement, such as the commission arrangement in _Fortune_. The worry about it is whether this limitation is sufficiently clear and precise to avoid conflict with employment at will.

5. _Opportunism and Reputations._ In _Jordan v. Duff & Phelps, Inc._, 815 F.2d 429 (7th Cir. 1987), an at-will employee of a close corporation resigned and sold his stock back to the company for book value as required under his compensation plan. The company's chairman accepted his resignation without telling him of a possible merger that would increase his shares' value from $23,000 to over $600,000. When Jordan learned of the merger, he filed a 10b-5 action alleging fraud in the purchase of corporate securities. The majority opinion by Judge Easterbrook reversed a summary judgment for the employer, distinguishing between an employer who is "thoughtless, nasty, and mistaken" from one who engages in "[a]vowedly opportunistic conduct." In his opinion Judge Easterbrook gave a hypothetical variation of the facts: Suppose the employer sent a note to the employee, saying:

> There will be a lucrative merger tomorrow. You have been a wonderful employee, but in order to keep the proceeds of the merger for ourselves, we are letting you go, effective this instant. Here is the $23,000 for your shares.

Judge Easterbrook said the court did not "suppose for a second" that the firm could fire an employee for this reason. Judge Posner, in dissent, noted that "the possibility that corporations will exploit their junior executives . . . may well be the least urgent problem facing our nation." Judge Posner argued that junior executives would rather rely on their employer's good will and interest in reputation, and on their own bargaining power, than "pay for contract rights that are difficult and costly to enforce."

MURPHY v. AMERICAN HOME PRODUCTS CORP.
Court of Appeals of New York
448 N.E.2d 86 (1983)

JONES, JUDGE.

This court has not and does not now recognize a cause of action in tort for abusive or wrongful discharge of an employee; such recognition must await action of the Legislature. Nor does the complaint here state a cause of action for intentional infliction of emotional distress, for _prima facie_ tort, or for breach of contract. These causes of action were, therefore, properly dismissed. Appellant's cause of action based on his claim of age discrimination, however, should be reinstated.

Plaintiff, Joseph Murphy, was first employed by defendant, American Home Products Corp., in 1957. He thereafter served in various accounting positions, eventually attaining the office of assistant treasurer, but he never had a formal contract of employment. On April 18, 1980, when he was 59 years old, he was discharged.

Plaintiff claims that he was fired for two reasons: because of his disclosure to top management of alleged accounting improprieties on the part of corporate personnel and because of his age. As to the first ground, plaintiff asserts that his firing was in retaliation for his revelation to officers and directors of defendant corporation that he had uncovered at least $50 million in illegal account manipulations of secret pension reserves which improperly inflated the company's growth in income and allowed high-ranking officers to reap unwarranted bonuses from a management incentive plan, as well as in retaliation for his own refusal to engage in the alleged accounting improprieties. He contends that the company's internal regulations required him to make the disclosure that he did. He also alleges that his termination was carried out in a humiliating manner. . . .

The complaint set up four causes of action. As his first cause of action, plaintiff alleged that his discharge "was wrongful, malicious and in bad faith" and that defendant was bound "not to dismiss its employees for reasons that are contrary to public policy." In his second cause of action, plaintiff claimed that his dismissal "was intended to and did cause plaintiff severe mental and emotional distress thereby damaging plaintiff." His third claim was based on an allegation that the manner of his termination "was deliberately and viciously insulting, was designed to and did embarrass and humiliate plaintiff and was intended to and did cause plaintiff severe mental and emotional distress thereby damaging plaintiff." In his fourth cause of action, plaintiff asserted that, although his employment contract was of indefinite duration, the law imposes in every employment contract "the requirement that an employer shall deal with each employee fairly and in good faith." On that predicate he alleged that defendant's conduct in stalling his advancement and ultimately firing him for his disclosures "breached the terms of its contract requiring good faith and fair dealing toward plaintiff and damaged plaintiff thereby." Plaintiff demanded compensatory and punitive damages.

With respect to his first cause of action, plaintiff urges that the time has come when the courts of New York should recognize the tort of abusive or wrongful discharge of an at-will employee. To do so would alter our long-settled rule that where an employment is for an indefinite term it is presumed to be a hiring at will which may be freely terminated by either party at any time for any reason or even for no reason. Plaintiff argues that a trend has emerged in the courts of other States to temper what is perceived as the unfairness of the traditional rule by allowing a cause of action in tort to redress abusive discharges. He accurately points out that this tort has elsewhere been recognized to hold employers liable for dismissal of employees in retaliation for employee conduct that is protected by public policy. . . . Plaintiff would have this court adopt this emerging view. We decline his invitation, being of the opinion that such a significant change in our law is best left to the Legislature.

Those jurisdictions that have modified the traditional at-will rule appear to have been motivated by conclusions that the freedom of contract underpinnings of the rule have become outdated, that individual employees in the modern work force do not have the bargaining power to negotiate security for the jobs on which they have grown to rely, and that the rule yields harsh results for those employees who do not enjoy the benefits of express contractual limitations on the power of dismissal. Whether these conclusions are supportable or whether for other compelling reasons employers should, as a matter of policy, be held liable to at-will employees discharged in circumstances for which no liability has existed at common law, are issues better left to resolution at the hands of the Legislature. In addition to the fundamental question whether such liability should be recognized in New York, of no less practical importance is the definition of its configuration if it is to be recognized.

Both of these aspects of the issue, involving perception and declaration of relevant public policy (the underlying determinative consideration with respect to tort liability in general) are best and more appropriately explored and resolved by the legislative branch of our government. The Legislature has infinitely greater resources and procedural means to discern the public will, to examine the variety of pertinent considerations, to elicit the views of the various segments of the community that would be directly affected and in any event critically interested, and to investigate and anticipate the impact of imposition of such liability. Standards should doubtless be established applicable to the multifarious types of employment and the various circumstances of discharge. If the rule of nonliability for termination of at-will employment is to be tempered, it should be accomplished through a principled statutory scheme, adopted after opportunity for public ventilation, rather than in consequence of judicial resolution of the partisan arguments of individual adversarial litigants.

Additionally, if the rights and obligations under a relationship forged, perhaps some time ago, between employer and employee in reliance on existing legal principles are to be significantly altered, a fitting accommodation of the competing interests to be affected may well dictate that any change should be given prospective effect only, or at least so the Legislature might conclude.

For all the reasons stated, we conclude that recognition in New York State of tort liability for what has become known as abusive or wrongful discharge should await legislative action.[1]

Plaintiff's second cause of action is framed in terms of a claim for intentional infliction of emotional distress. To survive a motion to dismiss, plaintiff's allegations must satisfy the rule set out in RESTATEMENT OF TORTS, SECOND, . . .: "One who by extreme and outrageous conduct intentionally or recklessly causes severe emotional distress to another is subject to liability for such

---

[1] Employees in New York have already been afforded express statutory protection from firing for engaging in certain protected activities (e.g., Judiciary Law, § 519 (prohibiting discharge of employee due to absence from employment for jury service); [laws barring discharge for opposing unlawful discriminatory practices or for filing a complaint or participating in a proceeding under Human Rights Law or Labor Law]). . . .

emotional distress" (§ 46, subd. [1]). Comment d to that section notes that: "Liability has been found only where the conduct has been so outrageous in character, and so extreme in degree, as to go beyond all possible bounds of decency, and to be regarded as atrocious, and utterly intolerable in a civilized community." The facts alleged by plaintiff regarding the manner of his termination fall far short of this strict standard. Further, in light of our holding above that there is now no cause of action in tort in New York for abusive or wrongful discharge of an at-will employee, plaintiff should not be allowed to evade that conclusion or to subvert the traditional at-will contract rule by casting his cause of action in terms of a tort of intentional infliction of emotional distress.

Plaintiff's third cause of action was also properly dismissed. If considered, as plaintiff would have us, as intended to allege a *prima facie* tort it is deficient inasmuch as there is no allegation that his discharge was without economic or social justification. Moreover, we held in *James v. Board of Educ.,* 340 N.E.2d 735 (N.Y. 1975), which also involved the exercise of an unrestricted right to discharge an employee, that: "Plaintiff cannot, by the device of an allegation that the sole reason for the termination of his employment by these public officials acting within the ambit of their authority was to harm him without justification (a contention which could be advanced with respect to almost any such termination), bootstrap himself around a motion addressed to the pleadings." Nor does the conclusory allegation of malice by plaintiff here supply the deficiency. As with the intentional infliction of emotional distress claim, this cause of action cannot be allowed in circumvention of the unavailability of a tort claim for wrongful discharge or the contract rule against liability for discharge of an at-will employee.

Plaintiff's fourth cause of action is for breach of contract. Although he concedes in his complaint that his employment contract was of indefinite duration (inferentially recognizing that, were there no more, under traditional principles his employer might have discharged him at any time), he asserts that in all employment contracts the law implies an obligation on the part of the employer to deal with his employees fairly and in good faith and that a discharge in violation of that implied obligation exposes the employer to liability for breach of contract. Seeking then to apply this proposition to the present case, plaintiff argues in substance that he was required by the terms of his employment to disclose accounting improprieties and that defendant's discharge of him for having done so constituted a failure by the employer to act in good faith and thus a breach of the contract of employment.

No New York case upholding any such broad proposition is cited to us by plaintiff (or identified by our dissenting colleague), and we know of none. New York does recognize that in appropriate circumstances an obligation of good faith and fair dealing on the part of a party to a contract may be implied and, if implied will be enforced. In such instances the implied obligation is in aid and furtherance of other terms of the agreement of the parties. No obligation can be implied, however, which would be inconsistent with other terms of the contractual relationship. Thus, in the case now before us, plaintiff's employment was at will, a relationship in which the law accords the employer an unfettered right to terminate the employment at any time. In the context of such an employment it would be incongruous to say that an inference may be drawn that the employer impliedly agreed to a provision which would be destructive of his right of termination. The parties may by express agreement limit or restrict the employer's right of discharge, but to imply such a limitation from the existence of an unrestricted right would be internally inconsistent. In sum, under New York law as it now stands, absent a constitutionally impermissible purpose, a statutory proscription, or an express limitation in the individual contract of employment, an employer's right at any time to terminate an employment at will remains unimpaired.

Of course, if there were an express limitation on the employer's right of discharge it would be given effect even though the employment contract was of indefinite duration. Thus, in *Weiner v. McGraw-Hill, Inc.,* 443 N.E.2d 441 (N.Y. 1982), cited by plaintiff, we recently held that, on an appropriate evidentiary showing, a limitation on the employer's right to terminate an employment of indefinite duration might be imported from an express provision therefore found in the employer's handbook on personnel policies and procedures. Plaintiff's attempts on this appeal to bring himself within the beneficial scope of that holding must fail, however. There is here no evidence of any such express limitation. Although general references are to be found in his brief in our court to an employer's "manual," no citation is furnished to any provision therein pertinent to the employer's right to terminate his employment, and the alleged manual was not submitted with his affidavit in opposition to the motion to dismiss his complaint.

Accordingly, the fourth cause of action should have been dismissed for failure to state a cause of action.[2]

[The court then held that the courts below improperly dismissed Murphy's age-discrimination claim as barred by the statute of limitations.]

MEYER, JUDGE (dissenting in part).

. . . I agree with the majority that we should not now adopt the tort remedies proposed in those writings, because such remedies are essentially grounded in public policy, the declaration of which is a function of both the Legislature and the courts, because the New York Legislature has not been reticent in the area, and because of the difficulty encountered by the courts adopting such remedies in articulating the exact nature of the public policy which will bring them into play.

---

2 . . . We reject the view of the dissenter that a good faith limitation should now be judicially engrafted on what in New York has been the unfettered right of termination lying at the core of an employment at will. We do so for precisely the reasons which persuade him as well as the other members of the court that we should now refrain from judicial recognition of the tort action for abusive discharge. As the dissenter is at pains to note, there has been much criticism of the traditional conception of the legal obligations and rights which attach to an employment at will. It may well be that in the light of modern economic and social considerations radical changes should be made. As all of us recognize, however, resolution of the critical issues turns on identification and balancing of fundamental components of public policy. Recognition of an implied-in-law obligation of good faith as restricting the employer's right to terminate is as much a part of this matrix as is recognition of the tort action for abusive discharge. We are of the view that this aggregate of rights and obligations should not be approached piecemeal but should be considered in its totality and then resolved by the Legislature.

. . . I cannot, however, accept the majority's refusal to follow precedent decisional law recognizing an implied-in-law obligation on the part of the employer not to discharge an employee for doing that which the employment contract obligated him to do or to differentiate between that existing contract obligation and the public policy laden tort of abusive discharge. Plaintiff's complaint alleges that "defendant's internal regulations . . . required that plaintiff report any deviation from proper accounting practice to defendant's top management" and that he was dismissed as a result of his doing just that. Because those allegations sufficiently state a cause of action for breach of contract not only under decisions of other States but as a matter of New York law as well, I dissent from the majority's affirmance of the dismissal of the fourth cause of action.

I do not gainsay that *Martin v. New York Life Ins. Co.,* 42 N.E. 416 (N.Y. 1895), however questionable its origin and continued existence, is the New York rule concerning employment contracts of unspecified duration. . . . But the policy reasons behind refusing to read a durational term into employment contracts do not require reading out of such contracts the "implied covenant of fair dealing and good faith" which "is implicit in all contracts" and is "a contractual obligation of universal force which underlies all written agreements."

I refer not to the promise that each party will use reasonable efforts to carry out the contract purpose, which may be implied-in-fact from the contract negotiations to establish consideration though the writing be "imperfectly expressed" in that respect, but to the covenant implied by the law that the parties will not "frustrate the contracts into which they have entered" and that one party will "not intentionally and purposely do anything to prevent the other party from carrying out the agreement on his part" or that may hinder or obstruct his doing that which the contract stipulates he should do. . . .

The principle, moreover, is espoused by the RESTATEMENT (SECOND) OF CONTRACTS, (§ 205), which flatly states that "Every contract imposes upon each party a duty of good faith and fair dealing in its performance and its enforcement," and which in Comment e and the Reporter's Notes thereto indicates its application to the "abuse of a power . . . to terminate the contract" including "an express power to terminate a contract at will." It is recognized as well in section 1-203 of the Uniform Commercial Code and by WILLISTON, CONTRACTS, which tells us that: "Wherever, therefore, a contract cannot be carried out in the way in which it was obviously expected that it should be carried out without one party or the other performing some act not expressly promised by him, a promise to do that act must be implied." The same reasoning that reads into an output contract the requirement that the manufacturing plant continue to perform in good faith and into the contract of an employee hired to invent that the resulting patent belongs to the employer though no express provision to such effect be contained in the contract requires reading into the contract the present plaintiff alleges a provision that he will not be terminated for doing that which the parties have expressly contracted he shall do.[7] To be borne in mind is the fact that we deal not with a contract which by its expressed term authorizes the employer to terminate without cause, but with one in which, because no durational term has been expressed, the law implies a right of termination. In the latter situation only the strongest of policy reasons can sustain reading the implied right of termination as a limitation upon the express obligation imposed upon the employee.

There is, moreover, no compelling policy reason to read the implied obligation of good faith out of contracts impliedly terminable at will. To do so belies the "universal force" of the good faith obligation which, as we have seen, the law reads into "all contracts." Nor can credence be given the *in terrorem* suggestion that to limit terminable-at-will contracts by good faith will drive industry from New York. That is no more than speculation and hardly appears acceptable in the face of (1) the recognition without apparent industrial exodus of the even more burdensome tort remedy for discharge of at-will employees by such industrial States as California, Connecticut, Illinois, Indiana, Maryland, Massachusetts, Michigan, New Jersey, Pennsylvania and Wisconsin, and (2) the responses reported in Ewing, *What Business Thinks About Employee Rights,* a Harvard Business Review survey of employers reprinted in INDIVIDUAL RIGHTS IN THE CORPORATION: A READER ON EMPLOYEE RIGHTS (Westin & Salisbury eds.), at page 21. The more particularly is this so because collective bargaining "just cause" provisions, which impose a greater burden on employers than does a good faith limitation, have not done so, and because employers can obtain a large measure of protection by expressly reserving in the employment contract the right to terminate without cause. . . .

NOTES

1. *Pigeonholes.* *Fortune* and *Murphy* illustrate the two classic fact patterns where the covenant of good faith and fair dealing is strongest. Generally stated, *Fortune* is a case of asymmetric performance where the employee performs first and the employer later. The covenant protects the employee against an opportunistic firing in this situation. *Murphy* is a situation where the employee is fired for performing the duties required by his job. The covenant, where it is accepted, protects an employee against the catch-22 of being fired for doing what his job requires him to do.

2. *Rejecting the Pigeonholes.* Fewer than a dozen states have accepted the covenant of good faith and fair dealing in employment. The biggest worry in other states is whether the covenant can be limited to definable situations, or whether it would inevitably become broader. *See Wagenseller v. Scottsdale Mem'l Hosp.,* 710 P.2d 1025, 1040 (Ariz. 1985) (accepting California's version of the covenant would "tread perilously close to abolishing completely the at-will doctrine. . . .;" the court adopted a narrower version). A halfway house,

---

[7] Ironically, the employer's implied absolute right to terminate at-will employment for any reason or for no reason had its origin in the necessity of according the employer mutuality with the right of the employee to quit his job at any time. Logically, of course, the same principle of mutuality requires that if, as plaintiff alleges and must prove in order to succeed, defendant's contract with him required him to report to defendant's top management any deviation from proper accounting practice, plaintiff's employment not be terminated because he did so.

adopted in some states, would permit the covenant to be used only to recover damages, but not to challenge discharge decisions themselves. *See Wakefield v. Northern Telecom, Inc.,* 769 F.2d 109, 112 (2d Cir. 1985) (Wakefield may not use covenant to challenge "his termination *per se,*" but may claim improperly denied commissions).

3. *Defining Good Faith.* In a leading essay on good faith in general contract and commercial law, Professor Robert Summers insists that good faith cannot be defined. As he says,

> [to ask what good faith means] misconceives good faith. Good faith, as judges generally use the term in matters contractual, is best understood as an "excluder" — a phrase with no general meaning or meanings of its own. Instead, it functions to rule out many different forms of bad faith. It is hard to get this point across to persons used to thinking that every word must have one or more general meanings of its own — must be either unequivocal or ambiguous.

> . . . In most cases the party acting in bad faith frustrates the justified expectations of another. . . . [T]he ways in which he may do this are numerous and radically diverse. Moreover, whether an aggrieved party's expectations are justified must inevitably vary with attendant circumstances. For these reasons it is not fruitful to try to generalize further. It is easy enough to formulate examples of bad faith and work from them. Besides, any general definition of good faith, if not vacuous, is sure to be unduly restrictive, especially if cast in statutory form.

Robert S. Summers, *"Good Faith" in General Contract Law and the Sales Provisions of the Uniform Commercial Code,* 54 VA. L. REV. 195, 262-63 (1968).*

4. *Damages in Wrongful-Termination Cases.* Wrongfully discharged employees, suing in either tort or contract, can generally recover lost wages, salary, commissions, and fringe benefits. Most courts will allow employees to be compensated for expected reductions in future income as well, if not too speculative. In *Goins v. Ford Motor Co.,* 347 N.W.2d 184 (Mich. Ct. App. 1983), for example, the court upheld a recovery of $270,440 for an employee wrongfully discharged after five months on the job for filing a workers' compensation claim with a prior employer. Lost future earnings were calculated as the difference between the discharged employee's current salary and the salary of the position for which he was being groomed prior to his discharge, multiplied by his forty years' life expectancy, and reduced to present value. It may be more appropriate, however, also to attempt to measure the likelihood that the employee would have later quit or been dismissed for cause, including a termination for business reasons. *See* Tyler J. Bowles, *Wrongful Discharge: The Time Horizon of Future Damages and the Economic Basis for Damages,* 4 J. LEGAL ECON. 75 (1994).

Employees suing in tort can additionally recover damages for pain and suffering, mental distress, loss of reputation, and other compensatory

---

* Reprinted with permission of the Virginia Law Review Association and Fred B. Rothman & Co.

damages such as the loss on the sale of a house. If the defendant's conduct is sufficiently outrageous, tort recoveries can also include punitive damages.

5. *Reinstatement in Wrongful-Discharge Cases.* Reinstatement is another possible remedy in tort and contract, but courts are reluctant to order reinstatement. As one court put it: "full redress for breach of the contract is available by an award of damages. Additionally, in light of the hostility between the parties, it would be inappropriate to order reinstatement of plaintiff to her employment position." *Zahler v. Niagara County Chapter of N.Y. State Ass'n for Retarded Children*, 491 N.Y.S.2d 880, 881 (N.Y. App. Div. 1985).

The reluctance of courts in wrongful-discharge cases to order reinstatement and willingness to award frontpay differs from the relief pattern in Title VII and other discrimination cases and in NLRA cases. In those cases, reinstatement is the preferred remedy and frontpay is given only where reinstatement is impossible or impracticable. To what extent might this difference be explained by the fact that wrongful-discharge plaintiffs tend to be high-level employees, and courts are more reluctant to order reinstatement to jobs perceived as requiring a personal relationship between employer and employee? *See* Martha West, *The Case Against Reinstatement in Wrongful Discharge,* 1988 U. Ill. L. Rev. 1, 53-54.

6. *The Tort-Contract Boundary.* Because tort damages can be more generous than contract damages, employees have an incentive to try to characterize their claims as tort claims. In *Hunter v. Up-Right*, 864 P.2d 88 (Cal. 1993), for example, a welder was falsely told by his supervisor that the company had decided to eliminate his position. After being refused a lesser position within the company, Hunter signed a resignation. When he realized the company had not eliminated his position, Hunter sued for fraud and deceit as well as breach of an implied contract not to dismiss without cause. The Court rejected his attempt to recover tort damages, declaring that a tort recovery is available only "when the plaintiff's fraud damages cannot be said to result from [the] termination itself." *Id.* at 89.

In *Lazar v. Superior Court (Rykoff-Sexton, Inc.)*, 909 P.2d 981 (Cal. 1996), the Court distinguished *Hunter* and allowed tort recovery for fraudulent inducement of an employment contract. Lazar had been the president of a family-owned company in New York for eighteen years, making $120,000. Rykoff-Sexton persuaded him to move with his family to California to accept a job as general manager for contract design, promising that his job would be secure and would involve significant pay increases. Lazar asked for a written employment contract, but was refused, Rykoff stating that a written contract was unnecessary because "our word is our bond." Lazar began work in May 1990 and was terminated two years later.

Lazar brought a fraud claim, alleging that Rykoff had a company policy limiting salary increases to 2-3% and was planning a merger that would eliminate his position, even while it was promising him large salary increases and job security. The California Supreme Court determined that Lazar made out a good claim of promissory fraud, because he properly alleged (a) misrepresentation; (b) knowledge of falsity; (c) intent to defraud, *i.e.*, to induce reliance; (d) justifiable reliance; and (e) resulting damage. The Court distinguished

Hunter, asserting that Hunter had failed to show detrimental reliance, because he would have been fired even had he not had been falsely lead to resign. Lazar, by contrast, relied to his detriment on the false promises when he left New York.

These cases illustrate the border war between tort and contract. In *Lazar*, the court recognizes a promissory-fraud action, even though the facts show a classic oral contract (complete with all the classic dangers of an oral contract). In addition to broader damages, a tort cause of action also avoids parol-evidence and statute-of-frauds problems. Typically, however, it has a different (and shorter) statute of limitations. But the deeper question is whether and when the common law should recognize a tort cause of action that overlaps substantially with a contract cause of action.

Chapter 7

THE FUTURE OF WRONGFUL-DISCHARGE LAW

A. A RETURN TO EMPLOYMENT AT WILL

RICHARD A. EPSTEIN, IN DEFENSE OF THE CONTRACT AT WILL, 51 UNIVERSITY OF CHICAGO LAW REVIEW 947, 951-69 (1984) *

There is . . . today a widely held view that the contract at will has outlived its usefulness. But this view is mistaken. The contract at will is not ideal for every employment relation. No court or legislature should ever command its use. Nonetheless, there are two ways in which the contract at will should be respected: one deals with entitlements against regulation and the other with presumptions in the event of contractual silence.

First, the parties should be permitted as of right to adopt this form of contract if they so desire. The principle behind this conclusion is that freedom of contract tends both to advance individual autonomy and to promote the efficient operation of labor markets.

Second, the contract at will should be respected as a rule of construction in response to the perennial question of gaps in contract language: what term should be implied in the absence of explicit agreement on the question of duration or grounds for termination? The applicable standard asks two familiar questions: what rule tends to lend predictability to litigation and to advance the joint interests of the parties? On both these points I hope to show that the contract at will represents in most contexts the efficient solution to the employment relation. To be sure, the stakes are lower where the outright prohibition is no longer in the offing. No rule of construction ever has the power of a rule of regulation, since the parties by negotiation can reverse what the law otherwise commands. Nonetheless, bad rules of contract construction have costs that should not be understated, here or elsewhere. The rule of construction is normally chosen because it reflects the dominant practice in a given class of cases and because that practice is itself regarded as making good sense for the standard transactions it governs. It is of course freely waivable by a joint expression of contrary intention. When the law introduces a just-cause requirement, it flies in the face of ordinary understandings and thus rests upon an assumption that just-cause arrangements are in the broad run of cases either more frequent or desirable than the contract at will, though neither is the case. Where this rule of construction is used, therefore, contracting-out will have to take place in the very large number of cases where the parties desire to conform to the norm by entering into a contract at will.

---

* Reprinted with permission of the University of Chicago Law Review.

Furthermore, it may be difficult to waive the for-cause requirement in fact, even if waiver is formally allowable as a matter of law, because of high standards for "informed" waiver that cannot be met after the fact. By degrees, the original presumption against the contract at will could so gain in strength that a requirement that is waivable in theory could easily become conclusive in fact. . . .

In this area of private-contracting autonomy, there are some exceptions, arising out of the infrequent cases in which discharge of the contract at will is inconsistent with the performance of some public duty or with the protection of some public right. Just as a contract to commit murder should not be enforceable, neither should one to pollute illegally or to commit perjury.[11] But these cases, however difficult in their own right, in no way require abandoning the basic common law presumption in favor of contracts at will. The recent efforts to undermine or abolish the contract at will should be evaluated not in terms of what they *hope* to achieve, whether stated in terms of worker participation, industrial harmony, fundamental fairness, or enlightened employment relations. Instead they should be evaluated for the generally harsh results that they actually produce. They introduce an enormous amount of undesirable complexity into the law of employment relations; they increase the frequency of civil litigation; and over the broad run of cases they work to the disadvantage of both the employers and the employees whose conduct they govern. . . .

The first way to argue for the contract at will is to insist upon the importance of freedom of contract as an end in itself. Freedom of contract is an aspect of individual liberty, every bit as much as freedom of speech, or freedom in the selection of marriage partners or in the adoption of religious beliefs or affiliations. Just as it is regarded as *prima facie* unjust to abridge these liberties, so too is it presumptively unjust to abridge the economic liberties of individuals. The desire to make one's own choices about employment may be as strong as it is with respect to marriage or participation in religious activities, and it is doubtless more pervasive than the desire to participate in political activity. Indeed for most people, their own health and comfort, and that of their families, depend critically upon their ability to earn a living by entering the employment market. If government regulation is

---

11 This problem has arisen where employees at will have refused to perjure themselves on behalf of the employer, *e.g., Petermann v. Teamsters Local 396*, 344 P.2d 25, 27-28 (Cal. 1959) (discharge for refusal to commit perjury held wrongful), or where workers have been dismissed because they have filed workers' compensation claims, *e.g., Frampton v. Central Ind. Gas Co.*, 297 N.E. 2d 425, 428 (Ind. 1973) (discharge for filing claim held wrongful). It seems clear that any contract to commit perjury should simply be treated as illegal. The workers' compensation case is more difficult both because there is less justification for the coercive character of compensation, since no third-party interests are at stake, and because in all events the worker is entitled to file his claim and will do so if its value exceeds the gains he expects from the employment contract. A common law court cannot, however, attack the soundness of a statutory compensation system, so that this restraint on freedom of contract should be as valid as one imposed for the protection of strangers. At this point the central question concerns the proper remedy. Typically, reinstatement of the plaintiff is ordered, which has the disadvantage of requiring the court to supervise an ongoing relationship. It may well be that the employer should be able to fire the worker, but nonetheless be required to pay damages, preferably fixed by statute, to the worker. . . .

inappropriate for personal, religious, or political activities, then what makes it intrinsically desirable for employment relations? . . .

The strong fairness argument in favor of freedom of contract makes short work of the various for-cause and good-faith restrictions upon private contracts. Yet the argument is incomplete in several respects. In particular, it does not explain why the presumption in the case of silence should be in favor of the contract at will. Nor does it give a descriptive account of why the contract at will is so commonly found in all trades and professions. Nor does the argument meet on their own terms the concerns voiced most frequently by the critics of the contract at will. Thus, the commonplace belief today (at least outside the actual world of business) is that the contract at will is so unfair and one-sided that it cannot be the outcome of a rational set of bargaining processes any more than, to take the extreme case, a contract for total slavery. . . .

In order to rebut this charge, it is necessary to do more than insist that individuals as a general matter know how to govern their own lives. It is also necessary to display the structural strengths of the contract at will that explain why rational people would enter into such a contract, if not all the time, then at least most of it. . . .

From this perspective, then, the task is to explain how and why the at-will contracting arrangement (in sharp contrast to slavery) typically works to the mutual advantage of the parties. . . . The inquiry into mutual benefit in turn requires an examination of the full range of costs and benefits that arise from collaborative ventures. It is just at this point that the nineteenth-century view is superior to the emerging modern conception. The modern view tends to lay heavy emphasis on the need to control employer abuse. Yet . . . the rights under the contract at will are fully bilateral, so that the employee can use the contract as a means to control the firm, just as the firm uses it to control the worker.

The issue for the parties, properly framed, is not how to minimize employer abuse, but rather how to maximize the gain from the relationship, which in part depends upon minimizing the sum of employer and employee abuse. Viewed in this way the private-contracting problem is far more complex. How does each party create incentives for the proper behavior of the other? How does each side insure against certain risks? How do both sides minimize the administrative costs of their contracting practices? . . .

Begin for the moment with the fears of the firm, for it is the firm's right to maintain at-will power that is now being called into question. In all too many cases, the firm must contend with the recurrent problem of employee theft and with the related problems of unauthorized use of firm equipment and employee kickback arrangements. As the analysis of partnerships shows, however, the proper concerns of the firm are not limited to obvious forms of criminal misconduct. The employee on a fixed wage can, at the margin, capture only a portion of the gain from his labor, and therefore has a tendency to reduce output. The employee who receives a commission equal to half the firm's profit attributable to his labor may work hard, but probably not quite as hard as he would if he received the entire profit from the completed sale, an arrangement that would solve the agency-cost problem only by undoing the firm. . . .

The problem of management then is to identify the forms of social control that are best able to minimize these agency costs. . . . Internal auditors may help control some forms of abuse, and simple observation by coworkers may well monitor employee activities. (There are some very subtle tradeoffs to be considered when the firm decides whether to use partitions or separate offices for its employees.) Promotions, bonuses, and wages are also critical in shaping the level of employee performance. But the carrot cannot be used to the exclusion of the stick. In order to maintain internal discipline, the firm may have to resort to sanctions against individual employees. It is far easier to use those powers that can be unilaterally exercised: to fire, to demote, to withhold wages, or to reprimand. These devices can visit very powerful losses upon individual employees without the need to resort to legal action, and they permit the firm to monitor employee performance continually in order to identify both strong and weak workers and to compensate them accordingly. The principles here are constant, whether we speak of senior officials or lowly subordinates, and it is for just this reason that the contract at will is found at all levels in private markets. . . .

Thus far, the analysis generally has focused on the position of the employer. Yet for the contract at will to be adopted *ex ante,* it must work for the benefit of workers as well. And indeed it does, for the contract at will also contains powerful limitations on employers' abuses of power. To see the importance of the contract at will to the employee, it is useful to distinguish between two cases. In the first, the employer pays a fixed sum of money to the worker and is then free to demand of the employee whatever services he wants for some fixed period of time. In the second case, there is no fixed period of employment. The employer is free to demand whatever he wants of the employee, who in turn is free to withdraw for good reason, bad reason, or no reason at all.

The first arrangement invites abuse by the employer, who can now make enormous demands upon the worker without having to take into account either the worker's disutility during the period of service or the value of the worker's labor at contract termination. A fixed-period contract that leaves the worker's obligations unspecified thereby creates a sharp tension between the parties, since the employer receives all the marginal benefits and the employee bears all the marginal costs.

Matters are very different where the employer makes increased demands under a contract at will. Now the worker can quit whenever the net value of the employment contract turns negative. As with the employer's power to fire or demote, the threat to quit (or at a lower level to come late or leave early) is one that can be exercised without resort to litigation. Furthermore, that threat turns out to be most effective when the employer's opportunistic behavior is the greatest because the situation is one in which the worker has least to lose. To be sure, the worker will not necessarily make a threat whenever the employer insists that the worker accept a less favorable set of contractual terms, for sometimes the changes may be accepted as an uneventful adjustment in the total compensation level attributable to a change in the market price of labor. This point counts, however, only as an additional strength of the contract at will, which allows for small adjustments *in both directions* in ongoing contractual arrangements with a minimum of bother and confusion. . . .

Another reason why employees are often willing to enter into at-will employment contracts stems from the asymmetry of reputational losses. Any party who cheats may well obtain a bad reputation that will induce others to avoid dealing with him. The size of these losses tends to differ systematically between employers and employees — to the advantage of the employee. Thus in the usual situation there are many workers and a single employer. The disparity in number is apt to be greatest in large industrial concerns, where the at-will contract is commonly, if mistakenly, thought to be most unsatisfactory because of the supposed inequality of bargaining power. The employer who decides to act for a bad reason or no reason at all may not face any legal liability under the classical common law rule. But he faces very powerful adverse economic consequences. If coworkers perceive the dismissal as arbitrary, they will take fresh stock of their own prospects, for they can no longer be certain that their faithful performance will ensure their security and advancement. The uncertain prospects created by arbitrary employer behavior is functionally indistinguishable from a reduction in wages unilaterally imposed by the employer. At the margin some workers will look elsewhere, and typically the best workers will have the greatest opportunities. By the same token the large employer has more to gain if he dismisses undesirable employees, for this ordinarily acts as an implicit increase in wages to the other employees, who are no longer burdened with uncooperative or obtuse coworkers. . . .

The reason why these contracts at will are effective is precisely that the employer must always pay an implicit price when he exercises his right to fire. He no longer has the right to compel the employee's service, as the employee can enter the market to find another job. The costs of the employer's decision therefore are borne in large measure by the employer himself, creating an implicit system of coinsurance between employer and employee against employer abuse. Nor, it must be stressed, are the costs to the employer light. It is true that employees who work within a firm acquire specific knowledge about its operation and upon dismissal can transfer only a portion of that knowledge to the new job. Nonetheless, the problem is roughly symmetrical, as the employer must find, select, and train a replacement worker who may not turn out to be better than the first employee. Workers are not fungible, and sorting them out may be difficult: résumés can be misleading, if not fraudulent; references may be only too eager to unload an unsuitable employee; training is expensive; and the new worker may not like the job or may be forced to move out of town. In any case, firms must bear the costs of voluntary turnover by workers who quit, which gives them a frequent reminder of the need to avoid self-inflicted losses. The institutional stability of employment contracts at will can now be explained in part by their legal fragility. The right to fire is exercised only infrequently because the threat of firing is effective. . . .

An examination of the contracting objectives of parties explains why contracts at will are common. The same set of considerations, however, also helps explain why contracts at will are *not* found in all employment contexts, but are instead sometimes displaced by more elaborate contractual mechanisms. The central point is that the contract at will works only where performance on both sides takes place in lockstep progression. This condition will be satisfied where neither side has performed or where the worker's past performance has been matched by appropriate payment from the employer. In these cases the contract at will provides both employer and employee with a simple, informal "bond" against the future misfeasance of the other side: fire or quit. Where the sequence of performance requires one side to perform in full before the other side begins performance, this bonding mechanism will break down because there are no longer two unperformed promises of roughly equal value to stand as security for each other. That is why an employee will have to resort to legal action if the employer simply refuses to pay wages for work that has already been done. It is also why a contract at will cannot handle the question of compensation for job-related personal injuries, for after injury the value of the right to quit no longer balances off the right to fire.

B. RATIONALIZING THE CONTEMPORARY CASES

STEWART J. SCHWAB, LIFE-CYCLE JUSTICE: ACCOMMODATING JUST CAUSE AND EMPLOYMENT AT WILL, 92 MICHIGAN LAW REVIEW 8-11, 39-50 (1993) *

Snapshot examinations of current unjust dismissal law have led employment law commentators to see only chaos, a set of cases with little internal coherence or rationale. A view of the decisions in their historical sweep causes commentators to see evolution: in the beginning was employment at will, now chaos exists, the natural ending point will be just cause. Most commentators applaud the trend, urge its completion, and bemoan any hesitation or backsliding by the courts. Their continual refrain is that the United States lags behind the rest of the world on this issue. At the other extreme, some conservatives, most prominently Richard Epstein, hearken back to the heyday of employment at will as the ideal state of employment law. Such observers lament every move away from a strict presumption that all employment contracts can be terminated at will by either party.

The fundamental problem with these perspectives is that they criticize current law but they do not understand or explain it, except in the crudest way. The just-cause boosters simply applaud every pro-employee decision and decry the others as backsliding responses to conservative political pressures. The at-will zealots simply cheer and boo the other way. Neither perspective appreciates the apparent vacillation of current courts, which erode the at-will presumption without rejecting it.

Current termination law does have an underlying coherence. We should recognize this coherence before we reject the contemporary common law system for either the Model Act's futuristic scheme of arbitrating just cause or a return to the heyday of employment at will. This paper attempts to

* Reprinted with permission of Michigan Law Review Association.

articulate the coherence of current doctrine. Reacting to the almost uniform polarization on this issue, I argue both positively and normatively for an intermediate position. The current intermediate position of the common law balances two conflicting problems. A career-employment relationship faces two types of opportunism: opportunistic firings by an unfettered employer and shirking by employees with job security. An extreme legal rule can handle either problem alone, but only by ignoring the other. Thus, a legal presumption of employment at will handles the shirking problem well but gives no protection against opportunistic firings. A just-cause regime has the opposite virtue and flaw. The legal challenge is to find an intermediate rule that provides the optimal check against both dangers.

The common law has groped towards such a rule by recognizing that the relative magnitudes of the two problems vary over the life cycle of the worker. The danger of employer opportunism is greatest for late-career workers, and it is also a problem for some beginning-career employees. By contrast, the greater problem at midcareer is shirking. In response, the courts have begun to offer contract protections for workers at the beginning and end of the life cycle, while maintaining a presumption of at-will employment for midcareer employees. In arguing for the wisdom of this approach, I, like the courts, refrain from making a categorical statement that at-will or just-cause employment should never — or should always — be the governing presumption. . . .

1. *Beginning-Career Opportunism*

Employees face a risk of opportunistic termination at the beginning of the life cycle. The risk arises because employees commit irretrievable investments to the relationship before the employer does. Usually the beginning-career cases involve employees who have moved to take a job or quit another job in reliance on a job offer.

[The article then discusses several cases, including *Grouse v. Group Health Plan* and *Veno v. Meredith*.]

We see, then, that courts sometimes allow claims by beginning-career employees who are arbitrarily fired after moving or quitting a prior job. Some courts use a promissory estoppel or reliance theory, some find an implied contract for a reasonable time to allow the employee to recoup his expenses, and some simply use the decision to move or to quit as evidence of an actual definite-term agreement. Regardless of the theory for recovery, one can explain these cases as attempts to regulate opportunistic firings early in the life cycle. Employers have not yet invested in the relationship and thus are not hurt if they arbitrarily dismiss the new employee. This means that the relationship is not self-enforcing, as it is when both parties have incurred sunk costs.

Nevertheless, protection for beginning-career employees is far from universal. Many or even most courts refuse to find that reliance on an at-will job offer is reasonable. In these cases, an employee quits another job or moves to a new job at his own risk.

The ambivalence of courts in this area is understandable. For at least three reasons, the opportunistic termination rationale for protecting employees is weaker in these beginning-career cases than it is later in the life cycle. First, very often the employer also makes substantial investments early in the relationship. Recruiting and training new employees can be a major cost to many firms.

Second, even if recruiting costs are insignificant — as they will be in many cases — so that arbitrarily firing the employee does not penalize the employer, the employer gains nothing from firing a person early in his career. Thus, while employees [sic] often suffer no penalty from an arbitrary beginning-career firing, they gain no benefit from them either. This fact distinguishes beginning-career from late-career firings, in which the employer can gain from firing employees whom it pays more than their current output.

A final problem with job protection for new employees is that employers often need a probationary period to sort out hiring mistakes, wherein they can fire employees without explanation or extensive documentation of their reasons. Relevant here is the fact that competitive firms, largely responding to the entry and exit of early-career employees, virtually always contract for at-will dismissal. Even the Model Employment Termination Act, which calls for general good-cause protection for employees, refuses to protect employees with less than a year of service.

In sum, in many situations employer opportunism against beginning employees is either a trivial threat or outweighed by legitimate needs to maintain employer flexibility. In these situations, courts do not scrutinize the sudden termination. Still, the potential for opportunistic employer offers is real. An employer engages in opportunistic behavior when it hires a better person before training anyone but after the first job applicant has relied on the offer. Courts protect beginning employees from such opportunism.

2. Late-Career Opportunism

Late-career employees face the greatest danger of opportunistic firings. At the end of their life cycle, they often earn more than their current productivity. If they do, the employer has a financial incentive to terminate them, even if it violates an implicit promise to allow the employee to reap the rewards of hard work earlier in his career.

The Age Discrimination in Employment Act provides one check against late-career opportunism. By prohibiting employers from firing workers above the age of forty because of their age, the ADEA protects older workers from discharges based upon stereotypes that lead employers to underestimate their productivity. "We need new blood" and "Doe is slowing down a notch" are classic statements that create age discrimination lawsuits.

However, the ADEA may offer only limited protection against the central concern of the life-cycle model — opportunistic firings when salary and forth-coming benefits outweigh current productivity. . . .

Greater protection may come from common law courts, which in recent years have begun policing opportunistic firings of late-career employees. The leading case is *Pugh v. See's Candies, Inc.*, in which a thirty-two-year employee was abruptly fired after working his way up from dishwasher to corporate vice president. The employee never had a clear agreement about job security, although managers had given him encouraging evaluations over the years. The court held that this career pattern, including the length of service and the policies and practices of the company, could establish an implied-in-fact promise against arbitrary dismissal. *Pugh* epitomizes the efficiency-wage story and its end-game dangers. Pugh committed himself to a single firm, worked hard to gain promotions to the promised easy life, but then was terminated. *Pugh* also demonstrates the effect of the arrival of new management on job security. In *Pugh*, new management arrived a year before Pugh's firing. Such major corporate changes may diminish the reputational check on firings of late-career employees.

Length of service is the key element that motivates courts to scrutinize a late-career firing. Most opinions, like *Pugh*, also examine oral statements and the company's general procedures. . . .

Occasionally, an employee faces the danger of beginning-career and late-career opportunism at the same time. This situation occurs when a long-time employee agrees to a job transfer. A prominent example is *Foley v. Community Oil Co.*, in which a thirty-year employee was fired three years after accepting a job transfer to another state. The court's explicit rationale in finding the employee had stated a claim tracks the life-cycle theory. The court first noted that "uprooting and moving a family" could give rise to a contractual claim. The court then declared that "longevity of service can also give rise to an implied contract right." Tracking the lock-in problem with which we have wrestled, the court explained that "the employee, in providing long-term employment to a single employer substantially diminishes his economic mobility."

In sum, one can explain these cases as attempts to monitor and enforce the implicit life-cycle employment contract. Late in an employee's career, the usual checks against opportunistic firings unravel. Courts enter to monitor the bargain. The bargain does not give late-career employees complete job security. They can be dismissed for cause, because otherwise the shirking problems would be immense, but the employer does not prove cause simply by proving that salary exceeds current productivity. That is the typical life-cycle pattern that both sides to career employment anticipate and, ex ante, it is in the interests of both sides.

3. *Midcareer Shirking*

Once the employer has begun to make substantial, asset-specific investments in an employee, the risk of arbitrary firing diminishes. The greater danger of opportunistic behavior — at least, behavior that an appropriate dismissal standard could limit — comes from the employee's side. Because the employer does not want to repeat recruiting and training costs with another employee, the incumbent employee has an opportunity to shirk without fear of dismissal. Shirking at midcareer can occur even if the employer has the right to dismiss at will, but the shirking problem can be exacerbated if the employer must also surmount the hurdle of proving just cause.

This is not to say that the employer cannot exploit the midcareer employee. Indeed, as I emphasized above, being trapped by investments in firm-specific capital and in community roots can make a midcareer employee ripe for exploitation. But the exploitation will not take the form of firing because the employer is making money from the relationship. Rather than fire a midcareer employee, an employer may pay him less than would be called for under a fair division of the gains from the long-term relationship or make his workload or working conditions more onerous. Just cause cannot protect the midcareer employee from these abuses. Better, then, for the law to focus on something it can handle, which is deterrence of shirking by midcareer employees.

The courts seem to have intuited this fact by refusing, in general, to create contract protections against arbitrary terminations for midcareer workers. Midcareer employees have made the fewest contributions to the doctrinal erosion of at-will employment. . . .

In summary, my argument is that the general pattern of good-faith and implied-contract cases reflects an intuitive understanding by the courts that employees are subject to opportunistic discharge at the end, and less consistently at the beginning, of the life cycle. Courts are reluctant, however, to give general protection against arbitrary dismissal to midcareer employees. The economic self-interest of employers should keep such dismissals in check. The greater concern is with employee shirking. . . .

NOTE

Judicial Interference with Social Norms. Even if a life-cycle arrangement is good for the employment relationship, it may be overly costly for the courts to enforce. Professors Rock and Wachter have argued that employers and employees often choose to operate under informal norms (often including the life-cycle model), rather than under more formal contracts or legal rules. If employees and employer so choose, Rock and Wachter contend that the courts should generally leave the parties alone because an important part of the value of norms is their low cost. If the courts start enforcing norms rather than allowing unilateral changes in the relationship, their value is diminished. Edward B. Rock & Michael L. Wachter, *The Enforceability of Norms and the Employment Relationship*, 144 U. PA. L. REV. 1913 (1996).

C. STATUTORY CHANGES TO THE AT-WILL DOCTRINE

Several scholars have argued that the vague, patchwork law of wrongful discharge as created by courts should be superseded by clear legislation. *See* Clyde W. Summers, *Individual Protection Against Unjust Dismissal: Time for a Statute*, 62 VA. L. REV. 481 (1976); Arthur S. Leonard, *A New Common Law of Employment Termination*, 66 N.C. L. REV. 631 (1987); Jack Steiber & Michael Murray, *Protection Against Unjust Discharge: The Need for a Federal Statute*, 16 U. MICH. J.L. REFORM 319 (1983). In 1987, Montana became the first state to pass a comprehensive statute mandating good cause for employment terminations.[*] In 1991, the Commissioners on Uniform State Laws (the same group that promulgated the Uniform Commercial Code), passed a Model Employment Termination Act[**] to serve as a model for legislatures

---

[*] The statute appears in the Statutory Appendix.

[**] The Model Act appears in the Statutory Appendix.

considering just-cause termination statutes. For an excellent overview by the principal draftsperson, see Theodore J. St. Antoine, *The Making of the Model Employment Termination Act*, 69 WASH. L. REV. 361 (1994). Among the many issues these statutes present are the following:

1. *Defining Good Cause.* Both the Montana statute and the Model Act use the term "good cause" rather than "just cause," the typical term in collective-bargaining contracts. Section 39-2-903(5) of the Montana statute defines good cause this way:

> "Good cause" means reasonable job-related grounds for dismissal based on a failure to satisfactorily perform job duties, disruption of the employer's operation, or other legitimate business reason.

Montana also prohibits discharges in retaliation for the employee's refusal to violate public policy or for reporting a violation of public policy. § 39-2-904(1), as defined in § 39-2-903(7).

The Model Act § 1(4) defines good cause in greater detail:

> "Good cause" means (i) a reasonable basis related to an individual employee for termination of the employee's employment in view of relevant factors and circumstances, which may include the employee's duties, responsibilities, conduct on the job or otherwise, job performance, and employment record, or (ii) the exercise of business judgment in good faith by the employer, including setting its economic or institutional goals and determining methods to achieve those goals, organizing or reorganizing operations, discontinuing, consolidating, or divesting operations or positions or parts of operations or positions, determining the size of its work force and the nature of the positions filled by its work force, and determining and changing standards of performance for positions.

2. *Reasonable or Correct Good Cause.* What happens when an employer fires a Montana worker in good faith after a reasonable investigation, but it turns out that the employer was wrong? Just as the common-law courts have wrestled with this issue (see notes 5 and 6 following the *Pugh* case in Chapter 4), courts have faced the question in interpreting the Montana statute. In *Marcy v. Delta Airlines*, 166 F.3d 1279 (9th Cir. 1999) (applying Montana law), the employer fired an employee for intentional falsification of payroll records. The worker claimed she had simply made a mistake. The worker sued under the Montana Wrongful Discharge from Employment Act (WDEA), and won before a jury. On appeal, the Ninth Circuit affirmed, declaring that "an employee discharged for a reason based on a mistaken interpretation of the facts has a valid claim under the WDEA, even if the employer acted in good faith." Judge Graber, dissenting, would have certified the question to the Montana Supreme Court, complaining that the majority was second-guessing a reasonable business decision by the employer. All sides in the case apparently agreed that, under the Montana statute, an employer cannot legally fire an employee if the employer knew that the "falsification" was unintentional.

3. *Courts or Arbitration?* A third issue is whether the tribunal that determines good cause should be a common-law court, arbitrator, or something else.[*] An arbitration system would lower the costs of each adjudicated case, but the lower cost would increase the number of discharges challenged by employees, perhaps increasing total costs of adjudication.

The Montana statute contemplates litigation of termination cases in state court, but it encourages the parties to arbitrate the dispute (§ 39-2-914(1)). If a party offers to arbitrate, the offer is rejected, and the offeror prevails in court, the other side must pay its attorney fees (§ 39-2-914(4)). If the employee wins in arbitration, the employer must pay the arbitrator's fee and all costs (§ 39-2-914(5)).

The Model Termination Act proposes a more thorough system of arbitration (§ 5), although it also proposes variations that would have a state agency (Alternative A) or courts (Alternative B) handle termination disputes.

4. *Remedies.* To obtain employer support for wrongful-discharge legislation, statutes generally limit the damages that a wrongfully terminated employee can recover. The tradeoff is similar to the classic one underlying workers' compensation laws: more certain recovery of smaller damages.

The Montana statute calls for an award of lost wages and fringe benefits for a period of four years from the date of discharge, together with interest (§ 39-2-905(1)). Interim earnings must be deducted. The Montana statute allows punitive damages only if the employee establishes "by clear and convincing evidence that the employer engaged in actual fraud or actual malice" (§ 39-2-905(2)). The statute expressly disallows any recovery for pain and suffering, emotional distress, and compensatory damages (§ 39-2-905(3)).

The Model Act contemplates reinstatement and backpay as the prime remedies (§§ 7(b)(1), 7(b)(2)). If reinstatement is not awarded, the Model Act authorizes an award of wages and fringe benefits for up to three years, taking into account such equitable considerations as the employee's length of service with the employer and the reasons for the termination (§ 7(b)(3)). Interim and likely alternative earnings must be deducted from the award. Like the Montana statute, the Model Act expressly prohibits the arbitrator from awarding "damages for pain and suffering, emotional distress, defamation, fraud, or other injury under the common law, punitive damages, compensatory damages, or any other monetary award." (§ 7(d)).

5. *Waiver.* The Montana statute does not apply to employees under collective-bargaining contracts or a written contract for a specific term (§ 39-2-912(2)). Similarly, the Model Act does not cover terminations at the end of a written or oral contract "of specified duration related to the completion of a specified task, project, undertaking, or assignment." (§ 4(d)).

The Model Act also allows the parties in writing to waive the good-cause requirement for termination, if the employer agrees that for any termination other than willful misconduct it will pay one month's severance pay for every full year of employment, up to thirty months (§ 4(c)).

---

[*] Professor Bellace suggests that unemployment-insurance tribunals should be used to determine wrongful-discharge claims. Janice R. Bellace, *A Right of Fair Dismissal: Enforcing a Statutory Guarantee*, 16 U. MICH. J.L. REFORM 207 (1983). As she points out, unemployment-insurance panels already decide comparable issues in determining whether a claimant was fired for job-related misconduct, which disqualifies them from benefits.

The Model Act leaves the term "willful misconduct" undefined. It is a term often used in unemployment-insurance law for determining whether a fired employee is ineligible for unemployment insurance. Generally, willful misconduct requires more than employee incompetence.

For what jobs are employers most likely to seek 4(c) waivers? The good-cause requirements will prove most burdensome in jobs in which it is difficult to document good cause. For example, should law firms and other employers of professionals seek 4(c) waivers in their employment contracts?

6. *Who Supports These Laws?* Do the Montana statute and the Model Termination Act clearly favor employees, by giving them general good-cause protection they did not have before? Or are the statutes a grand compromise (similar to workers' compensation statutes), whereby employers give up some defenses and employees give up some claims in exchange for a more streamlined process? What aspects of the law would be supported by employees, employers, or both?

Professor Krueger has empirically estimated the likelihood that unjust-dismissal legislation will be introduced in a state legislature. After controlling for such factors as the amount of union membership in manufacturing and the proportion of Democrats in the state legislature, he found that

> the probability that a state legislature proposes an unjust-dismissal law is increased by 6.7 percentage points if its court system has recognized the good faith exception, by 8.5 percentage points if the public policy exception has been recognized, and by 2.0 percentage points if the implied contract exception has been recognized. Put another way, the probability that a law is proposed is more than quadrupled if these causes of action have been allowed in a state.

Alan B. Krueger, *The Evolution of Unjust-Dismissal Legislation in the United States*, 44 INDUS. & LAB. REL. REV. 644, 655-56 (1991). Does this evidence suggest that legislatures consider wrongful-discharge statutes in order to curb expansive court decisions?

D. DISMISSAL STANDARDS IN OTHER COUNTRIES

The United States is unique in the industrialized world in having as its basic rule that workers can be fired for any reason without any notice. Even with the substantial erosions of employment at will we have studied, as well as the statutory prohibitions against discrimination examined later in this casebook, employers in the United States face fewer legal hurdles when terminating workers than do employers in most other countries. Other legal systems place many procedural and substantive checks both when employers fire an individual worker for alleged misconduct, and when employers reduce the size of the workforce due to economic restructuring. For a survey of termination laws, see Samuel Estreicher, *Unjust Dismissal Laws: Some Cautionary Notes*, 33 AM. J. COMP. L. 310 (1985).

To handle the larger caseload that comes when most terminations can face legal scrutiny, most countries have established specialized labor courts. Labor courts typically have representatives from both management and labor as judges. Their procedures are often less formal than the courts of general jurisdiction.

Whether the greater termination protections in Europe and elsewhere help or harm workers is a matter of great dispute. Many scholars argue that stringent employment protections are a major cause of "Eurosclerosis," a situation of high and lengthy unemployment as employers are afraid of hiring workers, knowing that it will be difficult to terminate them if conditions worsen. *See* Katherine Abraham & Susan N. Houseman, *Does Employment Protection Inhibit Labour Market Flexibility? Lessons from Germany, France, and Belgium, in* SOCIAL PROTECTION VERSUS ECONOMIC FLEXIBILITY: IS THERE A TRADE-OFF? 59 (Rebecca M. Blank ed., 1994).

Cross-country comparisons are notoriously difficult, however. For example, some commentators find that stringent employment-protection laws lead to more stable employment and unemployment in good and bad times, but the level of employment and unemployment is not clearly correlated to their stringency. Giuseppe Bertola et al., *Employment Protection in Industrialized Countries: The Case for New Indicators*, 139 INT'L LAB. REV. 5772 (2000). They conclude: "Empirical work provides mixed results in the evaluation of the influence of labour market regulation on labour market adjustment. Jurisprudence seems as important as the nominal strictness of regulations per se."

In 1982, the International Labour Organization adopted the Termination of Employment Convention (C158), which has since been signed by 34 nations, the United States obviously not among them. Its central provisions are set out below.

International Labour Organization Convention 158
Termination of Employment

Article 4: The employment of a worker shall not be terminated unless there is a valid reason for such termination connected with the capacity or conduct of the worker or based on the operational requirements of the undertaking, establishment or service.

Article 5: The following, inter alia, shall not constitute valid reasons for termination:

    (a)   union membership or participation in union activities outside working hours or, with the consent of the employer, within working hours;

    (b)   seeking office as, or acting or having acted in the capacity of, a workers' representative;

    (c)   the filing of a complaint or the participation in proceedings against an employer involving alleged violation of laws or regulations or recourse to competent administrative authorities;

    (d)   race, colour, sex, marital status, family responsibilities, pregnancy, religion, political opinion, national extraction or social origin;

    (e)   absence from work during maternity leave.

Article 6.1: Temporary absence from work because of illness or injury shall not constitute a valid reason for termination. . . .

Procedure Prior to or at the Time of Termination

Article 7: The employment of a worker shall not be terminated for reasons related to the worker's conduct or performance before he is provided an opportunity to defend himself against the allegations made, unless the employer cannot reasonably be expected to provide this opportunity.

Procedure of Appeal Against Termination

Article 8.1: A worker who considers that his employment has been unjustifiably terminated shall be entitled to appeal against that termination to an impartial body, such as a court, labour tribunal, arbitration committee or arbitrator. . . .

Article 9.1: The [impartial body] shall be empowered to examine the reasons given for the termination and the other circumstances relating to the case and to render a decision on whether the termination was justified. . . .

Article 9.3: In cases of termination stated to be for reasons based on the operational requirements of the undertaking, establishment or service, the [impartial body] shall be empowered to determine whether the termination was indeed for these reasons, but the extent to which they shall also be empowered to decide whether these reasons are sufficient to justify that termination shall be determined by [national law or practice].

NOTE

Exemptions from Termination Requirements. As with most legal issues, the devil is in the details. Article 2.2 allows member states to exclude from its protections workers with definite-term contracts, workers on probation, and workers engaged in casual work for a short period, although Article 3.3 admonishes states to protect against definite-term contracts "the aim of which is to avoid the protection resulting from this Convention." The Convention also allows states to exclude small firms from the termination requirements (Article 2.5).

Part III

EMPLOYEE PRIVACY

In this Part, we focus on privacy claims of workers. As we shall see, the common law often frames the issue against the backdrop of at-will employment, modified by the public-policy exception. While some privacy claims can fit within the public-policy exception, many cannot. Some employees attempt to apply the general common-law right to privacy to the workplace. Many of the privacy protections, however, have required statutory intervention by the legislature.

In general, our book covers the employment law of private-sector employees. In the case of privacy, however, the claims of government workers have been more thoroughly developed. Many of these rights have spilled over onto private workers, especially in the areas of free speech and freedom from drug testing. Whether the public-sector/private-sector divide should be porous is a highly contested topic in itself, as we shall see.

Chapter 8 examines the issues of politics and free speech. Chapter 9 begins by examining general privacy issues both at work and off the job. It then turns to the particular issues of drug testing and honesty testing. Chapter 10 examines issues arising from employer references, including the law of defamation and other torts.

Chapter 8

EMPLOYEE FREE SPEECH AND POLITICAL PROTECTIONS

In this chapter, we look first at the free-speech and political protections of government workers. The Constitution plays a major role here.

Except for the Thirteenth Amendment, which declares that "neither slavery nor involuntary servitude . . . shall exist within the United States," the federal Constitution only regulates state action. The Constitution does not restrict the actions of purely private employers, or give private employees any rights against their employers. The Constitution, particularly in its majestic due-process and equal-protection clauses, does restrict the actions of the Government as employer. In addition, Congress and state legislatures have given important civil-service protections to government workers.

The Constitution is consistent with at-will employment of government workers. As then-state Judge Oliver Wendell Holmes famously put it, in rejecting the constitutional claim of a police officer fired for engaging in political activity, a person "may have a constitutional right to talk politics, but he has no constitutional right to be a policeman." *McAuliffe v. Mayor & City of New Bedford*, 29 N.E. 517 (Mass. 1892). Government employment was regarded as a privilege, which the worker takes "on the terms which are offered to him." *Id.* But just as the common law has eroded employment at will in the private sector, the Supreme Court has found several important Constitutional limitations on an at-will rule for government employees. As Justice Brennan declared in *Keyishian v. Board of Regents*, 385 U.S. 589, 605-06 (1967), "the theory that public employment which may be denied altogether may be subjected to any conditions, regardless of how unreasonable, has been uniformly rejected. . . . It is too late in the day to doubt that the liberties of religion and expression may be infringed by the denial of or placing of conditions upon a benefit or privilege." The classic analysis of this shift is William Van Alstyne, *The Demise of the Right-Privilege Distinction in Constitutional Law*, 81 HARV. L. REV. 1439 (1968).

The first two cases examine Constitutional protections enjoyed by government workers. The Notes outline some of the statutory protections and regulation of government workers, which in practice are often more significant.

We then turn to free speech and political rights of private-sector workers. A major question will be the extent to which constitutional and statutory protections given public workers spill over to the private sector, or on the other hand the extent to which the at-will paradigm is thought to be inconsistent with free speech and other privacy rights.

A. POLITICAL AND SPEECH RIGHTS IN THE PUBLIC WORKPLACE

RUTAN v. REPUBLICAN PARTY
United States Supreme Court
497 U.S. 62 (1990)

JUSTICE BRENNAN delivered the opinion of the Court.

To the victor belong only those spoils that may be constitutionally obtained. *Elrod v. Burns*, 427 U.S. 347 (1976), and *Branti v. Finkel*, 445 U.S. 507 (1980), decided that the First Amendment forbids government officials to discharge or threaten to discharge public employees solely for not being supporters of the political party in power, unless party affiliation is an appropriate requirement for the position involved. Today we are asked to decide the constitutionality of several related political patronage practices — whether promotion, transfer, recall, and hiring decisions involving low-level public employees may be constitutionally based on party affiliation and support. We hold that they may not.

I

The petition and cross-petition before us arise from a lawsuit protesting certain employment policies and practices instituted by Governor James Thompson of Illinois. On November 12, 1980, the Governor issued an executive order proclaiming a hiring freeze for every agency, bureau, board, or commission subject to his control. The order prohibits state officials from hiring any employee, filling any vacancy, creating any new position, or taking any similar action. It affects approximately 60,000 state positions. More than 5,000 of these become available each year as a result of resignations, retirements, deaths, expansions, and reorganizations. The order proclaims that "no exceptions" are permitted without the Governor's "express permission after submission of appropriate requests to [his] office." . . .

Requests for the Governor's "express permission" have allegedly become routine. Permission has been granted or withheld through an agency expressly created for this purpose, the Governor's Office of Personnel (Governor's Office). Agencies have been screening applicants under Illinois' civil service system, making their personnel choices, and submitting them as requests to be approved or disapproved by the Governor's Office. Among the employment decisions for which approvals have been required are new hires, promotions, transfers, and recalls after layoffs.

By means of the freeze, according to petitioners and cross-respondents, the Governor has been using the Governor's Office to operate a political patronage system to limit state employment and beneficial employment-related decisions to those who are supported by the Republican Party. In reviewing an agency's request that a particular applicant be approved for a particular position, the Governor's Office has looked at whether the applicant voted in Republican primaries in past election years, whether the applicant has provided financial or other support to the Republican Party and its candidates, whether the applicant has promised to join and work for the Republican Party in the future, and whether the applicant has the support of Republican Party officials at state or local levels. . . .

II

A

In *Elrod*, we decided that a newly elected Democratic sheriff could not constitutionally engage in the patronage practice of replacing certain office staff with members of his own party "when the existing employees lack or fail to obtain requisite support from, or fail to affiliate with, that party." The plurality explained that conditioning public employment on the provision of support for the favored political party "unquestionably inhibits protected belief and association." It reasoned that conditioning employment on political activity pressures employees to pledge political allegiance to a party with which they prefer not to associate, to work for the election of political candidates they do not support, and to contribute money to be used to further policies with which they do not agree. The latter, the plurality noted, had been recognized by this Court as "tantamount to coerced belief." *Id.*, at 355 (citing *Buckley v. Valeo*, 424 U.S. 1, 19 (1976)). At the same time, employees are constrained from joining, working for, or contributing to the political party and candidates of their own choice. "[P]olitical belief and association constitute the core of those activities protected by the First Amendment," the plurality emphasized. . . .

The Court then decided that the government interests generally asserted in support of patronage fail to justify this burden on First Amendment rights because patronage dismissals are not the least restrictive means for fostering those interests. The plurality acknowledged that a government has a significant interest in ensuring that it has effective and efficient employees. It expressed doubt, however, that "mere difference of political persuasion motivates poor performance" and concluded that, in any case, the government can ensure employee effectiveness and efficiency through the less drastic means of discharging staff members whose work is inadequate. The plurality also found that a government can meet its need for politically loyal employees to implement its policies by the less intrusive measure of dismissing, on political grounds, only those employees in policymaking positions. Finally, although the plurality recognized that preservation of the democratic process "may in some instances justify limitations on First Amendment freedoms," it concluded that the "process functions as well without the practice, perhaps even better." Patronage, it explained, "can result in the entrenchment of one or a few parties to the exclusion of others" and "is a very effective impediment to the associational and speech freedoms which are essential to a meaningful system of democratic government."

Four years later, in *Branti*, we decided that the First Amendment prohibited a newly appointed public defender, who was a Democrat, from discharging assistant public defenders because they did not have the support of the Democratic Party. The Court rejected an attempt to distinguish the case from *Elrod*, deciding that it was immaterial whether the public defender had attempted to coerce employees to change political parties or had only dismissed them on the basis of their private political beliefs. . . .[5]

B

. . . Respondents urge us to view *Elrod* and *Branti* as inapplicable because the patronage dismissals at issue in those cases are different in kind from failure to promote, failure to transfer, and failure to recall after layoff. Respondents initially contend that the employee petitioners' and cross-respondents' First Amendment rights have not been infringed because they have no entitlement to promotion, transfer, or rehire. We rejected just such an argument in *Elrod* and *Branti*, as both cases involved state workers who were employees at will with no legal entitlement to continued employment. . . .

Likewise, we find the assertion here that the employee petitioners and cross-respondents had no legal entitlement to promotion, transfer, or recall beside the point.

Respondents next argue that the employment decisions at issue here do not violate the First Amendment because the decisions are not punitive, do not in any way adversely affect the terms of employment, and therefore do not chill the exercise of protected belief and association by public employees.[6] This is not credible. Employees who find themselves in dead-end positions due to their political backgrounds are adversely affected. They will feel a significant obligation to support political positions held by their superiors, and to refrain from acting on the political views they actually hold, in order to progress up the career ladder. Employees denied transfers to workplaces reasonably close to their homes until they join and work for the Republican Party will feel a daily pressure from their long commutes to do so. And employees who have been laid off may well feel compelled to engage in whatever political activity is necessary to regain regular paychecks and positions corresponding to their skill and experience. . . .

We find, however, that our conclusions in *Elrod* and *Branti* are equally applicable to the patronage practices at issue here. A government's interest in securing effective employees can be met by discharging, demoting, or transferring staff members whose work is deficient. A government's interest in securing employees who will loyally implement its policies can be adequately served by choosing or dismissing certain high-level employees on the basis of their political views. . . .

---

[5] *Branti* also refined the exception created by *Elrod* for certain employees. In *Elrod*, we suggested that policymaking and confidential employees probably could be dismissed on the basis of their political views. In *Branti*, we said that a State demonstrates a compelling interest in infringing First Amendment rights only when it can show that "party affiliation is an appropriate requirement for the effective performance of the public office involved." The scope of this exception does not concern us here as respondents concede that the five employees who brought this suit are not within it.

[6] Respondents' reliance on *Johnson v. Transportation Agency, Santa Clara County*, 480 U.S. 616 (1987), to this effect is misplaced. The question in *Johnson* was whether the Santa Clara County affirmative-action program violated the antidiscrimination requirement of Title VII of the Civil Rights Act of 1964. In that context, we said that the denial of a promotion did not unsettle any legitimate, firmly rooted expectations. We did not dispute, however, that it placed a burden on the person to whom the promotion was denied. . . .

We therefore determine that promotions, transfers, and recalls after layoffs based on political affiliation or support are an impermissible infringement on the First Amendment rights of public employees. In doing so, we reject the Seventh Circuit's view of the appropriate constitutional standard by which to measure alleged patronage practices in government employment. The Seventh Circuit proposed that only those employment decisions that are the "substantial equivalent of a dismissal" violate a public employee's rights under the First Amendment. We find this test unduly restrictive because it fails to recognize that there are deprivations less harsh than dismissal that nevertheless press state employees and applicants to conform their beliefs and associations to some state-selected orthodoxy. . . .

C

Petitioner James W. Moore presents the closely related question whether patronage hiring violates the First Amendment. Patronage hiring places burdens on free speech and association similar to those imposed by the patronage practices discussed above. A state job is valuable. Like most employment, it provides regular paychecks, health insurance, and other benefits. In addition, there may be openings with the State when business in the private sector is slow. There are also occupations for which the government is a major (or the only) source of employment, such as social workers, elementary school teachers, and prison guards. Thus, denial of a state job is a serious privation. . . .

The Court of Appeals reasoned that "rejecting an employment application does not impose a hardship upon an employee comparable to the loss of [a] job." *Ibid.*, citing *Wygant v. Jackson Bd. of Educ.*, 476 U.S. 267 (1986) (plurality opinion). Just as we reject the Seventh Circuit's proffered test, we find the Seventh Circuit's reliance on *Wygant* to distinguish hiring from dismissal unavailing. The court cited a passage from the plurality opinion in *Wygant* explaining that school boards attempting to redress past discrimination must choose methods that broadly distribute the disadvantages imposed by affirmative action plans among innocent parties. The plurality said that race-based layoffs placed too great a burden on individual members of the nonminority race, but suggested that discriminatory hiring was permissible, under certain circumstances, even though it burdened white applicants, because the burden was less intrusive than the loss of an existing job.

Wygant has no application to the question at issue here. The plurality's concern in that case was identifying the least harsh means of remedying past wrongs. It did not question that some remedy was permissible when there was sufficient evidence of past discrimination. In contrast, the Governor of Illinois has not instituted a remedial undertaking. It is unnecessary here to consider whether not being hired is less burdensome than being discharged, because the government is not pressed to do either on the basis of political affiliation. The question in the patronage context is not which penalty is more acute but whether the government, without sufficient justification, is pressuring employees to discontinue the free exercise of their First Amendment rights. . . .

JUSTICE STEVENS, concurring.

While I join the Court's opinion, these additional comments are prompted by . . . propositions advanced by JUSTICE SCALIA in his dissent. First, he implies that prohibiting imposition of an unconstitutional condition upon eligibility for government employment amounts to adoption of a civil service system. . . .

Denying the Governor of Illinois the power to require every state employee, and every applicant for state employment, to pledge allegiance and service to the political party in power is a far cry from a civil service code. The question in these cases is simply whether a Governor may adopt a rule that would be plainly unconstitutional if enacted by the General Assembly of Illinois. . . .

JUSTICE SCALIA, with whom THE CHIEF JUSTICE and JUSTICE KENNEDY join, and with whom JUSTICE O'CONNOR joins as to Parts II and III, dissenting.

Today the Court establishes the constitutional principle that party membership is not a permissible factor in the dispensation of government jobs, except those jobs for the performance of which party affiliation is an "appropriate requirement." It is hard to say precisely (or even generally) what that exception means, but if there is any category of jobs for whose performance party affiliation is not an appropriate requirement, it is the job of being a judge, where partisanship is not only unneeded but positively undesirable. It is, however, rare that a federal administration of one party will appoint a judge from another party. And it has always been rare. *See Marbury v. Madison*, 1 Cranch 137 (1803). Thus, the new principle that the Court today announces will be enforced by a corps of judges (the Members of this Court included) who overwhelmingly owe their office to its violation. Something must be wrong here, and I suggest it is the Court.

The merit principle for government employment is probably the most favored in modern America, having been widely adopted by civil service legislation at both the state and federal levels. But there is another point of view, described in characteristically Jacksonian fashion by an eminent practitioner of the patronage system, George Washington Plunkitt of Tammany Hall:

> I ain't up on sillygisms, but I can give you some arguments that nobody can answer.

> First, this great and glorious country was built up by political parties; second, parties can't hold together if their workers don't get offices when they win; third, if the parties go to pieces, the government they built up must go to pieces, too; fourth, then there'll be hell to pay.

W. RIORDON, PLUNKITT OF TAMMANY HALL 13 (1963).

It may well be that the Good Government Leagues of America were right, and that Plunkitt, James Michael Curley, and their ilk were wrong; but that is not entirely certain. As the merit principle has been extended and its effects increasingly felt; as the Boss Tweeds, the Tammany Halls, the Pendergast Machines, the Byrd Machines, and the Daley Machines have faded into history; we find that political leaders at all levels increasingly complain of the helplessness of elected government, unprotected by "party discipline," before the demands of small and cohesive interest groups.

The choice between patronage and the merit principle — or, to be more realistic about it, the choice between the desirable mix of merit and patronage principles in widely varying federal, state, and local political contexts — is not so clear that I would be prepared, as an original matter, to chisel a single, inflexible prescription into the Constitution. Fourteen years ago, in *Elrod*, the Court did that. *Elrod* was limited, however, as was the later decision of *Branti*, to patronage firings, leaving it to state and federal legislatures to determine when and where political affiliation could be taken into account in hirings and promotions. Today the Court makes its constitutional civil service reform absolute, extending to all decisions regarding government employment. Because the First Amendment has never been thought to require this disposition, which may well have disastrous consequences for our political system, I dissent.

NOTES

1. *Growth of the Non-Partisan Civil Service.* As Justice Scalia notes, the spoils system of political patronage has a long history in this country. *Marbury v. Madison*, 5 U.S. (1 Cranch) 137 (1803), the famous case establishing the power of judicial review, involved political patronage. Andrew Jackson, elected in 1828, explicitly introduced a spoils system into federal appointments to promote political responsiveness. Abraham Lincoln continued the practice with a vengeance, dismissing 1,457 of the 1,639 officers appointed by previous Presidents.

Support for a professional, independent civil service was galvanized by the assassination in 1881 of President James Garfield by a disappointed office seeker. The Pendleton Act, passed two years later, established a bipartisan Civil Service Commission to create competitive examinations as the basis for hiring federal workers. Originally covering only 10 percent of government workers, the "classified" service grew to 70 percent of the government workforce by 1919. Protections against arbitrary dismissal came later. The 1912 Lloyd-LaFollete Act prohibited a dismissal unless it would promote the "efficiency of the service," a standard that survives today. *See* 5 U.S.C. §§ 7503(a), 7513(a).

The efficiency of the independent bureaucracy was celebrated by Max Weber as "the most rational known means of exercising authority over human beings." 1 MAX WEBER, ECONOMY AND SOCIETY 223 (G. Roth & C. Wittich eds., 1978). Bureaucratic theory justified the apolitical civil service: "a merit-based system, staffed by professional experts and freed from the corrosive influence of politics by formal legal constraints on appointment and tenure, would provide the most efficient, rational tool for achieving the aims of public policy." *Developments in the Law: Public Employment*, 97 HARV. L. REV. 1611, 1629 (1984). *See generally* P. VAN RIPER, HISTORY OF THE UNITED STATES CIVIL SERVICE (1958).

2. *Civil Service Reform Act of 1978.* The elaborate protections given civil servants were increasingly criticized as causing and immunizing indifference or incompetence by government workers. The Watergate scandals showed, paradoxically, that the protections did not prevent manipulation of the civil service for political ends. The criticisms led to the Civil Service Reform Act of 1978 (CSRA), which the Senate Report declared to be "the most comprehensive reform of the Federal work force since passage of the Pendleton Act in 1883."

The CSRA dismantled the Civil Service Commission, which was criticized for combining the roles of manager, prosecutor, judge, and jury of the federal work force. Administrative and managerial functions were given to the Office of Personnel Management. A three-member Merit Systems Protection Board (MSPB) was created to hear appeals of personnel decisions by individual agencies. The MSPB has developed a highly formal, adversarial process modeled on the Federal Rules of Civil Procedure, complete with discovery and subpoena power. The MSPB will uphold an agency's decision to fire a worker if it rests on "substantial evidence," a lesser standard than the preponderance of the evidence. Employees claiming discrimination can get a de novo review of the MSPB's decision in federal district court. Review in all other cases is limited to whether the MSPB's decision was arbitrary or capricious, obtained without required procedures, or unsupported by substantial evidence.

The CSRA also created a new category of approximately 7,000 upper-level federal jobs, the Senior Executive Service (SES). Workers in the SES are evaluated on the basis of "performance," often by political appointees. SES workers have far fewer rights of appeal than ordinary civil servants. In return, merit bonuses are potentially available. The shift toward performance evaluations has led at least one commentator to declare that "the CSRA has sacrificed the goals of merit and political neutrality embedded in the bureaucratic vision that has dominated the development of the civil service in this century to the Jacksonian goal of political responsiveness." *Developments in the Law: Public Employment*, 97 HARV. L. REV. 1611, 1650 (1984).

3. Procedural Requirements for Government Employees with Property Interests in Their Jobs. The Constitution does not give a government worker a property interest in his job. A property interest must come from an independent source, such as a statute, municipal ordinance, or express or implied contract between the parties. For example, in *Perry v. Sindermann*, 408 U.S. 593 (1972), the Court found an implied entitlement to job tenure in a state college teacher who had completed ten one-year contracts.

Once a property interest in a job has been established, the Constitution regulates the process that is due before the Government may take it away. In *Cleveland Board of Education v. Loudermill*, 470 U.S. 532 (1985), the school board fired a security guard when it discovered that he had falsely claimed on his application that he was not a felon. The guard was a "classified civil servant." By state statute, such an employee could only be dismissed for cause and was entitled to administrative review after a dismissal. The guard filed suit, claiming an entitlement to respond to the charges before being dismissed. The District Court rejected the claim, reasoning that the very statute that created the property interest in the job also defined the procedures by which the government could take the job away. The Supreme Court rejected this "bitter with the sweet" theory. It held that the Constitution entitles government employees who cannot be fired without just cause to notice and an explanation of the charges, and an opportunity to respond before being terminated.

GARCETTI v. CEBALLOS
United States Supreme Court
126 S. Ct. 1951 (2006)

JUSTICE KENNEDY delivered the opinion of the Court.

It is well settled that "a State cannot condition public employment on a basis that infringes the employee's constitutionally protected interest in freedom of expression." *Connick v. Myers*, 461 U.S. 138, 142 (1983). The question presented by the instant case is whether the First Amendment protects a government employee from discipline based on speech made pursuant to the employee's official duties.

I

Respondent Richard Ceballos has been employed since 1989 as a deputy district attorney for the Los Angeles County District Attorney's Office. . . . In February 2000, a defense attorney contacted Ceballos about a pending criminal case. The defense attorney said there were inaccuracies in an affidavit used to obtain a critical search warrant. The attorney informed Ceballos that he had filed a motion to traverse, or challenge, the warrant, but he also wanted Ceballos to review the case. . . .

After examining the affidavit and visiting the location it described, Ceballos determined the affidavit contained serious misrepresentations. The affidavit called a long driveway what Ceballos thought should have been referred to as a separate roadway. Ceballos also questioned the affidavit's statement that tire tracks led from a stripped-down truck to the premises covered by the warrant. His doubts arose from his conclusion that the roadway's composition in some places made it difficult or impossible to leave visible tire tracks.

Ceballos spoke on the telephone to the warrant affiant, a deputy sheriff from the Los Angeles County Sheriff's Department, but he did not receive a satisfactory explanation for the perceived inaccuracies. He relayed his findings to his supervisors, petitioners Carol Najera and Frank Sundstedt, and followed up by preparing a disposition memorandum. The memo explained Ceballos' concerns and recommended dismissal of the case. . . .

Based on Ceballos' statements, a meeting was held to discuss the affidavit. Attendees included Ceballos, Sundstedt, and Najera, as well as the warrant affiant and other employees from the sheriff's department. The meeting allegedly became heated, with one lieutenant sharply criticizing Ceballos for his handling of the case.

Despite Ceballos' concerns, Sundstedt decided to proceed with the prosecution, pending disposition of the defense motion to traverse. The trial court held a hearing on the motion. Ceballos was called by the defense and recounted his observations about the affidavit, but the trial court rejected the challenge to the warrant.

Ceballos claims that in the aftermath of these events he was subjected to a series of retaliatory employment actions. The actions included reassignment from his calendar deputy position to a trial deputy position, transfer to another courthouse, and denial of a promotion. Ceballos initiated an employment grievance, but the grievance was denied based on a finding that he had not suffered any retaliation. Unsatisfied, Ceballos sued, [asserting a claim under 42 U.S.C. § 1983]. . . . He alleged petitioners violated the First and Fourteenth Amendments by retaliating against him based on his [disposition] memo.

. . . . Petitioners moved for summary judgment, and the District Court granted their motion. . . .

The Court of Appeals for the Ninth Circuit reversed, holding that "Ceballos's allegations of wrongdoing in the memorandum constitute protected speech under the First Amendment." In reaching its conclusion the court looked to the First Amendment analysis set forth in *Pickering v. Board of Ed.*, 391 U.S. 563 (1968), and *Connick*. *Connick* instructs courts to begin by considering whether the expressions in question were made by the speaker "as a citizen upon matters of public concern." The Court of Appeals determined that Ceballos' memo, which recited what he thought to be governmental misconduct, was "inherently a matter of public concern." . . .

Having concluded that Ceballos' memo satisfied the public-concern requirement, the Court of Appeals proceeded to balance Ceballos' interest in his speech against his supervisors' interest in responding to it. The court struck the balance in Ceballos' favor, noting that petitioners "failed even to suggest disruption or inefficiency in the workings of the District Attorney's Office" as a result of the memo. . . .

We granted certiorari, and we now reverse.

II

As the Court's decisions have noted, for many years "the unchallenged dogma was that a public employee had no right to object to conditions placed upon the terms of employment — including those which restricted the exercise of constitutional rights." *Connick*. That dogma has been qualified in important respects. The Court has made clear that public employees do not surrender all their First Amendment rights by reason of their employment. Rather, the First Amendment protects a public employee's right, in certain circumstances, to speak as a citizen addressing matters of public concern.

Pickering provides a useful starting point in explaining the Court's doctrine. There the relevant speech was a teacher's letter to a local newspaper addressing issues including the funding policies of his school board. "The problem in any case," the Court stated, "is to arrive at a balance between the interests of the teacher, as a citizen, in commenting upon matters of public concern and the interest of the State, as an employer, in promoting the efficiency of the public services it performs through its employees." The Court found the teacher's speech "neither [was] shown nor can be presumed to have in any way either impeded the teacher's proper performance of his daily duties in the classroom or to have interfered with the regular operation of the schools generally." Thus, the Court concluded that "the interest of the school administration in limiting teachers' opportunities to contribute to public debate is not significantly greater than its interest in limiting a similar contribution by any member of the general public."

Pickering and the cases decided in its wake identify two inquiries to guide interpretation of the constitutional protections accorded to public employee speech. The first requires determining whether the employee spoke as a citizen on a matter of public concern. If the answer is no, the employee has no First Amendment cause of action based on his or her employer's reaction to the speech. If the answer is yes, then the possibility of a First Amendment claim arises. The question becomes whether the relevant government entity had an adequate justification for treating the employee differently from any other member of the general public. This consideration reflects the importance of the relationship between the speaker's expressions and employment. A government entity has broader discretion to restrict speech when it acts in its role as employer, but the restrictions it imposes must be directed at speech that has some potential to affect the entity's operations.

. . . .

When a citizen enters government service, the citizen by necessity must accept certain limitations on his or her freedom. Government employers, like private employers, need a significant degree of control over their employees' words and actions; without it, there would be little chance for the efficient provision of public services. *Cf. Connick, supra,* at 143 ("[G]overnment offices could not function if every employment decision became a constitutional matter"). Public employees, moreover, often occupy trusted positions in society. When they speak out, they can express views that contravene governmental policies or impair the proper performance of governmental functions.

At the same time, the Court has recognized that a citizen who works for the government is nonetheless a citizen. The First Amendment limits the ability of a public employer to leverage the employment relationship to restrict, incidentally or intentionally, the liberties employees enjoy in their capacities as private citizens. So long as employees are speaking as citizens about matters of public concern, they must face only those speech restrictions that are necessary for their employers to operate efficiently and effectively.

The Court's employee-speech jurisprudence protects, of course, the constitutional rights of public employees. Yet the First Amendment interests at stake extend beyond the individual speaker. The Court has acknowledged the importance of promoting the public's interest in receiving the well-informed views of government employees engaging in civic discussion. *Pickering* again provides an instructive example. The Court characterized its holding as rejecting the attempt of school administrators to "limi[t] teachers' opportunities to contribute to public debate." It also noted that teachers are "the members of a community most likely to have informed and definite opinions" about school expenditures. The Court's approach acknowledged the necessity for informed, vibrant dialogue in a democratic society. It suggested, in addition, that widespread costs may arise when dialogue is repressed. The Court's more recent cases have expressed similar concerns. *See, e.g., San Diego v. Roe,* 543 U.S. 77, 82 (2004) *(per curiam)* ("Were [public employees] not able to speak on [the operation of their employers], the community would be deprived of informed opinions on important public issues. The interest at stake is as much the public's interest in receiving informed opinion as it is the employee's own right to disseminate it").

The Court's decisions, then, have sought both to promote the individual and societal interests that are served when employees speak as citizens on matters of public concern and to respect the needs of government employers attempting to perform their important public functions. Underlying our cases has been the premise that while the First Amendment invests public employees with certain rights, it does not empower them to "constitutionalize the employee grievance."

III

With these principles in mind we turn to the instant case. Respondent Ceballos believed the affidavit used to obtain a search warrant contained serious misrepresentations. He conveyed his opinion and recommendation in a memo to his supervisor. That Ceballos expressed his views inside his office, rather than publicly, is not dispositive. Employees in some cases may receive First Amendment protection for expressions made at work. Many citizens do much of their talking inside their respective workplaces, and it would not serve the goal of treating public employees like "any member of the general public," to hold that all speech within the office is automatically exposed to restriction.

The memo concerned the subject matter of Ceballos' employment, but this, too, is nondispositive. The First Amendment protects some expressions related to the speaker's job. As the Court noted in *Pickering:* "Teachers are, as a class, the members of a community most likely to have informed and definite opinions as to how funds allotted to the operation of the schools should be spent. Accordingly, it is essential that they be able to speak out freely on such questions without fear of retaliatory dismissal." The same is true of many other categories of public employees.

The controlling factor in Ceballos' case is that his expressions were made pursuant to his duties as a calendar deputy. That consideration — the fact that Ceballos spoke as a prosecutor fulfilling a responsibility to advise his supervisor about how best to proceed with a pending case — distinguishes Ceballos' case from those in which the First Amendment provides protection against discipline. We hold that when public employees make statements pursuant to their official duties, the employees are not speaking as citizens for First Amendment purposes, and the Constitution does not insulate their communications from employer discipline.

Ceballos wrote his disposition memo because that is part of what he, as a calendar deputy, was employed to do. It is immaterial whether he experienced some personal gratification from writing the memo; his First Amendment rights do not depend on his job satisfaction. The significant point is that the memo was written pursuant to Ceballos' official duties. Restricting speech that owes its existence to a public employee's professional responsibilities does not infringe any liberties the employee might have enjoyed as a private citizen. It simply reflects the exercise of employer control over what the employer itself has commissioned or created. Contrast, for example, the expressions made by the speaker in *Pickering*, whose letter to the newspaper had no official significance and bore similarities to letters submitted by numerous citizens every day.

Ceballos did not act as a citizen when he went about conducting his daily professional activities, such as supervising attorneys, investigating charges, and preparing filings. In the same way he did not speak as a citizen by writing a memo that addressed the proper disposition of a pending criminal case. When he went to work and performed the tasks he was paid to perform, Ceballos acted as a government employee. The fact that his duties sometimes required him to speak or write does not mean his supervisors were prohibited from evaluating his performance.

This result is consistent with our precedents' attention to the potential societal value of employee speech. Refusing to recognize First Amendment claims based on government employees' work product does not prevent them from participating in public debate. The employees retain the prospect of constitutional protection for their contributions to the civic discourse. This prospect of protection, however, does not invest them with a right to perform their jobs however they see fit.

Our holding likewise is supported by the emphasis of our precedents on affording government employers sufficient discretion to manage their operations. Employers have heightened interests in controlling speech made by an employee in his or her professional capacity. Official communications have official consequences, creating a need for substantive consistency and clarity. Supervisors must ensure that their employees' official communications are accurate, demonstrate sound judgment, and promote the employer's mission. Ceballos' memo is illustrative. It demanded the attention of his supervisors and led to a heated meeting with employees from the sheriff's department. If Ceballos' superiors thought his memo was inflammatory or misguided, they had the authority to take proper corrective action.

Ceballos' proposed contrary rule, adopted by the Court of Appeals, would commit state and federal courts to a new, permanent, and intrusive role, mandating judicial oversight of communications between and among government employees and their superiors in the course of official business. This displacement of managerial discretion by judicial supervision finds no support in our precedents. When an employee speaks as a citizen addressing a matter of public concern, the First Amendment requires a delicate balancing of the competing interests surrounding the speech and its consequences. When, however, the employee is simply performing his or her job duties, there is no warrant for a similar degree of scrutiny. To hold otherwise would be to demand permanent judicial intervention in the conduct of governmental operations to a degree inconsistent with sound principles of federalism and the separation of powers.

The Court of Appeals based its holding in part on what it perceived as a doctrinal anomaly. The court suggested it would be inconsistent to compel public employers to tolerate certain employee speech made publicly but not speech made pursuant to an employee's assigned duties. This objection misconceives the theoretical underpinnings of our decisions. Employees who make public statements outside the course of performing their official duties retain some possibility of First Amendment protection because that is the kind of activity engaged in by citizens who do not work for the government. The same goes for writing a letter to a local newspaper, see *Pickering*, or discussing politics with a co-worker, see *Rankin*, 483 U.S. 378. When a public employee speaks pursuant to employment responsibilities, however, there is no relevant analogue to speech by citizens who are not government employees.

The Court of Appeals' concern also is unfounded as a practical matter. The perceived anomaly, it should be noted, is limited in scope: It relates only to the expressions an employee makes pursuant to his or her official responsibilities, not to statements or complaints (such as those at issue in cases like *Pickering* and *Connick*) that are made outside the duties of employment. If, moreover, a government employer is troubled by the perceived anomaly, it has the means at hand to avoid it. A public employer that wishes to encourage its employees to voice concerns privately retains the option of instituting internal policies and procedures that are receptive to employee criticism. Giving employees an internal forum for their speech will discourage them from concluding that the safest avenue of expression is to state their views in public.

. . . We reject, however, the suggestion that employers can restrict employees' rights by creating excessively broad job descriptions. The proper inquiry is a practical one. Formal job descriptions often bear little resemblance to the duties an employee actually is expected to perform, and the listing of a given task in an employee's written job description is neither necessary nor sufficient to demonstrate that conducting the task is within the scope of the employee's professional duties for First Amendment purposes.

. . . .

IV

Exposing governmental inefficiency and misconduct is a matter of considerable significance. As the Court noted in *Connick*, public employers should, "as a matter of good judgment," be "receptive to constructive criticism offered by their employees." The dictates of sound judgment are reinforced by the powerful network of legislative enactments — such as whistle-blower protection laws and labor codes — available to those who seek to expose wrongdoing. Cases involving government attorneys implicate additional safeguards in the form of, for example, rules of conduct and constitutional obligations apart from the First Amendment. *See, e.g.*, Cal. Rule Prof. Conduct 5-110 (2005) ("A member in government service shall not institute or cause to be instituted criminal charges when the member knows or should know that the charges are not supported by probable cause"); *Brady v. Maryland*, 373 U.S. 83 (1963). These imperatives, as well as obligations arising from any other applicable constitutional provisions and mandates of the criminal and civil laws, protect employees and provide checks on supervisors who would order unlawful or otherwise inappropriate actions.

We reject, however, the notion that the First Amendment shields from discipline the expressions employees make pursuant to their professional duties. Our precedents do not support the existence of a constitutional cause of action behind every statement a public employee makes in the course of doing his or her job.

The judgment of the Court of Appeals is reversed, and the case is remanded for proceedings consistent with this opinion.

It is so ordered.

[JUSTICE STEVENS' dissenting opinion is omitted.]

JUSTICE SOUTER, with whom JUSTICE STEVENS and JUSTICE GINSBURG join, dissenting.

. . . .

I

As all agree, the qualified speech protection embodied in *Pickering* balancing resolves the tension between individual and public interests in the speech, on the one hand, and the government's interest in operating efficiently without distraction or embarrassment by talkative or headline-grabbing employees. The need for a balance hardly disappears when an employee speaks on matters his job requires him to address; rather, it seems obvious that the individual and public value of such speech is no less, and may well be greater, when the employee speaks pursuant to his duties in addressing a subject he knows intimately for the very reason that it falls within his duties.

As for the importance of such speech to the individual, it stands to reason that a citizen may well place a very high value on a right to speak on the public issues he decides to make the subject of his work day after day. Would anyone doubt that a school principal evaluating the performance of teachers for promotion or pay adjustment retains a citizen's interest in addressing the quality of teaching in the schools? (Still, the majority indicates he could be fired without First Amendment recourse for fair but unfavorable comment when the teacher under review is the superintendent's daughter.) Would anyone deny that a prosecutor like Richard Ceballos may claim the interest of any citizen in speaking out against a rogue law enforcement officer, simply because his job requires him to express a judgment about the officer's performance? (But the majority says the First Amendment gives Ceballos no protection, even if his judgment in this case was sound and appropriately expressed.)

Indeed, the very idea of categorically separating the citizen's interest from the employee's interest ignores the fact that the ranks of public service include those who share the poet's "object . . . to unite [m]y avocation and my vocation;"[1] these citizen servants are the ones whose civic interest rises highest when they speak pursuant to their duties, and these are exactly the ones government employers most want to attract. There is no question that public employees speaking on matters they are obliged to address would generally place a high value on a right to speak, as any responsible citizen would.

Nor is there any reason to raise the counterintuitive question whether the public interest in hearing informed employees evaporates when they speak

---

[1] R. FROST, TWO TRAMPS IN MUD TIME, COLLECTED POEMS, PROSE, & PLAYS 251, 252 (R. Poirier & M. Richardson eds., 1995).

as required on some subject at the core of their jobs. Two Terms ago, we recalled the public value that the *Pickering* Court perceived in the speech of public employees as a class: "Underlying the decision in *Pickering* is the recognition that public employees are often the members of the community who are likely to have informed opinions as to the operations of their public employers, operations which are of substantial concern to the public. Were they not able to speak on these matters, the community would be deprived of informed opinions on important public issues. The interest at stake is as much the public's interest in receiving informed opinion as it is the employee's own right to disseminate it." *San Diego v. Roe*, 543 U.S. 77, 82 (2004) *(per curiam)* (citation omitted). This is not a whit less true when an employee's job duties require him to speak about such things: when, for example, a public auditor speaks on his discovery of embezzlement of public funds, when a building inspector makes an obligatory report of an attempt to bribe him, or when a law enforcement officer expressly balks at a superior's order to violate constitutional rights he is sworn to protect. (The majority, however, places all these speakers beyond the reach of First Amendment protection against retaliation.)

Nothing, then, accountable on the individual and public side of the *Pickering* balance changes when an employee speaks "pursuant" to public duties. On the side of the government employer, however, something is different, and to this extent, I agree with the majority of the Court. The majority is rightly concerned that the employee who speaks out on matters subject to comment in doing his own work has the greater leverage to create office uproars and fracture the government's authority to set policy to be carried out coherently through the ranks . . . . Up to a point, then, the majority makes good points: government needs civility in the workplace, consistency in policy, and honesty and competence in public service.

But why do the majority's concerns, which we all share, require categorical exclusion of First Amendment protection against any official retaliation for things said on the job? Is it not possible to respect the unchallenged individual and public interests in the speech through a *Pickering* balance without drawing the strange line I mentioned before? . . . It is thus no adequate justification for the suppression of potentially valuable information simply to recognize that the government has a huge interest in managing its employees and preventing the occasionally irresponsible one from turning his job into a bully pulpit. Even there, the lesson of *Pickering* (and the object of most constitutional adjudication) is still to the point: when constitutionally significant interests clash, resist the demand for winner-take-all; try to make adjustments that serve all of the values at stake.

[T]he majority's position comes with no guarantee against factbound litigation over whether a public employee's statements were made "pursuant to . . . official duties." In fact, the majority invites such litigation by describing the enquiry as a "practical one," apparently based on the totality of employment circumstances. Are prosecutors' discretionary statements about cases addressed to the press on the courthouse steps made "pursuant to their official duties"? Are government nuclear scientists' complaints to their supervisors about a colleague's improper handling of radioactive materials made "pursuant" to duties?

. . . .

B

The majority [argues] that the First Amendment has little or no work to do here owing to an assertedly comprehensive complement of state and national statutes protecting government whistle-blowers from vindictive bosses. But even if I close my eyes to the tenet that " '[t]he applicability of a provision of the Constitution has never depended on the vagaries of state or federal law,' " *Board of Comm'rs, Wabaunsee Cty. v. Umbehr*, 518 U.S. 668, 680 (1996), the majority's counsel to rest easy fails on its own terms.

To begin with, speech addressing official wrongdoing may well fall outside protected whistle-blowing, defined in the classic sense of exposing an official's fault to a third party or to the public; the teacher in *Givhan*, for example, who raised the issue of unconstitutional hiring bias, would not have qualified as that sort of whistle-blower, for she was fired after a private conversation with the school principal. In any event, the combined variants of statutory whistle-blower definitions and protections add up to a patchwork, not a showing that worries may be remitted to legislatures for relief. *See* D. WESTMAN & N. MODESITT, WHISTLEBLOWING: LAW OF RETALIATORY DISCHARGE 67-75, 281-307 (2d ed. 2004). Some state statutes protect all government workers, including the employees of municipalities and other subdivisions; others stop at state employees. Some limit protection to employees who tell their bosses before they speak out; others forbid bosses from imposing any requirement to warn. As for the federal Whistleblower Protection Act of 1989, 5 U.S.C. § 1213 *et seq.*, current case law requires an employee complaining of retaliation to show " 'irrefragable proof' " that the person criticized was not acting in good faith and in compliance with the law, see *Lachance v. White*, 174 F.3d 1378, 1381 (Fed. Cir. 1999), *cert. denied*, 528 U.S. 1153 (2000). And federal employees have been held to have no protection for disclosures made to immediate supervisors or for statements of facts publicly known already. Most significantly, federal employees have been held to be unprotected for statements made in connection with normal employment duties, *Huffman v. Office of Personnel Management*, 263 F.3d 1341, 1352 (Fed. Cir. 2001), the very speech that the majority says will be covered by "the powerful network of legislative enactments . . . available to those who seek to expose wrongdoing." My point is not to disparage particular statutes or speak here to the merits of interpretations by other federal courts, but merely to show the current understanding of statutory protection: individuals doing the same sorts of governmental jobs and saying the same sorts of things addressed to civic concerns will get different protection depending on the local, state, or federal jurisdictions that happened to employ them.

JUSTICE BREYER, dissenting.

Like the majority, I understand the need to "affor[d] government employers sufficient discretion to manage their operations." And I agree that the Constitution does not seek to "displac[e] . . . managerial discretion by judicial supervision." Nonetheless, there may well be circumstances with special demand for constitutional protection of the speech at issue, where governmental justifications may be limited, and where administrable standards seem readily available — to the point where the majority's fears of department management by lawsuit are misplaced. In such an instance, I believe that courts should apply the *Pickering* standard, even though the government employee speaks upon matters of public concern in the course of his ordinary duties.

This is such a case. . . . The facts present two special circumstances that together justify First Amendment review.

First, the speech at issue is professional speech — the speech of a lawyer. Such speech is subject to independent regulation by canons of the profession. Those canons provide an obligation to speak in certain instances. And where that is so, the government's own interest in forbidding that speech is diminished. *Cf. Legal Services Corporation v. Velazquez*, 531 U.S. 533, 544 (2001) ("Restricting LSC [Legal Services Corporation] attorneys in advising their clients and in presenting arguments and analyses to the courts distorts the legal system by altering the traditional role of the attorneys"). *See also Polk County v. Dodson*, 454 U.S. 312, 321 (1981) ("[A] public defender is not amenable to administrative direction in the same sense as other employees of the State"). *See generally* Post, *Subsidized Speech*, 106 YALE L.J. 151, 172 (1996) ("[P]rofessionals must always qualify their loyalty and commitment to the vertical hierarchy of an organization by their horizontal commitment to general professional norms and standards"). The objective specificity and public availability of the profession's canons also help to diminish the risk that the courts will improperly interfere with the government's necessary authority to manage its work.

Second, the Constitution itself here imposes speech obligations upon the government's professional employee. A prosecutor has a constitutional obligation to learn of, to preserve, and to communicate with the defense about exculpatory and impeachment evidence in the government's possession. So, for example, might a prison doctor have a similar constitutionally related professional obligation to communicate with superiors about seriously unsafe or unsanitary conditions in the cellblock. There may well be other examples.

. . . .

NOTES

1. *Speech Outside of Official Duties.* *Ceballos* creates a new rule for speech as part of official job duties, but leaves other government-employee speech subject to the basic *Connick-Pickering* test. Consider how this situation should be analyzed. A police officer is terminated for selling sexually explicit videos of himself in a generic police uniform on Ebay. The officer challenges his superiors' decision, arguing that his private, off-duty actions are unrelated to employment and so protected by the First Amendment.

These are the facts of *City of San Diego v. Roe*, 543 U.S. 77 (2004), cited by both the majority and dissent in *Ceballos*. In a per curium opinion reversing the Ninth Circuit, the *Roe* Court held that the officer's expressions did not address a matter of public concern, defined as "a subject of general interest and of value and concern to the public at the time of publication," and thus were not subject to the *Pickering* balancing test.

2. *Job Descriptions.* *Ceballos* purports to provide a clear rule: "when public employees make statements pursuant to their official duties, the employees are not speaking as citizens for First Amendment purposes." *Rutan* also articulates a clear rule: no job discipline because of party affiliation except for policymaking or confidential employees. One value of a clear rule is that many employee-free-speech claims can be dismissed quickly by summary judgment, if they create litigation at all. But will the litigation simply turn to whether the speech was part of the official duties (*Ceballos*) or whether the employee is in a policymaking or confidential position (*Rutan*)?

To what degree should courts look to formal job descriptions in making these inquiries? The *Ceballos* majority emphasizes actual employment activity of individuals, rather than their formal job descriptions. Other courts, however, strongly disagree with this approach. In *Riley v. Blagojevich*, 425 F.3d 357, 360-62 (7th Cir. 2005) (holding that assistant prison wardens held policymaking jobs), Judge Posner argues that formal job descriptions should be used to evaluate employment duties whenever possible. As Posner sees it, formal job descriptions reduce the oversight responsibilities of courts, provide guidance to litigants, and reduce employees' "incentive to try and protect their jobs simply by not performing those [formal] duties." Nevertheless, Posner acknowledges that courts must still "focus on how the description was created; how it is updated and thus kept realistic rather than being allowed to drift far from the actual duties of the position; in short, on how reliable, how authoritative, the description is."

3. *Ceballos' Application to Professors.* In a deleted portion of the opinion, the *Ceballos* majority states: "There is some argument that expression related to academic scholarship or classroom instruction implicates additional constitutional interests that are not fully accounted for by this Court's customary employee-speech jurisprudence. We need not, and for that reason do not, decide whether the analysis we conduct today would apply in the same manner to a case involving speech related to scholarship or teaching." Justice Souter, however, was far more concerned: "This ostensible domain beyond the pale of the First Amendment is spacious enough to include even the teaching of a public university professor, and I have to hope that today's majority does not mean to imperil First Amendment protection of academic freedom in public colleges and universities, whose teachers necessarily speak and write 'pursuant to official duties.'" What are the likely effects of *Ceballos* on higher education? If a public-university professor is disciplined for taking a strong, controversial stance during lectures, will she be without constitutional protection? Or perhaps the protections should come from the tenure process rather than the Constitution?

4. *The Necessity of Constitutional Protections.* A basic point of Justice Kennedy in *Ceballos* is that not every public-employee grievance should become a constitutional claim. In Part IV of his opinion, Kennedy sketches other statutory protections given to government whistleblowers, suggesting a lesser need for First Amendment protection. Justice Souter in dissent emphasizes that whistleblower and civil-service protections vary widely in scope and effectiveness. In evaluating these competing claims, recall the Notes on Whistleblower Statutes in Chapter 5, *supra*.

5. *Going Public Versus Going Through the System.* The *Ceballos* majority seems well aware that its decision might encourage government employees to go outside their official duties by engaging in public, external whistleblowing. This bucks the trend of recent whistleblower statutes and decisions, which generally promote private, internal whistleblowing. Justice Stevens' dissent, not included here, picked up on this problem, calling it "perverse to fashion a new rule that provides employees with an incentive to voice their concerns publicly before talking frankly to their superiors."

6. *Statutory Restrictions on Employee Political Activity.* In 1939, Congress passed "An Act to prevent pernicious political activities," better known as the Hatch Act, 5 U.S.C. §§ 1501-1508, 7321-7327. It severely restricted the permissible political activity of federal civil-service workers. "Little Hatch Acts" placed similar restrictions on state workers. Controversial from its beginning, the purpose of the Hatch Act was to ensure that civil servants are politically unbiased and free of political coercion. The centerpiece of the Hatch Act prohibited covered federal workers from taking an "active part in political management or in political campaigns." 5 U.S.C. § 7324(a)(2). Detailed regulations attempted to distinguish between partisan and nonpartisan activities, active leadership and individual participation, and solicitation versus mere expression of opinion. The constitutionality of the Hatch Act was upheld in *United Public Workers v. Mitchell*, 330 U.S. 75 (1947), and reaffirmed in *United States Civil Service Commission v. National Association of Letter Carriers*, 413 U.S. 548 (1973).

In 1993, however, in The Hatch Act Reform Amendments, Congress dramatically loosened the political restrictions on civil service workers. As the preamble states, Congress passed the Amendments "to restore to Federal civilian employees their right to participate voluntarily, as private citizens, in the political processes of the Nation, to protect such employees from improper political solicitation, and for other purposes." 5 U.S.C. preface. In drawing the line between on-the-job and off-the-job political activity, these amendments dramatically cut back on the scope of the prohibition. Thus, while civil-service workers still cannot engage in political activity while on duty or run for a partisan political office, they are allowed to work actively on political campaigns and make campaign contributions. *See generally* Rafael Gely & Timothy D. Chandler, *Restricting Public Employees' Political Activities: Good Government or Partisan Politics?*, 37 HOUSTON L. REV. 775, 821-22 (2000) (arguing that "the regulation of political activities via Hatch Act legislation manipulates political processes as much as political patronage does," and urging the Supreme Court to be "more willing to question government efforts to limit political participation by public employees").

B. POLITICAL AND SPEECH RIGHTS IN THE PRIVATE WORKPLACE

NOVOSEL v. NATIONWIDE INSURANCE CO.
United States Court of Appeals, Third Circuit
721 F.2d 894 (1983)

Before ADAMS, HUNTER and GARTH, CIRCUIT JUDGES.

ADAMS, CIRCUIT JUDGE.

This appeal presents us with the task of determining under what circumstances a federal court sitting in diversity under Pennsylvania law may intercede in a non-union employment relationship and limit the employer's ability to discharge employees. . . .

Novosel was an employee of Nationwide from December 1966 until November 18, 1981. He had steadily advanced through the company's ranks in a career unmarred by reprimands or disciplinary action. At the time his employment was terminated, he was a district claims manager and one of three candidates for the position of division claims manager.

In late October 1981, a memorandum was circulated through Nationwide's offices soliciting the participation of all employees in an effort to lobby the Pennsylvania House of Representatives. Specifically, employees were instructed to clip, copy, and obtain signatures on coupons bearing the insignia of the Pennsylvania Committee for No-Fault Reform. This Committee was actively supporting the passage of House Bill 1285, the "No-Fault Reform Act," then before the state legislature.

The allegations of the complaint charge that the sole reason for Novosel's discharge was his refusal to participate in the lobbying effort and his privately stated opposition to the company's political stand. Novosel contends that the discharge for refusing to lobby the state legislature on the employer's behalf constituted the tort of wrongful discharge on the grounds it was willful, arbitrary, malicious and in bad faith, and that it was contrary to public policy. [The District Court dismissed the complaint, and this appeal followed.]

The circumstances of the discharge presented by Novosel fall squarely within the range of activity embraced by the emerging tort case law. As one commentator has written:

> The factual pattern alleged in these cases seldom varies. The employee objects to work that the employee believes is violative of state or federal law or otherwise improper; the employee protests to his employer that the work should not be performed; the employee expresses his intention not to assist the employer in the furtherance of such work and/or engages in "self-help" activity outside the work place to halt the work; and the employer discharges the employee for refusal to work or incompatibility with management.

Olsen, *Wrongful Discharge Claims Raised by At Will Employees: A New Legal Concern for Employers*, 32 LAB. L.J. 265, 276 (1981). In a landmark opinion, the Pennsylvania Supreme Court acknowledged that such a situation could give rise to a legal cause of action:

It may be granted that there are areas of an employee's life in which his employer has no legitimate interest. An intrusion into one of these areas by virtue of the employer's power of discharge might plausibly give rise to a cause of action, particularly where some recognized facet of public policy is threatened. The notion that substantive due process elevates an employer's privilege of hiring and discharging his employees to an absolute constitutional right has long since been discredited.

Geary v. United States Steel Corp., 319 A.2d 174, 180 (Pa. 1974). Under the particular facts of *Geary*, the court held:

[T]his case does not require us to define in comprehensive fashion the perimeters of this privilege [to employ-at-will], and we decline to do so. We hold only that where the complaint itself discloses a plausible and legitimate reason for terminating an at-will employment relationship and no clear mandate of public policy is violated thereby, an employee at will has no right of action against his employer for wrongful discharge.

319 A.2d at 180.

Applying the logic of *Geary*, we find that Pennsylvania law permits a cause of action for wrongful discharge where the employment termination abridges a significant and recognized public policy. The district court did not consider the question whether an averment of discharge for refusing to support the employer's lobbying efforts is sufficiently violative of such public policy as to state a cause of action. Nationwide, however, now proposes that "the only prohibition on the termination of an employee is that the termination cannot violate a *statutorily* recognized public policy," Brief of Appellee at 5 (emphasis added).

This Court has recognized that the "only Pennsylvania cases applying public policy exceptions have done so where no statutory remedies were available." *Bruffett* [*v. Warner Communications, Inc.*, 692 F.2d 910 (3d Cir. 1982)] at 919. . . . Given that there are no statutory remedies available in the present case and taking into consideration the importance of the political and associational freedoms of the federal and state Constitutions, the absence of a statutory declaration of public policy would appear to be no bar to the existence of a cause of action. Accordingly, a cognizable expression of public policy may be derived in this case from either the First Amendment of the United States Constitution or Article I, Section 7 of the Pennsylvania Constitution.

The key question in considering the tort claim is therefore whether a discharge for disagreement with the employer's legislative agenda or a refusal to lobby the state legislature on the employer's behalf sufficiently implicate a recognized facet of public policy. The definition of a "clearly mandated public policy" as one that "strikes at the heart of a citizen's social right, duties and responsibilities," set forth in *Palmateer v. International Harvester Co.*, 421 N.E.2d 876 (Ill. 1981), appears to provide a workable standard for the tort action. While no Pennsylvania law directly addresses the public policy question at bar, the protection of an employee's freedom of political expression would appear to involve no less compelling a societal interest than the fulfillment of jury service or the filing of a workers' compensation claim.

An extensive case law has developed concerning the protection of constitutional rights, particularly First Amendment rights, of government employees. As the Supreme Court has commented, "[f]or most of this century, the unchallenged dogma was that a public employee had no right to object to conditions placed upon the terms of employment — including those which restricted the exercise of constitutional rights." *Connick v. Myers*, 461 U.S. 138, 143 (1983). The Court in *Connick*, however, also observed the constitutional repudiation of this dogma: "[f]or at least 15 years, it has been settled that a state cannot condition public employment on a basis that infringes the employee's constitutionally protected interest in freedom of expression." *Id.* at 1687, *citing Branti v. Finkel*, 445 U.S. 507, 515-516 (1980); *Perry v. Sindermann*, 408 U.S. 593, 597 (1972); *Pickering v. Board of Education*, 391 U.S. 563 (1968); *Keyishian v. Board of Regents*, 385 U.S. 589, 605-606 (1967) . . . . Thus, there can no longer be any doubt that speech on public issues "has always rested on the highest rung of the hierarchy of First Amendment values." *NAACP v. Claiborne Hardware Co.*, 458 U.S. 886 (1982), *quoting Carey v. Brown*, 447 U.S. 455, 467 (1980).[7]

In striking down the use of patronage appointments for federal government employees, the Court further noted that one of its goals was to insure that "employees themselves are to be sufficiently free from improper influences." *CSC v. Letter Carriers*, 413 U.S. 548, 564 (1973). It was not, however, simply the abuse of state authority over public employees that fueled the Court's concern over patronage political appointments; no less central is the fear that the political process would be irremediably distorted. If employers such as federal, state or municipal governments are allowed coercive control of the scope and direction of employee political activities, it is argued, their influence will be geometrically enhanced at the expense of both the individual rights of the employees and the ability of the lone political actor to be effectively heard. . . .

Although Novosel is not a government employee, the public employee cases do not confine themselves to the narrow question of state action. Rather, these cases suggest that an important public policy is in fact implicated wherever the power to hire and fire is utilized to dictate the terms of employee political activities. In dealing with public employees, the cause of action arises directly from the Constitution rather than from common law developments. The protection of important political freedoms, however, goes well beyond the question whether the threat comes from state or private bodies. The inquiry before us is whether the concern for the rights of political expression and association which animated the public employee cases is sufficient to state a public policy under Pennsylvania law. While there are no Pennsylvania cases squarely on this point, we believe that the clear direction of the opinions promulgated by the state's courts suggests that this question be answered in the affirmative.

---

[7] Nor can there be any doubt that the right to petition or not petition the legislature is incorporated within protected speech on public issues. Thus, for example, in limiting the scope of the Sherman Act, the Supreme Court declared, "[t]he right of petition is one of the freedoms protected by the Bill of Rights, and we cannot, of course, lightly impute to Congress an intent to invade these freedoms." *Eastern RR Presidents' Conference v. Noerr Motor Freight, Inc.*, 365 U.S. 127, 138 (1961).

Having concluded thereby that an important public policy is at stake, we now hold that Novosel's allegations state a claim within the ambit of *Geary* in that Novosel's complaint discloses no plausible and legitimate reason for terminating his employment, and his discharge violates a clear mandate of public policy. The Pennsylvania Supreme Court's rulings . . . are thus interpreted to extend to a non-constitutional claim where a corporation conditions employment upon political subordination. This is not the first judicial recognition of the relationship between economic power and the political process:

> [T]he special status of corporations has placed them in a position to control vast amounts of economic power which may, if not regulated, dominate not only the economy but also the very heart of our democracy, the electoral process. . . . [The desired end] is not one of equalizing the resources of opposing candidates or opposing positions, but rather of preventing institutions which have been permitted to amass wealth as a result of special advantages extended by the State for certain economic purposes from using that wealth to acquire an unfair advantage in the political process. . . .

First National Bank of Boston v. Bellotti, 435 U.S. 765, 809 (1978) (White, J., dissenting).[9]

[O]n remand the district court should employ the four part inquiry the [Pennsylvania Supreme Court] derived from *Connick* and *Pickering*:

1. Whether, because of the speech, the employer is prevented from efficiently carrying out its responsibilities;

2. Whether the speech impairs the employee's ability to carry out his own responsibilities;

3. Whether the speech interferes with essential and close working relationships;

4. Whether the manner, time and place in which the speech occurs interferes with business operations.

Sacks [v. Commonwealth of Pennsylvania, Department of Public Welfare, 465 A.2d 981 (Pa. Sup. Ct. 1983)], at 988.

In weighing these issues, a court should employ the balancing test factors set forth for wrongful discharge cases by the Pennsylvania Superior Court in *Yaindl [v. Ingersoll-Rand Co.*, 422 A.2d 611 (Pa. Super. Ct. 1980)]:

---

[9] The district court relies heavily upon the majority opinion in *Bellotti* to support the proposition that so long as an employer's actions were "in furtherance of its normal and ordinary business interests," its political activities are beyond our scrutiny. By extending constitutional protection to corporate political activity, the district court precludes any common law tort claim. In our view, this reliance on *Bellotti* obscures the fact that there are two distinct issues present here: 1) whether a corporation may engage in the type of lobbying demonstrated by defendant; and 2) whether the economic power of such corporations (in this case the power to discharge) may be utilized to coerce individual employee assistance to the corporate political agenda. Although *Bellotti* does find that corporate speech is entitled to First Amendment protection, the opinion does not stand for the proposition that corporations in the political arena can neither do any wrong nor be regulated. . . . At the very least, it does not follow from *Bellotti* that the right of political expression of a corporation enjoys a transcendent constitutional position regardless of other societal or constitutional interests.

(a)   the nature of the actor's conduct,

(b)   the actor's motive,

(c)   the interests of the other with which the actor's conduct interferes,

(d)   the interests sought to be advanced by the actor,

(e)   the social interests in protecting the freedom of action of the actor and the contractual interests of the other,

(f)   the proximity or remoteness of the actor's conduct to the interference, and

(g)   the relations between the parties.

. . . .

Statement of Judge Becker sur the Denial of the Petition for Rehearing

Because this is a diversity case, the holding of the panel constitutes a mere prediction of the likely course of Pennsylvania law, one subject to revision by the Pennsylvania Supreme Court or the Pennsylvania General Assembly. While this fact would ordinarily render en banc consideration inappropriate, I nonetheless believe that the panel's decision is sufficiently important and sufficiently questionable to call for reconsideration by the en banc Court. . . .

My concern is that the panel has announced an extremely broad "public policy" exception to the law of at-will employment in Pennsylvania that threatens to engulf or "overrule" the holding of the Pennsylvania Supreme Court in *Geary v. U.S. Steel Corp.*, 319 A.2d 174 (Pa. 1974) — an action Pennsylvania itself has apparently shown no inclination to undertake. More specifically, I have three major problems with the panel opinion.

First, the opinion ignores the state action requirement of first amendment jurisprudence, particularly by its repeated, and, in my view, inappropriate citation of public employee cases, and by its implicit assumption that a public policy against government interference with free speech may be readily extended to private actors in voluntary association with another. Second, the opinion could be read to suggest that an explicit contractual provision authorizing an employer to dismiss a lobbyist for failure to undertake lobbying might be unenforceable or subject to a balancing test. Third, the opinion fails to consider other public policy interests, such as the economic interests of the public in efficient corporate performance, the first amendment interests of corporations, and the legitimate interests of a corporation in commanding the loyalty of its employees to pursue its economic well being.

NOTES

1. *Distorting the Legislative Process.* Is the problem with Nationwide's policy that it uses its power at the workplace to magnify its clout with the legislature "artificially"? Is this a third-party cost of at-will employment worthy of regulation by the tort system? And does it matter whether the employee's central job duties involve speaking for the employer? In *Korb v.*

Raytheon Corp., 574 N.E.2d 370 (Mass. 1991), a defense-contractor executive in charge of Washington operations was fired for criticizing increased defense spending at a news conference. The court rejected a claim that the firing interfered with his right to express himself, determining that his statements were directly contrary to the company's financial interests.

2. *The Public-Sector Analogy.* Judge Becker's complaint about relying on public-sector values in deciding private-employment claims is a familiar one, and courts are typically cautious about doing so. But consider the argument of Professor Issacharoff, who finds it natural that public-employment principles will influence private-employment common law:

> One of the key sources for modern developments in employment law has been the public sector, where the Bill of Rights provides a built-in general presumption against parity for relations between the citizenry and the state. Once constitutional doctrine jettisoned the strict rights/ privileges distinction and recognized entitlements to certain state benefits, public employment became a natural arena for the pioneering of substantive claims to employment rights. Since the 1960s, the public sector has been the source of dramatic expansions in employee rights to free expression, due process, and privacy.

> Weiler's discussion of the developing common law of wrongful termination overlooks the dramatic expansion of public-sector employment and the critical role that public-sector litigation has played in the development of the common law. Given that only recently has a subject denominated "employment law" emerged independent of "labor law," it is perhaps to be expected that commentators such as Weiler view the common law developments through the comparative prism of union-based labor law.

> If we return to the premise of the NLRA, however, the increased impact of the public sector fits with the expectation that the terms and conditions of employment set in the dominant economic sectors would spill over into the rest of the labor market. The public sector has come to rival, if not surpass, the private union sector in setting the terms and conditions of the current labor market. The proportion of the work force employed by government is roughly equal to the union sector. In addition, a substantial number of unionized employees are currently in the public sector, which has a unionization rate almost three times that of the private sector. The relative weight of public sector employment is even greater among professional and managerial employees, precisely the group most likely to initiate private wrongful-discharge claims. Thus, it is not surprising that courts seeking to redress wrongful-discharge claims routinely look to the public sector cases for guidance. . . .

> Unfortunately, reference to the public sector case law further exposes the limitations of the current common law developments. Although the public sector cases have developed a doctrinal overview based on the establishment of enforceable property rights for tenured employees, no equivalent development has taken hold in the common law cases. The defining feature of the common law retrenchment on

employment at will has been the use of tort and contract doctrines that define employee rights only transactionally, in relation to what a particular employer said or did or promised.

Samuel Issacharoff, *Reconstructing Employment*, 104 HARV. L. REV. 607, 616-17 (1990)* (reviewing PAUL C. WEILER, GOVERNING THE WORKPLACE (1990)).

3. *Local Office for Private-Sector Workers.* Suppose an employee decides to run for local office. Can the employer terminate him? In *Davis v. Louisiana Computing Corp.*, 394 So. 2d 678 (La. Ct. App. 1981), the court upheld a $24,000 jury verdict against a computer company, whose major clients were local governmental agencies, when it fired an employee for becoming a candidate for city council. The court recognized that the "candidacy would antagonize persons who could withdraw business from plaintiff's employer," but found the employee protected by a state statute that prohibited employers with more than twenty employees from preventing any employee from engaging in politics or becoming a candidate for public office. Should the type of job the employee performs be a consideration? What if a newspaper reporter covering the local government decides to run for city council?

The New Mexico Supreme Court was less sympathetic to a private-sector worker fired after being elected as (part-time) mayor. In *Shovelin v. Central New Mexico Electric Coop.*, 850 P.2d 996 (N.M. 1993), the court rejected a retaliatory-discharge claim, finding no violation of a "clear mandate of public policy." The court specifically declined to follow the approach of *Novosel*, declaring that "we have not found a single case adopting or endorsing the public policy recognized in *Novosel*."

TIMEKEEPING SYSTEMS, INC.
National Labor Relations Board
323 NLRB 244 (1997)

By CHAIRMAN GOULD and MEMBERS BROWNING and FOX.

On November 12, 1996, Administrative Law Judge Bernard Ries issued the attached decision. . . . The Board has considered the decision and the record in light of the exceptions and briefs and has decided to affirm the judge's rulings, findings, and conclusions and to adopt the recommended Order as modified. . . .

The sole issue presented is whether Respondent discharged Lawrence Leinweber on December 5, 1995, because of his protected concerted activities and therefore violated Section 8(a)(1) of the [National Labor Relations] Act. . . .

I. *The Facts*

Respondent is a small Cleveland, Ohio company which manufactures data collection products. The chief operational officer of Respondent is Barry Markwitz. . . . Larry Leinweber, the Charging Party, 1 of about 23 employees

---

located in two buildings, was hired by Respondent in April 1995 as a "software engineer" who prepared computer programs.

On December 1, Markwitz sent a message to all of Respondent's employees by electronic mail ("e-mail") regarding "proposed plans" for an incentive based bonus system (as to which employees were told to "reply with your comments or stop by to see me. A response to this is required.") and changes in vacation policy ("Your comments are welcome, but not required"). The incorporated memorandum regarding the proposed vacation policy changes, which are our only concern here, stated prefatorily, "Please give me your comments (send me an e-mail or stop in and talk to me) by Tuesday, 12/5." The particular suggested policy changes in which we are interested were to close the offices on December 23 and reopen on January 2 and to adjust the number of paid days off over a 5-year period, the effect of which, Markwitz asserted, was that the employees "actually get more days off each year, compared to our present system."

Markwitz received a number of employee responses regarding his vacation proposals, including one on December 1, by e-mail, from Leinweber. Leinweber's response demonstrated that, in fact, the change referred to above would result in the same number of vacation days per year, and less flexibility as to their use. On December 4, Leinweber, having checked his calculations over the weekend, discovered a minor error, and notified Markwitz by e-mail.

Markwitz did not reply to Leinweber's communications. On December 5, Tom Dutton, a member of the engineering team, sent an e-mail to Markwitz, with copies to other engineering team members (which would include Leinweber), reading, "In response to the proposed vacation plan, I have only one word, GREAT!" Promptly, Leinweber, according to his credible testimony, sent an e-mail to Dutton telling him that the proposed policy did not, in fact, redound to the advantage of the employees.

Also on December 5, Leinweber sent a lengthy e-mail message to all employees, including Markwitz. The message spelled out in detail Leinweber's calculations regarding the result of the proposed vacation policy change. It contained, as well, some flippant and rather grating language.

The salutation was "Greetings Fellow Traveler." In his initial remarks, Leinweber wrote, "The closing statement in Barry's memo: 'The effect of this is that you actually get more days off each year, compared to our present system,' will be proven false." This declaration is reiterated in the final thought of the memo: "Thus, the closing statement in Barry's memo . . . is proven false." The paragraph preceding that statement reads, "Assuming anyone actually cares about the company and being productive on the job, if Christmas falls on Tuesday or Wednesday (*sic*) as it will in 1996 and 1997, respectively, two work weeks of one and two days each will be produced by the proposed plan, and I wouldn't expect these to be any more productive than the fragmented weeks that they replace." In closing, Leinweber asked that the recipient "please send errata to the (*sic*) Larry."

Also on December 5, after reading the e-mail message from Leinweber, Dutton e-mailed again to Markwitz, and also the engineering team (as shown on the e-mail address), saying in part, "After reading Larry's E-mail(s) of this date[,] I realized I had made a mistake in calculating the vacation days and wish to change my comment from 'GREAT' to 'Not so Great' on the proposed vacation policy." Dutton also noted in his message that the proposals had "generated more E-mail than any other plan in the company."

At the hearing, Markwitz at first admitted that he was "angry that Mr. Leinweber sent his e-mail messages to all employees." He prepared on December 5 a memorandum to Leinweber which was conveyed to him by the engineering team leader. The memo stated that Markwitz was "saddened and disappointed" by Leinweber's e-mail, which was "inappropriate and intentionally provocative" and beneath "someone as talented and intelligent as you are." Markwitz then wrote:

> Our employment manual states: "Certain actions or types of behavior may result in immediate dismissal. These include, but are not limited to: Failure to treat others with courtesy and respect."

Markwitz went on to "direct" Leinweber to write him, by 5 p.m. that day: "In light of the above, why this e-mail message was inappropriate. How sending an e-mail message like this hurts the company. How this matter should have been handled."

Markwitz continued: "If your response is acceptable to me, you will post it by e-mail today to those who received your other message. If you decline to do so, or if your response is unacceptable to me, your employment will be terminated immediately. Otherwise, your employment will continue on a probationary basis for six months, during which time your employment may be terminated at any time and for any reason. Larry, I am very disappointed in you."

At the hearing, Markwitz testified that what upset him about the document was its "tone": it was a "slap in the face" of employees with good attitudes and a "personal attack" upon him. [Leinweber was then fired.]

II. *Discussion and Conclusion*

In *Meyers I*, the Board stated the principles applicable to an alleged discharge for protected concerted activity under Section 8(a)(1) of the Act, and *Meyers II* did not purport to change those principles:[9] Once the activity is found to be concerted, an 8(a)(1) violation will be found if, in addition, the employer knew of the concerted nature of the employee's activity, the concerted activity was protected by the Act, and the adverse employment action at issue (*e.g.*, discharge) was motivated by the employee's protected concerted activity.

Leinweber's e-mailings clearly constituted "concerted" activity . . . for the "purpose of mutual aid or protection," as required by Section 7 of the Act. Leinweber's effort to incite the other employees to help him preserve a vacation policy which he believed best served his interests, and perhaps the interests of other employees, unquestionably qualified his communication as

---

[9] *Meyers Industries*, 268 N.L.R.B. 493, 497 (1984), *remanded sub nom. Prill v. NLRB*, 755 N.L.R.B. 941 (D.C. Cir. 1987), *on remand, Meyers Industries*, 281 N.L.R.B. 882 (1986), *aff'd. sub nom. Prill v. NLRB*, 835 F.2d 1481 (D.C. Cir.).

being in pursuit of "mutual aid or protection." While the court in *New River Industries, Inc. v. NLRB*, 945 F.2d 1290 (4th Cir. 1991), may have thought, contrary to the Board, that a sarcastic letter was, in Respondent's words, intended "merely to belittle management," here there is no doubt that Leinweber had a specific objective in mind for which he hoped to elicit "mutual aid." . . .

While I have found that Markwitz was principally aggrieved by the tenor of Leinweber's e-mail and its perceived personal denigration of Markwitz, his December 9 message to employees establishes as well that a component of his anger was caused by the fact that Leinweber had attempted to enlist other employees in his cause. Although the law of "protected concerted activity" does not require the General Counsel to prove that the employer has disciplined an employee because he/she has engaged in concerted activity, but rather only requires that the employer knows that the conduct being disciplined is concerted, the evidence here shows that the concertedness of Leinweber's conduct also very likely infected Markwitz's decision to discharge.[11]

In considering the other elements of a *prima facie* protected concerted activity case, as outlined in *Meyer I* there is obviously no question that Markwitz was aware of the concerted activity, nor any doubt that it played the principal role in Leinweber's discharge.

The final question raised by the Respondent is whether Leinweber's December 5 message was "protected." Some concerted conduct can be expressed in so intolerable a manner as to lose the protection of Section 7. While the legal description of the sort of behavior which withdraws the protection of the Act from concerted activity has varied, *Dreis & Krump Mfg. Co., Inc. v. NLRB*, 544 F.2d 320, 329 (7th Cir. 1976), . . . has often been spotlighted for its statement of the test:

> [C]ommunications occurring during the course of otherwise protected activity remain likewise protected unless found to be 'so violent or of such serious character as to render the employee unfit for further service.'

In applying the foregoing or similar standards, the Board has invoked a forfeiture of the protection of the Act only in cases where the concerted behavior has been truly insubordinate or disruptive of the work process. It has generally been the Board's position that unpleasantries uttered in the course of otherwise protected concerted activity do not strip away the Act's protection. In *Postal Service*, 241 N.L.R.B. 389 (1979), a letter characterizing acting supervisors as "a-holes" was not beyond the pale. In *Harris Corp.*, 269 N.L.R.B. 733 (1984), a letter describing management with such words as "hypocritical," "despotic," and "tyrannical" was not disqualifying, despite its "boorish, ill-bred, and hostile tone." In *Churchill's Restaurant*, 276 N.L.R.B. 775 (1985), where an employer discharged an employee who, he believed, was

---

[11] I note that Respondent's employee manual lists as a ground for discharge "Discussing your rate of pay or your compensation arrangement with another employee." This would normally constitute an unfair labor practice, *see, e.g., Radisson Plaza Minneapolis*, 307 N.L.R.B. 94 (1992); *Heck's, Inc.*, 293 N.L.R.B. 1111, 1113 (1989). However, the complaint contains no such allegation and the General Counsel has not, on brief, sought a finding based on this statement. I shall therefore not address the matter further.

saying that the employer was "prejudiced," which the latter considered an "insult," the remarks were held not "so offensive as to threaten plant discipline." A statement to other employees that the chief executive officer was a "cheap son of a bitch" was considered to be protected concerted activity in *Groves Truck & Trailer*, 281 N.L.R.B. 1194, 1195 (1986).

The question of the protected nature of Leinweber's activity is controlled by the latter line of precedents. It is clear from Markwitz's correspondence and testimony that his ultimate decision to discharge Leinweber was based on two aspects of Leinweber's conduct. The major reason was the tone of the letter and the specific remarks about Markwitz. As I have noted previously, it is also evident that Markwitz was displeased by the fact that Weber had communicated the message to the other employees,[13] and that concern entwined with and aggravated, in Markwitz's mind, the first reaction.

Markwitz, like any other employer, wants a friction free working environment. But, as the court of appeals pointed out in *Thor Power Tool*, Section 7 activity may acceptably be accompanied by some "impropriety." And, in *Dreis & Krump Mfg. Co.*, the court of appeals laid down the rather stiff test of whether the questioned activity is "of such serious character as to render the employee unfit for further service." Surely, the words and phrases used by Leinweber in his message were not that egregious. The Leinweber message has arrogant overtones, but the language is less assaultive than the "boorish, ill-bred, and hostile" wording found not to be disqualifying in *Harris Corp.* Indeed, Markwitz was prepared to retain Leinweber if he would submit some sort of apology, which he failed to do. I find that the message itself was not couched in language sufficiently serious to warrant divestment of Section 7 protection. . . .

Finally, although unnecessarily, I address Respondent's contention that "[i]t would be wrong to saddle Respondent for many years into the future with the burden of a reinstated employee the likes of Leinweber." Leinweber is, I concede, a rather unusual person, perhaps one of the new breed of cyberspace pioneers who are attracting public attention, and at the same time — how else can I say it — a bit of a wise guy. Still, in his December 5 e-mail, Markwitz described Leinweber as "talented and intelligent," and he was willing to retain Leinweber after receipt of the offending message if Leinweber would publicly apologize. Markwitz also implored employee Heather Hudson on December 5 to urge Leinweber to write the apology because "he did not want to fire him." I do not gather from this that Markwitz would be totally distraught if he had to rehire Leinweber. In any event, Markwitz's feelings must take second place to the dictates of the statute; the employer who was called a "cheap son-of-a-bitch" by an employee in *Groves Truck & Trailer* was probably not entirely pleased either. . . .

[The Board ordered that Leinweber be reinstated with back pay, and that the company post a notice at its facility explaining the violation found and promising not to violate the National Labor Relations Act again.]

---

[13] As indicated earlier, Markwitz wrote the employees on December 6 that the "right way" to handle a "grievance, or a question, or a comment, or a complaint" was to speak to him or one of the other managers. This statement is itself probably violative of Sec. 8(a)(1), *see* fn. 11, *supra*, but, for the reasons there given, I will not consider the issue further. . . .

NOTES

1. *Denouement of Leinweber.* Leinweber accepted his back pay but refused reinstatement. Despite his legal vindication, Leinweber declared in an interview with the Wall Street Journal, "I'm totally gun-shy about e-mail." Michael J. McCarthy, *Sympathetic Ear: Your Manager's Policy On Employee's E-Mail May Have a Weak Spot*, WALL ST. J., Apr. 25, 2000, at A1.

2. *The NLRA in the Nonunion Workplace.* The National Labor Relations Act is the major statute regulating unions; indeed, the NLRA often is thought to have no relevance to nonunion establishments, except when a union is trying to organize. But § 7 of the NLRA, which defines the rights of employees under the Act, gives employees the right "to engage in other concerted activities for the purpose of . . . other mutual aid or protection." As the *Leinweber* case illustrates, § 7 rights are increasingly being applied to workplaces that have no thought of unionizing.

Professor Morris argues that Congress protects "pre-organizational" concerted activities by employees in part because they could evolve toward more formalized union activity, thus furthering the overall NLRA policy of "encouraging the practice and procedure of collective bargaining." But employees need not have a conscious goal of forming a union in order to be protected:

> In the early organizational stages of the process that Section 7 describes, employees need not be consciously aware that they are engaged in a concerted act. They need only be involved in an act of association, speech, or petition ("petition," in workplace terminology, being essentially the presentation of a grievance) that reasonably relates to "wages, hours, [or] other terms and conditions of employment." It is important, however, that the employer must not have unreasonably interfered with or denied their opportunity to engage in such activity. If equality of organizational power is to have a meaning consistent with the policy of the statute, then it follows that Section 7 guarantees (1) that employees will have the right to confer among themselves about any of the foregoing matters; (2) that several employees may each voice a common concern about such matters and thereby impliedly engage in concerted activity; (3) that a single employee has the right to turn to one or more fellow employees to seek mutual aid or protection as to such matters; and (4) that a single employee has the right to attempt to initiate an action or seek support, for the benefit of the employees as a group, with respect to such matters, regardless of whether she or he is ultimately successful in that endeavor. The only restrictions the employer should be able to place on such conduct are those for which there are "legitimate and substantial business justifications."

Charles J. Morris, *NLRB Protection in the Nonunion Workplace: A Glimpse at a General Theory of Section 7 Conduct*, 137 U. PENN. L. REV. 1673, 1701-02 (1989).

3. *Protected Concerted Activities.* Three inquiries must be satisfied before the NLRA will protect an employee's action.

(1) *Concerted*. The NLRA protects only group activities. Activities by an individual employee solely on his or her own behalf are not covered. In *Meyers I* and *II*, the NLRB held that a truck driver in a nonunion plant who refused to drive his vehicle and who complained to a state regulatory agency about allegedly unsafe brakes was not engaged in concerted activity. The Board in *Meyers II* emphasized that concerted activity "encompasses those circumstances where individual employees seek to initiate or to induce or to prepare for group action, as well as individual employees bringing truly group complaints to the attention of management." But the Board held that invocation of a safety statute cannot be regarded as an extension of concerted activity in any realistic sense. The Board in the *Meyers* cases distinguished *NLRB v. City Disposal System*, 465 U.S. 104 (1984), where the Supreme Court found that a unionized truck driver who refused to drive because of faulty brakes was engaged in concerted activity, because the collective-bargaining agreement entitled workers to refuse to operate unsafe equipment. The *Meyers II* Board declared that "invocation of employee contract rights is a continuation of an ongoing process of employee concerted activity, whereas employee invocation of statutory rights is not. We believe that we best effectuate the policies of the Act when we focus our resources on the protection of actions taken pursuant to that process."

(2) *Work-Related Object*. The action must be for mutual aid or protection reasonably related to wages, hours, and other terms and conditions of employment. In *Eastex, Inc. v. NLRB*, 437 U.S. 556 (1978), the Supreme Court gave a broad reading to the phrase. An employer refused to permit employees to circulate a union newsletter on company property during nonworking time that included material criticizing a presidential veto of a minimum-wage increase and urging employees to oppose a right-to-work provision in the state constitution. The Supreme Court found this to be an unfair labor practice because the newsletter was for "mutual aid or protection," even though the subject matter was outside the employer's immediate control. The union status of the workers appeared to be irrelevant to the decision.

(3) *Protected*. Even if the employees' act is concerted activity for work-related mutual aid or protection, it may still be unprotected if it is unlawful, violent, in breach of contract, or indefensible. The classic case finding indefensible conduct is *NLRB v. IBEW Local 1129 (Jefferson Standard Broadcasting Co.)*, 346 U.S. 464 (1953), where employees, without referring to an on-going dispute with the union, distributed handbills in the off-hours to the public that disparaged the company's product. *See generally* Calvin William Sharpe, *"By Any Means Necessary": Unprotected Conduct and Decisional Discretion Under the National Labor Relations Act*, 20 BERKELEY J. EMP. & LAB. L. 203 (1999).

The protected-activity requirement still bites workers. In *Endicott Interconnect Technologies, Inc. v. NLRB*, 453 F.3d 532 (D.C. Cir. 2006), IBM had sold a computer circuit-board manufacturing facility to EIT, which promptly laid off ten percent of its workforce. Employee Richard White was fired after being quoted in the local newspaper saying that the layoffs created "gaping holes in this business, because development and support people with specific knowledge of unique process were let go, leaving voids in the critical knowledge base for the highly technical business," and later attacking the EIT owner in an internet posting urging that EIT recognize the union, saying that the owner lacked "good ability to manage" EIT, was causing the business to be "tanked," and was going to "put it into the dirt." The NLRB General Counsel filed a complaint and the Board found a violation, but the D.C. Circuit held the Board had misapplied *Jefferson Standard.* The court found the employee's comments so obviously damaging and disloyal that the employer had good reason to terminate the employee, and the NLRB could not reasonably find the actions to be protected.

4. *Pluses and Minuses of NLRA Protection.* Invoking NLRA protection has both benefits and drawbacks. The General Counsel investigates the charge and decides whether to issue a complaint, so the employee does not have to pay for a private lawyer but also loses control of the litigation. In addition, remedies under the NLRA are more limited than in tort suits over public policy, generally only reinstatement with back pay. Finally, because the NLRA preempts state law, employers may have a defense to a retaliatory-discharge tort claim if it involves concerted action or a collective-bargaining agreement. *See Allis-Chalmers Corp. v. Lueck,* 471 U.S. 202 (1985) (state tort claim preempted where resolution depends on analysis of terms of a collective-bargaining agreement). *But see Lingle v. Norge Div. of Magic Chef, Inc.,* 486 U.S. 399 (1988) (state public-policy tort claim not preempted where resolution does not depend on interpretation of collective-bargaining agreement).

Chapter 9

EMPLOYEE PRIVACY RIGHTS ON AND OFF THE JOB

In this chapter, we look at general privacy claims of workers. Section A begins with on-the-job privacy claims that employers should not monitor some aspect of the workplace. Section B looks at off-work privacy claims of workers. Section C examines privacy claims surrounding drug testing, and Section D looks at privacy claims for honesty testing and other types of screening.

A. ON-THE-JOB PRIVACY CLAIMS

O'CONNOR v. ORTEGA
Supreme Court of the United States
480 U.S. 709 (1987)

O'CONNOR, J., announced the judgment of the Court and delivered an opinion in which REHNQUIST, C.J., and WHITE and POWELL, J.J., joined.

I

Dr. Magno Ortega, a physician and psychiatrist, held the position of Chief of Professional Education at Napa State Hospital (Hospital) for 17 years, until his dismissal from that position in 1981. As Chief of Professional Education, Dr. Ortega had primary responsibility for training young physicians in psychiatric residency programs.

In July 1981, Hospital officials, including Dr. Dennis O'Connor, the Executive Director of the Hospital, became concerned about possible improprieties in Dr. Ortega's management of the residency program. In particular, the Hospital officials were concerned with Dr. Ortega's acquisition of an Apple II computer for use in the residency program. The officials thought that Dr. Ortega may have misled Dr. O'Connor into believing that the computer had been donated, when in fact the computer had been financed by the possibly coerced contributions of residents. Additionally, the Hospital officials were concerned with charges that Dr. Ortega had sexually harassed two female Hospital employees, and had taken inappropriate disciplinary action against a resident.

On July 30, 1981, Dr. O'Connor requested that Dr. Ortega take paid administrative leave during an investigation of these charges. . . .

Dr. O'Connor selected several Hospital personnel to conduct the investigation, including an accountant, a physician, and a Hospital security officer. Richard Friday, the Hospital Administrator, led this "investigative team." At some point during the investigation, Mr. Friday made the decision to enter

Dr. Ortega's office. The specific reason for the entry into Dr. Ortega's office is unclear from the record. The petitioners claim that the search was conducted to secure state property. Initially, petitioners contended that such a search was pursuant to a Hospital policy of conducting a routine inventory of state property in the office of a terminated employee. At the time of the search, however, the Hospital had not yet terminated Dr. Ortega's employment; Dr. Ortega was still on administrative leave. Apparently, there was no policy of inventorying the offices of those on administrative leave. Before the search had been initiated, however, petitioners had become aware that Dr. Ortega had taken the computer to his home. Dr. Ortega contends that the purpose of the search was to secure evidence for use against him in administrative disciplinary proceedings.

The resulting search of Dr. Ortega's office was quite thorough. The investigators entered the office a number of times and seized several items from Dr. Ortega's desk and file cabinets, including a Valentine's Day card, a photograph, and a book of poetry all sent to Dr. Ortega by a former resident physician. These items were later used in a proceeding before a hearing officer of the California State Personnel Board to impeach the credibility of the former resident, who testified on Dr. Ortega's behalf. The investigators also seized billing documentation of one of Dr. Ortega's private patients under the California Medicaid program. The investigators did not otherwise separate Dr. Ortega's property from state property because, as one investigator testified, "[t]rying to sort State from non-State, it was too much to do, so I gave it up and boxed it up." Thus, no formal inventory of the property in the office was ever made. Instead, all the papers in Dr. Ortega's office were merely placed in boxes, and put in storage for Dr. Ortega to retrieve.

Dr. Ortega commenced this action against petitioners in Federal District Court under 42 U.S.C. § 1983, alleging that the search of his office violated the Fourth Amendment. . . .

II

The strictures of the Fourth Amendment, applied to the States through the Fourteenth Amendment, have been applied to the conduct of governmental officials in various civil activities. . . . Searches and seizures by government employers or supervisors of the private property of their employees, therefore, are subject to the restraints of the Fourth Amendment.

The Fourth Amendment protects the "right of the people to be secure in their persons, houses, papers, and effects, against unreasonable searches and seizures. . . ." Our cases establish that Dr. Ortega's Fourth Amendment rights are implicated only if the conduct of the Hospital officials at issue in this case infringed "an expectation of privacy that society is prepared to consider reasonable." *United States v. Jacobsen*, 466 U.S. 109, 113 (1984). We have no talisman that determines in all cases those privacy expectations that society is prepared to accept as reasonable. Instead, "the Court has given weight to such factors as the intention of the Framers of the Fourth Amendment, the uses to which the individual has put a location, and our societal understanding that certain areas deserve the most scrupulous protection from government invasion." *Oliver v. United States*, 466 U.S. 170, 178 (1984) (citations omitted).

Because the reasonableness of an expectation of privacy, as well as the appropriate standard for a search, is understood to differ according to context, it is essential first to delineate the boundaries of the workplace context. The workplace includes those areas and items that are related to work and are generally within the employer's control. At a hospital, for example, the hallways, cafeteria, offices, desks, and file cabinets, among other areas, are all part of the workplace. These areas remain part of the workplace context even if the employee has placed personal items in them, such as a photograph placed in a desk or a letter posted on an employee bulletin board.

Not everything that passes through the confines of the business address can be considered part of the workplace context, however. An employee may bring closed luggage to the office prior to leaving on a trip, or a handbag or briefcase each workday. While whatever expectation of privacy the employee has in the existence and the outward appearance of the luggage is affected by its presence in the workplace, the employee's expectation of privacy in the contents of the luggage is not affected in the same way. The appropriate standard for a workplace search does not necessarily apply to a piece of closed personal luggage, a handbag or a briefcase that happens to be within the employer's business address.

Within the workplace context, this Court has recognized that employees may have a reasonable expectation of privacy against intrusions by police. As with the expectation of privacy in one's home, such an expectation in one's place of work is "based upon societal expectations that have deep roots in the history of the Amendment." *Oliver v. United States*, *supra*, 466 U.S., at 178, n. 8.

Given the societal expectations of privacy in one's place of work . . . we reject the contention made by the Solicitor General and petitioners that public employees can never have a reasonable expectation of privacy in their place of work. Individuals do not lose Fourth Amendment rights merely because they work for the government instead of a private employer. The operational realities of the workplace, however, may make some employees' expectations of privacy unreasonable when an intrusion is by a supervisor rather than a law enforcement official. Public employees' expectations of privacy in their offices, desks, and file cabinets, like similar expectations of employees in the private sector, may be reduced by virtue of actual office practices and procedures, or by legitimate regulation. . . . The employee's expectation of privacy must be assessed in the context of the employment relation. An office is seldom a private enclave free from entry by supervisors, other employees, and business and personal invitees. Instead, in many cases offices are continually entered by fellow employees and other visitors during the workday for conferences, consultations, and other work-related visits. Simply put, it is the nature of government offices that others — such as fellow employees, supervisors, consensual visitors, and the general public — may have frequent access to an individual's office. . . . Given the great variety of work environments in the public sector, the question whether an employee has a reasonable expectation of privacy must be addressed on a case-by-case basis.

The Court of Appeals concluded that Dr. Ortega had a reasonable expectation of privacy in his office, and five Members of this Court agree with that determination. . . . Because the record does not reveal the extent to which Hospital officials may have had work-related reasons to enter Dr. Ortega's office, we think the Court of Appeals should have remanded the matter to the District Court for its further determination. But regardless of any legitimate right of access the Hospital staff may have had to the office as such, we recognize that the undisputed evidence suggests that Dr. Ortega had a reasonable expectation of privacy in his desk and file cabinets. The undisputed evidence discloses that Dr. Ortega did not share his desk or file cabinets with any other employees. Dr. Ortega had occupied the office for 17 years and he kept materials in his office, which included personal correspondence, medical files, correspondence from private patients unconnected to the Hospital, personal financial records, teaching aids and notes, and personal gifts and mementos. The files on physicians in residency training were kept outside Dr. Ortega's office. Indeed, the only items found by the investigators were apparently personal items because, with the exception of the items seized for use in the administrative hearings, all the papers and effects found in the office were simply placed in boxes and made available to Dr. Ortega. Finally, we note that there was no evidence that the Hospital had established any reasonable regulation or policy discouraging employees such as Dr. Ortega from storing personal papers and effects in their desks or file cabinets, although the absence of such a policy does not create an expectation of privacy where it would not otherwise exist.

On the basis of this undisputed evidence, we accept the conclusion of the Court of Appeals that Dr. Ortega had a reasonable expectation of privacy at least in his desk and file cabinets.

III

Having determined that Dr. Ortega had a reasonable expectation of privacy in his office, the Court of Appeals simply concluded without discussion that the "search . . . was not a reasonable search under the fourth amendment." But as we have stated in *T.L.O.*, "[t]o hold that the Fourth Amendment applies to searches conducted by [public employers] is only to begin the inquiry into the standards governing such searches. . . . [W]hat is reasonable depends on the context within which a search takes place." *New Jersey v. T.L.O.*, 469 U.S. 325, 337 (1985). . . . In the case of searches conducted by a public employer, we must balance the invasion of the employees' legitimate expectations of privacy against the government's need for supervision, control, and the efficient operation of the workplace. . . .

There is surprisingly little case law on the appropriate Fourth Amendment standard of reasonableness for a public employer's work-related search of its employee's offices, desks, or file cabinets. . . .

The legitimate privacy interests of public employees in the private objects they bring to the workplace may be substantial. Against these privacy interests, however, must be balanced the realities of the workplace, which strongly suggest that a warrant requirement would be unworkable. While police, and even administrative enforcement personnel, conduct searches for the primary purpose of obtaining evidence for use in criminal or other enforcement proceedings, employers most frequently need to enter the offices and desks of their employees for legitimate work-related reasons wholly unrelated to illegal conduct. Employers and supervisors are focused primarily on the need to complete the government agency's work in a prompt and efficient manner. An employer may have need for correspondence, or a file or report available only in an employee's office while the employee is away from the office. Or, as is alleged to have been the case here, employers may need to safeguard or identify state property or records in an office in connection with a pending investigation into suspected employee misfeasance.

In our view, requiring an employer to obtain a warrant whenever the employer wished to enter an employee's office, desk, or file cabinets for a work-related purpose would seriously disrupt the routine conduct of business and would be unduly burdensome. Imposing unwieldy warrant procedures in such cases upon supervisors, who would otherwise have no reason to be familiar with such procedures, is simply unreasonable. In contrast to other circumstances in which we have required warrants, supervisors in offices such as at the Hospital are hardly in the business of investigating the violation of criminal laws. Rather, work-related searches are merely incident to the primary business of the agency. . . .

Whether probable cause is an inappropriate standard for public employer searches of their employees' offices presents a more difficult issue. . . .

The governmental interest justifying work-related intrusions by public employers is the efficient and proper operation of the workplace. Government agencies provide myriad services to the public, and the work of these agencies would suffer if employers were required to have probable cause before they entered an employee's desk for the purpose of finding a file or piece of office correspondence. Indeed, it is difficult to give the concept of probable cause, rooted as it is in the criminal investigatory context, much meaning when the purpose of a search is to retrieve a file for work-related reasons. Similarly, the concept of probable cause has little meaning for a routine inventory conducted by public employers for the purpose of securing state property. To ensure the efficient and proper operation of the agency, therefore, public employers must be given wide latitude to enter employee offices for work-related, noninvestigatory reasons.

We come to a similar conclusion for searches conducted pursuant to an investigation of work-related employee misconduct. . . . Public employers have an interest in ensuring that their agencies operate in an effective and efficient manner, and the work of these agencies inevitably suffers from the inefficiency, incompetence, mismanagement, or other work-related misfeasance of its employees. Indeed, in many cases, public employees are entrusted with tremendous responsibility, and the consequences of their misconduct or incompetence to both the agency and the public interest can be severe. In contrast to law enforcement officials, therefore, public employers are not enforcers of the criminal law; instead, public employers have a direct and overriding interest in ensuring that the work of the agency is conducted in a proper and efficient manner. In our view, therefore, a probable cause requirement for searches of the type at issue here would impose intolerable burdens on public employers. The delay in correcting the employee misconduct caused by the need for probable cause rather than reasonable suspicion will be translated into tangible and often irreparable damage to the agency's work, and ultimately to the public interest. . . . It is simply unrealistic to expect supervisors in most government agencies to learn the subtleties of the probable cause standard. . . .

Balanced against the substantial government interests in the efficient and proper operation of the workplace are the privacy interests of government employees in their place of work which, while not insubstantial, are far less than those found at home or in some other contexts. . . . Government offices are provided to employees for the sole purpose of facilitating the work of an agency. The employee may avoid exposing personal belongings at work by simply leaving them at home.

In sum, we conclude that the "special needs, beyond the normal need for law enforcement make the . . . probable-cause requirement impracticable," for legitimate work-related, noninvestigatory intrusions as well as investigations of work-related misconduct. A standard of reasonableness will neither unduly burden the efforts of government employers to ensure the efficient and proper operation of the workplace, nor authorize arbitrary intrusions upon the privacy of public employees. We hold, therefore, that public employer intrusions on the constitutionally protected privacy interests of government employees for noninvestigatory, work-related purposes, as well as for investigations of work-related misconduct, should be judged by the standard of reasonableness under all the circumstances. Under this reasonableness standard, both the inception and the scope of the intrusion must be reasonable.

Ordinarily, a search of an employee's office by a supervisor will be "justified at its inception" when there are reasonable grounds for suspecting that the search will turn up evidence that the employee is guilty of work-related misconduct, or that the search is necessary for a noninvestigatory work-related purpose such as to retrieve a needed file. Because petitioners had an "individualized suspicion" of misconduct by Dr. Ortega, we need not decide whether individualized suspicion is an essential element of the standard of reasonableness that we adopt today. The search will be permissible in its scope when "the measures adopted are reasonably related to the objectives of the search and not excessively intrusive in light of . . . the nature of the [misconduct]." 469 U.S., at 342.

IV

[The] District Court was in error in granting petitioners summary judgment. There was a dispute of fact about the character of the search, and the District Court acted under the erroneous assumption that the search was conducted pursuant to a Hospital policy. Moreover, no findings were made as to the scope of the search that was undertaken.

On remand, therefore, the District Court must determine the justification for the search and seizure, and evaluate the reasonableness of both the inception of the search and its scope.

[The concurring opinion of JUSTICE SCALIA is omitted.]

[The dissenting opinion of JUSTICE BLACKMUN, joined by JUSTICES BRENNAN, MARSHALL, and STEVENS, is omitted.]

NOTES

1. *Ortega on Remand.* On remand, the Ninth Circuit affirmed the trial court's decision that Ortega's Fourth Amendment rights had been violated, holding that the employer's "purely indiscriminate fishing expedition through [Mr. Ortega's] most personal belongings" under the pretense of conducting an inventory of state property clearly exceeded the scope of a reasonable work-related search. *Ortega v. O'Connor*, 146 F.3d 1149, 1159 (9th Cir. 1998).

2. *Government as Employer.* As we saw in Chapter 8 when we considered free-speech and political protections, public employees enjoy constitutional protections not afforded their private-sector counterparts. At the same time, these protections may be weaker when the government acts as employer than when it enforces the criminal law or acts as a regulator.

3. *Reasonable Expectation of Privacy and Criminal Investigations.* The majority opinion in *Ortega* suggests that either the nature of a government employee's privacy interest, the nature of the government's interest when it acts as an employer, or both, justify suspending the usual Fourth-Amendment requirements of warrant and probable cause when the government conducts a search in its capacity as an employer. The employer need only demonstrate reasonable cause for making a noninvestigatory work-related intrusion or a search pursuant to an investigation of employee misconduct. What happens when an investigation of employee misconduct turns into a criminal investigation? In *United States v. Simons*, 29 F. Supp. 2d 324 (E.D. Va. 1998), the employer (the C.I.A.) searched an employee's workplace hard drive when it suspected him of downloading large amounts of pornographic material. Upon discovering the presence of child pornography, the employer entered the employee's office, seized his hard drive, and turned it over to the F.B.I. for a criminal investigation. Defendant argued that when the employer became aware of child pornography, the investigation became criminal in nature and any further search required a warrant. The court held that the CIA had a legitimate workplace interest in continuing the investigation as far as it did, and that "the actions an employer might take in response to an employee's misconduct most likely would differ depending on the magnitude of the employee's misconduct." *Id.* at 328.

K-MART CORP. STORE NO. 7441 v. TROTTI
Court of Appeals of Texas
677 S.W.2d 632 (1984)

Before EVANS, C.J., and COHEN and BULLOCK, JJ.

BULLOCK, JUSTICE.

K-Mart Corporation appeals from a judgment awarding the appellee, Trotti, $8,000.00 in actual damages and $100,000.00 in exemplary damages for invasion of privacy.

We reverse and remand.

The appellee was an employee in the hosiery department at the appellants' store number 7441. Her supervisors had never indicated any dissatisfaction with her work nor any suspicion of her honesty.

The appellants provided their employees with lockers for the storage of personal effects during working hours. There was no assignment of any given locker to any individual employee. The employees could, on request, receive locks for the lockers from the appellants, and if the appellants provided the lock to an employee they would keep either a copy of the lock's combination or a master key for padlocks. Testimony indicated that there was some problem in providing a sufficient number of locks to employees, and, as a result, the store's administrative personnel permitted employees to purchase and use their own locks on the lockers, but in these instances, the appellants did not require the employee to provide the manager with either a combination or duplicate key. The appellee, with appellants' knowledge, used one of these lockers and provided her own combination lock.

On October 31, 1981, the appellee placed her purse in her locker when she arrived for work. She testified that she snapped the lock closed and then pulled on it to make sure it was locked. When she returned to her locker during her afternoon break, she discovered the lock hanging open. Searching through her locker, the appellee further discovered her personal items in her purse in considerable disorder. Nothing was missing from either the locker or the purse. The store manager testified that, in the company of three junior administrators at the store, he had that afternoon searched the lockers because of a suspicion raised by the appellants' security personnel that an unidentified employee, not the appellee, had stolen a watch. The manager and his assistants were also searching for missing price-marking guns. The appellee further testified that, as she left the employee's locker area after discovering her locker open, she heard the manager suggest to his assistants, "Let's get busy again." The manager testified that none of the parties searched through employees' personal effects.

The appellee approached the manager later that day and asked if he had searched employees' lockers and/or her purse. The manager initially denied either kind of search and maintained this denial for approximately one month. At that time, the manager then admitted having searched the employees' lockers and further mentioned that they had, in fact, searched the appellee's purse, later saying that he meant that they had searched only her locker and not her purse.

The manager testified that during the initial hiring interviews, all prospective employees received verbal notification from personnel supervisors that it was the appellants' policy to conduct ingress-egress searches of employees and also to conduct unannounced searches of lockers. A personnel supervisor and an assistant manager, however, testified that, although locker searches did regularly occur, the personnel supervisors did not apprise prospective employees of this policy. . . .

The appellants requested the trial court to define an "invasion of privacy" as "the intentional intrusion upon the solitude or seclusion of another that is highly offensive to a reasonable person." This is the definition enunciated in *Gill v. Snow,* [644 S.W.2d 222 (Tex. Ct. App. 1982)], and in the RESTATE-MENT (SECOND) OF TORTS, Sec. 652B (1977). The court refused to include the part of the requested instruction, ". . . that is highly offensive to a reasonable person." The appellants argue that this refusal constituted an abuse of discretion because the Rules of Civil Procedure require such an instruction. TEX. R. CIV. P. 273 and 277. The appellee alleges that the record establishes that the intrusion was highly offensive as a matter of law, and that, therefore, the instruction was unnecessary. . . .

The definition of "invasion of privacy" that the appellant requested is one widely and repeatedly accepted. Although the Texas Supreme Court has not adopted a verbatim rendition of this definition, it is clear that, in Texas, an actionable invasion of privacy by intrusion must consist of an unjustified intrusion of the plaintiff's solitude or seclusion of such magnitude as to cause an ordinary individual to feel severely offended, humiliated, or outraged.

The appellants correctly point out that no Texas case yet reported has ever declined to include a requirement that the intrusion complained of be highly offensive to a reasonable person, and the appellee agrees with this statement. Nevertheless, the appellee urges that since the facts of this case established the highly objectionable nature of the intrusion as a matter of law, the requested instruction was unnecessary, and thus the trial court properly refused to include it.

We disagree with the appellee's contention. The record does indicate the appellee's outrage upon discovering the appellants' activities but fails to demonstrate that there could be no dispute as to the severity of the offensive-ness of the intrusion, thereby making it impossible for us to conclude that the facts established the disputed portion of the instruction as a matter of law.

Moreover, we note that the result of accepting this contention would be to raise the legal theory of invasion of privacy from the realm of intentional torts into the sphere of strict liability. It would make any wrongful intrusion actionable, requiring a plaintiff to establish merely that the intrusion occurred and that the plaintiff did not consent to it. Because of the stern form of liability which already stems from an invasion of privacy, discussed *infra*, accepting a definition of invasion of privacy which lacked a standard of high offensive-ness would result in fundamentally unfair assessments against defendants who offended unreasonably sensitive plaintiffs, but whose transgressions would not realistically fill either an ordinary person or the general society with any sense of outrage. A business executive, for example, could find himself liable for entering an associate's office without express permission; so could a beautician who opened a co-worker's drawer in order to find some supplies needed for a customer.

We hold that the element of a highly offensive intrusion is a fundamental part of the definition of an invasion of privacy, and that the term "invasion of privacy" is a highly technical, legal term, requiring, under Rule 277, an explanation to the jury. In the instant case, the definition of an invasion of privacy necessarily required the inclusion of the requested standard of offensiveness.

We sustain the appellant's first four points of error, and, since we are ordering a new trial, we find it appropriate to examine the sufficiency of the evidence supporting the jury's finding.

The lockers indisputably were the appellants' property, and in their un-locked state, a jury could reasonably infer that those lockers were subject to legitimate, reasonable searches by the appellants. This would also be true where the employee used a lock provided by the appellants, because in retaining the lock's combination or master key, it could be inferred that the appellants manifested an interest both in maintaining control over the locker and in conducting legitimate, reasonable searches. Where, as in the instant case, however, the employee purchases and uses his own lock on the lockers, with the employer's knowledge, the fact finder is justified in concluding that the employee manifested, and the employer recognized, an expectation that the locker and its contents would be free from intrusion and interference.

In the present case, there is evidence that the appellee locked the locker with her own lock; that when the appellee returned from a break, the lock was lying open; that upon searching her locker, the appellee discovered that someone had rifled her purse; that the appellants' managerial personnel initially denied making the search but subsequently admitted searching her locker and her purse. We find this is far more evidence than a "mere scintilla," and we hold that there is some evidence to support the jury's finding.

. . . We hold that the weight of the evidence indicates that the appellants' employees came upon a locker with a lock provided by an employee, disre-garded the appellee's demonstration of her expectation of privacy, opened and searched the locker, and probably opened and searched her purse as well; and, in so holding, we consider it is immaterial whether the appellee actually securely locked her locker or not. It is sufficient that an employee in this situation, by having placed a lock on the locker at the employee's own expense and with the appellants' consent, has demonstrated a legitimate expectation to a right of privacy in both the locker itself and those personal effects within it. We accordingly overrule appellants' fifth point of error. . . .

The judgment is reversed, and the case is remanded for new trial.

NOTES

1. Rationale for Privacy Claims. The privacy cause of action sounds in tort, but has loud contract or relational overtones. A traditional tort rationale — controlling the third party effects of employer actions — is difficult to find. In *Trotti*, the manager testified that all prospective employees were warned about unannounced searches of lockers. If this testimony were believed, would Trotti have a privacy claim? Would her expectation of privacy be reasonable? If she has no claim, is it because the parties implicitly agreed that their relationship would include unannounced locker searches? Consent is a critical factor in courts' analysis of whether a privacy invasion is actionable. But are there circumstances in which consent should be disregarded? For example, if a person refuses to consent to release of information that he has HIV, should the interests of individuals who have intimate contact with him override his lack of consent? Should interest in protecting the public from the intrusive use of lie detector tests override a particular individual's consent to take a test? For an argument that consent should be balanced against overriding third-party interests, see Steven L. Willborn, *Consenting Employees: Workplace Privacy and the Role of Consent*, 66 LA. L. REV. 975, 992-1001 (2006).

2. *Lockers, Telephones, and Beyond.* Today, employees have potential privacy interests in a wide variety of places at work, in addition to lockers. According to the American Management Association, 76% of major firms in the U.S. monitor workers' website connections, 50% store and review employees' computer files, 55% retain and review employee e-mail messages, and 51% monitor the amount of time employees spend on the phone and track the numbers called. Furthermore, "companies are increasingly putting teeth into technology policies": 26% have fired workers for misusing the internet and 25% have terminated employees for e-mail misuse. AMERICAN MGMT. ASS'N & ePOLICY INST., 2005 WORKPLACE MONITORING AND SURVEILLANCE (2005), *available at* http://www.amanet.org/research/pdfs/EMS_summary05.pdf. Another survey of large U.S. enterprises found that employer concern over litigation is an important part of their motivation in monitoring employee telecommunications activity. More than 25% of enterprises were ordered by a court or regulatory body to produce employee e-mail in the 12 months preceding the survey. PROOFPOINT, OUTBOUND EMAIL AND CONTENT SECURITY IN TODAY'S ENTERPRISE (2006), *available at* http://www.proofpoint.com.

3. *Phone Calls and the Wiretap Act.* Employees sometimes complain that a supervisor has invaded their privacy by listening to private phone calls made at work. While common-law invasion of privacy lawsuits are rare, employees have sought protection from an unlikely sounding source: Title III of the Omnibus Crime Control and Safe Streets Act of 1968, 18 U.S.C. §§ 2510-2520. In the Wiretap Act, as it is more commonly called, Congress focused on law enforcement's battle against organized crime. But the statute more broadly prohibits most electronic surveillance by private persons, including the interception of telephone calls. Employees can bring civil suits to recover actual damages or liquidated damages of the higher of $100 a day or $1,000, plus punitive damages and attorney's fees. Two significant exceptions are (1) when one of the parties to the communication has given express or implied consent to interception, and (2) when the interception occurs "in the ordinary course of . . . business."

Questions often arise about the extent to which employers can listen to or tape employee phone calls. In *Arias v. Mutual Central Alarm Services, Inc.*, 202 F.3d 553 (2d Cir. 2000), for example, the employer recorded all telephone calls at the office. The employees complained about the invasion of their privacy and filed suit under the Omnibus Crime Control Act, but the court rejected the claim. It held that the blanket recording of all telephone calls fell within the ordinary course of business exception because the alarm company received sensitive security information and such practices are standard within the industry.

Employees are more successful when the employer cannot show a legitimate business reason for listening to the employee's phone conversation. For example, suppose the employer monitors an employee's incoming call during lunch when she speaks with a friend about interviewing for another job. Does the statute forbid the employer from listening in on this call? In *Watkins v. L.M. Berry & Co.*, 704 F.2d 577 (11th Cir. 1983), the court reversed a summary judgment for the employer on these facts. The court recognized that the employer had a business interest in learning that an employee might quit, but declared that "[t]he phrase 'in the ordinary course of business' cannot be expanded to mean anything that interests a company." The court held:

> [A] personal call may not be intercepted in the ordinary course of business under the exemption in section 2510(5)(a)(i), except to the extent necessary to guard against unauthorized use of the telephone or to determine whether a call is personal or not. In other words, a personal call may be intercepted in the ordinary course of business to determine its nature but never its contents.

Id. at 583.

Sometimes it is difficult to distinguish a call in which the employer has a legitimate business interest from one that is personal in nature. In *Fischer v. Mt. Olive Lutheran Church, Inc.*, 207 F. Supp. 2d 914 (W.D. Wis. 2002), a church receptionist inadvertently intercepted a sexually graphic phone conversation between the church's youth minister and an adult male. The conversation included references to the parties having sex with each other. The receptionist alerted others, who then also listened in on the call. When the minister later sued the church under the Wiretap Act, the church argued that the interception fell within the ordinary course of business exception because the minister's job description included counseling youth and adult members of the congregation, and the contents of the conversation raised concerns about possible church liability for improper contact between an employee and a minor. The court dismissed the employer's motion for summary judgment, holding that the receptionist and other employees ought to have hung up the phone immediately upon determining that the minister's conversation was with an adult and personal in nature.

4. Electronic Communications. In 1986, Congress passed an amendment to the Wiretap Act, the Electronic Communications Privacy Act (ECPA). Title I of the ECPA bans the interception or disclosure of electronic communications. Title II of the statute, the Stored Communications Act, regulates access to stored wire and electronic communications and transaction records.

Interpreting the ECPA in light of the Internet, which was created after passage of the statute, has been very complex.

KONOP v. HAWAIIAN AIRLINES, INC.
United States Court of Appeals, Ninth Circuit
302 F.3d 868 (2002)

BOOCHEVER, CIRCUIT JUDGE:

Konop, a pilot for Hawaiian, created and maintained a website where he posted bulletins critical of his employer, its officers, and the incumbent union, Air Line Pilots Association ("ALPA"). Many of those criticisms related to Konop's opposition to labor concessions which Hawaiian sought from ALPA. Because ALPA supported the concessions, Konop, via his website, encouraged Hawaiian employees to consider alternative union representation.

Konop controlled access to his website by requiring visitors to log in with a user name and password. He created a list of people, mostly pilots and other employees of Hawaiian, who were eligible to access the website. Pilots Gene Wong and James Gardner were included on this list. Konop programmed the website to allow access when a person entered the name of an eligible person, created a password, and clicked the "SUBMIT" button on the screen, indicating acceptance of the terms and conditions of use. These terms and conditions prohibited any member of Hawaiian's management from viewing the website and prohibited users from disclosing the website's contents to anyone else.

In December 1995, Hawaiian vice president James Davis asked Wong for permission to use Wong's name to access Konop's website. Wong agreed. Davis claimed he was concerned about untruthful allegations that he believed Konop was making on the website. . . .

Later, Davis also logged in with the name of another pilot, Gardner, who had similarly consented to Davis' use of his name. Through April 1996, Konop claims that his records indicate that Davis logged in over twenty times as Wong, and that Gardner or Davis logged in at least fourteen more times as Gardner.

Konop filed suit alleging claims under the federal Wiretap Act, the Stored Communications Act, the Railway Labor Act, and state tort law, arising from Davis' viewing and use of Konop's secure website. Konop also alleged that Hawaiian placed him on medical suspension in retaliation for his opposition to the proposed labor concessions, in violation of the Railway Labor Act. The district court granted summary judgment to Hawaiian on all but the retaliatory suspension claim, and entered judgment against Konop on that claim after a short bench trial.

Konop appeals. . . .

B. *Wiretap Act*

Konop argues that Davis' conduct constitutes an interception of an electronic communication in violation of the Wiretap Act. The Wiretap Act makes it an offense to "intentionally intercept . . . any wire, oral, or electronic communication." 18 U.S.C. § 2511(1)(a). We must therefore determine whether Konop's website is an "electronic communication" and, if so, whether Davis "intercepted" that communication.

An "electronic communication" is defined as "any transfer of signs, signals, writing, images, sounds, data, or intelligence of any nature transmitted in whole or in part by a wire, radio, electromagnetic, photoelectronic or photooptical system." *Id.* § 2510(12). . . . [W]ebsite owners such as Konop transmit electronic documents to servers, where the documents are stored. If a user wishes to view the website, the user requests that the server transmit a copy of the document to the user's computer. When the server sends the document to the user's computer for viewing, a transfer of information from the website owner to the user has occurred. Although the website owner's document does not go directly or immediately to the user, once a user accesses a website, information is transferred from the website owner to the user via one of the specified mediums. We therefore conclude that Konop's website fits the definition of "electronic communication."

The Wiretap Act, however, prohibits only "interceptions" of electronic communications. "Intercept" is defined as "the aural or other acquisition of the contents of any wire, electronic, or oral communication through the use of any electronic, mechanical, or other device." *Id.* § 2510(4). Standing alone, this definition would seem to suggest that an individual "intercepts" an electronic communication merely by "acquiring" its contents, regardless of when or under what circumstances the acquisition occurs. Courts, however, have clarified that Congress intended a narrower definition of "intercept" with regard to electronic communications.

In *Steve Jackson Games, Inc. v. United States Secret Service*, 36 F.3d 457 (5th Cir. 1994), the Fifth Circuit held that the government's acquisition of email messages stored on an electronic bulletin board system, but not yet retrieved by the intended recipients, was not an "interception" under the Wiretap Act. The court observed that, prior to the enactment of the ECPA, the word "intercept" had been interpreted to mean the acquisition of a communication contemporaneous with transmission. The court further observed that Congress, in passing the ECPA, intended to retain the previous definition of "intercept" with respect to wire and oral communications, while amending the Wiretap Act to cover interceptions of electronic communications. The court reasoned, however, that the word "intercept" could not describe the exact same conduct with respect to wire and electronic communications, because wire and electronic communications were defined differently in the statute. Specifically, the term "wire communication" was defined to include storage of the communication, while "electronic communication" was not. The court concluded that this textual difference evidenced Congress' understanding that, although one could "intercept" a *wire* communication in storage, one could not "intercept" an *electronic* communication in storage. . . .

The Ninth Circuit endorsed the reasoning of *Steve Jackson Games* in *United States v. Smith*, 155 F.3d 1051 (1998). . . .

We agree with the *Steve Jackson* and *Smith* courts that the narrow definition of "intercept" applies to electronic communications. Notably, Congress has since amended the Wiretap Act to eliminate storage from the definition of wire communication, *see* USA PATRIOT Act § 209, 115 Stat. at 283, such that the textual distinction relied upon by the *Steve Jackson* and *Smith* courts no longer exists. This change, however, supports the analysis of those cases. By eliminating storage from the definition of wire communication, Congress essentially reinstated the pre-ECPA definition of "intercept" — acquisition contemporaneous with transmission — with respect to wire communications. The purpose of the recent amendment was to reduce protection of voice mail messages to the lower level of protection provided other electronically stored communications. *See* H.R. Rep. 107-236(I), at 158-59 (2001). When Congress passed the USA PATRIOT Act, it was aware of the narrow definition courts had given the term "intercept" with respect to electronic communications, but chose not to change or modify that definition. To the contrary, it modified the statute to make that definition applicable to voice mail messages as well. Congress, therefore, accepted and implicitly approved the judicial definition of "intercept" as acquisition contemporaneous with transmission.

We therefore hold that for a website such as Konop's to be "intercepted" in violation of the Wiretap Act, it must be acquired during transmission, not while it is in electronic storage. This conclusion is consistent with the ordinary meaning of "intercept," which is "to stop, seize, or interrupt in progress or course before arrival." WEBSTER'S NINTH NEW COLLEGIATE DICTIONARY 630 (1985). More importantly, it is consistent with the structure of the ECPA, which created the SCA for the express purpose of addressing "access to *stored* . . . electronic communications and transactional records." S. Rep. No. 99-541 at 3 (emphasis added). The level of protection provided stored communications under the SCA is considerably less than that provided communications covered by the Wiretap Act. Section 2703(a) of the SCA details the procedures law enforcement must follow to access the contents of stored electronic communications, but these procedures are considerably less burdensome and less restrictive than those required to obtain a wiretap order under the Wiretap Act. Thus, if Konop's position were correct and acquisition of a stored electronic communication were an interception under the Wiretap Act, the government would have to comply with the more burdensome, more restrictive procedures of the Wiretap Act to do exactly what Congress apparently authorized it to do under the less burdensome procedures of the SCA. Congress could not have intended this result. . . .

Because we conclude that Davis' conduct did not constitute an "interception" of an electronic communication in violation of the Wiretap Act, we affirm the district court's grant of summary judgment against Konop on his Wiretap Act claims.

C. Stored Communications Act

Konop also argues that, by viewing his secure website, Davis accessed a stored electronic communication without authorization in violation of the SCA. The SCA makes it an offense to "intentionally access without authorization a facility through which an electronic communication service is provided . . . and thereby obtain . . . access to a wire or electronic communication while it is in electronic storage in such system." 18 U.S.C. § 2701(a)(1). The SCA excepts from liability, however, "conduct authorized . . . by a user of that service with respect to a communication of or intended for that user." 18 U.S.C. § 2701(c)(2). The district court found that the exception in § 2701(c)(2) applied because Wong and Gardner consented to Davis' use of Konop's website. It therefore granted summary judgment to Hawaiian on the SCA claim.

The parties agree that the relevant "electronic communications service" is Konop's website, and that the website was in "electronic storage." In addition, for the purposes of this opinion, we accept the parties' assumption that Davis' conduct constituted "access without authorization" to "a facility through which an electronic communication service is provided."

The district court concluded that Wong and Gardner had the authority under § 2701(c)(2) to consent to Davis' use of the website because Konop put Wong and Gardner on the list of eligible users. This conclusion is consistent with other parts of the Wiretap Act and the SCA which allow intended recipients of wire and electronic communications to authorize third parties to access those communications. In addition, there is some indication in the legislative history that Congress believed "addressees" or "intended recipients" of electronic communications would have the authority under the SCA to allow third parties access to those communications. *See* H.R. Rep. No. 99-647, at 66-67 (explaining that "an addressee [of an electronic communication] may consent to the disclosure of a communication to any other person" and that "[a] person may be an 'intended recipient' of a communication . . . even if he is not individually identified by name or otherwise").

Nevertheless, the plain language of § 2701(c)(2) indicates that only a "user" of the service can authorize a third party's access to the communication. The statute defines "user" as one who 1) uses the service and 2) is duly authorized to do so. Because the statutory language is unambiguous, it must control our construction of the statute, notwithstanding the legislative history. The statute does not define the word "use," so we apply the ordinary definition, which is "to put into action or service, avail oneself of, employ." WEBSTER'S at 1299. . . .

Based on the common definition of the word "use," we cannot find any evidence in the record that Wong ever used Konop's website. There is some evidence, however, that Gardner may have used the website, but it is unclear when that use occurred. At any rate, the district court did not make any findings on whether Wong and Gardner actually used Konop's website it simply assumed that Wong and Gardner, by virtue of being eligible to view the website, could authorize Davis' access. The problem with this approach is that it essentially reads the "user" requirement out of § 2701(c)(2). Taking the facts in the light most favorable to Konop, we must assume that neither Wong nor Gardner was a "user" of the website at the time he authorized Davis to view it. We therefore reverse the district court's grant of summary judgment to Hawaiian on Konop's SCA claim.

[The court's discussion of the Railway Labor Act and retaliation claims is omitted.]

NOTES

1. *"Interception" as Acquisition Contemporaneous with Transmission.* The *Konop* court's narrow interpretation of the statutory term "interception" means that although (as we discussed above) an employer who listens in on an employee's telephone conversation after determining that the subject matter is private violates the Wiretap Act's prohibition on interception, an employer who reads the private contents of an employee's stored website does not because reading a stored electronic communication is not acquisition contemporaneous with transmission. This definition of interception has also been applied to e-mail. *Fraser v. Nationwide Mutual Insurance Co.*, 352 F.3d 107, 114 (3d Cir. 2003) (there can be no "intercept" as defined in the ECPA of an e-mail in storage). Given the speed of transmission of electronic communications, it seems likely that almost all intrusions into e-mail or internet communication will occur after the information is stored. The Stored

Communications Act (SCA), meanwhile, prohibits access to electronically stored communications, but exempts access authorized by a user of the service (§ 2701(c)(2)), who, as we see in *Konop*, may include any intended recipient of the communication. Section 2701(c)(1) of the SCA also exempts access by the *provider* of the electronic communications service — which of course is often the employer itself. *See, e.g., Bohach v. City of Reno*, 932 F. Supp. 1232 (D. Nev. 1996) (because the City of Reno was the "provider" of the electronic communications service that allowed employees to send and store messages, neither it nor its employees were liable under the SCA for reading employees' stored messages).

Finally, common-law protections such as the privacy tort typically offer no recourse for an employee whose employer has accessed stored electronic communications. Courts have rejected employee claims that measures one might think would create a reasonable expectation of privacy, such as individualized passwords, protect them from employer intrusion. In *Smyth v. Pillsbury Co.*, 914 F. Supp. 97 (E.D. Pa. 1996), for example, an employee found no recourse in his intrusion-on-seclusion claim after the employer fired him for transmitting unprofessional comments over company e-mail. The company had an express policy promising employees that all e-mail communications would remain confidential and privileged and that e-mail communications could not be intercepted by or used by the company against its employees as grounds for termination or reprimand. The court stated:

> [W]e do not find a reasonable expectation of privacy in e-mail communications voluntarily made by an employee to his supervisor over the company e-mail system notwithstanding any assurances that such communications would not be intercepted by management. Once plaintiff communicated the alleged unprofessional comments to a second person (his supervisor) over an e-mail system which was apparently utilized by the entire company, any reasonable expectation of privacy was lost.

Id. at 101. *See also Garrity v. Hancock Mutual Life Ins. Co.*, 2002 U.S. Dist. LEXIS 8343 (D. Mass.) (company instruction of employees on how to create individualized passwords and personal e-mail folders did not create a reasonable expectation of privacy).

2. *Duty to Monitor?* Employers frequently cite concern over litigation as a reason for monitoring employee e-mail and internet use. What are the obligations of an employer that becomes aware an employee is engaged in inappropriate activities? Consider the case of *Doe v. XYC Corp.*, 887 A.2d 1156 (N.J. Super. 2005), in which a company discovered that one of its employees had been visiting pornographic websites, including child-pornography sites. The company twice told the employee to stop, but took no other action during the nearly two years between its discovery and the employee's arrest on child-pornography charges. The police investigation found numerous child-pornography images on the employee's work computer and evidence of visits to child-pornography websites. Among the employee's activities were clandestinely photographing his wife's 10-year-old daughter in nude positions, and transmitting the photographs to websites from his work computer. The wife sued the company for negligence. The New Jersey Superior Court reversed summary judgment for the defendant and held that there was no expectation of privacy on the part of the employee to prevent the employer from accessing his workplace computer and the company was on notice that the employee was visiting child pornography websites. Therefore the company was under a duty to act, either by terminating the employee or reporting his activities to law enforcement authorities. The matter was returned to the jury for resolution of the question whether the company's breach of duty proximately caused harm to the 10-year-old daughter.

3. *Monitoring Movement.* Employers also use technology to monitor the movement of employees. For example, recent years have seen a sharp rise in the availability and sophistication of Global Positioning System (GPS) technology. While a 2005 survey reported that only 5% of employers used it to track company cell phones and 8% used it to track company vehicles (AMERICAN MANAGEMENT ASSOCIATION & ePOLICY INSTITUTE, *supra*), increased use of this practice seems very likely. Would requiring an employee to carry a GPS device throughout the work day intrude on his or her privacy interests? The limited decisional law on the matter suggests the answer is no. *See Elgin v. Coca-Cola Bottling Co.*, 2005 U.S. Dist. LEXIS 28976 (E.D. Mo. 2005) (use of GPS tracking device on company car, which revealed no more than highly public information as to the van's location, did not intrude on seclusion of employee or rise to the level of being highly offensive to a reasonable person).

What about constant video surveillance in employees' work areas? *See Vega-Rodriguez v. Puerto Rico Tel. Co.*, 110 F.3d 174 (1st Cir. 1997) (public employment case holding that since a company could assign humans to monitor the work station continuously without constitutional insult, the employer could choose instead to carry out that task by means of unconcealed video cameras not equipped with microphones, which record only what the human eye could observe).

4. *Government Intervention in the Rat Race.* One major issue in any government regulation of electronic monitoring (as in most employment privacy issues) is whether weighing the costs and benefits of electronic monitoring should be left to private employers and employees. If monitoring increases productivity, the employer can compensate workers for the stress and loss of autonomy with higher wages. Employers who engage in overly invasive monitoring will be at a competitive disadvantage by having to pay abnormally high compensating wages or by having difficulty in hiring workers. The argument, then, is that the private marketplace can reach an appropriate decision on the amount of monitoring.

What arguments can be made supporting government intervention in this decision? All the costs and benefits of monitoring seem to be borne by employers and employees themselves, so regulating third-party effects is an implausible justification for government intervention.

One possible model is to recognize that, to an extent, workers are in a rat race with each other. Workers are not only interested in their absolute standard of living, but in their relative standard of living as well, for many benefits accrue to being in the top percentiles of society. Thus, individuals may well agree to accept high-pressure, high-paying employment in an attempt to get into the upper-middle class. To keep up, other employees must likewise join the rat race. But, unless the Lake Wobegon effect operates, not everyone can be in the upper-middle class. Thus, everyone rationally accepts high-stress work even though (like in an arms race) we may all be better off by agreeing to less stressful jobs. For a general discussion of this problem, with many examples, see ROBERT H. FRANK, CHOOSING THE RIGHT POND (1985).

B. OFF-WORK PRIVACY CLAIMS

BRUNNER v. AL ATTAR
Court of Appeals of Texas
786 S.W.2d 784 (1990)

Before SAM BASS, DUNN and O'CONNOR, JJ.

SAM BASS, JUSTICE.

Brunner appeals from a summary judgment for Farouk Al Attar, Rima Al Attar, and Apollo Paint & Body. We affirm.

Farouk Al Attar and Rima Al Attar are husband and wife, and partners in a general partnership, known as Apollo Paint & Body. . . . Brunner alleged that Farouk terminated her, because he feared that she would catch and spread the Acquired Immune Deficiency Syndrome (AIDS) to employees. Appellees urged that Brunner was terminated because of her refusal to work during the hours required, her request to be terminated, and her failure, inability and/or refusal to perform the work expected of her.

Brunner stated that she had neither contracted AIDS, nor been infected with the human immunodeficiency virus which causes AIDS.

Appellees moved for summary judgment, alleging that Brunner did not state a cause of action, and could not amend her pleadings to state a cause of action.

Brunner testified by deposition that she was terminated from Apollo Paint & Body because she was a volunteer with the AIDS Foundation. Brunner had told Farouk that she would be volunteering in her free time on Saturdays and Sundays, and in the evenings. Brunner promised that her volunteer work would not interfere with her position at Apollo, and stated that there was no danger to the employees at Apollo Paint & Body, because Brunner could not catch AIDS from the patients' touching, sneezing, or breathing on her. She further stated that the only way to catch AIDS is through sexual contact or blood transfusions. Brunner told Farouk that his customers did not have to know about her volunteer work. Farouk responded by saying that he could not allow Brunner to perform volunteer work at the AIDS Foundation and work at Apollo. Farouk told Brunner that he did not want to place himself, his family, and the office workers in jeopardy. Farouk urged Brunner to resign, and she refused. . . .

In her first point of error, Brunner asserts that this Court should not permit her to be terminated for performing volunteer work for the AIDS Foundation because her termination violates the public policy exception to the employment-at-will doctrine.

Brunner does not allege that her employment was governed by a contract, or that it was for a definite term. The general rule is that employment for an indefinite term may be terminated at will and without cause. In *Sabine Pilot, Inc. v. Hauck*, 687 S.W.2d 733 (Tex. 1985), the Texas Supreme Court recognized a very narrow exception to the judicially-created employment-at-will doctrine. "That narrow exception covers only the discharge of an employee for the sole reason that the employee refused to perform an illegal act." . . . In *McClendon v. Ingersoll-Rand Co.*, 779 S.W.2d 69, 71 (Tex. 1989),[*] the supreme court announced another judicially-created exception to the employment-at-will doctrine, which permits recovery of lost future wages, mental anguish, and punitive damages, where the "plaintiff proves that the principal reason for his termination was the employer's desire to avoid contributing to or paying benefits under the employee's pension fund."

Brunner alleges that she was fired because she refused to quit her volunteer work with the AIDS Foundation; however, she has not alleged that she was terminated for refusing to perform an illegal act, or because her employer wished to avoid paying benefits under her pension fund. Brunner has failed to allege sufficient facts to place her within these two exceptions to the employment-at-will doctrine. *See Jennings v. Minco Technology Labs, Inc.*, 765 S.W.2d 497, 500-02 (Tex. App.-Austin 1989, *writ denied*) (court refused to create an exception to the doctrine on the grounds of public policy, to enable an employee to obtain declaratory and injunctive relief, restraining employer from administering random urinalysis drug tests on employees); *Berry v. Doctor's Health Facilities*, 715 S.W.2d 60, 61, 62-63 (Tex. App.-Dallas 1986, *no writ*) (court declined to create an exception to the employment-at-will doctrine on the grounds of public policy, to encompass a cause of action asserting wrongful termination, because the employee "knew too much" about alleged improprieties within the hospital administration); *Winters v. Houston Chronicle Publishing Company*, 781 S.W.2d 408 (Tex. App.-Houston [1st Dist.] 1989, *writ pending*) (court declined to extend *Sabine Pilot* exception to employment-at-will doctrine, where private employee alleged he was discharged for reporting to management that his upper level managers and supervisors were engaged in circulation fraud, inventory theft, and a "kickback" scheme). This Court cannot create another exception for performing volunteer work at the Houston AIDS Foundation. If such an exception is to be created, that is a matter within the province of the Texas Supreme Court. . . .

The judgment is affirmed.

NOTES

1. *Volunteering as Public Policy.* As this case shows, an employee who is fired for off-work conduct objectionable to the employer has difficulty fitting within one of the standard categories of wrongful discharge in violation of public policy. Texas at this time had not recognized a claim for wrongful discharge for fulfilling a public duty. Would Brunner have had greater success fitting into this pigeonhole? Or should the case be analyzed directly as a privacy claim, rather than a wrongful discharge case?

[*] This case was later reversed by the United States Supreme Court in *Ingersoll-Rand Co. v. McClendon*, 498 U.S. 133 (1990), which held that ERISA preempts a state law wrongful-discharge claim that an employer fired an employee to avoid contributing to a pension fund.

2. *Employer Interests.* Given contemporary medical information concerning the communicability of the AIDS virus, did the employer here have a business interest in Brunner's volunteer work at the AIDS clinic? Or is this simply an example of the hysteria surrounding AIDS? Does the employer have a legitimate concern if fellow employees are (irrationally) fearful of working with Brunner?

More generally, should the law police the firing of productive employees for off-work conduct? Are employers likely to do this often, or will they face marketplace penalties for firing productive employees?

3. *Night Law School.* In *Scroghan v. Kraftco Corp.*, 551 S.W.2d 811 (Ky. Ct. App. 1977), an at-will employee was fired when he announced that he planned to attend law school at night. The employee brought a suit for wrongful discharge, but the court upheld a summary judgment dismissing the claim, declaring that the employee's "attendance at night school was a private rather than a public concern." The employee had claimed a violation of the public policy in favor of continued education, as embodied in the National Defense Education Act of 1958, 20 U.S.C. § 401.

Was the court correct in asserting that education is a purely private matter? Although the court in *Scroghan* did not rely on this fact, Congress had stopped funding programs under the National Defense Education Act by the time the suit was brought. Does this weaken Scroghan's argument that the statute enunciated a clear public policy? Or does a focus on this obscure federal statute trivialize the claim that higher education of citizens is an important public policy?

Would the claim have been more powerful if characterized as an invasion of personal privacy rather than a violation of public policy? The case illustrates the tension between privacy rights and an insistence on public concern.

4. *Off-Work Conduct and Just Cause.* Arbitrators interpreting union contracts with just-cause provisions rarely uphold discharges for off-work conduct unless the employer can demonstrate a clear detriment to the workplace.

> Arbitrators have long held that what an employee does on his own time and off Company premises is not a proper basis for disciplinary action unless it can be shown that the employee's conduct has an adverse effect on the Company's business or reputation, the morale and well-being of other employees, or the employee's ability to perform his regular duties.

Indian Head, Inc., 71 Lab. Arb. (BNA) 82, 85 (1978) (Rimer, Arb.) (reinstating employee fired for off-work possession of marijuana).

Arbitrators have sometimes deviated from the off-work principle when the worker is fired for being a visible member of a repugnant group like the Ku Klux Klan, greatly upsetting co-workers. *See Baltimore Transit Co.*, 47 Lab. Arb. (BNA) 62 (1966) (Duff, Arb.) (bus operator publicly identified as grand dragon of KKK justifiably terminated for cause when fellow employees threatened wildcat strike). Is such a situation distinguishable from *Brunner*, apart from the fact the Brunner was an at-will employee so the employer did not need a good reason to terminate her?

5. *Legal Off-Work Activity — "Lifestyle" Statutes.* Several states, including Colorado, Nevada, New York, and North Dakota, have enacted statutes prohibiting employers from firing workers for legal off-work activity. N.D. CENT. CODE § 14-02.4-03 reads:

> It is a discriminatory practice for an employer to fail or refuse to hire a person; to discharge an employee; or to accord adverse or unequal treatment to a person or employee with respect to application, hiring, training, apprenticeship, tenure, promotion, upgrading, compensation, layoff, or a term, privilege, or condition of employment, because of . . . participation in lawful activity off the employer's premises during non-working hours.

6. *Smoking Off the Job.* One of the first areas where employees asserted off-work privacy rights was smoking. Employers have a clear business interest in rejecting job applicants who smoke, whether on or off the job. A study of Boston postal workers showed that smokers had 34% higher absenteeism, 29% higher risk of industrial accidents, 40% more occupational injuries, and 55% more disciplinary incidents. The debilitating effects of smoking remained after controlling for age, gender, race, job category, exercise habits, and drug abuse. *See* James Ryan et al., *Occupational Risks Associated With Cigarette Smoking: A Prospective Study*, 82 AM. J. PUB. HEALTH 29 (1992). One scholar reports that "the estimated costs borne by businesses for the average smoker — including health insurance, fire losses, workers' compensation, absenteeism, productivity losses, and health difficulties for nonsmokers — . . . may be as high as $1000 per worker." Mark A. Rothstein, *Refusing to Employ Smokers: Good Public Health or Bad Public Policy?*, 62 NOTRE DAME L. REV. 940, 944-46 (1987).

On the other hand, refusing to hire workers because they smoke at home raises privacy concerns. A 1992 National Consumers League poll found that 79% of workers said a prospective employer has no right to ask whether they smoke off the job. Monitoring whether an employee smokes at home would itself be problematic.

As with other employee privacy issues, including drug testing and polygraphs, public employees with constitutional claims were the first to challenge no-smoking-off-work policies. An early case challenged a public fire department's regulation prohibiting on-and off-duty smoking for firefighter trainees. Upholding the regulation against a due process challenge, the court applied a rational relationship test:

> We need look no further for a legitimate purpose and rational connection than the Surgeon General's warning on the side of every box of cigarettes sold in this country that cigarette smoking is hazardous to health. Further, we take notice that good health and physical conditioning are essential requirements for firefighters. We also note that firefighters are frequently exposed to smoke inhalation and that it might reasonably be feared that smoking increases this risk. We conclude that these considerations are enough to establish, *prima facie*, a rational basis for the regulation.

Grusendorf v. City of Okla. City, 816 F.2d 539, 543 (10th Cir. 1987).

Some state legislatures have protected private-employee smokers. In 1991, New Jersey passed a smokers' rights bill, which prohibits employers from making hiring, firing, compensation, or other personnel decisions based on whether a worker or job applicant smokes away from the job, "unless the employer has a rational basis for doing so which is reasonably related to the employment, including the responsibilities of the employee or prospective employee." The law specifically allows employers to offer better options and rates for non-smokers for life and health insurance benefits. Several other states, including Indiana and New Mexico, have also passed smokers' rights laws that restrict the ability of employers to discriminate against smokers.

RULON-MILLER v. INTERNATIONAL BUSINESS MACHINE CORP.
California Court of Appeal
208 Cal. Rptr. 524 (1984)

RUSHING, ASSOCIATE JUSTICE.

International Business Machines (IBM) appeals from the judgment entered against it after a jury awarded $100,000 compensatory and $200,000 punitive damages to respondent (Virginia Rulon-Miller) on claims of wrongful discharge and intentional infliction of emotional distress. Rulon-Miller was a low-level marketing manager at IBM in its office products division in San Francisco. Her termination as a marketing manager at IBM came about as a result of an accusation made by her immediate supervisor, defendant Callahan, of a romantic relationship with the manager of a rival office products firm, QYX. . . .

IBM is an employer traditionally thought to provide great security to its employees as well as an environment of openness and dignity. The company is organized into divisions, and each division is, to an extent, independent of others. The company prides itself on providing career opportunities to its employees, and respondent represents a good example of this. She started in 1967 as a receptionist in the Philadelphia Data Center. She was told that "career opportunities are available to [employees] as long as they are performing satisfactorily and are willing to accept new challenges." While she worked at the data center in Philadelphia, she attended night school and earned a baccalaureate degree. She was promoted to equipment scheduler and not long after received her first merit award. The company moved her to Atlanta, Georgia where she spent 15 months as a data processor. She was transferred to the office products division and was assigned the position of "marketing support representative" in San Francisco where she trained users (*i.e.*, customers) of newly-purchased IBM equipment. Respondent was promoted to "product planner" in 1973 where her duties included overseeing the performance of new office products in the marketplace. As a product planner, she moved to Austin, Texas and later to Lexington, Kentucky. Thereafter, at the urging of her managers that she go into sales in the office products division, she enrolled at the IBM sales school in Dallas. After graduation, she was assigned to San Francisco.

[Rulon-Miller continued to receive superb evaluations. In 1978 she was named a marketing manager in the office products branch, which sold typewriters and other office equipment.]

IBM knew about respondent's relationship with Matt Blum well before her appointment as a manager. Respondent met Blum in 1976 when he was an account manager for IBM. That they were dating was widely known within the organization. In 1977 Blum left IBM to join QYX, an IBM competitor, and was transferred to Philadelphia. When Blum returned to San Francisco in the summer of 1978, IBM personnel were aware that he and respondent began dating again. This seemed to present no problems to respondent's superiors, as Callahan confirmed when she was promoted to manager. Respondent testified: "Somewhat in passing, Phil said: I heard the other day you were dating Matt Blum, and I said: Oh. And he said, I don't have any problem with that. You're my number one pick. I just want to assure you that you are my selection." The relationship with Blum was also known to Regional Manager Gary Nelson who agreed with Callahan. Neither Callahan nor Nelson raised any issue of conflict of interest because of the Blum relationship.

Respondent flourished in her management position, and the company, apparently grateful for her efforts, gave her a $4,000 merit raise in 1979 and told her that she was doing a good job. A week later, her manager, Phillip Callahan, left a message that he wanted to see her.

When she walked into Callahan's office he confronted her with the question of whether she was *dating* Matt Blum. She wondered at the relevance of the inquiry and he said the dating constituted a "conflict of interest," and told her to stop dating Blum or lose her job and said she had a "couple of days to a week" to think about it.

The next day Callahan called her in again, told her "he had made up her mind for her," and when she protested, dismissed her.[3] IBM and Callahan claim that he merely "transferred" respondent to another division.

---

[3] Respondent stated the next day she was again summoned to his office where Callahan sat ominously behind a desk cleared of any paperwork, an unusual scenario for any IBM manager.

She further testified: "I walked into Phil's office, and he asked me to shut the door, and he said he was removing me from management effectively immediately. And I said: What?

"And he repeated it. And I was taken aback, I was a little startled, and I think I said: Well, gee, I thought I had a couple of days to a week to think over the situation that we discussed yesterday.

"And he said: I'm making the decision for you.

"And I said: Phil, you've told me that I'm doing a good job. You told me that we are not losing anybody to QYX because I am dating Matt Blum, that we are not losing any equipment to QYX. I just don't understand what bearing dating has to do with my job.

"And he said: We have a conflict of interest. . . .

"I said: Well, what kind of a job would it be?

"And he said: Well, I don't have it, but it will be non-management. You won't be a manager again.

"Pardon me? . . .

"And I think I was getting very upset so I think I said something because of that respect for the individual tenet of IBM's that I really believed in I didn't think that he was following what I thought IBM, really did believe in. And he just said: You know, you are removed from management effective immediately.

"And I said: I think you are dismissing me.

Respondent's claims of wrongful discharge and intentional infliction of emotional distress were both submitted to the jury. . . .

The initial discussion between Callahan and respondent of her relationship with Blum is important. We must accept the version of the facts most favorable to the respondent herein. When Callahan questioned her relationship with Blum, respondent invoked her right to privacy in her personal life relying on existing IBM policies. A threshold inquiry is thus presented whether respondent could reasonably rely on those policies for job protection. Any conflicting action by the company would be wrongful in that it would constitute a violation of her contract rights.

Under the common law rule codified in Labor Code section 2922, an employment contract of indefinite duration is, in general, terminable at "the will" of either party. This common law rule has been considerably altered by the recognition of the Supreme Court of California that implicit in any such relationship or contract is an underlying principle that requires the parties to deal openly and fairly with one another. . . . The duty of fair dealing by an employer is, simply stated, a requirement that like cases be treated alike. Implied in this, of course, is that the company, if it has rules and regulations, apply those rules and regulations to its employees as well as affording its employees their protection. . . .

In this case, there is a close question of whether those rules or regulations permit IBM to inquire into the purely personal life of the employee. If so, an attendant question is whether such a policy was applied consistently, particularly as between men and women. The distinction is important because the right of privacy, a constitutional right in California, could be implicated by the IBM inquiry. Much of the testimony below concerned what those policies were. The evidence was conflicting on the meaning of certain IBM policies. We observe ambiguity in the application but not in the intent. The "Watson Memo" (so called because it was signed by a former chairman of IBM) provided as follows:

TO ALL IBM MANAGERS:

> The line that separates an individual's on-the-job business life from his other life as a private citizen is at times well-defined and at other times indistinct. But the line does exist, and you and I, as managers in IBM, must be able to recognize that line.

> I have seen instances where managers took disciplinary measures against employees for actions or conduct that are not rightfully the company's concern. These managers usually justified their decisions by citing their personal code of ethics and morals or by quoting some fragment of company policy that seemed to support their position. Both arguments proved unjust on close examination. What we need, in every case, is balanced judgment which weighs the needs of the business and the rights of the individual.

"And he said: If you feel that way, give me your I.D. card and your key to the office. I want you to leave the premises immediately.

"And I was just about to burst into tears, and I didn't cry at work, so I basically fled his office.

"I felt he dismissed me."

Our primary objective as IBM managers is to further the business of this company by leading our people properly and measuring quantity and quality of work and effectiveness on the job against clearly set standards of responsibility and compensation. This is performance — and performance is, in the final analysis, the one thing that the company can insist on from everyone.

We have concern with an employee's off-the-job behavior only when it reduces his ability to perform regular job assignments, interferes with the job performance of other employees, or if his outside behavior affects the reputation of the company in a major way. When on-the-job performance is acceptable, I can think of few situations in which outside activities could result in disciplinary action or dismissal.

When such situations do come to your attention, you should seek the advice and counsel of the next appropriate level of management and the personnel department in determining what action — if any — is called for. Action should be taken only when a legitimate interest of the company is injured or jeopardized. Furthermore the damage must be clear beyond reasonable doubt and not based on hasty decisions about what one person might think is good for the company.

IBM's first basic belief is respect for the individual, and the essence of this belief is a strict regard for his right to personal privacy. This idea should never be compromised easily or quickly.

/s/ Tom Watson, Jr.

It is clear that this company policy insures to the employee both the right of privacy and the right to hold a job even though "off-the-job behavior" might not be approved of by the employee's manager.

IBM had adopted policies governing employee conduct. Some of those policies were collected in a document known as the "Performance and Recognition" (PAR) Manual. IBM relies on the following portion of the PAR Manual:

A conflict of interest can arise when an employee is involved in activity for personal gain, which for any reason is in conflict with IBM's business interests. Generally speaking, 'moonlighting' is defined as working at some activity for personal gain outside of your IBM job. If you do perform outside work, you have a special responsibility to avoid any conflict with IBM's business interests.

Obviously, you cannot solicit or perform in competition with IBM product or service offerings. Outside work cannot be performed on IBM time, including 'personal' time off. You cannot use IBM equipment, materials, resources, or 'inside' information for outside work. Nor should you solicit business or clients or perform outside work on IBM premises.

Employees must be free of any significant investment or association of their own or of their immediate family's [sic], in competitors or suppliers, which might interfere or be thought to interfere with the independent exercise of their judgment in the best interests of IBM.

This policy of IBM is entitled "Gifts" and appears to be directed at "moonlighting" and soliciting outside business or clients on IBM premises. It prohibits "significant investment" in competitors or suppliers of IBM. It also prohibits "association" with such persons "which might interfere or be thought to interfere with the independent exercise of their judgment in the best interests of IBM."

Callahan based his action against respondent on a "conflict of interest." But the record shows that IBM did not interpret this policy to prohibit a romantic relationship. Callahan admitted that there was no company rule or policy requiring an employee to terminate friendships with fellow employees who leave and join competitors.[4] Gary Nelson, Callahan's superior, also confirmed that IBM had no policy against employees socializing with competitors.

This issue was hotly contested with respondent claiming that the "conflict of interest" claim was a pretext for her unjust termination. Whether it was presented a fact question for the jury.

Do the policies reflected in this record give IBM a right to terminate an employee for a conflict of interest? The answer must be yes, but whether respondent's conduct constituted such was for the jury. We observe that while respondent was successful, her primary job did not give her access to sensitive information which could have been useful to competitors. She was, after all, a seller of typewriters and office equipment. Respondent's brief makes much of the concession by IBM that there was no evidence whatever that respondent had given any information or help to IBM's competitor QYX. It really is no concession at all; she did not have the information or help to give. Even so, the question is one of substantial evidence. The evidence is abundant that there was no conflict of interest by respondent.

It does seem clear that an overall policy established by IBM chairman Watson was one of no company interest in the outside activities of an employee so long as the activities did not interfere with the work of the employee. Moreover, in the last analysis, it may be simply a question for the jury to decide whether, in the application of these policies, the right was conferred on IBM to inquire into the personal or romantic relationships its managers had with others. This is an important question because IBM, in attempting to reargue the facts to us, casts this argument in other terms, namely: that it had a right to inquire even if there was no evidence that such a relationship interfered with the discharge of the employee's duties *because* it had the effect of diminishing the morale of the employees answering to the manager. This is the "Caesar's wife" argument; it is merely a recast of the principal argument and asks the same question in different terms.[5] The same answer holds in

---

[4] An interesting side issue to this point is that Blum continued to play on an IBM softball team while working for QYX.

[5] What we mean by that is that if you charge that an employee is passing confidential information to a competitor, the question remains whether the charge is true on the evidence available to the person deciding the issue, in this case, the respondent's managers at IBM. If you recast this argument in the form of the "Caesar's wife" argument attempted by IBM, it will be seen that exactly the same question arises, namely, "is it true?" Indeed, the import of the argument is that the rumor, or an unfounded allegation, could serve as a basis for the termination of the employee.

both cases: there being no evidence to support the more direct argument, there is no evidence to support the indirect argument.

Moreover, the record shows that the evidence of rumor was not a basis for any decline in the morale of the employees reporting to respondent. Employees Mary Hrize and Wayne Fyvie, who reported to respondent's manager that she was seen at a tea dance at the Hyatt Regency with Matt Blum and also that she was not living at her residence in Marin, did not believe that those rumors in any way impaired her abilities as a manager. In the initial confrontation between respondent and her superior the assertion of the right to be free of inquiries concerning her personal life was based on substantive direct contract rights she had flowing to her from IBM policies. Further, there is no doubt that the jury could have so found and on this record we must assume that they did so find. . . .

Intentional Infliction of Emotional Distress

The contract rights in an employment agreement or the covenant of good faith and fair dealing gives both employer and employee the right to breach and to respond in damages. Here, however, the question is whether if IBM elected to exercise that right it should also be liable for punitive damages, because of its intentional infliction of emotional distress. The issue is whether the conduct of the marketing manager of IBM was "extreme and outrageous," a question involving the objective facts of what happened in the confrontation between the employee and employer as well as the special susceptibility of suffering of the employee.

The general rule is that this tort, in essence, requires the defendant's conduct to be so extreme and outrageous as to go beyond all possible bounds of decency, and to be regarded as atrocious and utterly intolerable in a civilized community. . . .

The jury was entitled to consider the evidence of extreme and outrageous conduct in light of the June 7 exchange followed by Callahan's conduct and pretextual statements, as well as in light of express corporate policy as manifested by the Watson memo. Indeed, the concern of the Watson memo is also a right protected by law. As we earlier noted "the right of privacy is unquestionably a 'fundamental interest of our society' " (*City and County of San Francisco v. Superior Court*, 125 Cal. App. 3d 879, 883.) It is guaranteed to all people by article I, section 1, of the state Constitution. So the question is whether the invasion of plaintiff's privacy rights by her employer, in the setting of this case, constitutes extreme and outrageous conduct. The jury by special verdict so found.

To determine if Callahan's conduct could reach the level of extreme, outrageous, and atrocious conduct, requires detailed examination. First, there was a decided element of deception in Callahan acting as if the relationship with Blum was something new. The evidence was clear he knew of the involvement of respondent and Blum well before her promotion. Second, he acted in flagrant disregard of IBM policies prohibiting him from inquiring into respondent's "off job behavior." By giving respondent "a few days" to think about the choice between job and lover, he implied that if she gave up Blum she could have her job. He then acted without giving her "a few days to think about it" or giving her the right to choose.

So far the conduct is certainly unfair but not atrocious. What brings Callahan's conduct to an actionable level is the way he brought these several elements together in the second meeting with respondent. He said, after calling her in, "I'm making the decision for you." The implications of his statement were richly ambiguous, meaning she could not act or think for herself, or that he was acting in her best interest, or that she persisted in a romantic involvement inconsistent with her job. When she protested, he fired her.

The combination of statements and conduct would under any reasoned view tend to humiliate and degrade respondent. To be denied a right granted to all other employees for conduct unrelated to her work was to degrade her as a person. His unilateral action in purporting to remove any free choice on her part contrary to his earlier assurances also would support a conclusion that his conduct was intended to emphasize that she was powerless to do anything to assert her rights as an IBM employee. And such powerlessness is one of the most debilitating kinds of human oppression. The sum of such evidence clearly supports the jury finding of extreme and outrageous conduct.

Accordingly we conclude that the emotional distress cause of action was amply proved and supports the award of punitive damages.

The judgment is affirmed.

RACANELLI, P.J., and HOLMDAHL, J., concur.

NOTES

1. *Employer Respect for Privacy.* Why did IBM have the policy, described in the Watson memo, of respecting employee privacy rights? Does such a policy make good business sense? Without the memo, would Rulon-Miller have won her case? If not, does this suggest that the default rule is that employees have no right to date whomever they want without fear of discharge?

2. *Dating Cases.* Considerable litigation has surrounded the discharge of workers for relationships or affairs. Most cases, like *Rulon*, involve affairs with co-workers or competitors. Here, employers have at least an arguable interest in the relationship, and most courts have held against employees. In *Patton v. J.C. Penney Co.*, 719 P.2d 854 (Or. 1986), for example, a male employee was fired for continuing a "social relationship" with a female co-worker even though the employer had no general policy against socializing between employees. The court rejected a wrongful discharge claim, reasoning that "[i]t may seem harsh that an employer can fire an employee because of dislike of the employee's personal lifestyle, but because the plaintiff cannot show that the actions fit under an exception to the general rule, plaintiff is subject to the traditional doctrine of 'fire at will.'" *Id.* at 857.

Courts have similarly rejected claims for wrongful discharge when a worker was fired for having an affair with a subordinate, *Rogers v. I.B.M.*, 500 F. Supp. 867 (W.D. Pa. 1980); with a supervisor, *Trumbauer v. Group Health*

Coop., 635 F. Supp. 543 (W.D. Wash. 1986), and even for unwittingly discovering that the boss was having an affair with a secretary, *Hillenbrand v. City of Evansville*, 457 N.E.2d 236 (Ind. Ct. App. 1983).

Some employees discharged for dating have sought relief under state "lifestyle statutes," mentioned earlier, that purport to protect lawful off-duty conduct. New York Labor Law § 201-d(2)(c) forbids employer discrimination against employees because of their participation in "legal recreational activities." Courts have refused to find, however, that "dating" is a protected "recreational activity." *See State v. Wal-Mart Stores*, 207 A.D.2d 150 (N.Y. App. Div. 1995) (dismissing claim of employees fired for violating company policy against married employees dating employees other than their spouse); *McCavitt v. Swiss Reinsurance Am. Corp.*, 237 F.3d 166 (2d Cir. 2000) (dismissing claim of employee fired for having "personal relationship" with co-worker). Similarly unsuccessful was a California employee who relied on California Labor Code § 96(k) as a statutory source of public policy to support an action for wrongful discharge in violation of public policy after he was fired for dating a subordinate. Section 96(k) requires the California Labor Commissioner to take assignments of "[c]laims for loss of wages as a result of demotion, suspension, or discharge from employment for lawful conduct occurring during nonworking hours away from the employer's premises." The California Court of Appeal held that § 96(k) does not itself embody any new substantive rights for employees, but rather, simply delineates a procedural mechanism by which the Labor Commissioner shall exercise jurisdiction over independently recognized constitutional rights (which do not include the right of supervisors to date subordinates). *Barbee v. Household Automotive Finance Corp.*, 113 Cal. App. 4th 525 (2003).

Even when the employee is not dating a competitor or co-worker, courts are reluctant to second-guess a discharge. In *Staats v. Ohio National Life Insurance Co.*, 620 F. Supp. 118 (W.D. Pa. 1985) (applying Pennsylvania law), the court dismissed a wrongful discharge claim of an employee fired for attending a convention with a person who was not his spouse. The court reasoned that

> though freedom of association is an important social right, and one that ordinarily should not dictate employment decisions, . . . the right to "associate with" a non-spouse *at an employer's convention* is hardly the kind of threat to "some recognized facet of public policy" [contemplated by the tort of wrongful discharge].

And in *Karren v. Far West Federal Savings*, 717 P.2d 1271 (Or. Ct. App.), *review denied*, 725 P.2d 1293 (Or. 1986), the court upheld the dismissal of a wrongful-discharge claim where a bank loan coordinator was fired for becoming engaged to marry. The court found her claim was "based on a private right which is not related to her role as an employee."

One of the few successful cases in this area, besides *Rulon-Miller*, is *Slohoda v. United Parcel Service*, 475 A.2d 618 (N.J. Super. Ct. App. Div. 1984). There the court overturned a summary judgment against a married employee who was fired for having an affair. The court concluded that, if the company would not have fired an unmarried employee in a similar situation, the firing would discriminate on the basis of marital status in violation of state law.

C. DRUG TESTING

Both the executive and legislative branches of the federal government have attempted to promote drug-free workplaces. In 1986 President Reagan signed Executive Order 12,564 calling for executive agency heads to develop plans for a drug-free workplace. Each plan is to include a statement of policy, a counseling and rehabilitation program, supervisory training, treatment referral provisions, and a drug testing program for employees in sensitive positions. In addition, agencies are authorized to test any job applicant and to test employees upon reasonable suspicion of drug use, after an accident or unsafe practice, or to help with rehabilitation or counseling. The order also mandates procedural safeguards.

The Drug-Free Workplace Act of 1988, 41 U.S.C. §§ 701-707, extends beyond government employees to federal contractors and federal grant recipients. To receive a federal contract or grant, employers must certify they will provide a drug-free workplace by notifying employees that illegal drugs are prohibited in the workplace and establishing drug-free awareness programs. The act does not specifically refer to drug testing. An early survey of affected employers found the Act to be largely ineffective. Donald J. Peterson & Douglas Massengill, *Employer Response to the Drug-Free Workplace Act of 1988: A Preliminary Look*, LAB. L.J., March 1991, at 144, 149-50.

Drug testing is very prevalent in the private sector. Over 61% of major U.S. firms reported in a 2004 survey that they employed drug testing. AMERICAN MANAGEMENT ASSOCIATION, 2004 WORKPLACE TESTING SURVEY: MEDICAL TESTING.

Employers have justified drug testing programs on many grounds, including:

> (1) drug use is illegal and therefore employers have a responsibility to discover employees who may be breaking the law; (2) employees abusing drugs often need substantial sums of money to buy drugs and these employees are likely to steal from their employer or to accept bribes on the job; (3) employees using drugs are likely to have a reduction in their productivity; (4) maintaining a drug-free workplace is essential to an employer's public image; and (5) drug testing is essential to protect safety and health.

Mark A. Rothstein, *Drug Testing in the Workplace: The Challenge to Employment Relations and Employment Law*, 63 CHI.-KENT L. REV. 683, 736 (1987).

Are these concerns valid? Consider the following:

> If the underlying purpose of drug testing is safety, there is no reason why drug testing should be limited to illicit drugs. In terms of the number of people who abuse them and the fatalities, injuries, and property damage caused by their effects in the workplace, alcohol and prescription drugs (often in combination) pose a much greater threat than illicit drugs.

Id. at 740.

Is safety or productivity the true employer motivation in drug testing, or do employers want to be seen as being on the right side in the war on drugs?

Several studies have concluded that drug screening is not cost effective for most private employers. *See* DRUG TESTING: COST AND EFFECT, CORNELL/ SMITHERS REPORT ON WORKPLACE SUBSTANCE ABUSE POLICY (1992). A report by the ACLU contends that employee off-duty drug use has an insignificant effect on work performance, that the cost of testing is unjustifiable, and that maintaining a mandatory drug-testing program can actually lower productivity. AMERICAN CIVIL LIBERTIES UNION, DRUG TESTING: A BAD INVESTMENT (1999) (reporting that Texas Instruments spends $1 million to test 10,000 workers — about $100 per employee).

1. CONSTITUTIONAL CHALLENGES

The advent of widespread drug testing in the workplace has led to legal challenges in both the public and private sector. Public employees challenged drug-testing programs under the Fourth Amendment's prohibition on unreasonable search and seizure, culminating in two Supreme Court decisions. *Skinner v. Railway Labor Executives Association*, 489 U.S. 602 (1989), involved a challenge to Federal Railroad Administration regulations mandating that private railroads test for drugs or alcohol after major railroad accidents. Although the seven-member majority found that taking blood and urine samples to test them for drugs were "searches" under the Fourth Amendment, the Court dispensed with the usual requirements of probable cause and warrant for conducting such tests. The record contained evidence that drug and alcohol abuse were substantial problems in the railroad industry and had led to numerous accidents. Concluding that the government's "special needs" for suspicionless testing outweighed the individual liberty interests of railroad employees, whose privacy expectation was diminished by the pervasive safety regulations in the industry, the Court held that the program was reasonable under the Fourth Amendment.

In the companion case decided on the same day, *National Treasury Employees Union v. von Raab*, 489 U.S. 602 (1989), employees of the United States Customs service challenged the employer practice of mandatory urinalysis testing of all employees who sought a transfer or promotion to positions involving direct drug interdiction or requiring the employee to carry a firearm or handle classified material. The five-member majority held that individualized suspicion of drug use was not required because the government's interest in deterring drug use among those eligible for promotion to positions involving drug interdiction and the use of firearms outweighed the individual privacy interests of those employees. The Court remanded for determination whether all of the employees categorized as handling classified information did indeed handle sufficiently sensitive information to reduce their expectation of privacy and justify their inclusion in the urinalysis program. Justice Scalia wrote in a dissent that because of the speculativeness of the conclusions that there was a drug use problem in the Customs Service, and that there was a connection between drug use and harm, the program was nothing more than a symbolic opposition to drug use. Setting an example, in Scalia's view, was not sufficient reason to justify the impairment of individual liberties occasioned by the program.

The Supreme Court struck down a government drug-testing requirement for the first time in *Chandler v. Miller*, 520 U.S. 305 (1997). In finding unconstitutional a Georgia statute requiring candidates for high office to pass a drug test in order to qualify for state office, the court concluded that "where, as in this case, public safety is not genuinely in jeopardy, the Fourth Amendment precludes the suspicionless search, no matter how conveniently arranged." *Id.* at 323. Echoing Justice Scalia's dissent in *von Raab*, the Court declared that the only real purpose for the Georgia statute was symbolic, to "display[] its commitment to the struggle against drug abuse."

Because *Chandler* addresses only candidates for public office, lower courts continue to disagree whether suspicionless random testing of government employees violates the Fourth Amendment. *Compare American Fed'n of Gov't Employees v. Weinberger*, 651 F. Supp. 726 (S.D. Ga. 1986) (mandatory, periodic urinalysis of civilian police officers is unreasonable search and seizure), *and Romaguera v. Gegenheimer*, 162 F.3d 893 (5th Cir. 1998) (random drug testing of specified groups of employees at the Clerk's Office is unconstitutional), *with Hatley v. Dep't of the Navy*, 164 F.3d 602 (Fed. Cir. 1998) (random urinalysis of firefighters is not an illegal search and seizure), *and Stigile v. Clinton*, 110 F.3d 801 (D.C. Cir. 1997) (urinalysis of passholders to the Old Executive Office Building is not an unreasonable search). *Cf. Anchorage Police Dep't Employees Ass'n v. Municipality of Anchorage*, 24 P.3d 547 (Alaska 2001) (upholding suspicionless testing of police and fire department employees upon job application, promotion, demotion, transfer, and after a traffic accident, but striking down random suspicionless testing as violating the state constitution); *Peterson v. City of Mesa*, 83 P.3d 35 (Ariz. 2004) (unannounced and random, suspicionless, testing of firefighters violated both Arizona and federal constitution).

2. PRIVATE-EMPLOYEE CHALLENGES

a. The Fourth-Amendment Analogy

Most courts in drug-testing cases sharply distinguish public employees, protected to some degree by the Fourth Amendment as cases like *Skinner* and *von Raab* show, and private employees. In one outlying case, *Hennessey v. Coastal Eagle Point Oil Co.*, 6 Indiv. Empl. Rts. Cas. (BNA) 113 (N.J. Super. Ct. 1989), the New Jersey Superior Court upheld a wrongful-discharge claim by an employee fired after failing a random drug test. The court relied on cases upholding constitutional claims of public employees against drug testing, insisting that they "pronounced a standard of general public policy regarding drug screening throughout the workplace, which applies to public as well as private employment." The Appellate Division promptly reversed, declaring:

> We are reluctant to utilize constitutional values of privacy as a source of public policy [in a wrongful-discharge case] in a private employment context. Application of constitutional values such as individual privacy to private relationships carries the danger that those values will "expand like a gas to fill up the available space."

Hennessey v. Coastal Eagle Point Oil Co., 589 A.2d 170, 176 (N.J. Super. Ct. App. Div. 1991). The New Jersey Supreme Court affirmed the Appellate

Division, emphasizing the employee's safety responsibilities, but hinted in dicta that the Constitution could serve as a source of public policy even in the private sector. *Hennessey v. Coastal Eagle Point Oil Co.*, 609 A.2d 11 (N.J. 1992).

Although some state constitutions guarantee a right of privacy, those rights typically do not extend to private employees. *See, e.g., Luedtke v. Nabors Alaska Drilling, Inc.*, 768 P.2d 1123 (1989) (right to privacy in Alaska constitution does not extend to plaintiffs contesting private-employer drug-testing program). California is an exception. *See Luck v. Southern Pacific Transp. Co.*, 267 Cal. Rptr. 618 (Cal. Ct. App.), *cert. denied*, 498 U.S. 939 (1990) (private-sector employer's drug-testing program involving urinalysis intruded upon reasonable expectations of privacy thus triggering constitutional analysis under the California constitition).

b. Privacy as Public Policy?

Private employees typically rely on common-law torts and statutory protections against the intrusive effects of drug testing. An interesting question is whether privacy claims ever rise to the level of public policy, or by definition are private interests, not public. Consider again the case of *Luck v. Southern Pacific Transportation Co.*, where the court upheld a jury verdict that a railroad breached its implied covenant of good faith and fair dealing by firing a computer operator who refused to submit to urinalysis. The employee was pregnant and feared a test that revealed this would harm her career. The court refused to find a violation of public policy that would support tort damages:

> A termination that is against public policy must affect a duty which inures to the benefit of the public at large rather than to a particular employer or employee. Past cases recognizing a tort action for termination in violation of public policy seek to protect the public by protecting an employee who refused to commit a crime, reported criminal activity, or disclosed other illegal, unethical, or unsafe practices. However, even the reporting of improper conduct may not constitute a public policy interest; if, for example, an employee's duty to disclose information to his employer serves only the employer's private interest, the public policy rationale does not apply. . . . [T]he absence of a distinctly public interest is apparent when we consider that if an employer and employee expressly agreed that the employee had no obligation to, and should not, inform the employer of any adverse information the employee learned about a co-worker's background, no public policy would render the agreement void. If the employer and employee could have lawfully made such an agreement, *Foley* [*v. Interactive Data Corp.*, 765 P.2d 373 (Cal. 1988)] reasoned, it cannot be said that the employer, by discharging an employee on this basis, violated a fundamental duty imposed on all employers for the protection of the public interest.
>
> Measured against the *Foley* standard, Luck did not state a cause of action for wrongful termination in violation of public policy. The right to privacy is, by its very name, a private right, not a public one. The parties could have lawfully agreed that Luck would submit to

urinalysis without violating any public interest. Such an agreement between Luck and Southern Pacific would not have been against public policy. Therefore, under *Foley*, there was no violation of public policy.

Judge Poche, dissenting, complained that the majority missed the inherent public policy contained in a constitutional right:

> Unless we accept the perfectly logical and defensible position that inalienable personal rights inure by their very nature to the benefit of all Californians and thus to the public benefit, we accord no practical protection to the very rights given the greatest deference by our Constitution. The bizarre outcome of the majority's reasoning is evident here. Barbara Luck has, they acknowledge, an inalienable right to be free from an involuntary intrusion into her privacy by her employer's demand she submit to urinalysis. Had her employer not fired her for refusing the test, she presumably could have obtained injunctive relief from the testing. However, because her employer immediately fired her for insubordination before she could seek such judicial vindication of her rights she is deprived of her job and of any tortious claim for the employer's conduct.

Another California court of appeal decided a case in the same year as *Luck* with the opposite result. *See Semore v. Pool*, 266 Cal. Rptr. 280 (Cal. Ct. App. 1990) (employee fired for refusing to submit to random pupillary eye drug test has an action for wrongful discharge in violation of public policy under state constitutional right to privacy).

Justice Brotherton stated the tension inherent in privacy-as-public-policy cases succinctly when he dissented in *Twigg v. Hercules Corp.*, 406 S.E.2d 52 (W. Va. 1990), from the majority's holding that it is contrary to public policy in West Virginia for an employer to require an employee to submit to drug testing, unless it has reasonable suspicion of drug usage or the job involves public safety or the safety of others. He said:

> I dissent to the majority's opinion for one reason: How can an attempt to create a drug-free environment be against the public policy of this State?

For a thoughtful discussion of the tension between privacy claims and the at-will doctrine, see Pauline T. Kim, *The Story of Luck v. Southern Pacific Transportation Co.: The Struggle to Perfect Employee Privacy*, *in* EMPLOYMENT LAW STORIES (Samuel Estreicher & Gillian Lester eds., 2006).

c. Invasive Procedure or Results?

The core objections of employees who challenge drug testing may differ. Some are concerned about the invasive or embarrassing procedures used in collecting samples, while others worry that testing is overinclusive in the information it reveals to employers.

Kelley v. Schlumberger, 849 F.2d 41 (1st Cir. 1988) (applying Louisiana law), is one of the few cases upholding a claim that the collection of a urine specimen is overly invasive. There, the Court of Appeals upheld a jury verdict of $1 for violating the employee's right to privacy and $125,000 for negligently inflicted emotional distress. As the court described the claim: "Direct observation of employees urinating was at the core of the plaintiff's complaint. During the trial he described himself as being 'disgusted by the whole idea of someone being paid to look at [his] penis while [he] urinated.'" *But see Fowler v. New York City Dep't of Sanitation*, 704 F. Supp. 1264 (S.D.N.Y. 1989) (upholding urinalysis testing of public employees that required male employees to provide urine samples under the direct observation of female supervisors).

More common is for employees to emphasize the overinclusive results of drug testing. Drug tests not only supply information about illegal drug use but potentially provide employers with data on an employee's ingestion of legal drugs or other medical conditions. Questionnaires requiring employees to list all drugs they have ingested that might affect the test results, as well as the test itself, can reveal to the employer whether the employee is pregnant, epileptic, diabetic, or taking birth control pills, among other medical facts. In *Capua v. City of Plainfield*, 643 F. Supp. 1507 (D.N.J. 1986), the District Court emphasized these concerns:

> [C]ompulsory urinalysis forces plaintiffs to divulge private, personal medical information unrelated to the government's professed interest in discovering illegal drug abuse. Advances in medical technology make it possible to uncover disorders, including epilepsy and diabetes, by analyzing chemical compounds in urine. Plaintiffs have a significant interest in safeguarding the confidentiality of such information whereas the government has no countervailing legitimate need for access to this personal medical data. The dangers of disclosure as a result of telltale urinalysis range from embarrassment to improper use of such information in job assignments, security, and promotion.

Some judges are more skeptical about the privacy claims. For example, Judge Higginbotham wrote in the lower court opinion in *National Treasury Employees Union v. von Raab*, 808 F.2d 1057, 1061 (5th Cir. 1987) (denying stay pending appeal):

> The precise privacy interest asserted is elusive, and the plaintiffs are, at best, inexact as to just what that privacy interest is. Finding an objectively reasonable expectation of privacy in urine, a waste product, contains inherent contradictions. The district court found such a right of privacy, but, in fairness, plaintiffs do not rest there. Rather, it appears from the plaintiffs' brief that it is the manner of taking the samples that is said to invade privacy, because outer garments in which a false sample might be hidden must be removed and a person of the same sex remains outside a stall while the applicant urinates. Yet, apart from the partial disrobing (apparently not independently challenged) persons using public toilet facilities experience a similar lack of privacy. The right must then be a perceived indignity in the whole process, a perceived affront to personal identity by the presence in the same room of another while engaging in a private body function.
>
> It is suggested that the testing program rests on a generalized lack of trust and not on a developed suspicion of an individual applicant.

Necessarily there is a plain implication that an applicant is part of a group that, given the demands of the job, cannot be trusted to be truthful about drug use. The difficulty is that just such distrust, or equally accurate, care, is behind every background check and every security check; indeed the information gained in tests of urine is not different from that disclosed in medical records, for which consent to examine is a routine part of applications for many sensitive government posts. In short, given the practice of testing and background checks required for so many government jobs, whether any expectations of privacy by these job applicants were objectively reasonable is dubious at best. Certainly, to ride with the cops one ought to expect inquiry, and by the surest means, into whether he is a robber.

d. Statutory Regulation

About half of the states now have legislation regulating drug testing. Most statutes regulate test procedures, written policies, testing in certified laboratories, and by imposing requirements such as a second test to confirm initial positive results. Some statutes seem primarily concerned with employee privacy, e.g., VT. STAT. ANN. tit. 21, §§ 511-519 (restricting the permissible circumstances and procedures for testing employees for drugs), while others insulate employers from liability if they follow limited restrictions on drug testing. E.g., UTAH CODE ANN. §§ 34-38-1 to -15. The following case illustrates some of the issues that may arise under such a statute.

SANCHEZ v. GEORGIA GULF CORP.
Court of Appeal of Louisiana, First Circuit
853 So. 2d 697 (2003)

WHIPPLE, J.:

On June 15, 2000, Sanchez, an "at-will" employee of Georgia Gulf, submitted to a random drug screen urinalysis. He was subsequently terminated from employment on June 22, 2000, for allegedly testing positive for the presence of a cocaine metabolite, Benzoylecgonine. Thereafter, on September 26, 2000, Sanchez instituted this action against Georgia Gulf, contending that it had breached its statutory duties to him in dismissing him on the basis of a positive drug test without first allowing him the opportunity to provide information about prescription medication he was taking that could result in an erroneous positive result. Sanchez sought damages for physical and mental pain and suffering, loss of income, loss of reputation and medical expenses. . . .

Georgia Gulf responded by filing a motion for summary judgment, essentially contending that because it could fire Sanchez "for any reason or for no reason" pursuant to the at-will employment doctrine, Sanchez had no claim for damages for wrongful termination. . . .

Sanchez also filed a cross-motion for summary judgment, contending that he was entitled to judgment in his favor, declaring that "the 'positive' cocaine test result attributed to him was invalid as a matter of law." . . .

[Georgia Gulf appeals the trial-court decision to deny Georgia Gulf's motion for summary judgment and grant Sanchez's motion for summary judgment.]

Louisiana's Drug-Testing Statute

Prior to addressing Georgia Gulf's assignments of error herein, a brief overview of Louisiana's drug-testing statute is necessary for an understanding of the issues presented. In 1990, the Louisiana legislature adopted drug-testing procedures set forth in LSA-R.S. 49:1001 *et seq.* (the "drug-testing statute"), that are designed to protect individual constitutional rights. Pursuant to this legislation, drug testing of Louisiana residents and of all samples collected in this state shall be performed in accordance with the Mandatory Guidelines for Federal Workplace Drug Testing Programs, as issued by the National Institute on Drug Abuse Guidelines and published in the Federal Register ("NIDA guidelines"). The NIDA Guidelines specify collection and testing procedures in order to assure accurate and unadulterated tests, set out specific requirements for reviewing and interpreting positive results and require that a medical review officer review the drug tests prior to reporting the results to the employer.

Specifically, the statutory framework contemplates that the sample be collected by a trained individual known as the "collection site person." The transfer of the sample to an appropriate laboratory is then regulated to ensure a proper chain of custody.

Pursuant to the statute, an initial or screening test is then performed on the sample. This test is an immunoassay screen used to eliminate "negative" urine specimens from further consideration. The initial or screening test may be performed either by a NIDA-certified laboratory or laboratory certified for forensic urine drug testing by the College of American Pathologists ("CAP-FUDT-certified laboratory") or by a "screening laboratory," which is a facility that is state-certified, but not NIDA- or CAP-FUDT-certified.

The statute specifies that if the initial test is positive, a second test, called a confirmatory test shall be performed by a NIDA- or CAP-FUDT-certified laboratory. The confirmatory test uses a different technique and chemical principle from that of the initial test in order to ensure reliability and accuracy.

The drug-testing statute further provides that all confirmed positive drug test results shall be reported directly from the laboratory to a qualified "medical review officer" for review. A "medical review officer" ("MRO") is statutorily defined as a "licensed physician responsible for receiving laboratory results generated by [an employer's] drug testing program who has knowledge of substance abuse disorders and has appropriate medical training to interpret and evaluate an individual's positive test result together with his medical history and any other relevant biomedical information." LSA-R.S. 49:1001(10).

In reviewing the confirmed positive result, the employer's designated MRO shall contact the individual who submitted the specimen as outlined in the NIDA guidelines, before making a final decision to verify a positive result or report that result to the employer. LSA-R.S. 49:1007(B) & (C). With regard to the purpose of the requirement of review by an MRO, the NIDA guidelines provide as follows:

> An essential part of the drug testing program is the final review of results. A positive test result does not automatically identify an employee/applicant as an illegal drug user. An individual with a detailed knowledge of possible alternate medical explanations is essential to the review of results. This review shall be performed by the MRO prior to the transmission of results to agency officials [or, in this case, the employer]. . . .

In its first and second assignments of error, Georgia Gulf contends that the trial court erred in granting Sanchez's motion for summary judgment, and finding that the positive drug test result was invalid as a matter of law, contending . . . LSA-R.S. 49:1007 does not require the invalidation of positive drug test results if the results were not reviewed by an MRO. . . .

[W]e find no merit to [this argument.] While conceding that LSA-R.S. 49:1007 provides that a positive test result "shall" be reviewed by an MRO, Georgia Gulf argues that this statute is not mandatory, but, rather, is merely directory. . . .

The interpretation of a statute as directory or mandatory depends upon legislative intent. Although a statute may not prescribe the result that will follow from non-compliance, if the requirement of the statute is so essential to the statutory plan that the legislative intent would be frustrated by non-compliance, then it is mandatory. A significant consideration in determining whether a statutory requirement should be given mandatory or directory effect is a comparison of the results to which each such construction would lead.

The drug-testing statute represents a comprehensive procedure that employers must follow in conducting drug testing of its employees that is designed to assure accurate and unadulterated tests and results. As detailed above, the strict specimen collection procedures, chain of custody requirements, testing methods and review process are designed to achieve this goal of accuracy. As noted by the United States District Court for the Northern District of New York, a generally-held belief in the accuracy of drug tests may lead employers to place undue confidence in their results. *Santiago v. Greyhound Lines, Inc.*, 956 F. Supp. 144, 151 (N.D.N.Y. 1997). As the court further emphasized, the harm to employees falsely accused is significant, even devastating, noting as follows:

> An employee can be shut out of the job market as a result of a tainted or negligent test result or report. The stigma as a drug user can cast doubt on the future prospects of employment, even if the test is later discovered to be a false positive. In a company that is downsizing, a mark or suspicion of any kind may result in an employee's termination and long-term unemployment.

Santiago, 956 F. Supp. at 151 (quoting David W. Lockard, *Protecting Medical Laboratories from Tort Liability for Drug Testing*, 17 J. LEGAL MED. 427, 428 (1996)).

Although LSA-R.S. 49:1007 does not prescribe the specific result that will follow from non-compliance, we conclude that failure to comply with the provisions of this statute would defeat the purpose of the drug-testing statute. As the legislature correctly recognized, the requirement that a positive result be reviewed by an MRO and verified as positive after consultation with the employee regarding relevant prescription medication or health conditions is essential for the protection of employers, who want to ensure a drug-free work environment, and employees, who voluntarily submit to these drug screens. Absent a requirement that such results be reviewed by a qualified MRO, an employee who falsely tests positive is deprived of the ability to explain those results. As the legislature apparently recognized, the detrimental effect to the employee's career could be devastating. Indeed, in the instant case, Sanchez avers that he was a twenty-six year employee of Georgia Gulf who has never used illegal drugs, but was fired without being given the opportunity to discuss medication he was taking and any effect it may have had on the test results. This factual situation, if established at trial, is precisely the type of devastating result that may occur where an employee is deprived of the opportunity to explain the results.

Accordingly, we conclude that failure to comply with the provisions of LSA-R.S. 49:1007 would defeat the purpose of the drug-testing statute as a whole; thus, these requirements are mandatory. Georgia Gulf's argument to the contrary is without merit.

Because we conclude that the requirement of MRO review pursuant to LSA-R.S. 49:1007 is mandated by the statute, and there is no factual dispute that MRO review as contemplated therein did not occur in this case, we find no error in the trial court's granting of Sanchez's motion for summary judgment, finding that "the 'positive' cocaine test result attributed to [Sanchez] was invalid as a matter of law." . . .

NOTES

1. ***Job Protection for an At-Will Employee.*** Sanchez was an at-will employee, and yet the court rejected the employer's argument that it could fire Sanchez "for any reason or for no reason" and instead awarded Sanchez damages. Under the *Sanchez* court's reading, the Louisiana's drug-testing statute essentially gives at-will employees protection from discharge when employers do not comply with the statute's mandatory requirements.

2. ***The Dilemma of Consent.*** Suppose Sanchez had refused to take the test and was fired as a result. Many drug-testing statutes expressly permit an employer to take disciplinary action, including dismissal, if an employee refuses to provide a sample. *See, e.g.*, MISS. CODE ANN. § 71-7-7; ALASKA STAT. § 23.10.655. The common-law approach is more ambiguous. Some courts have refused to decide the legality of drug-testing programs if the employee refuses to take the test. The employee must make a choice: take the drug test and litigate its invasiveness later or refuse to take the test, retain privacy, but lose the job. *See, e.g., Luedtke v. Nabors Alaska Drilling, Inc.*, 768 P.2d 1123 (1989) (no cause of action for invasion of privacy arises where the intrusion is prevented from taking place) and *Everett v. Napper*, 632 F. Supp. 1481 (N.D. Ga. 1986) (no search under the Fourth Amendment when discharged employees refused to take urinalysis drug test). *But see American Fed'n of Gov't*

Employees v. Weinberger, 651 F. Supp. 726 (S.D. Ga. 1986) (advance consent ineffective when the drug-testing program is unreasonable search under the Fourth Amendment); *Luck v. Southern Pac. Transp. Co.*, 267 Cal. Rptr. 618 (Cal. Ct. App.), *cert. denied*, 498 U.S. 939 (1990) (right to refuse to submit to urinalysis a privacy interest protected by state constitution).

The issue was posed directly in *Jennings v. Minco Technology Labs,* 765 S.W.2d 497 (Tex. Ct. App. 1989), when an employee sought to enjoin a drug-testing plan under which the employer would ask employees on a random basis to give urine samples to be tested, with their consent, for evidence of illegal drug consumption. Employees would be fired for refusing to give a urine sample. While recognizing the common-law right to privacy, the court refused to find that the drug-testing program fit within the public policy exception to employment at will. The court continued:

> We cannot accept Jennings's theory for an additional reason. Jennings's employer threatens no *unlawful* invasion of any employee's privacy interest; therefore it threatens no act contrary to the public policy underlying the common-law right of privacy. The company's plan contemplates, rather, that an employee's urine will be taken and tested only if he consents. The plan therefore assumes, respects, and depends upon the central element of the right of privacy and its attendant public policy: the individual's exclusive right to determine the occasion, extent, and conditions under which he will disclose his private affairs to others. This consensual predicate to any test reduces Jennings's argument to her remaining contention.

> Jennings contends finally that she is poor and needs her salary to maintain herself and her family. Consequently, any "consent" she may give, in submitting to urinalysis, will be illusory and not real. For that practical reason, she argues, the company's plan does threaten a non-consensual, and therefore unlawful, invasion of her privacy. We disagree with the theory. A competent person's legal rights and obligations, under the common law governing the making, interpretation, and enforcement of contracts, cannot vary according to his economic circumstances. There cannot be one law of contracts for the rich and another for the poor. We cannot imagine a theory more at war with the basic assumptions held by society and its law. Nothing would introduce greater disorder into both. Because Jennings may not be denied the legal rights others have under the common law of contracts, she may not be given greater rights than they. The law views her economic circumstances as neutral and irrelevant facts insofar as her contracts are concerned.

3. *Applicants versus Employees.* A number of drug-testing statutes distinguish between applicants and employees, offering stronger protections for employees. *See, e.g.*, Vt. Stat. Ann. tit. 21, §§ 512-513, which requires an employer to have probable cause for testing employees and prohibits termination for a positive test if an employee successfully completes employer-provided rehabilitation counseling, but which requires only notice of the drug-testing procedure for applicants.

Courts have drawn a parallel distinction in interpreting common law and constitutional doctrine. An example is *Loder v. City of Glendale*, 927 P.2d 1200 (Cal. 1997). The city of Glendale required all applicants for new jobs and current employees seeking promotions to pass a drug and alcohol test. The court held that the federal Constitution prohibited the drug test for employees, but held that the federal and state Constitutions permitted the drug test for job applicants. It reasoned that the employer has a greater need to conduct suspicionless drug tests on applicants, and that the drug test was a lesser invasion of privacy on applicants than employees:

> [A]n employer generally need not resort to suspicionless drug testing to determine whether a current employee is likely to be absent from work or less productive or effective as a result of current drug or alcohol abuse: an employer can observe the employee at work, evaluate his or her work product and safety record, and check employment records to determine whether the employee has been excessively absent or late. If a current employee's performance and work record provides some basis for suspecting that the employee presently is abusing drugs or alcohol, the employer will have an individualized basis for requesting that the particular employee undergo drug testing, and current employees whose performance provides no reason to suspect that they currently are using drugs or abusing alcohol will not be compelled to sustain the intrusion on their privacy inherent in mandatory urinalysis testing. . . .

> When deciding whether to hire a job applicant, however, an employer has not had a similar opportunity to observe the applicant over a period of time. Although the employer can request information regarding the applicant's performance in past jobs or in nonemployment settings, an employer reasonably may lack total confidence in the reliability of information supplied by a former employer or other references. And although an employer will, of course, obtain the opportunity to make its own observations after it has hired the applicant, the hiring of a new employee frequently represents a considerable investment on the part of an employer, often involving the training of the new employee. Furthermore, once an applicant is hired, any attempt by the employer to dismiss the employee generally will entail additional expenses, including those relating to the hiring of a replacement. In view of these considerations, we believe that an employer has a greater need for, and interest in, conducting suspicionless drug testing of job applicants than it does in conducting such testing of current employees.

> Turning to the degree of the intrusion on reasonable expectations of privacy imposed by the city's drug testing program, we believe that the intrusion on privacy is significantly diminished because the drug testing urinalysis in this case was administered as part of a preemployment medical examination that the job applicant, in any event, would have been required to undergo. . . . Plaintiff in this case, however, has not contended that the city's examination procedure is unlawful insofar as it requires all job applicants who have been offered

employment to submit to a medical examination as a condition of their hiring, and plaintiff has not cited, and our independent research has not revealed, any authority suggesting it is impermissible for an employer to require all job applicants to submit to medical examinations without regard to the nature of the position in question.

927 P.2d at 1223-24.

Justice Kennard, dissenting, disputed the basic distinction between applicants and employees. First, she questioned "whether the government's purely economic considerations . . . can ever be sufficient 'to overcome the interests in vindicating human dignity' embodied in the constitutionally guaranteed right of privacy." Further, hiring applicants on a probationary basis would be an alternative, less intrusive means of determining whether an individual's performance is affected by substance abuse. Justice Kennard granted that the alternative "may impose certain costs on the employer," but declared that such costs would be partially offset by the greater accuracy of on-the-job observation.

Despite Justice Kennard's hesitations, greater judicial scrutiny of drug testing of employees may make sense under the internal labor markets model. Job applicants have not established roots with the company or made firm-specific investments, and thus are freer to reject invasive applications. Employers have more power to exploit existing employees, who because of their job specific capital have much more to lose if they refuse to consent to invasive testing.

Labor-law regulation of unionized employees also distinguishes between drug testing of job applicants and employees. Drug and alcohol testing of current employees is a mandatory subject of bargaining, thus requiring employers to bargain with the union before implementing a drug-testing program. *Johnson-Bateman Co. v. International Ass'n of Machinists, Local 1047*, 295 N.L.R.B. 180 (1989). Employers are free to test job applicants without consulting the union, however, because applicants are not employees within the meaning of the collective-bargaining obligations of the NLRA. *Cowles Media Co. v. Newspaper Guild, Local 2*, 295 N.L.R.B. 543 (1989).

D. HONESTY TESTS AND OTHER KINDS OF BACKGROUND SCREENING

The annual economic loss to American business from employee theft may be as high as $25 billion. *See* IRA M. SHEPARD & ROBERT L. DUSTON, THIEVES AT WORK: AN EMPLOYER'S GUIDE TO COMBATING WORKPLACE DISHONESTY 19 (1988). In addition to video and other forms of surveillance discussed earlier in this chapter, employers have employed a variety of techniques designed to screen job applicants for honesty and to investigate thefts.

In the 1970s and 1980s, the use of polygraph or "lie-detector" tests became popular. The legal response of the states to polygraphs varied widely, and many commentators perceived widespread employer abuse of the polygraph. In 1988 Congress passed the Employee Polygraph Protection Act of 1988, 29 U.S.C. §§ 2001-2009. The Act makes it unlawful for any employer directly or indirectly to require or request any employee or applicant to submit to a lie detector test, or to use the results of any lie detector test. § 2002. It provides for civil penalties up to $10,000 and authorizes private civil actions by employees or applicants. § 2005. It contains a number of exemptions, including public employers, national defense and security contractors, security guard firms, and drug manufacturers and distributors. § 2006. Although the statute has greatly restricted private employer use of polygraphs, the significant sphere in which the statute does not prohibit employer use of polygraphs is in an ongoing investigation involving economic loss or injury to the employer's business, such as theft, embezzlement, or misappropriation. §§ 2006(d), 2007. In such circumstances, the employer may request an employee to submit to a polygraph test so long as certain procedures are followed, such as giving the examinee the right to terminate the test at any time and to be exempted if a medical condition verified by a physician would produce abnormal responses. The examinee may also not be "asked questions in a manner designed to degrade, or needlessly intrude on, such examinee" or asked questions regarding religious, racial, political, sexual, or union beliefs. The Act does not preempt more restrictive state laws. § 2009.

NOTES

1. *Scope of the Ongoing-Investigation Exemption.* Suppose a worker accuses a supervisor of sexual assault when they were alone on a shift, which the supervisor vigorously denies. How should the employer resolve this situation? Could it ask the supervisor to take a polygraph examination, and fire him if he failed the test? Read § 2006(d).

Suppose the employer decides to forego any polygraph exam and simply fires the supervisor on the basis of the worker's accusation. Might the supervisor ask the employer to give him a polygraph test, so that if he passes he can keep his job? Read § 2002.

Suppose an employee is suspected of taking other employees' purses (or breaking into cars in the company parking lot). Can the employer ask the employee to submit to a polygraph test?

Suppose an employer suspects an employee was drunk when he had an accident in a company car while driving to deposit cash in the company account. Much of the cash is lost. Can the employer give a polygraph test to determine if the employee was drunk or was careless with the money?

2. *Paper-and-Pencil Honesty Testing.* As detailed in Chapter 10, employers are increasingly unwilling to divulge information about former employees for fear it will provide ammunition for a defamation suit. Now that pre-employment polygraph testing is largely illegal, employers have turned to honesty testing (also called paper-and-pencil testing or integrity testing).

The Department of Labor's final regulations make clear that paper-and-pencil honesty tests are not included in the definition of "lie detector" under the Employee Polygraph Protection Act of 1988. Most state anti-polygraph statutes likewise do not cover paper-and-pencil tests. For example, the Minnesota Supreme Court interpreted its statute banning a "polygraph, voice stress analysis, or any test purporting to test honesty" as covering only tests that measure physiological changes. *See State by Spannaus v. Century*

Camera, Inc., 309 N.W.2d 735 (Minn. 1981). Only a few states, including Massachusetts and Rhode Island, have statutorily restricted the use of honesty tests. An added consideration is the relatively low cost of honesty tests, which cost perhaps $5 to $20 each to give and score, compared with polygraph testing, which costs from $35 to $50. The upshot has been a dramatic increase in the use of honesty testing in recent years.

Honesty tests purport to measure dishonesty or general counterproductive behavior, which may include such acts as "participating in strikes, coming to work late, and abusing sick leave." OFFICE OF TECHNOLOGY ASSESSMENT, THE USE OF INTEGRITY TESTS FOR PRE-EMPLOYMENT SCREENING 25 (1990). This report concluded, however, that "the research on integrity tests has not yet produced data that clearly supports or dismisses the assertion that these tests can predict honest behavior." *Id.* at 8. Much of the research on honesty tests has so far been conducted by the test makers themselves.

SOROKA v. DAYTON HUDSON CORP.
California Court of Appeal
1 Cal. Rptr. 2d 77 (1991)

REARDON, ASSOCIATE JUSTICE.

Appellants Sibi Soroka, Sue Urry and William d'Arcangelo filed a class action challenging respondent Dayton Hudson Corporation's practice of requiring Target Store security officer applicants to pass a psychological screening. The trial court denied Soroka's motion for a preliminary injunction to prohibit the use of this screening pending the outcome of this litigation. . . . The American Civil Liberties Union (ACLU) filed an amicus brief in support of Soroka's constitutional right to privacy claims. We reverse the trial court's order denying a preliminary injunction and remand the matter to the trial court for further proceedings on class certification.

I. *Facts*

Respondent Dayton Hudson Corporation owns and operates Target Stores throughout California and the United States. Job applicants for store security officer (SSO) positions must, as a condition of employment, take a psychological test that Target calls the "Psychscreen." An SSO's main function is to observe, apprehend and arrest suspected shoplifters. An SSO is not armed, but carries handcuffs and may use force against a suspect in self-defense. Target views good judgment and emotional stability as important SSO job skills. It intends the Psychscreen to screen out SSO applicants who are emotionally unstable, who may put customers or employees in jeopardy, or who will not take direction and follow Target procedures.

The Psychscreen is a combination of the Minnesota Multiphasic Personality Inventory and the California Psychological Inventory. Both of these tests have been used to screen out emotionally unfit applicants for public safety positions such as police officers, correctional officers, pilots, air traffic controllers and nuclear power plant operators.[4] The test is composed of 704 true-false

---

[4] We view the duties and responsibilities of these public safety personnel to be substantially different from those of store security officers.

questions. At Target, the test administrator is told to instruct applicants to answer every question.

The test includes questions about an applicant's religious attitudes, such as: "¶ 67. I feel sure that there is only one true religion. . . . ¶ 201. I have no patience with people who believe there is only one true religion. . . . ¶ 477. My soul sometimes leaves my body. . . . ¶ 483. A minister can cure disease by praying and putting his hand on your head. . . . ¶ 486. Everything is turning out just like the prophets of the Bible said it would. . . . ¶ 505. I go to church almost every week. . . . ¶ 506. I believe in the second coming of Christ. . . . ¶ 516. I believe in a life hereafter. . . . ¶ 578. I am very religious (more than most people). . . . ¶ 580. I believe my sins are unpardonable. . . . ¶ 606. I believe there is a God. . . . ¶ 688. I believe there is a Devil and a Hell in afterlife."

The test includes questions that might reveal an applicant's sexual orientation, such as: "¶ 137. I wish I were not bothered by thoughts about sex. . . . ¶ 290. I have never been in trouble because of my sex behavior. . . . ¶ 339. I have been in trouble one or more times because of my sex behavior. . . . ¶ 466. My sex life is satisfactory. . . . ¶ 492. I am very strongly attracted by members of my own sex. . . . ¶ 496. I have often wished I were a girl. (Or if you are a girl) I have never been sorry that I am a girl. . . . ¶ 525. I have never indulged in any unusual sex practices. . . . ¶ 558. I am worried about sex matters. . . . ¶ 592. I like to talk about sex. . . . ¶ 640. Many of my dreams are about sex matters."[5]

An SSO's completed test is scored by the consulting psychologist firm of Martin-McAllister. The firm interprets test responses and rates the applicant on five traits: emotional stability, interpersonal style, addiction potential, dependability and reliability, and socialization — *i.e.*, a tendency to follow established rules. Martin-McAllister sends a form to Target rating the applicant on these five traits and recommending whether to hire the applicant. Hiring decisions are made on the basis of these recommendations, although the recommendations may be overridden. Target does not receive any responses to specific questions. It has never conducted a formal validation study of the Psychscreen, but before it implemented the test, Target tested 17 or 18 of its more successful SSO's.

Appellants Sibi Soroka, Susan Urry and William d'Arcangelo were applicants for SSO positions when they took the Psychscreen. All three were upset by the nature of the Psychscreen questions. Soroka was hired by Target. Urry — a Mormon — and d'Arcangelo were not hired. In August 1989, Soroka filed a charge that use of the Psychscreen discriminated on the basis of race, sex, religion and physical handicap with the Department of Fair Employment and Housing.

Having exhausted their administrative remedies, Soroka, Urry and D'Arcangelo filed a class action against Target in September 1989 to challenge its use of the Psychscreen. . . . Soroka alleged causes of action for violation

---

[5] Soroka challenges many different types of questions on appeal. However, we do not find it necessary to consider questions other than those relating to religious beliefs and sexual orientation.

of the constitutional right to privacy, invasion of privacy, disclosure of confidential medical information, fraud, negligent misrepresentation, intentional and negligent infliction of emotional distress, violation of the Fair Employment and Housing Act, violation of sections 1101 and 1102 of the Labor Code, and unfair business practices. . . .

In June 1990, Soroka moved for a preliminary injunction to prohibit Target from using the Psychscreen during the pendency of the action. A professional psychologist submitted a declaration opining that use of the test was unjustified and improper, resulting in faulty assessments to the detriment of job applicants. He concluded that its use violated basic professional standards and that it had not been demonstrated to be reliable or valid as an employment evaluation. For example, one of the two tests on which the Psychscreen was based was designed for use only in hospital or clinical settings. Soroka noted that two of Target's experts had previously opined that the Minnesota Multiphasic Personality Inventory was virtually useless as a preemployment screening device. It was also suggested that the Psychscreen resulted in a 61 percent rate of false positives — that is, that more than 6 in 10 qualified applicants for SSO positions were not hired.

Target's experts submitted declarations contesting these conclusions and favoring the use of the Psychscreen as an employment screening device. Some Target officials believed that use of this test has increased the quality and performance of its SSO's. However, others testified that they did not believe that there had been a problem with the reliability of SSO applicants before the Psychscreen was implemented. Target's vice president of loss prevention was unable to link changes in asset protection specifically to use of the Psychscreen. In rebuttal, Soroka's experts were critical of the conclusions of Target's experts. One rebuttal expert noted that some of the intrusive, non-job-related questions had been deleted from a revised form of the test because they were offensive, invasive and added little to the test's validity. . . .

The trial court . . . denied Soroka's motion for preliminary injunction. . . .

II. *Preliminary Injunction*

. . . .

1. *The Right to Privacy*

The California Constitution explicitly protects our right to privacy. Article I, section 1 provides: "All people are by nature free and independent and have inalienable rights. Among these are enjoying and defending life and liberty, acquiring, possessing, and protecting property, and pursuing and obtaining safety, happiness, and privacy." . . .

Target concedes that the Psychscreen constitutes an intrusion on the privacy rights of the applicants, although it characterizes this intrusion as a limited one. However, even the constitutional right to privacy does not prohibit all incursion into individual privacy. The parties agree that a violation of the right to privacy may be justified, but disagree about the standard to be used to make this determination. At trial, Target persuaded the court to apply a reasonableness standard because Soroka was an applicant, rather than a Target employee. On appeal, Soroka and the ACLU contend that Target must show more than reasonableness — that it must demonstrate a compelling interest — to justify its use of the Psychscreen.

2. *Applicants vs. Employees*

Soroka and the ACLU contend that job applicants are entitled to the protection of the compelling interest test, just as employees are. The trial court disagreed, employing a reasonableness standard enunciated in a decision of Division Three of this District which distinguished between applicants and employees. (*Wilkinson v. Times Mirror Corp.*, 215 Cal. App. 3d 1034.)

In *Wilkinson*, a book publisher required job applicants to submit to drug urinalysis as part of its preemployment physical examination. The appellate court rejected the applicants' contention that the compelling interest test should apply to determine whether the publisher's invasion of their privacy interests was justified under article I, section 1. Instead, the court fashioned and applied a lesser standard based on whether the challenged conduct was reasonable. When setting this standard, the most persuasive factor for the *Wilkinson* court appears to have been that the plaintiffs were applicants for employment rather than employees. "Any individual who chooses to seek employment necessarily also chooses to disclose certain personal information to prospective employers, such as employment and educational history, and to allow the prospective employer to verify that information." (*Id.*, at 1048.) This applicant-employee distinction was pivotal for the *Wilkinson* court. "Simply put, applicants for jobs . . . have a choice; they may consent to the limited invasion of their privacy resulting from the testing, or may decline both the test and the conditional offer of employment." (*Id.*, at 1049.)

Our review of the ballot argument satisfies us that the voters did not intend to grant less privacy protection to job applicants than to employees. The ballot argument specifically refers to job applicants when it states that Californians "are required to report some information, regardless of our wishes for privacy or our belief that there is no public need for the information. Each time we . . . *interview for a job*, . . . a dossier is opened and an informational profile is sketched." (Ballot Pamp., Proposed Amends. to Cal. Const. with arguments to voters, Gen. Elec. (Nov. 7, 1972) p. 27, emphasis added.) Thus, the major underpinning of *Wilkinson* is suspect.

Appellate court decisions predating *Wilkinson* have also applied the compelling interest standard in cases involving job applicants. (*See Central Valley Ch. 7th Step Foundation, Inc. v. Younger* (1989) 214 Cal. App. 3d 145, 151, 162-165 [arrest records distributed to public employers].) Target attempts to distinguish these cases as ones involving public, not private, employers, but that is a distinction without a difference in the context of the state constitutional right to privacy. Private and public employers alike are bound by the terms of the privacy provisions of article I, section 1. . . .

In conclusion, we are satisfied that any violation of the right to privacy of job applicants must be justified by a compelling interest. This conclusion is consistent with the voter's expression of intent when they amended article

I, section 1 to make privacy an inalienable right and with subsequent decisions of the California Supreme Court.

3. *Nexus Requirement*

Soroka and the ACLU also argue that Target has not demonstrated that its Psychscreen questions are job-related — *i.e.*, that they provide information relevant to the emotional stability of its SSO applicants. Having considered the religious belief and sexual orientation questions carefully, we find this contention equally persuasive.

Although the state right of privacy is broader than the federal right, California courts construing article I, section 1 have looked to federal precedents for guidance. Under the lower federal standard, employees may not be compelled to submit to a violation of their right to privacy unless a clear, direct nexus exists between the nature of the employee's duty and the nature of the violation. We are satisfied that this nexus requirement applies with even greater force under article I, section 1.

Again, we turn to the voter's interpretation of article I, section 1. The ballot argument — the only legislative history for the privacy amendment — specifically states that one purpose of the constitutional right to privacy is to prevent businesses "from collecting . . . *unnecessary* information about us. . . ." (*White v. Davis*, 13 Cal. 3d at 774, emphasis added; *see Wilkinson v. Times Mirror Corp., supra*, 215 Cal. App. 3d at 1040.) It also asserts that the right to privacy would "preclude the collection of *extraneous* or *frivolous* information." (Ballot Pamp., Proposed Amends. to Cal. Const. with arguments to voters, Gen. Elec. (Nov. 7, 1972) p. 28, emphasis added.) Thus, the ballot language requires that the information collected be *necessary* to achieve the purpose for which the information has been gathered. This language convinces us that the voters intended that a nexus requirement apply.

The California Supreme Court has also recognized this nexus requirement. When it found that public employees could not be compelled to take a polygraph test, it criticized the questions asked as both highly personal and unrelated to any employment duties. (*See Long Beach City Employees Assn. v. City of Long Beach*, 41 Cal. 3d 937, 945 (1986).) It found that a public employer may require its workers to answer *some* questions, but only those that specifically, directly and narrowly relate to the performance of the employee's official duties. (*Id.*, at 947.) This nexus requirement also finds support in the seminal case from our high court on the right to privacy, which characterizes as one of the principal mischiefs at which article I, section 1 was directed "the *overbroad* collection . . . of unnecessary personal information. . . ." (*White v. Davis, supra*, 13 Cal. 3d at 775, emphasis added.) If the information Target seeks is not job-related, that collection is overbroad, and the information unnecessary.

Wilkinson attempted to address this nexus requirement but its conclusion is inconsistent with federal law, which affords less protection than that provided by the state constitutional privacy amendment. *Wilkinson* held that an employer has a legitimate interest in not hiring individuals whose drug abuse may render them unable to perform their job responsibilities in a satisfactory manner. Federal courts have held that this sort of generalized justification is not sufficient to justify an infringement of an employee's Fourth Amendment rights. If this justification is insufficient to satisfy a lesser Fourth Amendment test, then it cannot pass muster under the more stringent compelling interest test.

4. *Application of Law*

Target concedes that the Psychscreen intrudes on the privacy interests of its job applicants. Having carefully considered *Wilkinson*, we find its reasoning unpersuasive. As it is inconsistent with both the legislative history of article I, section 1 and the case law interpreting that provision, we decline to follow it. Under the legislative history and case law, Target's intrusion into the privacy rights of its SSO applicants must be justified by a compelling interest to withstand constitutional scrutiny. Thus, the trial court abused its discretion by committing an error of law — applying the reasonableness test, rather than the compelling interest test.

While Target unquestionably has an interest in employing emotionally stable persons to be SSO's, testing applicants about their religious beliefs and sexual orientation does not further this interest. To justify the invasion of privacy resulting from use of the Psychscreen, Target must demonstrate a compelling interest and must establish that the test serves a job-related purpose. In its opposition to Soroka's motion for preliminary injunction, Target made no showing that a person's religious beliefs or sexual orientation have any bearing on the emotional stability or on the ability to perform an SSO's job responsibilities. It did no more than to make generalized claims about the Psychscreen's relationship to emotional fitness and to assert that it has seen an overall improvement in SSO quality and performance since it implemented the Psychscreen. This is not sufficient to constitute a compelling interest, nor does it satisfy the nexus requirement. Therefore, Target's inquiry into the religious beliefs and sexual orientation of SSO applicants unjustifiably violates the state constitutional right to privacy. Soroka has established that he is likely to prevail on the merits of his constitutional claims. . . .

B. *Statutory Claims*

1. *Fair Employment and Housing Act*

Soroka contends that the trial court abused its discretion by concluding that he was unlikely to prevail on his FEHA claims. These claims are based on allegations that the questions require applicants to divulge information about their religious beliefs. . . .

In California, an employer may not refuse to hire a person on the basis of his or her religious beliefs. Likewise, an employer is prohibited from making any non-job-related inquiry that expresses "directly or indirectly, any limitation, specification, or discrimination as to . . . religious creed. . . ." (Gov. Code, § 12940, subd. (d).) FEHA guidelines provide that an employer may make any preemployment inquiry that does not discriminate on a basis enumerated in FEHA. However, inquiries that identify an individual on the basis of religious creed are unlawful unless pursuant to a permissible defense. Job-relatedness is an affirmative defense. A means of selection that is facially neutral but that has an adverse impact on persons on the basis of religious creed is permissible only on a showing that the selection process is sufficiently related to an essential function of the job in question to warrant its use.

The trial court committed an error of law when it found that questions such as "I feel sure that there is only one true religion," "Everything is turning out just like the prophets of the Bible said it would," and "I believe in the second coming of Christ" were not intended to reveal religious beliefs. Clearly, these questions were intended to — and did — inquire about the religious beliefs of Target's SSO applicants. As a matter of law, these questions constitute an inquiry that expresses a "specification [of a] religious creed." (Gov. Code, § 12940, subd. (d).)

Once Soroka established a *prima facie* case of an impermissible inquiry, the burden of proof shifted to Target to demonstrate that the religious beliefs questions were job-related. As we have already determined, Target has not established that the Psychscreen's questions about religious beliefs have any bearing on that applicant's ability to perform an SSO's job responsibilities. Therefore, Soroka has established the likelihood that he will prevail at trial on this statutory claim.

2. *Labor Code Sections 1101 and 1102*

Soroka also argues that the trial court abused its discretion by concluding that he was unlikely to prevail on his claims based on sections 1101 and 1102 of the Labor Code. The trial court found that Soroka did not establish that the questions asked in the Psychscreen are designed to reveal an applicant's sexual orientation. It also found that Soroka did not establish that Target's hiring decisions are made on the basis of sexual orientation.

Under California law, employers are precluded from making, adopting or enforcing any policy that tends to control or direct the political activities or affiliations of employees. (Lab.Code, § 1101, subd. (b).) Employers are also prohibited from coercing, influencing, or attempting to coerce or influence employees to adopt or follow or refrain from adopting or following any particular line of political activity by threatening a loss of employment. (*Id.*, § 1102.) These statutes have been held to protect applicants as well as employees. (*Gay Law Students Assn. v. Pacific Tel. & Tel. Co.* (1979) 24 Cal. 3d 458, 487, fn. 16, 595 P.2d 592.)

Labor Code sections 1101 and 1102 protect an employee's fundamental right to engage in political activity without employer interference. (*Gay Law Students Assn. v. Pacific Tel. & Tel. Co., supra*, 24 Cal. 3d at 487.) The "struggle of the homosexual community for equal rights, particularly in the field of employment, must be recognized as a political activity." (*Id.*, at 488.) These statutes also prohibit a private employer from discriminating against an employee on the basis of his or her sexual orientation. (*See* 69 Ops. Cal. Atty. Gen. 80, 82 (1986).)

The trial court committed an error of law when it determined that Psychscreen questions such as "I am very strongly attracted by members of my own sex" were not intended to reveal an applicant's sexual orientation. On its face, this question directly asks an applicant to reveal his or her sexual orientation. One of the five traits that Target uses the Psychscreen to determine is "socialization," which it defines as "the extent to which an individual subscribes to traditional values and mores and feels an obligation to act in accordance with them." Persons who identify themselves as homosexuals may be stigmatized as "willing to defy or violate" these norms, which may in turn result in an invalid test.

As a matter of law, this practice tends to discriminate against those who express a homosexual orientation. (*See* Lab. Code, § 1101.) It also constitutes an attempt to coerce an applicant to refrain from expressing a homosexual orientation by threat of loss of employment. (*See id.*, § 1102.) Therefore, Soroka has established that he is likely to prevail at trial on this statutory basis, as well.

The order denying the preliminary injunction is reversed. . . .

POCHE, ACTING P.J., and PERLEY, J., concur.

NOTES

1. Settlement. The *Soroka* case eventually settled for over $2 million. The 2,500 applicants who had taken the invasive test split $1.3 million; $60,000 went to the four named plaintiffs; and the rest went for attorney's fees. *See* 89 Ind. Emp. Rts (BNA) No. 16 (July 20, 1993) and No. 22 (October 12, 1993). The California Supreme Court then dismissed the case as moot, robbing it of precedential value. *See Soroka v. Dayton Hudson Corp.*, 862 P.2d 148 (Cal. 1993).

2. Subsequent Legal Developments. The California Supreme Court later departed from *Soroka*'s approach to analyzing a privacy claim under the California constitution. In *Hill v. National Collegiate Athletic Ass'n*, 865 P.2d 633 (1994), a case involving drug testing of college athletes, the court held that a plaintiff alleging a violation of privacy must first establish a legally protected privacy interest, a reasonable expectation of privacy in the circumstances, and a serious invasion of privacy. If these threshold elements are satisfied, the defendant may prevail only by demonstrating that the intrusion is justified by one or more countervailing interests. The plaintiff may, in turn, rebut the defendant's assertion of countervailing interests by showing a less intrusive means by which the interests could be satisfied. Notably, *Hill* rejected the universal application of a "compelling" interest standard, stating instead that ordinary balancing tests will generally suffice.

3. Psychologically Naked. Professor Finkin finds the *Soroka* case to be a small victory.

> *Soroka*, seemingly a vindication of employee privacy, illustrates how narrow the idea of intrusion is even under a legal regime seemingly more generous than the common law. If the gravamen of the wrong is requiring an employee to answer certain intimate questions, it follows that privacy would not be implicated if the questions were non-intrusive. . . . This eludes the real privacy issue posed by a psychological assessment: It strips the "test subject" — note the dehumanization

inherent in the language — psychologically naked. Unlike an interview, where one confronts a human being whom one can attempt to persuade . . ., the individual is rendered helpless, depersonalized, transparent, an object of scientific scrutiny. . . .

This might be justified by the special circumstances of a particular employment, for example, in aviation or atomic energy. But in almost all jurisdictions, so long as members of protected classes are not disproportionately disadvantaged, these devices may be used with impunity, irrespective of the want of professional validation for such use.

Matthew W. Finkin, *Employee Privacy, American Values, and the Law*, 72 CHI.-KENT L. REV. 221, 234-35 (1996).

4. *Gay Rights and Political Activity.* While sometimes lost in the constitutional discussion, the *Soroka* court's discussion of the statutory claims is important. It expands on cases holding that California's Labor Code prohibits private employers from interfering with the political activity of employees, concluding that this prohibition includes discrimination on the basis of sexual orientation. Through the ban on interfering with political activity, the court holds as a matter of law that a private employer cannot inquire about sexual orientation.

5. *Privacy Claims of Job Applicants.* *Soroka* held that job applicants should have as much privacy protection as employees. This ruling probably does not survive *Loder v. City of Glendale*, 927 P.2d 1200 (Cal. 1997), discussed in Part C of this chapter.

6. *The MMPI.* One of the two tests upon which Psychscreen is based is the Minnesota Multiphasic Personality Inventory-2. This is a well-known and well-validated personality test originally designed to identify psychopathology in mental patients.

As Target pointed out to the court, the employer does not see the job applicant's answers to individual questions. Rather, it receives a checklist from the testing company summarizing the applicant's personality. These checklists have never been independently validated. Typical checklists highlight the validity and acceptability of the MMPI profile (*e.g.*, denied common, trivial moral faults), serious psychological-emotional problems (*e.g.*, overconcern about own health, potential medical absence, and disability problems), stability and judgment (*e.g.*, potential for overreactions and loss of judgment under stress), self-control and anger control (*e.g.*, could be dangerous to others), and work factors (*e.g.*, problems in handling criticism, rationalizer). *See* JAMES N. BUTCHER, NEW DEVELOPMENTS IN THE USE OF THE MMPI 189 (1979).

Unlike most honesty tests, the MMPI demonstrates extremely low rates of false positive error — less than one percent of persons diagnosed by the test as ill are free of psychopathology. It suffers from high rates of false negative error, however, which can lead to the mistaken hiring of individuals who are not psychologically suited for the job. This is an inversion of the usual public-policy concern with false positives. *See* OFFICE OF TECHNOLOGY ASSESSMENT, THE USE OF INTEGRITY TESTS FOR PRE-EMPLOYMENT SCREENING 39 n.47 (1990).

Regardless of its validity, use of the MMPI may violate the Americans with Disabilities Act (ADA) (analyzed in Chapter 14). The ADA expressly limits the ability of employers to use "medical examinations" as a condition of employment. 42 U.S.C. § 12101(b)(1). The purpose of this restriction is to prevent employers from making employment decisions based on information that reveals an impairment of an applicant's physical or mental health. In *Karraker v. Rent-A-Center, Inc.*, 411 F.3d 831 (7th Cir. 2005), plaintiffs were three brothers who brought an action on behalf of a class of individuals employed by Rent-A-Center. They claimed that Rent-A-Center violated the ADA when it used the results of MMPI tests in making promotional decisions. The MMPI measures traits such as depression, hysteria, paranoia, and mania. Elevated scores on the MMPI can be used in diagnosing certain psychiatric disorders. One of the issues before the Seventh Circuit was whether the District Court erred when it ruled that Rent-A-Center's use of the MMPI did not function as a "medical examination" under the ADA because its results were not interpreted by a psychologist, and because the scoring method used by Rent-A-Center focused on personality traits rather than disclosing mental illness. The Seventh Circuit reversed the District Court, holding that "the practical effect of the use of the MMPI is similar no matter how the test is used or scored — that is, whether or not [Rent-A-Center] used the test to weed out applicants with certain disorders, its use of the MMPI likely had the effect of excluding employees with disorders from promotions." *Id.* at 836-37.

7. Fakability. As veterans of many standardized tests, law students might think it particularly easy to know how to answer honesty questions if one wants the job. Will dishonest job applicants simply fake their answers? An American Psychological Association study suggests not:

> A common reaction to paper-and-pencil honesty tests is one of incredulity that they should work at all. Most of the questions seem quite transparent, and it seems obvious to many observers that job applicants would not willingly report undesirable behaviors that would ruin their chances for employment; surely they would lie. Although we would not like to discourage continued research on dissimulation, faking may not be as great a problem as most people fear. Some applicants may not regard the tests as very important, and hence are not motivated to lie to any great extent; others may think they can "outsmart" the tests by admitting to various transgressions. Still others may believe that companies can and will check up on what they say and therefore they should be truthful. Finally, at a more theoretical level, we know that people tend to assume that others are much the same as themselves; to the extent to which less honest applicants succumb to this "false consensus" effect, they will assume that their anti-social attitudes and behaviors are quite normal, and therefore they can express them freely.

LEWIS R. GOLDBERG ET AL., QUESTIONNAIRES USED IN THE PREDICTION OF TRUSTWORTHINESS IN PRE-EMPLOYMENT SELECTION DECISIONS: AN A.P.A. TASK FORCE REPORT 12-13 (1991).

Also consider the following experiment about honesty tests, which suggests that job applicants do not fake answers even when they could:

Two common employer concerns about pre-employment honesty testing were addressed: fakability and the test taker's reaction to such tests. Students, 84% with work experience in industries where honesty tests are common, took an honesty test under one of three instructional sets: respond honestly, fake good, and respond as if applying for a job. While subjects instructed to fake good could easily do so, the scores of subjects responding as job applicants more closely resembled those of subjects instructed to respond honestly. Strong negative reactions to honesty tests were not found; rather, most subjects felt that such tests were appropriate.

Ann Marie Ryan & Paul R. Sackett, *Pre-Employment Honesty Testing: Fakability, Reactions of Test Takers, and Company Image*, 1 J. Bus. & Psych. 248 (1987).

8. *Dangers of Misclassification.* While no one is pleased when they fail a test they should have passed, the dangers of false positives[*] in (dis)honesty testing may be particularly severe.

[M]isclassification of honest individuals is particularly onerous. First, honesty and integrity are highly value-laden concepts that cut to the core of basic concepts of morality. Identifying an individual as "at risk to commit dishonest acts" almost certainly carries a greater stigma than does the classification of an individual in other terms, *e.g.*, relatively low cognitive abilities: the latter may channel the individual toward certain kinds of jobs not requiring those specific cognitive skills, but there are virtually no jobs for which dishonesty would be either required or desired.

Office of Technology Assessment, *supra*, at 12. A broader question is whether "honesty" is indeed a fixed personality trait, or depends on the situation. Some have argued that one's honesty depends on the situation:

[T]here is disagreement among psychologists as to whether honesty is an individual trait or whether it is situationally determined. Some psychologists believe that honesty or dishonesty is more a function of the climate created by management than an individual's personality. If honesty is, in fact situationally determined, this suggests that problems with dishonesty could be addressed more effectively by management practices that support (encourage and reward) honest behavior.

Carolyn Wiley & Docia L. Rudly, *Managerial Issues and Responsibilities in the Use of Integrity Tests*, 42 Lab. L.J. 152, 154 (1991).

On the other hand, if dishonesty is an immutable trait then employees cannot learn to be honest. "Individuals who perform poorly on honesty tests could, presumably, seek professional counseling or somehow change their thinking. But the question is whether genuine changes in underlying character would be reflected in subsequent tests. For example, the answer to a

---

[*] The term "false positive" is confusing here because the term "honesty" testing is a misnomer. Like drug tests, honesty tests attempt to uncover bad traits in employees. For both types of tests, standard terminology calls a falsely accused person a false positive. A drug user or dishonest employee who escapes detection is a false negative. In a skills test that employees want to pass, a false positive would be an unskilled employee who somehow passed the test.

question like 'did you ever steal' would be the same despite an individual's successful transformation into an honest person. On a math test, however, an individual who has mastered a skill since failing the first test would, presumably, answer the relevant questions more successfully on subsequent attempts." OFFICE OF TECHNOLOGY ASSESSMENT, *supra*, at 13.

Some have found the very scientific cast of honesty tests to be troubling:

> [I]ntegrity tests carry a scientific imprimatur — they are marketed with literature proclaiming their "experimental validation" — therefore substantially intensifying an individual's burden of proving that misclassification has occurred. Thus, while a virtue of the tests is their attempt to reduce the prevalence of subjective biases that might contaminate other screening and selection processes, the result can be more severe for individuals who are misclassified.

OFFICE OF TECHNOLOGY ASSESSMENT, *supra*, at 14.

9. *Test Accuracy and the Base-Rate Problem.* A major factor in the debate over polygraph and honesty testing is the accuracy of tests. Reliable estimates are difficult to obtain. The OTA reviewed five studies that compared honesty test scores for retail employees and whether they were detected for theft. The results showed that, for employees detected for theft, the tests labeled 50% to 95% as dishonest. Of the (presumably honest) employees not detected for theft, the tests labeled between 35% and 84% as honest. This suggests a wide range in the accuracy of honesty tests.

Often overlooked in this debate is a greater problem in many contexts — the low base rate. If most people in the population to be tested are honest, even very accurate tests will falsely label people as dishonest more often than they correctly label them dishonest. False positives (labeling an honest person as dishonest) become a serious problem. *See generally* Kevin R. Murphy, *Detecting Infrequent Deception,* 72 J. APPLIED PSYCHOLOGY 611 (1987).

To see this, let us take the most generous results described above. Let us suppose that 95% of all dishonest test-takers will fail the honesty test. (This figure is sometimes called the sensitivity rate.) Let us suppose that 84% of honest test-takers will pass the honesty test. (This figure is sometimes called the selectivity rate.)

Most policymakers should not be directly interested in either of these numbers. Rather, the concern should be with the likelihood that one who fails a test is nevertheless honest. These are the innocent persons who will not receive the job because of the test. This number depends, however, not only on the sensitivity and selectivity rates of the test, but also on the base rate of dishonest people who will be given the test.

Suppose, as is plausible in an honesty test given to all job applicants (and consistent with the findings of the OTA study), that only 5% of the applicants are dishonest. Then, if 1,000 job applicants are given the test, we would expect the results shown in Table 9-1.

Table 9-1
EXPECTED RESULTS OF HONESTY TESTS
Sensitivity Rate = 95%, Selectivity Rate = 84%
Base Rate of Dishonest Test-takers = 5%

	TEST LABELS HONEST	TEST LABELS DISHONEST	TOTAL NUMBER
HONEST APPLICANTS	798	152 (false positives)	950
DISHONEST APPLICANTS	3 (false negatives)	47	50
TOTAL	801	199	1,000

The fairness issue, which focuses on the false positives, is stark. If the employer rejects all applicants failing the honesty test, over ¾ of rejected applicants (152/199) will be honest. This result obtains not because the test is inaccurate (we assumed a 95% sensitivity rate and 84% selectivity rate) but because so few applicants are dishonest.

On the other hand, the chart also reveals the incentives many employers have in using honesty tests for job applicants. If the employer did not screen for honesty, the chance of hiring a dishonest person is 5% (the base rate of dishonesty). If the employer only hires test passers, the chance of hiring a dishonest person is only 3/801, or 0.4%. In many situations, employers will be more concerned about hiring dishonest persons (false negatives) than rejecting honest persons (false positives). This is likely when an employer has many applications for job openings and honesty is important relative to other skills. It is no surprise, then, that retail trade employers were major users of polygraphs for job applicants, and continue to use honesty testing today, even though such tests exclude many qualified applicants.

If the base rate were as high as 50%, by contrast, the test seems much fairer. In that case, assuming the same selectivity and sensitivity rates as before, the test would label 555 of every 1,000 test-takers as dishonest. Of these 555, only 80 (17%), would actually be honest.

For example, suppose an employer only gives an honesty test upon reasonable (50/50) suspicion that the employee had stolen property. This would create a base rate of 50%, in that half of the test-takers would in fact be dishonest. If an employer fired every employee in such a case who failed the test, only 17% of the fired employees would be fired unfairly. The changing base rate may explain why Congress, in prohibiting most uses of the polygraph, allowed employers to use a polygraph to investigate economic losses.

10. *Genetic Screening.* Another type of employee testing — one with a specter of science run amok — is genetic screening. Using blood samples, the screening process can identify individuals who are genetically predisposed to diseases such as breast or colon cancer, sickle cell anemia, and Huntington's disease. Employers use this information to evaluate health insurance costs and to bar especially sensitive employees from positions with dangerous substances. Due to its high costs, only a few employers (mostly in the chemical industry) currently genetically test their employees. As the price declines, personnel directors may be more prone to use the tests in the future. *See generally* Sharona Hoffman, *Preplacement Examinations and Job-Relatedness: How to Enhance Privacy and Diminish Discrimination in the Workplace*, 49 U. Kan. L. Rev. 517 (2001).

As of 2006, at least half the states had laws protecting against genetic discrimination in the workplace. Wisconsin, for example, forbids employers from using genetic tests to affect terms of employment, but expressly allows the employer, with the employee's written consent, to use a genetic test to investigate a worker's compensation claim or to determine the employee's susceptibility to a potentially toxic substance. Wis. Stat. § 111.372.

One reason for banning genetic discrimination is its disparate impact along racial and ethnic lines, an impact that could also violate Title VII if not job related. In addition, genetic screening by employers raises similar issues to those from drug and alcohol testing. In particular, many people are concerned with the invasion of privacy and the accuracy of genetic testing in predicting harm. The American Medical Association's Council on Ethical and Judicial Affairs declared that genetic tests alone "do not have sufficient predictive value to be relied on as a basis for excluding workers." Council on Ethical and Judicial Affairs of the American Medical Association, *Use of Genetic Testing by Employers,* 266 J. Am. Med. Ass'n 1827, 1830 (1991).

The only federal statute directly addressing genetic discrimination is the 1996 Health Insurance Portability and Accountability Act (analyzed in Chapter 20). HIPAA prohibits group health plans from using any health-related factor, including genetic information, as a basis for denying or limiting eligibility for coverage or for charging an individual more for coverage. ERISA §§ 701(b)(1)(B), 702(a)(1)(F).

The Americans with Disabilities Act may also limit the employer's use of genetic tests. In 1995, the Equal Employment Opportunity Commission issued an enforcement guideline advising that an employer who makes an employment decision based on genetic information regards that individual as having a disability within the meaning of the ADA. II EEOC Compliance Manual § 902. The EEOC filed its first lawsuit challenging genetic screening in 2001, but the case quickly settled when the employer abandoned its practice. *See* Ilene V. Goldberg, *Genetic Testing of Railroad Workers Halted After EEOC Files Suit*, 17 Termination of Employment Bulletin (West) 1 (May 2001).

11. *Background Checking: The Rise of an Industry?* Another employer screening practice that is on the rise, particularly since 9/11, is the use of exhaustive background checks, often using a professional agency. The idea informing this practice is that an applicant's past behavior will predict their future behavior. Background reports may contain information such as criminal records, credit histories, driving records, Social Security records, military records, educational histories, and bankruptcy proceedings. The Fair Credit Reporting Act (FCRA), 15 U.S.C. § 1681 *et seq.*, requires employers who use an outside "consumer reporting agency" to obtain information about an applicant to disclose to the applicant that a report is being prepared, collect a signed release from the applicant before collecting various kinds of information, and provide a copy of any report produced to the applicant if the report is used to deny employment. If, on the other hand, an employer decides to conduct a background investigation using in-house resources, it is exempt from the FCRA notice and disclosure requirements.

The consumer reporting agency need not verify the authenticity of the source providing the information unless the subject of the report objects, in which case the agency must give notice to the employer of the dispute, re-investigate the source, and delete the disputed information if it cannot verify the accuracy of the information. § 1681i. If the credit agency is satisfied with the accuracy of the information and the subject still disputes the information, the subject's only recourse is to file a written objection that must be included in the report. As Professor Finkin dryly observes, "the prospective employer's willingness to hire under those circumstances remains to be seen." Matthew W. Finkin, *From Anonymity to Transparence: Screening the Workforce in an Information Age*, 2000 COLUM. BUS REV. 403, 443 (2000).

Inaccuracy of reports is not a trivial concern, given the potentially harmful consequences. One of the few cases litigated under the FCRA involved a job applicant, Lewis, who was offered a position as a product salesman contingent on the employer's completion of a background check. When he called the employer after not hearing back for two weeks, the employee he spoke with called him an "unsavory character" and told him that if he tried to contact them again they would notify law enforcement. Lewis was also fired abruptly from his existing job for "poor performance" despite having received a positive evaluation just two weeks earlier. Lewis hired a private investigator, who determined that his Social Security number showed a criminal record that included a murder conviction. This was the result of a data-entry error by a police officer who had keyed in the information about the actual criminal who committed the murder. Lewis sued the entities he alleged sold the information to his existing and prospective employers, claiming they violated numerous provisions of the FCRA. The case settled in 2003, after the Ohio District Court denied defendants' motions for summary judgment in which they claimed that they were not "credit reporting agencies" under the FCRA, and that even if they were, their actions did not cause harm to the plaintiff. *See Lewis v. Ohio Prof'l Elec. Network LLC*, 190 F. Supp. 2d 1049 (D. Ohio 2002).

NOTE ON NEGLIGENT HIRING

Suppose an employer hires an applicant despite questionable results on a psychological test. Might the employer face liability if the employee harms someone? The following case explores this issue.

THATCHER v. BRENNAN
United States District Court, S.D. Mississippi
657 F. Supp. 6 (1986)

TOM S. LEE, DISTRICT JUDGE.

. . . The plaintiff brought this action against Bert Brennan and Mead Johnson, jointly and severally, following an altercation between the plaintiff and Brennan which occurred on May 21, 1984. The alleged liability of Mead Johnson is predicated upon two theories: (1) respondeat superior and (2) negligent hiring. Mead Johnson has moved for summary judgment on both theories. . . .

Respondeat Superior

On May 21, 1984, Bert Brennan was an employee of Mead Johnson, having been hired February 8, 1982. As a medical sales specialist, Brennan was responsible for the sale of Mead Johnson pharmaceutical products, primarily through physician specifications. Although he lived in Covington, Louisiana, Brennan's sales territory included Hinds County, Mississippi. He was required by Mead Johnson to be in Jackson, Mississippi at least once every five weeks to make calls on physicians. Due to the travel required, Brennan was provided an automobile by his employer and was reimbursed for his travel expenses, including the expenses for his trips to Jackson.

On the morning of May 21, 1984, Brennan had made some physician sales calls in New Orleans, Louisiana. About 12:30 or 1:00 p.m., he left his home in Louisiana and drove to Jackson. Upon arrival, Brennan checked into a hotel, got some paper work "squared away," and then drove to the post office to mail it. Upon leaving the post office, Brennan turned his automobile right onto a street in front of Thatcher, and a disagreement began, which continued until the cars stopped and a fight took place in the parking lot of a jewelry store. After this incident, which occurred about 5:45 p.m., Brennan returned to his motel. For purposes of this motion, Mead Johnson has admitted that Brennan instigated the altercation without provocation from the plaintiff.

The paper work which Brennan mailed consisted of physician call cards and a sample inventory. The parties disagree as to whether Brennan was in fact *required* to mail these papers. Mead Johnson claims that these items could have been mailed at some other time and/or place, whereas the plaintiff asserts that Brennan was required by Mead Johnson to mail the call cards daily. The court is of the opinion that this is immaterial since, whether required or not, Brennan did mail the papers and, in doing so, was performing his work as a Mead Johnson sales representative.

When Brennan left the post office, he was returning to his hotel where he had planned to make dinner arrangements with a doctor friend. As such social interaction with physicians is encouraged by Mead Johnson, it may be reasonably inferred that Brennan was returning to the hotel to perform business-related activities. Nevertheless, the parties agree that while Brennan was in Jackson, he was not required by Mead Johnson to follow any specific schedule or agenda. Importantly, it is also agreed between the parties that nothing about Brennan's altercation promoted the sale of pharmaceuticals for Mead Johnson.

It is clear in Mississippi that an employer may be held liable for the intentional acts of its employees if the employer either authorized the act prior to or ratified the act after its commission, or the act was committed within the scope of employment. Since there is nothing to indicate that Mead Johnson either authorized or ratified Brennan's intentional assault and battery upon

Thatcher, Brennan must have been acting within the scope of his employment in order for Mead Johnson to be held liable.

In *Loper v. Yazoo & M.V.R. Co.*, 145 So. 743 (Miss. 1933), the Mississippi Supreme Court recognized that the phrase "scope of employment" which is used to determine an employer's liability for the acts of its employees has no fixed legal or technical meaning. Instead, the court has enunciated various tests for determining whether particular conduct of an employee is within the scope of employment. These tests include, for example,

(1) Whether the employee's conduct is "so unlike that authorized that it is substantially different";

(2) Whether the act complained of is committed in the prosecution of the employer's business and within the scope of the employee's authority;

(3) Whether such act is in the furtherance of the business of the master and as an incident to the performance of the duties of the character or kind which he was employed to perform; and

(4) Whether the act was done in the course of and as a means of accomplishing the purposes of the employment and, therefore, in furtherance of the master's business.

These "tests" provide some guidance, but often a fine line separates those acts which are within and those which are without the scope of employment. It has been noted that

> The most difficult questions arise where the servant, for strictly personal reasons and not in furtherance of his employment, loses his temper and attacks the plaintiff in a quarrel which arises out of the employment — as where, for example, a truck driver collides with the plaintiff, and an altercation follows. Here, unless some non-delegable duty can be found, the older rule denied recovery, and this is still the holding of the majority of the decisions. There has been a tendency in the later cases, however, to allow recovery on the ground that the employment has provided a peculiar opportunity and even incentive for such loss of temper[.]

Prosser and Keeton, The Law of Torts, 465-66 (5th ed. 1984).

. . . In the instant case, Brennan was authorized, expected, and even required to drive an automobile as part of his employment. However, he was not authorized to assault other persons, and there is nothing in the previous relationship between Brennan and Mead Johnson which would indicate that such conduct was acceptable. Moreover, the act is not one which is commonly performed by Mead Johnson sales personnel, nor can it be said to be a "normal" method of selling, or similar to acts which Brennan was authorized to perform. The most that can be said is that the assault was within the "time and place" of employment. The "purpose" of the assault was not to further any of Mead Johnson's interests but, rather, was intended to satisfy Brennan's purely personal objectives. . . .

Negligent Hiring

The plaintiff has also asserted a claim against Mead Johnson on the basis of negligent hiring. He contends that Mead Johnson either knew or should have known of Brennan's alleged propensity for violence but nevertheless employed Brennan, placed him in contact with residents of Hinds County and directed him to travel the streets of Jackson for the purpose of selling pharmaceutical products "even though he has violent and malicious personality traits."

. . . [T]he court concludes that in this case plaintiff must prove that (1) Brennan had a propensity for violence, (2) Mead Johnson knew or should have known of such propensity, and (3) Mead Johnson, in disregard for the rights of those persons with whom Brennan could reasonably be expected to come into contact, hired Brennan, either negligently or with callous disregard for the rights of such persons.

. . . The plaintiff herein has failed to demonstrate any propensity for, or likelihood of, violence on the part of Brennan and has further failed to produce sufficient evidence that Mead Johnson knew, or had reason to know, of any such propensity for violence. The only evidence of actual violent conduct by Brennan is the affray between him and the plaintiff which is the subject of this action. Plaintiff has directed the court's attention to no other incident, either preceding or following his being hired by Mead Johnson, which would tend to show that Brennan was a violent or vicious individual. Instead, plaintiff asserts that the results of a personality inventory test and an adaptability test taken by Brennan reveal his propensity for violence.

These tests were administered to Brennan by Mead Johnson personnel prior to his being hired in February 1982. An evaluation of the test results led Mead Johnson's personnel employees to the following conclusion:

> Bert has the potential to be a moody, opinionated and headstrong and early in his life might even have been considered spoiled or immature
>
> . . . Bert is a person of high aggression. . . .
>
> Overall profile appears to be significantly different from the temperament profile of most sales candidates we see. It appears to reflect a young person undergoing a great deal of emotional and personal stress and turmoil.

Plaintiff contends on the sole basis of this evaluation that Brennan, as a person of "high aggression," did indeed have a propensity for violence, and that Mead Johnson had knowledge of this propensity as a result of its own analysis of Brennan's personality inventory tests.

The plaintiff has supplied the court with an analysis of the test results by a clinical psychologist, J. Donald Matherne, Ph.D. Dr. Matherne states that upon review of the information provided him, it is "quite apparent that . . . Wilbert Brennan, manifests evidence of very serious emotional and personality instability." He further states that the "test findings clearly indicate an individual lacking in self-control, socialization skills and responsibility," and that Mead Johnson apparently hired Wilbert Brennan with full knowledge of his propensity for aggression as well as his propensity for violent behavior. He further opines that Wilbert Brennan should not have been employed by Mead Johnson as a pharmaceutical sales representative since "one would predict with a high degree of clinical probability that this individual would have manifested, within a period of time, significant adjustment problems, work inefficiency and problems involving self control." The court is of the opinion that the test results alone did not provide a sufficient basis to put Mead Johnson on notice of any purported violent tendencies of Brennan. While Brennan may have been accurately evaluated as a person of "high aggression," the term "aggression" is not synonymous with "violent."

The tests in question were administered in late 1981, and the evaluation by Mead Johnson personnel was rendered in January 1982. The altercation between Thatcher and Brennan did not occur until May 1984, after Brennan was hired, and during this two-year period there is no evidence that Brennan demonstrated any violent behavior whatsoever. One who is volatile and malicious and who has a propensity for violence would presumably have manifested such aberrant traits over a two-year period. Yet, during the interim between the time that Brennan was hired and the date of the altercation with Thatcher, there were no incidents of violent behavior. Therefore, even assuming Mead Johnson, at the time it hired Brennan, could have reasonably concluded on the basis of the tests that Brennan had a potential for violence, the total lack of evidence of any violent conduct by Brennan over the succeeding two years certainly belies any claim of negligent hiring under the circumstances of this case.

Accordingly, it is ordered that the motion for summary judgment of defendant Mead Johnson is granted.

NOTES

1. *Theories of Employer Liability.* Under the doctrine of *respondeat superior*, employers are held strictly liable for the torts of employees acting within the scope of their duties. *Respondeat superior* does not usually apply when an employee assaults a third person or otherwise acts beyond the scope of his duties. In such a case, the injured third party must show that the actions of the employer itself make it liable for the injury. Usually this is attempted by showing that the employer was negligent in hiring, training, or retaining the employee. Thus, direct negligence claims usually arise when an employee assaults some third party.

2. *Criminal Record of Employees.* The fact situation in *Thatcher* (negligent processing of the company's internal information) is relatively rare. A more common negligent-hiring claim is that the employer did not sufficiently check references or the background of an applicant, particularly whether the applicant had a criminal record that might indicate a likelihood to assault third parties. In *Malorney v. B&L Motor Freight, Inc.*, 496 N.E.2d 1086 (Ill. App. Ct. 1986), for example, a hitchhiker raped by a truck driver survived a summary judgment motion and was allowed to proceed to trial on the claim that the company had hired the truck driver despite the fact that he had been convicted of violent sex crimes.

What should the company in *B&L Motor Freight* have done? If it had asked the rapist's former employer, would that employer have told the truth? If the former employer had lied or given a bland reference, could the rape victim sue it as well? *See Randi W. v. Muroc Joint Unified Sch. Dist.*, 929 P.2d 582 (Cal. 1997) (employers giving good references with affirmative misrepresentations can be liable to third parties).

3. *Negligent Failure to Test.* One response of employers to cases like *Thatcher* is not to give personality tests. But the failure to test employees can lead to lawsuits as well. In *Southern Bell Telephone & Telegraph Co. v. Sharara*, 307 S.E.2d 129 (Ga. Ct. App. 1983), a telephone company employee physically attacked a woman after installing a phone in her home. The victim sued Southern Bell for negligence in hiring or retaining the attacker. She argued that the company should have given periodic psychological tests to employees who enter customers' homes. The trial court agreed that this claim could survive summary judgment, but the court of appeals reversed. In concurrence, Judge Deen wrote:

> While concurring fully with the majority opinion, it might be added the better practice, in cases as here, would be for installer-repairman employees who are required to enter into homes of customers be more closely checked, observed, screened and interviewed by employers as to any outward manifestation of dangerous propensities relating to aggression or violence. We know of no requirement of compulsory psychological periodic blanket testing and counseling of all of one's employees. In fact, were this to be done by employers, without the employees' consent, serious First Amendment individual rights of privacy and other employee constitutional and civil rights might be at issue.
>
> Even an owner of a dog is not liable for an injury to another unless knowledge of prior propensities or a penchant to bite or attack by the dog exists. The same type theory or a form of negligent entrustment obtains here with respect to hiring or retaining an employee without any prior knowledge of overaggressiveness, violent or criminal propensities or tendencies. Unless there exists present knowledge by the employer (owner) of prior propensities, aggression and violence (to bite), there can be no liability.
>
> In psychological interviews seeking to pinpoint the origin and sources of negative, antisocial, violent propensities of aggression of humans, most alleged experts usually concentrate in only two areas: Nature (instinctivism — heredity — innateness) or Nurture (behaviorism — environment — society). While nature-nurture norms may well influence what happens to us, the criminal law of Georgia recognizes a third area it considers of prime importance, that is, a consideration of and the presumption of voluntary free will and the resulting responsibility of paying the penalty for our wrongful criminal acts committed. Many times psychological testing by alleged experts obscures and ignores any reference to the latter area since the voluntary free will of humans is considered and thought by many as unpredictable and, therefore, empirically unscientific. The law presumes, on the other hand, that all humans know right from wrong, as to their acts committed; therefore, the latter area of voluntary will under our criminal code needs to be again emphasized, that the actor is to blame, in all psychological counseling as to aggression, and the former two nature-nurture norms need to be deemphasized, as they suggest someone else is to blame other than the actor. Concentrating

only on nature and nurture norms in psychological testing is counter productive to encouraging all citizens in upholding restrictions that certain conduct is wrong as set forth in our juvenile and criminal code and in the reduction of criminal acts of violence and aggression.

Id. at 132-33.

4. *Negligent Hiring in the Public Sector.* After a high-speed car chase, Jill Brown was caught and thrown to the ground by a deputy sheriff, suffering injuries that required four knee operations. The deputy sheriff was the great-nephew of the sheriff, and had a known propensity for violence. Brown sued the county under 42 U.S.C. § 1983, claiming that the inadequate hiring standards amounted to deliberate indifference to her constitutional right against excessive violence by law-enforcement officials. The Fifth Circuit upheld a $872,500 jury verdict for Brown, but the Supreme Court reversed in a 5-4 decision. *Board of County Comm'rs v. Brown*, 520 U.S. 397 (1997). Justice O'Connor, writing for the majority, declared that the evidence was insufficient to go to the jury because the causal connection between the negligence and the harm was too weak: The use of excessive force was not a "plainly obvious" consequence of the decision to hire, even though the officer was an extremely poor deputy candidate.

Chapter 10

EMPLOYER REFERENCES — DEFAMATION AND OTHER TORTS

In addition to claims of improper intrusion into one's private sphere, another category of privacy claims addresses the public disclosure of private facts. In the employment context, such claims often arise when personnel records are shown to others. For example, in *Bratt v. IBM Corp.*, 785 F.2d 352 (1st Cir. 1986), a supervisor recommended that an employee see a psychiatrist under contract with IBM. The psychiatrist later discussed her examination with several IBM managers. Balancing "the employer's legitimate business interest in disseminating the information against the nature and substantiality of the intrusion," the court upheld the employee's privacy claim.

A harsher view was taken in *Eddy v. Brown*, 715 P.2d 74 (Okla. 1986). There, the court rejected a privacy claim when a supervisor had told a "limited number" of co-workers that Eddy had been seeing a psychiatrist. The court rejected an intrusion upon privacy claim because the psychiatric visits were part of Eddy's employment medical records, and "hence of legitimate concern to his supervisor." The court rejected a claim of unreasonable publicity of private facts because only a small group of co-workers were made privy to Eddy's private affairs, while the tort requires disclosure to the general public.

Closely related to concerns of public disclosure of private facts is the tort of defamation. Employees often bring defamation claims when the reasons for a firing are made public. As the following cases illustrate, this complicated tort has common-law roots that have been modified in part by constitutional law. THE RESTATEMENT (SECOND) OF TORTS § 558 (1997) lays out the standard requirements for defamation:

To create liability for defamation there must be:

(a) a false and defamatory statement concerning another;

(b) an unprivileged publication to a third party;

(c) fault amounting at least to negligence on the part of the publisher; and

(d) either actionability of the statement irrespective of special harm or the existence of special harm caused by the publication.

ELBESHBESHY v. FRANKLIN INSTITUTE
United States District Court, E.D. Pennsylvania
618 F. Supp. 170 (1985)

BECHTLE, DISTRICT JUDGE.

Presently before the court is the motion for partial summary judgment of defendant The Franklin Institute. For the reasons stated herein, defendant's motion will be denied.

Plaintiff was employed by defendant in its nuclear structural mechanics unit from January 3, 1984 to April 17, 1984. Plaintiff's job description involved a technical aspect of drafting proposals after plaintiff reviewed the plans for nuclear power plants submitted by architects and engineers to the Nuclear Regulatory Commission, and a marketing aspect of submitting the proposals to the Nuclear Regulatory Commission. Plaintiff drafted two proposals, one concerning "overcooling transient" and one concerning "hydrogen blanketing." Plaintiff's proposals were reviewed by plaintiff's supervisor, Dr. Vu Con ("Dr. Con") and by Dr. Con's supervisor, Dr. Salvatore Carfagno ("Dr. Carfagno"). Dr. Con believed that the proposals contained substantive shortcomings. Plaintiff did not agree with Dr. Con's assessment. Dr. Carfagno did not express an opinion with respect to the substantive quality of plaintiff's work, but he did decide that the working relationship between Dr. Con and plaintiff was not pleasant.

On April 17, 1984, defendant terminated plaintiff's employment. The reason given for the termination in plaintiff's employment record was plaintiff's "lack of cooperation." . . .

Defendant argues first that its statement was not defamatory. A defamatory statement is one which tends "to harm the reputation of another as to lower him in the estimation of the community or to deter third persons from associating or dealing with him." *Thomas M. Merton Center v. Rockwell Int'l Corp.*, 442 A.2d 213 (Pa. 1981), citing RESTATEMENT (SECOND) OF TORTS § 559 (1977).

In the circumstances of the instant case, at this stage of the proceedings, the court believes that the assertion in plaintiff's employment record that plaintiff was terminated for "lack of cooperation" could be defamatory. It is not unreasonable that the assertion, standing alone, might lead members of the community and third persons to reasonably believe that plaintiff's nature was irremediably insubordinate, obnoxious, and antagonistic. Such a conclusion is especially likely where plaintiff was terminated after only three and a half months of employment. Additionally, the assertion that plaintiff was terminated because plaintiff lacked cooperation is quite different from an assertion that plaintiff was terminated due to a personality conflict between plaintiff and Dr. Con, or because he was not qualified to perform the work for which he was employed. It is one thing to say that plaintiff could not fit into the organization of the defendant, but it is very different to say that plaintiff cannot get along with management and disrupts the harmony of the workplace. Persons who are said to be disruptive, insubordinate, obnoxious, and antagonistic are persons with whom third persons tend not to want to deal or associate and whom members of the community tend to hold in low esteem.

Second, defendant argues that the statement that the reason behind plaintiff's termination was "lack of cooperation" was not published. Publication occurs, however, when the defamer communicates the statement to one other person, even if that one other person is the defamer's agent. RESTATEMENT (SECOND) OF TORTS § 577 cmt. c (1977). Since plaintiff presented evidence that the statement was communicated to Dr. Con, Dr. Carfagno, and members of defendant's personnel department, the publication element may be satisfied here.

Third, defendant argues that plaintiff's claim for defamation is barred by defendant's qualified privilege to evaluate the job performance of its employees. Plaintiff, however, presented some evidence that plaintiff was terminated for reasons of professional jealousy. Accordingly, the court holds that a genuine issue as to a material fact exists here as to whether defendant acted with malice or abused its privilege. . . .

In conclusion, the court will deny defendant's motion for partial summary judgment.

NOTES

1. *Libel and Slander.* Traditionally, slander is oral defamation and libel is written defamation. Employers are often charged with both. The importance of the common-law distinction is that plaintiffs cannot recover for slander without proving special damages, unless the statement is slander per se. In general, special damages are not needed to support a libel claim. Some states, however, further distinguish between libel per se, where the statement is defamatory on its face, and libel per quod, where the factfinder must look to facts beyond the statement itself to determine if it is defamatory. In these states, a libel per quod claim also requires a showing of special damages. Special damages are pecuniary losses directly caused by the reaction of others to the defamatory statement.

In practice, these distinctions are less important in the employment context than in other areas for two reasons. First, defamed employees often can show special damages, if the defamation causes them to lose a job opportunity. Second, oral statements damaging to one's business, trade, or profession are considered slander per se, for which recovery is possible without proving special damages. RESTATEMENT (SECOND) OF TORTS § 573 comment b explicitly declares that this slander per se rule "is equally applicable to artisans, mechanics and workmen generally, whether skilled or unskilled."

2. *Defamatory Acts.* Suppose an employer, eager to avoid a defamation claim, gives no explanation when firing an employee. Might this in itself be defamatory, in that it tends to harm the employee's reputation? In *Tyler v. Macks Stores*, 272 S.E.2d 633 (S.C. 1980), an employee and his manager were fired following a polygraph test. The court held that these acts supported a defamation claim sufficient to reach the jury, because they might have given "fellow employees and others the feeling that he had been discharged for some wrongful activity." *Accord Berg v. Consol. Freightways*, 421 A.2d 831 (Pa. Super. Ct. 1980) (firing employee in midst of criminal investigation into theft at work valid basis for slander suit).

3. *Publication.* *Elbeshbeshy* applies the majority rule that the publication element of defamation is satisfied even if the statement never goes outside the company, as long as a third person hears or reads it. *Accord Luttrell v. United Tel. Sys.*, 683 P.2d 1292 (Kan. Ct. App. 1984) (employer sufficiently protected by qualified privilege). Several courts have ruled, however, that intracorporate defamation is simply the corporation talking to itself and cannot be a publication. *See, e.g., Monahan v. Sims*, 294 S.E.2d 548 (Ga. Ct. App. 1982).

As with other acts of its agents, a corporation is liable for the defamatory statements of its employees made while acting within the scope of their authority. In *Tacket v. General Motors Corp.*, 836 F.2d 1042 (7th Cir. 1987) (applying Indiana law) (per Easterbrook, J.), an unknown person painted a small sign saying "TACKET TACKET WHAT A RACKET" on a factory wall. The sign was possibly defamatory because it reinforced rumors that Tacket, the night superintendent of the plant, had improperly subcontracted work to himself. The company painted over the sign after seven or eight months. The court, following RESTATEMENT § 577(2), held that a reasonable juror could conclude that the company intentionally and unreasonably failed to remove the sign and thereby published a defamatory statement. It therefore reversed a directed verdict for the employer.

On remand, Tacket prevailed at trial and was awarded $100,000 in damages. The judgment was reversed on appeal because Tacket had shown only psychological injury, and not the pecuniary damages required under Indiana defamation law. *Tacket v. General Motors Corp.*, 937 F.2d 1201 (7th Cir. 1991).

4. Self-Publication. Suppose a personnel director falsely fires an employee for gross insubordination, but tells no one other than the fired employee of the reason. Still, it is foreseeable that prospective employers will ask the employee why he was discharged, and he will be compelled to lie or publish the defamation. Should the employee have a defamation claim against the employer? *See Lewis v. Equitable Life Assur. Soc'y*, 389 N.W.2d 876 (Minn. 1986) (recognizing doctrine of compelled self-publication on these facts).

The self-publication doctrine has had a mixed reception by courts and legislatures. In *Olivieri v. Rodriguez*, 122 F.3d 406 (7th Cir. 1997), a probationary police officer was discharged without a hearing for sexual harassment. He alleged harm even though there was no evidence the reason for the discharge was disclosed to anyone other than the plaintiff:

> The doctrine [of compelled self-defamation] is inconsistent with the fundamental principle of mitigation of damages. . . . The principle of self-defamation . . . would encourage Olivieri to apply for a job to every police force in the nation, in order to magnify his damages; and to blurt out to each of them the ground of this discharge in the most lurid terms, to the same end.

Id. at 408-09.

In the legislatures, a 1987 Minnesota statute, enacted in response to *Lewis*, requires employers to provide a written, truthful reason for the termination at the employee's request, and prohibits a defamation action based on this statement. MINN. STAT. ANN. § 181.933. Colorado also enacted a statute in response to a case recognizing the doctrine of compelled self-publication; the statute eliminated the doctrine altogether. *See Churchey v. Adolph Coors Co.*, 759 P.2d 1336 (Colo. 1988); COLO. REV. STAT. ANN. § 13-25-125.5 (effective 1989). *See generally* Markita D. Cooper, *Between a Rock and a Hard Case: Time for a New Doctrine of Compelled Self-Publication*, 72 NOTRE DAME L. REV. 373 (1997) (urging a restructured claim that would require plaintiffs to show egregious employer conduct, an inquiry by a prospective employer, and efforts by plaintiff to mitigate damages by explaining the circumstances of the termination).

ZINDA v. LOUISIANA PACIFIC CORP.
Supreme Court of Wisconsin
440 N.W.2d 548 (1989)

BABLITCH, JUSTICE.

Allan D. "Rick" Zinda (Zinda) brought both a defamation and invasion of privacy action against his former employer, Louisiana Pacific Corporation (Louisiana Pacific), based on a statement concerning his discharge which was published in a company newsletter. . . .

The essential facts are undisputed. Approximately two years prior to his employment with Louisiana Pacific, Zinda was injured as a result of falling through "waferboard" on the roof of a garage he was constructing at his home. Zinda sustained numerous injuries, including a broken rib, a broken bone in the back, and a broken heel.

In connection with his application for employment with Louisiana Pacific in 1983, Zinda completed a standard application form as well as a medical history form. In the "personal health history" portion of the medical form, Zinda provided the following answers:

Upper Back Trouble — No.

Middle Back Trouble — No.

Low Back Trouble — No.

Back Injury or Disability — No

Fracture or Broken Bone — No.

Back X-ray — No.

In explaining a "yes" answer regarding previous hospitalizations and surgery, Zinda wrote: "[W]hen I was 15 years old for Hay Fever, Tonsil, Appendits [sic], and fall off roof." Later, during a pre-employment interview, Zinda clarified that he had previously fallen off a roof and broken some bones including his ribs and a heel, but that he had no present problems. Zinda signed both forms acknowledging that all answers were true and that any false statements or misrepresentations would result in immediate discharge, regardless of when such facts were discovered.

Approximately one year later, Zinda filed a products liability action against Louisiana Pacific, alleging that it negligently manufactured the "waferboard" involved in his fall off the roof. The complaint asserted that Zinda had suffered permanent disabilities as a result of the injuries, and sought substantial compensatory and punitive damages.

The complaint was served on the personnel manager of the Louisiana Pacific plant who compared the allegations against the answers Zinda gave on his application forms. Apparently concluding that Zinda had intentionally withheld adverse information concerning his physical condition, the personnel manager notified Zinda that his employment was suspended pending an investigation into possible fraud regarding his employment forms. Approximately three weeks later, Louisiana Pacific terminated Zinda's employment.

Subsequently, Louisiana Pacific published a notice regarding Zinda's termination on the seventh page of the plant newspaper, the "Waferboard Press," under the following heading:

COMINGS AND GOINGS

5/1/84	Death	Leland Thysen	
5/10/84	Voluntary Quit	Jeff Aiken	Back to Railroad
5/14/84	Hire	Paul Lueck	Electrician
5/25/84	Terminate	Al Christner	Falsification of Emp. forms
5/27/84	Hire	Bill Nordback	A crew
5/29/84	Hire	Dennis Voight	B crew
5/29/84	Terminate	Larry Radzak	Theft
5/29/84	Terminate	Al Zinda	Falsification of Emp. forms
5/31/84	Hire	Mike Hoskins	Panel Saw
5/31/84	Voluntary Quit	Mike Laronge	Personal reasons
5/31/84	Hire	Jeff Walker	C crew

Approximately 160 copies of the newsletter were distributed to employees by placement in the lunchroom. Employees were not restricted from taking the newsletter home, and employees regularly took the newsletters out of the workplace. Testimony indicates that a copy reached the local hospital, where Zinda's wife worked, and two of her co-workers read the reference to Zinda's termination.

Zinda amended his complaint to include allegations of defamation, invasion of privacy, and wrongful discharge. Louisiana Pacific answered, raising conditional privilege as a defense, asserting that it had no liability for good faith communications to employees concerning the reasons for the discharge of another employee.

The circuit court granted summary judgment dismissing Zinda's claim for wrongful discharge. Zinda then voluntarily dismissed the products liability claim. The defamation and invasion of privacy claims were tried to a jury. . . . Regarding the defamation and invasion of privacy claims, the trial court refused without explanation to submit Louisiana Pacific's requested instruction on conditional privilege.

The jury returned a verdict awarding $50,000.00 for defamation as well as $50,000.00 for invasion of privacy. The trial court denied all post verdict motions and granted judgment on the verdict. . . .

We turn first to the issue of liability for defamation. We conclude that the information published in the company newsletter was conditionally privileged as a communication of common interest concerning the employer-employee relationship. We further conclude that although the privilege may be lost if abused, a jury question was presented in this case as to whether the information was excessively published.

A communication is defamatory if it tends to harm the reputation of another so as to lower him in the estimation of the community or deter third persons from associating or dealing with him. If the statements are capable of a nondefamatory as well as a defamatory meaning, then a jury question is presented as to how the statement was understood by its recipients.

However, not all defamations are actionable. Some defamations fall within a class of conduct which the law terms privileged. The defense of privilege has developed under the public policy that certain conduct which would otherwise be actionable may escape liability because the defendant is acting in furtherance of some interest of societal importance, which is entitled to protection even at the expense of uncompensated harm to the plaintiff.

Privileged defamations may be either absolute or conditional. Absolute privileges give complete protection without any inquiry into the defendant's motives. This privilege has been extended to judicial officers, legislative proceedings, and to certain governmental executive officers.

The arguments in this case, however, are concerned only with conditional privilege. In the area of conditional privilege, we have endorsed the language of the RESTATEMENT OF TORTS. The RESTATEMENT recognizes the existence of a conditional privilege in a number of different situations. Among these are statements made on a subject matter in which the person making the statement and the person to whom it is made have a legitimate common interest.

Section 596 of the RESTATEMENT (SECOND) OF TORTS defines the "common interest" privilege:

> An occasion makes a publication conditionally privileged if the circumstances lead any one of several persons having a common interest in a particular subject matter correctly or reasonably to believe that there is information that another sharing the common interest is entitled to know.

The common interest privilege is based on the policy that one is entitled to learn from his associates what is being done in a matter in which he or she has an interest in common. Thus, defamatory statements are privileged which are made in furtherance of common property, business, or professional interests. The Restatement extends such privilege to "partners, fellow officers of a corporation for profit, fellow shareholders, and fellow servants. . . ." *See id.*, Comment d. at 597.

The common interest privilege is particularly germane to the employer-employee relationship. We have applied a conditional privilege to various communications between employers and persons having a common interest in the employee's conduct. For instance, in *Hett v. Ploetz*, 121 N.W.2d 270 (Wis. 1963), a defamatory letter of reference from an ex-employer to a prospective employer was held to be entitled to a conditional privilege. We stated that the prospective employer has an interest in receiving information concerning the character and qualifications of the former employee, and the ex-employer has an interest in giving such information in good faith to insure that he may receive an honest evaluation when he hires new employees.

Similarly, in *Johnson v. Rudolph Wurlitzer Co.*, 222 N.W. 451, 454 (Wis. 1928), we held that a conditional privilege applied to defamatory statements by a store manager to other employees in the office about an alleged embezzlement involving a fellow employee. We stated that because of their employment, the employees had a common interest in discovering the source of the shortage that was being investigated.

We conclude that the common interest privilege attaches to the employer-employee relationship in this case. Employees have a legitimate interest in knowing the reasons a fellow employee was discharged. Conversely, an employer has an interest in maintaining morale and quieting rumors which may disrupt business. Here, Louisiana Pacific's personnel manager testified that at the time of Zinda's termination, the plant had been going through a rather extensive retooling and reprocessing. During that time, normal crews had been broken apart and there were prevailing rumors that Louisiana Pacific was laying off employees. The company believed for this reason that it would be the best policy to immediately suppress rumors by being completely honest concerning employees who were no longer with the company.

Moreover, we conclude that truthfulness and integrity in the employment application process is an important common interest. An employer who asks questions such as those involved here is entitled to receive an honest answer, and reasonable communication in a plant newsletter concerning terminations for misrepresentations discourages other employees from engaging in similar conduct. In addition, the employees have an interest in knowing how the rules are enforced, and the type of conduct that may result in their discharge from employment. Accordingly, Louisiana Pacific's communication to its employees concerning Zinda's discharge was entitled to a conditional privilege.

However, conditional privilege is not absolute and may be forfeited if the privilege is abused. The RESTATEMENT (SECOND) OF TORTS lists five conditions which may constitute an abuse of the privilege, and the occurrence of any one causes the loss of the privilege. The privilege may be abused: (1) because of the defendant's knowledge or reckless disregard as to the falsity of the defamatory matter; (2) because the defamatory matter is published for some purpose other than that for which the particular privilege is given; (3) because the publication is made to some person not reasonably believed to be necessary for the accomplishment of the purpose of the particular privilege; (4) because the publication includes defamatory matter not reasonably believed to be necessary to accomplish the purpose for which the occasion is privileged; or (5) the publication includes unprivileged matter as well as privileged matter.

Zinda insists that any privilege which may have existed in this case was abused as a matter of law by excessive publication under condition (3). Essentially, Zinda argues that Louisiana Pacific made no attempt to restrict the publication to persons with a common interest in his termination. Zinda alludes to testimony elicited on cross-examination which purportedly indicates that the personnel manager had knowledge that employees routinely took the newsletters home. Furthermore, Zinda asserts that the content of the newsletter encouraged its removal from the plant.

We disagree that Louisiana Pacific abused its privilege as a matter of law. The question whether a conditional privilege has been abused is a factual question for the jury, unless the facts are such that only one conclusion can be reasonably drawn. RESTATEMENT (SECOND) OF TORTS, § 619(2), Cmt. b, at 316.

Contrary to Zinda's insistence, the evidence alluded to does not necessarily lead to the conclusion that Louisiana Pacific excessively published the statement concerning Zinda's discharge. Once it is determined by the court that the defamatory communication was made on an occasion of conditional privilege, the burden shifts to the plaintiff to affirmatively prove abuse. Here, despite allegations of widespread distribution throughout the community, Zinda's proof at trial was limited to the testimony of two unprivileged women who read the reference to Zinda's termination at the hospital where his wife worked.

An employer is entitled to use a method of publication that involves an incidental communication to persons not within the scope of the privilege. Often the only practical means of communicating defamatory information involves a probability or even a certainty that it will reach persons whose knowledge of it is of no value in accomplishing the purpose for which the privilege is given. In *Walters* [*v. Sentinel Co.*, 169 N.W. 564 (Wis. 1918)], this court stated that if "a newspaper, published primarily for a given constituency, such as county or state, church or lodge, have [sic] a small circulation outside such constituency, it is not deprived of its privilege in the discussion of matters of concern to its constituency because of such incidental outside circulation."

As previously discussed, Louisiana Pacific had an interest in informing each and every one of its employees about the subject of Zinda's discharge.[2] We cannot as a matter of law consider the communication in this case an unreasonable means to accomplish this purpose. Testimony indicates that the company attempted to correlate the number of copies printed to the number of employees in the plant. These copies were circulated only in the lunchroom, over the course of several days, so that every workshift would have an opportunity to read the newsletter. Thus, despite the company's alleged knowledge that employees often took the newsletter home, a jury could conclude that the great bulk of its readers had a direct and legitimate interest in the information regarding Zinda's termination, and that the outside communication was reasonably believed to be necessary to communicate the privileged information. Accordingly, the privilege was not abused as a matter of law, and it was error to refuse the requested instruction.

[The court then reversed and remanded the privacy judgment, holding that a claim for public disclosure of private facts, like a defamation claim, had a defense of conditional privilege.]

NOTE

Absolute Privilege. Parties and witnesses to judicial proceedings are absolutely privileged to publish defamatory statements, even if with malice

---

[2] To the extent that Zinda implies that the allegedly defamatory matter was indiscriminately taken home by the employees and communicated to various family members, we agree with courts of other jurisdictions which have held that defamatory communications made to family members are ordinarily subject to a conditional privilege.

they knowingly say something false. *See* RESTATEMENT (SECOND) OF TORTS §§ 587, 588 (1977). Several states have extended the privilege to administrative proceedings, including unemployment-compensation hearings. In those states, an employer can testify at an unemployment-compensation hearing about the reason for discharge without fear of a defamation suit. *See Blote v. First Fed. Sav. & Loan Ass'n*, 422 N.W.2d 834 (S.D. 1988).

SIGAL CONSTRUCTION CORP. v. STANBURY
District of Columbia Court of Appeals
586 A.2d 1204 (1991)

Before FERREN, BELSON, and FARRELL, ASSOCIATE JUDGES.

FERREN, ASSOCIATE JUDGE:

In this defamation case, a jury awarded appellee, Kenneth S. Stanbury, $370,440 against his former employer, appellant Sigal Construction Corporation. The jury found that a Sigal project manager, Paul Littman, had slandered Stanbury while giving an employment reference to another construction company after Sigal had terminated Stanbury's employment. The trial court denied Sigal's motion for judgment notwithstanding the verdict or for a new trial. The court, however, granted a remittitur ordering Stanbury to accept $250,000 or a new trial for damages. Stanbury accepted the $250,000. Sigal appeals the trial court's denial of its motion for judgment notwithstanding the verdict. . . .

Stanbury worked as a project manager for Sigal from May 1984 to June 1985. According to Sigal's personnel manager, Pamela Heiber, Sigal terminated Stanbury's employment because he "was not doing his job correctly." Sigal, however, told Stanbury he was let go for "lack of work or reduction in work." According to Heiber, "[w]e felt sympathy for Ken because of his age in life" (he was 63 when Sigal terminated his employment). Stanbury contacted Ray Stevens, a previous employer and Regional Manager at Daniel Construction, to find out whether any work was available. Some time later, Stevens called Stanbury about employment as a project manager on the Pentagon City project. Stanbury was eventually offered the job subject to approval by the owner of the project, Lincoln Properties.

William Janes, a Lincoln Properties general partner, had responsibility for investigating Stanbury's employment references. Janes called David Orr, a former Sigal project executive, who suggested that Janes contact Paul Littman, a current Sigal project executive. Janes did so, and Littman later memorialized the conversation:

> [Janes] claimed David [Orr] had told him not to hire Ken [Stanbury] and asked me what I thought. I told him.
>
> 1) Ken seemed detail oriented to the point of losing sight of the big picture.
>
> 2) He had a lot of knowledge and experience on big jobs.
>
> 3) With a large staff might be a very competent P.M. [project manager].

4) Obviously he no longer worked for us and that might say enough.

These paraphrase what I said nearly word for word.

At trial, Littman acknowledged and Stanbury confirmed that Littman had made these statements without having supervised, evaluated, read an evaluation of, or even worked with Stanbury (other than seeing Stanbury in the halls at the office). According to them both, their contact was entirely casual. More specifically, Stanbury testified without contradiction that he had talked to Littman only once during Stanbury's fourteen months with Sigal, and that this conversation was a general discussion about Stanbury's previous job. According to Littman, in evaluating Stanbury for Janes he relied entirely on the "general impression [he] had developed" from "hearing people talk about [Stanbury's] work at the job," perhaps at "casual luncheons" or "project executive meetings" or "over a beer on a Friday afternoon." Littman did nothing to verify the second-hand knowledge he had acquired about Stanbury. At trial, he could recall no facts or work-related incidents that would support the impressions he reported to Janes. When asked where his information about one of Stanbury's projects came from, Littman testified that "[t]here aren't any real specific instances I can point to. I think it was a general opinion I had just developed in the year or two [Stanbury] had been there." Littman thought that his opinion "possibly" came from "hearing people talk about [Stanbury's] work or job."

In contrast with Littman's acknowledgments at trial that his information about Stanbury was limited to vague hearsay, Janes testified at trial that Littman appeared to have knowledge of Stanbury's performance — indeed, that Littman told Janes he had worked with Stanbury on a project. Janes further testified that he could not recall whether Littman had acknowledged never supervising or seeing an evaluation of Stanbury. Littman's trial testimony substantially corroborated Janes' account of his interaction with Littman. Littman testified that Janes knew Littman was a project executive (who would supervise a project manager), that Stanbury was a project manager, and that Littman did not tell Janes he had never supervised, worked with, evaluated, or read an evaluation of Stanbury even though Littman knew Janes wanted to speak with someone who had "interact[ed]" with Stanbury. Littman also testified that, although he lacked explicit authority from Sigal to provide employment references, it was common in the construction industry for someone in his position to do so. Although the impact of Littman's statements on Janes was disputed at trial, Daniel Construction did not hire Stanbury for the Pentagon City project or for any other project. According to Stanbury, Stevens told him that Daniel Construction had not hired him because Lincoln Properties would not approve him. Stanbury further testified that, according to Stevens, Lincoln Properties (presumably Janes) had made "serious negative comments" about Stanbury and that Daniel Construction would have hired him but for Lincoln Properties' disapproval. Stanbury concluded, after further contacts, that Daniel Construction would not consider him for other projects because of Lincoln Properties' negative impression attributable to Littman's comments. . . .

Sigal first challenges the trial court's refusal to grant a judgment n.o.v. on the ground that the court erroneously characterized Littman's statements as purported facts, not opinions. This argument is attributable to *Gertz v. Robert Welch, Inc.*, 418 U.S. 323 (1974), where the Supreme Court stated in dictum:

> Under the First Amendment there is no such thing as a false idea. However pernicious an opinion may seem, we depend for its correction not on the conscience of judges and juries but on the competition of other ideas. But there is no constitutional value in false statements of fact.

Thereafter, a majority of the federal circuit courts of appeal have interpreted the *Gertz* dictum to mean that statements of fact can be actionable defamation; statements of opinion cannot. This court has joined the trend.

Recently, however, in *Milkovich v. Lorain Journal Co.*, 497 U.S. 1 (1990), the Supreme Court ruled that freedom of expression "is adequately secured by existing constitutional doctrine without creation of an artificial dichotomy between 'opinion' and fact." *Id.*, at 19. The Court said, in effect, that the lower courts had misinterpreted the *Gertz* dictum:

> Read in context, . . . the fair meaning of the passage is to equate the word "opinion" in the second sentence with the word "idea" in the first sentence. Under this view, the language was merely a reiteration of Justice Holmes' classic "marketplace of ideas" concept. (Citation omitted.)
>
> Thus we do not think this passage from *Gertz* was intended to create a wholesale defamation exemption for anything that might be labeled "opinion." (Citation omitted.) Not only would such an interpretation be contrary to the tenor and context of the passage, but it would also ignore the fact that *expressions of "opinion" may often imply an assertion of objective fact.*

Id., at 18 (emphasis added; citation omitted). . . .

Accordingly, while reserving a place for non-actionable "figurative or hyperbolic language" that could not reasonably be understood as a defamatory statement, the Court concluded that the perceived distinction between "opinion" and "fact" was an "artificial dichotomy," which did not advance constitutional analysis. Rather, according to *Milkovich*, any statement — even one expressed as an "opinion" — can amount to actionable defamation, unprotected by the First Amendment, if it reasonably implies a false assertion of fact and the statement is made with the level of fault required for recovery, respectively, by public figures or officials or by private figures.

This case, however, was tried, and appellate briefs were filed, on the premise that the opinion/fact dichotomy derived from *Gertz* and ensuing cases was the applicable law. . . . Because we conclude (as elaborated below) that Littman's statements about Stanbury were sufficiently factual under the pre-*Milkovich* standard to preclude constitutional protection as "opinion," we need not decide whether *Milkovich* applies. We therefore turn to the *Gertz* caselaw. . . .

[W]e conclude that — viewed (as they must be) in the light most favorable to Stanbury — Littman's statements were expressions of fact, not of constitutionally protected opinion. We look, first, at context. Littman told Janes that Stanbury was "detail oriented . . . to the point of losing sight of the big picture."[10] The context of this statement was an interview intended to help Janes (and thus Lincoln Properties) determine Stanbury's suitability for employment. In commenting on Stanbury's work habits, Littman must have known, or at least should have known, that Janes would interpret his statements as factual evaluations of Stanbury's approach to managing a construction project; otherwise, the information would have been meaningless in the context that had generated Janes' inquiry.

Furthermore, in considering the entire context of the statements — an employment reference — we note that, in the very conversation in which Littman made the allegedly defamatory remarks, he made several undisputed factual statements to Janes about Stanbury's history as a project manager, as well as a remark that "he no longer worked for us and that might say enough."[12] These remarks add still additional evidence to support the conclusion that Littman stated actionable facts, not protected opinion. Finally, the fact that Stanbury was not hired, apparently because of Littman's statements, could reasonably be taken as evidence of a factual content to the statements.

[Additionally], Littman's statements can be said to have implied "undisclosed defamatory facts." Stanbury testified, without contradiction, that "not seeing the big picture" meant in the construction trade that he did not perform his job properly, could not recognize unusual problems, and thus could not determine what is necessary to correct such problems so that the project would be properly completed on time. Stanbury also testified that "seeing the big picture" was critical to the job of project manager:

> It is important because unless you can visualize the whole project and determine whether it is normal or if it is unusual, and if it is unusual how it is unusual, what has to be done to fix it, it can serious[ly] affect your final completion and your cost. . . . [T]he project manager is the planner and the person that is responsible for the job, and he is the one that has to visualize and make the decisions.

Moreover, Littman's own testimony buttressed Stanbury's interpretation. Littman said he meant "as an outside observer that the project wasn't going well, and that in the end that was the big picture." Thus, a reasonable juror could find that Littman's statements to Janes implied undisclosed factual data.

[A third] criterion is the verifiability of the statements. Both parties introduced evidence to support either the truth or the falsity of Littman's statements. This evidence made clear that whether Stanbury was too detail oriented to complete the project properly and on time could be objectively evaluated and thus verified. Sigal has proffered no alternative meaning for

---

[10] The trial court ruled that "detail oriented," standing alone, was too vague to constitute a defamatory statement of fact but that it became defamatory when combined with Littman's statement about the "big picture."

[12] In addition to his editorial comment about Stanbury's termination of employment, Littman testified he told Janes that Stanbury had a lot of experience on big jobs and that with a large staff Stanbury might be competent. The trial court ruled that these three "statements in the surrounding context would signal to the average reader that the statements uttered by Littman were assertions of fact."

Littman's statement, either in the trial court or on appeal, that would suggest the words were subjective or vague. We agree with the trial court:

> While [Sigal] asserts that the meaning of the statement may vary from individual to individual, there was no evidence produced by [Sigal] which suggested that the statement made in the context in which it was made, meant anything different than what Plaintiff sought to prove it meant.

In fact, Janes — the person to whom the statement was made, and who was in the best position to interpret what it meant — testified that he derived from Littman's comments specific information concerning Stanbury's work. . . .

Given the context in which Littman aired his comments about Stanbury, and judged in their entirety, we conclude the statements were assertions of fact within the meaning of *Gertz* and *Myers*, not constitutionally protected opinions.

Although Littman's statements were actionable assertions of "fact," not constitutionally protected "opinion," Stanbury had the burden of proving Sigal (through Littman) was negligent, including the fact that Littman's statements were false. The trial court accordingly gave the jury a negligence instruction. Sigal does not contest, on appeal, either that the statements were false or were negligently made. Sigal does contend, however — and Stanbury does not dispute — that Littman's negligent statements were subject to a "qualified privilege." . . .

Once the privilege applies, the plaintiff has the burden of proving the defendant has abused, and thus lost, it. To defeat the privilege, a plaintiff must prove the defendant acted with "common law malice." Such malice implies a greater level of ill will than the mind-set reflected by mere negligence. . . .

There was sufficient evidence at trial, viewed in the light most favorable to Stanbury, from which a reasonable jury could find by clear and convincing evidence that Littman and Sigal had abused the qualified privilege under Virginia law by acting with "such gross indifference or recklessness as to amount to wanton and willful disregard of the rights of" Stanbury. Littman testified, and Stanbury's testimony confirmed, that Littman had never supervised, worked with, evaluated, or read an evaluation of Stanbury. Moreover, Littman testified that he had not received information from anyone in particular, let alone anyone who had had a work-related relationship with Stanbury. Littman's sources for his statements to Janes were observations in the company's halls and general office contacts with unnamed third parties, perhaps at "casual lunches" or "project executive meetings" or "over beer on a Friday afternoon." But he could recall none of the conversations or otherwise provide any concrete support for his statements, whether first-hand information or hearsay. Littman admitted that he had no facts to support any of his statements to Janes and that he had never sought to verify the information before giving his evaluation. Littman also testified that he knew Janes wanted to speak with someone who had "interacted" with Stanbury at Sigal, and yet Littman further testified that he did not tell Janes he had never done so. Nor did Littman tell Janes the altogether vague sources of his statements. To make matters worse, according to Janes testimony, Littman told Janes that he had worked with Stanbury on a project.

In short, this is a case of pure "rumor" or "gossip" or "scuttlebutt" conveyed as fact, without any disclaimer or explanation, coupled with Littman's erroneously leading the prospective employer to believe he had worked on a project with Stanbury. Reviewing the evidence in the light most favorable to Stanbury, as we must, we cannot say there was no record basis for the jury to find by clear and convincing evidence that Littman made the statements to Janes with gross indifference or recklessness amounting to wanton and willful disregard of Stanbury's rights under Virginia law.

In sustaining the conclusion that Sigal (through Littman) abused the qualified privilege, we do not mean to imply that employers are at serious risk when providing employment references in the normal course of business. Nor are we suggesting that employers, when providing such references, may not rely on information from the employee's co-workers, even when hearsay. Our analysis here is limited to an office gossip situation where the recommender (1) has conveyed information which cannot be traced to anyone with personal knowledge of the employee whose reputation is at stake, (2) has not qualified his statements by disclosing the nebulous source of his information, and (3) has led the prospective employer to believe he has worked on a project with the employee and thus has first-hand information. . . .

Affirmed.

NOTES

1. *Employer Policies on References.* Fear of legal liability has a significant effect on employers' willingness to provide references. In a recent survey of 345 human resources professionals, 53% said they were aware of someone in their organization refusing to provide information about a former employee for fear of legal liability. Fifty-four percent of those surveyed had a blanket company policy of refusing to provide any references or information about current or former employees. Of those willing to provide information, 25% limited it to verification of employment. SOCIETY FOR HUMAN RESOURCES MANAGEMENT, 2004 REFERENCE AND BACKGROUND CHECKING SURVEY REPORT 16-18 (2005).

2. *Encouraging the Flow of Reference Information.* A free rider problem may exist with references. The risks that a candidly negative reference will be found defamatory fall on the old employer, while the benefits accrue to the interviewing employer. As a result, a policy of refusing to give references may be wise for each individual employer, even though it would harm the public interest by limiting the flow of valuable information about prospective employees.

In the past decade, about half the states have responded to this problem by enacting statutes designed to provide employers with qualified immunity from defamation liability when providing reference information. One curious feature of these "immunity" statutes is that, in general, they tend to re-state the common law defamation standards that were in place before the statutes were enacted. *See* OKLA STAT. tit. 40, § 61 (enacted in 1995) (employer immune unless knowledge of falsity, malice, or reckless disregard of truth); TENN. CODE ANN. § 50-1-105 (enacted in 1995) (similar). Sometimes the statutes even cut in the other direction and increase the possibility of a defamation suit, for example, by requiring employers to provide copies of references to employees. *See* COLO. REV. STAT. § 8-2-114(b); IND. CODE § 22-5-3-1(c).

Ironically, however, these curious statutes may achieve the Legislatures' goal of encouraging employers to provide references. Professors Paetzold and Willborn contend that employers are refusing to give references based on an irrational or highly biased fear of defamation liability. Paetzold and Willborn found that, over the past two decades as more and more employers refused to give references because of fear of liability, their actual exposure to that type of liability declined. They speculate that employer perceptions have been based on reports of large defamation awards made by juries, which are widely reported, rather than on a full sample of cases in which most are dismissed and even large jury awards tend to be greatly reduced through remittitur or on appeal. Ramona L. Paetzold & Steven L. Willborn, *Employer (Ir)rationality and the Demise of Employment References,* 30 AM. BUS. L.J. 123 (1992). If this is true, the "immunity" statutes may increase reference-giving by correcting employer misperceptions about their exposure to defamation liability, even if they do not change the actual liability standard at all.

3. *Constitutional Overlay.* The Supreme Court has limited the scope of defamation actions that place an unconstitutional chill on free speech. As applied to employment cases, the constitutional limitations are unclear. One question is whether the employee must prove the employer was negligent in making the defamatory statement. At common law, defamation was a strict-liability tort, in that a speaker could be liable for publishing a defamatory statement even if he could not reasonably have known it was false. In *New York Times Co. v. Sullivan,* 376 U.S. 254 (1964), the Court held that public officials could maintain a defamation action only by proving "actual malice" — that the speaker had knowledge the statement was false or acted with reckless disregard of whether or not it was false. In *Gertz v. Robert Welch, Inc.,* 418 U.S. 323 (1974), the Court held that, in defamation suits by a private individual against a media defendant, states cannot impose liability without fault, and cannot impose presumed or punitive damages without a showing of knowledge of falsity or reckless disregard for the truth.

Most employment defamation claims, however, involve neither public officials or figures nor media defendants. The Court has not definitively declared whether a private plaintiff suing a nonmedia defendant must show any kind of fault. In *Dun & Bradstreet, Inc. v. Greenmoss Builders, Inc.,* 472 U.S. 749 (1985), five Justices said that the *Gertz* requirement on presumed or punitive damages — no recovery without malice — should extend to non-media defendants. But whether liability against non-media defendants requires fault remains unclear. As set out at the beginning of this section, the RESTATEMENT — extrapolating from *Gertz* — requires a showing of negligence in all actions.

Related to the issue of whether negligence is required is the standard for showing whether the employer abused its conditional privilege. *Stanbury* (which included negligence as part of the employee's basic case) reflects the standard view that the employee must show by clear and convincing evidence that the employer abused its privilege by acting recklessly. If the employee need only show negligence, the conditional privilege would add no protection. In those states that do not require negligence as an element of the basic tort of defamation, however, a lower standard may apply. In those states, perhaps it is sufficient for the employee to show that the employer abused the conditional privilege by proving negligence.

4. Bad References as Breach of Contract. Often, employees are asked to resign rather than be fired, and one reason for them to do so is that a resignation provides an opportunity to negotiate a contract specifying the reasons the employer will give for the resignation. Discrimination and other lawsuits that are settled often contain similar agreements, in which the employee agrees to go quietly in return for cash and an agreement that the employer will give only good or neutral references. To what degree should such contracts be enforceable?

A limited-reference agreement was held to be enforceable in *Resnik v. Blue Cross & Blue Shield*, 912 S.W.2d 567 (Mo. Ct. App. 1995). Upon termination, the parties agreed that "reference inquiries . . . will be limited to name, job title, and dates of employment only." The employee interviewed at a new company, which expressed serious interest in hiring him and then contacted his former supervisor. After a forty-five minute phone conversation between the two employers, the new employer never contacted the employee again. The court held that a jury could find that the first employer gave a bad reference, breaching the agreement, from circumstantial evidence including the lengthy telephone call.

On the other hand, an agreement was held non-enforceable on the painful facts of *Picton v. Anderson Union High School District*, 57 Cal. Rptr. 2d 829 (Cal. Ct. App. 1996). A teacher settled charges of sexual-misconduct towards students, including rape, by resigning in exchange for a withdrawal of all accusations and an agreement not to disclose the real reason for the separation. The rape victim agreed to the settlement. The school district then broke the agreement, sending documents to the state commission on teacher credentialing. The court rejected the teacher's breach of contract suit, holding that the Education Code and regulations made it illegal for the school district to agree to suppress the facts of discharge. The court also rejected a defamation claim, finding that communications to the commission were absolutely privileged. The court also rejected the teacher's claims of fraudulent inducement of contract as falling within the improper breach of contract claim. Finally, the court rejected claims of wrongful discharge, civil conspiracy, tortious interference with prospective economic advantage, and intentional and negligent infliction of emotional distress, because the part of the agreement whereby the parties agreed to release all claims was legally binding on the teacher. Had the employer been a private employer not subject to the Education Code — say a nursery school or YMCA — would the court have reached the same result on grounds of public policy?

5. Good References as Torts. In *Randi W. v. Muroc Joint Unified School District*, 929 P.2d 582 (Cal. 1997), a school district wrote a positive reference for an employee, even though it had forced him to resign because of sexual-misconduct allegations. Based in part on the reference, the employee was hired by another school district as an administrator. In that position, he sexually assaulted a thirteen-year-old student. The student sued the school district for the positive reference on fraud and negligent-misrepresentation theories. The California Supreme Court held that employers giving good references may be liable if they make affirmative misrepresentations that present a foreseeable and substantial risk of physical harm to third parties.

The Court declared that the school district would not have been liable if it had not provided any reference at all, but "having volunteered [positive] information, [the school district was] obliged to complete the picture by disclosing material facts regarding [the employee's] sexual improprieties." *Id.* at 592.

6. *Waiving Defamation Claims.* Suppose a prospective employer, wanting candid references, asks a job applicant to sign a release waiving any possible defamation claims against prior employers who may serve as references. In a 2005 survey, 22% of human resources professionals reported a company policy requiring employees to sign a waiver before a reference is given. SOCIETY FOR HUMAN RESOURCES MANAGEMENT, 2004 REFERENCE AND BACKGROUND CHECKING SURVEY REPORT 21 (2005). Can this contract shield prior employers from defamation claims against an applicant who fails to get a job? *See Cox v. Nasche*, 70 F.3d 1030 (9th Cir. 1995) (applying Alaskan law) (holding that signed release confers absolute privilege upon prior employers in defamation suit). *See also* RESTATEMENT (SECOND) OF TORTS § 583 (1977) ("the consent of another to the publication of defamatory matter concerning him is a complete defense to his action for defamation"). *But see Kellums v. Freight Sales Ctrs., Inc.*, 467 So. 2d 816 (Fla. Dist. Ct. App. 1985) (holding that a release waives claims of invasion of privacy or tortious interference with business relations, but does not waive claims against defamatory statements made "knowingly and maliciously," because a party cannot absolve itself by contract of an intentional or "quasi-intentional" tort claim).

Part IV

EMPLOYEE DUTIES AND PROMISES

Chapter 11

DUTY OF LOYALTY AND TRADE SECRETS

A. THE THEORY OF TRADE SECRETS AND NONCOMPETITION CLAUSES

Employees learn things on the job. Nobel-laureate Gary Becker has distinguished between two types of job training. On the one hand, employees may receive "specific" training that is only valuable to their particular employer. Employers should be willing to pay for this kind of training. They will be able to recoup the payments later as the employees perform work with the special training, but are paid wages a bit below full market value. The employer would only provide the training if it were valuable and, by definition, the employees can only perform that valuable work for the employer providing the training. Thus, the employer does not need to worry about laws or contracts to keep the employee from leaving and depriving it of the benefit of its investment.

On the other hand, employees may receive "general" training that is valuable to many employers. In this case, under Becker's model, an employer would not be willing to pay for any of the training. If it did, the employee could leave immediately after receiving the training to work for another employer who would be willing to pay the full market wage. Consequently, an employer paying for general training would never be able to recoup its investment by paying an employee less than full market value later because as soon as the training was completed, the employee would be able to go work for another employer who could pay full value (especially since the employee comes already trained at somebody else's expense). Thus, in theory still, *employees* must pay for the full value of general training, normally in lower wages than they would receive otherwise as they are receiving the training. If that is the case, laws or contracts to keep employees from leaving would still be unneeded or undesirable. Since employees have paid in lower wages for the full value of all their general training, they *should* be permitted to leave freely. GARY S. BECKER, HUMAN CAPITAL (1964).

But now consider an employee who receives general training (again, training valuable to many employers) that is simply too valuable for the employee to pay for in lower wages. If the full reduction in wages were made, the employee would have to pay the employer! One possibility here is that the employer may require employees to get and pay for the general training before they are hired. Consider, for example, the nature of the training you are receiving at this moment and who is paying for it. Alternatively, the employer may pay for the training even though it is general, but attempt to limit the employee's ability to leave until the employee has worked long enough to repay the employer for its investment. Similarly, if we think of "job training" broadly to include valuable business information, an employer may want to disclose that information to an employee on her first day of employment, yet protect it from being disclosed to other employers. For example, imagine an employee who is provided with the probably apocryphal Coca-Cola formula on her first day of employment. The employer needs to disclose the information to the employee so the Coke can be manufactured, but does not want the formula disclosed. Again, the employer will want to limit the employee's ability to leave immediately with the information. These latter two situations, then, are ones in which there may be a role for laws or contracts that impose limits on the ability of employees to leave employment and take their job training with them. Restrictions may be justified when employers provide job training that is too expensive for the employee to pay for ahead of time or at the same time the training is being provided. Paul H. Rubin & Peter Shedd, *Human Capital & Covenants Not to Compete*, 10 J. LEGAL STUD. 93 (1981).

The justification for restrictions on employee mobility in this model is that it encourages employers to produce valuable business information and to provide expensive general training to employees. If employers could not protect the information or their investments in job training, employers would not invest as much in these valuable activities, or they would have to take inefficient steps to protect the information (for example, by dividing tasks up between many employees so no individual employee could leave with useful information). The task for courts under this model is to distinguish between two types of restrictions: 1) restrictions that protect employers when they disclose valuable information to employees or make expensive investments in training and 2) restrictions that prevent employees from using general on-the-job training that they have already paid for themselves. That task would be complicated enough even if everyone accepted the model. But, as always, the real world is more complicated, and more interesting.

ALAN HYDE, TRADE SECRETS PRACTICE IN SILICON VALLEY [*]

High-technology companies often share trade secrets with competitors, treating information very differently than the theory suggests. New start-up companies are typically founded by managers leaving established companies. The new companies may make products that work with the products of the old company, or may compete with them by making versions of the same product. But either way, the old company rarely sues departing employees.

For example, consider the manufacture of hard drives (mostly in Silicon Valley, California). Successful firms are founded by departing employees of existing firms. Of sixty-eight firms entering that industry over a twenty-year period (1977-97), forty were started by former employees of existing firms, and those forty included all but four of the start-ups that generated revenue, accounting for 99.4 percent of the total revenues of the start-up group. (Of course, most of the "established" firms that gave birth to employee start-ups had themselves been spun out of even older firms). The more valuable a company's technology, the more its employees will leave to start new, success-ful firms. It doesn't matter how big the old firm is. The greater its technological

---

[*] This Note was prepared for this book by Professor Alan Hyde. It is adapted from his book, WORKING IN SILICON VALLEY: ECONOMIC AND LEGAL ANALYSIS OF A HIGH-VELOCITY LABOR MARKET (2003).

know-how (measured by the range and capacities of its products), the greater the likelihood of employees leaving to start a start-up, and the longer the start-up will survive. Start-ups included both innovators and firms that basically imitated the older firm. The result was that the price of disk drives fell while firm profits increased.[1]

Company secrets also pass to competitors because production involves networks of related firms. Companies often outsource as much production as they can. Bringing a new product to market requires the cooperation of a network of subcontractors handling design or production. Because employees change jobs frequently and rarely make entire careers inside one firm, they know people at other firms and can put together networks of cooperating individuals and firms.[2] Engineers frequently call friends and former co-workers at competing firms to chat about mutual problems and possible solutions.[3] Customers will demand "second sources" of key components, so companies must license or share their technology.

These patterns are found in many high technology industries, but are particularly common in Silicon Valley, California, the high technology industries around Stanford University. Many observers attribute the extraordinary technological and economic growth of the Valley to its networks of production and the rapid passage of information among firms. Some employers share this analysis. Cisco, for example, has a policy of never suing departing employees. Cisco's high-end routers compete with the products of Juniper and Redback, both founded by former Cisco employees (without any litigation by Cisco). Cisco does have a policy of not reemploying employees who have worked at Juniper or Redback, but I was told that exceptions have been made to this policy. When I asked for an example, I was told: "When we think they've learned something."

Law has both facilitated and adjusted to the pattern of networked production and information sharing. California does not enforce covenants not to compete. The statutory ban on them dates from nineteenth century codification and was not adopted with any reference to high technology. But today it takes away the most important weapon that employers might use against employees who leave to join, or start, competitors. According to Professor Ronald Gilson, Massachusetts employees (unlike California employees) fear lawsuits if they form start-ups or change employers, and this results in larger, fewer firms.[4]

California employers may still sue those employees if they disclose trade secrets. However, they rarely do this. Many have concluded that such suits are difficult to win and usually hurt the employer who brings them. The

---

[1] April Mitchell Franco & Darren Filson, *Knowledge Diffusion Through Employee Mobility*, Federal Reserve Bank of Minneapolis, Research Department Staff Report 272 (July 2000).

[2] AnnaLee Saxenian, Regional Advantage: Culture and Competition in Silicon Valley and Route 128 (1994).

[3] Eric von Hippel, The Sources of Innovation (1988); Sim B. Sitkin, *Secrecy in Organizations: Determinants of Secrecy Behavior among Engineers in Three Silicon Valley Semiconductor Firms.* (1986) (unpublished Ph.D. dissertation, Graduate School of Business, Stanford University).

[4] Ronald J. Gilson, *The Legal Infrastructure of High Technology Industrial Districts: Silicon Valley, Route 128, and Covenants not to Compete*, 74 N.Y.U. L. Rev. 575 (1999).

difficulty in winning trade secrets suits does not reflect unique features of California statute or case law. California has the same Uniform Trade Secrets Act as forty other jurisdictions. (California does not give any independent weight to negotiated trade secret agreements; plaintiffs must show the threatened disclosure of information that the statute makes a trade secret.)[5] There certainly are California cases that enjoin departing employees from disclosing trade secrets on their new job.[6]

Intel has recently tried and failed to make use of trade secret law. In the mid-90s, Intel cultivated a reputation as an aggressive litigator in defense of its trade secrets. One such suit was its pursuit of ULSI Technologies, a rival chip manufacturer to which a former Intel employee brought the specifications of an Intel chip in progress. Although ULSI immediately notified Intel and offered to open its files to show that it had no other Intel secrets, Intel chose instead to pursue both civil and criminal penalties. These accomplished little for Intel. The criminal and civil juries found for the defendants on the grounds that Intel's supposed secrets were mostly known in the industry anyway.[7] Meanwhile, the litigation and similar litigation at the time hurt Intel's recruiting. As a high Intel official told me, "Chat groups lit up all over the Valley. Every engineer we interviewed that year wanted to know if we would sue him when he left."

Intel sued no departing employees until 2000, when it sued four executives and engineers who left for a competitor making fast ethernet equipment. The court denied relief as to the three key individuals, finding that they were "trustworthy" and wouldn't disclose any Intel secrets on the new job.[8] The court also read California's statutory ban on covenants not to compete to stand for a broader "strong public policy against limitations on employment mobility." (The court did find that the competitor's questions to a fourth, lower-level applicant went too far in trying to find out what Intel was working on). The case then settled, so never went to any appellate court, but the lawyers to whom I spoke expect it to be influential.

The Silicon Valley pattern combines high employee mobility, high information spreading, low litigation, and rapid economic growth. It raises — but does not answer — the question of whether American law on covenants not to compete and trade secrets should be more like California's, forbidding enforcement of covenants and making trade secrets suits difficult for plaintiffs.

Economists would normally describe this choice as a trade-off. If employers can protect their secrets, they have good incentives to create information but the incentives to spread information are weak. If employees can usually leave to compete with their former employer, this may weaken the incentives to create information but creates good incentives for information to spread. But economists cannot tell us which arrangement is better for society as a whole, partly because few have given much attention to the economic value of information that is nobody's property.

---

[5] *State Farm Mut. Auto Ins. Co. v. Dempster*, 344 P.2d 821, 825-26 (Cal. Ct. App. 1959) (dictum).

[6] *By-Buk Co. v. Printed Cellophane Tape Co.*, 329 P.2d 147 (Cal. Ct. App. 1958).

[7] Tim Jackson, Inside Intel 284-93 (1988).

[8] *Intel Corporation v. Broadcom Corporation*, California Superior Court, County of Santa Clara (unpublished order, No. CV 788310, May 25, 2000).

An exception is Paul M. Romer, whose New Growth Theory makes information the central element in economic growth. Information becomes more important when shared among many users than when held as private property by Intel. "To see why extremely strong property rights might be a problem," writes Romer,[9] "imagine that Bell Labs had been given a nonexpiring, ironclad patent on the discovery of the transistor. Or even worse, imagine that such a patent had gone to an organization such as IBM or General Motors. Think of how different the digital electronics and consumer electronics industries would be if every inventor who improved on the design of the transistor and every person who applied the transistor in a new setting had to negotiate with one of these large, bureaucratic organizations for permission to proceed."

Under Romer's model, Intel will have adequate incentives to innovate without special devices permitting it to keep those innovations secret, while society will be better off the quicker such technical information diffuses. Romer's innovation is to separate two kinds of knowledge that are often combined as "human capital": "rivalrous" knowledge where the use by one person precludes the use by another; and "nonrivalrous" knowledge that can be reused infinitely at no additional cost, such as programs, instructions, protocols, designs, or other know-how. Nonrivalrous information is not limited to "public domain" knowledge like chemical compounds. It includes information like the specifications of Intel's forthcoming basic processing chip.[10] In Romer's model, production has four basic inputs: capital, labor, rivalrous human capital, and nonrivalrous knowledge to which everyone has equal access. Capital is assumed to grow by the amount of foregone consumption, and labor and rivalrous human capital are assumed for simplicity to be fixed.

Under these assumptions, Romer derives a solution in which nonrivalrous information can grow without bound and becomes the most important factor of production for growth. The limitless growth of nonrivalrous information is crucial and distinguishes it from other factors of production. Raw materials, water, and workers' bodies can become used up, overfished, or worn out, particularly if held in common without strong property rights. Information, by contrast, is not a common pond that can be overfished. It never wears out and private actors use it over and over again. Firms nevertheless invest in research, even though they will not be able to exclude rivals from the information eventually produced, because they can still charge more for their products than the costs of production.

---

[9] Paul M. Romer, *Implementing a National Technology Strategy with Self-Organizing Industry Investment Boards*, 1993 BROOKINGS PAPERS ON ECONOMIC ACTIVITY: MICROECONOMICS 345, 358.

[10] Paul M. Romer, *Endogenous Technological Change*, 98 J. POL. ECON. S71 (1990). In Romer's model, information like "the specifications of a forthcoming Intel chip" is nonrivalrous, but it may be "excludable." His theory is limited to information that is nonrivalrous and nonexcludable. "Rivalry is a purely technological attribute. A purely rival good has the property that its use by one firm or person precludes its use by another; a purely nonrival good has the property that its use by one firm or person in no way limits its use by another. Excludability is a function of both the technology and the legal system. A good is excludable if the owner can prevent others from using it." *Id.* S73-74. Most information is "nonrivalrous" in Romer's terminology. The exception is information that is lodged in one human body that can only be in one place at one time.

Romer's appears to be the economic theory that explains much of the difference between Silicon Valley and Route 128 observed by AnnaLee Saxenian. Saxenian is not able to compare direct investment in the production of information by California and Massachusetts employers during the years of her study, but the differences, if any, seem unlikely to account for Silicon Valley's much greater growth. Silicon Valley produces more growth from employer investment in information because more of that information is nonexcludable. Rapid employee turnover turns information that firms and lawyers otherwise might consider proprietary (such as specifications of forthcoming products) into Romer-like nonrivalrous, nonexcludable information. Yet firms do not, in general, stop investing in the production of technological change merely because they know, in a high-velocity labor market, that this information will soon pass to competitors or even enable employees to start their own competitor.

Employers benefit in at least four ways from a regime of weak trade secrets protection. First, they are hirers as well as losers of labor. Second, shared information lowers their own production costs.[11] Third, innovations do not just require incentives for employers; they also require incentives for employees. Employees have maximum incentives to produce innovations, in a labor market in which they are able to start their own companies (or move around), and trade on what they learned on their last job.[12] Fourth, an implied promise not to interfere with future employability is the price that employers pay in order to induce employees to accept highly contingent work relations.[13]

NOTES

1. Silicon Valley and Route 128. Scholars such as Hyde, Gilson, and Saxenian contrast the fabulous growth of Silicon Valley with the more modest growth of Boston's Route 128, both centers of the new high-technology economy. Silicon Valley is the paradigm high-velocity market, to use Hyde's evocative phrase, with much movement by workers between many specialized firms. Route 128, by contrast, is dominated by a few large corporations such as Honeywell and Digital Equipment Corporation, whose goal was independence. As sociologist AnnaLee Saxenian describes it,

The industrial structure of Route 128 was defined by the search for corporate self-sufficiency or autarky. As they grew, local companies built self-contained and vertically integrated structures, just as Silicon Valley firms were experimenting with openness and specialization. The desire for self-sufficiency was largely a product of local executives' inherited ideas about how to organize production. The region's new technology start-ups drew most of their managers from the diversified electrical and consumer electronics products of the Northeast such as

---

[11] David P. Cooper, *Innovation and Reciprocal Externalities: Information Transmission via Job Mobility*, 45 J. ECON. BEHAV. & ORG. 403 (2001).

[12] GILLIAN L.L. LESTER & ERIC L. TALLEY, TRADE SECRETS AND MUTUAL INVESTMENTS, U.S.C. Law School, Olin Research Paper No. 00-15 (2000).

[13] Tracy R. Lewis & Dennis Yao, Innovation, Knowledge Flow, and Worker Mobility (2001) (unpublished manuscript).

Sylvania, General Electric, and RCA. Their notions of appropriate business strategies and structures were shaped by these models.

AnnaLee Saxenian, Regional Advantage: Culture and Competition in Silicon Valley and Route 128 (1994).

A key question for lawyers is the degree to which law on the books and law in action contributes to these economic outcomes. California is distinctive in refusing to enforce covenants not to compete except in limited situations, such as the sale of a business. But as Hyde emphasizes, the reluctance of Silicon Valley firms to bring trade-secret claims, and the reluctance of courts to enforce them, also contributes to the success of the high-velocity market.

2. *General Training and Temporary Help Firms.* In a careful empirical study, Professor Autor has found that temporary help supply (THS) firms pay for general training for their workers, contrary to the Becker model. They do so to attract and retain the most desirable workers:

> THS firms [offer workers] free skills training in subjects such as word processing, data entry, and in some cases computer programming. Manpower, Inc., the nation's largest THS employer, estimates that it trains more than 100,000 temporaries per year in the use of office automation software. The Bureau of Labor Statistics [survey] found that 89 percent of temporary workers are employed by establishments that provide some form of nominally free skills training. . . .

> [T]he training provided by temporary help employers — primarily end user computer skills — is inherently general. Furthermore, because workers typically receive training up-front during unpaid hours prior to taking any paid assignments, productivity is inherently zero during the training period. It is therefore clear that the direct, up-front costs of skills training, which include computer equipment, instructional materials, and training staff, are borne by THS firms.

> While THS firms offer a variety of benefits to attract workers, training is distinct among them because it is thought to differentially attract desirable workers. . . . Closely related to the recruiting function is the idea that skills training facilitates worker assessment. . . . This screening role has three components: pre-training exams measure the skills that workers possess; tests before and after training permit firms to gauge workers' ability to acquire new skills; and workers' motivation to take training is itself considered an emblem of skill or desirability.

> [T]he dual roles played by training . . . — self-selection and information acquisition — are complementary. By inducing self-selection of high ability workers, training improves the firm's worker pool. By revealing private information about worker ability, training then allows the firm to profit from this pool.

David H. Autor, *Why Do Temporary Help Firms Provide Free General Skills Training?*, 116 Q.J. Econ. 1409 (2001).

3. *Universities and Free Trade.* Determining the correct balance between allowing workers and information to move freely vs. encouraging innovation by imposing restrictions is very difficult. Consider this comment by another Nobel-laureate and his co-author:

> Intellectual property provides innovators with temporary monopoly power. Monopoly power always results in economic inefficiency. There is accordingly a high cost of granting even temporary monopoly power, but the benefit is that by doing so, greater motivation is provided for inventive activity. The dynamic gains, it is hoped, exceed the static losses.
>
> Much of the most important innovative activity is outside the realm of intellectual property. Behind the innovations associated with atomic energy or lasers were basic discoveries in physics. Behind the computer were basic discoveries in mathematics. The basic research which underlies practical innovation in almost all arenas occurs in universities and government research laboratories, and few of these discoveries are protected by intellectual property. . . . [T]here is little evidence that stronger intellectual property protection would generate a greater flow of basic ideas.

JOSEPH E. STIGLITZ & ANDREW CHARLTON, FAIR TRADE FOR ALL: HOW TRADE CAN PROMOTE DEVELOPMENT 141-42 (2005).

Is this merely a descriptive statement: We "know" that trade restrictions are not necessary to create incentives for important research because universities do important research without those restrictions. If so, are universities a fair test case given the large public investment in their research efforts and their insulation from normal profit-and-loss concerns? And what should we make of the statement as universities become more entrepreneurial and begin to protect the intellectual property produced by their faculty and other researchers aggressively? DEREK BOK, UNIVERSITIES IN THE MARKETPLACE: THE COMMERCIALIZATION OF HIGHER EDUCATION (2003). Should we applaud this development because universities will be able to produce more and better basic research with the extra resources at their disposal? Or condemn it (or even prevent it legally) because it will limit the quick and beneficial dispersion of basic research ideas?

B. TAKING CUSTOMERS AND EMPLOYEES

We now turn to the case law on duty of loyalty, asking under what circumstances the law prevents an employee from starting a competing business using customers or fellow employees of the old employers.

JET COURIER SERVICE v. MULEI
Supreme Court of Colorado, en banc
771 P.2d 486 (1989)

LOHR, JUSTICE.

I

Jet is an air courier company engaged principally in supplying a specialized transportation service to customer banks. Jet provides air and incidental ground courier service to carry canceled checks between banks to facilitate rapid processing of those checks through the banking system. Shortened processing time enables the banks at which the checks are cashed to make use of the funds sooner. Because the sums involved are large, substantial amounts of daily interest are at stake. As a result, the ability to assure speedy deliveries is essential to compete effectively in the air courier business.

In 1981 Jet was an established family-owned corporation headed by Donald W. Wright. The principal offices of the corporation were in Cincinnati, Ohio. Jet had no office in Denver. Anthony Mulei at that time was working in Denver for another air courier service in a management capacity. Mulei had worked in the air courier business for a number of years and was very familiar with it. He had numerous business connections in the banking industry in Denver and other cities. On February 18, 1981, Wright and Mulei agreed that Mulei would come to work for Jet and would open a Denver office and manage Jet's Western Zone operations from that office. They orally agreed that Mulei would be vice president and general manager for the Western Zone and would have autonomy in matters such as the solicitation of business, the operation of the business, and personnel policies. The parties further agreed that Mulei would be paid $36,000 per year, plus a bonus of ten percent of the net profits of the Western Zone, to be calculated and paid every three months. Based in part on Mulei's business relationships with several regional banks, Wright and Mulei expected that Mulei would be able to expand Jet's business.

Late in 1981 Wright sent Mulei a written employment agreement containing the same terms as the oral agreement with the addition of a noncompetition covenant whereby Mulei would agree not to compete with Jet for two years after termination of his employment, without any geographic restriction. Mulei signed the written agreement. At some time before this litigation commenced, Wright also signed the agreement on behalf of Jet.

Mulei performed services as agreed and was successful in significantly increasing the business of Jet in the Western Zone as well as other areas of the United States. Although Jet regularly paid Mulei his monthly salary, and paid him additional sums from time to time totaling $31,000 over the period of his employment, Jet never computed or paid the quarterly bonuses in the manner contemplated by the contract. From time to time Mulei requested payments and accountings but was not successful in obtaining them.

Mulei became progressively dissatisfied with his inability to resolve the bonus issue and with what he believed to be intrusions into his promised areas of autonomy in personnel and operational matters. Toward the end of 1982 he began to look for other work in the air courier field and sought legal advice concerning the validity of the noncompetition covenant in his employment contract.

In the course of seeking other employment opportunities and while still employed by Jet, Mulei began to investigate setting up another air courier company that would compete with Jet in the air courier business. In January 1983, Mulei spoke with John Towner, a Kansas air charter operator who was in the business of supplying certain air transportation services, about going into business together. In February 1983, Mulei met with Towner and two

Jet employees to discuss setting up this new business and obtaining customers.

On February 27, 1983, Mulei, while still employed by Jet and on Jet business in Phoenix, talked to two of Jet's customer banks to inform them he would be leaving Jet in mid-March and to tell them he "would try to give them the same service." He engaged in similar discussions with two bank customers of Jet in Dallas while still employed by Jet. Early in March 1983, Mulei met with representatives of three of Jet's Denver customers, First Interstate Bank of Denver, Central Bank of Denver, and United Bank of Denver, and discussed the new air courier company that Mulei and Towner were forming. Mulei told the United Bank of Denver float manager that "if they wished to give us [ACT] the business," then ACT would be able to serve them without any break in the service, and that ACT would be able to take over their business and fully satisfy their air courier service needs. Mulei further told United Bank of Denver that "by minimizing expenses, I would be in a position, sometime later, to reduce cost." Mulei had similar conversations with representatives of First Interstate Bank of Denver.

Prior to the termination of Mulei's employment by Jet on March 10, 1983, Mulei met with nine pilots who were flying for Jet to discuss his formation of ACT. Before his termination, Mulei also met with Jet's Denver office staff and with its ground couriers[4] to discuss potential future employment with ACT. Mulei offered Jet's office staff better working conditions, including health and dental insurance and part ownership of ACT, if they were to join ACT. Mulei did not inform Wright of any of these activities with respect to Jet customers, contractors or employees.

ACT was incorporated on February 28, 1983. Mulei was elected president at the first shareholders meeting. On behalf of Jet, Wright fired Mulei on March 10, 1983, when Wright first learned of Mulei's organization of a competing enterprise. On that same day Mulei caused ACT to become operational and compete with Jet.[6] Five Denver banks that had been Jet customers became ACT customers at that time. Additionally, when Mulei was fired, three of the four other employees in Jet's Denver office also left Jet and joined ACT. All of Jet's ground carriers in Denver immediately left Jet and joined ACT. All nine of Jet's pilots in Denver either quit or were fired. Jet was able to

---

[4] The trial court's findings indicate that it considered the Jet pilots and ground couriers to be independent contractors and not employees of Jet, [but] did not focus on this distinction in reaching its conclusion. The court of appeals also did not discuss any employee/independent contractor distinction. . . . We agree that any distinction as to whether the personnel, other than Mulei, . . . were employees or independent contractors is not pertinent to [this case.] The record indicates that the Jet pilots and ground carriers were an integral and necessary part of Jet's operation. Therefore, the various personnel are simply referred to as "employees" for purposes of this opinion.

[6] Mulei had intended to make ACT operational on March 14 at the beginning of a business week. Mulei advanced the date to March 10 when Wright "prematurely" learned of Mulei's activities in setting up a competing business and discharged him from his employment with Jet. Activity on March 10 was frenzied. Mulei ran ACT from a Denver hotel room and attempted to obtain the business of Jet's bank customers and to assure them that ACT could provide uninterrupted quality service. At the same time, Wright brought in personnel from Cincinnati and other cities and attempted to keep the Denver office operational and to persuade Jet's customers to continue to obtain air courier service from Jet.

maintain its Denver operations only through a rapid and massive transfer of resources, including chartered aircraft and ground couriers, from Jet's other offices. . . .

II

The court of appeals affirmed the trial court's conclusion that Mulei did not breach his duty of loyalty to Jet by his activities prior to the time he was fired by Jet. Specifically, the court of appeals concluded that Mulei did not breach his duty of loyalty either by meeting with Jet's customers to discuss ACT's future operating plans or by meeting with Jet's employees to discuss future employment opportunities with ACT. We conclude that the court of appeals applied improper legal standards in reviewing the trial court's conclusions as to what actions constitute a breach of an employee's duty of loyalty to his employer. . . .

Section 387 of the RESTATEMENT (SECOND) OF AGENCY (1957) provides that "[u]nless otherwise agreed, an agent is subject to a duty to his principal to act solely for the benefit of the principal in all matters connected with his agency." . . . Underlying the duty of loyalty arising out of the employment relationship is the policy consideration that commercial competition must be conducted through honesty and fair dealing. "Fairness dictates that an employee not be permitted to exploit the trust of his employer so as to obtain an unfair advantage in competing with the employer in a matter concerning the latter's business." *Maryland Metals, Inc. v. Metzner,* 382 A.2d 564, 568 (Md. 1978).

Thus, one facet of the duty of loyalty is an agent's "duty not to compete with the principal concerning the subject matter of his agency." RESTATEMENT (SECOND) OF AGENCY § 393. A limiting consideration in delineating the scope of an agent's duty not to compete is society's interest in fostering free and vigorous economic competition. In attempting to accommodate the competing policy considerations of honesty and fair dealing on the one hand and free and vigorous economic competition on the other, courts have recognized "a privilege in favor of employees which enables them to prepare or make arrangements to compete with their employers prior to leaving the employ of their prospective rivals without fear of incurring liability for breach of their fiduciary duty of loyalty." *Maryland Metals,* 382 A.2d at 569. Previous decisions have acknowledged that "the line separating mere preparation from active competition may be difficult to discern in some cases." *Id.* at 569 n.3. Thus, "[i]t is the nature of [the employee's] preparations which is significant" in determining whether a breach has occurred. *Bancroft-Whitney Co. v. Glen,* 411 P.2d 921, 935 (Cal. 1966).

Given the employee's duty of loyalty to and duty not to compete with his employer and the employee's corresponding privilege to make preparations to compete after termination of his employment, the issue here is whether Mulei's pre-termination meetings with Jet's customers and his co-employees to discuss ACT's future operations constituted violations of his duty of loyalty or whether these meetings were merely legally permissible preparations to compete.

A

We first apply the principles outlined above to determine whether the court of appeals erred in concluding that Mulei's meetings with Jet's customers did not breach Mulei's duty of loyalty. . . .

While still employed by Jet, Mulei was subject to a duty of loyalty to act solely for the benefit of Jet in all matters connected with his employment. Jet was entitled to receive Mulei's undivided loyalty. The fact that ACT did not commence operations and begin competing with Jet until after Mulei's departure from Jet is not dispositive. Instead, the key inquiry is whether Mulei's meetings amounted to solicitation, which would be a breach of his duty of loyalty. Generally, under his privilege to make preparations to compete after the termination of his employment, an employee may advise current customers that he will be leaving his current employment. However, any pre-termination solicitation of those customers for a new competing business violates an employee's duty of loyalty. Accordingly, we conclude that the court of appeals and the trial court applied an unduly narrow legal standard in holding that Mulei's pre-termination customer meetings were not a breach of Mulei's duty of loyalty simply because ACT did not commence competing with Jet until after Mulei had been discharged.

[The Court then remanded for a retrial on whether Mulei's conversations with some of Jet's customers violated his duty of loyalty to Jet.]

B

We next consider whether the court of appeals erred in concluding that Mulei's meetings with Jet employees did not breach his duty of loyalty. An employee's duty of loyalty applies to the solicitation of co-employees, as well as to the solicitation of customers, during the time the soliciting employee works for his employer. Generally, an employee breaches his duty of loyalty if prior to the termination of his own employment, he solicits his co-employees to join him in his new competing enterprise.

In the case now before us, the court of appeals affirmed the trial court's conclusion that Mulei did not breach his duty of loyalty by meeting with other Jet employees prior to the termination of his own employment with Jet. In concluding that there was no breach of Mulei's duty of loyalty, the court of appeals relied on its previous decision in *Electrolux Corp. v. Lawson,* 654 P.2d 340 (Colo. Ct. App. 1982). The court of appeals cited *Electrolux* for the proposition that an employee will not be liable for a breach of his duty of loyalty unless he causes co-employees to breach a contract. We disagree with this proposition, and we again conclude that the court of appeals and the trial court applied an unduly restrictive legal standard in determining whether Mulei's pre-termination discussions with co-employees breached his duty of loyalty.

In *Electrolux,* an Electrolux branch manager solicited a number of his co-workers to join him in a new distributorship he was opening. Six of the co-workers then left Electrolux to join the new firm. The court of appeals read the RESTATEMENT (SECOND) OF AGENCY § 393 comment e as imposing liability for breach of an employee's duty not to compete only when "he causes his fellow employees to breach a contract." 654 P.2d at 341. Because the Electrolux workers' employment contracts were terminable at will, their resignations did not constitute a breach of their employment contracts. Thus, reasoned the court of appeals, since there was no breach of any employment contracts there was no breach of the manager's duty not to compete.

Comment e to section 393 of the Restatement notes that the "limits of proper conduct with reference to securing the services of fellow employees are not well marked." The comment goes on to state that an "employee is subject to liability if, before or after leaving the employment, he causes fellow employees to break their contracts with the employer." However, the Restatement neither implies nor explicitly states, as did the court of appeals in *Electrolux* and *Mulei,* that causing co-employees to break their contracts is the only instance where an employee will be liable for breaching his duty of loyalty by soliciting co-employees. For instance, the Restatement notes that "a court may find that it is a breach of duty for a number of the key officers or employees to agree to leave their employment simultaneously and without giving the employer an opportunity to hire and train replacements." *Id.*

The distinction between breaching contracts terminable at will and those not terminable at will is the standard applied in the RESTATEMENT (SECOND) OF TORTS for determining liability for the tort of intentional interference with contractual relations. *See Memorial Gardens, Inc. v. Olympian Sales & Management Consultants, Inc.,* 690 P.2d 207, 210-11 (Colo. 1984) (noting that the RESTATEMENT (SECOND) OF TORTS "provides less protection for contracts terminable at will because an interference with a contract terminable at will is an interference with a future expectancy, not a legal right"). However, we conclude that the distinction between contracts terminable at will and those not terminable at will is not dispositive in a breach of duty of loyalty analysis. Although inducing another to breach a contract terminable at will may not lead to liability for tortious interference with contractual relations under the RESTATEMENT (SECOND) OF TORTS, it does not follow that the same standard is dispositive of whether an employee breached his duty of loyalty by soliciting co-employees to leave their employ and join a new enterprise.

To adopt the holding of the court of appeals would be to conclude that the scope of an employee's duty of loyalty with respect to solicitation of co-employees is limited to his duty to refrain from tortious interference with his employer's contractual relations with the co-employees. The court of appeals' holding thus fails to apply applicable principles of agency law and finds liability only for a breach of duties imposed by tort law. This result is readily apparent in the court of appeals' opinion in the present case, which applied the same terminable-at-will analysis to both Jet's breach of duty of loyalty counterclaim and its counterclaim for tortious interference with contractual relations. Such an analytical approach is fundamentally inconsistent with the broad duty of loyalty imposed on an agent/employee by the principles of agency law as stated in the Restatement. By virtue of the agency relationship, the duty of loyalty and noncompetition placed on the agent is necessarily greater than the duty imposed on all persons by tort law to refrain from wrongful interference with contract relations.

[W]e conclude that a court should focus on the following factors in determining whether an employee's actions amount to impermissible solicitation of co-workers. A court should consider the nature of the employment relationship, the impact or potential impact of the employee's actions on the employer's operations, and the extent of any benefits promised or inducements made to co-workers to obtain their services for the new competing enterprise. No single factor is dispositive; instead, a court must examine the nature of an employee's preparations to compete to determine if they amount to impermissible solicitation. Additionally, an employee's solicitation of co-workers need not be successful in order to establish a breach of his duty of loyalty. . . .

Again, based on the trial court's findings and the record before us, we are unable to determine whether Mulei's pre-termination meetings with his Jet co-employees were permissible preparations for competition or whether these actions constituted solicitation of co-employees that amounted to a breach of his duty of loyalty. Accordingly, this case must be returned to the trial court for retrial for the additional purpose of determining whether under the standards of an employee's duty of loyalty set forth in this opinion, Mulei's pre-termination meetings with Jet co-employees amounted to impermissible solicitation in violation of his duty of loyalty.

C

The trial court concluded that Mulei did not violate any duty of loyalty to Jet in part because he "continued to operate the Western Zone on a profitable, efficient and service-oriented basis." Mulei now contends that this finding regarding his profitable operation of Jet's Western Zone precludes a determination that he breached any duty of loyalty to Jet. We disagree. . . .

The key inquiry in determining whether Mulei breached his duty of loyalty is not whether Jet's Western Zone was profitable. Instead, the focus is on whether Mulei acted solely for Jet's benefit in all matters connected with his employment, and whether Mulei competed with Jet during his employment, giving due regard to Mulei's right to make preparations to compete. Accordingly, the fact that Mulei operated Jet's Western Zone efficiently and profitably does not preclude a determination that he breached his duty of loyalty to Jet by his pre-termination actions.

D

Neither does the fact that Jet failed to make the agreed-upon quarterly bonus payments excuse Mulei from being subject to a duty of loyalty to Jet. . . .

Assuming, without deciding, that Jet's nonpayment amounted to a material breach of Mulei's employment agreement, then Mulei had the option of renouncing his authority and leaving Jet's employ. However, there is no evidence in the record indicating that Mulei renounced his authority; instead, the record shows he continued to act for Jet and to operate the Western Zone despite Jet's failure to make the quarterly bonus payments. If the trial court finds on retrial that Mulei did not renounce his agency/employment relation with Jet, then he had a duty to continue that relationship and a corresponding duty of loyalty. Thus, Jet's breach of the employment agreement would not excuse Mulei from being subject to a continuing duty of loyalty to act solely for Jet's benefit in all matters connected with his employment until the time his employment with Jet was terminated on March 10, 1983.

III

[The Court then held that Mulei would not be entitled to any compensation or bonus payments for the period in which he was disloyal.]

The general rule is that an employee is not entitled to any compensation for services performed during the period he engaged in activities constituting a breach of his duty of loyalty even though part of these services may have been properly performed. . . .

However, if Mulei breached any duty of loyalty, he could still recover compensation for services properly rendered during periods in which no such breach occurred and for which compensation is apportioned in his employment agreement.

Mulei's employment contract provided that his salary was to be paid on a monthly basis, and that his bonus was to be calculated and paid on a quarterly basis. Applying the principles outlined above, if on retrial the trial court concludes that Mulei breached his duty of loyalty to Jet, then Mulei would be entitled to compensation for services properly performed during periods in which no such breach occurred and for which compensation is apportioned in the employment agreement. Moreover, under this apportionment approach, Mulei would not be entitled to any salary compensation for any month during which he engaged in acts breaching his duty of loyalty, nor would he be entitled to any bonus payments for any quarter during which he engaged in acts breaching his duty of loyalty.

NOTES

1. *Irrelevance of Contract.* Some six months after starting work, Mulei signed an employment agreement in which he agreed not to compete with Jet for two years after termination of his employment. Would the court's analysis have differed had he not signed this agreement?

2. *Corporate Opportunities.* In addition to the duty of loyalty that constrains all employees, high-level fiduciaries of a corporation are constrained by the related principle of corporate opportunity. This principle prohibits a corporation's directors, officers, and controlling shareholders from usurping a corporate opportunity for themselves. A corporate opportunity has been defined as "a business opportunity in which the corporation has an *interest* or *expectancy* or which is *essential* to the corporation." ROBERT C. CLARK, CORPORATE LAW § 7.2.1 (1986). A broader definition would include as corporate opportunities "any business opportunities that are within the subject corporation's line of business." *Id.* at § 7.2.2. A fiduciary can defend his action on the grounds that the corporation was financially or legally unable to take the opportunity, rejected or abandoned the opportunity, or had approved of the fiduciary's action. Dean Clark has urged a greater recognition of differences between public versus closely held corporations, with the corporate-opportunity doctrine being used more forcefully to restrict fiduciaries of public corporations.

If Mulei is treated as an officer of Jet Courier Service, would the corporate-opportunity principle be an additional ground preventing him from grabbing the Jet Courier business for himself? What if Mulei acquired a competing business?

3. *Duty of Loyalty When Masking as an Employee.* In *Food Lion v. Capital Cities/ABC,* 194 F.3d 505 (4th Cir. 1999), two ABC television reporters used false resumes to get jobs at a Food Lion supermarket and secretly videotaped unwholesome food-handling practices. Some of the videotape was used by ABC in a PrimeTime Live broadcast, showing Food Lion employees repackaging and redating fish that had passed its expiration date, grinding expired beef with fresh beef, and applying barbecue sauce to chicken past its expiration date to mask the smell and selling it as fresh in the gourmet food section. Food Lion sued ABC and the reporters. Food Lion did not sue for defamation, but focused on the methods by which ABC gathered its information in bringing claims for fraud, breach of duty of loyalty, trespass, and unfair trade practices. The court of appeals reversed the lower court's judgment that the ABC defendants committed fraud and unfair trade practices, but affirmed the judgment that the reporters breached their duty of loyalty to Food Lion. In holding that the reporters committed the tort of disloyalty against Food Lion, the court of appeals explained:

> Our holding on this point is not a sweeping one. An employee does not commit a tort simply by holding two jobs or by performing a second job inadequately. For example, a second employer has no tort action for breach of the duty of loyalty when its employee fails to devote adequate attention or effort to her second (night shift) job because she is tired. That is because the inadequate performance is simply an incident of trying to work two jobs. There is no intent to act adversely to the second employer for the benefit of the first. . . . Because [the reporters] had the requisite intent to act against the interests of their second employer, Food Lion, for the benefit of their main employer, ABC, they were liable in tort for their disloyalty.

Id. at 516 (applying North Carolina law). *But see Dalton v. Camp*, 548 S.E.2d 704 (N.C. 2001) (specifically disapproving of *Food Lions'* interpretation of state law, holding that breach of duty in North Carolina is not recognized as an independent cause of action, but can be used only by an employer as a defense in a wrongful termination case).

MAI SYSTEMS CORP. v. PEAK COMPUTER, INC.
United States Court of Appeals, Ninth Circuit
991 F.2d 511 (1993)

BRUNETTI, CIRCUIT JUDGE:

Peak Computer, Inc. and two of its employees appeal the district court's order issuing a preliminary injunction pending trial as well as the district court's order issuing a permanent injunction following the grant of partial summary judgment.

I. *Facts*

MAI Systems Corp., until recently, manufactured computers and designed software to run those computers. The company continues to service its computers and the software necessary to operate the computers. MAI software includes operating system software, which is necessary to run any other program on the computer.

Peak Computer, Inc. is a company organized in 1990 that maintains computer systems for its clients. Peak maintains MAI computers for more than one hundred clients in Southern California. This accounts for between fifty and seventy percent of Peak's business.

Peak's service of MAI computers includes routine maintenance and emergency repairs. Malfunctions often are related to the failure of circuit boards inside the computers, and it may be necessary for a Peak technician to operate the computer and its operating system software in order to service the machine.

In August, 1991, Eric Francis left his job as customer service manager at MAI and joined Peak. Three other MAI employees joined Peak a short time later. Some businesses that had been using MAI to service their computers switched to Peak after learning of Francis's move.

II. *Procedural History*

On March 17, 1992, MAI filed suit in the district court against Peak, Peak's president Vincent Chiechi, and Francis. The complaint includes counts alleging copyright infringement, misappropriation of trade secrets, trademark infringement, false advertising, and unfair competition.

MAI asked the district court for a temporary restraining order and preliminary injunction pending the outcome of the suit. The district court issued a temporary restraining order on March 18, 1992 and converted it to a preliminary injunction on March 26, 1992. On April 15, 1992, the district court issued a written version of the preliminary injunction along with findings of fact and conclusions of law. . . .

V. *Misappropriation of Trade Secrets*

The district court granted summary judgment in favor of MAI on its misappropriation of trade secrets claims and issued a permanent injunction against Peak on these claims. The permanent injunction prohibits Peak from "misappropriating, using in any manner in their business, including advertising connected therewith, and/or disclosing to others MAI's trade secrets," including: (1) MAI Customer Database; (2) MAI Field Information Bulletins ("FIB"); and, (3) MAI software. . . .

A. Customer Database

California has adopted the Uniform Trade Secrets Act ("UTSA") which codifies the basic principles of common law trade secret protection. To establish a violation under the UTSA, it must be shown that a defendant has been unjustly enriched by the improper appropriation, use or disclosure of a "trade secret."

Peak argues both that the MAI Customer Database is not a "trade secret," and that even if it is a trade secret, that Peak did not "misappropriate" it. The UTSA defines a "trade secret" as:

> information, including a formula, pattern, compilation, program, device, method, technique, or process, that:
>
> > (1) Derives independent economic value, actual or potential, from not being generally known to the public or to other persons who can obtain economic value from its disclosure or use; and
> >
> > (2) Is the subject of efforts that are reasonable under the circumstances to maintain its secrecy.

MAI contends its Customer Database is a valuable collection of data assembled over many years that allows MAI to tailor its service contracts and pricing to the unique needs of its customers and constitutes a trade secret.

We agree that the Customer Database qualifies as a trade secret. The Customer Database has potential economic value because it allows a competitor like Peak to direct its sales efforts to those potential customers that are already using the MAI computer system. Further, MAI took reasonable steps to insure the secrecy to this information as required by the UTSA. MAI required its employees to sign confidentiality agreements respecting its trade secrets, including the Customer Database. Thus, under the UTSA, the MAI Customer Database constitutes a trade secret.

We also agree with MAI that the record before the district court on summary judgment establishes that Peak misappropriated the Customer Database. "Misappropriation" is defined under the UTSA as:

> > (1) Acquisition of a trade secret of another by a person who knows or has reason to know that the trade secret was acquired by improper means;[7] or
> >
> > (2) Disclosure or use of a trade secret of another without express or implied consent by a person who:
> >
> > > (A) Used improper means to acquire knowledge of the trade secret; or
> > >
> > > (B) At the time of disclosure or use, knew or had reason to know that his or her knowledge of the trade secret was: (i) Derived from or through a person who had utilized improper means to acquire it; (ii) Acquired under circumstances giving rise to a duty to maintain its secrecy or limit its use; or (iii) Derived from or through a person who owed a duty to the person seeking relief to maintain its secrecy or limit its use; or
> > >
> > > (C) Before a material change of his or her position knew or had reason to know that it was a trade secret and that knowledge of it had been acquired by accident or by mistake.

---

[7] The UTSA defines "improper means," as "theft, bribery, misrepresentation, breach or inducement of a breach of a duty to maintain secrecy, or espionage through electronic or other means."

Peak contends that Francis never physically took any portion of MAI's customer database and that neither Francis nor anyone under his direction put information he had obtained from working at MAI in the Peak database. However, to find misappropriation under the UTSA, this need not be established.

The UTSA definition of "misappropriation" has been clarified by case law which establishes that the right to announce a new affiliation, even to trade secret clients of a former employer, is basic to an individual's right to engage in fair competition, and that the common law right to compete fairly and the right to announce a new business affiliation have survived the enactment of the UTSA. However, misappropriation occurs if information from a customer database is used to solicit customers.

Merely informing a former employer's customers of a change of employment, without more, is not solicitation. However, in this case, Francis did more than merely announce his new affiliation with Peak. When Francis began working for Peak, he called MAI customers whose names he recognized. Additionally, Francis personally went to visit some of these MAI customers with proposals to try and get them to switch over to Peak. These actions constituted solicitation and misappropriation under the UTSA definition. We affirm the district court's grant of summary judgment in favor of MAI on its claim that Peak misappropriated its Customer Database and affirm the permanent injunction as it relates to this issue.

B. Field Information Bulletins

MAI argues summary judgment was properly granted on its claim of misappropriation of the FIBs because the FIBs are a valuable trade secret of MAI and the evidence showed that the FIBs were being used by Peak to operate a business competing unfairly with MAI.

We agree that the FIBs constitute trade secrets. It is uncontroverted that they contain technical data developed by MAI to aid in the repair and servicing of MAI computers, and that MAI has taken reasonable steps to insure that the FIBs are not generally known to the public.

However, whether Peak has misappropriated the FIBs remains a genuine issue of material fact. The only evidence introduced by MAI to establish Peak's use of the FIBs is Peak's advertisements claiming that "Peak's system specialists are specifically trained on the latest hardware releases on MAI Basic Four." MAI asserts that if Peak did not use FIBs that this claim would have to be false. However, Weiner and Boulanger testified in their depositions that they had never seen a FIB at Peak. Similarly, Boulanger, Robert Pratt and Michael McIntosh[8] each testified that they did not have any FIB information when they left MAI. Weighing this evidence in the light most favorable to Peak, whether Peak used any of the FIBs remains a genuine issue of material fact, and the district court's grant of summary judgment on this claim of trade secret misappropriation is reversed and the permanent injunction is vacated as it relates to this issue.

---

[8] Pratt and Boulanger are both computer technicians who left MAI to work at Peak.

C. Software

MAI contends the district court properly granted summary judgment on its claim of misappropriation of software because its software constitutes valuable unpublished works that allow its machines to be maintained. MAI argues that Peak misappropriated the software by loading it into the RAM.

We recognize that computer software can qualify for trade secret protection under the UTSA. However, a plaintiff who seeks relief for misappropriation of trade secrets must identify the trade secrets and carry the burden of showing that they exist.

Here, while MAI asserts that it has trade secrets in its diagnostic software and operating system, and that its licensing agreements constitute reasonable efforts to maintain their secrecy, MAI does not specifically identify these trade secrets. Since the trade secrets are not specifically identified, we cannot determine whether Peak has misappropriated any trade secrets by running the MAI operating software and/or diagnostic software in maintaining MAI systems for its customers, and we reverse the district court's grant of summary judgment in favor of MAI on its claim that Peak misappropriated trade secrets in its computer software and vacate the permanent injunction as it relates to this issue.

VI. *Breach of Contract*

The district court granted summary judgment in favor of MAI on its breach of contract claim against Eric Francis. It is clear from the depositions of Francis and Chiechi that Francis solicited customers and employees of MAI in breach of his employment contract with MAI, and we affirm the district court's grant of summary judgment on this issue and affirm the permanent injunction as it relates to this claim.

VIII. *Conclusion*

. . . The permanent injunction issued by the district court . . . is vacated as it relates to MAI's software and MAI's Field Information Bulletins.

The remainder of the permanent injunction shall remain in effect. . . .

The district court's grant of summary judgment is AFFIRMED in part and REVERSED in part. This case is REMANDED for proceedings consistent with this opinion.

NOTES

1. *Memorized Customer Lists.* One recurring trade-secrets pattern involves customer lists. In general, the common law allows ex-employees to contact customers of their old employer. As one court put it: "an employee's recollection of information pertaining to specific needs and business habits of particular customers is not confidential." *Walter Karl, Inc. v. Wood*, 528 N.Y.S.2d 94, 98 (App. Div. 1988). On the other hand, courts will find a trade-secrets violation if the employer can show the customer list was developed at great expense over a period of years and could not be replicated without great expense. *See Allen v. Johar, Inc.*, 823 S.W.2d 824 (Ark. 1992) (enjoining employee from using memorized customer list).

2. *Trade-Secrets Common Law and the UTSA.* Trade-secrets law has a long history in common law. Like many other common-law doctrines, it has been criticized for being unduly vague and malleable. For example, one court enjoined a cookie bakery from using the "trade secret" of sweeping the nut dust into the chocolate chip cookie batter, when the bakery learned of this technique from an employee who had learned it at his prior employer's business. *Peggy Lawton Kitchens, Inc. v. Hogan*, 466 N.E.2d 138 (Mass. App. Ct. 1984). Now forty-four states, including California and Colorado but not Massachusetts or New York, have adopted Uniform Trade Secrets Acts (UTSAs) and no longer operate under the common law. Professor Hyde, however, sees little difference between common law and UTSA doctrine:

> Courts read [their state's UTSA] as if it simply codified their state's common law. . . . [They] do not look for ways in which the statute's language might be said to change the law. They do not make any effort to make the law uniform among the states that have adopted the Uniform Act.

ALAN HYDE, WORKING IN SILICON VALLEY: ECONOMIC AND LEGAL ANALYSIS OF A HIGH-VELOCITY LABOR MARKET 30-31 (2003).

C. TRADE SECRETS IN INFORMATION

In this part we move away from customer lists and examine the restrictions on employees in passing on trade secrets when they change jobs.

PEPSICO, INC. v. REDMOND
United States Court of Appeals, Seventh Circuit
54 F.3d 1262 (1995)

FLAUM, CIRCUIT JUDGE.

Plaintiff PepsiCo, Inc., sought a preliminary injunction against defendants William Redmond and the Quaker Oats Company to prevent Redmond, a former PepsiCo employee, from divulging PepsiCo trade secrets and confidential information in his new job with Quaker and from assuming any duties with Quaker relating to beverage pricing, marketing, and distribution. The district court agreed with PepsiCo and granted the injunction. We now affirm that decision.

I.

The facts of this case lay against a backdrop of fierce beverage-industry competition between Quaker and PepsiCo, especially in "sports drinks"[1] and

---

[1] Sports drinks are also called "isotonics," implying that they contain the same salt concentration as human blood, and "electrolytes," implying that the substances contained in the drink have dissociated into ions.

"new age drinks."[2] Quaker's sports drink, "Gatorade," is the dominant brand in its market niche. PepsiCo introduced its Gatorade rival, "All Sport," in March and April of 1994, but sales of All Sport lag far behind those of Gatorade. Quaker also has the lead in the new-age-drink category. Although PepsiCo has entered the market through joint ventures with the Thomas J. Lipton Company and Ocean Spray Cranberries, Inc., Quaker purchased Snapple Beverage Corp., a large new-age-drink maker, in late 1994. PepsiCo's products have about half of Snapple's market share. Both companies see 1995 as an important year for their products: PepsiCo has developed extensive plans to increase its market presence, while Quaker is trying to solidify its lead by integrating Gatorade and Snapple distribution. Meanwhile, PepsiCo and Quaker each face strong competition from Coca Cola Co., which has its own sports drink, "PowerAde," and which introduced its own Snapple-rival, "Fruitopia," in 1994, as well as from independent beverage producers.

William Redmond, Jr., worked for PepsiCo in its PepsiCola North America division ("PCNA") from 1984 to 1994. Redmond became the General Manager of the Northern California Business Unit in June, 1993, and was promoted one year later to General Manager of the business unit covering all of California, a unit having annual revenues of more than 500 million dollars and representing twenty percent of PCNA's profit for all of the United States.

Redmond's relatively high-level position at PCNA gave him access to inside information and trade secrets. Redmond, like other PepsiCo management employees, had signed a confidentiality agreement with PepsiCo. That agreement stated in relevant part that he

> w[ould] not disclose at any time, to anyone other than officers or employees of [PepsiCo], or make use of, confidential information relating to the business of [PepsiCo] . . . obtained while in the employ of [PepsiCo], which shall not be generally known or available to the public or recognized as standard practices.

Donald Uzzi, who had left PepsiCo in the beginning of 1994 to become the head of Quaker's Gatorade division, began courting Redmond for Quaker in May, 1994. . . .

On November 8, 1994, Uzzi extended Redmond a written offer for the position of Vice President-Field Operations for Gatorade and Redmond accepted. Later that same day, Redmond called William Bensyl, the Senior Vice President of Human Resources for PCNA, and told him that he had an offer from Quaker to become the Chief Operating Officer of the combined Gatorade and Snapple company but had not yet accepted it. Redmond also asked whether he should, in light of the offer, carry out his plans to make calls upon certain PCNA customers. Bensyl told Redmond to make the visits.

Redmond also misstated his situation to a number of his PCNA colleagues, including Craig Weatherup, PCNA's President and Chief Executive Officer, and Brenda Barnes, PCNA's Chief Operating Officer and Redmond's immediate superior. As with Bensyl, Redmond told them that he had been offered

---

[2] "New age drink" is a catch-all category for noncarbonated soft drinks and includes such beverages as ready-to-drink tea products and fruit drinks. Sports drinks may also fall under the new-age-drink heading.

the position of Chief Operating Officer at Gatorade and that he was leaning "60/40" in favor of accepting the new position.

On November 10, 1994, Redmond met with Barnes and told her that he had decided to accept the Quaker offer and was resigning from PCNA. . . .

PepsiCo filed this diversity suit on November 16, 1994, seeking a temporary restraining order to enjoin Redmond from assuming his duties at Quaker and to prevent him from disclosing trade secrets or confidential information to his new employer. The district court granted PepsiCo's request that same day but dissolved the order *sua sponte* two days later, after determining that PepsiCo had failed to meet its burden of establishing that it would suffer irreparable harm. The court found that PepsiCo's fears about Redmond were based upon a mistaken understanding of his new position at Quaker and that the likelihood that Redmond would improperly reveal any confidential information did not "rise above mere speculation."

From November 23, 1994, to December 1, 1994, the district court conducted a preliminary injunction hearing on the same matter. At the hearing, PepsiCo offered evidence of a number of trade secrets and confidential information it desired protected and to which Redmond was privy. First, it identified PCNA's "Strategic Plan," an annually revised document that contains PCNA's plans to compete, its financial goals, and its strategies for manufacturing, production, marketing, packaging, and distribution for the coming three years. Strategic Plans are developed by Weatherup and his staff with input from PCNA's general managers, including Redmond, and are considered highly confidential. The Strategic Plan derives much of its value from the fact that it is secret and competitors cannot anticipate PCNA's next moves. PCNA managers received the most recent Strategic Plan at a meeting in July, 1994, a meeting Redmond attended. PCNA also presented information at the meeting regarding its plans for Lipton ready-to-drink teas and for All Sport for 1995 and beyond, including new flavors and package sizes.

Second, PepsiCo pointed to PCNA's Annual Operating Plan ("AOP") as a trade secret. The AOP is a national plan for a given year and guides PCNA's financial goals, marketing plans, promotional event calendars, growth expectations, and operational changes in that year. The AOP, which is implemented by PCNA unit General Managers, including Redmond, contains specific information regarding all PCNA initiatives for the forthcoming year. The AOP bears a label that reads "Private and Confidential — Do Not Reproduce" and is considered highly confidential by PCNA managers.

. . . PepsiCo introduced evidence that Redmond had detailed knowledge of PCNA's pricing architecture and that he was aware of and had been involved in preparing PCNA's customer development agreements with PCNA's California and California-based national customers. Indeed, PepsiCo showed that Redmond, as the General Manager for California, would have been responsible for implementing the pricing architecture guidelines for his business unit.

PepsiCo also showed that Redmond had intimate knowledge of PCNA "attack plans" for specific markets. Pursuant to these plans, PCNA dedicates extra funds to supporting its brands against other brands in selected markets. To use a hypothetical example, PCNA might budget an additional $500,000 to spend in Chicago at a particular time to help All Sport close its market gap with Gatorade. Testimony and documents demonstrated Redmond's awareness of these plans and his participation in drafting some of them.

Finally, PepsiCo offered evidence of PCNA trade secrets regarding innovations in its selling and delivery systems. . . .

Having shown Redmond's intimate knowledge of PCNA's plans for 1995, PepsiCo argued that Redmond would inevitably disclose that information to Quaker in his new position, at which he would have substantial input as to Gatorade and Snapple pricing, costs, margins, distribution systems, products, packaging and marketing, and could give Quaker an unfair advantage in its upcoming skirmishes with PepsiCo. Redmond and Quaker countered that Redmond's primary initial duties at Quaker as Vice President-Field Operations would be to integrate Gatorade and Snapple distribution and then to manage that distribution as well as the promotion, marketing and sales of these products. Redmond asserted that the integration would be conducted according to a pre-existing plan and that his special knowledge of PCNA strategies would be irrelevant. The defendants also pointed out that Redmond had signed a confidentiality agreement with Quaker preventing him from disclosing "any confidential information belonging to others," as well as the Quaker Code of Ethics, which prohibits employees from engaging in "illegal or improper acts to acquire a competitor's trade secrets." Redmond additionally promised at the hearing that should he be faced with a situation at Quaker that might involve the use or disclosure of PCNA information, he would seek advice from Quaker's in-house counsel and would refrain from making the decision.

PepsiCo responded to the defendants' representations by pointing out that the evidence did not show that Redmond would simply be implementing a business plan already in place. On the contrary, as of November, 1994, the plan to integrate Gatorade and Snapple distribution consisted of a single distributorship agreement and a two-page "contract terms summary." Such a basic plan would not lend itself to widespread application among the over 300 independent Snapple distributors. Since the integration process would likely face resistance from Snapple distributors and Quaker had no scheme to deal with this probability, Redmond, as the person in charge of the integration, would likely have a great deal of influence on the process. PepsiCo further argued that Snapple's 1995 marketing and promotion plans had not necessarily been completed prior to Redmond's joining Quaker, that Uzzi disagreed with portions of the Snapple plans, and that the plans were open to re-evaluation. Uzzi testified that the plan for integrating Gatorade and Snapple distribution is something that would happen in the future. Redmond would therefore likely have input in remaking these plans, and if he did, he would inevitably be making decisions with PCNA's strategic plans and 1995 AOP in mind. Moreover, PepsiCo continued, diverging testimony made it difficult to know exactly what Redmond would be doing at Quaker. Redmond described his job as "managing the entire sales effort of Gatorade at the field level, possibly including strategic planning." . . . Thus, PepsiCo asserted, Redmond would have a high position in the Gatorade hierarchy, and PCNA trade secrets and confidential information would necessarily influence his decisions. Even if Redmond could somehow refrain from relying on this information, as he promised he would, his actions in leaving PCNA, Uzzi's actions in hiring Redmond, and the varying testimony regarding Redmond's new responsibilities, made Redmond's assurances to PepsiCo less than comforting.

On December 15, 1994, the district court issued an order enjoining Redmond from assuming his position at Quaker through May, 1995, and permanently from using or disclosing any PCNA trade secrets or confidential information. The court entered its findings of fact and conclusions of law on January 26, 1995, *nunc pro tunc* December 15, 1994. The court, which completely adopted PepsiCo's position, found that Redmond's new job posed a clear threat of misappropriation of trade secrets and confidential information that could be enjoined under Illinois statutory and common law. The court also emphasized Redmond's lack of forthrightness both in his activities before accepting his job with Quaker and in his testimony as factors leading the court to believe the threat of misappropriation was real. This appeal followed.

II.

Both parties agree that the primary issue on appeal is whether the district court correctly concluded that PepsiCo had a reasonable likelihood of success on its various claims for trade secret misappropriation and breach of a confidentiality agreement.[3] . . .

A.

The Illinois Trade Secrets Act ("ITSA"), which governs the trade secret issues in this case, provides that a court may enjoin the "actual or threatened misappropriation" of a trade secret. A party seeking an injunction must therefore prove both the existence of a trade secret and the misappropriation. The defendants' appeal focuses solely on misappropriation; although the defendants only reluctantly refer to PepsiCo's marketing and distribution plans as trade secrets, they do not seriously contest that this information falls under the ITSA.

The question of threatened or inevitable misappropriation in this case lies at the heart of a basic tension in trade secret law. Trade secret law serves to protect "standards of commercial morality" and "encourage[] invention and innovation" while maintaining "the public interest in having free and open competition in the manufacture and sale of unpatented goods." Yet that same law should not prevent workers from pursuing their livelihoods when they leave their current positions. It has been said that federal age discrimination law does not guarantee tenure for older employees. Similarly, trade secret law does not provide a reserve clause for solicitous employers.

This tension is particularly exacerbated when a plaintiff sues to prevent not the actual misappropriation of trade secrets but the mere threat that it

---

[3] The district court concluded that PepsiCo satisfied the other requirements for a preliminary injunction: whether PepsiCo has an adequate remedy at law or will be irreparably harmed if the injunction does not issue; whether the threatened injury to PepsiCo outweighs the threatened harm the injunction may inflict on Quaker and Redmond; and whether the granting of the preliminary injunction will disserve the public interest. Quaker and Redmond do not challenge these holdings on appeal.

will occur. While the ITSA plainly permits a court to enjoin the threat of misappropriation of trade secrets, there is little law in Illinois or in this circuit establishing what constitutes threatened or inevitable misappropriation. Indeed, there are only two cases in this circuit that address the issue: *Teradyne, Inc. v. Clear Communications Corp.*, 707 F. Supp. 353 (N.D. Ill. 1989) and *AMP Inc. v. Fleischhacker*, 823 F.2d 1199 (7th Cir. 1987).

In *Teradyne,* Teradyne alleged that a competitor, Clear Communications, had lured employees away from Teradyne and intended to employ them in the same field. In an insightful opinion, Judge Zagel observed that "threatened misappropriation can be enjoined under Illinois law" where there is a "high degree of probability of inevitable and immediate . . . use of . . . trade secrets." *Teradyne*, 707 F. Supp. at 356. Judge Zagel held, however, that Teradyne's complaint failed to state a claim because Teradyne did not allege "that defendants have in fact threatened to use Teradyne's secrets or that they will inevitably do so." Teradyne's claims would have passed Rule 12(b)(6) muster had they properly alleged inevitable disclosure, including a statement that Clear intended to use Teradyne's trade secrets or that the former Teradyne employees had disavowed their confidentiality agreements with Teradyne, or an allegation that Clear could not operate without Teradyne's secrets. . . .

In *AMP*, we affirmed the denial of a preliminary injunction on the grounds that the plaintiff AMP had failed to show either the existence of any trade secrets or the likelihood that defendant Fleischhacker, a former AMP employee, would compromise those secrets or any other confidential business information. AMP, which produced electrical and electronic connection devices, argued that Fleishhacker's new position at AMP's competitor would inevitably lead him to compromise AMP's trade secrets regarding the manufacture of connectors. *AMP*, 823 F.2d at 1207. In rejecting that argument, we emphasized that the mere fact that a person assumed a similar position at a competitor does not, without more, make it "inevitable that he will use or disclose . . . trade secret information" so as to "demonstrate irreparable injury." *Id.*

It should be noted that *AMP*, which we decided in 1987, predates the ITSA, which took effect in 1988. The ITSA abolishes any common law remedies or authority contrary to its own terms. The ITSA does not, however, represent a major deviation from the Illinois common law of unfair trade practices. The ITSA mostly codifies rather than modifies the common law doctrine that preceded it. Thus, we believe that *AMP* continues to reflect the proper standard under Illinois's current statutory scheme.[7]

The ITSA, *Teradyne,* and *AMP* lead to the same conclusion: a plaintiff may prove a claim of trade secret misappropriation by demonstrating that defendant's new employment will inevitably lead him to rely on the plaintiff's trade secrets. . . .

---

[7] The ITSA has overruled *AMP*'s implications regarding the durability of an agreement to protect trade secrets. *AMP* followed a line of Illinois cases questioning the validity of agreements to keep trade secrets confidential where those agreements did not have durational or geographical limits. The ITSA, in reversing those cases, provides that "a contractual or other duty to maintain secrecy or limit use of a trade secret shall not be deemed to be void or unenforceable solely for lack of durational or geographical limitation on the duty."

PepsiCo presented substantial evidence at the preliminary injunction hearing that Redmond possessed extensive and intimate knowledge about PCNA's strategic goals for 1995 in sports drinks and new age drinks. The district court concluded on the basis of that presentation that unless Redmond possessed an uncanny ability to compartmentalize information, he would necessarily be making decisions about Gatorade and Snapple by relying on his knowledge of PCNA trade secrets. It is not the "general skills and knowledge acquired during his tenure with" PepsiCo that PepsiCo seeks to keep from falling into Quaker's hands, but rather "the particularized plans or processes developed by [PCNA] and disclosed to him while the employer-employee relationship existed, which are unknown to others in the industry and which give the employer an advantage over his competitors." The *Teradyne* and *AMP* plaintiffs could do nothing more than assert that skilled employees were taking their skills elsewhere; PepsiCo has done much more.

Admittedly, PepsiCo has not brought a traditional trade secret case, in which a former employee has knowledge of a special manufacturing process or customer list and can give a competitor an unfair advantage by transferring the technology or customers to that competitor. PepsiCo has not contended that Quaker has stolen the All Sport formula or its list of distributors. Rather PepsiCo has asserted that Redmond cannot help but rely on PCNA trade secrets as he helps plot Gatorade and Snapple's new course, and that these secrets will enable Quaker to achieve a substantial advantage by knowing exactly how PCNA will price, distribute, and market its sports drinks and new age drinks and being able to respond strategically. This type of trade secret problem may arise less often, but it nevertheless falls within the realm of trade secret protection under the present circumstances.

Quaker and Redmond assert that they have not and do not intend to use whatever confidential information Redmond has by virtue of his former employment. They point out that Redmond has already signed an agreement with Quaker not to disclose any trade secrets or confidential information gleaned from his earlier employment. They also note with regard to distribution systems that even if Quaker wanted to steal information about PCNA's distribution plans, they would be completely useless in attempting to integrate the Gatorade and Snapple beverage lines.

The defendants' arguments fall somewhat short of the mark. Again, the danger of misappropriation in the present case is not that Quaker threatens to use PCNA's secrets to create distribution systems or coopt PCNA's advertising and marketing ideas. Rather, PepsiCo believes that Quaker, unfairly armed with knowledge of PCNA's plans, will be able to anticipate its distribution, packaging, pricing, and marketing moves. Redmond and Quaker even concede that Redmond might be faced with a decision that could be influenced by certain confidential information that he obtained while at PepsiCo. In other words, PepsiCo finds itself in the position of a coach, one of whose players has left, playbook in hand, to join the opposing team before the big game. Quaker and Redmond's protestations that their distribution systems and plans are entirely different from PCNA's are thus not really responsive.

The district court also concluded from the evidence that Uzzi's actions in hiring Redmond and Redmond's actions in pursuing and accepting his new job demonstrated a lack of candor on their part and proof of their willingness to misuse PCNA trade secrets, findings Quaker and Redmond vigorously challenge. The court expressly found that:

> Redmond's lack of forthrightness on some occasions, and out and out lies on others, in the period between the time he accepted the position with defendant Quaker and when he informed plaintiff that he had accepted that position leads the court to conclude that defendant Redmond could not be trusted to act with the necessary sensitivity and good faith under the circumstances in which the only practical verification that he was not using plaintiff's secrets would be defendant Redmond's word to that effect.

. . . .

Thus, when we couple the demonstrated inevitability that Redmond would rely on PCNA trade secrets in his new job at Quaker with the district court's reluctance to believe that Redmond would refrain from disclosing these secrets in his new position (or that Quaker would ensure Redmond did not disclose them), we conclude that the district court correctly decided that PepsiCo demonstrated a likelihood of success on its statutory claim of trade secret misappropriation. . . .

C.

For the same reasons we concluded that the district court did not abuse its discretion in granting the preliminary injunction on the issue of trade secret misappropriation, we also agree with its decision on the likelihood of Redmond's breach of his confidentiality agreement should he begin working at Quaker. Because Redmond's position at Quaker would initially cause him to disclose trade secrets, it would necessarily force him to breach his agreement not to disclose confidential information acquired while employed in PCNA.

III.

. . . .

For the foregoing reasons, we affirm the district court's order enjoining Redmond from assuming his responsibilities at Quaker through May, 1995, and preventing him forever from disclosing PCNA trade secrets and confidential information.

Affirmed.

NOTES

1. *Importance of Preliminary Injunction.* In *Pepsico*, like many other trade-secrets cases, the issue is whether the court should grant plaintiff-employer's motion for a preliminary injunction. In theory, this is just the first step in the litigation trail. But in practice it is the crucial stage. In theory, an employer may be able to recover damages, but they are exceedingly difficult to prove and obtain. As a practical matter, if an employer is to protect its trade secrets, it must prevent the employee from using them elsewhere in the first place.

2. Federal Statutory Law. In 1996, Congress turned the misappropriation of trade secrets into a federal criminal offense. Economic Espionage Act of 1996, 18 U.S.C. § 1831 *et seq.* The Act protects a wider range of information than most state statutes do. "Trade secret" is defined to include:

> all forms and types of financial, business, scientific, technical, economic, or engineering information, including patterns, plans, compilations, program devices, formulas, designs, prototypes, methods, techniques, processes, procedures, programs, or codes, whether tangible or intangible, and whether or how stored, compiled, or memorialized physically, electronically, graphically, photographically, or in writing if —
>
> > (A)   the owner thereof has taken reasonable measures to keep such information secret; and
> >
> > (B)   the information derives independent economic value, actual or potential, from not being generally known to, and not being readily ascertainable through proper means by, the public. . . .

18 U.S.C. § 1839(3). The Act provides significant penalties. Misappropriations that benefit foreign governments can result in fines of up to $500,000 or imprisonment for up to fifteen years (or, for organizations, fines of up to $10 million). Misappropriations for commercial purposes can result in imprisonment for up to ten years (or, for organizations, fines of up to $5 million).

In *United States v. Martin*, 228 F.3d 1 (1st Cir. 2000), a chemist, bored and dissatisfied with her job at a veterinary product lab in Maine, applied for a job at a start-up competing firm in Wyoming. Over the next six months, while still working for the first employer, the chemist sent information about products, test kits, and projects of the Maine lab to the potential employer in Wyoming. Unfortunately, she later inadvertently sent an e-mail detailing the information she was sending to Wyoming to a manager at the first employer. The first employer alerted the FBI, who promptly investigated. Ultimately, both the employee and the second employer were convicted of conspiracy to steal trade secrets in violation of the Act as well as wire fraud, mail fraud, and conspiracy to transport stolen property in interstate commerce.

3. Negative Information. Suppose an employee knows the trial-and-error steps her former employer took in trying to develop a product. Can this be a trade secret? On the one hand, this kind of negative information seems hard to distinguish from general knowledge that employers acquire through on-the-job training. On the other hand, this kind of information could help a competitor avoid the same kinds of mistakes. A number of courts have accepted negative information as a trade secret. *See Morton v. Rank America, Inc.*, 812 F. Supp. 1062, 1073-74 (C.D. Cal. 1993) (holding that the names of potential customers who did not place orders constitute a trade secret).

Chapter 12
ENFORCEMENT OF NONCOMPETITION CLAUSES

Many employers are not content to rely on the common law of trade secrets or duty of loyalty to protect their investment in workers. One alternative is to extract a promise that the employee will work for the employer for a specified period. Such a definite-term contract cannot be a complete solution, however, because courts will not specifically enforce a promise to work. In addition to the practical problem of judicially monitoring whether the employee is adequately performing the court-mandated work, compelling someone to work may violate the Thirteenth Amendment's prohibition of involuntary servitude. *See Beverly Glen Music, Inc. v. Warner Communications, Inc.,* 224 Cal. Rptr. 260 (Cal. Ct. App. 1986) (thirteenth amendment prohibits specific enforcement of singer's contract). *Cf. Bailey v. Alabama,* 219 U.S. 219 (1911) (Thirteenth Amendment prohibits criminal remedies for breaches of promise to work).

Instead, employers often negotiate noncompetition clauses whereby employees promise not to compete against the employer if they leave. Such clauses indirectly protect employer's investments in training their workers and revealing trade secrets to them. The employer's interest is easy to see. A 1979 survey of Los Angeles employers, for example, found that recruitment and initial training costs ranged from over $2,000 for each office worker, to over $3,500 for production workers, to over $10,000 for salary-exempt workers. On the other hand, employers can use noncompetition clauses opportunistically to exploit workers.

As we saw in the last chapter, there is a close relation between trade-secrets law and the enforceability of covenants not to compete (CNCs). Indeed, some cases seem to limit CNCs to protection of trade secrets, while other cases speak more broadly.

REM METALS CORP. v. LOGAN
Supreme Court of Oregon
565 P.2d 1080 (1977)

Before Tongue, Linde and Campbell, JJ.

Tongue, Justice.

This is a suit in equity to enforce "noncompetition" provisions of two employment agreements between plaintiff and defendant, who had been employed by plaintiff as a welder of precision titanium castings. Defendant appeals from a decree enjoining him from engaging in such work for a period of six months in Oregon for Precision Castparts Corporation, a competitor of plaintiff. We reverse.

The primary question presented for decision in this case, according to plaintiff Rem, is whether, as an employer, it had a sufficient "protectible interest" in the skills and knowledge of defendant as a skilled craftsman engaged as a repair welder of precision titanium castings, so as to justify enforcement of such a "noncompetition" agreement as a "reasonable restraint" upon defendant.

The titanium castings on which defendant Logan worked as a repair welder were produced by his employer, the plaintiff, under contract with Pratt & Whitney Aircraft Division for use as bearing housings for jet aircraft engines under exceedingly strict specifications. Only three companies are engaged in the production of such castings for Pratt & Whitney. These include plaintiff, Precision Castparts (its principal competitor) and Misco of Michigan (a smaller company).

In the process of the production of such castings any defects are repaired by welding performed by skilled welders who are "certified" by Pratt & Whitney inspectors as being sufficiently skilled to be entrusted with this important work. There was also some evidence that titanium is a "rare" or "reactive" metal and is difficult to weld.

Defendant was one of two or three "certified" welders employed by plaintiff and was plaintiff's best welder, with a proficiency rating of 98.3 per cent. Other welders rated below 95 per cent. There was testimony, however, that three other welders had been able to become sufficiently qualified so as to be "certified" for Pratt & Whitney work after 20 hours of training and that during 1966 seven of plaintiff's welders (including defendant) were so "certified."

Defendant Logan had been previously employed by Wah Chang Corporation, where he learned to weld electrodes of titanium. He was employed by plaintiff in 1969 and subsequently signed two employment contracts, as did nearly all Rem employees, including provisions to the effect that for a period of one year after termination he would not engage in any business in competition with Rem within the United States, "whether as principal, agent, employer, consultant or otherwise."

In 1972 defendant was transferred to the welding department. He testified that he became "certified" in "less than two weeks," and that no one gave him "any instruction before he took the certification test" for the welding of titanium.

Plaintiff offered testimony describing its training program for welders. When asked whether Rem had any "trade secrets in the welding department that are not generally known in the industry," that witness answered that "Rem was able to do a better job," to ship ahead of its schedules, and with fewer "rejects" from Pratt & Whitney than its competitors, so that "there is something we must be doing that our competitors are not doing." Rem's president testified that defendant received job training at Rem and "extensive written procedures prepared by Rem" which enable him to weld titanium castings. He also testified, however, that it was nevertheless not surprising that defendant Logan was able to become "certified" within "a matter of a few days," as testified by Logan.

Rem's supervisor of welding testified that:

I don't think it's a matter of disclosing inasmuch as it is its instructional nature. If a welder's in the tank doing the work, we're qualifying it and giving what instructions we are capable of.

There was also testimony by another former Rem titanium welder, since employed by Precision Castparts, that he observed no differences in the welding procedures and techniques at Rem and at PCP except that Rem uses a "vacuum tank," while PCP uses a "plastic bubble," both of which are standard techniques.

On September 18, 1976, defendant Logan, after being refused a wage increase of 50 cents per hour by Rem, went to work at that increased rate for Precision Castparts. Plaintiff offered evidence that, as a result, it was unable for a period of two weeks to ship castings worth approximately $25,000 to Pratt & Whitney and that it then had difficulty in maintaining its shipping schedules of such titanium castings because it did not have welders who were "able to complete the weld repair cycle in a satisfactory manner." It appears, however, that Rem was then able to train two welders who "shortly thereafter were able to pass the qualification test of Pratt & Whitney." Plaintiff's witnesses also testified to their concern over Rem's continued ability to compete with Precision Castparts, its principal competitor, which by then had 14 or 15 titanium welders, including defendant Logan.[2] . . .

In our judgment, this case falls within the rule as stated in Blake, *Employee Agreements Not to Compete,* 73 Harv. L. Rev. 625, 652 (1960), as follows:

> . . . It has been uniformly held that general knowledge, skill, or facility acquired through training or experience while working for an employer appertain exclusively to the employee. The fact that they were acquired or developed during the employment does not, by itself, give the employer a sufficient interest to support a restraining covenant, even though the on-the-job training has been extensive and costly. In the absence of special circumstances the risk of future competition from the employee falls upon the employer and cannot be shifted, even though the possible damages is greatly increased by experience gained in the course of the employment.

To the same effect, although under different facts, it was held in *McCombs v. McClelland,* 354 P.2d 311 (Or. 1960) that:

> . . . The fact that defendant may have gained considerable experience while in plaintiff's employ is not grounds for injunctive relief. An employer cannot by contract prevent his employee upon termination of the employment from using skill and intelligence acquired or increased and improved through experience or through instruction received in the course of employment. . . .

We recognize, however, as does Blake, *supra* (at 653), that on any given set of facts it may be difficult to "draw a line" between "training in the general skills and knowledge of the trade, and training which imparts information pertaining especially to the employer's business" and that this is the "central problem" in such cases. In other words, as stated by Blake, *supra* (at 647):

---

[2] It also appears that Precision Castparts is "underwriting" the cost of Mr. Logan's defense.

. . . Its objective is not to prevent the competitive use of the unique personal qualities of the employee — either during or after the employment — but to prevent competitive use, for a time, of information or relationships which pertain peculiarly to the employer and which the employee acquired in the course of the employment. . . .[6]

In such a case, however, the burden of proof is upon the employer to establish the existence of "trade secrets," "information or relationships which pertain peculiarly to the employer," or other "special circumstances" sufficient to justify the enforcement of such a restrictive covenant.

Based upon our examination of this record, which we review de novo, and under the facts and circumstances of this case, we hold that this employer failed to sustain that burden of proof. Although defendant received training and experience while employed by plaintiff which developed his skill as a repair welder of titanium castings, plaintiff did not, in our judgment, establish by sufficient and credible evidence "special circumstances" of such a nature as to entitle Rem to demand the enforcement upon this defendant by injunction of this "noncompetition" clause as a "reasonable restraint."

For these reasons, the decree of the trial court is reversed.

NOTES

1. General Training and Exceptional Talent. *Rem Metals* is a classic example of an employer who provides general training that makes an employee valuable to other employers as well. The court applied the rule that recouping the costs of general training or preventing competition is insufficient to justify a noncompetition clause. That Logan was the most talented welder in the company seems irrelevant. The Becker model of human capital predicts that Logan would receive lower wages than he otherwise would during his general training. The training was so short, however, that this prediction would be difficult to test here.

Occasionally, courts find that an employer has a protectible interest in employees whose services are special, unique, or extraordinary. For example, when the soul singer James Brown breached his agreement with King Records "not to perform for the purpose of making phonographic records with any person other than us," by recording on the Mercury label, a New York court enforced the covenant because of Brown's special, unique, and extraordinary skills. *King Records, Inc. v. Brown*, 252 N.Y.S.2d 988 (N.Y. App. Div. 1964). *See also Matuszak v. Houston Oilers, Inc.*, 515 S.W.2d 725 (Tex. Civ. App. 1974) (upholding preliminary injunction preventing a number-one draft choice from defecting to rival football league, in part because of player's uniqueness). *But see* ARTHUR L. CORBIN, 6A CORBIN ON CONTRACTS § 1391B (Supp. 1991) ("Princeton could not have enjoined Albert Einstein from leaving to take a position at Harvard just because he was famous and his scientific writings enhanced Princeton's reputation").

---

[6] As stated in *Sarkes Tarzian, Inc. v. Audio Devices, Inc.*, 166 F. Supp. 250, 265 (S.D. Cal. 1958): ". . . Trade secrets must be 'the particular secrets of the employer as distinguished from the general secrets of the trade in which he is engaged'. . . ."

2. *Recovering Training Expenses.* Suppose a truck driver signs a three-year employment contract in which he agrees to pay $1,500 to reimburse the employer for training expenses if he quits during the term. Is this contract distinguishable from the one in *Rem Metals*? *See Becker v. Blair*, 361 N.W.2d 434 (Minn. Ct. App. 1985) (enforcing promise as part of fixed-term employment contract rather than as a "restrictive employment covenant"). *See also New York State United Teachers v. Thompson*, 459 F. Supp. 677 (N.D.N.Y. 1978) (employer has cause of action for breach of contract when teacher refuses to return to job after educational leave of absence); *Milwaukee Area Joint Apprenticeship Training Comm. v. Howell*, 67 F.3d 1333 (7th Cir. 1995) (finding no violation of ERISA or state law regulating restrictive covenants when an apprenticeship program costing over $10,000 requires participants to accept employment with contributing employers or repay the costs). *But see Sands Appliance Servs., Inc. v. Wilson*, 615 N.W.2d 241 (Michigan 2000) (a "tuition contract" requiring employee to pay employer $50 per week for three years as tuition for training violates the statute prohibiting employment contracts from requiring remuneration from an employee).

3. *Parol Evidence and Consideration.* The various contract-law doctrines regulating enforceability often pose problems in noncompetition cases, as they do in employment-termination cases. For example, should oral promises not to compete be enforceable? *See Metcalfe Investments, Inc. v. Garrison*, 919 P.2d 1356 (Alaska 1996) (an employee's oral promise to refrain from using customer lists in a new business for an unlimited period of time is not subject to statute of frauds and therefore enforceable). What about the argument that noncompetition clauses signed after the employee begins work are unenforceable because the employer has given no extra consideration for the promise? *Compare Poole v. Incentives Unlimited, Inc.*, 548 S.E.2d 207 (S.C. 2001) (refusing to enforce noncompetition covenant signed three and a half years after employee began work because promise to continue already existing at-will employment is insufficient consideration, even though the same promise at the initial hiring would be sufficient to enforce noncompetition covenant), *with Curtis 1000, Inc. v. Suess*, 24 F.3d 941 (7th Cir. 1994) (holding that at-will employment can support valid noncompetition clause because employee gets an "expectation of continued employment," even if expectation is not legally enforceable).

KARPINSKI v. INGRASCI
Court of Appeals of New York
268 N.E.2d 751 (1971)

FULD, CHIEF JUDGE.

This appeal requires us to determine whether a covenant by a professional man not to compete with his employer is enforceable and, if it is, to what extent.

The plaintiff, Dr. Karpinski, an oral surgeon, had been carrying on his practice alone in Auburn — in Cayuga County — for many years. In 1953, he decided to expand and, since nearly all of an oral surgeon's business stems from referrals, he embarked upon a plan to "cultivate connections" among dentists in the four nearby Counties of Tompkins, Seneca, Cortland and Ontario. The plan was successful, and by 1962 twenty per cent of his practice consisted of treating patients referred to him by dentists located in those counties. In that year, after a number of those dentists had told him that some of their patients found it difficult to travel from their homes to Auburn, the plaintiff decided to open a second office in centrally-located Ithaca. He began looking for an assistant and, in the course of his search, met the defendant, Dr. Ingrasci, who was just completing his training in oral surgery at the Buffalo General Hospital and was desirous of entering private practice. Dr. Ingrasci manifested an interest in becoming associated with Dr. Karpinski and, after a number of discussions, they reached an understanding; the defendant was to live in Ithaca, a locale with which he had no prior familiarity, and there work as an employee of the plaintiff.

A contract, reflecting the agreement, was signed by the defendant in June, 1962. It was for three years and, shortly after its execution, the defendant started working in the office which the plaintiff rented and fully equipped at his own expense. The provision of the contract with which we are concerned is a covenant by the defendant not to compete with the plaintiff. More particularly, it recited that the defendant

> promises and covenants that while this agreement is in effect and forever thereafter, he will never practice dentistry and/or Oral Surgery in Cayuga, Cortland, Seneca, Tompkins or Ontario counties except: (a) In association with the [plaintiff] or (b) If the [plaintiff] terminates the agreement and employs another oral surgeon.

In addition, the defendant agreed, "in consideration of the . . . terms of employment, and of the experience gained while working with" the plaintiff, to execute a $40,000 promissory note to the plaintiff, to become payable if the defendant left the plaintiff and practiced "dentistry and/or Oral Surgery" in the five enumerated counties.[1]

When the contract expired, the two men engaged in extended discussions as to the nature of their continued association — as employer and employee or as partners. Unable to reach an accord, the defendant, in February, 1968, left the plaintiff's employ and opened his own office for the practice of oral surgery in Ithaca a week later. The dentists in the area thereupon began referring their patients to the defendant rather than to the plaintiff, and in two months the latter's practice from the Ithaca area dwindled to almost nothing and he closed the office in that city. In point of fact, the record discloses that about 90% of the defendant's present practice comes from referrals from dentists in the counties specified in the restrictive covenant, the very same dentists who had been referring patients to the plaintiff's Ithaca office when the defendant was working there.[2]

The plaintiff, alleging a breach of the restrictive covenant, seeks not only an injunction to enforce it but also a judgment of $40,000 on the note. The

---

[1] Either party was privileged to terminate the agreement on 60 days' notice within the three-year period and, if the plaintiff were to do so, the contract recited, the defendant was released from the restrictive covenant and the note.

[2] There are two other oral surgeons, in addition to the plaintiff and the defendant, serving the Ithaca area.

Supreme Court, after a nonjury trial, decided in favor of the plaintiff and granted him both an injunction and damages as requested. On appeal, however, the Appellate Division reversed the resulting judgment and dismissed the complaint; it was that court's view that the covenant was void and unenforceable on the ground that its restriction against the practice of both dentistry *and* oral surgery was impermissibly broad.

There can be no doubt that the defendant violated the terms of the covenant when he opened his own office in Ithaca. But the mere fact of breach does not, in and of itself, resolve the case. Since there are "powerful considerations of public policy which militate against sanctioning the loss of a man's livelihood," the courts will subject a covenant by an employee not to compete with his former employer to an "overriding limitation of 'reasonableness.'" Such covenants by physicians are, if reasonable in scope, generally given effect. "It is a firmly established doctrine," it has been noted, "that a member of one of the learned professions, upon becoming assistant to another member thereof, may, upon a sufficient consideration, bind himself not to engage in the practice of his profession upon the termination of his contract of employment, within a reasonable territorial extent, as such an agreement is not in restraint of trade or against public policy."

Each case must, of course, depend, to a great extent, upon its own facts. It may well be that, in some instances, a restriction not to conduct a profession or a business in two counties or even in one, may exceed permissible limits. But, in the case before us, having in mind the character and size of the counties involved, the area restriction imposed is manifestly reasonable. The five small rural counties which it encompasses comprise the very area from which the plaintiff obtained his patients and in which the defendant would be in direct competition with him. Thus, the covenant's coverage coincides precisely with "the territory over which the practice extends," and this is proper and permissible. In brief, the plaintiff made no attempt to extend his influence beyond the area from which he drew his patients, the defendant being perfectly free to practice as he chooses outside the five specified counties.

Nor may the covenant be declared invalid because it is unlimited as to time, forever restricting the defendant from competing with the plaintiff. It is settled that such a covenant will not be stricken merely because it "contains no time limit or is expressly made unlimited as to time." "According to the weight of authority as applied to contracts by physicians, surgeons and others of kindred profession . . . relief for violation of these contracts will not be denied merely because the agreement is unlimited as to time, where as to area the restraint is limited and reasonable." In the present case, the defendant opened an office in Ithaca, in competition with the plaintiff, just one week after his employment had come to an end. Under the circumstances presented, we thoroughly agree with the trial judge that it is clear that nearly all of the defendant's practice was, and would be, directly attributable to his association with his former employer.

This brings us to the most troublesome part of the restriction imposed upon the defendant. By the terms of the contract, he agreed not to practice "dentistry and/or Oral Surgery" in competition with the plaintiff. Since the plaintiff practices only "oral surgery," and it was for the practice of that limited type of "dentistry" that he had employed the defendant, the Appellate Division concluded that the plaintiff went beyond permissible limits when he obtained from the defendant the covenant that he would not engage in any "dentistry" whatsoever. The restriction, *as formulated,* is, as the Appellate Division concluded, too broad; it is not reasonable for a man to be excluded from a profession for which he has been trained when he does not compete with his former employer by practicing it.

The plaintiff seeks to justify the breadth of the covenant by urging that, if it had restricted only the defendant's practice of oral surgery and permitted him to practice "dentistry" — that is, to hold himself out as a dentist generally — the defendant would have been permitted, under the Education Law, to do all the work which an oral surgeon could. We have no sympathy with this argument; the plaintiff was not privileged to prevent the defendant from working in an area of dentistry in which he would not be in competition with him. The plaintiff would have all the protection he needs if the restriction were to be limited to the practice of oral surgery, and this poses the question as to the court's power to "sever" the impermissible from the valid and uphold the covenant to the extent that it is reasonable.

. . . As Professor Blake put it (73 Harv. L. Rev., at pp. 674-675), "If in balancing the equities the court decides that his [the employee's] activity would fit within the scope of a reasonable prohibition, it is apt to make use of the tool of severance, paring an unreasonable restraint down to appropriate size and enforcing it." In short, . . . "we find it just and equitable to protect appellant [employer] by injunction to the extent necessary to accomplish the basic purpose of the contract insofar as such contract is reasonable." Accordingly, since his practice is solely as an oral surgeon, the plaintiff gains all the injunctive protection to which he is entitled if effect be given only to that part of the covenant which prohibits the defendant from practicing oral surgery.

The question arises, however, whether injunctive relief is precluded by the fact that the defendant's promissory note for $40,000 was to become payable if he breached the agreement not to compete. We believe not. The mere inclusion in a covenant of a liquidated damages provision does not automatically bar the grant of an injunction. As this court wrote in the *Diamond Match Co.* case (13 N.E., at p. 424), "It is a question of intention, to be deduced from the whole instrument and the circumstances; and if it appear that the performance of the covenant was intended, and not merely the payment of damages in case of a breach, the covenant will be enforced." The covenant under consideration in this case may not reasonably be read to render "the liquidated damages provision . . . the sole remedy." On the other hand, it would be grossly unfair to grant the plaintiff, in addition to an injunction, the full amount of damages ($40,000) which the parties apparently contemplated for a total breach of the covenant, since the injunction will halt any further violation. The proper approach is that taken in *Wirth* (192 N.E. 297). The court, there faced with a similar situation, granted the injunction sought and, instead of awarding the amount of liquidated damages specified, remitted the matter for determination of the *actual* damages suffered during the period of the breach.

The hardship necessarily imposed on the defendant must be borne by him in view of the plaintiff's rightful interest in protecting the valuable practice of oral surgery which he built up over the course of many years. The defendant is, of course, privileged to practice "dentistry" generally in Ithaca or continue to practice "oral surgery" anywhere in the United States outside of the five small rural counties enumerated. The covenant, part of a contract carefully negotiated with no indication of fraud or overbearing on either side, must be enforced, insofar as it reasonably and validly may, according to its terms. In sum, then, the plaintiff is entitled to an injunction barring the defendant from practicing oral surgery in the five specified counties and to damages actually suffered by him in the period during which the defendant conducted such a practice in Ithaca after leaving the plaintiff's employ.

NOTES

1. Lifetime and Worldwide Bans. Enforcing a lifetime ban, even with a limited geographic restriction, is highly unusual. Courts seem increasingly receptive, however, to arguments that the increasing geographic scope of competition justifies nationwide or even worldwide bans. *See Briggs v. R.R. Donnelley & Sons*, 446 F. Supp. 153 (D. Mass. 1978) (enforcing do-not-compete clause with no explicit geographic term to prohibit contacts with customers worldwide).

2. Court Decrees and Reality. More than twenty years after the court injunction, Dr. Ingrasci continued to advertise in the Ithaca Yellow Pages for a practice limited to oral surgery. How can this be explained? Suppose an oral surgery practice in Ithaca was worth more to Dr. Ingrasci than it cost Dr. Karpinski. If so, both dentists would be better off if Ingrasci paid Karpinski to waive the injunction. This may be an example of the Coase Theorem's assertion that, if transaction costs are sufficiently low, initial legal entitlements will not affect the final outcome.

A major argument against noncompetition clauses is that, by restricting employees from changing employers, they prevent workers from moving to jobs where they would be most productive. Does the Ingrasci "reality" noted above undermine this argument? Professor Kitch has argued that it does:

> [T]he parties to the transaction can always retransact. If an employee has a higher valued activity in some other employment, he can offer a payment to his employer to obtain release from his contract, as is done in professional sports. . . . The question is not whether there will be competition but whether such contracts would serve a useful purpose in permitting firms to capture the returns from investments in human capital and, thus, create the appropriate incentives to make such investments.

Edmund W. Kitch, *The Law and Economics of Rights in Valuable Information,* 9 J. LEGAL STUD. 683, 688 (1980).

3. Vagaries in a Reasonableness Inquiry. The court in *Karpinski* emphasizes that each case must depend upon its own facts. This makes it difficult for lawyers to advise their clients on whether a do-not-compete clause will be enforceable. For a vivid illustration of this, compare the following cases which involve the same employer suing on nearly identical noncompetition agreements. *Compare Welcome Wagon, Inc. v. Morris*, 224 F.2d 693 (4th Cir.

1955) (refusing to enforce five-year nationwide noncompetition agreement when defendant locates in same city), *and Briggs v. Boston*, 15 F. Supp. 763 (N.D. Iowa 1936) (same), *with Welcome Wagon Int'l, Inc. v. Pender*, 120 S.E.2d 739 (N.C. 1961) (enforcing five-year noncompetition agreement when defendant locates in same city), *Briggs v. Butler*, 45 N.E.2d 757 (Ohio 1942) (same), *and Briggs v. Glover*, 3 N.Y.S.2d 979 (N.Y. Sup. Ct. 1939) (same).

4. *Protecting a Monopoly Position.* What is the significance of footnote 2's statement that two other oral surgeons practiced in Ithaca? If Karpinski and Ingrasci were the only oral surgeons in the area, should the case come out differently? Would the residents of Ithaca then face a monopoly, if the noncompetition clause was enforced?

In *Iredell Digestive Disease Clinic v. Petrozza*, 373 S.E.2d 449 (N.C. Ct. App. 1988), *aff'd,* 377 S.E.2d 750 (N.C. 1989), a noncompetition clause forbade a gastroenterologist from working for three years within a twenty-mile radius of a rural clinic. The court refused to enforce the clause, despite its limited geographical and time restrictions, emphasizing the importance of patients having freedom to choose between personal physicians and that the defendant was the only practitioner capable of performing certain emergency services. Consider *Dick v. Geist*, 693 P.2d 1133 (Idaho Ct. App. 1985), wherein the court refused to enforce a covenant that would have prevented the region's only neonatologist from continuing to work in the area. The court made no reference to the covenant's monopolistic effects, instead emphasizing the serious adverse public health implications of forcing the doctor to leave the area.

5. *Lawyers and Noncompetition Clauses.* Rule 5.6 of the ABA MODEL RULES OF PROFESSIONAL CONDUCT prohibits partnership or employment agreements from restricting the right to practice law after a relationship ends. The principal rationale is that such restrictions may infringe upon the ability of clients to choose their lawyers. In *Howard v. Babcock*, 863 P.2d 150 (Cal. 1993), the California Supreme Court upheld a law firm partnership agreement that allowed the firm to withhold funds from a departing partner who intends to compete in the same market. The court reasoned that the agreement left the partner free to "practice at a price" while compensating the firm for the loss of clients, and thus did not restrict the practice of law. The court observed that a revolution in the practice of law now requires economic interests of the law firm to be protected as they are in other business enterprises. Justice Kennard, dissenting, refused to admit "that a new reality in the practice of law justifies its erosion of legal ethical standards." *Id.* at 161. For a contrary position, see *Jacob v. Norris, McLaughlin & Marcus*, 607 A.2d 142 (N.J. 1992) (invalidating an agreement requiring departing lawyers to give up compensation if they continued to represent firm clients).

6. *Contracting Beyond the Common Law.* As we saw in the previous chapter, the common-law duty of loyalty prevents employees from exploiting trade secrets after leaving work, even in the absence of a noncompetition promise. Some courts and commentators have suggested that noncompetition clauses cannot go beyond the common law in restricting employees. For example, in *Curtis 1000 Inc. v. Suess*, 24 F.3d 941 (7th Cir. 1994), a salesman had signed a covenant promising not to call on any former customers for two years after leaving his employer. The court refused to issue a preliminary injunction, finding that Illinois law limited the interests that a noncompete clause may protect to trade secrets, confidential information, and relations with "near permanent" customers of the employer. *See also Reed, Roberts Assocs. v. Strauman*, 353 N.E.2d 590 (N.Y. 1976) (requiring existence of trade secrets or a unique skill for the enforcement of a non-solicitation promise). Why would an employer want a contract clause if it cannot exceed the restriction the employer already has under the common law?

7. Trimming Overbroad Clauses. Courts have developed three responses to an overly broad noncompetition clause. Some will rewrite an offensive clause. For example, in *Dean Van Horn Consulting Assocs. v. Wold*, 395 N.W.2d 405 (Minn. Ct. App. 1986), the court reduced a three-year noncompetition clause to one year and enforced a one-year CNC. Others adopt a "blue pencil" rule, enforcing the reasonable parts of the clause only if they are grammatically separable from the invalid parts. *See Timenterial, Inc. v. Dagata*, 277 A.2d 512 (Conn. Super. Ct. 1971). Finally, some courts refuse to sever objectionable portions or rewrite the covenant, reasoning that this would encourage employers to write "truly ominous covenants" knowing that courts would pare them down if found overbroad. *White v. Fletcher/Mayo/Assocs.*, 303 S.E.2d 746 (Ga. 1983). *Accord CAE Vanguard, Inc. v. Newman*, 518 N.W.2d 652 (Neb. 1994).

OUTSOURCE INTERNATIONAL, INC. v. BARTON & BARTON STAFFING SOLUTIONS
United States Court of Appeals, Seventh Circuit
192 F.3d 662 (1999)

BAUER, CIRCUIT JUDGE.

In May 1998, Outsource International, Inc. ("Outsource," "OSI," or the "EMPLOYER") filed a temporary restraining order (a "TRO") and preliminary injunction against former OSI employee George Barton and Barton's Staffing Solutions, Inc. ("BSSI") (collectively referred to as the "defendants") based upon Barton's alleged violations of a confidentiality clause and a non-compete clause in the Employment Agreement between Barton and OSI. The district court granted the TRO, and on June 12, 1998, after a two-day evidentiary hearing, the district court entered a modified preliminary injunction against Barton and BSSI. Barton and BSSI appeal from the entry of the modified preliminary injunction order. We affirm.

I. Background

OSI provides temporary industrial staffing and employment consulting services to industrial customers located throughout the United States, including the Chicago suburban area. OSI has been a prominent fixture in the temporary staffing industry for many years and has developed a strong reputation for its quality and dependable services.

Like other businesses in the temporary staffing industry, OSI's product is temporary workers. OSI attempts to develop and market its product by keeping extensive computerized records on its workers. These records include information such as each worker's previous work environments, pay rates, billing rates, and worker compensation rates. OSI also attempts to provide superior service to its customers by providing more qualified workers, which in turn, makes its product more reliable throughout the temporary industrial labor staffing industry. OSI puts considerable time into developing its employee files and its customer relations and, therefore, attempts to protect this information from outside competitors. It also requires that its staffing consultants enter into certain restrictive covenants, such as a non-compete clause and a confidential information clause. These restrictive covenants are embodied in each consultant's Employment Agreement with the company.

In 1992, Barton became a labor staffing consultant at L.M. Investors, Inc. ("LM") [which was later acquired by OSI]. In 1993, Barton signed an Employment Agreement with LM. The Employment Agreement contained confidentiality and non-compete clauses as conditions of his employment. The agreement also provided that these clauses would remain in effect for one year after the termination of his employment with OSI. Specifically, Barton's Employment Agreement contained the following noncompete clause and confidentiality agreement:

> During the term of the Agreement and for a period of one (1) year immediately following the termination of EMPLOYEE's employment, for any cause whatsoever, so long as EMPLOYER continues to carry on the same business, said EMPLOYEE shall not, for any reason whatsoever, directly or indirectly, for himself or on behalf of, or in conjunction with, any other person, persons, company, partnership, corporation or business entity:
>
> (i) Call upon, divert, influence or solicit or attempt to call upon, divert, influence or solicit any customer or customers of EMPLOYER;
>
> (ii) Divulge the names and addresses or any information concerning any customer of EMPLOYER;
>
> (iii) Disclose any information or knowledge relating to EMPLOYER, including but not limited to, EMPLOYER's system or method of conducting business to any person, persons, firms, corporations or other entities unaffiliated with EMPLOYER, for any reason or purpose whatsoever;
>
> (iv) Own, manage, operate, control, be employed by, participate in or be connected in any manner with the ownership, management, operation or control of the same, similar or related line of business as that carried on by EMPLOYER within a radius of twenty-five (25) miles from EMPLOYEE's home office or within a radius equivalent to EMPLOYEE's defined territory, whichever is greater.

By its terms, the Employment Agreement could be enforced only through injunctive relief. By signing the Employment Agreement, Barton agreed to waive his right to a jury trial if a dispute should arise and he agreed that he would be liable to pay all costs and expenses of the action, including attorney fees.

From 1993 until April 7, 1998, Barton was the exclusive staffing consultant for LM in his territory. In February 1998, OSI acquired LM. On April 7, 1998,

Barton resigned from OSI. At the time of his resignation, he was the staffing consultant for four of OSI's Illinois offices: Aurora East, Aurora West, Joliet, and University Park. Barton's home base was the Aurora East office.

Immediately after Barton resigned from OSI, he opened BSSI, a temporary industrial labor staffing company, in West Chicago, Illinois. BSSI's office is approximately 12 miles from OSI's Aurora East office. To staff BSSI, Barton hired former OSI employees that had worked with him while he was at OSI. Within weeks after starting his business, Barton and BSSI had acquired twelve former OSI customers that Barton had serviced while he was employed at OSI. . . .

On appeal, the defendants admit that Barton violated the restrictive covenant in his Employment Agreement; they argue, however, that the restrictions are unenforceable and, therefore, that the district court erred in entering the preliminary injunction order. They also challenge the scope of the injunction.

II. *Discussion* . . .

B. The Non-Compete Agreement

The basic test applied by Illinois courts in determining the enforceability of restrictive covenants is "whether the terms of the agreement are reasonable and necessary to protect a legitimate business interest of the employer." . . . Illinois courts long have recognized two situations in which an employer has a legitimate business interest to justify enforcement of a covenant not to compete: (1) where the customer relationships are near-permanent and but for the employee's association with the employer the employee would not have had contact with the customers; and (2) where the former employee acquired trade secrets or other confidential information through his employment and subsequently tried to use it for his own benefit. Here, the district court applied both tests and determined that they were alternative grounds that supported its decision to grant a preliminary injunction. We will affirm the district court's decision if we find that either of the two alternative grounds was sufficient to enforce the covenant not to compete.

1. Near-Permanent Relationship Test

. . . .

In the present case, the district court considered the nature of OSI's business (the industrial staffing industry) and determined that the customer loyalty OSI enjoyed and the unique product OSI offered in the industry (as opposed to a general sales product) created a near-permanent relationship with its customers. Specifically, the district court stated:

> [In this case,] I believe that the existence of multiple suppliers to a single user is not an indication that any one supplier is as good as another. I believe it is because from the user's perspective the user simply does not wish to be in a position of seeking temporary industrial workers and not having them when and where the user wants them.

And I think that this is a key finding because the courts, as I read the prior cases, deal with prior fact situations in terms of — and I paraphrase — "There are many suppliers; ergo, there is nothing unique or special [about the product or service]."

I do not believe that inference can be drawn here and I do not draw it. It is, in fact, I think difficult to consider that relationships are not nearpermanent, not only for the above reasons, but for all of the facts which show that the need for reliability is paramount in this particular industry; and common sense would lead one to the conclusion that if any suppliers of temporary industrial workers have shown to any buyer of these services that their services are reliable . . . [then] the user will continue to go back to that supplier absent some extraordinary incentives in terms of prices. . . .

So I believe that the near[-]permanent relationships do exist. I find that they do exist in this business.

This finding is supported by record evidence. The record reflects that OSI (and LM, its predecessor company) enjoyed a brand name recognition throughout the industry which gave it a certain level of dependability and prominence. The record also reflects that OSI had strong customer loyalty and that it set itself apart from other staffing businesses in the industry through an elaborate employee screening and customer service system. Thus, the district court did not abuse its discretion in finding that a near-permanent relationship existed between OSI and its customers.

We also must briefly consider the second part of the near-permanence test — we must determine whether "but for" Barton's association with OSI, he would not have had contact with the customers that he obtained from OSI after he left its employ. In concluding that the "but for" element of the near-permanence test was met, the district court held that but for OSI's good name and substantial resources, Barton could not have "sold" his customers on his industrial staffing services. Specifically, the court held that:

> Outsource added substantial value to the product that Barton was selling in several ways, one of which was for potential customers to agree to meet with Barton. . . . He needed Outsource's resources, not to consummate sales, but to get to the initial contact stage of his deals with companies in need of temporary services.

This factual finding is supported by record evidence as well. Barton testified that he acquired all twelve of BSSI's customers by telephoning the primary contacts he had developed while he was working for OSI. Thus, the district court did not abuse its discretion in finding that but for Barton's association with OSI, he would not have had contact with the customers.

Based on the evidence in the record, the district court's findings regarding the nature of OSI's business and its ability to meet the nearpermanency test were within the court's discretion.

2. Confidential Information Test

The defendants also contend that the district court erred in finding that the confidential information test served as a valid basis for enforcing the restrictive covenant. . . . Here, in making its determination, the district court stated:

> The value of the confidential information I think is shown by the speed in which Mr. Barton acquired the business of former [OSI] customers. He may have extraordinary power as a salesperson, but it is doubtful to me that extraordinary power could have — in fact, I find that it is really quite incredible that even the most powerful sales person could have acquired that business with the speed with which he acquired it if he were not assisted at least by cost and price figures and such data as the comp rates. . . .

> Because he spent so long with Outsource . . . it is impossible to say that any of these clients with which he's dealing are Barton's and Barton's alone.

The record shows that OSI put considerable effort into developing a workforce and keeping data on the workforce secret. Furthermore, OSI maintained classified records on its customers, to which Barton had access. Shortly after Barton left OSI and opened BSSI, most of his staff consisted of former OSI employees. All of BSSI's clients were OSI clients when Barton was employed by OSI. Thus, the district court did not abuse its discretion in determining that Barton took confidential information while in OSI's employ and used it for his own benefit.

C. Geographic and Activity Restrictions

The defendants also contend that the geographic and activity restrictions in the restrictive covenant must be modified if we determine that the covenant is enforceable. While we agree with the defendants' general premise that restrictive covenants should be narrowly tailored so as only to protect a legitimate business interest of the employer, in the immediate case, the defendants' argument is underdeveloped and unsupported by law and, therefore, it is waived.

Conclusion

The district court did not abuse its discretion in entering the preliminary injunction order or in finding that the restrictive covenant was enforceable. We Affirm.

Posner, Chief Judge, dissenting.

I regret my inability to agree with the court's disposition of the case, because it is the right disposition from the standpoint of substantive justice. Mr. Barton is an adult of sound mind who made an unequivocal promise, for which he was doubtless adequately compensated, not to compete with his employer within 25 miles for a year after he ceased being employed. He quit of his own volition — quit in fact to set up in competition with his employer. And all the customers whom he obtained for his new company, before the preliminary injunction which the court affirms today put him temporarily out of business, were customers of his former employer. So he broke his contract. But Illinois law, to which we must of course bow in this diversity suit, is hostile to covenants not to compete found in employment contracts. An Illinois court would not enforce this covenant.

There is no longer any good reason for such hostility, though it is nothing either new or limited to Illinois. The English common law called such covenants "restraints of trade" and refused to enforce them unless they were adjudged "reasonable" in time and geographical scope. The original rationale had nothing to do with restraint of trade in its modern, antitrust sense. It was paternalism in a culture of poverty, restricted employment, and an exiguous social safety net. The fear behind it was that workers would be tricked into agreeing to covenants that would, if enforced, propel them into destitution. This fear, though it continues to be cited, has no basis in current American conditions.

Later, however, the focus of concern shifted to whether a covenant not to compete might have anticompetitive consequences, since the covenant would eliminate the covenantor as a potential competitor of the covenantee within the area covered by, and during the term of, the covenant. This concern never had much basis, as recognized in *Consultants & Designers, Inc. v. Butler Service Group, Inc.*, 720 F.2d 1553, 1562-64 (11th Cir. 1983), especially when the covenant was found in an employment contract. It would be unlikely for the vitality of competition to depend on the ability of a former employee to compete with his former employer. So unlikely that it would make little sense to place a cloud of suspicion over such covenants, rather than considering competitive effects on a case by case basis.

At the same time that the concerns behind judicial hostility to covenants not to compete have waned, recognition of their social value has grown. The clearest case for such a covenant is where the employee's work gives him access to the employer's trade secrets. The employer could include in the employment contract a clause forbidding the employee to take any of the employer's trade secrets with him when he left the employment, as in fact the employer did in this case. Such clauses are difficult to enforce, however, as it is often difficult to determine whether the former employee is using his former employer's trade secrets or using either ideas of his own invention or ideas that are in the public domain. A covenant not to compete is much easier to enforce, and to the extent enforced prevents the employee, during the time and within the geographical scope of the covenant, from using his former employer's trade secrets.

A related function of such a covenant is to protect the employer's investment in the employee's "human capital," or earning capacity. Paul H. Rubin & Peter Shedd, *Human Capital and Covenants Not to Compete*, 10 J. LEGAL STUD. 93, 96-97 (1981). The employer may give the employee training that the employee could use to compete against the employer. If covenants not to compete are forbidden, the employer will pay a lower wage, in effect charging the employee for the training. There is no reason why the law should prefer this method of protecting the employer's investment to a covenant not to compete.

I can see no reason in today's America for judicial hostility to covenants not to compete. It is possible to imagine situations in which the device might be abused, but the doctrines of fraud, duress, and unconscionability are available to deal with such situations. A covenant's reasonableness in terms of duration and geographical scope is merely a consideration bearing on such defenses. . . . Had Barton signed a covenant in which he agreed that if he ever left the employ of Outsource he would never again work in the business of providing temporary industrial labor anywhere in the world, there would be at least a suspicion that he had been forced or tricked into signing the covenant and therefore that it should not be enforced. There is no suggestion of that here, and so if I were writing on a clean slate I would agree wholeheartedly with the district court's granting a preliminary injunction against Barton's violating the covenant.

But the Illinois courts approach covenants not to compete in a different way, not radically different perhaps but different enough to require a reversal in this case. Their view is that a covenant not to compete that is contained in an employment contract is enforceable in only two circumstances — either where the covenant protects a "near permanent" relationship between the former employer and his customers, or where it protects "confidential information" (that is, trade secrets) of the former employer. The latter circumstance is straightforward; as I noted earlier, a covenant not to compete is easier to enforce than a covenant that forbids the former employee to use confidential information.

The reason given for protecting "near permanent relationships" between the former employer and its customers is that if the customer was locked into its relationship with the former employer, the former employee could not have enticed the customer away without using skills or contacts that he had obtained in the course of his employment. This is welcome recognition that a covenant not to compete can be a proper method of protecting an employer's investment in the employee's human capital. The significance of "near" permanent may be to make clear that if the employer and the customer have an actual contract which the employee induces the customer to break, and thus a relationship that is "permanent" for the duration of the contract, the covenant not to compete would be academic; the employee would be liable in tort for inducing the breach of a contract. Without either a contract with the customer or a covenant with the employee, the employee's action in "stealing" the customer would be privileged unless the employee used independently tortious means, such as a violation of fiduciary duty, to accomplish the "theft."

The Illinois courts appear to place the burden of proving that the covenant meets one of the two criteria of validity on the employer. In effect Illinois requires the employer to prove that the covenant not to compete serves a social purpose. Such a requirement is inconsistent with the idea of freedom of contract, which animates contract law and a corollary of which is that courts do not limit the enforcement of contracts to those the social point of which the court can see. They enforce a contract unless there is some reason to think it imposes heavy costs on third parties, offends the moral code, fails to comply with formal requirements (such as those imposed on some contracts by the statute of frauds), or doesn't embody an actual deal between competent consenting adults.

Still, we must take the Illinois law as we find it, and apply it as best we can to the facts of the case. Barton was employed by Outsource as a salesman, soliciting orders for temporary industrial workers that Outsource would supply. These are skilled and semi-skilled factory workers — packers, assemblers, fork-lift operators, and the like. They are employed by Outsource and in effect "rented" to industrial firms as temporary workers. Barton had been in the business for many years before his employment by Outsource. Deciding to go out on his own, he quit Outsource and quickly obtained business from a dozen customers of Outsource with whom he had dealt. There is no question that he violated the covenant not to compete in his employment contract, which barred him for one year after his employment ended from competing with Outsource in the Chicago area. But there is no evidence that he stole any of Outsource's trade secrets. . . . Outsource's customer list, which Barton may have used to get customers for himself, was not secret. Nor is it likely that Barton relied on the list; these were people he had been dealing with for years. The wages that Outsource pays its workers are not secret either. Barton did not take the list of workers on Outsource's roster, but obtained workers for his customers in the same way that Outsource does, by radio and newspaper advertisements. Many of these workers had been working for Outsource, but that is no surprise; competing local suppliers of temporary labor hire from the same pool, and temporary workers often register with multiple agencies.

Outsource screens the workers whom it hires and sorts them into different job categories so that it knows whom to dispatch when it receives an order from one of its customers. This information — the list of workers screened for reliability and the jobs that they can do — is a genuine trade secret, and so Outsource would have a strong case if Barton had taken this information with him when he quit and set up on his own. But there is no evidence that he did this. Regardless of that, if Outsource does the screening and sorting function better than other suppliers of temporary industrial labor, it may have established "near permanent" relationships with its customers, but of this there is no evidence either. The only users of temp labor who testified at the preliminary injunction hearing agreed that such users have no sense of loyalty to particular suppliers. Both witnesses used multiple agencies. It was feasible for Barton to use standard selling techniques, rather than any techniques that he had learned from Outsource or information that he took with him when he left Outsource, to get customers for his new business.

The district judge said that Barton "gets credibility in terms of the reliability issue from the testing, screening and transport services that were provided when he was at Outsource." I don't get this. The customers whom Barton obtained when he left Outsource knew that he was no longer with Outsource and that they were dealing not with Outsource but with a startup. If they trusted him, it was for his personal qualities.

The cases in which Illinois courts (or federal courts applying Illinois law in diversity cases) uphold covenants not to compete found in employment contracts are cases in which the former employer was supplying a specialized, complex product or (more usually) service, often a professional service such as veterinary care. Those are settings in which the former employee is likely to be using information or training acquired from his former employer. Enforcement is denied when the former employer is supplying a fungible or standardized product or service. As we explained in *Curtis 1000, Inc. v. Suess*, 24 F.3d 941, 948 (1994) (citations omitted), "the Illinois cases distinguish between sellers of services, especially professional services such as accounting and consulting, and sellers of ordinary goods. In the former class, where the quality of the seller's service is difficult to determine by simple inspection, customers come to repose trust in a particular seller, and that trust is a valuable business asset, created by years of careful management, that the employee is not allowed to take away with him. In the latter class, involving the sale of goods, the element of trust is attenuated, particularly where . . . the good is a simple and common one sold under competitive conditions. In these cases Illinois law does not permit the seller to claim a protectable interest in his relations with his customers. . . . For here current price and quality, rather than a past investment in meeting customers' needs, are the decisive factors in the continued success of the firm, and they of course are not appropriated by the departing employee."

Human beings are not fungible; skilled and semi-skilled workers differ along such dimensions as reliability, experience, know-how, and wage demands. But Barton, who had worked in the business of supplying temporary industrial labor for many years before going to work for Outsource, knew all this. He did not know the specifics about the workers whom Outsource screened and sorted, but he did not take those specifics with him when he left, either. To repeat, as far as this record shows, all he used in signing up customers for his new venture were the standard sales techniques used in this business.

Since the irreparable harm to Barton from the grant of a preliminary injunction to Outsource exceeds the irreparable harm that Outsource would experience from the denial of the injunction (as a start-up, Barton would find it difficult to prove damages from being frozen out of business for a year as a result of the enforcement of the covenant), Outsource must prove not just that it has a better case than Barton but that it has a much better case. . . .

NOTES

1. *Suing the Second Employer*. An employer whose employee violates a noncompetition clause is not limited to suing that employee, but may also sue the subsequent employer. In *United Labs., Inc. v. Kuykendall*, 403 S.E.2d 104 (N.C. Ct. App. 1991), the second employer promised a job applicant that it would pay legal costs for any lawsuit by the first employer based upon a noncompetition clause. In a subsequent lawsuit, the original employer recovered $11,700 against the employee for breach of contract and over $145,000 in compensatory and punitive damages against the second employer on theories of interference with restrictive covenants and unfair trade practices.

2. *Enforcing Noncompetition Covenants Against Fired Employees*. In *Karpinski*, the parties failed to agree on a new contract when the definite-term contract expired. In *Outsource*, Judge Posner declared that substantive justice should require enforcement of a noncompetition clause when the employee "quit[s] of his own volition." But, in contrast with these cases, suppose an employee is fired, with or without just cause. Should an otherwise valid noncompetition clause be enforceable in this situation? *Compare Wark v. Ervin Press Corp.*, 48 F.2d 152 (7th Cir. 1931) (enforcing noncompetition clause against fired employee), *and Robert S. Weiss & Assoc. v. Wiederlight*, 546 A.2d 216 (Conn. 1988) (stating that "the reasonableness of a restrictive covenant of employment does not turn on whether the employee subject to the covenant left his position voluntarily or was dismissed by the employer"), *with Ma & Pa, Inc. v. Kelly*, 342 N.W.2d 500 (Iowa 1984) (stating that termination is a factor opposing injunction), *and Insulation Corp. v. Brobston*, 667 A.2d 729 (Pa. Super. Ct. 1995) (refusing to enforce noncompetition clause against employee fired for poor performance because such a bad worker cannot pose the same competitive threat as one who voluntarily joins another business). One argument for enforcement is to prevent moral hazard: employees wanting to compete for another employer may try to get fired if noncompetition covenants can only be enforced against employees who quit.

Chapter 13

EMPLOYEE INVENTIONS

FRANCKLYN v. GUILFORD PACKING CO.
United States Court of Appeals, Ninth Circuit
695 F.2d 1158 (1983)

Before WRIGHT, SKOPIL and ALARCON, CIRCUIT JUDGES.

ALARCON, CIRCUIT JUDGE:

Guilford [Packing Company] has been in the fishing and fish processing business for a number of years. Francklyn was hired to harvest clams on beds leased by Guilford. Francklyn was paid on a piecework basis, and he was required to deliver all of his catch to Guilford. Guilford also owned the boat and harvester that Francklyn used in harvesting the clams. Although Francklyn's work schedule was flexible, Guilford expected him to harvest clams when the tide and weather permitted. In the interim periods Francklyn was to maintain the boat and harvester in good repair. At the end of each clamming season, Francklyn returned the boat and harvester to Guilford. The district court found that the arrangement between Guilford and Francklyn also contemplated that Francklyn would be making modifications to the clam harvester in an attempt to improve its performance; Guilford also agreed to reimburse Francklyn for expenses incurred in modifying the harvester.

Francklyn became dissatisfied with the operation of Guilford's harvester. Over a two-year period, while employed by Guilford, he perfected and completed a modified version of the harvester which he used on Guilford's clam boat, the LITTLE JERK. The district court found that much or all the early work in modifying the harvester was done at the Guilford Packing Company plant, with the company's tools. The district court also found that pursuant to their agreement, Guilford reimbursed Francklyn for all materials used to modify the harvester for which Francklyn asked payment, although at some point Francklyn unilaterally determined not to seek further reimbursement.

In 1969, Francklyn obtained a patent for the modified harvester. Francklyn told Wilbur Harms (appellee and officer of Guilford) that Guilford could use his harvester without paying royalties on the "Little Jerk or any other clam boat you may have. . . ." The parties agree that Francklyn gave Guilford a royalty-free license to the harvester used on the LITTLE JERK.

In 1972, Guilford retired this boat and harvester. Subsequently, Guilford manufactured a second harvester, based on the Francklyn invention, and used it on a different boat, the SIDEWINDER. Francklyn now claims that Guilford's manufacture and use of this second harvester infringed his patent.

In 1968, . . . Carr built a harvester which was owned by the partnership of Lowman and Carr. It is undisputed that the harvester infringed Francklyn's patented invention. In October, 1969, Francklyn sent Lowman a notice of infringement. Lowman and Carr consulted a patent attorney who advised them that Francklyn's patent was invalid and that even if it was valid, Guilford had a shop right to the patent. The attorney also advised Lowman and Carr that Guilford could utilize its shop right by buying the harvester from Lowman and Carr and leasing it back to them. Lowman and Carr then sold the harvester to Guilford and Guilford leased it back to them. Lowman continued to use the device in harvesting clams for Guilford. In February, 1975, Francklyn served Lowman with a second notice of infringement. Thereafter, this action was filed.

The district court found that Guilford and its officers had a shop right to Francklyn's invention. . . . The district court [also determined] that neither Lowman nor Guilford infringed Francklyn's patent when they entered into the sale and leaseback transaction. . . .

Francklyn contends that Guilford could not acquire shop rights in his invention because he was not an employee of Guilford's. In our view, this reflects too narrow a view of the nature of a shop right.

This court has indicated that while a shop right generally arises out of an employer-employee relationship, it is not necessarily limited to such a relationship. The full nature of the parties' relationship must be examined to determine whether a shop right exists, not merely whether that relationship is characterized as an employment or as an independent contractual arrangement.

As this court noted in *Kierulff,* the doctrine of the shop right is of equitable origin:

> The principle involved is that where an inventor or owner of an invention *acquiesces* in the use of the invention by another, particularly where he *induces* and *assists* in such use without demand for compensation or other notice of restriction of the right to continue, he will be deemed to have vested the user with an irrevocable, equitable license to use the invention.

Kierulff v. Metropolitan Stevedore Co., 315 F.2d 839, 841 (9th Cir. 1963) (*quoting Gate-Way, Inc. v. Hillgren,* 82 F. Supp at 555) (emphasis added).

In this case, the factual findings made by the district court fully support the conclusion that Guilford acquired a shop right to Francklyn's invention broad enough to cover its manufacture and use of the second harvester. First, the district court found that Francklyn knew, after his patent was issued, that Guilford was utilizing his harvester on the SIDEWINDER; nevertheless, Francklyn did not seek royalties from Guilford or otherwise attempt to enforce his patent against it until he instituted this suit in 1975. Such a finding clearly supports the conclusion that Francklyn knowingly acquiesced in Guilford's manufacture and use of a copy of his invention on the SIDEWINDER.

Moreover, the findings of the district court support the conclusion that Francklyn induced Guilford to manufacture and use a copy of his invention on the SIDEWINDER. Francklyn testified at trial that he told Wilbur Harms "you will also be able to use the LITTLE JERK or any other clam boat that you may have free of any royalties as long as my patent is valid." Francklyn's testimony certainly supports the district court's finding that "Francklyn offered Guilford Packing Company free use of the LITTLE JERK or any other clam boat with the harvesting rig for the life of his patent without payment of royalties." The district court also found that "Francklyn consistently told Wilbur and Richmond Harms that they could operate using the patented invention without payment of royalties." These findings, supported by credible evidence, are not clearly erroneous, and fully support the ruling below. On the basis of both Francklyn's statements and his silence, Guilford could certainly have reasonably inferred, and apparently did infer, that Francklyn consented to its manufacture and use of his invention on the SIDEWINDER. Under these facts, the finding of a shop right was clearly correct.

Francklyn also argues that under *United States v. Dubilier Condenser Corp.*, 289 U.S. 178 (1933), he is entitled as a matter of law to a finding that Guilford did not have a shop right in his invention. Again, we disagree.

According to *Dubilier* a shop right may arise where the conception and perfection of the invention occurs during the hours of employment and is accomplished while working with the employer's tools and appliances. Here, the evidence adduced at trial supports the conclusion that Francklyn tested and perfected the modified harvester during his hours of work. Francklyn argues that the modifications were made on his own time, and not during his hours of employment, *i.e.,* when he was actually harvesting clams. However, as noted earlier, the work agreement between Francklyn and Guilford contemplated that Francklyn would be making modifications to the harvester in an attempt to improve its performance; the time Francklyn spent modifying the harvester can therefore reasonably be considered as part of his work time. As Francklyn candidly stated at trial, "if it hadn't been for him [Wilbur Harms] I would never have had the opportunity to develop what I developed on the boat in the first place because I would never have had the job to do it." It is also apparent that Francklyn tested the modified harvester while he was harvesting clams for Guilford.

Francklyn also contends that the second aspect of the *Dubilier* test has not been met, since modifications to the harvester were not done with Guilford's materials or appliances. He bases his argument on the fact that the modifications took place at his boat house rather than at Guilford's factory, and that he used his own tools. The district court, however, found that early work on the modification of the harvester took place at Guilford's factory, with Guilford's tools. Moreover, Guilford presented evidence, and the district court found, that Guilford agreed to underwrite all expenses incurred by Francklyn in his modifications of the harvester. Indeed, Francklyn testified that during a May 27, 1975 deposition he had stated that "Mr. Harms told me that if I did anything to the machine [harvester], worked on it, he said that he would pay for the materials that I used and in hopes that we could come up with something that would make it work better, which he did up to a certain point." Francklyn thus conceded that Harms had offered to pay for materials, and that he had been reimbursed for at least a portion of his expenses. The court found that Francklyn unilaterally chose not to seek reimbursement for most of his expenses. Under these circumstances, Guilford's offer to pay for the expenses incurred in the modification of the harvester substantially complies with *Dubilier*'s requirement that the employer supply materials and appliances necessary to perfect the inventions.

We conclude that the district court correctly found that Guilford had a shop right that Francklyn's invention was broad enough to cover its manufacture and use of invention.

We must next decide whether a third party such as Lowman can avoid paying royalties to an inventor by selling an infringing device to the holder of a shop right, such as Guilford, and then leasing the device back from the holder of the right. We hold that a third party cannot evade liability for patent infringement pursuant to such a transaction.

The court below found that the harvester manufactured and used by Lowman applied the teachings of claims 3 and 6 of Francklyn's patent. The parties do not dispute this finding. Moreover, both prior and subsequent to the sale of the harvester to Guilford, Lowman had used that harvester to gather clams to sell to various fish processing plants, including Guilford's. It is therefore clear that Lowman's manufacture and use of this harvester would constitute an infringement of Francklyn's patent unless otherwise privileged. The issue, then, is whether Lowman can evade liability for infringement by entering into a sale and lease back transaction with Guilford, the holder of a shop right to Francklyn's invention. We hold that he cannot.

As noted above, Guilford's shop right was broad enough to encompass the manufacture of Francklyn's invention. The sale and lease back of the device manufactured by Lowman, however, was an attempt by Guilford to assign its shop right to manufacture Francklyn's invention to Lowman. This it cannot do. It is a well established principle that shop right is personal to the employer; it cannot be assigned or transferred by contract to a third person.

The agreement between Guilford and Lowman could not affect Lowman's duty to pay royalties or damages to Francklyn for his infringement of Francklyn's patented invention. Guilford and Lowman could not contract between themselves to abrogate Lowman's duty to pay royalties to Francklyn.

We conclude that Guilford had a shop right to Francklyn's invention. That right is personal to Guilford. It cannot be transferred to Lowman to give him a defense to a claim of patent infringement based on his manufacture and use of a product which is a copy of Francklyn's invention.

NOTE

Shop Rights Preventing Holdups. *Franklyn* illustrates the general rule that applies when an employee not specifically hired for research and development develops an invention with firm resources: the employee gets the patent and the firm gets the shop right. Professor Merges defends this divided ownership because it prevents holdups by employer and employee:

> In awarding shop rights, the law asks primarily whether the employee used firm resources. Given that these resources typically include firm machinery, labs, processes, and personnel, the legal test appears to be a fair proxy for the complementarity between the invention and the firm's other assets. Certainly it is true that inventions created with

firm resources are more likely to be complementary: inventions completely unrelated to a firm's business can just as easily be made away from the job site, and many employees seem to know, or at least intuit, that developing ideas at work subjects them to stronger firm ownership claims. [I]t is precisely when inventions are complementary to a firm's assets that divided ownership is most likely to create holdups[, because an employee who owns the right to one part of a complex, multicomponent product can often demand (or "hold out" in negotiations) for far more than the value of the invention standing alone.] The shop rights doctrine addresses this concern by giving the firm a partial interest in the invention — enough of an interest to use it without negotiating with the ex-employee. This prevents the possibility of a holdup by the employee and consequent underinvestment in R&D by the firm. By the same token, courts recognize that without a shop right employees would have some worrisome ex ante incentives. . . . The law precludes holdup, in other words, by granting an entitlement that leaves neither party at the mercy of the other.

Robert P. Merges, *The Law and Economics of Employee Inventions*, 13 Harv. J.L. & Tech. 1, 12-13, 17-18 (1999).*

INGERSOLL-RAND CO. v. CIAVATTA
Supreme Court of New Jersey
542 A.2d 879 (1988)

Garibaldi, J.

. . . .

Ingersoll-Rand is engaged in the research, development, manufacture, and sale of products for use in various heavy industries. It does business through more than thirty divisions, which are organized into eleven business groups that cover a broad range of technology, including air compressors, construction equipment, mining machinery, oil field products, and tools. Ingersoll-Rand's sales exceed $2 billion and the company dedicates approximately 3.5% to 4.0% of its revenues, or $70-80 million, to research and development.

Historically, one of the dangers of underground mining is the potential collapse of a mine's rock roof. Several methods and devices have been employed to stabilize the strata of rock layers in the roof of a mine. In 1973, Dr. James Scott, a Professor of Mining Engineering at the University of Missouri, conceived of the friction stabilizer roof support system and communicated with Ingersoll-Rand regarding the development of this concept. Ingersoll-Rand, working with Dr. Scott, expended substantial sums on the research and development of the product. On December 2, 1975, the United States Patent Office issued the first patent for Dr. Scott's friction stabilizer. Dr. Scott subsequently assigned the patent to Ingersoll-Rand. In February 1977 Ingersoll-Rand began marketing its stabilizer under an agreement with Dr. Scott. . . .

The split set stabilizer has been a very successful product for Ingersoll-Rand. It represented over half of all stabilizer units sold in the United States

---

* Reprinted with permission of the Harvard Journal of Law & Technology.

for metal and non-metal mines, with over one million units sold in 1984. Ingersoll-Rand controls over ninety percent of the submarket for friction stabilizers. . . .

Defendant, Armand Ciavatta, is a 57-year-old engineer. . . . Since 1950, Ciavatta has held a number of technical engineering positions involving a variety of engineering principles. . . .

In the fall of 1974 . . . he became Program Manager with Ingersoll-Rand Research, Inc. As a condition of his employment with Ingersoll-Rand Research, he executed an "Agreement Relating to Proprietary Matter" (Proprietary Agreement) in which he agreed, in pertinent part:

> 1. To assign and I hereby do assign, to the COMPANY, its successors and assigns, my entire right, title and interest in and to all inventions, copyrights and/or designs I have made or may hereafter make, conceive, develop or perfect, either solely or jointly with others either
>
> (a) during the period of such employment, if such inventions, copyrights and/or designs are related, directly or indirectly, to the business of, or to the research or development work of the COMPANY or its affiliates, or
>
> (b) with the use of the time, materials or facilities of the COMPANY or any of its affiliates, or
>
> (c) within one year after termination of such employment if conceived as a result of and is attributable to work done during such employment and relates to a method, substance, machine, article of manufacture or improvements therein within the scope of the business of the COMPANY or any of its affiliates.

Additionally, in Paragraph 4 of the Agreement, Ciavatta agreed:

> 4. Not to divulge, either during my employment or thereafter to any person, agency, firm or corporation, any secret, confidential or other proprietary information of the COMPANY or any of its affiliates which I may obtain through my employment without first obtaining written permission from the COMPANY.

Ciavatta signed this Agreement on October 1, 1974, and at that time he had read and understood its terms.

While employed by Ingersoll-Rand Research as a Program Manager from October 1974 through March 1978, Ciavatta worked on a variety of development projects, other than those relevant to this litigation, including a tunneling device and the development of coal haulage machinery. As a result of his participation in these development projects, Ciavatta became interested in underground mining and read extensively the industry literature on the subject. From 1974 to 1978, Ciavatta never was formally involved in or assigned to research or development relevant to the friction stabilizer. Nevertheless, Dr. McGahan, the Director of Research, encouraged the research staff to be creative, to discuss ideas for projects or potential projects beyond those to which they had been assigned. These ideas were to be submitted on disclosure forms. Through 1975, Ciavatta submitted thirteen patent disclosures to his employer for mining technology and instrumentation. Five of the thirteen proposals were for devices to support or stabilize roofs of underground mines. Four of the five invention disclosures were not friction stabilizers, but one was an improvement to Ingersoll-Rand's split-set. Ciavatta's work during this period was his first exposure to mining support equipment. Ingersoll-Rand chose not to pursue any of his concepts. Thereafter, defendant claims, he lost his motivation to invent and did not originate any additional concepts while employed by Ingersoll-Rand.

In March 1978, the company transferred Ciavatta to the Split Set Division of Ingersoll-Rand Equipment Corp. While there, he served as Manufacturing Manager and Quality Control Manager. Ingersoll-Rand does not fabricate the stabilizer in any of its plants. Rather, it contracts with two vendors who manufacture the Split Set roof stabilizers, which Ingersoll-Rand then sells to the mining industry. As manager of manufacturing, it was Ciavatta's position to administer the manufacturing program. His responsibilities in that post included supervising the manufacture, production, quality control, and distribution of Ingersoll-Rand's Split Set roof stabilizers. During this period, the company did not employ Ciavatta to design, invent, or modify the basic configuration of its Split Set roof stabilizer, and in fact he did not do so. Ciavatta did, however, have access to Ingersoll-Rand's manufacturing drawings, materials, and specifications. Ingersoll-Rand considers all of that information confidential, although the information had been published in industry trade publications. At the Ingersoll-Rand Research Center the company maintains a security system in order to ensure the confidentiality of its information. Drawings are stamped proprietary, visitors are escorted while in the Ingersoll-Rand Research Center, vendors must sign proprietary information agreements, and all employees must enter into a Proprietary Master Agreement similar to that at issue in this case.

In the spring of 1979, as a result of certain quality control problems, Ciavatta stopped certain shipments of the stabilizer and recommended that the vendors modify their production process. Ciavatta's superior countermanded this directive and directed the vendors to make their scheduled shipments. Subsequently, in June of that year, Ingersoll-Rand terminated Ciavatta's employment. Ciavatta claims that the company did not offer any explanation for his termination; the company claims it terminated his employment because of unsatisfactory performance and his poor relations with fellow employees.

Ciavatta asserts, and the trial court found, that he first conceived of the invention in dispute in the summer of 1979 while unemployed and off the Ingersoll-Rand payroll. Apparently, he was installing a light fixture in his home when he first conceived of his invention, an elliptical metal tube designed to stabilize the roofs of mines. While searching for employment following his discharge from Ingersoll-Rand, Ciavatta intermittently worked on his design. He completed his first sketch of the stabilizing device on August 25, 1979, approximately two months after Ingersoll-Rand fired him. Ciavatta's stabilizer differs from Ingersoll-Rand's in two respects: its tubular portion is closed rather than split, and the tube is elliptical in shape.

Ciavatta . . . began refining the system in a more systematic manner. Although still looking for employment, he "started to go through significantly more calculations," and obtained sample tubing to run experimental tests. In March 1980, nine months after his termination, Ciavatta filed for a United States patent on the device and was awarded U.S. Patent No. 4316677 in February 1982. Subsequently, in March 1982, Ciavatta received a second patent, U.S. Patent No. 4322183, which involved an improvement to the roof stabilizer protected by Ciavatta's first patent.

In July 1980, Ciavatta prepared a business plan and . . . used his life savings and borrowed over $125,000 from his brother and a bank to take his invention to the marketplace. Ciavatta exhibited his now-patented invention at a trade show in October 1982, and sales of his product then began. He made his first sale in January 1983. Sales for 1983 totalled approximately $30,000. By the time that the trial of this case commenced in June 1985 his total sales approximated $270,000. Ciavatta's stabilizer sells for approximately 15% less than Ingersoll-Rand's stabilizer. The trial court observed "[t]he market place has begun to accept defendant's product and his device appears to be a competitive threat to plaintiff's device."

. . . In July 1982, Ciavatta received a letter from Ingersoll-Rand's patent counsel requesting that he assign his patent to the company. Ciavatta communicated to Ingersoll-Rand that his lawyer had advised him that he was not obligated to assign his patent to his former employer. . . .

In September 1983, after Ciavatta had sold his product to several Ingersoll-Rand customers, the company decided to lower the price of its split set stabilizer and to commence this lawsuit. . . .

The issue of Ciavatta's liability for breach of contract was tried without a jury. Ingersoll-Rand attempted to prove that Ciavatta had stolen his invention and that he had relied on Ingersoll-Rand's trade secrets or other confidential information in conceiving his product. Ciavatta argued that the "holdover" clause is unenforceable in the absence of a finding that the invention was based on the employer's trade secrets or other confidential information. . . .

[The trial court found that Ciavatta did not pirate any trade secrets or confidential information in conceiving his invention, but nevertheless enforced the agreement. The trial court] articulated a general reasonableness test and determined that the balance tilted in favor of Ingersoll-Rand because Ciavatta's "knowledge of the underground mining industry was based entirely on his employment experience with Ingersoll-Rand," and he had been "enriched" by the company's non-confidential ideas and by his access to Ingersoll-Rand's "information, experience, expertise and ideas and the creative interaction gleaned from his employment with the company." The court also determined that Ciavatta's engineering experience was so diverse that "assignment of this specific invention did not unreasonably preclude realistic employment opportunities in other fields." . . .

The Appellate Division accepted the trial court's factual determination but reversed the judgment. . . .

II

Paragraph 1(c) of Ciavatta's Proprietary Agreement with Ingersoll-Rand comprises a one-year so-called "holdover" agreement under which the employee promises to assign his or her "entire right, title and interest" in any invention he or she creates during a one-year period following termination of employment if that invention is "conceived as a result of and is attributable to work done during such employment." The central question presented in this case is the enforceability of that covenant.

The common law regards an invention as the property of the inventor who conceived, developed, and perfected it. The Supreme Judicial Court of Massachusetts accurately summarized the common-law position in *National Development Co. v. Gray*, 55 N.E.2d 783, 786 (Mass. 1944):

> One by merely entering an employment requiring the performance of services of a noninventive nature does not lose his rights to any inventions that he may make during the employment . . . and this is true even if the patent is for an improvement upon a device or process used by the employer or is of such great practical value as to supersede the devices or processes with which the employee became familiar during his employment. . . . The law looks upon an invention as the property of the one who conceived, developed and perfected it, and establishes, protects and enforces the inventor's rights in his invention unless he has contracted away those rights.

Generally, where an employer hires an employee to design a specific invention or solve a specific problem, the employee has a duty to assign the resulting patent. Where the employee is not hired specifically to design or invent, but nevertheless conceives of a device during working hours with the use of the employer's materials and equipment, the employer is granted an irrevocable but non-exclusive right to use the invention under the "shop right rule." A shop right is an employer's royalty or fee, a non-exclusive and nontransferable license to use an employee's patented invention.

Since the common-law doctrines are vague and ambiguous in defining the rights of employers and employees in employees' inventions, most employers use written contracts to allocate invention rights. Such contracts requiring an employee to assign to the employer inventions designed or conceived during the period of employment are valid.

The contractual allocation of invention rights between employers and employees is especially critical given the fact that 80% to 90% of all inventions in the United States are made by employed inventors. The United States is not alone in this regard. In West Germany, 60% to 75% of all inventions come from employed inventors; in France the figure is 70% to 75%. In both countries, 90% of all useful inventions are made by employees.

Most large, technologically advanced companies today require their employees by contract to assign their patents to their employers. Courts, however, will not enforce invention assignment contracts that unreasonably obligate an employee in each and every instance to transfer the ownership of the employee's invention to the employer. Additionally, several states have recently adopted legislation that delimits employer-employee invention assignment agreements. Those statutes restrict the instances in which employers may compel the assignment of employee inventions. *See* Minn. Stat. Ann. §§ 181.78 (1980); N.C. Gen. Stat. §§ 66-57.1 to 57-2 (1981); Wash. Rev. Code

Ann. § 49.44.140 (1987); Cal. Lab. Code § 2870 (West 1987). All of these statutes provide that any employee invention assignment agreement that purports to give employers greater rights than they have under the statute is against public policy and, consequently, unenforceable.

In the instant case, the contract involves the assignment of future or post-employment inventions. Contractual provisions requiring assignment of post-employment inventions are commonly referred to as "trailer" or "holdover" clauses. The public policy issues involved in the enforceability of these holdover clauses reflect the dichotomy of our views on the rights of an inventor and rights of an employer. Our society has long recognized the intensely personal nature of an invention and the importance of providing stimulation and encouragement to inventors. Some commentators believe that the existing patent system does not present sufficient motivation to an employee-inventor. These commentators allege that the United States is in danger of losing its position as technology leader of the world. They cite for support that America is experiencing a declining patent balance and is less patent-productive than many foreign countries. More and more United States patents are not issued to United States citizens and companies but to foreigners. Interestingly, Japan, which began tying employed inventors' compensation to the market value of the invention in 1959, has witnessed a dramatic increase in the number of inventions generated by employed inventors.

To encourage an inventor's creativity, courts have held that on terminating his employment, an inventor has the right to use the general skills and knowledge gained through the prior employment. Nonetheless, it is acknowledged that the inventive process is increasingly being supported and subsidized by corporations and governments. It is becoming a more collective research process, the collective product of corporate and government research laboratories instead of the identifiable work of one or two individuals. Employers, therefore, have the right to protect their trade secrets, confidential information, and customer relations. Thus, employees and employers both have significant interests warranting judicial attention.

In view of the competing interests involved in holdover agreements, courts have not held them void per se. Rather, the courts apply a test of reasonableness. Moreover, courts strictly construe contractual provisions that require assignment of post-employment inventions; they must be fair, reasonable, and just. Generally, a clause is unreasonable if it: (1) extends beyond any apparent protection that the employer reasonably requires; (2) prevents the inventor from seeking other employment; or (3) adversely impacts on the public.

New Jersey courts previously have not specifically addressed the enforceability of a "holdover" clause. We have, however, addressed the enforceability of analogous employee noncompetition contracts. We find that our determination of the enforceability of those post-contracts is applicable to our determination in this case of the enforceability of "holdover" clauses.

In [*Solari Industries, Inc. v. Malady*, 264 A.2d 53 (N.J. 1970), and *Whitmyer Bros., Inc. v. Doyle*, 274 A.2d 577 (N.J. 1971)] we articulated a three-part test to determine the validity of a noncompetition covenant in an employment contract. Under those cases, a court will find a noncompetition covenant reasonable if it "simply protects the legitimate interests of the employer, imposes no undue hardship on the employee and is not injurious to the public." *Solari* and *Whitmyer* both recognize as legitimate the employer's interest in protecting trade secrets, confidential information, and customer relations. Since adopting the three-part *Solari/Whitmyer* test, New Jersey courts have addressed similar questions with respect to lawyers; doctors; accountants; and management and consulting firms.

[The Court then discussed several cases from various jurisdictions.]

IV

The cases thus support the enforceability of holdover agreements if they are reasonable. In assessing the reasonableness of holdover agreements, this Court will follow the *Solari/Whitmyer* test of reasonableness. By applying the reasonableness test, the judicial analysis of holdover agreements will parallel the judicial analysis of contracts requiring an employee to assign to the employer inventions made or conceived of by an employee *during* his or her employment. We have held such contracts to be enforceable when reasonable. Likewise, we will enforce holdover agreements to the same extent that we will enforce similar post-employment restrictive agreements, giving employers "that limited measure of relief within the terms of the noncompetitive agreement which would be reasonably necessary to protect his 'legitimate interests,' would cause 'no undue hardship' on the employee, and would 'not impair the public interest.'" *Whitmyer*, 274 A.2d at 582; *Solari*, 264 A.2d at 61.

The first two parts of the *Solari/Whitmyer* test focus on the protection of the legitimate interests of the employer and the extent of the hardship on the employee. Plainly, the court must balance these competing interests. In cases where the employer's interests are strong, such as cases involving trade secrets or confidential information, a court will enforce a restrictive agreement. Conversely, in cases where the employer's interests do not rise to the level of a proprietary interest deserving of judicial protection, a court will conclude that a restrictive agreement merely stifles competition and therefore is unenforceable. Courts also recognize that knowledge, skill, expertise, and information acquired by an employee during his employment become part of the employee's person. . . .

Ciavatta urges that holdover agreements also should be enforced only when the former employee has used the trade secrets or confidential information of the employer in developing his post-termination invention. Since it is undisputed that he did not do so in inventing his stabilizer, he argues, paragraph 1(c), the holdover clause, should not be enforced against him.

Ingersoll-Rand, however, argues that it is inequitable to limit an employer's "protectable interest" solely to trade secrets and other confidential information. Today, large corporations maintain at great expense modern research and development programs that involve synergistic processes. Such "think tanks" require the free and open exchange of new ideas among the members of a research staff using the employer's body of accumulated information and experiences. This creative process receives its impetus and inspiration from the assimilation of an employer's advanced knowledge and a spontaneous interaction among colleagues, co-employees, and superiors. Ingersoll-Rand argues that it maintains this creative atmosphere in its research and development effort at great expense and that it should be allowed to protect itself against a former employee who invents a unique, competing concept attributable to such brainstorming. Ingersoll-Rand contends that such creative brainstorming enriched Ciavatta and led to his invention and therefore that paragraph 1(c) of the proprietary agreement should be enforced.

We agree with Ingersoll-Rand that the protection afforded by holdover agreements such as the one executed by the parties in this lawsuit may under certain circumstances exceed the limitation of trade secrets and confidential information. We recognize that employers may have legitimate interests in protecting information that is not a trade secret or proprietary information, but highly specialized, current information not generally known in the industry, created and stimulated by the research environment furnished by the employer, to which the employee has been "exposed" and "enriched" solely due to his employment. We do not attempt to define the exact parameters of that protectable interest.

We expect courts to construe narrowly this interest, which will be deemed part of the "reasonableness" equation. The line between such information, trade secrets, and the general skills and knowledge of a highly sophisticated employee will be very difficult to draw, and the employer will have the burden to do so. Nevertheless, we do not hesitate to recognize what appears to us a business reality that modern day employers are in need of some protection against the use or disclosure of valuable information regarding the employer's business, which information is passed on to certain employees confidentially by virtue of the positions those employees hold in the employer's enterprise.

Courts, however, must be aware that holdover agreements impose restrictions on employees. Such agreements clearly limit an employee's employment opportunities and in many instances probably interfere with an employee securing a position in which he could most effectively use his skills, at the same time depriving society of a more productive worker. How restrictive the clause is on a particular employee depends, of course, on the facts and circumstances of the case. Indeed, in many instances, the employee may have little choice but to sign a holdover agreement in order to secure employment. Conversely, some very talented or experienced individuals, pursued by several corporations, may bargain for highly lucrative positions in exchange for their promise to be bound by a holdover agreement. Accordingly, courts must evaluate the reasonableness of holdover agreements in light of the individual circumstances of the employer and employee. Courts must balance the employer's need for protection and the hardship on the employee that may result.

The third prong of the *Solari/Whitmyer* test relates to the public interest. Throughout this opinion, we have analyzed the relevant competing public interests. We reiterate that the public has a clear interest in safeguarding fair commercial practices and in protecting employers from theft or piracy of trade secrets, confidential information, or, more generally, knowledge and technique in which the employer may be said to have a proprietary interest.

The public has an equally clear and strong interest in fostering creativity and invention and in encouraging technological improvement and design enhancement of all goods in the marketplace.

In sum, we conclude that holdover agreements are enforceable when reasonable, and that in determining if the post-termination restriction is reasonable, we will apply the three-prong test of *Solari/Whitmyer*. Thus, resolution of each case will depend on its own facts and circumstances. Courts must not go too far in construing holdover agreements to insulate employers from competition from former employees. That courts should not be overly zealous in protecting employers should not, however, dissuade a court from analyzing the reasonableness of a holdover covenant or from enforcing it where it is reasonable. Thus, here, we must balance the interests of Ingersoll-Rand and Ciavatta on the basis of the facts to determine whether the enforcement of the holdover agreement in this instance would be reasonable.

VI

We conclude that on the facts of this case, Ingersoll-Rand is not entitled to an assignment of the patent on Ciavatta's friction stabilizer. We find that Ingersoll-Rand has not substantiated that Ciavatta invented his friction stabilizer in violation of his contractual obligation under the holdover clause. Ingersoll-Rand has not established that Ciavatta "conceived" of his invention as a result of his employment at Ingersoll-Rand. The facts convince us that the holdover clause does not apply here however liberally we are willing to construe the protection afforded employers by such clauses. Furthermore, we also find that enforcement of the holdover agreement in this case would be unreasonable even if the contract by its terms applied to Ciavatta's invention.

The record shows that Armand Ciavatta was not hired to invent or to work on design improvements or other variations of the split set friction stabilizer. He was not directed by his employer into its research and development department, and even though Ciavatta himself submitted numerous product ideas to Ingersoll-Rand, the company never developed any of those ideas. Indeed, Ciavatta testified that as a result of plaintiffs' rejection of his submitted ideas, he was discouraged from creating or using his ingenuity to develop new ideas or suggest adaptations to existing Ingersoll-Rand products. Ingersoll-Rand did not assign Ciavatta to a "think tank" division in which he would likely have encountered on a daily basis the ideas of fellow Ingersoll-Rand personnel regarding how the split set stabilizer could be improved or how a more desirable alternative stabilizer might be designed.

More importantly, the information needed to invent the split set stabilizer is not that unique type of information that we would deem protectable even under our expanded definition of a protectable interest. All of the specifications and capabilities of the Ingersoll-Rand split set stabilizer were widely publicized throughout industry and trade publications. In fact, the general design of Atlas Copco's friction stabilizer, the leading competitor of the Ingersoll-Rand stabilizer, is identical to the general design of the Ingersoll-Rand product. Moreover, Ingersoll-Rand openly advertised the characteristics of its split set product. The uses of the product were well known throughout the mining industry as were the names of the particular users of the product. Production cost figures and pricing schedules were known in the industry as well. Furthermore, the technology behind the split set was no mystery; there was trial testimony that the technology behind the production of the split set was over fifty years old. Thus, it is clear that Ingersoll-Rand has done little to guard the details of its friction stabilizer or maintain a secretive atmosphere surrounding corporate development and marketing of the product. Instead, the company deliberately created and perpetuated an open, public posture in the mining industry submarket in which it operated and in which it enjoyed a commanding market share. Matters of general knowledge throughout an industry cannot be claimed as secrets nor as "unique information" derived as a result of current, ongoing research of the employer.

Ciavatta did not develop his stabilizer on the basis of valuable information about the Ingersoll-Rand product imparted to him because he held a special position with the company. His departure from Ingersoll-Rand and subsequent invention and development of his own competing product do not suggest that he purposefully left to develop a competing product on the basis of the knowledge he gained from his employment. We do not hold that the manner of an employee's departure is dispositive. It is a factor that the court should consider, however, and, in this case, that factor weighs heavily in defendant's favor. Ciavatta was fired from Ingersoll-Rand and testified that he conceived of his invention while installing a light fixture at his home some months after he was terminated. Thereafter, he performed further, independent calculations to test and refine his concept. He worked intermittently on the product as he searched for employment. He developed the product based on his general skill, expertise, and knowledge. While Ciavatta employed certain skills and knowledge he undoubtedly gained during his employment by Ingersoll-Rand, his invention was not the result of any research currently being done by the company or any company research in which he personally was involved. Indeed, the technology Ciavatta employed was developed over fifty years ago and well known in the industry. Nor did he use any of Ingersoll-Rand's capital or materials in the development of his invention. . . .

These facts lead us to believe that the factors of the *Solari/Whitmyer* balancing test weigh heavily in favor of defendant, even assuming that paragraph 1(c) applies. Although we specifically hold today that reasonable holdover agreements may be enforceable, we decline to enforce the agreement between Ingersoll-Rand and Ciavatta because, as it relates to the patented invention in dispute, the restriction is unreasonable under *Solari/Whitmyer*. We recognize that employers may have a protectable interest in certain proprietary information that former employees may use to invent competing products. We also recognize that the range of the employer's proprietary information that may be protected by contract may narrowly exceed the specific types of information covered by the law of trade secrets and confidential information. Here, however, when we apply the reasonableness test of *Solari/Whitmyer,* we conclude that enforcement of the holdover agreement would work an undue hardship on defendant. Thus, we conclude that the restraint in this specific case is unreasonable and hence unenforceable.

Accordingly, we affirm the judgment of the Appellate Division.

NOTES

1. *Works of Authorship.* Under the federal Copyright Act of 1976, 17 U.S.C. § 201(b), an employer is presumed to be the author of any work made for hire:

> In the case of a work made for hire, the employer or other person for whom the work was prepared is considered the author for purposes of this title, and unless the parties have expressly agreed otherwise in a written instrument signed by them, owns all the rights comprised in the copyright.

The Supreme Court addressed § 201(b) in *Community for Creative Non-Violence v. Reid*, 490 U.S. 730 (1989). A nonprofit organization sponsored a nativity scene of contemporary homeless people for the annual Christmastime Pageant of Peace in Washington, D.C. The group hired James Earl Reid to build the sculpture, called "Third World America." Reid donated his labor to the project. C.C.N.V. built a pedestal for the statue and made several suggestions which Reid incorporated into his work. After the pageant was completed, the parties could not agree about what should be done with the statue, and each party then filed a copyright claim. The case eventually reached the Supreme Court.

The Supreme Court held that federal common law of agency, rather than state law, should be used to determine whether the creator of a copyrighted work is an employee. It found that Reid was an independent contractor rather than an employee, and that "Third World America" thus was not a "work made for hire" within the meaning of 17 U.S.C. § 201(b). The Court remanded the case for a determination of whether C.C.N.V. and Reid prepared the work "with the intention that their contributions be merged into inseparable or interdependent parts of a unitary whole," in which case the "joint work" doctrine would apply.

2. *Independent Contractors and Works for Hire.* Suppose a corporation hires independent computer programmers to create software for its workplace. Even if the corporation closely supervises the development of the program, the independent contractors are the authors and owners of the copyright. Unless they have waived their rights by contract, they have the right to make modifications and sell the software to others. This is an example where workers have greater rights as independent contractors than as employees. *See generally* Charles D. Ossola, *"Joint Work" Theory Raises New Questions on Authors' Rights*, NATIONAL L.J. S10 (Jan. 18, 1993).

The copyrights of independent contractors were at issue in *New York Times Co. v. Tasini*, 533 U.S. 483 (2001). Freelance writers had contributed stories to the *New York Times*, retaining the copyright, while the *Times* owned the copyright for the collection. The freelancers sued when the *Times* allowed Lexis/Nexis to reproduce and distribute the articles in its electronic database. The Court held that both the print publisher and the electronic publishers had infringed the copyrights of the freelance authors. The Court emphasized that the freelancers were not employees and had not otherwise contracted to make the stories "works for hire" within the meaning of 17 U.S.C. § 201(b). *Id.* at 497 n.7.

3. *Fear of R&D Employee Holdups.* Professor Merges supports the rule that employees in R&D departments are generally not entitled to their inventions, arguing that employee ownership of inventions would create large transaction costs:

> At the most basic level, the difference between employer and employee ownership is a matter of transaction costs. Employer ownership is more efficient for two transaction-related reasons: (1) it occurs at the commencement of employment and thus is far simpler than deals struck after an employee makes a specific invention; and (2) it eliminates the possibility of holdups by employee-inventors, thereby making it more attractive for a firm to invest in R&D by employees in the first place.

> In the conventional arrangement, employee contracts function as "pre-assignments": they are signed at the commencement of employment and therefore before any inventions have been made. Thus, when employees do come up with inventions, under the law the employer firm already owns the invention.

> Pre-assignment to a single entity avoids holdup costs. A "holdup," in economic parlance, occurs whenever one person extorts abnormally large amounts of money from another person. The classic example is the owner of one parcel of land in the middle of a large tract comprising many individual, identical parcels. The potential for holdup emerges when a developer comes up with a plan to aggregate all the parcels into a single tract that is more valuable than the sum of the values of the individual parcels. If the developer acquires all but the last parcel needed to realize the valuable development project, the owner of that last parcel can extract from the developer an amount much larger than what the single parcel would have fetched in a normal transaction. The price of the last parcel will approach the greater of (1) the developer's expected profit from the project and (2) the amount the developer would lose if he had to abandon the project and begin again somewhere else. In such a case, the owner of the last parcel has a "holdup right."

> Holdups are common in the intellectual property context because discrete intellectual property rights often cover individual components of a complex, multicomponent product. An individual intellectual property rightsholder can follow the same strategy as the owner of the last parcel of land in the earlier example: if a manufacturer wants to develop a new product, the rightsholder can extract much of the value of the final product by waiting until all the other rightsholders have granted licenses to the manufacturer. Many employee inventions fit this pattern: they are one component of a complex, multicomponent product whose total market value often far exceeds the value of the component standing alone. As a result, the associated patents could serve as the basis of a holdup strategy *if* the patents were owned by individual employees. The prevailing rule of employer ownership prevents this result, and thus makes good economic sense.

If employees were able to hold up the employer firm, the ex ante consequence might be underinvestment in R&D. A holdup right depends on a high degree of complementarity between the assets owned by the investing party and the key input owned by the person with the holdup right. Research and development creates highly complementary assets and thus increases the risk of holdup. Common ownership of complementary assets solves the holdup problem and promotes socially beneficial activities, such as R&D.

Robert P. Merges, *The Law and Economics of Employee Inventions*, 13 HARV. J.L. & TECH. 1, 12-13 (1999).[*]

---

[*] Reprinted with permission of the Harvard Journal of Law & Technology.

Part V

PROHIBITIONS ON STATUS DISCRIMINATION

Chapter 14

LEGAL MODELS OF DISCRIMINATION

Many laws prohibit employment discrimination. At the federal level, Title VII of the Civil Rights Act of 1964 is the central statute. It prohibits discrimination because of race, color, religion, sex, and national origin. But a number of other federal statutes also prohibit employment discrimination. Some prohibit other types of discrimination, such as age discrimination or discrimination against persons with disabilities, while others overlap with Title VII in substance, but differ in procedure and remedy. These latter include the Equal Pay Act of 1963; the Civil Rights Act of 1866, 42 U.S.C. § 1981; and the Ku Klux Klan Act of 1871, 42 U.S.C. § 1983. In addition to these federal statutes, literally hundreds of state and local laws exist. These laws often increase the types of status protected (for example, many prohibit discrimination based on sexual orientation and marital status) and the number of employers covered (for example, many cover employers with fewer than 15 employees). In addition, these state and local laws always provide their own procedures and remedies.

Despite this multitude of laws, only three basic models exist for proving employment discrimination. The three models — disparate treatment, disparate impact, and reasonable accommodation — rely on different underlying theories and impose different burdens of proof on employers and employees, but together they define the range of what is legally cognizable as employment discrimination in this country.

A. DISPARATE TREATMENT

1. INDIVIDUAL DISPARATE TREATMENT

McDONNELL DOUGLAS CORP. v. GREEN
United States Supreme Court
411 U.S. 792 (1973)

MR. JUSTICE POWELL delivered the opinion of the Court.

The case before us raises significant questions as to the proper order and nature of proof in actions under Title VII of the Civil Rights Act of 1964.

Petitioner, McDonnell Douglas Corp., is an aerospace and aircraft manufacturer headquartered in St. Louis, Missouri, where it employs over 30,000 people. Respondent, a black citizen of St. Louis, worked for petitioner as a mechanic and laboratory technician from 1956 until August 28, 1964 when he was laid off in the course of a general reduction in petitioner's work force.

Respondent, a long-time activist in the civil rights movement, protested vigorously that his discharge and the general hiring practices of petitioner were racially motivated. As part of this protest, respondent and other members of the Congress on Racial Equality illegally stalled their cars on the main roads leading to petitioner's plant for the purpose of blocking access to it at the time of the morning shift change. The District Judge described the plan for, and respondent's participation in, the "stall-in" as follows:

> [F]ive teams, each consisting of four cars would "tie up" five main access roads into McDonnell at the time of the morning rush hour. The drivers of the cars were instructed to line up next to each other completely blocking the intersections or roads. The drivers were also instructed to stop their cars, turn off the engines, pull the emergency brake, raise all windows, lock the doors, and remain in their cars until the police arrived. The plan was to have the cars remain in position for one hour.
>
> Acting under the "stall in" plan, plaintiff [respondent in the present action] drove his car onto Brown Road, a McDonnell access road, at approximately 7:00 a.m., at the start of the morning rush hour. Plaintiff was aware of the traffic problems that would result. He stopped his car with the intent to block traffic. The police arrived shortly and requested plaintiff to move his car. He refused to move his car voluntarily. Plaintiff's car was towed away by the police, and he was arrested for obstructing traffic. Plaintiff pleaded guilty to the charge of obstructing traffic and was fined.

318 F. Supp. 846, 849.

On July 2, 1965, a "lock-in" took place wherein a chain and padlock were placed on the front door of a building to prevent the occupants, certain of petitioner's employees, from leaving. Though respondent apparently knew beforehand of the "lock-in," the full extent of his involvement remains uncertain.

Some three weeks following the "lock-in," on July 25, 1965, petitioner publicly advertised for qualified mechanics, respondent's trade, and respondent promptly applied for re-employment. Petitioner turned down respondent, basing its rejection on respondent's participation in the "stall-in" and "lock-in." Shortly thereafter, respondent filed a formal complaint with the Equal Employment Opportunity Commission, claiming that petitioner had refused to rehire him because of his race. . . .

The critical issue before us concerns the order and allocation of proof in a private, non-class action challenging employment discrimination. . . . The broad, overriding interest [protected by Title VII and] shared by employer, employee, and consumer, is efficient and trustworthy workmanship assured through fair and racially neutral employment and personnel decisions. In the implementation of such decisions, it is abundantly clear that Title VII tolerates no racial discrimination, subtle or otherwise.

In this case respondent, the complainant below, charges that he was denied employment "because of his involvement in civil rights activities" and "because of his race and color." Petitioner denied discrimination of any kind, asserting that its failure to re-employ respondent was based upon and justified by his participation in the unlawful conduct against it. Thus, the issue at the trial on remand is framed by those opposing factual contentions. . . .

The complainant in a Title VII trial must carry the initial burden under the statute of establishing a *prima facie* case of racial discrimination. This may be done by showing (i) that he belongs to a racial minority; (ii) that he applied and was qualified for a job for which the employer was seeking applicants; (iii) that, despite his qualifications, he was rejected; and (iv) that, after his rejection, the position remained open and the employer continued to seek applicants from persons of complainant's qualifications.[13] In the instant case, we agree with the Court of Appeals that respondent proved a *prima facie* case. Petitioner sought mechanics, respondent's trade, and continued to do so after respondent's rejection. Petitioner, moreover, does not dispute respondent's qualifications[14] and acknowledges that his past work performance in petitioner's employ was "satisfactory."

The burden then must shift to the employer to articulate some legitimate, nondiscriminatory reason for the employee's rejection. We need not attempt in the instant case to detail every matter which fairly could be recognized as a reasonable basis for a refusal to hire. Here petitioner has assigned respondent's participation in unlawful conduct against it as the cause for his rejection. We think that this suffices to discharge petitioner's burden of proof at this stage and to meet respondent's *prima facie* case of discrimination.

The Court of Appeals intimated, however, that petitioner's stated reason for refusing to rehire respondent was a "subjective" rather than objective criterion which "carr[ies] little weight in rebutting charges of discrimination." This was among the statements which caused the dissenting judge to read the opinion as taking "the position that such unlawful acts as Green committed against McDonnell would not legally entitle McDonnell to refuse to hire him, even though no racial motivation was involved. . . ." Regardless of whether this was the intended import of the opinion, we think the court below seriously underestimated the rebuttal weight to which petitioner's reasons were entitled. Respondent admittedly had taken part in a carefully planned "stall-in," designed to tie up access to and egress from petitioner's plant at a peak traffic hour. Nothing in Title VII compels an employer to absolve and rehire one who has engaged in such deliberate, unlawful activity against it. . . .[17]

Petitioner's reason for rejection thus suffices to meet the *prima facie* case, but the inquiry must not end here. While Title VII does not, without more, compel rehiring of respondent, neither does it permit petitioner to use

---

[13] The facts necessarily will vary in Title VII cases, and the specification above of the *prima facie* proof required from respondent is not necessarily applicable in every respect to differing factual situations.

[14] We note that the issue of what may properly be used to test qualifications for employment is not present in this case. Where employers have instituted employment tests and qualifications with an exclusionary effect on minority applicants, such requirements must be "shown to bear a demonstrable relationship to successful performance of the jobs" for which they were used, *Griggs v. Duke Power Co.*, 401 U.S. 424, 431 (1971).

[17] The unlawful activity in this case was directed specifically against petitioner. We need not consider or decide here whether, or under what circumstances, unlawful activity not directed against the particular employer may be a legitimate justification for refusing to hire.

respondent's conduct as a pretext for the sort of discrimination prohibited by § 703(a)(1). On remand, respondent must, as the Court of Appeals recognized, be afforded a fair opportunity to show that petitioner's stated reason for respondent's rejection was in fact pretext. Especially relevant to such a showing would be evidence that white employees involved in acts against petitioner of comparable seriousness to the "stall-in" were nevertheless retained or rehired. Petitioner may justifiably refuse to rehire one who was engaged in unlawful, disruptive acts against it, but only if this criterion is applied alike to members of all races.

Other evidence that may be relevant to any showing of pretext includes facts as to the petitioner's treatment of respondent during his prior term of employment; petitioner's reaction, if any, to respondent's legitimate civil rights activities; and petitioner's general policy and practice with respect to minority employment. On the latter point, statistics as to petitioner's employment policy and practice may be helpful to a determination of whether petitioner's refusal to rehire respondent in this case conformed to a general pattern of discrimination against blacks.[19] In short, on the retrial respondent must be given a full and fair opportunity to demonstrate by competent evidence that the presumptively valid reasons for his rejection were in fact a coverup for a racially discriminatory decision. . . .

In sum, respondent should have been allowed to pursue his claim under § 703(a)(1). If the evidence on retrial is substantially in accord with that before us in this case, we think that respondent carried his burden of establishing a *prima facie* case of racial discrimination and that petitioner successfully rebutted that case. But this does not end the matter. On retrial, respondent must be afforded a fair opportunity to demonstrate that petitioner's assigned reason for refusing to re-employ was a pretext or discriminatory in its application. If the District Judge so finds, he must order a prompt and appropriate remedy. In the absence of such a finding, petitioner's refusal to rehire must stand.

NOTES

1. *Life After the Supreme Court.* Despite this victory in the Supreme Court, Percy Green eventually lost the case. On remand, the District Court held he was rejected because of his illegal activities, not because of his race or participation in legitimate civil rights activities. *Green v. McDonnell Douglas Corp.*, 390 F. Supp. 501 (1975), *aff'd*, 528 F.2d 1102 (8th Cir. 1976). Instead of life as a mechanic, Green finished his education and became a social activist. By his own count, he has been arrested over 100 times in protest demonstrations. David B. Oppenheimer, *The Story of Green v. McDonnell Douglas, in* EMPLOYMENT DISCRIMINATION STORIES 13, 34 (Joel Wm. Friedman ed., 2006).

---

[19] The District Court may, for example, determine, after reasonable discovery that "the [racial] composition of defendant's labor force is itself reflective of restrictive or exclusionary practices." We caution that such general determinations, while helpful, may not be in and of themselves controlling as to an individualized hiring decision, particularly in the presence of an otherwise justifiable reason for refusing to rehire.

2. *Framing the Factual Inquiry.* In *Texas Department of Community Affairs v. Burdine*, 450 U.S. 248, 253-56 (1981), the Supreme Court discussed the underlying rationale of the *McDonnell Douglas* framework for analyzing individual disparate treatment cases:

> The burden of establishing a *prima facie* case of disparate treatment is not onerous. The plaintiff must prove by a preponderance of the evidence that she applied for an available position for which she was qualified, but was rejected under circumstances which give rise to an inference of unlawful discrimination. The *prima facie* case serves an important function in the litigation: it eliminates the most common nondiscriminatory reasons for the plaintiff's rejection, [lack of qualifications and no job vacancy]. Establishment of the *prima facie* case in effect creates a presumption that the employer unlawfully discriminated against the employee. If the trier of fact believes the plaintiff's evidence, and if the employer is silent in the face of the presumption, the court must enter judgment for the plaintiff because no issue of fact remains in the case.[7]
>
> The burden that shifts to the defendant, therefore, is to rebut the presumption of discrimination by producing evidence that the plaintiff was rejected, or someone else was preferred, for a legitimate, nondiscriminatory reason. The defendant need not persuade the court that it was actually motivated by the proffered reasons. It is sufficient if the defendant's evidence raises a genuine issue of fact as to whether it discriminated against the plaintiff.[8] To accomplish this, the defendant must clearly set forth, through the introduction of admissible evidence, the reasons for the plaintiff's rejection. The explanation provided must be legally sufficient to justify a judgment for the defendant. If the defendant carries this burden of production, the presumption raised by the *prima facie* case is rebutted, and the factual inquiry proceeds to a new level of specificity. Placing this burden of production on the defendant thus serves simultaneously to meet the plaintiff's *prima facie* case by presenting a legitimate reason for the action and to frame the factual issue with sufficient clarity so that the plaintiff will have a full and fair opportunity to demonstrate pretext. The sufficiency of the defendant's evidence should be evaluated by the extent to which it fulfills these functions.
>
> The plaintiff retains the burden of persuasion. She now must have the opportunity to demonstrate that the proffered reason was not the

---

[7] The phrase "prima facie case" not only may denote the establishment of a legally mandatory, rebuttable presumption, but also may be used by courts to describe the plaintiff's burden of producing enough evidence to permit the trier of fact to infer the fact at issue. *McDonnell Douglas* should have made it apparent that in the Title VII context we use "prima facie case" in the former sense.

[8] This evidentiary relationship between the presumption created by a *prima facie* case and the consequential burden of production placed on the defendant is a traditional feature of the common law. . . . Usually, assessing the burden of production helps the judge determine whether the litigants have created an issue of fact to be decided by the jury. In a Title VII case, the allocation of burdens and the creation of a presumption by the establishment of a *prima facie* case is intended progressively to sharpen the inquiry into the elusive factual question of intentional discrimination.

true reason for the employment decision. This burden now merges with the ultimate burden of persuading the court that she has been the victim of intentional discrimination. She may succeed in this either directly, by persuading the court that a discriminatory reason more likely motivated the employer, or indirectly, by showing that the employer's proffered explanation is unworthy of credence.

3. The Ultimate Issue. In *St. Mary's Honor Center v. Hicks*, 509 U.S. 502 (1993), the Supreme Court held that a plaintiff could not prevail under the *McDonnell Douglas* model simply by convincing the trier of fact that the reasons the employer gave for its adverse employment decisions were not true. In addition, the plaintiff has to prove the "ultimate fact of intentional discrimination." *Id.* at 510.

In *Hicks*, the employer claimed that it demoted and then discharged the plaintiff because of the severity and number of times he had violated the employer's rules. The District Court found that the adverse employment decisions were not made because of the plaintiff's rules violations, but held for the employer anyway. Despite the weakness of the employer's purported reasons for its decisions, the plaintiff had not convinced the Court that race was the real reason. The Supreme Court held that this was permissible. Under the *McDonnell Douglas* model, proof of a *prima facie* case and disproof of the employer's proffered reasons for the adverse action *permit* a trier of fact to make a finding of illegal discrimination, but it does not *require* such a finding. The plaintiff "at all times" bears the "ultimate burden" of convincing the trier of fact of intentional discrimination. *Id.* at 510.

PRICE WATERHOUSE v. HOPKINS
United States Supreme Court
490 U.S. 228 (1989)

JUSTICE BRENNAN announced the judgment of the Court and delivered an opinion, in which JUSTICE MARSHALL, JUSTICE BLACKMUN, and JUSTICE STEVENS join.

Ann Hopkins had worked at Price Waterhouse[, a nationwide professional accounting partnership,] for five years when the partners in [her] office proposed her as a candidate for partnership. Of the 662 partners at the firm at that time, 7 were women. Of the 88 persons proposed for partnership that year, only 1 — Hopkins — was a woman. Forty-seven of these candidates were admitted to the partnership, 21 were rejected, and 20 — including Hopkins — were "held" for reconsideration the following year. . . .[1]

In a jointly prepared statement supporting her candidacy, the partners in Hopkins' office showcased her successful 2-year effort to secure a $25 million contract with the Department of State, labeling it "an outstanding performance" and one that Hopkins carried out "virtually at the partner level." . . .

---

[1] Before the time for reconsideration came, two of the partners in Hopkins' office withdrew their support for her, and the office informed her that she would not be reconsidered for partnership. Hopkins then resigned. Price Waterhouse does not challenge the Court of Appeals' conclusion that the refusal to repropose her for partnership amounted to a constructive discharge.

Judge Gesell[, the District Court judge,] specifically found that . . . "[n]one of the other partnership candidates at Price Waterhouse that year had a comparable record in terms of successfully securing major contracts for the partnership."

The partners in Hopkins' office praised her character as well as her accomplishments, describing her in their joint statement as "an outstanding professional" who had a "deft touch," a "strong character, independence and integrity." Clients appear to have agreed with these assessments. At trial, one official from the State Department described her as "extremely competent, intelligent," "strong and forthright, very productive, energetic and creative." . . .

On too many occasions, however, Hopkins' aggressiveness apparently spilled over into abrasiveness. Staff members seem to have borne the brunt of Hopkins' brusqueness. . . . Although later evaluations indicate an improvement, Hopkins' perceived shortcomings in this important area eventually doomed her bid for partnership. Virtually all of the partners' negative remarks about Hopkins — even those of partners supporting her — had to do with her "interpersonal skills." Both "[s]upporters and opponents of her candidacy," stressed Judge Gesell, "indicated that she was sometimes overly aggressive, unduly harsh, difficult to work with and impatient with staff."

There were clear signs, though, that some of the partners reacted negatively to Hopkins' personality because she was a woman. One partner described her as "macho"; another suggested that she "overcompensated for being a woman"; a third advised her to take "a course at charm school." Several partners criticized her use of profanity; in response, one partner suggested that those partners objected to her swearing only "because it's a lady using foul language." Another supporter explained that Hopkins "ha[d] matured from a tough-talking somewhat masculine hard-nosed mgr to an authoritative, formidable, but much more appealing lady ptr candidate." But it was the man who . . . bore responsibility for explaining to Hopkins the reasons for the Policy Board's decision to place her candidacy on hold who delivered the coup de grace: in order to improve her chances for partnership, Thomas Beyer advised, Hopkins should "walk more femininely, talk more femininely, dress more femininely, wear make-up, have her hair styled, and wear jewelry."

Dr. Susan Fiske, a social psychologist and Associate Professor of Psychology at Carnegie-Mellon University, testified at trial that the partnership selection process at Price Waterhouse was likely influenced by sex stereotyping. Her testimony focused not only on the overtly sex-based comments of partners but also on gender-neutral remarks, made by partners who knew Hopkins only slightly, that were intensely critical of her. One partner, for example, baldly stated that Hopkins was "universally disliked" by staff, and another described her as "consistently annoying and irritating"; yet these were people who had had very little contact with Hopkins. According to Fiske, Hopkins' uniqueness (as the only woman in the pool of candidates) and the subjectivity of the evaluations made it likely that sharply critical remarks such as these were the product of sex stereotyping — although Fiske admitted that she could not say with certainty whether any particular comment was the result of stereotyping. . . .

Judge Gesell found that Price Waterhouse legitimately emphasized inter-personal skills in its partnership decisions, and also found that the firm had not fabricated its complaints about Hopkins' interpersonal skills as a pretext for discrimination. . . . The judge went on to decide, however, that some of the partners' remarks about Hopkins stemmed from an impermissibly cabined view of the proper behavior of women, and that Price Waterhouse had done nothing to disavow reliance on such comments. He held that Price Waterhouse had unlawfully discriminated against Hopkins on the basis of sex by con-sciously giving credence and effect to partners' comments that resulted from sex stereotyping. Noting that Price Waterhouse could avoid equitable relief by proving by clear and convincing evidence that it would have placed Hopkins' candidacy on hold even absent this discrimination, the judge decided that the firm had not carried this heavy burden.

The Court of Appeals affirmed the District Court's ultimate conclusion, but departed from its analysis in one particular: it held that even if a plaintiff proves that discrimination played a role in an employment decision, the defendant will not be found liable if it proves, by clear and convincing evidence, that it would have made the same decision in the absence of discrimi-nation. Under this approach, an employer is not deemed to have violated Title VII if it proves that it would have made the same decision in the absence of an impermissible motive, whereas under the District Court's approach, the employer's proof in that respect only avoids equitable relief. We decide today that the Court of Appeals had the better approach, but that both courts erred in requiring the employer to make its proof by clear and convincing evidence.

II

The specification of the standard of causation under Title VII is a decision about the kind of conduct that violates that statute. According to Price Waterhouse, an employer violates Title VII only if it gives decisive consider-ation to an employee's gender, race, national origin, or religion in making a decision that affects that employee. On Price Waterhouse's theory, even if a plaintiff shows that her gender played a part in an employment decision, it is still her burden to show that the decision would have been different if the employer had not discriminated. In Hopkins' view, on the other hand, an employer violates the statute whenever it allows one of these attributes to play any part in an employment decision. Once a plaintiff shows that this occurred, according to Hopkins, the employer's proof that it would have made the same decision in the absence of discrimination can serve to limit equitable relief but not to avoid a finding of liability. We conclude that, as often happens, the truth lies somewhere in-between.

A

In passing Title VII, Congress made the simple but momentous announce-ment that sex, race, religion, and national origin are not relevant to the selection, evaluation, or compensation of employees. Yet, the statute does not purport to limit the other qualities and characteristics that employers *may* take into account in making employment decisions. The converse, therefore, of "for cause" legislation, Title VII eliminates certain bases for distinguishing among employees while otherwise preserving employers' freedom of choice. This balance between employee rights and employer prerogatives turns out to be decisive in the case before us.

Congress' intent to forbid employers to take gender into account in making employment decisions appears on the face of the statute. In now-familiar language, the statute forbids an employer to "fail or refuse to hire or to discharge any individual, or otherwise to discriminate with respect to his compensation, terms, conditions, or privileges of employment," or to "limit, segregate, or classify his employees or applicants for employment in any way which would deprive or tend to deprive any individual of employment opportunities or otherwise adversely affect his status as an employee, *because of* such individual's . . . sex." [Title VII, §§ 703(a)(1), (2)] (emphasis added). We take these words to mean that gender must be irrelevant to employment decisions. To construe the words "because of" as colloquial shorthand for "but-for causation," as does Price Waterhouse, is to misunderstand them.

But-for causation is a hypothetical construct. In determining whether a particular factor was a but-for cause of a given event, we begin by assuming that that factor was present at the time of the event, and then ask whether, even if that factor had been absent, the event nevertheless would have transpired in the same way. The present, active tense of the operative verbs of § 703(a)(1) ("to fail or refuse"), in contrast, turns our attention to the actual moment of the event in question, the adverse employment decision. The critical inquiry, the one commanded by the words of § 703(a)(1), is whether gender was a factor in the employment decision *at the moment it was made.* Moreover, since we know that the words "because of" do not mean "*solely* because of,"[7] we also know that Title VII meant to condemn even those decisions based on a mixture of legitimate and illegitimate considerations. When, therefore, an employer considers both gender and legitimate factors at the time of making a decision, that decision was "because of" sex and the other, legitimate considerations — even if we may say later, in the context of litigation, that the decision would have been the same if gender had not been taken into account.

To attribute this meaning to the words "because of" does not, as the dissent asserts, divest them of causal significance. A simple example illustrates the point. Suppose two physical forces act upon and move an object, and suppose that either force acting alone would have moved the object. As the dissent would have it, *neither* physical force was a "cause" of the motion unless we can show that but for one or both of them, the object would not have moved; apparently both forces were simply "in the air" unless we can identify at least one of them as a but-for cause of the object's movement. Events that are causally overdetermined, in other words, may not have any "cause" at all. This cannot be so.

We need not leave our common sense at the doorstep when we interpret a statute. It is difficult for us to imagine that, in the simple words "because of," Congress meant to obligate a plaintiff to identify the precise causal role

---

[7] Congress specifically rejected an amendment that would have placed the word "solely" in front of the words "because of." 110 Cong. Rec. 2728, 13837 (1964).

played by legitimate and illegitimate motivations in the employment decision she challenges. We conclude, instead, that Congress meant to obligate her to prove that the employer relied upon sex-based considerations in coming to its decision. . . .

To say that an employer may not take gender into account is not, however, the end of the matter, for that describes only one aspect of Title VII. The other important aspect of the statute is its preservation of an employer's remaining freedom of choice. We conclude that the preservation of this freedom means that an employer shall not be liable if it can prove that, even if it had not taken gender into account, it would have come to the same decision regarding a particular person. . . .

The central point is this: while an employer may not take gender into account in making an employment decision (except in those very narrow circumstances in which gender is a BFOQ), it is free to decide against a woman for other reasons. We think these principles require that, once a plaintiff in a Title VII case shows that gender played a motivating part in an employment decision, the defendant may avoid a finding of liability[10] only by proving that it would have made the same decision even if it had not allowed gender to play such a role. This balance of burdens is the direct result of Title VII's balance of rights.

Our holding casts no shadow on *Burdine,* in which we decided that, even after a plaintiff has made out a *prima facie* case of discrimination under Title VII, the burden of persuasion does not shift to the employer to show that its stated legitimate reason for the employment decision was the true reason. We stress, first, that neither court below shifted the burden of persuasion to Price Waterhouse on this question, and in fact, the District Court found that Hopkins had not shown that the firm's stated reason for its decision was pretextual. Moreover, since we hold that the plaintiff retains the burden of persuasion on the issue whether gender played a part in the employment decision, the situation before us is not the one of "shifting burdens" that we addressed in *Burdine.* Instead, the employer's burden is most appropriately deemed an affirmative defense: the plaintiff must persuade the factfinder on one point, and then the employer, if it wishes to prevail, must persuade it on another.

Price Waterhouse's claim that the employer does not bear any burden of proof (if it bears one at all) until the plaintiff has shown "substantial evidence that Price Waterhouse's explanation for failing to promote Hopkins was not the 'true reason' for its action" merely restates its argument that the plaintiff in a mixed-motives case must squeeze her proof into *Burdine*'s framework. Where a decision was the product of a mixture of legitimate and illegitimate motives, however, it simply makes no sense to ask whether the legitimate reason was "*the* 'true reason'" (emphasis added) for the decision — which is

---

10 Hopkins argues that once she made this showing, she was entitled to a finding that Price Waterhouse had discriminated against her on the basis of sex; as a consequence, she says, the partnership's proof could only limit the relief she received. [The Court rejected this argument and said no liability would result if the employer could carry its burden. This portion of the decision was overturned by Congress in the Civil Rights Act of 1991. *See* Note 2 following the *Desert Palace* case.]

the question asked by *Burdine*.[12] Oblivious to this last point, the dissent would insist that *Burdine*'s framework perform work that it was never intended to perform. It would require a plaintiff who challenges an adverse employment decision in which both legitimate and illegitimate considerations played a part to pretend that the decision, in fact, stemmed from a single source — for the premise of *Burdine* is that *either* a legitimate *or* an illegitimate set of considerations led to the challenged decision. To say that *Burdine*'s evidentiary scheme will not help us decide a case admittedly involving *both* kinds of considerations is not to cast aspersions on the utility of that scheme in the circumstances for which it was designed. . . .

C

In saying that gender played a motivating part in an employment decision, we mean that, if we asked the employer at the moment of the decision what its reasons were and if we received a truthful response, one of those reasons would be that the applicant or employee was a woman. In the specific context of sex stereotyping, an employer who acts on the basis of a belief that a woman cannot be aggressive, or that she must not be, has acted on the basis of gender. . . .

Remarks at work that are based on sex stereotypes do not inevitably prove that gender played a part in a particular employment decision. The plaintiff must show that the employer actually relied on her gender in making its decision. In making this showing, stereotyped remarks can certainly be *evidence* that gender played a part. . . .

As to the employer's proof, in most cases, the employer should be able to present some objective evidence as to its probable decision in the absence of an impermissible motive.[14] Moreover, proving " 'that the same decision would have been justified . . . is not the same as proving that the same decision would have been made.' " An employer may not, in other words, prevail in a mixed-motives case by offering a legitimate and sufficient reason for its decision if that reason did not motivate it at the time of the decision. Finally, an employer may not meet its burden in such a case by merely showing that at the time of the decision it was motivated only in part by a legitimate reason. The very premise of a mixed-motives case is that a legitimate reason was present. . . . The employer instead must show that its legitimate reason, standing alone, would have induced it to make the same decision.

---

12 Nothing in this opinion should be taken to suggest that a case must be correctly labeled as either a "pretext" case or a "mixed-motives" case from the beginning in the District Court; indeed, we expect that plaintiffs often will allege, in the alternative, that their cases are both. Discovery often will be necessary before the plaintiff can know whether both legitimate and illegitimate considerations played a part in the decision against her. At some point in the proceedings, of course, the District Court must decide whether a particular case involves mixed motives. If the plaintiff fails to satisfy the factfinder that it is more likely than not that a forbidden characteristic played a part in the employment decision, then she may prevail only if she proves, following *Burdine,* that the employer's stated reason for its decision is pretextual. . . .

14 JUSTICE WHITE's suggestion that the employer's own testimony as to the probable decision in the absence of discrimination is due special credence where the court has, contrary to the employer's testimony, found that an illegitimate factor played a part in the decision, is baffling.

III

The courts below held that an employer who has allowed a discriminatory impulse to play a motivating part in an employment decision must prove by clear and convincing evidence that it would have made the same decision in the absence of discrimination. We are persuaded that the better rule is that the employer must make this showing by a preponderance of the evidence.

Conventional rules of civil litigation generally apply in Title VII cases and one of these rules is that parties to civil litigation need only prove their case by a preponderance of the evidence. . . .

IV

The District Court found that sex stereotyping "was permitted to play a part" in the evaluation of Hopkins as a candidate for partnership. Price Waterhouse disputes both that stereotyping occurred and that it played any part in the decision to place Hopkins' candidacy on hold. In the firm's view, in other words, the District Court's factual conclusions are clearly erroneous. We do not agree.

In finding that some of the partners' comments reflected sex stereotyping, the District Court relied in part on Dr. Fiske's expert testimony. . . . We are not inclined to accept petitioner's belated and unsubstantiated characterization of Dr. Fiske's testimony as "gossamer evidence" based only on "intuitive hunches" and of her detection of sex stereotyping as "intuitively divined." Nor are we disposed to adopt the dissent's dismissive attitude toward Dr. Fiske's field of study and toward her own professional integrity.

Indeed, we are tempted to say that Dr. Fiske's expert testimony was merely icing on Hopkins' cake. It takes no special training to discern sex stereotyping in a description of an aggressive female employee as requiring "a course at charm school." Nor, turning to Thomas Beyer's memorable advice to Hopkins, does it require expertise in psychology to know that, if an employee's flawed "interpersonal skills" can be corrected by a soft-hued suit or a new shade of lipstick, perhaps it is the employee's sex and not her interpersonal skills that has drawn the criticism. . . .

V

We hold that when a plaintiff in a Title VII case proves that her gender played a motivating part in an employment decision, the defendant may avoid a finding of liability only by proving by a preponderance of the evidence that it would have made the same decision even if it had not taken the plaintiff's gender into account. Because the courts below erred by deciding that the defendant must make this proof by clear and convincing evidence, we reverse the Court of Appeals' judgment against Price Waterhouse on liability and remand the case to that court for further proceedings.

It is so ordered.

JUSTICE WHITE, concurring in the judgment. . . .

I concur in the judgment reversing this case in part and remanding. With respect to the employer's burden, however, the plurality seems to require, at least in most cases, that the employer submit objective evidence that the same result would have occurred absent the unlawful motivation. In my view, however, there is no special requirement that the employer carry its burden by objective evidence. In a mixed-motives case, where the legitimate motive found would have been ample grounds for the action taken, and the employer credibly testifies that the action would have been taken for the legitimate reasons alone, this should be ample proof. . . .

JUSTICE O'CONNOR, concurring in the judgment. . . .

[T]he rule we adopt today is at least a change in direction from some of our prior precedents. . . . Such a departure requires justification, and its outlines should be carefully drawn.

First, *McDonnell Douglas* itself dealt with a situation where the plaintiff presented no direct evidence that the employer had relied on a forbidden factor under Title VII in making an employment decision. . . . In the face of [the] inferential proof [contemplated by *McDonnell Douglas*], the employer's burden was deemed to be only one of production. . . . I do not think that the employer is entitled to the same presumption of good faith where there is direct evidence that it has placed substantial reliance on factors whose consideration is forbidden by Title VII. . . .

Second, the facts of this case . . . convince me that the evidentiary standard I propose is necessary to make real [Title VII's] promise of [non-discrimination.] . . . Ann Hopkins had taken her proof as far as it could go. . . . It is as if Ann Hopkins were sitting in the hall outside the room where partnership decisions were being made. As the partners filed in to consider her candidacy, she heard several of them make sexist remarks in discussing her suitability for partnership. As the decisionmakers exited the room, she was *told* by one of those privy to the decisionmaking process that her gender was a major reason for the rejection of her partnership bid. If . . . "[p]resumptions shifting the burden of proof are often created to reflect judicial evaluations of probabilities and to conform with a party's superior access to the proof," one would be hard pressed to think of a situation where it would be more appropriate to require the defendant to show that its decision would have been justified by wholly legitimate concerns. . . .

Moreover . . . [p]articularly in the context of the professional world, where decisions are often made by collegial bodies on the basis of largely subjective criteria, requiring the plaintiff to prove that *any* one factor was the definitive cause of the decisionmakers' action may be tantamount to declaring Title VII inapplicable to such decisions. . . .

In my view, in order to justify shifting the burden on the issue of causation to the defendant, a disparate treatment plaintiff must show by direct evidence that an illegitimate criterion was a substantial factor in the decision. . . . Requiring that the plaintiff demonstrate that an illegitimate factor played a substantial role in the employment decision identifies those employment situations where the deterrent purpose of Title VII is most clearly implicated.

As an evidentiary matter, where a plaintiff has made this type of strong showing of illicit motivation, the factfinder is entitled to presume that the employer's discriminatory animus made a difference to the outcome, absent proof to the contrary from the employer. Where a disparate treatment plaintiff has made such a showing, the burden then rests with the employer to convince the trier of fact that it is more likely than not that the decision would have been the same absent consideration of the illegitimate factor. The employer need not isolate the sole cause for the decision; rather it must demonstrate that with the illegitimate factor removed from the calculus, sufficient business reasons would have induced it to take the same employment action. . . .

Thus, stray remarks in the workplace, while perhaps probative of sexual harassment, cannot justify requiring the employer to prove that its hiring or promotion decisions were based on legitimate criteria. Nor can statements by nondecisionmakers, or statements by decisionmakers unrelated to the decisional process itself, suffice to satisfy the plaintiff's burden in this regard. In addition, in my view testimony such as Dr. Fiske's in this case, standing alone, would not justify shifting the burden of persuasion to the employer. Race and gender always "play a role" in an employment decision in the benign sense that these are human characteristics of which decisionmakers are aware and about which they may comment in a perfectly neutral and nondiscriminatory fashion. For example, in the context of this case, a mere reference to "a lady candidate" might show that gender "played a role" in the decision, but by no means could support a rational factfinder's inference that the decision was made "because of" sex. What is required is what Ann Hopkins showed here: direct evidence that decisionmakers placed substantial negative reliance on an illegitimate criterion in reaching their decision. . . .

JUSTICE KENNEDY, with whom the CHIEF JUSTICE and JUSTICE SCALIA join, dissenting. . . .

The plurality begins by noting the quite unremarkable fact that Title VII is written in the present tense. . . . This observation, however, tells us nothing of particular relevance to Title VII or the cause of action it creates. I am unaware of any federal prohibitory statute that is written in the past tense. Every liability determination, including the novel one constructed by the plurality, necessarily is concerned with the examination of a past event. The plurality's analysis of verb tense serves only to divert attention from the causation requirement that is made part of the statute by the "because of" phrase. That phrase, I respectfully submit, embodies a rather simple concept that the plurality labors to ignore.[2] . . .

I would adhere to [the] established evidentiary framework [of *McDonnell Douglas* and *Burdine*], which provides the appropriate standard for this and other individual disparate-treatment cases. . . . The Court's attempt at

---

[2] The plurality's discussion of overdetermined causes only highlights the error of its insistence that but-for is not the substantive standard of causation under Title VII. The opinion discusses the situation where two physical forces move an object, and either force acting alone would have moved the object. Translated to the context of Title VII, this situation would arise where an employer took an adverse action in reliance both on sex and on legitimate reasons, and *either* the illegitimate or the legitimate reason standing alone would have produced the action. If this state of affairs is proved to the factfinder, there will be no liability under the plurality's own test, for the same decision would have been made had the illegitimate reason never been considered.

refinement provides limited practical benefits at the cost of confusion and complexity, with the attendant risk that the trier of fact will misapprehend the controlling legal principles and reach an incorrect decision. . . .

The potential benefits of the new approach, in my view, are overstated. First, the Court makes clear that the *Price Waterhouse* scheme is applicable only in those cases where the plaintiff has produced direct and substantial proof that an impermissible motive was relied upon in making the decision at issue. The burden shift properly will be found to apply in only a limited number of employment discrimination cases. The application of the new scheme, furthermore, will make a difference only in a smaller subset of cases. . . .

Although the *Price Waterhouse* system is not for every case, almost every plaintiff is certain to ask for a *Price Waterhouse* instruction, perhaps on the basis of "stray remarks" or other evidence of discriminatory animus. Trial and appellate courts will therefore be saddled with the task of developing standards for determining when to apply the burden shift. One of their new tasks will be the generation of a jurisprudence of the meaning of "substantial factor." Courts will also be required to make the often subtle and difficult distinction between "direct" and "indirect" or "circumstantial" evidence. Lower courts long have had difficulty applying *McDonnell Douglas* and *Burdine*. Addition of a second burden-shifting mechanism, the application of which itself depends on assessment of credibility and a determination whether evidence is sufficiently direct and substantial, is not likely to lend clarity to the process. . . .

NOTE

Life After the Supreme Court. On remand, the District Court found that Price Waterhouse did not carry its burden of proving it would have reached the same decision in the absence of discrimination. Consequently, it found for Hopkins and ordered the firm to make her a partner and pay her $371,000 in backpay. *Hopkins v. Price Waterhouse*, 737 F. Supp. 1202 (D.D.C.), *aff'd*, 920 F.2d 967 (D.C. Cir. 1990). Hopkins accepted the partnership position. She reports that occasionally young staff members have asked her for advice about how to become partner. She replies that "I'd be happy to help, but I don't think [you'd] want to do it the way I did." Amy Saltzman, *Life After the Lawsuit*, U.S. NEWS & WORLD REPORT, Aug. 19, 1996, at 42.

DESERT PALACE, INC. v. COSTA
United States Supreme Court
539 U.S. 90 (2003)

JUSTICE THOMAS delivered the opinion of the Court.

The question before us in this case is whether a plaintiff must present direct evidence of discrimination in order to obtain a mixed-motive instruction under Title VII of the Civil Rights Act of 1964, as amended by the Civil Rights Act of 1991 (1991 Act). We hold that direct evidence is not required.

I

A

Since 1964, Title VII has made it an "unlawful employment practice for an employer . . . to discriminate against any individual . . ., *because of* such individual's race, color, religion, sex, or national origin." Title VII § 703(a)(1) (emphasis added). In *Price Waterhouse v. Hopkins*, 490 U.S. 228 (1989), the Court considered whether an employment decision is made "because of" sex in a "mixed-motive" case, *i.e.*, where both legitimate and illegitimate reasons motivated the decision. The Court concluded that, under § 703(a)(1), an employer could "avoid a finding of liability . . . by proving that it would have made the same decision even if it had not allowed gender to play such a role." The Court was divided, however, over the predicate question of when the burden of proof may be shifted to an employer to prove the affirmative defense.

Justice Brennan, writing for a plurality of four Justices, would have held that "when a plaintiff . . . proves that her gender played a *motivating* part in an employment decision, the defendant may avoid a finding of liability only by proving by a preponderance of the evidence that it would have made the same decision even if it had not taken the plaintiff's gender into account." *Id.*, at 258 (emphasis added). The plurality did not, however, "suggest a limitation on the possible ways of proving that [gender] stereotyping played a motivating role in an employment decision." *Id.*, at 251-252.

Justice White and Justice O'Connor both concurred in the judgment. Justice White would have held that the case was governed by *Mt. Healthy City Bd. of Ed. v. Doyle*, 429 U.S. 274 (1977), and would have shifted the burden to the employer only when a plaintiff "show[ed] that the unlawful motive was a substantial factor in the adverse employment action." *Price Waterhouse, supra*, at 259. Justice O'Connor, like Justice White, would have required the plaintiff to show that an illegitimate consideration was a "substantial factor" in the employment decision. 490 U.S., at 276. But, under Justice O'Connor's view, "the burden on the issue of causation" would shift to the employer only where "a disparate treatment plaintiff [could] show by *direct evidence* that an illegitimate criterion was a substantial factor in the decision." *Ibid.* (emphasis added).

Two years after *Price Waterhouse*, Congress passed the 1991 Act. In particular, § 107 of the 1991 Act, which is at issue in this case, "respond[ed]" to *Price Waterhouse* by "setting forth standards applicable in 'mixed motive' cases" in two new statutory provisions.[1] The first establishes an alternative for proving that an "unlawful employment practice" has occurred:

> Except as otherwise provided in this subchapter, an unlawful employ-ment practice is established when the complaining party demonstrates that race, color, religion, sex, or national origin was a motivating factor for any employment practice, even though other factors also motivated the practice. Title VII § 703(m).

---

[1] This case does not require us to decide when, if ever, § 107 applies outside of the mixed-motive context.

The second provides that, with respect to "a claim in which an individual proves a violation under section 703(m)," the employer has a limited affirmative defense that does not absolve it of liability, but restricts the remedies available to a plaintiff. The available remedies include only declaratory relief, certain types of injunctive relief, and attorney's fees and costs. Title VII § 706(g)(2)(B). In order to avail itself of the affirmative defense, the employer must "demonstrat[e] that [it] would have taken the same action in the absence of the impermissible motivating factor." *Ibid.*

Since the passage of the 1991 Act, the Courts of Appeals have divided over whether a plaintiff must prove by direct evidence that an impermissible consideration was a "motivating factor" in an adverse employment action. Relying primarily on Justice O'Connor's concurrence in *Price Waterhouse*, a number of courts have held that direct evidence is required to establish liability under § 703(m). In the decision below, however, the Ninth Circuit concluded otherwise.

B

Petitioner Desert Palace, Inc., employed respondent Catharina Costa as a warehouse worker and heavy equipment operator. Respondent was the only woman in this job and in her local Teamsters bargaining unit.

Respondent experienced a number of problems with management and her co-workers that led to an escalating series of disciplinary sanctions, including informal rebukes, a denial of privileges, and suspension. Petitioner finally terminated respondent after she was involved in a physical altercation in a warehouse elevator with fellow Teamsters member Herbert Gerber. Petitioner disciplined both employees because the facts surrounding the incident were in dispute, but Gerber, who had a clean disciplinary record, received only a 5-day suspension.

Respondent subsequently filed this lawsuit against petitioner in the United States District Court for the District of Nevada, asserting claims of sex discrimination and sexual harassment under Title VII. The District Court dismissed the sexual harassment claim, but allowed the claim for sex discrimination to go to the jury. At trial, respondent presented evidence that (1) she was singled out for "intense 'stalking'" by one of her supervisors, (2) she received harsher discipline than men for the same conduct, (3) she was treated less favorably than men in the assignment of overtime, and (4) supervisors repeatedly "stack[ed]" her disciplinary record and "frequently used or tolerated" sex-based slurs against her.

Based on this evidence, the District Court denied petitioner's motion for judgment as a matter of law, and submitted the case to the jury with instructions, two of which are relevant here. First, without objection from petitioner, the District Court instructed the jury that "[t]he plaintiff has the burden of proving . . . by a preponderance of the evidence that she suffered adverse work conditions and that her sex was a motivating factor in any such work conditions imposed upon her."

Second, the District Court gave the jury the following mixed-motive instruction:

You have heard evidence that the defendant's treatment of the plaintiff was motivated by the plaintiff's sex and also by other lawful reasons. If you find that the plaintiff's sex was a motivating factor in the defendant's treatment of the plaintiff, the plaintiff is entitled to your verdict, even if you find that the defendant's conduct was also motivated by a lawful reason.

However, if you find that the defendant's treatment of the plaintiff was motivated by both gender and lawful reasons, you must decide whether the plaintiff is entitled to damages. The plaintiff is entitled to damages unless the defendant proves by a preponderance of the evidence that the defendant would have treated plaintiff similarly even if the plaintiff's gender had played no role in the employment decision.

Petitioner unsuccessfully objected to this instruction, claiming that respondent had failed to adduce "direct evidence" that sex was a motivating factor in her dismissal or in any of the other adverse employment actions taken against her. The jury rendered a verdict for respondent, awarding backpay, compensatory damages, and punitive damages. The District Court denied petitioner's renewed motion for judgment as a matter of law.

The Court of Appeals initially vacated and remanded, holding that the District Court had erred in giving the mixed-motive instruction because respondent has failed to present [direct evidence of discrimination. After rehearing en banc, the entire Court of Appeals affirmed the District Court holding that direct evidence of discrimination was not necessary for respondent to receive a mixed-motives instruction.]

II

This case provides us with the first opportunity to consider the effects of the 1991 Act on jury instructions in mixed-motive cases. Specifically, we must decide whether a plaintiff must present direct evidence of discrimination in order to obtain a mixed-motive instruction under § 703(m). Petitioner's argument on this point proceeds in three steps: (1) Justice O'Connor's opinion is the holding of *Price Waterhouse*; (2) Justice O'Connor's *Price Waterhouse* opinion requires direct evidence of discrimination before a mixed-motive instruction can be given; and (3) the 1991 Act does nothing to abrogate that holding. Like the Court of Appeals, we see no need to address which of the opinions in *Price Waterhouse* is controlling: the third step of petitioner's argument is flawed, primarily because it is inconsistent with the text of § 703(m).

Our precedents make clear that the starting point for our analysis is the statutory text. And where, as here, the words of the statute are unambiguous, the "judicial inquiry is complete." Section 703(m) unambiguously states that a plaintiff need only "demonstrat[e]" that an employer used a forbidden consideration with respect to "any employment practice." On its face, the statute does not mention, much less require, that a plaintiff make a heightened showing through direct evidence. Indeed, petitioner concedes as much.

Moreover, Congress explicitly defined the term "demonstrates" in the 1991 Act, leaving little doubt that no special evidentiary showing is required. Title VII defines the term "demonstrates" as to "mee[t] the burdens of production and persuasion." § 701(m). If Congress intended the term "demonstrates" to require that the "burdens of production and persuasion" be met by direct evidence or some other heightened showing, it could have made that intent clear by including language to that effect in § 701(m). Its failure to do so is significant, for Congress has been unequivocal when imposing heightened proof requirements in other circumstances, including in other provisions of Title 42. *See, e.g.,* 8 U.S.C. § 1158(a)(2)(B) (stating that an asylum application may not be filed unless an alien "demonstrates by clear and convincing evidence" that the application was filed within one year of the alien's arrival in the United States); 42 U.S.C. § 5851(b)(3)(D) (providing that "[r]elief may not be ordered" against an employer in retaliation cases involving whistle-blowers under the Atomic Energy Act where the employer is able to "*demonstrat[e] by clear and convincing evidence* that it would have taken the same unfavorable personnel action in the absence of such behavior" (emphasis added)); *cf. Price Waterhouse,* 490 U.S., at 253 (plurality opinion) ("Only rarely have we required clear and convincing proof where the action defended against seeks only conventional relief").

In addition, Title VII's silence with respect to the type of evidence required in mixed-motive cases also suggests that we should not depart from the "[c]onventional rul[e] of civil litigation [that] generally appl[ies] in Title VII cases." That rule requires a plaintiff to prove his case "by a preponderance of the evidence," using "direct or circumstantial evidence," *Postal Service Bd. of Governors v. Aikens,* 460 U.S. 711, 714, n. 3 (1983). We have often acknowledged the utility of circumstantial evidence in discrimination cases. For instance, in *Reeves v. Sanderson Plumbing Products, Inc.,* 530 U.S. 133 (2000), we recognized that evidence that a defendant's explanation for an employment practice is "unworthy of credence" is "one form of *circumstantial evidence* that is probative of intentional discrimination." *Id.,* at 147 (emphasis added). The reason for treating circumstantial and direct evidence alike is both clear and deep-rooted: "Circumstantial evidence is not only sufficient, but may also be more certain, satisfying and persuasive than direct evidence." *Rogers v. Missouri Pacific R. Co.,* 352 U.S. 500, 508, n. 17 (1957).

The adequacy of circumstantial evidence also extends beyond civil cases; we have never questioned the sufficiency of circumstantial evidence in support of a criminal conviction, even though proof beyond a reasonable doubt is required. And juries are routinely instructed that "[t]he law makes no distinction between the weight or value to be given to either direct or circumstantial evidence." It is not surprising, therefore, that neither petitioner nor its *amici curiae* can point to any other circumstance in which we have restricted a litigant to the presentation of direct evidence absent some affirmative directive in a statute.

Finally, the use of the term "demonstrates" in other provisions of Title VII tends to show further that § 703(m) does not incorporate a direct evidence requirement. *See, e.g.,* §§ 703(k)(1)(A)(i), 706(g)(2)(B). For instance, § 706(g)(2)(B) requires an employer to "demonstrat[e] that [it] would have taken the same action in the absence of the impermissible motivating factor" in order to take advantage of the partial affirmative defense. Due to the similarity in structure between that provision and § 703(m), it would be logical to assume that the term "demonstrates" would carry the same meaning with respect to both provisions. But when pressed at oral argument about whether direct evidence is required before the partial affirmative defense can be invoked, petitioner did not "agree that . . . the defendant or the employer has any heightened standard" to satisfy. Absent some congressional indication to the contrary, we decline to give the same term in the same Act a different meaning depending on whether the rights of the plaintiff or the defendant are at issue.

For the reasons stated above, we agree with the Court of Appeals that no heightened showing is required under § 703(m).

. . . .

In order to obtain an instruction under § 703(m), a plaintiff need only present sufficient evidence for a reasonable jury to conclude, by a preponderance of the evidence, that "race, color, religion, sex, or national origin was a motivating factor for any employment practice." Because direct evidence of discrimination is not required in mixed-motive cases, the Court of Appeals correctly concluded that the District Court did not abuse its discretion in giving a mixed-motive instruction to the jury. Accordingly, the judgment of the Court of Appeals is affirmed.

It is so ordered.

[JUSTICE O'CONNOR filed a concurring opinion.]

NOTES

1. *Did McDonnell Douglas Survive the Desert?* Most academic commentators see little role for *McDonnell Douglas* after *Desert Palace. See, e.g.*, Henry L. Chambers, Jr., *The Effect of Eliminating Distinctions Among Title VII Disparate Treatment Cases*, 57 SMU L. REV. 83, 102-103 (2004) ("Over time, . . . the motivating-factor test will apply to all disparate treatment cases"); William R. Corbett, *An Allegory of the Cave and the* Desert Palace, 41 HOUS. L. REV. 1549, 1551 ("*McDonnell Douglas* . . . is dead"). The courts, however, have been more cautious. For example, in *Rachid v. Jack in the Box, Inc.*, 376 F.3d 305, 312 (5th Cir. 2004), the Court applied a "modified" *McDonnell Douglas* framework. Under this interpretation of the decisions, the plaintiff still presents the standard *prima facie* case from *McDonnell Douglas*, which shifts the burden to the defendant to articulate a legitimate, non-discriminatory reason for its decision. At that point, however, the plaintiff can either proffer the standard *McDonnell Douglas* argument that the employer's reason is pretext and not the true basis of its decision, or it can proffer the argument that, even though the employer's reason is true, it is only one of the reasons for the employer's actions and that discrimination was an additional motivating factor. One reason for judicial cautiousness is that the Supreme Court did not even mention *McDonnell Douglas* in its *Desert Palace* decision; it would have been odd for the Supreme Court to abrogate the long-standing *McDonnell Douglas* framework without any comment.

2. *Price Waterhouse or the Civil Rights Act of 1991?* The Civil Rights Act of 1991 codified the mixed-motives method of proof only within Title VII (and not within other statutes, such as the Age Discrimination in Employment Act) and only with respect to race, color, religion, sex, and national origin discrimination. Title VII § 703(m). Because of this, the courts often still apply an unmodified version of *Price Waterhouse* to other types of claims. *See, e.g., Glanzman v. Metropolitan Management Corp.*, 391 F.3d 506, 512 (4th Cir. 2004) (*Price Waterhouse*, and not statutory version, applies to an ADEA claim); *Matima v. Celli*, 228 F.3d 68, 81 (2d Cir. 2000) (*Price Waterhouse* applies to a retaliation claim under Title VII). The major distinction between the two varieties of mixed-motives claims is that an employer/defendant incurs *no* liability at all under *Price Waterhouse* if it proves it would have made the same decision even if the improper factor had not been considered, while under the Civil Rights Act of 1991, the employer merely limits its liability.

3. *After-Acquired Evidence.* In *Price Waterhouse*, the Court considered how to evaluate a case when the employer may have been influenced by both legitimate and illegitimate factors at the time the decision was made. In *McKennon v. Nashville Banner Publishing Co.*, 513 U.S. 352 (1995), the Supreme Court considered what should happen when the timing is different. In *McKennon*, the employer fired the plaintiff because of her age. During discovery, however, the employer learned that the plaintiff had engaged in misconduct at work that would have resulted in her immediate discharge had the employer known about it at the time.

A unanimous Court held that after-acquired evidence of wrongdoing can be a defense, but only if the employer can establish that it "was of such severity that the employee in fact would have been terminated on those grounds alone if the employer had known of it at the time of the discharge." *Id.* at 362-63. The defense operates not as a complete bar, but as a limitation on the relief available:

> The proper boundaries of remedial relief in [these] cases must be addressed by the judicial system in the ordinary course of further decisions, for the factual permutations and the equitable considerations they raise will vary from case to case. We do conclude that here, and as a general rule in cases of this type, neither reinstatement nor front pay is an appropriate remedy. It would be both inequitable and pointless to order the reinstatement of someone the employer would have terminated, and will terminate, in any event and upon lawful grounds.

> The proper measure of backpay presents a more difficult problem. . . . The beginning point in the trial court's formulation of a remedy should be calculation of backpay from the date of the unlawful discharge to the date the new information was discovered. In determining the appropriate order for relief, the court can consider taking into further account extraordinary equitable circumstances that affect the legitimate interests of either party.

Id. at 361-62.

The Court worried that employers might "as a routine matter undertake extensive discovery into an employee's background or performance" in an attempt to establish the defense, but indicated that the availability of attorney's fees and Rule 11 sanctions would be sufficient to "deter most abuses." *Id.* at 363.

2. SYSTEMIC DISPARATE TREATMENT

HAZELWOOD SCHOOL DISTRICT v. UNITED STATES
United States Supreme Court
433 U.S. 299 (1977)

Mr. Justice Stewart delivered the opinion of the Court.

The petitioner Hazelwood School District covers 78 square miles in the northern part of St. Louis County, Mo. In 1973 the Attorney General brought this lawsuit against Hazelwood and various of its officials, alleging that they were engaged in a "pattern or practice" of employment discrimination in violation of Title VII of the Civil Rights Act of 1964. . . .

Hazelwood was formed from 13 rural school districts between 1949 and 1951 by a process of annexation. By the 1967-1968 school year, 17,550 students were enrolled in the district, of whom only 59 were Negro; the number of Negro pupils increased to 576 of 25,166 in 1972-1973, a total of just over 2%.

From the beginning, Hazelwood followed relatively unstructured procedures in hiring its teachers. [An application file was kept and when an opening occurred, 3 to 10 applicants would be selected for interviews, generally those who had submitted applications most recently.]

Interviews were conducted by a department chairman, program coordinator, or the principal at the school where the teaching vacancy existed. [E]ach school principal possessed virtually unlimited discretion in hiring teachers for his school. The only general guidance given to the principals was to hire the "most competent" person available, and such intangibles as "personality, disposition, appearance, poise, voice, articulation, and ability to deal with people" counted heavily. The principal's choice was routinely honored by Hazelwood's Superintendent and the Board of Education.

In the early 1960's Hazelwood found it necessary to recruit new teachers, and for that purpose members of its staff visited a number of colleges and universities in Missouri and bordering States. All the institutions visited were predominantly white, and Hazelwood did not seriously recruit at either of the two predominantly Negro four-year colleges in Missouri.[4] As a buyer's market began to develop for public school teachers, Hazelwood curtailed its recruiting efforts. For the 1971-1972 school year, 3,127 persons applied for only 234 teaching vacancies; for the 1972-1973 school year, there were 2,373 applications for 282 vacancies. A number of the applicants who were not hired were Negroes.

---

[4] One of those two schools was never visited even though it was located in nearby St. Louis. The second was briefly visited on one occasion, but no potential applicant was interviewed.

Hazelwood hired its first Negro teacher in 1969. The number of Negro faculty members gradually increased in successive years: 6 of 957 in the 1970 school year; 16 of 1,107 by the end of the 1972 school year; 22 of 1,231 in the 1973 school year. By comparison, according to 1970 census figures, of more than 19,000 teachers employed in that year in the St. Louis area, 15.4% were Negro. That percentage figure included the St. Louis City School District, which in recent years has followed a policy of attempting to maintain a 50% Negro teaching staff. Apart from that school district, 5.7% of the teachers in the county were Negro in 1970. . . .

Drawing upon these historic facts, the Government mounted its "pattern or practice" attack in the District Court upon four different fronts. It adduced evidence of (1) a history of alleged racially discriminatory practices, (2) statistical disparities in hiring, (3) the standardless and largely subjective hiring procedures, and (4) specific instances of alleged discrimination against 55 unsuccessful Negro applicants for teaching jobs. Hazelwood offered virtually no additional evidence in response, relying instead on evidence introduced by the Government, perceived deficiencies in the Government's case, and its own officially promulgated policy "to hire all teachers on the basis of training, preparation and recommendations, regardless of race, color or creed."

The District Court ruled that the Government had failed to establish a pattern or practice of discrimination. The court was unpersuaded by the alleged history of discrimination, noting that no dual school system had ever existed in Hazelwood. The statistics showing that relatively small numbers of Negroes were employed as teachers were found nonprobative, on the ground that the percentage of Negro pupils in Hazelwood was similarly small. The court found nothing illegal or suspect in the teacher-hiring procedures that Hazelwood had followed. Finally, the court reviewed the evidence in the 55 cases of alleged individual discrimination, and after stating that the burden of proving intentional discrimination was on the Government, it found that this burden had not been sustained in a single instance. Hence, the court entered judgment for the defendants.

The Court of Appeals for the Eighth Circuit reversed. . . . We granted certiorari. . . .

This Court's recent consideration in *International Brotherhood of Teamsters v. United States,* 431 U.S. 324 (1977), of the role of statistics in pattern-or-practice suits under Title VII provides substantial guidance in evaluating the arguments advanced by the petitioners. In that case we stated that it is the Government's burden to "establish by a preponderance of the evidence that racial discrimination was the [employer's] standard operating procedure, the regular rather than the unusual practice." We also noted that statistics can be an important source of proof in employment discrimination cases, since

"absent explanation, it is ordinarily to be expected that nondiscriminatory hiring practices will in time result in a work force more or less representative of the racial and ethnic composition of the population in the community from which employees are hired. Evidence of long-lasting and gross disparity between the composition of a work force and that of the general population thus may be significant even though

§ 703(j) makes clear that Title VII imposes no requirement that a work force mirror the general population." *Id., at* 340 n.20.

Where gross statistical disparities can be shown, they alone may in a proper case constitute *prima facie* proof of a pattern or practice of discrimination. *Teamsters, supra,* 431 U.S. at 339.

There can be no doubt, in light of the *Teamsters* case, that the District Court's comparison of Hazelwood's teacher work force to its student population fundamentally misconceived the role of statistics in employment discrimination cases. The Court of Appeals was correct in the view that a proper comparison was between the racial composition of Hazelwood's teaching staff and the racial composition of the qualified public school teacher population in the relevant labor market.[13] The percentage of Negroes on Hazelwood's teaching staff in 1972-1973 was 1.4% and in 1973-1974 it was 1.8%. By contrast, the percentage of qualified Negro teachers in the area was, according to the 1970 census, at least 5.7%.[14] Although these differences were on their face substantial, the Court of Appeals erred in substituting its judgment for that of the District Court and holding that the Government had conclusively proved its "pattern or practice" lawsuit.

The Court of Appeals totally disregarded the possibility that this *prima facie* statistical proof in the record might at the trial court level be rebutted by statistics dealing with Hazelwood's hiring after it became subject to Title VII. Racial discrimination by public employers was not made illegal under Title VII until March 24, 1972. A public employer who from that date forward made

---

[13] In *Teamsters,* the comparison between the percentage of Negroes on the employer's work force and the percentage in the general areawide population was highly probative, because the job skill there involved — the ability to drive a truck — is one that many persons possess or can fairly readily acquire. When special qualifications are required to fill particular jobs, comparisons to the general population (rather than to the smaller group of individuals who possess the necessary qualifications) may have little probative value. The comparative statistics introduced by the Government in the District Court, however, were properly limited to public school teachers. . . .

Although the petitioners concede as a general matter the probative force of the comparative work-force statistics, they object to the Court of Appeals' heavy reliance on these data on the ground that applicant-flow data, showing the actual percentage of white and Negro applicants for teaching positions at Hazelwood, would be firmer proof. . . . [T]here was no clear evidence of such statistics. We leave it to the District Court on remand to determine whether competent proof of those data can be adduced. If so, it would, of course, be very relevant.

[14] As is discussed below, the Government contends that a comparative figure of 15.4%, rather than 5.7%, is the appropriate one. But even assuming, *arguendo,* that the 5.7% figure urged by the petitioners is correct, the disparity between that figure and the percentage of Negroes on Hazelwood's teaching staff would be more than fourfold for the 1972-1973 school year, and threefold for the 1973-1974 school year. A precise method of measuring the significance of such statistical disparities was explained in *Castaneda v. Partida,* 430 U.S. 482, 496-497, n.17. It involves calculation of the "standard deviation" as a measure of predicted fluctuations from the expected value of a sample. Using the 5.7% figure as the basis for calculating the expected value, the expected number of Negroes on the Hazelwood teaching staff would be roughly 63 in 1972-1973 and 70 in 1973-1974. The observed number in those years was 16 and 22, respectively. The difference between the observed and expected values was more than six standard deviations in 1972-1973 and more than five standard deviations in 1973-1974. The Court in *Castaneda* noted that "[a]s a general rule for such large samples, if the difference between the expected value and the observed number is greater than two or three standard deviations," then the hypothesis that teachers were hired without regard to race would be suspect. 430 U.S., at 497 n.17.

all its employment decisions in a wholly nondiscriminatory way would not violate Title VII even if it had formerly maintained an all-white work force by purposefully excluding Negroes.[15] For this reason, the Court cautioned in the *Teamsters* opinion that once a *prima facie* case has been established by statistical work-force disparities, the employer must be given an opportunity to show that "the claimed discriminatory pattern is a product of pre-Act hiring rather than unlawful post-Act discrimination." 431 U.S., at 360.

The record in this case showed that for the 1972-1973 school year, Hazelwood hired 282 new teachers, 10 [of] whom (3.5%) were Negroes; for the following school year it hired 123 new teachers, 5 of whom (4.1%) were Negroes. Over the two-year period, Negroes constituted a total of 15 of the 405 new teachers hired (3.7%). Although the Court of Appeals briefly mentioned these data in reciting the facts, it wholly ignored them in discussing whether the Government had shown a pattern or practice of discrimination. And it gave no consideration at all to the possibility that post-Act data as to the number of Negroes hired compared to the total number of Negro applicants might tell a totally different story.

What the hiring figures prove obviously depends upon the figures to which they are compared. The Court of Appeals accepted the Government's argument that the relevant comparison was to the labor market area of St. Louis County and the city of St. Louis, in which, according to the 1970 census, 15.4% of all teachers were Negro. The propriety of that comparison was vigorously disputed by the petitioners, who urged that because the city of St. Louis has made special attempts to maintain a 50% Negro teaching staff, inclusion of that school district in the relevant market area distorts the comparison. Were that argument accepted, the percentage of Negro teachers in the relevant labor market area (St. Louis County alone) as shown in the 1970 census would be 5.7% rather than 15.4%.

The difference between these figures may well be important; the disparity between 3.7% (the percentage of Negro teachers hired by Hazelwood in 1972-1973 and 1973-1974) and 5.7% may be sufficiently small to weaken the Government's other proof, while the disparity between 3.7% and 15.4% may be sufficiently large to reinforce it.[17] In determining which of the two figures

---

[15] This is not to say that evidence of pre-Act discrimination can never have any probative force. Proof that an employer engaged in racial discrimination prior to the effective date of Title VII might in some circumstances support the inference that such discrimination continued, particularly where relevant aspects of the decisionmaking process had undergone little change. And, of course, a public employer even before the extension of Title VII in 1972 was subject to the command of the Fourteenth Amendment not to engage in purposeful racial discrimination.

[17] Indeed, under the statistical methodology explained in *Castaneda,* [*supra* note 14,] the difference between using 15.4% and 5.7% as the areawide figure would be significant. If the 15.4% figure is taken as the basis for comparison, the expected number of Negro teachers hired by Hazelwood in 1972-1973 would be 43 (rather than the actual figure of 10) of a total of 282, a difference of more than five standard deviations; the expected number of 1973-1974 would be 19 (rather than the actual figure 5) of a total of 123, a difference of more than three standard deviations. For the two years combined, the difference between the observed number of 15 Negro teachers hired (of a total of 405) would vary from the expected number of 62 by more than six standard deviations. Because a fluctuation of more than two or three standard deviations would undercut the hypothesis that decisions were being made randomly with respect to race, each of these statistical comparisons would reinforce rather than rebut the Government's other proof.

or, very possibly, what intermediate figure provides the most accurate basis for comparison to the hiring figures at Hazelwood, it will be necessary to evaluate such considerations as (i) whether the racially based hiring policies of the St. Louis City School District were in effect as far back as 1970, the year in which the census figures were taken; (ii) to what extent those policies have changed the racial composition of that district's teaching staff from what it would otherwise have been; (iii) to what extent St. Louis' recruitment policies have diverted to the city, teachers who might otherwise have applied to Hazelwood; (iv) to what extent Negro teachers employed by the city would prefer employment in other districts such as Hazelwood; and (v) what the experience in other school districts in St. Louis County indicates about the validity of excluding the City School District from the relevant labor market.

It is thus clear that a determination of the appropriate comparative figures in this case will depend upon further evaluation by the trial court. As this Court admonished in *Teamsters*: "[S]tatistics . . . come in infinite variety. . . . [T]heir usefulness depends on all of the surrounding facts and circumstances." 431 U.S., at 340. Only the trial court is in a position to make the appropriate determination after further findings. And only after such a determination is made can a foundation be established for deciding whether or not Hazelwood engaged in a pattern or practice of racial discrimination in its employment practices in violation of the law.

We hold, therefore, that the Court of Appeals erred in disregarding the post-Act hiring statistics in the record, and that it should have remanded the case to the District Court for further findings as to the relevant labor market area and for an ultimate determination of whether Hazelwood engaged in a pattern or practice of employment discrimination after March 24, 1972. Accordingly, the judgment is vacated, and the case is remanded to the District Court for further proceedings consistent with this opinion.

It is so ordered.

Mr. Justice White, concurring in [the opinion.]

I join the Court's opinion . . . but with reservations with respect to the relative neglect of applicant pool data in finding a *prima facie* case of employment discrimination and heavy reliance on the disparity between the areawide percentage of black public school teachers and the percentage of blacks on Hazelwood's teaching staff. Since the issue is whether Hazelwood discriminated against blacks in hiring after Title VII became applicable to it

---

If, however, the 5.7% areawide figure is used, the expected number of Negro teachers hired in 1972-1973 would be roughly 16, less than two standard deviations from the observed number of 10; for 1973-1974, the expected value would be roughly seven, less than one standard deviation from the observed value of 5; and for the two years combined, the expected value of 23 would be less than two standard deviations from the observed total of 15. A more precise method of analyzing these statistics confirms the results of the standard deviation analysis. *See* F. Mosteller, R. Rourke, & G. Thomas, Probabilty with Statistical Applications 494 (2d ed. 1970).

These observations are not intended to suggest that precise calculations of statistical significance are necessary in employing statistical proof, but merely to highlight the importance of the choice of the relevant labor market area.

in 1972, perhaps the Government should have looked initially to Hazelwood's hiring practices in the 1972-1973 and 1973-1974 academic years with respect to the available applicant pool, rather than to history and to comparative workforce statistics from other school districts. Indeed, there is evidence in the record suggesting that Hazelwood, with a black enrollment of only 2%, hired a higher percentage of black applicants than of white applicants for these two years. The Court's opinion, of course, permits Hazelwood to introduce applicant pool data on remand in order to rebut the prima facie case of a discriminatory pattern or practice. This may be the only fair and realistic allocation of the evidence burden, but arguably the United States should have been required to adduce evidence as to the applicant pool before it was entitled to its *prima facie* presumption. At least it might have been required to present some defensible ground for believing that the racial composition of Hazelwood's applicant pool was roughly the same as that for the school districts in the general area, before relying on comparative work-force data to establish its prima facie case.

[MR. JUSTICE BRENNAN also filed a concurring opinion.]

MR. JUSTICE STEVENS, dissenting.

The basic framework in a pattern-or-practice suit brought by the Government under Title VII of the Civil Rights Act of 1964 is the same as that in any other lawsuit. The plaintiff has the burden of proving a *prima facie* case; if he does so, the burden of rebutting that case shifts to the defendant. In this case, since neither party complains that any relevant evidence was excluded, our task is to decide (1) whether the Government's evidence established a *prima facie* case; and (2), if so, whether the remaining evidence is sufficient to carry Hazelwood's burden of rebutting that *prima facie* case.

The first question is clearly answered by the Government's statistical evidence, its historical evidence, and its evidence relating to specific acts of discrimination.

One-third of the teachers hired by Hazelwood resided in the city of St. Louis at the time of their initial employment. . . . [I]t was therefore appropriate to treat the city, as well as the county, as part of the relevant labor market. In that market, 15% of the teachers were black. In the Hazelwood District at the time of trial less than 2% of the teachers were black. An even more telling statistic is that after Title VII became applicable to it, only 3.7% of the new teachers hired by Hazelwood were black. Proof of these gross disparities was in itself sufficient to make out a *prima facie* case of discrimination.

As a matter of history, Hazelwood employed no black teachers until 1969. Both before and after the 1972 amendment making the statute applicable to public school districts, petitioner used a standardless and largely subjective hiring procedure. Since "relevant aspects of the decisionmaking process had undergone little change," it is proper to infer that the pre-Act policy of preferring white teachers continued to influence Hazelwood's hiring practices.[3]

---

[3] . . . Since Hazelwood's hiring before 1972 was so clearly discriminatory, there is some irony in its claim that "Hazelwood continued [after 1972] to select its teachers on the same careful basis that it had relied on before in staffing its growing system." Brief for Petitioners 29-30.

The inference of discrimination was corroborated by post-Act evidence that Hazelwood had refused to hire 16 qualified black applicants for racial reasons. Taking the Government's evidence as a whole, there can be no doubt about the sufficiency of its *prima facie* case. . . .

Hazelwood "offered virtually no additional evidence in response." It challenges the Government's statistical analysis by claiming that the city of St. Louis should be excluded from the relevant market and pointing out that only 5.7% of the teachers in the county (excluding the city) were black. It further argues that the city's policy of trying to maintain a 50% black teaching staff diverted teachers from the county to the city. There are two separate reasons why these arguments are insufficient: they are not supported by the evidence; even if true, they do not overcome the Government's case.

The petitioners offered no evidence concerning wage differentials, commuting problems, or the relative advantages of teaching in an inner-city school as opposed to a suburban school. Without any such evidence in the record, it is difficult to understand why the simple fact that the city was the source of a third of Hazelwood's faculty should not be sufficient to demonstrate that it is a part of the relevant market. . . .

But even if it were proper to exclude the city of St. Louis from the market, the statistical evidence would still tend to prove discrimination. With the city excluded, 5.7% of the teachers in the remaining market were black. On the basis of a random selection, one would therefore expect 5.7% of the 405 teachers hired by Hazelwood in the 1972-1973 and 1973-1974 school years to have been black. But instead of 23 black teachers, Hazelwood hired only 15, less than two-thirds of the expected number. Without the benefit of expert testimony, I would hesitate to infer that the disparity between 23 and 15 is great enough, in itself, to prove discrimination.[5] It is perfectly clear, however, that whatever probative force this disparity has, it tends to prove discrimination and does absolutely nothing in the way of carrying Hazelwood's burden of overcoming the Government's *prima facie* case.

Absolute precision in the analysis of market data is too much to expect. We may fairly assume that a nondiscriminatory selection process would have resulted in the hiring of somewhere between the 15% suggested by the Government and the 5.7% suggested by petitioners, or perhaps 30 or 40 black teachers, instead of the 15 actually hired.[6] On that assumption, the Court of Appeals' determination that there were 16 individual cases of discriminatory refusal to hire black applicants in the post-1972 period seems remarkably accurate.

In sum, the Government is entitled to prevail on the present record. It proved a *prima facie* case, which Hazelwood failed to rebut. [We should not] burden a busy federal court with another trial. . . . It is always possible to

---

[5] After I had drafted this opinion, one of my law clerks advised me that, given the size of the two-year sample, there is only about a 5% likelihood that a disparity this large would be produced by a random selection from the labor pool. If his calculation (which was made using the method described in H. BLALOCK, SOCIAL STATISTICS 151-173 (1972)) is correct, it is easy to understand why Hazelwood offered no expert testimony.

[6] Some of the other school districts in the county have a 10% ratio of blacks on their faculties.

imagine more evidence which could have been offered, but at some point litigation must come to an end.

NOTES

1. *The Inexorable Zero.* In *Teamsters v. United States*, 431 U.S. 324 (1977), the government challenged an employer's record of hiring blacks and Spanish-surnamed persons to positions as line drivers. The employer's actual record of hiring these minorities approached "the inexorable zero": 0.4% of the line drivers were black and 0.3% were Spanish-surnamed. The Court compared that record in the line-driver position to the proportion of minorities employed by the company overall (5% for blacks and 4% for Spanish-surnamed persons) and to the proportion of minorities in the areas from which the company hired (in Atlanta, for example, 22% of the metropolitan area and 51% of the city proper was black). In addition to the statistical evidence, the government presented over forty specific instances of discrimination. The Court held that this evidence was sufficient to support a finding of systemic disparate treatment discrimination.

2. *The Analytical Framework.* *Hazelwood* discusses the three analytical steps in a systemic disparate treatment case. First, the *actual treatment* of the plaintiff group must be determined. In *Hazelwood*, how many black teachers were employed by the school district? Second, the *ideal treatment* of the group — the treatment one would expect in the absence of discrimination — must be determined. In the absence of discrimination, how many black teachers would you expect to see? And third, the actual and ideal treatment must be compared to determine whether any difference is large enough to create an inference of discrimination.

3. *Actual Treatment.* Assume that you represent a rejected female candidate for a tenure-track position on the law school faculty who is claiming that the law school engages in systemic disparate treatment discrimination when hiring faculty. How would you determine the actual treatment of women by the law school? What time frame would you use? What law school employees would you include? Would you include a head law librarian who is a tenured member of the faculty, but who does not teach? How about clinical faculty who have a separate tenure track with different hiring and promotion criteria? Visiting faculty? Legal writing instructors? Adjuncts?

4. *Ideal Treatment.* *Hazelwood* and *Teamsters* identify different pools that can be used to determine ideal treatment. *Teamsters* used the employer's hiring statistics for other positions and general population statistics as indicators of ideal treatment, while one issue in *Hazelwood* was whether the proportion of black teachers in St. Louis City and County or just in the County alone should be used. Justice White argued that the proportion of blacks who *applied* to teach at Hazelwood should be used instead of more general population statistics.

In *Local 28, Sheet Metal Workers' International Ass'n v. EEOC*, 478 U.S. 421 (1986), the Supreme Court accepted a very precise figure (29.23%) as the ideal treatment for a union alleged to have discriminated against black and Hispanic applicants to an apprenticeship program designed to teach sheet metal skills. The expert who produced the precise figure later described her process for determining the ideal treatment:

> Defining a labor pool involves identifying all persons who are ready, willing and able to perform the duties required by the hiring (or admitting) organization. One of the first decisions to make is what the geographic boundaries of the labor pool should be. Having drawn these borders, the analyst may take into account characteristics such as age, labor-force status, education and experience in order to separate those who belong in the labor pool for the given position from those who do not.

> It is reasonable, and therefore conventional, to assume that the relevant labor market for low-to middle-level jobs is fairly local, while the labor market for high-level jobs is national or, perhaps, regional in scope. . . .

> Given the characteristics of the positions under analysis, I decided that the relevant labor pool was a fairly local one, and I considered the New York SMSA [standard metropolitan statistical area] together with several nearby New Jersey SMSAs to be the best measure of it. The defendants' expert agreed that the labor pool was relatively local, and the area he used to define it closely approximated the SMSAs I used. . . .

> We did disagree, however, on whether some counties within the defined boundaries should be given more weight than others. I saw no reason to do so. After all, Manhattan was no farther from the general area of the union's work activity than Suffolk County; the Bronx was no farther than Essex County. Hence, I applied no weighting scheme in calculating the combined SMSAs' availability rate. The defendants' expert, on the other hand, argued that some counties should be given greater weight than others in the calculation of the minority availability rate. Moreover, he argued that each county's weight in the calculation should depend on the portion of the union's journeymen membership residing there.

> The effect of applying such a weighting scheme was to depress seriously the estimated proportion of minorities in the labor pool. Since the membership of the sheet metal workers' union was largely white, and since the sheet metal workers lived in counties with relatively low minority populations, the counties given the heaviest weights in the opposing expert's availability-rate calculation were the counties with the lowest minority availability rates. . . .

> The next question concerned the age dimensions of the pool. Including only those over 25 would have biased the estimated minority availability rate downward. None of the locals allowed individuals over 25 into their apprentice programs. . . . (Because the age distribution of minorities and non-minorities tends to differ, the choice of the relevant labor pool's age dimensions is seldom neutral in its effect on the calculated minority availability rate.)

> A third issue was the labor-force status and occupational dimensions of the relevant labor pool. After defining the pool in terms of its

geographical and age dimension, the expert must decide whether everyone in the specified area and age interval should be included in the labor pool, or whether only some portion of this population should be included. . . .

Economists generally exclude from the relevant pool those classified by the Census Bureau as not in the labor force because individuals so classified have reported themselves as not seeking work. They are not "ready" and "willing," although, for all we know, they are "able." Since it is inaccurate to include those who report themselves as unavailable for work in the labor pool used to calculate the availability rate, only labor-force statistics, not population counts, should be used for such a calculation.

Nor is it sufficiently accurate to use the entire labor force in the specified area and age interval. Some degree of occupational specificity is generally necessary as an indicator of ability and willingness to perform the duties of the position in question. For example, bank tellers do not belong in the relevant labor pool for financial analysts. While they might be ready and willing to do the job, they would generally not be able; they lack the necessary skills. On the other hand, corporate lawyers don't belong in the relevant labor pool for paralegals. While they have the skills for the jobs, they have superior opportunities available to them and would not, in general, supply themselves to it; though "able," they would not generally be "ready" and "willing."

In line with these considerations, I defined the labor pool as consisting only of persons in the labor force. I also chose to specify occupational boundaries narrow enough to exclude those who were not likely to supply themselves as apprentices in sheet metal work and broad enough to include those who might reasonably do so. The category of blue-collar workers satisfied these conditions.

Including the entire population in the area and age group previously specified would have included individuals who were not ready, willing and able to work. Including only sheet metal workers would also have been inappropriate [because, since] minorities were a much smaller proportion of sheet metal workers than of blue-collar workers as a group[, it would have] seriously biased the estimated minority availability rate downward.

The district court accepted a labor-pool specification that included blue-collar workers in the labor force, and only these workers.

Harriet Zellner, *Defining Labor Pools Proves No Easy Task*, NAT'L L.J., Oct. 27, 1986, at 15, 42-43. *

How would you determine the ideal treatment figure in our law school hypothetical?

5. *Analyzing the Difference Between Actual and Ideal Treatment.* As *Hazelwood* indicates, statistics are often used to determine whether the

---

* Reprinted with the permission of *The National Law Journal,* copyright 1986. The New York Law Publishing Company.

difference between actual and ideal treatment is large enough to be probative of discriminatory intent. The binomial distribution formula discussed by the Court tells us how often one would expect to see the actual treatment (or worse) if random selections were made from the ideal treatment pool. The less probable the actual treatment, the more likely it resulted from discrimination. The "two or three standard deviations" rule announced by the Court means that the difference between actual and ideal treatment will be recognized as probative of discrimination if the actual treatment would be seen less than about 1% to 5% of the time, assuming hiring was random as to race.

The binomial distribution formula is:

$$Z = \frac{A - NP}{\sqrt{NP(1 - P)}}$$

where   Z = number of standard deviations
         A = actual number of blacks hired (actual treatment)
         N = total number of people hired   } (N times P is the
         P = proportion of blacks in population   } ideal treatment)

Although this type of analysis is well-accepted in systemic disparate treatment cases, significant questions remain about its appropriateness. *See* David H. Kaye, *Is Proof of Statistical Significance Relevant?*, 61 WASH. L. REV. 1333 (1986); Ramona Paetzold, *Problems With Statistical Significance in Employment Discrimination Litigation*, 26 NEW ENG. L. REV. 395 (1991).

6. *Lawyers, Numbers, and Law Clerks.* Lawyers are not often noted for their expertise in statistics and Supreme Court Justices are no exception. So how were the Justices able to produce an opinion like *Hazelwood*? Justice Blackmun's papers reveal that it was likely the result of happenstance. One of his law clerks that term happened to have a Ph.D. in applied physics (as well as a law degree, of course) and he initiated the sophisticated statistical approach first in *Casteneda*, a jury discrimination case which is cited in *Hazelwood*, and then again in *Hazelwood* itself. The Justices, obviously, had to be convinced that it was correct, but not without some misgivings. For example, when Justice Stewart notified the other Justices that he was adding a citation to the Mosteller statistics book to footnote 17, his concluding sentence was "Please do not ask me to explain it." Stewart J. Schwab & Steven L. Willborn, *The Story of Hazelwood: Employment Discrimination by the Numbers, in* EMPLOYMENT DISCRIMINATION STORIES 37, 46-52 (Joel Wm. Friedman ed., 2006).

Despite the normal wariness of lawyers about numbers, the statistical analysis is not very difficult or mysterious. Using the formula above, and plugging in A = 15 (the actual number of black teachers hired during the relevant time period), N = 405 (the total number of teachers hired), and P = .057 (the percentage of blacks in the pool of teachers, excluding the city), one gets Z = 1.73 standard deviations. One can look up this Z score in a statistical table and discover that there is about an 8% likelihood that a disparity at least this large would occur by random selection. Thus, Justice Stevens' law clerk exaggerated slightly in footnote 5 of the Justice's dissenting opinion, but was basically correct.

If one assumes that P = .154 (the percentage of blacks in the labor pool including the city), the resulting Z score is 6.52 standard deviations. The Court majority did this math in footnote 17, and concluded that this was a sufficient difference to be probative of discrimination.

7. *Individual Relief.* A finding of systemic discrimination creates a presumption that the employer has discriminated against individual members of the protected class. Consequently, individual class members who can show that they were "potential victims" (for example, that they unsuccessfully applied for a job with the employer) are entitled to individual relief, unless the employer can demonstrate that it did not discriminate against them. *See Teamsters v. United States*, 431 U.S. 324, 362 (1977). If a systemic case could be made out in *Hazelwood*, for example, an individual black applicant who could prove that she unsuccessfully applied for a teaching position with Hazelwood during the relevant time period would be presumptively entitled to individual relief such as backpay. The employer could avoid this liability only if it could demonstrate that it did not discriminate against this particular individual — by proving, for example, that there were no job openings at the time, that the applicant was not qualified, or that there was no discrimination for other reasons.

Determining the appropriate remedy after a finding of systemic discrimination is especially problematic in situations where the individual victims either can no longer be identified or no longer desire employment with the discriminating employer. *See, e.g., Hameed v. Iron Workers, Local 396*, 637 F.2d 506 (8th Cir. 1980) (allocating damages across all class members when court could not determine which ones would have received positions in the absence of discrimination); *Local 28, Sheet Metal Workers' Int'l Ass'n v. EEOC*, 478 U.S. 421 (1986) (permitting preferences for minorities who were not actual victims of discrimination when union engaged in egregious discrimination and actual victims could no longer be identified).

8. *Hazelwood and Social Change.* *Hazelwood* opens up the possibility of large-scale litigation and the promise of significant institutional and maybe even social change. Instead of pursuing discrimination individual by individual, *Hazelwood* permits discrimination to be addressed at a structural level. When problems are identified, it might be possible to craft broad-scale remedies that would change corporate culture, open up opportunities, and in the process create significant social change. The actual results, however, appear to be much more limited. Professor Michael Selmi has found that employment-discrimination class actions do not generally have any significant impact on corporate value, do not benefit class members very much, and do little to deter corporate wrong-doing. The winners from these lawsuits, according to Professor Selmi, are plaintiffs' attorneys and groups associated with the diversity industry (such as minority-owned businesses and organizations providing diversity training). Michael Selmi, *The Price of Discrimination: The Nature of Class Action Employment Discrimination Litigation and Its Effects*, 81 Texas L. Rev. 1249 (2003).

3. THE BONA FIDE OCCUPATIONAL QUALIFICATION DEFENSE

The antidiscrimination statutes do not prohibit every instance of employer disparate-treatment discrimination. This section will consider one of the two major exceptions to the general rule of nondiscrimination: employers may rely on suspect criteria when they are very closely related to ability to do the job, the so-called bona fide occupational qualification (BFOQ) defense. The other major exception (affirmative-action programs) will be considered later.

WESTERN AIR LINES, INC. v. CRISWELL
United States Supreme Court
472 U.S. 400 (1985)

JUSTICE STEVENS delivered the opinion of the Court.

The petitioner, Western Air Lines, Inc., requires that its flight engineers retire at age 60. Although the Age Discrimination in Employment Act of 1967 (ADEA) generally prohibits mandatory retirement, . . . the Act provides an exception "where age is a bona fide occupational qualification [BFOQ] reasonably necessary to the normal operation of the particular business." [ADEA, § 4(f)(1).] A jury concluded that Western's mandatory retirement rule did not qualify as a BFOQ even though it purportedly was adopted for safety reasons. The question here is whether the jury was properly instructed on the elements of the BFOQ defense.

I

In its commercial airline operations, Western operates a variety of aircraft, including the Boeing 727 and the McDonnell-Douglas DC-10. These aircraft require three crew members in the cockpit: a captain, a first officer, and a flight engineer. "The 'captain' is the pilot and controls the aircraft. He is responsible for all phases of its operation. The 'first officer' is the copilot and assists the captain. The 'flight engineer' usually monitors a side-facing instrument panel. He does not operate the flight controls unless the captain and the first officer become incapacitated."

A regulation of the Federal Aviation Administration (FAA) prohibits any person from serving as a pilot or first officer on a commercial flight "if that person has reached his 60th birthday." . . . At the same time, the FAA has refused to establish a mandatory retirement age for flight engineers. . . .

In 1978, respondents Criswell and Starley were captains operating DC-10s for Western. Both men celebrated their 60th birthdays in July 1978. Under the collective-bargaining agreement in effect between Western and the union, cockpit crew members could obtain open positions by bidding in order of seniority. In order to avoid mandatory retirement under the FAA's under-age-60 rule for pilots, Criswell and Starley applied for reassignment as flight engineers. Western denied both requests. . . . [R]espondent Ron, a career flight engineer, was also retired in 1978 after his 60th birthday.

Criswell, Starley, and Ron brought this action against Western contending that the under-age-60 qualification for the position of flight engineer violated the ADEA. In the District Court, Western defended, in part, on the theory that the age-60 rule is a BFOQ "reasonably necessary" to the safe operation of the airline. . . .

As the District Court summarized, the evidence at trial established that the flight engineer's "normal duties are less critical to the safety of flight than those of a pilot." The flight engineer, however, does have critical functions in emergency situations and, of course, might cause considerable disruption in the event of his own medical emergency.

The actual capabilities of persons over age 60, and the ability to detect disease or a precipitous decline in their faculties, were the subject of conflicting medical testimony. Western's expert witness, a former FAA Deputy Federal Air Surgeon, was especially concerned about the possibility of a "cardiovascular event" such as a heart attack. He testified that "with advancing age the likelihood of onset of disease increases and that in persons over age 60 it could not be predicted whether and when such diseases would occur."

The plaintiffs' experts, on the other hand, testified that physiological deterioration is caused by disease, not aging, and that "it was feasible to determine on the basis of individual medical examinations whether flight deck crew members, including those over age 60, were physically qualified to continue to fly." . . .

III

In *Usery v. Tamiami Trail Tours, Inc.,* 531 F.2d 224 (1976), the Court of Appeals for the Fifth Circuit was called upon to evaluate the merits of a BFOQ defense to a claim of age discrimination. Tamiami Trail Tours, Inc., had a policy of refusing to hire persons over-age-40 as intercity bus drivers. At trial, the bus company introduced testimony supporting its theory that the hiring policy was a BFOQ based upon safety considerations — the need to employ persons who have a low risk of accidents. In evaluating this contention, the Court of Appeals drew on its Title VII precedents, and concluded that two inquiries were relevant.

First, the court recognized that some job qualifications may be so peripheral to the central mission of the employer's business that *no* age discrimination can be "reasonably *necessary* to the normal operation of the particular business."[18] [ADEA, § 4(f)(1).] The bus company justified the age qualification for hiring its drivers on safety considerations, but the court concluded that this claim was to be evaluated under an objective standard:

> [T]he job qualifications which the employer invokes to justify his discrimination must be *reasonably necessary* to the essence of his business — here, the *safe* transportation of bus passengers from one point

---

[18] *Diaz v. Pan American World Airways, Inc.,* 442 F.2d 385 (5th Cir.), *cert. denied,* 404 U.S. 950 (1971), provided authority for this proposition. In *Diaz* the court had rejected Pan American's claim that a female-only qualification for the position of in-flight cabin attendant was a BFOQ under Title VII. The District Court had upheld the qualification as a BFOQ finding that the airline's passengers preferred the "pleasant environment" and the "cosmetic effect" provided by female attendants, and that most men were unable to perform effectively the "non-mechanical functions" of the job. The Court of Appeals rejected the BFOQ defense concluding that these considerations "are tangential to the essence of the business involved."

to another. The greater the safety factor, measured by the likelihood of harm and the probable severity of that harm in case of an accident, the more stringent may be the job qualifications designed to insure safe driving.

This inquiry "adjusts to the safety factor" by ensuring that the employer's restrictive job qualifications are "reasonably necessary" to further the overriding interest in public safety. In *Tamiami,* the court noted that no one had seriously challenged the bus company's safety justification for hiring drivers with a low risk of having accidents.

Second, the court recognized that the ADEA requires that age qualifications be something more than "convenient" or "reasonable"; they must be "reasonably necessary . . . to the particular business," and this is only so when the employer is compelled to rely on age as a proxy for the safety-related job qualifications validated in the first inquiry.[19] This showing could be made in two ways. The employer could establish that it " 'had reasonable cause to believe, that is, a factual basis for believing, that all or substantially all [persons over the age qualifications] would be unable to perform safely and efficiently the duties of the job involved.' " In *Tamiami,* the employer did not seek to justify its hiring qualification under this standard.

Alternatively, the employer could establish that age was a legitimate proxy for the safety-related job qualifications by proving that it is " 'impossible or highly impractical' " to deal with the older employees on an individualized basis. "One method by which the employer can carry this burden is to establish that some members of the discriminated-against class possess a trait precluding safe and efficient job performance that cannot be ascertained by means other than knowledge of the applicant's membership in the class." In *Tamiami,* the medical evidence on this point was conflicting, but the District Court had found that individual examinations could not determine which individuals over the age of 40 would be unable to operate the buses safely. The Court of Appeals found that this finding of fact was not "clearly erroneous," and affirmed the District Court's judgment for the bus company on the BFOQ defense. . . .

Every Court of Appeals that has confronted a BFOQ defense based on safety considerations has analyzed the problem consistently with the *Tamiami* standard. An EEOC regulation embraces the same criteria. Considering the narrow language of the BFOQ exception, the parallel treatment of such questions under Title VII, and the uniform application of the standard by the federal courts, the EEOC, and Congress, we conclude that this two-part inquiry properly identifies the relevant considerations for resolving a BFOQ defense to an age-based qualification purportedly justified by considerations of safety.

---

19 *Weeks v. Southern Bell Telephone & Telegraph Co.,* 408 F.2d 228 (5th Cir. 1969), provided authority for this proposition. In *Weeks* the court rejected Southern Bell's claim that a male-only qualification for the position of switchman was a BFOQ under Title VII. Southern Bell argued, and the District Court had found, that the job was "strenuous," but the court observed that that "finding is extremely vague." The court rejected the BFOQ defense concluding that "using these class stereotypes denies desirable positions to a great many women perfectly capable of performing the duties involved." Moreover, the employer had made no showing that it was "impossible or highly impractical to deal with women on an individualized basis."

IV

In this Court, Western . . . acknowledges that the *Tamiami* standard identifies the relevant general inquiries that must be made in evaluating the BFOQ defense. However, Western claims that in several respects the instructions given below were insufficiently protective of public safety. . . .

Reasonably Necessary Job Qualifications

Western relied on two different kinds of job qualifications to justify its mandatory retirement policy. First, it argued that flight engineers should have a low risk of incapacitation or psychological and physiological deterioration. At this vague level of analysis respondents have not seriously disputed — nor could they — that the qualification of good health for a vital crew member is reasonably necessary to the essence of the airline's operations. Instead, they have argued that age is not a necessary proxy for that qualification.

On a more specific level, Western argues that flight engineers must meet the same stringent qualifications as pilots, and that it was therefore quite logical to extend to flight engineers the FAA's age-60 retirement rule for pilots. Although the FAA's rule for pilots, adopted for safety reasons, is relevant evidence in the airline's BFOQ defense, it is not to be accorded conclusive weight. The extent to which the rule is probative varies with the weight of the evidence supporting its safety rationale and "the congruity between the . . . occupations at issue." In this case, the evidence clearly established that the FAA, Western, and other airlines all recognized that the qualifications for a flight engineer were less rigorous than those required for a pilot.[28]

In the absence of persuasive evidence supporting its position, Western nevertheless argues that the jury should have been instructed to defer to "Western's selection of job qualifications for the position of [flight engineer] that are reasonable in light of the safety risks." This proposal is plainly at odds with Congress' decision, in adopting the ADEA, to subject such management decisions to a test of objective justification in a court of law. The BFOQ standard adopted in the statute is one of "reasonable necessity," not reasonableness.

In adopting that standard, Congress did not ignore the public interest in safety. That interest is adequately reflected in instructions that track the language of the statute. When an employer establishes that a job qualification has been carefully formulated to respond to documented concerns for public safety, it will not be overly burdensome to persuade a trier of fact that the qualification is "reasonably necessary" to safe operation of the business. The uncertainty implicit in the concept of managing safety risks always makes it "reasonably necessary" to err on the side of caution in a close case. The employer cannot be expected to establish the risk of an airline accident "to a certainty, for certainty would require running the risk until a tragic accident

---

[28] As the Court of Appeals noted, the "jury heard testimony that Western itself allows a captain under the age of sixty who cannot, for health reasons, continue to fly as a captain or co-pilot to downbid to a position as second officer. [In addition,] half the pilots flying in the United States are flying for major airlines which do not require second officers to retire at the age of sixty, and . . . there are over 200 such second officers currently flying on wide-bodied aircraft."

would prove that the judgment was sound." *Usery v. Tamiami Trail Tours, Inc.*, 531 F.2d, at 238. When the employer's argument has a credible basis in the record, it is difficult to believe that a jury of laypersons — many of whom no doubt have flown or could expect to fly on commercial air carriers — would not defer in a close case to the airline's judgment. Since the instructions in this case would not have prevented the airline from raising this contention to the jury in closing argument, we are satisfied that the verdict is a consequence of a defect in Western's proof rather than a defect in the trial court's instructions. . . .

Age as a Proxy for Job Qualifications

Western contended below that the ADEA only requires that the employer establish "a rational basis in fact" for believing that identification of those persons lacking suitable qualifications cannot occur on an individualized basis. This "rational basis in fact" standard would have been tantamount to an instruction to return a verdict in the defendant's favor. Because that standard conveys a meaning that is significantly different from that conveyed by the statutory phrase "reasonably necessary," it was correctly rejected by the trial court.

Western argues that a "rational basis" standard should be adopted because medical disputes can never be proved "to a certainty" and because juries should not be permitted "to resolve bona fide conflicts among medical experts respecting the adequacy of individualized testing." The jury, however, need not be convinced beyond all doubt that medical testing is impossible, but only that the proposition is true "on a preponderance of the evidence." Moreover, Western's attack on the wisdom of assigning the resolution of complex questions to 12 laypersons is inconsistent with the structure of the ADEA. Congress expressly decided that problems involving age discrimination in employment should be resolved on a "case-by-case basis" by proof to a jury.

The "rational basis" standard is also inconsistent with the preference for individual evaluation expressed in the language and legislative history of the ADEA.[36] Under the Act, employers are to evaluate employees between the ages of 40 and 70[*] on their merits and not their age. In the BFOQ defense, Congress provided a limited exception to this general principle, but required that employers validate any discrimination as "reasonably necessary to the normal operation of the particular business." It might well be "rational" to require mandatory retirement at *any* age less than 70, but that result would not comply with Congress' direction that employers must justify the rationale for the age chosen. Unless an employer can establish a substantial basis for believing that all or nearly all employees above an age lack the qualifications required for the position, the age selected for mandatory retirement less than 70 must be an age at which it is highly impractical for the employer to insure by individual testing that its employees will have the necessary qualifications for the job. . . .

---

[36] Indeed, under a "rational basis" standard a jury might well consider that its "inquiry is at an end" with an expert witness' articulation of any "plausible reaso[n]" for the employer's decision.

[*] Subsequent to this case, in 1987, the ADEA was amended to expand its protections beyond age 70. As a result, the ADEA currently protects all covered employees age 40 and older.

When an employee covered by the Act is able to point to reputable businesses in the same industry that choose to eschew reliance on mandatory retirement earlier than age 70, when the employer itself relies on individualized testing in similar circumstances, and when the administrative agency with primary responsibility for maintaining airline safety has determined that individualized testing is not impractical for the relevant position, the employer's attempt to justify its decision on the basis of the contrary opinion of experts — solicited for the purposes of litigation — is hardly convincing on any objective standard short of complete deference. Even in cases involving public safety, the ADEA plainly does not permit the trier of fact to give complete deference to the employer's decision.

The judgment of the Court of Appeals is

Affirmed.

Justice Powell took no part in the decision of this case.

NOTES

1. *Uses and Limits of the BFOQ Defense.* The BFOQ defense applies only when an employer explicitly relies on an otherwise prohibited status to make an employment decision. In *Criswell*, for example, the employer explicitly relied on age (a prohibited status) to decide who was eligible for flight engineer positions. As a practical matter, the BFOQ defense does not arise in cases in which the employer denies the existence of discrimination. An employer, for example, would be hard put to prove that only males could do a particular job, while at the same time claiming that sex was not a factor in its hiring decisions.

Discrimination on the basis of race or color cannot be justified using the BFOQ defense. *See* Title VII, § 703(e). In practice, most BFOQ cases involve either age or sex discrimination.

2. *The Essence of the Job.* The basic rationale for the BFOQ defense becomes most apparent through extreme examples — employers who need sperm or egg donors or wet nurses. Determining the relevance of sex to the essence of the job in such cases is not hard. Obviously, the problems occur at other points on the continuum. How persuasive would you find the following justification by an employer who refused to hire female guards in a male, maximum-security penitentiary?

> The likelihood that inmates [all of whom are deprived of a normal heterosexual environment and some of whom have criminally assaulted women in the past] would assault a woman because she was a woman would pose a real threat not only to the victim of the assault but also to the basic control of the penitentiary and protection of its inmates and the other security personnel. The employee's very womanhood would thus directly undermine her capacity to provide the security that is the essence of a correctional counselor's responsibility.

Dothard v. Rawlinson, 433 U.S. 321, 336 (1977) (permitting prison to hire only males).

3. *Customer Preferences.* Many of the difficult cases involve the preferences of customers for employees of a particular sex or age. In one of the early cases, relied on in *Criswell*, a court rejected the claim by an airline that its practice of hiring only female stewardesses was justified because of the preferences of airline passengers. *Diaz v. Pan Am. World Airways, Inc., supra.* But to what extent should employers be allowed to rely on customer preferences:

(a) When there is a close tie to job performance? *Compare Fernandez v. Wynn Oil Co.*, 653 F.2d 1273 (9th Cir. 1981) (reluctance of Latin American and Southeast Asian customers to conduct business with women did not justify company's failure to promote woman to international marketing position), *with EEOC v. University of Tex. Health Science Ctr.*, 710 F.2d 1091 (5th Cir. 1983) (employer could hire only people under age forty-five as campus police officers because they are better able to deal with students).

(b) When privacy interests of the customer are present? *Compare Fesel v. Masonic Home of Del., Inc.*, 447 F. Supp. 1346 (D. Del. 1978), *aff'd,* 591 F.2d 1334 (3d Cir. 1979) (employer refusal to assign male nursing aides to attend to female nursing home residents justified by BFOQ because of privacy interests of residents), *with Spragg v. Shore Care*, 679 A.2d 685 (N.J. Super. Ct. App. Div. 1996) (upholding jury verdict that BFOQ did not justify policy of assigning male home health aides to male patients only, despite privacy interests of female patients).

(c) When a protected status relates to authenticity? *See* EEOC's Sex Discrimination Guidelines, 29 C.F.R. § 1604.2 (sex can be a BFOQ if "necessary for the purpose of authenticity or genuineness . . . *e.g.*, for an actor or actress"). *Cf. Cook v. Babbitt*, 819 F. Supp. 1, 16 (D.D.C. 1993) (if asserted, interest in authenticity may have justified policy of excluding women from portraying soldiers in Civil War reenactments).

(d) When customers are especially adamant about their preferences? *Kern v. Dynalectron Corp.*, 577 F. Supp. 1196 (N.D. Tex. 1983), *aff'd,* 746 F.2d 810 (5th Cir. 1984) (employer requirement that pilots be Moslem justified by BFOQ because pilots were required to fly to Mecca in Saudi Arabia where non-Moslem pilots, if caught, are beheaded).

(e) When employers claim they need to be especially sensitive to customer preferences? *Ferrill v. Parker Group, Inc.*, 967 F. Supp. 472 (N.D. Ala. 1997) (Title VII violated when company making "get out the vote" calls for political candidates matched white callers to white voters and black callers to black voters); *Wilson v. Southwest Airlines Co.*, 517 F. Supp. 292 (N.D. Tex. 1981) (no BFOQ for female flight attendants even though company claims they were an important part of its marketing strategy).

4. *"Protecting" Women from Harm.* Applying the BFOQ also becomes problematic when employers exclude a protected class for "good" reasons that do not relate to ability to do the job. In *UAW v. Johnson Controls*, 499 U.S. 187 (1991), for example, the employer barred all women, except those whose infertility was medically documented, from jobs involving exposure to lead at levels that might be dangerous to fetuses. The Court held that the BFOQ defense did not apply; it only permits employers to discriminate against women who are unable to perform their job duties. Here the women could perform their job duties, albeit at some added risk to their fetuses should they become pregnant.

B. DISPARATE IMPACT

GRIGGS v. DUKE POWER CO.
United States Supreme Court
401 U.S. 424 (1971)

MR. CHIEF JUSTICE BURGER delivered the opinion of the Court.

We granted the writ in this case to resolve the question whether an employer is prohibited by the Civil Rights Act of 1964, Title VII, from requiring a high school education or passing of a standardized general intelligence test as a condition of employment in or transfer to jobs when (a) neither standard is shown to be significantly related to successful job performance, (b) both requirements operate to disqualify Negroes at a substantially higher rate than white applicants, and (c) the jobs in question formerly had been filled only by white employees as part of a longstanding practice of giving preference to whites.

Congress provided, in Title VII of the Civil Rights Act of 1964, for class actions for enforcement of provisions of the Act and this proceeding was brought by a group of incumbent Negro employees against Duke Power Company. All the petitioners are employed at the Company's Dan River Steam Station, a power generating facility located at Draper, North Carolina. At the time this action was instituted, the Company had 95 employees at the Dan River Station, 14 of whom were Negroes; 13 of these are petitioners here.

The District Court found that prior to July 2, 1965, the effective date of the Civil Rights Act of 1964, the Company openly discriminated on the basis of race in the hiring and assigning of employees at its Dan River plant. The plant was organized into five operating departments: (1) Labor, (2) Coal Handling, (3) Operations, (4) Maintenance, and (5) Laboratory and Test. Negroes were employed only in the Labor Department where the highest paying jobs paid less than the lowest paying jobs in the other four "operating" departments in which only whites were employed. Promotions were normally made within each department on the basis of job seniority. Transferees into a department usually began in the lowest position.

In 1955 the Company instituted a policy of requiring a high school education for initial assignment to any department except Labor, and for transfer from the Coal Handling to any "inside" department (Operations, Maintenance, or Laboratory). When the Company abandoned its policy of restricting Negroes to the Labor Department in 1965, completion of high school also was made a prerequisite to transfer from Labor to any other department. From the time the high school requirement was instituted to the time of trial, however, white employees hired before the time of the high school education requirement continued to perform satisfactorily and achieve promotions in the "operating" departments. Findings on this score are not challenged.

The Company added a further requirement for new employees on July 2, 1965, the date on which Title VII became effective. To qualify for placement in any but the Labor Department it became necessary to register satisfactory scores on two professionally prepared aptitude tests, as well as to have a high school education. Completion of high school alone continued to render employees eligible for transfer to the four desirable departments from which Negroes had been excluded if the incumbent had been employed prior to the time of the new requirement. In September 1965 the Company began to permit incumbent employees who lacked a high school education to qualify for transfer from Labor or Coal Handling to an "inside" job by passing two tests — the Wonderlic Personnel Test, which purports to measure general intelligence, and the Bennett Mechanical Comprehension Test. Neither was directed or intended to measure the ability to learn to perform a particular job or category of jobs. The requisite scores used for both initial hiring and transfer approximated the national median for high school graduates.[3] . . .

The objective of Congress in the enactment of Title VII is plain from the language of the statute. It was to achieve equality of employment opportunities and remove barriers that have operated in the past to favor an identifiable group of white employees over other employees. Under the Act, practices, procedures, or tests neutral on their face, and even neutral in terms of intent, cannot be maintained if they operate to "freeze" the status quo of prior discriminatory employment practices.

The Court of Appeals' opinion, and the partial dissent, agreed that, on the record in the present case, "whites register far better on the Company's alternative requirements" than Negroes.[6] This consequence would appear to be directly traceable to race. Basic intelligence must have the means of articulation to manifest itself fairly in a testing process. Because they are Negroes, petitioners have long received inferior education in segregated schools. . . . Congress did not intend by Title VII, however, to guarantee a job to every person regardless of qualifications. In short, the Act does not command that any person be hired simply because he was formerly the subject of discrimination, or because he is a member of a minority group. Discriminatory preference for any group, minority or majority, is precisely and only what Congress has proscribed. What is required by Congress is the removal of artificial, arbitrary, and unnecessary barriers to employment when the barriers operate invidiously to discriminate on the basis of racial or other impermissible classification.

Congress has now provided that tests or criteria for employment or promotion may not provide equality of opportunity merely in the sense of the fabled offer of milk to the stork and the fox. On the contrary, Congress has now required that the posture and condition of the job-seeker be taken into account. It has — to resort again to the fable — provided that the vessel in which the

---

[3] The test standards are thus more stringent than the high school requirement, since they would screen out approximately half of all high school graduates.

[6] In North Carolina, 1960 census statistics show that, while 34% of white males had completed high school, only 12% of Negro males had done so. Similarly, with respect to standardized tests, the EEOC in one case found that use of a battery of tests, including the Wonderlic and Bennett tests used by the Company in the instant case, resulted in 58% of whites passing the tests, as compared with only 6% of the blacks.

milk is proffered be one all seekers can use. The Act proscribes not only overt discrimination but also practices that are fair in form, but discriminatory in operation. The touchstone is business necessity. If an employment practice which operates to exclude Negroes cannot be shown to be related to job performance, the practice is prohibited.

On the record before us, neither the high school completion requirement nor the general intelligence test is shown to bear a demonstrable relationship to successful performance of the jobs for which it was used. Both were adopted, as the Court of Appeals noted, without meaningful study of their relationship to job-performance ability. Rather, a vice president of the Company testified, the requirements were instituted on the Company's judgment that they generally would improve the overall quality of the work force. The evidence, however, shows that employees who have not completed high school or taken the tests have continued to perform satisfactorily and make progress in departments for which the high school and test criteria are now used. . . .

The Court of Appeals held that the Company had adopted the diploma and test requirements without any "intention to discriminate against Negro employees." We do not suggest that either the District Court or the Court of Appeals erred in examining the employer's intent; but good intent or absence of discriminatory intent does not redeem employment procedures or testing mechanisms that operate as "built-in headwinds" for minority groups and are unrelated to measuring job capability.

The Company's lack of discriminatory intent is suggested by special efforts to help the undereducated employees through Company financing of two-thirds the cost of tuition for high school training. But Congress directed the thrust of the Act to the consequences of employment practices, not simply the motivation. More than that, Congress has placed on the employer the burden of showing that any given requirement must have a manifest relationship to the employment in question. . . .

Nothing in the Act precludes the use of testing or measuring procedures; obviously they are useful. What Congress has forbidden is giving these devices and mechanisms controlling force unless they are demonstrably a reasonable measure of job performance. Congress has not commanded that the less qualified be preferred over the better qualified simply because of minority origins. Far from disparaging job qualifications as such, Congress has made such qualifications the controlling factor, so that race, religion, nationality, and sex become irrelevant. What Congress has commanded is that any tests used must measure the person for the job and not the person in the abstract.

The judgment of the Court of Appeals is, as to that portion of the judgment appealed from, reversed.

Mr. Justice Brennan took no part in the consideration or decision of this case.

NOTES

1. *The Elements of a Disparate-Impact Claim.* *Griggs* presents the three basic elements of a disparate-impact claim. The plaintiff must a) identify a

facially neutral factor used to make an employment decision and b) prove that the factor has a disparate impact on a protected group. If the plaintiff can prove those elements, the employer may defend by c) proving that the factor is justified by business necessity. Subsequent cases articulated a final element: Where a factor with a disparate impact *is* justified by business necessity, a plaintiff can still prevail by demonstrating that "other selection processes that have a lesser discriminatory effect could also suitably serve the employer's business needs." *Watson v. Fort Worth Bank & Trust*, 487 U.S. 977, 1006 (1988) (Blackmun, J., concurring). *See Albemarle Paper Co. v. Moody*, 422 U.S. 405, 425 (1975). In the Civil Rights Act of 1991, Congress amended Title VII to include these elements in the statutory language of Title VII. Title VII § 703(k).

2. *Identifying the Facially Neutral Factor.* Plaintiffs must identify the "particular employment practice" causing the disparate impact. Title VII § 703(k)(1)(A)(i). Thus, a plaintiff generally cannot make out a *prima facie* case by demonstrating that a group of factors used by an employer to make a hiring decision (for example, a college degree requirement, adequate performance on a written test, and a successful interview) had a disparate impact on black applicants. Rather, the plaintiff would have to prove that one (or more) of the factors individually had a disparate impact. The only exception to this is when the plaintiff can prove that the factors are not "capable of separation for analysis" (perhaps because the employer did not keep adequate records of their separate effects). Only then can a plaintiff establish a *prima facie* case by demonstrating that the factors together produced a disparate impact. Title VII § 703(k)(1)(B)(i).

This requirement raises several difficult issues. Most obviously, it requires identifying "particular employment practices." If an employer requires employees to be at least 5 feet, 2 inches tall and weigh at least 120 pounds, is there one employment practice, or two? Intuition would indicate two (a height requirement and a weight requirement), but the legislative history indicates that there is only one because the two are "functionally integrated" to measure strength. The distinction is very hazy at the margins.

The distinction can also be extremely important because the independent effect of separate practices does not bear any necessary relationship to the combined effect of the practices. It is possible, for example, that no practice considered individually has a disparate impact on a protected group, but that the practices in combination have a severe adverse impact. On the other hand, it is also possible that each practice considered individually has an adverse impact, but that the practices in combination do not. For many examples and suggestions on how to analyze these situations, see Ramona L. Paetzold & Steven L. Willborn, *Deconstructing Disparate Impact: A View of the Model Through New Lenses*, 74 N.C. L. REV. 325 (1996).

3. *How Disparate Must the Impact Be?* The EEOC has proposed a rough-and-ready rule for determining how large the disparate effect must be to be probative of illegal discrimination:

> A selection rate for any race, sex, or ethnic group which is less than four-fifths (⅘) (or eighty percent) of the rate for the group with the highest rate will generally be regarded by the Federal enforcement

agencies as evidence of adverse impact, while a greater than four-fifths rate will generally not be regarded by the Federal enforcement agencies as evidence of adverse impact.

29 C.F.R. § 1607.4(D).

Using the four-fifths rule, how disparate was the impact of the high school diploma requirement in *Griggs*?

Although the four-fifths rule is attractive because it is easy to apply, some have argued that more sophisticated statistical analyses should be used. *See* Anthony E. Boardman & Aidan R. Vining, *The Role of Probative Statistics in Employment Discrimination Cases,* 46 LAW & CONTEMP. PROBS. 189 (1983); Elaine W. Shoben, *Differential Pass-Fail Rates in Employment Testing: Statistical Proof Under Title VII,* 91 HARV. L. REV. 793 (1978). *But see* Paul Meier et al., *What Happened in Hazelwood: Statistics, Employment Discrimination and the 80% Rule,* 1984 AM. B. FOUND. RES. J. 139 (four-fifths rule is superior to other statistical models).

4. *Business Necessity.* To justify an employment practice with a disparate impact, an employer must demonstrate that it is "job related for the position in question and consistent with business necessity." Title VII, § 702 (k)(1)(A)(i). As one might expect, the courts have not consistently applied the standard. Consider, for example, two cases examining the legitimacy of a rule that the employer would not employ spouses of current employees. Both cases found that the rule had a disparate impact on women and both discussed the same types of business justifications (problems with supervision and scheduling, morale problems with other employees, etc.), but the courts reached different results. In *Yuhas v. Libbey-Owens-Ford Co.,* 562 F.2d 496, 500 (7th Cir. 1977), the court found that the no-spouse rule was justified by business necessity, because it "plausibly improves the work environment and because it does not penalize women on the basis of their environmental or genetic background," while in *EEOC v. Rath Packing Co.,* 787 F.2d 318, 332 (8th Cir. 1986), the court found that the rule was *not* justified by business necessity, because it was not "essential" for eliminating a "concrete and demonstrable" problem.

5. *The Seniority Exception.* Seniority systems often have a disparate impact on African-Americans and women. Seniority systems, by their very nature, allocate benefits such as wages and vacation time disproportionately to workers with longer job tenures. Often this means disproportionate benefits to white male workers who have more years of work experience because of past discrimination against other groups, fewer interruptions in their work lives, or other factors.

Title VII, however, exempts seniority systems from the normal operation of the disparate impact model. Section 703(h) provides that:

> it shall not be an unlawful employment practice for an employer to apply different standards of compensation, or different terms, conditions or privileges of employment pursuant to a bona fide seniority . . . system, . . . provided that such differences are not the result of an intention to discriminate because of race, color, religion, sex or national origin. . . .

Thus, seniority systems violate Title VII only if plaintiffs can prove that the employer uses the system with explicit intention to discriminate. *Teamsters v. United States*, 431 U.S. 324, 348-56 (1977). The principal issues under section 703(h) are what constitutes a seniority system entitled to the section's protection, *California Brewers Ass'n v. Bryant*, 444 U.S. 598 (1980), and how one proves that an employer is intentionally using a seniority system to discriminate. Mark S. Brodin, *Role of Fault and Motive in Defining Discrimination: The Seniority Question Under Title VII*, 62 N.C. L. Rev. 943 (1984).

6. *The Relationship Between Systemic Disparate Treatment and Disparate Impact.* Suppose an employer receives applications from 1,000 prospective employees, 200 of whom are black persons. The applicant pool provides the best available evidence of the treatment one would expect in the absence of discrimination. The employer hires 200 of the applicants, including twenty black employees. Can a rejected black applicant present a *prima facie* case of systemic disparate treatment discrimination?

The employer rebuts by showing that it requires applicants to have a college diploma to be considered for the jobs in issue, which eliminated 100 of the black applicants but none of the white applicants from consideration. Has the employer successfully rebutted the systemic disparate treatment claim? Could the rejected black applicant now use the disparate-impact model to challenge the employer's practices?

What if the employer rebutted instead by showing that it requires a college diploma, five years of experience, a good job reference, and a passing score on a written examination to be hired and those factors combined eliminated 100 of the black applicants, but none of the white applicants? How would this change your analysis of the disparate impact claim?

7. *The Nineteenth Century Civil Rights Acts.* The disparate-impact model cannot be used to establish liability under the nineteenth century civil rights acts, 42 U.S.C. §§ 1981 & 1983. *See General Bldg. Contrs. Ass'n v. Pennsylvania*, 458 U.S. 375 (1982). * The disparate treatment model must be used instead.

Section 1981 prohibits racial discrimination in making and enforcing contracts. Since employment is a contractual relationship, employers who engage in intentional racial discrimination may violate section 1981. All employers except the federal government (even employers too small to be covered by Title VII) are covered by section 1981. About 86% of establishments (employing 14-22% of all workers) have fewer than fifteen employees and thus are covered by section 1981 but not Title VII. *See* Theodore Eisenberg & Stewart Schwab, *The Importance of Section 1981*, 73 Cornell L. Rev. 596, 602 & n.42 (1988). Eleventh Amendment immunity, however, significantly complicates the coverage of state instrumentalities. *See* Charles A. Sullivan et al., Employment Discrimination §§ 21.1, 23.5 (2d ed. 1988).

---

* Section 1983 protects rights that are found in the Constitution and other federal laws. Consequently, the disparate-impact theory would be available in a section 1983 action if the underlying law permitted liability based on that theory. In status-discrimination cases, however, section 1983 is generally used to enforce the equal-protection clause, which requires a showing of discriminatory intent. *Washington v. Davis*, 426 U.S. 229 (1976).

Section 1983 provides a cause of action against every person who under color of state law deprives another person of rights secured by the Constitution or federal laws. Thus, section 1983 may provide an independent cause of action against *public* employers that engage in status discrimination.

Sections 1981 and 1983 have long been considered important components of the web of federal laws prohibiting status discrimination primarily because of their procedural and remedial advantages. Compensatory damages (such as damages for pain and suffering) are available under sections 1981 and 1983, as are punitive damages. The availability of legal damages also means that jury trials are available under these laws. Until enactment of the Civil Rights Act of 1991, these types of damages and jury trials were not available under Title VII and, even after the Act, compensatory damages are capped for Title VII claims but not for claims under sections 1981 and 1983. 42 U.S.C. § 1981A(b)(3). The nineteenth century civil rights acts are also valued by plaintiffs because they differ from Title VII in their coverage, statutes of limitations, and procedural exhaustion requirements.

C. REASONABLE ACCOMMODATION

The reasonable-accommodation model applies to discrimination against individuals with disabilities under the Americans with Disabilities Act (ADA) and the Rehabilitation Act and to religious discrimination under Title VII. Our focus here will be on disability discrimination. In general terms, the model requires employers to make reasonable accommodations to individuals with disabilities if the individuals can perform the essential functions of the job with the accommodations. Employers, however, need not make any accommodations that would impose an undue hardship on the employer.

The reasonable-accommodation model requires more of employers than the disparate-treatment and impact models. All the models require employers to refrain from discriminating against protected persons when they can be as productive as others, but only the reasonable-accommodation model requires employers to take affirmative (and sometimes costly) steps to assist protected persons who would not be as productive as others without the extra measures. Another way of thinking about this is that the treatment and impact models permit employers to consider applicants and employees as presented — if an applicant is not as qualified as another applicant or cannot meet justifiable job requirements, the models do not limit the employer's ability to reject the applicant. The reasonable-accommodation model, in contrast, requires the employer to consider what steps it can reasonably take to enhance the ability of applicants and employees to be productive or meet justifiable job requirements — if a disabled applicant cannot meet a justifiable job requirement without some accommodation, the model requires the employer to consider what it can do to enable the applicant to meet the requirement.

In this section, the first case examines the definition of "individual with a disability." The following case explores the nature and extent of the duty of reasonable accommodation.

SUTTON v. UNITED AIR LINES, INC.
United States Supreme Court
527 U.S. 471 (1999)

JUSTICE O'CONNOR delivered the opinion of the Court. . . .

I

Petitioners are twin sisters, both of whom have severe myopia. Each petitioner's uncorrected visual acuity is 20/200 or worse in her right eye and 20/400 or worse in her left eye, but "[w]ith the use of corrective lenses, each . . . has vision that is 20/20 or better." Consequently, without corrective lenses, each "effectively cannot see to conduct numerous activities such as driving a vehicle, watching television or shopping in public stores," but with corrective measures, such as glasses or contact lenses, both "function identically to individuals without a similar impairment."

In 1992, petitioners applied to respondent for employment as commercial airline pilots. They met respondent's basic age, education, experience, and FAA certification qualifications. After submitting their applications for employment, both petitioners were invited by respondent to an interview and to flight simulator tests. Both were told during their interviews, however, that a mistake had been made in inviting them to interview because petitioners did not meet respondent's minimum vision requirement, which was uncorrected visual acuity of 20/100 or better. Due to their failure to meet this requirement, petitioners' interviews were terminated, and neither was offered a pilot position. [Petitioners then filed a charge of disability discrimination under the Americans with Disabilities Act and, subsequently, this lawsuit.]

II

The ADA prohibits discrimination by covered entities, including private employers, against qualified individuals with a disability. Specifically, it provides that no covered employer "shall discriminate against a qualified individual with a disability because of the disability of such individual in regard to job application procedures, the hiring, advancement, or discharge of employees, employee compensation, job training, and other terms, conditions, and privileges of employment." 42 U.S.C. § 12112(a); *see also* § 12111(2) ("The term 'covered entity' means an employer, employment agency, labor organization, or joint labor-management committee"). A "qualified individual with a disability" is identified as "an individual with a disability who, with or without reasonable accommodation, can perform the essential functions of the employment position that such individual holds or desires." § 12111(8). In turn, a "disability" is defined as:

"(A) a physical or mental impairment that substantially limits one or more of the major life activities of such individual;

"(B) a record of such an impairment; or

"(C) being regarded as having such an impairment." § 12102(2).

Accordingly, to fall within this definition one must have an actual disability (subsection (A)), have a record of a disability (subsection (B)), or be regarded as having one (subsection (C)). . . .

No agency . . . has been given authority to issue regulations implementing the generally applicable provisions of the ADA which fall outside Titles I-V. Most notably, no agency has been delegated authority to interpret the term "disability." . . . The EEOC has, nonetheless, issued regulations to provide additional guidance regarding the proper interpretation of this term. [T]he EEOC regulations define the three elements of disability: (1) "physical or mental impairment," (2) "substantially limits," and (3) "major life activities." Under the regulations, a "physical impairment" includes "[a]ny physiological disorder, or condition, cosmetic disfigurement, or anatomical loss affecting one or more of the following body systems: neurological, musculoskeletal, special sense organs, respiratory (including speech organs), cardiovascular, reproductive, digestive, genito-urinary, hemic and lymphatic, skin, and endocrine." [29 C.F.R.] § 1630.2(h)(1). The term "substantially limits" means, among other things, "[u]nable to perform a major life activity that the average person in the general population can perform;" or "[s]ignificantly restricted as to the condition, manner or duration under which an individual can perform a particular major life activity as compared to the condition, manner, or duration under which the average person in the general population can perform that same major life activity." § 1630.2(j). Finally, "[m]ajor [l]ife [a]ctivities means functions such as caring for oneself, performing manual tasks, walking, seeing, hearing, speaking, breathing, learning, and working." § 1630.2(i). Because both parties accept these regulations as valid, and determining their validity is not necessary to decide this case, we have no occasion to consider what deference they are due, if any.

The [EEOC] also issued interpretive guidelines to aid in the implementation of their regulations. For instance, at the time that it promulgated the above regulations, the EEOC issued an "Interpretive Guidance," which provides that "[t]he determination of whether an individual is substantially limited in a major life activity must be made on a case by case basis, without regard to mitigating measures such as medicines, or assistive or prosthetic devices." 29 CFR pt. 1630, App. § 1630.2(j) (1998) (describing § 1630.2(j)). . . . Although the parties dispute the persuasive force of these interpretive guidelines, we have no need in this case to decide what deference is due.

III

With this statutory and regulatory framework in mind, we turn first to the question whether petitioners have stated a claim under subsection (A) of the disability definition, that is, whether they have alleged that they possess a physical impairment that substantially limits them in one or more major life activities. Because petitioners allege that with corrective measures their vision "is 20/20 or better," they are not actually disabled within the meaning of the Act if the "disability" determination is made with reference to these measures. Consequently, with respect to subsection (A) of the disability definition, our decision turns on whether disability is to be determined with or without reference to corrective measures. . . .

We conclude that . . . the approach adopted by the agency guidelines — that persons are to be evaluated in their hypothetical uncorrected state — is an impermissible interpretation of the ADA. Looking at the Act as a whole, it is apparent that if a person is taking measures to correct for, or mitigate, a physical or mental impairment, the effects of those measures — both positive and negative — must be taken into account when judging whether that person is "substantially limited" in a major life activity and thus "disabled" under the Act. The dissent relies on the legislative history of the ADA for the contrary proposition that individuals should be examined in their uncorrected state. Because we decide that, by its terms, the ADA cannot be read in this manner, we have no reason to consider the ADA's legislative history.

Three separate provisions of the ADA, read in concert, lead us to this conclusion. The Act defines a "disability" as "a physical or mental impairment that *substantially limits* one or more of the major life activities" of an individual. Because the phrase "substantially limits" appears in the Act in the present indicative verb form, we think the language is properly read as requiring that a person be presently — not potentially or hypothetically — substantially limited in order to demonstrate a disability. A "disability" exists only where an impairment "substantially limits" a major life activity, not where it "might," "could," or "would" be substantially limiting if mitigating measures were not taken. A person whose physical or mental impairment is corrected by medication or other measures does not have an impairment that presently "substantially limits" a major life activity. To be sure, a person whose physical or mental impairment is corrected by mitigating measures still has an impairment, but if the impairment is corrected it does not "substantially limi[t]" a major life activity.

The definition of disability also requires that disabilities be evaluated "with respect to an individual" and be determined based on whether an impairment substantially limits the "major life activities of such individual." § 12102(2). Thus, whether a person has a disability under the ADA is an individualized inquiry. *See Bragdon v. Abbott*, 524 U.S. 624, 641-42 (1998) (declining to consider whether HIV infection is a per se disability under the ADA); 29 CFR pt. 1630, App. § 1630.2(j) ("The determination of whether an individual has a disability is not necessarily based on the name or diagnosis of the impairment the person has, but rather on the effect of that impairment on the life of the individual").

The agency guidelines' directive that persons be judged in their uncorrected or unmitigated state runs directly counter to the individualized inquiry mandated by the ADA. The agency approach would often require courts and employers to speculate about a person's condition and would, in many cases, force them to make a disability determination based on general information about how an uncorrected impairment usually affects individuals, rather than on the individual's actual condition. For instance, under this view, courts would almost certainly find all diabetics to be disabled, because if they failed to monitor their blood sugar levels and administer insulin, they would almost certainly be substantially limited in one or more major life activities. A diabetic whose illness does not impair his or her daily activities would therefore be considered disabled simply because he or she has diabetes. Thus, the guidelines approach would create a system in which persons often must be treated as members of a group of people with similar impairments, rather than as individuals. This is contrary to both the letter and the spirit of the ADA.

The guidelines approach could also lead to the anomalous result that in determining whether an individual is disabled, courts and employers could not consider any negative side effects suffered by an individual resulting from the use of mitigating measures, even when those side effects are very severe. *See, e.g.*, Johnson, *Antipsychotics: Pros and Cons of Antipsychotics*, RN (Aug.1997) (noting that antipsychotic drugs can cause a variety of adverse effects, including neuroleptic malignant syndrome and painful seizures); *Liver Risk Warning Added to Parkinson's Drug*, FDA CONSUMER (Mar. 1, 1999) (warning that a drug for treating Parkinson's disease can cause liver damage); Curry & Kulling, *Newer Antiepileptic Drugs*, AMERICAN FAMILY PHYSICIAN (Feb. 1, 1998) (cataloging serious negative side effects of new antiepileptic drugs). This result is also inconsistent with the individualized approach of the ADA.

Finally, and critically, findings enacted as part of the ADA require the conclusion that Congress did not intend to bring under the statute's protection all those whose uncorrected conditions amount to disabilities. Congress found that "some 43,000,000 Americans have one or more physical or mental disabilities, and this number is increasing as the population as a whole is growing older." § 12101(a)(1). This figure is inconsistent with the definition of disability pressed by petitioners.

Although the exact source of the 43 million figure is not clear, the corresponding finding in the 1988 precursor to the ADA was drawn directly from a report prepared by the National Council on Disability. That report detailed the difficulty of estimating the number of disabled persons due to varying operational definitions of disability. It explained that the estimates of the number of disabled Americans ranged from an overinclusive 160 million under a "health conditions approach," which looks at all conditions that impair the health or normal functional abilities of an individual, to an underinclusive 22.7 million under a "work disability approach," which focuses on individuals' reported ability to work. It noted that "a figure of 35 or 36 million [was] the most commonly quoted estimate." The 36 million number included in the 1988 bill's findings thus clearly reflects an approach to defining disabilities that is closer to the work disabilities approach than the health conditions approach.

Regardless of its exact source, however, the 43 million figure reflects an understanding that those whose impairments are largely corrected by medication or other devices are not "disabled" within the meaning of the ADA. The estimate is consistent with the numbers produced by studies performed during this same time period that took a similar functional approach to determining disability. . . . By contrast, nonfunctional approaches to defining disability produce significantly larger numbers. As noted above, the 1986 National Council on Disability report estimated that there were over 160 million disabled under the "health conditions approach."

Because it is included in the ADA's text, the finding that 43 million individuals are disabled gives content to the ADA's terms, specifically the term "disability." Had Congress intended to include all persons with corrected physical limitations among those covered by the Act, it undoubtedly would have cited a much higher number of disabled persons in the findings. That it did not is evidence that the ADA's coverage is restricted to only those whose impairments are not mitigated by corrective measures.

The dissents suggest that viewing individuals in their corrected state will exclude from the definition of "disab[led]" those who use prosthetic limbs or take medicine for epilepsy or high blood pressure. This suggestion is incorrect. The use of a corrective device does not, by itself, relieve one's disability. Rather, one has a disability under subsection A if, notwithstanding the use of a corrective device, that individual is substantially limited in a major life activity. For example, individuals who use prosthetic limbs or wheelchairs may be mobile and capable of functioning in society but still be disabled because of a substantial limitation on their ability to walk or run. The same may be true of individuals who take medicine to lessen the symptoms of an impairment so that they can function but nevertheless remain substantially limited. Alternatively, one whose high blood pressure is "cured" by medication may be regarded as disabled by a covered entity, and thus disabled under subsection C of the definition. The use or nonuse of a corrective device does not determine whether an individual is disabled; that determination depends on whether the limitations an individual with an impairment actually faces are in fact substantially limiting. . . .

Accordingly, because we decide that disability under the Act is to be determined with reference to corrective measures, we agree with the courts below that petitioners have not stated a claim that they are substantially limited in any major life activity.

IV

Our conclusion that petitioners have failed to state a claim that they are actually disabled under subsection (A) of the disability definition does not end our inquiry. Under subsection (C), individuals who are "regarded as" having a disability are disabled within the meaning of the ADA. Subsection (C) provides that having a disability includes "being regarded as having," § 12102(2)(C), "a physical or mental impairment that substantially limits one or more of the major life activities of such individual," § 12102(2)(A). There are two apparent ways in which individuals may fall within this statutory definition: (1) a covered entity mistakenly believes that a person has a physical impairment that substantially limits one or more major life activities, or (2) a covered entity mistakenly believes that an actual, nonlimiting impairment substantially limits one or more major life activities. In both cases, it is neces-sary that a covered entity entertain misperceptions about the individual — it must believe either that one has a substantially limiting impairment that one does not have or that one has a substantially limiting impairment when, in fact, the impairment is not so limiting. These misperceptions often "resul[t] from stereotypic assumptions not truly indicative of . . . individual ability." *See* 42 U.S.C. § 12101(7). *See also School Bd. of Nassau Cty. v. Arline*, 480 U.S. 273, 284 (1987) ("By amending the definition of 'handicapped individual' to include not only those who are actually physically impaired, but also those who are regarded as impaired and who, as a result, are substantially limited in a major life activity, Congress acknowledged that society's accumulated myths and fears about disability and disease are as handicapping as are the physical limitations that flow from actual impairment").

There is no dispute that petitioners are physically impaired. Petitioners do not make the obvious argument that they are regarded due to their impairments as substantially limited in the major life activity of seeing. They contend only that respondent mistakenly believes their physical impairments substantially limit them in the major life activity of working. To support this claim, petitioners allege that respondent has a vision requirement, which is allegedly based on myth and stereotype. Further, this requirement substantially limits their ability to engage in the major life activity of working by precluding them from obtaining the job of global airline pilot, which they argue is a "class of employment." In reply, respondent argues that the position of global airline pilot is not a class of jobs and therefore petitioners have not stated a claim that they are regarded as substantially limited in the major life activity of working.

Standing alone, the allegation that respondent has a vision requirement in place does not establish a claim that respondent regards petitioners as substantially limited in the major life activity of working. By its terms, the ADA allows employers to prefer some physical attributes over others and to establish physical criteria. An employer runs afoul of the ADA when it makes an employment decision based on a physical or mental impairment, real or imagined, that is regarded as substantially limiting a major life activity. Accordingly, an employer is free to decide that physical characteristics or medical conditions that do not rise to the level of an impairment — such as one's height, build, or singing voice — are preferable to others, just as it is free to decide that some limiting, but not substantially limiting, impairments make individuals less than ideally suited for a job.

Considering the allegations of the amended complaint in tandem, petitioners have not stated a claim that respondent regards their impairment as substantially limiting their ability to work. The ADA does not define "substantially limits," but "substantially" suggests "considerable" or "specified to a large degree." *See* WEBSTER'S THIRD NEW INTERNATIONAL DICTIONARY 2280 (1976) (defining "substantially" as "in a substantial manner" and "substantial" as "considerable in amount, value, or worth" and "being that specified to a large degree or in the main"). The EEOC has codified regulations interpreting the term "substantially limits" in this manner, defining the term to mean "[u]nable to perform" or "[s]ignificantly restricted." *See* 29 CFR §§ 1630.2(j)(1)(i), (ii) (1998).

When the major life activity under consideration is that of working, the statutory phrase "substantially limits" requires, at a minimum, that plaintiffs allege they are unable to work in a broad class of jobs. Reflecting this requirement, the EEOC uses a specialized definition of the term "substantially limits" when referring to the major life activity of working:

"significantly restricted in the ability to perform either a class of jobs or a broad range of jobs in various classes as compared to the average person having comparable training, skills and abilities. The inability to perform a single, particular job does not constitute a substantial limitation in the major life activity of working." § 1630.2(j)(3)(i).

The EEOC further identifies several factors that courts should consider when determining whether an individual is substantially limited in the major life activity of working, including the geographical area to which the individual has reasonable access, and "the number and types of jobs utilizing similar training, knowledge, skills or abilities, within the geographical area, from which the individual is also disqualified." §§ 1630.2(j)(3)(ii)(A), (B). To be substantially limited in the major life activity of working, then, one must be precluded from more than one type of job, a specialized job, or a particular job of choice. If jobs utilizing an individual's skills (but perhaps not his or her unique talents) are available, one is not precluded from a substantial class of jobs. Similarly, if a host of different types of jobs are available, one is not precluded from a broad range of jobs.

Because the parties accept that the term "major life activities" includes working, we do not determine the validity of the cited regulations. We note, however, that there may be some conceptual difficulty in defining "major life activities" to include work, for it seems "to argue in a circle to say that if one is excluded, for instance, by reason of [an impairment, from working with others] . . . then that exclusion constitutes an impairment, when the question you're asking is, whether the exclusion itself is by reason of handicap." Indeed, even the EEOC has expressed reluctance to define "major life activities" to include working and has suggested that working be viewed as a residual life activity, considered, as a last resort, only "[i]f an individual is *not* substantially limited with respect to any other major life activity." 29 CFR pt. 1630, App. § 1630.2(j) (1998) (emphasis added) ("If an individual is substantially limited in *any other* major life activity, no determination should be made as to whether the individual is substantially limited in working" (emphasis added)).

Assuming without deciding that working is a major life activity and that the EEOC regulations interpreting the term "substantially limits" are reasonable, petitioners have failed to allege adequately that their poor eyesight is regarded as an impairment that substantially limits them in the major life activity of working. They allege only that respondent regards their poor vision as precluding them from holding positions as a "global airline pilot." Because the position of global airline pilot is a single job, this allegation does not support the claim that respondent regards petitioners as having a substantially limiting impairment. *See* 29 CFR § 1630.2(j)(3)(i) ("The inability to perform a single, particular job does not constitute a substantial limitation in the major life activity of working"). Indeed, there are a number of other positions utilizing petitioners' skills, such as regional pilot and pilot instructor to name a few, that are available to them. Even under the EEOC's Interpretative Guidance, to which petitioners ask us to defer, "an individual who cannot be a commercial airline pilot because of a minor vision impairment, but who can be a commercial airline co-pilot or a pilot for a courier service, would not be substantially limited in the major life activity of working." 29 CFR pt. 1630, App. § 1630.2.

Petitioners also argue that if one were to assume that a substantial number of airline carriers have similar vision requirements, they would be substantially limited in the major life activity of working. Even assuming for the sake of argument that the adoption of similar vision requirements by other carriers would represent a substantial limitation on the major life activity of working, the argument is nevertheless flawed. It is not enough to say that if the physical criteria of a single employer were imputed to all similar employers one would be regarded as substantially limited in the major life activity of working only as a result of this imputation. An otherwise valid job requirement, such as a height requirement, does not become invalid simply because it would limit a person's employment opportunities in a substantial way if it were adopted by a substantial number of employers. Because petitioners have not alleged, and cannot demonstrate, that respondent's vision requirement reflects a belief that petitioners' vision substantially limits them, we agree with the decision of the Court of Appeals affirming the dismissal of petitioners' claim that they are regarded as disabled. . . .

[JUSTICE GINSBURG filed a concurring opinion.]

JUSTICE STEVENS, with whom JUSTICE BREYER joins, dissenting. . . .

The three parts of th[e] definition [of disability in the ADA] do not identify mutually exclusive, discrete categories. On the contrary, they furnish three overlapping formulas aimed at ensuring that individuals who now have, or ever had, a substantially limiting impairment are covered by the Act.

An example of a rather common condition illustrates this point: There are many individuals who have lost one or more limbs in industrial accidents, or perhaps in the service of their country in places like Iwo Jima. With the aid of prostheses, coupled with courageous determination and physical therapy, many of these hardy individuals can perform all of their major life activities just as efficiently as an average couch potato. If the Act were just concerned with their present ability to participate in society, many of these individuals' physical impairments would not be viewed as disabilities. Similarly, if the statute were solely concerned with whether these individuals viewed themselves as disabled — or with whether a majority of employers regarded them as unable to perform most jobs — many of these individuals would lack statutory protection from discrimination based on their prostheses.

The sweep of the statute's three-pronged definition, however, makes it pellucidly clear that Congress intended the Act to cover such persons. The fact that a prosthetic device, such as an artificial leg, has restored one's ability to perform major life activities surely cannot mean that subsection (A) of the definition is inapplicable. Nor should the fact that the individual considers himself (or actually is) "cured," or that a prospective employer considers him generally employable, mean that subsections (B) or (C) are inapplicable. But under the Court's emphasis on "the present indicative verb form" used in subsection (A), that subsection presumably would not apply. And under the Court's focus on the individual's "presen[t] — not potentia[l] or hypothetica[l]" — condition, and on whether a person is "precluded from a broad range of jobs," subsections (B) and (C) presumably would not apply. . . .

Subsection (B) of the definition . . . sheds a revelatory light on the question whether Congress was concerned only about the corrected or mitigated status of a person's impairment. If the Court is correct that "[a] 'disability' exists only where" a person's "present" or "actual" condition is substantially impaired, there would be no reason to include in the protected class those who were once disabled but who are now fully recovered. Subsection (B) of the Act's definition, however, plainly covers a person who previously had a serious hearing impairment that has since been completely cured. *See School Bd. of Nassau Cty. v. Arline*, 480 U.S. 273, 281 (1987). Still, if I correctly understand the Court's opinion, it holds that one who continues to wear a hearing aid that she has worn all her life might not be covered — fully cured impairments are covered, but merely treatable ones are not. The text of the Act surely does not require such a bizarre result. . . .

If a narrow reading of the term "disability" were necessary in order to avoid the danger that the Act might otherwise force United to hire pilots who might endanger the lives of their passengers, it would make good sense . . . to confine its coverage. There is, however, no such danger in this case. If a person is "disabled" within the meaning of the Act, she still cannot prevail on a claim of discrimination unless she can prove that the employer took action "because of" that impairment, and that she can, "with or without reasonable accommodation, . . . perform the essential functions" of the job of a commercial airline pilot. Even then, an employer may avoid liability if it shows that the criteria of having uncorrected visual acuity of at least 20/100 is "job-related and consistent with business necessity" or if such vision (even if correctable to 20/20) would pose a health or safety hazard.

This case, in other words, is not about whether petitioners are genuinely qualified or whether they can perform the job of an airline pilot without posing an undue safety risk. The case just raises the threshold question whether petitioners are members of the ADA's protected class. . . . Hence, this particular case, at its core, is about whether, assuming that petitioners can prove that they are "qualified," the airline has any duty to come forward with some legitimate explanation for refusing to hire them because of their uncorrected eyesight, or whether the ADA leaves the airline free to decline to hire petitioners on this basis even if it is acting purely on the basis of irrational fear and stereotype. . . .

I do not mean to suggest, of course, that the ADA should be read to prohibit discrimination on the basis of, say, blue eyes, deformed fingernails, or heights of less than six feet. Those conditions, to the extent that they are even "impairments," do not substantially limit individuals in any condition and thus are different in kind from the impairment in the case before us. While not all eyesight that can be enhanced by glasses is substantially limiting, having 20/200 vision in one's better eye is, without treatment, a significant hindrance. Only two percent of the population suffers from such myopia. Such acuity precludes a person from driving, shopping in a public store, or viewing a computer screen from a reasonable distance. Uncorrected vision, therefore, can be "substantially limiting" in the same way that unmedicated epilepsy or diabetes can be. Because Congress obviously intended to include individuals with the latter impairments in the Act's protected class, we should give petitioners the same protection. . . .

The Court claims that [its] rule is necessary to avoid requiring courts to "speculate" about a person's "hypothetical" condition and to preserve the Act's focus on making "individualized inquiries" into whether a person is disabled. [But v]iewing a person in her "unmitigated" state simply requires examining that individual's abilities in a different state, not the abilities of every person who shares a similar condition. It is just as easy individually to test petitioners' eyesight with their glasses on as with their glasses off.[5] . . .

It has also been suggested that if we treat as "disabilities" impairments that may be mitigated by measures as ordinary and expedient as wearing eyeglasses, a flood of litigation will ensue. The suggestion is misguided. Although vision is of critical importance for airline pilots, in most segments of the economy whether an employee wears glasses — or uses any of several other mitigating measures — is a matter of complete indifference to employers. It is difficult to envision many situations in which a qualified employee who needs glasses to perform her job might be fired — as the statute requires — "because of" the fact that she cannot see well without them. Such a proposition would be ridiculous in the garden-variety case. On the other hand, if an accounting firm, for example, adopted a guideline refusing to hire any incoming accountant who has uncorrected vision of less than 20/100 — or, by the same token, any person who is unable without medication to avoid having seizures — such a rule would seem to be the essence of invidious discrimination. . . .

Accordingly, although I express no opinion on the ultimate merits of petitioners' claim, I am persuaded that they have a disability covered by the ADA. I therefore respectfully dissent.

[JUSTICE BREYER filed a dissenting opinion.]

NOTES

1. *Hypertension and Monocularity.* The Supreme Court reinforced its decision in *Sutton* through two other decisions issued the same day. In *Murphy v. United Parcel Service*, 527 U.S. 516 (1999), an employee whose mechanics position required him to drive commercial vehicles was fired when his employer discovered that his blood pressure exceeded Department of Transportation (DOT) requirements. The Court applied *Sutton* to hold that the employee was not an individual with a disability under the ADA because 1) the determination was to be made taking the employee's mitigating measures into consideration; 2) with medication, the employee's blood pressure was controlled and did not substantially limit any of his major life activities; and 3) disqualification from mechanics jobs requiring him to drive commercial vehicles did not interfere with the major life activity of working since a wide

---

[5] For much the same reason, the Court's concern that the agencies' approach would "lead to the anomalous result" that courts would ignore "negative side effects suffered by an individual resulting from the use of mitigating measures," is misplaced. It seems safe to assume that most individuals who take medication that itself substantially limits a major life activity would be substantially limited in some other way if they did not take the medication. The Court's examples of psychosis, Parkinson's disease, and epilepsy certainly support this presumption. To the extent that certain people may be substantially limited only when taking "mitigating measures," it might fairly be said that just as contagiousness is symptomatic of a disability because an individual's "contagiousness and her physical impairment each [may result] from the same underlying condition," *School Bd. of Nassau Cty. v. Arline*, 480 U.S. 273, 282 (1987), side effects are symptomatic of a disability because side effects and a physical impairment may flow from the same underlying condition.

range of other jobs were available, including mechanics jobs that did not require driving.

In *Albertson's, Inc. v. Kirkingburg*, 527 U.S. 555 (1999), an employee was fired from his job as a truck driver after he failed to meet the DOT's basic vision standards and was not rehired even though he later obtained a waiver. The Court refined the *Sutton* analysis in holding that the employee was not an individual with a disability. First, the Court held that the appropriate focus is not on *differences* between the employee's ability to see compared to other people, but rather on whether the employee was substantially limited. Second, the Court held that the lower court had failed to consider mitigating measures appropriately. Interestingly, the mitigating measure in *Albertson's* was the employee's own brain which had subconsciously adjusted to his monocularity. The Court held that, like eyeglasses or drugs in the other two cases, brain adjustment was a type of mitigating factor which must be taken into consideration. Finally, the Court held that monocularity especially must be analyzed on a case-by-case basis because it varies considerably on factors such as the degree of visual acuity in the weaker eye, the extent of the compensating adjustments, and the ultimate scope of the restrictions on visual ability. The Court also held that the employer was justified in relying on the DOT's eyesight requirements as essential job qualifications, even though the DOT occasionally, as in this case, grants waivers.

2. Impairments and Disabilities. A later Supreme Court decision considered whether someone with carpal tunnel syndrome was an individual with a disability. In *Toyota Motor Manufacturing v. Williams*, 534 U.S. 184 (2002), the Court made it clear that merely having an impairment does not mean that one has a disability. In addition, the impairment must be permanent or long term and it must substantially interfere with a "major life activity," that is, an activity of "central importance to daily life," such as walking, seeing, or hearing. *Id.* at 196. The Supreme Court reversed the Court of Appeals which found that the plaintiff was an individual with a disability. The Court of Appeals had focused too much on the plaintiff's inability to perform manual tasks at work and too little on her ability to perform everyday tasks such as brushing her teeth, washing her face, tending her flower garden, and picking up around the house.

3. The Definition of Disability. Consider whether the following people are individuals with disabilities:

(a) An applicant for a flight-attendant position who exceeds the airline's weight limitations because he is an avid bodybuilder. *See Tudyman v. United Airlines*, 608 F. Supp. 739 (C.D. Cal. 1984) (no). What if the applicant were simply overweight? *See Andrews v. Ohio*, 104 F.3d 803 (6th Cir. 1997) (no). What if the applicant were severely overweight? *Cook v. Rhode Island,* 10 F.3d 17 (1st Cir. 1993) (upholding jury verdict that morbidly obese person is an individual with a disability). *See* Lisa E. Key, *Voluntary Disabilities and the ADA: A Reasonable Interpretation of "Reasonable Accommodation,"* 48 HASTINGS L.J. 75 (1996).

(b) A person infected with the HIV virus, but who is currently asymptomatic. *Compare Bragdon v. Abbott*, 524 U.S. 624 (1998) (yes, because of limitations on ability to engage in major life activity of reproduction), *with Blanks v.*

Southwestern Bell Communications, Inc., 310 F.3d 398 (5th Cir. 2002) (no, where plaintiff and wife had decided not to have any more children and wife was unable to do so).

(c) A person whose disability prevents him from lifting more than 25 pounds. *Compare Williams v. Channel Master Satellite Sys., Inc.*, 101 F.3d 346 (4th Cir. 1996) (no, because not a substantial limitation compared with the average person), *with Burns v. Coca-Cola Enters., Inc.*, 222 F.3d 247 (6th Cir. 2000) (yes, because limitation eliminated 50% of available jobs given plaintiff's educational background and experience).

(d) A bus driver who took drugs for hypertension and pain which caused drowsiness. *See Hill v. Kansas City Area Transp. Auth.*, 181 F.3d 891 (8th Cir. 1999) (no, because insufficient evidence plaintiff was required to take this particular combination of drugs). Or a person who could have taken drugs to treat a condition, but who refused. *See Tangires v. Johns Hopkins Hosp.*, 79 F. Supp. 2d 587 (D. Md.), *aff'd*, 230 F.3d 1354 (4th Cir. 2000) (no).

4. *Exclusions From the ADA's Definition of Disability.* The ADA also contains specific exclusions from its definition of disability including homosexuality, transvestism, and compulsive gambling. *See* §§ 508, 511. Some of the exclusions merely confirm what almost certainly would have been the result under the general definition of disability, *Blackwell v. United States Dep't of Treasury*, 830 F.2d 1183 (D.C. Cir. 1987) (homosexuality not a disability under general definition of Rehabilitation Act), but others narrow the scope of the general definition. *Blackwell v. United States Dep't of Treasury*, 639 F. Supp. 289 (D.D.C. 1986) (transvestitism is a disability under the general definition of the Rehabilitation Act).

The ADA (and the Rehabilitation Act) also exclude from coverage *current* users of illegal drugs; former users who are rehabilitated are covered. ADA §§ 104, 510; Rehabilitation Act § 8(C). Employers have expressed some concern with this distinction: "Rehabilitated could mean someone who's been off drugs for a year, a month, two days, or someone who just decided this morning not to use drugs anymore." William Current, Director, Institute for a Drug-Free Workplace, 251 DAILY LAB. REP. C-1 (Dec. 31, 1991). *But see Shafer v. Preston Mem. Hosp. Corp.*, 107 F.3d 274 (4th Cir. 1997) (use of drugs one month before discharge constitutes "current" use); *Zenor v. El Paso Healthcare Sys.*, 176 F.3d 847 (5th Cir. 1999) (to be rehabilitated individuals must be drug free for a significant period of time).

5. *Pre-employment Inquiries About Disabilities.* The ADA prohibits pre-employment medical examinations and, indeed, all pre-employment inquiries about disabilities. § 102(d). Medical examinations are permissible *after* a conditional offer of employment is made, but only if certain conditions are met. § 102(d)(3). In practice, these provisions mean that employers will first learn of their duty to accommodate either when applicants disclose that they may have difficulty in performing job duties or after a conditional offer of employment is made.

6. *The ADA and the Rehabilitation Act.* The drafters of the ADA relied heavily on the experience under the Rehabilitation Act. Most of the central concepts of the ADA were borrowed from the Rehabilitation Act and its regulations, including the three-part definition of disability and the notions of reasonable accommodation and undue hardship. On substantive issues, the courts rely on cases under the two statutes almost interchangeably.

The two Acts differ mainly in coverage and procedure. The Rehabilitation Act applies only to a narrow range of employers (the federal government, federal contractors, and recipients of federal funds) and its enforcement mechanisms are complex and limited. The ADA's coverage extends to all employers with fifteen or more employees and it incorporates the enforcement provisions of Title VII. ADA §§ 101(4), 107(a).

US AIRWAYS, INC. v. BARNETT
United States Supreme Court
535 U.S. 391 (2002)

JUSTICE BREYER delivered the opinion of the Court.

The Americans with Disabilities Act of 1990 (ADA or Act) prohibits an employer from discriminating against an "individual with a disability" who, with "reasonable accommodation," can perform the essential functions of the job. This case, arising in the context of summary judgment, asks us how the Act resolves a potential conflict between: (1) the interests of a disabled worker who seeks assignment to a particular position as a "reasonable accommodation," and (2) the interests of other workers with superior rights to bid for the job under an employer's seniority system. In such a case, does the accommodation demand trump the seniority system?

In our view, the seniority system will prevail in the run of cases. As we interpret the statute, to show that a requested accommodation conflicts with the rules of a seniority system is ordinarily to show that the accommodation is not "reasonable." Hence such a showing will entitle an employer/defendant to summary judgment on the question — unless there is more. The plaintiff remains free to present evidence of special circumstances that make "reasonable" a seniority rule exception in the particular case. And such a showing will defeat the employer's demand for summary judgment. FED. RULE CIV. PROC. 56(e).

I

In 1990, Robert Barnett, the plaintiff and respondent here, injured his back while working in a cargo-handling position at petitioner U.S. Airways, Inc. He invoked seniority rights and transferred to a less physically demanding mailroom position. Under U.S. Airways' seniority system, that position, like others, periodically became open to seniority-based employee bidding. In 1992, Barnett learned that at least two employees senior to him intended to bid for the mailroom job. He asked U.S. Airways to accommodate his disability-imposed limitations by making an exception that would allow him to remain in the mailroom. After permitting Barnett to continue his mailroom work for five months while it considered the matter, U.S. Airways eventually decided not to make an exception. And Barnett lost his job.

Barnett then brought this ADA suit claiming, among other things, that he was an "individual with a disability" capable of performing the essential functions of the mailroom job, that the mailroom job amounted to a "reasonable accommodation" of his disability, and that U.S. Airways, in refusing to assign him the job, unlawfully discriminated against him. US Airways moved for summary judgment . . . contending that its "well-established" seniority system granted other employees the right to obtain the mailroom position.

[The District Court granted summary judgment to U.S. Airways. An en banc panel of the United States Court of Appeals for the Ninth Circuit reversed.]

The Circuits have reached different conclusions about the legal significance of a seniority system. We agreed to answer U.S. Airways' question.

II

In answering the question presented, we must consider the following statutory provisions. First, the ADA says that an employer may not "discriminate against a qualified individual with a disability." 42 U.S.C. § 12112(a). Second, the ADA says that a "qualified" individual includes "an individual with a disability who, *with* or without *reasonable accommodation,* can perform the essential functions of" the relevant "employment position." § 12111(8) (emphasis added). Third, the ADA says that "discrimination" includes an employer's "*not making reasonable accommodations* to the known physical or mental limitations of an otherwise qualified . . . employee, *unless* [the employer] can demonstrate that the accommodation would impose an *undue hardship* on the operation of [its] business." § 12112(b)(5)(A) (emphasis added). Fourth, the ADA says that the term " 'reasonable accommodation' may include . . . reassignment to a vacant position." § 12111(9)(B).

The parties interpret this statutory language as applied to seniority systems in radically different ways. In U.S. Airways' view, the fact that an accommodation would violate the rules of a seniority system always shows that the accommodation is not a "reasonable" one. In Barnett's polar opposite view, a seniority system violation never shows that an accommodation sought is not a "reasonable" one. Barnett concedes that a violation of seniority rules might help to show that the accommodation will work "undue" employer "hardship," but that is a matter for an employer to demonstrate case by case. We shall initially consider the parties' main legal arguments in support of these conflicting positions.

A

US Airways' claim that a seniority system virtually always trumps a conflicting accommodation demand rests primarily upon its view of how the Act treats workplace "preferences." Insofar as a requested accommodation violates a disability-neutral workplace rule, such as a seniority rule, it grants the employee with a disability treatment that other workers could not receive. Yet the Act, U.S. Airways says, seeks only "equal" treatment for those with disabilities. *See, e.g.,* 42 U.S.C. § 12101(a)(9). It does not, it contends, require an employer to grant preferential treatment. *Cf.* H.R.Rep. No. 101-485, pt. 2, p. 66 (1990), U.S.Code Cong. & Admin.News 1990, pp. 303, 348-349; S.Rep. No. 101-116, pp. 26-27 (1989) (employer has no "obligation to prefer *applicants* with disabilities over other *applicants*" (emphasis added)). Hence it does not require the employer to grant a request that, in violating a disability-neutral rule, would provide a preference.

While linguistically logical, this argument fails to recognize what the Act specifies, namely, that preferences will sometimes prove necessary to achieve the Act's basic equal opportunity goal. The Act requires preferences in the form of "reasonable accommodations" that are needed for those with disabilities to obtain the *same* workplace opportunities that those without disabilities automatically enjoy. By definition any special "accommodation" requires the employer to treat an employee with a disability differently, *i.e.,* preferentially. And the fact that the difference in treatment violates an employer's disability-neutral rule cannot by itself place the accommodation beyond the Act's potential reach.

Were that not so, the "reasonable accommodation" provision could not accomplish its intended objective. Neutral office assignment rules would automatically prevent the accommodation of an employee whose disability-imposed limitations require him to work on the ground floor. Neutral "break-from-work" rules would automatically prevent the accommodation of an individual who needs additional breaks from work, perhaps to permit medical visits. Neutral furniture budget rules would automatically prevent the accommodation of an individual who needs a different kind of chair or desk. Many employers will have neutral rules governing the kinds of actions most needed to reasonably accommodate a worker with a disability. *See* 42 U.S.C. § 12111(9)(b) (setting forth examples such as "job restructuring," "part-time or modified work schedules," "acquisition or modification of equipment or devices," "and other similar accommodations"). Yet Congress, while providing such examples, said nothing suggesting that the presence of such neutral rules would create an automatic exemption. Nor have the lower courts made any such suggestion. *Cf. Garcia-Ayala v. Lederle Parenterals, Inc.*, 212 F.3d 638, 648 (1st Cir. 2000) (requiring leave beyond that allowed under the company's own leave policy); *Hendricks-Robinson v. Excel Corp.*, 154 F.3d 685, 699 (7th Cir. 1998) (requiring exception to employer's neutral "physical fitness" job requirement).

In sum, the nature of the "reasonable accommodation" requirement, the statutory examples, and the Act's silence about the exempting effect of neutral rules together convince us that the Act does not create any such automatic exemption. The simple fact that an accommodation would provide a "preference" — in the sense that it would permit the worker with a disability to violate a rule that others must obey — cannot, *in and of itself,* automatically show that the accommodation is not "reasonable." As a result, we reject the position taken by U.S. Airways and Justice Scalia to the contrary.

US Airways also points to the ADA provisions stating that a " 'reasonable accommodation' may include . . . reassignment to a *vacant* position." § 12111(9)(B) (emphasis added). And it claims that the fact that an established seniority system would assign that position to another worker automatically and always means that the position is not a "vacant" one. Nothing in the Act, however, suggests that Congress intended the word "vacant" to have a specialized meaning. And in ordinary English, a seniority system can give employees seniority rights allowing them to bid for a "vacant" position. The position in this case was held, at the time of suit, by Barnett, not by some other worker; and that position, under the U.S. Airways seniority system, became an "open" one. Moreover, U.S. Airways has said that it "reserves the right to change any and all" portions of the seniority system at will. Consequently, we cannot agree with U.S. Airways about the position's vacancy; nor do we agree that the Act would automatically deny Barnett's accommodation request for that reason.

B

Barnett argues that the statutory words "reasonable accommodation" mean only "effective accommodation," authorizing a court to consider the requested accommodation's ability to meet an individual's disability-related needs, and nothing more. On this view, a seniority rule violation, having nothing to do with the accommodation's effectiveness, has nothing to do with its "reasonableness." It might, at most, help to prove an "undue hardship on the operation of the business." But, he adds, that is a matter that the statute requires the employer to demonstrate, case by case.

In support of this interpretation Barnett points to Equal Employment Opportunity Commission (EEOC) regulations stating that "reasonable accommodation means . . . [m]odifications or adjustments . . . that *enable* a qualified individual with a disability to perform the essential functions of [a] position." 29 CFR § 1630(*o*)(ii) (2001) (emphasis added). *See also* H.R.Rep. No. 101-485, pt. 2, at 66, U.S. Code Cong. & Admin. News 1990, pp. 303, 348-349; S.Rep. No. 101-116, at 35 (discussing reasonable accommodations in terms of "effectiveness," while discussing costs in terms of "undue hardship"). Barnett adds that any other view would make the words "reasonable accommodation" and "undue hardship" virtual mirror images — creating redundancy in the statute. And he says that any such other view would create a practical burden of proof dilemma.

The practical burden of proof dilemma arises, Barnett argues, because the statute imposes the burden of demonstrating an "undue hardship" upon the employer, while the burden of proving "reasonable accommodation" remains with the plaintiff, here the employee. This allocation seems sensible in that an employer can more frequently and easily prove the presence of business hardship than an employee can prove its absence. But suppose that an employee must counter a claim of "seniority rule violation" in order to prove that an "accommodation" request is "reasonable." Would that not force the employee to prove what is in effect an absence, *i.e.,* an absence of hardship, despite the statute's insistence that the employer "demonstrate" hardship's presence?

These arguments do not persuade us that Barnett's legal interpretation of "reasonable" is correct. For one thing, in ordinary English the word "reasonable" does not mean "effective." It is the word "accommodation," not the word "reasonable," that conveys the need for effectiveness. An *ineffective* "modification" or "adjustment" will not *accommodate* a disabled individual's limitations. Nor does an ordinary English meaning of the term "reasonable accommodation" make of it a simple, redundant mirror image of the term "undue hardship." The statute refers to an "undue hardship on the operation of the business." 42 U.S.C. § 12112(b)(5)(A). Yet a demand for an effective accommodation could prove unreasonable because of its impact, not on business operations, but on fellow employees — say because it will lead to dismissals, relocations, or modification of employee benefits to which an employer, looking at the matter from the perspective of the business itself, may be relatively indifferent.

Neither does the statute's primary purpose require Barnett's special reading. The statute seeks to diminish or to eliminate the stereotypical thought processes, the thoughtless actions, and the hostile reactions that far too often bar those with disabilities from participating fully in the Nation's life, including the workplace. *See generally* §§ 12101(a) and (b). These objectives demand unprejudiced thought and reasonable responsive reaction on the part of employers and fellow workers alike. They will sometimes require affirmative conduct to promote entry of disabled people into the workforce. They do not, however, demand action beyond the realm of the reasonable.

Neither has Congress indicated in the statute, or elsewhere, that the word "reasonable" means no more than "effective." The EEOC regulations do say that reasonable accommodations "enable" a person with a disability to perform the essential functions of a task. But that phrasing simply emphasizes the statutory provision's basic objective. The regulations do not say that "enable" and "reasonable" mean the same thing. And as discussed below, no circuit court has so read them.

Finally, an ordinary language interpretation of the word "reasonable" does not create the "burden of proof" dilemma to which Barnett points. Many of the lower courts, while rejecting both U.S. Airways' and Barnett's more absolute views, have reconciled the phrases "reasonable accommodation" and "undue hardship" in a practical way.

They have held that a plaintiff/employee (to defeat a defendant/employer's motion for summary judgment) need only show that an "accommodation" seems reasonable on its face, *i.e.,* ordinarily or in the run of cases. *See, e.g., Barth v. Gelb*, 2 F.3d 1180, 1187 (D.C. Cir. 1993) (interpreting parallel language in Rehabilitation Act, stating that plaintiff need only show he seeks a "*method of accommodation* that is reasonable in the run of cases" (emphasis in original)).

Once the plaintiff has made this showing, the defendant/employer then must show special (typically case-specific) circumstances that demonstrate undue hardship in the particular circumstances. *See Barth, supra,* at 1187 ("undue hardship inquiry focuses on the hardships imposed . . . in the context of the particular agency's operations").

Not every court has used the same language, but their results are functionally similar. In our opinion, that practical view of the statute, applied consistently with ordinary summary judgment principles, avoids Barnett's burden of proof dilemma, while reconciling the two statutory phrases ("reasonable accommodation" and "undue hardship").

III

The question in the present case focuses on the relationship between seniority systems and the plaintiff's need to show that an "accommodation" seems reasonable on its face, *i.e.,* ordinarily or in the run of cases. We must assume that the plaintiff, an employee, is an "individual with a disability." He has requested assignment to a mailroom position as a "reasonable accommodation." We also assume that normally such a request would be reasonable within the meaning of the statute, were it not for one circumstance, namely, that the assignment would violate the rules of a seniority system. *See* § 12111(9) ("reasonable accommodation" may include "reassignment to a vacant position"). Does that circumstance mean that the proposed accommodation is not a "reasonable" one?

In our view, the answer to this question ordinarily is "yes." The statute does not require proof on a case-by-case basis that a seniority system should prevail. That is because it would not be reasonable in the run of cases that the assignment in question trump the rules of a seniority system. To the contrary, it will ordinarily be unreasonable for the assignment to prevail.

A

Several factors support our conclusion that a proposed accommodation will not be reasonable in the run of cases. Analogous case law supports this conclusion, for it has recognized the importance of seniority to employee-management relations. This Court has held that, in the context of a Title VII religious discrimination case, an employer need not adapt to an employee's special worship schedule as a "reasonable accommodation" where doing so would conflict with the seniority rights of other employees. *Trans World Airlines, Inc. v. Hardison*, 432 U.S. 63, 79-80 (1977). The lower courts have unanimously found that collectively bargained seniority trumps the need for reasonable accommodation in the context of the linguistically similar Rehabilitation Act. And several Circuits, though differing in their reasoning, have reached a similar conclusion in the context of seniority and the ADA. All these cases discuss *collectively bargained* seniority systems, not systems (like the present system) which are unilaterally imposed by management. But the relevant seniority system advantages, and related difficulties that result from violations of seniority rules, are not limited to collectively bargained systems.

For one thing, the typical seniority system provides important employee benefits by creating, and fulfilling, employee expectations of fair, uniform treatment. These benefits include "job security and an opportunity for steady and predictable advancement based on objective standards." They include "an element of due process," limiting "unfairness in personnel decisions." And they consequently encourage employees to invest in the employing company, accepting "less than their value to the firm early in their careers" in return for greater benefits in later years.

Most important for present purposes, to require the typical employer to show more than the existence of a seniority system might well undermine the employees' expectations of consistent, uniform treatment — expectations upon which the seniority system's benefits depend. That is because such a rule would substitute a complex case-specific "accommodation" decision made by management for the more uniform, impersonal operation of seniority rules. Such management decisionmaking, with its inevitable discretionary elements, would involve a matter of the greatest importance to employees, namely, layoffs; it would take place outside, as well as inside, the confines of a court case; and it might well take place fairly often. *Cf.* ADA, 42 U.S.C. § 12101(a)(1) (estimating that some 43 million Americans suffer from physical or mental disabilities). We can find nothing in the statute that suggests Congress intended to undermine seniority systems in this way. And we consequently conclude that the employer's showing of violation of the rules of a seniority system is by itself ordinarily sufficient.

B

The plaintiff (here the employee) nonetheless remains free to show that special circumstances warrant a finding that, despite the presence of a seniority system (which the ADA may not trump in the run of cases), the requested "accommodation" is "reasonable" on the particular facts. That is because special circumstances might alter the important expectations described above. The plaintiff might show, for example, that the employer, having retained the right to change the seniority system unilaterally, exercises that right fairly frequently, reducing employee expectations that the system will be followed — to the point where one more departure, needed to accommodate an individual with a disability, will not likely make a difference. The plaintiff might show that the system already contains exceptions such that, in the circumstances, one further exception is unlikely to matter. We do not mean these examples to exhaust the kinds of showings that a plaintiff might make. But we do mean to say that the plaintiff must bear the burden of showing special circumstances that make an exception from the seniority system reasonable in the particular case. And to do so, the plaintiff must explain why, in the particular case, an exception to the employer's seniority policy can constitute a "reasonable accommodation" even though in the ordinary case it cannot.

IV

In its question presented, U.S. Airways asked us whether the ADA requires an employer to assign a disabled employee to a particular position even though another employee is entitled to that position under the employer's "established seniority system." We answer that *ordinarily* the ADA does not require that assignment. Hence, a showing that the assignment would violate the rules of a seniority system warrants summary judgment for the employer — unless there is more. The plaintiff must present evidence of that "more," namely, special circumstances surrounding the particular case that demonstrate the assignment is nonetheless reasonable.

Because the lower courts took a different view of the matter, and because neither party has had an opportunity to seek summary judgment in accordance with the principles we set forth here, we vacate the Court of Appeals' judgment and remand the case for further proceedings consistent with this opinion.

It is so ordered.

JUSTICE STEVENS, concurring.

While I join the Court's opinion, my colleagues' separate writings prompt these additional comments. . . .

Although the Court of Appeals did not apply the standard that the Court endorses today, it correctly rejected the *per se* rule that petitioner has pressed upon us and properly reversed the District Court's entry of summary judgment for petitioner. The Court of Appeals also correctly held that there was a triable issue of fact precluding the entry of summary judgment with respect to whether petitioner violated the statute by failing to engage in an interactive process concerning respondent's three proposed accommodations. This latter holding is untouched by the Court's opinion today.

Among the questions that I have not been able to answer on the basis of the limited record that has been presented to us are: (1) whether the mailroom position held by respondent became open for bidding merely in response to a routine airline schedule change, or as the direct consequence of the layoff of several thousand employees; (2) whether respondent's requested accommodation should be viewed as an assignment to a vacant position, or as the maintenance of the status quo; and (3) exactly what impact the grant of respondent's request would have had on other employees. As I understand the Court's opinion, on remand, respondent will have the burden of answering these and other questions in order to overcome the presumption that petitioner's seniority system justified respondent's discharge.

JUSTICE O'CONNOR, concurring.

I agree with portions of the opinion of the Court, but I find problematic the Court's test for determining whether the fact that a job reassignment violates a seniority system makes the reassignment an unreasonable accommodation under the Americans with Disabilities Act of 1990 (ADA or Act). Although a seniority system plays an important role in the workplace, for the reasons I explain below, I would prefer to say that the effect of a seniority system on the reasonableness of a reassignment as an accommodation for purposes of the ADA depends on whether the seniority system is legally enforceable. [I]n order that the Court may adopt a rule, and because I believe the Court's rule will often lead to the same outcome as the one I would have adopted, I join the Court's opinion despite my concerns.

The ADA specifically lists "reassignment to a vacant position" as one example of a "reasonable accommodation." 42 U.S.C. § 12111(9)(B). In deciding whether an otherwise reasonable accommodation involving a reassignment is unreasonable because it would require an exception to a seniority system, I think the relevant issue is whether the seniority system prevents the position in question from being vacant. The word "vacant" means "not filled or occupied by an incumbent [or] possessor." WEBSTER'S THIRD NEW INTERNATIONAL DICTIONARY 2527 (1976). In the context of a workplace, a vacant position is a position in which no employee currently works and to which no individual has a legal entitlement. For example, in a workplace without a seniority system, when an employee ceases working for the employer, the employee's former position is vacant until a replacement is hired. Even if the replacement does not start work immediately, once the replacement enters into a contractual agreement with the employer, the position is no longer vacant because it has a "possessor." In contrast, when an employee ceases working in a workplace with a legally enforceable seniority system, the employee's former position does not become vacant if the seniority system entitles another employee to it. Instead, the employee entitled to the position under the seniority system immediately becomes the new "possessor" of that position. In a workplace with an unenforceable seniority policy, however, an employee expecting assignment to a position under the seniority policy would not have any type of contractual right to the position and so could not be said to be its "possessor." The position therefore would become vacant.

Given this understanding of when a position can properly be considered vacant, if a seniority system, in the absence of the ADA, would give someone other than the individual seeking the accommodation a legal entitlement or contractual right to the position to which reassignment is sought, the seniority system prevents the position from being vacant. If a position is not vacant, then reassignment to it is not a reasonable accommodation. The Act specifically says that "reassignment to a *vacant* position" is a type of "reasonable accommodation." § 12111(9)(B) (emphasis added). . . .

Petitioner's Personnel Policy Guide for Agents, which contains its seniority policy, specifically states that it is "*not* intended to be a contract (express or implied) or otherwise to create legally enforceable obligations," and that petitioner "reserves the right to change any and all of the stated policies and procedures in [the] Guide at any time, without advanc[e] notice." . . . Because the policy did not give any other employee a right to the position respondent sought, the position could be said to have been vacant when it became open for bidding, making the requested accommodation reasonable.

In Part II of its opinion, the Court correctly explains that "a plaintiff/employee (to defeat a defendant/employer's motion for summary judgment) need only show that an 'accommodation' seems reasonable on its face, *i.e.,* ordinarily or in the run of cases." In other words, the plaintiff must show that the method of accommodation the employee seeks is reasonable in the run of cases. As the Court also correctly explains, "[o]nce the plaintiff has made this showing, the defendant/employer then must show special . . . circumstances that demonstrate undue hardship" in the context of the particular employer's operations. These interpretations give appropriate meaning to both the term "reasonable," 42 U.S.C. § 12112(b)(5)(A), and the term "undue hardship," *ibid.,* preventing the concepts from overlapping by making reasonableness a general inquiry and undue hardship a specific inquiry. When the Court turns to applying its interpretation of the Act to seniority systems, however, it seems to blend the two inquiries by suggesting that the plaintiff should have the opportunity to prove that there are special circumstances in the context of that particular seniority system that would cause an exception to the system to be reasonable despite the fact that such exceptions are unreasonable in the run of cases.

Although I am troubled by the Court's reasoning, I believe the Court's approach for evaluating seniority systems will often lead to the same outcome as the test I would have adopted. Unenforceable seniority systems are likely to involve policies in which employers "retai[n] the right to change the system," and will often "permi[t] exceptions." They will also often contain disclaimers that "reduc[e] employee expectations that the system will be followed." Thus, under the Court's test, disabled employees seeking accommodations that would require exceptions to unenforceable seniority systems may be able to show circumstances that make the accommodation "reasonable in the[ir] particular case." Because I think the Court's test will often lead to the correct outcome, and because I think it important that a majority of the Court agree on a rule when interpreting statutes, I join the Court's opinion.

JUSTICE SCALIA, with whom JUSTICE THOMAS joins, dissenting.

The question presented asks whether the "reasonable accommodation" mandate of the Americans with Disabilities Act of 1990 (ADA or Act) requires reassignment of a disabled employee to a position that "another employee is entitled to hold . . . under the employer's bona fide and established seniority system." Indulging its penchant for eschewing clear rules that might avoid litigation, the Court answers "maybe." It creates a presumption that an exception to a seniority rule is an "unreasonable" accommodation, but allows that presumption to be rebutted by showing that the exception "will not likely make a difference."

The principal defect of today's opinion, however, goes well beyond the uncertainty it produces regarding the relationship between the ADA and the infinite variety of seniority systems. The conclusion that any seniority system can ever be overridden is merely one consequence of a mistaken interpretation of the ADA that makes all employment rules and practices — even those which (like a seniority system) pose no *distinctive* obstacle to the disabled — subject to suspension when that is (in a court's view) a "reasonable" means of enabling a disabled employee to keep his job. That is a far cry from what I believe the accommodation provision of the ADA requires: the suspension (within reason) of those employment rules and practices *that the employee's disability prevents him from observing.*

I

The Court begins its analysis by describing the ADA as declaring that an employer may not "discriminate against a qualified individual with a disability." In fact the Act says more: an employer may not "discriminate against a qualified individual with a disability *because of the disability* of such individual." 42 U.S.C. § 12112(a) (emphasis added). It further provides that discrimination includes "not making reasonable accommodations *to the known physical or mental limitations* of an otherwise qualified individual with a disability." § 12112(b)(5)(A) (emphasis added).

Read together, these provisions order employers to modify or remove (within reason) policies and practices that burden a disabled person "because of [his] disability." In other words, the ADA eliminates workplace barriers only if a disability prevents an employee from overcoming them — those barriers that would not be barriers *but for* the employee's disability. These include, for example, work stations that cannot accept the employee's wheelchair, or an assembly-line practice that requires long periods of standing. But they do not include rules and practices that bear no more heavily upon the disabled employee than upon others — even though an exemption from such a rule or practice might in a sense "make up for" the employee's disability. It is not a required accommodation, for example, to pay a disabled employee more than others at his grade level — even if that increment is earmarked for massage or physical therapy that would enable the employee to work with as little physical discomfort as his co-workers. That would be "accommodating" the disabled employee, but it would not be "making . . . accommodatio[n] *to the known physical or mental limitations*" of the employee, § 12112(b)(5)(A), because it would not eliminate any workplace practice that constitutes an obstacle *because of* his disability.

So also with exemption from a seniority system, which burdens the disabled and nondisabled alike. In particular cases, seniority rules may have a harsher effect upon the disabled employee than upon his co-workers. If the disabled employee is physically capable of performing only one task in the workplace, seniority rules may be, for him, the difference between employment and unemployment. But that does not make the seniority system a disability-related obstacle, any more than harsher impact upon the more needy disabled employee renders the salary system a disability-related obstacle. When one departs from this understanding, the ADA's accommodation provision becomes a standardless grab bag — leaving it to the courts to decide which workplace preferences (higher salary, longer vacations, reassignment to positions to which others are entitled) can be deemed "reasonable" to "make up for" the particular employee's disability.

Some courts, including the Ninth Circuit in the present case, have accepted respondent's contention that the ADA demands accommodation even with respect to those obstacles that have nothing to do with the disability. Their principal basis for this position is that the definition of "reasonable accommodation" includes "reassignment to a vacant position." § 12111(9)(B). This accommodation would be meaningless, they contend, if it required only that the disabled employee be *considered* for a vacant position. The ADA already prohibits employers from discriminating against the disabled with respect to "hiring, advancement, or discharge . . . and other terms, conditions, and privileges of employment." § 12112(a). Surely, the argument goes, a disabled employee must be given preference over a nondisabled employee when a vacant position appears.

This argument seems to me quite mistaken. The right to be given a vacant position so long as there are no obstacles to that appointment (including another candidate who is better qualified, if "best qualified" is the workplace rule) is of considerable value. If an employee is hired to fill a position but fails miserably, he will typically be fired. Few employers will search their organization charts for vacancies to which the low-performing employee might be suited. The ADA, however, prohibits an employer from firing a person whose disability is the cause of his poor performance without first seeking to place him in a vacant job where the disability will not affect performance. Such reassignment is an accommodation *to the disability* because it removes an obstacle (the inability to perform the functions of the assigned job) arising solely from the disability.

The phrase "reassignment to a vacant position" appears in a subsection describing a variety of potential "reasonable accommodation[s]":

> "(A) making existing facilities used by employees readily accessible to and usable by individuals with disabilities; and

> "(B) job restructuring, part-time or modified work schedules, *reassignment to a vacant position,* acquisition or modification of equipment or devices, appropriate adjustment or modifications of examinations, training materials or policies, the provision of qualified readers or interpreters, and other similar accommodations for individuals with disabilities." § 12111(9) (emphasis added).

Subsection (A) clearly addresses features of the workplace that burden the disabled *because of* their disabilities. Subsection (B) is broader in scope but equally targeted at disability-related obstacles. Thus it encompasses "modified work schedules" (which may accommodate inability to work for protracted periods), "modification of equipment and devices," and "provision of qualified readers or interpreters." There is no reason why the phrase "reassignment to a vacant position" should be thought to have a uniquely different focus. It envisions elimination of the obstacle of the *current position* (which requires activity that the disabled employee cannot tolerate) when there is an alternate position freely available. If he is qualified for that position, and no one else is seeking it, or no one else who seeks it is better qualified, he *must* be given the position. But "reassignment to a vacant position" does *not* envision the elimination of obstacles to the employee's service in the new position that have nothing to do with his disability — for example, another employee's claim to that position under a seniority system, or another employee's superior qualifications.

Sadly, this analysis is lost on the Court, which mistakenly and inexplicably concludes that my position here is the same as that attributed to U.S. Airways. In rejecting the argument that the ADA creates no "automatic exemption" for neutral workplace rules such as "break-from-work" and furniture budget rules, the Court rejects an argument I have not made.

II

Although, as I have said, the uncertainty cast upon bona fide seniority systems is the least of the ill consequences produced by today's decision, a few words on that subject are nonetheless in order. Since, under the Court's interpretation of the ADA, *all* workplace rules are eligible to be used as vehicles of accommodation, the one means of saving seniority systems is a judicial finding that accommodation through the suspension of *those* workplace rules would be unreasonable. The Court is unwilling, however, to make that finding categorically, with respect to all seniority systems. Instead, it creates (and "creates" is the appropriate word) a *rebuttable presumption* that exceptions to seniority rules are not "reasonable" under the ADA, but leaves it free for the disabled employee to show that *under the "special circumstances" of his case,* an exception would be "reasonable." The employee would be entitled to an exception, for example, if he showed that "one more departure" from the seniority rules "will not likely make a difference."

I have no idea what this means. When is it possible for a departure from seniority rules to "not likely make a difference"? Even when a bona fide seniority system has multiple exceptions, employees expect that these are the *only* exceptions. One more unannounced exception will undermine the values ("fair, uniform treatment," "job security," "predictable advancement," etc.) that the Court cites as its reasons for believing seniority systems so important that they merit a presumption of exemption.

One is tempted to impart some rationality to the scheme by speculating that the Court's burden-shifting rule is merely intended to give the disabled employee an opportunity to show that the employer's seniority system is in fact a sham — a system so full of exceptions that it creates no meaningful employee expectations. The rule applies, however, even if the seniority system is "bona fide and established." And the Court says that "to require the typical employer to show more than the existence of a seniority system might well undermine the employees' expectations of consistent, uniform treatment. . . ." How could deviations from a sham seniority system "undermine the employees' expectations"?

I must conclude, then, that the Court's rebuttable presumption does not merely give disabled employees the opportunity to unmask sham seniority systems; it gives them a vague and unspecified power (whenever they can show "special circumstances") to undercut *bona fide* systems. The Court claims that its new test will not require exceptions to seniority systems "in the run of cases," but that is belied by the disposition of this case. The Court remands to give respondent an opportunity to show that an exception to petitioner's seniority system "will not likely make a difference" to employee expectations, despite the following finding by the District Court:

> "[T]he uncontroverted evidence shows that [petitioner's] seniority system has been in place for 'decades' and governs over 14,000 . . . Agents. Moreover, seniority policies such as the one at issue in this case are common to the airline industry. Given this context, it seems clear that [petitioner's] employees were justified in relying upon the policy. As such, any significant alteration of that policy would result in undue hardship to both the company and its non-disabled employees."

. . . .

Because the Court's opinion leaves the question whether a seniority system must be disregarded in order to accommodate a disabled employee in a state of uncertainty that can be resolved only by constant litigation; and because it adopts an interpretation of the ADA that incorrectly subjects all employer rules and practices to the requirement of reasonable accommodation; I respectfully dissent.

JUSTICE SOUTER, with whom JUSTICE GINSBURG joins, dissenting . . .

Nothing in the ADA insulates seniority rules from the "reasonable accommodation" requirement, in marked contrast to Title VII of the Civil Rights Act of 1964 and the Age Discrimination in Employment Act of 1967, each of which has an explicit protection for seniority. *See* 42 U.S.C. § 2000e-2(h) ("Notwithstanding any other provision of this subchapter, it shall not be an unlawful employment practice for an employer to [provide different benefits to employees] pursuant to a bona fide seniority . . . system. . . ."); 29 U.S.C. § 623(f) ("It shall not be unlawful for an employer . . . to take any action otherwise prohibited [under previous sections] . . . to observe the terms of a bona fide seniority system [except for involuntary retirement] . . ."). Because Congress modeled several of the ADA's provisions on Title VII, its failure to replicate Title VII's exemption for seniority systems leaves the statute ambiguous, albeit with more than a hint that seniority rules do not inevitably carry the day.

In any event, the statute's legislative history resolves the ambiguity. The Committee Reports from both the House of Representatives and the Senate explain that seniority protections contained in a collective-bargaining agreement should not amount to more than "a factor" when it comes to deciding whether some accommodation at odds with the seniority rules is "reasonable" nevertheless. H.R. Rep. No. 101-485, pt. 2, p. 63 (1990), U.S.Code Cong. & Admin.News 1990, pp. 303, 345, (existence of collectively bargained protections for seniority "would not be determinative" on the issue whether an accommodation was reasonable); S. Rep. No. 101-116, p. 32 (1989) (a collective-bargaining agreement assigning jobs based on seniority "may be considered as a factor in determining" whether an accommodation is reasonable). Here, of course, it does not matter whether the congressional committees were right or wrong in thinking that views of sound ADA application could reduce a collectively bargained seniority policy to the level of "a factor," in the absence of a specific statutory provision to that effect. In fact, I doubt that any interpretive clue in legislative history could trump settled law specifically making collective bargaining agreements enforceable. The point in this case, however, is simply to recognize that if Congress considered that sort of agreement no more than a factor in the analysis, surely no greater weight was meant for a seniority scheme like the one before us, unilaterally imposed by the employer, and, unlike collective bargaining agreements, not singled out for protection by any positive federal statute.

This legislative history also specifically rules out the majority's reliance on *Trans World Airlines, Inc. v. Hardison*, 432 U.S. 63 (1977), a case involving a request for a religious accommodation under Title VII that would have broken the seniority rules of a collective-bargaining agreement. We held that such an accommodation would not be "reasonable," and said that our conclusion was "supported" by Title VII's explicit exemption for seniority systems. The committees of both Houses of Congress dealing with the ADA were aware of this case and expressed a choice against treating it as authority under the ADA, with its lack of any provision for maintaining seniority rules. *E.g.,* H.R. Rep. No. 101-485, pt.2, at 68 ("The Committee wishes to make it clear that the principles enunciated by the Supreme Court in *TWA v. Hardison* . . . are not applicable to this legislation"); S. Rep. No. 101-116, at 36 (same).

Because a unilaterally-imposed seniority system enjoys no special protection under the ADA, a consideration of facts peculiar to this very case is needed to gauge whether Barnett has carried the burden of showing his proposed accommodation to be a "reasonable" one despite the policy in force at U.S. Airways. The majority describes this as a burden to show the accommodation is "plausible" or "feasible," and I believe Barnett has met it.

He held the mailroom job for two years before learning that employees with greater seniority planned to bid for the position, given U.S. Airways's decision to declare the job "vacant." Thus, perhaps unlike ADA claimants who request accommodation through reassignment, Barnett was seeking not a change but a continuation of the status quo. All he asked was that U.S. Airways refrain from declaring the position "vacant"; he did not ask to bump any other employee and no one would have lost a job on his account. There was no evidence in the District Court of any unmanageable ripple effects from Barnett's request, or showing that he would have overstepped an inordinate number of seniority levels by remaining where he was.

In fact, it is hard to see the seniority scheme here as any match for Barnett's ADA requests, since U.S. Airways apparently took pains to ensure that its seniority rules raised no great expectations. In its policy statement, U.S. Airways said that "[t]he Agent Personnel Policy Guide is *not* intended to be a contract" and that "USAir reserves the right to change any and all of the stated policies and procedures in this Guide at any time, without advanced notice." While I will skip any state-by-state analysis of the legal treatment of employee handbooks (a source of many lawyers' fees) it is safe to say that the contract law of a number of jurisdictions would treat this disclaimer as fatal to any claim an employee might make to enforce the seniority policy over an employer's contrary decision.

With U.S. Airways itself insisting that its seniority system was noncontractual and modifiable at will, there is no reason to think that Barnett's accommodation would have resulted in anything more than minimal disruption to U.S. Airways's operations, if that. Barnett has shown his requested accommodation to be "reasonable," and the burden ought to shift to U.S. Airways if it wishes to claim that, in spite of surface appearances, violation of the seniority scheme would have worked an undue hardship. I would therefore affirm the Ninth Circuit.

NOTES

1. *The Limits of Reasonable Accommodation.* Determining the precise boundaries of the duty of reasonable accommodation is very difficult. *Barnett* is the leading case on the topic, and the only guidance provided by the Supreme Court. *Barnett* considered an accommodation which would have imposed costs mostly on other workers in the form of lost opportunities. But that is only one of a wide variety of possible costs.

More commonly, the issue is more direct: how much must an employer spend before an accommodation becomes unreasonable? The leading study indicates that most accommodations tend to be inexpensive. A study of Sears, Roebuck, and Co. found that between 1993 and 1996, seventy-two percent of the company's accommodations for individuals with disabilities required no cost, twenty-seven percent cost less than $500, and only one percent cost more than $500. The average cost of an accommodation was $45. By comparison, the average cost of replacing an employee who was not accommodated was $1,800 to $2,400. Peter David Blanck, *Transcending Title I of the Americans With Disabilities Act: A Report on Sears, Roebuck and Co.*, 20 MENTAL & PHYSICAL DISABILITY L. REP. 278 (1996). But, of course, that does not mean that all accommodations are cheap. One of the leading early cases on reasonable accommodation required an employer to hire half-time readers for blind social workers at an annual cost of more than $6,500 per worker. *Nelson v. Thornburgh*, 567 F. Supp. 369 (E.D. Pa. 1983), *aff'd*, 732 F.2d 146 (3d Cir. 1984), *cert. denied*, 469 U.S. 1188 (1985) (decided under the Rehabilitation Act).

Costs can also appear in many other forms. For example:

(a) Does reasonable accommodation ever require employers to grant a leave of absence? *Compare Garcia-Ayala v. Lederle Parenterals, Inc.*, 212 F.3d 638 (1st Cir. 2000) (employer may be required to extend leave five months beyond one-year leave provided under employer's leave policies), *with Cisneros v. Wilson*, 226 F.3d 1113 (10th Cir. 2000) (employer not required to grant requested three-month leave where employee's ability to return to work at end of leave uncertain).

(b) Does reasonable accommodation ever require an employer to permit an employee to work from home? *Compare Vande Zande v. State of Wisconsin*, 44 F.3d 538 (7th Cir. 1995) (work at home only required in "extraordinary" case because most jobs require team work and supervision), *with Humphrey v. Memorial Hosps. Ass'n*, 239 F.3d 1128 (9th Cir. 2000), *cert. denied*, 535 U.S. 1011 (2002) (work at home may be required for medical transcriptionist with obsessive-compulsive disorder).

2. *The Procedural Aspect of Reasonable Accommodation.* The evolving concept of reasonable accommodation has a procedural component as well as a substantive one. The courts generally agree that employers must explore accommodation possibilities with individuals with disabilities and those individuals, in turn, have a correlative duty to aid in this exploration. A failure to engage in this type of interactive process may itself violate the employer's duty of reasonable accommodation. *See, e.g., Canny v. Dr. Pepper/Seven-Up Bottling Group, Inc.*, 439 F.3d 894 (8th Cir. 2006); *Cutrera v. Board of Supervisors*, 429 F.3d 108 (5th Cir. 2005). The Court in *Barnett* had granted certiorari on this issue, so it was interesting that only Justice Stevens mentioned it in his opinion.

3. *Reasonable Accommodation under Title VII.* As the dissenters in *Barnett* point out, the accommodations required for religious beliefs and practices under Title VII are more limited than the accommodations required under the ADA and the Rehabilitation Act. In *Trans World Airlines v. Hardison*, 432 U.S. 63 (1977), the plaintiff's religious tenets required that he refrain from work from sunset on Friday until sunset on Saturday. TWA eventually discharged him for failing to work during his scheduled shifts during those times. The Supreme Court held that TWA had not violated Title VII because both of the possible accommodations in the case would have imposed an "undue hardship." One accommodation that TWA could have made would have been to circumvent the seniority system and schedule another employee to work during the time Hardison's religious tenets prevented him from working. The Court held that TWA was not required to make that accommodation, because it would be anomalous under a statute prohibiting religious discrimination to deprive another employee of her shift preference because she did not adhere to a religion with a Saturday Sabbath. Thus, narrowly read, *Hardison* means that employers need not make accommodations if they would result in any interference with a seniority system. More broadly read, *Hardison* may mean that accommodations need not be made if they would result in any interference with the preferences of other employees. TWA could also have accommodated Hardison by encouraging other employees to work on Hardison's shift by paying them overtime. The Court held, however, that anything more than a "de minimis cost" is an undue hardship. Thus, that accommodation was not required by Title VII either. In a later case, the Supreme Court indicated that if two or more reasonable accommodations are possible, employers need not select the one that is most favorable to the employee; employers meet their obligation by offering *any* reasonable accommodation. *Ansonia Bd. of Educ. v. Philbrook*, 479 U.S. 60 (1986).

Do you think the courts apply a less stringent version of the reasonable accommodation model to religious discrimination because they perceive that problem to be less serious than discrimination against persons with disabilities? Or are there other reasons? *See Protos v. Volkswagen of Am. Inc.*, 797 F.2d 129 (3d Cir.), *cert. denied*, 479 U.S. 972 (1986) (religious-accommodation requirement does not violate First Amendment).

4. *The Uneasy Status of Undue Hardship.* The relationship between reasonable accommodation and undue hardship is problematic. The undue hardship issue is reached only after an accommodation has been proven to be reasonable. But how can a *reasonable* accommodation ever impose an undue hardship? Wouldn't the accommodation be unreasonable if it imposed an undue hardship? But that interpretation would read the undue hardship stage of the analysis out of the statute, which violates standard canons of statutory construction.

The majority in *Barnett* articulates the standard distinction. Reasonable accommodation refers to whether the accommodation would be reasonable in the "ordinary" case or "in the run of cases," while undue hardship refers to special burdens the accommodation might impose given the employer's particular circumstances. In her concurring opinion, Justice O'Connor worries that the Court blended these two inquiries in its analysis or, worse, applied them backwards by permitting special circumstances to render reasonable accommodations that would be unreasonable in the run of cases.

5. *Qualified Individual with a Disability.* Employers are only required to accommodate "qualified" individuals with disabilities, but this requirement is intimately connected to the accommodation duty. "Qualified" individuals with disabilities are those who *"with or without reasonable accommodation, can perform the essential functions of the employment position."* ADA § 101(8). The notions of qualification and essential functions are also difficult and evolving:

(a) When is regular attendance an essential job function? *Compare Ward v. Massachusetts Health Research Inst.* 209 F.3d 29 (5th Cir. 2000) (regular attendance may not be required for data entry position), *with Buckles v. First Data Resources, Inc.*, 176 F.3d 1098 (8th Cir. 1999) (regular attendance an essential function of most jobs).

(b) How should courts evaluate jobs with many functions? *See, e.g., Stone v. City of Mount Vernon*, 118 F.3d 92 (2d Cir. 1997), *cert. denied*, 522 U.S. 1112 (1998) (paraplegic may be qualified for a fire department job because not all employees engage in fire fighting and department may be able to absorb one individual who cannot perform that function); *Lujan v. Pacific Maritime Ass'n*, 165 F.3d 738 (9th Cir. 1999) (improper to bundle all possible types of longshoremen assignments into position; plaintiff may be qualified if he can perform some, but not all functions).

(c) To what extent should courts rely on the employer's articulation of the essential functions of a job? ADA § 101(8) ("consideration shall be given to the employer's judgment as to what functions of a job are essential"). *See Davis v. Florida Power & Light Co.*, 205 F.3d 1301 (11th Cir. 2000), *cert. denied*, 531 U.S. 927 (2000) (overtime is an essential function of the job even though employer failed to include it in job description) *Milton v. Scrivner, Inc.*, 53 F.3d 1118 (10th Cir. 1995) (speed an essential function of job based on employer's production standards even though the standards are new and operate to exclude disabled employees currently performing job).

6. *A New Type of Discrimination?* Consider two bare-bones hypotheticals comparing the reasonable-accommodation model with the other two major models of discrimination:

(a) *Disparate Treatment.*

An employer entertains job applications and rejects two applicants, the first because she is a woman, the second because she is disabled. Do the rejected applicants have good claims?

The woman has a good claim. This is explicit, intentional discrimination because of sex. The only defense under Title VII would be whether sex was a bona fide occupational qualification (BFOQ) and that defense is narrowly construed to prevent it from swamping Title VII's general command to ignore the sex of workers. Importantly, cost considerations are not a part of the BFOQ defense.

The disabled worker may also have a good claim, but it is much more fragile than the woman's. The ADA prohibits employers from considering disability in an invidious or stereotypical way. But the ADA contemplates that employers will often consider disability in a legitimate way. Indeed, the procedural aspect of the accommodation duty *requires* employers to consider disability. The employer can avoid ADA liability for its reliance on disability if the worker cannot perform the essential requirements of the job, if an unreasonable accommodation would be required, or if the accommodation would impose an undue hardship on the employer. These inquiries are different in kind from the BFOQ inquiry. Most importantly, cost considerations are the heart of the matter under the ADA, while they are banned under Title VII. Mere consideration of sex exposes an employer to considerable risk of a Title VII violation.

Consideration of disability, on the other hand, merely opens the door to ADA analysis; reasonable accommodation and undue hardship often provide a defense to liability.

(b) *Disparate Impact.*

Suppose a job requires frequent lifting of 80 pound sacks. The employer screens out job applicants by asking them to lift an 80 pound sack. Two applicants are rejected because they could not lift the sack: a woman and a person in a wheelchair. How do their claims fare?

The woman has only a weak claim because, even though the requirement may have a disparate impact on women, the employer is likely to be able to defend successfully by demonstrating that the test is job related and consistent with business necessity. The woman cannot argue that the 80 pound sacks should be split into 40 pound sacks to make it easier for women to hold the jobs. Title VII examines the test, not the job. By contrast, the rejected disabled applicant can challenge the job itself. The ADA's reasonable accommodation requirement requires the employer to consider dividing the 80 pound sacks as a method of accommodation.

These comparisons between reasonable accommodation, on the one hand, and the disparate treatment and impact models, on the other hand, have lead some commentators to argue that the ADA is a distinct model of discrimination which, even though it may be justified, places heavier burdens on employers than do prior antidiscrimination statutes, such as Title VII. *See* Stewart J. Schwab & Steven L. Willborn, *Reasonable Accommodation of Workplace Disabilities*, 44 WM. & MARY L. REV. 1197 (2003) (ADA imposes hard preferences on employers requiring direct expenditures to comply, while Title VII only imposes soft, nondiscrimination preferences); Samuel Issacharoff & Justin Nelson, *Discrimination With a Difference: Can Employment Discrimination Law Accommodate the Americans With Disabilities Act?*, 79 N.C. L. REV. 307 (2001) (Title VII is primarily focused on nondiscrimination with redistribution as a byproduct; the ADA, in contrast, is primarily redistributive and is not constrained by the nondiscrimination obligation). This view has been challenged by Professor Christine Jolls who argues within an economic framework that Title VII's "nondiscrimination" mandates are broadly similar to the accommodation mandates of the ADA. Christine Jolls, *Accommodation Mandates*, 53 STAN. L. REV. 223 (2000).

Chapter 15

APPLYING THE LEGAL MODELS OF DISCRIMINATION

A. SEX DISCRIMINATION

1. SEXUAL HARASSMENT

HARRIS v. FORKLIFT SYSTEMS, INC.
United States Supreme Court
510 U.S. 17 (1993)

JUSTICE O'CONNOR delivered the opinion for a unanimous Court.

In this case we consider the definition of a discriminatorily "abusive work environment" (also known as a "hostile work environment") under Title VII of the Civil Rights Act of 1964.

I

Teresa Harris worked as a manager at Forklift Systems, Inc., an equipment rental company, from April 1985 until October 1987. Charles Hardy was Forklift's president.

The Magistrate found that, throughout Harris' time at Forklift, Hardy often insulted her because of her gender and often made her the target of unwanted sexual innuendos. Hardy told Harris on several occasions, in the presence of other employees, "You're a woman, what do you know" and "We need a man as the rental manager"; at least once, he told her she was "a dumb ass woman." Again in front of others, he suggested that the two of them "go to the Holiday Inn to negotiate [Harris'] raise." Hardy occasionally asked Harris and other female employees to get coins from his front pants pocket. He threw objects on the ground in front of Harris and other women, and asked them to pick the objects up. He made sexual innuendos about Harris' and other women's clothing.

In mid-August 1987, Harris complained to Hardy about his conduct. Hardy said he was surprised that Harris was offended, claimed he was only joking, and apologized. He also promised he would stop, and based on this assurance Harris stayed on the job. But in early September, Hardy began anew: While Harris was arranging a deal with one of Forklift's customers, he asked her, again in front of other employees, "What did you do, promise the guy . . . some [sex] Saturday night?" On October 1, Harris collected her paycheck and quit.

Harris then sued Forklift, claiming that Hardy's conduct had created an abusive work environment for her because of her gender. The United States District Court for the Middle District of Tennessee, adopting the report and

473

recommendation of the Magistrate, found this to be "a close case," but held that Hardy's conduct did not create an abusive environment. The court found that some of Hardy's comments "offended [Harris], and would offend the reasonable woman," but that they were not

> so severe as to be expected to seriously affect [Harris'] psychological well-being. A reasonable woman manager under like circumstances would have been offended by Hardy, but his conduct would not have risen to the level of interfering with that person's work performance.

> Neither do I believe that [Harris] was subjectively so offended that she suffered injury. . . . Although Hardy may at times have genuinely offended [Harris], I do not believe that he created a working environment so poisoned as to be intimidating or abusive to [Harris]. . . .

We granted certiorari to resolve a conflict among the Circuits on whether conduct, to be actionable as "abusive work environment" harassment (no *quid pro quo* harassment issue is present here), must "seriously affect [an employee's] psychological well-being" or lead the plaintiff to "suffe[r] injury."

II

Title VII of the Civil Rights Act of 1964 makes it "an unlawful employment practice for an employer . . . to discriminate against any individual with respect to his compensation, terms, conditions, or privileges of employment, because of such individual's race, color, religion, sex, or national origin." 42 U.S.C. § 2000e-2(a)(1). As we made clear in *Meritor Savings Bank v. Vinson*, 477 U.S. 57 (1986), this language "is not limited to 'economic' or 'tangible' discrimination. The phrase 'terms, conditions, or privileges of employment' evinces a congressional intent 'to strike at the entire spectrum of disparate treatment of men and women' in employment," which includes requiring people to work in a discriminatorily hostile or abusive environment. *Id.*, at 64. When the workplace is permeated with "discriminatory intimidation, ridicule, and insult," 477 U.S., at 65, that is "sufficiently severe or pervasive to alter the conditions of the victim's employment and create an abusive working environment," *id.*, at 67, Title VII is violated.

This standard, which we reaffirm today, takes a middle path between making actionable any conduct that is merely offensive and requiring the conduct to cause a tangible psychological injury. As we pointed out in *Meritor*, "mere utterance of an . . . epithet which engenders offensive feelings in a employee" does not sufficiently affect the conditions of employment to implicate Title VII. Conduct that is not severe or pervasive enough to create an objectively hostile or abusive work environment — an environment that a reasonable person would find hostile or abusive — is beyond Title VII's purview. Likewise, if the victim does not subjectively perceive the environment to be abusive, the conduct has not actually altered the conditions of the victim's employment, and there is no Title VII violation.

But Title VII comes into play before the harassing conduct leads to a nervous breakdown. A discriminatorily abusive work environment, even one that does not seriously affect employees' psychological well-being, can and often will detract from employees' job performance, discourage employees from remaining on the job, or keep them from advancing in their careers. Moreover, even without regard to these tangible effects, the very fact that the discriminatory conduct was so severe or pervasive that it created a work environment abusive to employees because of their race, gender, religion, or national origin offends Title VII's broad rule of workplace equality. The appalling conduct alleged in *Meritor*, and the reference in that case to environments "so heavily polluted with discrimination as to destroy completely the emotional and psychological stability of minority group workers," merely present some especially egregious examples of harassment. They do not mark the boundary of what is actionable.

We therefore believe the District Court erred in relying on whether the conduct "seriously affect[ed] plaintiff's psychological well-being" or led her to "suffe[r] injury." Such an inquiry may needlessly focus the factfinder's attention on concrete psychological harm, an element Title VII does not require. Certainly Title VII bars conduct that would seriously affect a reasonable person's psychological well-being, but the statute is not limited to such conduct. So long as the environment would reasonably be perceived, and is perceived, as hostile or abusive, there is no need for it also to be psychologically injurious.

This is not, and by its nature cannot be, a mathematically precise test. We need not answer today all the potential questions it raises. . . . But we can say that whether an environment is "hostile" or "abusive" can be determined only by looking at all the circumstances. These may include the frequency of the discriminatory conduct; its severity; whether it is physically threatening or humiliating, or a mere offensive utterance; and whether it unreasonably interferes with an employee's work performance. The effect on the employee's psychological well-being is, of course, relevant to determining whether the plaintiff actually found the environment abusive. But while psychological harm, like any other relevant factor, may be taken into account, no single factor is required.

III

Forklift, while conceding that a requirement that the conduct seriously affect psychological well-being is unfounded, argues that the District Court nonetheless correctly applied the *Meritor* standard. We disagree. Though the District Court did conclude that the work environment was not "intimidating or abusive to [Harris]," it did so only after finding that the conduct was not "so severe as to be expected to seriously affect plaintiff's psychological well-being," and that Harris was not "subjectively so offended that she suffered injury." The District Court's application of these incorrect standards may well have influenced its ultimate conclusion, especially given that the court found this to be a "close case."

We therefore reverse the judgment of the Court of Appeals, and remand the case for further proceedings consistent with this opinion.

So ordered.

JUSTICE SCALIA, concurring.

Meritor Savings Bank v. Vinson, 477 U.S. 57 (1986), held that Title VII prohibits sexual harassment that takes the form of a hostile work environment. The Court stated that sexual harassment is actionable if it is "sufficiently severe or pervasive 'to alter the conditions of [the victim's] employment and create an abusive work environment.'" *Id.*, at 67. Today's opinion elaborates that the challenged conduct must be severe or pervasive enough "to create an objectively hostile or abusive work environment — an environment that a reasonable person would find hostile or abusive."

"Abusive" (or "hostile," which in this context I take to mean the same thing) does not seem to me a very clear standard — and I do not think clarity is at all increased by adding the adverb "objectively" or by appealing to a "reasonable person's" notion of what the vague word means. Today's opinion does list a number of factors that contribute to abusiveness, but since it neither says how much of each is necessary (an impossible task) nor identifies any single factor as determinative, it thereby adds little certitude. As a practical matter, today's holding lets virtually unguided juries decide whether sex-related conduct engaged in (or permitted by) an employer is egregious enough to warrant an award of damages. One might say that what constitutes "negligence" (a traditional jury question) is not much more clear and certain than what constitutes "abusiveness." Perhaps so. But the class of plaintiffs seeking to recover for negligence is limited to those who have suffered harm, whereas under this statute "abusiveness" is to be the test of whether legal harm has been suffered, opening more expansive vistas of litigation.

Be that as it may, I know of no alternative to the course the Court today has taken. One of the factors mentioned in the Court's nonexhaustive list — whether the conduct unreasonably interferes with an employee's work performance — would, if it were made an absolute test, provide greater guidance to juries and employers. But I see no basis for such a limitation in the language of the statute. Accepting *Meritor*'s interpretation of the term "conditions of employment" as the law, the test is not whether work has been impaired, but whether working conditions have been discriminatorily altered. I know of no test more faithful to the inherently vague statutory language than the one the Court today adopts. For these reasons, I join the opinion of the Court.

JUSTICE GINSBURG, concurring.

Today the Court reaffirms the holding of *Meritor Savings Bank v. Vinson*, 477 U.S. 57, 66 (1986): "[A] plaintiff may establish a violation of Title VII by proving that discrimination based on sex has created a hostile or abusive work environment." The critical issue, Title VII's text indicates, is whether members of one sex are exposed to disadvantageous terms or conditions of employment to which members of the other sex are not exposed. *See* 42 U.S.C. § 2000e-2(a)(1) (declaring that it is unlawful to discriminate with respect to, *inter alia*, "terms" or "conditions" of employment). As the Equal Employment Opportunity Commission emphasized, the adjudicator's inquiry should center, dominantly, on whether the discriminatory conduct has unreasonably interfered with the plaintiff's work performance. To show such interference, "the plaintiff need not prove that his or her tangible productivity has declined as a result of the harassment." *Davis v. Monsanto Chemical Co.*, 858 F.2d 345, 349 (6th

Cir. 1988). It suffices to prove that a reasonable person subjected to the discriminatory conduct would find, as the plaintiff did, that the harassment so altered working conditions as to "ma[k]e it more difficult to do the job." . . .

The Court's opinion, which I join, seems to me in harmony with the view expressed in this concurring statement.

NOTES

1. *Quid Pro Quo vs. Hostile Environment.* There are two general categories of sexual harassment cases: quid pro quo cases and hostile environment cases. Quid pro quo cases are those in which the harassment has resulted in a "tangible employment action," that is, one in which there has been "a significant change in employment status, such as hiring, firing, failing to promote, reassignment with significantly different responsibilities, or a decision causing a significant change in benefits." *Burlington Indus., Inc. v. Ellerth*, 524 U.S. 742, 761 (1998). In contrast, *Harris* is a hostile environment case — there has been no tangible employment action, but the harassing conduct has been sufficiently severe or pervasive to alter the working environment.

The distinction between the two types of sexual harassment cases has two primary consequences. First, as discussed in *Faragher, infra*, employers are always liable for *quid pro quo* discrimination, but not for hostile environment discrimination. Second, the requirement that the harassment be "severe or pervasive" applies only in hostile environment cases.

2. *The Hardy and the Susceptible.* *Harris* requires plaintiffs to prove that the work environment is both objectively and subjectively hostile. Thus, if the environment would not have been hostile to a reasonable person, a particularly susceptible plaintiff would fail to make out a claim even if she suffered severe personal injury. At the other end of the spectrum, even if a reasonable person would have considered the environment to be quite hostile, a particularly hardy plaintiff would fail if she could not prove that she personally perceived the environment to be hostile.

3. *Unwelcomeness.* In its first consideration of sexual harassment, the Supreme Court said that the "gravamen of any sexual harassment claim is that the alleged sexual advances were 'unwelcome.'" *Meritor Savings Bank v. Vinson*, 477 U.S. 57, 68 (1986). The Supreme Court has de-emphasized the element in subsequent cases, and did not mention it at all in *Harris*. Nevertheless, it remains a standard element of the cause of action as applied in the lower courts.

The unwelcomeness element has bite in two kinds of cases. First, the element excludes crude horseplay cases in which the purported victim was an active participant in the horseplay. *See, e.g., Reed v. Shepard*, 939 F.2d 484 (7th Cir. 1991) (woman's claim failed because, although she was subjected to crude and disgusting behavior, she also participated actively in it). Second, the element excludes "romance" cases in which a plaintiff claims discrimination because the employer has favored another worker with whom s/he is having a consensual sexual relationship. *See, e.g., DeCintio v. Westchester County Med. Ctr.*, 807 F.2d 304 (2d Cir. 1986) (no claim where man did not get promotion because it was given to woman who was romantically involved with supervisor). *But see Miller v. Department of Corrections*, 115 P.3d 77 (Cal. 2005) (although no cause of action for isolated incidents of preferential treatment of a sexual partner, a widespread pattern of sexual favoritism can infect the work environment sufficiently to create a hostile environment).

Although universally accepted in the courts, scholars have criticized the unwelcomeness element. Susan Estrich, for example, argues that it will focus the case on the victim's conduct, rather than the perpetrator's, and all too often on what a woman wears, how she talks, or with whom she sleeps. *Sex at Work*, 43 STAN. L. REV. 813, 826-34 (1991). Vicki Schultz says that unwelcomeness simply is irrelevant to what should be the core purpose of sexual harassment law, preventing attempts to undermine the competence of women in the workplace. *Reconceptualizing Sexual Harassment*, 107 YALE L.J. 1683, 1702 (1998). And Steven Willborn argues that unwelcomeness should play no role in *quid pro quo* cases because it focuses on the wrong party and improperly incorporates a consent defense to discrimination, but that it may have a modest role in helping to determine whether hostile environment discrimination is sufficiently severe or pervasive to alter the work environment. *Taking Discrimination Seriously:* Oncale *and the Fate of Exceptionalism in Sexual Harassment Law*, 7 WM. & MARY BILL RTS. J. 677, 694-96 (1999).

ONCALE v. SUNDOWNER OFFSHORE SERVICES, INC.
United States Supreme Court
523 U.S. 75 (1998)

JUSTICE SCALIA delivered the opinion of the Court.

This case presents the question whether workplace harassment can violate Title VII's prohibition against "discriminat[ion] . . . because of . . . sex" when the harasser and the harassed employee are of the same sex.

I

. . . .

In late October 1991, Oncale was working for respondent Sundowner Offshore Services on a Chevron U.S.A., Inc., oil platform in the Gulf of Mexico. He was employed as a roustabout on an eight-man crew which included respondents John Lyons, Danny Pippen, and Brandon Johnson. Lyons, the crane operator, and Pippen, the driller, had supervisory authority. On several occasions, Oncale was forcibly subjected to sex-related, humiliating actions against him by Lyons, Pippen and Johnson in the presence of the rest of the crew. Pippen and Lyons also physically assaulted Oncale in a sexual manner, and Lyons threatened him with rape.

Oncale's complaints to supervisory personnel produced no remedial action; in fact, the company's Safety Compliance Clerk, Valent Hohen, told Oncale that Lyons and Pippen "picked [on] him all the time too," and called him a name suggesting homosexuality. Oncale eventually quit — asking that his pink slip reflect that he "voluntarily left due to sexual harassment and verbal abuse." When asked at his deposition why he left Sundowner, Oncale stated

"I felt that if I didn't leave my job, that I would be raped or forced to have sex."

Oncale filed a complaint against Sundowner in the United States District Court for the Eastern District of Louisiana, alleging that he was discriminated against in his employment because of his sex. [The District Court and Fifth Circuit Court of Appeals dismissed his action, holding that same-sex harassment was not cognizable under Title VII.] We granted certiorari.

II

Title VII of the Civil Rights Act of 1964 provides, in relevant part, that "[i]t shall be an unlawful employment practice for an employer . . . to discriminate against any individual with respect to his compensation, terms, conditions, or privileges of employment, because of such individual's race, color, religion, sex, or national origin." We have held that this not only covers "terms" and "conditions" in the narrow contractual sense, but "evinces a congressional intent to strike at the entire spectrum of disparate treatment of men and women in employment." *Meritor Savings Bank, FSB v. Vinson*, 477 U.S. 57 (1986) (citations and internal quotation marks omitted). "When the workplace is permeated with discriminatory intimidation, ridicule, and insult that is sufficiently severe or pervasive to alter the conditions of the victim's employment and create an abusive working environment, Title VII is violated." *Harris v. Forklift Systems, Inc.*, 510 U.S. 17, 21 (1993) (citations and internal quotation marks omitted).

Title VII's prohibition of discrimination "because of . . . sex" protects men as well as women, *Newport News Shipbuilding & Dry Dock Co. v. EEOC*, 462 U.S. 669 (1983), and in the related context of racial discrimination in the workplace we have rejected any conclusive presumption that an employer will not discriminate against members of his own race. "Because of the many facets of human motivation, it would be unwise to presume as a matter of law that human beings of one definable group will not discriminate against other members of that group." *Castaneda v. Partida*, 430 U.S. 482, 499 (1977). In *Johnson v. Transportation Agency, Santa Clara Cty.*, 480 U.S. 616 (1987), a male employee claimed that his employer discriminated against him because of his sex when it preferred a female employee for promotion. Although we ultimately rejected the claim on other grounds, we did not consider it significant that the supervisor who made that decision was also a man. If our precedents leave any doubt on the question, we hold today that nothing in Title VII necessarily bars a claim of discrimination "because of . . . sex" merely because the plaintiff and the defendant (or the person charged with acting on behalf of the defendant) are of the same sex.

Courts have had little trouble with that principle in cases like *Johnson*, where an employee claims to have been passed over for a job or promotion. But when the issue arises in the context of a "hostile environment" sexual harassment claim, the state and federal courts have taken a bewildering variety of stances. Some, like the Fifth Circuit in this case, have held that same-sex sexual harassment claims are never cognizable under Title VII. Other decisions say that such claims are actionable only if the plaintiff can prove that the harasser is homosexual (and thus presumably motivated by sexual desire). *Compare McWilliams v. Fairfax County Board of Supervisors*, 72 F.3d 1191 (4th Cir. 1996), *with Wrightson v. Pizza Hut of America*, 99 F.3d 138 (4th Cir. 1996). Still others suggest that workplace harassment that is sexual in content is always actionable, regardless of the harasser's sex, sexual orientation, or motivations. *See Doe v. Belleville*, 119 F.3d 563 (7th Cir. 1997).

We see no justification in the statutory language or our precedents for a categorical rule excluding same-sex harassment claims from the coverage of Title VII. As some courts have observed, male-on-male sexual harassment in the workplace was assuredly not the principal evil Congress was concerned with when it enacted Title VII. But statutory prohibitions often go beyond the principal evil to cover reasonably comparable evils, and it is ultimately the provisions of our laws rather than the principal concerns of our legislators by which we are governed. Title VII prohibits "discriminat[ion] . . . because of . . . sex" in the "terms" or "conditions" of employment. Our holding that this includes sexual harassment must extend to sexual harassment of any kind that meets the statutory requirements.

Respondents and their *amici* contend that recognizing liability for same-sex harassment will transform Title VII into a general civility code for the American workplace. But that risk is no greater for same-sex than for opposite-sex harassment, and is adequately met by careful attention to the requirements of the statute. Title VII does not prohibit all verbal or physical harassment in the workplace; it is directed only at *"discriminat[ion] . . . because of . . . sex."* We have never held that workplace harassment, even harassment between men and women, is automatically discrimination because of sex merely because the words used have sexual content or connotations. "The critical issue, Title VII's text indicates, is whether members of one sex are exposed to disadvantageous terms or conditions of employment to which members of the other sex are not exposed." *Harris, supra*, at 25 (Ginsburg, J., concurring).

Courts and juries have found the inference of discrimination easy to draw in most male-female sexual harassment situations, because the challenged conduct typically involves explicit or implicit proposals of sexual activity; it is reasonable to assume those proposals would not have been made to someone of the same sex. The same chain of inference would be available to a plaintiff alleging same-sex harassment, if there were credible evidence that the harasser was homosexual. But harassing conduct need not be motivated by sexual desire to support an inference of discrimination on the basis of sex. A trier of fact might reasonably find such discrimination, for example, if a female victim is harassed in such sex-specific and derogatory terms by another woman as to make it clear that the harasser is motivated by general hostility to the presence of women in the workplace. A same-sex harassment plaintiff may also, of course, offer direct comparative evidence about how the alleged harasser treated members of both sexes in a mixed-sex workplace. Whatever evidentiary route the plaintiff chooses to follow, he or she must always prove that the conduct at issue was not merely tinged with offensive sexual connotations, but actually constituted *"discrimina[tion] . . . because of . . . sex."*

And there is another requirement that prevents Title VII from expanding into a general civility code: As we emphasized in *Meritor* and *Harris*, the statute does not reach genuine but innocuous differences in the ways men and women routinely interact with members of the same sex and of the opposite sex. The prohibition of harassment on the basis of sex requires neither asexuality nor androgyny in the workplace; it forbids only behavior so objectively offensive as to alter the "conditions" of the victim's employment. "Conduct that is not severe or pervasive enough to create an objectively hostile or abusive work environment — an environment that a reasonable person would find hostile or abusive — is beyond Title VII's purview." *Harris*, 510 U.S., at 21, citing *Meritor*, 477 U.S., at 67. We have always regarded that requirement as crucial, and as sufficient to ensure that courts and juries do not mistake ordinary socializing in the workplace — such as male-on-male horseplay or intersexual flirtation — for discriminatory "conditions of employment."

We have emphasized, moreover, that the objective severity of harassment should be judged from the perspective of a reasonable person in the plaintiff's position, considering "all the circumstances." *Harris, supra*, at 23. In same-sex (as in all) harassment cases, that inquiry requires careful consideration of the social context in which particular behavior occurs and is experienced by its target. A professional football player's working environment is not severely or pervasively abusive, for example, if the coach smacks him on the buttocks as he heads onto the field — even if the same behavior would reasonably be experienced as abusive by the coach's secretary (male or female) back at the office. The real social impact of workplace behavior often depends on a constellation of surrounding circumstances, expectations, and relationships which are not fully captured by a simple recitation of the words used or the physical acts performed. Common sense, and an appropriate sensitivity to social context, will enable courts and juries to distinguish between simple teasing or roughhousing among members of the same sex, and conduct which a reasonable person in the plaintiff's position would find severely hostile or abusive.

III

Because we conclude that sex discrimination consisting of same-sex sexual harassment is actionable under Title VII, the judgment of the Court of Appeals for the Fifth Circuit is reversed, and the case is remanded for further proceedings consistent with this opinion. . . .

JUSTICE THOMAS, concurring.

I concur because the Court stresses that in every sexual harassment case, the plaintiff must plead and ultimately prove Title VII's statutory requirement that there be discrimination "because of . . . sex."

NOTES

1. *Severe or Pervasive*. *Oncale* clarifies that this element is intended to prevent sexual harassment law from becoming a "general civility code" in the workplace. But where precisely is the line to be drawn? In single-incident cases, the standard is fairly high. In one of President Clinton's contributions to the area, a district court held that the element was not satisfied even accepting Paula Jones' allegations that then-Governor Clinton invited her to his hotel room, exposed himself to her, and requested oral sex. *Jones v. Clinton*, 990 F. Supp. 657 (E.D. Ark. 1998). Similarly, the Supreme Court has held that no reasonable person would find the standard met when an employee participated in a meeting with co-workers who joked about a job applicant who had said, "I hear making love to you is like making love to the Grand Canyon." *Clark County Sch. Dist. v. Breeden*, 532 U.S. 268 (2001). Generally, to meet this element in single-incident cases, the conduct has to be serious and involve physical contact. *See, e.g., Smith v. Sheahan*, 189 F.3d 529 (7th Cir. 1999) (physical assault); *Tomka v. Seiler Corp.*, 66 F.3d 1295 (2d Cir. 1995) (sexual assault).

2. *The Discrimination Element.* Both Justice Scalia in his unanimous majority opinion and Justice Thomas in his brief concurrence emphasize that discrimination is an element of a harassment claim. Is this a change in the law of sexual harassment? Would there be harassment, for example, where both men and women in a workplace are exposed to sexually suggestive nude pictures of women? *See Robinson v. Jacksonville Shipyards, Inc.*, 760 F. Supp. 1486 (M.D. Fla. 1991) (before *Oncale*, yes). Would there be harassment where both men and women are exposed to very rough and sexually suggestive language? *See Steiner v. Showboat Operating Co.*, 25 F.3d 1459 (9th Cir. 1994) (before *Oncale*, yes). In addressing these questions, does it matter that the harassment is to be judged from the perspective of a reasonable person in the plaintiff's position and that men and women may have different reactions to nude pictures in the workplace or to rough, sexually suggestive language?

3. *Sexual Orientation.* As *Oncale* illustrates, plaintiffs have had some success in attacking harassment based on sexual orientation by characterizing it as a type of gender discrimination. *See Rene v. MGM Grand Hotel, Inc.*, 305 F.3d 1061 (9th Cir. 2002) (en banc), *cert. denied*, 538 U.S. 922 (2003); *Nichols v. Azteca Restaurant Enters.*, 256 F.3d 864 (9th Cir. 2001). This does not mean, however, that Title VII generally prohibits discrimination based on sexual orientation or even sexual harassment based on sexual orientation. The word "sex" in Title VII is uniformly interpreted to prohibit only discrimination based on gender and not to extend to discrimination because of sexual orientation. *See, e.g., Simonton v. Runyon*, 232 F.3d 33 (2d Cir. 2000); *Wrightson v. Pizza Hut, Inc.*, 99 F.3d 138 (4th Cir. 1996).

In addition, harassment based on sexual orientation must be re-characterized as gender discrimination to be cognizable; sexual orientation is not a disability covered by the ADA or the Rehabilitation Act; and distinctions based on sexual orientation receive the lowest level of scrutiny under the Equal Protection Clause. *High Tech Gays v. Defense Indus. Sec. Clearance Office*, 895 F.2d 563 (9th Cir. 1990). *But cf. Romer v. Evans*, 517 U.S. 620 (1996) (state constitutional provision prohibiting any state action intended to protect gays or lesbians struck down under the Equal Protection Clause's rational-basis test).

Many state and local discrimination laws, however, provide protections. Thirteen states prohibit discrimination based on sexual orientation in both public and private employment; an additional eight states prohibit this type of discrimination in the public sector only; and over 100 counties and municipalities have local laws restricting the practice.

LYLE v. WARNER BROTHERS TELEVISION PRODUCTIONS
Supreme Court of California
132 P.3d 211 (2006)

Baxter, J.:

Plaintiff was a comedy writers' assistant who worked on the production of a popular television show called *Friends*. The show revolved around a group of young, sexually active adults, featured adult-oriented sexual humor, and typically relied on sexual and anatomical language, innuendo, wordplay, and physical gestures to convey its humor. Before plaintiff was hired, she had been forewarned that the show dealt with sexual matters and that, as an assistant to the comedy writers, she would be listening to their sexual jokes and discussions about sex and transcribing the jokes and dialogue most likely to be used for scripts. After four months of employment, plaintiff was fired because of problems with her typing and transcription. She then filed this action against three of the male comedy writers and others, asserting among other things that the writers' use of sexually coarse and vulgar language and conduct, including the recounting of their own sexual experiences, constituted harassment based on sex within the meaning of the Fair Employment and Housing Act (the FEHA) (Gov. Code, § 12900 *et seq.*; all further statutory references are to this code unless otherwise indicated). . . .

We granted review to address whether the use of sexually coarse and vulgar language in the workplace can constitute harassment based on sex within the meaning of the FEHA, and if so, whether the imposition of liability under the FEHA for such speech would infringe on defendants' federal and state constitutional rights of free speech. . . .

Factual Background

In her deposition, plaintiff testified she had no recollection of any employee on the *Friends* production ever saying anything sexually offensive about her directly to her. No one on the production ever asked her out on a date or sexually propositioned her. Likewise, no one ever demanded sexual favors of her or physically threatened her.

Plaintiff testified, however, that a number of offensive discussions and actions occurred in the writers' meetings she was required to attend. The writers regularly discussed their preferences in women and sex in general. Chase spoke of his preferences for blonde women, a certain bra cup size, "get[ting] right to sex" and not "mess[ing] around with too much foreplay." Malins had a love of young girls and cheerleaders. Some of the sex-based discussions occurred outside the writers' room, that is, in the breakroom and in the hallways.

Also during the writers' meetings, Malins constantly spoke of his oral sex experiences and told the group that when he and his wife fought, he would "get naked" and then they would never finish the argument. Malins had a "coloring book" depicting female cheerleaders with their legs spread open; he would draw breasts and vaginas on the cheerleaders during the writers' meetings. The book was left on his desk or sometimes on writers' assistants' desks. Malins frequently used a pencil to alter portions of the name "*Friends*" on scripts so it would read "penis." Malins also spoke of his fantasy about an episode of the show in which the *Friends* character "Joey" enters the bathroom while the character "Rachel" is showering and has his way with her. And, during each of the four months plaintiff worked on the *Friends* production, some writers made masturbatory gestures.

In addition, plaintiff heard the writers talk about what they would like to do sexually to different female cast members on *Friends*. Malins remarked to Chase that Chase could have "f***" one of the actresses on the show a couple of years before, and the two constantly bantered about the topic and how Chase had missed his chance to do so. Chase, Malins, and Reich spoke demeaningly about another actress on the show, making jokes about whether she was competent in sexually servicing her boyfriend. They also referred to her infertility once and joked she had "dried twigs" or "dried branches in her vagina." . . . [The plaintiff] also submitted two of her own declarations, in which she reiterated and more particularly described the graphic nature of the writers' alleged comments and conduct.[2] . . .

In this court, defendants argue the facts shown in the summary judgment proceeding do not establish actionable harassment under the FEHA because: (1) use of sexual speech, standing alone, does not violate the FEHA's prohibition against harassment because of sex; and (2) the conduct did not amount to severe or pervasive conduct that altered the terms or conditions of plaintiff's employment.

The FEHA and its Prohibitions

With certain exceptions not implicated here, the FEHA makes it an unlawful employment practice for an employer, "because of the . . . sex . . . of any person . . . to discriminate against the person in compensation or in terms, conditions, or privileges of employment." § 12940, subd. (a). Likewise, it is an unlawful employment practice for an employer, "because of . . . sex, . . . to harass an employee." § 12940, subd. (j)(1). Under the statutory scheme, " 'harassment' because of sex" includes sexual harassment and gender harassment. § 12940, subd. (j)(4)(C). . . .

Like the FEHA, title VII of the federal Civil Rights Act of 1964 (Title VII), 42 U.S.C. § 2000e *et seq.*, prohibits sexual harassment, making it an unlawful employment practice for an employer, among other things, "to discriminate against any individual with respect to his compensation, terms, conditions, or privileges of employment, because of such individual's . . . sex[.]" 42 U.S.C. § 2000e-2(a)(1). Because the workplace environment is one of the terms, conditions, or privileges of employment, a plaintiff may establish a violation of Title VII by showing that discrimination because of sex has created a hostile

---

[2] [In the case, this footnote contains a long list of very crude and offensive statements and actions.]

or abusive work environment. *See Meritor Savings Bank v. Vinson*, 477 U.S. 57, 64-66 (1986). Thus, while the wording of Title VII and the FEHA differs in some particulars, both statutory schemes regard the prohibition against sexual harassment as part and parcel of the proscription against sexual discrimination, and "the antidiscriminatory objectives and overriding public policy purposes of the two acts are identical." *Beyda v. City of Los Angeles*, 76 Cal. Rptr. 2d 547 (1998).

In light of these similarities, California courts frequently seek guidance from Title VII decisions when interpreting the FEHA and its prohibitions against sexual harassment. . . .

Under Title VII, a hostile work environment sexual harassment claim requires a plaintiff employee to show she was subjected to sexual advances, conduct, or comments that were (1) unwelcome; (2) because of sex; and (3) sufficiently severe or pervasive to alter the conditions of her employment and create an abusive work environment. In addition, she must establish the offending conduct was imputable to her employer. California courts have adopted the same standard for hostile work environment sexual harassment claims under the FEHA.

Sufficiency of Plaintiff's Factual Showing

[A] defendant moving for summary judgment meets its burden of showing that a cause of action has no merit by establishing that one or more elements of the cause of action cannot be established.

Here, defendants met that burden in their moving papers. First, they pointed to plaintiff's concessions that none of the three male writers' offensive conduct involved or was aimed at her. Second, considering the totality of the circumstances, especially the nature of the writers' work, the facts largely forming the basis of plaintiff's sexual harassment action — (1) the writers' sexual antics, including their pantomiming of masturbation, their drawing in the cheerleader coloring book, their altering words on scripts and calendars to spell out male and female body parts, (2) their graphic discussions about their personal sexual experiences, sexual preferences, and preferences in women, and (3) their bragging about their personal sexual exploits with girlfriends and wives — did not present a triable issue whether the writers engaged in harassment "because of . . . sex."

There is no dispute *Friends* was a situation comedy that featured young sexually active adults and sexual humor geared primarily toward adults. Aired episodes of the show often used sexual and anatomical language, innuendo, wordplay, and physical gestures to create humor concerning sex, including oral sex, anal sex, heterosexual sex, gay sex, "talking dirty" during sex, premature ejaculation, pornography, pedophiles, and "threesomes." The circumstance that this was a creative workplace focused on generating scripts for an adult-oriented comedy show featuring sexual themes is significant in assessing the existence of triable issues of facts regarding whether the writers' sexual antics and coarse sexual talk were aimed at plaintiff or at women in general, whether plaintiff and other women were singled out to see and hear what happened, and whether the conduct was otherwise motivated by plaintiff's gender.

Here, the record shows that the instances of sexual antics and sexual discussions did not involve and were not aimed at plaintiff or any other female employee. It further confirms that such "nondirected" conduct was undertaken in group sessions with both male and female participants present, and that women writers on the *Friends* production also discussed their own sexual experiences to generate material for the show. That the writers commonly engaged in discussions of personal sexual experiences and preferences and used physical gesturing while brainstorming and generating script ideas for this particular show was neither surprising nor unreasonable from a creative standpoint. Indeed, plaintiff testified that, when told during her interview for the *Friends* position that "the humor could get a little lowbrow in the writers' room," she responded she would have no problem because previously she had worked around writers and knew what to expect. Although plaintiff contends the writers "sorely understated the actual climate" of the writers' room in her interview, these types of sexual discussions and jokes (especially those relating to the writers' personal experiences) did in fact provide material for actual scripts.[9] The fact that certain discussions did not lead to specific jokes or dialogue airing on the show merely reflected the creative process at work and did not serve to convert such nondirected conduct into harassment because of sex.

Moreover, although plaintiff contended in her deposition that much of the three writers' vulgar discussions and conduct wasted her time, there was no indication the conduct affected the work hours or duties of plaintiff and her male counterparts in a disparate manner. Accordingly, while the conduct certainly was tinged with "sexual content" and sexual "connotations," a reasonable trier of fact could not find, based on the facts presented here, that "members of one sex [were] exposed to disadvantageous terms or conditions of employment to which members of the other sex [were] not exposed," *Oncale v. Sundowner Offshore Services, Inc.*, 523 U.S. 75, 80 (1998), or that if plaintiff "had been a man she would not have been treated in the same manner" *Accardi v. Superior Court*, 21 Cal. App. 2d 292, 296 (1993).

The circumstances surrounding the nondirected sexual antics and sexual talk are plainly distinguishable from the circumstances concerning somewhat similar conduct found actionable in *Ocheltree v. Scollon Productions, Inc.*, 335 F.3d 325 (4th Cir. 2003). In *Ocheltree*, a case involving employees working at a costume production shop, the record showed that the plaintiff's male coworkers engaged in a daily stream of sexually explicit discussions and conduct: they spoke in crude terms of their sexual exploits with their wives and girlfriends; they used a female-form mannequin to demonstrate sexual techniques; one sang a vulgar song to the plaintiff; and another showed the plaintiff a magazine with graphic photographs of men with pierced genitalia to get her reaction. In that case, the appellate court affirmed an award of compensatory damages to the plaintiff because "[a] reasonable jury could find that much of the sex-laden and sexist talk and conduct in the production shop was aimed at [the plaintiff] because of sex — specifically, that the men

---

[9] Of course, explicit sexual references typically were replaced with innuendos, imagery, similes, allusions, puns, or metaphors in order to convey sexual themes in a form suitable for broadcast on network television. For example, "motherf***" was replaced with "mother kisser," "testicles" with "balls," and "anal sex" with "in the stern."

behaved as they did to make her uncomfortable and self-conscious as the only woman in the workplace." *Id.* at 332-333.

Unlike the situation presented in *Ocheltree*, the record here reflects a workplace where comedy writers were paid to create scripts highlighting adult-themed sexual humor and jokes, and where members of both sexes contributed and were exposed to the creative process spawning such humor and jokes. In this context, the defendant writers' nondirected sexual antics and sexual talk did not contribute to an environment in which women and men were treated disparately. Moreover, there was nothing to suggest defendants engaged in this particular behavior to make plaintiff uncomfortable or self-conscious, or to intimidate, ridicule, or insult her, as was the case in *Ocheltree*.

During the discovery process, plaintiff testified her FEHA claim additionally was predicated on what the writers said they would like to do sexually to the different female cast members on *Friends*, and jokes that defendant Chase had missed a sexual opportunity with one of the actresses. The writers also made demeaning comments about another of the actresses, asking whether she was competent in sexually servicing her boyfriend and remarking she probably had "dried twigs" or "dried branches" in her vagina.

Unlike the writers' nondirected conduct, these particular comments support at least an inference that certain women working on the production of *Friends* were targeted for personal insult and derogation because of their sex, while the men working there were not. The question remains, however, whether the comments were sufficiently severe or pervasive to create a sexually hostile work environment.

The evidence in the summary judgment proceeding showed that plaintiff named the two actresses as the only women on the production about whom the writers specifically made these offensive sex-based comments. As far as the two actresses were concerned, the conduct was not severe or pervasive: no sexual assault, threat of assault, sexual propositioning, or unwelcome physical contact occurred; nor did the conduct amount to verbal abuse or harassment, inasmuch as the actresses were not even present to hear the writers' offensive remarks and, apparently, had no awareness of what had been said.

Because the derogatory comments did not involve plaintiff, she was obligated to set forth specific facts from which a reasonable trier of fact could find the conduct "permeated" her direct workplace environment and was "pervasive and destructive." In this connection, plaintiff points to her deposition testimony that she was too appalled, mortified, and offended by these comments (and the other conduct complained of) to speak, and to her later declaration that the conduct caused her "severe distress." Other parts of her testimony, however, revealed she viewed the writers and their conduct as puerile and annoying, rather than extreme or destructive: she testified the writers' room was "like being in a junior high locker room" and described the writers as "pimply-faced teenagers" and "silly little boys" who engaged in "very juvenile, counterproductive behavior" when they "spen[t] their time doing drawings" in the cheerleader coloring book and "discussing lewd things." But even where seemingly contradictory testimony like this is offered regarding a plaintiff's subjective perceptions, courts will not hesitate to find in favor of a defendant where the record does not establish an objectively hostile work environment.

Plaintiff acknowledged the writers made references to the one actress's fertility and the "dried branches in her vagina" on only one occasion. Plaintiff did not, however, offer specific facts regarding how often or on how many occasions the writers engaged in the graphic sexual jokes and talk about the other actress. Although plaintiff testified that, in the four months she worked on *Friends*, Malins and Chase constantly bantered about Chase's missed sexual opportunity with that actress, her declarations indicated that some of more graphic comments were made only once or "at least twice." Without more, a reasonable trier of fact could not conclude that these reported comments concerning the two actresses "permeated" plaintiff's direct work environment, or that they were "pervasive and destructive of [that] environment," so as to allow recovery despite the fact plaintiff was not personally subjected to offensive remarks or touchings and did not suffer a tangible job detriment.

In opposing defendants' summary judgment motion, plaintiff offered additional evidence of offensive gender-related language. Specifically, she submitted two declarations in which she claimed to have heard defendants Chase, Malins, and Reich refer to women who displeased them or made them mad as "cunts" and "bitches." But plaintiff made no claim the writers ever referred to her by those terms, either to her face or to others, and she gave no indication whether the writers used gender-related epithets with reference to men in comparable situations.[11]

Even when we consider this belated presentation of epithets in the workplace, we find it insufficient to warrant reversal of the summary judgment order. . . . Although plaintiff was reasonably specific in describing the one telephone reference to Marta Kauffman, she otherwise was not, merely indicating the writers used the epithets when they were displeased or mad. The missing context is especially significant here, because one of the reported epithets ("bitch") was not a term that was necessarily misogynistic or even unsuitable for broadcast television. Indeed, in one *Friends* episode, the character Chandler addressed the character Monica by that term. . . .

Considering the totality of the circumstances, whether we view the epithet evidence by itself, or in conjunction with the evidence of the actress-related comments, we are unable to conclude a reasonable trier of fact could, on the meager facts shown, find the conduct of the three male writers was sufficiently severe or pervasive to create a hostile work environment.

[P]laintiff contends there is a triable issue of material fact as to whether the writers' offensive conduct was part of the creative process leading to scripts and a necessary part of their work, or whether it was undertaken purely for their own personal sexual gratification. In support of this point, she cites the evidence that defendants engaged in vulgar behavior outside of the writers' room, for example, in the hallways or near her desk. . . . But summary

---

[11] Although plaintiff's evidence also showed the writers regularly referred to women's anatomies by certain vulgar terms, her evidence further disclosed the writers regularly referred to men's anatomies with comparable vulgar terms. No disparity of treatment on this point appears.

judgment was proper here because none of the offensive conduct complained of meets both the "because of sex" and "severe or pervasive" requirements for establishing a hostile work environment sexual harassment claim. That is, while the record conceivably reflects a triable issue of fact as to whether some of defendants' offensive comments were directed at women because of their sex and hence unnecessary to the work (i.e., the reported gender-related epithets and the comments involving the actresses), the facts plaintiff offered simply are insufficient to establish that any such conduct was severe enough or sufficiently pervasive to be actionable. Moreover, assuming arguendo the incidents taking place in the hallways somehow could be deemed unnecessary to the work generated inside the writers' room, there is no indication these other incidents involved or were aimed at plaintiff or any other female employee, or that they appeared materially different from the type of sexual joking and discussions occurring in the writers' room that actually led to material for scripts. . . .

Constitutional Rights of Free Speech

In affirming the grant of summary judgment in favor of defendants, we have concluded plaintiff's factual showing of the writers' sexually coarse and vulgar language does not establish a prima facie case of hostile work environment sexual harassment. In light of that conclusion, we have no occasion to determine whether liability for such language might infringe on defendants' rights of free speech under the First Amendment to the federal Constitution or the state Constitution.

Conclusion and Disposition

When we apply the legal principles governing sexual harassment claims, and give plaintiff the benefit of the rules governing review of summary judgment orders, we conclude defendants have shown that plaintiff has not established, and cannot reasonably expect to establish, a prima facie case of hostile workplace environment sexual harassment.

In reaching this conclusion, we do not suggest the use of sexually coarse and vulgar language in the workplace can never constitute harassment because of sex; indeed, language similar to that at issue here might well establish actionable harassment depending on the circumstances. Nor do we imply that employees generally should be free, without employer restriction, to engage in sexually coarse and vulgar language or conduct at the workplace. We simply recognize that, like Title VII, the FEHA is "not a 'civility code' and [is] not designed to rid the workplace of vulgarity." While the FEHA prohibits harassing conduct that creates a work environment that is hostile or abusive on the basis of sex, it does not outlaw sexually coarse and vulgar language or conduct that merely offends. . . .

CHIN, J., Concurring.:

I agree that the trial court properly granted summary judgment in favor of defendants under the relevant statutes. I write separately to explain that any other result would violate free speech rights under the First Amendment of the United States Constitution and its California counterpart, article I, section 2, of the California Constitution (hereafter collectively the First Amendment).

This case has very little to do with sexual harassment and very much to do with core First Amendment free speech rights. The writers of the television show, *Friends*, were engaged in a *creative process* — writing adult comedy — when the alleged harassing conduct occurred. The First Amendment protects creativity. *Friends* was entertainment, but entertainment is fully entitled to First Amendment protection. "There is no doubt that entertainment, as well as news, enjoys First Amendment protection." *Zacchini v. Scripps-Howard Broadcasting Co.*, 433 U.S. 562, 578 (1977). . . .

Balancing the compelling need to protect employees from sexual harassment with free speech rights can, in some contexts, present very difficult questions. For example, a potential, and sometimes real, tension between free speech and antiharassment laws exists even in the ordinary workplace. . . .

But the issue here is quite different. In *Aguilar, supra*, 21 Cal.4th 121, the workplace was a car rental company. Creative expression was not the company's product. Here, by contrast, the product, a comedy show, was itself expression. Questions regarding free speech rights in the ordinary workplace — where speech is not an integral part of the product — can be difficult, as the five separate opinions in *Aguilar* attest. I need not, and do not, go into these questions here, because this case presents an entirely different and, to my mind, rather straightforward constitutional question. When, as here, the workplace product is the creative expression itself, free speech rights are paramount. The *Friends* writers were not renting cars and talking about sex on the side. They were writing adult comedy; sexual repartee was an integral part of the process. . . .

The writers here did at times go to extremes in the creative process. They pushed the limits — hard. Some of what they did might be incomprehensible to people unfamiliar with the creative process. But that is what creative people sometimes have to do. As explained in an amicus curiae brief representing the Writers Guild of America, "the process creators go through to capture the necessary magic is inexact, counterintuitive, nonlinear, often painful — and above all, delicate. And the problem is even more complicated for group writing." "Group writing," the brief explains, "requires an atmosphere of complete trust. Writers must feel not only that it's all right to fail, but also that they can share their most private and darkest thoughts without concern for ridicule or embarrassment or legal accountability." The brief quotes Steven Bochco, cocreator of *Hill Street Blues*, *L.A. Law*, and *NYPD Blue*, and one of the individuals the brief represents, as explaining that a "certain level of intimacy is required to do the work at its best, and so there is an implicit contract among the writers: what is said in the room, stays in the room." The brief further explains that "with adult audiences in particular, the characters, dialogue, and stories must ring true. That means on shows like *Law and Order*, *ER*, or *The Sopranos*, writers must tap into places in their experience or psyches that most of us are far too polite or self-conscious to bring up."

The creative process must be unfettered, especially because it can often take strange turns, as many bizarre and potentially offensive ideas are suggested, tried, and, in the end, either discarded or used. As the Writers Guild brief notes, "*All in the Family* pushed the limits in its day, but with race rather than sex." The brief quotes Norman Lear, *All in the Family*'s creator, and another of the individuals on whose behalf the brief was filed, as saying, "We were dealing with racism and constantly on dangerous ground. . . . We cleaned up a lot of what was said in the room, and some people *still* found it offensive." It is hard to imagine *All in the Family* having been successfully written if the writers and others involved in the creative process had to fear lawsuits by employees who claimed to be offended by the process of discovering what worked and did not work, what was funny and what was not funny, that led to the racial and ethnic humor actually used in the show. . . .

For this reason, it is meaningless to argue, as plaintiff does, that much of what occurred in this process did not make its way into the actual shows. The First Amendment also protects attempts at creativity that end in failure. That which ends up on the cutting room floor is also part of the creative process. . . .

Does this mean that anything that occurs while writing a television show is permissible? Do employees involved in that process receive no protection? Of course not. Just as criminal threats are not protected, just as no one has the right to falsely shout fire in a crowded theater, limits exist as to what may occur in the writers' room. [E]ven in this context, speech that is *directed*, or "aimed at a particular employee because of her race, sex, religion, or national origin," is not protected. Speech directed towards plaintiff *because* of her sex could not further the creative process.

Accordingly, I agree with the general test proposed in the amicus curiae brief of the California Newspaper Publishers Association et al.: "Where, as here, an employer's product is protected by the First Amendment — whether it be a television program, a newspaper, a book, or any other similar work — the challenged speech should not be actionable if the court finds that the speech arose in the context of the creative and/or editorial process, and it was not directed at or about the plaintiff."

This test presents the proper balance. Often, free speech cases involve the very difficult balancing of important competing interests. But here, in the creative context, free speech is critical while the competing interest — protecting employees involved in the creative process against offensive language and conduct *not directed at them* — is, in comparison, minimal. Neither plaintiff nor anyone else is required to become part of a creative team. But those who choose to join a creative team should not be allowed to complain that some of the creativity was offensive or that behavior not directed at them was unnecessary to the creative process. . . .

NOTES

1. *Sexual Harassment in the Classroom.* The concurrence views even very crude speech as protected so long as the employer's product is protected by the First Amendment and the language is not directed at anyone personally. In part, this is because "those who choose to join a creative team should not be allowed to complain that some of the creativity was offensive . . . or unnecessary to the creative process." Does this give your Professor free rein to speak in a very crude and offensive way during this part of the course? *See Bonnell v. Lorenzo*, 241 F.3d 800, *cert. denied* 534 U.S. 951 (2001) (use of crude and profane language in classroom not protected by First Amendment or academic freedom).

2. *Sexual Harassment and the First Amendment.* By its terms, sexual harassment law could be used to restrict speech in the workplace. Theoretically, a case could be established based solely on speech which was unwelcome, of a sexual nature, and severe or pervasive. This has lead to a lively debate, even though in practice few real-life cases involve speech alone. Ann Juliano & Stewart J. Schwab, *The Sweep of Sexual Harassment Cases*, 86 CORNELL L. REV. 548, 588-89 (2001) (out of the 650 sexual harassment cases between 1986 and 1996, only one case involved "allegations of pornography and graffiti in the absence of any other conduct, and the plaintiff lost").

Some scholars contend that the law on its face violates the First Amendment; others say that harassment law is consistent with the First Amendment if it is interpreted in certain ways; and still others defend harassment law as entirely consistent with the First Amendment. For examples of each position, see Kingsley Browne, *Title VII as Censorship: Hostile-Environment Harassment and the First Amendment*, 52 OHIO ST. L.J. 481 (1991) (unconstitutional); Eugene Volokh, Comment, *Freedom of Speech and Workplace Harassment*, 39 UCLA L. REV. 1791 (1992) (constitutional if harassment law interpreted to restrict only personally-directed harassing speech); Mary Becker, *How Free is Speech at Work?*, 29 U.C. DAVIS. L. REV. 815 (1996) (consistent with the First Amendment).

FARAGHER v. CITY OF BOCA RATON
United States Supreme Court
524 U.S. 775 (1998)

JUSTICE SOUTER delivered the opinion of the Court.

This case calls for identification of the circumstances under which an employer may be held liable under Title VII of the Civil Rights Act of 1964 for the acts of a supervisory employee whose sexual harassment of subordinates has created a hostile work environment amounting to employment discrimination. We hold that an employer is vicariously liable for actionable discrimination caused by a supervisor, but subject to an affirmative defense looking to the reasonableness of the employer's conduct as well as that of a plaintiff victim.

I

Between 1985 and 1990, while attending college, petitioner Beth Ann Faragher worked part time and during the summers as an ocean lifeguard for the Marine Safety Section of the Parks and Recreation Department of respondent, the City of Boca Raton, Florida (City). During this period, Faragher's immediate supervisors were Bill Terry, David Silverman, and Robert Gordon. In June 1990, Faragher resigned. . . .

The lifeguards and supervisors were stationed at the city beach and worked out of the Marine Safety Headquarters, a small one-story building containing an office, a meeting room, and a single, unisex locker room with a shower. Their work routine was structured in a "paramilitary configuration," with a clear chain of command. Lifeguards reported to lieutenants and captains, who reported to Terry. He was supervised by the Recreation Superintendent, who in turn reported to a Director of Parks and Recreation, answerable to the City Manager. The lifeguards had no significant contact with higher city officials like the Recreation Superintendent.

In February 1986, the City adopted a sexual harassment policy, which it stated in a memorandum from the City Manager addressed to all employees. In May 1990, the City revised the policy and reissued a statement of it. Although the City may actually have circulated the memos and statements to some employees, it completely failed to disseminate its policy among employees of the Marine Safety Section, with the result that Terry, Silverman, Gordon, and many lifeguards were unaware of it.

From time to time over the course of Faragher's tenure at the Marine Safety Section, between 4 and 6 of the 40 to 50 lifeguards were women. During that 5-year period, Terry repeatedly touched the bodies of female employees without invitation, would put his arm around Faragher, with his hand on her buttocks, and once made contact with another female lifeguard in a motion of sexual simulation. He made crudely demeaning references to women generally and once commented disparagingly on Faragher's shape. During a job interview with a woman he hired as a lifeguard, Terry said that the female lifeguards had sex with their male counterparts and asked whether she would do the same.

Silverman behaved in similar ways. He once tackled Faragher and remarked that, but for a physical characteristic he found unattractive, he would readily have had sexual relations with her. Another time, he pantomimed an act of oral sex. Within earshot of the female lifeguards, Silverman made frequent, vulgar references to women and sexual matters, commented on the bodies of female lifeguards and beachgoers, and at least twice told female lifeguards that he would like to engage in sex with them.

Faragher did not complain to higher management about Terry or Silverman. Although she spoke of their behavior to Gordon, she did not regard these discussions as formal complaints to a supervisor but as conversations with a person she held in high esteem. Other female lifeguards had similarly informal talks with Gordon, but because Gordon did not feel that it was his place to do so, he did not report these complaints to Terry, his own supervisor, or to any other city official. Gordon responded to the complaints of one lifeguard by saying that "the City just [doesn't] care." . . .

On the basis of these findings, the District Court concluded that the conduct of Terry and Silverman was discriminatory harassment sufficiently serious to alter the conditions of Faragher's employment and constitute an abusive working environment. The District Court then ruled that [the City was] liable for the harassment of its supervisory employees. . . . The District Court then awarded Faragher one dollar in nominal damages on her Title VII claim.

[The Court of Appeals for the Eleventh Circuit reversed, holding that the City was not liable for the conduct of its supervisors because they were not acting within the scope of their employment, they were not aided in their actions by the agency relationship, and the City had no constructive knowledge of the harassment.]

II

A

While [our prior cases such as *Harris* and *Oncale* have indicated] the substantive contours of the hostile environments forbidden by Title VII, our cases have established few definite rules for determining when an employer will be liable for a discriminatory environment that is otherwise actionably abusive. Given the circumstances of many of the litigated cases, including some that have come to us, it is not surprising that in many of them, the issue has been joined over the sufficiency of the abusive conditions, not the standards for determining an employer's liability for them. There have, for example, been myriad cases in which [lower courts] have held employers liable on account of actual knowledge by the employer, or high-echelon officials of an employer organization, of sufficiently harassing action by subordinates, which the employer or its informed officers have done nothing to stop. In such instances, the combined knowledge and inaction may be seen as demonstrable negligence, or as the employer's adoption of the offending conduct and its results, quite as if they had been authorized affirmatively as the employer's policy.

Nor was it exceptional that standards for binding the employer were not in issue in *Harris*. In that case of discrimination by hostile environment, the individual charged with creating the abusive atmosphere was the president of the corporate employer, who was indisputably within that class of an employer organization's officials who may be treated as the organization's proxy.

Finally, there is nothing remarkable in the fact that claims against employers for discriminatory employment actions with tangible results, like hiring, firing, promotion, compensation, and work assignment, have resulted in employer liability once the discrimination was shown. *See Meritor*, 477 U.S., at 70-71 (noting that "courts have consistently held employers liable for the discriminatory discharges of employees by supervisory personnel, whether or not the employer knew, should have known, or approved of the supervisor's actions").

A variety of reasons have been invoked for this apparently unanimous rule. Some courts explain, in a variation of the "proxy" theory discussed above, that when a supervisor makes such decisions, he "merges" with the employer, and his act becomes that of the employer. Other courts have suggested that vicarious liability is proper because the supervisor acts within the scope of his authority when he makes discriminatory decisions in hiring, firing, promotion, and the like. Others have suggested that vicarious liability is appropriate because the supervisor who discriminates in this manner is aided by the agency relation. Finally, still other courts have endorsed both of the latter two theories.

The soundness of the results in these cases (and their continuing vitality), in light of basic agency principles, was confirmed by this Court's only discussion to date of standards of employer liability, in *Meritor*, which involved a claim of discrimination by a supervisor's sexual harassment of a subordinate over an extended period. In affirming the Court of Appeals's holding that a hostile atmosphere resulting from sex discrimination is actionable under Title VII, we also anticipated proceedings on remand by holding agency principles relevant in assigning employer liability and by rejecting three per se rules of liability or immunity. We observed that the very definition of employer in Title VII, as including an "agent," expressed Congress's intent that courts look to traditional principles of the law of agency in devising standards of employer liability in those instances where liability for the actions of a supervisory employee was not otherwise obvious, and although we cautioned that "common-law principles may not be transferable in all their particulars to Title VII," we cited the Restatement §§ 219-237, with general approval.

We then proceeded to reject two limitations on employer liability, while establishing the rule that some limitation was intended. We held that neither the existence of a company grievance procedure nor the absence of actual notice of the harassment on the part of upper management would be dispositive of such a claim; while either might be relevant to the liability, neither would result automatically in employer immunity. Conversely, we held that Title VII placed some limit on employer responsibility for the creation of a discriminatory environment by a supervisor, and we held that Title VII does not make employers "always automatically liable for sexual harassment by their supervisors," contrary to the view of the Court of Appeals, which had held that "an employer is strictly liable for a hostile environment created by a supervisor's sexual advances, even though the employer neither knew nor reasonably could have known of the alleged misconduct."

Meritor's statement of the law is the foundation on which we build today. . . .

B

The Court of Appeals identified, and rejected, three possible grounds drawn from agency law for holding the City vicariously liable for the hostile environment created by the supervisors. It considered whether the two supervisors were acting within the scope of their employment when they engaged in the harassing conduct. The court then enquired whether they were significantly aided by the agency relationship in committing the harassment, and also considered the possibility of imputing Gordon's knowledge of the harassment to the City. Finally, the Court of Appeals ruled out liability for negligence in failing to prevent the harassment. Faragher relies principally on the latter three theories of liability.

1

A "master is subject to liability for the torts of his servants committed while acting in the scope of their employment." RESTATEMENT § 219(1). This doctrine has traditionally defined the "scope of employment" as including conduct "of the kind [a servant] is employed to perform," occurring "substantially within the authorized time and space limits," and "actuated, at least in part, by a purpose to serve the master," but as excluding an intentional use of force "unexpectable by the master." *Id.*, § 228(1).

Courts of Appeals have typically held, or assumed, that conduct similar to the subject of this complaint falls outside the scope of employment. *See, e.g., Harrison [v. Eddy Potash, Inc.]*, 112 F.3d [1437], 1444 [10th Cir. 1997] (sexual harassment " 'simply is not within the job description of any supervisor or any other worker in any reputable business' "). In so doing, the courts have emphasized that harassment consisting of unwelcome remarks and touching is motivated solely by individual desires and serves no purpose of the employer. For this reason, courts have likened hostile environment sexual harassment to the classic "frolic and detour" for which an employer has no vicarious liability.

These cases ostensibly stand in some tension with others arising outside Title VII, where the scope of employment has been defined broadly enough to hold employers vicariously liable for intentional torts that were in no sense inspired by any purpose to serve the employer. In *Ira S. Bushey & Sons, Inc. v. United States*, 398 F.2d 167 (1968), for example, the Second Circuit charged the Government with vicarious liability for the depredation of a drunken sailor returning to his ship after a night's carouse, who inexplicably opened valves that flooded a drydock, damaging both the drydock and the ship. Judge Friendly acknowledged that the sailor's conduct was not remotely motivated by a purpose to serve his employer, but relied on the "deeply rooted sentiment that a business enterprise cannot justly disclaim responsibility for accidents which may fairly be said to be characteristic of its activities," and imposed vicarious liability on the ground that the sailor's conduct "was not so 'unforeseeable' as to make it unfair to charge the Government with responsibility." *Id.*, at 171. Other examples of an expansive sense of scope of employment are readily found, *see, e.g., Leonbruno v. Champlain Silk Mills*, 128 N.E. 711 (N.Y. 1920) (opinion of Cardozo, J.) (employer was liable under worker's compensation statute for eye injury sustained when employee threw an apple at another; the accident arose "in the course of employment" because such horseplay should be expected). Courts, in fact, have treated scope of employment generously enough to include sexual assaults. *See, e.g., Samuels v. Southern Baptist Hospital*, 594 So.2d 571, 574 (La. App. 1992) (nursing assistant raped patient). The rationales for these decisions have varied, with some courts echoing *Bushey* in explaining that the employees's acts were foreseeable and that the employer should in fairness bear the resulting costs of doing business and others finding that the employee's sexual misconduct arose from or was in some way related to the employee's essential duties. *See, e.g., Samuels, supra*, at 574 (tortious conduct was "reasonably incidental" to the performance of the nursing assistant's duties in caring for a "helpless" patient in a "locked environment").

An assignment to reconcile the run of the Title VII cases with those just cited would be a taxing one. Here it is enough to recognize that their disparate results do not necessarily reflect wildly varying terms of the particular employment contracts involved, but represent differing judgments about the desirability of holding an employer liable for his subordinates' wayward behavior. . . . Older cases, for example, treated smoking by an employee during working hours as an act outside the scope of employment, but more recently courts have generally held smoking on the job to fall within the scope. It is not that employers formerly did not authorize smoking but have now begun to do so, or that employees previously smoked for their own purposes but now do so to serve the employer. We simply understand smoking differently now and have revised the old judgments about what ought to be done about it.

The proper analysis here, then, calls not for a mechanical application of indefinite and malleable factors set forth in the Restatement, *see, e.g.*, §§ 219, 228, 229, but rather an enquiry into the reasons that would support a conclusion that harassing behavior ought to be held within the scope of a supervisor's employment, and the reasons for the opposite view. The Restatement itself points to such an approach, as in the commentary that the "ultimate question" in determining the scope of employment is "whether or not it is just that the loss resulting from the servant's acts should be considered as one of the normal risks to be borne by the business in which the servant is employed." *Id.*, § 229, Comment a.

In the case before us, a justification for holding the offensive behavior within the scope of Terry's and Silverman's employment was well put in Judge Barkett's dissent: "[A] pervasively hostile work environment of sexual harassment is never (one would hope) authorized, but the supervisor is clearly charged with maintaining a productive, safe work environment. The supervisor directs and controls the conduct of the employees, and the manner of doing so may inure to the employer's benefit or detriment, including subjecting the employer to Title VII liability." 111 F.3d, at 1542 (opinion dissenting in part and concurring in part). It is by now well recognized that hostile environment sexual harassment by supervisors (and, for that matter, co-employees) is a persistent problem in the workplace. An employer can, in a general sense, reasonably anticipate the possibility of such conduct occurring in its workplace, and one might justify the assignment of the burden of the untoward behavior to the employer as one of the costs of doing business, to be charged to the enterprise rather than the victim. As noted, developments like this occur from time to time in the law of agency.

Two things counsel us to draw the contrary conclusion. First, there is no reason to suppose that Congress wished courts to ignore the traditional distinction between acts falling within the scope and acts amounting to what the older law called frolics or detours from the course of employment. Such a distinction can readily be applied to the spectrum of possible harassing conduct by supervisors, as the following examples show. First, a supervisor might discriminate racially in job assignments in order to placate the prejudice pervasive in the labor force. Instances of this variety of the heckler's veto would be consciously intended to further the employer's interests by preserving peace in the workplace. Next, supervisors might reprimand male employees for workplace failings with banter, but respond to women's shortcomings in harsh or vulgar terms. A third example might be the supervisor who, as here, expresses his sexual interests in ways having no apparent object whatever of serving an interest of the employer. If a line is to be drawn between scope and frolic, it would lie between the first two examples and the third, and it thus makes sense in terms of traditional agency law to analyze the scope issue, in cases like the third example, just as most federal courts addressing that issue have done, classifying the harassment as beyond the scope of employment.

The second reason goes to an even broader unanimity of views among the holdings of District Courts and Courts of Appeals thus far. Those courts have held not only that the sort of harassment at issue here was outside the scope of supervisors' authority, but, by uniformly judging employer liability for co-worker harassment under a negligence standard, they have also implicitly treated such harassment as outside the scope of common employees' duties as well. If, indeed, the cases did not rest, at least implicitly, on the notion that such harassment falls outside the scope of employment, their liability issues would have turned simply on the application of the scope-of-employment rule.

It is quite unlikely that these cases would escape efforts to render them obsolete if we were to hold that supervisors who engage in discriminatory harassment are necessarily acting within the scope of their employment. The rationale for placing harassment within the scope of supervisory authority would be the fairness of requiring the employer to bear the burden of foreseeable social behavior, and the same rationale would apply when the behavior was that of co-employees. The employer generally benefits just as obviously from the work of common employees as from the work of supervisors; they simply have different jobs to do, all aimed at the success of the enterprise. As between an innocent employer and an innocent employee, if we use scope of employment reasoning to require the employer to bear the cost of an actionably hostile workplace created by one class of employees (*i.e.*, supervisors), it could appear just as appropriate to do the same when the environment was created by another class (*i.e.*, co-workers).

The answer to this argument might well be to point out that the scope of supervisory employment may be treated separately by recognizing that supervisors have special authority enhancing their capacity to harass, and that the employer can guard against their misbehavior more easily because their numbers are by definition fewer than the numbers of regular employees. But this answer happens to implicate an entirely separate category of agency law (to be considered in the next section), which imposes vicarious liability on employers for tortious acts committed by use of particular authority conferred as an element of an employee's agency relationship with the employer. Since the virtue of categorical clarity is obvious, it is better to reject reliance on misuse of supervisory authority (without more) as irrelevant to scope-of-employment analysis.

2

The Court of Appeals also rejected vicarious liability on the part of the City insofar as it might rest on the concluding principle set forth in § 219(2)(d) of the Restatement, that an employer "is not subject to liability for the torts of his servants acting outside the scope of their employment unless . . . the servant purported to act or speak on behalf of the principal and there was reliance on apparent authority, or he was aided in accomplishing the tort by the existence of the agency relation." Faragher points to several ways in which the agency relationship aided Terry and Silverman in carrying out their harassment. She argues that in general offending supervisors can abuse their authority to keep subordinates in their presence while they make offensive statements, and that they implicitly threaten to misuse their supervisory powers to deter any resistance or complaint. Thus, she maintains that power conferred on Terry and Silverman by the City enabled them to act for so long without provoking defiance or complaint. . . .

We . . . agree with Faragher that in implementing Title VII it makes sense to hold an employer vicariously liable for some tortious conduct of a supervisor made possible by abuse of his supervisory authority, and that the aided-by-agency-relation principle embodied in § 219(2)(d) of the Restatement provides an appropriate starting point for determining liability for the kind of harassment presented here. Several courts, indeed, have noted what Faragher has argued, that there is a sense in which a harassing supervisor is always assisted in his misconduct by the supervisory relationship. *See, e.g., Rodgers v. Western-Southern Life Ins. Co.*, 12 F.3d 668, 675 (7th Cir. 1993). The agency relationship affords contact with an employee subjected to a supervisor's sexual harassment, and the victim may well be reluctant to accept the risks of blowing the whistle on a superior. When a person with supervisory authority discriminates in the terms and conditions of subordinates' employment, his actions necessarily draw upon his superior position over the people who report to him, or those under them, whereas an employee generally cannot check a supervisor's abusive conduct the same way that she might deal with abuse from a co-worker. When a fellow employee harasses, the victim can walk away or tell the offender where to go, but it may be difficult to offer such responses to a supervisor, whose "power to supervise — [which may be] to hire and fire, and to set work schedules and pay rates — does not disappear . . . when he chooses to harass through insults and offensive gestures rather than directly with threats of firing or promises of promotion." Estrich, *Sex at Work*, 43 STAN. L. REV. 813, 854 (1991). Recognition of employer liability when discriminatory misuse of supervisory authority alters the terms and conditions of a victim's employment is underscored by the fact that the employer has a greater opportunity to guard against misconduct by supervisors than by common workers; employers have greater opportunity and incentive to screen them, train them, and monitor their performance.

In sum, there are good reasons for vicarious liability for misuse of supervisory authority. That rationale must, however, satisfy one more condition. We are not entitled to recognize this theory under Title VII unless we can square it with *Meritor*'s holding that an employer is not "automatically" liable for harassment by a supervisor who creates the requisite degree of discrimination,[4] and there is obviously some tension between that holding and the

---

[4] We are bound to honor *Meritor* on this point not merely because of the high value placed on stare decisis in statutory interpretation, but for a further reason as well. With the amendments enacted by the Civil Rights Act of 1991, Congress both expanded the monetary relief available under Title VII to include compensatory and punitive damages and modified the statutory grounds

position that a supervisor's misconduct aided by supervisory authority subjects the employer to liability vicariously; if the "aid" may be the unspoken suggestion of retaliation by misuse of supervisory authority, the risk of automatic liability is high. To counter it, we think there are two basic alternatives, one being to require proof of some affirmative invocation of that authority by the harassing supervisor, the other to recognize an affirmative defense to liability in some circumstances, even when a supervisor has created the actionable environment.

There is certainly some authority for requiring active or affirmative, as distinct from passive or implicit, misuse of supervisory authority before liability may be imputed. That is the way some courts have viewed the familiar cases holding the employer liable for discriminatory employment action with tangible consequences, like firing and demotion. And we have already noted some examples of liability provided by the Restatement itself, which suggests that an affirmative misuse of power might be required. *See supra* (telegraph operator sends false messages, a store manager cheats customers, editor publishes libelous editorial).

But neat examples illustrating the line between the affirmative and merely implicit uses of power are not easy to come by in considering management behavior. Supervisors do not make speeches threatening sanctions whenever they make requests in the legitimate exercise of managerial authority, and yet every subordinate employee knows the sanctions exist; this is the reason that courts have consistently held that acts of supervisors have greater power to alter the environment than acts of co-employees generally. How far from the course of ostensible supervisory behavior would a company officer have to step before his orders would not reasonably be seen as actively using authority? Judgment calls would often be close, the results would often seem disparate even if not demonstrably contradictory, and the temptation to litigate would be hard to resist. We think plaintiffs and defendants alike would be poorly served by an active-use rule.

The other basic alternative to automatic liability would avoid this particular temptation to litigate, but allow an employer to show as an affirmative defense to liability that the employer had exercised reasonable care to avoid harassment and to eliminate it when it might occur, and that the complaining employee had failed to act with like reasonable care to take advantage of the employer's safeguards and otherwise to prevent harm that could have been avoided. This composite defense would, we think, implement the statute sensibly, for reasons that are not hard to fathom.

Although Title VII seeks "to make persons whole for injuries suffered on account of unlawful employment discrimination," *Albemarle Paper Co. v. Moody*, 422 U.S. 405, 418 (1975), its "primary objective," like that of any statute meant to influence primary conduct, is not to provide redress but to

---

of several of our decisions. The decision of Congress to leave *Meritor* intact is conspicuous. We thus have to assume that in expanding employers' potential liability under Title VII, Congress relied on our statements in *Meritor* about the limits of employer liability. To disregard those statements now (even if we were convinced of reasons for doing so) would be not only to disregard stare decisis in statutory interpretation, but to substitute our revised judgment about the proper allocation of the costs of harassment for Congress's considered decision on the subject.

avoid harm. As long ago as 1980, the Equal Employment Opportunity Commission (EEOC), charged with the enforcement of Title VII, adopted regulations advising employers to "take all steps necessary to prevent sexual harassment from occurring, such as . . . informing employees of their right to raise and how to raise the issue of harassment," 29 C.F.R. § 1604.11(f) (1997), and in 1990 the Commission issued a policy statement enjoining employers to establish a complaint procedure "designed to encourage victims of harassment to come forward [without requiring] a victim to complain first to the offending supervisor." EEOC Policy Guidance on Sexual Harassment, 8 FEP Manual 405:6699 (Mar. 19, 1990) (internal quotation marks omitted). It would therefore implement clear statutory policy and complement the Government's Title VII enforcement efforts to recognize the employer's affirmative obligation to prevent violations and give credit here to employers who make reasonable efforts to discharge their duty. Indeed, a theory of vicarious liability for misuse of supervisory power would be at odds with the statutory policy if it failed to provide employers with some such incentive.

The requirement to show that the employee has failed in a coordinate duty to avoid or mitigate harm reflects an equally obvious policy imported from the general theory of damages, that a victim has a duty "to use such means as are reasonable under the circumstances to avoid or minimize the damages" that result from violations of the statute. *Ford Motor Co. v. EEOC,* 458 U.S. 219, 231, n. 15 (1982) (quoting C. McCormick, Law of Damages 127 (1935)) (internal quotation marks omitted). An employer may, for example, have provided a proven, effective mechanism for reporting and resolving complaints of sexual harassment, available to the employee without undue risk or expense. If the plaintiff unreasonably failed to avail herself of the employer's preventive or remedial apparatus, she should not recover damages that could have been avoided if she had done so. If the victim could have avoided harm, no liability should be found against the employer who had taken reasonable care, and if damages could reasonably have been mitigated no award against a liable employer should reward a plaintiff for what her own efforts could have avoided.

In order to accommodate the principle of vicarious liability for harm caused by misuse of supervisory authority, as well as Title VII's equally basic policies of encouraging forethought by employers and saving action by objecting employees, we adopt the following holding in this case and in *Burlington Industries, Inc. v. Ellerth,* [524 U.S. 742 (1998),] also decided today. An employer is subject to vicarious liability to a victimized employee for an actionable hostile environment created by a supervisor with immediate (or successively higher) authority over the employee. When no tangible employment action is taken, a defending employer may raise an affirmative defense to liability or damages, subject to proof by a preponderance of the evidence, *see* Fed. R. Civ. P. 8(c). The defense comprises two necessary elements: (a) that the employer exercised reasonable care to prevent and correct promptly any sexually harassing behavior, and (b) that the plaintiff employee unreasonably failed to take advantage of any preventive or corrective opportunities provided by the employer or to avoid harm otherwise. While proof that an employer had promulgated an antiharassment policy with complaint procedure is not necessary in every instance as a matter of law, the need for a stated policy suitable to the employment circumstances may appropriately be addressed in any case when litigating the first element of the defense. And while proof that an employee failed to fulfill the corresponding obligation of reasonable care to avoid harm is not limited to showing an unreasonable failure to use any complaint procedure provided by the employer, a demonstration of such failure will normally suffice to satisfy the employer's burden under the second element of the defense. No affirmative defense is available, however, when the supervisor's harassment culminates in a tangible employment action, such as discharge, demotion, or undesirable reassignment.

Applying these rules here, we believe that the judgment of the Court of Appeals must be reversed. . . .

While the City would have an opportunity to raise an affirmative defense if there were any serious prospect of its presenting one, it appears from the record that any such avenue is closed. The District Court found that the City had entirely failed to disseminate its policy against sexual harassment among the beach employees and that its officials made no attempt to keep track of the conduct of supervisors like Terry and Silverman. The record also makes clear that the City's policy did not include any assurance that the harassing supervisors could be bypassed in registering complaints. Under such circumstances, we hold as a matter of law that the City could not be found to have exercised reasonable care to prevent the supervisors' harassing conduct. Unlike the employer of a small workforce, who might expect that sufficient care to prevent tortious behavior could be exercised informally, those responsible for city operations could not reasonably have thought that precautions against hostile environments in any one of many departments in far-flung locations could be effective without communicating some formal policy against harassment, with a sensible complaint procedure. . . .

The City points to nothing that might justify a conclusion by the District Court on remand that the City had exercised reasonable care. Nor is there any reason to remand for consideration of Faragher's efforts to mitigate her own damages, since the award to her was solely nominal. . . .

The judgment of the Court of Appeals for the Eleventh Circuit is reversed, and the case is remanded for reinstatement of the judgment of the District Court.

[JUSTICE GINSBURG filed a concurring opinion.]

JUSTICE THOMAS, with whom JUSTICE SCALIA joins, dissenting.

The Court today manufactures a rule that employers are vicariously liable if supervisors create a sexually hostile work environment, subject to an affirmative defense that the Court barely attempts to define. [Instead of this rule, an] employer should be liable if, and only if, the plaintiff proves that the employer was negligent in permitting the supervisor's conduct to occur. . . .

When a supervisor inflicts an adverse employment consequence upon an employee who has rebuffed his advances, the supervisor exercises the specific authority granted to him by his company. His acts, therefore, are the company's acts and are properly chargeable to it.

If a supervisor creates a hostile work environment, however, he does not act for the employer. As the Court concedes, a supervisor's creation of a hostile work environment is neither within the scope of his employment, nor part of his apparent authority. Indeed, a hostile work environment is antithetical to the interests of the employer. In such circumstances, an employer should be liable only if it has been negligent. That is, liability should attach only if the employer either knew, or in the exercise of reasonable care should have known about the hostile work environment and failed to take remedial action.[3]

NOTES

1. *Applying the Standard.* Consider an employer who does everything reasonably possible to avoid and respond to harassment. It has an express policy prohibiting harassment and posts it broadly. When an employee is harassed by a supervisor and complains, the employer responds immediately by separating the two and, after a prompt investigation, confronts the supervisor who immediately resigns. Is the employer liable for the supervisor's harassment? *See Corcoran v. Shoney's Colonial, Inc.*, 24 F. Supp. 2d 601 (W.D. Va. 1998) (yes, because employer cannot meet second prong of affirmative defense that employee failed to take advantage of employer's corrective opportunities).

2. *Employer Liability for Harassment by Non-Supervisors.* The standard of employer liability in *Faragher* applies to harassment by supervisors. But harassment can also occur through the actions of others, such as co-workers, independent contractors, and customers. For harassment by non-supervisors, the courts use a negligence standard. *See, e.g., Lockard v. Pizza Hut*, 162 F.3d 1062 (10th Cir. 1998) (employer liable for customer harassment of a waitress where supervisor ordered her to serve customers after being placed on notice that harassment was likely).

Dunn v. Washington County Hosp., 429 F.3d 689 (7th Cir. 2005), provides a particularly interesting and provocative discussion of this principle. In *Dunn*, the District Court had held that a hospital could not be liable when a nurse was harassed by an independent contractor, the physician responsible for obstetric and emergency services. Judge Easterbrook disagreed:

> [For non-supervisors,] it makes no difference whether the person whose acts are complained of is an employee, an independent contractor, or for that matter a customer. Ability to "control" the actor plays no role. Employees are not puppets on strings; employers have an arsenal of incentives and sanctions (including discharge) that can be applied to affect conduct. It is the use (or failure to use) these options

---

[3] I agree with the Court that the doctrine of *quid pro quo* sexual harassment is irrelevant to the issue of an employer's vicarious liability. I do not, however, agree that the distinction between hostile work environment and *quid pro quo* sexual harassment is relevant "when there is a threshold question whether a plaintiff can prove discrimination in violation of Title VII." A supervisor's threat to take adverse action against an employee who refuses his sexual demands, if never carried out, may create a hostile work environment, but that is all. Cases involving such threats, without more, should therefore be analyzed as hostile work environment cases only. If, on the other hand, the supervisor carries out his threat and causes the plaintiff a job detriment, the plaintiff may have a disparate treatment claim under Title VII.

that makes an employer responsible — and in this respect independent contractors are no different from employees. Indeed, it makes no difference whether the actor is human. Suppose a patient kept a macaw in his room, that the bird bit and scratched women but not men, and that the Hospital did nothing. The Hospital would be responsible for the decision to expose women to the working conditions affected by the macaw, even though the bird (a) was not an employee, and (b) could not be controlled by reasoning or sanctions. It would be the Hospital's responsibility to protect its female employees by excluding the offending bird from the premises.

Id. at 691.

3. Perils of Reporting Harassment. In *Jordan v. Alternative Resources Corp.*, 458 F.3d 332 (4th Cir. 2006), Robert Jordan overheard a fellow employee make an extremely crude and racist statement. He reported the incident to management and was fired. The court dismissed Mr. Jordan's discrimination and retaliation claims because no objectively reasonable person could have believed that "an isolated racial slur, which is always and everywhere inappropriate, [constitutes] the sort of severe or pervasive conduct that creates a hostile work environment." *Id.* at 342. The dissenter argued that *Faragher* and other cases require plaintiffs to report harassing conduct early to preserve their claims, yet this case permits them to be fired if they do so too early. "As a result of today's decision, employees. who experience racially harassing conduct are faced with a 'Catch-22.' They may report such conduct to their employer at their peril (as Jordan did), or they may remain quiet and work in a racially hostile and degrading work environment, with no legal recourse beyond resignation." *Id.* at 355 (King, J., dissenting).

4. Harassment as a General Type of Discrimination. Although sexual harassment is by far the most litigated type, the harassment concept applies across the range of discrimination statutes. *See, e.g., Fox v. General Motors Corp.*, 247 F.3d 169 (4th Cir. 2001) (recognizing disability harassment); *Crawford v. Medina Gen. Hosp.*, 96 F.3d 830 (6th Cir. 1996) (recognizing harassment under the Age Discrimination in Employment Act). Indeed, the first case recognizing harassment as cognizable under Title VII involved racial harassment. *Rogers v. EEOC*, 454 F.2d 234 (5th Cir. 1971).

2. SEX-BASED SOCIAL CONVENTIONS

JESPERSEN v. HARRAH'S OPERATING COMPANY
United States Court of Appeals, Ninth Circuit
444 F.3d 1104 (2006) (en banc)

SCHROEDER, CHIEF JUDGE:

The plaintiff, Darlene Jespersen, was terminated from her position as a bartender at the sports bar in Harrah's Reno casino not long after Harrah's began to enforce its comprehensive uniform, appearance and grooming standards for all bartenders. The standards required all bartenders, men and women, to wear the same uniform of black pants and white shirts, a bow tie,

and comfortable black shoes. The standards also included grooming requirements that differed to some extent for men and women, requiring women to
wear some facial makeup and not permitting men to wear any. Jespersen
refused to comply with the makeup requirement and was effectively terminated for that reason. . . .

I. *Background*

Plaintiff Darlene Jespersen worked successfully as a bartender at Harrah's
for twenty years and compiled what by all accounts was an exemplary record.
During Jespersen's entire tenure with Harrah's, the company maintained a
policy encouraging female beverage servers to wear makeup. The parties
agree, however, that the policy was not enforced until 2000. In February 2000,
Harrah's implemented a "Beverage Department Image Transformation"
program at twenty Harrah's locations, including its casino in Reno. Part of
the program consisted of new grooming and appearance standards, called the
"Personal Best" program. The program contained certain appearance standards that applied equally to both sexes, including a standard uniform of black
pants, white shirt, black vest, and black bow tie. Jespersen has never objected
to any of these policies. The program also contained some sex-differentiated
appearance requirements as to hair, nails, and makeup.

In April 2000, Harrah's amended that policy to require that women wear
makeup. Jespersen's only objection here is to the makeup requirement. The
amended policy provided in relevant part:

> All Beverage Service Personnel, in addition to being friendly, polite,
> courteous and responsive to our customer's needs, must possess the
> ability to physically perform the essential factors of the job as set forth
> in the standard job descriptions. They must be well groomed, appeal-
> ing to the eye, be firm and body toned, and be comfortable with
> maintaining this look while wearing the specified uniform. Additional
> factors to be considered include, but are not limited to, hair styles,
> overall body contour, and degree of comfort the employee projects
> while wearing the uniform.
>
> . . . .
>
> Beverage Bartenders and Barbacks will adhere to these additional
> guidelines:
>
> - Overall Guidelines (applied equally to male/female):
>   - Appearance: Must maintain Personal Best image por-
>   trayed at time of hire.
>   - Jewelry, if issued, must be worn. Otherwise, tasteful and
>   simple jewelry is permitted; no large chokers, chains or
>   bracelets. . . .
> - Males:
>   - Hair must not extend below top of shirt collar. Ponytails
>   are prohibited. . . .
>   - Eye and facial makeup is not permitted. . . .

- Females:
  - Hair must be teased, curled, or styled every day you work. Hair must be worn down at all times, no exceptions. . . .
  - *Make up (face powder, blush and mascara) must be worn and applied neatly in complimentary colors. Lip color must be worn at all times.* (emphasis added).

Jespersen did not wear makeup on or off the job, and in her deposition stated that wearing it would conflict with her self-image. It is not disputed that she found the makeup requirement offensive, and felt so uncomfortable wearing makeup that she found it interfered with her ability to perform as a bartender. Unwilling to wear the makeup, and not qualifying for any open positions at the casino with a similar compensation scale, Jespersen left her employment with Harrah's. . . .

II. *Unequal Burdens*

In order to assert a valid Title VII claim for sex discrimination, a plaintiff must make out a prima facie case establishing that the challenged employment action was either intentionally discriminatory or that it had a discriminatory effect on the basis of gender. *McDonnell Douglas Corp. v. Green*, 411 U.S. 792, 802 (1973). Once a plaintiff establishes such a prima facie case, "the burden then must shift to the employer to articulate some legitimate, nondiscriminatory reason for the employee's rejection." *Id.* at 802.

In this case, Jespersen argues that the makeup requirement itself establishes a prima facie case of discriminatory intent and must be justified by Harrah's as a bona fide occupational qualification. Our settled law in this circuit, however, does not support Jespersen's position that a sex-based difference in appearance standards alone, without any further showing of disparate effects, creates a prima facie case.

In *Gerdom v. Cont'l Airlines, Inc.*, 692 F.2d 602 (9th Cir. 1982), we considered the Continental Airlines policy that imposed strict weight restrictions on female flight attendants, and held it constituted a violation of Title VII. We did so because the airline imposed no weight restriction whatsoever on a class of male employees who performed the same or similar functions as the flight attendants. Indeed, the policy was touted by the airline as intended to "create the public image of an airline which offered passengers service by thin, attractive women, whom executives referred to as Continental's 'girls.' " In fact, Continental specifically argued that its policy was justified by its "desire to compete [with other airlines] by featuring attractive female cabin attendants[,]" a justification which this court recognized as "discriminatory on its face." The weight restriction was part of an overall program to create a sexual image for the airline.

In contrast, this case involves an appearance policy that applied to both male and female bartenders, and was aimed at creating a professional and very similar look for all of them. All bartenders wore the same uniform. The policy only differentiated as to grooming standards.

In *Frank v. United Airlines, Inc.*, 216 F.3d 845 (9th Cir. 2000), we dealt with a weight policy that applied different standards to men and women in a facially unequal way. The women were forced to meet the requirements of a medium body frame standard while men were required to meet only the more generous requirements of a large body frame standard. In that case, we recognized that "an appearance standard that imposes different but essentially equal burdens on men and women is not disparate treatment." The United weight policy, however, did not impose equal burdens. On its face, the policy embodied a requirement that categorically "applied less favorably to one gender[,]" and the burdens imposed upon that gender were obvious from the policy itself.

This case stands in marked contrast, for here we deal with requirements that, on their face, are not more onerous for one gender than the other. Rather, Harrah's "Personal Best" policy contains sex-differentiated requirements regarding each employee's hair, hands, and face. While those individual requirements differ according to gender, none on its face places a greater burden on one gender than the other. Grooming standards that appropriately differentiate between the genders are not facially discriminatory.

We have long recognized that companies may differentiate between men and women in appearance and grooming policies. . . . The material issue under our settled law is not whether the policies are different, but whether the policy imposed on the plaintiff creates an "unequal burden" for the plaintiff's gender. . . . Under established equal burdens analysis, when an employer's grooming and appearance policy does not unreasonably burden one gender more than the other, that policy will not violate Title VII.

Jespersen asks us to take judicial notice of the fact that it costs more money and takes more time for a woman to comply with the makeup requirement than it takes for a man to comply with the requirement that he keep his hair short, but these are not matters appropriate for judicial notice. Judicial notice is reserved for matters "generally known within the territorial jurisdiction of the trial court" or "capable of accurate and ready determination by resort to sources whose accuracy cannot reasonably be questioned." Fed. R. Evid. 201. The time and cost of makeup and haircuts is in neither category. The facts that Jespersen would have this court judicially notice are not subject to the requisite "high degree of indisputability" generally required for such judicial notice. Fed. R. Evid. 201 advisory committee's note.

Our rules thus provide that a plaintiff may not cure her failure to present the trial court with facts sufficient to establish the validity of her claim by requesting that this court take judicial notice of such facts. Those rules apply here. Jespersen did not submit any documentation or any evidence of the relative cost and time required to comply with the grooming requirements by men and women. As a result, we would have to speculate about those issues in order to then guess whether the policy creates unequal burdens for women. This would not be appropriate.

Having failed to create a record establishing that the "Personal Best" policies are more burdensome for women than for men, Jespersen did not present any triable issue of fact. The district court correctly granted summary judgment on the record before it with respect to Jespersen's claim that the makeup policy created an unequal burden for women.

III. *Sex Stereotyping*

In *Price Waterhouse*, the Supreme Court considered a mixed-motive discrimination case. 490 U.S. 228 (1989). There, the plaintiff, Ann Hopkins, was denied partnership in the national accounting firm of Price Waterhouse because some of the partners found her to be too aggressive. While some partners praised Hopkins's " 'strong character, independence and integrity[,]' " others commented that she needed to take " 'a course at charm school[.]' " *Id.* at 234-35. The Supreme Court determined that once a plaintiff has established that gender played "a motivating part in an employment decision, the defendant may avoid a finding of liability only by proving by a preponderance of the evidence that it would have made the same decision even if it had not taken the plaintiff's gender into account." *Id.* at 258. Consequently, in establishing that "gender played a motivating part in an employment decision," a plaintiff in a Title VII case may introduce evidence that the employment decision was made in part because of a sex stereotype. . . .

The stereotyping in *Price Waterhouse* interfered with Hopkins' ability to perform her work; the advice that she should take "a course at charm school" was intended to discourage her use of the forceful and aggressive techniques that made her successful in the first place. Impermissible sex stereotyping was clear because the very traits that she was asked to hide were the same traits considered praiseworthy in men.

Harrah's "Personal Best" policy is very different. The policy does not single out Jespersen. It applies to all of the bartenders, male and female. It requires all of the bartenders to wear exactly the same uniforms while interacting with the public in the context of the entertainment industry. It is for the most part unisex, from the black tie to the non-skid shoes. There is no evidence in this record to indicate that the policy was adopted to make women bartenders conform to a commonly-accepted stereotypical image of what women should wear. The record contains nothing to suggest the grooming standards would objectively inhibit a woman's ability to do the job. The only evidence in the record to support the stereotyping claim is Jespersen's own subjective reaction to the makeup requirement.

Judge Pregerson's dissent improperly divides the grooming policy into separate categories of hair, hands, and face, and then focuses exclusively on the makeup requirement to conclude that the policy constitutes sex stereotyping. This parsing, however, conflicts with established grooming standards analysis. The requirements must be viewed in the context of the overall policy. . . .

We respect Jespersen's resolve to be true to herself and to the image that she wishes to project to the world. We cannot agree, however, that her objection to the makeup requirement, without more, can give rise to a claim of sex stereotyping under Title VII. If we were to do so, we would come perilously close to holding that every grooming, apparel, or appearance requirement that an individual finds personally offensive, or in conflict with his or her own self-image, can create a triable issue of sex discrimination.

This is not a case where the dress or appearance requirement is intended to be sexually provocative, and tending to stereotype women as sex objects.

See, e.g., EEOC v. Sage Realty Corp., 507 F. Supp. 599 (S.D.N.Y. 1981). In *Sage Realty*, the plaintiff was a lobby attendant in a hotel that employed only female lobby attendants and required a mandatory uniform. The uniform was an octagon designed with an opening for the attendant's head, to be worn as a poncho, with snaps at the wrists and a tack on each side of the poncho, which was otherwise open. The attendants wore blue dancer pants as part of the uniform but were prohibited from wearing a shirt, blouse, or skirt under the outfit. There, the plaintiff was required to wear a uniform that was "short and revealing on both sides [such that her] thighs and portions of her buttocks were exposed." *Id.* Jespersen, in contrast, was asked only to wear a unisex uniform that covered her entire body and was designed for men and women. The "Personal Best" policy does not, on its face, indicate any discriminatory or sexually stereotypical intent on the part of Harrah's. . . .

We emphasize that we do not preclude, as a matter of law, a claim of sex-stereotyping on the basis of dress or appearance codes. Others may well be filed, and any bases for such claims refined as law in this area evolves. This record, however, is devoid of any basis for permitting this particular claim to go forward, as it is limited to the subjective reaction of a single employee, and there is no evidence of a stereotypical motivation on the part of the employer. This case is essentially a challenge to one small part of what is an overall apparel, appearance, and grooming policy that applies largely the same requirements to both men and women. [T]he touchstone is reasonableness. A makeup requirement must be seen in the context of the overall standards imposed on employees in a given workplace.

Affirmed.

PREGERSON, CIRCUIT JUDGE, with whom JUDGES KOZINSKI, GRABER, and W. FLETCHER join, dissenting:

. . . . I part ways with the majority . . . inasmuch as I believe that the "Personal Best" program was part of a policy motivated by sex stereotyping and that Jespersen's termination for failing to comply with the program's requirements was "because of" her sex. Accordingly, I dissent from Part III of the majority opinion and from the judgment of the court.

The majority contends that it is bound to reject Jespersen's sex stereotyping claim because she presented too little evidence — only her "own subjective reaction to the makeup requirement." I disagree. Jespersen's evidence showed that Harrah's fired her because she did not comply with a grooming policy that imposed a facial uniform (full makeup) on only female bartenders. Harrah's stringent "Personal Best" policy required female beverage servers to wear foundation, blush, mascara, and lip color, and to ensure that lip color was on at all times. Jespersen and her female colleagues were required to meet with professional image consultants who in turn created a facial template for each woman. Jespersen was required not simply to wear makeup; in addition, the consultants dictated where and how the makeup had to be applied.

Quite simply, her termination for failing to comply with a grooming policy that imposed a facial uniform on only female bartenders is discrimination "because of" sex. Such discrimination is clearly and unambiguously impermissible under Title VII, which requires that "gender must be *irrelevant* to employment decisions." *Price Waterhouse v. Hopkins*, 490 U.S. 228, 240 (1989) (plurality opinion) (emphasis added).[2]

Notwithstanding Jespersen's failure to present additional evidence, little is required to make out a sex-stereotyping — as distinct from an undue burden — claim in this situation. In *Price Waterhouse*, the Supreme Court held that an employer may not condition employment on an employee's conformance to a sex stereotype associated with their gender. As the majority recognizes, *Price Waterhouse* allows a Title VII plaintiff to "introduce evidence that the employment decision was made in part because of a sex stereotype." It is not entirely clear exactly what this evidence must be, but nothing in *Price Waterhouse* suggests that a certain type or quantity of evidence is required to prove a prima facie case of discrimination. Moreover, *Price Waterhouse* recognizes that gender discrimination may manifest itself in stereotypical notions as to how women should dress and present themselves, not only as to how they should behave. . . .

Because I believe that we should be careful not to insulate appearance requirements by viewing them in broad categories, such as "hair, hands, and face," I would consider the makeup requirement on its own terms. Viewed in isolation — or, at the very least, as part of a narrower category of requirements affecting employees' faces — the makeup or facial uniform requirement becomes closely analogous to the uniform policy held to constitute impermissible sex stereotyping in *Carroll v. Talman Federal Savings & Loan Ass'n of Chicago*, 604 F.2d 1028, 1029 (7th Cir. 1979). In *Carroll*, the defendant bank required women to wear employer-issued uniforms, but permitted men to wear business attire of their own choosing. The Seventh Circuit found this rule discriminatory because it suggested to the public that the uniformed women held a "lesser professional status" and that women could not be trusted to choose appropriate business attire.

Just as the bank in *Carroll* deemed female employees incapable of achieving a professional appearance without assigned uniforms, Harrah's regarded women as unable to achieve a neat, attractive, and professional appearance without the facial uniform designed by a consultant and required by Harrah's. The inescapable message is that women's undoctored faces compare unfavorably to men's, not because of a physical difference between men's and women's faces, but because of a cultural assumption — and gender-based stereotype — that women's faces are incomplete, unattractive, or unprofessional without full makeup. We need not denounce all makeup as inherently offensive, just as there was no need to denounce all uniforms as inherently offensive in *Carroll*, to conclude that *requiring* female bartenders to wear full makeup is an impermissible sex stereotype and is evidence of discrimination because of sex. . . .

Therefore, I respectfully dissent.

---

[2] Harrah's has not attempted to defend the "Personal Best" makeup requirement as a BFOQ. In fact, there is little doubt that the "Personal Best" policy is not a business necessity, as Harrah's quietly disposed of this policy after Jespersen filed this suit. . . .

KOZINSKI, CIRCUIT JUDGE, with whom JUDGES GRABER and W. FLETCHER join, dissenting:

I agree with Judge Pregerson and join his dissent — subject to one caveat: I believe that Jespersen also presented a triable issue of fact on the question of disparate burden.

The majority is right that "the [makeup] requirements must be viewed in the context of the overall policy." But I find it perfectly clear that Harrah's overall grooming policy is substantially more burdensome for women than for men. Every requirement that forces men to spend time or money on their appearance has a corresponding requirement that is as, or more, burdensome for women: short hair v. "teased, curled, or styled" hair; clean trimmed nails v. nail length and color requirements; black leather shoes v. black leather shoes. The requirement that women spend time and money applying full facial makeup has no corresponding requirement for men, making the "overall policy" more burdensome for the former than for the latter. The only question is how much.

It is true that Jespersen failed to present evidence about what it costs to buy makeup and how long it takes to apply it. But is there any doubt that putting on makeup costs money and takes time? Harrah's policy requires women to apply face powder, blush, mascara and lipstick. You don't need an expert witness to figure out that such items don't grow on trees.

Nor is there any rational doubt that application of makeup is an intricate and painstaking process that requires considerable time and care. Even those of us who don't wear makeup know how long it can take from the hundreds of hours we've spent over the years frantically tapping our toes and pointing to our wrists. It's hard to imagine that a woman could "put on her face," as they say, in the time it would take a man to shave — certainly not if she were to do the careful and thorough job Harrah's expects. Makeup, moreover, must be applied and removed every day; the policy burdens men with no such daily ritual. While a man could jog to the casino, slip into his uniform, and get right to work, a woman must travel to work so as to avoid smearing her makeup, or arrive early to put on her makeup there.

It might have been tidier if Jespersen had introduced evidence as to the time and cost associated with complying with the makeup requirement, but I can understand her failure to do so, as these hardly seem like questions reasonably subject to dispute. We could — and should — take judicial notice of these incontrovertible facts.

Alternatively, Jespersen did introduce evidence that she finds it burdensome to *wear* makeup because doing so is inconsistent with her self-image and interferes with her job performance. My colleagues dismiss this evidence, apparently on the ground that wearing makeup does not, as a matter of law, constitute a substantial burden. This presupposes that Jespersen is unreasonable or idiosyncratic in her discomfort. Why so? Whether to wear cosmetics — literally, the face one presents to the world — is an intensely personal choice. Makeup, moreover, touches delicate parts of the anatomy—the lips, the eyes, the cheeks — and can cause serious discomfort, sometimes even allergic reactions, for someone unaccustomed to wearing it. If you are used to wearing makeup — as most American women are — this may seem like no big deal. But those of us not used to wearing makeup would find a requirement that we do so highly intrusive. Imagine, for example, a rule that all judges wear face powder, blush, mascara and lipstick while on the bench. Like Jespersen, I would find such a regime burdensome and demeaning; it would interfere with my job performance. I suspect many of my colleagues would feel the same way.

Everyone accepts this as a reasonable reaction from a man, but why should it be different for a woman? It is not because of anatomical differences, such as a requirement that women wear bathing suits that cover their breasts. Women's faces, just like those of men, can be perfectly presentable without makeup; it is a cultural artifact that most women raised in the United States learn to put on — and presumably enjoy wearing — cosmetics. But cultural norms change; not so long ago a man wearing an earring was a gypsy, a pirate or an oddity. Today, a man wearing body piercing jewelry is hardly noticed. So, too, a large (and perhaps growing) number of women choose to present themselves to the world without makeup. I see no justification for forcing them to conform to Harrah's quaint notion of what a "real woman" looks like.

Nor do I think it appropriate for a court to dismiss a woman's testimony that she finds wearing makeup degrading and intrusive, as Jespersen clearly does. Not only do we have her sworn statement to that effect, but there can be no doubt about her sincerity or the intensity of her feelings: She quit her job — a job she performed well for two decades — rather than put on the makeup. That is a choice her male colleagues were not forced to make. To me, this states a case of disparate burden, and I would let a jury decide whether an employer can force a woman to make this choice.

Finally, I note with dismay the employer's decision to let go a valued, experienced employee who had gained accolades from her customers, over what, in the end, is a trivial matter. Quality employees are difficult to find in any industry and I would think an employer would long hesitate before forcing a loyal, long-time employee to quit over an honest and heart-felt difference of opinion about a matter of personal significance to her. Having won the legal battle, I hope that Harrah's will now do the generous and decent thing by offering Jespersen her job back, and letting her give it her personal best — without the makeup.

NOTES

1. Working Mothers. Elana Back was denied tenure as a school psychologist after her supervisors made a number of comments about her role as a mother. For example, they said they "did not know how she could perform [her] job with little ones" and that it was "not possible for [her] to be a good mother and have this job." The Second Circuit said this evidence was sufficient to survive a motion for summary judgment. If proven, this type of gender stereotyping is illegal even without any evidence that the employer treated male employees with young children differently and even though 85% of the teachers employed by the school district were women and 71% of those women had children. *Back v. Hastings on Hudson Union Free School District*, 365 F.3d 107 (2d Cir. 2004).

Consider how meaningful this victory against a sex-based social convention really is. First, a primary effect of decisions like Back may well be to drive these kinds of comments underground. Early in the history of Title VII, there were many cases with explicit racist and sexist statements. *See, e.g., Newman v. Avco Corp.*, 491 F. Supp. 89 (M.D. Tenn. 1973) (finding of discrimination supported by evidence of racial epithets). Those cases have largely disappeared, even though there is no doubt that the underlying motivations still exist too often. Second, the underlying motivations in situations like Back's are likely to persist as long as women bear the bulk of childcare responsibilities and the workplace remains poorly structured to accommodate those responsibilities. There is little reason to think either of these factors will change soon. Third, these cases are difficult to win even when there is strong evidence of bias. Even though Elana Back survived a motion for summary judgment, she eventually lost her case. *Back v. Hastings on Hudson*, 161 Fed. Appx. 96 (2d Cir. 2005) (upholding a verdict for the school district).

2. *Real Differences and the Structural Move.* Some of the differences between men and women are real, not merely conventions. Women get pregnant; men do not. As with sex-based social conventions, the basic approach of discrimination law is not well suited to these kinds of problems. What is equal treatment when the comparators are different? With pregnancy, the basic rule of Title VII is that employers must treat pregnancy as they treat other types of temporary disabilities. Title VII § 701(k). The limits of this basic rule are apparent. *Troupe v. May Dep't Stores Co.* 20 F.3d 734, 738 (7th Cir. 1994) ("Employers can treat pregnant women just as badly as they treat similarly affected but nonpregnant employees"). In addition, the rule can be difficult to apply in practice. *See, e.g., Reeves v. Swift Transp. Co.*, 446 F.3d 637 (6th Cir. 2006) (holding no pregnancy discrimination when a woman was denied light-duty work and discharged even though light-duty work was available to workers who were injured on the job).

Thus, in these situations, an antidiscrimination approach alone is likely to be ineffective. Instead, the very structure of the workplace needs to be addressed. Some moves have been made in this direction. For example, the federal government and many states have enacted statutes that require employers to provide unpaid leaves of absence upon the birth or adoption of a child or in the event of family illness. *See* Family and Medical Leave Act, 29 U.S.C. §§ 2601 *et seq.* (discussed in Chapter 18). But in general, both legislatures and courts have resisted these types of structural changes. The central message, however, is not that legislatures and courts are recalcitrant, but rather that the ability of antidiscrimination law to effect change is limited. Antidiscrimination law is likely to be effective when like can be compared to like and when unequal treatment or outcomes can be clearly assigned to an individual employer. When comparisons become difficult and responsibility becomes more diffuse, the law loses force. *See* Samuel R. Bagenstos, *The Structural Turn and the Limits of Antidiscrimination Law*, 94 Cal. L. Rev. 1 (2006).

B. AGE DISCRIMINATION

SMITH v. CITY OF JACKSON
United States Supreme Court
544 U.S. 228 (2005)

MR. JUSTICE STEVENS announced the judgment of the Court and delivered the opinion of the Court with respect to Parts I, II, and IV, and an opinion with respect to Part III, in which SOUTER, GINSBURG, and BREYER join.

Petitioners, police and public safety officers employed by the city of Jackson, Mississippi (hereinafter City), contend that salary increases received in 1999 violated the Age Discrimination in Employment Act of 1967 (ADEA) because they were less generous to officers over the age of 40 than to younger officers. Their suit raises the question whether the "disparate-impact" theory of recovery announced in *Griggs v. Duke Power Co.*, 401 U.S. 424 (1971), for cases brought under Title VII of the Civil Rights Act of 1964, is cognizable under the ADEA. Despite the age of the ADEA, it is a question that we have not yet addressed.

I

On October 1, 1998, the City adopted a pay plan granting raises to all City employees. The stated purpose of the plan was to "attract and retain qualified people, provide incentive for performance, maintain competitiveness with other public sector agencies and ensure equitable compensation to all employees regardless of age, sex, race and/or disability." On May 1, 1999, a revision of the plan, which was motivated, at least in part, by the City's desire to bring the starting salaries of police officers up to the regional average, granted raises to all police officers and police dispatchers. Those who had less than five years of tenure received proportionately greater raises when compared to their former pay than those with more seniority. Although some officers over the age of 40 had less than five years of service, most of the older officers had more.

Petitioners are a group of older officers who filed suit under the ADEA claiming both that the City deliberately discriminated against them because of their age (the "disparate-treatment" claim) and that they were "adversely affected" by the plan because of their age (the "disparate-impact" claim). The District Court granted summary judgment to the City on both claims. The Court of Appeals held that the ruling on the former claim was premature because petitioners were entitled to further discovery on the issue of intent, but it affirmed the dismissal of the disparate-impact claim. Over one judge's dissent, the majority concluded that disparate-impact claims are categorically unavailable under the ADEA. Both the majority and the dissent assumed that the facts alleged by petitioners would entitle them to relief under the reasoning of *Griggs*.

We granted the officers' petition for certiorari and now hold that the ADEA does authorize recovery in "disparate-impact" cases comparable to *Griggs*. Because, however, we conclude that petitioners have not set forth a valid disparate-impact claim, we affirm.

II

. . . As enacted in 1967, § 4(a)(2) of the ADEA, now codified as 29 U.S.C. § 623(a)(2), provided that it shall be unlawful for an employer "to limit, segregate, or classify his employees in any way which would deprive or tend to deprive any individual of employment opportunities or otherwise adversely affect his status as an employee, because of such individual's age. . . ." Except for substitution of the word "age" for the words "race, color, religion, sex, or national origin," the language of that provision in the ADEA is identical to that found in § 703(a)(2) of the Civil Rights Act of 1964 (Title VII). Other provisions of the ADEA also parallel the earlier statute. Unlike Title VII, however, § 4(f)(1) of the ADEA contains language that significantly narrows its coverage by permitting any "otherwise prohibited" action "where the differentiation is based on reasonable factors other than age" (hereinafter RFOA provision).

III

In determining whether the ADEA authorizes disparate-impact claims, we begin with the premise that when Congress uses the same language in two statutes having similar purposes, particularly when one is enacted shortly after the other, it is appropriate to presume that Congress intended that text to have the same meaning in both statutes. . . . Our unanimous interpretation of § 703(a)(2) of Title VII in *Griggs* is therefore a precedent of compelling importance.

In *Griggs*, a case decided four years after the enactment of the ADEA, we considered whether § 703 of Title VII prohibited an employer "from requiring a high school education or passing of a standardized general intelligence test as a condition of employment in or transfer to jobs when (a) neither standard is shown to be significantly related to successful job performance, (b) both requirements operate to disqualify Negroes at a substantially higher rate than white applicants, and (c) the jobs in question formerly had been filled only by white employees as part of a longstanding practice of giving preference to whites." Accepting the Court of Appeals' conclusion that the employer had adopted the diploma and test requirements without any intent to discriminate, we held that good faith "does not redeem employment procedures or testing mechanisms that operate as 'built-in headwinds' for minority groups and are unrelated to measuring job capability."

We explained that Congress had "directed the thrust of the Act to the consequences of employment practices, not simply the motivation." We relied on the fact that history is "filled with examples of men and women who rendered highly effective performance without the conventional badges of accomplishment in terms of certificates, diplomas, or degrees. Diplomas and tests are useful servants, but Congress has mandated the commonsense proposition that they are not to become masters of reality." And we noted that the Equal Employment Opportunity Commission (EEOC), which had enforcement responsibility, had issued guidelines that accorded with our view. We thus squarely held that § 703(a)(2) of Title VII did not require a showing of discriminatory intent.[5]

While our opinion in *Griggs* relied primarily on the purposes of the Act, buttressed by the fact that the EEOC had endorsed the same view, we have subsequently noted that our holding represented the better reading of the statutory text as well. Neither § 703(a)(2) nor the comparable language in the ADEA simply prohibits actions that "limit, segregate, or classify" persons; rather the language prohibits such actions that "deprive any individual of employment opportunities or otherwise adversely affect his status as an employee, because of such individual's" race or age. Thus the text focuses on the effects of the action on the employee rather than the motivation for the action of the employer.[6]

Griggs, which interpreted the identical text at issue here, thus strongly suggests that a disparate-impact theory should be cognizable under the ADEA.[7]

---

[5] The congressional purposes on which we relied in *Griggs* have a striking parallel to two important points made in the *Wirtz Report*[, a 1965 report by the Secretary of Labor which advised Congress on the need for the ADEA]. Just as the *Griggs* opinion ruled out discrimination based on racial animus as a problem in that case, the *Wirtz Report* concluded that there was no significant discrimination of that kind so far as older workers are concerned. And just as *Griggs* recognized that the high school diploma requirement, which was unrelated to job performance, had an unfair impact on African-Americans who had received inferior educational opportunities in segregated schools, the *Wirtz Report* identified the identical obstacle to the employment of older workers. "Any formal employment standard which requires, for example, a high school diploma will obviously work against the employment of many older workers — unfairly if, despite his limited schooling, an older worker's years of experience have given him the relevant equivalent of a high school education." Thus, just as the statutory text is identical, there is a remarkable similarity between the congressional goals we cited in *Griggs* and those present in the *Wirtz Report*.

[6] In reaching a contrary conclusion, Justice O'Connor ignores key textual differences between § 4(a)(1), which does not encompass disparate-impact liability, and § 4(a)(2). Paragraph (a)(1) makes it unlawful for an employer "to fail or refuse to hire . . . *any individual* . . . because of *such individual's* age." (Emphasis added.) The focus of the paragraph is on the employer's actions with respect to the targeted individual. Paragraph (a)(2), however, makes it unlawful for an employer "to limit . . . his *employees* in any way which would deprive or tend to deprive *any individual* of employment opportunities or otherwise adversely affect *his* status as an employee, because of *such individual's* age." (Emphasis added.) Unlike in paragraph (a)(1), there is thus an incongruity between the employer's actions — which are focused on his employees generally — and the individual employee who adversely suffers because of those actions. Thus, an employer who classifies his employees without respect to age may still be liable under the terms of this paragraph if such classification adversely affects the employee because of that employee's age — the very definition of disparate impact. Justice O'Connor is therefore quite wrong to suggest that the textual differences between the two paragraphs are unimportant.

[7] Justice O'Connor reaches a contrary conclusion based on the text of the statute, the legislative history, and the structure of the statute. As we explain above, her textual reasoning is not persuasive. Further, while Congress may have intended to remedy disparate-impact type situations through "noncoercive measures" in part, there is nothing to suggest that it intended such measures to be the sole method of achieving the desired result of remedying practices that had an adverse effect on older workers. Finally, we agree that the differences between age and the classes protected in Title VII are relevant, and that Congress might well have intended to treat the two differently. However, Congress obviously considered those classes of individuals to be sufficiently similar to warrant enacting identical legislation, at least with respect to employment practices it sought to prohibit. While those differences, *coupled with a difference in the text of the statute* such as the RFOA provision, may warrant addressing disparate-impact claims in the two statutes differently, it does not justify departing from the plain text and our settled interpretation of that text.

. . . The Court of Appeals' categorical rejection of disparate-impact liability, like Justice O'Connor's, rested primarily on the RFOA provision.

The RFOA provision provides that it shall not be unlawful for an employer "to take any action otherwise prohibited under subsectio[n] (a) . . . where the differentiation is based on reasonable factors other than age discrimination. . . ." In most disparate-treatment cases, if an employer in fact acted on a factor other than age, the action would not be prohibited under subsection (a) in the first place. In those disparate-treatment cases, . . . the RFOA provision is simply unnecessary to avoid liability under the ADEA, since there was no prohibited action in the first place. The RFOA provision is not, as Justice O'Connor suggests, a "safe harbor from liability," since there would be no liability under § 4(a).

In disparate-impact cases, however, the allegedly "otherwise prohibited" activity is not based on age. It is, accordingly, in cases involving disparate-impact claims that the RFOA provision plays its principal role by precluding liability if the adverse impact was attributable to a nonage factor that was "reasonable." Rather than support an argument that disparate impact is unavailable under the ADEA, the RFOA provision actually supports the contrary conclusion.[8]

Finally, we note that both the Department of Labor, which initially drafted the legislation, and the EEOC, which is the agency charged by Congress with responsibility for implementing the statute, 29 U.S.C. § 628, have consistently interpreted the ADEA to authorize relief on a disparate-impact theory. The initial regulations, while not mentioning disparate impact by name, nevertheless permitted such claims if the employer relied on a factor that was not related to age. 29 CFR § 860.103(f)(1)(i) (1970) (barring physical fitness requirements that were not "reasonably necessary for the specific work to be performed"). *See also* § 1625.7 (2004) (setting forth the standards for a disparate-impact claim).

The text of the statute, as interpreted in *Griggs*, the RFOA provision, and the EEOC regulations all support petitioners' view. We therefore conclude that it was error for the Court of Appeals to hold that the disparate-impact theory of liability is categorically unavailable under the ADEA.

IV

Two textual differences between the ADEA and Title VII make it clear that even though both statutes authorize recovery on a disparate-impact theory, the scope of disparate-impact liability under ADEA is narrower than under Title VII. The first is the RFOA provision, which we have already identified. The second is the amendment to Title VII contained in the Civil Rights Act of 1991. One of the purposes of that amendment was to modify the Court's holding in *Wards Cove Packing Co. v. Atonio*, 490 U.S. 642 (1989), a case in

---

[8] We note that if Congress intended to prohibit all disparate-impact claims, it certainly could have done so. For instance, in the Equal Pay Act of 1963, 29 U.S.C. § 206(d)(1), Congress barred recovery if a pay differential was based "on any other factor" — reasonable or unreasonable — "other than sex." The fact that Congress provided that employees could use only *reasonable* factors in defending a suit under the ADEA is therefore instructive.

which we narrowly construed the employer's exposure to liability on a disparate-impact theory. While the relevant 1991 amendments expanded the coverage of Title VII, they did not amend the ADEA or speak to the subject of age discrimination. Hence, *Wards Cove*'s pre-1991 interpretation of Title VII's identical language remains applicable to the ADEA.

Congress' decision to limit the coverage of the ADEA by including the RFOA provision is consistent with the fact that age, unlike race or other classifications protected by Title VII, not uncommonly has relevance to an individual's capacity to engage in certain types of employment. To be sure, Congress recognized that this is not always the case, and that society may perceive those differences to be larger or more consequential than they are in fact. However, as Secretary Wirtz noted in his report, "certain circumstances . . . unquestionably affect older workers more strongly, as a group, than they do younger workers." Thus, it is not surprising that certain employment criteria that are routinely used may be reasonable despite their adverse impact on older workers as a group. Moreover, intentional discrimination on the basis of age has not occurred at the same levels as discrimination against those protected by Title VII. While the ADEA reflects Congress' intent to give older workers employment opportunities whenever possible, the RFOA provision reflects this historical difference.

Turning to the case before us, we initially note that petitioners have done little more than point out that the pay plan at issue is relatively less generous to older workers than to younger workers. They have not identified any specific test, requirement, or practice within the pay plan that has an adverse impact on older workers. As we held in *Wards Cove*, it is not enough to simply allege that there is a disparate impact on workers, or point to a generalized policy that leads to such an impact. Rather, the employee is "responsible for isolating and identifying the specific employment practices that are allegedly responsible for any observed statistical disparities." Petitioners have failed to do so. Their failure to identify the specific practice being challenged is the sort of omission that could "result in employers being potentially liable for 'the myriad of innocent causes that may lead to statistical imbalances. . . .'" In this case not only did petitioners thus err by failing to identify the relevant practice, but it is also clear from the record that the City's plan was based on reasonable factors other than age.

The plan divided each of five basic positions — police officer, master police officer, police sergeant, police lieutenant, and deputy police chief — into a series of steps and half-steps. The wage for each range was based on a survey of comparable communities in the Southeast. Employees were then assigned a step (or half-step) within their position that corresponded to the lowest step that would still give the individual a 2% raise. Most of the officers were in the three lowest ranks; in each of those ranks there were officers under age 40 and officers over 40. In none did their age affect their compensation. The few officers in the two highest ranks are all over 40. Their raises, though higher in dollar amount than the raises given to junior officers, represented a smaller percentage of their salaries, which of course are higher than the salaries paid to their juniors. They are members of the class complaining of the "disparate impact" of the award.

Petitioners' evidence established two principal facts: First, almost two-thirds (66.2%) of the officers under 40 received raises of more than 10% while less than half (45.3%) of those over 40 did. Second, the average percentage increase for the entire class of officers with less than five years of tenure was somewhat higher than the percentage for those with more seniority. Because older officers tended to occupy more senior positions, on average they received smaller increases when measured as a percentage of their salary. The basic explanation for the differential was the City's perceived need to raise the salaries of junior officers to make them competitive with comparable positions in the market.

Thus, the disparate impact is attributable to the City's decision to give raises based on seniority and position. Reliance on seniority and rank is unquestionably reasonable given the City's goal of raising employees' salaries to match those in surrounding communities. In sum, we hold that the City's decision to grant a larger raise to lower echelon employees for the purpose of bringing salaries in line with that of surrounding police forces was a decision based on a "reasonable factor other than age" that responded to the City's legitimate goal of retaining police officers.

While there may have been other reasonable ways for the City to achieve its goals, the one selected was not unreasonable. Unlike the business necessity test, which asks whether there are other ways for the employer to achieve its goals that do not result in a disparate impact on a protected class, the reasonableness inquiry includes no such requirement.

Accordingly, while we do not agree with the Court of Appeals' holding that the disparate-impact theory of recovery is never available under the ADEA, we affirm its judgment.

It is so ordered.

The Chief Justice took no part in the decision of this case.

Justice Scalia, concurring in part and concurring in the judgment.

I concur in the judgment of the Court, and join all except Part III of its opinion. As to that Part, I agree with all of the Court's reasoning, but would find it a basis, not for independent determination of the disparate-impact question, but for deferral to the reasonable views of the Equal Employment Opportunity Commission (EEOC or Commission) pursuant to *Chevron U.S.A. Inc. v. Natural Resources Defense Council, Inc.*, 467 U.S. 837 (1984). . . .

The EEOC has express authority to promulgate rules and regulations interpreting the ADEA. It has exercised that authority to recognize disparate-impact claims. And, for the reasons given by the plurality opinion, its position is eminently reasonable. In my view, that is sufficient to resolve this case.

Justice O'Connor, with whom Justices Kennedy and Thomas join, concurring in the judgment. . . .

I would . . . affirm the judgment below on the ground that disparate impact claims are not cognizable under the ADEA.

The plurality . . . reads paragraph 4(a)(2) [of the ADEA] to prohibit employer actions that "adversely affect [an individual's] status as an employe[e] because of such individual's age." Under this reading, "because of . . . age" refers to the cause of the adverse effect rather than the motive for the employer's action. This reading is unpersuasive for two reasons. First, it ignores the obvious parallel between paragraphs (a)(1) and (a)(2) by giving the phrase "because of such individual's age" a different meaning in each of the two paragraphs. And second, it ignores the drafters' use of a comma separating the "because of . . . age" clause from the preceding language. That comma makes plain that the "because of . . . age" clause should not be read, as the plurality would have it, to modify only the "adversely affect" phrase. Rather, the "because of . . . age" clause is set aside to make clear that it modifies the entirety of the preceding paragraph: An employer may not, because of an individual's age, limit, segregate, or classify his employees in a way that harms that individual.

The plurality also argues that its reading is supported by the supposed "incongruity" between paragraph (a)(2)'s use of the plural in referring to the employer's actions ("limit, segregate, or classify his *employees*") and its use of the singular in the "because of such *individual's* age" clause. (Emphases added.) Not so. For the reasons just stated, the "because of . . . age" clause modifies all of the preceding language of paragraph (a)(2). That preceding language is phrased in both the plural (insofar as it refers to the employer's actions relating to employees) and the singular (insofar as it requires that such action actually harm an individual). The use of the singular in the "because of . . . age" clause simply makes clear that paragraph (a)(2) forbids an employer to limit, segregate, or classify his employees if that decision is taken because of even one employee's age and that individual (alone or together with others) is harmed. . . .

While § 4(a)(2) of the ADEA makes it unlawful to intentionally discriminate because of age, § 4(f)(1) clarifies that "[i]t shall not be unlawful for an employer . . . to take any action otherwise prohibited under subsections (a), (b), (c), or (e) of this section . . . where the differentiation is based on reasonable factors other than age. . . ." 29 U.S.C. § 623(f)(1). This "reasonable factors other than age" (RFOA) provision "insure[s] that employers [are] permitted to use neutral criteria" other than age, even if this results in a disparate adverse impact on older workers. The provision therefore expresses Congress' clear intention that employers not be subject to liability absent proof of intentional age-based discrimination. That policy, in my view, cannot easily be reconciled with the plurality's expansive reading of § 4(a)(2).

The plurality however, reasons that the RFOA provision's language instead confirms that § 4(a) authorizes disparate impact claims. If § 4(a) prohibited only intentional discrimination, the argument goes, then the RFOA provision would have no effect because any action based on a factor other than age would not be "otherwise prohibited" under § 4(a). Moreover, the plurality says, the RFOA provision applies only to employer actions based on reasonable factors other than age — so employers may still be held liable for actions based on unreasonable nonage factors.

This argument misconstrues the purpose and effect of the RFOA provision. Discriminatory intent is required under § 4(a), for the reasons discussed above. The role of the RFOA provision is to afford employers an independent safe harbor from liability. It provides that, where a plaintiff has made out a prima facie case of intentional age discrimination under § 4(a) — thus "creat[ing] a presumption that the employer unlawfully discriminated against the employee" — the employer can rebut this case by producing evidence that its action was based on a reasonable nonage factor. Thus, the RFOA provision codifies a safe harbor analogous to the "legitimate, nondiscriminatory reason" (LNR) justification later recognized in Title VII suits. *McDonnell Douglas Corp. v. Green*, 411 U.S. 792, 802 (1973).

Assuming the *McDonnell Douglas* framework applies to ADEA suits, this "rebuttal" function of the RFOA provision is arguably redundant with the judicially established LNR justification. But, at most, that merely demonstrates Congress' abundance of caution in codifying an express statutory exemption from liability in the absence of discriminatory intent. It is noteworthy that even after *McDonnell Douglas* was decided, lower courts continued to rely on the RFOA exemption, in lieu of the LNR justification, as the basis for rebutting a prima facie case of age discrimination.

In any event, the RFOA provision also plays a distinct (and clearly nonredundant) role in "mixed-motive" cases. In such cases, an adverse action taken in substantial part because of an employee's age may be "otherwise prohibited" by § 4(a). *See Desert Palace, Inc. v. Costa*, 539 U.S. 90, 93 (2003); *Price Waterhouse v. Hopkins*, 490 U.S. 228, 262-266 (1989) (O'CONNOR, J., concurring in judgment). The RFOA exemption makes clear that such conduct is nevertheless lawful so long as it is "based on" a reasonable factor other than age.

Finally, the RFOA provision's reference to "reasonable" factors serves only to prevent the employer from gaining the benefit of the statutory safe harbor by offering an irrational justification. Reliance on an unreasonable nonage factor would indicate that the employer's explanation is, in fact, no more than a pretext for intentional discrimination. . . .

Although I would not read the ADEA to authorize disparate impact claims, I agree with the Court that, if such claims are allowed, they are strictly circumscribed by the RFOA exemption. That exemption requires only that the challenged employment practice be based on a "reasonable" nonage factor — that is, one that is rationally related to some legitimate business objective. I also agree with the Court that, if disparate impact claims are to be permitted under the ADEA, they are governed by the standards set forth in our decision in *Wards Cove Packing Co. v. Atonio*, 490 U.S. 642 (1989). That means, as the Court holds, that "a plaintiff must demonstrate that it is the application of a specific or particular employment practice that has created the disparate impact under attack." It also means that once the employer has produced evidence that its action was based on a reasonable nonage factor, the plaintiff bears the burden of disproving this assertion. Even if petitioners' disparate impact claim were cognizable under the ADEA, that claim clearly would fail in light of these requirements.

NOTES

1. *Age Discrimination and the Life-Cycle Model.* The life-cycle model helps to explain the special vulnerabilities of older workers. Under the life-cycle model, workers at the end of their careers receive wages in excess of their marginal productivity. This is not a gift from the employer, but a deferred payment for earlier periods when marginal productivity exceeded wages. This pattern, however, exposes older workers to distinct risks:

> The primary risk is that an employer under financial stress may come to see an expensive senior employee as an unaffordable luxury, regardless of implicit contractual obligations. . . . [A second risk] directly tied to the first is that if an employee were to lose her employment, there would be a strong disincentive to any subsequent employer hiring her. . . . An older employee already at (or near) the end stage of the employment cycle would present an unduly expensive investment for a new employer. The employer would have to invest in firm-specific training of the older worker, the worker would expect a high wage, and the older employee might be retiring within a few years. For an employer to hire an older employee at the wage such an employee would normally command within the firm's employment scale simply would be economically irrational. Further, because a reduction in pay to a level approximating productivity would appear to be a dignitary affront to the employee and would be potentially disruptive within the firm, the life-cycle wage pattern has the predictable effect of freezing unemployed older workers out of the job market altogether.

Samuel Issacharoff & Erica Worth, *Is Age Discrimination Really Age Discrimination?: The ADEA's Unnatural Solution*, 72 N.Y.U. L. REV. 780, 791-92 (1997).

2. *Age Discrimination and Statistics.* Statistical analysis under the ADEA poses special problems, primarily because age is a continuous variable. Consider two consequences of this, using sex discrimination as our comparison. First, with sex, discrimination *within* the protected class can generally be treated as nondiscrimination. An employer who favors some women over others is generally making distinctions on factors other than sex; as a result, the analysis can focus on differences in treatment *between* men and women. But that is not true with age discrimination. Differences in treatment *within* the protected class (those at least 40 years old) may be as probative of discrimination as differences *between* the protected and unprotected (those under age 40) classes. An employer, for example, would be acting illegally if it refused to hire people over age 70 even if everyone the employer hired instead was also within the protected class (that is, at least age 40).

Second, the proper groups to use for comparison through statistical analysis are harder to identify. For sex discrimination, statistical analysis compares the treatment of men and women. But what are the proper comparison groups for a 50-year-old plaintiff alleging systemic disparate treatment discrimination? Should the plaintiff group be those exactly 50 years old? Those 40 years old and over? Everyone 50 years old and over? The 50- to 60-year old group? And for each of these groups, who should make up the comparator group? Should it include only those in the unprotected class, that is, those under 40 years old? All those under 50 years old? All those outside the 50- to 60-year-old group, including those older? For consideration of these issues and the approaches courts have taken to them, see RAMONA L. PAETZOLD & STEVEN L. WILLBORN, THE STATISTICS OF DISCRIMINATION §§ 7.01-7.11 (1999).

3. *Sexual Harassment and Age Discrimination.* Should employer attempts to deal with allegations of sexual harassment be given special deference in age discrimination cases? In *Elrod v. Sears, Roebuck & Co.,* 939 F.2d 1466 (11th Cir. 1991), the plaintiff was discharged and replaced with a younger worker. The plaintiff claimed age discrimination and won a jury verdict. The employer claimed the plaintiff was discharged because of allegations of sexual harassment. The Court of Appeals affirmed a judgment notwithstanding the verdict for the employer:

> We can assume for purposes of this opinion that [the female] employees [alleging harassment] were lying through their teeth. The inquiry of the ADEA is limited to whether [the company] *believed* that Elrod was guilty of harassment, and if so, whether this belief was the reason behind Elrod's discharge. . . .
>
> Elrod may have convinced the jury that the allegations against him were untrue, but he certainly did not present evidence that Sears' asserted belief in those allegations was unworthy of credence.

Id. at 1470-71.

SOLON v. GARY COMMUNITY SCHOOL CORP.
United States Court of Appeals, Seventh Circuit
180 F.3d 844 (1999)

ILANA DIAMOND ROVNER, CIRCUIT JUDGE.

Since 1984, the Gary Community School Corporation ("Gary Schools") has offered early retirement incentives to teachers aged 58 to 61. Eligible teachers who elect to retire early receive monthly payments until they turn 62. Teachers who retire on their 58th birthday receive the maximum forty-eight months of benefits available under this plan; teachers who retire later receive the same monthly payments but fewer of them, as the payments terminate at age 62. A similar plan is in place for school administrators. The plaintiffs in this case are teachers and administrators who were eligible for the early retirement incentives but chose not to retire at age 58. They contend that the incentive plan is inconsistent with the Age Discrimination in Employment Act because the plan doles out unequal benefits based on age. . . .

I.

Between 1970 and 1984, the student enrollment within the Gary public school system dropped by one-third, precipitating lay-offs among teachers and administrators. In 1982, the Gary Teacher's Union proposed that the school system adopt an early retirement incentive plan. The aim of the plan was to induce teachers at the top of the pay scale to retire sooner than they would otherwise, thereby enabling the school system to retain more teachers who were lower in seniority and earned smaller salaries.

After study and negotiations, an early retirement incentive plan ("ERIP") was included in the collective bargaining agreement ("CBA") that the union and the school system adopted in 1983 for the 1984 calendar year. The ERIP specified the following eligibility criteria for teachers wishing to participate: (1) a minimum of fifteen years of creditable service, with at least ten of those years earned in the Gary Community School Corporation; (2) a Bachelor's Degree; and (3) a minimum age of 58 and a maximum age of 61. Teachers who met these criteria could receive early retirement incentive pay for up to forty-eight months, ending at age 62. These payments were calculated with reference to the starting salary paid to a teacher with a Bachelor's Degree during the year that the early retiree became eligible to participate in the ERIP. On an annual basis, early retirees with a Master's Degree would receive fifty percent of that starting salary, while those with a Bachelor's Degree alone would receive forty percent. Early retirees were also eligible under the ERIP to continue participating in the school system's group health and life insurance programs. Both the monthly payments and the right to continued insurance coverage were benefits offered in addition to, rather than in lieu of, any and all severance and retirement benefits that the early retirees had earned in the course of their employment.

This ERIP for teachers has been included in each collective bargaining agreement negotiated since 1983. The terms have never been modified or renegotiated. [Later, a similar early retirement plan was adopted for administrators.]

The thirty-four plaintiffs in this case were all employees of Gary Schools when the ERIPs for teachers and administrators were first implemented in 1984. Each was below the age of 58 when the plans were adopted and subsequently remained employed through at least June 1995, shortly before this suit was filed. During that time period, each of the plaintiffs became eligible to participate in the ERIPs upon turning 58 years old and thus had the option to retire at that age and receive the maximum benefits available. Each chose instead to continue working beyond age 58, foregoing some or all of the incentives provided for in the ERIP. At the time this case was tried, twelve of the plaintiffs had retired, most after they had reached the age of 62 (meaning they received no early retirement benefits at all). One had died before trial while still in the school district's employ. The remaining twenty-one plaintiffs were still working for Gary Schools when the trial commenced.

Asserting that the age-based nature of the Gary Schools ERIPs was discriminatory, the plaintiffs filed suit under the ADEA. . . .

II.

The ADEA bars an employer from discriminating against any individual in the "compensation, terms, conditions, or privileges of employment, because of such individual's age[.]" 29 U.S.C. § 623(a)(1). That bar, Congress has now made clear, extends to "virtually *all* employee benefits and benefit plans," S. Rep. No. 101-263, at 5 (1990), *reprinted in* 1990 U.S.C.C.A.N. 1509, 1510 (emphasis ours), including early retirement plans. *See* 29 U.S.C. § 630(*l*).[2]

---

[2] The Supreme Court held in *Public Employees Retirement Sys. of Ohio v. Betts*, 492 U.S. 158 (1989), that the provisions of a bona fide employee benefit plan were beyond the scope of the ADEA "so long as the plan is not a method of discriminating in other, nonfringe-benefit aspects of the

Thus, although an employer of course has no duty to offer early retirement incentives, once the employer elects to do so it must make those benefits available on nondiscriminatory terms, just as it must with any other fringe benefit.

A.

. . . .

Gary Schools insists that none of the plaintiffs has standing to maintain this action . . . . All of the plaintiffs were eligible for early retirement and, had they retired at age 58, would have received the full four years of incentive pay. Relying on our opinion in *Henn v. National Geographic Society*, 819 F.2d 824 (7th Cir.), *cert. denied*, 484 U.S. 964 (1987), Gary Schools emphasizes that the offer of these retirement incentives was a *benefit* to older workers, and that eligible employees were free to take it or leave it as they chose. Having weighed their options and chosen to continue working, the plaintiffs cannot claim to have been injured, as Gary Schools sees it; the school system points out that each of the plaintiffs either testified or stipulated that he or she earned more in wages from Gary Schools than he or she would have received in early retirement benefits. Moreover, any harm that the plaintiffs did suffer was instead traceable to their own unfettered choices, in Gary Schools' view, not the terms of the ERIPs.

The explicit terms of the early retirement incentives at issue in this case make it relatively easy for the plaintiffs to establish standing, however. The thrust of the plaintiffs' claims is that the ERIPs define "early" retirement wholly in terms of an employee's age, without reference to his need or desire to work. In other words, because the incentive payments under the plans commence at age 58 and end at age 62, only retirement prior to the latter age is deemed "early." No benefits under the ERIPs are offered to an individual who retires after reaching the age of 62, even if he agrees to retire in advance of his own target retirement date. It is in this respect that persons who retire outside the time frame of the ERIPs suffer an injury that gives them standing to sue.

A simple comparison illustrates the disparity. The ERIPs would permit a 58-year-old teacher with plans to retire at age 62 to retire immediately instead and receive four years of incentive payments. Yet a 66-year-old teacher with plans to retire at age 70, but otherwise identically situated with her younger colleague (same number of years of creditable service, same accumulated pension benefits, and so on), would receive nothing if she chose to retire at once, notwithstanding that her retirement would be just as premature as that of her 58-year-old colleague. Individuals like this more senior teacher, for whom early retirement comes later than their 62nd birthday, suffer a concrete injury

---

employment relationship[.]" *Id.* at 177. That holding left most pension and early retirement incentive plans free from scrutiny under the ADEA. Congress overruled *Betts* the following year when it enacted the Older Workers Benefit Protection Act of 1990, Pub. L. No. 101-433, 104 Stat. 978. That act, among other things, clarified that the ADEA's proscription against age discrimination in the "compensation, terms, conditions, or privileges of employment" included "*all* employee benefits, including such benefits provided pursuant to a bona fide employee benefit plan." 29 U.S.C. § 630(*l*) (emphasis ours).

by virtue of the express terms of the ERIPs, just as surely as they would if their age disqualified them from receiving performance bonuses, wage increases, or promotions.

Our opinion in *Henn* does not suggest otherwise. The question we addressed there was not whether the plaintiffs had standing to challenge their employer's early retirement incentive program, but whether they had made out a prima facie case of discrimination. The program at issue in *Henn* was a one-time offer made to all advertising salesmen over the age of 55. Those who elected to retire at that time received a severance payment of one year's salary, retirement benefits calculated as if the retiree had quit at age 65, medical coverage for life, and supplemental life insurance. Each of the four plaintiffs had accepted the offer and received all of the benefits he was promised. Nonetheless, they filed suit, contending that their separation, as induced by the early retirement package, violated the ADEA. We rejected the notion . . . that retirement under an early retirement plan by itself gives rise to a *prima facie* case of age discrimination. We emphasized the significant value that a benign offer of early retirement carries for the employee to whom it is extended:

> Provided the employee may decline the offer and keep working under lawful conditions, the offer makes him better off. He has an additional option, one that may be (as it was here) worth a good deal of money. He may retire, receive the value of the package, and either take a new job (increasing his income) or enjoy new leisure. He may also elect to keep working and forfeit the package.

819 F.2d at 826. Persons eligible for early retirement are, therefore, "the beneficiar[ies] of any distinction on the basis of age." *Id.* at 827. "None can claim to be adversely affected by discrimination in the design or offer of the early retirement package." *Id.* We concluded that the retirees in *Henn* could prevail on a claim of discrimination "only by showing that [their employer] manipulated the options so that they were driven to early retirement not by its attractions but by the terror of the alternative." *Id.* at 829. In other words, the relevant question was "whether the existing [employment] conditions (ignoring the offer of early retirement) violate the ADEA." *Id.*

Henn's inquiry does not answer the question posed in this case. The plaintiffs here are not contending that they were pressured to retire early, or that they suffered some affirmative detriment (a cut in pay, for example) as a result of their decisions to continue working. Their claim is that the way in which eligibility for participation in the ERIPs is defined by age is in itself discriminatory. This was a claim we did not confront in *Henn*. In that case, *anyone* over the age of 55 was able to take advantage of the offer. Beyond the minimum-age requirement — something that the ADEA sanctions, *see* 29 U.S.C. § 623(*l*)(1)(A) — the terms of the plan incorporated no age-based assumptions as to when retirement is "early" and when it is not; a 75-year old could retire on the same terms as a 55-year old.

B.

Having resolved the standing question, we can turn to the merits. The principal issue we must consider is whether the plaintiffs successfully established a *prima facie* case of age discrimination. [T]he district court concluded that Gary Schools had waived the affirmative defenses set out in 29 U.S.C. § 623(f). Gary Schools does not challenge that ruling and therefore cannot resort to the statutory defenses in the effort to avoid liability. Instead, it insists that the plaintiffs have not even made out a *prima facie* case of discrimination, obviating any need to mount a defense. However, our opinion in *Karlen v. City Colleges of Chicago*[, 837 F.2d 314 (7th Cir.), *cert. denied*, 486 U.S. 1044 (1988),] makes short work of that argument.

The early retirement plan at issue in *Karlen* was in significant respects similar to the Gary Schools ERIPs. The plan was designed in part to encourage more senior teachers, who were of course employed at higher salaries, to retire early and enable the municipal college system to hire new teachers at lower salaries. The plan was open to any faculty member between the ages of 55 and 69[3] who had been employed on a full-time basis for at least ten continuous years. An individual who retired under the plan would receive a pension based on his highest four years of salary and the length of his service. That component of the plan, which was not keyed to the employee's age, was not challenged. Two other aspects were. First, upon retirement, the employee would also receive a lump sum equal to a certain percentage of his accumulated sick pay. Those retiring at ages 55 to 58 would receive fifty percent, those retiring at 59 would receive sixty percent, and those retiring at 60 to 64 would be paid eighty percent. Those who retired at 65 to 70, however, would receive only forty-five percent of their accumulated sick pay. In addition, faculty members who retired between the ages of 55 and 64 continued to be covered by the colleges' comprehensive group insurance plan until they reached the age of 70, while those who retired at age 65 or later would lose that coverage unless they elected to shoulder the premiums themselves. Thus, employees who retired at age 64 or earlier received significantly greater benefits than those who waited until age 65.

We found the terms of this plan sufficient to establish a *prima facie* case of age discrimination. We emphasized that this was not a case like *Henn*, in which the retirement incentives were offered to everyone over a given age on the same terms. *Karlen*, 837 F.2d at 318.

> In the present case, . . . there is discrimination against the older worker. Everyone between 55 and 69 is eligible for early retirement, but those between 64 and 69 — an older age group — are disfavored relative to the younger employees in the eligible group. If the City Colleges said to their faculty, at age 65 you lose your free parking space (or dental insurance, or any other fringe benefit), they would be guilty, *prima facie*, of age discrimination. Early-retirement benefits are another fringe benefit — and they plummet at age 65.

Id. We proceeded to consider the City Colleges' arguments in defense of the plan disparities, and in the course of that discussion firmly rejected the notion that establishing a presumptive age of "early" retirement is permissible under the ADEA:

---

[3] At that time, the mandatory retirement age for teachers was 70 — the ADEA applied only to employees aged 40 to 69. In 1987, the upper age limit was removed from the statute, effectively eliminating mandatory retirement for most employees. *See* 29 U.S.C. § 631(a).

A feature common to both the sick-pay and insurance components of the Early Retirement Plan is the sharp drop in benefits at age 65. . . . The Colleges cannot and do not argue that the drop in benefits at age 65 is justified by the higher cost of benefits to a 65-year-old retiree as compared to a 64-year-old one (because of more accumulated sick leave, valued at a higher base pay, and because of higher insurance costs). They argue that in order to induce early retirement of faculty members in the 65-69 year bracket they have to make 65 a breaking point. They say that if the decline in benefits with age were gradual, as it would have to be to reflect accurately the changing cost of the retirement package, no one would retire before 70. The small annual decline in sick-pay distribution and in insurance coverage would be more than offset by the growth in the pension component of the retirement package as a result of salary raises and additional years of service. So the purpose of the Early Retirement Program — to induce early retirement — would be defeated.

This strikes us as a damaging admission rather than a powerful defense. To withhold benefits from older persons in order to induce them to retire seems precisely the form of discrimination at which the Age Discrimination in Employment Act is aimed. Rather than offering a carrot to all workers 55 years and older, as in the *Henn* case, the City Colleges are offering the whole carrot to workers 55 to 64 and taking back half for workers 65 to 69. The reason is that the Colleges want to induce workers to retire by 65. In effect they have two early retirement programs; a munificent one for workers 55 to 64 and a chintzy one for workers 65 to 69. . . .

Id. at 320.

In this case, there is an equally obvious difference in the benefits that retirees will receive under the ERIPs depending upon their age. Those retiring at age 58 will receive four years of incentive payments, those retiring at age 60 only two years, and those retiring at age 62 or later, nothing. Those employees who elect to retire at 62 or later are put at a disadvantage for not retiring when they were 58 to 61, no matter how "early" their later separation may be in terms of their length of service or previous retirement plans. And even for those within the 58 to 61 age group, we have exactly the situation that we did in *Karlen* — a full "carrot" for those aged 58, and an increasingly smaller piece of that carrot (25 percent less per year) for those closer to age 62. The amount of the benefits varies depending upon the retiree's age, nothing else. Just as in *Karlen*, the terms of the ERIPs establish a *prima facie* case of age discrimination.

That the disadvantage employees over the age of 58 experience is the withdrawal of a "carrot" rather than the sting of a "stick" makes no difference to the analysis. It may well be true that teachers and administrators who choose not to retire suffer no loss in position, salary, or other benefits; indeed they will almost certainly earn more in salary and benefits by continuing to work than they have forfeited by declining to retire at age 58 to 61. The same was no doubt true in *Karlen*. But once they have reached the age of 62, all early retirement incentives are withheld, no matter how ahead of schedule the employee elects to retire in terms of his years of service, for example — and no matter that any employee who retires ahead of schedule confers a benefit on Gary Schools by reducing its salary obligations and opening a position for a junior employee. Later-retiring employees will thus have to work longer to make up for the early retirement benefits they would have received at age 58 to 61, incurring substantial opportunity costs as a result. In this respect, employees who retire at a younger age are treated more favorably than those who retire later, based not on years of service or some other nondiscriminatory factor, but solely on their age at retirement. This is the point of *Karlen*: the "carrot" of early retirement incentives cannot be extended based solely on the age of the retiree.

Nor does it matter that each of the plaintiffs could have retired within the framework of the ERIPs and received the maximum available benefits. The point of the plaintiffs' case is not that they were never eligible for the incentives, but that the terms of the plans put them to an unlawful choice. Employees are offered incentives to retire sooner than they otherwise plan, but "early" retirement is defined exclusively in terms of age. Yet one's ability to retire is typically dependent on a host of factors other than age: one's years of service with the employer (which will typically affect pension benefits), savings, dependents, health, and so on. Consequently, not all 58-year-olds will be equally situated to retire. One 58-year-old might have already completed thirty years of service with Gary Schools, for example, and as a result have earned the level of pension benefits that allows him to retire, but it might take a more recent employee who is also 58 and has similar financial needs another several years to reach that same level. The first could elect to retire at once and receive four years of incentive payments; the second would have to continue working and as a result forfeit some or all of the early retirement payments. In this way the ERIPs treat employees who are similarly situated in terms of their preparedness to retire differently, depending on their age.

Of course, the disparity of which the plaintiffs complain results from the maximum age (62) that the ERIPs impose on the receipt of early retirement benefits, and Gary Schools reminds us that we found such a maximum lawful in *Dorsch v. L.B. Foster Co.*, 782 F.2d 1421, 1428 (7th Cir. 1986). The plan under scrutiny there offered employees whose age plus years of service totaled 75 or more incentive payments of $600 per month until they reached the age of 62. By virtue of the age cap, qualified younger retirees would receive the monthly payments for a greater number of years and would therefore earn greater total benefits than older workers. Nonetheless, we found nothing in that arrangement inconsistent with the ADEA. *Id.* at 1427-28. "Obviously a man of 67 cannot retire at 55 and obtain benefits provided for persons of that age. And to effect the purpose of encouraging early retirement, the sliding scale of diminishing benefits is manifestly appropriate." *Id.* at 1428 (quoting *Patterson v. Independent School Dist. No. 709*, 742 F.2d 465, 468-69 (8th Cir. 1984)).

It was several years after we decided *Dorsch*, however, that Congress enacted the Older Workers Benefit Protection Act, which made substantial revisions to the ADEA, including changes to the provisions concerning early retirement plans. *See* n. 2, *supra*. Among the new provisions is one stating that it is not a prima facie violation of the Act for a "defined benefit plan"[4] to offer "social security supplements for plan participants that commence before the age and terminate at the age (specified by the plan) when participants are eligible to receive reduced or unreduced old-age insurance benefits under title II of the Social Security Act . . . and that do not exceed such old-age insurance benefits." 29 U.S.C. § 623(*l*)(1)(B)(ii). The ADEA thus sanctions "bridge" payments which span the gap between an employee's age upon early retirement and the age at which she first becomes eligible for reduced or unreduced social security benefits. Those payments might look something like the $600 monthly payments we examined in *Dorsch*, which terminated when an employee reached age 62 — the minimum eligibility age for reduced social security benefits. In fact, the legislative history of the OWBPA explicitly addresses *Dorsch*, and limits its rationale to these types of bridge payments. S. Rep. No. 101-263, at 21 (1990), *reprinted in* 1990 U.S.C.C.A.N. 1509, 1526-27.[5] Thus, as amended by the OWBPA, the ADEA does permit an employer to offer, as an early retirement incentive, monthly payments which terminate at a specified age, even though younger workers will stand to receive greater benefits under that arrangement than older workers. However, those payments must satisfy the criteria specified in the statute, key among them being the requirement that the payments not exceed the payments that the retiree is likely to receive once she is eligible for social security benefits. 29 U.S.C. § 623(*l*)(1)(B)(ii). Here, the record reveals no connection between the ERIP payments and the social security benefits that early retirees could be expected to receive at age 62, when the incentive payments cease. On the contrary, the assistant superintendent for fiscal integrity conceded that Gary Schools never undertook any type of analysis as to the age at which early retirees actually opt to begin receiving social security payments or the specific dollar amounts of the social security payments that teachers and administrators would receive. Consequently, neither *Dorsch* (as limited by the OWBPA) nor the narrow provision of the statute permitting social security bridge payments is of any help to Gary Schools.

C.

When it granted summary judgment in favor of the plaintiffs on the question of liability, the district court observed that because the terms of the ERIPs were discriminatory on their face, the plaintiffs were not required to prove that Gary Schools *intended* to discriminate on the basis of age; that intent could instead be presumed. Gary Schools argues that the court erred in relieving the plaintiffs of this obligation. Even if it is appropriate to presume discriminatory intent in other contexts, Gary Schools argues, it is improper to do so in the context of early retirement incentives. It steers us back to *Henn*

---

[4] Broadly speaking, a defined benefit plan is one consisting of a general pool of assets (rather than individualized accounts) from which an employee, upon retirement, is periodically paid a fixed amount.

[5] *Compare* S. Rep. No. 101-263, at 27, 1990 U.S.C.C.A.N. at 1533 ("Early retirement incentive plans that deny or reduce benefits to older workers while continuing to make them available to younger workers may encourage premature departure from employment by older workers. This not only conflicts with the purpose of eliminating age discrimination in employee benefits; it also frustrates (rather than promotes) the employment of older persons.").

in which we noted that because an "offer of early retirement is beneficial to the recipient, there is no reason to treat every early retirement as presumptively an act of age discrimination," and also to *Karlen*, where we pointed out that to the extent early retirement incentives discriminate, often "the discrimination seems to be in favor of rather than against older employees, by giving them an additional option and one prized by many older employees." In view of the beneficial choices that early retirement plans make available to senior employees, Gary Schools reasons, it is impermissible to presume discriminatory intent based on the terms of the plans alone. Only if the plaintiffs can show that the terms of the plan make "arbitrary" distinctions based on age and that the school system *intentionally* discriminated against them, can they establish liability, Gary Schools insists.

The district court was correct to presume discriminatory intent in this case, however. The terms of the ERIPs themselves explicitly establish an employee's eligibility for the early retirement incentives in terms of his age. The plans are therefore discriminatory on their face and independent proof of an illicit motive is unnecessary. We recognized as much in *Karlen*, when we concluded that the terms of the City Colleges' early retirement plans, which sharply reduced the benefits offered to employees aged 65 and older, themselves established a *prima facie* case of age discrimination. The reasons for the drop-off, we noted, would be relevant not to the *prima facie* case, but to the affirmative defenses specified by the statute. Here, of course, Gary Schools was found to have waived those defenses.

The age-based distinctions drawn by the ERIPs are also arbitrary, as we have already discussed. Harkening now to the provision of the statute that permits an employer to offer "bridge" payments which will run until the retiree attains eligibility for social security, Gary Schools argues that the age cap of 62 that it imposed on the early retirement incentives is not arbitrary and hence not discriminatory. At that age, it reasons, a retiree can begin to collect reduced social security payments and therefore no longer needs a financial incentive to retire. The flaw in that argument, as we have already mentioned, is that the incentive payments that Gary Schools offers are in no way keyed to the payments that an employee can be expected to receive from the Social Security Administration, as the statute requires. 29 U.S.C. § 623(*l*)(1)(B)(ii). So far as the record reveals, then, these payments offered a retirement incentive entirely unrelated to an employee's expectations as to the social security income he might begin to receive at age 62. The statutory approval of social security bridge payments therefore does not endorse the age cap that Gary Schools has imposed on the incentives.

D.

Finally, Gary Schools suggests that the plaintiffs have been given a windfall by having been awarded the benefits (or the right to receive the benefits) offered by the ERIPs without having to retire at the age specified by the plans. In effect, the plaintiffs' victory has transformed the early retirement incentives into severance payments made to *all* employees upon retirement. That argument has some intuitive appeal. None of the plaintiffs who testified, for example, indicated that she retired sooner than she otherwise planned or was prepared to do. There is no way to know on this record, then, whether any of the plaintiffs "earned" the incentives by retiring "early." That may simply be the price Gary Schools has to pay, however, for establishing an early retirement plan which turns on the employee's age. Once that discriminatory criterion is removed, there is nothing left in the terms of the plan (but for the criteria as to the employee's minimum years of service) to objectively assess any given employee's eligibility for the incentives. In any case, Gary Schools has not appealed the terms of the judgment entered in the plaintiffs' favor. We therefore need not consider whether there were any alternative remedies available to rectify the discrimination.

NOTES

1. *The Statutory Affirmative Defense.* The ADEA contains an explicit exception for "voluntary" early-retirement plans that are "consistent with the relevant purpose[s]" of the ADEA. ADEA § 623(f)(2)(B)(ii). A plan would not be "voluntary" if "under the circumstances, a reasonable person would have concluded that there was no choice but to accept the offer." *Auerbach v. Board of Educ.*, 136 F.3d 104, 113 (2d Cir. 1998). Practically, a scheme would not be voluntary if the employer threatened retaliation for a refusal to participate or failed to provide adequate information. Generally, a plan would not be consistent with the purposes of the ADEA if it relies on age stereotypes or if it withholds benefits when employees reach a certain age. *See, e.g., EEOC v. Crown Point Cmty. Sch. Corp.*, 72 FEP Cases 1803 (N.D. Ind. 1997) (holding plan illegal because it relied on stereotype that employees would retire at age 65, even after employer presented evidence that most employees retired at age 65). Gary Schools did not attempt to fit within this exception, probably because it thought it could not satisfy the second requirement.

2. *Permissible Early-Retirement Programs.* *Solon* indicates that an early retirement program which makes an offer of benefits only to employees up to a certain age (age sixty-two in *Solon*) is unlikely to pass muster under the ADEA because it discriminates against workers older than the cutoff age. But this poses a problem for employers. If employees can receive the benefits *whenever* they retire (over a certain age), the benefits do not provide much of an incentive to retire *early*. So what are employers to do?

One option suggested by the legislative history of the Older Workers Benefit Protection Act is to offer the extra benefits only for a "window" period — workers over age 60, say, can receive the extra benefits only if they retire within the next 18 months. After that, the offer disappears. Would such a temporally conditioned incentive violate the ADEA? *See Auerbach, supra* (no). Professor Harper agrees that this is the correct legal result, but disagrees with the underlying policy: "The only practical way to prevent employers from using retirement incentives to effect the termination of particular workers selected on the basis of age . . . is to prohibit age-based incentives from being temporally or otherwise conditioned." Michael C. Harper, *Age-Based Exit Incentives, Coercion, and the Prospective Waiver of ADEA Rights: The Failure of the Older Workers Benefit Protection Act*, 79 VA. L. REV. 1271, 1329 (1993).

Alternatively, employers might eschew early-retirement programs altogether. If the work force needs to be reduced, employers might simply discharge employees. Would an employer violate the ADEA if it reduced its work force by discharging the highest paid employees? *See Bay v. Times Mirror Magazines, Inc.,* 936 F.2d 112 (2d Cir. 1991) (no). *But see* Christine Jolls, *Hand-Tying and the Age Discrimination in Employment Act,* 74 TEX. L. REV. 1813 (1996) (one justification for the ADEA is that it permits employers to commit credibly to higher wages for senior employees).

3. *Waiver of ADEA Rights.* Employers offering early-retirement incentive plans risk ADEA challenges. One employer response to this risk has been to obtain waivers of ADEA claims from employees accepting the retirement offer. The OWBPA specifies several minimum conditions for these waivers to be effective. For example, the agreement must advise the employee to consult with an attorney and must provide consideration "in addition to anything of value to which the [employee] is already entitled." ADEA § 7(f)(1)(A)-(H). If an employee accepts a hefty retirement bonus as an incentive to retire, but the waiver agreement fails to meet all the OWBPA requirements, should the employee be able to keep the money and sue? Or should the employee be required to return the bonus before being allowed to forward an ADEA claim? *See Oubre v. Entergy Operations, Inc.,,* 522 U.S. 422 (1998) (employee can keep the money and sue).

4. *Retirement and the Life-Cycle Model.* The life-cycle model predicts that employees will receive wages in excess of marginal productivity at the end of their careers. Prior to the ADEA, that period had a finite endpoint: Employers could require employees to retire at a certain age, usually 65. When the 1986 amendments to the ADEA eliminated mandatory retirement, employers turned to retirement incentive programs to try to limit the period, but OWBPA's changes made implementing such programs more costly and risky. Viewed in this light, the ADEA and OWBPA changes are problematic. In the short run, current employees at the end of their careers will receive a windfall. When they began their careers, they expected the beneficial final period to end at age 65. Now it can continue indefinitely, unless the employer provides extra benefits to induce retirement. In the long run, the changes threaten the life-cycle model. Employers will be less willing to enter into such arrangements if the costs at the final stage cannot be predicted. If that occurs, the benefits of the life-cycle employment arrangement, such as reduced employer monitoring and a gradually upward-sloping salary path, would be lost. *See* Samuel Issacharoff & Erica Worth, *Is Age Discrimination Really Age Discrimination?: The ADEA's Unnatural Solution,* 72 N.Y.U. L. REV. 780 (1997); Erica Worth, Note, *In Defense of Targeted ERIPs: Understanding the Interaction of Life-Cycle Employment and Early Retirement Incentive Plans,* 74 TEX. L. REV. 411 (1995).

C. AFFIRMATIVE ACTION AND THE PROBLEMS OF REMEDIES

JOHNSON v. TRANSPORTATION AGENCY
United States Supreme Court
480 U.S. 616 (1987)

JUSTICE BRENNAN delivered the opinion of the Court.

Respondent, Transportation Agency of Santa Clara County, California, unilaterally promulgated an Affirmative Action Plan applicable, *inter alia,* to promotions of employees. In selecting applicants for the promotional position of road dispatcher, the Agency, pursuant to the Plan, passed over petitioner Paul Johnson, a male employee, and promoted a female employee applicant, Diane Joyce. The question for decision is whether in making the promotion the Agency impermissibly took into account the sex of the applicants in violation of Title VII of the Civil Rights Act of 1964. . . .[2]

I

In December 1978, the Santa Clara County Transit District Board of Supervisors adopted an Affirmative Action Plan (Plan) for the County Transportation Agency. The Plan . . . provides that, in making promotions to positions within a traditionally segregated job classification in which women have been significantly underrepresented, the Agency is authorized to consider as one factor the sex of a qualified applicant.

In reviewing the composition of its work force, the Agency noted in its Plan that women were represented in numbers far less than their proportion of the county labor force in both the Agency as a whole and in five of seven job categories. Specifically, while women constituted 36.4% of the area labor market, they composed only 22.4% of Agency employees. Furthermore, women working at the Agency were concentrated largely in EEOC job categories traditionally held by women: women made up 76% of Office and Clerical Workers, but only 7.1% of Agency Officials and Administrators, 8.6% of Professionals, 9.7% of Technicians, and 22% of Service and Maintenance workers. As for the job classification relevant to this case, none of the 238 Skilled Craft Worker positions was held by a woman. . . .

The Agency stated that its Plan was intended to achieve "a statistically measurable yearly improvement in hiring, training and promotion of minorities and women throughout the Agency in all major job classifications where they are underrepresented." As a benchmark by which to evaluate progress, the Agency stated that its long-term goal was to attain a work force whose composition reflected the proportion of minorities and women in the area labor force. Thus, for the Skilled Craft category in which the road dispatcher

---

[2] No constitutional issue was either raised or addressed in the litigation below. We therefore decide in this case only the issue of the prohibitory scope of Title VII. Of course, where the issue is properly raised, public employers must justify the adoption and implementation of a voluntary affirmative action plan under the Equal Protection Clause. *See Wygant v. Jackson Board of Education,* 476 U.S. 267 (1986).

position at issue here was classified, the Agency's aspiration was that eventually about 36% of the jobs would be occupied by women. . . .

The Plan acknowledged that a number of factors might make it unrealistic to rely on the Agency's long-term goals in evaluating the Agency's progress in expanding job opportunities for minorities and women. Among the factors identified were low turnover rates in some classifications, the fact that some jobs involved heavy labor, the small number of positions within some job categories, the limited number of entry positions leading to the Technical and Skilled Craft classifications, and the limited number of minorities and women qualified for positions requiring specialized training and experience. . . .

The Agency's Plan thus set aside no specific number of positions for minorities or women, but authorized the consideration of ethnicity or sex as a factor when evaluating qualified candidates for jobs in which members of such groups were poorly represented. One such job was the road dispatcher position that is the subject of the dispute in this case.

On December 12, 1979, the Agency announced a vacancy for the promotional position of road dispatcher in the Agency's Roads Division. Dispatchers assign road crews, equipment, and materials, and maintain records pertaining to road maintenance jobs. . . .

Twelve County employees applied for the promotion, including Joyce and Johnson. Joyce had worked for the County since 1970, serving as an account clerk until 1975. She had applied for a road dispatcher position in 1974, but was deemed ineligible because she had not served as a road maintenance worker. In 1975, Joyce transferred from a senior account clerk position to a road maintenance worker position, becoming the first woman to fill such a job. During her four years in that position, she occasionally worked out of class as a road dispatcher.

Petitioner Johnson began with the county in 1967 as a road yard clerk, after private employment that included working as a supervisor and dispatcher. He had also unsuccessfully applied for the road dispatcher opening in 1974. In 1977, his clerical position was downgraded, and he sought and received a transfer to the position of road maintenance worker. He also occasionally worked out of class as a dispatcher while performing that job.

Nine of the applicants, including Joyce and Johnson, were deemed qualified for the job, and were interviewed by a two-person board. Seven of the applicants scored above 70 on this interview, which meant that they were certified as eligible for selection by the appointing authority. The scores awarded ranged from 70 to 80. Johnson was tied for second with score of 75, while Joyce ranked next with a score of 73. . . .

[James Graebner was Director of the Agency and authorized to select any of the seven persons deemed eligible.] After deliberation, Graebner concluded that the promotion should be given to Joyce. As he testified: "I tried to look at the whole picture, the combination of her qualifications and Mr. Johnson's qualifications, their test scores, their expertise, their background, affirmative action matters, things like that . . . I believe it was a combination of all those."

[Petitioner Johnson then commenced this action.]

II

As a preliminary matter, we note that petitioner bears the burden of establishing the invalidity of the Agency's Plan. Only last term in *Wygant v. Jackson Board of Education,* 476 U.S. 267, 277-78 (1986), we held that "[t]he ultimate burden remains with the employees to demonstrate the unconstitutionality of an affirmative-action program," and we see no basis for a different rule regarding a plan's alleged violation of Title VII. This case also fits readily within the analytical framework set forth in *McDonnell Douglas Corp. v. Green,* 411 U.S. 792 (1973). Once a plaintiff establishes a *prima facie* case that race or sex has been taken into account in an employer's employment decision, the burden shifts to the employer to articulate a nondiscriminatory rationale for its decision. The existence of an affirmative action plan provides such a rationale. If such a plan is articulated as the basis for the employer's decision, the burden shifts to the plaintiff to prove that the employer's justification is pretextual and the plan is invalid. As a practical matter, of course, an employer will generally seek to avoid a charge of pretext by presenting evidence in support of its plan. That does not mean, however, as petitioner suggests, that reliance on an affirmative action plan is to be treated as an affirmative defense requiring the employer to carry the burden of proving the validity of the plan. The burden of proving its invalidity remains on the plaintiff.

The assessment of the legality of the Agency Plan must be guided by our decision in [*Steelworkers v.*] *Weber,* 443 U.S. 193 (1979). In that case, the Court addressed the question whether the employer violated Title VII by adopting a voluntary affirmative action plan designed to "eliminate manifest racial imbalances in traditionally segregated job categories." The respondent employee in that case challenged the employer's denial of his application for a position in a newly established craft training program, contending that the employer's selection process impermissibly took into account the race of the applicants. The selection process was guided by an affirmative action plan, which provided that 50% of the new trainees were to be black until the percentage of black skilled craftworkers in the employer's plant approximated the percentage of blacks in the local labor force. Adoption of the plan had been prompted by the fact that only 5 of 273, or 1.83%, of skilled craftworkers at the plant were black, even though the work force in the area was approximately 39% black. Because of the historical exclusion of blacks from craft positions, the employer regarded its former policy of hiring trained outsiders as inadequate to redress the imbalance in its work force.

We upheld the employer's decision to select less senior black applicants over the white respondent, for we found that taking race into account was consistent with Title VII's objective of "break[ing] down old patterns of racial segregation and hierarchy." As we stated:

> "It would be ironic indeed if a law triggered by a Nation's concern over centuries of racial injustice and intended to improve the lot of those who had 'been excluded from the American dream for so long' constituted the first legislative prohibition of all voluntary, private, race-conscious efforts to abolish traditional patterns of racial segregation

and hierarchy." *Id.* at 204 (quoting remarks of Sen. Humphrey, 110 Cong. Rec. 6552 (1964)).

We noted that the plan did not "unnecessarily trammel the interests of the white employees," since it did not require "the discharge of white workers and their replacement with new black hirees." Nor did the plan create "an absolute bar to the advancement of white employees," since half of those trained in the new program were to be white. Finally, we observed that the plan was a temporary measure, not designed to maintain racial balance, but to "eliminate a manifest racial imbalance." As Justice Blackmun's concurrence made clear, *Weber* held that an employer seeking to justify the adoption of a plan need not point to its own prior discriminatory practices, nor even to evidence of an "arguable violation" on its part. Rather, it need point only to a "conspicuous . . . imbalance in traditionally segregated job categories." Our decision was grounded in the recognition that voluntary employer action can play a crucial role in furthering Title VII's purpose of eliminating the effects of discrimination in the workplace, and that Title VII should not be read to thwart such efforts.[8]

In reviewing the employment decision at issue in this case, we must first examine whether that decision was made pursuant to a plan prompted by concerns similar to those of the employer in *Weber*. Next, we must determine whether the effect of the plan on males and non-minorities is comparable to the effect of the plan in that case.

The first issue is therefore whether consideration of the sex of applicants for Skilled Craft jobs was justified by the existence of a "manifest imbalance" that reflected underrepresentation of women in "traditionally segregated job categories." In determining whether an imbalance exists that would justify taking sex or race into account, a comparison of the percentage of minorities or women in the employer's work force with the percentage in the area labor market or general population is appropriate in analyzing jobs that require no special expertise, see *Teamsters,* or training programs designed to provide expertise, see *Weber*. Where a job requires special training, however, the comparison should be with those in the labor force who possess the relevant qualifications. *See Hazelwood*. The requirement that the "manifest imbalance" relate to a "traditionally segregated job category" provides assurance both that

---

[8] Justice Scalia's suggestion that an affirmative action program may be adopted only to redress an employer's past discrimination was rejected in *Steelworkers v. Weber* because the prospect of liability created by such an admission would create a significant disincentive for voluntary action. As Justice Blackmun's concurrence in that case pointed out, such a standard would "plac[e] voluntary compliance with Title VII in profound jeopardy. The only way for the employer and the union to keep their footing on the 'tightrope' it creates would be to eschew all forms of voluntary affirmative action." . . .

Contrary to Justice Scalia's contention, our decision last term in . . . *Sheet Metal Workers v. EEOC,* 478 U.S. 421 (1986), provide[s] no support for a standard more restrictive than that enunciated in *Weber*. . . . In *Sheet Metal Workers,* the issue we addressed was the scope of judicial remedial authority under Title VII, authority that has not been exercised in this case. Justice Scalia's suggestion that employers should be able to do no more voluntarily than courts can order as remedies ignores the fundamental difference between volitional private behavior and the exercise of coercion by the State. Plainly, "Congress' concern that federal courts not impose unwanted obligations on employers and unions," reflects a desire to preserve a relatively large domain for voluntary employer action.

sex or race will be taken into account in a manner consistent with Title VII's purpose of eliminating the effects of employment discrimination, and that the interests of those employees not benefiting from the plan will not be unduly infringed.

A manifest imbalance need not be such that it would support a prima facie case against the employer, as suggested in Justice O'Connor's concurrence, since we do not regard as identical the constraints of Title VII and the federal constitution on voluntarily adopted affirmative action plans. Application of the "prima facie" standard in Title VII cases would be inconsistent with *Weber's* focus on statistical imbalance,[10] and could inappropriately create a significant disincentive for employers to adopt an affirmative action plan. *See Weber,* [443 U.S.,] at 204 (Title VII intended as a "catalyst" for employer efforts to eliminate vestiges of discrimination). A corporation concerned with maximizing return on investment, for instance, is hardly likely to adopt a plan if in order to do so it must compile evidence that could be used to subject it to a colorable Title VII suit.[11]

It is clear that the decision to hire Joyce was made pursuant to an Agency plan that directed that sex or race be taken into account for the purpose of remedying underrepresentation. The Agency Plan acknowledged the "limited opportunities that have existed in the past," for women to find employment in certain job classifications "where women have not been traditionally employed in significant numbers." As a result, observed the Plan, women were concentrated in traditionally female jobs in the Agency, and represented a lower percentage in other job classifications than would be expected if such traditional segregation had not occurred. Specifically, 9 of the 10 Para-Professionals and 110 of the 145 Office and Clerical Workers were women.

---

[10] The difference between the "manifest imbalance" and "prima facie" standards is illuminated by *Weber.* Had the Court in that case been concerned with past discrimination by the employer, it would have focused on discrimination in hiring skilled, not unskilled, workers, since only the scarcity of the former in Kaiser's work force would have made it vulnerable to a Title VII suit. In order to make out a prima facie case on such a claim, a plaintiff would be required to compare the percentage of black skilled workers in the Kaiser work force with the percentage of black skilled craft workers in the area labor market.

Weber obviously did not make such a comparison. Instead, it focused on the disparity between the percentage of black skilled craft workers in Kaiser's ranks and the percentage of blacks in the area labor force. Such an approach reflected a recognition that the proportion of black craft workers in the local labor force was likely as miniscule as the proportion in Kaiser's work force. The Court realized that the lack of imbalance between these figures would mean that employers in precisely those industries in which discrimination has been most effective would be precluded from adopting training programs to increase the percentage of qualified minorities. Thus, in cases such as *Weber,* where the employment decision at issue involves the selection of unskilled persons for a training program, the "manifest imbalance" standard permits comparison with the general labor force. By contrast, the "prima facie" standard would require comparison with the percentage of minorities or women qualified for the job for which the trainees are being trained, a standard that would have invalidated the plan in *Weber* itself.

[11] In some cases, of course, the manifest imbalance may be sufficiently egregious to establish a prima facie case. However, as long as there is a manifest imbalance, an employer may adopt a plan even where the disparity is not so striking, without being required to introduce the non-statistical evidence of past discrimination that would be demanded by the "prima facie" standard. Of course, when there is sufficient evidence to meet the more stringent "prima facie" standard, be it statistical, non-statistical, or a combination of the two, the employer is free to adopt an affirmative action plan.

By contrast, women were only 2 of the 28 Officials and Administrators, 5 of the 58 Professionals, 12 of the 124 Technicians, none of the Skilled Craft Workers, and 1 — who was Joyce — of the 110 Road Maintenance Workers. The Plan sought to remedy these imbalances through "hiring, training and promotion of . . . women throughout the Agency in all major job classifications where they are underrepresented." . . .

As the Agency Plan recognized, women were most egregiously underrepresented in the Skilled Craft job category, since *none* of the 238 positions was occupied by a woman. . . . The promotion of Joyce thus satisfies the first requirement enunciated in *Weber,* since it was undertaken to further an affirmative action plan designed to eliminate Agency work force imbalances in traditionally segregated job categories.

We next consider whether the Agency Plan unnecessarily trammeled the rights of male employees or created an absolute bar to their advancement. In contrast to the plan in *Weber,* which provided that 50% of the positions in the craft training program were exclusively for blacks, and to the consent decree upheld last term in *Firefighters v. Cleveland,* 478 U.S. 501 (1986), which required the promotion of specific numbers of minorities, the Plan sets aside no positions for women. The Plan expressly states that "[t]he 'goals' established for each Division should not be construed as 'quotas' that must be met." Rather, the Plan merely authorizes that consideration be given to affirmative action concerns when evaluating qualified applicants. As the Agency Director testified, the sex of Joyce was but one of numerous factors he took into account in arriving at his decision. The Plan thus resembles the "Harvard Plan" approvingly noted by Justice Powell in *University of California Regents v. Bakke,* 438 U.S. 265, 316-319 (1978), which considers race along with other criteria in determining admission to the college. . . . Similarly, the Agency Plan requires women to compete with all other qualified applicants. *No* persons are automatically excluded from consideration; *all* are able to have their qualifications weighed against those of other applicants.

In addition, petitioner had no absolute entitlement to the road dispatcher position. Seven of the applicants were classified as qualified and eligible, and the Agency Director was authorized to promote any of the seven. Thus, denial of the promotion unsettled no legitimate firmly rooted expectation on the part of the petitioner. Furthermore, while the petitioner in this case was denied a promotion, he retained his employment with the Agency, at the same salary and with the same seniority, and remained eligible for other promotions.[15]

Finally, the Agency's Plan was intended to *attain* a balanced work force, not to maintain one. The Plan contains ten references to the Agency's desire to "attain" such a balance, but no reference whatsoever to a goal of maintaining it. . . .

The Agency acknowledged the difficulties that it would confront in remedying the imbalance in its work force, and it anticipated only gradual increases

[15] Furthermore, from 1978 to 1982 Skilled Craft jobs in the Agency increased from 238 to 349. . . . Of the 111 new Skilled Craft jobs during this period, 105, or almost 95%, went to men. . . . While this degree of employment expansion by an employer is by no means essential to a plan's validity, it underscores the fact that the Plan in this case in no way significantly restricts the employment prospects of such persons. . . .

in the representation of minorities and women. It is thus unsurprising that the Plan contains no explicit end date, for the Agency's flexible, case-by-case approach was not expected to yield success in a brief period of time. Express assurance that a program is only temporary may be necessary if the program actually sets aside positions according to specific numbers. This is necessary both to minimize the effect of the program on other employees, and to ensure that the plan's goals "[are] not being used simply to achieve and maintain . . . balance, but rather as a benchmark against which" the employer may measure its progress in eliminating the underrepresentation of minorities and women. In this case, however, substantial evidence shows that the Agency has sought to take a moderate, gradual approach to eliminating the imbalance in its work force, one which establishes realistic guidance for employment decisions, and which visits minimal intrusion on the legitimate expectations of other employees. Given this fact, as well as the Agency's express commitment to "attain" a balanced work force, there is ample assurance that the Agency does not seek to use its Plan to maintain a permanent racial and sexual balance.

III

. . . We therefore hold that the Agency appropriately took into account as one factor the sex of Diane Joyce in determining that she should be promoted to the road dispatcher position. The decision to do so was made pursuant to an affirmative action plan that represents a moderate, flexible, case-by-case approach to effecting a gradual improvement in the representation of minorities and women in the Agency's work force. Such a plan is fully consistent with Title VII, for it embodies the contribution that voluntary employer action can make in eliminating the vestiges of discrimination in the workplace. Accordingly, the judgment of the Court of Appeals is

Affirmed.

JUSTICE STEVENS, concurring.

While I join the Court's opinion, I write separately to explain my view of this case's position in our evolving antidiscrimination law and to emphasize that the opinion does not establish the permissible outer limits of voluntary programs undertaken by employers to benefit disadvantaged groups. . . .

The logic of antidiscrimination legislation requires that judicial constructions of Title VII leave "breathing room" for employer initiatives to benefit members of minority groups. . . . As construed in *Weber* and in *Firefighters,* the statute does not absolutely prohibit preferential hiring in favor of minorities; it was merely intended to protect historically disadvantaged groups *against* discrimination and not to hamper managerial efforts to benefit members of disadvantaged groups that are consistent with that paramount purpose. . . .

Whether a voluntary decision of the kind made by respondent would ever be prohibited by Title VII is a question we need not answer until it is squarely presented. Given the interpretation of the statute the Court adopted in *Weber,* I see no reason why the employer has any duty, prior to granting a preference to a qualified minority employee, to determine whether his past conduct might constitute an arguable violation of Title VII. Indeed, in some instances the employer may find it more helpful to focus on the future. [Employers might give the following forward-looking justifications for affirmative action programs: improving their services to black constituencies, averting racial tension over the allocation of jobs in a community, or increasing the diversity of a work force, to name but a few examples.]

The Court today does not foreclose other voluntary decisions based in part on a qualified employee's membership in a disadvantaged group. Accordingly, I concur.

JUSTICE O'CONNOR, concurring in the judgment. . . .

In my view, the proper initial inquiry in evaluating the legality of an affirmative action plan by a public employer under Title VII is no different from that required by the Equal Protection Clause. In either case, consistent with the congressional intent to provide some measure of protection to the interests of the employer's nonminority employees, the employer must have had a firm basis for believing that remedial action was required. An employer would have such a firm basis if it can point to a statistical disparity sufficient to support a prima facie claim under Title VII by the employee beneficiaries of the affirmative action plan of a pattern or practice claim of discrimination. . . .

While employers must have a firm basis for concluding that remedial action is necessary, neither *Wygant* nor *Weber* places a burden on employers to prove that they actually discriminated against women or minorities. . . . [A] contemporaneous finding of discrimination should not be required because it would discourage voluntary efforts to remedy apparent discrimination. A requirement that an employer actually prove that it had discriminated in the past would also unduly discourage voluntary efforts to remedy apparent discrimination. . . . Evidence sufficient for a prima facie Title VII pattern or practice claim against the employer itself suggests that the absence of women or minorities in a work force cannot be explained by general societal discrimination alone and that remedial action is appropriate. . . .

In this case, I am . . . satisfied that the respondent had a firm basis for adopting an affirmative action program. Although the District Court found no discrimination against women in fact, at the time the affirmative action plan was adopted, there were *no* women in its skilled craft positions. The petitioner concedes that women constituted approximately 5% of the local labor pool of skilled craft workers in 1970. Thus, when compared to the percentage of women in the qualified work force, the statistical disparity would have been sufficient for a prima facie Title VII case brought by unsuccessful women job applicants. . . . Accordingly, I concur in the judgment of the Court.

JUSTICE SCALIA, with whom THE CHIEF JUSTICE joins, and with whom JUSTICE WHITE joins in Parts I and II, dissenting. . . .

The most significant proposition of law established by today's decision is that racial or sexual discrimination is permitted under Title VII when it is intended to overcome the effect, not of the employer's own discrimination, but of societal attitudes that have limited the entry of certain races, or of a particular sex, into certain jobs. . . . [T]his holding . . . contradict[s] a decision of this Court rendered only last Term. *Wygant v. Jackson Board of Education,* 476 U.S. 267 (1986), held that the objective of remedying societal discrimination cannot prevent remedial affirmative action from violating the Equal Protection Clause. Because, therefore, those justifications (*e.g.*, the remedying of past societal wrongs) that are inadequate to insulate discriminatory action from the racial discrimination prohibitions of the Constitution are also inadequate to insulate it from the racial discrimination prohibitions of Title VII; and because the portions of Title VII at issue here treat race and sex equivalently; *Wygant,* which dealt with race discrimination, is fully applicable precedent, and is squarely inconsistent with today's decision.[4]

[The majority also argues that the Plan does not "unnecessarily trammel" the interests of male and nonminority employees.] The majority emphasizes, as though it is meaningful, that *"No* persons are automatically excluded from consideration; *all* are able to have their qualifications weighed against those of other applicants." . . .

Johnson was indeed entitled to have his qualifications weighed against those of other applicants — but more to the point, he was virtually assured that, after the weighing, if there was any minimally qualified applicant from one of the favored groups, he would be rejected. . . .

[I]n many contexts[, the practical effect of today's decision will be to *require*] employers, public as well as private, to engage in intentional discrimination on the basis of race or sex. This Court's prior interpretations of Title VII, especially the decision in *Griggs v. Duke Power Co.*, 401 U.S. 424 (1971), subject employers to a potential Title VII suit whenever there is a noticeable imbalance in the representation of minorities or women in the employer's work force. Even the employer who is confident of ultimately prevailing in such a suit must contemplate the expense and adverse publicity of a trial. . . . If, however, employers are free to discriminate through affirmative action, without fear of "reverse discrimination" suits by their nonminority or male victims, they are offered a threshold defense against Title VII liability premised on numerical disparities. Thus, after today's decision the *failure* to engage in reverse discrimination is economic folly, and arguably a breach of duty to shareholders or taxpayers, wherever the cost of anticipated Title VII

---

[4] Justice O'Connor's concurrence at least makes an attempt to bring this term into accord with last. Under her reading of Title VII, an employer may discriminate affirmatively, so to speak, if he has a "firm basis" for believing that he might be guilty of (nonaffirmative) discrimination under the Act, and if his action is designed to remedy that suspected prior discrimination. This is something of a half-way house between leaving employers scot-free to discriminate against disfavored groups, as the majority opinion does, and prohibiting discrimination, as do the words of Title VII. In the present case, although the District Court found that in fact no sex discrimination existed, Justice O'Connor would find a "firm basis" for the agency's *belief* that sex discrimination existed in the "inexorable zero": the complete absence, prior to Diane Joyce, of any women in the Agency's skilled positions. There are two problems with this: First, even positing a "firm basis" for the Agency's belief in prior discrimination, . . . the plan was patently not *designed to remedy* that prior discrimination, but rather to establish a sexually representative work force. Second, even an absolute zero is not "inexorable." While it may inexorably provide "firm basis" for belief in the mind of an outside observer, it cannot conclusively establish such a belief *on the employer's part,* since he may be aware of the particular reasons that account for the zero. . . . The question is in any event one of fact, which, if it were indeed relevant to the outcome, would require a remand to the District Court rather than an affirmance.

litigation exceeds the cost of hiring less capable (though still minimally capable) workers. . . . A statute designed to establish a color-blind and gender-blind workplace has thus been converted into a powerful engine of racism and sexism, not merely *permitting* intentional race-and sex-based discrimination, but often making it, through operation of the legal system, practically compelled.

NOTES

1. *A Framework for Thinking About Remedies.* Discrimination remedies, and remedies generally, can be thought of as mechanisms for shifting losses from injured parties to parties legally responsible for the losses. For this loss-shifting model to apply easily, one needs to be able to 1) identify the injured party; 2) isolate and quantify the loss; and 3) identify the responsible party to whom the loss should be shifted. Remedies in discrimination cases are difficult, because it is not uncommon for one or more of the elements needed to apply the loss-shifting model to be missing. Indeed, one of the reasons *Johnson* is a difficult case is that *none* of the elements are satisfied. Consider the following variations:

(a) A black plaintiff proves that an employer would have hired him except for his race. The courts, except in rare circumstances, award the plaintiff backpay; require the employer to hire the plaintiff (or at least to make an offer); and require the employer to grant to the plaintiff the seniority the plaintiff would have had had he been hired initially. The backpay award is easy to justify using the loss-shifting model; the award simply shifts the wage loss caused by the employer's discriminatory refusal to hire from the injured party (the black plaintiff) to the responsible party (the employer). Retroactive seniority, although well-accepted, is more difficult to justify, because the loss (seniority) is not shifted to the employer, but to the employer's current employees, whose seniority expectations are diminished because of the remedy. The obligation to hire the black plaintiff is also well-accepted, even though it may shift losses to people other than the responsible party; assuming the employer hires the plaintiff instead of someone else, that someone else is bearing a portion of the cost of the remedy. *See Albemarle Paper Co. v. Moody*, 422 U.S. 405 (1975) (backpay an appropriate remedy); *Franks v. Bowman Transp. Co.*, 424 U.S. 747 (1976) (retroactive seniority an appropriate remedy).

(b) A union discriminatorily denies blacks admission to an apprenticeship program. Using the systemic disparate treatment model, the court determines that forty-five more blacks would have been admitted to the program had the union not discriminated. One hundred and eighty blacks prove that they applied for and were denied admission. How should the remedy be structured? *See Hameed v. Iron Workers, Local 396*, 637 F.2d 506 (8th Cir. 1980) (attempt to determine which blacks would have been hired; if not possible, estimate total wage loss caused by failure to admit forty-five blacks and require employer to pay that amount to 180 black applicants on pro rata basis). *Cf. EEOC v. Enterprise Ass'n Steamfitters Local 638*, 542 F.2d 579 (2d Cir. 1976), *cert. denied,* 430 U.S. 911 (1977) (backpay denied to black applicants because their injuries too remote and speculative).

(c) The Alabama Department of Public Safety discriminated against blacks who applied to be state troopers and against blacks who applied for promotions. The discrimination continued even after a court ordered it to stop. Eventually, the court ordered the Department to promote one black trooper for each white trooper promoted, provided qualified black applicants were available, until blacks constituted 25% (the proportion of blacks in the relevant labor market) of the persons in a rank. Using the loss-shifting model, why is this a problematic remedy? The Supreme Court has held that this type of remedy is appropriate, provided that the discrimination against which it is addressed is long-standing and egregious and that the remedy is temporary and flexible and does not have too adverse an effect on non-minority interests. *See United States v. Paradise*, 480 U.S. 149 (1987) (case the problem is based on); *Local 28, Sheet Metal Workers' Int'l Ass'n v. EEOC*, 478 U.S. 421 (1986).

2. Affirmative Action and the Constitution. *Johnson* involved a public employer, but no constitutional issues were raised. Constitutional analysis requires consideration of the same two general sets of issues considered in *Johnson* — is the employer's preference justified and narrowly tailored? — but it may heighten the level of scrutiny. *See Adarand Constrs., Inc. v. Pena*, 515 U.S. 200 (1995) (strict scrutiny to be applied to race-based preferences); *Associated Gen. Contractors of Cal., Inc. v. San Francisco*, 813 F.2d 922 (9th Cir. 1987) (striking down racial preferences under strict scrutiny, while upholding gender preference under intermediate scrutiny).

TAXMAN v. BOARD OF EDUCATION
United States Court of Appeals, Third Circuit (en banc)
91 F.3d 1547 (3d Cir. 1996), *cert. granted*, 521 U.S. 1117,
cert. dismissed, 522 U.S. 1010 (1997)

MANSMANN, CIRCUIT JUDGE. . . .

In 1975, the Board of Education of the Township of Piscataway, New Jersey, developed an affirmative action policy applicable to employment decisions. . . . In 1983 the Board also adopted a one page "Policy", entitled "Affirmative Action — Employment Practices."

The 1975 document states that the purpose of the Program is "to provide equal educational opportunity for students and equal employment opportunity for employees and prospective employees," and "to make a concentrated effort to attract . . . minority personnel for all positions so that their qualifications can be evaluated along with other candidates." The 1983 document states that its purpose is to "ensure[] equal employment opportunity . . . and prohibit discrimination in employment because of . . . race. . . ."

The operative language regarding the means by which affirmative-action goals are to be furthered is identical in the two documents. "In all cases, the most qualified candidate will be recommended for appointment. However, when candidates appear to be of equal qualification, candidates meeting the criteria of the affirmative action program will be recommended." The phrase "candidates meeting the criteria of the affirmative action program" refers to members of racial, national origin or gender groups identified as minorities for statistical reporting purposes by the New Jersey State Department of

Education, including Blacks. The 1983 document also clarifies that the affirmative action program applies to "every aspect of employment including . . . layoffs. . . ."

The Board's affirmative action policy did not have "any remedial purpose"; it was not adopted "with the intention of remedying the results of any prior discrimination or identified underrepresentation of minorities within the Piscataway Public School System." At all relevant times, Black teachers were neither "underrepresented" nor "underutilized" in the Piscataway School District work force. Indeed, statistics in 1976 and 1985 showed that the percentage of Black employees in the job category which included teachers exceeded the percentage of Blacks in the available work force.

In May, 1989, the Board accepted a recommendation from the Superintendent of Schools to reduce the teaching staff in the Business Department at Piscataway High School by one. At that time, two of the teachers in the department were of equal seniority, both having begun their employment with the Board on the same day nine years earlier. One of those teachers was intervenor plaintiff Sharon Taxman, who is White, and the other was Debra Williams, who is Black. Williams was the only minority teacher among the faculty of the Business Department.

Decisions regarding layoffs by New Jersey school boards are highly circumscribed by state law; nontenured faculty must be laid off first, and layoffs among tenured teachers in the affected subject area or grade level must proceed in reverse order of seniority. . . . Thus, local boards lack discretion to choose between employees for layoff, except in the rare instance of a tie in seniority between the two or more employees eligible to fill the last remaining position.

The Board determined that it was facing just such a rare circumstance in deciding between Taxman and Williams. In prior decisions involving the layoff of employees with equal seniority, the Board had broken the tie through "a random process which included drawing numbers out of a container, drawing lots or having a lottery."[4] In none of those instances, however, had the employees involved been of different races.

In light of the unique posture of the layoff decision, Superintendent of Schools Burton Edelchick recommended to the Board that the affirmative action plan be invoked in order to determine which teacher to retain. Superintendent Edelchick made this recommendation "because he believed Ms. Williams and Ms. Taxman were tied in seniority, were equally qualified, and because Ms. Williams was the only Black teacher in the Business Education Department."

While the Board recognized that it was not bound to apply the affirmative action policy, it made a discretionary decision to invoke the policy to break

---

[4] The dissent of Chief Judge Sloviter characterizes the use of a random process as "a solution that could be expected of the state's gaming tables." We take issue with this characterization, noting that those wiser than we have advised that "the lot puts an end to disputes and is decisive in a controversy between the mighty." *Proverbs* 18:18 (New American). Furthermore, the use of a random process is not something which the court has imposed upon the Board but is instead a mechanism adopted by the Board itself in reaching a decision in prior employment matters.

the tie between Williams and Taxman. As a result, the Board "voted to terminate the employment of Sharon Taxman, effective June 30, 1988. . . ."

At his deposition Theodore H. Kruse, the Board's President, explained his vote to apply the affirmative action policy as follows:

> A. Basically I think because I had been aware that the student body and the community which is our responsibility, the schools of the community, is really quite diverse and there — I have a general feeling during my tenure on the board that it was valuable for the students to see in the various employment roles a wide range of background, and that it was also valuable to the work force and in particular to the teaching staff that they have — they see that in each other.

Asked to articulate the "educational objective" served by retaining Williams rather than Taxman, Kruse stated:

> A. In my own personal perspective I believe by retaining Mrs. Williams it was sending a very clear message that we feel that our staff should be culturally diverse, our student population is culturally diverse and there is a distinct advantage to students, to all students, to be made — come into contact with people of different cultures, different background, so that they are more aware, more tolerant, more accepting, more understanding of people of all background.
>
> Q. What do you mean by the phrase you used, culturally diverse?
>
> A. Someone other than — different than yourself. And we have, our student population and our community has people of all different background, ethnic background, religious background, cultural background, and it's important that our school district encourage awareness and acceptance and tolerance and, therefore, I personally think it's important that our staff reflect that too.

[The District Court granted a summary judgment for Taxman on liability and held a trial on damages. The Court awarded Taxman $134,015 in damages for backpay and interest and a jury awarded her an additional $10,000 for emotional suffering.]

IV.

A.

Title VII was enacted to further two primary goals: to end discrimination on the basis of race, color, religion, sex or national origin, thereby guaranteeing equal opportunity in the workplace, and to remedy the segregation and underrepresentation of minorities that discrimination has caused in our Nation's work force.

Title VII's first purpose is set forth in section 2000e-2's several prohibitions, which expressly denounce the discrimination which Congress sought to end. 42 U.S.C. § 2000e-(2(a)-(d), (l); *McDonnell Douglas [Corp. v. Green,* 411 U.S. 792,] 800 [(1973)] ("The language of Title VII makes plain the purpose of Congress to assure equality of employment opportunities and to eliminate those discriminatory practices and devices which have fostered racially stratified job environments to the disadvantage of minority citizens."). . . .

Title VII's second purpose, ending the segregative effects of discrimination, is revealed in the congressional debate surrounding the statute's enactment. In [*Steelworkers v.*] *Weber*, [443 U.S. 193 (1979),] the Court carefully catalogued the comments made by the proponents of Title VII which demonstrate the Act's remedial concerns. *Weber*, at 202-04. By way of illustration, we cite Senator Clark's remarks to the Senate:

> The rate of Negro unemployment has gone up consistently as compared with white unemployment for the past 15 years. This is a social malaise and a social situation which we should not tolerate. That is one of the principal reasons why the bill should pass.

Id. (quoting 110 Cong. Rec. at 7220) (statement of Sen. Clark). . . .

The significance of this second corrective purpose cannot be overstated. It is only because Title VII was written to eradicate not only discrimination per se but the *consequences* of prior discrimination as well, that racial preferences in the form of affirmative action can co-exist with the Act's antidiscrimination mandate.

Thus, based on our analysis of Title VII's two goals, we are convinced that unless an affirmative action plan has a remedial purpose, it cannot be said to mirror the purposes of the statute, and, therefore, cannot satisfy the first prong of the *Weber* test.

We see this case as one involving straightforward statutory interpretation controlled by the text and legislative history of Title VII as interpreted in *Weber* and *Johnson*. The statute on its face provides that race cannot be a factor in employer decisions about hires, promotions, and layoffs, and the legislative history demonstrates that barring considerations of race from the workplace was Congress' primary objective. If exceptions to this bar are to be made, they must be made on the basis of what Congress has said. The affirmative action plans at issue in *Weber* and *Johnson* were sustained only because the Supreme Court, examining those plans in light of congressional intent, found a secondary congressional objective in Title VII that had to be accommodated — *i.e.*, the elimination of the effects of past discrimination in the workplace. Here, there is no congressional recognition of diversity as a Title VII objective requiring accommodation.

Accordingly, it is beyond cavil that the Board, by invoking its affirmative action policy to lay off Sharon Taxman, violated the terms of Title VII. While the Court in *Weber* and *Johnson* permitted some deviation from the antidiscrimination mandate of the statute in order to erase the effects of past discrimination, these rulings do not open the door to additional non-remedial deviations. Here, as in *Weber* and *Johnson*, the Board must justify its deviation from the statutory mandate based on positive legislative history, not on its idea of what is appropriate.

B.

The Board recognizes that there is no positive legislative history supporting its goal of promoting racial diversity "for education's sake", and concedes that there is no caselaw approving such a purpose to support an affirmative action plan under Title VII. "[T]he Board would have [us] infer the propriety of this purpose from fragments of other authority." . . .

We find the Board's reliance on Fourteenth Amendment caselaw misplaced. . . . We are acutely aware, as is the Board, that the federal courts have never decided a "pure" Title VII case where racial diversity for education's sake was advanced as the sole justification for a race-based decision. The Board argues that in deciding just such a case, we should look to the Supreme Court's endorsement of diversity as a goal in the Equal Protection context. This argument, however, is based upon a faulty premise. . . .

We are . . . unpersuaded by the Board's contention that Equal Protection cases arising in an education context support upholding the Board's purpose in a Title VII action. These Equal Protection cases, unlike the case at hand, involved corrective efforts to confront racial segregation or chronic minority underrepresentation in the schools. In this context, we are not at all surprised that the goal of diversity was raised. While we wholeheartedly endorse any statements in these cases extolling the educational value of exposing students to persons of diverse races and backgrounds, given the framework in which they were made, we cannot accept them as authority for the conclusion that the Board's non-remedial racial diversity goal is a permissible basis for affirmative action under Title VII. *See, e.g., Wygant* [*v. Jackson Board of Education*], 476 U.S. at 267 [(1986)] (Marshall, J., dissenting) (noting that the racially-conscious layoff provision at issue was aimed at preserving the faculty integration achieved by the Jackson, Michigan Public Schools in the early 1970s through affirmative action; minority representation went from 3.9% in 1969 to 8.8% in 1971); *Regents of the University of California v. Bakke*, 438 U.S. 265 (1978) (Powell, J., announcing the judgment of the Court) (observing that the 1968 class of the Medical School of the University of California at Davis contained three Asians, no Blacks, no Mexican-Americans and no American Indians).

More specifically, [the principal] Supreme Court case upon which the Board relies, *Bakke*, 438 U.S. at 265, [is] inapposite. *Bakke* involved a rejected White applicant's challenge under the Constitution and Title VI of the Civil Rights Act of 1964 to a special admissions program instituted by the Medical School of the University of California at Davis which essentially set aside 16 places for minority candidates. Justice Powell, whose vote was necessary both to establish the validity of considering race in admission decisions and to invalidate the racial quota before the Court, was of the opinion that the attainment of a "diverse student body" is a constitutionally permissible goal for an institution of higher education. . . .

[However,] *Bakke*'s factual and legal setting, as well as the diversity that universities aspire to in their student bodies, are, in our view, so different from the facts, relevant law and the racial diversity purpose involved in this case that we find little in *Bakke* to guide us.

. . . .

V.

Since we have not found anything in the Board's arguments to convince us that this case requires examination beyond statutory interpretation, we return to the point at which we started: the language of Title VII itself and the . . . cases reviewing affirmative action plans in light of that statute. Our analysis of the statute and the caselaw convinces us that a non-remedial affirmative action plan cannot form the basis for deviating from the antidiscrimination mandate of Title VII.

The Board admits that it did not act to remedy the effects of past employment discrimination. The parties have stipulated that neither the Board's adoption of its affirmative action policy nor its subsequent decision to apply it in choosing between Taxman and Williams was intended to remedy the results of any prior discrimination or identified underrepresentation of Blacks within the Piscataway School District's teacher workforce as a whole. Nor does the Board contend that its action here was directed at remedying any *de jure* or *de facto* segregation. Even though the Board's race-conscious action was taken to avoid what could have been an all-White faculty within the Business Department, the Board concedes that Blacks are not underrepresented in its teaching workforce as a whole or even in the Piscataway High School.

Rather, the Board's sole purpose in applying its affirmative action policy in this case was to obtain an educational benefit which it believed would result from a racially diverse faculty. While the benefits flowing from diversity in the educational context are significant indeed, we are constrained to hold, as did the district court, that inasmuch as "the Board does not even attempt to show that its affirmative action plan was adopted to remedy past discrimination or as the result of a manifest imbalance in the employment of minorities," the Board has failed to satisfy the first prong of the *Weber* test.

We turn next to the second prong of the *Weber* analysis. This second prong requires that we determine whether the Board's policy "unnecessarily trammel[s] . . . [nonminority] interests. . . ." Under this requirement, too, the Board's policy is deficient.

We begin by noting the policy's utter lack of definition and structure. While it is not for us to decide how much diversity in a high school facility is "enough," the Board cannot abdicate its responsibility to define "racial diversity" and to determine what degree of racial diversity in the Piscataway School is sufficient. . . . The affirmative action plans that have met with the Supreme Court's approval under Title VII had objectives, as well as benchmarks which served to evaluate progress, guide the employment decisions at issue and assure the grant of only those minority preferences necessary to further the plans' purpose. By contrast, the Board's policy, devoid of goals and standards, is governed entirely by the Board's whim, leaving the Board free, if it so chooses, to grant racial preferences that do not promote even the policy's claimed purpose. Indeed, under the terms of this policy, the Board, in pursuit of a "racially diverse" work force, could use affirmative action to discriminate against those whom Title VII was enacted to protect. Such a policy unnecessarily trammels the interests of nonminority employees.

Moreover, both *Weber* and *Johnson* unequivocally provide that valid affirmative action plans are "temporary" measures that seek to "attain", not "maintain" a "permanent racial . . . balance." The Board's policy, adopted in 1975, is an established fixture of unlimited duration, to be resurrected from time to time whenever the Board believes that the ratio between Blacks and Whites in any Piscataway School is skewed. On this basis alone, the policy contravenes *Weber*'s teaching.

Finally, we are convinced that the harm imposed upon a nonminority employee by the loss of his or her job is so substantial and the cost so severe that the Board's goal of racial diversity, even if legitimate under Title VII, may not be pursued in this particular fashion. This is especially true where, as here, the nonminority employee is tenured. In *Weber* and *Johnson*, when considering whether nonminorities were unduly encumbered by affirmative action, the Court found it significant that they retained their employment. We, therefore, adopt the plurality's pronouncement in Wygant that "[w]hile hiring goals impose a diffuse burden, often foreclosing only one of several opportunities, layoffs impose the entire burden of achieving racial equality on particular individuals, often resulting in serious disruption of their lives. That burden is too intrusive." *Wygant*, 476 U.S. at 283.

Accordingly, we conclude that under the second prong of the Weber test, the Board's affirmative action policy violates Title VII. In addition to containing an impermissible purpose, the policy "unnecessarily trammel[s] the interests of the [nonminority] employees." . . .

VII.

Having found the Board liable under Title VII, we turn our attention to the issue of damages, addressing first the district court's order that Taxman be awarded one hundred percent backpay for the entire period of her layoff. The Board argues that where a backpay award is appropriate, the court's goal should be to restore "the conditions and relationships that would have been had there been no" unlawful discrimination. According to the Board, the district court's award of one hundred percent backpay was plainly unfair. Had it not invoked the affirmative action plan, the Board would have followed its usual procedure, using a coin toss or other random process to break the seniority tie between Williams and Taxman. Taxman, therefore, would have stood no more than a fifty percent chance of keeping her job had there been no unlawful discrimination.

We disagree. In deciding backpay issues, a district court has wide latitude to "locate 'a just result'" and to further the "make whole remedy of Title VII in light of the circumstances of a particular case." *Albemarle Paper Co. v. Moody*, 422 U.S. 405 (1975). While Taxman cannot be returned to the position that she held prior to her layoff — one of virtually precise equality with Williams in terms of the factors relevant to the decision — she can be returned to a position of financial equality with Williams through a one hundred percent backpay award. We are convinced that this award most closely approximates the conditions that would have prevailed in the absence of discrimination. . . .

Given the law and the circumstances presented in this case, we are convinced that the district court's analysis with respect to backpay reflects the sound exercise of judicial discretion and we will affirm the award. . . .

VIII.

While we have rejected the argument that the Board's non-remedial application of the affirmative action policy is consistent with the language and intent of Title VII, we do not reject in principle the diversity goal articulated by the Board. Indeed, we recognize that the differences among us underlie the richness and strength of our Nation. Our disposition of this matter, however, rests squarely on the foundation of Title VII. Although we applaud the goal of racial diversity, we cannot agree that Title VII permits an employer to advance that goal through non-remedial discriminatory measures.

SLOVITER, CHIEF JUDGE, dissenting, with whom JUDGES LEWIS and MCKEE join.

[T]he narrow question posed by this appeal can be restated as whether Title VII requires a New Jersey school or school board, which is faced with deciding which of two equally qualified teachers should be laid off, to make its decision through a coin toss or lottery, a solution that could be expected of the state's gaming tables, or whether Title VII permits the school board to factor into the decision its bona fide belief, based on its experience with secondary schools, that students derive educational benefit by having a Black faculty member in an otherwise all-White department. Because I believe that the area of discretion left to employers in educational institutions by Title VII encompasses the School Board's action in this case, I respectfully dissent.

The posture in which the legal issue in this case is presented is so stripped of extraneous factors that it could well serve as the question for a law school moot court. I emphasize at the outset issues that this case does not present. We need not decide whether it is permissible for a school to lay off a more qualified employee in favor of a less qualified employee on the basis of race, because that did not happen here. Nor need we consider what requirements Title VII may impose on unwilling employers, or how much racial diversity in a high school faculty may be "enough." . . .

II.

It was the Board's decision to include the desire for a racially diverse faculty among the various factors entering into its discretionary decision that the majority of this court brands a Title VII violation as a matter of law. *No Supreme Court case compels that anomalous result.* Notwithstanding the majority's literal construction of the language of Title VII, no Supreme Court case has ever interpreted the statute to preclude consideration of race or sex for the purpose of insuring diversity in the classroom as *one of many* factors in an employment decision, the situation presented here. Moreover, in the only two instances in which the Supreme Court examined under Title VII, without the added scrutiny imposed by the Equal Protection Clause, affirmative action plans voluntarily adopted by employers that gave preference to race or sex as a determinative factor, the Court upheld both plans. . . .

The majority presents *Weber* and *Johnson* as if their significance lies in the obstacle course they purportedly establish for any employer adopting an affirmative action program. But . . . the significance of each of those cases is that the Supreme Court sustained the affirmative action plans presented, and in doing so deviated from the literal interpretation of Title VII precluding use of race or gender in any employment action. . . .

It is "ironic indeed" that the promotion of racial diversity in the classroom, which has formed so central a role in this country's struggle to eliminate the causes and consequences of racial discrimination, is today held to be at odds with the very Act that was triggered by our "Nation's concern over centuries of racial injustice." *Weber*, 443 U.S. at 204. Nor does it seem plausible that the drafters of Title VII intended it to be interpreted so as to require a local school district to resort to a lottery to determine which of two qualified teachers to retain, rather than employ the School Board's own educational policy undertaken to insure students an opportunity to learn from a teacher who was a member of the very group whose treatment motivated Congress to enact Title VII in the first place. In my view, the Board's purpose of obtaining the educational benefit to be derived from a racially diverse faculty is entirely consistent with the purposes animating Title VII and the Civil Rights Act of 1964. . . .

I therefore respectfully disagree with the majority, both in its construction of *Weber* and *Johnson* as leaving no doors open for any action that takes race into consideration in an employment situation other than to remedy past discrimination and the consequential racial imbalance in the workforce, and in what appears to be its limited view of the purposes of Title VII. I would hold that a school board's bona fide decision to obtain the educational benefit to be derived from a racially diverse faculty is a permissible basis for its voluntary affirmative action under Title VII scrutiny.

III.

It is undeniable that, in the abstract, a layoff imposes a far greater burden on the affected employee than a denial of promotion or even a failure to hire. In this case, however, it cannot be said with any certainty that Taxman would have avoided the layoff had the Board's decision not been race-conscious. If a random selection had been made, Taxman would have had no more than a fifty-percent chance of not being laid off. Thus, this was not a situation where Taxman had a "legitimate and firmly rooted expectation" of no layoff. *Johnson*, 480 U.S. at 638.

This differs from the situation of an employee who is next in line for a promotion by the objective factor of seniority. Taxman's qualifications were merely equal to those of her competitor for this purpose. In *Johnson* the Court held that because there were six other employees who also met the qualifications for the job, Johnson had no "entitlement" or "legitimate firmly rooted expectation" in the promotion, even though he had scored higher than the others on the qualifying test. Moreover, just as the plaintiff in *Johnson* remained eligible for promotion in the future, Taxman retained recall rights after her layoff, and did in fact regain her job. . . .

I return to the question raised at the outset: whether Title VII requires that the Board toss a coin to make the layoff selection between equally situated employees. . . .[T]he majority . . . points to no language in Title VII to suggest that a lottery is required as the solution to a layoff decision in preference to a reasoned decision by members of the School Board, some of whom are experienced educators, that the race of a faculty member has a relevant educational significance if the department would otherwise be all White. While it may seem fairer to some, I see nothing in Title VII that requires use of a lottery.

Because I cannot say that faculty diversity is not a permissible purpose to support the race-conscious decision made here and because the Board's action was not overly intrusive on Taxman's rights, I would reverse the grant of summary judgment for Taxman under Title VII and direct that summary judgment be granted to the School Board.[1]

NOTES

1. *The Final Resolution.* The *Taxman* case was settled after the Supreme Court had granted certiorari. Sharon Taxman received $433,500. The settlement was unusual because it was made possible when the Black Leadership Forum agreed to contribute $308,500 (or about 70% of the total amount) towards the settlement. The School Board paid the rest. The Black Leadership Forum is a coalition of national civil rights organizations which includes the Urban League, the NAACP, and the Rainbow Coalition.

2. *Would Taxman Win After Grutter?* In *Grutter v. Bollinger*, 539 U.S. 306 (2003), the Supreme Court held that diversity is a compelling interest that justified the use of race in making student admission decisions at the University of Michigan Law School. The Court deferred to the Law School's considered judgment that diversity was essential to the Law School's educational mission. In a companion case, the Court struck down the undergraduate affirmative-action program because it favored minority applicants too mechanically. *Gratz v. Bollinger*, 539 U.S. 244 (2003).

The application of *Grutter* to other settings, and especially to employment, is uncertain. The majority in *Taxman* seemed to anticipate *Grutter* when it said "the diversity that universities aspire to in their student bodies [is,] in our view, [very] different from the . . . racial diversity purpose involved in this case." But that, of course, is the question. *Grutter* determined that a diverse student body can be a compelling interest for a law school. Does that also mean that a diverse teaching staff is a compelling interest in a public school? *See, e.g., Parents Involved in Community Schools v. Seattle School District No. 1*, 426 F.3d 1162 (2005), *cert. granted*, 126 S. Ct. 2351 (2006) (compelling interest in diversity justified school district's use of race as a tie-breaker in assigning students to schools); *Petit v. City of Chicago*, 352 F.3d 1111 (7th Cir. 2003), *cert. denied*, 541 U.S. 1074 (2004) (court defers to city's judgment that a diverse police force is a compelling interest).

---

[1] Because I think the school board is not liable I will not dwell on the issue of damages. I note simply that there is much logic to the Board's argument that Taxman should be awarded fifty percent rather than one hundred percent of the backpay she would have received had she not been laid off. The record shows that, had the Board not based its decision on race, it would have chosen between Taxman and Williams by means of a coin toss or lottery. Since in such circumstances Taxman would have stood only a fifty-percent chance of retaining her job, a fifty-percent backpay award most accurately "recreate[s] the conditions and relationships that would have been had there been no" consideration of race.

Similarly, *Grutter* would not resolve the issue of whether the program in *Taxman* was sufficiently narrowly tailored, in particular, whether it imposed an undue burden. *Grutter* held that the admissions program at the Michigan Law School did not impose an undue burden on nonminority candidates because diversity was construed broadly to include not only race, but "all the qualities valued by the university" and each candidate's application was evaluated individually to consider possible diversity contributions. 539 U.S. at 340-41. Those notions do not apply very well to *Taxman* where race was the key consideration and the burden fell on an individual who could be clearly and easily identified.

3. Symbolism. Affirmative action is controversial, not only because of its real-world consequences, but also because of its symbolism:

> [A]ffirmative action has meant racial progress for two generations of African Americans. That is its symbolic significance. The dramatic act of eliminating it now carries with it an undeniably negative message to and about its potential beneficiaries. Our original decision to adopt affirmative action as the lynchpin of American race policy may have been wrong. It may have been right, but for reasons that were not the basis for the original decision. But too much time has gone by, too many reasonable expectations have been built upon it, to change courses now.

Deborah C. Malamud, *Values, Symbols, and Facts in the Affirmative Action Debate*, 95 MICH. L. REV. 1668, 1712 (1997).

Part VI

REGULATION OF COMPENSATION

Chapter 16

WAGES AND HOURS LEGISLATION

A. THE HISTORY OF WAGE AND HOUR REGULATION IN THE UNITED STATES

LOCHNER v. NEW YORK
United States Supreme Court
198 U.S. 45 (1905)

MR. JUSTICE PECKHAM . . . delivered the opinion of the court.

The indictment charges . . . that the plaintiff in error . . . wrongfully and unlawfully required and permitted an employé working for him to work more than sixty hours in one week.* . . . The mandate of the statute, that "no employé shall be required or permitted to work," is the substantial equivalent of an enactment that "no employé shall contract or agree to work," more than ten hours per day, and as there is no provision for special emergencies the statute is mandatory in all cases. It is not an act merely fixing the number of hours which shall constitute a legal day's work, but an absolute prohibition upon the employer permitting, under any circumstances, more than ten hours' work to be done in his establishment. The employé may desire to earn the extra money which would arise from his working more than the prescribed time, but this statute forbids the employer from permitting the employé to earn it.

The statute necessarily interferes with the right of contract between the employer and employés, concerning the number of hours in which the latter may labor in the bakery of the employer. The general right to make a contract in relation to his business is part of the liberty of the individual protected by the Fourteenth Amendment of the Federal Constitution. Under that provision no State can deprive any person of life, liberty or property without due process of law. The right to purchase or to sell labor is part of the liberty protected by this amendment, unless there are circumstances which exclude the right. There are, however, certain powers, existing in the sovereignty of each State in the Union, somewhat vaguely termed police powers, the exact description and limitation of which have not been attempted by the courts. Those powers, broadly stated, and without, at present, any attempt at a more specific limitation, relate to the safety, health, morals, and general welfare

---

* The section of the New York statute under which the indictment was found reads as follows:

§ 110. *Hours of labor in bakeries and confectionery establishments.* No employé shall be required or permitted to work in a biscuit, bread or cake bakery or confectionery establishment more than sixty hours in any one week, or more than ten hours in any one day, unless for the purpose of making a shorter work day on the last day of the week; nor more hours in any one week than will make an average of ten hours per day for the number of days during such week in which such employé shall work.

of the public. Both property and liberty are held on such reasonable conditions as may be imposed by the governing power of the State in the exercise of those powers, and with such conditions the Fourteenth Amendment was not designed to interfere.

The State, therefore, has power to prevent the individual from making certain kinds of contracts, and in regard to them the Federal Constitution offers no protection. If the contract be one which the State, in the legitimate exercise of its police power, has the right to prohibit, it is not prevented from prohibiting it by the Fourteenth Amendment. Contracts in violation of a statute, either of the Federal or state government, or a contract to let one's property for immoral purposes, or to do any other unlawful act, could obtain no protection from the Federal Constitution, as coming under the liberty of person or of free contract. Therefore, when the State, by its legislature, in the assumed exercise of its police powers, has passed an act which seriously limits the right to labor or the right of contract in regard to their means of livelihood between persons who are *sui juris* (both employer and employé), it becomes of great importance to determine which shall prevail — the right of the individual to labor for such time as he may choose, or the right of the State to prevent the individual from laboring or from entering into any contract to labor, beyond a certain time prescribed by the State.

This court has recognized the existence and upheld the exercise of the police powers of the States in many cases which might fairly be considered as border ones, and it has, in the course of its determination of questions regarding the asserted invalidity of such statutes, on the ground of their violation of the rights secured by the Federal Constitution, been guided by rules of a very liberal nature, the application of which has resulted, in numerous instances, in upholding the validity of state statutes thus assailed. Among the later cases where the state law has been upheld by this court is that of *Holden v. Hardy,* 169 U.S. 366 [1898]. A provision in the act of the legislature of Utah was there under consideration, the act limiting the employment of workmen in all underground mines or workings, to eight hours per day, "except in cases of emergency, where life or property is in imminent danger." It also limited the hours of labor in smelting and other institutions for the reduction or refining of ores or metals to eight hours per day, except in like cases of emergency. The act was held to be a valid exercise of the police powers of the State. It was held that the kind of employment, mining, smelting, etc., and the character of the employés in such kinds of labor, were such as to make it reasonable and proper for the state to interfere to prevent the employés from being constrained by the rules laid down by the proprietors in regard to labor. . . .

It will be observed that, even with regard to that class of labor, the Utah statute provided for cases of emergency wherein the provisions of the statute would not apply. The statute now before this court has no emergency clause in it, and, if the statute is valid, there are no circumstances and no emergencies under which the slightest violation of the provisions of the act would be innocent. There is nothing in *Holden v. Hardy* which covers the case now before us. . . .

It must, of course, be conceded that there is a limit to the valid exercise of the police power by the State. . . . Otherwise the Fourteenth Amendment would have no efficacy and the legislatures of the States would have un-bounded power, and it would be enough to say that any piece of legislation was enacted to conserve the morals, the health, or the safety of the people; such legislation would be valid, no matter how absolutely without foundation the claim might be. . . . In every case that comes before this court, therefore, where legislation of this character is concerned, and where the protection of the Federal Constitution is sought, the question necessarily arises: Is this a fair, reasonable, and appropriate exercise of the police power of the State, or is it an unreasonable, unnecessary, and arbitrary interference with the right of the individual to his personal liberty, or to enter into those contracts in relation to labor which may seem to him appropriate or necessary for the support of himself and his family? Of course the liberty of contract relating to labor includes both parties to it. The one has as much right to purchase as the other to sell labor. . . .

The question whether this act is valid as a labor law, pure and simple, may be dismissed in a few words. There is no reasonable ground for interfering with the liberty of person or the right of free contract, by determining the hours of labor, in the occupation of a baker. There is no contention that bakers as a class are not equal in intelligence and capacity to men in other trades or manual occupations, or that they are not able to assert their rights and care for themselves without the protecting arm of the State, interfering with their independence of judgment and of action. They are in no sense wards of the State. Viewed in the light of a purely labor law, with no reference whatever to the question of health, we think that a law like the one before us involves neither the safety, the morals, nor the welfare, of the public, and that the interest of the public is not in the slightest degree affected by such an act. The law must be upheld, if at all, as a law pertaining to the health of the individual engaged in the occupation of a baker. It does not affect any other portion of the public than those who are engaged in that occupation. Clean and wholesome bread does not depend upon whether the baker works but ten hours per day or only sixty hours a week. The limitation of the hours of labor does not come within the police power on that ground. . . .

There is, in our judgment, no reasonable foundation for holding this to be necessary or appropriate as a health law to safeguard the public health, or the health of the individuals who are following the trade of a baker. If this statute be valid, and if, therefore, a proper case is made out in which to deny the right of an individual, *sui juris,* as employer or employé, to make contracts for the labor of the latter under the protection of the provisions of the Federal Constitution, there would seem to be no length to which legislation of this nature might not go. . . .

We think that there can be no fair doubt that the trade of a baker, in and of itself, is not an unhealthy one to that degree which would authorize the legislature to interfere with the right to labor, and with the right of free contract on the part of the individual, either as employer or employé. In looking through statistics regarding all trades and occupations, it may be true that the trade of a baker does not appear to be as healthy as some other trades, and is also vastly more healthy than still others. To the common understand-ing the trade of a baker has never been regarded as an unhealthy one. Very likely physicians would not recommend the exercise of that or of any other trade as a remedy for ill health. Some occupations are more healthy than others, but we think there are none which might not come under the power of the legislature to supervise and control the hours of working therein, if the mere fact that the occupation is not absolutely and perfectly healthy is to confer that right upon the legislative department of the government. It might be safely affirmed that almost all occupations more or less affect the health. There must be more than the mere fact of the possible existence of some small amount of unhealthiness to warrant legislative interference with liberty. It is unfortunately true that labor, even in any department, may possibly carry with it the seeds of unhealthiness. But are we all, on that account, at the mercy of legislative majorities? A printer, a tinsmith, a locksmith, a carpenter, a cabinetmaker, a dry goods clerk, a bank's, a lawyer's, or a physician's clerk, or a clerk in almost any kind of business, would all come under the power of the legislature, on this assumption. No trade, no occupation, no mode of earning one's living, could escape this all-pervading power, and the acts of the legislature in limiting the hours of labor in all employments would be valid, although such limitation might seriously cripple the ability of the laborer to support himself and his family. . . .

It is also urged, pursuing the same line of argument, that it is to the interest of the State that its population should be strong and robust, and therefore any legislation which may be said to tend to make people healthy must be valid as health laws, enacted under the police power. If this be a valid argument and a justification for this kind of legislation, it follows that the protection of the Federal Constitution from undue interference with liberty of person and freedom of contract is visionary, wherever the law is sought to be justified as a valid exercise of the police power. Scarcely any law but might find shelter under such assumptions, and conduct, properly so called, as well as contract, would come under the restrictive sway of the legislature. Not only the hours of employés, but the hours of employers, could be regulated, and doctors, lawyers, scientists, all professional men, as well as athletes and artisans, could be forbidden to fatigue their brains and bodies by prolonged hours of exercise, lest the fighting strength of the State be impaired. We mention these extreme cases because the contention is extreme. We do not believe in the soundness of the views which uphold this law. . . . Statutes of the nature of that under review, limiting the hours in which grown and intelligent men may labor to earn their living, are mere meddlesome interferences with the rights of the individual, and they are not saved from condemnation by the claim that they are passed in the exercise of the police power and upon the subject of the health of the individual whose rights are interfered with, unless there be some fair ground, reasonable in and of itself, to say that there is material danger to the public health, or to the health of the employés, if the hours of labor are not curtailed. . . . All that [the Legislature] could properly do has been done by it with regard to the conduct of bakeries, as provided for in the other sections of the act, above set forth. These several sections provide for the inspection of the premises where the bakery is carried on, with regard to furnishing proper wash rooms and waterclosets, apart from the bake room, also with regard to providing proper drainage, plumbing, and painting; the sections, in addition, provide for the height of the ceiling, the cementing or tiling of floors, where necessary in the opinion of the factory inspector, and for other things of that nature; alterations are also provided for, and are to be made where necessary in the opinion of the inspector, in order to comply with the provisions of the statute. These various sections may be wise and valid regulations, and they certainly go to the full extent of providing for the cleanliness and the healthiness, so far as possible, of the quarters in which bakeries are to be conducted. Adding to all these requirements a prohibition to enter into any contract of labor in a bakery for more than a certain number of hours a week is, in our judgment, so wholly beside the matter of a proper, reasonable and fair provision as to run counter to that liberty of person and of free contract provided for in the Federal Constitution.

It was further urged on the argument that restricting the hours of labor in the case of bakers was valid because it tended to cleanliness on the part of the workers, as a man was more apt to be cleanly when not overworked, and if cleanly then his "output" was also more likely to be so. What has already been said applies with equal force to this contention. We do not admit the reasoning to be sufficient to justify the claimed right of such interference. . . . In our judgment it is not possible in fact to discover the connection between the number of hours a baker may work in the bakery and the healthful quality of the bread made by the workman. The connection, if any exist, is too shadowy and thin to build any argument for the interference of the legislature. If the man works ten hours a day it is all right, but if ten and a half or eleven his health is in danger and his bread may be unhealthy, and, therefore, he shall not be permitted to do it. This, we think, is unreasonable and entirely arbitrary. When assertions such as we have adverted to become necessary in order to give, if possible, a plausible foundation for the contention that the law is a "health law," it gives rise to at least a suspicion that there was some other motive dominating the legislature than the purpose to subserve the public health or welfare. . . .

It is impossible for us to shut our eyes to the fact that . . . laws of this character, while passed under what is claimed to be the police power for the purpose of protecting the public health or welfare, are, in reality, passed from other motives. . . . It seems to us that the real object and purpose were simply to regulate the hours of labor between the master and his employés (all being men, *sui juris*), in a private business, not dangerous in any degree to morals, or in any real and substantial degree to the health of the employés. Under such circumstances the freedom of master and employé to contract with each other in relation to their employment, and in defining the same, cannot be prohibited or interfered with, without violating the Federal Constitution. . . .

Reversed.

Mr. Justice Harlan, with whom Mr. Justice White and Mr. Justice Day concurred, dissenting. . . .

It is plain that [the] statute [in question] was enacted in order to protect the physical well-being of those who work in bakery and confectionery establishments. It may be that the statute had its origin, in part, in the belief that employers and employés in such establishments were not upon an equal footing, and that the necessities of the latter often compelled them to submit to such exactions as unduly taxed their strength. Be this as it may, the statute must be taken as expressing the belief of the people of New York that, as a general rule, and in the case of the average man, labor in excess of sixty hours during a week in such establishments may endanger the health of those who thus labor. Whether or not this be wise legislation it is not the province of the court to inquire. Under our systems of government the courts are not concerned with the wisdom or policy of legislation. So that in determining the question of power to interfere with liberty of contract, the court may inquire whether the means devised by the State are germane to an end which may be lawfully accomplished and have a real or substantial relation to the protection of health, as involved in the daily work of the persons, male and female, engaged in bakery and confectionery establishments. But when this inquiry is entered upon I find it impossible, in view of common experience, to say that there is here no real or substantial relation between the means employed by the State and the end sought to be accomplished by its legislation. . . .

Professor Hirt in his treatise on the "Diseases of the Workers" has said: "The labor of the bakers is among the hardest and most laborious imaginable. . . . It is hard, very hard work, not only because it requires a great deal of physical exertion in an overheated workshop and during unreasonably long hours, but more so because of the erratic demands of the public, compelling the baker to perform the greater part of his work at night, thus depriving him of an opportunity to enjoy the necessary rest and sleep, a fact which is highly injurious to his health." Another writer says: "The constant inhaling of flour dust causes inflammation of the lungs and of the bronchial tubes. The eyes also suffer through this dust, which is responsible for the many cases of running eyes among the bakers. The long hours of toil to which all bakers are subjected produce rheumatism, cramps, and swollen legs. The intense heat in the workshops induces the workers to resort to cooling drinks, which together with their habit of exposing the greater part of their bodies to the change in the atmosphere, is another source of a number of diseases of various organs. Nearly all bakers are pale-faced and of more delicate health than the workers of other crafts, which is chiefly due to their hard work and their irregular and unnatural mode of living, whereby the power of resistance against disease is greatly diminished. The average age of a baker is below that of other workmen; they seldom live over their fiftieth year, most of them dying between the ages of forty and fifty. During periods of epidemic diseases the bakers are generally the first to succumb to the disease, and the number swept away during such periods far exceeds the number of other crafts in comparison to the men employed in the respective industries. When, in 1720, the plague visited the city of Marseilles, France, every baker in the city succumbed to the epidemic, which caused considerable excitement in the neighboring cities and resulted in measures for the sanitary protection of the bakers." . . .

Statistics show that the average daily working time among workingmen in different countries is, in Australia, 8 hours; in Great Britain, 9; in the United States, 9¾; in Denmark, 9¾; in Norway, 10; Sweden, France, and Switzerland, 10½; Germany, 10¼; Belgium, Italy, and Austria, 11; and in Russia, 12 hours.

We judicially know that the question of the number of hours during which a workman should continuously labor has been, for a long period, and is yet, a subject of serious consideration among civilized peoples, and by those having special knowledge of the laws of health. Suppose the statute prohibited labor in bakery and confectionery establishments in excess of eighteen hours each day. No one, I take it, could dispute the power of the State to enact such a statute. But the statute before us does not embrace extreme or exceptional cases. It may be said to occupy a middle ground in respect of the hours of labor. What is the true ground for the State to take between legitimate protection, by legislation, of the public health and liberty of contract is not a question easily solved, nor one in respect of which there is or can be absolute certainty. . . .

We also judicially know that the number of hours that should constitute a day's labor in particular occupations involving the physical strength and safety of workmen has been the subject of enactments by Congress and by nearly all of the States. Many, if not most, of those enactments fix eight hours as the proper basis of a day's labor.

I do not stop to consider whether any particular view of this economic question presents the sounder theory. What the precise facts are it may be difficult to say. It is enough for the determination of this case, and it is enough for this court to know, that the question is one about which there is room for debate and for an honest difference of opinion. There are many reasons of a weighty, substantial character, based upon the experience of mankind, in support of the theory that, all things considered, more than ten hours' steady work each day, from week to week, in a bakery or confectionery establishment, may endanger the health and shorten the lives of the workmen, thereby diminishing their physical and mental capacity to serve the State, and to provide for those dependent upon them.

If such reasons exist that ought to be the end of this case, for the State is not amenable to the judiciary, in respect of its legislative enactments, unless such enactments are plainly, palpably, beyond all question, inconsistent with the Constitution of the United States. . . . Our duty, I submit, is to sustain the statute as not being in conflict with the Federal Constitution, for the reason — and such is an all-sufficient reason — it is not shown to be plainly and palpably inconsistent with that instrument. Let the State alone in the management of its purely domestic affairs, so long as it does not appear beyond all question that it has violated the Federal Constitution. . . .

MR. JUSTICE HOLMES dissenting. . . .

This case is decided upon an economic theory which a large part of the country does not entertain. If it were a question whether I agreed with that theory, I should desire to study it further and long before making up my mind. But I do not conceive that to be my duty, because I strongly believe that my agreement or disagreement has nothing to do with the right of a majority to embody their opinions in law. It is settled by various decisions of this court that state constitutions and state laws may regulate life in many ways which we as legislators might think as injudicious or if you like as tyrannical as this, and which equally with this interfere with the liberty to contract. Sunday laws and usury laws are ancient examples. A more modern one is the prohibition of lotteries. The liberty of the citizen to do as he likes so long as he does not interfere with the liberty of others to do the same, which has been a shibboleth for some well-known writers, is interfered with by school laws, by the Post Office, by every state or municipal institution which takes his money for purposes thought desirable, whether he likes it or not. The Fourteenth Amendment does not enact Mr. Herbert Spencer's Social Statics. [We have upheld a number of laws that cut down on the liberty to contract.] Some of these laws embody convictions or prejudices which judges are likely to share. Some may not. But a constitution is not intended to embody a particular economic theory, whether of paternalism and the organic relation of the citizen to the State or of *laissez faire*. It is made for people of fundamentally differing views, and the accident of our finding certain opinions natural and familiar or novel and even shocking ought not to conclude our judgment upon the question whether statutes embodying them conflict with the Constitution of the United States.

General propositions do not decide concrete cases. The decision will depend on a judgment or intuition more subtle than any articulate major premise. But I think that the proposition just stated, if it is accepted, will carry us far toward the end. Every opinion tends to become a law. I think that the word liberty in the Fourteenth Amendment is perverted when it is held to prevent the natural outcome of a dominant opinion, unless it can be said that a rational and fair man necessarily would admit that the statute proposed would infringe fundamental principles as they have been understood by the traditions of our people and our law. It does not need research to show that no such sweeping condemnation can be passed upon the statute before us. A reasonable man might think it a proper measure on the score of health. Men whom I certainly could not pronounce unreasonable would uphold it as a first instalment of a general regulation of the hours of work. Whether in the latter aspect it would be open to the charge of inequality I think it unnecessary to discuss.

NOTES

1. *Early Wage and Hour Laws.* Laws regulating wages and hours have a long lineage in America, dating back to restrictions on *maximum* wages in the Massachusetts Bay Colony in 1630. Legislation setting maximum hours of work was in place in a number of states by the mid-nineteenth century, while minimum-wage legislation made its first appearance in this country after the turn of the twentieth century.

The first maximum-hours laws in the United States limited a day's work to ten hours. The early laws, however, all permitted the statutory limit on hours to be waived by contract, and none of the laws contained enforcement provisions. The language of the first act, the New Hampshire law, is illustrative:

> In all contracts for or relating to labor, ten hours of actual labor shall be taken to be a day's work, unless otherwise agreed by the parties; and no person shall be required or holden to perform more than ten

hours labor in any one day, except in pursuance of an express contract requiring a greater time.

NEW HAMPSHIRE LAWS, 1847, ch. 488, § 1.

Forty years later, when states began to enact non-waivable and enforceable limits on hours of work, the first rumblings of the *Lochner* era began to be felt. In 1891 in Nebraska, for example, the Populist legislature enacted a law that set the legal work day at eight hours, enforced by a provision that required employers to pay double the time paid for the previous hour for each hour worked over eight hours (that is, double time for the ninth hour, quadruple time for the tenth hour, and so on). In one of the first volleys of the *Lochner* era, the Nebraska Supreme Court held the statute to be unconstitutional. *Low v. Rees Printing Co.*, 59 N.W. 362 (Neb. 1894).

2. *The Effects and Demise of Lochner.* The *Lochner* era extended into the mid-1930s. The Supreme Court struck down nearly two hundred state statutes during that time. But *Lochner* was by no means a complete bar to state regulation — many statutes were also upheld. The Court regularly upheld statutes regulating the labor of women and children and hours of labor for employees in dangerous occupations. Thus, in *Muller v. Oregon*, 208 U.S. 412 (1908), the Court upheld a statute limiting the working hours of women, saying that it "is impossible to close one's eyes to the fact that she still looks to her brother and depends on him." *Id.* at 422. And the Court occasionally upheld other labor statutes. In *Bunting v. Oregon*, 243 U.S. 426 (1917), for example, the Court, without even mentioning *Lochner*, applied a deferential standard to uphold an Oregon statute that limited hours of work in manufacturing establishments to thirteen hours per day and that required premium pay for all work over ten hours. During the *Lochner* era, then, the courts engaged in probing inquiries into the bases of state regulation, but the results of the inquiries were by no means preordained.

The demise of *Lochner* resulted in a deferential standard. State statutes would almost always be upheld in the face of a challenge under the Due Process Clause:

> So far as the requirement of due process is concerned, and in the absence of other constitutional restriction, a state is free to adopt whatever economic policy may reasonably be deemed to promote public welfare, and to enforce that policy by legislation adapted to its purpose. The courts are without authority either to declare such policy, or, when it is declared by the legislature, to override it. If the laws are seen to have a reasonable relation to a proper legislative purpose, and are neither arbitrary nor discriminatory, the requirements of due process are satisfied. . . . With the wisdom of the policy adopted, with the adequacy or practicability of the law enacted to forward it, the courts are both incompetent and unauthorized to deal.

Nebbia v. New York, 291 U.S. 502, 537 (1934) (upholding a New York statute authorizing an agency to establish minimum milk prices).

JONATHAN GROSSMAN, FAIR LABOR STANDARDS ACT OF 1938: MAXIMUM STRUGGLE FOR A MINIMUM WAGE, 101 MONTHLY LABOR REVIEW 22, 22-29 (1978)

New Deal promise. In 1933, under the "New Deal" program, Roosevelt's advisers developed a National Industrial Recovery Act (NRA).[4] The act suspended antitrust laws so that industries could enforce fair-trade codes resulting in less competition and higher wages. On signing the bill, the President stated: "History will probably record the National Industrial Recovery Act as the most important and far-reaching legislation ever enacted by the American Congress." The law was popular, and one family in Darby, Penn., christened a newborn daughter Nira to honor it.

As an early step of the NRA, Roosevelt promulgated a President's Reemployment Agreement "to raise wages, create employment, and thus restore business." Employers signed more than 2.3 million agreements, covering 16.3 million employees. Signers agreed to a workweek between 35 and 40 hours and a minimum wage of $12 to $15 a week and undertook, with some exceptions, not to employ youths under 16 years of age. Employers who signed the agreement displayed a "badge of honor," a blue eagle over the motto "We do our part." Patriotic Americans were expected to buy only from "Blue Eagle" business concerns.

In the meantime, various industries developed more complete codes. The Cotton Textile Code was the first of these and one of the most important. It provided for a 40-hour workweek, set a minimum weekly wage of $13 in the North and $12 in the South, and abolished child labor. The President said this code made him "happier than any other one thing . . . since I have come to Washington, for the code abolished child labor in the textile industry." He added: "After years of fruitless effort and discussion, this ancient atrocity went out in a day."

A crushing blow. On "Black Monday," May 27, 1935, the Supreme Court disarmed the NRA as the major depression-fighting weapon of the New Deal. The 1935 case of [*A.L.A. Schechter Poultry Corp. v. United States*, 295 U.S. 495,] tested the constitutionality of the NRA by questioning a code to improve the sordid conditions under which chickens were slaughtered and sold to retail kosher butchers. All nine justices agreed that the act was an unconstitutional delegation of government power to private interests. Even the liberal Benjamin Cardozo thought it was "delegation running riot." Though the "sick chicken" decision seems an absurd case upon which to decide the fate of so sweeping a policy, it invalidated not only the restrictive trade practices set by the NRA-authorized codes, but the codes' progressive labor provisions as well.

As if to head off further attempts at labor reform, the Supreme Court, in a series of decisions, invalidated both State and Federal labor laws. Most notorious was the 1936 case of Joseph Tipaldo.[5] The manager of a Brooklyn,

---

[4] The proper initials for the Law are NIRA. The initials for the National Recovery Administration created by the act are NRA. Following a common practice, the initials NRA are used here for both the law and the administration.

[5] *Morehead v. Tipaldo*, 298 U.S. 587 (1936).

N.Y., laundry, Tipaldo had been paying nine laundry women only $10 a week, in violation of the New York State minimum wage law. When forced to pay his workers $14.88, Tipaldo coerced them to kick back the difference. When Tipaldo was jailed on charges of violating the State law, forgery, and conspiracy, his lawyers sought a writ of habeas corpus on grounds the New York law was unconstitutional. The Supreme Court, by a 5-to-4 majority, voided the law as a violation of liberty of contract.

The *Tipaldo* decision was among the most unpopular ever rendered by the Supreme Court. Even bitter foes of President Roosevelt and the New Deal criticized the Court. Ex-President Herbert Hoover said the Court had gone to extremes. Conservative Republican Congressman Hamilton Fish called it a "new Dred Scott decision" condemning 3 million women and children to economic slavery.

A switch in time. . . . When Roosevelt won the 1936 election by 523 electoral votes to 8, he interpreted his landslide victory as support for the New Deal and was determined to overcome the obstacle of Supreme Court opposition as soon as possible. In February 1937, he struck back at the "nine old men" of the Bench: He proposed to "pack" the Court by adding up to six extra judges, one for each judge who did not retire at age 70. Roosevelt further voiced his disappointment with the Court at the victory dinner for his second inauguration, saying if the "three-horse team [of the executive, legislative, and judicial branches] pulls as one, the field will be ploughed," but that "the field will not be ploughed if one horse lies down in the traces or plunges off in another direction."

However, Roosevelt's metaphorical maverick fell in step. On "White Monday," March 29, 1937, the Court reversed its course when it decided the case of *West Coast Hotel Company v. Parrish*[, 300 U.S. 379]. Elsie Parrish, a former chambermaid at the Cascadian Hotel in Wenatchee, Wash., sued for $216.19 in back wages, charging that the hotel had paid her less than the State minimum wage. In an unexpected turnaround, Justice Owen Roberts voted with the four-man liberal minority to uphold the Washington minimum wage law.

As other close decisions continued to validate social and economic legislation, support for Roosevelt's Court "reorganization" faded. Meanwhile, Justice Roberts felt called upon to deny that he had switched sides to ward off Roosevelt's court-packing plan. He claimed valid legal distinctions between the *Tipaldo* case and the *Parrish* case. Nevertheless, many historians subscribe to the contemporary view of Roberts' vote, that "a switch in time saved nine."

Back to the drawing board

Justice Roberts' "Big Switch" is an important event in American legal history. It is also a turning point in American social history, for it marked a new legal attitude toward labor standards. To be sure, validating a single State law was a far cry from upholding general Federal legislation, but the *Parrish* decision encouraged advocates of fair labor standards to work all the harder to develop a bill that might be upheld by the Supreme Court.

An ardent advocate. No top government official worked more ardently to develop legislation to help underpaid workers and exploited child laborers than Secretary of Labor Frances Perkins. Almost all her working life, Perkins fought for pro-labor legislation. . . .

When, in 1933, President Roosevelt asked Frances Perkins to become Secretary of Labor, she told him that she would accept if she could advocate a law to put a floor under wages and a ceiling over hours of work and to abolish abuses of child labor. When Roosevelt heartily agreed, Perkins asked him, "Have you considered that to launch such a program . . . might be considered unconstitutional?" Roosevelt retorted, "Well, we can work out something when the time comes."

During the constitutional crisis over the NRA, Secretary Perkins asked lawyers at the Department of Labor to draw up two wage-hour and child-labor bills which might survive Supreme Court review. She then told Roosevelt, "I have something up my sleeve. . . . I've got two bills . . . locked in the lower left-hand drawer of my desk against an emergency." Roosevelt laughed and said, "There's New England caution for you. . . . You're pretty unconstitutional, aren't you?"

Earlier Government groundwork. One of the bills that Perkins had "locked" in the bottom drawer of her desk was used before the 1937 "Big Switch." The bill proposed using the purchasing power of the Government as an instrument for improving labor standards. . . .

The Roosevelt-Perkins . . . initiative resulted in the Public Contracts Act of 1936 (Walsh-Healey)[, which] required most government contractors to adopt an 8-hour day and a 40-hour week, to employ only those over 16 years of age if they were boys or 18 years of age if they were girls, and to pay a "prevailing minimum wage" to be determined by the Secretary of Labor. . . . Though limited to government supply contracts and weakened by amendments and court interpretations, the Walsh-Healey Public Contracts Act was hailed as a token of good faith by the Federal Government — that it intended to lead the way to better pay and working conditions.

A broader bill is born

President Roosevelt had postponed action on a fair labor standards law because of his fight to "pack" the Court. After the "switch in time," when he felt the time was ripe, he asked Frances Perkins, "What happened to that nice unconstitutional bill you had tucked away?"

The bill — the second that Perkins had "tucked" away — was a general fair labor standards act. To cope with the danger of judicial review, Perkins' lawyers had taken several constitutional approaches so that, if one or two legal principles were invalidated, the bill might still be accepted. The bill provided for minimum-wage boards which would determine, after public hearing and consideration of cost-of-living figures from the Bureau of Labor Statistics, whether wages in particular industries were below subsistence levels. . . .

An early form of the bill being readied for Congress affected only wages and hours. To that version Roosevelt added a child-labor provision based on the political judgment that adding a clause banning goods in interstate commerce produced by children under 16 years of age would increase the chance of getting a wage-hour measure through both Houses, because child-labor limitations were popular in Congress.

Congress — round I

On May 24, 1937, President Roosevelt sent the bill to Congress with a message that America should be able to give "all our able-bodied working men and women a fair day's pay for a fair day's work." He continued: "A self-supporting and self-respecting democracy can plead no justification for the existence of child labor, no economic reason for chiseling workers' wages or stretching workers' hours." Though States had the right to set standards within their own borders, he said, goods produced under "conditions that do not meet rudimentary standards of decency should be regarded as contraband and ought not to be allowed to pollute the channels of interstate trade." He asked Congress to pass applicable legislation "at this session." . . .

Organized labor supported the bill but was split on how strong it should be. . . . William Green of the American Federation of Labor (AFL) and John L. Lewis of the Congress of Industrial Organizations (CIO), on one of the rare occasions when they agreed, both favored a bill which would limit labor standards to low-paid and essentially unorganized workers. Based on some past experiences, many union leaders feared that a minimum wage might become a maximum and that wage boards would intervene in areas which they wanted reserved for labor-management negotiations. They were satisfied when the bill was amended to exclude work covered by collective bargaining.

The weakened bill passed the Senate July 31, 1937, by a vote of 56 to 28 and would have easily passed the House if it had been put to a vote. But a coalition of Republicans and conservative Democrats bottled it up in the House Rules Committee. After a long hot summer, Congress adjourned without House action on fair labor standards.

Congress — round II

An angry President Roosevelt decided to press again for passage of the . . . bill. Having lost popularity and split the Democratic Party in his battle to "pack" the Supreme Court, Roosevelt felt that attacking abuses of child labor and sweatshop wages and hours was a popular cause that might reunite the party. A wage-hour, child-labor law promised to be a happy marriage of high idealism and practical politics.

On October 12, 1937, Roosevelt called a special session of Congress to convene on November 15. The public interest, he said, required immediate Congressional action: "The exploitation of child labor and the undercutting of wages and the stretching of the hours of the poorest paid workers in periods of business recession has a serious effect on buying power."

Despite White House and business pressure, the conservative alliance of Republicans and Southern Democrats that controlled the House Rules Committee refused to discharge the bill as it stood. Congresswoman Mary Norton of New Jersey, now chairing the House Labor Committee, made a valiant attempt to shake the bill loose. . . . [B]y December 2, the bill's supporters had rounded up enough signers to give the petition the 218 signatures necessary to bring the bill to a vote on the House floor.

With victory within grasp, the bill became a battleground in the war raging between the AFL and the CIO. The AFL accused the Roosevelt Administration of favoring industrial over craft unions and opposed wage-board determination of labor standards for specific industries. Accordingly, the AFL fought for a substitute bill with a flat 40-cent-an-hour minimum wage and a maximum 40-hour week.

In the ensuing confusion, shortly before the Christmas holiday of 1937, the House by a vote of 218 to 198 unexpectedly sent the bill back to the Labor Committee. In her memoir of President Roosevelt, Frances Perkins wrote:

> This was the first time that a major administration bill had been defeated on the floor of the House. The press took the view that this was the death knell of wage-hour legislation as well as a decisive blow to the President's prestige.

Roosevelt tries again

Again, Roosevelt returned to the fray. In his annual message to Congress on January 3, 1938, he said he was seeking "legislation to end starvation wages and intolerable hours." He paid deference to the South by saying that "no reasonable person seeks a complete uniformity in wages." He also made peace overtures to business by pointing out that he was forgoing "drastic" change, and he appeased organized labor, saying that "more desirable wages are and should continue to be the product of collective bargaining." . . .

Reworking the bill

In the meantime, Department of Labor lawyers worked on a new bill. Privately, Roosevelt had told Perkins that the length and complexity of the bill caused some of its difficulties. "Can't it be boiled down to two pages?" he asked. Lawyers trying to simplify the bill faced the problem that, although legal language makes legislation difficult to understand, bills written in simple English are often difficult for the courts to enforce. And because the wage-hour, child-labor bill had been drafted with the Supreme Court in mind, Solicitor of Labor Gerard Reilly could not meet the President's two-page goal; however, he succeeded in cutting the bill from 40 to 10 pages.

In late January 1938, Reilly and Perkins brought the revision to President Roosevelt. He approved it, and the new bill went to Congress. . . .

Norton appointed Representative Robert Ramspeck of Georgia to head a subcommittee to bridge the gap between various proposals. The subcommittee's efforts resulted in the Ramspeck compromise which Perkins felt "contained the bare essentials she could support." The compromise retained the 40-cent minimum hourly wage and the 40-hour maximum workweek. . . .

Congress — The final round

The House Labor Committee voted down the Ramspeck compromise, but, by a 10-to-4 vote, approved an even more "barebones" bill presented by Norton. Her bill, following the AFL proposal, provided for a 40-cent hourly minimum wage . . . .

Braving the floor battle

Proponents of the wage-hour, child-labor bill pressed the attack. They continued to point to "horror stories." One Congressman quoted a magazine article entitled "All Work and No Pay" which told how, in a company that paid wages in scrip for use in the company store, pay envelopes contained nothing for a full week's work after the deduction of store charges.

The most bitter controversy raged over labor standards in the South. "There are in the State of Georgia," one Indiana Congressman declaimed, "canning factories working . . . women 10 hours a day for $4.50 a week. Can the canning factories of Indiana and Connecticut or New York continue to exist and meet such competitive labor costs?" Southern Congressmen, in turn, challenged the Northern "monopolists" who hypocritically "loll on their tongues" words like "slave labor" and "sweatshops" and support bills which sentence Southern industry to death. Some Southern employers told the Department of Labor that they could not live with a 25-cent-an-hour minimum wage. They would have to fire all their people, they said. Adapting a biblical quotation, Representative John McClellan of Arkansas rhetorically asked, "What profiteth the laborer of the South if he gain the enactment of a wage and hour law — 40 cents per hour and 40 hours per week — if he then lose the opportunity to work?"

Partly because of Southern protests, provisions of the act were altered so that the minimum wage was reduced to 25 cents an hour for the first year of the act. Southerners gained additional concessions, such as a requirement that wage administrators consider lower costs of living and higher freight rates in the South before recommending wages above the minimum. . . .

The bill was voted upon May 24, 1938, with a 314-to-97 majority. After the House had passed the bill, the Senate-House Conference Committee made still more changes to reconcile differences. During the legislative battles over fair labor standards, members of Congress had proposed 72 amendments. Almost every change sought exemptions, narrowed coverage, lowered standards, weakened administration, limited investigation, or in some other way worked to weaken the bill.

The surviving proposal as approved by the conference committee finally passed the House on June [14], 1938, by a vote of 291 to 89. Shortly thereafter, the Senate approved it without a record of the votes. Congress then sent the bill to the President. On June 25, 1938, the President signed the Fair Labor Standards Act to become effective on October 24, 1938. . . .

The Fair Labor Standards Act of 1938 marked a turning point in American social policy. It substituted for the "rugged individualism" of an earlier era a social responsibility of the Federal Government toward American wage earners. Referring to the FLSA the night before signing the bill into law, President

Roosevelt declared that, "Except perhaps for the Social Security Act, it is the most far-reaching, the most far-sighted program for the benefit of workers ever adopted."

NOTES

1. *Regional Effects.* Grossman recounts regional differences in the reactions to the Fair Labor Standards Act proposals. On the ultimate vote in the House, representatives from former Confederate states provided 40% of the votes against the bill, but only 16% of the votes for the bill. Although the motivations were undoubtedly more complex, in broad terms, as the excerpt indicates, the North supported the bill to protect its industries from "unfair" low-wage competition, while the South opposed it because of fears that jobs would be lost.

These concerns are by no means outdated. Although the argument these days tends to revolve around free trade rather than minimum-wage levels, the United States in recent years has found itself on both sides of the debate. With average hourly wages in manufacturing of $17.86 in 2004, the United States has been both the low-wage competitor of countries such as Denmark ($30.17) and Germany ($25.10) and the high-wage competitor worried about job loss to countries such as Mexico ($2.23) and Sri Lanka ($0.44 in 2003). In some cases, American companies respond to competition by setting up their own factories overseas or south of the border, where wages and regulatory taxes are less onerous than if they employed American workers in the United States.

How is one to evaluate these conflicting concerns? Consider two arguments:

(a) *Labor Migration.* The wage differences between the North and the South result from imbalances in the supply of and demand for labor in the two regions. In the absence of a minimum wage, the two markets will balance out fairly quickly. The lower wages in the South will cause workers to leave for higher paying jobs elsewhere and will induce outside employers to enter the region in search of lower wage costs. Those two forces will increase wages in the South. In the North the opposite is occurring: Workers are arriving from the South and employers are leaving. Wages will go down. Eventually, labor and capital will end up where they can be most productive. A minimum wage law should not be enacted; it would only slow this natural correction process.

(b) *Social Costs and Lost Jobs.* Low-wage employers do not pay for all the costs of the labor they employ. They do not, for example, pay enough for adequate medical care, so either society must step in and pay or the workers must simply do without. Minimum-wage laws should be enacted to force employers to pay enough to cover all of these social costs; employers should not be permitted to externalize these costs to society or to workers. If some employers cannot bear these costs (if instead of raising wages to the new minimum, some employers go out of business and jobs are lost), society is better off without those jobs. They are jobs that were not valuable enough to bear all the costs of the workers needed to perform them. Society benefits when the capital of these employers is redirected to support more productive enterprises.

2. Union Attitudes. The attitude of unions to the Fair Labor Standards Act is not without its own complexities. On the one hand, a minimum-wage law should make it more difficult for unions to organize low-paid workers. The law provides these workers with a wage increase without the need to pay any union dues. On the other hand, a minimum-wage law might make it easier for unions to negotiate higher wages for the employees it already represents. Employers with whom the unions are negotiating should be less resistant to wage increases if they know that their non-union competitors have to pay at least the minimum wage. Why do you think the AFL was concerned about wage boards that would determine labor standards by industry?

B. THE FAIR LABOR STANDARDS ACT

More than a half century after its initial enactment, and after numerous amendments, the Fair Labor Standards Act (FLSA) is still the centerpiece of this country's wage and hour laws. The Act has three principal substantive obligations. First, it establishes a minimum wage. The current minimum wage is $5.15 per hour, although a lower subminimum wage of $4.25 per hour can be paid to some workers. Second, the Act requires premium pay for overtime work — work over forty hours in any week must be paid at a rate one-and-one-half times the regular rate of pay. And third, the Act restricts the ability of employers to employ children. Although exceptions exist, as a general matter, employers may not hire children at all until they are fourteen years old, and various restrictions are placed on their employment until they are eighteen years old.[*]

This section will begin by discussing each of these substantive obligations. The minimum wage, maximum hour, and child labor provisions of the FLSA are each intended to pursue broad social objectives, so for each we will talk first about what those objectives are, how the Act is structured to address them, and the promise and limitations of the FLSA in achieving them. Then we will talk about the difficult implementation problems raised by the obligations in practice.

We will then discuss the coverage of the FLSA. In common with most of the laws we discuss in this book, the FLSA applies only when there is an employer-employee relationship. Even when there is an employer-employee relationship, however, the FLSA does not cover all employers, nor does it cover all of the employees of covered employers. We will discuss issues raised by these additional coverage limitations. Throughout we focus on policy issues: Why is coverage limited? Why not cover all employers and employees? What are the consequences of limited coverage?

---

[*] The Fair Labor Standards Act also requires equal pay for men and women performing the same work. That important substantive obligation, incorporated into the FLSA by the Equal Pay Act of 1963, is better viewed as a non-discrimination obligation than as a wage-and-hour requirement.

1. SUBSTANTIVE OBLIGATIONS OF THE FLSA

a. Minimum Wages

The minimum wage today is no longer a living wage. . . . [It must be increased] if we are to succeed in our national efforts to encourage the poor, the disadvantaged, the young, and the unemployed to achieve a larger measure of self reliance. The reward of fair wages for a job well done is the foundation upon which this nation has built its fortune.

—H.R. REP. NO. 101-260, 101st Cong., 1st Sess. 14-15 (1989)

A [$20.00] industrial minimum wage would go a long way toward perpetuating the family farm.

—ROBERT EVENSON, ORAL TRADITION *

The minimum-wage provisions of the FLSA are intended to address the problems of poverty faced by the working poor, to ensure that they can earn a wage that will allow them to live a decent life. The difficulty is that a minimum wage may also mean that some working poor will lose their jobs and be forced back onto the family farm, or worse. In this section, we will first describe the minimum-wage provisions of the FLSA and then evaluate them by considering both the people who might be helped by the laws and the people who might be hurt.

The minimum wage, as its name implies, sets a level below which wages cannot fall. The minimum wage in nominal terms has gradually increased over time, from 25 cents an hour when the Act was first enacted in 1938 to $5.15 an hour today. In *real* terms, however, the minimum has gone up and down. Generally, it has been between 45% and 55% of the average hourly earnings in manufacturing. When the minimum wage has reached the low end of the range in real terms, Congress has amended the Act to increase the minimum. As of 2006, the real level of the minimum wage is at its all-time low — 31% of average hourly earnings for private sector nonsupervisory workers.

The $5.15 per hour minimum wage does not apply to all workers. Some workers are not covered by the minimum-wage provisions of the Act. (We will discuss coverage of the FLSA later in this chapter.) When it was first enacted, the minimum-wage provisions of the FLSA covered about 43% of nonsupervisory employees; today they cover about 88%. In addition, the Act permits workers under twenty years old to be paid a subminimum wage of $4.25 per hour for their first ninety days of employment.

The percentage of workers that actually receives the minimum wage has declined over time. In 1979, 13.4 percent of all wage and salary workers were paid at or below the federal minimum wage, whereas in 2004 the figure was only 2.7 percent. BUREAU OF LABOR STATISTICS, CHARACTERISTICS OF MINI-MUM WAGE WORKERS: 2004, tbl. 10 (2005).

To begin our evaluation of the minimum wage, consider Figure 16-1, which presents a model of the labor market for unskilled workers. Because the

---

* Cited in Finis Welch, *Minimum Wage Legislation in the United States, in* EVALUATING THE LABOR-MARKET EFFECTS OF SOCIAL PROGRAMS 1 (Orley Ashenfelter & James Blum eds., 1976) (the amount of the minimum wage has been increased to correct for inflation).

minimum-wage provisions of the FLSA do not cover all employees, the market is divided into two sectors, one covered by a minimum-wage law and one not covered. Employees can move back and forth between the sectors seeking higher wages. In the absence of a minimum-wage law, wages and employment would be at equilibrium, W_E and E_E respectively. Wages should be about the same in both sectors; otherwise, employees would shift from the lower-paying sector to the other.

Figure 16-1. The Effects of a Minimum Wage Law

(a) Covered Sector   **(b) Uncovered Sector**

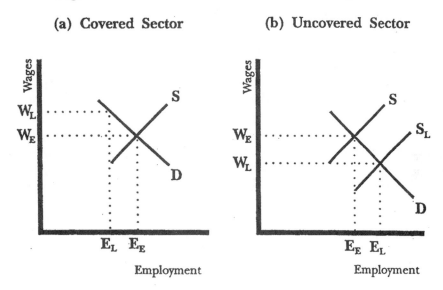

Employment   Employment

Now assume the existence of a minimum wage of W_L in the covered sector. To have any effect, the minimum wage must be higher than the equilibrium wage. If it were lower, employers would continue to pay the equilibrium wage and no one would benefit from the law or be hurt by it — the law would simply be irrelevant. As illustrated by Figure 16-1(a), higher wages in the covered sector will have one of two effects on workers in that sector. First, they may keep their jobs and earn the higher wages or, second, because the higher wages result in less demand for workers, they may lose their jobs.

Workers who lose their jobs in the covered sector would have some options. First, they could move to the uncovered sector. As Figure 16-1(b) illustrates, that would mean that the supply of workers to that sector would increase (the new supply curve is S_L). As a result, the number of jobs in the uncovered sector would increase, but the wages would be lower than they would have been in the absence of a minimum-wage law. Second, workers who lose their jobs in the covered sector could decide to wait for a job opening to occur in the higher-paying covered sector. That would mean that the unemployment rate would increase. Or third, workers could drop out of the labor market and do other things. They might, for example, return to school.

In theory, then, the minimum-wage provisions of the FLSA help some people and hurt others. The people who are helped directly are the workers in the covered sector who keep their jobs and, as a result, earn higher wages. The people who are hurt are the workers who lose their jobs in the covered sector. They may take jobs in the uncovered sector that pay lower wages because of the minimum wage, suffer periods of unemployment, or be forced to pursue activities outside of the labor market that they would not pursue otherwise. The minimum wage would also help and hurt other workers more indirectly. The minimum wage, for example, might help a worker who would earn slightly more than the minimum wage even without a law. A minimum wage is likely to have a ripple effect which would increase her wages a bit to maintain a differential between her wages and the wages of minimum wage workers. It might also help a worker who responds to losing her job by returning to school or obtaining other training because she should then earn more when she re-enters the labor market. Similarly, the minimum wage may hurt other workers indirectly. Workers in the uncovered sector when the minimum wage law is enacted, for example, will find their real wages lowered because of the increased supply of workers to the sector.

Given these types of possible gains and losses, how does one evaluate the minimum wage provisions of the FLSA? One approach is simply to attempt to add up the gains and losses and see which is greater. The Congressional Budget Office (CBO) did that for one of the proposals that eventually resulted in the 1989 amendments to the FLSA. It determined that the proposal would help low-wage workers because the extra earnings received by those who would receive higher wages would exceed the losses caused by lower employment. *Minimum Wage Legislation,* 68 Cong. Dig. 131, 135 (1989).

The CBO approach, however, does not do a very good job of evaluating the effectiveness of the minimum wage as an aid to the working poor. To do that, we would want to know more about who was helped and who was hurt. Consider two possible minimum wage workers: (1) the teenage son of one of your professors working part-time at a fast-food restaurant, and (2) a single mother of three working full-time as a salesperson. If all of the workers who are helped by the minimum wage fall into the first category and all who are hurt fall into the second, we might reject the minimum wage as appropriate public policy even if the CBO conclusions about the effect of the minimum wage overall were correct. If the reverse were true, we might favor the minimum wage even if the losses overall were greater than the gains.

The real world, as usual, does not present clear choices. On the overall balance of gains and losses, some economists believe that modest increases in the minimum wage may not result in any employment losses at all or, indeed, may actually increase employment. David Card & Alan B. Krueger, Myth and Measurement: The New Economics of the Minimum Wage (1995). If this is true, the overall balance of gains and losses would support a minimum wage and we should seriously re-evaluate the standard economic model that predicts employment losses. This is a controversial view, however. Most economists still believe that the minimum wage produces employment losses consistent with the standard model, although with sharp disagreement about the magnitude and distribution of the losses. For a good review of the issues, see Daniel Shaviro, *The Minimum Wage, the Earned Income Tax Credit, and Optimal Subsidy Policy,* 64 U. Chi. L. Rev. 405 (1997).

On the issue of who is helped, the minimum wage is a fairly blunt anti-poverty instrument: Most of the people who are helped by the law are not poor. According to analysis of public survey data by opponents of minimum wage increases, in 2003, only 17% of low-wage workers were living in poor households. A major reason for this was that most minimum-wage workers lived in households that contained other workers. Perhaps even more significantly, approximately 79% of people living in poverty are not in the workforce, and 23% of poor families have no working members. RICHARD V. BURKHAUSER & JOSEPH J. SABIA, EMPLOYMENT POLICIES INSTITUTE, RAISING THE MINIMUM WAGE, ANOTHER EMPTY PROMISE TO THE WORKING POOR (2005), *available at* www.epionline.org/studies/burkhauser_08-2005.pdf; BUREAU OF LABOR STATISTICS, U.S. DEP'T OF LABOR, REPORT NO. 994, A PROFILE OF THE WORKING POOR, 2004 (2006). Even proponents of the minimum wage acknowledge that increases have only a modest positive effect on overall poverty rates, if any. CARD & KRUEGER, *supra*, at 305-07. Nevertheless, this modest help to the poor may well be justified if the minimum wage does no harm. But, as indicated above, the extent and distribution of employment losses are still very contested issues.

NOTES

1. *The Youth Subminimum Wage.* The youth subminimum wage responds to the adverse employment effects of the minimum wage on young workers. Young workers, since they are the least skilled even in the pool of low-wage workers, bear a disproportionate share of any job losses resulting from increases in the minimum wage. Many economists offer estimates on the decline of teenage employment relative to minimum wage. An opinion survey of labor economists in 1996 produced the median estimate of a one percent decrease in teenage employment for every ten percent increase in the median wage. Victor R. Fuchs et al., *Economists' Views about Parameters, Values, and Policies: Survey Results in Labor and Public Economics*, 36 J. ECON. LIT. 1387 (1998). The subminimum wage, which can be paid only to workers under twenty years of age, should ease those effects to some extent. But consider:

> One of the goals of the minimum wage is to reduce youth employment. The youth subminimum wage interferes with that goal and, as a result, is bad public policy for two reasons. First, the subminimum wage will mean that teenage workers will get jobs that otherwise would go to adults. Since only 13% of teenage minimum-wage workers are poor, compared with 22% of adult minimum-wage workers, the subminimum wage blunts even more the ability of the minimum wage to reduce poverty. Second, the subminimum wage means that more youth will get low-paying jobs that provide relatively poor training. That is something we should discourage, not encourage. Teenagers would be better off going to school to train for better jobs, and they *do* go to school when increases in the minimum wage limit their ability to get jobs.

Is this argument countered by Section 206(g)(2) of the FLSA which prohibits employers from displacing other workers in favor of those eligible for the subminimum wage?

2. *Reductions in Employment.* A uniform national minimum wage is unlikely to have the same effects across the country:

> [I]n the long run some of the reduction in employment may result from a reduction in the number of firms in the market rather than from changes in the number of workers employed by each firm. Such cases might occur where the firms in question competed in the product market with firms in other labor markets paying wages higher than [the minimum wage] for superior labor. The minimum wage would then raise wages in the low-wage market without improving the quality of its labor. If the firms in question had been competing on even terms before the minimum-wage law, they would now be at a disadvantage and might have to move out of the local labor market or go out of business.

DANIEL S. HAMERMESH & ALBERT REES, THE ECONOMICS OF WORK AND PAY 105-06 (3d ed. 1984). Thus, a minimum wage might cause employment losses in one area of the country, while another area of the country was experiencing gains.

3. *Another Look at Reductions in Employment.* Wages are only one part of an employee's compensation package. In return for their work, employees might also receive a variety of fringe benefits (such as health insurance or contributions to a pension plan) or valuable on-the-job training. Employment losses would be minimized if employers responded to increases in the minimum wage by reducing other parts of the compensation package. If this occurs, and some researchers have found that it does, should legislatures be more hesitant to pass minimum wage laws?

Or perhaps we should not be concerned about employment losses at all:

> [B]y downplaying the number of jobs destroyed by a statutory minimum wage, proponents unwittingly undermine the most cogent grounds for supporting it — namely, that the jobs it destroys are low-wage and unproductive. . . . Thus the appropriate response to the argument that the minimum wage hurts the very people it is supposed to protect is: the minimum wage helps those marginal workers by forcing their inefficient employers either to rationalize or to be driven out of business by more efficient competitors paying higher wages.

Marc Linder, *The Minimum Wage as Industrial Policy: A Forgotten Role,* 16 J. LEGIS. 151, 155-56 (1990).

4. *Alternatives to the Minimum Wage.* If minimum wages are such a blunt anti-poverty tool, should we try something else? Consider these alternatives:

Wage Subsidies. Wage subsidies would be a direct way to increase wages. Heads of low-wage families, for example, might be entitled to a pay subsidy from the government that would be equal to half the difference between their actual wage and a decent wage, say eight dollars per hour. Thus, someone who was earning six dollars per hour would get a wage subsidy of one dollar per hour. "In principle, a wage subsidy could be an ideal tool. It could be carefully targeted to just those persons in families who need their wages boosted. It would increase the rewards of work and, if anything, it would increase employment, rather than diminish it, as raising the minimum wage could do." DAVID ELLWOOD, POOR SUPPORT: POVERTY IN THE AMERICAN FAMILY 113 (1988).

The Earned Income Tax Credit (EITC). Under the EITC, individuals with low earnings receive tax credits for each dollar they earn. If the tax credits exceed tax liability, the credits are treated as overpayments so they can be received in cash as a refund. Under current law, the tax credit can be as high as $3,556 — an individual with two or more children may receive a 40% tax credit on earnings up to $8,890. At higher income levels, the tax credit phases out — for the individual with two children, the credit is reduced by 21 cents for every dollar earned over $11,610 so that it is completely phased out when the individual earns $28,495. (These amounts vary depending on family size; amounts are indexed for inflation.) I.R.C. § 32. The EITC could be expanded to do more, for example, by making it more generous for individuals without children (the maximum credit for these individuals is $323), by increasing the earnings on which the credit is paid, or by slowing the phase-out.

> The EITC helps the working poor while mainly avoiding the conun-
> drums. The rewards of work are increased, not diminished. Benefits
> go only to those with an earned income. . . . And employers would
> have no reason to change their hiring practices. . . . Moreover, the
> EITC [can] be adjusted to vary according to the size of a family so that
> the biggest raise in pay would go to families with the most children
> and the greatest need.

Id. at 115-116. *See also* Daniel Shaviro, *The Minimum Wage, the Earned Income Tax Credit, and Optimal Subsidy Policy*, 64 U. CHI. L. REV. 405 (1997) (arguing that the EITC is much better than the minimum wage for both progressive redistribution and encouraging workforce participation among the poor). *But see* Anne L. Alstott, *Work vs. Freedom: A Liberal Challenge to Employment Subsidies*, 108 YALE L.J. 967 (1999) (unconditional cash grants to the poor would be even better: easier to administer, less chance that employers would capture benefits, more freedom for the poor).

With these advantages over the minimum wage, why do you think these alternatives are less central to governmental policy on low-wage workers? *See* THE WHITE HOUSE, *Budget of the United States Government, FY 2007*, Table 25-413 (2006) (in FY 2005, the EITC cost the federal government over $35 billion, and is projected to pass $40 billion by 2011).

5. *Other Federal Wage Statutes.* Although the Fair Labor Standards Act is the most important federal wage statute, a number of other laws impose minimum-wage obligations on entities that are performing work for the federal government. The most important of these other laws are the Davis-Bacon Act, 40 U.S.C. §§ 3141-44, 3146, 3147, which applies to contracts in excess of $2,000 for work on federal buildings or other public works; the Walsh-Healey Public Contracts Act, 41 U.S.C. §§ 35-45, which applies to employers that provide materials, supplies, and equipment to the United States under contracts exceeding $10,000; and the Service Contract Act, 41 U.S.C. §§ 351-358, which applies to contracts in excess of $2,500 to provide services to the federal government. These statutes all require contracting entities to pay workers at least the prevailing wage in the locality.

b. Premium Pay for Overtime Hours

Remember, the long struggle for the 8-hour day was not a struggle for 8 hours of work. It was a struggle for 16 hours away from work.

—Maurice Sugar, General Counsel, UAW[*]

Because most factory workers are working . . . longer hours, they have been able to maintain their spendable earnings and to save.

—N. Arnold Tolles, Bureau of Labor Statistics[**]

The FLSA requires employers to pay premium pay when employees work more than forty hours in any workweek. Employers are required to pay for overtime hours at a rate one-and-one-half times the "regular" rate of pay. (Problems with determining the regular rate of pay, and hence the overtime rate, will be discussed later.) The FLSA does not limit the number of hours adult employees can work — it only requires that they be paid at a higher rate if they work more than forty hours per week.

The overtime provisions of the FLSA were primarily intended to spread work: to reduce unemployment by encouraging employers to hire more workers, rather than to add hours, when they need additional labor. Secondarily, the provisions were intended to protect individual employees from employers who might require them to work unreasonably long hours or, at least, to compensate employees for the burdens of the long hours.

Consider the work-spreading argument first. Say that an employer has forty employees and needs forty extra hours to be worked each week. The employer needs to decide whether to have each of its forty current employees work an extra hour each week or whether it should hire an additional worker. Because of the overtime provisions of the FLSA, the employer would have to pay its current employees one-and-one-half times their regular rate of pay for the extra forty hours. An additional worker could be paid at the regular rate. Thus, the premium-pay requirement should result in an extra employee being hired more often than would occur without the requirement.

So why do employers *ever* have employees work overtime? The principal answer is that even though employers can pay a new employee less for the extra hours, the new employee may be more expensive overall. An employer would have to advertise for, hire, and train a new employee and may incur extra expenses for benefits such as health insurance. If current employees did the work, they obviously would not have to be hired again and their health-insurance costs would not go up. Indeed, many of the costs of employees are quasi-fixed in this sense — once an employee is hired they do not increase as the number of hours worked increases. An employer may have employees work overtime because the quasi-fixed costs of hiring a new employee are greater than the amount of the wage premium that needs to be paid to current employees.

---

[*] *The Truth About "Portal to Portal,"* 7 LAW. GUILD REV. 23, 35 (1947).

[**] *Spendable Earnings of Factory Workers, 1941-43,* 58 MONTHLY LAB. REV. 477, 478 (1944).

Is the overtime premium effective at spreading work? As usual, it is hard to tell. Say that because of the overtime premium, an employer hires a new employee to do additional work rather than having current employees work overtime. At first glance, this would seem to further the work-spreading goal of the FLSA. But if the new employee was a moonlighter, the goal would not be furthered. Instead of spreading work, the overtime premium would mean only that employees work long hours for two or more employers rather than for a single employer.

The work-spreading goal may also be frustrated in another way. The overtime premium encourages work-spreading by increasing the cost of overtime. The goal is furthered when employers, because of the extra cost of overtime, decide to hire additional employees instead. But employers have other common responses when the cost of labor increases. They may reduce the hourly wage of workers who work overtime in order to offset the premium. *See* Stephen J. Trejo, *Does the Statutory Overtime Premium Discourage Long Workweeks?* 56 INDUS. & LAB. REL. REV. 530 (2003) (reporting data consistent with this phenomenon). They may decide to spend money on labor-saving machines so they do not need the additional hours *or* the additional workers. Or they may decide that at the increased cost, the additional labor simply is not justified. To the extent employers respond to the increased cost of overtime in these ways, the overtime premium would not spread work very well: less work would exist to spread. *Cf.* Dora L. Costa, *Hours of Work and the Fair Labor Standards Act: A Study of Retail and Wholesale Trade, 1938-1950,* 53 INDUS. & LAB. REL. REV. 648 (2000) (FLSA reduced the standard work week by 5% and the proportion of workers working more than 40 hours per week by 18%, but did not result in any increased employment).

The overtime provisions of the FLSA also are intended to protect the leisure time of workers, to encourage employers to allow them sixteen hours away from work each day. But some workers, obviously, might prefer to work more than forty hours per week, even at straight-time rates, especially during economic periods when real wage levels are not increasing and they must increase their hours to increase their earnings. Why limit the ability of these workers to work the number of hours they would prefer?

One response is that the FLSA is necessary to protect the health of workers. In the absence of the FLSA, workers may injure their health by agreeing to work too many hours. Workers may work too much because they do not have full information about the long-term health consequences of working long hours. Even if they had that information, they would work too much if they discounted the future too much. That is, they may be too willing to sacrifice future health and productivity for current income. And even if they had full information and discounted the future properly, they may work too much because many of the costs of bad health can be externalized. The state will absorb much of the cost of poor health, both by subsidizing health care and by subsidizing disabled workers. Thus, the FLSA may be necessary to correct for these types of market failures.

NOTES

1. *Changes in Quasi-Fixed Costs.* In the last three decades, fringe benefits have approximately doubled as a proportion of total compensation. Many of these costs (such as the costs for health insurance) are quasi-fixed in the sense that they are per-employee costs that do not increase as hours of work increase. Thus, the FLSA is probably not as effective in spreading work today as it was before the relative increases in quasi-fixed costs: One-and-one-half times the regular rate of pay is a lower proportion of total compensation today than it was three decades ago. Proposals have been made periodically in Congress to address this problem by increasing the premium for overtime work to double the regular rate of pay.

2. *The History of Hours and Overtime Premiums.* During the *Lochner* era, legislation that attempted to limit the number of working hours for broad categories of workers was generally struck down as unconstitutional. Nevertheless, during that time, the hours actually worked by employees went down dramatically, from an average of fifty-nine hours per week in 1900, to fifty hours per week before the onset of the depression, to thirty-eight hours per week in 1937 shortly before the FLSA was enacted. DAVID R. ROEDIGER & PHILLIP S. FONER, OUR OWN TIME: A HISTORY OF AMERICAN LABOR AND THE WORKING DAY x (1989). Similarly, many employers offered overtime premiums during the 1920s without any statutory mandate. Does this information mean that the FLSA was unnecessary because the labor market was capable of achieving the goals of the FLSA on its own?

3. *Dual-Earner Families and the "Time Crunch."* Although there has been a long-term reduction overall in hours of work, women's market work has increased over the past 100 years as they have joined the paid workforce. The rise of dual-earner families has given rise to a new concern: that the demands of market work compete with time previously devoted to families and communities. Many workers report that pressure to earn more money or satisfy their employer leads them to spend more time on market work, at the expense of family time, than they would like. Some scholars argue that we ought to reduce the standard 40-hour workweek as a way to moderate this "time crunch" phenomenon. *See e.g.*, Vicki Schultz & Allison Hoffman, *The Need for a Reduced Workweek in the United States*, *in* PRECARIOUS WORK, WOMEN AND THE NEW ECONOMY: THE CHALLENGE TO LEGAL NORMS 131-51 (Judy Fudge & Rosemary Owens eds., 2006).

4. *Long Hours and Earnings Inequality.* When the FLSA limits long hours, it may increase earnings inequality. Because of the exemption for executive, administrative, and professional employees, the FLSA often does not apply to the highest-paid workers. Therefore, their hours are not restricted by the overtime premium requirement. But the FLSA does restrict hours of the lowest-paid workers. Thus, the FLSA tends to magnify earnings inequality: workers with higher wages to begin with can also work more hours. Between 1973 and 1991, 26% of the increase in earnings inequality for men, and *all* of the increase for women, can be explained by changes in hours worked. Dora L. Costa, *The Wage and the Length of the Work Day: From the 1890s to 1991*, 18 J. LAB. ECON. 156 (2000).

Think about it also from the other direction: the effect of earnings inequality on the incentive to work long hours. In the United States, someone working long hours may move up in a very wide wage distribution and avoid a layoff with meager unemployment benefits and loss of health insurance. In Germany, by contrast, the wage distribution is much narrower, unemployment benefits better, and health insurance guaranteed. Thus, even though Americans already work more hours than Germans, they are also more likely to want to work even more hours. Earnings inequality means greater rewards for those longer hours. So without a reduction in earnings inequality, Americans are likely to remain workaholics compared to Germans. Linda Bell & Richard Freeman, *The Incentive for Working Hard: Explaining Hours Worked Differences in the U.S. & Germany*, 8 LAB. ECON. 181 (2001). The overtime provisions of the FLSA struggle against this high demand for long hours.

c. Restrictions on the Use of Child Labor

Stooped over a row of squash, . . . Alfedo Diaz, aged fourteen, is helping his parents bring in the last of an October harvest they have "sharecropped" for a local grower. The pickings are slim. Together, they hope to earn $50 this day. In adjoining patches of squash, other families are working too. Soon they will all move to winter strawberries.

"I don't think I'll be able to return to school until the strawberries are in," Alfedo says, not stopping to look up. "Maybe then, in a month or so." In truth, he hasn't been to school for eight months. Likely he will never go back. His parents, Jesus and Clementina, are in their late fifties and say they need him to work. "We are too old to work alone," Diaz says, watching his son. "We cannot make the money we need to live if we do not have help."

—THE BOSTON GLOBE, April 22, 1990

The FLSA limits the use of "oppressive" child labor. What is oppressive under the Act and Department of Labor regulations depends on the age of the child. First, it is oppressive to employ children under age fourteen at all, unless they fall within one of a few, narrow exceptions. Children as young as ten, however, can work under the exceptions. Second, children who are fourteen and fifteen years old may work, but there are limits both on the types of occupations in which they can engage and in the number of hours they can work. When school is in session, these children can work no more than three hours per day and no more than eighteen hours per week. When school is not in session, they can work up to eight hours per day and forty hours per week. The work must be performed between 7 a.m. and 7 p.m., except in the summer (June 1 to Labor Day) when evening work can extend to 9 p.m. Third, children who are sixteen and seventeen years old may work under the same FLSA minimum-wage and maximum-hour conditions as adults, except that they are prohibited from working in occupations that have been determined to be hazardous by the Secretary of Labor. To date, the Secretary has found seventeen occupations to be hazardous. At eighteen years of age, employees are regarded as adults under the FLSA.

The child-labor provisions of the FLSA, obviously, are intended in part to protect the interests of children. Portions of the FLSA (most predominantly the prohibition on work in hazardous occupations) are intended to protect the physical safety of children. Prior to the FLSA, there was certainly cause for concern:

> It is a sorry but indisputable fact that where children are employed, the most unhealthful work is generally given them. In . . . cotton and woolen mills, where large number of children are employed, clouds of lint-dust fill the lungs and menace the health. . . . In bottle factories . . . the atmosphere is constantly charged with microscopic particles of glass. In the wood-working industries . . . the air is laden with fine sawdust. Children employed in soap and soap-powder factories work, many of them, in clouds of alkaline dust which inflames the eyelids and nostrils. . . . In the coal-mines the breaker boys breathe air that is heavy and thick with particles of coal, and their lungs become black in consequence. In the manufacture of felt hats, little girls are often employed at the machines which tear the fur from the skins of rabbits and other animals. Recently, I stood and watched a young girl working at such a machine; she wore a newspaper pinned over her head and a handkerchief tied over her mouth. She was white with dust from head to feet, and when she stooped to pick anything from the floor the dust would fall from her paper headcovering in little heaps. About seven feet from the mouth of the machine was a window through which poured thick volumes of dust as it was belched out from the machine. I placed a sheet of paper on the inner sill of the window and in twenty minutes it was covered with a layer of fine dust, half an inch deep. Yet that girl works midway between the window and the machine, in the very centre of the volume of dust, sixty hours a week. These are a few of the occupations in which the dangers arise from the forced inhalation of dust.

JOHN SPARGO, THE BITTER CRY OF THE CHILDREN 175-80 (1907).

Today, the FLSA's importance and effectiveness in protecting the physical safety of children is less clear. The Occupational Safety and Health Act and related safety laws (which will be discussed later in this volume) have made work safer for *all* workers, so the need for special protection for young workers has declined. Moreover, the FLSA's effectiveness in protecting children who are at risk of physical injury is questionable. Over 90% of FLSA child-labor violations are in the trade and service industries, among the safest of the eight major industrial groups, while agriculture, one of the most dangerous industries, especially for children, is largely unregulated by the Act.[*] *See* 29 U.S.C. § 213(c).

The child-labor provisions of the FLSA are also intended to protect the interests of children by promoting education. The rationale is that if their work opportunities are limited, children will be more likely to attend and do well in school. Once again, this was unquestionably a forceful rationale in the first half of the twentieth century when child factory workers generally did not

---

[*] In 2003, the death rates per 100,000 workers for the eight major industrial groups were mining and quarrying (22.3), agriculture (20.9), construction (11.4), transportation and utilities (10.0), manufacturing (2.8), government (2.0), trade (1.3), and services (1.1). NATIONAL SAFETY COUNCIL, INJURY FACTS 48 (2006). That year, agriculture, with 1.5 percent of the workforce, accounted for 60 percent of the workplace deaths of youths under 16 years old. *Id.* at 67, 71.

go to school at all and, as a result, were three to four times more likely to be illiterate than other children. Alexander J. McKelway, *The Needs of the Cotton Mill Operatives, in* CHILDREN AND YOUTH IN AMERICA, Vol. II, at 659-61 (Robert Bremner ed., 1971). But is it still a forceful rationale today? Modern research indicates that a potential conflict between work and education still exists, but its nature has changed. Today, children who work usually go to school, too. But children who work a lot (twenty hours per week or more) tend to earn lower grades, cheat more frequently, skip school more often, and use drugs and alcohol more frequently. LAURENCE STEINBERG, BEYOND THE CLASSROOM: WHY SCHOOL REFORM HAS FAILED AND WHAT PARENTS NEED TO DO 163-73 (1996). About half of all high-school seniors who work, and about one-third of all juniors who work, spend more than twenty hours per week on the job. *Id.* at 170. Thus, while the issue is still relevant, the ability of the FLSA to address current problems created by potential conflicts between work and school is suspect.

Finally, the child-labor restrictions are intended to protect the interests of adults. By limiting the supply of workers, the FLSA should increase the pay of adults and may increase the number of jobs available to them.

NOTES

1. ***The History of Federal Child-Labor Legislation.*** Early attempts to deal with child labor at the federal level were not able to survive the searching judicial inquiries of the *Lochner* era. The Child Labor Act of 1916, 39 Stat. 675, would have prevented interstate commerce in the products of child labor, but it was ruled unconstitutional by the Supreme Court in *Hammer v. Dagenhart*, 247 U.S. 251 (1918), because it intruded too deeply into a matter reserved for state and local control. Congress tried again by imposing a 10% tax on all products of child labor, Child Labor Tax Act, 40 Stat. 1148 (1918), but the Supreme Court struck that statute down, too, holding that it exceeded the federal taxing power. *Child Labor Tax Case*, 259 U.S. 20 (1922). Congress then approved and submitted to the states a constitutional amendment which would have authorized it to regulate child labor, 43 Stat. 670 (1924), but the proposal met with resounding disapproval by the states. The roadblock to federal legislation was removed with the demise of *Lochner*. In *United States v. Darby*, 312 U.S. 100 (1941), the Supreme Court upheld the constitutionality of the Fair Labor Standards Act, expressly overruling *Hammer v. Dagenhart* in the process.

2. ***Child Labor and Free Trade.*** Child labor is an international issue. The International Labor Organization estimates that 120 million children world-wide work full-time, with at least 40 million of them working in hazardous conditions. Free-trade agreements, such as the General Agreement on Tariffs and Trade (GATT), ensure that the products of this labor can flow easily to markets world-wide. Concern that free trade will lead to a race to the bottom, undermining "core" labor standards, such as restrictions on child labor, is a major issue in international trade.

The United States has attempted to have international trade organizations, such as the World Trade Organization (WTO), study the relationship between trade and core labor standards. *See* 19 U.S.C. § 3551 (President required to seek establishment of a working party in the WTO to examine worker rights). The United States' efforts to date, however, have been largely unsuccessful. Many other countries view these initiatives skeptically. They suspect that the initiatives may be intended primarily to protect U.S. workers from competition, rather than foreign children from exploitation, and they fear that, if implemented, the initiatives would compromise the principal comparative advantage of developing countries: low-wage labor.

3. *Are Child-Labor Laws Necessary at All?* Consider the following argument:

> The child-labor laws are superfluous. Everything that they try to accomplish is already covered by other laws. They try to protect the physical safety of children, encourage them to go to school, and protect the jobs and wages of adults. But all of those purposes are already adequately dealt with through safety and health laws, compulsory-education laws, and minimum-wage laws. But the child-labor laws are worse than superfluous. They also interfere with the good judgment of parents in raising their children. Parents know best whether their children can do better by going to school or working, or combining the two in some way, but child-labor laws limit the options available to parents and their children.

Convinced?

d.   Problems With Implementing the Substantive Obligations

Implementation of the minimum-wage and maximum-hour provisions of the FLSA requires two basic types of information: wages and hours. How much does the employee make and how many hours does she work? When employers pay strictly by the hour for normal shifts, for example by establishing a wage rate of $10.00 per hour for an 8-to-5 job, implementation is usually easy. The base wage rate in our example is greater than the minimum wage requirement of $5.15 per hour and the employee must be paid $15.00 per hour for any hours worked in excess of 40 each week (that is, at a rate one-and-one-half times the "regular" rate). But any variation from this simple pattern may cause problems, and most employers vary in one way or another. Is an employee working for FLSA purposes when her employer requires her to be on call and available for work, but she is not actually working? Should bonuses or incentive pay be added into the regular rate of pay? What if an employer pays less than the minimum wage but allows the employee free use of a company car — should the car be treated as wages and, if so, what is it worth? The possible variations are almost infinite. This section will introduce some of the implementation issues raised by the FLSA.

BRIGHT v. HOUSTON NORTHWEST MEDICAL CENTER SURVIVOR, INC.
United States Court of Appeals, Fifth Circuit (en banc)
934 F.2d 671 (1991)

GARWOOD, CIRCUIT JUDGE. . . .

This is a former employee's suit for overtime compensation under section 7(a)(1) of the Fair Labor Standards Act (FLSA), 29 U.S.C. § 207(a)(1). The question presented is whether "on-call" time the employee spent at home, or at other locations of his choosing substantially removed from his employer's place of business, is . . . working time in instances where the employee was not actually "called." [The district court granted Northwest's motion for summary judgment. A divided panel of this court reversed and remanded for trial. 888 F.2d 1059 (5th Cir. 1989). Upon reconsideration *en banc*, this court now affirms the district court decision.]

Bright went to work for Northwest at its hospital in Houston in April 1981 as a biomedical equipment repair technician, and remained in that employment until late January 1983 when, for reasons wholly unrelated to any matters at issue here, he was in effect fired. . . . [Beginning in February 1982, Bright] was required to wear an electronic paging device or "beeper" [during his off-duty hours] and to be "on call" to come to the hospital to make emergency repairs on biomedical equipment. . . .

Bright was not compensated for his on-call time, and knew this was the arrangement. . . .[2] During the "on-call" time, if Bright were called, and came to the hospital, he was compensated by four hours compensatory time at his then regular hourly rate (which apparently was some $9 or $10 per hour) for each such call. . . . This case does not involve any claim respecting entitlement to compensation (overtime or otherwise) for time that Bright actually spent pursuant to a call from Northwest received while he was on call.

It is undisputed that during the on-call time at issue Bright was not required to, and did not, remain at or about the hospital or any premises of or designated by his employer. He was free to go wherever and do whatever he wanted, subject *only* to the following three restrictions: (1) he must not be intoxicated or impaired to the degree that he could not work on medical equipment if called to the hospital, although total abstinence was not required (as it was during the daily workshift); (2) he must always be reachable by the beeper; (3) and he must be able to arrive at the hospital within, in Bright's words, "approximately twenty minutes" from the time he was reached on the beeper. . . . On deposition Bright admitted while on call he not only stayed at home and watched television and the like, but also engaged in other activities away from home, including his "normal shopping" (including supermarket and mall shopping) and "occasionally" going out to restaurants to eat. . . . Bright also testified on deposition that he was "called" on "average"

---

[2] Bright was told that efforts were being made to have a future hospital budget contain provision for some unspecified character of compensation in respect to his on-call and beeper status; but it was clear that this would only apply to periods after such a budget were approved (and would not be "retroactive"); as Bright knew all along, no such budget was ever approved.

two times during the working week (Monday through Friday) and "ordinarily two to three times" on the weekend.

At issue here is whether the time Bright spent on call, but uncalled on, is working time under section [207 of the FLSA. The two leading Supreme Court cases on the issue, *Armour & Co. v. Wantock*, 323 U.S. 126 (1944), and *Skidmore v. Swift & Co.*, 323 U.S. 134 (1944)] clearly stand for the proposition that, in a proper setting, on-call time may be working time for purposes of section [207]. . . .

In *Armour* the plaintiffs were firemen who worked a regular 8:00 a.m. to 5:00 p.m. shift, and then were on call at the employer's premises from 5:00 p.m. until 8:00 a.m. of the following day, after which they had 24 wholly unrestricted hours, and then repeated the cycle. The Court observed that

> "[t]he litigation concerns the time [5:00 p.m. to 8:00 a.m.] during which these men were required to be on the employer's premises, to some extent amenable to the employer's discipline, subject to call, but not engaged in any specific work. The Company provided cooking equipment, beds, radios, and facilities for cards and amusements with which the men slept, ate, or entertained themselves pretty much as they chose. They were not, however, at liberty to leave the premises except that, by permission of the watchman, they might go to a nearby restaurant for their evening meal." [323 U.S. at 128.]

Armour sustained the district court's determination, which had been affirmed by the Seventh Circuit, that all this time (apart from hours presumably devoted to sleeping or eating, a matter that the plaintiffs did not appeal) was working time.[6]

Bright's case is wholly different from *Armour* and *Skidmore* and similar cases in that Bright did not have to remain on or about his employer's place of business, or some location designated by his employer, but was free to be at his home or at any place or places he chose, without advising his employer, subject only to the restrictions that he be reachable by beeper, not be intoxicated, and be able to arrive at the hospital in "approximately" twenty minutes.[7] Bright was not only able to carry on his normal personal activities

---

[6] In *Skidmore* the facts were similar and [the lower court] concluded that "the time plaintiffs spent in the [employer's] fire hall subject to call to answer fire alarms does not constitute hours worked." The Supreme Court reversed and remanded for reconsideration because the lower court determination apparently rested on the erroneous notion that "waiting time may not be work." [*Skidmore*, however, differed from *Armour* in several respects.] In *Armour* there was no agreement or payment for on-call time actually spent answering an alarm (although in the suit the employer did not contest liability for such alarm answering time); but in *Skidmore* there was agreed compensation in case the employees received such a call. Further, in *Skidmore* the men apparently did not have to remain strictly on the employer's premises, so long as they were "within hailing distance" thereof, while no such accommodation appears to have been present in *Armour*.

[7] The administrative interpretations reflect the difference in kind between situations where the on-call employee has to remain at or about the employer's place of business and those where the on-call employee can be at home or other accessible places of his choosing. *See* 29 CFR § 785.17:

> "An employee who is required to remain on call on the employer's premises or so close thereto that he cannot use the time effectively for his own purposes is working while 'on call.' An employee who is not required to remain on the employer's premises but is merely required to leave word at his home or with company officials where he may be reached is not working while on call." . . .

at his own home, but could also do normal shopping, eating at restaurants, and the like, as he chose.

To hold that Bright's on-call time was working time would be inconsistent with several of our own prior decisions, as well as those in other circuits, which have determined that considerably more restrictive on-call status did not result in work time.

In *Brock* [*v. El Paso Natural Gas Co.,* 826 F.2d 369 (5th Cir. 1987)] . . . the employee claimants lived relatively near their employer's pumping stations where their regular work day was 7:30 a.m. to 4:00 p.m. However, during the nonworking hours of 4:00 p.m. to 7:30 a.m. every day, one employee was required to remain "on call"; this required the employee to remain at his home where he could hear an alarm; if it went off, he would go to the station to correct the problem. We noted that "[o]therwise, the on-call employee is free to eat, sleep, entertain guests, watch television, or engage in any other personal recreational activity, alone or with his family, as long as he is within hailing distance of the alarm and the station." *Id.* at 370 (footnote omitted). The employees were compensated for this time only in instances where they were actually called. We held that as a matter of law the on-call time was not work time for purposes of the FLSA.

In *Halferty* [*v. Pulse Drug Co.,* 864 F.2d 1185 (5th Cir. 1989)] . . . the employee time in question was spent at home from 5:00 p.m. to 8:00 a.m. to be available for telephone calls as an ambulance dispatcher. We stated that in these cases "the critical issue . . . is whether the employee can use the time effectively for his or her own purposes." *Id.* at 1189. We held that as a matter of law the plaintiff there could use the time effectively for her own purposes and that she was hence not entitled to recover, stating:

> "The facts show that Halferty could visit friends, entertain guests, sleep, watch television, do laundry, and babysit. We, therefore, conclude that she could use the time for her own purposes and that she is not entitled to compensation for her idle time. . . ." *Id.*

We noted that "[e]mployees who have received compensation for idle time generally have had almost no freedom at all." *Id.* at 1190. And, we cited and relied on, among other cases, . . . *Pilkenton v. Appalachian Regional Hospitals, Inc.,* 336 F. Supp. 334 (W.D. Va. 1971). . . .

In *Pilkenton,* the on-call employees had beepers and had to remain within an "approximately twenty minutes" drive from their employer's hospital during their on-call time. That time was held noncompensable (except for instances where they were called).

Also to be considered are our decisions in *Allen v. Atlantic Richfield Co.,* 724 F.2d 1131 (5th Cir. 1984), and *Rousseau* [*v. Teledyne Movible Offshore, Inc.,* 805 F.2d 1245 (5th Cir. 1986)]. In *Allen,* guards at a plant under strike from early January to the end of March were required to remain at the plant twenty-four hours a day, during twelve of which they were on duty, and during the other twelve they "were free to sleep, eat at no expense, watch movies, play pool or cards, exercise, read, or listen to music. . . ." 724 F.2d at 1137. They were not compensated for this off-duty time (except that if, in an emergency, they were called to work during the off-duty time they were paid for that work). We upheld a verdict for the defendant that this off-duty time was not compensable.

In *Rousseau,* the claimant employees worked on derrick barges for seven-day shifts, twelve hours each day; during the other "off" twelve hours, however, they were required to remain on the barges and to be available for emergency work. They were compensated only for the time they actually worked, not for any of the twelve-hour waiting time (except for such actual work as they might do during that time) spent on the barges. [We affirmed the district court's decision that the waiting time was not working time,] relying on the statement in the district court's opinion that "[t]he stipulated facts and evidence show that during their off duty time on the barges, the plaintiffs were free to sleep, eat, watch television, watch VCR movies, play pingpong or cards, read, listen to music, etc." *Id.* at 1248.

As noted, we have described "the critical issue" in cases of this kind as being "whether the employee can use the [on-call] time effectively for his or her own purposes." *Halferty,* 864 F.2d at 1189. This does not imply that the employee must have substantially the same flexibility or freedom as he would if not on call, else all or almost all on-call time would be working time, a proposition that the settled case law and the administrative guidelines clearly reject. Only in the very rarest of situations, if ever, would there be any point in an employee being on call if he could not be reached by his employer so as to shortly thereafter — generally at least a significant time before the next regular workshift could take care of the matter — be able to perform a needed service, usually at some particular location.

Within such accepted confines, Bright was clearly able to use his on-call time effectively for his own personal purposes. Indeed, it is evident that he was *much more* able to do so than the employees in the above discussed cases whose on-call time was held to be nonworking time. Unlike the employees in *Brock* (restricted to home or plant), *Halferty* (restricted to home), *Rousseau* (restricted to barge), and *Allen* (restricted to plant), Bright was not restricted to any one or a few fixed locations, but could go virtually anywhere within approximately twenty minutes of the hospital. . . . Within that limit, anything was permissible, except excessive alcohol consumption. An approximately twenty minute radius was involved in *Pilkenton.* . . . We have found no unreversed decision holding compensable on-call time that afforded even nearly as much freedom for personal use as did Bright's. Had the twenty to thirty minute "leash" been longer, Bright would, of course, have been able to do *more* things, but that does not mean that within the applicable restrictions he could not effectively use the on-call time wholly for his own private purposes. Millions of employees go for weeks at a time without traveling more than seventeen miles from their place of employment.

The panel majority did not disagree with our prior decisions. Rather, it placed crucial reliance on the fact that Bright throughout the nearly one year in issue never had any relief from his on-call status during his nonworking hours. The panel majority states that Bright's case "differs from . . . other cases in one important respect: Bright . . . never had any reprieve from on-call duties," *Bright,* 888 F.2d at 1061; "the restrictions only applied to the workers in *Rousseau* for seven days at a time," which it described as "the critical fact," *id.* at 1063; *Allen* was distinguished because "of critical importance is the fact that the arrangement was a temporary one, lasting only the length of the strike," *id.* (footnote omitted). In essence, the panel majority inferentially conceded that for any given day or week of on-call time, Bright was as free to use the time for his own purposes as were the employees in the above-cited cases where the time was held nonworking. But the panel majority claims that a different result should apply here because Bright's arrangement lasted nearly a year.

We are aware of no authority that supports this theory, and we decline to adopt it. . . . [T]he FLSA is structured on a workweek basis. Section [207,] at issue here, requires time and a half pay "for a workweek longer than forty hours." What Bright was or was not free to do in the last week in September is wholly irrelevant to whether he worked any overtime in the first week of that month. As we said in *Halferty,* the issue "is whether the employee can use the time effectively for his or her own purposes," and that must be decided, under the statutory framework, on the basis of each workweek at the most.

We do not deny the obvious truth that the long continued aspect of Bright's on-call status made his job highly undesirable and arguably somewhat oppressive. Clearly, it would have been vastly more pleasant from Bright's point of view had he only been on call the first week of every month, for example. But the FLSA's overtime provisions are more narrowly focused than being simply directed at requiring extra compensation for oppressive or confining conditions of employment. A Texan working 8:30 p.m. to 3:00 a.m. six days a week (thirty-nine hours), fifty-two weeks a year, at a remote Alaska location has a most restrictive and oppressive job that as a practical matter prevents, *inter alia,* vacations, visiting relatives, and attending live operatic performances or major league sporting events, but it seems obvious that the FLSA overtime provisions provide no relief for those oppressive and confining conditions. Bright's job was oppressive and confining in many of the same ways, but it, too, did not involve more than forty hours work a week.[8]

The district court properly granted summary judgment for Northwest, and that judgment is accordingly

Affirmed.

Jerre S. Williams, Circuit Judge, with whom Johnson, Circuit Judge, joins, dissenting:

I dissent from the decision of the en banc court in this case. . . . The facts as stated in the opinion for the Court are accurate insofar as they go. They need supplementation by way of emphasis. The panel opinion and this dissent are grounded wholly on the circumstance which must be accepted as true that for a period of approximately eleven months from February 1982 until January 1983, employee Bright's life was significantly circumscribed by his employer without compensation. There was no relief by way of other employees sharing the duties so that Bright would have periods of being free from

---

[8] Except in instances, not at issue here, where the extra work was compensated consistently with section [207].

the restrictions. There were no free weekends, there was no vacation, there were no free days or nights. This is the core issue in the case. . . .

I do not go into detail to comment upon the cases discussed and treated as controlling by the majority opinion of the en banc court. None of them control. Every single one of them, without exception, involves a situation where the employer had more than one employee sharing the oppressive schedule or there was some other means of "covering the employee" so that the employee was not committed and under serious limitations without respite over a substantial period of time. . . .

The nearest case to the facts of this case has to do with the employee Pilkenton, who was on a schedule with virtually the identical restrictions as Bright. *Pilkenton v. Appalachian Regional Hosps., Inc.,* 336 F. Supp. 334 (W.D. Va. 1971). But in *Pilkenton* another employee shared the on-call duty so that each employee was freed of the duty and personal limitations for half of his or her overall time. Thus, the employees were not being held on a permanent 20 minute leash.

At the end, the opinion for the Court falls back, as it must, upon the proposition that Bright was in the same situation as someone holding a job in a remote part of Alaska where, after an eight hour day, the use of his or her own time obviously is limited. This reliance is wholly foreign to the thrust of the Fair Labor Standards Act. Admittedly, there are jobs which because of location are in isolated areas. That is in the nature of the jobs. But the isolation is not the result of an employer's direction requiring employee on-call availability during off-duty hours. The employer has nothing to do with the restricted recreational and living accommodations in an isolated job. That is not an on-call situation at all. In contrast, here it is the employer who is enforcing a unique restriction upon a particular employee as part of the particular on-call work assignment. This is of the essence of the thrust of potential work time under the Fair Labor Standards Act.

This distinction can be seen more clearly if in an extreme case the employer directed a particular employee permanently to remain behind on the hospital campus for an hour each day after the workshift was over in case some problem arose about the changeover from one shift to another. The employee would be free to read a book, watch television, walk around the grounds, but would be required to remain on the grounds for an hour in case the employee was needed. It would be exceedingly difficult to hold that that particular hour was not work time. It would be an additional on-call restriction for the benefit of the employer placed upon the employee for an extra hour every day but without compensation.

Bright's case, of course, is not that extreme in its restriction. But it is not a remote location case caused by the nature of the work applicable to all jobs. It is an on-call isolation case caused by the employer's own orders defining the particular work assignment. Thus, we are left, as the panel opinion said, with the circumstance in which Bright "was not far removed from a prisoner serving a sentence under slightly relaxed house arrest terms. He never could go to downtown Houston, he never could go to Galveston and see the ocean. He never could go to a baseball or football game in the Astrodome. An out of town event, even a visit to relatives or friends in San Antonio or Austin, was totally out of the question." *Bright,* 888 F.2d at 1064. Further, the employer had a relatively simple and humane means of avoiding this restriction which was akin to and rather close to house arrest. The remedy is found in every single one of the cases cited by the majority opinion and relied upon by the majority opinion. The employer could have set up a system under which this onerous restrictive duty could be shared or certain periods of relief could be afforded.

Finally, the opinion for the Court asserts that all overtime issues under the statute must be based upon a week by week analysis. . . . While the FLSA calls for the calculation of the payment of overtime on a weekly basis, it does not require that each individual week be a wholly separate entity in determining whether an employee is working or not.

In *Allen v. Atlantic Richfield Co.,* 724 F.2d 1131 (5th Cir. 1981) (cited in the en banc opinion), we considered a case in which security personnel because of a strike were required to remain on the grounds of the industrial establishment for 24 hours every day for a period of what was apparently the first few weeks of an eleven week strike. Later, arrangements were made during the strike to rotate the 24 hour duty. The jury found that the security employees were not working during this period when they were off duty although they were required to remain at the plant. We upheld the jury verdict.

We can draw two authoritative conclusions from our decision in this case. First, the opinion makes no reference to a week by week limitation but instead assumed that the entire time during which the 24 hour requirement was in effect was relevant to the work time issue. Second, the case shows that we can and should trust juries in these cases to deny bonanzas to unfounded claims of extra work. The jury found no additional work time in that relatively short period of a few weeks involved in *Allen.*

Bright may not be able to prove to a jury that he was entitled to any additional work time credit. . . . But I dissent because this is not a case for summary judgment. A trial is necessary to assess the facts of this case. . . .

NOTES

1. *Should Bright Move to Kansas?* In *Renfro v. City of Emporia,* 948 F.2d 1529 (10th Cir. 1991), the court affirmed a summary judgment requiring the city to pay overtime and liquidated damages to firefighters for on-call time. In *Renfro,* firefighters were regularly required to be on call for 24-hour periods. While on call, the city required the firefighters to carry a pager and be able to return to work within twenty minutes of being called. They were paid only when called and were called on average three to five times per 24-hour period. Firefighters were able to trade their on-call duties with other firefighters and, while on call, firefighters had "participated in sports activities, socialized with friends and relatives, attended business meetings, gone shopping, gone out to eat, babysat, and performed maintenance or other activities around their home." *Id.* at 1532. Indeed, one-third of the firefighters were able to maintain second jobs despite the uncertainties created by the on-call time.

2. *Pay for On-Call Time.* On-call time presents a problem under the Fair Labor Standards Act in part because of the dichotomous nature of work time under the Act: Either an employee is or is not working. The firefighters in *Renfro* were awarded overtime pay and liquidated damages for all their on-call hours. One firefighter, for example, was awarded $122,000 in backpay and liquidated damages. In contrast, Bright was found not to be working during his on-call time, so he was entitled to nothing for his inconveniences. Neither outcome seems quite right.

3. *How Should Employers Respond?* Employers have two primary ways of responding to the problem of on-call time. First, they can attempt to structure the on-call time so that it is not work time that is compensable under the Act. *Bright* and *Renfro* provide some clues on how to do that — longer response time, limiting the number of calls to work, and so forth. Second, employers can attempt to adjust wages so that treating the on-call time as compensable is not too burdensome. That is, by reducing the regular hourly rate, the employer may be able to offset most of the cost of treating the on-call time as compensable. Do you think an employer should be able to pay a lower rate for on-call time than for regular work time? *See Townsend v. Mercy Hosp.*, 862 F.2d 1009 (3d Cir. 1988) (yes, under certain conditions). *Cf. Dinges v. Sacred Heart St. Mary's Hosp., Inc.*, 164 F.3d 1056 (7th Cir. 1999) (less than minimum-wage pay for on-call time a factor in deciding that it was not work time under the FLSA).

4. *The Broader Issue of Compensable Time.* The issue of what hours are compensable under the FLSA reaches far beyond on-call time. Is time during coffee breaks compensable? How about meal periods? Time spent walking from the timeclock to the area where the work is actually performed? Time spent walking to the production floor after donning protective gear? Driving to work? Driving from home to a customer's business to perform emergency services? The possible circumstances are virtually endless. The regulations, which merely seem to be endless, answer many of the questions. (The answers to the questions above, for example, are yes, no, no, yes, no, and yes.)

The Portal-to-Portal Act of 1947 was enacted primarily in response to these types of issues. Although it is known only to labor-law specialists today, the Act was a major political issue when it was enacted. For a good history, see Marc Linder, *Class Struggle at the Door: The Origins of the Portal-to-Portal Act of 1947,* 39 BUFF. L. REV. 53 (1991).

Perhaps the most interesting question here is not how these issues are resolved (for example, is time spent on coffee breaks compensable or not?), but rather why they are important at all. Let us say that the rule on coffee breaks changes — before, time spent on coffee breaks was not compensable, now it is. Why might that change be important? Consider the following argument:

> For most employees, the change in the coffee-break rule will not result in any long-term increase in their income. Employers will merely lower the base wage rate (or other parts of the compensation package) to compensate for the extra compensable time. But the change will be important for minimum-wage workers. Since employers cannot lower the base wage rate for these workers, the change would

result in an increase in income. The increase, however, may also cause some employment losses for minimum-wage workers.

MARSHALL v. SAM DELL'S DODGE CORP.
United States District Court, N.D. New York
451 F. Supp. 294 (1978)

PORT, SENIOR DISTRICT JUDGE.

Defendant Sam Dell's Dodge Corp. is an automobile dealership in Syracuse, New York. . . . The hours and wages of 117 salespersons who were employed at Sam Dell's Dodge . . . are at issue. . . .

The defendants paid their salespeople under a series of rather complex plans. Total compensation included combinations of base pay, commissions, and bonuses. . . . The plans varied from time to time but can be summarized as follows. Each salesperson received base pay of $56.00 per week for most of the period covered by this action. The base pay was received free and clear without regard to sales made. Commissions were paid on the sales of just about everything, new cars, used cars, trucks, accessories and finance agreements. At times the commissions were fixed amounts paid for the sale of each new car. For used cars and, more recently, for new cars the commissions were a percentage of either the sales price or the dealer's profits. On top of commissions, salespersons were paid bonuses as an incentive for increased sales. For selling four or more cars during one week, a salesperson would receive a weekly bonus in the next pay check. If he or she sold over 20 cars during one month, a monthly bonus would be received at the end of that month. Similarly, annual bonuses were paid for the sale of over a given number of cars during a calendar year. For a good salesperson, these bonuses could be substantial compared to the base pay.

Some salesmen testified, however, that they would stagger receipt of their commissions so as to spread out or average their income during the year. In this way, they would not get a disproportionately large pay check after a highly successful selling week. Nevertheless, there were some weeks during each year when each salesperson received only the base salary $56.00 . . . and failed to earn any commissions or bonuses.

Many of the salespeople were furnished by defendants with demonstrator cars or "demos." Primarily, these cars were used in connection with the salespersons' duties at Sam Dell's Dodge Corp. . . . Salespeople used them for demonstration rides for their customers. . . . Salespersons were permitted to drive the cars for personal use when not working; however, they were specifically told that the cars were not for their families. . . . The value of the use of the "demos" was never included on the employee's W-2 tax statements or the employer's pay records. After April, 1976, defendants' pay plans indicated that a Form 1099 would be given to each employee listing the value of the "demo" car at $20.00 each month. However, defendants failed to introduce any evidence that the 1099 Forms were ever provided.

The bulk of the testimony received at trial concerned the number of hours worked each week by the sales staff. Defendants' showroom and car lots, referred to throughout the trial as the "store" were open six days a week. On Mondays, Tuesdays and Thursdays, the store was open from 9:00 A.M. to 9:30 P.M. Wednesdays, Fridays and Saturdays the store was open from 9:00 A.M. to 6:30 P.M. Thus, defendants' posted operating time for the store totaled 66 hours per week. . . .

The average workweek for defendants' salespersons . . . was 55 hours. The store was open 66 hours each week but eliminating 1½ hours each for early departure, . . . four hours for lunch, two for dinner, and another two for personal time leaves a 55 hour workweek.

This is not a precise figure. It is my inference based on the evidence I regarded as credible. The deductions from the scheduled workweek are probably generous to the defendants; certainly they cannot be considered niggardly toward an employer whose deliberately contrived time records made precision impossible.

Despite the fact that defendants encouraged their employees to work long hours, defendants kept time records which grossly understated the number of hours actually worked. While the sales staff was working, on the average, a 55 hour or more week, defendants required their employees to sign time slips which purported to show that the employees were working only 36 hours per week.

The defendants' practice of knowingly maintaining inaccurate time records which greatly understated the number of hours worked by their sales personnel [means that] the violations of the Act were willful.

III. Conclusions of Law and Discussion

A. *The Workweek Is the Relevant Pay Period*

Defendants' salespersons worked on the average 55 hours per week. For weeks during which they made no sales and, therefore, earned no commissions or bonuses, they would receive only the base pay [of] $56 per week which was less than the minimum wage. [The minimum wage ranged from $1.60 to $2.65 per hour during the relevant time period.] Plaintiff contends that, by not paying the guaranteed minimum wage for each hour worked in each week, defendants violated section [206] of the Act. Defendants concede that they paid their employees only $56 in some weeks and that simple multiplication of the required minimum wage times the hours worked in those weeks exceeds the amounts paid. They contend, however, that some period other than the week should be used in assessing compliance with the minimum wage requirements of the Act. . . .

The defendants herein established, by their own practice, the workweek as the customary pay period. Their salespersons were paid each week for earnings which accrued during that week. While car sales may be seasonal, defendants' pay practice . . . was regular. Having established the week as the applicable pay period, defendants cannot now argue that any other time period measures compliance with the Act.

Further support for this conclusion comes from the Secretary's own interpretations of section [206] of the Act. "Section [206(b)] of the Act . . . is applicable on a workweek basis and *requires payment* of the prescribed minimum wages to each employee who 'in any workweek' is employed in a covered enterprise." Likewise, the Secretary's regulations implementing section [207] of the Act base compliance on the workweek. "The Act takes a single workweek as its standard and does not permit averaging of hours over two or more weeks." 29 C.F.R. § 778.104.[9] Clearly, the Secretary's interpretations of the Act, although not binding on the court, are entitled to great weight.

The Supreme Court has emphasized the importance of paying an employee's minimum wage on a weekly basis. In considering the rationale behind the liquidated damages provision of the Act, 29 U.S.C. § 216(b), the Court noted that

> failure to pay the statutory minimum on time may be . . . detrimental to maintenance of the minimum standard of living "necessary for health, efficiency and general well-being of workers." . . . Employees receiving less than the statutory minimum are not likely to have sufficient resources to maintain their well-being and efficiency until such sums are paid at a future date.

Brooklyn Savings Bank v. O'Neil, 324 U.S. 697, 707-08 (1945). The defendants may see this rationale as applicable only to workers with annual incomes in the minimum wage range. However, in the period with which we are dealing even the better paid salesman with a family would be hard pressed if he were obliged to suffer a few weeks at less than minimum wages. Plaintiff has shown that at least four of defendants' salesmen failed to receive the minimum wage during periods of nine to twelve consecutive weeks. This is the precise danger which the Fair Labor Standards Act sought to meet. . . .

In this case the relevant period for analyzing compliance with section [206] of the Act is the workweek. Regardless of the total pay received by an employee, the Act requires that each employee receive, each week, an amount equal to the minimum wage times the number of hours worked. Defendants have, therefore, violated section [206] of the Act by paying less than minimum wage to certain employees in certain weeks. However, because of the nature of defendants' pay plans, it is necessary to inquire whether compensation other than the weekly pay check can be allocated among the various workweeks.

B. *Bonuses*

In addition to their base salary and commissions, defendants' salespersons received weekly, monthly and annual bonuses. The bonuses served as an incentive plan for higher sales and were paid if a salesperson sold over a given number of vehicles during any week, month or year. . . .

---

[9] This regulation is part of the Secretary's regulations concerning overtime compensation. *See* 29 C.F.R. §§ 778.0-778.603. The workweek is clearly the relevant time period for measuring overtime, since maximum hours are defined in relation to a single week. *See* 29 U.S.C. § 207(a). Arguably the significance of the workweek is not as strong in relation to minimum wage, as long as the employee ultimately receives minimum wage for the hours worked. However, since the courts have noted the importance of the workweek, even when calculating minimum wage, *see, e.g., Brooklyn Savings Bank v. O'Neil*, 324 U.S. 697 (1945), the cited regulation is relevant to the case at bar. This conclusion is buttressed by defendants' own practice of paying their employees weekly.

[T]he payment of bonuses can only be considered in connection with the minimum wages for the week in which they are paid. Under the facts in this case, any other recognition of the bonus payments would obviously be a deferred payment of wages which could not be credited against the minimum wage requirement for any prior week. That is not to say that circumstances other than these present here may not arise which would require different treatment.

C. *Demonstrator Cars*

Although they did not argue the question in their briefs, defendants introduced evidence suggesting that they compensated their salespersons by providing them with demonstrator cars or "demos." The reasonable cost of facilities customarily furnished to employees may be considered part of their wages. 29 C.F.R. § 531.30. However facilities which are "primarily for the benefit or convenience of the employer" do not qualify as wages. 29 C.F.R. § 531.32(c).

Defendants' employees were given "demos" and were permitted to drive them for personal use when not working; their family members were forbidden from driving the cars. The evidence suggested that mileage accumulated by the salespeople when driving for personal use was not insignificant when compared with business use. Nevertheless, it is plain that these "demos" were furnished primarily for the benefit of defendants. Clearly, the cars were valuable and necessary tools.

> It is obvious that a salesman of an automobile should have an automobile in his possession at all times that would be one of those products that his employer was engaged in selling. The very nature of his duties as a car salesman would require his possession and use of an automobile, even on personal business, and that the business of his employer would suffer if this were not the case.

Brennan v. Modern Chevrolet Co.,, 363 F. Supp. 327, 333 (N.D. Tex. 1973), *aff'd,* 491 F.2d 1271 (5th Cir. 1974). Furthermore, neither defendants nor their employees treated the cars as wages. Although a sum was deducted from each pay check for insurance, the value of the use of the cars was not indicated on defendants' pay records. Nor did the W-2 tax statements reflect the value of the use of the "demos" furnished.

In *Brennan v. Modern Chevrolet Co.*, the district court conceded that personal use of the cars accounted for 90% of the mileage accumulated. Still, because of the primary benefit to the employer, the cars were not wages. The reasoning . . . applies at least as strongly to the facts of the instant case. Under the circumstances, the value of the demonstrator cars cannot be counted as wages. . . .

E. *Unpaid Minimum Wages*

Defendants' salespersons are due unpaid minimum wages in amounts to be calculated by the parties in accordance with this Memorandum-Decision and Order.

Defendants must pay minimum wages due from June 21, 1973 until the present. The basic minimum wage which defendants were obligated to pay their salespersons can be calculated by multiplying the applicable statutory hourly minimum wage by the number of hours worked during each week. The number of hours worked by each employee . . . was 55 hours per week. . . .

The amount of back wages due to the salespersons is the deficiency between the minimum wage and the amount of pay received in each week that pay fell short of the minimum. Two adjustments must be made to this calculation: Vacation time must be considered, and interest added.

Where defendants' pay records indicate a vacation, the employee is entitled to no recovery for that period. Interest at the lawful rate in effect at the time in New York State is payable from the date of each deficiency on the amount found due. *Hodgson v. Wheaton Glass Co.*, 446 F.2d 527, 535 (3d Cir. 1971). . . .

NOTES

1. *FLSA Calculus.* The actual minimum-wage rate varied during the time of this lawsuit, but for our purposes, let's say the rate was $2.00/hour. Also, to keep things simple, let's ignore interest payments. According to the Court, how much should Employee A recover for the month of February (covering four weeks) when she received the normal base salary each week ($56) plus a bonus at the end of the month of $400? (Note: The court found that employees worked 55 hours per week.) If the facts were the same except that furniture was sold rather than cars, would the employer have been in compliance with the FLSA if it had paid Employee A that amount? *See* 29 U.S.C. § 213(b)(10) (sellers of automobiles exempt from overtime provisions).

2. *Demonstrator Cars as Wages.* The FLSA recognizes that wages can be paid in forms other than cash. Wages are defined by the Act to include the reasonable cost to the employer of providing "board, lodging, or other facilities" if they are "customarily furnished" to employees. 29 U.S.C. § 203(m). The Secretary of Labor interprets this language to permit in-kind payments to be included in FLSA wages only if they are primarily for the benefit or convenience of the employee, accepted voluntarily by the employee, and of a kind customarily furnished by the employer or by other employers engaged in similar activities. The amount included in wages may not be more than the actual cost of the in-kind good to the employer. 29 C.F.R. § 531.3. *But see Herman v. Collis Foods, Inc.*, 176 F.3d 912 (6th Cir. 1999) (invalidating part of regulation requiring employee to accept in-kind goods voluntarily; employer may *require* employees to accept meals and treat them as FLSA wages).

Why are there such limitations on treating in-kind payments as wages? *Cf.* 29 C.F.R. § 531.32(c) (employers cannot count as FLSA wages cost of electricity used in the plant, company fire and police protection, or taxes and insurance on employer's buildings). Why might some employees want cars to be treated as wages? *See* 29 C.F.R. § 778.116 (in-kind payments to be included in "regular rate" for determining overtime).

3. Employer Response. How would you expect Sam Dell's Dodge to pay its sales force in the future?

DUNLOP v. GRAY-GOTO, INC.
United States Court of Appeals, Tenth Circuit
528 F.2d 792 (1976)

McWILLIAMS, CIRCUIT JUDGE.

This is a Fair Labor Standards case. The trial court . . . found that though certain employees of the defendant had worked overtime for which no overtime premium was paid, the defendant had nonetheless not violated the overtime requirements of the Act because the defendant had paid its employees certain fringe benefits, including paid vacations and holidays, and biannual bonuses, the value of which equalled or exceeded the amount of overtime compensation otherwise due under the Act. These so-called fringe benefits the trial court allowed to be "set off" against unpaid overtime compensation otherwise due defendant's employees. In so holding the trial court relied on its finding that the defendant and its employees had expressly agreed that such fringe benefits would take the place of overtime pay. . . .

Our study of the matter leads us to conclude that the trial court erred in finding that the so-called fringe benefits could be deemed as the equivalent of overtime pay. . . .

29 U.S.C. § 207(a) provides that an employee who works in interstate commerce in excess of 40 hours per week shall for the excess hours be paid at a rate no less than "one and one-half times the regular rate at which he is employed." Perhaps the primary purpose of the overtime compensation requirement is to "spread employment" by putting pressure on the employer through the overtime pay requirement. A secondary purpose is to compensate an employee in a specific manner "for the strain of working longer than forty hours." *Bay Ridge Co. v. Aaron*, 334 U.S. 446, 470 (1948).

29 U.S.C. § 207(e) defines what "regular rate" of pay is by stating that such term "include[s] all remuneration for employment paid to, or on behalf of, the employee. . . ." That same section goes on to declare that seven categories of employer payments are not to be taken into consideration in determining what an employee's "regular rate" of pay is. 29 U.S.C. § 207(h) provides that the extra compensation described in subsections (5), (6), and (7) in 29 U.S.C. § 207(e) "shall be creditable toward overtime compensation payable pursuant to this section." Implicit therein is that the extra compensation described in subsections (1), (2), (3) and (4) is not to be credited towards overtime payments required by the Act.

The fringe benefits as found by the trial court are "in the form of paid vacations, six holidays with pay each year, biannual bonuses, and the extension of benefits of a group life, health and accident insurance program." Paid vacations and pay for holidays would appear to be included in subsection (2) of 29 U.S.C. § 207(e), which refers to "payments made for occasional periods when no work is performed due to vacation, holiday. . . ." The bonuses would appear to fall into subsection (1) of 29 U.S.C. § 207(e), which refers to "payments in the nature of gifts made at Christmas time or other special occasions, as a reward for service. . . ." The "insurance benefits" found by the trial court would appear to fall within subsection (4) of 29 U.S.C. § 207(e), which refers to "life, accident [and] health insurance or similar benefits for employees." So, under 29 U.S.C. § 207(e) the fringe benefits found by the trial court are not to be included in ascertaining an employee's "regular rate" of pay. At the same time, however, as we read 29 U.S.C. § 207(h) such benefits as were found here by the trial court may not be credited toward overtime compensation due under the Act.

Our holding that the fringe benefits with which we are here concerned may not be credited against overtime pay required by the Act would appear to be in accord with the general case law on the subject. . . . In *Rigopoulos v. Kervan*, 140 F.2d 506, 507 (2d Cir. 1943) the Second Circuit stated that 29 U.S.C. § 207 "plainly contemplates that overtime compensation shall be paid in the course of employment and not accumulated beyond the regular pay day." And in *Brennan v. Heard,*, 491 F.2d 1, 4 (5th Cir. 1974) the Fifth Circuit observed that "[s]et-offs against back pay awards deprive the employee of the 'cash in hand' contemplated by the Act. . . ."

The trial court laid particular emphasis on its finding that in the instant case the employees involved and the defendant employer had an express understanding before any employer-employee relationship was ever entered into that there would be no overtime pay for hours worked in excess of forty hours per week, and that in lieu thereof they would receive the fringe benefits above referred to. In our view any such private agreement or understanding between the parties cannot circumvent the overtime pay requirements of the Act. In this regard see *Brooklyn Bank v. O'Neil*, 324 U.S. 697, 704 (1945), where the Supreme Court held that "[w]here a private right is granted in the public interest to effectuate a legislative policy, waiver of a right so charged or colored with public interest will not be allowed when it would thwart the legislative policy which it was designed to effectuate." *See also Mitchell v. Greinetz*, 235 F.2d 621 (10th Cir. 1956), where we held that waiver of statutory wages under the Fair Labor Standards Act is not permissible. It is on this basis then that we conclude that the trial court erred in permitting fringe benefits to be set off against overtime pay otherwise due. . . .

NOTES

1. *FLSA Calculus II.* Consider our furniture retailer again. The employer agrees to pay employees $10/hour for non-overtime hours, $15/hour for overtime hours, and a $100 bonus if the employee sells more than $5,000 worth of furniture in a week. Employee A works 50 hours in a week and sells $7,500 worth of furniture. The employer pays her $650 — $10/hour for the first 40 hours ($400), $15/hour for the next 10 hours ($150), and the $100 bonus for selling more than $5,000 worth of furniture. Why has the employer violated the FLSA? What can the employer do if it wants to retain its incentive bonus and yet limit its weekly wage bill for productive employees to about $650?

2. *Compensatory Time Off in Lieu of Overtime Pay.* In the public sector, employers can do part of what Gray-Goto attempted to do. Section 207(o) of the FLSA permits public employers to provide compensatory time off instead of overtime pay, if several conditions are met. For example, the arrangement must be set forth in an agreement arrived at before the overtime work is performed, the employee must receive one-and-one-half hours of compensatory time off for each overtime hour worked, an employee cannot accrue more than a certain number of compensatory hours (240 hours for most employees), and employers must grant employee requests to use their compensatory time unless it would "unduly disrupt" the workplace. Bills are regularly introduced in Congress to extend to all employers the option of providing compensatory time off instead of overtime pay.

3. *A Mirror Image.* *Gray-Goto* held that an employer could not satisfy its FLSA obligations by making benefit contributions in lieu of cash payments. How should a court handle the converse: An employer who makes cash payments to plaintiffs in lieu of increased contributions to benefit programs? In *Theisen v. City of Maple Grove*, 41 F. Supp. 2d 932 (D. Minn. 1992), the collective-bargaining agreement required the employer to make flat monthly payments to employees in lieu of increased contributions for insurance. The Court held that these cash payments need not be included in the regular rate because they did not depend on the number of hours employees worked, relying on Sections 207(e)(1) and (2). Did the Court read the statute correctly?

4. *The FLSA as a Response to Onerous Work Conditions?* Tew works as a meat market manager for Food Lion, a grocery store. Food Lion has a scheduling system which minimizes overtime hours and performance standards which are difficult to meet by working only during scheduled work time. As a result, Tew decides to work overtime "off the clock" to avoid discipline for substandard performance, even though Food Lion also has a firm policy against working "off the clock." Later, Tew leaves his employment with Food Lion and files a lawsuit to recover unpaid overtime compensation for the "off the clock" hours. Should he be able to recover? If so, should Food Lion be successful on a counterclaim against Tew for violation of his employment contract (in which he agreed to abide by all company rules) or for violation of his fiduciary duties as manager of the meat market? *Lyle v. Food Lion, Inc.*, 954 F.2d 984 (4th Cir. 1992) (Tew recovers; counterclaims dismissed).

2. COVERAGE

Congress clearly intended coverage under the Fair Labor Standards Act to be broad, and so it is. *See Powell v. United States Cartridge Co.*, 339 U.S. 497, 516 (1950) ("Breadth of coverage was vital to [the Act's] mission"). Broad coverage, however, is merely a guiding principle. In its details, the Act presents three general types of coverage issues.

First, the Act only applies when there is an employer-employee relationship. We have already discussed that issue through the *Lauritzen* case in Chapter 2.

Second, the Act only applies to certain employees. An employee is covered only if she is personally engaged in commerce (individual coverage) or if she works for an enterprise that is engaged in commerce (enterprise coverage). Individual employees are covered if they are engaged in interstate or foreign commerce or in the production of goods for commerce. Although individual coverage is not as broad as the commerce clause might permit, the coverage is nevertheless very broad and the distinctions, as you might expect, are quite fine-grained. For example, employees providing water or seeds to a farmer who is intending to sell his crops in interstate commerce are sufficiently engaged in commerce to be covered by the Act (because the water and seeds become a part of the product in commerce), but employees providing fertilizer to the farmer are not sufficiently engaged in commerce to be covered (because the fertilizer becomes a part of the soil, rather than the product in commerce). For this and other examples, see 29 C.F.R. § § 776, 776.19(b)(4).

Even if employees are not covered individually, they may be covered if their employer (or, more precisely, their enterprise) is covered. A covered enterprise is one that has employees who are engaged in commerce or the production of goods for commerce, or that has employees who handle goods or materials that someone else has moved or produced for commerce. *See* 29 U.S.C. § 203(s)(1)(A)(i). The entity must also have a gross volume of business of at least $500,000 per year. Because of the broad interpretation of "commerce," enterprises that meet the monetary requirement are usually covered by the statute. The dollar volume limitation means that employees of smaller companies may not be covered by the FLSA. To prevent employers from organizing themselves into small business units in order to avoid FLSA liability, the statute will aggregate multiple establishments if they are operated or controlled by a person who is using them for a common business purpose. *See* 29 U.S.C § 203(r)(1); *Brennan v. Arnheim & Neely Inc.*, 410 U.S. 512 (1973). Hospitals, schools, and public agencies are covered regardless of the commerce test or the dollar volume requirement. 29 U.S.C. § 203(s)(1)(B).

Third, the Act has many exemptions from coverage. Thus, even if employees are engaged in commerce and, hence, fall within the general coverage of the Act, they may not be entitled to the Act's protections because they fit within one of the exemptions. The *Davis* case below considers one of the most important exemptions, the exemption for executive, administrative, and professional employees.

DAVIS v. MOUNTAIRE FARMS, INC.
United States District Court, District of Delaware
2005 WL 1522609 (2005)

JORDAN, J.

On June 21, 2004, Plaintiffs commenced this action filing a three count complaint asserting violations of the [Fair Labor Standards Act (the "FLSA" or the "Act"), 29 U.S.C. § 201 *et. seq.*] by Defendants for misclassifying Plaintiffs as exempt employees, failing to pay overtime, and retaliation. . . .

Defendants are engaged in the business of producing, processing, and distributing poultry products for consumers. Defendants contract with over 300 farmers (referred to as "Growers") to grow chickens. Plaintiffs are or were employed by Defendants. They worked as the leaders of chicken catching crews. A chicken catching crew consists of one crew leader, seven or eight catchers and one forklift operator. Defendants' human resource department is not involved in recruiting and hiring chicken catchers and does not advertise for chicken catcher positions.

A crew leader supervises the catchers and the forklift driver in the catching process, and is responsible for staffing and maintaining a full crew. A crew leader is also responsible for properly training the members of his crew. A crew leader transports members of his crew to and from the assigned farm each work day. On the farm, a crew leader directs and observes the catching process, and is responsible for ensuring compliance with the Live Haul Guidelines, which generally describe the Growers' responsibilities, the crew leaders' duties, and the catching methods and ventilation procedures. The crew leader decides when the crew takes a break. Furthermore, crew leaders are responsible for the safety of their crew, and for completion of the "farm ticket," which tracks information on the conditions and particularities of each farm. Additionally, crew leaders have the authority to discipline their crew members. . . .

III. *Discussion*

The parties agree on the operative facts regarding the duties of a crew leader but dispute whether the crew leaders' responsibilities fall within the executive exemptions of the FLSA, 29 U.S.C. § 213(A). More specifically, they dispute whether their "primary duty" was management and whether "particular weight" was given to their suggestions and recommendations as to the hiring and firing, advancement, promotion or any other change in status of employees.

A. *FLSA's Executive Exemption*

Under the FLSA, an employer may not employ any worker "for a workweek longer than forty hours unless such employee receives compensation . . . at a rate not less than one and one-half times the regular rate at which [the employee] is employed." 29 U.S.C. § 207(a)(1). However, the Act exempts "any employee in a bona fide executive . . . capacity. . . ." 29 U.S.C. § 213(a)(1). The regulations promulgated to give effect to the Act state four elements defining an "employee in a bona fide executive capacity."

The term "employee employed in a bona fide executive capacity" in section 13(a)(1) of the Act shall mean any employee:

(1) Compensated on a salary basis at a rate of not less than $455 per week . . . exclusive of board, lodging or other facilities;

(2) Whose primary duty is management of the enterprise in which the employee is employed or of a customarily recognized department or subdivision thereof;

(3) Who customarily and regularly directs the work of two or more other employees; and

(4) Who has the authority to hire or fire other employees or whose suggestions and recommendations as to the hiring, firing, advancement, promotion or any other change of status of other employees are given particular weight.

29 C.F.R. § 541.100. "An employer has the burden of establishing that the exemption applies to its employee[s], and such exemptions are narrowly construed against the employer." *Sansoucie v. Reproductive Associates*, 2005 WL 1075596 (2005) (D. Del. 2005) (citing *Idaho Sheet Metal Works, Inc. v. Wirtz*, 383 U.S. 190 (1966); *Mitchell v. Kentucky Finance Co.*, 359 U.S. 290 (1959)).

Plaintiffs concede that they were compensated on a salary basis sufficient to satisfy section (a)(1) of the regulation. Further, Plaintiffs concede that they customarily and regularly directed the work of two or more employees and, therefore, section (a)(3) of the regulation is satisfied. Thus, at issue is whether their primary duty was management, as required by section (a)(2), and whether their "hire or fire" suggestions were given sufficient weight to satisfy section (a)(4) of the regulation.

1. *Plaintiffs' Primary Duty is Management*

Plaintiffs . . . concede that they "were involved in the management of the enterprise . . ." because they had to ensure that the requisite number of chickens were caught, properly loaded, transported and delivered to Defendants' processing plant. Plaintiffs assert, however, that management of the enterprise was not their primary duty. . . .

Under the FLSA regulations, "primary duty" is defined as follows:

> The term "primary duty" means the principal, main, major or most important duty that the employee performs. Determination of an employee's primary duty must be based on all the facts in a particular case, with the major emphasis on the character of the employee's job as a whole. Factors to consider when determining the primary duty of an employee include, but are not limited to, the relative importance of the exempt duties as compared with other types of duties; the amount of time spent performing exempt work; the employee's relative freedom from direct supervision; and the relationship between the employee's salary and the wages paid to other employees for the kind of nonexempt work performed by the employee.

29 C.F.R. § 541.700(a). To determine whether Plaintiffs' primary duty was management, a court must consider the listed factors, along with any "facts unique to this case. . . ." *See Baldwin v. Trailer Inns, Inc.*, 266 F.3d 1104, 1113-14 (9th Cir. 2001).

Plaintiffs' only argument in support of their claim that management was not their "primary duty" is that, despite their responsibilities of handling issues at the farms and interacting with the Growers, the "crew leaders [were] only following company guidelines and needed to obtain higher supervisory approval for any deviation from the company guidelines." Defendants counter that crew leaders have substantial discretion over each step in the chicken catching process and that, "while the [c]rew [l]eaders are responsible for ensuring that the [c]rew follows [Defendants'] Live Haul Guidelines, the Plaintiffs testified that the procedure could not always be followed and that it was within their discretion to deviate from these procedures when they deemed necessary."

That Defendants have "well-defined policies, and that tasks are spelled out in great detail," is insufficient to negate the conclusion that the Plaintiffs' primary duty was management. *See Donovan v. Burger King Corp.*, 672 F.2d 221, 223, 226 (1st Cir. 1982) (holding that the assistant managers' primary duty was management despite their tasks being "governed by highly detailed, step-by-step instructions contained in Burger King's [manual]"). Indeed, "ensuring that company policies are carried out constitutes the very essence of supervisory work." *Id.* at 226 (internal quotations omitted).

Here, Plaintiffs confirmed that Defendants' Live Haul Guidelines describe the crew leaders' responsibilities. Plaintiff Walters described that it was within his discretion to deviate from the guidelines "up to a point," that it was not always possible to follow the guidelines exactly, and that he deviated from the procedures depending on the circumstances encountered on the farm. Plaintiffs Briddell and Gibbs confirmed a crew leader's ability to deviate from the guidelines. A crew leader is "directing all the responsibilities on the farm . . ." and is regarded "the leader out there [on the farm]." Thus the Plaintiffs' primary duty was management. *See, e.g., Baldwin*, 266 F.3d at 1116 (concluding that defendant's "employment meets the primary duty requirement because [defendant] had authority and discretion to manage the park on a day-to-day basis without supervision and control from [management]"); *Donovan*, 672 F.2d at 226 (holding assistant manager' primary duty is management despite performing non-exempt tasks); *Guthrie v. Lady Jane Collieries, Inc.*, 722 F.2d 1141, 1144-47 (3d Cir. 1983) (holding coal mine's foremen primary duty is management because of their independence from supervision and their safety and supervisory responsibilities).

Even if Plaintiffs were generally required to follow company policies and thus had diminished discretionary freedom, they fell within the accepted definition of employees whose primary duty is management. Therefore, section (a)(2) of the pertinent regulation is satisfied. 29 C.F.R. § 541.100(a)(2).

2. *Plaintiffs' Input into Hiring and Firing*

Plaintiffs contend that crew leaders are non-exempt under the FLSA because they lack the authority to hire or fire and that recommendations and suggestions made to Defendants were not given "particular weight" as required by section (a)(4). Plaintiffs say that their job responsibilities did not include the hiring of chicken catchers and that their involvement with the hiring process was minimal because it was limited to sending a potential candidate to a gentlemen named Lynch to go through Defendants' hiring procedure. Mr. Lynch is the Live Haul Manager for the Mountaire Selbyville Plant where Plaintiffs are or were employed. Furthermore, Plaintiffs suggest that they "had no impact at all as to who was hired by Defendant[s]," and that they did not have the authority to hire or fire or recommend the promotion of a catcher to forklift driver.

Defendants respond that those arguments are not supported by the facts in this case. Plaintiff Garrison testified in his deposition that the crew leader is responsible for staffing and maintaining a full crew, including suggesting new catchers for hire to Mr. Lynch. Garrison, in need of additional crew members, sent three people to Mr. Lynch telling him "I [would] like you [to] look to hire this guy." Defendants declined to hire one of the suggested individuals because the individual had worked for Defendants in the past and did not maintain a good work record. Plaintiff Gibbs stated that he brought his entire crew to work for Defendants when he was hired and that he also suggested two or three other individuals to be hired, of whom all but one were actually hired. Gibbs also effectuated the promotion of a catcher to a forklift driver by affirming a catcher's performance upon an inquiry by Mr. Lynch. Plaintiff Briddell testified that he selected at least four individuals who joined his crew as catchers.

Even though catchers typically quit before they are terminated, Garrison recommended that a catcher named Heath be terminated, and Heath was terminated. Briddell recommended the termination of a catcher named Hitchens, and Hitchens was terminated. Crew leaders also have the authority to discipline their crew members. Plaintiffs Garrison and Walters each issued six disciplinary warnings. Defendants argue that the "imposition of disciplinary action" is equivalent to changing an employee's status.

The question comes down to whether Defendants gave "particular weight" to Plaintiffs' suggestions and recommendations about hiring, firing, and discipline. The pertinent DOL regulations provide guidance on how to determine whether "particular weight" was given:

> To determine whether an employee's suggestions and recommendations are given "particular weight," factors to be considered include, but are not limited to, whether it is part of the employee's job duties to make such suggestions and recommendations; the frequency with which such suggestions and recommendations are made or requested; and the frequency with which the employee's suggestions and recommendations are relied upon. Generally, an executive's suggestions and recommendations must pertain to employees whom the executive customarily and regularly directs. It does not include an occasional suggestion with regard to the change in status of a co-worker. An employee's suggestions and recommendations may still be deemed to have "particular weight" even if a higher level manager's recommendation has more importance and even if the employee does not have authority to make the ultimate decision as to the employee's change in status.

29 C.F.R. § 541.105.

In *Haines v. Southern Retailers*, 939 F. Supp. 441, 450 (E.D. Va. 1996), the plaintiff argued that her employment lacked discretionary powers because "she was closely supervised by senior management . . . [,] could not hire or fire without outside management's approval . . . [,] performed many of her duties pursuant to strict guidelines . . . [,] was not permitted to discipline employees without the approval of her supervisor, and . . . was subject to rigid supervision and regular visits by upper management." *Id.* The court rejected her argument, stating that employees in similar positions have been held "vested with enough discretionary power and freedom from supervision to qualify for the executive exemption," even if those employees have only limited ability to hire and fire and whose managerial duties are regulated by strict guidelines. *Id.* The same is true for Plaintiffs in this case. *See* 939 F. Supp. at 451. In other words, "nothing in the governing regulations or relevant case law requires that a supervisor must have unfettered discretion in the performance of his management duties in order to be deemed an executive." *Beauchamp*, 357 F. Supp. 2d at 1017 (holding that production supervisor qualifies for executive exemption despite limited authority to hire and fire because the defendant company was using a temporary worker agency as an initial source of new employees).

Viewing the record most favorably to the Plaintiffs, as I must while considering Defendants' motion for summary judgment, I nevertheless conclude that Plaintiffs' work as crew leaders satisfies the requirement of 29 C.F.R. § 541.100(a)(4). Thus, Plaintiffs, in their positions as crew leaders met all four of the regulatory prerequisites and were "employee[s] in a bona fide executive . . . capacity. . . ." Therefore, no overtime pay is owed to them pursuant to the FLSA. 29 U.S.C. § 213(a)(1). . . .

[Discussion of retaliation and other claims is omitted].

NOTES

1. *Third Circuit Reversal.* Plaintiffs appealed to the Third Circuit Court of Appeals on the issue of whether the fourth prong of the test for the executive exemption was satisfied as a matter of law (there was no dispute that the other prongs were satisfied). The Third Circuit reversed and remanded on grounds that issues of fact existed as to whether the crew leaders were responsible for hiring and firing, and whether their recommendations on such issues were given particular weight. *Davis v. Mountaire Farms, Inc.*, 453 F.3d 554 (3d Cir. 2006).

2. *The Salary Test.* To fit within the exemption for executive, administrative, and professional employees, an employee must both perform certain duties and be paid a salary. The principal case discusses the duties test. The salary test can also be problematic. Do employees meet the salary test if they are generally paid a salary, but their pay is docked for working less than eight hours in a day? *See Martin v. Malcolm Pirnie, Inc.*, 949 F.2d 611 (2d Cir. 1991) (no). What if the employer imposes a disciplinary sanction of suspension without pay? *See* C.F.R. § 541.602(5) (salary test met if unpaid disciplinary sanction of one or more full days is imposed in good faith for serious workplace misconduct). What if no employee's pay has ever been docked, but the employer has a clear policy saying that such deductions will be made? *See Auer v. Robbins*, 519 U.S. 452 (1997) (salary test not met). What if, instead of docking salary, the employer requires employees who miss work for part of the day to make up the work later in the week? *See Cowart v. Ingalls Shipbuilding, Inc.*, 213 F.3d 261 (5th Cir. 2000) (salary test met). What if the employer docks salary for absences taken under the Family and Medical Leave Act? *See Rowe v. Laidlaw Transit, Inc.*, 244 F.3d 1115 (9th Cir. 2001) (salary test met; deductions from salary for FMLA leaves do not affect exempt status).

3. *Exemptions From Coverage.* Executive, administrative, and professional employees are exempted from coverage under the minimum-wage and overtime provisions of the FLSA, but are still covered by the equal pay and child-labor provisions. The FLSA contains other exemptions that apply to one or more of the Act's requirements. *See* 29 U.S.C. §§ 207, 213. It is easier to see a rationale for some of the exemptions than for others. The basic question once again, however, is why not simply cover all employees?

The exemptions, rather than limits on individual employee and enterprise coverage, account for the bulk of the uncovered sector. In 2003, of the approximately 124 million wage and salary earners in the United States, about 8 million were not covered by the FLSA because of coverage limits and 28 million were not covered because of the exemptions (including 20 million of the 31 million white collar workers who were subject to the salary test). The Department of Labor estimates that the new regulations will provide protection to an additional 6.7 million salaried workers, as well as over 3 million hourly workers. *Defining and Delimiting the Exemptions for Executive, Administrating, Professional, Outside Sales and Computer Employees*, 69 Fed. Reg. 22,122, 22,213 (Apr. 23, 2003), *available at* www.dol.gov/esa/regs/fedreg/final/2004009016.pdf.

4. *Lawyers and Law Clerks.* Lawyers are ordinarily considered exempt employees as "learned professionals," whose work requires "advanced knowledge . . . customarily acquired by a prolonged course of specialized intellectual instruction." 29 C.F.R. § 541.3(a)(1). *See also* 29 C.F.R. § 541.301. *See Kavanagh v. City of Phoenix*, 87 F. Supp. 2d 958 (D. Ariz. 2000) (head of police department's legal unit is an exempt professional); *Jackson Co. Assistant Prosecutors Ass'n v. County of Jackson*, No. 90-CU-70409-DT, 1991 U.S. Dist. LEXIS 2789 (E.D. Mich. Jan. 31, 1991) (county prosecutors are exempt professionals).

Should law clerks also be exempt? Or paralegals? *Cf. Quirk v. Baltimore Co.*, 895 F. Supp. 773 (D. Md. 1995) (paramedics are not exempt professionals); *Owsley v. San Antonio Indep. Sch. Dist.*, 187 F.3d 521 (5th Cir. 1999) (athletic trainers are exempt professionals).

C. WAGE-PAYMENT LAWS

BECKWITH v. UNITED PARCEL SERVICE
United States Court of Appeals, First Circuit
889 F.2d 344 (1989)

Coffin, Senior Circuit Judge. . . .

Plaintiff Daniel Beckwith, a driver for appellant United Parcel Service, was terminated for gross negligence for violating UPS delivery policies and causing substantial loss of merchandise.[1] In a meeting with his UPS supervisors and his union representative, Beckwith offered to pay back the losses he caused if UPS would reinstate him. UPS agreed, and the parties entered into a written payroll deduction agreement providing that $50 per week would be

---

[1] Plaintiff apparently released packages in circumstances not permitted by UPS policies. This resulted in the misdelivery of approximately $8,000 worth of computer equipment and approximately $1,400 worth of other merchandise, including video equipment. This merchandise was never recovered by UPS or its intended recipients.

deducted from Beckwith's paycheck until a total of $7,814 was repaid.[2] The weekly deductions began in April 1986.

About eighteen months later, Beckwith filed this action claiming that payroll deduction agreements such as the one he signed are prohibited by Maine law, and that UPS therefore was required to return to him the total amount deducted from his paychecks. Beckwith relied on 26 M.R.S.A. § 629, which states in pertinent part:

> No person, firm or corporation shall require or permit any person as a condition of securing or retaining employment to work without monetary compensation or when having an agreement, verbal, written or implied that a part of such compensation should be returned to the person, firm or corporation for any reason other than for the payment of a loan, debt or advance made to the person. . . .

> For purposes of this subchapter, the word "debt" means a benefit to the employee. Debt does not include items incurred by the employee in the course of the employee's work . . ., such as cash shortages, inventory shortages . . ., damages to the employer's property in any form or any merchandise purchased by a customer.

> An employer shall be liable to the employees for the amount returned to the employer as prohibited in this section.

Beckwith also sought liquidated damages, interest and attorney's fees under 26 M.R.S.A. § 626-A. . . .

The district court [held that Beckwith was entitled to the return of the withheld money, but] rejected Beckwith's claim for liquidated damages and attorney's fees, concluding that the Maine legislature intended to limit an employee's remedy under § 629 to recoupment of the deducted wages. . . .

[Section 629] does not prohibit *all* voluntary agreements between employers and employees for the reimbursement of employee debts. In our view, it simply bars the use of one method, payroll deductions, for doing so. We recognize that § 629 does not explicitly refer to pay withholding agreements. We believe, however, that the statute's reference to the *return of monetary compensation for work* is intended to refer to a direct payment to the employer from one's wages rather than to any payment at all. It is unlikely that the legislature would have chosen these specific words if its purpose was to prohibit employers entirely from securing agreements for the payment of debts caused by an employee's admitted negligence. *Cf. Male v. Acme Markets, Inc.*, 264 A.2d 245 (N.J. Super. Ct. App. Div. 1970) (declining to construe New Jersey statute prohibiting wage withholding to bar voluntary reimbursement of funds).[6]

The legislature undoubtedly viewed the payroll deduction as harmful and unfair because it deprives the worker of wages earned before he has had a

---

[2] UPS agreed to forgive the other losses caused by Beckwith's violations.

[6] Thus, § 629 would not foreclose an employee from agreeing, as a condition for reinstatement, to reimburse his employer for damages caused at a specified rate per month — so long as the amount of reimbursement does not come directly out of the employee's paycheck. Of course, any agreement that required the equivalent of a payroll deduction would be invalid. An employer could not, for example, require an employee to pay $50 per week as a condition of receiving his "full" paycheck.

chance to decide on a given payday how best to allocate his available resources. With a payroll deduction, an employee suffering an unexpected financial crisis loses the flexibility to pay his debt a little late so that he has enough money for that week's food. In addition, if funds are withheld automatically, the employee who seeks to challenge a particular deduction — for example, because he thinks the debt already is repaid — would nevertheless first lose access to his money. . . .

[T]he district court ruled that the wage withholding agreement was "null and void" and unenforceable against Beckwith. In its reply brief to us, UPS argues for the first time that only the payroll deduction provision should be invalidated and that the remainder of the agreement should be held enforceable. UPS claims that it has not urged this approach previously because Beckwith had not previously argued that it was only the payroll deduction provision that violated § 629. It apparently has been UPS's assumption that *any* agreement to pay back employment-related losses incurred by employees is barred by the statute if made a condition of employment.

We decline to consider whether the agreement is severable. It was UPS's obligation to argue to the district court that some remedy short of invalidating the agreement would satisfy Maine law. Although its failure to do so stems from mistaken assumptions about the scope of § 629, UPS had adequate notice of the theory that the *wage withholding* provision, and not the payback agreement itself, violated Maine law. Beckwith's complaint alleged that "[t]he actions of Defendant *in withholding weekly sums from Plaintiff's pay* are in violation of 26 M.R.S.A. § 629." (Emphasis added.) . . . The district court's opinion also suggests a focus on the payroll deduction element of the agreement: "The facts here do not fit within any of the section 629 exceptions permitting *paycheck deductions* as a condition of employment."

The company was not deceived by Beckwith's arguments, but merely taken unawares. In these circumstances, we see no reason to depart from the well-established principle that issues not raised below will not be considered on appeal. We therefore affirm the judgment of the district court invalidating the wage withholding agreement.

[The Court also affirmed the district court's remedy which required UPS to return to Beckwith the amount wrongly withheld from his pay, but denied Beckwith's request for liquidated damages and attorney's fees.]

NOTES

1. *Recovering Losses.* Employers generally can sue to recover losses caused by an employee's negligence or dishonesty. RESTATEMENT SECOND OF AGENCY § 401. *But see Fried v. Aftec, Inc.*, 587 A.2d 290 (N.J. Super. Ct. App. Div. 1991) (employer can recover for dishonesty, but not for negligence or ineptness; employer's remedy for the latter concerns is to fire the employee). Thus, UPS could have sued Beckwith to recover its losses. Wage-payment laws, however, generally restrict UPS's ability to recover its losses more directly by withholding the lost amounts from Beckwith's check. This restriction in wage-payment laws furthers both procedural and substantive goals. Procedurally, it is intended to force UPS to sue if it wants to recover to ensure that

Beckwith has a fair opportunity to defend against the alleged negligence or dishonesty. Substantively, the restriction is intended to limit the ability of employers to shift to employees costs that should be the employer's responsibility, such as losses from bad checks or robberies.

   2. When Employees Want Losses Withheld From Their Checks. As *Beckwith* illustrates, sometimes employees *want* to be able to guarantee payments for losses: Beckwith was going to lose his job unless he could guarantee payment in some way. Even without the interest in his job, Beckwith may have preferred a private settlement to a public lawsuit seeking recovery.

   Could UPS and Beckwith have agreed:

   (1) That UPS would pay Beckwith with two checks each week, one for $50 and the other for the rest of Beckwith's pay, and that upon receipt Beckwith would immediately endorse the $50 check to UPS? *See Male v. Acme Mkts.*, 264 A.2d 245 (N.J. Super. Ct. App. Div. 1970) (no).

   (2) That Beckwith would make a $50 payment each week until the lost amount was repaid? *Compare id.* (implies no) *with Stoll v. Goodnight Corp.*, 469 So. 2d 1072 (La. Ct. App. 1985) (yes).

   (3) That Beckwith would be reemployed at a rate of pay $50 per week less than he had been paid previously with an understanding that his pay would be increased after the amount saved in wage payments equaled the losses? *See Salter v. Freight Sales Co.*, 357 N.W.2d 38 (Iowa Ct. App. 1984) (no).

   Concern about the voluntariness of employee agreements to repay is a principal reason that the wage-payment cases generally make it difficult for an employer to seek to recover losses without filing a lawsuit against the employee. In *Stoll v. Goodnight Corp., supra,* for example, a travel agent agreed to repay the employer in installments for a $778 bad check she had accepted. She had not been negligent in accepting the check, but agreed to the repayment because she understood that she would lose her job if she refused. Two weeks after the repayment was completed, she was fired. No violation of the wage-payment statute was found, in part because she had voluntarily agreed to make the repayment.

   3. Other Common Provisions in Wage-Payment Laws. Wage-payment laws vary considerably across the states. Most require wage payments to be made in cash or by check (rather than in scrip, for example) and to be made periodically (such as every week or month). Most statutes also regulate the payment of wages upon termination of employment, requiring payment within a certain period of time after the relationship is ended. Often, the period is shorter when the employee is discharged than it is when the employee quits. Most statutes also impose restrictions on the assignment of wages. For example, some states prohibit assignments, while others require the employer and the worker's spouse to consent to any assignment. Many states also restrict the garnishment of wages and restrict the ability of employers to discharge workers for having their wages garnished. The federal government has also regulated garnishment. Consumer Credit Protection Act, 15 U.S.C. §§ 1673-1674 (limiting the amount that can be garnished and prohibiting discharge for one garnishment). The statutory supplement contains examples of state wage-payment laws on each of these topics.

Chapter 17

UNEMPLOYMENT AND UNEMPLOYMENT INSURANCE

A. SKETCHES OF THE UNEMPLOYED

LOUIS UCHITELLE, THE DISPOSABLE AMERICAN: LAYOFFS AND THEIR CONSEQUENCES 108-11 (2006) *

Stephen A. Holthausen . . . still cannot believe that his success as a bank loan officer, and his standing in his community, failed to protect him from the layoff that took him by surprise on Monday morning, August 13, 1990. What happened to him was the age of layoffs at its cruelest, theatrically cruel. Here was a vice president for business lending at the New England Savings Bank in New London, Connecticut, the co-chairman of the board of trustees of the Congregational church in nearby Westbrook, his hometown, the vice chairman of the police advisory board, a past president of the Junior Chamber of Commerce, just forty-six years old, who got swept away in a staff reduction to save money.

The ax fell on his first day back from a two-week family vacation in Maine. His immediate boss wanted him gone that very Monday morning, but a higher officer granted Holthausen's request for a two-week reprieve so that he could respond to the mail that had piled up during the vacation and clean up pending matters with customers. He was told that his position as vice president for business lending was eliminated, and he was too. But toward the end of the two weeks, he met the twenty-two-year-old who had taken over his duties, and who was earning less than Holthausen. "I was costing them $50,000 plus health insurance plus group life insurance plus stock options; I had all that stuff," he said. "I was not terminated for failure, or putting my hand in the cookie jar. They just took the most expensive people and tossed them out. I was on the wrong end of the numbers."

It was a classic downsizing in which the victim, Holthausen, after twenty-two years in banking, sporting a resume that chronicled successes, was told in effect that his cost outstripped his value, and he had to go. . . .

As a banker, he had survived two mergers, and the cost-cutting that inevitably followed. He attributed his survival to the strengths that he brought to his work. These were a combination of salesmanship and civic involvement, including the many shallow relationships that good salesmen cultivate. "I have the gift of gab," Holthausen explained, obviously pleased to possess that talent. His civic activities brought him borrowers from his community, and his status in banking gave him standing in Westbrook, a small southern Connecticut town of mostly middle-income families like the Holthausens. He thought he had survived the third merger, in October 1988. That merger made New England Savings the owner of his employer, First Federal Savings. But banks everywhere in the country were in trouble, in many cases in danger of folding. They had made too many bad loans in the eighties, and the nation soon tipped into recession, compounding the pressure on them. New England Savings, in response, continued to cut costs, and when Holthausen lost his job, the stature that he had acquired from his mixture of banking and civic activity collapsed. But not right away.

He had thought that he could take his customers with him to another bank; their regard for him would keep them loyal. "They did not care what bank's name was on the loan documents or on their deposit slips as long as I was their banker," he said. The recession and the banking crisis blocked that strategy before he could test it; he could not get another job in banking. After his severance ran out, he did work for a while as a consultant to the Saybrook Bank and Trust Company, giving advice on how to deal with loans in default, but Saybrook failed in December 1991. At home, his already shaky marriage collapsed, brought down finally by the layoff. To this day, Holthausen remains critical of his ex-wife, Diane, for failing to provide emotional support and faith in her husband's skills, just as he is forever critical of New England Savings for failing to value his earning power as a loan officer.

Feeling panicky, Diane Holthausen solicited food packages from the Westbrook Congregational Church, although her husband was then cochairman of the board of trustees, and compounded this humiliation by asking the minister and several parishioners for money, telling them the family was destitute. Years later, their daughter, Gretchen, by then out of college and working as a research assistant at Yale University's School of Medicine, in the psychiatry department, offered a more nuanced explanation of that devastating period in which neither parent gave comfort to the other. "My father's job and income and health benefits were so much a part of our lives that we did not recognize where they came from until they ended," she told me. "My mother was so shocked by the layoff and she blamed my father because she did not know anyone else to blame. She could not be angry at the bank because it was not part of our lives any longer. She was frustrated with herself because she had no other source of income, and she blamed him because he was putting the family through so much hardship. . . ."

[Holthausen] slid steadily down the economic ladder. He pumped gas for a while at a station owned by a former bank customer, drove a car for a salesman who had lost his license for drunken driving, got paid to be a guinea pig in the testing of a prescription drug, and did odd jobs as a handyman until a ladder fell while he was trimming trees and he broke his arm. For a while, he was treated at a Veterans Administration hospital for depression.

H.G. KAUFMAN, PROFESSIONALS IN SEARCH OF WORK: COPING WITH THE STRESS OF JOB LOSS AND UNDEREMPLOYMENT 53-55 (1982) *

[T]he degree of stress created by job loss is comparable to that of other losses in life, such as divorce and the death of a spouse or a close friend. The epidemiological evidence also indicates that joblessness has a widespread impact on mental and physical health. The rise in unemployment has been associated with subsequent increases in mental hospitalization, suicides, murders, and alcoholism. Infant mortality and deaths from stroke, heart, and kidney diseases have also risen following periods of high unemployment. Stress created during recession periods appears quite pervasive, affecting not only the unemployed, but also those who are still working.

There does not seem to be any doubt that work is much more central to the identity of professionals than of other workers. Therefore, since work becomes a greater potential source of both frustration and satisfaction for professionals, they would be more likely to experience severe stress as a result of unemployment than would other workers. Furthermore, jobless professionals have consistently been found to exhibit significantly more stress than their colleagues who remain employed, with perhaps as many as two-fifths experiencing psychological impairment extreme enough to require mental assistance. Those professionals who are affected by unemployment stress are likely to manifest at least some of the following psychological changes and symptoms:

1. Low self-esteem.
2. High anxiety.
3. Anomie.
4. Self-blame.
5. Depression.
6. Social isolation.
7. Anger and resentment.
8. Aggression toward others.
9. Psychosomatic disorders.
10. Occupational rigidity.
11. Professional obsolescence.
12. Low motivation to work.
13. Low achievement motivation.
14. External locus of control.
15. Helplessness.
16. Premature death from suicide or illness.

A factor analysis revealed that the unemployed professional may undergo stress which is either general in nature or more specific, involving symptoms of psychopathology or work inhibition. It is likely that those who exhibit the more extreme psychopathological characteristics would be more prone to experience intrapunitive symptoms manifested by psychosomatic disorders and even premature death from either stress-induced illness or suicide. In fact, failure in the work role for males precipitates the basic suicide syndrome. Applied to job loss, this syndrome involves failure in a work role to which one is strongly committed, followed by occupational rigidity or inability to change roles, feelings of shame, and finally, social isolation as a defense to protect oneself against such feelings. Although job loss and other types of failure in the work role are apparently the most important cause of male suicides, clearly most unemployed professionals do not resort to this self-destructive path in dealing with their failure. Responses such as withdrawal and work inhibition are much more likely to occur, but as defense mechanisms these become highly dysfunctional in dealing with the problem of finding a job.

There is some evidence that unemployment can have an "ecological" effect on the whole family. Wives of unemployed men have been found to experience psychophysiological stress accompanying that of their husbands. Older children particularly may also suffer psychological effects, such as a loss of self-esteem as a result of their father being out of work. Furthermore, the stress created by unemployment has been identified as the highest risk factor predisposing parents to child abuse.

The drastic psychological changes that some professionals experience as a result of job loss may be explained as resulting from the need to bring their cognitions about themselves into balance and thereby reduce cognitive inconsistencies. Accordingly, a reduction in the motivation to work would reflect an attempt to lower one's level of aspiration to be more congruent with a diminished self-esteem. Nevertheless, despite their devalued self-esteem, professionals for whom work remains an important part of their identity appear to maintain a high motivation to return to work for restoration of their self-esteem.

The reactions of many professionals to unemployment can also be understood in terms of a societal model in which an environment that devalues self-esteem and diminishes the individual's control can result in low levels of achievement and satisfaction, in addition to aggression toward oneself and others. Widespread unemployment creates just such an environment and it is the resulting loss of self-esteem and the emergence of helplessness that appears to be central to the psychological consequences of joblessness among professionals. This helps explain why unemployment has been found to be the best economic predictor of mental health, whereas inflation appears totally unrelated.

B.   THE UNEMPLOYMENT INSURANCE PROGRAM

Unemployment insurance in the United States is provided by a unique blend of federal and state government programs, created during the Great Depression with a fascinating constitutional history. It is a major government transfer program, accounting in recession years for some 15% of all government transfer payments to individuals. In 1939, its first full year of operation, the UI system paid a half-billion dollars in benefits. Over a half century later, in 2005, UI programs paid over $31.3 billion to 7.9 million unemployed workers. They collected $36.7 billion from employers, thus generating a net surplus, and imposed an average tax rate of 0.8% on total wages. 2005 was a year of low unemployment, 5%. At other points in the business cycle, UI benefits can greatly exceed current UI taxes. In 1983, for example, when the unemployment rate was 10.1%, UI paid regular benefits of over $20 billion to nearly 10 million workers, plus another $8 billion in extended benefits. Federal and state tax collections were about $18 billion in 1983. At other times, UI programs run a surplus.

1.   HISTORY AND FINANCIAL STRUCTURE OF UNEMPLOYMENT INSURANCE

In 1932, Wisconsin became the first state to enact an unemployment insurance program, and it remained the only state program prior to passage of federal laws in 1935. The "principal obstacle" to state UI legislation, declared the House Ways and Means Committee in 1935, was that the payroll tax used to finance the system would put the enacting state's employers at a competitive disadvantage. With some 25% of the workforce unemployed, a national mandatory unemployment insurance program soon became a major priority of the New Deal. In particular, Frances Perkins, Roosevelt's Secretary of Labor, placed a high priority on unemployment insurance. One concern, however, was that the Supreme Court would strike down any nationally administered system.

There is a story, perhaps apocryphal, that Supreme Court Justice Louis Brandeis whispered to Perkins at a dinner party, "use the taxing power." (Brandeis's daughter was an administrator of Wisconsin's UI program, and Brandeis was clearly a proponent of a nationwide UI program.) Whether Brandeis was the catalyst or not, in the summer of 1934 the Commission on Economic Security, chaired by Perkins, drafted an unemployment insurance program as part of the Social Security Act that used the federal taxing power to skirt the Supreme Court threat. The federal tax would "encourage" states to adopt an unemployment insurance program. One advantage of the tax approach, thought the drafters, was that even if the Supreme Court struck down the federal law, the state programs would be up and running.

Under the Social Security Act of 1935, as amended, the federal government imposes an employer payroll tax on every covered employee. Currently, the tax is 6.2% of the first $7,000 in wages.* However, if the employer operates

---

* The original Social Security Act of 1935 taxed all wages of covered workers. This decision was consistent with the goal of imposing a uniform tax throughout the country so no state would have an advantage over another. In the 1939 amendments, Congress limited the tax base to the

in a state with a qualified state unemployment insurance program, the federal government offsets the federal tax with any state taxes the employer has paid up to 5.4%. The federal tax credit is not simply a wash. If the state has an approved UI plan that charges some employers less than 5.4% for good experience, they still get credit for the entire 5.4%. Additionally, the federal government uses part of the remaining 0.8% federal tax to fund the administrative costs of state plans.

The incentive for employers to lobby their state government to create a qualified UI program was tremendous. Without a qualified state program, employers would pay a substantial federal tax that would give their state's workers no benefits. With a state program, employers would pay the same or lower taxes and their workers would receive benefits. By 1937, all states had enacted unemployment insurance laws. That same year, the Supreme Court upheld the constitutionality of the UI taxing scheme. *Steward Machine Co. v. Davis*, 301 U.S. 548 (1937).

Initially, federal law had modest requirements for a state program to "qualify" for the tax credit. States had to pay benefits through public employment offices (rather than, say, the mails). State administrators had to be hired on a merit basis rather than through political patronage. States were required to deposit all UI tax receipts in the unemployment trust fund in the United States Treasury and could withdraw funds only to pay benefits. States could not deny benefits because a claimant refused a job that (1) was vacant because of a strike; (2) paid less than the prevailing wage; or (3) required membership in a company union or prohibited membership in a "bona fide" labor union.

Nevertheless, the federal program informally created a more uniform pattern than these modest requirements might suggest. The Social Security Board** drafted model guidelines in 1936 for states that wanted to be sure they enacted a qualified program. The Board also issued opinion letters on such issues as methods of experience rating. In the early days, Federal grants to states for administration were based on detailed, line-item budgets submitted by the states.

The result is that all state UI programs have significant common elements, with considerable variations at the margins. In every state, eligibility depends on earning a certain amount, working a certain number of weeks, or some combination, during a preceding base period. These eligibility requirements are intended to measure the worker's prior attachment to the work force. In most states, claimants must wait a week before collecting benefits. Full-time workers commonly are eligible for twenty-six weeks of benefits. Benefits typically are 50% of weekly wages up to a statutory maximum. Most states set their cap as one-half to two-thirds of the average weekly wages in the state. Because of the cap on benefits, average UI benefits replace only one-third of

---

first $3,000 of wages, a ceiling that exceeded the annual wages of 98% of workers. The federal tax rate at the time was 3%. The FUTA tax base has not kept pace with the rise in payrolls. Today, with the $7,000 federal base (and somewhat higher state bases), only about 30% of total payroll of taxable employers is subject to the tax. Had the 1939 ceiling been continually indexed for wage growth, the current ceiling would be over $50,000 instead of $7,000.

** The federal regulatory authority for unemployment insurance was later shifted to the Unemployment Insurance Service of the Department of Labor.

prior wages. Thirteen states give additional benefits for dependents, generally $10 or less per week. The smallest minimum benefit is $5 in Hawaii; the largest maximum is $496 in Washington.

On the tax side, as of 2006, forty-two states have adopted tax bases higher than the $7,000 federal base, ranging as high as Hawaii's $34,000. Because states attempt to charge higher taxes to those employers with frequent layoffs, tax rates vary widely among employers. In 2005, minimum tax rates ranged from zero percent in several states to a high of 2.9% in Arizona. Massachusetts charges the highest maximum rate — 15.4% of taxable payroll. In 2005, state taxes averaged 2.8% of taxable payroll, or 0.8% of total payroll. The average UI tax burden varies widely between states, however. It ranges from 0.48 to 5.1% of taxable payroll, or 0.2 to 1.48% of total payroll.

In 2005, 7.9 million unemployed workers received UI benefits. Their average weekly benefit was $266.69 and the average duration was 15.3 weeks. 35.9% of the recipients exhausted their regular benefits. All these figures vary widely with the business cycle.

Since 1969, the federal unemployment trust fund has been treated as part of the federal budget. Thus, whenever benefits paid exceed UI taxes received (the usual situation in a recession), the UI program adds to the federal budget deficit. In 1982, for example, the unemployment trust fund added almost $7.5 billion to the federal deficit, an increase in the deficit of 6.2%. In 1987, by contrast, the UI fund reduced the deficit by $7.3 billion, keeping the deficit from being 4.6% higher than it was. Importantly, any changes in eligibility and coverage will also affect the federal budget. In part because of UI's inclusion in the federal budget, Congress has become more active in recent decades in amending the UI system. The 1980 National Commission on Unemployment Compensation (NCUC) was formed by both houses of Congress and the President to re-examine the federal-state unemployment insurance system, and unanimously recommended removing UI from the federal unified budget. As Wilbur Cohen, the Chair of the NCUC explained, "[t]he [congressional] emphasis on cost cutting indicates lack of understanding of the intended countercyclical nature of the UI program which is aimed at having an excess of benefits over income during periods of higher-than-normal unemployment." Cohen, *Reflections on the Work of the National Commission on Unemployment Compensation,* 59 U. Detroit J. Urb. L. 486, 496 (1982).

In a series of amendments in the 1970s, Congress greatly expanded the coverage of UI. One major addition was the coverage of state and local government employees. Congress was not so bold as to impose a federal tax on local school boards. Instead, one of the conditions for a qualifying state plan is that it must cover state and local government workers, even though the FUTA tax only covers private-sector employees. Further, states must permit governmental entities (and nonprofit organizations) to finance benefit costs by reimbursing the Trust Fund rather than by paying state taxes. Today, UI programs cover all employers that have at least one employee for at least twenty weeks of the year, or with a payroll of at least $1,500 in any calendar quarter. As a result of these program extensions, coverage of wage and salary workers rose from 65% in 1970 to nearly 90% today.

In 1970, Congress also established a permanent extended benefit program, which grants claimants who exhaust their regular state benefits an additional thirteen weeks of benefits. The extended benefit program is triggered whenever state insured unemployment rates reach specified high levels. The extended benefit program is jointly funded by federal and state payroll taxes.

In addition to the regular UI program and the extended benefit program, in the nine major recessions since World War II, Congress has enacted temporary supplemental programs for unemployed workers. Unlike the regular and extended programs, these temporary programs are funded from general federal revenues.

The expanded coverage created financial difficulties in the UI programs of several states for the first time since World War II. This has led to congressional battles to force states to tighten eligibility requirements. In recent years, Congress has dramatically increased the number of requirements for an approved state program qualifying for the federal tax credit offset. For example, state programs must deny benefits to illegal aliens, to professional athletes between seasons, and to schoolteachers between terms. State programs must offset benefits by the amount of pension benefits a claimant receives and the amount of child support he owes. State agencies must give wage records to welfare agencies determining eligibility of needy families. State programs must disqualify ex-service members who declined the option to reenlist.

2. CAUSES OF UNEMPLOYMENT AND THE ROLE OF UI

One of the most unpleasant consequences of a free-market economy is that some persons desiring work cannot find it. The causes of unemployment are several. Economies periodically have recessions where consumer demand and production falls, leading to cyclical unemployment. Even in a full-employment economy, some workers will be between jobs and therefore unemployed. Information about job vacancies is limited, and it simply takes time for workers to find appropriate jobs. Some frictional unemployment, as this has been called, is perhaps inevitable. Unemployment insurance, by subsidizing job search costs, can extend the length of frictional unemployment. To help reduce this friction, many states tie their UI programs to a state employment service. UI claimants are required to register with the employment service, which serves as a job bank and reference service.

More serious is structural unemployment, which arises from a geographic or skill mismatch between workers and available jobs. Structural unemployment is an acute problem when a major employer in a community goes out of business. Many workers, particularly older workers, are unwilling or unable to learn new skills or relocate to new jobs. Many young workers, particularly those with little education, likewise face structural unemployment, in that appropriate jobs simply do not exist. The federal government has initiated many job training programs, such as the Job Training Partnership Act of 1982, in an attempt to combat structural unemployment. Unemployment insurance programs seem less effective in helping workers combat structural unemployment. Indeed, in recent years several states have disqualified participants in training programs from UI benefits, on the ground they are not currently available for work.

Another type of unemployment has been termed wait unemployment. Many unemployed workers are on temporary layoff and do not actively look for other work, preferring to wait for a recall. Such workers generally are covered by unemployment insurance, and in most states are not subject to the usual requirement that UI claimants actively search for work. We deal more fully with the effect of UI benefits on wait unemployment below.

A continual debate centers on whether unemployment insurance should attempt to combat or alleviate all of the various forms of unemployment. The general policy has been for unemployment insurance to be a limited response to the problem of unemployment. In the main, unemployment insurance is designed to provide temporary, partial wage replacement to experienced workers who become unemployed through no fault of their own. Teenagers who have trouble finding a first job, homemakers returning to the job market, and the long-term unemployed who have exhausted UI benefits are generally ineligible for unemployment insurance. For an explanation of this limited aim of UI, consider the following article.

GILLIAN LESTER, UNEMPLOYMENT INSURANCE AND WEALTH REDISTRIBUTION, 49 UCLA L. Rev. 335 (2001) [*]

In recent years, legal scholars and policymakers have increasingly advocated the expansion and liberalization of unemployment insurance (UI) beyond its traditional bounds. Proposals range from increasing the number of workers who are eligible for UI, to eliminating traditional reasons for disqualifying workers from benefits, to increasing the amount of benefits.

In spite of their diverse nature, most expansionist proposals share two pivotal and related claims about unemployment insurance. First, reformers argue that the structure of UI has failed to keep pace with the evolving complexity of modern labor markets. Indeed, UI was designed to provide wage replacement benefits to workers employed in traditional long-term jobs in the event of unexpected, involuntary unemployment. The postwar influx of women and younger workers into the paid workforce dramatically and permanently altered this occupational paradigm, introducing a significant segment of part-time, temporary, contract, and other types of "contingent" workers into the regulatory landscape.

Because UI explicitly links eligibility to "labor force attachment," and narrowly construes what counts as involuntary unemployment, it may exclude nontraditional workers from benefits. As it happens, "UI recipiency" has declined by approximately 40 percent since the 1950s. Reformers lament this drop in the proportion of unemployed workers who receive benefits. They are concerned that the system no longer fully achieves its original goals of protecting a broad base of workers from wage loss and from downward mobility in the event of involuntary unemployment, while stabilizing the economy by injecting funds into it during downturns.

---

[*] Excerpted with permission of the author and UCLA Law Review.

[Second, some] reformers further argue that unemployment insurance has failed in its potential to be a more active instrument of wealth redistribution. . . . Consequently, they argue, we should reform UI so that it better achieves its progressive potential: Relaxing eligibility rules would draw current "misfits" into the scope of coverage, thereby ameliorating the burdens on low-income workers and workers with conflicting family caregiving obligations.

I share reformers' normative commitments. Eradicating poverty among low-wage and marginal workers ought to be a central concern for American labor policy. Moreover, the law can and should play an important role in providing feasible ways for families to balance the conflicting demands of work and caregiving obligations, particularly as women continue to seek full participation in the workforce. Despite my sympathies for these *normative* goals, however, in this Article I question whether expanding UI is the best *prescriptive* mechanism for accomplishing them.

My analysis is both theoretical and empirical. Theoretically, I argue that expanding UI does not logically follow from a moral commitment to redistribute wealth to less well-off individuals (such as poor workers or workers who bear substantial caregiving obligations). Indeed, at its core, UI is a scheme to provide compensation for involuntary unemployment. No amount of tweaking, clarifying, or redefining of terms can alter the fact that job loss is the critical moment for triggering recipiency. As such, it is inevitable that such a system will suffer from both overinclusiveness (providing benefits for well-off unemployed workers) and underinclusiveness (failing to provide benefits for more deserving employed workers) relative to a redistributional goal. Simply put, if we wish to transfer wealth to poorer workers, we should use a more direct surrogate for need than involuntary job loss. Low family income, for example, might be a more suitable criterion for redistribution. Similarly, if we want to ease the financial burdens of caring for dependent children and elders, we should target needs associated with such caregiving, rather than unexpected job loss, as criteria for transferring wealth.

Empirically, as well, a number of reformist positions suffer under close scrutiny. Proposals to pull more nontraditional workers into the UI framework, for example, involve more than modest institutional modifications. Including a broader swath of workers in UI, particularly workers with very low wages or hours, may result in lower employment, wages, or other nonpecuniary benefits for these workers. Whether and to what extent such repercussions would follow from expanding UI eligibility is a critical and complex empirical question that deserves far greater attention than reformers have given it. . . .

[D]irect tax and transfer programs designed to subsidize workers with low income may be a better fit for reformers' redistributional goals, as might a tailored program of family leave insurance, based on a non-experience-rated tax of all employers, designed to smooth income of individuals whose work-family conflicts lead to interruptions in paid employment. . . .

If we aspire to provide subsidies to the working poor, or to alleviate the burdens of caring for dependent family members, UI is a clumsy vehicle.

As Professor Lester emphasizes, unemployment insurance is not a successful welfare program and was not intended to serve that function. Most importantly, there is no income test (or "means" testing, as it is often called) for benefits: whether non-work income (perhaps from other family members) is $1,000 or $100,000 does not affect a claimant's eligibility. As Table 17-1 shows, most UI recipients are prime-age white males.

Table 17-1
Demographic Characteristics of Unemployed Persons and UI Recipients, Calendar Year 1994 (in percents)

Characteristic	Distribution of			Percent of Unemployed Receiving UI Benefits[a] (4)
	Civilian Labor Force (1)	Total Unemployed (2)	UI Claimants (3)	
Age				
16 to 34	43	60	38	21
35 to 54	45	32	45	47
55 and over	12	8	12	51
N.A.[b]			5	
Gender				
Men	54	55	57	35
Women	46	45	40	30
N.A.[b]			3	
Race				
White	85	74	65	30
Black/Hispanic	11	21	26	41
Other	4	5	5	32
N.A.[b]			5	

[a] Data from fourth quarter only.

[b] "N.A." indicates data not available.

Sources: Advisory Council on Unemployment Insurance, Defining Federal and State Roles in Unemployment Insurance (1996); United States Department of Labor, Unemployment Insurance Service, Division of Actuarial Services, UI Data Summary (March 1997); United States Department of Labor, Unemployment Insurance Service, Data Retrieval Request (run Feb. 20, 1998).

Fewer than 40 percent of all unemployed persons receive unemployment benefits, as shown by Table 17-2. The majority of unemployed workers are ineligible for UI benefits, because they did not have a job before becoming unemployed or because they voluntarily quit their job. Most job losers are eligible for UI benefits, unless they were fired for job-related misconduct or have exhausted their period of benefits. Even among job losers, only two-thirds receive benefits.

Table 17-2
Reasons for Unemployment
July 2006 (seasonally adjusted)

Reason for Unemployment*	No. of Workers	% of All Unemployed
New Entrants to the Labor Force (not eligible for UI)	629,000	8.4%
Reentrants (generally not eligible)	2,358,000	32.2%
Job Leavers (generally not eligible)	857,000	11.0%
Job Losers (generally eligible)	3,370,000	48.4%
Total Unemployment	7,214,000	100%
Workers Receiving UI Benefits**	2,653,600	36%

* Source: Bureau of Labor Statistics web page (http://www.bls.gov/).

**Source: UI Data Summary, U.S. Department of Labor, Office of Workforce Security, Division of Fiscal and Actuarial Services. Data for 12 months preceding end of 1st quarter of 2006.

a. UI and Job Search Behavior

Many studies have shown that unemployment insurance actually increases unemployment. An unemployed worker receiving UI benefits has an income cushion that reduces the urgency of finding another job. This rise in unemployment is not necessarily a loss for society. By allowing workers to prolong their job search, UI benefits enable workers to reject poor jobs and wait for a better job match that increases their productivity. One study of this tradeoff concluded that raising the UI benefit rate from 40% to 50% of income would prolong unemployment by 1.5 weeks, but would increase post-unemployment wages by 7%. Ronald G. Ehrenberg & Ronald L. Oaxaca, *Unemployment Insurance, Duration of Unemployment, and Subsequent Wage Gain,* 66 Am. Econ. Rev. 754 (1976). This job-search effect did not apply for men who returned to their previous employer or who quit voluntarily. Older women responded similarly but less dramatically to increases in UI benefits. Younger workers increased the length of unemployment slightly when UI benefits were increased, but did not receive higher post-unemployment wages as a result.

Spillover effects influence the job search even of workers ineligible for UI. Estimates suggest that, because covered workers stay unemployed longer than they otherwise would, uncovered job seekers (typically new entrants and reentrants to the labor force) find work faster than they would in an economy without unemployment insurance.

b. Experience Rating and Employer Layoff Behavior

An important feature of unemployment insurance is its imperfect experience rating. The system tries to force individual employers to recognize the costs to the system of terminating a worker by increasing the tax rate of those employers whose employees frequently receive UI benefits. But the experience rating is imperfect, meaning that an employer's tax payments do not go up by the full amount of the benefits its terminated employees receive. The following excerpt sketches the methods of experience rating, and explains why it is imperfect.

ADVISORY COUNCIL ON UNEMPLOYMENT COMPENSATION, UNEMPLOYMENT INSURANCE IN THE UNITED STATES 73-82 (1995)

The fundamental method of financing the U.S. system of Unemployment Insurance has been a contentious issue since the system was established. During the debates in the 1930s that shaped the basic structure of the system, some argued that it should be funded through an "experience-rated" tax that imposes the highest tax rates on employers that generate the most cost to the system. Others argued that the system should be financed by a flat tax on employers.

Proponents of experience rating eventually prevailed. They argued that experience rating had the following three fundamental advantages, which are still offered today as reasons for its continuance: (1) the encouragement of stable employment, (2) the attribution of the costs of unemployment insurance benefits to the employer responsible for the unemployment, and (3) the creation of an incentive for employers to participate actively in policing the UI program.

Despite these apparent advantages, the United States is the only nation that chooses to finance its UI system through an experience-rated tax. As a result, experience rating has come under close scrutiny and has been the subject of ongoing debate. To some, experience rating is the root problem with the UI system, in that its strict allocation of costs tends to limit benefits as employers seek to minimize their costs. To others, experience rating is an essential component in making unemployment benefits one of the costs of doing business. . . .

Systems of Experience Rating

Over the years, states' experience rating provisions have become increasingly varied and complex. Although these systems vary substantially in many ways, the incentives that they create are generally similar. Under each of these methods, employers are ranked annually against one another and are assigned a specific tax rate based on that ranking, with employers who generate more costs to the system assigned a higher rate.

In all states, employers pay an assigned UI tax rate on the amount of their taxable wages, which are those annual wages for each employee that fall below a prescribed base level. The actual ranges of employer tax rates . . . vary substantially from state to state. In the 1993 tax year, the states' minimum tax rate varied from 0 percent (in 7 states) to a high of 2.5 percent in New York. The maximum tax rate on taxable wages varied from 5.4 percent (in 13 states) to a high of 10.5 percent in Pennsylvania. As a result of the range in tax rates and taxable wage bases, taxes paid range from zero for some employers to more than $900 per worker for other employers. Within a state, the entire schedule of tax rates is often adjusted up or down, depending on the balance in the state trust fund.

In general, the states' current systems of experience rating can be classified in one of four categories: reserve ratio, benefit ratio, benefit-wage ratio, and payroll decline. . . .

Reserve Ratio

The reserve ratio formula, which is used by 33 states [includes District of Columbia, U.S. Virgin Islands and Puerto Rico], is the most common method of experience rating. An account is established for each employer; contributions are credit to the account and benefits paid to former employees are charged against the account. The balance is carried over from year to year for the duration of the employer's activity.

The reserve ratio is defined as the account's balance relative to the employer's annual taxable payroll. The higher an employer's reserve ratio, the lower the assigned tax rate. Conversely, the lower an employer's reserve ratio (which can be negative), the higher the assigned tax rate.

Benefit Ratio

The benefit ratio formula is used by 17 states to experience rate UI benefits. Under this formula, firms pay taxes in proportion to the ratio of *benefits* paid relative to taxable wages, without directly taking contributions into account. Because this ratio uses only the most recent 3 years of data to assign tax rates, the benefit ratio formula is more short term in its focus than is the reserve ratio formula, which incorporates the entire life span of an employer's account.

[The benefit-wage ratio formula is now used by only two states — Oklahoma and Delaware. The payroll decline method is now used only by Alaska.]

Factors Affecting the Degree of Experience Rating

The degree to which an experience rating system succeeds in assigning UI benefit costs to the employer who generates an individual cost depends on the details of the system. If a number of provisions allow assignable UI costs to be paid for by entities other than the responsible employer, then the degree of overall experience rating in the system declines. . . .

Noncharged Benefits

All states provide that, in some circumstances, certain benefits paid are not charged to the account of an individual employer, but instead are shared among all UI taxpayers. The purpose of adopting a noncharging provision is often to reduce employer opposition to a particular kind of benefit. Common forms of noncharged benefits include these: (1) payments to workers who quit their last job, (2) dependents' benefits, (3) payments to workers who are enrolled in approved training, (4) erroneous benefit payments that are not recovered, and (5) the state share of the Extended Benefits program. Differences among the states in the use of noncharged benefits are substantial, ranging in 1993 from 1 percent in the District of Columbia to 32 percent in Washington.

Ineffectively Charged Benefits

Ineffectively charged benefits develop when an individual employer's tax rate is too low to cover the benefits paid to that employer's former employees, which happens when employers are at a state's maximum tax rate. Under these circumstances, benefits charged against the employer neither draw on accumulated past taxes nor trigger additional current taxes. Such ineffective charges become a drain to the system which must be made up in some way through taxes paid by other employers.

During 1993, average ineffective charges in the United States ranged from less than 1 percent in Montana to 39 percent in Oklahoma. As expected, the average maximum tax rate was higher in states with fewer ineffective charges. Among the 10 states with the lowest ineffective charges, the average maximum tax rate was 6.7 percent. The 10 states with the highest ineffective charges had an average maximum tax rate of 6.0 percent.

At the end of each fiscal year, several states also automatically reduce the size of an employer's negative balance to a maximum percentage of the employer's payroll. As a result, employers at those states' maximum tax rates routinely benefit from outright tax forgiveness. In those states, employers with large negative balances are never required to make tax payments on those balances, and their costs are shifted permanently to other employers.

Inactive Charges

Inactive charges result when an employer goes out of business and, therefore, stops paying payroll taxes. Benefits collected by former employees result in inactive charges, which also reduce the degree of experience rating in the system.

Changes in the State Taxable Wage Base

Some states change the level of their taxable wage bases relatively frequently. The impact of such changes on the degree of experience rating is complex [but often can result in less perfect experience rating]. . . .

It is by changing the *distribution* of employer tax rates across the tax schedule in a state, that a change in the taxable wage base most directly affects the degree of experience rating in a state. This distribution varies greatly across states. Raising the taxable wage base *reduces* the degree of experience rating to the extent that it moves more employers down to the minimum tax rate. Raising the taxable wage base *increases* the degree of experience rating for employers who were at the maximum tax rate prior to the increase, but below the maximum rate after the increase. (The reason for this is that these employers then have to contribute a higher percentage toward costs attributed to them.) Without detailed information on the distribution of employers at the minimum and maximum tax rates on a state-by-state basis, therefore, it is difficult to determine in advance the overall extent to which an increase in the taxable wage base would raise or lower the overall degree of experience rating.

Benefit Charging for Multiple Employers

States differ as to how they charge benefits to employers' accounts when there are multiple employers. Only nine states charge the most recent or principal employer exclusively. This is a particularly effective mechanism for preserving the degree to which the funding of the system is experience-rated.

To illustrate the influence of UI on the employer's decision to lay off workers, consider the examples outlined in Table 17-3.

Table 17-3
Firm A — Constant Employment Strategy

Per Worker amounts	Quarter 1	Quarter 2	Quarter 3	Quarter 4	Total
(1) Quarterly Gross Profit (all costs but wages)	$180	$20	$20	$180	$400
(2) Wages	$180	$20	$20	$180	$400
(3) Net Profit	$0	$0	$0	$0	$0

Firm B — Layoff Strategy Using UI Benefits

	Quarter 1	Quarter 2	Quarter 3	Quarter 4	Total
(1) Quarterly Gross Profit (all costs but wages)	$180	$0 (on layoff)	$0 (on layoff)	$180	$360
(2) Wages	$140	$0 (on layoff)	$0 (on layoff)	$140	$280
(3) UI Benefits	$0 (at work)	$70	$70	$0 (at work)	$140
(4) Extra UI Costs	$0	$20	$20	$0	$40
(5) Net Profit	+$40	-$20	-$20	+$40	$40

Both firms face the same fluctuating revenues and other costs. Firm A responds with a constant employment strategy, paying its workers what they are worth in each quarter.

Firm B adopts a temporary layoff strategy. Firm B workers receive wages of $140 when working, but are laid off when demand for the product declines. When laid off, workers receive UI benefits of $70 (half their wage) for two quarters. Because of imperfect experience rating, however, the cost to the firm of temporarily laying off workers is only $20. In effect, other firms and their workers are subsidizing Firm B and its workers $50 for each quarter of layoff. The firm can share this subsidy with its workers, making Firm B and its workers better off than Firm A and its workers. Firm B is better off because it nets $40 more in profits than Firm A. Firm B's workers are better off because they receive $20 more per year in compensation (wages + UI benefits) than Firm A's workers. Overall, society loses $40 per year in output from Firm B's strategy.

Considerable empirical evidence confirms that the UI system causes about one-half of all temporary layoff unemployment. Temporary layoffs, in turn, are responsible for about half of all the persons classified as unemployed job losers. The use of temporary layoffs in manufacturing is even higher, with about 75% of those laid off returning to their original employers. *See* Martin Feldstein, *The Effect of Unemployment Insurance on Temporary Layoff Unemployment,* 68 AM. ECON. REV. 834 (1978). The challenge for the system is to discourage excessive use of temporary layoffs while fulfilling worthwhile goals of income support and job search.

Until 1987, UI benefits were not fully taxable income, which increased the incentive for employers to adopt a high wage, temporary layoff policy. Using the example of Table 17-3, Firm A workers would have $400 of total income, all taxable, while Firm B workers would have $420 of total income, but only $280 would be fully taxable. In an influential article, Martin Feldstein pointed out the perverse incentives this had on unemployment. Feldstein, *Unemployment Compensation: Adverse Incentives and Distributional Anomalies,* 27 NAT'L TAX J. 231 (1974). In response, Congress phased out the tax-exempt status of UI benefits. Since 1987, the federal government has taxed all unemployment benefits as ordinary income. Many states also subject UI benefits to state taxes.

Imperfect experience rating creates distortions between industries as well. Industries with stable employment pay far more into the system than they take out. For example, in the construction industry, where layoffs are common, workers receive $1.66 in UI benefits for every $1 construction employers pay in UI taxes. On the other hand, workers in finance, insurance, and real estate receive only 40 cents for every $1 paid in taxes by employers. Manufacturing employees receive slightly more ($1.07) for every dollar their employers contribute to the system. Donald R. Deere, *Unemployment Insurance and Employment,* 9 J. LAB. ECON. 307 (1991).

NOTE

The desire to avoid UI tax costs has led some business entities that have heavy lay-offs to engage in opportunistic "dumping" of employees under their state unemployment tax acts ("SUTA dumping"). For example, Company "A" may set up a shell Company "B" that has no employees, and therefore no layoffs, and thus a low, possibly zero, tax rate. Company A then transfers all of its employees to Company B. When Company B's tax rate rises due to layoffs, the employees are transferred to yet another shell corporation. This practice leads to depletion of the UI trust fund by SUTA dumpers without any compensating contribution of revenues. In 2004 Congress passed legislation, the SUTA Dumping Prevention Act of 2004, P.L. 108-295, designed to prevent this practice. The law requires that by 2006 all states must have in place anti-SUTA dumping legislation, including meaningful civil and criminal penalties for violating the new laws.

3. WORK SEARCH REQUIREMENTS

All states require that UI claimants actively search for work and accept suitable employment when found. A classic statement of the requirement comes from *Fly v. Industrial Commission*, 359 S.W.2d 481 (Mo. Ct. App. 1962):

> Claimant is not entitled to draw pay because she lost her job. The compensation is payable because she can't get another one. She must really and sincerely look for the job, not wait for the job to seek her out. Nor will a lackadaisical, half-hearted, or occasional effort suffice.

States differ in how they scrutinize the job search of claimants. Many states have customized search requirements, whereby agency staff assess the claimant's occupation and local labor-market conditions and assign the claimant a specific number of employer contacts to make (usually between zero and five per week). Often, claimants must come to the unemployment office weekly or biweekly to receive their benefits check, and at the same time fill out a form listing employers they have contacted and other steps taken to find a job. Whether such scrutiny is effective is questionable. One study showed that, out of every 10,000 claims for UI benefits, only two were denied for refusing suitable work.

The job search issue is most difficult for workers on layoff who hope to return to their employer. Unemployed workers with a definite recall date generally are eligible for UI benefits without actively searching for another job. Major problems arise when the recall is more speculative, as the following case illustrates.

KNOX v. UNEMPLOYMENT COMPENSATION BOARD OF REVIEW
Commonwealth Court of Pennsylvania
315 A.2d 915 (1974)

KRAMER, JUDGE.

This is an appeal by William J. Knox, Jr. (Knox) from an order of the Unemployment Compensation Board of Review (Board) which affirmed the referee's denial of benefits to Knox.

Knox had been employed by H. K. Porter Company (Porter) for 17 years when he was laid off due to the permanent closing of the plant in which he worked. Knox applied for and received unemployment compensation for approximately two and one-half months. His unemployment compensation was terminated after the following incident. Knox was given a job referral by the local office of the Bureau of Employment Security. The job referral was for a position similar to his former employment with Porter and paid approximately the same wage. Knox accepted the referral and reported to the personnel office of the prospective employer for an interview. During the interview, Knox mentioned that he might be recalled by the successor to Porter's plant and that he would return to work there if recalled. As a result, he was not hired.

Section 402(a) of the Unemployment Compensation Law is the applicable controlling statutory provision. It reads:

> An employee shall be ineligible for compensation for any week — (a) in which his unemployment is due to failure, *without good cause,* either to apply for suitable work at such time and in such manner as the department may prescribe, or to accept suitable work when offered to him by the employment office or by any employer, irrespective of whether or not such work is in 'employment' as defined in this act: Provided, That such employer notifies the employment office of such offer within three (3) days after the making thereof. (Emphasis added.)

The words "good cause" found in Section 402(a) have been interpreted to be synonymous with "good faith." In his brief, Knox concedes that conduct which discourages a prospective employer from employing a claimant evidences a lack of good faith and constitutes proper grounds for denying benefits under Section 402(a). He urges, however, that such conduct must indicate that the claimant would be irresponsible, lackadaisical or unreliable, whereas he merely was being honest. While we sympathize with Knox, we cannot agree.

In *Paisley v. Commonwealth of Pennsylvania, Unemployment Compensation Board of Review,* 315 A.2d 908, 908-909 (Pa. Commw. Ct. 1974), we stated:

> The law on this matter is clear that a claimant cannot attach such conditions to his acceptance of work as to render himself unavailable for suitable work. "A claimant is required at all times to be ready, able, and willing to accept suitable employment, temporary or full time. . . . But one may render himself unavailable for work by conditions and limitations as to employment. Willingness to be employed conditionally does not necessarily meet the test of availability. The determination of availability is largely a question of fact for the Board." *Pinto Unemployment Compensation Case,* 79 A.2d 802, 803 (Pa. Super. Ct. 1951). The statement by a claimant to a prospective employer that he expects to be recalled to his former job at an indefinite time in the future and that he intends to return when recalled limits the claimant's availability for work so as to render him ineligible for benefits. . . .

Knox's desire to protect his 17 years of seniority is understandable, but, nonetheless, he presented the prospective employer with an unacceptable condition of employment.

Our scope of review in unemployment cases is limited, absent fraud, to questions of law and whether or not the findings of the Board are supported by the evidence. The Board's findings in this case are supported by the evidence and we find no error of law. Therefore, . . . the order of the Unemployment Compensation Board of Review denying benefits to William J. Knox, Jr., is hereby affirmed.

NOTES

1. **Lying in Good Faith.** Knox jumped through the hoops of a job search, but honestly told prospective employers that he planned to return to his former employer if recalled. This statement obviously makes him less desirable to other employers: why should they incur the time and expense of hiring someone who is likely to leave soon? The court declares that such statements, even if honest, indicate a lack of good faith. To meet the good faith job search standard, must Knox lie during job interviews?

2. **UI Benefits and Temporary Layoffs.** From the claimant's perspective, denying benefits because he wants to preserve his seventeen years' job seniority at his former job seems harsh. But is this tight standard justifiable to discourage employers from excessive use of temporary layoffs?

3. **Definite Recall Dates.** UI claimants with a definite recall date usually are not required to search for other work. In Michigan, for example, an unemployed person can receive UI benefits without seeking work if the employer promptly "notifies the commission in writing that . . . work is expected to be available for the individual within a declared number of days, not to exceed 45 calendar days following the last day the individual worked." If the employer does not notify the commission, the seeking-work requirement can nevertheless be waived "if an individual is on a short-term layoff with a definite return to work date which is not later than 15 consecutive calendar days beginning with the first day of scheduled unemployment resulting from the layoff." Rule 216(3) of the Michigan Employment Security Act.

4. **Work Search Rules.** A telephone survey of some 2,500 former UI claimants in ten states attempted to see whether UI recipients looked harder for work in states with stricter work-search rules:

> Our analysis of the effects of work-search rules on the work-search behavior of claimants tends to provide the expected pattern of results. Claimants from states whose work-search rules are strict are generally more likely to search for work, devote more hours to work search, and contact more employers than is true of claimants from moderately strict and lenient states. Conversely, claimants from states whose work-search rules are lenient are the least likely to search, devote the fewest hours to work search, and contact the fewest number of employers. Thus, it would appear that differences in the work-search rules, or perhaps the overall work-search policy or climate, of states do influence the work-search behavior of claimants.

> An unexpected pattern of results emerges when we divide the sample into those claimants who expected to be recalled to their former jobs and those who did not. The results for the latter group of

claimants, who are typically the primary job searchers, do not consistently show the expected relationship between the strictness of work-search rules and work-search behavior. Instead, the pattern found for the entire sample appears to be due to the effects of work-search rules on the behavior of claimants who regard themselves as job-attached. It may be that claimants who are not job-attached are sufficiently self-motivated to search fairly rigorously regardless of state rules, but those who expect to be recalled are likely to fail to search rigorously unless they are compelled to do so by state rules. . . .

The analysis of the effects of work-search rules on the job-finding success of claimants produces the unexpected result that claimants from states whose work-search rules are the strictest are less successful at leaving the UI rolls and becoming reemployed. In addition, once they become reemployed, claimants from states whose work-search rules are strict are less likely to work full time, less likely to work for their former employers, and more likely to earn less than claimants from states whose rules are moderate or lenient.

These results appear to stem from the more serious labor-market problems found in the sample states whose work-search rules are strict. We could not control completely for these economic differences, and it seems that the effects of economic conditions on job-finding success dominate the effects of work-search rules.

WALTER CORSON ET AL., WORK SEARCH AMONG UNEMPLOYMENT INSURANCE CLAIMANTS: AN INVESTIGATION OF SOME EFFECTS OF STATE RULES AND ENFORCEMENT 164-66 (1987).

A later study tried to separate economic conditions from work-search rules by giving special scrutiny to the search behavior of randomly selected claimants. The results provided "no support for the view that the failure to actively seek work has been a cause of overpayment in the UI system." Orley Ashenfelter, et al., *Do Unemployment Insurance Recipients Actively Seek Work? Randomized Trials in Four U.S. States*, 125 J. ECONOMETRICS 53 (2005).

5. *Available-for-Work Requirement.* Suppose the claimant has difficulty searching for work because of problems finding a reliable babysitter. Should she be considered unavailable for work and therefore denied unemployment benefits? *See In re Paula Williams*, 574 N.Y.S.2d 416 (N.Y. App. Div. 1991) (yes).

C. DISQUALIFICATIONS FROM UI BENEFITS

The general premise of unemployment insurance is that workers who lose their jobs through no fault of their own should receive governmental assistance to tide them over while looking for a new job. The corollary is that workers who voluntarily quit their jobs without good cause, or who were terminated for willful misconduct, are generally disqualified from benefits.

Disqualified is a term of art in unemployment insurance. In many states, a disqualified worker receives no benefits for the entire spell of unemployment. The Department of Labor, however, urges states to disqualify workers only for the length of time the average worker in an ordinary labor market needs to find suitable work, which is generally about six weeks. Unemployment spells longer than this average are thought to be due to market forces beyond the worker's control, rather than due to the disqualifying act. Many states have followed this recommendation and grant reduced or postponed benefits to workers who voluntarily quit or are fired for misconduct.

Determining whether a worker should be disqualified for UI benefits raises many of the same issues prominent in wrongful discharge or discrimination lawsuits. Indeed, a UI hearing is the prime forum where low-status, low-paid workers bring such claims. These workers are unlikely to hire a lawyer and file a lawsuit over the employer's action, because monetary damages are likely to be modest. But such workers do want UI benefits while they search for another job, and often represent themselves in appealing a denial of benefits. In New York, for example, lawyers can only charge $500 to represent a UI claimant, and the agency must approve in advance the amount charged. The following cases illustrate the range of issues that can arise:

(1) *Harassment Based on Sexual Orientation*: A hair stylist quit his job after being harassed by the owner of the salon because he was gay. Should this be a voluntary quit, disqualifying him from UI benefits? *See Hanke v. Safari Hair Adventure*, 512 N.W.2d 614 (Minn. Ct. App. 1994) (reversing denial of benefits).

(2) *Public Safety / Internal Whistleblower*: A hospital hired a hystotechnician to prepare tissue samples for microscopic analysis by pathologists. She refused to perform gross-cutting on tissue from live patients because she feared her limited training would impair the accuracy of the diagnosis, which in turn would risk the patient's life or health. Eventually the hospital fired her for incompetence and insubordination. Should she receive UI benefits because her termination was due to her sincere (but perhaps misguided) concern for public safety? *See Amador v. Unemployment Ins. Appeals Bd.*, 677 P.2d 224 (Cal. 1984) (reversing denial of benefits).

(3) *Drug Testing*: An engineering company employee doing work for a nuclear power plant was fired for refusing to submit to a random drug test. Should he receive UI benefits, perhaps on a privacy rationale? *See Halbert v. City of Columbus*, 722 So. 2d 522 (Miss. 1998) (upholding denial of benefits). *But see Andrews v. Unemployment Dep't*, 998 P.2d 769 (Or. Ct. App. 1999) (holding that refusing an unreasonable drug test is not disqualifying misconduct); *Glide Lumber Prods. Co. v. Employment Div.*, 741 P.2d 907 (Or. Ct. App. 1987) (upholding award of UI benefits to an employee who failed a random drug test when there was no evidence that his drug use affected his work performance).

(4) *Free Speech Toward Employer*: A machinist and union shop steward was fired when he threatened to publish a newsletter criticizing management policies and calling the corporation "brain dead." Should he receive UI benefits? *See Meehan v. Lull Corp.*, 466 N.W.2d 14 (Minn. Ct. App. 1991) (reversing denial of UI benefits because mere statement of intended misconduct is not disqualifying "willful or wanton" conduct).

(5) *Free Speech Toward Co-Worker*: An employee was fired for espousing his religious beliefs in the workplace. Should he receive UI benefits? *See In*

Re Harvey, 689 N.Y.S.2d 789 (App. Div. 1999) (upholding denial of benefits because employee knew or should have known that continued injection of his religious beliefs at work could lead to his termination).

(6) *Smoking on the Job*: A sixty-five-year-old life-long smoker quit her job when the employer changed its policy to permit smoking only outside the building. Should she receive UI benefits? *See Quinn, Gent, Buseck & Leemhuis v. Unemployment Comp. Bd.*, 606 A.2d 1300 (Pa. Commw. Ct. 1992) (reversing an award of benefits because employee could have quit smoking or gone outside to smoke). On the other hand, should a non-smoker who quits when his employer refuses to provide him with a smoke-free environment receive UI benefits? *See Halpern v. Chapedelaine Corporate Sec.*, 696 N.Y.S.2d 581 (App. Div. 1999) (upholding award of benefits).

(7) *Honesty Testing*: An employee was fired after refusing to take the Reid psychiatric profile pertaining to employee honesty. Is he eligible for UI benefits? *See Heins v. Commonwealth*, 534 A.2d 592 (Pa. Commw. Ct. 1987) (upholding denial of benefits because employer's request to take test was reasonable).

(8) *Off-Work Conduct*: A Catholic school fired a teacher because she married a divorced man. The school had a written policy that prohibited teachers from publicly rejecting doctrine of the Catholic church. Should she receive UI benefits? *See Bishop Leonard Reg'l Catholic Sch. v. Unemployment Comp. Bd. of Review*, 593 A.2d 28 (Pa. Commw. Ct. 1991) (reversing award of benefits).

(9) *Drinking Off the Job*: A worker accepts employment with a firm that has a rule prohibiting employees from using tobacco, alcohol, or drugs at any time, on or off work. The employee is fired after confessing that he several times consumed alcohol off work. Should he receive UI benefits? *See Best Lock Corp. v. Review Bd.*, 572 N.E.2d 520 (Ind. Ct. App. 1991) (affirming award of benefits because employer failed to prove its rule was reasonable).

(10) *Consulting a Lawyer*: An employee was fired for refusing to answer his employer's questions about a potential workers' compensation claim without an attorney present. Should he receive UI benefits? *See Baca v. Unique Originals, Inc.*, 724 So. 2d 628 (Fla. Dist. Ct. App. 1998) (reversing denial of benefits).

(11) *Domestic Violence.* An employee quits because her abusive former partner is stalking her and she feels compelled to relocate. Should she receive UI benefits? In recent years numerous states (28 as of 2006) pay unemployment insurance to victims of domestic or sexual violence who must leave a job due to threats to their personal or family safety.

NOTE

UI Benefits and Wrongful-Discharge Damages. The general rule of damages in a wrongful discharge suit is that the plaintiff must mitigate losses by seeking employment. Wages actually earned, and wages that could have been earned with reasonable diligence, are deducted from any award. Income from collateral sources, such as UI benefits, however, is not deducted from the award. *See generally* HOWARD A. SPECTER & MATTHEW W. FINKIN, INDIVIDUAL EMPLOYMENT LAW AND LITIGATION § 15.08, at 310 (1989).

As the cases above indicate, UI disqualification issues arise in a variety of contexts. In the following cases, we focus on how women are treated by the UI system.

1. VOLUNTARY QUITS

WIMBERLY v. LABOR & INDUSTRIAL RELATIONS COMMISSION
United States Supreme Court
479 U.S. 511 (1987)

JUSTICE O'CONNOR delivered the opinion of the Court.

The Missouri Supreme Court concluded that the Federal Unemployment Tax Act, 26 U.S.C. § 3304(a)(12), does not prohibit a State from disqualifying unemployment compensation claimants who leave their jobs because of pregnancy, when the State imposes the same disqualification on all claimants who leave their jobs for a reason not causally connected to their work or their employer. We granted certiorari because the court's decision conflicts with that of the Court of Appeals for the Fourth Circuit in *Brown v. Porcher,* 660 F.2d 1001 (1981), *cert. denied,* 459 U.S. 1150 (1983), on a question of practical significance in the administration of state unemployment compensation laws.

I

In August 1980, after having been employed by the J.C. Penney Company for approximately three years, petitioner requested a leave of absence on account of her pregnancy. Pursuant to its established policy, the J.C. Penney Company granted petitioner a "leave without guarantee of reinstatement," meaning that petitioner would be rehired only if a position was available when petitioner was ready to return to work. Petitioner's child was born on November 5, 1980. On December 1, 1980, when petitioner notified J.C. Penney that she wished to return to work, she was told that there were no positions open.

Petitioner then filed a claim for unemployment benefits. The claim was denied by the Division of Employment Security (Division) pursuant to Mo. Rev. Stat. § 288.050.1(1) (Supp. 1984), which disqualifies a claimant who "has left his work voluntarily without good cause attributable to his work or to his employer." A deputy for the Division determined that petitioner had "quit because of pregnancy," and therefore had left work "voluntarily and without good cause attributable to [her] work or to [her] employer." Petitioner appealed the decision to the Division's appeals tribunal, which, after a full evidentiary hearing, entered findings of fact and conclusions of law affirming the deputy's decision. The Labor and Industrial Relations Commission denied petitioner's petition for review.

Petitioner then sought review in the Circuit Court of Jackson County, Missouri. The court concluded that § 288.050.1(1) was inconsistent with 26 U.S.C. § 3304(a)(12) as construed in *Brown v. Porcher, supra,* and therefore could not be enforced. Following *Brown,* the Circuit Court held that § 3304(a)(12) "banned the use of pregnancy or its termination as an excuse for denying benefits to otherwise eligible women," and accordingly reversed the Commission's decision and remanded for entry of an award. The Missouri Court of Appeals affirmed. Although the Court of Appeals expressed "reservations concerning the soundness of the ruling in *Brown,*" it felt constrained to follow the Fourth Circuit's construction of § 3304(a)(12).

The Missouri Supreme Court reversed, with three judges dissenting. The court held that previous state appellate decisions had correctly interpreted Mo. Rev. Stat. § 288.050.1(1) (Supp. 1984) as disqualifying all claimants who, like petitioner, leave work "for reasons that, while perhaps legitimate and necessary from a personal standpoint, were not causally connected to the claimant's work or employer." 688 S.W.2d, at 346. Rejecting the notion that it was bound by *Brown v. Porcher, supra,* the court determined that § 288.050.1(1) was consistent with the federal statute. The court held that the plain language of § 3304(a)(12) only prohibits state laws from singling out pregnancy for unfavorable treatment. The Missouri scheme does not conflict with this requirement, the court found, because the state law does not expressly refer to pregnancy; rather, benefits are denied only when claimants leave work for reasons not attributable to the employer or connected with the work. The court noted that the Department of Labor, the agency charged with enforcing the statute, consistently has viewed § 3304(a)(12) as prohibiting discrimination rather than mandating preferential treatment. We now affirm.

II

The Federal Unemployment Tax Act (Act), 26 U.S.C. § 3301 *et seq.*, envisions a cooperative federal-state program of benefits to unemployed workers. The Act establishes certain minimum federal standards that a State must satisfy in order for a State to participate in the program. *See* 26 U.S.C. § 3304(a). The standard at issue in this case, § 3304(a)(12), mandates that "no person shall be denied compensation under such State law solely on the basis of pregnancy or termination of pregnancy."

Apart from the minimum standards reflected in § 3304(a), the Act leaves to state discretion the rules governing the administration of unemployment compensation programs. State programs, therefore, vary in their treatment of the distribution of unemployment benefits, although all require a claimant to satisfy some version of a three-part test. First, all States require claimants to earn a specified amount of wages or to work a specified number of weeks in covered employment during a 1-year base period in order to be entitled to receive benefits. Second, all States require claimants to be "eligible" for benefits, that is, they must be able to work and available for work. Third, claimants who satisfy these requirements may be "disqualified" for reasons set forth in state law. The most common reasons for disqualification under state unemployment compensation laws are voluntarily leaving the job without good cause, being discharged for misconduct, and refusing suitable work. *See* Note, *Denial of Unemployment Benefits to Otherwise Eligible Women on the Basis of Pregnancy: Section 3304(a)(12) of the Federal Unemployment Tax Act,* 82 MICH. L. REV. 1925, 1928-1929 (1984).

The treatment of pregnancy-related terminations is a matter of considerable disparity among the States. Most States regard leave on account of pregnancy as a voluntary termination for good cause. Some of these States have specific statutory provisions enumerating pregnancy-motivated termination as good cause for leaving a job, while others, by judicial or administrative decision, treat pregnancy as encompassed within larger categories of good cause such as illness or compelling personal reasons. A few States, however, like Missouri, have chosen to define "leaving for good cause" narrowly. In these States, all persons who leave their jobs are disqualified from receiving benefits unless they leave for reasons directly attributable to the work or to the employer.

Petitioner does not dispute that the Missouri scheme treats pregnant women the same as all other persons who leave for reasons not causally connected to their work or their employer, including those suffering from other types of temporary disabilities. She contends, however, that § 3304(a)(12) is not simply an antidiscrimination statute, but rather that it mandates preferential treatment for women who leave work because of pregnancy. According to petitioner, § 3304(a)(12) affirmatively requires States to provide unemployment benefits to women who leave work because of pregnancy when they are next available and able to work, regardless of the State's treatment of other similarly situated claimants.

Contrary to petitioner's assertions, the plain import of the language of § 3304(a)(12) is that Congress intended only to prohibit States from singling out pregnancy for unfavorable treatment. The text of the statute provides that compensation shall not be denied under state law "solely on the basis of pregnancy." The focus of this language is on the basis for the State's decision, not the claimant's reason for leaving her job. Thus, a State could not decide to deny benefits to pregnant women while at the same time allowing benefits to persons who are in other respects similarly situated: the "sole basis" for such a decision would be on account of pregnancy. On the other hand, if a State adopts a neutral rule that incidentally disqualifies pregnant or formerly pregnant claimants as part of a larger group, the neutral application of that rule cannot readily be characterized as a decision made "solely on the basis of pregnancy." For example, under Missouri law, all persons who leave work for reasons not causally connected to the work or the employer are disqualified from receiving benefits. To apply this law, it is not necessary to know that petitioner left because of pregnancy: all that is relevant is that she stopped work for a reason bearing no causal connection to her work or her employer. Because the State's decision could have been made without ever knowing that petitioner had been pregnant, pregnancy was not the "sole basis" for the decision under a natural reading of § 3304(a)(12)'s language.

We have, on other occasions, construed language similar to that in § 3304(a)(12) as prohibiting disadvantageous treatment, rather than as mandating preferential treatment. In *Monroe v. Standard Oil Co.,* 452 U.S. 549 (1981), for example, the Court considered 38 U.S.C. § 2021(b)(3), a provision of the Vietnam Era Veterans' Readjustment Assistance Act of 1974, which provides that a person "shall not be denied retention in employment . . . because of any obligation" as a member of the Nation's Reserve Forces. The *Monroe* Court concluded that the intent of the provision was to afford reservists "the same treatment afforded their co-workers without military obligations," 452 U.S., at 560; it did not create an "employer responsibility to provide preferential treatment." *Id.,* at 562. Similarly, in *Southeastern Community College v. Davis,* 442 U.S. 397 (1979), we considered § 504 of the Rehabilitation Act of 1973, 29 U.S.C. § 794, which provides that an "otherwise qualified handicapped individual" shall not be excluded from a federally funded program "solely by reason of his handicap." We concluded that the statutory language was only intended to "eliminate discrimination against otherwise qualified individuals," and generally did not mandate "affirmative efforts to overcome the disabilities caused by handicaps." 442 U.S., at 410.

Even petitioner concedes that § 3304(a)(12) does not prohibit States from denying benefits to pregnant or formerly pregnant women who fail to satisfy neutral eligibility requirements such as ability to work and availability for work. Nevertheless, she contends that the statute prohibits the application to pregnant women of neutral *disqualification* provisions. But the statute's plain language will not support the distinction petitioner attempts to draw. The statute does not extend only to disqualification rules. It applies, by its own terms, to any decision to deny compensation. In both instances, the scope of the statutory mandate is the same: the State cannot single out pregnancy for disadvantageous treatment, but it is not compelled to afford preferential treatment.

The legislative history cited by petitioner does not support her view that § 3304(a)(12) mandates preferential treatment for women on account of pregnancy.

[The Court then examines wording changes in the drafting process and discussions in the House Report of various state statutes.]

The Senate Report also focuses exclusively on state rules that single out pregnant women for disadvantageous treatment. In *Turner v. Department of Employment Security,* [423 U.S. 44 (1975),] this Court struck down on due process grounds a Utah statute providing that a woman was disqualified for 12 weeks before the expected date of childbirth and for 6 weeks after childbirth, even if she left work for reasons unrelated to pregnancy. The Senate Report used the provision at issue in *Turner* as representative of the kind of rule that § 3304(a)(12) was intended to prohibit:

> "In a number of States, an individual whose unemployment is related to pregnancy is barred from receiving any unemployment benefits. In 1975 the Supreme Court found a *provision of this type* in the Utah unemployment compensation statute to be unconstitutional. . . . A number of other States have similar provisions although most appear to involve somewhat shorter periods of disqualification." S. Rep. No. 94-1265, at 19, 21 (emphasis added).

In short, petitioner can point to nothing in the Committee Reports, or elsewhere in the statute's legislative history, that evidences congressional intent to mandate preferential treatment for women on account of pregnancy.

There is no hint that Congress disapproved of, much less intended to prohibit, a neutral rule such as Missouri's. Indeed, the legislative history shows that Congress was focused only on the issue addressed by the plain language of § 3304(a)(12): prohibiting rules that single out pregnant women or formerly pregnant women for disadvantageous treatment. . . .

Because § 3304(a)(12) does not require States to afford preferential treatment to women on account of pregnancy, the judgment of the Missouri Supreme Court is affirmed.

It is so ordered.

JUSTICE BLACKMUN took no part in the decision of this case.

NOTE

Family and Medical Leave Act. The Family and Medical Leave Act of 1993, passed after this case was decided, now gives workers like Wimberly the right to take twelve weeks unpaid leave because of pregnancy and childbirth. The FMLA would not have helped Wimberly, however, because she took more than twelve weeks leave.

MacGREGOR v. UNEMPLOYMENT INSURANCE APPEALS BOARD
Supreme Court of California
689 P.2d 453 (1984)

REYNOSO, JUSTICE.

When a worker leaves her employment to accompany her "nonmarital partner" to another state in order to maintain the familial relationship they have established with their child does she voluntarily leave work with good cause within the meaning of the statute governing eligibility for unemployment insurance benefits? We left open the possibility that a claimant might show good cause in such circumstances when we decided *Norman v. Unemployment Insurance Appeals Board*, 663 P.2d 904 (Cal. 1983), less than two years ago. We now hold that Patricia MacGregor has established that her quitting was motivated by the need to preserve the family she had established with her nonmarital partner and their child, and that this need constituted good cause for her voluntary departure from work. We therefore affirm the judgment of the Santa Clara County Superior Court ordering the Unemployment Insurance Appeals Board to reconsider its decision and to award benefits to plaintiff if she meets other eligibility requirements.

Plaintiff Patricia MacGregor worked as a waitress at the Ramada Inn in Santa Clara, California from July 7, 1978, through December 31, 1979. On January 1, 1980, she began a six-month pregnancy leave of absence. According to the terms of her leave, she was to return to work in June of 1980.

MacGregor was engaged to and lived with Dick Bailey, the father of her expected child. Their daughter Leanna was born February 29, 1980. The three continued to live together as a family. Bailey acknowledged that he was Leanna's father.

In April, Bailey decided the family should move to New York to live with and care for his 76-year-old father. At the time, his father was under medical care for a variety of serious ailments and anticipated surgery later that summer. Because of his ill health he no longer wished to live alone. No relatives lived nearby and Bailey was the only child. Bailey's father asked if Bailey, MacGregor and their daughter would come to live with and care for him. In May MacGregor informed her employer that she would not be returning to work.

MacGregor, Bailey and their daughter moved into Bailey's father's home in June. When MacGregor was unable to find work, she applied for unemployment insurance benefits. Her claim was referred to the California Employment Development Department (Department), which determined that she had quit voluntarily without good cause and was thus ineligible for benefits. (Unemp. Ins. Code, § 1256.)

MacGregor appealed this decision. A hearing was conducted before a referee in Massena, New York. The transcript was referred to the Department where it was considered by an administrative law judge. The judge determined MacGregor had left her most recent work voluntarily without good cause and was thus disqualified from receiving benefits. Although the judge found evidence in the record indicating that Bailey had to return to New York to care for his father who was ill, the judge concluded that "it [was] not apparent why it was essential for the claimant to follow." Since there was no marriage, no plans to marry at a certain future date, and no assurance the relationship would continue for any particular period of time, the judge found there was no family unit to be preserved.

MacGregor again appealed. The California Unemployment Insurance Appeals Board (Board) adopted as its own the administrative law judge's decision and statement of facts and reasons. Plaintiff then sought a writ of mandate from the Santa Clara Superior Court pursuant to Code of Civil Procedure section 1094.5.

After considering the record of the administrative proceeding, the superior court found plaintiff had good cause for leaving her employment. The court found as facts that MacGregor had lived with Bailey for three years, that she and Bailey had established a family unit with their child, that Bailey had decided to move to New York, and that plaintiff had chosen to leave her employment and relocate to New York in order to maintain and preserve their family unit. The court concluded that these underlying facts established good cause for plaintiff's quitting pursuant to section 1256 and that she was therefore entitled to receive benefits if otherwise qualified.

The court issued a peremptory writ of mandate directing the Board to set aside its decision and to reconsider its action in light of the court's findings of fact and conclusions of law. The Board appealed. While the Board's appeal was pending, this court decided *Norman v. Unemployment Insurance Appeals Board, supra.*

In *Norman* we discussed the meaning of "good cause" under section 1256. Section 1256 provides that "an individual is disqualified for unemployment compensation benefits if the director finds that he or she left his or her most recent work voluntarily without good cause or that he or she has been discharged for misconduct connected with his or her most recent work. . . ."

Whether or not there is "good cause" within the meaning of section 1256 is a question of law which must be answered in relation to the particular facts of each case. Good cause may exist for reasons which are personal and not connected to the employment situation, but those reasons must be imperative and compelling in nature. Several Courts of Appeal have defined "good cause" as used in section 1256 to mean "such a cause as justifies an employee's voluntarily leaving the ranks of the employed; . . . such a cause as would, in a similar situation, reasonably motivate the average able-bodied and qualified worker to give up his or her employment with its certain wage rewards in order to enter the ranks of the unemployed." (*Evenson v. Unemployment Ins. Appeals Bd., supra,* 62 Cal. App. 3d at p. 1016; *Zorrero v. Unemployment Ins. Appeals Bd.* (1975) 47 Cal. App. 3d 434 [120 Cal. Rptr. 855].)

Precedent decisions of the Board have long recognized that the circumstances attendant upon a worker's decision to leave employment in order to accompany a spouse and family to a new home may be so compelling as to constitute good cause for quitting within section 1256. Thus, in *In re Dipre* (Cal. Unemp. Ins. App. Bd. Precedent Benefit Dec. No. P-B-230 (1976)), a husband had decided to return to a former home in Pennsylvania after his wife informed him that she planned to leave California with their three minor children and make her home in Pennsylvania regardless of his desires. The Board determined that the husband acted under compelling circumstances. His decision to leave employment in order to preserve his marriage and the family unit was a reasonable one, which constituted good cause under section 1256.

In 1982 the Legislature added the fourth paragraph to section 1256 which recognizes that the desire to preserve a marital relationship, or a relationship in which marriage is imminent, may constitute good cause within the meaning of the statute.[3] The Legislature explicitly stated that the amendment was intended to overturn the Court of Appeal decision in *Norman v. Unemployment Insurance Appeals Board* (which had found good cause based on a nonmarital relationship) and to "endorse the policy of the Employment Development Department, as expressed in its regulations, which distinguishes persons who are married or whose marriage is imminent from others in determining whether a person has left his or her most recent work without good cause. . . ."

The Court of Appeal's decision in *Norman* was vacated when this court granted a hearing. This court's opinion issued subsequent to the amendment of section 1256. While not specifically addressing or construing the newly enacted statutory presumption, the opinion did reach a result consistent with the statute. We found that a claimant who had left California to preserve her relationship with the man she planned to marry had not established good cause. The record contained no indication that the couple's marriage was imminent and lacked sufficient indications of the need to preserve a permanent and lasting familial relationship. Citing a line of appellate decisions

---

[3] The fourth paragraph of section 1256 provides: "An individual may be deemed to have left his or her most recent work with good cause if he or she leaves employment to accompany his or her spouse to a place from which it is impractical to commute to the employment."

declining to equate nonmarital relationships with marriage for all purposes, the *Norman* opinion concluded that "[the] Legislature's decision to give weight to marital relationships in the determination of 'good cause' supports public policy encouraging marriage and is a reasonable method of alleviating otherwise difficult problems of proof." (34 Cal. 3d at p. 8.) "The inevitable questions would include issues such as the factors deemed relevant, the length of the relationship, the parties' eventual plans as to marriage, and the sincerity of their beliefs as to whether they should ever marry." (*Id.*, at p. 10.)

Nevertheless, this court explained there was nothing about Norman's lack of a legally recognized marriage which *precluded* her from receiving benefits if she could establish that compelling circumstances made her voluntary leaving "akin to involuntary departure." (*Ibid.*) Using a hypothetical which foresaw the claim now before us, the *Norman* court suggested that some significant factor in addition to the nonmarital relationship might provide the necessary compelling circumstance: "Thus, for example, where there are children of a nonformalized relationship, and an employee leaves his or her position to be with a nonmarital loved one and their children, good cause might be shown." (*Ibid.*)

It is apparent from the *Norman* decision's treatment of the subject that the presumption which attaches to a couple that is legally married is not the exclusive means of demonstrating good cause based on compelling family circumstances. Regulations of the Department itself recognize the "existing or prospective marital status of the claimant" as but one of three kinds of domestic obligations which might compel a person to leave work with good cause.[4] . . .

The evidence here amply supports the trial court's findings that MacGregor had "established a family unit consisting of herself, her fiancé and their child" and that she "chose to relocate to New York with her fiancé and their child in order to maintain and preserve their family unit." The record shows that MacGregor and Bailey had maintained a common household for over two years prior to the birth of their daughter. When the child was born the parents received her into that home and gave her Bailey's surname. It is clear that both MacGregor and Bailey intend to and do provide a stable and secure home for their daughter. . . .

Leanna was only two months old when Bailey decided his father's illness required him to move to New York. The need for MacGregor to follow — which

---

[4] The parties agree that the regulations, which became effective May 18, 1980, are not controlling in this case. They nevertheless provide guidance as to the kinds of familial obligations that the board generally considers compelling. In addition to obligations arising out of the existing or prospective marital status of the claimant, legal or moral obligations relating to the health, care, or welfare of the claimant's family, or to the exercise of parental control over a claimant who is an unemancipated minor may also give rise to a voluntary leaving with good cause. Family is broadly defined to include "the spouse of the claimant, or any parent, child, brother, sister, grandparent, grandchild, son-in-law, or daughter-in-law, of the claimant or of the claimant's spouse, including step, foster, and adoptive relationships, or any guardian or person with whom the claimant has assumed reciprocal rights, duties, and liabilities of a parent-child, or a grandparent-grandchild relationship, whether or not the same live in a common household." Compelling circumstances may be found where a minor child of the claimant requires care and supervision and there is no reasonable alternative and where there is a need to preserve family unity.

the administrative law judge could not fathom — is in our view manifest. The intimate nature of the family bond among these three individuals would have been forever altered had MacGregor decided that she, or she and Leanna, should not accompany Bailey to New York.

The Board's arguments here, like the administrative decisions below, focus on the lack of a legal marriage relationship between plaintiff and Bailey. The Board urges that leaving work to join a spouse should be deemed good cause only where there is a marriage to be preserved. This rule, according to the Board, is consistent with the public policy favoring marriage and with laws which afford special benefits and protections to that institution. The rule would also avoid the difficulties and dangers which would accompany a requirement that administrative agencies and the courts make individualized determination of the "true nature" of intimate personal relationships.

This court considered similar arguments in *Norman v. Unemployment Ins. Appeals Bd., supra*. There, although we declined to find good cause based solely on a nonmarital relationship in which marriage was not imminent, we explicitly declined to hold that a legal marriage is a prerequisite for establishing good cause where other indices of compelling familial obligations exist. Today we reaffirm the principle that the lack of a legally recognized marriage does not prevent a claimant from demonstrating that compelling familial obligations provided good cause for leaving employment.[5]

The state's policy in favor of maintaining secure and stable relationships between parents and children is equally as strong as its interest in preserving the institution of marriage. The Legislature has declared that the rights and obligations of parents and children exist regardless of the marital status of the parents. The purposes of the conciliation statutes relied on by the Board include the protection of the rights of children as well as the protection of the institution of matrimony. The courts have recognized the family as a basic unit of our society.

The problems of proof which concerned this court in the *Norman* case are not substantial in this situation where the basis for the familial relationship is clear and objectively verifiable. Plaintiff and her fiancé share a home with their natural child. Both have acknowledged the child as theirs and have assumed the responsibilities of providing for her care and support, as well as the benefits of her company and companionship.

The Board asserts that a claimant who leaves employment to accompany a spouse to a different locality must show that the spouse was forced to establish the new domicile by "compelling circumstances" which would constitute good cause. Prior decisions of the Board recognize, however, that even if one spouse's reason for relocating appears arbitrary, the importance of preserving the marital or familial relationship may provide good cause for the other spouse's decision to follow.

In this case the decisions of the administrative law judge and the Board conceded that Bailey had a good reason for relocating: the care of his elderly and ill father. This would constitute a compelling circumstance under the

---

[5] In light of this decision we need not resolve plaintiff's contention that a nonmarital rule unconstitutionally infringes her right of privacy in the matters of marriage and reproduction.

Department's own regulations. The trial court found as matters of fact that Bailey made the decision to move and that plaintiff chose to go with him in order to preserve their family unit. The court's findings are supported by substantial, credible and competent evidence. The conclusion that MacGregor had "such a cause as would, in a similar situation, reasonably motivate the average able-bodied and qualified worker to give up his or her employment with its certain wage rewards in order to enter the ranks of the unemployed" is entirely consistent with the laws and public policies of the State of California.

As the record clearly supports the trial court's finding that plaintiff had good cause for leaving work, the judgment is affirmed.

NOTES

1. Statutory Definition of Family. Other state courts have interpreted "family" obligations more narrowly. In *Davis v. Employment Security Dep't*, 737 P.2d 1262 (Wash. 1987), the court declared it would take "immediate family" literally. The court saw no fundamental right to live in a meretricious relationship, and held it not to be good cause for UI purposes to move in order to continue such a relationship.

2. Constitutional Issues. By deciding for the UI claimant on statutory grounds, the Court avoided the lurking constitutional issue. In *Austin v. Berryman*, 878 F.2d 786 (4th Cir. 1989) (en banc), the Fourth Circuit was forced to face similar constitutional claims in light of a Virginia UI statute (since repealed) that expressly declared "the voluntary leaving of work with an employer to accompany or to join his or her spouse in a new locality" is not good cause for leaving work. The claimant testified she quit work to follow her husband (who had moved some 150 miles to take care of his elderly mother), because her religion commanded that she follow her husband wherever he might go. The court unanimously rejected her claim that the denial of UI benefits infringed her fundamental marital rights protected by the Fourteenth Amendment. In a subsequent opinion, the court rejected her equal-protection claim. *Austin v. Berryman*, 955 F.2d 223 (4th Cir. 1992). The claimant showed that 86.8% of persons disqualified from UI for quitting to accompany a spouse were women. The court found this insufficient to prove that the statute had a gender-based discriminatory purpose.

The court also rejected, four judges dissenting, her claim that the denial of UI benefits burdened her first-amendment right to the free exercise of her religion. In doing so, the court distinguished several Supreme Court decisions that upheld free-exercise claims by workers who were terminated for being unable to work for religious reasons. *See Frazee v. Illinois Dep't of Emp. Sec.*, 489 U.S. 829 (1989) (denial of UI benefits unconstitutionally burdens free exercise of religion when unemployment due to claimant's refusal to work on his Sabbath); *Thomas v. Review Bd.*, 450 U.S. 707 (1981) (same result when worker dismissed for refusing to help build military tanks for religious reasons). The Fourth Circuit found those cases to turn on a conflict between the circumstances of work and the employee's religious beliefs, whereas here the proximate cause of Austin's unemployment was geographic distance, not religious beliefs.

3. Trailing Military Spouses. Despite the decision in *MacGregor*, most states disqualify workers who quit to accompany a spouse who relocates. Several states (Colorado, Georgia, Nebraska, New Mexico, and Florida) have recently passed legislation that excepts claimants who leave their job due to a spouse's military transfer. Currently, only six states (Indiana, Kentucky, Maine, Nebraska, Oklahoma, and Texas) have legislation that allows benefits following any kind of family transfer.

JONES v. REVIEW BOARD OF INDIANA EMPLOYMENT SECURITY DIVISION
Court of Appeals of Indiana
399 N.E.2d 844 (1980)

GARRARD, PRESIDING JUDGE.

Appellant Tenner R. Jones appeals from a decision of the Review Board of the Indiana Employment Security Division (Board) which denied her unemployment compensation on the basis that she voluntarily left her employment without good cause in connection with her work.

Jones worked for Marian Hill as a cook from December 12, 1977 through March 24, 1978. When she was offered the position she informed her supervisor that she could only work the hours of 9:00 a.m. to 3:00 p.m. because she had family responsibilities. In March 1978, Jones was told that her hours would be changed to 9:00 a.m. to 6:00 p.m. When Jones protested the change she was told that if she did not work the new hours, someone would be hired that would. *Jones then agreed to accept the change of hours.* The next day, however, Jones informed her supervisor that she could not work the hours because she had four children at home to care for. Jones agreed to continue working until a replacement was found.

Jones contends on appeal that the Board's decision was contrary to law since the reason for termination, a change in her working conditions contrary to an existing employment contract, constituted good cause.

Generally, an employer has the prerogative of setting business hours, working schedules and working conditions in the absence of a specific agreement. However, an employee has the right to place conditions or limitations on his employment. If such conditions are made known to the employer and are agreed to by it, these conditions become contractual working conditions. If the working conditions are unilaterally changed by the employer and the employee chooses to terminate the employment rather than accept the change, the employee will be entitled to unemployment benefits since the reason for termination was a change in work agreed to be performed by the employee. Such reason constitutes good cause. *Wade v. Hurly,* 515 P.2d 491 (Colo. Ct. App. 1973); *Gray v. Dobbs House, Inc.,* 357 N.E.2d 900 (Ind. Ct. App. 1976) (concurring opinion). Likewise, if the employee is discharged for refusal to accept a unilateral change in the agreed upon working conditions, the employee would be entitled to benefits as the discharge would not be for just cause as it is defined in IC 22-4-15-1.[1] However, if the employee chooses to

---

[1] IC 22-4-15-1 provides in pertinent part,

"Discharge for just cause" as used in this section is defined to include but not be limited to

remain in the employment under the changed conditions, the prior agreed upon condition will be deemed to have been abandoned and will no longer be considered part of the working conditions.

In the case at hand, the record supports a Board determination that Jones agreed to the change in the theretofore agreed upon working conditions. Therefore, she was not entitled to good cause status for terminating her employment because of the change. Additionally we note that leaving employment because of family responsibilities constitutes leaving without good cause. *Gray v. Dobbs House, Inc.,* 357 N.E.2d 900 (Ind. Ct. App. 1976).

Jones also contends that the Board's decision is contrary to law because the evidence before the Board shows conclusively that the termination was not voluntary. Jones characterizes the employer's statements that she would be replaced if she did not work the hours as coercive threats rendering her termination involuntary. We do not agree. While it is apparent that Jones would have been discharged had she failed to work the additional three hours, she was not thereby forced into tendering her resignation. She was able to choose, of her own free will, to remain employed by working the additional three hours as she had agreed to do. Furthermore, the record reveals that the spectre of discharge was not the cause of her termination. Jones' motivation to leave her employment was induced by her parental responsibilities and her husband's demands that she not work the hours.

The decision of the Board denying benefits is affirmed.

NOTES

1. *Work and Parental Responsibilities.* Jones has four children at home. Does the court take seriously the limits of her choices? Could she truly choose, of her own free will, to work the additional three hours? While for many men a shift change from 3 p.m. to 6 p.m. may not be a major change, for many working mothers it is an impossible change. *See generally* Martin H. Malin, *Unemployment Compensation in a Time of Increasing Work-Family Conflicts,* 29 U. Mich. J.L. Reform 131 (1996).

2. *Fine Lines.* The court suggests that the critical fact was that Jones initially agreed to the shift change, but after discussing it with her husband that night, changed her mind and quit. If she had initially rejected the change and quit, would she be eligible for UI benefits? *See Indianapolis Osteopathic Hosp. v. Jones,* 669 N.E.2d 431 (Ind. Ct. App. 1996) (upholding award of benefits).

Suppose that instead of quitting Jones had continued to work her old shift and was fired for leaving early every day. Would she have been eligible for

---

separation initiated by an employer for falsification of an employment application to obtain employment through subterfuge; knowing violation of a reasonable and uniformly enforced rule of an employer; unsatisfactory attendance, if the individual cannot show good cause for absences or tardiness; damaging the employer's property through wilful negligence; refusing to obey instructions; reporting to work under the influence of alcohol or drugs or consuming alcohol or drugs on employer's premises during working hours; conduct endangering safety of self or coworkers; incarceration in jail following conviction of a misdemeanor or felony by a court of competent jurisdiction or for any breach of duty in connection with work which is reasonably owed employer by an employee.

UI benefits? *See Mississippi Emp. Sec. Comm'n v. Bell*, 584 So. 2d 1270 (Miss. 1991) (upholding award benefits to an employee who agreed to a shift change but was fired for continual lateness because of childcare difficulties). Are these fine lines defensible?

2. WILLFUL MISCONDUCT

McCOURTNEY v. IMPRIMIS TECHNOLOGY, INC.
Court of Appeals of Minnesota
465 N.W.2d 721 (1991)

Considered and decided by KALITOWSKI, P.J., and SHORT and POPOVICH, JJ.

KALITOWSKI, JUDGE.

Relator Diane McCourtney seeks review of a decision by the Commissioner of Jobs and Training which denied her claim for unemployment compensation benefits. McCourtney argues her persistent absences due to a sick baby did not constitute disqualifying misconduct. McCourtney also challenges the Commissioner's decision on equal protection grounds. . . . We reverse the Commissioner's decision denying benefits.

Facts

McCourtney was employed by Imprimis as a full-time accounts payable clerk for over 10½ years. McCourtney's ending salary was $1,360 per month. Her scheduled hours were 6:30 a.m. to 3:00 p.m. Monday through Friday. McCourtney was an excellent employee, and until January 1990 she had no attendance problems.

On September 30, 1989, McCourtney gave birth to an infant who suffered from numerous illnesses. The baby's father and other members of McCourtney's family were unable to assist her with child care.

Due to her baby's illnesses, McCourtney was frequently absent from work between January and May 1990. She was absent 71% of the time between January 1 and February 25; 36% of the time between February 25 and March 11; 31% of the time between March 12 and March 25; and 13% of the time between March 26 and April 8. Between April 9 and April 12 she was absent for four straight days, and during that same two-week pay period, she missed another eight hours. When she missed 10½ hours of work the following week, she was suspended pending termination. Imprimis issued McCourtney two written warnings before finally discharging her for excessive absenteeism.

McCourtney does not challenge her employer's right to terminate her due to absenteeism. McCourtney applied for unemployment compensation benefits, but the Department of Jobs and Training denied her claim. McCourtney appealed to a Department referee, who conducted a hearing.

The evidence at the hearing demonstrated 99.9% of McCourtney's absences were due to her sick baby. Although each of McCourtney's absences was excused, Imprimis issued a written warning in February requiring McCourtney to develop a written plan to solve her child care problem.

In response to this warning, McCourtney prepared a memo to her manager, discussing two possible options for care of her baby when she was unable to take him to her regular baby sitter: (1) professional in-home care; and (2) back-up day care facilities. McCourtney agreed to determine what services were available in her community.

McCourtney looked through the yellow pages, contacted Hennepin County, and called family members. She investigated the possibility of hiring a nanny, but could not afford the cost.

McCourtney contacted ten local child care facilities, and discovered that "Tender Care" was the only provider which would care for sick infants on short notice. However, Tender Care could not guarantee a caregiver would always be available, and would not allow McCourtney to interview a caregiver before he or she entered her home. Other problems with Tender Care services included the cost and the caregiver's inflexible starting time.

Following the hearing, the referee concluded McCourtney was discharged for misconduct because she had some control over her absences and her conduct constituted a violation of behavior which Imprimis had a right to expect of its employees. McCourtney appealed, and the Commissioner's representative affirmed the referee's decision. McCourtney filed this writ of certiorari, seeking review of the decision of the Commissioner's representative.

Issue

Do McCourtney's frequent absences constitute misconduct disqualifying her from receiving unemployment compensation benefits?

Analysis

An individual who is discharged for misconduct is disqualified from receiving unemployment compensation benefits. Minn. Stat. § 268.09, subd. 1(b) (Supp. 1989). The Minnesota Supreme Court has adopted the following definition of "misconduct":

> The intended meaning of the term "misconduct" is limited to conduct evincing such wilful or wanton disregard of an employer's interests as is found in deliberate violations or disregard of standards of behavior which the employer has the right to expect of his employee, or in carelessness or negligence of such degree or recurrence as to manifest equal culpability, wrongful intent or evil design, or to show an intentional and substantial disregard of the employer's interests or of the employee's duties and obligations to his employer. On the other hand mere inefficiency, unsatisfactory conduct, failure in good performance as the result of inability or incapacity, inadvertencies or ordinary negligence in isolated instances, or good-faith errors in judgment or discretion are not to be deemed misconduct.

In re Claim of Tilseth, 204 N.W.2d 644, 646 (Minn. 1973). In *Feia v. St. Cloud State College*, 244 N.W.2d 635 (Minn. 1976), the court summarized the *Tilseth* definition of misconduct as "conduct evincing a willful or wanton disregard for the employer's interests or conduct demonstrating a lack of concern by the employee for her job." *Id.* at 636. . . .

The unemployment compensation statutes are "humanitarian in nature and are liberally construed." *Group Health Plan, Inc. v. Lopez*, 341 N.W.2d 294, 296 (Minn. App. 1983). The intent of the unemployment compensation statutes is to assist those who are unemployed "through no fault of their own." Minn. Stat. § 268.03 (1988). The issue is not whether an employer was justified in discharging an employee, but rather, whether the employee committed "misconduct" disqualifying the employee from receiving benefits.

Each of McCourtney's absences was excused and was due to circumstances beyond her control. *Cf. Winkler v. Park Refuse Service, Inc.*, 361 N.W.2d 120, 124 (Minn. App. 1985) ("Absence from work under circumstances *within the control of the employee* has been determined to be misconduct sufficient to deny benefits. . . . The critical factor is whether the employee's behavior caused his failure to report to work.") (emphasis added). McCourtney made substantial efforts to find care for her child so she could work. Respondents argue McCourtney could have utilized the services of Tender Care. We disagree. The hours offered by Tender Care personnel were incompatible with McCourtney's work schedule.

In light of McCourtney's good faith efforts, her inability to find care for her child is not "misconduct" within the meaning of Minn. Stat. § 268.09, subd. 1(b). McCourtney's actions were motivated by a willful regard for her child's interests and not a wanton disregard of her employer's interest or lack of concern for her job.

We recognize that in some circumstances misconduct may be demonstrated by excessive absenteeism alone. Where the circumstances do not overwhelmingly demonstrate that an employee's absences are deliberate, willful, or equally culpable, we may also examine the employee's history, conduct, and underlying attitude. While McCourtney's absences were undeniably excessive, her work history and good faith attempts to find care for her child weigh against a determination that her absences demonstrated the culpability required by *Tilseth*.

We conclude that under the specific facts and circumstances of this case, Imprimis has failed to meet its burden of proving McCourtney's actions constitute misconduct as intended by the legislature and further defined by *Tilseth*. Therefore, McCourtney is entitled to unemployment compensation benefits. The economic burden this conclusion places on the employer is a necessary cost of the legislature's humanitarian concern for the welfare of persons unemployed through no fault of their own. . . .

Reversed.

POPOVICH, JUDGE (dissenting).

I respectfully dissent and would affirm the decision of the Commissioner's representative for the following reasons:

1. As the majority recognizes, Diane McCourtney's absences were frequent and excessive. She received two warnings yet her absences continued. We have

previously said that excessive absenteeism alone may demonstrate misconduct. I believe McCourtney's frequent absences evidenced a "disregard of standards of behavior which an employer has a right to expect of its employees." *Tilseth v. Midwest Lumber Co.*, 204 N.W.2d 644, 646 (Minn. 1973).

2. Under the majority's analysis, an employer becomes the victim of an employee's personal problems with obtaining child care. An employer is forced to (1) put up with the employee's extensive absences or (2) pay for the resulting unemployment at potentially great expense. I do not believe it was the legislature's intent to force employers into this Catch 22 position. Rather, as respondents point out, other social welfare programs have been developed to handle the child care issue. . . .

NOTES

1. *Goodness of Character.* The court emphasizes that McCourtney, before having children, had been an excellent employee and has a good "underlying attitude" about the problems she is creating for her employer. Should benefit decisions hinge on the Unemployment Commission's determination of an employee's attitude? Is such a criterion manageable for a state agency designed to process thousands of claims quickly and cheaply?

2. *Voluntarily Quit Versus Firings.* Suppose McCourtney, feeling bad about not pulling her weight at work, quit instead of being fired. If she continues to take steps to resolve her child-care problem, should she be eligible for UI benefits?

3. *Work Versus Family.* McCourtney, like many working mothers, faces deep conflict between being a good worker and a good parent. Even the majority's presentation of the issue as whether McCourtney is guilty of "misconduct" illustrates that the UI system emphasizes the difference between working mothers and male workers who rarely are asked to choose between work and family. UI's emphasis on giving benefits only to those fully committed to the labor force again reveals that working men are the model for the system. An award of UI benefits to McCourtney perhaps can be justified by lessening the immediacy of a choice between work and family. UI benefits can give her a financial cushion to sort out her situation.

4. *Uncharged Benefits.* Judge Popovich focuses on the employer's plight, and accuses the majority of putting the employer in a Catch-22 position: put up with the absences, or be charged with UI benefits. One response might be to decouple the alternatives by awarding benefits but not charging them to the employer. McCourtney should receive UI benefits, because she fits squarely within UI's purpose of financially supporting workers who involuntarily lose their jobs and need time to find more suitable work. But the employer's UI taxes should not increase, because it cannot control the problem.

Of course, uncharged benefits are a major cause for imperfect experience rating, which in turn leads to inefficiently high unemployment. Further, are worker's child-care problems really beyond the employer's control? Some firms are much better than others at accommodating the needs of working parents.

5. *Alcoholism and Involuntary Misconduct.* Suppose a worker's alcoholism leads to excessive absences, for which he is fired. In what ways is this situation like McCourtney's? *See In Re Pluckhan,*, 683 N.Y.S.2d 326 (App. Div. 1998) (holding that otherwise disqualifying misconduct is excused when alcoholism causes the misconduct and the claimant is available for and capable of employment); *City & County of Denver v. Industrial Comm'n*, 756 P.2d 373 (Colo. 1988) (holding that alcoholism is not disqualifying misconduct for UI if condition has progressed to point where it is non-volitional).

6. *Typical Incompetent Employees.* Willful misconduct consists of considerably more than simply being a lousy employee. An employee dismissed for incompetence generally will receive unemployment insurance. For example, a nurse who was fired for failing his licensing exam received UI benefits. *Primecare Med., Inc. v. Unemployment Comp. Bd. of Review*, 760 A.2d 483 (Pa. 2000). But a nurse who was fired for failing to obtain in-house approval for the use of soft wrist restraints on a patient returning from eye surgery as ordered by the surgeon was denied UI benefits. She had already been reprimanded several times for failing to follow proper procedures before being fired. Even though the in-house doctor later determined that she had appropriately used restraints, the court decided that her cumulative errors constituted willful misconduct. *Giordani v. Unemployment Appeals Comm'n*, 706 So. 2d 897 (Fla. Dist. Ct. App. 1998).

D. FEDERAL REGULATION OF PLANT CLOSINGS

When the major plant in a town closes, the community faces mass unemployment. The impact on the community can be extremely severe. The following excerpt summarizes studies on the impact of plant closings on the health of workers and their families.

BARRY BLUESTONE & BENNETT HARRISON, THE DEINDUSTRIALIZATION OF AMERICA 61-72 (1982) [*]

Families who fall victim to brief periods of lost earnings are frequently able to sustain their standards of living through unemployment insurance and savings. Unfortunately for the victims of plant closings, the consequences are often much more severe, ranging from a total depletion of savings to mortgage foreclosures and reliance on public welfare. Families sometimes lose not only their current incomes, but their total accumulated assets as well.

During the Great Depression, the waves of plant closings that spread across the country drove millions of families into poverty. A study completed in 1934 of Connecticut River Valley textile workers showed that two years after the mills closed down, 75 percent of the families affected were living in poverty, compared with 11 percent before the shutdown. More than one in four families was forced to move in order to find lower rents. Some families lost their houses when they fell behind on mortgages. Thirty-five percent reported no new purchases of clothing, and the consumption of other items was reduced significantly.

This experience did not die out with the end of the Depression. A similar fate is faced by workers and their families who suffer permanent layoff today.

---

[*] Reprinted with permission.

When the Plainfield, New Jersey, Mack Truck facility shut down in 1960, workers had to reduce their food and clothing consumption substantially, and they turned to borrowing and installment credit for other necessities. Aircraft workers in Hartford County, Connecticut — the jet engine capital of the world — responded to the loss of their jobs in the mid-1970's by sharply reducing their expenditures on food, clothing, and medical care in addition to a long list of "luxury" items such as recreation and house repair. Out of the eighty-one workers interviewed in a study by Rayman and Bluestone, three of these displaced jet engine workers lost their houses to foreclosure. Among participants in the upstate New York study conducted by Aronson and McKersie, 11 percent reported cutting back on housing expenses, 16 percent reduced their food consumption, 31 percent bought less clothing, and 43 percent spent less on recreation. In what could lead to a mortgaging of their families' health, one in seven reduced their expenditures for medical care. These figures are remarkably close to those found in the Hartford County research. . . .

Impacts on Physical and Mental Health

The loss of personal assets places families in an extraordinarily vulnerable position; for when savings run out, people lose the ability to respond to short-run crises. The first unanticipated financial burden that comes along — an unexpected health problem, a casualty or fire loss, or even a minor automobile accident — can easily hurl the family over the brink of economic solvency. The trauma associated with this type of loss extends well beyond the bounds of household money matters.

Medical researchers have found that acute economic distress associated with job loss causes a range of physical and mental health problems, the magnitudes of which are only now being assessed. Simply measuring the direct employment and earnings losses of plant closings therefore tends to seriously underestimate the total drain on families caught in the midst of capital shift.

Dr. Harvey Brenner of Johns Hopkins University, along with Sidney Cobb at Brown University and Stanislav Kasl at Yale University, have done careful studies in this area. Writing in Psychometric Medicine, Kasl and Cobb report high or increased blood pressure (hypertension) and abnormally high cholesterol and blood-sugar levels in blue-collar workers who lost their jobs due to factory closure. These factors are associated with the development of heart disease. Other disorders related to the stress of job loss are ulcers, respiratory diseases, and hyper-allergic reactions. Higher levels of serum glucose, serum pepsinogen, and serum uric acid found in those experiencing job termination relative to levels in a control group of continuously employed workers suggest unduly high propensities to diabetes and gout. Compounding these problems is the fact that economically deprived workers are often forced to curtail normal health care and suffer from poorer nutrition and housing.

The Kasl and Cobb findings are by no means unique. Aronson and McKersie write that two-fifths of their sample reported deterioration in their physical and emotional well-being since their termination. Headaches, upset stomachs, and feelings of depression were the most widely-reported health problems.

Aggressive feelings, anxiety, and alcohol abuse were the observed psychological consequences of the Youngstown steel closings. Similar conditions were widely reported among the aircraft workers in the Hartford County study. In most of these cases, the factor of time seems to be essential. Those who need much of it to find another job suffer the most. . . .

Special psychological problems arise when a plant closing occurs in a small community, especially when the establishment was the locality's major employer. Writing about the closing of a plant in southern Appalachia, Walter Strange notes that the people

> lost the central focus which had held the community together — its reason for existence — a focus which was held in common as community property, one which provided not only for economic needs but . . . a structural framework which gave coherence and cohesion to their lives.

These effects typically lessen or disappear following successful reemployment. Yet, "stressful situations" caused by a plant closing can linger long after the final shutdown has occurred. Moreover, feelings of lost self-esteem, grief, depression, and ill health can lessen the chances of finding reemployment; this failure, in turn, can exacerbate the emotional distress, generating a cycle of destruction. Ultimately a debilitating type of "blaming the victim" syndrome can evolve, causing dislocated workers to feel that the plant closing was their own fault. Strange argues "that those feelings of self-doubt can create fear of establishing a new employment relationship or complicate the adjustment process to a new job." As the sociologist Alfred Slote put it, in his seminal work on job termination:

> The most awful consequence of long-term unemployment is the development of the attitude, "I couldn't hold a job even if I found one," which transforms a man from unemployed to unemployable.

The "Ripple Effects" in the Community

While the impact of disinvestment on individual workers and their families, is probably the correct place to begin any inquiry into the social costs of unregulated deindustrialization, it cannot be the end of such an inquiry. For when mills or department stores or supermarket chains shut down, many other things can happen to a community. These can be extraordinarily costly as they ripple through the economy.

The primary effects are, of course, visited on those closest to the production unit that ceases operations. The unit's own employees lose salaries and wages, pensions, and other fringe benefits; supplier firms lose contracts; and the various levels of government lose corporate income and commercial property tax revenue. These in turn result in a series of secondary shocks including decreased retail purchases in the community, a reduction in earnings at supplier plants, and increased unemployment in other sectors. Finally, these events produce tertiary effects in the form of increased demand for public assistance and social services, reduced personal tax receipts, and eventually layoffs in other industries, including the public sector. What begins as a behind-closed-doors company decision to shut down a particular production facility ends up affecting literally everyone in town, including the butcher, the baker, and the candlestick maker. By the time all of these "ripple effects" spread throughout the economy, workers and families far removed from the original plant closing can be affected, often with dramatic consequences.

Some of these ripple (or multiplier) effects are felt immediately, while others take time to work through the economy. Some will dissipate quickly (especially if the local economy is expanding), while others may become a permanent part of the local economic environment. The extent of the impact of any particular closing will depend also on whether the plant or store was a major employer in the area, or an important purchaser of goods and services produced by other area businesses. All of these indirect impacts will be multiplied if a number of closings or cutbacks occur in the area simultaneously. . . .

When the company in the classic "company town" closes down, all of these effects are magnified tremendously. The case of Anaconda, Montana provides a perfect example. Anaconda Copper & Mining Co. had operated a huge copper smelter there for over seventy-five years when the Los Angeles-based Atlantic Richfield Co. (ARCO) acquired it. Two years later, on September 29, 1980, ARCO announced that it was abandoning the smelter, thus eliminating 80 percent of the entire annual payroll in this community of 12,000 people. Needless to say, the announcement sent a Richter scale shock wave through the town.

The action erased 1,000 jobs in Anaconda and 500 more in neighboring Great Falls. The fallout was immediate. In two weeks, new unemployment claims added 691 recipients to the rolls and before long, one in six in the work force was out of work. The food-stamp rolls grew by 190, to 434 families. About 170 workers chose early retirement rather than the $3,500 in severance pay. . . .

In all these ways, the ARCO smelter closing "echoed through the city." By December, the Chamber of Commerce found that thirty-six businesses it surveyed (excluding the railroad) had laid off, on the average, 20 percent of their employees. One fourth of the businesses said they anticipated further layoffs, and one third had canceled expansion plans. Most reported their business had dropped 10-50 percent, despite both the severance payments made by ARCO to its recently "pink-slipped" workers and the various forms of unemployment insurance and public aid supplied to those directly and indirectly affected.

The secondary victims of the smelter closing often had recourse to fewer public and private benefits than the smelter workers themselves. "The businessmen are getting the brunt of it right now," the town's Chevrolet dealer told a Los Angeles Times reporter. "They gave [the smelter workers] $3,500 in severance pay — I got caught with $500,000 in cars."

The physical and emotional trauma associated with this particular closing was also striking. Workers sold their $55,000 houses for $35,000 in order to take jobs elsewhere. Businesses that normally would have provided a comfortable retirement for their owners went bankrupt, leaving them with nothing more than Social Security for their old age. Visits to the Alcohol Service Center increased by 52 percent, and there was a 150-percent increase in the number of persons seeking drug counseling. The patient load at the Mental Health Center jumped 62 percent. To add injury to insult, on the day the smelter closing was announced, the local water company raised its rates. No one in town overlooked the fact that the water company was also owned by ARCO.

With the immense size of some industries like automobile and steel, entire regions behave as though they were company towns. The key losses flowing from the recent automobile layoffs are felt in steel, ferrous castings, aluminum, synthetic rubber, glass, plastics, textiles, and machine tools. The U.S. Department of Labor (DOL) has estimated that for every 100 jobs in the motor vehicle industry, 105 jobs are wiped out in the direct supplier network.

Economists talk about these indirect losses in terms of "employment multipliers." In this case, the DOL study reveals a multiplier of 2.05, since an initial loss of 100 jobs leads to an eventual total loss of 205. In studies of the automobile industry that were performed by the Transportation Systems Center of the U.S. Department of Transportation, the value of the multiplier was estimated to be even higher — in the range of 2.4 to 3.0.

Our own estimates using the M.I.T. Multiregional Input-Output Model (MRIO) suggests a multiplier in the same range. Beginning with a potential loss of 5,000 jobs in automobile assembly in Michigan, the MRIO permits a measurement of the effect of such a cut on all other industries in the United States on a state-by-state basis. According to this analysis, the original displacement of the assembly workers would eventually affect over 8,000 auto workers in all, as parts suppliers in Michigan and elsewhere eliminate jobs due to reduced orders. Along with Michigan, the midwestern states share the heaviest burden, with Ohio losing over 1,000 auto industry jobs, Indiana another 630, and Illinois and Wisconsin each losing at least 200.

In all, the 8,000 jobs potentially lost nationwide in the automobile industry would ultimately cause a decline in employment among all industries of more than 20,600. In other words, more than 12,000 non-auto industry jobs would be affected. For example, iron-ore miners in Minnesota — probably working in that state's northern "iron range" — will lose their jobs because, with fewer domestic cars produced, there is less need for sheet steel and consequently less demand for iron ore. Indeed, because of the staggering complexity and interrelatedness of the economy, nearly every industry will be touched sooner or later by the layoffs in the Michigan plants. Somewhere in the production chain — either in the direct manufacture of automobiles or, for that matter, in the weaving of the cloth that goes into the upholstery — workers will suffer short work weeks or temporary layoffs. Some will lose their jobs permanently. The biggest losers in this instance are those who work in closely allied industries such as steel, rubber, metalworking machinery, and metal stampings.

Of course, non-manufacturing workers are deeply affected as well. Over 1,000 jobs throughout the nation in transportation and warehousing would potentially disappear as a consequence of the original cutback in automobile assembly operations in Michigan. Nearly 1,800 wholesale and retail trade jobs and over 500 jobs in related business services will be affected. Presumably auto dealers, advertisers, truckers, and accountants will feel the pinch when some Detroit assembly lines close down for good. The same is obviously true when a steel or tire factory shuts down or even a major chain of supermarkets or discount department stores. The employment multipliers will differ from industry to industry depending on how well an industry is integrated into the entire production chain. But no instance of a plant, store, or office shutdown is an island unto itself.

Worker Adjustment and Retraining Notification Act of 1988

In 1988, Congress passed the federal Worker Adjustment and Retraining Notification Act (WARN Act), which requires employers with 100 or more full-time employees to give their workers and local government officials 60 days' advance notice of plant closings or mass layoffs. The key term in the WARN Act is "employment loss," which is defined as a termination of employment (other than through discharge for cause, voluntary resignation, or retirement), a layoff for more than six months, or a greater than 50% reduction in hours over a six-month period. With this term defined, the WARN Act then requires notice for any plant closing or mass layoff, which it defines as follows:

> "plant closing" is a temporary or permanent shutdown of a single site that causes an "employment loss" for 50 or more employees during a 30-day period.

> "mass layoff" is a reduction in force other than a plant closing that causes an "employment loss" during a 30-day period for 50 employees and one-third of the workforce, or for 500 employees even if less than one-third of the workforce.

The WARN Act has two major exceptions. The first is a "faltering company" exception, which applies to plant closings and not layoffs. A faltering company can give less than 60 days' notice if it had been actively seeking new financing to keep the plant open and in good faith believed that notice would jeopardize the negotiations. The second exception is for "unforeseeable business circumstances," and applies both to plant closings and mass layoffs. Such circumstances include a client's sudden and unexpected termination of a major contract, and natural disasters such as floods and earthquakes.

Violators are liable for up to 60 days of backpay and benefits for each employee, as well as attorney fees, and are subject to a civil penalty of $500 per day. At least one district court has held that punitive damages are unavailable under the act. The WARN Act does not preempt employees' rights under state law or union contracts.

Not surprisingly, the WARN Act's requirements have led to complex regulations and disputes over such issues as part-time employees, adequate notice, and the like. The following case demonstrates some of the complexity.

ROQUET v. ARTHUR ANDERSEN LLP
United States Court of Appeals, Seventh Circuit
398 F.3d 585 (2005)

TERENCE T. EVANS, CIRCUIT JUDGE.

This case involves the Worker Adjustment and Retraining Notification Act, 29 U.S.C. § 2101-2109, better known by its shortened name, the WARN Act. The Act became law in 1989, and its purpose is to soften the economic blow suffered by workers who unexpectedly face plant closings or mass layoffs. Among other things, the Act requires that companies subject to its reach (generally large employers) give employees 60 days notice in advance of any mass layoffs or plant closings. The notice gives affected workers a little time to adjust to a job loss, find new employment, or, if necessary, obtain retraining.

Our case, however, is not your typical WARN Act fare as it involves hot-button topics like "Enron," "document shredding," and "indictment." And it concerns an exception to the WARN Act's notification requirement: the Act's 60-day-notice obligation is eliminated, or reduced to a shorter term, if a mass layoff or plant closing is "caused by business circumstances that were not reasonably foreseeable as of the time that notice would have been required." *Id.* § 2102(b)(2)(A). The defendant here, the giant accounting and consulting firm Arthur Andersen LLP, convinced the district court that its failure to comply with the Act was excused by the exception we just quoted. The plaintiffs, a purported class of former Andersen employees, are here challenging that decision on appeal.

First, a little background. As of early 2002, Andersen had over 27,000 employees in 80 locations throughout the country. In addition to providing direct accounting and consulting services for clients, Andersen performed administrative support services for approximately 80 international practice firms that used the Andersen name. One of the firm's major clients was the Enron Corporation, the infamous Houston, Texas, energy marketer that fell like a house of cards in 2001 when it came to light that the company had grossly misstated its earnings. Andersen was at the center of Hurricane Enron — it audited the company's publicly filed financial statements and provided internal counseling.

In November of 2001, Andersen received bad news in the form of a subpoena from the SEC requesting Enron-related documents. During the course of its investigation, the SEC discovered that Andersen employees destroyed thousands of relevant documents in the 6 weeks leading up to its receipt of the subpoena. Over the next few months, the media began to speculate about Andersen's continuing viability. Stories also circulated that Andersen's employees were concerned about layoffs and that some of the company's clients were contemplating defection.

During this time, Andersen worked hard to try to resolve its Enron-related ills with the SEC and the Department of Justice (DOJ). As of February 22, 2002, Andersen had not suffered a significant loss of business nor was it giving any thought to a mass layoff. That day, Andersen's lawyers met with lawyers from the DOJ. The next day, counsel briefed Andersen's management team, and a participating manager e-mailed the following update to employees:

> At our meeting on Saturday, February 23, the current status of the investigation into document destruction was presented by the outside lawyers from Davis Polk. They are moving forward as quickly as possible to bring this matter to a conclusion as it relates to the Firm with the Department of Justice. Our desired timetable is to be in a position at the end of February to have the desired conclusion and an agreement in principle with the DOJ, so that we can finalize our disciplinary actions and prepare an internal announcement followed closely by a public announcement of the resolution of this investigation.

Discussions continued over the next few days.

On March 1, the DOJ delivered dire news — it was going to seek an indictment of the company. Andersen tried to convince the DOJ to change its mind, but to no avail. On March 7, an Andersen managing partner, Terry Hatchett, sent an e-mail informing employees that the firm was "presently engaged in discussions with the Department of Justice regarding the parties' respective views" and that "[n]o final conclusions have been reached." That very day, however, the DOJ filed a sealed indictment charging the firm with obstructing the SEC investigation by destroying and withholding documents On March 13, Andersen's lawyers asked the DOJ to defer prosecution of the company and focus instead on culpable individual employees. The DOJ refused to budge, and on March 14 the indictment was unsealed.

To the surprise of no one, news of the indictment triggered massive client defection. From March 15 to the 31st, Andersen lost $300 million in business. During this time period, the practice group on West Monroe Street in Chicago alone lost $57 million, roughly 14 percent of its fees. To put the gravity of these losses in perspective, the firm had lost only $5 million, or 1 percent, in the 10 weeks preceding the indictment. On March 28, Andersen announced that it was eliminating support services for its international network, which would result in additional revenue loss.

In light of these setbacks, and with additional hemorrhaging expected, Andersen decided to lay off thousands of employees. On April 8, management at West Monroe gave notices of termination to 560 employees, including Nancy Roquet and Coretta Robinson, the named plaintiffs in this suit. After receiving notice, Roquet remained on the payroll for 2 weeks and Robinson for 5 weeks. Andersen also made major cuts at its North Michigan Avenue site in Chicago as well as at its training facility in St. Charles, Illinois.

Roquet and Robinson filed a class-action complaint in federal district court alleging that Andersen violated the WARN Act by failing to give 60 days notice to its workers before laying them off. They sought back pay and lost benefits. In August of 2002, the court certified a class consisting of workers from the two Chicago sites and the St. Charles facility. Both sides eventually moved for summary judgment on the issue of whether Andersen's workforce reduction qualified as a "mass layoff" under the Act. The court concluded that it did and granted the plaintiffs' motion.

The parties then moved for summary judgment on the question of whether Andersen was exempt from liability under the WARN Act's "unforeseen business circumstances" exception. The district court concluded that the need for layoffs was not reasonably foreseeable 60 days before the decision was made and entered summary judgment in favor of Andersen. The plaintiffs appeal that decision, which we review *de novo*.

In evaluating this appeal, we note that the Department of Labor has provided some guidance regarding when the "unforeseen business circumstances" exception applies. In doing so, however, the agency eschewed *per se* rules and instead encouraged a case-by-case examination of the facts. A business circumstance may be reasonably unforeseeable if it was caused by some sudden, dramatic, and unexpected action, or by conditions outside the employer's control. 20 C.F.R. § 639.9(b)(1). When determining whether a mass layoff was caused by unforeseeable business circumstances, courts evaluate whether a similarly situated employer exercising reasonable judgment could have foreseen the circumstances that caused the layoff. *Id.* § 639.9(b)(2). Thus, a company will not be liable if, when confronted with potentially devastating occurrences, it reacts the same way that other reasonable employers within its own market would react. *Watson v. Mich. Indus. Holdings, Inc.*, 311 F.3d 760 (6th Cir. 2002).

The parties dispute whether Andersen established either element of the exception — causation and foreseeability. The district court concluded that the need for mass layoffs was caused by the public announcement of the indictment on March 14. We agree. Up until then, Andersen suffered no marked loss of business despite a spate of negative publicity. It is clear that economic hemorrhaging really did not begin until word of the indictment got out. The plaintiffs contend that Andersen's felonious misconduct caused the layoffs, not the indictment. But, while it is true that the illegal acts of some Andersen employees were the root cause of the firm's ultimate downfall, not until the indictment became public did it feel the pain. Had the DOJ indicted only individual Andersen employees instead of the firm as a whole, or targeted only the Houston office, the layoffs here may never have occurred.

The heart of the dispute in this case centers on foreseeability. In determining whether a crippling business circumstance is foreseeable, we must bear in mind that "it is the 'probability of occurrence that makes a business circumstance "reasonably foreseeable,"' rather than the 'mere possibility of such a circumstance.'" *Watson*, 311 F.3d at 765. The layoffs began on April 23, which means that Andersen was required to notify employees 60 days earlier, or February 22. The plaintiffs argue that the indictment was reasonably foreseeable on that date because "the DOJ disclosed to Andersen that an indictment was highly probable." But the record does not support this position. The plaintiffs point to Andersen's meeting with the DOJ on February 22 and its subsequent efforts to fight off an indictment. The February 23 e-mail summarizing that meeting, however, makes no mention of the firm being indicted. And Andersen's subsequent negotiations with the government do not mean that it knew an indictment was likely. Possible? Certainly. But probable? No. Indeed, as of February 22 it was not a foregone conclusion that Andersen would be indicted as a company — in the past, the government typically went after culpable individuals, not companies as a whole. By all accounts, this was an unusual move by the DOJ. There is evidence in the record suggesting that Andersen could have reasonably foreseen the indictment by March 1 — the date it was told by the DOJ that it was being indicted. But hope still remained that the dreaded act could be stalled if not avoided.

We believe that a reasonable company in Andersen's position would have reacted as it did. Confronted with the possibility of an indictment that threatened its very survival, the firm continued to negotiate with the government until the very end and turned to layoffs only after the indictment became public. The plaintiffs argue that Andersen should have notified employees of layoffs on February 22. We do not agree. At that point, Andersen had not yet lost business or been indicted. Indeed, in our view, a mass layoff at that point would have been a poor business decision. What if the government decided not to indict the firm as a whole, or waited 6 months to make the decision? The only reason for providing notice so early would be to ward off potential WARN Act liability. But, as the Sixth Circuit explained in *Watson,* the WARN Act is not intended to deter companies from fighting to stay afloat:

> WARN was not intended to force financially fragile, yet economically viable, employers to provide WARN notice and close its doors when there is a *possibility* that the business may fail at some undetermined time in the future. Such a reading of the Act would force many employers to lay off their employees prematurely, harming precisely those individuals WARN attempts to protect. A company that is struggling to survive financially may be able to continue on for years and it was not Congress's intent to force such a company to close its doors to comply with WARN's notice requirement.

311 F.3d at 765. These same concerns were at play here. Thus, Andersen's failure to notify employees earlier than it did was not unreasonable.

The plaintiffs argue that the layoffs were foreseeable as a matter of law under 20 C.F.R. § 639.9(b)(1) because the indictment was not sudden, dramatic, and unexpected nor outside the employer's control. In their view, Andersen was long aware of its misconduct, and punishment for that misconduct was inherently foreseeable. But the indictment was certainly sudden and dramatic in that Andersen did not know if it would be indicted as a firm. Nor did Andersen really know when the indictment would be returned until the act occurred. Again, the WARN Act deals in reasonable probabilities, not possibilities. Moreover, an employer does not have to be caught completely off guard by a dire business circumstance for it to be "sudden, dramatic, or unexpected." Case law reveals that WARN Act defendants need not show that the circumstances which caused a plant closing or mass layoff arose from out of the blue to qualify for the exception.

Our dissenting colleague tells us that "Andersen knew enough 'long before' April 8, 2002, to give the required statutory notice to its employees." (We've added the internal quotation marks.) That's an odd statement, for the statutory notice requires 60 days, and the dissent goes on to tell us in the same paragraph that the "impending catastrophe" was not foreseeable as of February 22, 2002. So, by that count alone, "long before" April 8 (when notice was given) is at best 45, not 60, days. And "long before" eventually becomes shorter still as the dissent settles on March 1, 38 days before the April 8 notice actually went out, as the trigger date. While we concede that an argument could be made that March 14, the date the indictment was unsealed, *could* be viewed as a WARN Act trigger date (which would further shorten the "long before" window to 25 days), we don't think it should be so viewed. We think the company, faced with this unprecedented cataclysmic event, reasonably needed a little time to assess how things would shake out. And it was not unreasonable for the company to think it could survive the carnage until early April, when on the 8th it ran up the white flag of surrender and gave the bad news to its employees.

The lead time in the notice Andersen ended up giving varied from employee to employee. Our two named plaintiffs, for example, got 2 (Roquet) and 5 (Robinson) weeks notice before they were out of work. Given the situation here, and the "business circumstances" exception in § 2102(b)(2)(A), Andersen, although deserving of no roses for the acts of some of its agents in the Enron mess, did not violate the WARN Act by giving the notice as it did on April 8.

We also reject the notion that the timing of the notice was under Andersen's control. The plaintiffs are confusing Andersen's responsibility and culpability for its misbehavior with its "control" over the indictment within the meaning of the regulation. Stated simply, Andersen could not indict itself. Andersen was not like a company that secretly plotted for a long time to move its operation to Mexico and closed up shop without any notice to its employees.

Andersen has appealed the district court's entry of summary judgment for the plaintiffs on the question of whether its workforce reduction constituted a "mass layoff" under the Act. But because we agree with the court's dismissal of the suit under the WARN Act's "unforeseen business circumstances" exception, we need not address the contention.

The judgment of the district court is Affirmed.

WOOD, CIRCUIT JUDGE, dissenting.

. . . The majority finds here that Andersen was entitled to take advantage of the unforeseen circumstances exception to the obligation to notify affected workers 60 days prior to a mass layoff or plant closing. In so holding, it either finds that notice was impossible right up to April 8, 2002, when the employees finally received the bad news, or it finds that the statute as a matter of law takes an all-or-nothing approach — if 60 days' notice is impossible, then no notice at all is required. . . .

Taking into account the language and purpose of the WARN Act, we should hold that the 60-day period is merely reduced, not eliminated, when the necessity for a mass layoff or plant closing becomes apparent within that time period. Indeed, immediately after describing the unforeseen circumstances exception, the statute reads: "An employer relying on this subsection shall give as much notice as is practicable and at that time shall give a brief statement of the basis for reducing the notification period." 29 U.S.C. § 2102(b)(3). . . .

The crucial date under the WARN Act is not the date when the company *knows* that a mass layoff is imminent, nor is it the date when the company finally gets around to identifying the exact employees affected by the mass layoff. The Act states plainly that the trigger date is the date when a mass layoff is "reasonably foreseeable." As soon as it is probable that a mass layoff will occur, the employer must provide notice as soon as is practicable. Here, Andersen knew of the indictment on March 1, yet it waited over five weeks before providing any notice to its employees. . . .

For these reasons, I would reverse and remand for further proceedings. I respectfully dissent.

NOTES

1. *Sale of Business.* Should the WARN Act be limited to loss of employment, or should employers be required to give advance notice when a major decision can foreseeably cause a loss of wages or benefits? In *International Alliance of Theatrical & Stage Employees v. Compact Video Services, Inc.*, 50 F.3d 1464 (9th Cir. 1995), a company sold its business to a nonunion entity. Almost all the employees continued working for the new entity, but with lower wages and benefits. The union sued for a violation of the WARN Act, arguing they were effectively laid off without advance notice. In a 2-1 decision, the court held that the sale of the business and a reduction in wages was not a WARN event. If the buying company had laid off workers, it, rather than the selling company, would be responsible for giving the WARN notice. Judge Ferguson, dissenting, complained that the decision "eviscerates the protections against unprecipitated termination which WARN was enacted to guarantee." *Id.* at 1471.

2. *Details Matter.* Even law firms as employers can fail to comply with WARN Act requirements. The law firm of Lord Day & Lord sent a letter to employees thirty days before closing, explaining in the letter that the firm could not give greater advance notice "since this termination arises from unforeseeable business circumstances." Citing the Act's requirement that an employer relying on the unforeseeable-business-circumstances exception must give as much notice as practicable and "give a brief statement of the basis for reducing the notification period," a New York district court held that the letter lacked sufficient detail to qualify for the exception. *Grimmer v. Lord Day & Lord*, 937 F. Supp. 255 (S.D.N.Y. 1996).

3. *WARN Lacks Enforcement Tools.* In enacting the WARN Act, Congress required the General Accounting Office to assess the effectiveness of the Act. In its 1993 report, the GAO found that more than half of the employers who laid off workers were not required under the law to give notice, primarily because the layoff or plant closure did not affect enough workers. Even where layoffs met the WARN triggers, half the employers gave no notice and another 29% gave fewer than sixty days' notice. The GAO concluded that private enforcement in the courts appears not to be working, and suggested that Congress give the Department of Labor the responsibility and authority to enforce the law.

Part VII

EMPLOYEE BENEFITS

Employee benefits are forms of employee compensation other than cash. Generally, they can be classified as either deferred compensation or in-kind payments. Deferred compensation consists of payments that are earned now but will not be available to the employee until later. Pensions are the best example. In-kind payments are compensation that is usable in the short-term but provided in a form other than money. Health insurance, leave time, and even government-mandated payments (such as those for unemployment insurance or workers' compensation coverage) fall into this category.

Employee benefits have become such a significant part of the compensation package that the common term for them — fringe benefits — has become anachronistic. As a percentage of wages and salaries, employee benefits have grown dramatically over the past century to their current level of about 40% of total wages and salaries, or more than $20,000 per employee. Table VII-1. As a result, large numbers of employees have a significant proportion of their income subject to the special risks posed by this form of compensation.

Table VII-1
Employee Benefits as a Percentage of Wages and
Salaries, 1929-2004

	1929	1955	1975	1995	2004
Total Benefits	3.0%	17.0%	30.0%	41.8%	40.3% ($20,158)
Pensions	0.2	2.2	3.6	6.7	8.0 ($4,161)
Insurance	0.1	1.1	3.4	8.3	11.9 ($5,789)
Legally Required	0.8	3.3	8.4	12.0	9.1 ($4,474)
Miscellaneous	1.9	10.4	14.6	14.8	11.2 ($5,734)

a   Amounts include only employer share of benefits. Employees also contribute significant amounts, especially for pensions and insurance.

b   Includes health and life insurance (more than 90% is attributable to health insurance).

c   Includes Social Security and Medicare taxes, unemployment compensation, and worker's compensation.

d   Includes benefits such as payments for time not worked, including vacations, holidays, and sick leave; severance pay; child care benefits; etc.

Source: Adapted from U.S. Chamber Research Center, Employee Benefits 40, Table 17 (1996); U.S. Chamber of Commerce, Employee Benefits Study 10 (2005).

The Functions of Employee Benefits

Employee benefits expose employees to more risk than simple wage payments made in cash. For deferred compensation, the employee is relying on a promise by the employer to make payments years or even decades in the future. For in-kind payments, the risks include misunderstandings about what is actually promised and the firmness of the employer's commitment. Has the employer really agreed to cover this type of medical procedure? To grant a leave under these circumstances? Will the employer really cover those expensive medical bills, or will it attempt to make changes to minimize its liability?

Given the extra risks of employee benefits, why are they such an important component of employee compensation? Even without the extra risk, other things being equal, one would expect compensation to be in cash rather than employee benefits. Employers should be neutral between providing an employee $1,000 per year in cash and contributing $1,000 per year for that employee in a pension fund. But employees should prefer cash. With cash, the employee could decide whether to save the money for use at retirement or to use it in other ways; the retirement contribution forces the employee to save it. Any extra risk associated with pensions should increase the preference for cash.

Employee benefits are an important component of compensation because other things are not equal: employee benefits serve several purposes that cannot be met, or cannot be met as well, through cash payments. First and most obviously, employee benefits provide tax advantages. Consider health insurance. If an employee in a 15% tax bracket is paid $1,000 in cash, she ends up with $850 after taxes to use towards the purchase of health insurance.

But if the employer provides the same amount in health insurance as an employee benefit, it can be paid for with pretax dollars, so the entire $1,000 is available.

These tax benefits are targeted to employees. The employer is entitled to a $1,000 deduction, whether it pays the employee in cash or provides her with health insurance. The employee, however, is required to declare a cash payment as income and pay taxes on it, but is entitled to exclude from her income, and hence avoid taxes on, monies paid for her health insurance. I.R.C. § 106. Who actually captures the tax benefits, however, is difficult to determine. If an employer offers $1,000 in cash or $875 in health insurance to an employee in a 15% tax bracket who wants health insurance, the employee should prefer the insurance. After taxes, the employee could only purchase $850 of insurance with the $1,000 in cash, but she will get $875 worth of insurance if she accepts the employer's alternative offer. But when the employee takes the insurance rather than the cash, the employer captures $125 of the $150 in tax benefits. Thus, employers and employees are likely to share the tax benefits in proportions that are determined by the complex workings of the labor market, rather than by whom the tax code targets as the beneficiary.

For pension payments, the advantage is tax deferral. For our hypothetical employee, a cash payment of $1,000 would be taxed immediately, and investment income on the remaining $850 would be taxed as it was earned. For qualified pension plans, neither the $1,000 nor its income would be taxed until they were withdrawn, usually at retirement. I.R.C. § 402. Table VII-2 illustrates the value of these tax advantages. The table assumes that a fifty-five year old person has $1,000 in wages and wishes to save it for fifteen years for use at retirement at age seventy, and that the market interest rate during the fifteen years is 8%. Several points from the table are worth noting. First, the tax advantages are greater for persons in higher tax brackets. The percent gain over the regular account increases from 18% to 37% as our hypothetical employee moves from the 15% tax bracket to the 28% tax bracket. Second, the tax advantages increase significantly if the retirement tax rate is lower than the tax rate during an employee's working years. The percent gain increases from 37% to 62% when the tax rate falls from 28% in working years to 15% in retirement. Third, a tax advantage may remain even if the tax rate is higher in retirement than during working years. Our hypothetical employee comes out ahead marginally when the tax rate increases from 15% during working years to 28% in retirement. The gain would be greater if the money has been invested for more than fifteen years, if the tax rate had increased sometime prior to retirement, or if the market interest rate had been higher than 8%.

Table VII-2
Tax Advantages of a $1,000 Contribution to a
Qualified Retirement Plan

	Tax Rate 15% in Working Years		Tax Rate 28% in Working Years	
	Regular Account	Qualified Plan	Regular Account	Qualified Plan
Wage Payment	$1,000	$1,000	$1,000	$1,000
Tax on Wage	150	0	280	0
Deposit	850	1,000	720	1,000
Value at Withdrawal	2,280	3,172	1,668	3,172
Retirement Tax Rate (No Change)	15%	15%	28%	28%
Tax on Withdrawal	0	476	0	888
Net Withdrawal	2,280	2,696	1,668	2,284
Gain Over Regular Account	—	416	—	616
Percent Gain	—	18%	—	37%
Retirement Tax Rate (Change)	28%	28%	15%	15%
Tax on Withdrawal	0	888	0	476
Net Withdrawal	2,280	2,284	1,668	2,696
Gain	—	4	—	1,028
Percent Gain	—	0%	—	62%

a   Amounts in a regular account compound at effective (after-tax) rates of 6.80% for taxpayers in the 15% tax bracket and 5.76% for taxpayers in the 28% tax bracket. Amounts in qualified plans compound at 8%.

Source: Adapted from CBO, Tax Policy for Pensions and Other Retirement Saving 3-5 (1987).

The tax advantages available for employee benefits are in place to encourage employers and employees to include benefits in the compensation package. And no one doubts that they work. One study indicated that removing the tax advantages would reduce the demand for pensions by about 39% and the demand for health insurance by about 12%. (Since employee benefits are a substitute for wages, the study also indicated that the decrease in pensions and health insurance would be accompanied by a 3.4% increase in wages.) STEPHEN A. WOODBURY & WEI-JANG HUANG, THE TAX TREATMENT OF FRINGE BENEFITS 140 (1991).

The increased coverage, however, is quite costly. The tax advantages provided to employer-sponsored pension plans resulted in lost tax revenues of $118 billion in fiscal year 2006. The revenues lost because of tax advantages provided for employer-provided health benefits were even more: $126 billion. By comparison, the tax revenues lost because of the deduction for home mortgage interest were $76 billion in 2006. ANALYTICAL PERSPECTIVES, BUDGET OF THE UNITED STATES GOVERNMENT, FISCAL YEAR 2006, Table 19-1, 317-319 (2005). (Figures are estimates and, because of differences in the nature of the programs and the ways in which the losses are calculated, they are only roughly comparable.)

While tax considerations are important, they are not the only reason for the increasing prominence of employee benefits. Employee benefits have several additional functions in addition to capturing tax benefits. They may, for example, help employers attract particular employees. Employers that provide child care and have generous parental leave policies may be more successful at attracting and retaining female employees with families than employers that pay more in wages. Indeed, employee benefit packages can be used to accomplish goals that might be difficult to pursue directly:

> [S]uppose a firm prefers to hire mature adults, preferably those with children, in the hopes of acquiring a stable, dependable work force. An employer attempting to attract these people by offering them higher wages than single, younger, or much older adults would risk charges of discrimination. Instead, the firm can accomplish the same effect by offering its employees fringe benefits that are of much more value to workers with families than to others. For example, offering family coverage under a health insurance plan has the effect of compensating those with families more than others, because single or childless people cannot really take advantage of the full benefit. . . . Thus, at times fringe benefits allow the firm to give preferential treatment to a group it wants to attract without running afoul of discrimination laws.

ROBERT J. FLANAGAN ET AL., ECONOMICS OF THE EMPLOYMENT RELATIONSHIP 244 (1989).

Similarly, employee benefits, and especially pensions, may enhance the ability of employers to retain employees. To the extent a pension is forfeited if the employee leaves the firm too soon, the pension can be used to encourage employees to stay. When this type of bonding works to increase employee tenure, the costs to employers of recruiting and training employees are reduced. The bonding may also serve employee interests. Employers should be more willing to provide costly training to employees if they can be assured employees will remain with the firm long enough for the firm to recoup its investment. Thus, employees may have more on-the-job training opportunities available to them than they would if pensions were not a compensation option.

Somewhat ironically, pensions may also assist employers in getting rid of employees at the end of their careers. Traditionally, employers have required employees to retire at a certain age, presumably when it was thought that productivity would begin to decline. The Age Discrimination in Employment Act, however, now makes it illegal for employers to require employees to retire. Pensions, though, can be used to encourage employees to retire. Most directly, pensions can help ensure that an employee's finances permit retirement without undue hardship. More subtly, pension plans can be structured so that the present value of lifetime pension benefits begins to decline with age, so that, in effect, the employee suffers a financial penalty by delaying retirement. In one study, for example, the present value of pension benefits for a thirty-year employee with a $25,000 annual salary was $172,000 if the employee retired ten years before the normal retirement age, $91,000 for retirement at the normal age, and only $26,000 for retirement ten years after the normal age. Edward P. Lazear, *Pensions as Severance Pay, in* FINANCIAL ASPECTS OF

THE UNITED STATES PENSION SYSTEM 57, 78 (Zvi Bodie & John B. Shoven eds., 1983).

Finally, employee benefits may be made a part of the compensation package because employers have a comparative advantage in providing them. Economies of scale, for example, may mean that employers are able to do a better job of investing retirement savings than individual employees, so it may make sense to have the savings placed in a pension fund administered by the employer rather than paid out to individual employees in current income. Similarly, some employee benefits present adverse selection problems when individual employees attempt to purchase them. Individuals seeking annuities at retirement, for example, are not likely to be offered generous annuities, because they are in a pool with people who expect to live a long time. Individuals seeking health insurance might be hiding health problems. Employers can ease these types of selectivity biases and, as a result, get better deals than individual employees for annuities, health insurance, and other types of employee benefits.

NOTES

1. Ensuring Tax Benefits for Low-Income Workers. For several reasons, employees with higher incomes have a stronger preference for pensions. First, the value of the tax benefits is greater for employees with higher incomes; deferring taxes is worth more for people who are in higher tax brackets. Second, employees with higher incomes are in a better position to set money aside for retirement; they do not need the money as much to pay for current needs. And third, Social Security will replace a lower proportion of the pre-retirement income of high income employees, so they need to save more to ensure a retirement at close to the same income level they enjoyed before retirement.

Because of these employee preferences (and employer incentives to respond to them), if the Internal Revenue Code did not provide some restraints, one would expect a very large proportion of the significant tax advantages for retirement savings to flow to people with high incomes. Because of this concern, the I.R.C. contains complicated "antidiscrimination" rules designed to require employers who offer pensions to extend their benefits to employees who are not highly compensated. Generally, for pension plans to be qualified for tax advantages, employers must ensure 1) that non-highly compensated employees participate in plans at a rate that is comparable to the rate of participation for highly compensated employees, and 2) that the ratio of contributions or benefits to salary for the two groups is equal. I.R.C. §§ 401(a)(4), 401(a)(26), 410(b).

Employer decisions about whether to offer pension plans are made more complicated by the antidiscrimination rules:

> From its own income tax viewpoint, the employer is theoretically indifferent to the plan's creation. Whether as a $1,000 wage payment or as a $1,000 contribution to a qualified retirement plan, the employer can deduct the total amount as a business expense. Yet by contributing to the plan, the employer channels a government subsidy to the plan participants. Providing

this subsidy is not cost free. Establishment and maintenance of a qualified plan involve significant administrative costs. . . .

At first glance it might appear that, as long as the potential subsidy to an employee exceeded the administrative costs of including the employee in the plan, the employer would choose to include the employee in the plan. This ignores the fact that savings and consumption patterns are not identical across the compensation spectrum. . . .

[Because low-paid employees have lower preferences for retirement savings,] a mere dollar-for-dollar substitution of retirement savings for wages would not maintain their level of satisfaction; wages would have to be increased. For example, an employee who was paid $10,000 before the plan's establishment might demand $9,500 after establishment even though the employer contributes an additional $1,000 to the plan. . . .

[On the other hand, for high-wage employees,] a dollar of retirement contribution is worth more than a dollar of compensation. Thus, such employees would be willing to accept some level of actual wage reduction as a cost of plan participation. For example, an employee who was paid $50,000 before the plan's establishment might only demand a salary of $44,500 if an additional $5,000 is contributed to the retirement plan. The total wage cost to the employer would therefore actually drop from $50,000 to $49,500. . . .

As the [anti]discrimination rules require more in the way of contributions for lower paid employees, the employer's costs increase. For any given employer, the costs may eventually exceed the benefits of covering the highly paid employees. At that point, the employer would decline to establish or continue a retirement plan.

Bruce Wolk, *Discrimination Rules for Qualified Retirement Plans: Good Intentions Confronting Economic Reality*, 70 VA. L. REV. 419, 430-33 (1984).

2. *Thinking Again About the Tax Advantages.* These antidiscrimination rules do not apply to health insurance, even though employees with higher incomes also benefit more from these tax advantages. Higher-income employees are more likely to have health insurance and to have better health insurance, and they benefit more even when they have the same health plan as lower-income employees. Paul Fronstin, *The Tax Treatment of Health Insurance and Employment-Based Health Benefits*, EBRI Issue Brief No. 294, June 2006, at 7-9 (assuming the same health plan, families earning $250,000 annually receive 1½ to 2½ times the tax benefits of families earning $45,000 annually).

The high cost of the tax advantages and these kinds of distributional effects for employee benefits have caused some to reconsider. For example, the President's Advisory Panel on Federal Tax Reform recently recommended that the tax exclusion for health insurance be limited to $5,000 annually for employee-only coverage or $11,500 for family coverage. SIMPLE, FAIR AND PRO-GROWTH: PROPOSALS TO FIX AMERICA'S TAX SYSTEM 78-82 (2005). Others have suggested eliminating the tax advantage entirely and using the extra tax revenues to provide government-sponsored health insurance to low-income workers. GAO, EFFECTS OF CHANGING THE TAX TREATMENT OF FRINGE BENE-FITS 3 (1992). But these kinds of changes would involve trade-offs. Employers would be less likely to offer health insurance and the poor and ill would have the most difficulty finding insurance elsewhere. Worker productivity may decline if they do not have the same access to health care. If overall spending on health care goes down, the pace of technological innovation may slow. Thus, "[a]ny honest debate of overhauling the federal tax treatment of health care in the United States needs to address [both] what a new system might do, [and] what the trade-offs and unintended consequences might be . . . ." Fronstin, *supra*, at 26.

Legal Regulation of Employee Benefits

The Employee Retirement Income Security Act of 1974 (ERISA) is the most important law regulating employee benefits. It is an interesting example of labor regulation, in part because of its indecisiveness. On the one hand, ERISA recognizes the voluntary and contractual nature of employee benefits. ERISA does not require employers to provide even a minimal package of employee benefits, and some of its provisions, such as the reporting and disclosure requirements, are intended to address problems that might interfere with the contracting process. On the other hand, ERISA is skeptical of the contractual regime. When employee benefits are provided, ERISA requires certain provisions to be included in the agreement, regardless of the parties' desires. ERISA applies to a broad range of employer-provided benefits, including pensions, health insurance, child care, prepaid legal services, and a variety of others. But ERISA makes an important distinction between pension plans and other types of employee benefit programs. ERISA §§ 3(1), (2). Pension plans involve saving for retirement during an employee's work life, followed by distribution of the savings to the employee during retirement. Both periods of time (for saving and for distribution) may be decades long. The other types of employee benefit plans, known as welfare plans, are more short-term in nature. At any point in time, employees either use or do not use the available health care, child care, or legal services, but the benefits do not accumulate over time. Viewed from the employer's perspective, welfare plans are paid for on a pay-as-you-go basis (the revenues and liabilities arise at about the same time), in contrast to pension plans which entail a long-term program of savings and distribution.

The distinction between pension and welfare plans is important, because some of ERISA's provisions apply only to pensions with their long-term promises, while other provisions apply to both types of plans. Only pension plans are subject to ERISA provisions intended to protect employees from the forfeiture of pensions that have been building over a number of years (vesting protections), to ensure that contributions adequate to pay the pensions promised at retirement are made during the working lives of employees, and to provide pension insurance when plans are unable to pay promised pension benefits. ERISA §§ 201-11, 301-08, 4001-02. Both pension and welfare plans are subject to ERISA provisions requiring information about plans to be reported to the government and disclosed to employee-participants, imposing fiduciary responsibilities on those making decisions for the plan, and providing remedies and enforcement mechanisms. ERISA §§ 101-11, 401-14, 501-15. In addition to this traditional distinction between pension and welfare plans,

Congress in recent years has increasingly amended ERISA to address the special problems of one type of welfare plan, employer-provided health insurance.

Despite its breadth, ERISA does not apply to all employee benefits. Some types of benefits are explicitly excluded from coverage, such as unemployment and workers' compensation benefits. ERISA § 4(b)(3). In addition, ERISA regulates only employee benefit "plans". ERISA § 4(a). In general, a "plan" requires an administrative structure, identification of intended benefits and beneficiaries, a funding arrangement, and procedures for receiving benefits. This means that ERISA does not apply to some important employee benefits, including most leave programs. But this certainly does not mean that these non-ERISA employee benefits are not regulated at all. Leave programs, in particular, are heavily regulated by a potpourri of laws, as are unemployment and workers' compensation. Indeed, in contrast to ERISA, these laws often *require* employers to provide these types of benefits.

We consider unemployment and workers' compensation elsewhere. In this part, we will begin by discussing leave time and then proceed to discuss pensions and health care, by far the most significant employee benefit plans regulated by ERISA.

Chapter 18

LEAVE TIME

Leave time is a very important type of employee benefit. Employees have been fired for missing work for many reasons that are personally compelling, but not legally protected. For example, Audrey Seidle was fired when she stayed home to care for her four-year-old son who had an ear infection, *Seidle v. Provident Mutual Life Ins. Co.*, 871 F. Supp. 238 (E.D. Pa. 1994); Kimberly Miller was fired when she stayed home because she had a bad case of the flu herself, *Miller v. AT&T Corp.*, 250 F.3d 820 (4th Cir. 2001); Kimberly Troupe was fired when she was often tardy and absent from work because of morning sickness during her pregnancy, *Troupe v. May Dep't Stores Co.*, 20 F.3d 734 (7th Cir. 1994); and Anthony Fioto was fired when he left work to be with his mother while she had emergency brain surgery. *Fioto v. Manhattan Woods Golf Enters., LLC*, 270 F. Supp. 2d 401 (S.D.N.Y. 2003).

Leave time is also important because it plays a role across a variety of broader workplace issues. As the examples above illustrate, women tend to request leaves more often than men. Thus, leave time is central to the effort to create a more level playing field for female workers. Similarly, the availability of leaves is often very important to the ability of individuals with disabilities to participate fully and actively in the labor market. Leaves have also become increasingly important in addressing family/work conflicts as more and more workers are either single parents or members of two-worker families.

Employer practices on leave time are extremely varied. A key variable is whether the leave is with or without pay. Most employers provide paid leave for at least some reasons, such as sickness (58%), vacation (77%), personal reasons (36%), funerals (68%), and family obligations (7%). U.S. BUREAU OF LABOR STATISTICS, NATIONAL COMPENSATION SURVEY: EMPLOYEE BENEFITS IN PRIVATE INDUSTRY IN THE UNITED STATES 22 (March 2005) (numbers are percentage of private-sector workers who are eligible for paid benefit).

Leave time is generally not governed by the Employee Retirement Income Security Act of 1974 (ERISA). Because ERISA is so complex, one might think this would simplify regulation of leave programs. But that is not the case. First, because ERISA does not apply, the leave programs provided voluntarily by employers are governed by state contract law, which varies from state to state. Even more importantly, however, when ERISA applies, it does not require employers to provide benefits, such as pensions and health insurance. Rather, it merely provides uniform federal regulation for those benefits when employers voluntarily decide to offer them. Leave time, in contrast, is regulated by many different state and federal laws, and many of those laws *require* employers to provide this type of employee benefit.

A. THE RIGHT TO LEAVE TIME

The most important law granting employees a right to leave time is the Family and Medical Leave Act of 1993 (the FMLA). In general, it requires employers with fifty or more employees to grant up to twelve weeks of unpaid leave each year to eligible workers who have serious health conditions themselves, who need to care for a newly born or adopted child, or who need to care for a spouse, child, or parent with a serious health condition. 28 U.S.C. § 2612. The FMLA protects the right to take a leave, to retain health insurance benefits while on leave, and to return to the same or an equivalent position after the leave. It also prohibits retaliation for requesting an FMLA leave.

But the FMLA is only one of many federal and state laws that provide employees with a right to leave time. At the federal level, for example, an employee may also have a right to leave time if:

- She is an individual with a disability who needs a leave as a reasonable accommodation to her disability. Americans with Disabilities Act, 42 U.S.C. §§ 12101 *et seq.*

- She is pregnant and the employer provides leave for other types of temporary disabilities. Pregnancy Discrimination Act, 42 U.S.C. § 701(k).

- She reports for military duty. Uniformed Services Employment and Reemployment Rights Act, 38 U.S.C. §§ 4301 *et seq.*

In addition to these federal laws, many states have their own laws that expand FMLA rights. For example, seventeen states have leave laws that apply to smaller employers, ten states require employers to grant leaves for parents who want to participate in a child's educational activities, and eight states provide for longer leaves. NATIONAL PARTNERSHIP FOR WOMEN & FAMILIES, STATE FAMILY LEAVE LAWS THAT ARE MORE EXPANSIVE THAN FMLA (2002). One state, California, even provides partial wage replacement during family leaves. CAL. UNEMP. INS. CODE § 3301.

WHITAKER v. BOSCH BRAKING SYSTEMS DIVISION

United States District Court, W.D. Michigan
180 F. Supp. 2d 922 (2001)

QUIST, J.

Plaintiff [Tami Whitaker's] job consisted of standing on her feet at all times, constant moving, and inserting screws and plugs with a rivet gun. In December 1998, Plaintiff became pregnant. She experienced considerable "morning sickness" — nausea, vomiting, and cramping — because of the pregnancy. Plaintiff's physician, Dr. Robert Brown, advised Plaintiff to limit her working hours and get more rest. Dr. Brown was concerned that if Plaintiff spent too much time on her feet at work she would risk hypertension and premature delivery . . . .

[Plaintiff sought an FMLA leave for release] from working overtime which, from time to time, could be assigned to her under a collective bargaining agreement. She could and would continue to work forty hours per week. Plaintiff gave Defendant only a note signed by Dr. Brown which states:

> 14 Jan 1999
>
> To whom it may concern
>
> Tami Whitaker is pregnant and her work should be limited to 8 hours/day 40 hours/week . . . .

Dennis Crossno, a human resources manager for Defendant, told Plaintiff that she had to fill out a leave form and bring in a doctor's note. Thereupon, Plaintiff presented Defendant with an "Application for Family Leave of Absence" and a "Certification of Health Care Provider." The Certification is signed by Dr. Brown. Among other things, the certification says:

> 4. Describe the medical facts which support your certification, including a brief statement as to how the medical facts meet the criteria of one of these categories:
>
> *This patient is pregnant with a EDC of 9-14-99. The patient is required to complete all prenatal visit [sic] for a healthy pregnancy.*
>
> 5. a. State the approximate date the condition commenced, and the probable duration of the condition (and also the probable duration of the patient's present incapacity if different):
>
> *LMP 12-7-98 with a EDC of 9-14-99. 40 wks. to completed pregnancy.*
>
> b. Will it be necessary for the employee to take work only intermittently or to work on a less than full schedule as a result of the condition (including for treatment described in Item 6 below)?
>
> Yes [x] No [ ] If yes, give the probable duration:
>
> *To attend prenatal visits.*
>
> c. If the condition is a chronic condition (condition #4) or pregnancy, state whether the patient is presently incapacitated and the likely duration and frequency of episodes of incapacity.
>
> *Normal pregnancy at this time. Due to pregnancy 8 hours a day, 40/wk should be allowed.*

Defendant denied Plaintiff FMLA leave . . . . After [the denial], Plaintiff refused to work overtime anyway. Crossno called Plaintiff into his office and told Plaintiff that if she did not get a doctor's slip stating that she could work overtime she would have to take short term disability leave. Plaintiff took the short term disability leave. She is suing for the difference between the wages and bonus she would have earned working forty hours per week less the amount she received from short term disability. . . .

The FMLA was enacted in 1993 to "help men and women balance the conflicting demands of work and personal life." *Price v. City of Fort Wayne*, 117 F.3d 1022, 1024 (7th Cir. 1997); 29 U.S.C. § 2601(b). Coverage is afforded to employees who have been employed by a covered employer for at least a year and have worked at least 1,250 hours during the twelve month period in question. 29 U.S.C. § 2611(2)(A). The FMLA provides eligible employees with a maximum of twelve weeks of unpaid leave in a given twelve month period to attend to certain family and medical matters. 29 U.S.C. § 2612(a). Leave may be taken for specified reasons, including medical reasons, childbirth or adoption, or for the care of a spouse, parent, or child who suffers from a serious health condition. *Id.* An employee seeking leave for medical reasons or to care for a family member may take leave either intermittently or on a reduced schedule when medically necessary. 29 U.S.C. § 2612(b). Upon return from FMLA leave, an employer must restore an employee to her former job or another position with equivalent pay, benefits, and conditions of employment. 29 U.S.C. § 2614(a)(1). An employer who fails to provide an employee FMLA leave may be held liable for compensatory damages, liquidated damages, and interest. 29 U.S.C. § 2617.

An employee seeking FMLA leave is obligated to give the employer notice sufficient to alert the employer leave is FMLA-qualifying leave. 29 U.S.C. § 2612(e). The regulations issued by the Department of Labor provide that the employee need not mention the FMLA by name, but is only required to give sufficient information to put the employer on notice that the leave may be FMLA-qualifying leave. 29 C.F.R. § 825.302(c). If an employee's request is unclear, the employer is required to inquire further to obtain the necessary details of the leave to be taken in order to ascertain whether the requested leave qualifies as FMLA leave. *Id.* An employer may require that an employee's request for leave be supported by a certification from the employee's health care provider. *See* 29 U.S.C. § 2613(a). The certification may request the health care provider to provide "appropriate medical facts" regarding the employee's serious health condition. 29 U.S.C. § 2613(b)(3).

In this case, Plaintiff claims that she was entitled to FMLA leave pursuant to 26 U.S.C. § 2612(a)(1)(D), which grants leave based on "a serious health condition that makes the employee unable to perform the functions of the position of such employee." To prevail on her claim, Plaintiff must show that: (1) she had a serious health condition; (2) that prevented her from performing her job duties; and (3) she gave Defendant reasonable notice of her need to take leave and the reasons for doing so . . . .

A. *Did Plaintiff Have A "Serious Health Condition"?*

The FMLA defines "serious health condition" as "an illness, injury, impairment, or physical or mental condition that involves — (A) inpatient care in a hospital, hospice, or residential medical care facility; or (B) continuing treatment by a health care provider." 29 U.S.C. § 2611(11). Because Plaintiff was not an inpatient in a hospital, hospice, or residential medical care facility, the inquiry is whether Plaintiff had a physical condition involving continuing treatment by a health care provider. The statute does not provide further guidance on what constitutes continuing treatment by a health care provider. However, the Secretary of Labor has authority to promulgate regulations to implement the FMLA. 29 U.S.C. § 2654. Pursuant to that authority, the Secretary has issued regulations that address what constitutes continuing treatment by a health care provider. With regard to pregnancy, the pertinent regulation states:

> (2) *Continuing treatment* by a health care provider. A serious health condition involving continuing treatment by a health care provider includes any one or more of the following:

. . . .

(ii) Any period of incapacity due to pregnancy, or for prenatal care.

29 C.F.R. § 825.114(a)(2)(ii). A period of incapacity includes "inability to work, attend school or perform other regular daily activities due to the serious health condition, treatment therefor, or recovery therefrom." 29 C.F.R. § 825.114(a)(2)(i).

Plaintiff contends that the condition of pregnancy, without more, is a serious health condition. Plaintiff asserts that in enacting the FMLA, Congress intended all pregnancies, not just "abnormal pregnancies", to constitute a serious health condition. There is some support for this argument. The legislative history of the FMLA contains language that "ongoing pregnancy" is a serious health condition.

Defendant argues that pregnancy is a serious health condition only if it renders an employee incapacitated or otherwise unable to perform her job. Defendant relies on 29 C.F.R. § 825.114(a)(2)(ii), quoted above, and 29 C.F.R. § 825.112(c), which states: "Circumstances may require that FMLA leave begin before the actual date of birth of a child. An expectant mother may take FMLA leave . . . before the birth of the child for prenatal care if her condition makes her unable to work." Other legislative history supports Defendant's position. In particular, the Senate Report states that, "with respect to an employee, the term 'serious health condition' is intended to cover conditions or illnesses that affect an employee's health to the extent that he or she must be absent from work on a recurring basis or for more than a few days for treatment or recovery."

. . . .

This Court agrees with [Defendant] that pregnancy "per se" is not a serious health condition. The regulations, which this Court finds to be reasonable and a valid exercise of the Secretary of Labor's authority, explicitly provide that pregnancy can be a serious health condition based upon continuing treatment by a health care provider only if the pregnancy produces a period of incapacity or if prenatal care is sought. 29 C.F.R. § 825.114(a)(2)(ii). The regulations acknowledge that pregnancy is treated differently from other conditions because in most cases, the employee must establish incapacity for more than three consecutive calendar days, and either treatment two or more times by a health care provider or at least one treatment by a health care provider resulting in a regimen of treatment under the supervision of the health care provider, while a pregnant employee need not establish those conditions. However, "incapacity" is a requirement all FMLA plaintiffs must show.

Because the Court has determined that pregnancy per se does not constitute a serious health condition, Plaintiff can succeed in establishing her claim only if she can establish a period of incapacity due to her pregnancy. Defendant asserts that Plaintiff cannot establish a serious health condition because the Certification and notes submitted by Dr. Brown indicated that Plaintiff was having a normal pregnancy, there were no facts showing that her pregnancy rendered her unable to work overtime, and there were no physical restrictions. According to Defendant's view, if Plaintiff was having a normal pregnancy and was otherwise not physically unable to perform her job duties, she did not have a serious health condition under the FMLA.

In *Gudenkauf* [*v. Stauffer Communications*, 922 F. Supp. 465 (D. Kan. 1996),] the court concluded that the plaintiff's own deposition testimony and affidavit regarding back pain, nausea, headaches and swelling during her pregnancy failed to show that she suffered from a serious health condition because neither the plaintiff's obstetrician nor her registered nurse practitioner either "directed or authorized" the employee to take leave for her pregnancy, and her obstetrician testified that the plaintiff's medical records did not show that the plaintiff requested or that the obstetrician gave any authorization to take leave prior to the delivery. . . .

Gudenkauf . . . hold[s] that a plaintiff may prove "incapacity" [only] through evidence that a health care provider determined that the plaintiff was unable to work because of the injury or illness. As one court has stated:

> Under this standard, in order to show that he or she was "required" to miss work for more than three days, a plaintiff employee must show that he or she was prevented from working *because of* the injury or illness based on a medical provider's assessment of the claimed condition. . . . [I]t means that a "health care provider" has determined that, in his or her professional medical judgment, the employee *cannot* work (or could not have worked) *because* of the illness.

Olsen v. Ohio Edison Co., 979 F. Supp. 1159, 1166 (N.D. Ohio 1997) (*citing Seidle v. Provident Mut. Life Ins. Co.*, 871 F. Supp. 238, 244 (E.D. Pa. 1994)). Plaintiff's evidence meets this standard. In fact, it is undisputed that Plaintiff's physician, Dr. Brown, examined Plaintiff and advised her that due to her pregnancy, she should not work more than eight hours per day due to the fact that her job involved continuous standing. In fact, Dr. Brown testified that prolonged standing (periods of greater than eight hours during the first twenty-four weeks of pregnancy and greater than four hours after that time) could result in early termination of the pregnancy or, later in the pregnancy, premature labor. Moreover, Dr. Brown confirmed that the requirement that Plaintiff work overtime presented an unacceptable risk to the pregnancy.

Defendant's primary argument is that Plaintiff cannot establish a serious health condition because she had a normal pregnancy and was physically able to perform her job. While Defendant's argument is factually correct, it fails as a matter of law because nothing in the FMLA provides that a pregnancy can constitute a serious health condition only if the pregnancy is abnormal or if the employee is physically unable to perform her job. . . . What Defendant's argument fails to take into account is that two women with normal pregnancies may be exposed to different risks because of different job duties. A pregnant legal secretary, for example, with ordinary secretarial duties, is unlikely to be exposed to any special risks to her pregnancy (other than those posed by working for a lawyer) in the course of her job. On the other hand, extreme heat may pose a risk to the pregnancy of a woman working on a road crew. . . . In the instant case, the unacceptable risk was requiring a pregnant woman to stand on her feet for more than eight hours per day. Plaintiff may have been physically able to perform her job, but she was prevented from doing so by Dr. Brown's restriction. What Defendant's argument really boils down to is this: a pregnant woman exposed to a job-related risk to her pregnancy does not have a serious health condition under the FMLA until the injury occurs to the mother or the unborn child. This Court does not believe that Congress intended such a result. Therefore, Plaintiff has established a serious medical condition.

B. *Did Plaintiff Provide Sufficient Proof of a Serious Health Condition?*

Defendant also asserts that Plaintiff's claim must fail because she failed to provide adequate documentation of a serious health condition. As mentioned above, an employer may require that a request for leave under 29 U.S.C. § 2612(a)(1)(D) be "supported by a certification issued by the health care provider." The certification must state, among other things: (1) the date on which the serious health condition commenced; (2) the probable duration of the condition; (3) the appropriate medical facts within the knowledge of the health care provider regarding the condition; (4) if leave is sought under 29 U.S.C. § 2612(a)(1)(D), a statement that the employee is unable to perform the functions of the position of the employee; and (5) in the case of certification for intermittent leave, or leave on a reduced leave schedule, under 29 U.S.C. § 2612(a)(1)(D), a statement of the medical necessity for the intermittent leave or leave on a reduced leave schedule, and the expected duration of the intermittent leave or reduced leave schedule. *See* 29 U.S.C. § 2613(b). If the employer is dissatisfied with the certification, it may require, at its own expense, second and third certifications. *See* 29 U.S.C. § 2613(c), (d).

Plaintiff asserts that because Plaintiff complied with Defendant's request for a medical certification and Defendant chose not to assert its right to obtain a second certification, Defendant is barred from challenging the findings in the first certification. The Court need not rule upon Plaintiff's estoppel/waiver argument, however, because Plaintiff fully complied with Defendant's request by submitting a completed certification and Defendant has not presented any evidence undermining the conclusions of Dr. Brown's certification. On the certification, Dr. Brown checked category 3 under question number 3, which indicated that Plaintiff had a serious health condition because she had a period of incapacity due to pregnancy. Under question number 4, which requests the medical facts, Dr. Brown stated that the patient was pregnant. In answer to question 5c., which asks whether the patient is presently incapacitated, Dr. Brown wrote, "Normal pregnancy at this time. Due to Pregnancy 8 hours a day, 40/wk should be allowed."

Defendant's only objection to the sufficiency of the certification is that it indicated that Plaintiff was having a normal pregnancy and there was no indication Plaintiff was physically unable to perform her job. However, in light of the restrictions indicated on the form and given Defendant's knowledge that Plaintiff's job involved almost continuous standing for eight hours, Defendant should have understood the reason for the restrictions. Moreover, Plaintiff provided Defendant with two notes from Dr. Brown indicating that Plaintiff's work should be limited to eight hours per day/forty hours per week due to her pregnancy. If the reasons for Dr. Brown's restrictions were not clear to Defendant, it could have sought clarification, with Plaintiff's permission, by having its own health care provider contact Dr. Brown. Instead, it chose to deny the request on the grounds that a normal pregnancy is not a serious health condition. . . .

C. Was Plaintiff Unable to Perform the Functions of Her Job?

Merely having a serious health condition does not, by itself, entitle an employee to FMLA leave. The serious health condition must be one "that makes the employee unable to perform the functions of the position of such employee." 29 U.S.C. § 2612(a)(1)(D). The regulations provide:

> An employee is "unable to perform the functions of the position" where the health care provider finds that the employee is unable to work at all or is unable to perform any one of the essential functions of the employee's position within the meaning of the Americans with Disabilities Act.

29 C.F.R. § 825.115. In the instant case, working overtime was an essential function of Plaintiff's position in that Plaintiff was, in essence, given a choice of taking short term disability or being disciplined for refusing overtime. Given Defendant's requirement that Plaintiff either obtain a note from Dr. Brown certifying her fitness for overtime work or take short term disability, there can be no dispute that working overtime was an essential function of Plaintiff's job.

Plaintiff has shown that there is no genuine issue of material fact with respect to her entitlement to leave. Once a party has demonstrated by a preponderance of the evidence entitlement to disputed FMLA leave, then the party's employer is liable for any deprivation of the right to take that leave. The employer's intent is irrelevant. Therefore, Defendant is liable for violating Plaintiff's rights under the FMLA. . . .

NOTES

1. *Too Much Leave.* An interesting aspect of Tami Whitaker's claim is that she used the FMLA to get *less* leave time. The employer granted her a short-term disability leave while she was pregnant. Her preference, however, was not to have a total leave (at lower pay), but rather to continue to work her regular hours without having to work overtime, which the employer normally required. The FMLA regulations clearly contemplate intermittent leave when necessary, as in this case. 29 C.F.R. § 825.203. In a case like Whitaker's, this means that the leave can extend over a much longer period of time than merely twelve calendar weeks. Whitaker's FMLA leave time would only have included the overtime hours she would have worked except for the required leave. 29 C.F.R. § 825.205. Thus, for example, if she normally would have worked ten hours of overtime per week, she would have been entitled to the no-overtime arrangement for 48 weeks. As we will discuss later, the employer cannot claim under the FMLA (as it could if a claim were made under the ADA) that this would cause an undue hardship on the employer.

2. *Whitaker and the Pregnancy Discrimination Act.* Tami Whitaker was provided with a short-term disability leave. The employer was probably required to provide this leave by the Pregnancy Discrimination Act (PDA), which requires employers to treat pregnancy as they treat other types of temporary disabilities. 42 U.S.C. § 701(k). It is possible that Whitaker may also have had a claim under the PDA for an exemption from overtime. If she could have proven that the employer did or would have granted such an exemption to another employee with a similar type of temporary disability, then the PDA would have required the employer to treat Whitaker in the same way. Indeed, the PDA could have provided greater benefits than the FMLA. For example, if the employer would have provided another employee with this type of exemption from overtime indefinitely, then Whitaker would also have been entitled to the exemption indefinitely, and would not have been restricted to the FMLA's twelve (or 48) weeks.

3. *The Limitations of the PDA.* The limitation of the basic rule of the PDA is obvious. As Judge Posner famously put it in upholding the discharge of a pregnant woman for excessive absences the day before her maternity leave was scheduled to begin, "[e]mployers can treat pregnant women just as badly as they treat similarly affected but nonpregnant employees." *Troupe v. May Dep't Stores Co.*, 20 F.3d 734, 738 (7th Cir. 1994). For examples of this limitation, see *Marafino v. St. Louis Cty. Circuit Ct.*, 707 F.2d 1005 (8th Cir. 1983) (not violation of PDA to refuse to hire pregnant applicant when employer proves that it would have refused to hire any applicant who needed to take a leave of absence shortly after beginning work); *Fleming v. Ayers & Assocs.*, 948 F.2d 993 (6th Cir. 1991) (although a violation of ERISA, discharge of mother of sick newborn to avoid paying health care costs of baby not a violation of Title VII); *Piantanida v. Wyman Ctr., Inc.*, 116 F.3d 340 (8th Cir. 1997) (PDA protects only pregnancy; discrimination because of plaintiff's status as a "new mom" not protected).

4. *Whitaker and the ADA.* Whitaker probably did not have a claim for leave time under the ADA for several reasons. First, pregnancy is seldom a disability under the ADA. Second, as the Court notes at the end of the decision, to qualify for leave under the FMLA, Whitaker had to prove that she was unable to perform at least one of the essential functions of her job. But if she cannot perform an essential function of her job, she is not a qualified individual entitled to relief under the ADA. (There is a twist here that we will explore in the next principal case; the ADA and FMLA may consider different time frames.) Third, even if she had been entitled to an exemption from overtime under the ADA, the employer might have been able to claim that offering the exemption from normal seniority rules would have required a greater-than-reasonable accommodation or imposed an undue hardship. *US Airways, Inc. v. Barnett*, 535 U.S. 391 (2002) (seniority rules generally take precedence over employer's duty to accommodate).

BYRNE v. AVON PRODUCTS, INC.
United States Court of Appeals, Seventh Circuit
328 F.3d 379 (2003)

EASTERBROOK, J.:

After more than four years of highly regarded service as the only stationary engineer on the night shift at Avon Products, John Byrne started to read and sleep on the job. Early in November 1998 a co-worker reported finding Byrne asleep in the carpenter's shop, which night employees sometimes use as a break room. Avon checked security logs (employees need a coded card to enter the carpenter's shop) and learned that Byrne had begun to frequent it. To investigate further, Avon installed a camera, which on its first night of operation revealed that Byrne spent about three hours of his shift reading or sleeping. The following shift Byrne lingered about six hours in the carpenter's shop, most of that time asleep with the lights off. Managers tried to discuss matters with Byrne on his next scheduled shift (November 16-17) but were unable to do so because he left work early, telling a co-worker that he was not feeling well and would be out the rest of the week. Calls were answered by one of his sisters, who told Avon that Byrne was "very sick". James Sparks, Avon's facilities engineer, finally reached Byrne, who mumbled several odd phrases but agreed to attend a meeting the afternoon of November 17. When Byrne did not appear, he was fired for that omission plus sleeping on the job. Byrne was in no shape for a conference, however, as he was suffering from depression. Relatives took him to the hospital after talking him out of a room in which he had barricaded himself. A psychiatrist concluded that by November 16 Byrne had begun to hallucinate; he attempted suicide on November 17 and during another panic attack tried to flush his head down a toilet. But two months of treatment enabled Byrne to surmount his mental difficulties. When Avon would not take him back, Byrne filed this suit under the Americans with Disabilities Act and the Family and Medical Leave Act. The district court granted summary judgment to Avon, ruling that neither statute excuses misconduct on the job.

The ADA forbids employers to discriminate against any "qualified individual with a disability because of the disability." 42 U.S.C. § 12112(a). "Qualified individual with a disability" is a defined term: "an individual with a disability who, with or without reasonable accommodation, can perform the essential functions of the employment position that such individual holds or desires." 42 U.S.C. § 12111(8). From November 1998 through mid-January 1999 Byrne could not stay awake (sleep disturbance is a common symptom of depression's onset) and had become too suspicious of his co-workers to tolerate them. As a result he was incapable of working. Byrne acknowledges this but contends that he should have been accommodated by being allowed *not* to work. That is not what the ADA says. The sort of accommodation contemplated by the Act is one that will allow the person to "perform the essential functions of the employment position." Not working is not a means to perform the job's essential functions. An inability to do the job's essential tasks means that one is not "qualified;" it does not mean that the employer must excuse the inability.

Time off may be an apt accommodation for intermittent conditions. Someone with arthritis or lupus may be able to do a given job even if, for brief periods, the inflammation is so painful that the person must stay home. *See Haschmann v. Time Warner Entertainment Co.*, 151 F.3d 591 (7th Cir. 1998). *Cf. Pals v. Schepel Buick & GMC Truck, Inc.*, 220 F.3d 495, 498 (7th Cir. 2000) (part-time work may accommodate a person recovering from a medical problem). But Byrne did not want a few days off or a part-time position; his only proposed accommodation is not working for an extended time, which as far as the ADA is concerned confesses that he was not a "qualified individual" in late 1998. "The rather common-sense idea is that if one is not able to be at work, one cannot be a qualified individual." *Waggoner v. Olin Corp.*, 169 F.3d 481, 482 (7th Cir. 1999). Spotty attendance by itself may show lack of qualification. *See EEOC v. Yellow Freight System, Inc.*, 253 F.3d 943 (7th Cir. 2001) (en banc). Inability to work for a multi-month period removes a person from the class protected by the ADA.

Although the ADA applies only to those who can do the job, the FMLA affords those who can't work as a result of a "serious health condition" up to 12 weeks of leave in a year. Byrne's condition was serious, and he was ready to work again before the 12 weeks ran out.

FMLA leave depends on the employer's knowledge of a qualifying condition, and Byrne contends that his sister's statement on November 17 that he was "very sick" plus news of his hospitalization, which reached Avon the next day, provided the necessary information. *Contrast Collins v. NTN-Bower Corp.*, 272 F.3d 1006 (7th Cir. 2001) (employee's claim to be "sick" is not enough). But the district judge thought that notice on November 17 came too late. For the preceding ten days or so, Byrne had been sleeping on the job, which justified his discharge. (The district judge added, and we agree, that the record would not permit a reasonable trier of fact to conclude that Avon discharged Byrne because of, rather than in spite of, the information about Byrne's mental health that it received on November 17 and 18.)

Perhaps, however, Byrne's unusual behavior (recall that he had been a model employee until November 1998) was *itself* notice that something had gone medically wrong, or perhaps notice was excused — for the statute requires notice only if the need for leave is foreseeable. *See* 29 U.S.C. § 2612(e). It is not beyond the bounds of reasonableness to treat a dramatic change in behavior as notice of a medical problem. That's clear enough if a worker collapses: an employer might suspect a stroke, or a heart attack, or insulin deficiency, or some other serious condition. It would be silly to require the unconscious worker to inform the employer verbally or in writing. Unusual behavior gives all the notice required, and no employer would be allowed to say "I fired this stricken person for shirking on company time, and by the time a physician arrived and told me why the worker was unconscious it was too late to claim FMLA leave." A sudden change may supply notice even if the employee is lucid: someone who breaks an arm obviously requires leave. It is enough under the FMLA if the employer knows of the employee's need for leave; the employee need not mention the statute or demand its benefits.

Byrne's situation is more complex because he hid in the carpenter's shop for several days running. This is consistent with onset of a disabling mental condition but also could be no more than malingering. Why, one might ask, did Byrne not notify supervisors and seek time off earlier — or just leave word with a co-worker and go home, as he did on November 17? That poses a medical question: Was someone in Byrne's state *able* to give notice? Medical information in the record would permit (though not compel) a jury to conclude that by early November 1998 Byrne not only was unable to regulate his sleep cycles but also had become suspicious of other people and was powerless to communicate his condition effectively. A person unable to give notice is excused from doing so.

When the approximate timing of the need for leave is not foreseeable, an employee should give notice to the employer of the need for FMLA leave as soon as practicable under the facts and circumstances of the particular case. It is expected that an employee will give notice to the employer within no more than one or two working days of learning of the need for leave, *except in extraordinary circumstances where such notice is not feasible.* In the case of a medical emergency requiring leave because of an employee's own serious health condition or to care for a family member with a serious health condition, written advance notice pursuant to an employer's internal rules and procedures may not be required when FMLA leave is involved.

29 C.F.R. § 825.303(a) (emphasis added). If a person with "major depression" (the psychiatrist's description of Byrne's condition) could not have told his employer about the problem and requested leave, then notice was not "feasible" and was unnecessary even if the change in behavior was not enough to alert Avon to a need for medical leave.

If a trier of fact believes either (a) that the change in behavior was enough to notify a reasonable employer that Byrne suffered from a serious health condition, or (b) that Byrne was mentally unable either to work or give notice early in November 1998, then he would be entitled to FMLA leave covering the period that Avon treats as misconduct. These are independent possibilities. Either one would entitle Byrne to reinstatement, *see* 29 U.S.C. § 2614(a), when the "serious health condition" had abated. Instead of treating Byrne's final two weeks as goldbricking, Avon should have classified this period as medical leave — if Byrne indeed was unable to give verbal or written notice, or if the sudden change in his behavior was itself notice of his mental problem. In either event, the FMLA would require adjustment of Byrne's pay status, for leave under this act is unpaid except to the extent that an employee has accrued medical or vacation leave available. 29 U.S.C. § 2612(c), (d). A judge would be entitled, under circumstances such as these, to require the employee to agree, as a condition of pursuing relief under the FMLA, that unproductive time preceding the discharge be reclassified as unpaid leave (with restitution of wages received) or taken as vacation or medical leave if any is available. Because the district court did not consider the possibility that Byrne's last two weeks should be reclassified as FMLA leave, it did not consider what adjustments along these lines may be appropriate. That subject should be handled promptly on remand.

NOTES

1. *What About the Duty to Accommodate?* Judge Easterbrook recognizes that an employee with arthritis or lupus may be unable to work for short periods of time and thus require a short-term leave, but nevertheless remain a qualified individual with a disability. So why is Byrne different? The Court seems to hold that two months is just too long under the ADA.

But the definition of qualified individual with a disability under the ADA says that one determines ability to work *with reasonable accommodation.* ADA, 42 U.S.C. § 12111(8). It was undisputed that Byrne was able to work after his two-month leave. Thus, the unspoken basis of the Court's decision must be that a two-month leave was an unreasonable accommodation or would have imposed an undue hardship on the employer. Since twelve weeks of leave are required by the FMLA, it would be hard to argue without some extra evidence that eight weeks of leave is unreasonable as a matter of law. Judge Easterbrook may have dismissed Byrne's ADA claim too quickly. *See Swanson v. Senior Resource Connection*, 254 F. Supp. 2d 945 (S.D. Ohio 2003) (holding that employee may have been entitled to *both* FMLA leave and ADA protection by proving that she could not perform essential functions of job *during* her two-week leave, but would have been able to perform the essential functions upon her return to work).

2. *Accommodating Employers.* Leaves are not costless for employers. If they were, employers would grant them freely and there would be no need for statutes like the FMLA, the ADA, and the PDA. It is interesting, however, that the statutes address this employer concern in three different ways.

Consider an employee whose leave would cause great problems for an employer. Under the ADA, this employee would not be entitled to a leave even if she were a qualified individual with a disability. Under the ADA, employers do not have to provide leaves if they would require more than a reasonable accommodation or impose an undue hardship. Thus, the ADA attends to employer concerns by requiring only leaves that are reasonable and that do not impose an undue hardship.

But neither of those is a defense under the FMLA. The employer would have to provide a leave of up to 12 weeks regardless of the problems for the employer. The FMLA, however, only applies to large employers with 50 or more employees (compared to 15 employees for the ADA and PDA). The general idea is that large employers will be able to adjust to leaves (and therefore must adjust), even if they might impose significant hardships on smaller employers.

The PDA adopts still a third approach. The PDA requires the employer to grant the leave only if it would grant the leave to another employee with a similar type of temporary disability. Thus, the PDA permits employers to set their own rules about what might be reasonable, but then requires employers to apply those rules to leaves required by pregnancy, too.

3. *What's a Disability Again?* The FMLA provides for leave to care for adult children with serious health conditions, but only if the conditions are the result of a mental or physical disability. 29 U.S.C. § 101(12)(B). The FMLA regulations use exactly the same language as the ADA to define "mental or physical disability" and refer specifically to the ADA and its regulations. 29 C.F.R. § 825.113(c)(2).

In *Navarro v. Pfizer Corp*, 261 F.3d 90 (1st Cir. 2001), the plaintiff was claiming a leave under the FMLA to care for her adult daughter who was having a difficult pregnancy. The District Court had held that the plaintiff was not entitled to a leave because a difficult pregnancy does not qualify as a disability under the ADA. This is the general rule under the ADA, primarily because pregnancy is thought to be too temporary a condition to qualify as a disability. Despite a vigorous dissent, the Court held that even though the difficult pregnancy would not be a disability under the ADA, it would qualify as one under the FMLA:

> A worker who seeks to take FMLA leave to care for a child often does so in response to a crisis situation. . . . If a hard-and-fast durational requirement is enforced, an employee will be effectively prevented from taking family leave to care for an adult child until it can be established that the child's problem will have an adequate duration. By then, the crisis may well have passed.
>
>   Such a scenario would place an employee with a sick adult child between a rock and a hard place, forcing him or her to choose between employment demands and family needs. This would run at cross purposes with the FMLA's goal of reassuring workers that ". . . they will not be asked to choose between continuing their employment, and meeting their personal and family obligations."

Id. at 102-03.

B. THE CONDITIONS OF THE LEAVE

ROGERS v. CITY OF SAN ANTONIO
United States Court of Appeals, Fifth Circuit
392 F.3d 758 (2004)

DENNIS, CIRCUIT JUDGE:

Plaintiffs, fifteen employees of the San Antonio fire department, who are members of either the United States military reserves or the National Guard ("Uniformed Services"), brought this civil action under the Uniform Services Employment and Reemployment Rights Act of 1994 ("USERRA")[1] against the City of San Antonio, Texas. . . . The plaintiffs contend that the City violated USERRA by denying them employment benefits because of their absences from work while performing their military duties in the Uniformed Services. . . . Plaintiffs assert that under USERRA § 4311(a) "the City . . . unlawfully discriminates against them by deeming them 'absent' from work whenever they are on leave fulfilling their military reserve duties, as opposed to viewing them as 'constructively present at work.'" The City contends that, because § 4316(b)(1) provides that persons absent from civilian employment by reason of military service are entitled only to such non-seniority rights and benefits as the employer provides to employees when they are on non-military leaves of absence, plaintiffs cannot recover since they were treated equally as to such rights with all employees absent on non-military leave.

Facts

Plaintiffs are employed by the City fire department in its Fire Suppression division and Emergency Medical Services division ("Firefighters"). The CBA between the City and the employees' Union governs the working conditions of all City firefighters. Plaintiffs, as members of the Uniformed Services

---

[1] 38 U.S.C. § 4301 *et seq.*

("reservists"), typically must take leave of absence for military training a minimum of one weekend per month and one annual two week session. . . .

[Plaintiffs claim the City violated USERRA by denying them several benefits. They claim they were improperly denied 1) straight-time pay for time absent while on military leave; 2) unscheduled overtime and training opportunities because they were on military leave when the opportunities were offered and, thus, the opportunities were extended instead to the next person on the seniority list; 3) extra leave time referred to as "bonus day" and "perfect attendance" leave because they could not meet the attendance requirements due to their military obligations; and 4) a twenty-seven hour cap on lost overtime. The cap on lost overtime provided that employees would be paid for overtime opportunities even though they did not work the overtime hours, provided they had already "lost" 27 hours of overtime previously. Time absent for military leave did not count as "lost overtime;" time absent for other reasons (such as vacation and FMLA leaves) did count.]

The district court granted the employees' motion as to liability on substantially all claims and denied the City's cross-motion. . . .

The threshold question of law is one of statutory construction, viz., namely which provision of USERRA, § 4311(a) or § 4316(b)(1), governs the adjudication of the employees' claims. The employees contend that the district court correctly applied only § 4311(a), which prohibits private employers from denying employment benefits to employees on the basis or their membership, service or obligations related to the United States military forces. The City contends that the district court erred in basing its decision on § 4311(a) because this case is appropriately governed only by § 4316(b)(1), which regulates the civilian employment non-seniority rights of persons who are required to be absent from jobs for service in the military forces. We review the decision of the district court on this issue of law *de novo*. . . .

A. *USERRA Overview*

The purposes of USERRA, enacted in 1994, are: (1) "to encourage noncareer service in the uniformed services[6] by eliminating or minimizing the disadvantages to civilian employment which can result from such service"; (2) to provide for "the prompt reemployment" of persons returning to civilian jobs from military service and to "minimize the disruption [of their] lives . . . as well as [to those of] their employers, fellow employees and communities"; and (3) "to prohibit discrimination against persons because of their service in the uniformed services." 38 U.S.C. § 4301. . . .

USERRA's anti-discrimination provision prohibits an employer from denying initial employment, reemployment, retention in employment, promotion, or any benefit of employment to a person on the basis of membership, application for membership, performance of service, application for service,

---

[6] "The term 'uniformed services' means the Armed Forces, the Army National Guard and the Air National Guard when engaged in active duty for training, inactive duty training, or full-time National Guard duty, the commissioned corps of the Public Health Service, and any other category of persons designated by the President in time of war or national emergency." 38 U.S.C. § 4303(16).

or obligation of service. 38 U.S.C. § 4311(a). Also, an employer must not retaliate against a person by taking adverse employment action against that person because he or she has taken an action to enforce a protection afforded under USERRA. *Id.* at § 4311(b).

Any person whose absence from a position of employment is necessitated by reason of service in the uniformed services is entitled to the reemployment rights and benefits of USERRA. *Id.* at 4312(a). The returning uniform services member ("reservist") seeking reemployment must make a timely return to or application for reinstatement in the reservist's employment position. *Id.* at 4312(a)(3). The employee reporting back to the employer following a period of less than 31 days must report not later than the beginning of the first full shift on the first full day following the completion of service. *Id.* at § 4312(e)(1)(A)(i). If the service period is between 31 and 180 days, the individual must report within 14 days of completion of service. *Id.* at § 4312(c). If the service was more than 180 days, the individual must request reemployment no more than 90 days after completion. *Id.* at § 4312(e)(1)(D).

An employer must promptly reemploy a person returning from a period of service if the person meets the Act's eligibility criteria. *Id.* at § 4312(f)(4). "Prompt employment" means as soon as practicable under the circumstances of the case. For example, prompt reinstatement after "weekend National Guard duty generally means the next regularly scheduled working day." However, prompt reinstatement after "several years of active duty may require more time, because [the] employer may have to reassign or give notice to another employee who occupied [the] position."

In construing a precursor to USERRA, the Supreme Court in *Fishgold v. Sullivan Drydock & Repair Corp.*, 328 U.S. 275 (1946), invented the "escalator" principle in stating that a returning service member "does not step back on the seniority escalator at the point he stepped off. He steps back on at the precise point he would have occupied had he kept his position continuously during the war." *Id.* at 284-285. Although *Fishgold* was mainly a seniority case, the escalator principle applies to the employment position, and rate of pay, as well as the seniority rights to which the returning service member is entitled.

Thus, USERRA requires that the service member be reemployed in the escalator job position comparable to the position he would have held had he remained continuously in his civilian employment. 38 U.S.C. § 4313. After service of 90 days or less, the person is entitled to reinstatement in the position of employment in which she or he would have been but for the interruption of employment by uniformed service. *Id.* at § 4313(a)(1)(A). If the service period was longer than 90 days, the service member is entitled to reemployment in the escalator position, but the employer may also reinstate the member in any position of like seniority status and pay for which he is qualified. 38 U.S.C. § 4313(a)(2)(A). If the service member is unable to qualify for either the escalator position or a comparable position, despite reasonable employer efforts, he is entitled to reemployment in a position that is the nearest approximation to the escalator position. *Id.* at § 4313(a)(2)(A), (B).

A person who is reemployed under USERRA is entitled to the seniority and other rights and benefits determined by seniority that the person had on the date of the beginning of service plus the additional seniority and rights and benefits that he or she would have attained if the person had remained continuously employed.[16] *Id.* at § 4316(a). This section states the basic escalator principle as it applies to seniority and seniority-based rights and benefits. An employer is not required to have a seniority system. USERRA requires only that employers who do have a seniority system restore the returning service member to the proper place on the seniority ladder. An employee's rate of pay after an absence from work due to uniformed service is also determined by application of the escalator principle.

USERRA does not grant escalator protection to service members' non-seniority rights and benefits but provides only that the employer treat employees absent because of military service equally with employees having similar seniority, status, and pay who are on comparable non-military leaves of absence under a contract, agreement, policy, practice, or plan in effect at anytime during that uniformed service. § 4316(b)(1).

B. *Legislative History and Jurisprudence*

The nation's first peacetime draft law, the Selective Training and Service Act of 1940 was designed to provide reemployment for veterans returning to civilian life in positions of "like seniority, status, and pay." [To understand the current provisions of USERRA, we need to consider § 2021(b)(3) of the Vietnam Era Veterans' Readjustment Assistance Act of 1974 (VRRA)] which, in pertinent part, provided that "any person who [is employed by a private employer] shall not be denied retention in employment or any promotion or other incident or advantage of employment because of any obligation as a member of a reserve component of the Armed Forces."

Senate Report No. 1477 explained the purpose of § 2021(b)(3) as follows:

> Employment practices that discriminate against employees with reserve obligations have become an increasing problem in recent years. Some of these employees have been denied promotions because they must attend weekly drills or summer training and others have been discharged because of these obligations. . . . The bill is intended to protect members of the Reserve components of the Armed Forces from such practices. . . . [Under it] reservists will be entitled to the same treatment afforded their coworkers not having such military obligations. . . .

As the Sixth Circuit noticed in *Monroe v. Standard Oil Co.*, 613 F.2d 641, 646 (6th Cir. 1980), however, VRRA § 2021(b)(3) was subject to two different interpretations:

---

[16] Section 4303(12) of USERRA defines "seniority" as: "longevity in employment together with any benefits of employment which accrue with, or are determined by, longevity in employment." The summary for USERRA's Proposed Regulations explains that:

> This definition imposes two requirements: first, the benefit must be provided as a reward for length of service rather than a form of short-term compensation for services rendered; second, the service member's receipt of the benefit, but for his or her absence due to service, must have been reasonably certain.

Proposed Regulation, summary 69 F.R. No. 181 at 56276.

First, it can be read to mean that any time an employee's forced absence for reserve duty requires him to forgo a benefit that would have accrued to him only if he had been present for work, he has been "denied" an incident or advantage of employment "because of" his military obligation.

Or, it can be read to "merely require that reservists be treated equally or neutrally with their fellow employees without military obligations" and "to meet this requirement, collective bargaining agreements and employment rules must be facially neutral and must be applied uniformly and equally to all employees." *Id.* . . .

In *West v. Safeway Stores, Inc.*, 609 F.2d 147 (5th Cir. 1980), the Fifth Circuit [adopted the first interpretation. It] construed § 2021(b)(3) "to require that employers, in applying collective bargaining agreements, treat reservists as if they were constructively present during their reserve duty in similar contexts." 609 F.2d at 150. The employee, a meat cutter, had contended that, since the collective bargaining agreement guaranteed a 40 hour work week and because the only reason that he was not receiving a 40 hour work week was due to his National Guard obligations, he was being denied an advantage of employment. The court agreed and held that the employer must provide him with his guaranteed 40 hour work week despite the fact that the collective bargaining agreement specifically provided that an employee's absence for weekend reserve or National Guard duty was excluded or negated from the guarantee.

The Sixth Circuit in a virtually identical situation, involving a 40 hour work week guarantee, however, disagreed with *West*, holding that § 2021(b)(3) merely required that reservists be treated no differently than other employees who are absent for non-military reasons. *Monroe v. Standard Oil Co.* [, 613 F.2d 641 (6th Cir. 1980)]. The employee's collective bargaining agreement right to work a 40 hour week, as in *West*, was contingent on the employee being present for work or arranging to switch shifts, as permitted by the agreement. Thus, the court held, because the employee was treated the same as his coworkers regarding absences and exchanging shifts, that right did not vest when the employee failed to do either, and the employer was required to do no more than grant him a leave of absence without pay to comply with his military reserve obligation. . . .

The Supreme Court granted certiorari in *Monroe*, affirmed the Sixth Circuit's decision, and substantially agreed with its reasoning. 452 U.S. 549. The Supreme Court concluded that the "legislative history . . . indicates that § 2021(b)(3) was enacted for the significant but limited purpose of protecting the employee-reservist against discrimination like discharge and demotion," by reason of reserve status. Further, the Court found nothing in § 2021(b)(3) or its legislative history to indicate that Congress even considered imposing an obligation on employers to provide a special work-scheduling preference, but rather that the history suggests that Congress did not intend employers to provide special benefits to employee-reservists not generally made available to other employees. Because the Supreme Court's interpretation of § 2021(b)(3) is contrary to the Fifth Circuit's decision in *West*, and the high court noted the "apparent inter-circuit conflict on this issue" between *West* and the Sixth

Circuit's decision, we conclude that *West*'s "constructive presence" interpretation was disapproved by *Monroe*. . . .

The Senate report on the bill that became [USERRA] § 4316(b)(1) stated that it "would codify court decisions that have interpreted current law as providing a statutorily-mandated leave of absence for military service that entitles service members to participate in benefits that are accorded other employees." The Report explained that:

> An individual who serves in the uniformed services will be considered to be on furlough or leave of absence while in the service [and] will be entitled to the same rights and benefits not determined by seniority that are generally provided to the employer's other employees with similar seniority, status, and pay who are on furlough or leave of absence[,] under a practice, policy, agreement, or plan in force at the beginning of the period of uniformed service or which becomes effective during the period of service. *Id.*

Although the legislative history of the bill that became § 4316(b)(1) does not mention *Monroe*, Congress necessarily intended for that section to codify *Monroe*'s interpretation of § 2021(b)(3) with respect to the effects upon the non-seniority rights of uniformed service members by their absences from civilian employment by reason of their military obligations. . . .

The legislative history of §§ 4311(a) and 4316(b)(1) does not mention *West*. On the other hand, that legislative history expresses an intent to codify in § 4316(b)(1) the *Monroe* [and subsequent lower court] cases with respect to non-seniority rights and benefits to which persons absent from civilian employment by reason of service in the uniformed services are entitled. *West* is inconsistent with and was expressly disapproved by *Monroe*. Therefore, we must conclude that USERRA's codification of *Monroe* . . . legislatively overruled *West*.

C. *Section 4316(b)(1) Governs This Case*

Section 4316(b)(1) of USERRA provides that an employee who is absent from employment for military service is deemed to be on leave of absence and "entitled to such rights and benefits not determined by seniority . . . generally provided by the employer to employees having similar seniority, status, and pay who are on furlough or leave of absence under a contract, agreement, policy, practice or plan . . . ." Reading § 4316(b)(1) together with § 4311(a), . . . we conclude that Congress intended § 4316(b)(1) to clarify and codify the interpretation of VRRA § 2021(b)(3) by the Supreme Court in *Monroe* . . . requiring employers, with respect to rights and benefits not determined by seniority, to treat employees taking military leave, equally, but not preferentially, in relation to peer employees taking comparable non-military leaves generally provided under the employer's contract, policy, practice or plan. Although, the "equal, but not preferential" requirement arose out of the Courts' interpretation of VRRA § 2021(b)(3)'s prohibition against denial of employment rights because of military obligations, which has been enhanced and continued by USERRA § 4311(a), Congress decided to adopt new § 4316(b)(1) to provide more specifically and affirmatively for the accrual of non-seniority rights and benefits by employees while on military duty, rather than continue to rely on the general prohibition against service-related denials of benefits for that purpose. Congress sought by § 4316(b)(1) to guarantee a measure of equality of treatment with respect to military and non-military leaves and to strike an appropriate balance between benefits to employee-service persons and costs to employers. USERRA does not authorize the courts to add to or detract from that guarantee or to restrike that balance.

For these reasons, we conclude that the district court erred in deciding that § 4311(a), rather than § 4316(b)(1), must be applied in this case. Because the district court gave several reasons for its interpretation, we will set them forth before commenting on each.

The district court decided that "section 4316 is inapplicable to this case [because] it only applies to a person who is reemployed under this chapter or who is absent on furlough or leave of absence." The district court stated that § 4316 "is specifically tailored to apply to a reservist or veteran returning to employment from active duty rather than reservists . . . who have been away for relatively short periods [for] drilling and training[.]" Furthermore, the court stated, "the anti-discrimination provisions (§§ 4311(a-c)) were specifically added 'to protect the rights of reservists which had been found to be inadequately protected' under the provision cited by the City (§ 4316, formerly VRRA § 2024(d))." Concluding that this case should be analyzed and decided under USERRA's § 4311(a) anti-discrimination provision, the district court identified *West,* decided under VRRA § 2021(b)(3), as our Circuit precedent that must be applied in deciding claims under the USERRA for non-seniority benefits by employees returning from service in the uniformed services. The district court read *West* to hold that VRRA § 2021(b)(3) "requires that employers, in applying collective bargaining agreements which grant a benefit of employment based on 'presence' rather than on 'hours actually worked,' should treat reservists as if they were 'constructively present' during their reserve duty."

We believe that the district court was mistaken in each of its reasons for deciding that § 4311(a) must be applied in this case and, consequently, also mistaken in using the *West* "constructive presence" theory to decide the firefighters' claims. . . .

First, § 4316(b)(1) is fully applicable to reservists' short absences from civilian employment for weekend drills or two-week annual training. In USERRA, the term "service in the uniformed services" means "the performance of duty on a voluntary or involuntary basis in a uniformed service under competent authority." 38 U.S.C. § 4303(13). It includes "active duty, active duty for training, initial active duty for training, inactive duty training, full-time National Guard duty," medical examinations to determine fitness for duty, and performance of funeral honors duty. *Id.* The term "uniformed services" means "the Armed Forces, the Army National Guard and the Air National Guard when engaged in active duty for training, inactive duty training, or full-time National Guard duty[.]" 38 U.S.C. § 4303(16). Thus, both of these terms apply to members of the uniformed services who participate in inactive duty training for weekend drills and two-week annual training. Consequently, § 4316(b)(1), which applies to "a person who is absent from a position of employment by reason of service in the uniformed services" is fully applicable to reservists during their weekend and two-week military duty sessions.

Second, "reemployment" is not formally defined in § 4303, but §§ 4312-4313, providing for USERRA reemployment rights and positions, plainly apply to "any person whose absence from a position of employment is necessitated by reason of service in the uniformed services." 38 U.S.C. § 4312. As noted in the previous paragraph, the terms "service in the uniformed services" and "uniformed services" apply to "inactive duty training," which refers to reservists and their two week and weekend training periods. Further, USERRA makes specific provisions for the reemployment of a person whose period of service in the uniformed services was less than 31 days. 38 U.S.C. § 4312(e)(1)(A); 4313(a)(1). Thus, a reservist who returns to his or her job after weekend drill is "reemployed" just as much as one who is reinstated after a period of service of two years . . . .

Finally, as we have noted, *West* and its "constructively present" theory of interpretation was disapproved by the Supreme Court in *Monroe* and legislatively overruled in the codification of *Monroe* . . . by USERRA § 4316(b)(1).

. . . .

Applying § 4316(b)(1) to the summary judgment record in this case, we conclude that the district court's judgment must be reversed and summary judgment granted for the City on the following claims: (1) lost straight-time pay; (2) lost overtime opportunities; and (3) missed upgrading opportunities. From our review of the record we have determined that there is no type of non-military leave available to any employee under which an employee can accrue or receive the foregoing kinds of benefits. Hence, insofar as the record shows, there is no type of leave under which these benefits may accrue that is comparable to any military leave.

We further conclude that the district court's summary judgment with respect to: (1) bonus day leave; (2) perfect attendance leave; and (3) the twenty-seven hour cap on lost overtime must be reversed and the case remanded for further proceedings on these claims. There are genuinely disputable issues as to the material facts of whether involuntary non-military leaves, not generally for extended durations, for jury duty, bereavement, and line of duty injury leave (provided that the employee returns to work in the following shift), under which employees may accrue or receive bonus day leave and perfect attendance leave benefits, are comparable to each plaintiff's military leaves taken for service in the uniformed services. For the same reason, there is a disputable issue as to whether sick leave, under which employees receive the benefit of the twenty-seven hour cap for the first shift of sick leave they use, is comparable to military leave. Thus, we reverse and remand on this claim also. . . .

NOTES

1. ***Leave and Reemployment Rights Under USERRA.*** USERRA contains a stronger right to leave and reemployment than the ADA, FMLA, and the PDA. USERRA applies to *all* employers, not only those of a certain size, 38

U.S.C. § 4303(a); the situations when an employer does not need to provide reemployment are much narrower than under the other statutes, 38 U.S.C. § 4312(d); and the right to a leave and reemployment will apply even if the employer does not provide any comparable leave to other employees, in contrast to the PDA.

2. *Conditions of the Leave.* Providing an employee with a right to leave and reemployment is only one part of the analysis. The other part is to specify the conditions of the leave. Consider, for example, these differences between the conditions of FMLA and USERRA leaves:

(a) ***Vacation Time***. Under the FMLA, an employer can require an employee to use her vacation time as part of her FMLA leave. 29 U.S.C. § 2612(d)(2). An employer would violate USERRA if it required an employee to use vacation or other paid time as part of her leave; under USERRA, it is the employee's choice. 38 U.S.C. § 4316(d).

(b) ***Health Insurance***. FMLA requires an employer to continue the employee's health-care benefits during the leave, but can attempt to recover its portion of the premium if the employee does not return to work after the leave. 29 U.S.C. § 2614(c). USERRA requires continued health-care coverage, but permits the employer to charge the employee 102% of the full premium under the plan (both employer and employee portions). 38 U.S.C. § 4317. (Thus, the USERRA provision is similar to COBRA continuation coverage, which we will discuss later in Chapter 20.)

(c) ***Seniority***. FMLA does not require employers to continue to credit employees with seniority accrual for time on leave. 28 U.S.C. § 2614(a)(3). USERRA requires employers to grant seniority for time on leave. 38 U.S.C. § 4316(a).

(d) ***Discharge Rights***. Upon return from leave under USERRA, employees can be discharged only "for cause" for up to one year. 38 U.S.C. § 4316(c) (one year of protection if leave for more than 180 days; 180 days of protection if leave was between 30 and 180 days). FMLA does not have an equivalent provision.

(e) ***Pensions***. Employees on USERRA leave must be treated as if they are working for purposes of pension eligibility, vesting, and benefit accrual. For defined-benefit plans, employers must also treat employees as if they received compensation during their leaves. For defined-contribution plans, employees must be given an opportunity to catch up on missed contributions. IRC § 414(u). FMLA does not have any equivalent protections.

3. *Leave and Workers' Compensation.* Problems with leave time may also arise at the intersection between an employer's leave policies and the requirements of social-insurance programs. For example, courts are split on whether employees obtain rights to leave time under workers' compensation laws. A minority of states require employers to provide leave time during periods of temporary disability caused by work-related injuries, regardless of the employer's own leave policies. *See Coolidge v. Riverdale Local Sch. Dist.*, 797 N.E.2d 61, 69 (Ohio 2003) (holding that "employees who are temporarily and totally disabled as a result of their work-related injuries have a right not only to the compensation provided in the act, but also to whatever period of absence from work is deemed medically necessary to complete their recovery or stabilize their injuries"). Most states, however, do not interpret their workers' compensation laws to exempt workers with work-related injuries from the provisions of an employer's neutral absenteeism policies or practices, so long as they are applied evenhandedly to all employees. *See Haggar Clothing Co. v. Hernandez*, 164 S.W.3d 386 (Tex. 2005) (upholding the discharge of an employee with a work-related injury whose leave extended beyond the one-year maximum allowed by the employer's leave-of-absence policy).

Chapter 19

PENSIONS

A. THE PROBLEM WITH PENSIONS

McNEVIN v. SOLVAY PROCESS CO.
New York Supreme Court, Appellate Division
53 N.Y.S. 98 (1898), *aff'd per curiam,*
60 N.E. 1115 (N.Y. 1901)

FOLLETT, J. This action was begun May 14, 1897, to recover $52.54, alleged to be due from the defendant to the plaintiff as his share of a pension fund established by the defendant for the benefit of a class of its employés. . . . The plaintiff entered the service of the defendant June 18, 1890, and continued therein until April 6, 1895, when he was discharged. January 1, 1892, the defendant established what is known as a "pension fund" for the benefit of a class of its employés, and at the same time established a set of rules . . . providing how the fund should be established, for whose benefit, how administered, and how applied for the benefit of the employés entitled to participate therein.

[The rules established a pension fund "to provide a means of support when by reason of accident, sickness, or advanced age labor must cease." The defendant was under no obligation to put any amounts into the pension fund and, when amounts were put into the fund, the rules provided that they were "gifts" that remained the sole property of the defendant and absolutely subject to its control. Each employé signed a pass book that contained the rules and a pledge by the employé "to faithfully perform the work entrusted to me with a true loyalty to the interests of the company." Amounts credited to the employé's account were written into the pass book. The rules provided that no employé could demand payment of the sum credited to his account, except when the defendant adjudged the account to be payable and that the fund's trustees were authorized to decide all questions concerning the rights of employés "without appeal." The rules said that payments would be made to employés at retirement or when employés were discharged without cause of dissatisfaction. Sums could be taken out of the pension fund only to pay allotments to employés. If an amount credited to an employé was not paid for some reason, the amount would go to an "additional fund" which eventually would be paid out to other employés or their survivors.]

It is conceded that this pension fund has been created voluntarily, and is a gift by the defendant, and the question upon which this case turns is whether, when a sum is credited to an employé on the pass book furnished by the defendant, the employé has a vested right in the sum so credited, or whether, under the terms by which the fund is established, the employé acquires no vested right until the gift is completed by actual payment to the employé. It must be conceded at the outset that a person or a corporation proposing to give a sum for the benefit of any person or any set of persons has the right to fix the terms of his bounty, and provide under what circumstances the gift shall become vested and absolute. Under the regulations established, it seems to me that none of the employés have a vested interest in any part of this fund, even though credited upon their pass books until the gift is completed by actual payment. Until that time it is an inchoate gift. The articles provide that an employé cannot, in any case, demand payment of the sum credited to his account, except when the defendant shall adjudge the account to be payable, in whole or in part, according to the rules and regulations established; and it is also provided that the sums credited shall remain the property of the defendant until actually paid, and that the fund shall be and remain under the sole control of the defendant's trustees, who are authorized to decide all questions concerning it without appeal. In this case the defendant's trustees decided, after a hearing of the plaintiff, that the plaintiff was not, when the action was begun, entitled to payment of any portion of the fund credited to him, and it seems to me that under the terms of the gift this decision is final, unless, within the discretion of the defendant's trustees, it shall be modified in the future. In case it shall be held that this plaintiff had a vested right in the fund credited to his account, it would necessarily follow that it might be reached by his creditors through proceedings supplementary to execution, and thus the very object of creating the fund would be destroyed. . . . It seems to me that the scheme by which this fund is created is simply a promise on the part of the defendant to give to its employés a certain sum in the future, with an absolute reservation that it may at any time determine not to complete the gift, and, if it does so determine, an employé has no right of action to recover the sum standing to his credit on the books of the pension fund. Whether the disposition and management of this fund may or may not be the subject of control in an equity action, in case it should be alleged and proved that the defendant's trustees were squandering the fund, or were guilty of bad faith in its management, is a question not before the court, this being a simple legal action to recover the sum standing to the plaintiff's credit on the theory that when he left the employment of the defendant he acquired an absolute vested right in the sum credited, which he has the right to recover.

The judgement and order should be reversed, and a new trial granted, with costs to the appellant to abide the event. All concur, except GREEN and WARD, JJ., dissenting.

GREEN, J. (dissenting). . . . In April, 1895, the plaintiff was dismissed from the service of the defendant by its foreman without any explanation being given for the reason of his dismissal, or any cause of dissatisfaction expressed. Afterwards he appeared before the trustees of the fund, and made application for payment of the amount allotted to him on his pass book. . . . He was subsequently notified that the trustees had voted that they would not pay off his allotment. . . . In the minutes of the trustees' meeting it was stated that plaintiff was discharged "for shirking," but the truth of this declaration was not supported by any evidence.

The court . . . charged the jury, in substance, that the plaintiff was entitled to recover, unless they found that he had . . . so negligently performed his services that there existed reasonable cause for dissatisfaction therewith, and reasonable ground for his discharge on account thereof. Exceptions were duly taken by the defendant. The defendant's contention is that . . . the trustees are the sole and exclusive judges of the existence and the sufficiency of the cause of dissatisfaction. Indeed, the argument amounts to this: that the plaintiff has conferred upon the trustees an arbitrary power to determine that they are dissatisfied with his services, and to forfeit his rights and interest created by the contract, without assigning any cause whatsoever. In the first place, it should be remarked that the provision . . . that sums to be paid are to be deemed gifts, and not transferable, cannot alter or impair the true character of the instrument or its legal effect and operation. A promise, founded upon a valuable consideration inuring to the benefit of a promisor, to pay a sum of money upon specified contingencies, is not a promise to make a gift, even though the parties call it so. To have that effect the agreement must annul the obligation to fulfill the promise, and leave it optional with the promisor. There is no such stipulation in this instrument, and the counsel for the defendant admits what cannot be denied — that it constitutes a contract founded upon a valuable consideration. . . . And therefore, in ascertaining the rights of the respective parties from the terms in which their understanding is expressed, we must start with the proposition that the plaintiff acquired, by virtue of the agreement, a vested legal interest in the pension fund, or a legal right to compel the defendant to fulfill its obligations; and the question is whether the plaintiff has incurred a forfeiture of such right or interest by reason of the nonperformance or misperformance of an essential obligation imposed upon him by the contract. In the determination of this question it is all important to observe the general principle that in the construction of all contracts under which forfeitures are claimed it is the duty of the court to interpret them strictly, in order to avoid such a result, for a forfeiture is not favored in the law. And though it may have been competent for the employés of the defendant to so contract that their rights in the pension fund shall depend upon the determination of a tribunal of their own choice, and to make the decision final and conclusive, yet, when one of the parties or its representatives are sought to be made the final judge, the courts will not give such a construction to the contract as to have that effect, if it be possible to give any other. . . .

Defendant contends that the provision . . . that in no case can the employés demand payment of the sums credited to their account except when the company shall adjudge the same to be payable, must be construed as a condition precedent to the right of recovery, and therefore, as a logical consequence, the trustees are vested with an arbitrary discretion in determining whether any cause of dissatisfaction existed, and the legal sufficiency of such cause. In other words, it is sufficient to say that they feel dissatisfied, and their utterance shall be final and conclusive, although there is no such stipulation contained in the contract. In answer to this it should be observed that . . . there must be cause for the dissatisfaction to justify a discharge, . . . but there is no provision in that or in any other article that the trustees shall be the sole, final, and exclusive judges of the cause, or that a particular act or omission on the part of the employé constituted a breach of the contract "to faithfully perform the work entrusted to me with a true loyalty to the interests of the company." In short, the plaintiff has not, in express terms, nor by necessary implication, constituted the trustees as a tribunal to determine, absolutely and without appeal to the courts, that he has committed a breach of the contract warranting his discharge, and a forfeiture of all rights conferred by it. There is no stipulation that the defendant may relieve itself of its obligation simply by a statement that the plaintiff has failed to perform his. The language of the instrument does not confer upon the defendant an arbitrary power to declare itself dissatisfied, and thereupon to terminate the contract and declare the forfeiture.

Defendant further contends that the authority conferred upon the trustees to decide all questions concerning the funds without appeal . . . renders their determination final and conclusive, and precludes an appeal to judicial tribunals for redress. . . . The answer to this argument is that the courts will not give such a construction to the contract as to have that effect, if any other construction may reasonably and properly be adopted. Now, it is obvious there are many questions that may arise concerning the funds and their application to which [this] provision . . . may properly be applied, and therefore [the] article does not necessarily require that it should be construed as an agreement to make the company the final arbiter upon the question whether the employé has been guilty of a breach of contract. For instance, the trustees may decide that only a portion of the allotment made shall be placed to an employés credit, whenever they judge it necessary as a matter of discipline (article 6); they may purchase an annuity for an employé permanently disabled, in their discretion (article 9); they may retain for a period the moneys due a retiring employé, or one discharged without cause, as security for the agreement not to injure the company after leaving its service (article 11); they shall decide the proportion to be paid to the widow and children of a deceased employé (article 12); they may decide other questions in respect of the additional fund, and so forth. We are therefore of the opinion that the plaintiff has not agreed that the trustees shall be the sole and exclusive arbitrators of his rights under the contract.

Defendant lays stress upon the fact that the company itself will gain nothing by a decision in its favor, since the amount withheld from the plaintiff must be transferred to the additional fund, thereby increasing the amount of that fund to be distributed among the widows and children or relatives of deserving employés. . . . That is true, but we are unable to perceive that it has any pertinent bearing upon the construction of the contract and its legal effect. The agreement was that, if the plaintiff should be discharged for cause of dissatisfaction, his account should be transferred to the additional fund for the benefit of deserving participants therein; otherwise it must be paid to him. It should be observed, by the way, that the employés have no security or protection against the application by the company of all the funds to the uses and purposes of its business; so that, in case of insolvency, a large part of the funds may be lost to them. . . .

In the absence of any adequate proof of the cause of discharge, or cause of dissatisfaction, it must be held that there is no proof that the plaintiff has violated his agreement by the commission of some act that he ought not to have done, or that he omitted to do something required of him, that justified a dismissal. . . . [T]he plaintiff has earned the moneys placed to his account, and it was incumbent upon the defendant to show some just cause or reason for depriving him of it. He is not claiming damages as for a breach of a purely executory contract, but is seeking to recover moneys due him upon a contract executed. . . .

It is an important observation to make that an adverse decision to the plaintiff in this case would justify the discharge of employés who may have loyally and faithfully performed their duties to the company for a long period of years simply upon a mere declaration that the company had cause for dissatisfaction, and the employé would be deprived of the moneys that he had fairly earned, without any remedy for their recovery in a court of justice. The cause was fairly and properly tried by the court below upon correct principles, and the judgement and order should be affirmed, with costs.

NOTES

1. *The Gratuity Theory of Pensions.* The majority's theory came to be known as the gratuity theory of pensions: the pension was merely a gift that the employer could grant or withhold at its discretion. This theory meshed well with the early employment at will cases. In one case, for example, an employer induced a thirty-seven year employee to retire by promising that his resignation would not result in a forfeiture of his pension payments. Then the employer refused to pay the pension. The court held for the employer, reasoning that since the employee could be discharged without cause, he could also be induced to retire with any representation. *Abbott v. International Harvester Co.*, 36 ERIE CO. L.J. 271 (Pa. Ct. C.P. 1953). Would employers want a regime similar to *Skagerberg* in which the law made it virtually impossible to make binding promises to pay pensions?

2. *The Dissent's Theory.* The dissent sees a contract rather than a gift. The contract, however, said that the trustees were to decide all issues under the contract "without appeal." The dissent avoids that language by construing it strictly against the employer. This approach encourages employers to explain their plans in clear and unambiguous language, but, as the next excerpt illustrates, it does not require the plans to contain any substantive provisions to protect employees against potential problems, nor does it ensure that employees will read and understand their plans.

RALPH NADER & KATE BLACKWELL, YOU AND YOUR PENSION 4-7 (1973) *

Charlie Reed thought he was going to get a pension. He went to work when he was twenty-one as a coal miner for Jones & Laughlin Steel Corporation, and after twenty-three years in the mines, he was laid off. He waited for a recall, but none came. Numbers of small mines were closing under the pressures of mechanization, and thousands of miners were looking for work wherever they could find it. Like many others, Reed finally found a job outside the coal industry to keep him and his family going.

---

* Reprinted with permission.

Thirteen years later, Reed applied for the pension he thought he had been earning during his twenty-three years in the mines. He found there wasn't one; instead, there was a rule Reed didn't know about: he had to have twenty years of service *within the thirty years preceding his application for benefits.* The rules made no exception for miners who had been laid off.

Reed was incensed. He began looking for other miners in southwestern Pennsylvania who had worked for at least twenty years and then found they weren't eligible for pensions when they retired. He has found 1200 of them.

The pension plan booklet that told Reed he would receive a pension said nothing about the possibility that he might be laid off, or that eligibility rules would disqualify him, or that new technology would leave thousands in the industry without jobs or pensions. Your pension description probably doesn't deal with such possibilities either, but they exist in every line of work for every employee who is counting on getting a pension someday. . . .

If you are inclined to say, "It can't happen to me," meet some of the people who found out it could. They aren't merely the short-term employees who quit after a couple of years or jumped from job to job; many have worked thirty years or more, often for the same company. In fact, many of them are exactly the people you thought pensions were set up to help. Most of them thought so, too.

James Tyler, a construction worker from Lakewood, California, paid his union dues for thirty-one years. He worked under the same union local for a number of years and then was told that in order to take a job six miles from his home, he had to join another local. He did. Later, when he applied for a pension, he found he wasn't eligible. After thirty-one years in the same industry, he didn't have enough years of continuous service under either local. He didn't know that *you may not get a pension if you change unions or even union locals.*

Joseph Mintz, fifty-six, of Buena Park, California, has been in aerospace work for over thirty years and has no pension coming to him. For twenty-seven years he worked for three different companies. At each job, he was laid off before he had the ten-year minimum service requirement for a pension. One company laid him off after nine years and ten months. He always got another job, but not a pension. He didn't know that *you may not get a pension if you are laid off or change jobs.*

A glass worker was employed for thirty-two years by the same company in Salem, New Jersey. When he was forty-eight, he had a stroke and was forced to quit work. He never received a pension: he had to reach age fifty before he was eligible. He didn't know that *you may not get a pension if you become disabled before a certain age.*

A foundry worker in Cleveland, Ohio, was fifty-one and had worked for the same employer for twenty-one years when the company closed down. By that time, the worker had contracted emphysema and was partially disabled, with little chance for another job. He found he didn't have a chance for a pension either. When the plant closed, the pension plan was terminated without enough money to pay him even part of the benefit he had earned. He didn't know that *you may not get a pension if your company goes out of business or if the plan terminates for any other reason.*

Harry Oakes of St. Paul, Minnesota, worked for a large department store for fifty-two years before he retired at the age of sixty-six. He received his pension benefit for thirteen months. The company went bankrupt and the pension fund — including payments to retirees — was terminated. He didn't know that *you may lose your benefits sometime after you retire if the pension fund terminates.*

The Employee Retirement Income Security Act of 1974

ERISA was the legislative response to the kinds of problems discussed in *McNevin* and in the Nader and Blackwell excerpt. ERISA distinguishes between two basic varieties of pension plans — defined benefit plans and defined contribution plans. ERISA §§ 3(34), (35). In defined benefit plans, employers promise employees a "defined benefit" at retirement. The amount of the benefit is determined by a formula specified by the plan which, in most plans, uses length of service and final salary as variables. For example, the formula may promise an annual benefit equal to .02 (the generosity factor) times years of service times the employee's average salary over her last three years of employment. Thus, if a thirty-year employee had an average salary of $50,000 over her last three years of employment, she would be entitled to an annual pension of $30,000 (.02 × 30 × $50,000). Employees do not have individual accounts established for them in defined benefit plans. Instead, the employer is responsible for making contributions to a trust adequate to ensure that the promised pensions can be paid from the pooled fund. The amount of contributions required will depend on a complex actuarial analysis which takes into consideration factors such as the age and length of service of employees, projections of future salary increases, and the rate of return on plan investments.

In defined contribution plans, employers promise only to pay a defined amount into an account established for each employee. The employer makes no promise about the amount of the employee's benefit at retirement, which will depend entirely on the amounts contributed into her individual account and on her account's investment experience. Today's ubiquitous 401(k) plans, named after a provision of the Internal Revenue Code, are defined contribution plans.

Defined benefit and defined contribution plans allocate investment risk differently. Employers offering defined benefit plans have promised a certain benefit at retirement. If the pension fund's investments do poorly, or if the fund is short for other reasons, the employer is liable for the shortfall. On the other hand, if the fund's investments do very well, the employer may be able to reduce its level of contributions to the fund or, even better, recoup the excess. Under defined contribution plans, in contrast, the employer has only promised to make certain contributions into individual employee accounts. If the investment experience is poor, the amounts employees will receive at retirement will go down; if the investment experience is good, employees will receive more in retirement than they initially expected.

Because of these differences between the two types of pension plans, some of ERISA's provisions apply only to defined benefit plans. ERISA, for example, contains a scheme to insure employer promises to pay pension benefits. The scheme, however, does not cover defined contribution plans because, by definition, employers offering that type of plan do not promise any particular pension benefit. Instead, employers merely promise to pay to employees their individual account balances. ERISA § 4021(b)(1). Similarly, ERISA contains provisions designed to require employers to make contributions adequate to fund the promised pension benefits when they become due. Once again, since employers offering defined contribution plans do not promise any particular benefit, but instead only promise to pay to employees the amounts contributed to their accounts plus earnings, ERISA's funding provisions do not generally apply to that type of plan. ERISA § 301(a)(8).

Historically, defined benefit plans were the predominant form of pension plan. As recently as 1992, more families participated in defined benefit plans than defined contribution plans (40% vs. 37%, with the remainder having both types of plans). By 2004, more than twice as many families participated in defined contribution plans (52% vs. 24%). Craig Copeland, *Individual Account Retirement Plans*, EBRI Issue Brief No. 293 (May 2006). This shift towards defined contribution plans has occurred, in large part, because both employers and employees prefer them. Employers prefer them because they can be structured to reward individual employee performance and because they reduce the employer's investment risk. Employees prefer them because they permit greater job mobility and control over assets.

NOTES

1. *Cash Balance Plans.* A cash balance plan is a relatively new type of "hybrid" pension plan. This type of plan creates a "hypothetical" account for each employee which is credited each year with an annual payment (*e.g.*, 10% of salary) and an interest amount (*e.g.*, 7% of the balance in the account). The employee's pension benefit is the amount in this account. The account is "hypothetical" because the interest amount is credited at a set amount, rather than based on the investment earnings of the pension trust. Technically, a cash balance plan is a defined benefit plan because the benefit is determined by a formula in the plan, rather than by the amount in an individual account. But to workers it looks like a defined contribution account because of the hypothetical individual accounts.

Cash balance plans are both popular (about one-fourth of large companies now offer them) and controversial. They are popular for a number of reasons: The benefits are more portable than those of traditional defined benefit plans, so they attend to a more mobile workforce; they are flexible for employers; they are insured by the Pension Benefit Guarantee Corporation; they are easier for employees to understand and monitor. They are controversial primarily because of the effect on older workers when employers convert from a traditional defined benefit plan to a cash balance plan. The conversion often results in a significant reduction in the projected benefits of older workers. *See Cooper v. IBM Personal Pension Plan*, 457 F.3d 636 (7th Cir. 2006) (holding that cash balance plan did not illegally discriminate on the basis of age even though it reduced the expected benefits of older workers); Pension Protection Act of 2006 § 701, Pub. L. No. 109-280, 120 Stat. 780 (2006) (cash balance conversions after June, 2005, that meet certain standards are exempt from age discrimination challenges). For a good discussion of cash balance plans, see Jonathan Barry Forman & Amy Nixon, *Cash Balance Pension Plan Conversions*, 25 OKLA. CITY U. L. REV. 379 (2000).

2. *ERISA and Public Pension Plans.* Governmental pension plans are not covered by ERISA. ERISA § 4(b)(1). Governmental pension plans are very large, managing in excess of $1 trillion in assets, and pose most of the problems to which ERISA is addressed. Some governmental plans, for example, have vesting schedules which are significantly longer than the ERISA standards and some are severely underfunded. NATIONAL EDUCATION ASS'N, CHARACTERISTICS OF 100 LARGE PUBLIC PENSION PLANS 11-15, 66-69 (2002) (twenty-eight of the plans had vesting schedules of ten years or longer; ten of the plans had assets sufficient to fund 75% or less of their expected pension obligations; the least funded plan had assets sufficient to cover only 21% of its expected liability). *See also, e.g.,* MONT. CODE ANN. §§ 19-17-401, 19-18-602 (twenty-year vesting period for certain fire fighters). Comprehensive bills modeled after ERISA to regulate public pension plans have been introduced periodically in Congress, but have only served to enrich our library of acronyms. *See, e.g.,* Public Employee Pension Plan Reporting and Accountability Act, H.R. 3127, 99th Cong. (1985) (PEPPRA). The National Conference of Commissioners on Uniform State Laws promulgated a uniform law to regulate the fiduciary duties and reporting and disclosure obligations of public funds. The proposed act, however, is limited in its scope; it does not, for example, cover vesting or funding issues. Uniform Management of Public Employee Retirement Systems Act, 7A U.L.A. 510 (1997). What do you think accounts for the reluctance of the federal government and the Uniform Law Commissioners to deal with the entire range of ERISA issues? *See* Joe Donohue & Ron Marsico, *Bond Plan Muscles Past Last Obstacles*, STAR-LEDGER (Newark, N.J.), June 6, 1997, at A1 (describing how $2.76 billion bond issue to finance state pensions frees up $1.6 billion in state budget over next six years).

B. PROTECTING EMPLOYEES FROM FORFEITURE

HUMMELL v. S.E. RYKOFF & CO.
United States Court of Appeals, Ninth Circuit
634 F.2d 446 (1980)

EUGENE A. WRIGHT, CIRCUIT JUDGE:

[R]ykoff established a profit-sharing plan for its employees in 1966. It contained a forfeiture or "bad boy" provision which required forfeiture of all of a participating employee's accrued benefits if he or she became a business competitor with Rykoff within two years after leaving Rykoff.

Congress passed ERISA in 1974. The Act provides minimum vesting standards for employee benefits and defines permissible forfeitures. [ERISA § 203]. One of the primary purposes of the Act is to insure that plan participants do not lose vested benefits because of "unduly restrictive" forfeiture provisions. . . .

Rykoff amended its plan to comply with ERISA. It narrowed the anticompetitive forfeiture provision to provide that if Rykoff learns that any former plan participant is employed by a competitor, the Plan Advisory Committee may direct the plan trustee to forfeit a percentage of the participant's benefits derived from company contributions. . . . The provision applies only to participants with less than six years experience with Rykoff. Those with six years or more are fully vested, regardless of any competitive activity.

Section 9.10 includes a vesting schedule to establish what percentage of a participant's interest derived from Rykoff's contribution is forfeited if he or she engages in competitive work.[*]

Years of Service With Employer	Forfeited % of Interest from Employer
2	50%
3	40
4	30
5	20
6	0

A different vesting schedule applies to benefits of plan participants with less than six years of service who terminate but do not engage in competitive activity. Section 9.05. Their interests are 100% vested after three years.

Years of Service With Employer	Forfeited % of Interest from Employer
less than 1 year	40%
less than 2 years	30
less than 3 years	10
3 or more years	0

Appellee Burton Hummell (Hummell) terminated his employment with Rykoff after 3½ years of service on September 23, 1976. He left to work for a competitor.

On October 21, 1977, the Advisory Committee directed the plan trustee to forfeit 40% (or $28,982.74) of Hummell's accrued benefits because of his post-employment competitive activity. The Committee arrived at the 40% figure by reference to the vesting schedule in Section 9.10.

[*] *Hummell* arose when ERISA permitted ten-year cliff vesting and fifteen-year graduated vesting. The employer relied on those requirements in drafting its plan and Hummell terminated his employment after eleven years, between the two sets of requirements. The case has been edited to reflect ERISA's current three-year cliff and six-year graduated vesting requirements for defined-contribution plans. ERISA § 203(a)(2)(B). (For defined-benefit plans, ERISA's minimum vesting standards are either five-year cliff or seven-year graduated. § 203(a)(2)(A).) The employer's plan and the timing of Hummell's termination have been changed to reflect the ERISA amendments. The substantive holding of the case remains the same.

Hummell appealed the decision to the Advisory Committee and lost. He then sued in district court which granted him summary judgment, holding the forfeiture provision violated ERISA. . . .

ERISA requires private pension plans to provide that an employee's right to his or her normal retirement benefit is nonforfeitable upon the attainment of normal retirement age. [§ 203(a)]. In addition, an employee's rights in his accrued benefit derived from his contributions must be nonforfeitable, [§ 203(a)(1)], and the plan must satisfy one of [the] minimum vesting schedules [for defined-contribution plans. § 203(a)(2)(B)].

The first alternative vesting schedule provides that an employee with at least three years of service must have "a nonforfeitable right to 100% of [the employee's] accrued benefit derived from employer contributions." [§ 203(a)(2)(B)(ii)]. There is no requirement for vesting of any lesser percentage of benefits before the required three years of service.

The schedule in subparagraph (a)(2)(B)(iii) provides graduated vesting. An employee . . . must have

a nonforfeitable right to a percentage of [the employee's] accrued benefit derived from employer contributions . . . determined under the following table:

Years of Service	Nonforfeitable%
2	20
3	40
4	60
5	80
6	100

Permitted forfeitures of accrued benefits from employer contributions are in paragraphs (A)-(D) of [§ 203(a)(3)]. They do not include anticompetitive forfeiture provisions or refer to the forfeitability of benefits which exceed the minimum vesting requirements in [§ 203(a)(2)(B)(ii) & (iii)].

The legislative history indicates that with these limited exceptions, *vested* employee rights cannot be forfeited for any reason.

The district court construed the statute to prohibit any anticompetitive forfeiture provision. . . . [T]his interpretation is erroneous.

A Treasury Regulation provides . . . ["t]o the extent that rights are not required to be nonforfeitable to satisfy the minimum vesting standards, . . . they may be forfeited without regard to the limitations on forfeitability required by this section.["] 26 C.F.R. § 1.411(a)-4.[3] . . .

We hold ERISA does not prohibit forfeiture of benefits in excess of the minimum vesting requirements in [§ 203].

Our holding that ERISA permits limited forfeitures does not resolve the validity of Rykoff's plan. The question remains whether Rykoff may apply the

---

[3] This Treasury Regulation [was] issued under the Internal Revenue Code's requirements for pension plans. ERISA provides they apply to analogous provisions of ERISA.

six-year graded vesting schedule to employees who violate the anticompetitive clause and the three-year 100% vesting schedule to all other employees.

The statute says that *a plan* must satisfy the requirements of subparagraph [§ 203(a)(2)(B). . . . It says nothing about applying option (ii) to some employees and (iii) to others. . . .

A Treasury Regulation says that composite arrangements are permissible as long as the plan satisfies all requirements of *one* vesting option for all of *an employee's* years of service. 26 C.F.R. § 1.411(a)-3(a)(2).

> A plan which, for example, satisfies the [three-year cliff vesting requirements of subparagraph ii, but not the six-year graduated vesting requirements of subparagraph iii] for an employee's first [two] years of service and satisfies the requirements of [sub]paragraph [iii but not ii] for all his remaining years of service, does not satisfy the requirements of this section. . . .

Taken together, the statute . . . and Treasury Regulations indicate that Congress intended to determine forfeitable benefits by referring to the same statutory schedule with which the plan's vesting schedule complies. For example, a plan with a minimum vesting schedule satisfying the three-year 100% option in [§ 203(a)(2)(B)(ii)] may forfeit 100% of an employee's employer-derived accrued benefits until the employee completes three years of service. A plan with a vesting schedule satisfying the requirements of [§ 203(a)(2)(B)(iii)] may forfeit employer-derived accrued benefits in accordance with the six-year graded schedule in the statute. . . .

We . . . should if possible construe Rykoff's plan to make it legal. Applying our interpretation to Rykoff's plan, we find the forfeiture clause must be altered to comply with ERISA. Rykoff's graduated three-year vesting schedule tracks [§ 203(a)(2)(B)(ii)].[7]

The forfeiture provision must be adjusted to apply only to that percentage of the vested contributions that may be forfeited lawfully under [§ 203(a)(2)(B)(ii)]. This means employees with less than three years experience who violate the forfeiture provision forfeit 100% of employer contributed accrued benefits. Those with three or more years experience are 100% vested in their benefits.

Hummell had 3½ years of service. Accordingly, he was 100% vested in his benefits and not subject to the anticompetitive forfeiture provision. He is entitled to reinstatement of $28,982.74 to his account. . . .

NOTES

1. *Analyzing Hummell.* At the time he resigned, Hummell had $72,457 attributable to employer contributions in his account. The court found Hummell was entitled to the total amount, despite his violation of the "bad boy" clause. The court's analysis, however, would not always favor employees. For

---

[7] Although Rykoff's schedule is more liberal than § [203(a)(2)(B)(ii)] requires because it allows vesting to accumulate before three years of service, we need not alter it. ERISA's legislative history and the Treasury Regulations indicate a plan may provide a vesting schedule more liberal than the statutory minimum.

example, if Hummell had left to work for a competitor after 2½ years of service, he would not have been entitled to any of the employer's contributions using the court's analysis, but he would have been entitled to 50% of them using a plain reading of the "bad boy" forfeiture provision in the plan. Was the court justified in changing the forfeiture called for by the "bad boy" clause to align with ERISA's three-year cliff vesting provision? Note that both Rykoff forfeiture provisions also meet or exceed ERISA's six-year vesting schedule.

2. *Public Policy and Nonforfeiture Provisions.* If protecting employees against forfeiture is a good idea, why allow total forfeiture of employer contributions for the first three years or partial forfeiture for the first six years? Why not require employer contributions to be vested immediately?

ERISA's vesting rules have a high degree of precision — they are specific and relatively easy to apply. One cost of that precision is that compliance with the rules may be a *defense* in situations where the underlying public policy against forfeiture seems to be at risk. In *Phillips v. Alaska Hotel & Restaurant Employees Pension Fund*, 944 F.2d 509 (9th Cir. 1991), for example, a plan's vesting rules, in combination with a highly transient workforce, operated to exclude 97% of the plan's participants from benefits. The plan, however, complied with ERISA's vesting requirements. Non-vested participants in the plan filed a lawsuit claiming that the plan was not being operated for the sole and exclusive benefit of employees, in violation of ERISA and the Labor Management Relations Act. ERISA § 404(a)(1); LMRA § 302(c)(5). The Court held for the plan, relying in part on the plan's compliance with ERISA's vesting rules.

3. *The Inevitable Complexity of Regulation.* Many avenues exist for attempting to avoid the antiforfeiture provisions of ERISA. A plan, for example, could have a three-year cliff vesting provision and yet guarantee very little if 1) the plan's definition of "years of service" made it difficult for employees to build up years ("a 'year of service' is a year in which an employee works 3,000 hours") or 2) the plan had benefits accrue significantly only after a long period of service ("benefits will accrue at a rate of $1.00 per year for the first twenty-five years of service and at a rate of $25,000 per year thereafter"). ERISA has many detailed provisions designed to make it difficult to avoid the basic policy of the vesting provisions. It has provisions, for example, which define "year of service" and others which regulate the rate of benefit accrual. *See* ERISA §§ 203(b), 204.

4. *Anti-discrimination and Section 510.* Section 510 is one of the web of ERISA provisions intended to protect employee access to pension funds:

> It shall be unlawful for any person to discharge, fine, suspend, expel, discipline, or discriminate against a participant or beneficiary for exercising any right to which he is entitled under the provisions of an employee benefit plan [or under Title I of ERISA], *or for the purpose of interfering with the attainment of any right to which such participant may become entitled under the plan [or Title I].*

Section 510 applies most directly to prohibit employers from discharging employees shortly before vesting to avoid pension liabilities. In *Reichman v. Bonsignore, Brignati & Mazzotta P.C.*, 818 F.2d 278 (2d Cir. 1987), for example, the employer was found to have violated section 510 by discharging an employee ten months before her pension rights fully vested. Full vesting would have increased the employee's pension benefits by $60,000. As the next case illustrates, however, applying section 510 is not always an easy task.

NEMETH v. CLARK EQUIPMENT CO.
United States District Court, W.D. Michigan
677 F. Supp. 899 (1987)

ENSLEN, DISTRICT JUDGE.

Clark Equipment Company ("Clark") is a manufacturer of material handling equipment, construction machinery, and components. Until February 1983, Clark operated a construction machinery plant at Benton Harbor, Michigan. Plaintiffs are eighteen (18) former Clark employees who lost their jobs, and their full pensions, when Clark closed its Benton Harbor plant in February, 1983. Each plaintiff's employment was terminated when the plant closed. Clark transferred the production formerly accomplished at Benton Harbor to the two remaining plants in its construction machinery division, located in St. Thomas, Ontario and Asheville, North Carolina.

In 1982 Clark's President and Chief Executive Officer, James Reinhart, determined that Clark was in serious financial trouble. . . . Reinhart determined that Clark might go bankrupt by the end of 1982 unless the company took drastic steps to reduce its production capacity and overhead costs.

To that end, Clark began to consolidate its operations. In order to determine which plants, if any, to close, Clark conducted a series of plant capacity studies. . . .

The construction machinery division had three plants: Benton Harbor, St. Thomas and Asheville. The company decided it could not close St. Thomas since duty restrictions would prevent it from competing in the Canadian market if it did not manufacture a portion of its product in Canada. The plant capacity study evaluated both Clark's options (eliminate Benton Harbor or eliminate Asheville) against a base case, or "do nothing" scenario. On the basis of this study, Clark decided to close the Benton Harbor plant. It announced this decision to the Benton Harbor workforce in early October, 1982. The plant actually closed in February, 1983.

Plaintiffs claim that Clark chose to close Benton Harbor instead of Asheville because of the increased pension expense Clark would incur if it allowed the Benton Harbor workforce to work until normal retirement age. . . . The plaintiffs in this case were within months or years of full retirement under [the Benton Harbor Pension Plan]. As a result of the plant closing, each plaintiff lost the right to qualify for full retirement benefits. . . .

Section 510 of ERISA prohibits employer conduct taken against an employee who participates in a pension benefit plan for "the purpose of interfering with the attainment of any right to which such participant may become entitled under the plan." . . . [T]his prohibition was "aimed primarily at preventing unscrupulous employers from discharging their employees in order to keep them from obtaining vested pension rights." In order to prevail under this section, plaintiffs must prove that the defendant made the decision to discharge them from employment with the specific intent to violate ERISA. *Gavalik v. Continental Can Co.*, 812 F.2d 834, 851 [(3d Cir. 1987)].

Plaintiffs need not prove that defendant's desire to interfere with their pension benefits was the *sole* reason for their termination. Rather, "§ 510 of ERISA requires no more than proof that the desire to defeat pension eligibility is 'a determinative factor' in the challenged conduct." *Gavalik* at 860. Once the plaintiffs establish that the desire to avoid pension liability was a determining factor in the decision to terminate their employment, the defendant, in order to avoid liability, must prove, "that it would have reached the same conclusion or engaged in the same conduct in any event, *i.e.*, in the absence of the impermissible consideration. . . ." *Id.* at 863. If the employer carries its burden to prove an alternative nondiscriminatory justification, the plaintiffs must then demonstrate that the proffered justification is a mere pretext, or that the discriminatory reason more likely motivated the defendant's action. *Id.* at 853.

In this case, plaintiffs' proof that Clark made the decision to close the Benton Harbor plant in order to prevent plaintiffs from obtaining their full retirement benefits consisted primarily of documents comparing payroll, pension expenses and other costs at the Benton Harbor and Asheville plants. Pension expenses at Benton Harbor would have amounted to $7.005 million over the relevant five (5) year period,[3] while those at Asheville would have come to only $1.096 million. According to plaintiffs' expert, the difference in pension costs, before accounting for union cost-cutting proposals and differences in efficiency between the two plants, amounts to 26.79% of the total difference in direct labor costs between the two plants. The overall difference in operating costs between the two plants was $26.9 million. Pension costs amounted to slightly less than 22% of this difference.[5] Pension costs thus amounted to slightly more than one-fifth of the cost difference between the two plants.

Plaintiffs' offered other evidence to show that Clark's decision to close the Benton Harbor plant was motivated by its desire to prevent plaintiffs from obtaining their full retirement benefits. Ken Ward, a former Clark employee, testified that Paul Schultz, former manager of the Benton Harbor plant, told him that "the pension costs were killing us." This comment was made during discussions about the possibility that Clark would close the plant. . . .

The Court finds that this evidence is sufficient to make out a *prima facie* case of pension discrimination in violation of section 510 of ERISA. Pension expenses were a significant item of cost making Benton Harbor more expensive to operate than Asheville. It is undisputed that the defendants considered these costs in making its decision to close the Benton Harbor plant. The Court cannot say that an expense amounting to more than twenty (20%) percent of the difference in operating expenses between the two plants was not a determining factor in Clark's decision to close the Benton Harbor plant,

---

[3] Defendant's decision was based on an estimate of costs over the five year period from 1983 to 1987.

[5] The difference in pension costs between Benton Harbor and Asheville, for the years 1983-1987, . . . is $5.909 million. This is 22% of the $26.9 million difference in operating costs.

although obviously it was not the sole reason for that decision. The evidence regarding transfer rights further demonstrates Clark's attempts to consolidate those savings by preventing the older and more senior employees from transferring to the Asheville plant and accruing the years of service necessary to obtain full pension benefits. Clark denied transfers to disabled, medically restricted and laid-off employees even though it had the ability to employ many of these individuals.[9] Even the employees who qualified for transfer had to . . . hastily move themselves and their families to North Carolina in order to obtain work. These facts, taken together with plaintiffs' direct evidence, are sufficient to show that Clark's decision was motivated, at least in part, by its desire to avoid paying full retirement benefits to the Benton Harbor workforce.

The Court must now determine whether the defendant met its burden of showing that it had a legitimate, nondiscriminatory reason for its actions. *Gavalik* at 853. The Court finds that Clark has met that burden. Clark produced an enormous amount of documentary evidence to establish its alternative justification for the decision to close Benton Harbor. Clark claims that it based its decision on a number of economic considerations, and that no one item of cost was singled out as the cost responsible for Benton Harbor's closure. Clark argues that it considered only "the bottom line," an elusive accounting concept which defied definition by any witness. For Charles Kiopes, General Manager for Construction Machinery, the bottom line was net gross margin. The plant capacity study showed a $33 million advantage in favor of closing Benton Harbor. James Reinhart and Raymond Pirrone said they also considered other items, including pretax income ($30 million advantage in favor of closing Benton Harbor), return on sales (1.3% advantage), return on assets (2.8% advantage), and operating expenses ($26.9 million advantage). Each Clark witness testified that his decision to recommend closing the Benton Harbor plant was based on a consideration of the entire study, and not solely upon a consideration of pension costs or even of direct labor costs.

While the Court is persuaded by Clark's evidence, it believes that Clark has overstated its case on the law. Clark's first argument is that a plaintiff cannot prevail under section 510 where, "elimination of jobs and termination of benefits were attributable to mounting economic losses, plant closures or winding up of a business." This is simply not the law. ERISA was intended to prevent employers from making employment decisions based upon their desire to avoid pension liability. Whether the defendant's motive is cost-saving or ill-will toward a particular employee, the employer will violate ERISA if it makes an employment decision solely, or even substantially, for the purpose of avoiding pension liability. Pensions cost money; money and "economic losses" are essentially synonymous. Allowing an employer to defend an ERISA claim solely on the ground that its pension program was too expensive to

---

[9] Defendant employed up to one hundred (100) temporary employees at the Asheville plant. These positions could have been made available to plaintiffs. There was no evidence that Clark was financially unable to fill these positions with permanent employees. In fact, Robert Johnson, employee relations manager at Asheville, testified that Clark hired temporary employees in part to keep the positions open for full-time workers and that Clark did not have enough transferees to fill those slots for at least one year after Benton Harbor closed.

maintain would defeat the purpose of § 510, which is to prohibit employers from making employment decisions based upon pension costs. . . .

Certainly, as defendant points out, plaintiffs must establish that Clark acted with the purpose of interfering with their attainment of benefits under the plan. Plaintiffs may not prevail if the loss of benefits was "a mere consequence of, but not a motivating factor behind a termination of employment." *Baker v. Kaiser Aluminum & Chemical Corp.,* 608 F. Supp. 1315, 1319 (N.D. Cal. 1984). Plaintiffs must show "more than . . . that the termination of [their] employment 'meant a monetary savings to defendants,' for otherwise an ERISA violation would automatically occur every time an employer terminated a fully-vested employee. . . ." *Donohue v. Custom Management Corp.,* 634 F. Supp. 1190, 1197 (W.D. Pa. 1986). The "something more" referred to in *Donohue* is the requisite causal link between pension benefits and an adverse employment action. Plaintiffs must prove by a preponderance of the evidence that the defendant's desire to avoid pension liability was a determining factor in motivating the challenged conduct. If plaintiffs establish that they lost work because of their pension benefits, plaintiffs will prevail. . . .

If Clark had made the decision based primarily on the costs of the pension plan, Clark would have acted with the purpose of interfering with plaintiffs' rights under that plan. The resulting loss of benefits would not have been an "incidental" result of the decision to terminate plaintiffs' employment, it would have been the motivating factor behind that decision, the cause of their termination. *Gavalik* at 860. The difficulty for plaintiffs in this case is that Clark's witnesses testified that pension costs were one of many considerations in their decision, and that no single factor standing alone motivated or dominated their decision to close the Benton Harbor plant. Combined with the documentary evidence provided by the defendant, this testimony establishes that the decision to close the Benton Harbor plant was not motivated, or caused, by Clark's consideration of pension costs at that plant.

The defendant next argues that "the 'invidious intent' to interfere with participants' ERISA rights is not found where termination cuts along independently established lines. . . . Section 510 addresses discriminatory conduct directed against individuals, not actions involving a plan in general such as the winding up of a plant or division." . . .

Taken to its logical extension, defendant's argument essentially means that an employer violates ERISA only when the employer discharges or otherwise discriminates against a single employee, rather than a class or group of employees. Again, Clark misstates the law. . . . ERISA does not distinguish between the termination of one employee and the termination of 100 employees. Either action is illegal if taken with the purpose of avoiding pension liability. Rather, ERISA distinguishes between the intent to interfere with vested pension rights and the intent to terminate employment for other, nondiscriminatory reasons. While termination of employees in order to reduce labor costs is not always illegal, ERISA prohibits such actions if the primary reason for high labor costs is pension liability.

Defendant's final argument is that ERISA does not provide a remedy for employees whose pension rights have vested and whose only injury is the "lost opportunity to accrue additional benefits." While Clark correctly points out that some courts have denied ERISA claims where the plaintiff's rights under a pension plan have vested, other courts have held that the question of whether an employee's rights were vested is irrelevant to the § 510 cause of action.

[S]ection 510 would make little sense if given the interpretation defendant urges. Employees whose pensions have vested, but whose right to retire has not yet accrued, often rely more heavily upon the promise of an adequate pension than do their younger, unvested colleagues. Older employees, like the plaintiffs in this case, are virtually unemployable if they lose their current jobs and, even if they could find work, would have a shorter working life in which to accrue new retirement benefits. Younger, unvested employees can find new work more easily than older displaced workers. They have a better chance of working long enough to earn a pension simply because they are younger and have a longer working life in which to accrue these rights. Employers also have a greater incentive to discriminate against older, vested employees since these employees are closer to retirement and the employer is closer to having to pay out the benefits it has promised. The employer can make good its promises to younger employees by investing smaller amounts of money over a longer period of time, thus reducing the strain of pension benefits on employers and reducing the incentive to discriminate against younger employees. For these reasons, section 510 would be essentially unnecessary were it intended to protect only unvested employees. Not only are unvested employees in less need of protection, but employers generally lack incentives to discriminate against them. Vested employees, on the other hand, are often in greater need of the statute's protection and the employer's incentive to violate it is often greatest with respect to those employees. . . .

ERISA protects against employer action taken to prevent the accrual of additional rights or benefits under a qualified plan. . . . [I]n *Folz v. Marriott Corp.*, 594 F. Supp. 1007 (W.D. Mo. 1984) the court found liability under § 510 where an employer discharged an employee suffering from multiple sclerosis for the purpose of preventing him from using the employer's health insurance benefits. In that case, the court held, "The allegation that an employee was terminated from his employment for the purpose of depriving him of *continued participation* in the employer's . . . insurance program states a cognizable claim under section 510 of ERISA."

In this case, plaintiffs make a similar claim. They argue that Clark terminated their employment in order to prevent them from accruing additional years of service and from obtaining full retirement benefits. This is exactly the sort of claim ERISA was intended to redress, as . . . *Folz* indicate[s]. If Clark terminated the plaintiffs' employment in order to prevent them from obtaining additional benefits under the pension plan, Clark violated ERISA.

While the Court views defendant's legal arguments with some distaste, it must agree with defendant's interpretation of the evidence in this case. The defendant has shown that it had a legitimate, non-discriminatory reason for terminating the plaintiffs' employment. Each Clark witness testified that he made the decision to recommend closure of the Benton Harbor plant based on a review of all the financial data available. No single item of cost or consideration was given more weight than any other. Direct testimony from at least three witnesses (James Reinhart, Raymond Pirrone and Charles Kiorpes) established that pension benefits were not a significant consideration in the decision. . . .

Plaintiffs' highest credible estimation of the significance of pension benefits was slightly less than 40% of the difference in labor costs between Benton Harbor and Asheville. At most, pension costs amounted to 20% of the total difference in cost between the two plants. Although this is a substantial amount, the Court finds that Clark would have made the decision to close Benton Harbor even if it had ignored the cost of the pension plan altogether. Had Clark eliminated consideration of all pension costs, there would still have been a $19.9 million difference in cost between Benton Harbor and Asheville. Even after adjusting these figures for the union's cost-cutting proposals, a difference in cost of $7.44 per standard hour exists, amounting to a difference of approximately $77,376.00 per employee over five years. These figures, together with the testimony of Clark executives, show that while Clark considered the cost of current pension benefits, and that this cost was substantial, it did not make the difference in Clark's decision to close the Benton Harbor plant.

Clark also successfully rebutted the inference of discrimination arising from its transfer policies. Michael Hanesworth, Clark's General Counsel for Labor Relations, testified that he recommended a restrictive interpretation of the Benton Harbor employees' transfer rights in order to protect both the seniority and the pension rights of workers at the Asheville plant. As a fiduciary for the Asheville workers' pension plan, Hanesworth had to consider the effect of transfers on the financial viability of the Asheville plant's pension plan. As he noted, if large numbers of Benton Harbor employees transferred to Asheville, they would place a great deal of strain on the Asheville pension plan. Since that plan was funded with the assumption that few, if any, employees would collect benefits from it for at least ten years . . . the plan would have been imperiled by the unanticipated retirement of workers before that date.

After reviewing the evidence, the Court finds that Clark . . . would have made the same decision, even if it had factored pension benefits out of the study entirely, because the evidence showed that Clark was looking for the least costly alternative. . . . Thus the Court concludes, somewhat reluctantly, that defendants should prevail on the ERISA claim.

NOTES

1. *A Natural Extension or Bad Economics?* On the one hand, *Nemeth* is a natural extension of the antiforfeiture protections of ERISA. When ERISA prohibits an employer from denying pension benefits *for any reason* after five years of service, it seems only fair also to prohibit that employer from firing an employee *specifically to avoid pension liabilities* after four years and eleven months of service. And it would seem to make no difference if the employer avoids the near-future pension liabilities one employee at a time or, as in *Nemeth,* simultaneously to large numbers of employees.

On the other hand, *Nemeth* counsels employers to blind themselves to an important set of costs when they make important decisions. If pension costs are significant enough to affect a decision, *Nemeth* holds that it is a violation of § 510 to consider them. (Ironically, if the costs are too small to matter — or even large, but not large enough to tip the decision — the employer can consider them.) Why do you think employee benefits are privileged over wages in this way? Because benefits, but not wages, are deferred compensation that has already been earned? Because benefits are more difficult to replace than wages?

2. *The Breadth of § 510.* Everytime an employer discharges an employee, and often when it takes lesser measures, the employee's pension benefits are affected. If the employee's rights have not yet vested, the discharge may eliminate any right of the employee to recover pension benefits. Even when employee rights have vested, the discharge prevents the accrual of additional benefits. *Nemeth* specifically holds that § 510's protections apply even after employee rights have vested. Indeed, § 510 is not limited to pension benefits. Welfare benefits, such as health insurance, can never vest and, unless the employer restricts itself in some way, can be changed by the employer virtually at will. Nevertheless, § 510's protections apply. *See Inter-Modal Rail Employees Ass'n v. Atchison, Topeka & Santa Fe Ry.*, 520 U.S. 510 (1997). Employers, however, can defend against § 510 actions by demonstrating that they have legitimate reasons for their adverse employment actions. Viewed in this way, § 510 seems to require employers to justify every adverse employment action. Is § 510 a general wrongful discharge statute masquerading as a statute protecting pension rights? *See* Terry Collingsworth, *ERISA Section 510 — A Further Limitation on Arbitrary Discharges,* 10 INDUS. REL. L.J. 319 (1988) (yes). *But see Meredith v. Navistar Int'l Transp. Co.,* 935 F.2d 124 (7th Cir. 1991) (no § 510 action where loss of benefits is mere consequence of, as opposed to motivating factor behind, the termination). *Accord Dytrt v. Mountain State Tel. & Tel. Co.,* 921 F.2d 889 (9th Cir. 1990).

Should the *Nemeth* rationale be extended to situations where the employee is not yet a participant in the pension plan? For example, consider an employer who offers an employee either a $21,000 annual salary with a 15% contribution to a pension plan or a $24,000 annual salary with no pension contribution. The employee demands a $24,000 annual salary with a 15% pension contribution, and sues when the employer refuses. Has the employer violated § 510 by basing its decision on pension costs? *See Garratt v. Walker,* 164 F.3d 1249 (10th Cir. 1998) (en banc) (ordering trial to determine if employer decision was made for legitimate business reasons or to avoid employer's obligation to fund pension plan).

3. *The Necessity of § 510.* Consider an employee who is deciding whether to accept current wages or a pension promise in return for her services. The employee presumably compares the current wages (W) she could receive to the present value of the anticipated pension (V) times the probability of receiving the pension (p). If $pV > W$, the employee accepts the pension promise in lieu of the wages. If not, she takes the wages.

In a world without § 510, employees would have a broader range of choices with respect to the trade-off between p and V. Employees who prefer a higher V at the cost of a higher risk of forfeiture (a lower p) would accept pensions from employers who did not have a provision equivalent to § 510 in their pension plans. Employees who prefer a lower V and a lower risk of forfeiture could accept pensions under plans with § 510 equivalents. Viewed in this way, § 510 is unnecessary. Employees who do not have § 510-type protections in their pension plans and, because of that, never receive pensions, have not been swindled — instead, they have gambled for higher pension payments and lost. Indeed, § 510 may frustrate the preferences of some employees. Section 510, when it has any effect at all, operates to increase p. Thus, employees who would prefer higher pensions, albeit at a higher risk that they might receive nothing, are frustrated.

Convinced?

C. GENDER EQUITY

LORENZEN v. EMPLOYEES RETIREMENT PLAN OF THE SPERRY & HUTCHINSON CO.
United States Court of Appeals, Seventh Circuit
896 F.2d 228 (1990)

POSNER, CIRCUIT JUDGE.

This is a suit under the Employee Retirement Income Security Act of 1974 (ERISA) by the widow of an employee of S & H, claiming that S & H's Retirement Plan, an ERISA plan, violated its fiduciary duties to her husband and herself, causing a loss of retirement benefits. The district judge granted summary judgment for Mrs. Lorenzen, awarding her some $192,000 and the plan appeals. . . .

Warren Lorenzen, a sales manager and long-time employee of S & H, was eligible to retire on February 1, 1987, having turned 65. As he was in the midst of managing a company project, the company requested him to postpone his retirement until July 1, and he agreed. At the same time he decided that when he did retire he would take his retirement benefits as a lump sum, rather than as a series of monthly payments for his life followed by monthly payments half as large to his wife for her life should she outlive him (the "50 percent joint and survivor option," as it was called). The taking of retirement benefits in a lump sum was an option expressly permitted by the plan, provided the spouse executed a written consent form, which Mrs. Lorenzen did. Since death is not retirement, in order to receive any retirement benefit at all, lump sum or annuity, the employee must live to the date of his retirement. If he dies before then, his spouse is entitled to a pre-retirement benefit but it is much smaller than the retirement benefit. On June 15, two weeks before his extended retirement date, Lorenzen suffered cardiac arrest and was hospitalized in grave condition. On June 27, he suffered cardiac arrest again and was plugged into life-support machinery. His condition was believed to be hopeless and his physicians advised Mrs. Lorenzen to request that the machinery be disconnected. She did so, it was disconnected, and Mr. Lorenzen died that day.

The plan documents do not define death, but the parties and the district judge assume that if Mrs. Lorenzen had not requested the removal of the life-support apparatus Mr. Lorenzen would have survived, within the meaning of the plan, until his retirement on July 1. In that event he would have received, pursuant to his earlier election, the lump-sum retirement benefit. Assuming he would then have been taken off life support, the lump sum would have passed to his widow. . . . And this was the amount the district court ordered the plan to pay her. The plan argues that since Lorenzen died before he retired, the widow is entitled only to the pre-retirement death benefit — in present-value terms and rounded off, $89,000 versus $192,000. Of course if Lorenzen had received the lump sum, frittered it away at the gaming tables, and then died, Mrs. Lorenzen would be even worse off than she is (it is against this possibility that the spouse is required to sign a consent form, as she did), but the plan has not argued this possibility as a ground for reducing her damages.

In holding for Mrs. Lorenzen the district judge appears to have been moved by the human appeal of her case. This is understandable. To have to decide whether to order the removal of life support from a loved one is painful enough without having to incur an enormous financial penalty in the bargain. The equities are not all on one side, however. (They rarely are; the tension between formal justice and substantive justice is often, and perhaps here, illusory.) Life-support equipment is expensive and, to a considerable degree, futile and degrading. It should not be used to secure retirement benefits. If the parties to retirement plans envisaged such a use, they probably would define death as inability to "live" without life-support machinery — at least if permitted by state law, which might forbid the guardian of a patient even in a hopeless vegetative state to disconnect the patient's life-support machinery. *Cruzan v. [Director, Missouri Dept. of Health,* 497 U.S. 261 (1990).] By postponing his retirement Mr. Lorenzen took a risk that if he died his widow would obtain less money than if he retired as soon as he was eligible. But he was compensated for bearing this risk by being paid his full salary (which exceeded his retirement benefit, lump sum or annuity, evaluated on a comparable basis, *i.e.* as a monthly payment) for a longer time, and by having an expectation of slightly increased retirement benefits, for they rose with the length of time that he was employed, although not steeply. This "compensation" was, to be sure, ex ante rather than ex post — had Lorenzen been gifted with pre-vision he would have retired. But a gamble is not unfair merely because the gambler loses. Nor was the plan unjustly enriched at the Lorenzens' expense. "A pension plan is not 'unjustly enriched' where a pensioner dies early with no benefits payable to his survivor. That eventuality simply offsets cases where a pensioner lives well into old age and more benefits are paid to him than were statistically predictable." Finally, the record contains no evidence of what it would have cost Mrs. Lorenzen to maintain her husband on life-support machinery for an additional three days. It could have been a considerable sum, depending on the scope and terms of his hospital insurance.

Mrs. Lorenzen had no contractual entitlement to retirement benefits — this much is clear — since her husband did not survive until retirement. ERISA, however, requires that a retirement or welfare plan make clear to the participants what the plan's terms and conditions are. [ERISA § 101.] Mrs. Lorenzen claims that the plan did not adequately apprise her husband of the consequences of his electing the lump-sum rather than annuity form of retirement benefits and of his electing to keep on working rather than retire at the earliest possible opportunity. The first claim is frivolous; regardless of which election Lorenzen would have made if fully informed, his death nullified any retirement benefits to which he and his wife might have been entitled had he lived to retirement. If he had elected the annuity form, then even though Mrs. Lorenzen would have been entitled — had he retired and she outlived him — to an annuity that would outlast his death, this entitlement would have been contingent on his retiring; and before he retired he died.

The second claim is that the plan should have advised Mr. Lorenzen more clearly than it did that if he postponed his retirement he was risking a net loss of benefits, since pre-retirement death benefits were lower than retirement benefits. There was no want of clarity, however. The plan summary explains that "if you should die either before retirement or after retirement but before benefits begin . . . your spouse or other beneficiary will receive a benefit. . . . [I]f you die after age 55 and your legal spouse is your beneficiary, this benefit will be the larger of 40% of the lump sum equivalent of the benefits you have earned under the plan or the amount he or she [*i.e.*, the legal spouse] would receive if you had retired on the day before your death under the 50% joint-and-survivor option." Mr. Lorenzen could have been under no illusion that if he died before his extended retirement date arrived, his widow would receive one hundred percent of his lump-sum retirement benefits rather than 50 percent of his retirement annuity. The risk he took in not retiring as soon as he could was an informed, a calculated, one. . . .

Mrs. Lorenzen [does not] argue that the plan summary was defective for failing to advise participants of the consequences of finding themselves on life-support machinery shortly before the scheduled date of retirement. She is wise not to make that argument, for the law is clear that the plan summary is not required to anticipate every possible idiosyncratic contingency that might affect a particular participant's or beneficiary's status. If it were, the summaries would be choked with detail and hopelessly confusing. Clarity and completeness are competing goods. . . .

The judgment is reversed and the case is remanded with directions to award Mrs. Lorenzen only the pre-retirement death benefit to which she is entitled under her husband's retirement plan. . . .

CUDAHY, CIRCUIT JUDGE, dissenting:

[W]ith respect to the merits, I do not quarrel with the essentials of the majority's analysis. . . . But I am at a loss to understand some of the majority's proffered justifications for its result. Mr. Lorenzen deferred his retirement for six months for the convenience of his employer. There is nothing to suggest that anyone brought to his or his wife's attention the possibility that she would suffer drastic financial penalties if he happened to die in the interim. Nor certainly is there any indication that he "gambled" six months' additional compensation against his wife's taking the risk of pension loss. The "rational bookmaker's" approach to problems is singularly out of place here.

By the same token there is no evidence that Mrs. Lorenzen knew she would suffer financially if she allowed life supports to be withdrawn from her husband "too soon." The human costs of this kind of decision are so overwhelming, economics is the wrong analysis to bring to the problem. And a cost-benefit study is beside the point. Fate claimed Mr. Lorenzen in a period when he was doing his employer a favor. And fate pressed on Mrs. Lorenzen a tragic choice which, quite by chance from her point of view, resulted in losing half her pension benefit. [District Court] Judge Evans thought these fortuities too cruel and decided the case in favor of the widow. Judge Evans, I believe, stepped back from the remorseless logic of the law with respect both to the time-to-appeal question and to the merits. [However, because I do not believe] that we have jurisdiction to hear the Plan's appeal, . . . I . . . do not reach the merits of the district court's award.

NOTES

1. ***The District Court Decision.*** The following excerpt is from Judge Evans' opinion in the *Lorenzen* case:

> Mrs. Lorenzen . . . argues that she is entitled to summary judgment awarding her the lump sum payment her husband was entitled to. She contends that neither the plan language nor the spousal consent form adequately informed her of the possible effects of her consent, in violation of [ERISA § 205(c)(3)(A)]. She further contends that the plan is contrary to the intention of Congress in protecting surviving spouses and that the court has power to fashion an equitable remedy to keep within the purpose and intent of ERISA. . . .

> The cause of what seems to be a very unfortunate result in this case is not that Delvina Lorenzen consented to a lump sum payment over joint and survivor benefits but that she was not aware that the lump sum payment would not be made unless her husband lived to retire. It is impossible to know what Warren Lorenzen knew on that point. It is clear that none of the letters he received provided him with the information. . . . [N]either the letters nor the spousal consent form gave any warning that the lump sum payment would be paid only if Mr. Lorenzen lived to his retirement date. This is a poignant situation both because Mr. Lorenzen, apparently out of some loyalty to the company, worked past his normal retirement date, and because his life in all probability could have been sustained until his postponed retirement date.

> In this situation, certain of defendants' arguments seem cold-hearted. S & H argues that by calling a toll-free number, Mrs. Lorenzen could have found out that she would not collect the lump sum payment if her husband died before retirement. Perhaps. But a woman confronted with a decision to remove her husband from life-support systems probably was not thinking about calling a benefits supervisor, toll free or not. . . .

> I am . . . convinced that a person who elects a lump sum benefit (and the spouse who agrees to the election) and then continues to work after his normal retirement day should be informed that if he dies before retirement, his wife is not entitled to the full lump sum. . . .

> Had Lorenzen refused to continue to work, he would have retired prior to his death and these problems would not have arisen. Had Mrs.

Lorenzen been informed that her husband had to live until he retired in order for the payment to be made, she would not, as she states in her affidavit, have agreed to remove the life-support systems. [Given the complexity of, and indeed contradictions in,] the plan documents, it is extremely unfair to expect Mrs. Lorenzen to have figured out anything about her rights.

Lorenzen v. Employees Ret. Plan, 699 F. Supp. 1367, 1369-71 (W.D. Wis. 1988), *rev'd*, 896 F.2d 228 (7th Cir. 1990).

2. *ERISA's Protection of Spousal Interests When the Participant Dies.* The Retirement Equity Act of 1984 (REAct) amended ERISA to provide two types of protections for spousal interests when a participant dies. When the participant survives until retirement, the default form of benefits is a qualified joint and survivor annuity (QJSA), which usually provides an annuity of x until the death of one spouse and 50% of x thereafter. ERISA § 205(a), (d). This form of benefit can be changed (so the benefit can be paid out as a lump sum or even as a single life annuity for the life of the participant), but only if the spouse consents to the change in writing. § 205(c). In the principal case, Mrs. Lorenzen consented to a change to a lump sum benefit. The lump sum figure of $192,000 in the case was equal to what it would have cost to purchase a joint and survivor annuity at the time of Mr. Lorenzen's retirement.

If the participant dies before retirement, the surviving spouse is entitled to a qualified preretirement survivor annuity (QPSA), commencing when the participant would have retired and equal to one-half the amount the participant would have received at retirement (equal, in other words, to the survivor annuity under the QJSA). ERISA § 205(a), (e). The QPSA can also be waived, but once again only with the written consent of the spouse. § 205(c). Mrs. Lorenzen did not waive her preretirement annuity; the $89,000 that Mrs. Lorenzen eventually received in the principal case was the QPSA, converted into a lump sum. If Mrs. Lorenzen had not signed any consents and Mr. Lorenzen had died the day after retiring, approximately what would have been the value of Mrs. Lorenzen's pension?

3. *ERISA's Protection of Spousal Interests Upon Divorce.* ERISA has strong provisions that prevent alienation of interests in pension benefits and that broadly preempt state laws that affect pension plans. ERISA §§ 206(d), 514. On anti-alienation, see *Patterson v. Schumate*, 504 U.S. 753 (1992) (anti-alienation provision permitted debtor to exclude $250,000 in pension assets from his bankruptcy estate); *Guidry v. Sheet Metal Workers Nat'l Pension Fund*, 493 U.S. 365 (1990) (anti-alienation provision protected union pension benefits of member who had embezzled $377,000 from the union). On preemption, see *Boggs v. Boggs*, 520 U.S. 833 (1997) (ERISA preempted state community property laws which would have permitted deceased spouse of a participant to make testamentary transfer of interests in a retirement plan); *Ingersoll-Rand Co. v. McClendon*, 498 U.S. 133 (1990) (ERISA preempts state-law claim of wrongful discharge in violation of public policy when employee discharged to prevent his pension from vesting).

On divorce, the nonparticipant spouse who wants to claim a portion of the participant spouse's pension benefits is seeking an alienation of pension benefits under state domestic relations law. REAct created exceptions to the anti-alienation and preemption provisions of ERISA that permit pension benefits to be allocated between the spouses at divorce through qualified domestic relations orders (QDROs). ERISA §§ 206(d)(3), 514(b)(7). REAct permits QDROs to provide that the nonparticipant spouse is to be treated as a surviving spouse for purposes of QJSAs and QPSAs (and that subsequent spouses, as a result, would not be considered spouses for those purposes). REAct, however, does not establish that, or anything else, as a default regime; divorcing parties can use the option, or not, and the terms of the QDRO (within certain limitations designed to protect the plan from confusion and conflicting claims) are up to the parties. ERISA, then, provides a procedural framework that permits divorcing parties to divide pensions, but does not deal with the difficult issue of how pension wealth should be allocated upon divorce.

4. *Protections for Women as Pension Plan Participants.* *Lorenzen* discusses ERISA protections for the interests of spouses in pensions, interests that are disproportionately held by women. But women, of course, can also have interests as employees/participants. For example, since women live longer than men, when male and female employees make the same contributions into a pension fund while they are working and receive equal annuities at retirement, a disproportionate share of the benefits will go to women. To correct for this, many employers used to require either that women make higher contributions into the fund or that they receive smaller annuities at retirement. The Supreme Court has ruled that both of these practices violate Title VII. *City of Los Angeles, Dep't of Water & Power v. Manhart*, 435 U.S. 702 (1978); *Arizona Governing Comm'n v. Norris*, 463 U.S. 1073 (1983).

The protections provided by *Manhart* and *Norris* are less salient today because of the strong trend away from defined benefit plans. Whether women will do better or worse as participants in defined contribution plans is an open question. On the one hand, defined contribution plans tend to be better for workers who change jobs more often, which benefits women. Women are more likely to participate in defined contribution plans and to accumulate more assets in them. On the other hand, when women retire and annuitize the amounts in their defined contribution plans, they will receive lower annuities than men because of their longer longevity. It is still too early to know "whether the good news in the accumulation of benefits sufficiently outweighs the bad news in the payout of benefits" to improve the retirement security of female workers. Alicia H. Munnell & Steven A. Sass, *401(k) Plans and Women: A "Good News/Bad News" Story*, CENTER FOR RETIREMENT RESEARCH (Jan. 2005).

D. FIDUCIARY DUTIES

BEACH v. COMMONWEALTH EDISON COMPANY
United States Court of Appeals, Seventh Circuit
382 F.3d 656 (2004)

EASTERBROOK, J.:

After 31 years on the job, Randall Beach retired from Commonwealth Edison in June 1997 and moved to Idaho. He was 52 at the time. By leaving before age 55, Beach gave up entitlement to future health benefits, though he retained his vested pension. Before taking this extra-early retirement, Beach asked his supervisor, plus ComEd's human resources staff, whether there was any immediate prospect that the firm would offer a voluntary separation package in his department, the Transmission and Distribution Organization. Beach knew that ComEd was reorganizing department by department and that it sometimes offered sweeteners, such as severance pay and health benefits, to those who agreed to depart. As Beach remembers these conversations, "everybody said absolutely it's not going to happen. You're not going to get the package. The company is not going to offer your department a package. It just will not happen. That was the essence of everything I got." Six weeks after Beach's retirement, however, ComEd did offer a separation package to 240 of the 4,700 employees in his department. Had he been employed on August 7, 1997, Beach would have been eligible for these benefits. When ComEd declined to treat him as if he had departed in August or September rather than May (when he gave notice and stopped working) or June (when he left the payroll), Beach filed this suit under the Employee Retirement Income Security Act. After a bench trial on stipulated facts, the district judge concluded that ComEd had violated its fiduciary duty to a participant in an ERISA plan by giving incorrect advice. Even though no one had intended to deceive Beach — ComEd's senior managers did not begin to consider separation benefits for the Transmission and Distribution Organization until after Beach's retirement, and no one in the human resources staff knew what was coming — the district judge held that ComEd must treat Beach as if he had stayed through August and qualified for all benefits then on offer.

The district court's major premise is that ComEd owed Beach a fiduciary duty with respect to future fringe-benefit plans, because he was a participant in the firm's pension plan. The court's minor premise is that any material inaccuracy, even an unintentional error, violates that fiduciary duty. The minor premise is problematic given this court's [prior] decisions, though it has some support elsewhere. *See Martinez v. Schlumberger, Ltd.*, 338 F.3d 407 (5th Cir. 2003); *Bins v. Exxon Co.*, 220 F.3d 1042 (9th Cir. 2000) (en banc). We need not consider the minor premise, however, because the district court's major premise is mistaken.

Duties under ERISA are plan-specific. The statute defines a "fiduciary" as a person who exercises authority or discretion over the administration of a plan, but only when performing those functions. ERISA §§ 3(21)(A). Thus an employer is not a fiduciary when considering whether to establish a plan in the first place, or what specific benefits to offer when creating or amending a plan. *See Hughes Aircraft Co. v. Jacobson*, 525 U.S. 432 (1999); *Lockheed Corp. v. Spink*, 517 U.S. 882 (1996). Otherwise by adopting a pension plan an employer would become its employees' fiduciary for all purposes and would be obliged, for example, to maximize its workers' salaries or to design plans that maximize fringe benefits. As *Hughes Aircraft* and similar decisions show, that is not ERISA's command. Beach was (and is) a participant in ComEd's pension plan but does not contend that he has received less than his due under it. He also was a participant in some welfare-benefit plans, such as ComEd's health-care plan; once again, however, he does not complain that ComEd wrongfully denied him any of those benefits or misled him in any way about them. He knew that if he left before age 55 those benefits would end; that decision was made with eyes open. What he wants — and what the district court gave him — is benefits under a separate plan that was not established until after he quit.

Throughout his briefs, Beach proceeds as if the separation incentives were created by amendment of a plan in which he was already a participant. That enables him to invoke *Varity Corp. v. Howe*, 516 U.S. 489 (1996), which held that ERISA prohibits a plan fiduciary from deceiving participants in an existing pension plan about the value of its benefits compared with those under a successor or substitute plan. Yet the plan under which Beach wants (and was awarded) benefits does not amend or modify any of ComEd's other plans — nor did Beach have to choose between its benefits and those of the plans in which he was a participant. The "Voluntary Separation Plan for Designated Transmission and Distribution Management Employees of Commonwealth Edison Company" dated August 7, 1997, is in the record: it is a stand-alone welfare-benefit plan that does not amend, supplement, or replace any other plan. As it did not come into existence until after Beach's retirement, ComEd did not owe him any fiduciary duty concerning its benefits.

Doubtless federal common law prohibits fraud with respect to pension and welfare benefits, apart from any need to invoke ERISA's fiduciary duty. ERISA preempts state law relating to pension plans, and federal courts regularly create federal common law (based on contract and trust law, see *Firestone Tire & Rubber Co. v. Bruch*, 489 U.S. 101 (1989)) to fill the gap. As we have emphasized, however, Beach does not contend that anyone defrauded him. Fraud requires knowledge of the truth and an intent to conceal or mislead. The people Beach consulted failed to foresee events, which is understandable because no plan had been proposed, let alone adopted, at the time. The district judge did not find the advice to have been either malicious or reckless. Even in retrospect it does not look wildly inaccurate. Beach worked in a division with 4,700 employees, only 240 of whom received an offer of special voluntary-separation benefits. By and large, employees in that division would have done well to make plans on the assumption that the pension and welfare systems already in place were the only ones they need consider. It turns out that Beach would have been among the fortunate 5% in his division, but just as there can be no fraud by hindsight, so a prediction that pans out for 95% of the concerned employees is hard to condemn just because it misses the mark for the rest. The staff should have let Beach know the limits of their information. (Perhaps they did so; it is hard to reconstruct oral advice after the fact, especially when one side does not remember anything. Only Beach recollects the conversations, and he got only the gist; he does not remember the precise words anyone used.) Negligent failure to add disclaimers and cautions is some distance from fraud, however.

A number of decisions address the question whether ERISA requires plan sponsors to give accurate information about potential amendments to existing plans. *Varity* shows that candid and complete information is required if two plans are in existence, and the sponsor tries to persuade employees to give up benefits under one in exchange for benefits under the other. These follow-on decisions conclude that a similar approach governs when a single plan is in the process of amendment. The majority view is that a duty of accurate disclosure begins "when (1) a specific proposal (2) is being discussed for purposes of implementation (3) by senior management with the authority to implement the change." *Fischer v. Philadelphia Elec. Co.*, 96 F.3d 1533, 1539 (3d Cir. 1996). At that point details of the amendment become material; until then there is only speculation. Two circuits conclude that the duty of disclosure arises sometime before the change is under "serious consideration" — though just what must be disclosed, and when, these circuits have struggled to pin down. *See Ballone v. Eastman Kodak Co.*, 109 F.3d 117 (2d Cir. 1997); *Martinez, supra*.

This debate mirrors (though the decisions do not acknowledge) a controversy in corporate and securities law. How soon must issuers of securities tell investors, or their employees, that merger discussions or other potentially substantial corporate transactions are afoot? We know from *Basic Inc. v. Levinson*, 485 U.S. 224 (1988), that firms cannot commit fraud about such transactions at any stage, but the time at which the information becomes so important that it must be disclosed accurately (if the issuer says anything), even if there is no intent to deceive, has been hard to determine. We have taken the view that accurate disclosure is not required until the price and structure of the deal have been resolved, see *Flamm v. Eberstadt*, 814 F.2d 1169 (7th Cir. 1987), though earlier disclosure may be required in closely held corporations, see *Jordan v. Duff & Phelps, Inc.*, 815 F.2d 429 (7th Cir. 1987). No court has held, however, that there is a duty in corporate or securities laws to predict accurately events that lie ahead. There is no reason why ERISA should require more.

The majority rule, reflected in *Fischer*, has the better of this debate. Giving firms a duty to forecast accurately, if the benefits staff says anything at all, could not help plan participants. It would just induce employers to tell the human resources staff to say nothing at all — to make no predictions and to refer employees to the printed plan descriptions. Yet chancy predictions may be better than silence; think of the 95% of the employees in ComEd's Transmission and Distribution Organization who would have received exactly the right advice, which could have facilitated their retirement planning. The alternative to enforced silence would be a declaration in the employee handbook that no one should rely on any oral information about the plans. That might or might not curtail legal risks — some workers would be bound to ask why the firm even had a benefits advisory staff, if it was insisting that everything the staff said was worthless — but again would do little to help people in Beach's position. It does not take familiarity with Bayes's Theorem to see that even potentially fallacious news may be better than no news. If the benefits staff must clam up, then rumor and office scuttle-butt come to the fore, and it is likely to be less accurate than the staff's educated guesses. So we are not persuaded by *Ballone* or *Martinez*.

ComEd did not amend any of its plans. We need not decide whether *Fischer*'s approach would apply to the establishment of a new plan, because none was under consideration when Beach resigned. There was no proposal at all, let alone a specific proposal under review by senior managers. It is undisputed that ComEd did not begin internal discussion of the details about the Transmission and Distribution Organization's reorganization until mid-June 1997, a month after Beach had given notice (and about the same time as his last day on the payroll). ComEd concluded that a small net reduction in staff would be required — about 30 of the 4,700 positions were to be eliminated. At a meeting on July 22 or 23, 1997, managers began to discuss whether it would make sense to use separation incentives, as opposed to other means, to achieve this reduction. Sometime late in July or early in August, Howard Nelson, ComEd's "Strategic Staffing Director," drafted a separation-incentives plan covering only 5% of the division's staff (240 employees, in the hope that 30 would take the bait). This plan was approved by Paul McCoy, Vice President for the Transmission and Distribution Organization, on August 6, and was announced to employees the next day. None of the circuits following the *Fischer* approach would conclude that this plan was under "serious consideration" before Beach retired. So even if we were to apply this approach to new plans — a question that we do not resolve today — Beach could not benefit.

Beach was not the victim of fraud, and ComEd did not have a duty of accurate disclosure in the period preceding the plan's adoption. The human relations staff might have been careless, but it did not violate any duty of loyalty owed to Beach. Accordingly, the judgment of the district court is reversed.

RIPPLE, J. dissenting:

A single principle controls this case. "[A] fiduciary may not materially mislead those to whom the duties of loyalty and prudence described in [ERISA § 404] are owed." *Berlin v. Michigan Bell Tel. Co.*, 858 F.2d 1154, 1163 (6th Cir. 1988). Mr. Beach was a participant in ComEd's retirement pension plan and its health-care plan; ComEd and Mr. Beach were in a fiduciary relationship with respect to these plans. The Voluntary Severance Plan ("VSP"), in essence, supplemented the retirement pension plan and the health-care plan. Therefore, when ComEd misrepresented the status of the VSP and its future plan-related benefits, it was "administer[ing]" these plans under the rationale of *Varity Corporation v. Howe*, 516 U.S. 489 (1996). Because, in its administration, ComEd made material misrepresentations in violation of its fiduciary duties, I would affirm the judgment of the district court.

1.

My colleagues hold that ComEd's misrepresentations were not made in a fiduciary capacity and thus are not actionable. Their view rests on the conclusion that ERISA's fiduciary duties are plan-specific. That proposition is unassailable, as far as it goes. . . . ERISA's fiduciary duties attach to an employer such as ComEd when it is a "fiduciary" with respect to an "established" plan and "manage[s]" or "administers" that established plan. ERISA §§ 3(1), (2)(A), (21)(A).

ComEd submits that ERISA's plan-specific nature means that an employer-administrator speaks as a fiduciary *only* when it speaks about new benefits that come in the form of an *amendment* to an established plan under which the employer and employee have a preexisting fiduciary relationship, as opposed to when that employer-administrator speaks about benefits in a *new* plan. At times, the majority appears inclined to that view. Such a limited review, however, is at odds with *Varity Corporation*, 516 U.S. 489. In *Varity*, officials deliberately misled Varity employees, who were participants in an existing ERISA plan and in a fiduciary relationship with Varity regarding that plan (Plan 1), to transfer out of Plan 1 and into a new plan (Plan 2); this new plan was established in an undercapitalized subsidiary, which eventually went into receivership. The Supreme Court held that Varity was acting in a fiduciary status — specifically, it was "administer[ing]" Plan 1 — when it made material misrepresentations regarding the future of plan benefits, which were found in Plan 2. . . . At the least, *Varity* stands for the proposition that, when a company such as ComEd becomes a fiduciary to an employee as to an ERISA "plan" (e.g., Plan 1), then its fiduciary duties of loyalty and care *can* attach to representations made regarding new plans under which the employer and employee do not have a pre-existing fiduciary relationship (e.g., Plan 2). *Varity* gave no hint, and neither have subsequent cases, that the critical distinction a court must draw in determining whether an employer-administrator spoke in a fiduciary status is whether the employer spoke about an "amendment" to an existing plan or to a "new" plan.

This interpretation also makes good sense. It would be intolerable to allow an employer-administrator to avoid the ramifications of its fiduciary status by simply attaching the label "new plan" — as opposed to "plan amendment" — to the subject of its misrepresentations. Furthermore, at least in the situation in which an employer-administrator is offering enhanced, sweetened benefits to induce early retirement or separation, the line between a plan "amendment" and a "new" plan is indeed blurry and easily distracts from the critical issue. The enhanced benefits can form the basis of a totally "new" plan; they can be added as "amendments" to an existing plan; or they can be part of a plan that "supplements" an existing plan. Regardless of the label, under *Varity's* reasoning, the critical factor is that there is a nexus between the new benefits about which the employer speaks and the existing plan under which an employer-employee fiduciary relationship already exists. When an employer speaks about new benefits that are related to benefits in a plan under which the employer and employee already have a fiduciary relationship, . . . the employer speaks about the future of plan-related benefits and thus is speaking in a fiduciary capacity.

[M]y colleagues . . . envision an artificially tight nexus between . . . new, future benefits and the benefits in the existing plan. *See supra* (rejecting that ComEd was operating as a fiduciary when it made misrepresentations to Mr. Beach because "the plan under which Beach wants (and was awarded) benefits does not amend or modify any of ComEd's other plans . . ."). I cannot subscribe to that limited view because it elevates form over substance. It may produce a conceptual bright-line, but it does so at the expense of limiting, as a practical matter, the effectiveness of the Congressional policy choices embodied in the statute. The facts of this case make the point starkly. At the time of ComEd's misstatements about the VSP, Mr. Beach was a participant in ComEd's retirement pension plan and its health-care plan, although he was not eligible for benefits under ComEd's retirement medical plan. The benefits in the retirement plan and the health-care plan cannot be untied from the VSP, which offered, inter alia, severance pay that would supplement his pension benefits and health benefits that would replace, upon retirement, his benefits under the health-care plan. In this circumstance, *Varity* fully supports the conclusion that ComEd was "administering" the retirement pension plan and health-care plan, and thus acting in a fiduciary capacity, when it furnished Mr. Beach with misinformation about the new VSP, which, in essence, supplemented or amended his existing plans with further retirement benefits.[1]

Before this court, ComEd also advances a temporal argument to cabin its fiduciary status. ComEd argues that, "as a matter of law," no fiduciary obligations should arise until a new plan such as the VSP is under "serious consideration." My colleagues appear to be inclined to that argument, albeit in dicta.

The "serious consideration" threshold arises from a group of cases from other circuits that have held that "material misrepresentations about a future plan offering do not constitute a breach of fiduciary duty unless the misrepresentations are made after the employer has 'seriously considered' the future offering." *Hockett v. Sun Co.*, 109 F.3d 1515, 1522 (10th Cir. 1997). A plan is under "serious consideration" when "(1) a specific proposal (2) is being discussed for purposes of implementation (3) by senior management with the authority to implement the change." *Fischer v. Philadelphia Elec. Co.*, 96 F.3d 1533, 1539 (3d Cir. 1996) (*"Fischer II"*). If the "serious consideration" litmus test were the appropriate one, Mr. Beach's claim would fail because at the time the relevant misinformation was communicated ComEd did not have a "specific proposal" for a severance package before senior management.

The "serious consideration" test is simply a line drawn in an attempt to balance "Congress' competing desires, in enacting ERISA, to safeguard employee benefit plans, and yet not make such plans so burdensome or threatening that employers would shy away from offering them." *Hockett*, 109 F.3d at 1522. The Tenth Circuit has elaborated:

> In our view, the [serious consideration test] appropriately narrows the range of instances in which an employer must disclose, in response to employees' inquiries, its tentative intentions regarding an ERISA plan. Employers frequently review retirement and benefit plans as part of ongoing efforts to succeed in a competitive and volatile marketplace. If *any* discussion by management regarding possible change to an ERISA plan triggered disclosure duties, the employer could be

---

[1] This is not to say that, once an employer becomes a fiduciary with respect to one plan, it becomes a "fiduciary for all purposes." Compare the situation in this case to the following hypothetical. Imagine that an employer-administrator with respect to a "pension plan," ERISA § 3(2)(A), gathered employees, who were also beneficiaries of that retirement plan, to discuss a new "prepaid legal services" plan, *id.* § 3(1). Imagine further that, in that meeting, the employer-administrator made material misrepresentations about the legal services plan. It would be difficult to say in that circumstance, that the employer's fiduciary status with respect to the retirement plan means that its statements regarding the *unconnected* legal services plan were made in a fiduciary capacity. Again turning back to *Varity*, it would be quite difficult to say that the employer was "administering" the "pension plan" when it made the misrepresentations.

burdened with providing a constant, ever-changing stream of information to inquisitive plan participants. And, most of such information actually would be useless, if not misleading, to employees, considering that many corporate ideas and strategies never reach maturity, or else metamorphose so dramatically along the way, that early disclosure would be of little value. Furthermore, requiring employers to reveal too soon their internal deliberations to inquiring beneficiaries could seriously "impair the achievement of legitimate business goals" by allowing competitors to know that the employer is considering a labor reduction, a site-change, a merger, or some other strategic move.

Even more importantly, we believe the [serious consideration] standard protects employees' access to material information without discouraging employers from improving their ERISA plans in the first place. As recognized by the Sixth Circuit, "changing circumstances, such as the need to reduce labor costs, might require an employer to sweeten its severance package, and an employer should not be forever deterred from giving its employees a better deal merely because it did not clearly indicate to a previous employee that a better deal might one day be proposed." Moreover, employers often decide to "sweeten" an early retirement plan only after the employer has determined that not enough employees are opting to retire under the existing one. . . . Thus, precipitous liability could push employers in the direction of involuntary lay-offs, a common alternative to early retirement inducements. The [serious consideration] standard minimizes this possibility.

Id. at 1522 (citations omitted).

The opposite view originated in the Second Circuit and has come to be known as the "materiality test." In *Ballone v. Eastman Kodak Co.*, 109 F.3d 117 (2d Cir. 1997), the Second Circuit rejected that "serious consideration of a future plan is a prerequisite to liability for misstatements regarding the availability of future pension benefits." The key inquiry, that court explained, is whether misrepresentations are "material," and they are "material if they would induce reasonable reliance"; "serious consideration" is but one factor in that inquiry. Courts that have rejected the "serious consideration" prerequisite for misrepresentations, and instead have adopted the "materiality" test, reflect the concern that the serious consideration prerequisite would give an employer-administrator "a free zone for lying" and misleading employees about the availability of a future plan that is just around the corner but not yet on senior management's desk for approval. *Martinez v. Schlumberger, Ltd.*, 338 F.3d 407, 428 (5th Cir. 2003). . . .

In my view, cases that have adopted this latter view reflect a far more profound appreciation of Congressional concerns in this area and a more realistic understanding of the practicalities of the situation. The circuits that have subscribed to this materiality test have held that an employer-administrator does not have a duty *affirmatively to disclose* deliberations regarding a new plan absent "serious consideration" of that plan, *but* it cannot make material *affirmative misrepresentations* regarding a plan in formation but not yet under "serious consideration." *See id.* at 429-31. In short, these circuits hold that the employer-administrator can choose not to speak until a plan is under "serious consideration," but if it does speak, it cannot mislead. . . .

In sum, I take the view that the proper course for an employer to follow is not to affect the employee's decision whether to retire in any way — not by lying to them to induce them to retire before implementation of an enhanced early retirement program, nor by being forced to tip off the employees to its business strategies to aid them in taking best advantage of the company's future plans. This middle road will allow the company to make its business decisions without hindrance while prohibiting it from tricking its employees into retirement by making guarantees it knows to be false. . . .

2.

ComEd made affirmative representations to Mr. Beach. Employing the materiality test, I would uphold the district court's determination that the misrepresentations made to Mr. Beach were material. "Where an ERISA fiduciary makes guarantees regarding future benefits that misrepresent present facts, the misrepresentations are material if they would induce a reasonable person to rely upon them." *Ballone*, 109 F.3d at 122. In addition to considering the "serious consideration" given to a plan, the following factors are utilized in deciding materiality:

> [1] how significantly the statement misrepresents the present status of internal deliberations regarding future plan changes, [2] the special relationship of trust and confidence between the plan fiduciary and beneficiary, [3] whether the employee was aware of other information or statements from the company tending to minimize the importance of the misrepresentation or should have been so aware . . ., and [4] the specificity of the assurance.

Id. at 125 (citations omitted).

Mr. Beach was repeatedly told that "absolutely" the company was not going to offer his department (Transmission & Distribution or T&D) a package and even if ComEd were considering a package, T&D would not be included. Contrary to ComEd's assertions, these representations significantly "misrepresent[ed] the [then-]present status of internal deliberations." *Ballone*, 109 F.3d at 125. There is no evidence in the record that ComEd definitively had decided it *would not*, after reorganization, offer a severance plan; indeed, there are not even any facts that would suggest that conclusion. On the other hand, evidence supports that there was a possibility that the reorganization study in T&D would ultimately result in the offering of a severance plan to some employees in T&D. For example, it is undisputed that documents in the record indicate that, as of June 1997, the reorganization plan called for excess employees in T&D, and that between 1994 and 1997, ComEd dealt with excess employees through involuntary and voluntary severance packages on twenty to thirty occasions. Of course, the record supports that, at the time of the misrepresentations, there was a possibility that no severance plan would be offered in T&D, but as Mr. Beach explained: "ComEd does not explain how the *possibility* that a package might not be offered could render a specific assurance that a package for his department was an *impossibility* a truthful and complete statement of then existing fact."

Moreover, these misstatements were more than co-employee "mispredictions." *Ballone*, 109 F.3d at 125 ("Whereas mere mispredictions are not actionable, false statements about future benefits may be material if couched as a guarantee, especially where, as alleged here, the guarantee is supported by specific statements of fact.") (citations omitted)). Mr. Beach was not given mere unadorned speculation regarding the company and its future benefits; rather, he was told specifically that *his department* would not, under any circumstances, be receiving a severance plan. Given the numerous, concrete assurances from several human resources staff, Mr. Beach understandably believed that the staff had not given him their *personal opinions* on the future, but that they had relayed to him the *fact* that ComEd had made a corporate decision that T&D would not be considered for a package. Further, the misrepresentations did not contain any indication of a lack of finality or that the decision was subject to change, and the record is without any indication that ComEd released "other information or statements" that rebutted or "tended to minimize the importance of the misrepresentation[s]." *Ballone*, 109 F.3d at 125.

At the end of the day, in a case such as this, materiality ultimately turns on whether the misrepresentations would induce a reasonable person in Mr. Beach's situation to rely or, in the words of the Third Circuit, the likelihood that the misrepresentations would mislead a reasonable employee in Mr. Beach's situation "in making an adequately informed decision about if and when to retire." *Fischer v. Philadelphia Elec. Co.*, 994 F.2d 130, 135 (3d Cir. 1993) ("*Fischer I*"). Although only a small percentage of T&D employees were ultimately offered the VSP, the undisputed evidence is that Mr. Beach left "his final commitment to retire open until the last possible day, June 19, 1997, in case there [sic] the chance for a *possible* VSP arose." Moreover, it is important to remember that, due to his wife's ailment, Mr. Beach had a special need for the health benefits offered in the VSP. Finally, the probability of a severance plan being offered in T&D — like the twenty to thirty severance plans offered before by ComEd — was not so small that it reasonably could not have affected Mr. Beach's retirement calculation. Given the record in this case, the district court's determination of materiality should remain undisturbed. . . .

One final issue remains to be addressed. It is undisputed that ComEd's employees did not intend to deceive Mr. Beach when they told him that no severance plan in T&D would be offered. ComEd argued to this court that this lack of scienter by ComEd's human resources representatives demands judgments in its favor, and the majority hints, in dicta, ComEd is correct. However, importing the intent to deceive requirement — synonymous in tort law with fraud or deceit — into this type of ERISA fiduciary duty case lacks any grounding. . . .

The plain language of ERISA's fiduciary duty provision points in the opposite direction. ERISA §§ 404(a) is entitled "Prudent man standard of care," and its duty of care portion, §§ 404(a)(1)(B), requires that the fiduciary discharge its duties "with the care, skill, prudence, and diligence under the circumstances then prevailing that a prudent man acting in a like capacity and familiar with such matters. . . ." "ERISA requires more of a fiduciary in discharging such duties than that he or she simply refrain from outright lying." *Hudson v. Gen. Dynamics Corp.*, 118 F. Supp. 2d 226, 246 (D. Conn. 2000).

To the extent ComEd's argument for requiring intent focuses only on the fiduciary plan administrator's non-fiduciary agents (i.e., the benefits representatives) and not the fiduciary itself, that too is unconvincing. First, this and other courts have held that an ERISA fiduciary can be liable for the misrepresentations of its non-fiduciary agents under the apparent authority doctrine. The apparent authority doctrine focuses on the reasonable reliance of the employee; it is irrelevant to the subjective intent of the agent. Moreover, shielding fiduciary/principals from liability because their non-fiduciary agents were without knowledge or intent would allow an employer-administrator to keep benefits representatives "out of the loop" and then avoid liability by saying their agents responded "ignorantly but truthfully." *Bins v. Exxon Co.*, 220 F.3d 1042, 1049 n. 6 (9th Cir. 2000) (en banc); *Fischer I*, 994 F.2d at 135 ("These obligations cannot be circumvented by building a 'Chinese wall' around those employees on whom plan participants reasonably rely for important information and guidance about retirement."). Furthermore, in this circumstance, it is not unreasonable to place the burden on the employer-administrator, the party with the information, to provide correct information to its front-line staff so that they do not mislead and injure employee beneficiaries.

For these reasons, I would hold that when an employer-administrator speaks — either directly or through its benefits representatives — it violates its fiduciary duties when it affirmatively misinforms a beneficiary knowing its statement is false, when it recklessly misinforms not knowing whether its statement "is true or not," and when it misinforms under circumstances indicating it should have known the falsity of its statement. This is not a "duty of prevision" or a "standard of absolute liability," rather, it is a standard which is consistent with the common law of trusts . . . and, in my opinion, appropriately balances the relative interests ERISA was intended to oblige. In this case, this standard is easily satisfied: ComEd's human resources personnel had absolutely no basis for their misrepresentations; at the least, they should have known better.

NOTE

Liability and Preemption. *Varity Corp.* made it clear that individual relief was available for fiduciary violations. *Varity Corp. v. Howe*, 516 U.S. 1075, 1075-79 (limiting *Massachusetts Mut. Life Ins. Co. v. Russell*, 473 U.S. 134 (1985)). Thus, to the extent a fiduciary breaches fiduciary duties by misleading plaintiffs in a situation like *Beach*, they will be able to recover individual damages under ERISA.

The plaintiffs will be in a more difficult position, however, if only non-fiduciaries mislead the plaintiffs. There is no non-fiduciary liability under ERISA. *Mertens v. Hewitt Assocs.*, 508 U.S. 248 (1993); *Reich v. Rowe*, 20 F.3d

25 (1st Cir. 1994). Plaintiffs could attempt to allege state law claims instead, but those claims may be preempted. We will consider preemption issues in the next chapter.

DONOVAN v. BIERWIRTH
United States Court of Appeals, Second Circuit
680 F.2d 263 (1982)

FRIENDLY, CIRCUIT JUDGE:

This action was brought on October 19, 1981, by the Secretary of Labor (the Secretary) under § 502(e)(1) of the Employee Retirement Income Security Act of 1974 (ERISA) in the District Court for the Eastern District of New York, against John C. Bierwirth, Robert G. Freese and Carl A. Paladino, Trustees of the Grumman Corporation Pension Plan (the Plan). The action stems from the unsuccessful tender offer by LTV Corporation (LTV) in the fall of 1981 for some 70% of the outstanding common stock and convertible securities of Grumman Corporation (Grumman) at $45 per share. At the time of the offer the Plan owned some 525,000 shares of Grumman common stock, which it had acquired in the mid-1970's. As hereafter recounted, the Plan not only declined to tender its stock but purchased an additional 1,158,000 shares at an average price of $38.27 per share, at a total cost of $44,312,380. These acts, the Secretary's complaint alleged, constituted a violation of §§ 404(a) and 406(b) of ERISA. . . .

A number of participants in the Plan were allowed to intervene as defendants; a supporting affidavit of one of the Plan participants alleged that:

> [S]pontaneously and within days after this suit was commenced, Grumman employees at all levels and in all departments began to circulate petitions expressing their approval of the trustees' actions, as participants in the Pension Plan. To date, petitions have been signed by approximately 17,000 of the 22,000 employees who are Plan participants and beneficiaries. . . .

The LTV tender offer followed a scenario that has become familiar. On September 21, 1981, in the absence of defendant Bierwirth, Chairman of the Board of Grumman, who was on vacation, Joseph O. Gavin, Jr., President of Grumman, received a telephone call from Paul Thayer, Chairman of the Board and Chief Executive Officer of LTV, inviting him to discuss a possible merger. Gavin rejected the invitation. Evidently unsurprised, LTV, prior to the opening of trading on the New York Stock Exchange on September 23, issued a press release announcing that it was planning to make a cash tender offer at $45 per share for up to 70% of Grumman's common stock and securities representing or convertible into common stock. According to the press release, the offer constituted "the first step in a plan to acquire 100% of the voting equity of the Grumman Corporation." On September 21 and 22 Grumman stock had sold on the New York Stock Exchange at prices ranging between 23⅞ and 27¼. . . .

The LTV offer was made on September 24. It was conditioned upon the tender of a minimum of 50.01% of Grumman's common stock and securities representing or convertible into common stock. The withdrawal/proration date was 12:01 A.M. on October 16, 1981; the termination date was 12:01 A.M. on October 23. Bierwirth cut short his vacation and reached the Grumman office at midday on September 24.

Although SEC Rule 14e-2 gave the Grumman board 10 business days from the commencement of the offer to communicate its position, if any, the board lost no time in going into action. It met on September 25. By then the LTV offer had caused the price of Grumman stock to rise to a range of 32⅝ to 34¼. The board had before it a two page letter of Dillon, Read & Co., Inc., which had served Grumman as investment banker, stating in a conclusory fashion that it was "of the opinion that the offer is inadequate from a financial point of view to holders of the Grumman securities." The letter said this conclusion was based on certain information of a business and financial nature regarding Grumman which was either publicly available or furnished to us by Grumman and [on] discussions with the management of Grumman regarding its business and prospects. The letter made no attempt at quantification of these factors, and no representative of Dillon, Read attended the meeting for questioning, although apparently there were some supporting financial materials available. Defendant Robert G. Freese had also prepared some projections which are not in the record. The board unanimously adopted a resolution to oppose the tender offer, and issued a press release to that effect, saying that the board had concluded that "the offer is inadequate, and not in the best interests of Grumman, its shareholders, employees or the United States."

On September 28 Grumman began [an action alleging inadequate disclosure and violation of § 7 of the Clayton Act] which was to lead to the injunction of the tender offer. On the same day defendant Bierwirth, Chairman of the Board of Grumman, sent a letter to the company's shareholders seeking their help in defeating the offer. The letter stated:

> We're very optimistic about our chances of defeating the takeover bid. About a third of all shares are held by Grumman's employee investment and pension plans. These plans are managed by Grummanites who will look long and hard at how well their fellow members would be served by selling off Grumman stock. Much of the rest is owned by Grumman people who, I believe, understand their future is worth more than a quick return on a block of shares.

The reasons given for opposing LTV's offer were the inadequacy of the price and others, relating to the pension fund, set forth in the margin.[3] The letter concluded by announcing that "Grumman's management is totally committed to defeating this takeover attempt," and by pleading "If you own Grumman shares, don't sell out to LTV."

On September 30, at the invitation of George Petrilak, President of the Grumman Retirees Club, Bierwirth met with 300 retirees to discuss the LTV offer. An affidavit of Petrilak avers that "there was great concern expressed

---

[3] "There's one other factor to keep in mind: your pension fund. It's Grumman's policy to fully fund its employee pension fund. In contrast, LTV's pension fund right now is underfunded by almost a quarter of a billion dollars. Grumman people could lose if the two funds were to be merged."

by the members as to the possible impact of LTV succeeding in their tender offer upon their pensions," and said that "[t]he overwhelming attitude of the retirees was 'what is good for Grumman is good for retirees.'" The Club purchased an advertisement appearing in Newsday, a Long Island newspaper, on October 13, headed

Grumman retirees protect your pension.
Do not tender your stock to LTV. . . .

The Grumman Pension Plan, established in 1943, is a "defined benefit plan" . . . covering both salaried and hourly employees. Initially banking institutions had acted as trustees of the Plan. However, in 1973 Grumman adopted a policy of having officers of Grumman or its affiliates serve as trustees, as permitted by § 408(c)(3) of ERISA. The trustees in the fall of 1981 were Bierwirth; Freese, chief financial officer of Grumman since 1972; and Carl A. Paladino, Treasurer of Grumman Aerospace Corporation since 1969. John Mullan, associate general counsel of Grumman, has served as counsel to the trustees and regularly attended their meetings. Sometime prior to January 1, 1975, the Plan had acquired 525,000 Grumman shares.

On September 28 Freese mentioned to Bierwirth that the trustees "are going to have to get together here at some point and decide what [to] do in regard to the holdings of Grumman stock." Bierwirth agreed. . . . During the next ten days, the three trustees had casual conversations as they happened to meet each other. Nothing was said about the Plan's buying Grumman shares and no financial data were assembled for the meeting. Bierwirth had been informed by Mullan that if LTV succeeded, it could "merge the pension Plan though it may take them some time" and also "could cancel the Plan to the extent that they eliminate the Fund although of course they would retain the corporate obligation to pay," and by unidentified other sources that changing the presumed earnings rate would permit the declaration of some of the fund as surplus and recapture for the corporation.

[T]he Plan trustees' meeting . . . was held on October 7. . . . Mullan made a ten minute presentation dealing with ERISA, pointing out that the trustees' decisions "as far as the Grumman stock was concerned had to be predicated solely upon the best interests of the participants of the Plan." There was then a general discussion of how the trustees felt about LTV, the Dillon, Read opinion letter, and Freese's five year financial projections for Grumman. Elaborating on the discussion of LTV, Freese mentioned concern about the underfunding of "their pension plan," LTV's highly leveraged debt situation which would be aggravated by the need for borrowing to finance the acquisition of Grumman, contingent liability with respect to environmental problems and a large number of pending lawsuits and alleged SEC violations, all of which was revealed in a recent LTV prospectus. . . . Freese expressed concern that the assumed rate of return used by LTV's pension plan was higher than that used by other companies and that LTV would have trouble making contributions to their pension plan. Bierwirth testified that the trustees "were aware of" a report about Grumman by Lehman Brothers Kuhn Loeb Inc. (Lehman Brothers). This report, dated July 8, 1981, which recommended purchase of Grumman common stock, then selling at $28 per share, projected a

1981-84 earnings progression of $2.75, $5.00, $6.50 and $7.50, and contained financial analysis supporting the estimates. . . .

After a half hour's discussion the trustees voted not to tender the 525,000 Grumman shares held by the Plan. According to Bierwirth the trustees "then discussed whether we should take a second step. If we did not want to tender the stock at $45 a share, should we then consider buying additional shares, the market then being in the 30's?" A merit of such a purchase would be in making it more difficult for LTV to gain control of the pension fund. However, "it was also important that a further investment in Grumman shares be the right thing for us to do." "[A] number of fortuitous events had occurred during the summer and early in September which greatly enhanced the outlook for Grumman" and had made Bierwirth "feel earlier that a further investment in Grumman was desirable and should be recommended to the Trustees come this fall." While it had been "very difficult to accumulate substantial positions in Grumman stock," which ordinarily traded at volumes of 20,000 shares a day, the daily volume of half a million shares induced by the LTV offer made it "possible to accumulate a major position in Grumman stock without affecting the price all that much." Bierwirth was then of the view that "probably a majority of the stock would not be tendered" but could not feel confident about it. He recognized that if the LTV tender offer were abandoned, selling by arbitrageurs would push the price down. Following their discussion of these ideas, the trustees concluded that purchases of Grumman stock up to the maximum of 10% of the value of the Plan's assets permitted by § 407(a)(2) of ERISA would be prudent. . . .

The trustees met briefly on Monday, October 12, and authorized the Plan's purchase of 1,275,000 additional Grumman shares — just short of ERISA's 10% limitation. A press release issued on October 13 stated that use of the authorization would increase the Plan's ownership of Grumman stock from 3.8% to approximately 8% of the outstanding fully diluted shares. The Plan, acting through Dillon, Read, purchased 958,000 shares at an average price of $38.61 per share on October 12 and an additional 200,000 shares on October 13 at an average price of $36.62, for a total cost of $44,312,380.

On the next day, October 14 . . . the district court temporarily enjoined the LTV offer, thereby drastically reducing its chances for success. The price of Grumman stock fell on October 15 to a range of 28¼-29½. After this court affirmed the temporary injunction, the price of Grumman shares was 28–28¾; the market value of the newly purchased shares was approximately $32,500,000. As this is written, the price is 26¼-26⅜. . . .

IV. *The Legal Standard . . .*

Sections 404(a)(1)(A) and (B) impose three different although overlapping standards. A fiduciary must discharge his duties "solely in the interests of the participants and beneficiaries." He must do this "for the exclusive purpose" of providing benefits to them. And he must comply "with the care, skill, prudence, and diligence under the circumstances then prevailing" of the traditional "prudent man."

The trustees urge that the mandates of § 404(a)(1)(A) and (B) must be interpreted in the light of two other sections of ERISA. One is § 408(c)(3) which permits the appointment of officers of the sponsoring corporation as trustees. The other is § 407(a)(3) which, as here applicable, permitted the Plan to acquire Grumman stock having an aggregate fair market value not exceeding 10% of the fair market value of the assets of the Plan. This provision, the trustees point out, was the result of a lengthy debate in which the Department of Labor played an important role; they rely especially on the following passage from its statement to the Senate Finance Committee:

> Especially significant among the expressly allowed transactions is that which permits, in most types of plans, investment of up to ten percent of the fund assets in securities issued by the employer of the employees who are participants in the plan. Since such an employer will often be an administrator of his plan, or will function as a trustee or in some other fiduciary capacity, this provision creates a limited exception to the listed proscription against self-dealing. The exception is made in recognition of *the symbiotic relationship* existing between the employer and the plan covering his employees. (Emphasis supplied).

Appellants do not contend that these provisions relieve corporate officers or directors who are trustees of a plan of the duties imposed by § 404(a) when dealing with stock of the corporation which is an asset of the Plan. They argue rather that, despite the words "sole" and "exclusive," such officers or directors do not violate their duties by following a course of action with respect to the plan which benefits the corporation as well as the beneficiaries.

We accept the argument but not the conclusion which appellants seem to think follows from it. Although officers of a corporation who are trustees of its pension plan do not violate their duties as trustees by taking action which, after careful and impartial investigation, they reasonably conclude best to promote the interests of participants and beneficiaries simply because it incidentally benefits the corporation or, indeed, themselves, their decisions must be made with an eye single to the interests of the participants and beneficiaries. RESTATEMENT (SECOND) OF TRUSTS § 170 (1959). This, in turn, imposes a duty on the trustees to avoid placing themselves in a position where their acts as officers or directors of the corporation will prevent their functioning with the complete loyalty to participants demanded of them as trustees of a pension plan.

There is much to be said for the Secretary's argument that the participation of Bierwirth and Freese in the directors' decision of September 25 press release announcing the unanimous decision of the board to do this on the ground, *inter alia,* of its inadequacy; the sending of Bierwirth's letter of September 28 repeating this and also announcing that the LTV offer was a threat to the pension fund; and the other activities of Bierwirth and Freese in opposing the offer precluded their exercising the detached judgment required of them as trustees of the Plan, and that the only proper course was for the trustees immediately to resign so that a neutral trustee or trustees could be swiftly appointed to serve for the duration of the tender offer. Looking at the matter realistically we find it almost impossible to see how Bierwirth and Freese, after what they had said and done between September 24 and October 7, could have voted to tender or even to sell the Plan's stock, no matter how compelling the evidence for one or the other of those courses might have been.[9] Grumman shareholders who had acted in accordance with the company's pleas would have had every reason to consider such action a breach of faith. . . .

The record contains specific instances of the trustees' failure to observe the high standard of duty placed upon them. Bierwirth and Freese should have been immediately aware of the difficult position which they occupied as a result of having decided as directors some of the same questions they would have to decide as trustees, and should have explored where their duty lay. Instead the question of a trustees' meeting was treated quite casually — something to be attended to when the hectic pace of fighting the tender offer would permit. One way for the trustees to inform themselves would have been to solicit the advice of independent counsel; Mullan, a junior Grumman employee, was under disabilities similar to those of the trustees themselves. He could hardly have been expected to tell the trustees that the better course would be to resign or even to suggest investigations which might alter the judgment of total commitment to defeating the LTV offer that management had already expressed. We do not mean by this either that trustees confronted with a difficult decision need always engage independent counsel or that engaging such counsel and following their advice will operate as a complete whitewash which, without more, satisfies ERISA's prudence requirement. But this was, and should have been perceived to be, an unusual situation peculiarly requiring legal advice from someone above the battle.

The trustees also failed to measure up to the standard required of them in failing to do a more thorough job in ascertaining the facts with respect to the LTV pension funds, the unfunded liabilities of which were to be a principal ground for their action, and investigating whether anything could be done to protect the Grumman pension fund in the event of an acquisition of Grumman by LTV. So far as the record shows, the sole knowledge the trustees had of the LTV pension plans came from two portions of the prospectus for the May 28, 1981, LTV stock offering. . . . The September 28 letter from Bierwirth to Grumman's shareholders drew on the prospectus' statement about unfunded liabilities but eliminated the phrase "which relates primarily to unfunded vested pension liabilities assumed in the purchase of Lykes." The omission of this clause was important because it created the false impression, on the basis of which the trustees could well have acted, that LTV had a single pension fund which had unfunded liabilities in the considerable amount stated. If, as the prospectus foreshadowed and investigation would have confirmed, the unfunded liabilities were principally in pension funds covering hourly employees of LTV's steel operations, the danger of these plans being

---

[9] We are not impressed with the defendants' argument that they, and particularly Bierwirth, had nothing to fear from the LTV offer in light of LTV's announced intention to make Grumman's office the headquarters of its aerospace division and to retain Bierwirth as C.E.O. of that division. No offer was made with respect to Freese or Paladino. Even as to Bierwirth there have been countless instances where, even when a proposal to retain the chief executive of the target was wholly sincere, he will have disappeared within a year or so. Moreover, being C.E.O. of a division of LTV was not the same thing as being C.E.O. of an independent Grumman. The press currently recounts how high corporate executives are equipping themselves with "golden parachutes" providing large benefits in the event that the executive is dismissed or even if he quits on his own volition after a takeover.

merged with Grumman's was considerably less than if LTV had a single underfunded pension fund.

The trustees' perception of danger would have been reduced yet further had they known that LTV treated a number of the 21 pension plans which it sponsored quite well. For example, the pension plan for salaried Vought employees was extremely well-funded, with an excess of current assets over vested liabilities of approximately $78,000,000. Other Vought plans, including one covering hourly workers, had not been treated so favorably, but nonetheless were in better financial condition than LTV's plans for employees in the steel industry. . . . Further inquiry in these areas . . . might well have changed the trustees' views regarding both the danger presented by LTV's offer to the Plan and their ability to obtain satisfactory protections from LTV for the Plan. In addition, even if the trustees' beliefs regarding the financial condition of LTV's pension plans and LTV's policies towards its plans had been entirely accurate, we see little in the record to indicate that they attempted to determine just what LTV could have done and could not have done to inflict financial harm upon the participants in Grumman's Plan.[14] The trustees easily could have retained an expert on ERISA to advise them on this subject. . . .

An even more telling point against the trustees is their swift movement from a decision not to tender or sell the shares already in the fund to a decision to invest more than $44,000,000 in the purchase of additional Grumman shares up to the 10% maximum permitted by § 407(a)(2) of ERISA. Their argument is that once they had reasonably decided not to tender the shares already in the fund since success of the offer would run counter to the interests of the beneficiaries, it followed that they should do everything else they lawfully could do to thwart the offer. This, however, should have involved a calculation of the risks and benefits involved. . . . Although Grumman shares may have seemed attractive when selling in the high 20's, with what appeared a good chance of appreciation, they were not necessarily attractive when, under the impetus of the tender offer, they had risen to the high 30's. Moreover, and even more important, in purchasing additional shares when they did, the trustees were buying into what, from their own point of view, was almost certainly a "no-win" situation. If the LTV offer succeeded, the Plan would be left as a minority stockholder in an LTV-controlled Grumman — a point that seems to have received no consideration. If it failed, as the Plan's purchase of additional 8% of the outstanding Grumman stock made more likely, the stock was almost certain to sink to its pre-offer level, as the trustees fully appreciated. Given the trustees' views as to the dim future of an LTV-controlled Grumman, it is thus exceedingly difficult to accept Bierwirth's testimony that the purchase of additional shares was justified from an investment standpoint — or even to conclude that the trustees really believed this. Investment considerations dictated a policy of waiting. If LTV's offer were accepted, the

---

[14] Counsel for the trustees argue that LTV could have merged the Grumman plan with an LTV plan, appointed new trustees, terminated the Grumman plan, and so forth. ERISA, of course, contains elaborate safeguards to protect employees from the financial consequences of such actions. Counsel for the trustees have not suggested how LTV could have avoided such safeguards, much less that the trustees seriously considered these factors in making their decision at the October 7 meeting.

trustees would not want more Grumman shares; if it failed, the shares would be obtainable at prices far below what was paid. Mid-October 1981 was thus the worst possible time for the Plan to buy Grumman stock as an investment.[16] It is almost impossible to believe that the trustees did not realize this and that their motive for purchasing the additional shares was for any purpose other than blocking the LTV offer. Moreover, even if we were to make the dubious assumption that a purchase for this purpose would have been permissible despite all the investment risks that it entailed, the trustees should at least have taken all reasonable steps to make sure the purchase was necessary. As indicated, Bierwirth was under the impression that the necessary 50.01% would not be tendered — an expectation not unnatural in view of the fact that Grumman's investment and pension plans already owned nearly a third of the shares — although he could not be sure. The record gives no explanation why, if additional shares were to be purchased, this could not have been done by Grumman, in some way that would not reduce the number of outstanding shares, with the bank credit Freese had negotiated in part for that very purpose, rather than by the Plan. There is also nothing to indicate that the trustees, or other Grumman officers or directors, had been willing to risk their own funds in buying additional Grumman shares. . . .

We do not join in all of the district judge's pejorative adjectives concerning the trustees. They were caught in a difficult and unusual situation — apparently, so far as shown in the briefs, one that had not arisen before. We accept that they were honestly convinced that acquisition of Grumman by the debt-ridden LTV would mean a less bright future for Grumman and also that an LTV acquisition posed some special dangers to the participants of the Plan.[17]

However, they should have realized that, since their judgment on this score could scarcely be unbiased, at the least they were bound to take every feasible precaution to see that they had carefully considered the other side, to free themselves, if indeed this was humanly possible, from any taint of the quick negative reaction characteristic of targets of hostile tender offers displayed at the September 24 board meeting, and particularly to consider the huge risks attendant on purchasing additional Grumman shares at a price substantially elevated by the tender offer. We need not decide whether even this would have sufficed; perhaps, after the events of late September, resignation was the only

---

[16] The judge was not bound to accept the trustees' claim that purchases of considerable amounts of Grumman stock could not be made (and that their failure to purchase Grumman stock earlier although their belief in its attractiveness was claimed to go back to the summer of 1981 was thereby explained) on the ground that, with a daily volume of only 20,000 shares, substantial purchases would have greatly increased the price. No expert testified to that effect and no explanation was offered how the Plan had managed to accumulate 525,000 shares when, as Bierwirth stated, the market had been much thinner. Even if we assume that a carefully executed buying program would have somewhat boosted the price, there was no testimony that this would have been anything like the increase of ten points that had resulted from LTV's $45 offer.

[17] These dangers included the low level of pension benefits allegedly maintained by LTV; the fact that while LTV complied only with the minimum funding requirements of ERISA, Grumman contributed the impliedly higher amount of the maximum amount deductible under the IRC; the fact that LTV could merge or terminate the Plan; the near certainty that LTV would appoint new trustees for the Plan; and the danger that, even if it had the best of intentions towards the Grumman Plan, LTV's financial condition might preclude it from treating the Plan favorably.

proper course. It is enough that, for the reasons we have indicated . . . the district judge was warranted in concluding, on the materials before him, that the trustees had not measured up to the high standards imposed by § 404(a)(1)(A) and (B) of ERISA. How the situation will appear after a trial is a different matter which we cannot now decide.

NOTES

1. *An Eye Single.* The court held that the trustees were to make their decisions with "an eye single to the interests of the participants and beneficiaries." More than three-quarters of the participants and beneficiaries signed petitions *supporting* the trustees' decisions. Why? With this backing from the group to be protected, why didn't the "eye single" standard cause the trustees' decisions to be upheld despite their "no win" financial prospects?

One reading of *Bierwirth* is that it adopted an "eye single with blinders" standard. The trustees were to act with only the interests of participants and beneficiaries in mind, but not with *all* of their interests in mind; their interests in continuing employment were not to be considered. Ironically, this resulted in protection for parties other than the participants and beneficiaries. Since this was a defined benefit plan, Grumman stockholders were the parties primarily interested in the financial prospects of the pension fund; they were the ones who would be liable if the fund ran short.

2. *Social Investing.* Social investing occurs when pension fund trustees make investments based on factors other than investment return. Social investing takes many forms, including investments that involve moral or political issues, investments targeted to improve the economic well-being of a State or region, and investments intended to enhance the non-retirement well-being of participants (such as below-market-rate housing loans).

Bierwirth's "eye single" interpretation of ERISA's fiduciary duties implies that social investing is improper. Investment decisions made primarily to benefit someone in South Africa or someone in the local economy generally conflict with the duty under ERISA to act solely in the interest of participants and beneficiaries. § 404. At the same time, however, fiduciaries may take social goals into consideration in making an investment decision if they are "costless" to participants and beneficiaries. If a trustee is presented with two investments with equal risk and return characteristics, the trustee may select one over the other *because* it provides greater social benefits. *See* 29 C.F.R. § 2509.94-1; Uniform Management of Public Employee Retirement Systems Act, § 8(a)(5), 7A U.L.A. 510 (1997). Do you think that standard provides trustees with sufficient discretion to engage in socially responsible investing? Or too much discretion? *Compare* Joel C. Dobris, *Arguments in Favor of Fiduciary Divestment of "South African" Securities*, 65 NEB. L. REV. 209 (1986), *with* John H. Langbein & Richard A. Posner, *Social Investing and the Law of Trusts*, 79 MICH. L. REV. 72 (1980).

3. *The Standard of Judicial Review.* In *Firestone Tire & Rubber Co. v. Bruch*, 489 U.S. 101 (1989), Firestone sold five of its plants to Occidental. Employees who worked at the plants claimed severance pay benefits when Firestone terminated them, even though they were immediately rehired by

Occidental at the same pay and position. Firestone denied the claims and the employees sued. The issue in *Firestone* was what standard should the courts use in reviewing decisions like these? On the one hand, a deferential standard of review, such as the arbitrary and capricious standard, would promote efficient plan administration, discourage litigation, and, hence, encourage employers to provide benefits. On the other hand, the administrators making benefits determinations are often operating under a conflict of interest. In *Firestone*, for example, the administrators making the severance pay determination were company employees who probably owed their primary loyalties to their employer and, since the plan was unfunded, the company stood to gain directly from a denial of benefits. *See* ERISA § 408(c)(3) (specifically permitting employers to appoint officers and employees to fiduciary positions). The Supreme Court held in *Firestone* that the courts should use a *de novo* standard in reviewing benefits decisions made by ERISA fiduciaries, unless the plan provides for a narrower standard of judicial review by giving the fiduciary discretionary authority to make benefit determinations and construe the plan. Since the severance pay plan in *Firestone* did not provide for a narrower standard of review, the Court held that the *de novo* standard applied.

The *Firestone* decision has been harshly criticized. *See* John H. Langbein, *The Supreme Court Flunks Trusts,* 1990 SUP. CT. REV. 207 (calling the decision "a crude piece of work" and "doctrinal hash"). The predictable result of *Firestone* has been that plan sponsors have amended their plans to provide for narrower standards of review. One court has gone so far as to draft model "safe harbor" language to facilitate these efforts. *Herzberger v. Standard Ins. Co.,* 205 F.3d 327, 331 (7th Cir. 2000). But what standard of review should courts apply when the plan provides for a narrower standard, but the fiduciary is operating under some type of conflict? *Firestone* provides no guidance. Lower courts have generally held that a conflict justifies stricter judicial scrutiny, but have differed on the details. *Compare Anderson v. Blue Cross & Blue Shield,* 898 F.2d 1556 (11th Cir. 1990) (conflict of interest means actions of fiduciary are "presumptively void" and must be affirmatively justified), *with Vega v. National Life Ins. Servs., Inc.,* 188 F.3d 287 (5th Cir. 1999) (en banc) (conflict of interest means court should use a "sliding scale" standard of review which reduces deference in proportion to fiduciary's conflict of interest).

4. ***Other Protection Against Conflicts.*** Do conflicts between the interests of a plan administrator and participants and beneficiaries always mean that a strict standard of judicial review is necessary? Perhaps not. Plan participants and beneficiaries may be adequately protected from non-neutral decisionmakers by factors other than strict standards of judicial review. For example, benefit plan decisions are sometimes made in the context of repeat players involved in long-term relationships. In these circumstances, employers would not want to develop reputations for sharp practices that might reduce morale or, indeed, decrease the value employees place on benefit programs. Similarly, unions are often available as monitors. *See* Daniel Fischel & John H. Langbein, *ERISA's Fundamental Contradiction: The Exclusive Benefit Rule,* 55 U. CHI. L. REV. 1105, 1131-32 (1988). A strict standard of review, such as the *de novo* standard, might be reserved for situations where these types of alternative protections against abuse are not present.

E. PLANS OF DISTRESSED EMPLOYERS

Safeguarding pensions when employers are distressed is another component of ERISA's broader goal of protecting the retirement security of employees. ERISA's vesting and fiduciary protections would be meaningless if employers could effectively forfeit employee interests at any time by terminating or abandoning their plans.

1. DEFINED-BENEFIT PLANS

PENSION BENEFIT GUARANTY CORP. v. LTV CORP.
United States Supreme Court
496 U.S. 633 (1990)

JUSTICE BLACKMUN delivered the opinion of the Court.

In this case we must determine whether the decision of the Pension Benefit Guaranty Corporation (PBGC) to restore certain pension plans under § 4047 of the Employee Retirement Income Security Act of 1974 (ERISA) was, as the Court of Appeals concluded, arbitrary and capricious or contrary to law, within the meaning of § 706 of the Administrative Procedure Act (APA).

I

Petitioner PBGC is a wholly owned United States Government corporation. . . . The PBGC administers and enforces Title IV of ERISA. Title IV includes a mandatory Government insurance program that protects the pension benefits of over 30 million private-sector American workers who participate in plans covered by the Title. In enacting Title IV, Congress sought to ensure that employees and their beneficiaries would not be completely "deprived of anticipated retirement benefits by the termination of pension plans before sufficient funds have been accumulated in the plans."

When a plan covered under Title IV terminates with insufficient assets to satisfy its pension obligations to the employees, the PBGC becomes trustee of the plan, taking over the plan's assets and liabilities. The PBGC then uses the plan's assets to cover what it can of the benefit obligations. The PBGC then must add its own funds to ensure payment of most of the remaining "nonforfeitable" benefits, *i.e.*, those benefits to which participants have earned entitlement under the plan terms as of the date of termination. ERISA does place limits on the benefits PBGC may guarantee upon plan termination, however, even if an employee is entitled to greater benefits under the terms of the plan.[*] In addition, benefit increases resulting from plan amendments adopted within five years of the termination are not paid in full. Finally, active plan participants (current employees) cease to earn additional benefits under

---

[*] The maximum monthly pension benefit insured by the PBGC was $3,972 in 2006. The amount is inflation-indexed.

the plan upon its termination, and lose entitlement to most benefits not yet fully earned as of the date of plan termination.

The cost of the PBGC insurance is borne primarily by employers that maintain ongoing pension plans. Sections 4006 and 4007 of ERISA require these employers to pay annual premiums.** The insurance program is also financed by statutory liability imposed on employers who terminate underfunded pension plans. Upon termination, the employer becomes liable to the PBGC for the benefits that the PBGC will pay out. Because the PBGC historically has recovered only a small portion of that liability, Congress repeatedly has been forced to increase the annual premiums. Even with these increases, the PBGC in its most recent Annual Report noted liabilities of $4 billion and assets of only $2.4 billion, leaving a deficit of over $1.5 billion.***

As noted above, plan termination is the insurable event under Title IV. Plans may be terminated "voluntarily" by an employer or "involuntarily" by the PBGC. An employer may terminate a plan voluntarily in one of two ways. It may proceed with a "standard termination" only if it has sufficient assets to pay all benefit commitments. A standard termination thus does not implicate PBGC insurance responsibilities. If an employer wishes to terminate a plan whose assets are insufficient to pay all benefits, the employer must demonstrate that it is in financial "distress" as defined in [Section 4041(c) of ERISA]. Neither a standard nor a distress termination by the employer, however, is permitted if termination would violate the terms of an existing collective-bargaining agreement.

The PBGC, though, may terminate a plan "involuntarily," notwithstanding the existence of a collective-bargaining agreement. Section 4042 of ERISA provides that the PBGC may terminate a plan [because, among other reasons, "the] possible long-run loss of the [PBGC] with respect to the plan may reasonably be expected to increase unreasonably if the plan is not terminated."

Termination can be undone by PBGC. Section 4047 of ERISA [permits the PBGC to] "restore the plan to its pretermination status, including, but not limited to, the transfer to the employer or a plan administrator of control of part or all of the remaining assets and liabilities of the plan." When a plan is restored, full benefits are reinstated, and the employer, rather than the PBGC, again is responsible for the plan's unfunded liabilities.

II

This case arose after respondent The LTV Corporation (LTV Corp.) and many of its subsidiaries, including LTV Steel Company Inc., (LTV Steel) (collectively LTV), in July 1986 filed petitions for reorganization under Chapter 11 of the Bankruptcy Code. At that time, LTV Steel was the sponsor of three

---

** The basic premium is $30 per participant per year for single-employer plans. After 2006, this amount will be inflation-indexed. Underfunded plans must also pay a supplemental premium. In addition, pension plan sponsors who have plans taken over by the PBGC and then later emerge from bankruptcy must pay termination premiums of $1,250 per participant for up to three years.

*** The 2005 Annual Report noted assets of $56 billion and liabilities of $79 billion and, hence, a net deficit of $23 billion. Five years earlier, the PBGC had noted a net surplus of about $10 billion. As this suggests, these numbers vary greatly depending on the economy.

defined benefit pension plans (the Plans) covered by Title IV of ERISA. Two of the Plans were the products of collective-bargaining negotiations with the United Steelworkers of America. The third was for nonunion salaried employees. Chronically underfunded, the Plans, by late 1986, had unfunded liabilities for promised benefits of almost $2.3 billion. Approximately $2.1 billion of this amount was covered by PBGC insurance.

It is undisputed that one of LTV Corp.'s principal goals in filing the Chapter 11 petitions was the restructuring of LTV Steel's pension obligations, a goal which could be accomplished if the Plans were terminated and responsibility for the unfunded liabilities was placed on the PBGC. LTV Steel then could negotiate with its employees for new pension arrangements. LTV, however, could not voluntarily terminate the Plans because two of them had been negotiated in collective bargaining. LTV therefore sought to have the PBGC terminate the Plans.

To that end, LTV advised the PBGC in 1986 that it could not continue to provide complete funding for the Plans. PBGC estimated that, without continued funding, the Plans' $2.1 billion underfunding could increase by as much as $65 million by December 1987 and by another $63 million by December 1988, unless the Plans were terminated. Moreover, extensive plant shutdowns were anticipated. These shutdowns, if they occurred before the Plans were terminated, would have required the payment of significant "shutdown benefits." The PBGC estimated that such benefits could increase the Plans' liabilities by as much as $300 million to $700 million, of which up to $500 million was covered by PBGC insurance. Confronted with this information, the PBGC, invoking § 4042(a)(4) of ERISA, determined that the Plans should be terminated in order to protect the insurance program from the unreasonable risk of large losses, and commenced termination proceedings in the District Court. With LTV's consent, the Plans were terminated effective January 13, 1987.

Because the Plans' participants lost some benefits as a result of the termination, the Steelworkers filed an adversary action against LTV in the Bankruptcy Court, challenging the termination and seeking an order directing LTV to make up the lost benefits. This action was settled, with LTV and the Steelworkers negotiating an interim collective-bargaining agreement that included new pension arrangements intended to make up benefits that plan participants lost as a result of the termination. New payments to retirees were based explicitly upon "a percentage of the difference between the benefit that was being paid under the Prior Plans and the amount paid by the PBGC." Retired participants were thereby placed in substantially the same positions they would have occupied had the old Plans never been terminated. The new agreements respecting active participants were also designed to replace benefits under the old Plans that were not insured by the PBGC, such as early-retirement benefits and shutdown benefits. With respect to shutdown benefits, LTV stated in Bankruptcy Court that the new benefits totaled "75% of benefits lost as a result of plan termination." With respect to some other kinds of benefits for active participants, the new arrangements provided 100% or more of the lost benefits.

The PBGC objected to these new pension agreements, characterizing them as "follow-on" plans. It defines a follow-on plan as a new benefit arrangement designed to wrap around the insurance benefits provided by the PBGC in such a way as to provide both retirees and active participants substantially the same benefits as they would have received had no termination occurred. The PBGC's policy against follow-on plans stems from the agency's belief that such plans are "abusive" of the insurance program and result in the PBGC's subsidizing an employer's ongoing pension program in a way not contemplated by Title IV. . . .

LTV ignored the PBGC's objections to the new pension arrangements and asked the Bankruptcy Court for permission to fund the follow-on plans. The Bankruptcy Court granted LTV's request. In doing so, however, it noted that the PBGC "may have legal options or avenues that it can assert administratively . . . to implement its policy goals. Nothing done here tonight precludes the PBGC from pursuing these options. . . ."

In early August 1987, the PBGC determined that the financial factors on which it had relied in terminating the Plans had changed significantly. Of particular significance to the PBGC was its belief that the steel industry, including LTV Steel, was experiencing a dramatic turnaround. As a result, the PBGC concluded it no longer faced the imminent risk, central to its original termination decision, of large unfunded liabilities stemming from plant shutdowns. . . . [B]ased upon LTV's improved financial circumstances and its follow-on plans, . . . the PBGC's Executive Director . . . decided to restore the Plans [under the PBGC's § 4047 powers]. . . .

LTV refused to comply with the restoration decision. This prompted the PBGC to initiate an enforcement action. . . .

III

A

The Court of Appeals first held that the restoration decision was arbitrary and capricious under § 706(2)(A) [of the Administrative Procedure Act] because the PBGC did not take account of all the areas of law the court deemed relevant to the restoration decision. The court expressed the view that "[b]ecause ERISA, bankruptcy and labor law are all involved in the case at hand, there must be a showing on the administrative record that PBGC, before reaching its decision, considered all of these areas of law, and to the extent possible, honored the policies underlying them." The court concluded that the administrative record did not reflect thorough and explicit consideration by the PBGC of the "policies and goals" of each of the three bodies of law. As the court put it, the PBGC "focused inordinately on ERISA." The Court of Appeals did not hold that the PBGC's decision *actually conflicted* with any provision in the bankruptcy or labor laws. . . . Rather the court held that because labor and bankruptcy law are "involved in the case at hand," the PBGC had an affirmative obligation, which had not been met, to address them.

The PBGC contends that the Court of Appeals misapplied the general rule that an agency must take into consideration all relevant factors by requiring the agency explicitly to consider and discuss labor and bankruptcy law. We agree.

First, and most important, we do not think that the requirement imposed by the Court of Appeals upon the PBGC can be reconciled with the plain language of § 4047, under which the PBGC is operating in this case. This section gives the PBGC the power to restore terminated plans in any case in which the PBGC determines such action to be "appropriate and consistent with its duties *under this title, [i.e.,* Title IV of ERISA]" (emphasis added). The statute does not direct the PBGC to make restoration decisions that further the "public interest" generally, but rather empowers the agency to restore when restoration would further the interests that Title IV of ERISA is designed to protect. Given this specific and unambiguous statutory mandate, we do not think that the PBGC did or could focus "inordinately" on ERISA in making its restoration decision.

Even if Congress' directive to the PBGC had not been so clear, we are not entirely sure that the Court of Appeals' holding makes good sense as a general principle of administrative law. The PBGC points up problems that would arise if federal courts routinely were to require each agency to take explicit account of public policies that derive from federal statutes other than the agency's enabling act. To begin with, there are numerous federal statutes that could be said to embody countless policies. If agency action may be disturbed whenever a reviewing court is able to point to an arguably relevant statutory policy that was not explicitly considered, then a very large number of agency decisions might be open to judicial invalidation.

The Court of Appeals' directive that the PBGC give effect to the "policies and goals" of other statutes, apart from what those statutes actually provide,[7] is questionable for another reason as well. Because the PBGC can claim no expertise in the labor and bankruptcy areas, it may be ill-equipped to undertake the difficult task of discerning and applying the "policies and goals" of those fields. . . .

For these reasons, we believe the Court of Appeals erred in holding that the PBGC's restoration decision was arbitrary and capricious because the agency failed adequately to consider principles and policies of bankruptcy law and labor law.

B

The Court of Appeals also rejected the grounds for restoration that the PBGC *did* assert and discuss. The court found that the first ground the PBGC proffered to support the restoration — its policy against follow-on plans — was contrary to law because there was no indication in the text of the restoration provision, § 4047, or its legislative history that Congress intended the PBGC to use successive benefit plans as a basis for restoration. The PBGC argues that in reaching this conclusion the Court of Appeals departed from traditional principles of statutory interpretation and judicial review of agency construction of statutes. Again, we must agree. . . .

---

[7] It is worth noting that the provisions of ERISA itself do take account of other areas of federal law. For example, as noted above, an employer may not voluntarily terminate a plan if to do so would violate the terms of a collective-bargaining agreement.

Here, the PBGC has interpreted § 4047 as giving it the power to base restoration decisions on the existence of follow-on plans. Our task . . . is to determine whether any clear congressional desire to avoid restoration decisions based on successive pension plans exists, and, if the answer is in the negative, whether the PBGC's policy is based upon a permissible construction of the statute.

Turning to the first half of the inquiry, we observe that the text of § 4047 does not evince a clear congressional intent to deprive the PBGC of the ability to base restoration decisions on the existence of follow-on plans. To the contrary, the textual grant of authority to the PBGC embodied in this section is broad. As noted above, the section authorizes the PBGC to restore terminated plans "in any such case in which [the PBGC] determines such action to be appropriate and consistent with its duties under [Title IV of ERISA]." The PBGC's duties consist primarily of furthering the statutory purposes of Title IV identified by Congress. These are:

> (1) to encourage the continuation and maintenance of voluntary private pension plans for the benefit of their participants;

> (2) to provide for the timely and uninterrupted payment of pension benefits to participants and beneficiaries under plans to which this subchapter applies; and

> (3) to maintain premiums established by [the PBGC] under [ERISA § 4006] at the lowest level consistent with carrying out the obligations of this subchapter. [ERISA § 4002(a)].

On their face, of course, none of these statutorily identified purposes has anything to say about the precise question at issue — the use of follow-on plans as a basis for restoration decisions.

Nor do any of the other traditional tools of statutory construction compel the conclusion that Congress intended that the PBGC not base its restoration decisions on follow-on plans. [The legislative history relied on by the Court of Appeals — a listing of the possible reasons for restoration in the 1974 legislative history that did not mention follow-on plans and the consideration and rejection of an amendment to ERISA in 1987 that would have explicitly permitted the PBGC to rely on follow-on plans — does not meet the "clear congressional intent" standard.]

Having determined that the PBGC's construction is not contrary to clear congressional intent, we still must ascertain whether the agency's policy is based upon a "permissible" construction of the statute, that is, a construction that is "rational and consistent with the statute." Respondents argue that the PBGC's anti-follow-on plan policy is irrational because, as a practical matter, no purpose is served when the PBGC bases a restoration decision on something other than the improved financial health of the employer. According to respondents, "financial improvement [is] both a necessary and a sufficient condition for restoration. The agency's asserted abuse policy . . . is *logically irrelevant* to the restoration decision." We think not. The PBGC's anti-follow-on policy is premised on the belief, which we find eminently reasonable, that employees will object more strenuously to a company's original decision to terminate a plan (or to take financial steps that make termination likely) if the company cannot use a follow-on plan to put the employees in the same (or a similar) position after termination as they were in before. The availability of a follow-on plan thus would remove a significant check — employee resistance — against termination of a pension plan.

Consequently, follow-on plans may tend to frustrate one of the objectives of ERISA that the PBGC is supposed to accomplish — the "continuation and maintenance of voluntary private pension plans." In addition, follow-on plans have a tendency to increase the PBGC's deficit and increase the insurance premiums all employers must pay, thereby frustrating another related statutory objective — the maintenance of low premiums. In short, the PBGC's construction based upon its conclusion that the existence of follow-on plans will lead to more plan terminations and increased PBGC liabilities is "assuredly a permissible one." Indeed, the judgments about the way the real world works that have gone into the PBGC's anti-follow-on policy are precisely the kind that agencies are better equipped to make than are courts.[8] This practical agency expertise is one of the principal justifications behind deference [to administrative agencies].

None of this is to say that financial improvement will never be relevant to a restoration decision. Indeed, if an employer's financial situation remains so dire that restoration would lead inevitably to immediate retermination, the PBGC may decide not to restore a terminated plan even where the employer has instituted a follow-on plan.[9] For present purposes, however, it is enough for us to decide that where, as here, there is no suggestion that immediate retermination of the plans will be necessary, it is rational for the PBGC to disfavor follow-on plans.

[JUSTICE WHITE, joined by JUSTICE O'CONNOR, wrote an opinion concurring in part and dissenting in part.]

JUSTICE STEVENS, dissenting.

In my opinion, at least with respect to ERISA plans that the PBGC has terminated involuntarily, the use of its restoration power under § 4047 to prohibit "follow-on" plans is contrary to the agency's statutory mandate. Unless there was a sufficient improvement in LTV's financial condition to justify the restoration order, I believe it should be set aside. I, therefore, would remand the case for a determination of whether that ground for the agency decision is adequately supported by the record.

---

[8] JUSTICE STEVENS suggests that the possibility of follow-on plans will make employees "no less likely to object to the financial steps that will lead to [an involuntary] plan termination because they would have no basis for belief that a union will insist on [the adoption of follow-on plans] when, perhaps years later, the PBGC involuntarily terminates the plan." There is no reason to believe, however, that financial decisions that lead to an involuntary termination always or ordinarily occur far in advance of the termination itself. Thus, as JUSTICE STEVENS himself acknowledges with respect to a voluntary termination, "those who could object to [the events resulting in an involuntary termination may also be] reasonably assured of receiving benefits when the insurance is paid." Moreover, even when an involuntary termination does not occur until well after the financial decisions that lead to termination are made, we think the PBGC's apparent belief that employee resistance to those financial decisions will be lessened to some degree by the prospect of follow-on plans after termination is not an unreasonable one.

[9] For example, the PBGC did not restore a fourth LTV plan that had been terminated because, among other things, the plan had insufficient assets to pay benefits when due.

A company that is undergoing reorganization under Chapter 11 of the Bankruptcy Code continues to operate an ongoing business and must have a satisfactory relationship with its work force in order to complete the reorganization process successfully. If its previous pension plans have been involuntarily terminated with the consequence that the PBGC has assumed the responsibility for discharging a significant share of the company's pension obligations, that responsibility by PBGC is an important resource on which the company has a right to rely during the reorganization process. It may use the financial cushion to fund capital investments, to pay current salary, or to satisfy contractual obligations, including the obligation to pay pension benefits. As long as the company uses its best efforts to complete the reorganization (and, incidentally, to reimburse PBGC for payments made to its former employees to the extent required by ERISA),[1] the PBGC does not have any reason to interfere with managerial decisions that the company makes and the bankruptcy court approves. Whether the company's resources are dedicated to current expenditures or capital investments and whether the package of employee benefits that is provided to the work force is composed entirely of wages, vacation pay, and health insurance, on the one hand, or includes additional pension benefits, on the other, should be matters of indifference to the PBGC. Indeed, if it was faithful to the statement of congressional purposes in ERISA, it should favor an alternative that increases the company's use and maintenance of pension plans and that provides for continued payment to existing plan beneficiaries. The follow-on plans, in my opinion, are wholly consistent with the purposes of ERISA.

According to the Court, the PBGC policy is premised on the belief that if the company cannot adopt a follow-on plan, the employees will object more strenuously (1) in the case of a voluntary termination, to the "company's original decision to terminate a plan"; and (2) in the case of an involuntary termination, to the company's decision "to take financial steps that make termination likely." That belief might be justified in the case of a voluntary termination of an ERISA plan. Since the follow-on plan would be adopted immediately after plan termination, those who could object to the insurable event are also reasonably assured of receiving benefits when the insurance is paid. That view is wholly unwarranted, however, in the case of an involuntary termination. The insurable event, plan termination, is within the control of the PBGC, which presumably has determined that the company does not have the financial resources to meet its current pension obligations. Even if the company could adopt a follow-on plan, the employees will be no less likely to object to the financial steps that will lead to plan termination because they would have no basis for belief that a union will insist on that course when, perhaps years later, the PBGC involuntarily terminates the plan. The safety that comes from a healthy pension plan will not be overcome by the hope that a future union will remember the interests of its retirees and former employees. Plan restoration in these circumstances is not a legitimate curative to

---

[1] At the time of the termination of the LTV plans, PBGC was entitled to recover only 75 percent of the amounts expended to discharge LTV's pension obligations. The statute has since been amended to authorize a 100 percent recovery. LTV represents that if the restoration order is upheld, and if — as seems highly probable — it is promptly followed by another termination, the PBGC bankruptcy claim will increase from about $2 billion to more than $3 billion. PBGC, of course, does not assert this change as a justification for the restoration order.

the problem of moral hazard, but rather constitutes punishment of both labor and management for the imprudence of their predecessors.

In the case of an involuntary termination, if a mistake in the financial analysis is made, or if there is a sufficient change in the financial condition of the company to justify a reinstatement of the company's obligation, the PBGC should use its restoration powers. Without such a financial justification, however, there is nothing in the statute to authorize the PBGC's use of that power to prevent a company from creating or maintaining the kind of employee benefit program that the statute was enacted to encourage.

Accordingly, I respectfully dissent.

NOTES

1. *Pension Termination Strategies.* The Pilots Retirement Plan for Delta Airlines permits pilots to retire with very short notice and to exit with a lump sum payment. As Delta became financially distressed and fell into bankruptcy, pilots began to retire. In October, 2005, the lump-sum option was suspended by ERISA rules designed to protect plans against liquidity shortfalls, but Delta was emerging from this situation in the summer of 2006. If the lump-sum option opened up again, Delta was convinced it would face a massive wave of pilot retirements for several reasons: the lump-sum payments would be large (many over $500,000 and some over $1 million), the pilots had taken large pay cuts that reduced the rewards of continuing to work, and the pilots knew that the lump sums would no longer be available if the plan were terminated in the future.

Delta's most pressing concern related to employment. Delta estimated that it would have to cancel thousands of flights if pilots retired as expected when the lump sums became available again. Many of the cancellations would be on short notice as the rules permitted pilots to provide notice of their retirement as late as the day before they retired. Of course, there were also serious concerns about the pension plan itself. If the expected retirements occurred and the lump-sum payments were made, Delta estimated it would owe the Pilots Retirement Plan about $1.5 billion when it emerged from bankruptcy less than a year later. ERISA contains anti-cutback rules that prohibited Delta from modifying or eliminating the lump-sum payment option itself, even if the pilots and their union agreed to the change.

What was Delta to do? Delta moved to terminate the pension plan which, among other things, would eliminate the favorable lump-sum payout option. This move was made in August, 2006, as this book is being prepared, so we do not yet know the ultimate resolution. The general point, however, is clear. Pensions and terminations are not only about retirement — they also have vital day-to-day consequences in the workplace.

2. *The Limits of Employee Protection.* Employees obviously receive some protections from the ERISA pension insurance scheme. But the protections are not absolute. *LTV Corp.* discusses some of the limits: a cap on the total amount of benefits insured, only partial coverage for benefits resulting from recent plan amendments, and no coverage for unvested and unearned benefits.

ERISA also fails to protect employee expectations of an inflation-resistant pension benefit. The promised benefit under a defined benefit plan is usually determined by multiplying a worker's final salary times years of service times a generosity factor (usually between .01 and .02). The final salary component is a rough inflation index. Terminating the plan removes the inflation index.

To illustrate, consider two employees. Both always work for employers with this defined benefit formula: $(.02) \times$ (years of service) $\times$ (final salary). Both work for twenty years. Employee A works for the same employer for the entire period. Employee B, however, works for one employer for ten years, but then that employer goes bankrupt and the plan is terminated, so Employee B works for a second employer for the remaining ten years. The inflation rate during the entire period is about 8% and wage increases have matched inflation. The salaries of both employees are $20,000 at the end of the first ten years and $40,000 at the end of their work lives. These are the pension benefits for the two employees:

<u>Employee A</u>

$(.02)\ (20)\ (\$40,000) = \$16,000$

<u>Employee B</u>

From first employer — $(.02)\ (10)\ (\$20,000) = \$\ 4,000$

From second employer — $(.02)\ (10)\ (\$40,000) = \underline{\$\ 8,000}$

Total $\$12,000$

Employee B receives less, because the plan termination deprived her of the inflation-indexing effect of the final salary component of the benefit formula for her first ten years of employment. (Note that this example also illustrates why pensions bond employees to particular firms. The result would be the same if Employee B voluntarily left her first employer after the first ten years.)

3. Allocating the Costs of Pension Insurance. As the *LTV Corp.* case indicates, the PBGC can seek to recover the cost of any benefits it pays from the employers whose plans are terminated. If all of the PBGC's expenses could be recovered in that way, the PBGC would provide only short-term insurance; the PBGC's primary role would be as an agency that enforces employer promises to pay pensions. But, of course, the PBGC does more than that. Many of the employers whose plans are terminated cannot pay, so the PBGC also fulfills a long-term insurance function.

The costs of this insurance are imposed on all plans covered by the PBGC insurance scheme. The *LTV Corp.* case discusses the current premium structure, which requires higher premiums from plans that pose a higher risk of claims upon the fund (as measured by unfunded vested benefits). Until the Pension Protection Act of 1987, the PBGC premiums did not reflect risk; instead, they were flat rate premiums which ranged over the years from $1 per plan participant in 1974 to $8.50 per plan participant in 1987.

4. The Opposite of Distress. Defined benefit plans can also become over-funded. When that occurs, employers, employees, and the government all have plausible claims to the excess benefits. Between 1980 and 1987, there was an explosion of voluntary plan terminations; to recoup excess funds, employers terminated more than 1,500 plans with reversions of at least $1 million each. Then Congress acted to discourage reversions by imposing nondeductible excise taxes of up to 50% on these types of reversion to employers. I.R.C. § 4980.

So what is an employer with a highly overfunded plan to do? Many options remain. For example:

- Quit making contributions to the plan until the overfunding disappears. *See* Richard A. Ippolito, *Reversion Taxes: Contingent Benefits, and the Decline in Pension Funding*, 77 J.L. & Econ. 199 (2001) (reversion tax has caused employers to reduce pension funding dramatically).

- Create new retirement benefits to use the surplus, while simultaneously serving other employer interests. For example, an employer interested in reducing its workforce might fund a generous early retirement program out of the surplus assets. *See Hughes Aircraft Co. v. Jacobson*, 525 U.S. 432 (1999) (ERISA not violated when employer used surplus assets to fund early retirement benefits).

- Use the surplus to cover unfunded liabilities for retiree health care benefits. The tax code specifically permits surplus pension assets to be used for this purpose. I.R.C. § 420.

- Acquire another company with an underfunded pension plan and merge the two plans. *Cf. Malia v. General Elec. Co.*, 23 F.3d 828 (3rd Cir.), *cert. denied*, 513 U.S. 956 (1994) (employees have no right to surplus assets when their plan merged with another plan).

2. DEFINED-CONTRIBUTION PLANS

JOHN H. LANGBEIN, THE ENRON PENSION INVESTMENT CATASTROPHE: WHY IT HAPPENED AND HOW CONGRESS SHOULD FIX IT, United States Senate, Committee on Governmental Affairs (Jan. 24, 2002)*

Enron Corp. sponsored a 401(k) pension plan for its employees. The plan permitted the employee to contribute up to 15 percent of his or her salary, subject to a ceiling. Enron made a matching contribution of half of what the employee contributed. The sums contributed by both employee and employer were tax deferred under Sections 401(a) and 401(k) of the Internal Revenue Code. The plan provided that Enron's contribution would be entirely in Enron stock. The employee participant could choose to invest his or her contribution among a menu of options, including leading well-diversified mutual funds or more Enron Stock.

The plan required the employee-participant to hold the employer-contributed Enron shares until age fifty. Only at that age could he or she direct that the Enron shares be sold and the proceeds redirected into other investments. With respect to these match shares, the plan made the employee-participants into involuntary Enron shareholders until age 50.

---

* Reprinted by permission of the author.

As Enron's financial difficulties began to be revealed in the fall of 2001, the value of Enron shares, including those held in the pension plan accounts, declined precipitously. Shares that had traded above $80 per share at the apogee are now effectively worthless. As a result, many Enron employees have lost huge portions of their expected retirement funds — both the employer match shares and those Enron shares that many employees elected to purchase with their own contributed funds.

Although some of the alleged financial skullduggery of Enron's managers, directors, and accountants may have violated ERISA fiduciary law, it is vital for Congress to understand that the key feature of the Enron plan that made it possible for these losses to occur — the large concentration of employer stock in the plan's investments — was permitted under ERISA, the federal pension regulatory law. . . .

401(k) plans such as Enron's are known as defined contribution (DC) plans, or in the language of ERISA, as "individual account plans." DC plans "provide for an individual account for each participant;" the participant's "benefits are based solely upon the amount contributed to the participant's account," plus the investment experience (dividends, gains or losses) of the account. ERISA § 3(34).

The distinctive feature of any DC plan is that investment risk rests entirely upon the account of each participating employee. The employee captures market gains, the employee suffers market declines.

By contrast, in a traditional defined benefit (DB) plan of the sort that prevails among large employers in manufacturing and transportation industries and utilities, the employer (or other sponsor) bears the investment risk. In a DB plan the employer promises the employee a certain benefit on retirement, and if the investments in the pension fund don't produce enough to pay the benefit, the employer must make up the shortfall from company assets. . . .

As ERISA now stands, the high concentration of employer stock that allowed the catastrophic losses to the Enron employees could only have occurred in a DC plan, because ERISA's diversification requirements (discussed below) would have prevented these concentrations in a DB plan. It would be a fallacy, however, to conclude that the problem lies in the nature of DC plans. The truth is that it is as easy to avoid over-concentration in a single stock in a DC plan as in a DB plan. For example, most of us who are employed in academia participate in DC plans operated by TIAA-CREF. TIAA-CREF diversifies its stock and bond investments across literally thousands of issues.

The ERISA failure that allowed the Enron employees' loss to occur is that ERISA contains an exception to its diversification requirement. ERISA allows certain types of DC plans, including 401(k) plans, to permit and/or require employees to hold these large concentrations of employer stock in their plan accounts.

Over the past two decades that 401(k) plans have been allowed there has been a huge increase in the use of DC plans, especially 401(k) plans. The Employee Benefits Research Institute (EBRI) reports that as of the year 2000, there were more than 327,000 401(k) plans in effect, covering more than 43 million active participants, holding assets of $1.8 trillion. There are many reasons for this complex development.

DC plans do have disadvantages, but they have two great advantages for employees that help explain their popularity.

First, DC plans offset the lack of portability in the private pension system. DC plans produce better results for the employee who works for several employers across his or her career than does a DB plan, because DB plans use career-average service formulas that favor long-service employees. DC plans are a response to the increasing mobility of the workforce.

Second, DC plans encourage employees to engage in more pension saving than usually occurs under DB plans, both because the transparency of the individual account mechanism is easier for the employee to understand and to value than a distant benefit formula; and because there are ways to arrange that any money in a DC account that the employee and his or her spouse do not turn out to need for their retirement will pass to their heirs. The ability to transfer the account balance on death encourages employees to make more ample provision for their retirement, secure in the knowledge that they will not forfeit the cushion.

Accordingly, the lesson to learn from the Enron debacle is not that DC plans should be restricted, but that the diversification standards that Congress wisely imposed on DB plans need to be extended to DC plans. . . .

The duty to diversify investments is a standard principle of good fiduciary investing practice, which was long ago absorbed into the trust investment law. ERISA has from its enactment in 1974 imposed this duty to diversify pension fund investments. ERISA § 404(a)(1)(C).

ERISA's duty to diversify does not, however, apply to all pension plans. Rather, Congress allowed an exception for certain types of DC plans. ERISA §§ 404(a)(2), 407(d)(3). That exception is a major mistake of pension policy, and until Congress fixes it, I can predict to you with utter certainty that cases like Enron will continue to occur.

Let me say a quick word about the underlying economics of the duty to diversify. The importance of diversification is by far the most important finding in the entire field of financial economics. Over the past 40 years, we have had a stream of empirical and theoretical studies, which have led so far to six Nobel prizes in economics, conclusively showing that there are large and essentially costless gains to diversifying an investment portfolio thoroughly.

Investment risk has three distinct components: market risk, industry risk, and firm risk. Market risk is common to all securities; it reflects general economic and political conditions, interest rates, and so forth, hence cannot be eliminated. Industry risk, by contrast, is specific to all the firms in each industry or industry grouping. Firm risk refers to factors that affect the fortunes only of the particular firm. My favorite illustration is the example of the international oil companies. All of them suffered from the 1973 Arab embargo (industry risk). By contrast, only Exxon incurred the liabilities arising from the great Alaskan oil spill of March 1989 (firm risk). Holding shares in other industries helped prudent investors to offset the decline of the oils in 1973; holding shares of other oils helped offset the decline in Exxon.

Only about 30 percent of the risk of security ownership is market risk, that is, risk that cannot be eliminated by diversification. By contrast, industry risk amounts to about 50 percent of investment risk, and firm risk comprises the remaining 20 percent. Thus, effective diversification can eliminate roughly 70 percent of investment risk.

And that is why, from the standpoint of good investment practice, a portfolio such as the Enron pension fund, so heavily concentrated in a single stock, any stock, is pure folly. But there are many plans sitting out there with even more employer stock than Enron. For example, as of January 2000, Proctor and Gamble had a DC plan with 96 percent in employer stock, Pfizer has one with 88 percent, Abbot Laboratories with 87 percent. . . .

A pension fund portfolio holding a massive part of its assets in any one stock is bad; but holding such a concentration in the stock of the employer is worse. For the employees of any firm, diversification away from the stock of that employer is even more important. The simple reason is that the employee is already horrifically underdiversified by having his or her human capital tied up with the employer. The employee is necessarily exposed to the risks of the employer by virtue of the employment relationship. The last thing in the world that the employee needs is to magnify the intrinsic underdiversification of the employment relationship, by taking his or her diversifiable investment capital and tying that as well to the fate of the employer.

The Enron debacle illustrates this point poignantly. Just when many of the employees have lost their jobs, they have also lost their pension savings, which in a 401(k) plan they could have borrowed against (or with a penalty, withdrawn) in order to tide them over. . . .

What's the case for having employer stock in pension funds? The argument is that employers want to incentivize employees to identify with the stockholders of the firm. Making employees into stockholders will motivate them to care about the firm's profitability.

There's a simple answer to that argument: Don't do it in the pension fund. If you want to sell stock to your employees for such sound business reasons, go right ahead and do so (subject to adequate disclosure of the risks — a subject to which I shall return). But you should not be able to treat such a program as a pension fund, for two very good reasons: It abuses the pension tax subsidy and it misleads employee-participants.

Congress provides two huge tax subsidies for qualified pension plans: Employee and employer contributions to such plans are tax deferred, and so is any investment buildup. Congress grants this subsidy in order to promote pension saving, hence to promote retirement income security. That policy is concerned to protect the employee and his spouse in their post-employment years. The policy has nothing to do with promoting employer interests. To the contrary, the most fundamental principle of ERISA fiduciary law is the so-called exclusive benefit rule, requiring that pension plan investing and administration must be done "solely in the interest of the participants and beneficiaries and . . . for the exclusive purpose of providing benefits" to them.

ERISA § 404(a)(1)(A). Ordinarily, therefore, subordinating the interests of the employees to those of the employer is a breach of the fiduciary duty to avoid such conflicts of interest under ERISA. Apart from the statutory exception that allows employer stock in pension plans, the message of ERISA is: pension plans are for employees, not for employers. Congress provides the pension tax subsidy for employee interests.

Another way to make that point is to remind ourselves that the employee has earned the pension. Employers do not offer pension plans in order to be nice guys — indeed, employers have a fiduciary duty to their shareholders not to waste the company's assets by giving those assets away to people, even employees. These plans are not gratuities. Employers offer pension plans as part of the compensation package, as what we call deferred compensation. Pensions are the employee's earnings, channelled into retirement saving at the source. We should not let supposed employer preferences interfere with the best interests of the employee.

As the Enron calamity shows, employees do not understand the risks involved in holding employer stock in their pension accounts. They rely on these accounts for their retirement. Many of the employees do not have enough years left in the workforce to be able to replace the losses in subsequent employment. . . .

The other claim on behalf of the status quo is that in our voluntary private pension system, if you don't let employers stuff employer stock in these plans, they won't offer the plans at all. This is highly unlikely.

In competitive markets, if one employer won't offer a pension plan while others do, that employer will be at a disadvantage in competing for workers. The employers who offer pensions today do so in order to be competitive for workers who are pension-sensitive, and such employers will continue to want to be competitive for such workers by offering pensions even if the employers are forbidden to stuff the plans with company stock.

We heard the same argument when Congress imposed vesting rules in ERISA in 1974, and when congress mandated spousal shares in 1984. The truth is that sensible pension regulation does not discourage plan formation. To the contrary, by making pension promises more reliable, it increases the attractiveness of pension plans to employees, and causes firms to offer more of them. . . .

If there is one bright spot for the future in the Enron pension catastrophe, it is that we know exactly how to prevent such cases from occurring again. We not only know the cause, we also know the cure.

The losses have been caused by allowing DC plans to be underdiversified. The cure is to require diversification. Congress has successfully insisted on diversifying plan investments in DB plans for a quarter century. What is needed is to extend that regime across the DC universe, to cover all tax-qualified plans.

Congress should not prohibit employer stock from pension plans altogether, because there are situations in which a prudent fiduciary investor may choose to hold some. For example, it is common for pension investment managers to buy index funds in fiduciary accounts. Index funds hold shares in all the companies in the index, and the employer may be one of those companies.

In ERISA § 407(a)(2), Congress set a ceiling on employer stock, saying that a plan may never hold more than ten percent, but Congress then left it to the prudence and diversification rules of ERISA § 404(a) to govern the question of how much less than 10 percent is appropriate. The normal answer will be little or none. The one time a DB plan tried to approach the 10 percent limit, in the most famous of all ERISA investment cases, *Donovan v. Bierwirth*, the Second Circuit held that the investment in employer stock was imprudent. *Bierwirth* stands for the proposition that the prudence and diversification norms of ERISA § 404(a) govern the exercise of the up-to-ten-percent authority in ERISA § 407(a)(2). . . .

The paradox of ERISA is that it contains both the problem and the solution to the Enron mess. ERISA contains a diversification regime that would prevent such cases from ever happening again if extended from DB to all DC plans. (Obviously, were Congress to take that step, it would be important to provide a transition period to assure orderly compliance.) . . .

If Congress lacks the political will to take that step, or to take it across the entirety of the DC plan universe, I would offer a weaker alternative: Congress should at least insist upon alerting employees about the risks of holding employer stock. My source of inspiration is the Surgeon General's warnings on cigarette packages. The thinking behind those warnings is that people need to be aware of the risks, so that they can alter their behavior. Transferred to the pension arena, the point is that if employees were warned about the risks of employer stock, they would be in a better position (1) to avoid electing to buy more of it in plans that offer it as an employee option, and (2) to pressure employers . . . to discontinue using employer stock in the match feature of 401(k) plans.

ERISA § 102 presently requires employers or other plan sponsors to send to employees annually a summary plan description (SPD), describing key features of each plan. I would recommend that Congress require that the SPD for any plan that contains an employer stock option or employer stock match contain a Surgeon General's warning, something like this:

WARNING

Under commonly accepted principles of good investment practice, a retirement account should be invested in a broadly diversified portfolio of stocks and bonds. It is particularly unwise for employees, who are already subject to the risks incident to employment, to hold significant concentrations of employer stock in an account that is meant for retirement saving.

A disclosure solution of this sort is, I repeat, a second best solution. The best solution is for Congress to mandate diversification across the entire universe of pension plans, as a condition of the tax subsidy that Congress grants these plans. By taking that step, Congress could tell the American worker with confidence that Congress has done what is necessary to assure that there will never again be another Enron-type pension calamity.

NOTES

1. *Real Losses.* The insurance provided by the PBGC for defined benefit plans has its limitations. But there is *no* insurance for defined contribution plans. The millions of dollars lost by Enron pension participants and beneficiaries are real losses. The participants and beneficiaries can attempt to recoup some of the losses by suing those who caused the losses, but this type of litigation is slow, expensive, and uncertain. *In re Enron Corporation Securities, Derivative & "ERISA" Litigation*, 284 F. Supp. 2d 511 (S.D. Tex. 2003) (173-page opinion denying summary judgment to defendants on most claims against Enron, individual officers and directors, plan trustees, accountants, lawyers, and investment banks).

2. *A Third-Best Solution.* Congress addressed the employer stock problem in the Pension Protection Act of 2006. Section 204(j) of ERISA now provides that employees in defined-contribution plans must be permitted to replace employer securities with other investments. (As with everything ERISA, there are some technical exceptions, including a phase-in period.) This amendment does less than either of Professor Langbein's suggestions. Professor Langbein's preferred solution was to *require* defined-contribution plans to be diversified by applying the same diversification standards that apply to defined-benefit plans. His second-best solution was to provide employees with a scary notice. Congress's solution prevents employers from requiring employees to have employer stock in their portfolio, but it does not require either diversification or a scary notice.

3. *Blackout Periods.* As its stock was dropping precipitously in October, 2001, Enron implemented a one-month blackout period for one of its major plans during which participants could not make any changes in their accounts. This was done to permit a change in the administrator of the plan. Participants were notified of the blackout one day before it began. The legality of this blackout period is one of the issues in the Enron litigation.

The Sarbanes-Oxley Act addressed this part of the Enron problem. The Act requires plan administrators to provide a thirty-day notice of blackout periods along with information about the dates of the blackout and reasons for it, and a statement advising participants to evaluate their investments in light of the limits on their ability to make changes. ERISA § 101(i); 29 C.F.R. § 2520-101(3).

4. *Notice as Solution.* A common solution to investment problems with defined-contribution plans is to provide participants with more information so they can make better decisions. That is the approach of Sarbanes-Oxley on the blackout issue and it is both Professor Langbein's second-best solution and Congress's actual solution (albeit without the scary notice) to the company stock problem. But is it likely to be effective?

Retirement decisions occur in precisely the kinds of circumstances where behavioral economics would indicate that participants will have difficulty making proper decisions, even if they have complete information. For example, participants have to consider complex financial information, over long time horizons, and within a complicated environment. This has caused some commentators to suggest that retirement policy should de-emphasize employee choice and become more paternalistic. Deborah M. Weiss, *Paternalistic*

Pension Policy: Psychological Evidence & Economic Theory, 58 U. CHI. LAW
REV. 1275 (1991). *See also* Colleen M. Medill, *Transforming the Role of the
Social Security Administration,* 92 CORNELL L. REV. __ (forthcoming 2006).

Ironically, at the same time Congress was rejecting a more paternalistic
approach on employer stock, it called on the lessons of behavior economics
elsewhere to try to increase retirement savings. The Pension Protection Act
of 2006 amended the Internal Revenue Code to permit employers to offer plans
in which employees were automatically enrolled in defined contribution plans,
unless they opt out. I.R.C. § 401(k)(13). *See* Brigitte C. Madrian & Dennis
F. Shea, *The Power of Suggestion: Inertia in 401(k) Participation & Savings
Behavior,* 116 Q.J. ECON. 1149 (2001) (reporting that retirement savings
increase with this type of default rule).

F. RETIREMENT SECURITY AND EMPLOYER-SPONSORED PENSIONS

MICHAEL J. GRAETZ, THE TROUBLED MARRIAGE OF RETIREMENT SECURITY AND TAX POLICIES, 135 U. PA. LAW REV. 851, 852-59 (1987) *

Commentators typically describe a tripartite system that enables and
encourages the provision of income security for individuals in the years
following their retirement from the workforce: Social Security, employer-
provided pensions, and individual savings. . . .

An effort to analyze these three aspects of retirement security policy as a
unified system is inherently complex. It is difficult to conceive of a wider
spectrum of public policy mechanisms intended to implement a single goal.
At one extreme is Social Security, a mandatory national public program
financed by the federal government's power to tax, fulfilled by the government's power to spend, and explicitly redistributional in both purpose and
effect — redistributional both across generations and within the same generation. At the opposite extreme is reliance on individual savings as a source of
retirement security, a predominantly private program, with the individual (or
the family) composing the relevant unit. . . . Bridging these two public/
private extremes are employer-provided pensions, voluntary private programs
encouraged through income tax reductions, regulated by government, both
directly and as to the many requirements that must be met to qualify for tax
benefits, and backed, at least in a limited way, by an insurance system of
national scope. Taken together, then, these three retirement security sources
reflect a full spectrum of policy initiatives: a federal social program for all
Americans, an individualistic program dependent principally upon familial
self-reliance, and a pluralistic communitarian program involving both employers and employees. . . .

At the outset one should describe the goals of retirement security policy in
order to measure the success or failure of the current mix of public and private
programs and to determine whether these programs comprise a coherent

whole in addressing the retirement security problem. The shortfall in income upon retirement is lost income from labor. Thus, while there are no doubt disagreements at the margin, replacement of some significant portion of preretirement wages must be the fundamental goal of retirement security policy. Retirement security also implies that the replacement of preretirement labor income will ensure for the retiree the maintenance of an adequate retirement income that will both protect the elderly from widespread poverty and generally ensure against an abrupt decline in a retiree's lifestyle. . . .

Delineating the retirement security goal as a wage-replacement goal helps to clarify the suitable functions of the various elements of our tripartite retirement security system. Social Security — a completely public program — might serve fully to meet the basic income adequacy goal for poorer workers, contribute substantially toward ensuring an adequate threshold retirement income for moderate income workers, and assist somewhat in post-retirement lifestyle maintenance for all workers. This vision of a public Social Security function would require at least all individuals who have enough earnings to satisfy current basic needs to substitute future for current consumption, for example by taxing current wages in exchange for subsequent wage-replacement retirement benefits. In addition, such a view regards as appropriate the redistributional aspects of Social Security and dismisses the contention that a public social security program should resemble an actuarially sound retirement insurance plan for all workers, even those at the highest income levels. The dominant public role of retirement income security policy should be to ensure post-retirement income adequacy for low- and moderate-income workers.

At the other end of the income scale, private individual savings are most likely to ensure retirement income security for those workers who have earned sufficiently high lifetime wages (or who otherwise have sufficient investment assets) to enable them to use current savings to protect themselves from a substantial decline in living standard upon retirement. The public role in this context should obviously permit, and perhaps facilitate, private savings for retirement, but the individual savings component of retirement security for higher-income workers should be a primarily private matter. Once basic income adequacy during retirement is assured, the government might well remain generally neutral about individual decisions by high-income workers regarding the tradeoff between their own current and future consumption, except to the extent that this tradeoff may affect the tendency of employers to create and maintain pension plans that will benefit low- and moderate-income workers as well.

The appropriate role of the social security and individual savings elements of the tripartite retirement security program thus fits easily within this Article's articulation of retirement security goals. Private pensions present more of a problem. While it is clear that these employer-provided pensions often contribute to basic income adequacy, especially for low- and moderate-income workers, it is not nearly so clear to what extent employer-provided plans should serve to facilitate post-retirement lifestyle maintenance for all workers. Specification of the appropriate role for employer-sponsored pension plans depends both on the overall ambitions of the national retirement security program and on the adequacy of Social Security. The voluntariness of such plans links them to individual savings, while their collective nature with respect to benefits and risks as well as with respect to employer and regulatory limitations on employee choices, suggests a public nature. Dominant reliance on income tax incentives as the public stimulus for employer plans necessarily confounds retirement security and income tax policies. . . .

[T]he necessary function of employer-provided pension plans in bridging the public antipoverty/basic income adequacy function of Social Security and the private lifestyle maintenance function of individual savings creates substantial tensions in the formulation of public policy regarding such plans. Typically, the tensions are manifested by debates over the appropriate conditions that must be met by private pensions in order to qualify for income tax benefits and over the propriety and effects of extending similar benefits to private individual retirement savings plans. Viewing employer pensions as an integral part of a coherent national retirement security policy, however, also requires coordinating the significant features of employer plans with the distribution of the benefits and burdens of both Social Security and the public aspects of individual savings. Ultimately, this raises questions about the ability of voluntary employer plans to fulfill their critical function in national retirement security policy.

NOTES

1. *An Adequate Replacement Rate.* Professor Graetz identifies replacement of pre-retirement wages as the central goal of retirement policy. But what is an adequate replacement rate? For several reasons, people do not need as much money after they retire to maintain their standard of living. For example, their taxes tend to go down significantly, they no longer need to save for retirement, and they no longer have work-related expenses, such as commuting costs. A recent estimate indicates that low-income couples (pre-retirement earnings of $20,000) need to replace about 83% of their pre-retirement income to maintain their living standards, while high-income couples ($90,000) need to replace about 75%. Alicia H. Munnell & Mauricio Soto, *What Replacement Rates Do Households Actually Experience in Retirement?*, Center for Retirement ResearchWorking Paper No. 10, at 30 (2005).

2. *Current Replacement Rates.* Replacement rates can vary widely depending on the precise analysis, and there are many choices to be made in making the analysis. Retirement income (the numerator) can be based on any combination of social security income, pension income, and/or income from other financial assets. Pre-retirement income (the denominator) can include only social security wages (which are capped), all wages, or income from all sources. The results will also vary depending on the population analyzed (*e.g.*, the time frame, men or women, couples or individuals). With those caveats, a recent analysis showed the following replacement rates for workers retiring between 1992 and 2004:

| | Couples | | Single Individuals | |
	Without Pensions	With Pensions	Without Pensions	With Pensions
Social Security	34.4%	29.5%	32.8%	27.8%
S.S. + pensions	34.4	51.5	32.8	55.7
S.S. + pensions + finan. assets	45.4	60.1	44.4	66.9

Alicia H. Munnell & Mauricio Soto, *supra*, at 35 (the denominator is an estimate of all earnings immediately prior to retirement).

3. *Redistribution Through Social Security.* Professor Graetz says that the dominant role for social security should be to ensure an adequate income for low- and moderate-income workers, which would justify redistribution. As with replacement rates, determining the actual distribution of social security benefits is complicated. Benefits vary based on earnings, marital status, mortality, and a host of other factors. Results are often different depending on whether the focus is on absolute dollars or replacement rates. But in general, lower-income workers receive higher replacement rates, as do women and couples (especially if the spouse does not work). Yet some groups that might be expected to benefit from these distributions do not. For example, although African-Americans earn less and therefore might be expected to receive higher social security benefits, they often lose more because of mortality differences and lesser access to spousal and survival benefits than they benefit from the progressive benefit formula. Lee Cohen et al., Social Security Redistribution by Education, Race, and Income: How Much and Why? (2001), *available at* www.mrrc.isr.umich.edu/publications/conference/pdf/cp01_carasso.pdf.

4. *Privatizing Social Security.* Privatizing social security, an important current political issue, would make these types of redistribution more difficult. Some people would see this as a positive development, others would not:

> We typically think that giving people choice is optimal since people can decide what is best for them. Thus the economic bias is to believe that, if people want to opt out of social security, they should be allowed to do so. In the context of social security privatization, however, this analysis is not right. Allowing people to opt out of social security to avoid adverse redistribution is not efficient; it just destroys what society is trying to accomplish. If rich people and two-worker families opt out of social security, for example, we will no longer be able to redistribute from rich to poor or from dual earners to single earners. One of the purposes of social security will have been defeated.

David Cutler, *Comment, in* Privatizing Social Security 358 (Martin Feldstein ed., 1998).

The movement for social security privatization is similar to efforts in employee benefit law generally to move from a more socialized, collectivized vision of economic security to one more dependent on individual responsibility. For pensions, this trend is evident in the movement away from defined benefit plans and towards defined contribution plans and in the rapid growth in various types of individual retirement options, such as IRAs. *See* Colleen E. Medill, *The Individual Responsibility Model of Retirement Plans Today: Conforming ERISA Policy to Reality*, 49 EMORY L. REV. 1 (2000). For health care, Health Savings Accounts would be the principal example of this trend.

Chapter 20

EMPLOYER-PROVIDED HEALTH INSURANCE

ERISA applies not only to pension plans, but also to "welfare" plans. The principal distinction between the two is that pension plans provide benefits upon retirement, while welfare plans provide benefits for other types of contingencies. Health insurance is the most important of the welfare plans, and we will focus on it. The statutory definition, however, also includes plans that provide disability, life, or unemployment insurance; vacation benefits; apprenticeship or other training programs; day-care centers; scholarship funds; and prepaid legal services. ERISA § 3(1).

Although ERISA has always covered welfare plans, originally they were only minimally regulated by the Act. When ERISA was first enacted in 1974, the only provisions that applied to welfare plans were the reporting and disclosure requirements, the fiduciary rules, and the enforcement provisions. When combined with ERISA's broad preemption of state law, this meant employer-provided health insurance was very lightly regulated given its importance and complexity.

Since then, however, Congress has amended ERISA several times to deal with specific problems. Today, employers providing health insurance must comply with COBRA, OBRA, HIPAA, NMHPA, MHPA, and WHCRA.[1] Predictably, this piecemeal approach to regulation has created compliance and enforcement problems. U.S. Dep't of Labor, Health Disclosure & Claims Issues: Fiscal Year 2001 Compliance Project Report (2003) (45% of employer health plans surveyed failed to comply fully with all these laws). Nevertheless, Congress has never moved away from this country's general approach to health care, embedded in ERISA, which depends primarily on private, employer-provided health insurance.

This chapter will discuss this general approach while maintaining a focus on the employment law underpinnings of the system. It will begin by discussing the rationale for a system that depends heavily on employer-provided insurance, and the special problems presented by such a system. Then it will discuss a number of important aspects of the system: preemption of state law, problems with enforcement under ERISA, portability of benefits, and the special problems of those with disabilities and retirees. Finally, the chapter will conclude with a general discussion of the appropriate role for government in this complex area.

---

[1] Consolidated Omnibus Budget Reconciliation Act of 1985 (COBRA); Omnibus Budget Reconciliation Act of 1985 (OBRA); Health Insurance Portability & Accountability Act of 1996 (HIPAA); Newborns' & Mothers' Health Protection Act of 1996 (NMPHA); the Mental Health Parity Act of 1996 (MHPA); Women's Health & Cancer Rights Act of 1998 (WHCRA). Practitioners refer to these as the "alphabet soup" requirements; we will discuss each of them later.

A. THINKING ABOUT AN EMPLOYMENT-BASED HEALTH CARE SYSTEM

Most Americans under age 65 receive health insurance through their employment. Of those with private health insurance, 91% receive their coverage through an employment-based health plan. Viewed another way, 62% of *all* nonelderly Americans receive health insurance through an employer, 18% are uninsured, and the remainder are insured under government programs or through individual or small-group insurance. (The elderly, of course, receive health insurance through Medicare, a governmental program.) Paul Fronstin, *Sources of Health Insurance & Characteristics of the Uninsured*, EBRI Issue Brief No. 287, Nov. 2005, at 4 (citing statistics for 2004).

Internationally, this is a highly unusual way of providing health insurance. Most of the rest of the world provides health care through a publicly financed national health care system covering the entire population although, as we will discuss below, the division between public and private systems is not as clean as many people think.

TIMOTHY STOLTZFUS JOST, PRIVATE OR PUBLIC APPROACHES TO INSURING THE UNINSURED: LESSONS FROM INTERNATIONAL EXPERIENCE WITH PRIVATE INSURANCE, 76 N.Y.U. L. Rev. 419, 472-83 (2001)[*]

[P]rivate health insurance is highly regulated and often government subsidized wherever it is relied upon as a primary means for purchasing essential health care services for a significant portion of a nation's population. Insurance also seems to be more highly regulated and subsidized where individual, as compared to group, policies predominate. What explains the pervasiveness of private insurance regulation in these examples? . . .

In competitive insurance markets, no single insurer can choose to offer the same price to all purchasers of insurance (*i.e.*, to "community rate" voluntarily). Any insurer that tried to do so obviously would have to charge a rate high enough to break even — that is, a rate high enough to cover the costs anticipated from extraordinarily expensive cases as well as the cost of a much higher number of more moderately expensive services. The distribution of health care costs over a population in any given year, however, is extraordinarily skewed. The most expensive one percent of the insured population accounts for thirty percent of all medical care costs, while the least expensive fifty percent are responsible for only three percent of costs. Thus, for an insurer dedicated to community rating to cover the costs it will face from extraordinarily expensive insureds, it will have to charge hefty premiums to many insureds who in fact will incur no insured expenses over the course of the year, many of whom will not anticipate any health care expenses at the outset.

Faced with sizeable premiums and little anticipation of need for insurance, some low-risk insureds undoubtedly will decline insurance coverage, choosing to self-insure. . . . High-risk insureds, on the other hand, will find community-rated insurance very attractive. In other words, insurers will be at risk for

---

[*] Reprinted with permission.

"adverse selection" (the preferential election to insure by high-risk individuals).

If, however, as would be expected in competitive markets, at least one insurer offers insurance at a lower price, low-risk insureds will abandon the high-cost insurer and flock to the new entrant. But high-risk insureds will do so as well, seriously threatening the viability of the lower-cost insurer. The lower-cost insurer may try to discourage some high-risk insureds by offering a less generous product, for example, a product subject to lower caps or higher cost sharing, or covering fewer services. If the lower cost insurer succeeds, however, high-risk insureds discouraged from moving to the low-cost insurer will remain with the higher-cost, higher-coverage insurer, which will now need to raise its premiums to cover the ever more expensive population it has retained. As it does so, however, its policies will become even less attractive to those low-risk insureds who had remained loyal to it. An insurer who community rates voluntarily, in the end, will slip into the insurance "death spiral," as it is left with an ever less favorable risk pool and must charge ever higher rates. High-option plans will be driven out of the market by adverse selection. In short, a stable "pooling equilibrium," in which every insured remains in a common pool paying the same amount for insurance is not possible in competitive health insurance markets.

If however, at least one insurer risk underwrites or "experience rates," offering higher rates for higher-risk applicants and lower rates for lower-risk applicants, the market will sort itself out into a "separation equilibrium." Low-risk insureds will leave high-cost, one-rate-fits-all insurance plans for lower-cost alternatives calibrated to their level of risk. Community-rated plans will be forced to move to risk underwriting or be priced out of the market. This is precisely what happened in the United States during the middle of the last century, as Blue Cross plans, many of which originally were community rated, lost the low-risk end of their business to experience-rated commercial insurers, who offered more attractive rates, and eventually adopted experience rating themselves.

Low-risk insureds, however, may not only find community-rated plans a bad deal, but they simply may be unable to afford them. Low-risk insureds in the United States are often young persons who have just entered the job market, and many may not yet have even a permanent or fulltime job. One-size-fits-all insurance rates set high enough to cover the expenses of all insureds simply may be too high to fit into their budgets. In fact, in the four years following the adoption by New York of required community rating in the individual market in 1993, individual enrollment dropped by at least thirty-eight percent and possibly by as much as fifty percent. During the same four years, one major New York insurer reported that the average age of its individual indemnity pool increased by 11.5 years. . . .

However, when plans underwrite based on individual, or even small group, risk and experience, they may charge premiums that high-risk individuals and groups find simply unaffordable, or plans simply may refuse to sell to some high-risk individuals when they are not required legally to do so. Insurers in the United States that sell in the individual market often exclude or limit coverage for maternity care, mental health, substance abuse treatment, or

HIV-related expenses; charge high deductibles and coinsurance amounts; and impose lengthy preexisting condition exclusions where permitted to do so. They charge rates as much as 50% to 200% higher than their standard rates for conditions such as obesity, tobacco use, and hypertension, and may deny coverage for a history of angina, stroke, or rheumatoid arthritis. Insurers compelled under HIPAA [the Health Insurance Portability and Accountability Act] to offer individual insurance policies to individuals who lost group insurance charged rates up to 600% above standard rates. Many individuals or employers therefore have had to pass up health insurance simply because of its cost. Regardless of whether plans are community-rated or experience-rated, therefore, some individuals will not be able to find coverage at an affordable price.

Moreover, insurers have means other than risk underwriting to control adverse selection. Preexisting condition exclusions or coverage waiting periods make insurance plans less appealing to high-cost insureds. Caps on coverage (either lifetime, enrollment period, or condition-specific coverage caps) likewise can discourage those in ill health from purchasing insurance. These devices, sometimes referred to as "postclaims underwriting," discourage adverse selection, but also limit the risks faced by insurers when it occurs. Finally, benefit packages can be designed to include or exclude benefits or providers of particular interest to low-or high-risk groups. . . .

The exclusionary effects of risk-underwritten private insurance are mitigated to a considerable degree when insurance is sold to employment-related groups. Employment-related groups, especially large groups, are able to spread risk broadly, making insurance more affordable to higher-risk individuals. In effect, they community rate at the group level rather than the insurer level. As only persons healthy enough to work and their dependents are included in such groups, the risk exposure faced by an insurer or self-insured employer who insures a group is controlled to some extent. If the employer covers most of the cost of the insurance itself as a business expense, moreover, low-risk employees may not be aware of the extent to which they are subsidizing their higher-risk coworkers. Where employment-related insurance is tax subsidized, as it long has been in the United States, insureds may be troubled even less by cross-subsidization. . . .

Because unregulated private health insurance markets leave high-risk individuals with very costly, often simply unaffordable, premiums, or apply other terms and conditions, such as lengthy preexisting condition exclusions, that make affordable insurance of little value, nations that rely on individual private insurance policies for providing primary cover to portions of their populations almost inevitably regulate (usually quite extensively) and often subsidize private insurance markets to mitigate these results. In other words, they conscript private insurance to serve the public goal of equitable access.

Regulation in some nations begins with attempts to require community rating, or at least to limit the extent of risk underwriting and experience rating. . . . Most countries also restrict or prohibit insurers from canceling or refusing to renew insurance for individuals or groups as they become higher risk with time or in fact incur substantial expenses. In many places, rating restrictions grow more complex over time, as insurers adjust to them and figure out ways to avoid them.

Simply requiring that all insurance purchasers be offered the same rates . . . will not suffice, however, to assure access to insurance. As noted above, by excluding preexisting conditions for long periods of time, barring coverage for high-cost or chronic conditions, or imposing low maximum coverage limitations (including disease-specific caps), insurers can defeat the whole purpose of government efforts to extend coverage to high-risk individuals. Private insurance coverage effectively will be denied to high-risk persons unless the use of these limitations is restricted, or perhaps even outlawed. Most nations in which private insurance plays an important role, therefore, including . . . the United States, . . . place limits on the extent to which insurers can impose these clauses and restrictions.

Insurers denied the use of these obvious restraints on coverage, however, can resort to still more subtle devices to skim the cream from markets and to avoid high-risk insureds. Insurers compelled to community rate can expect one-third of their insureds to be unprofitable, with the maximum predictable loss exceeding eight times overall average per capita expenditures. This creates significant incentives for cream skimming through whatever avenues are open. Some private insurers in Australia, required to sell policies on a community-rated basis, reportedly opened offices on the upper floors of buildings without elevators to limit accessibility by those in frail health.

Insurers may shape their benefit packages to include health club dues or discounts on running shoes, or to exclude long-term care or mental health care, in an effort to encourage low-risk and discourage high-risk applicants. They may refuse to pay commissions to agents who sell certain types of insurance or who sell insurance to certain types of customers, and may encourage "field underwriting," where agents simply do not sell insurance to certain potential consumers. If reforms grandfather in existing policies, insurers may close their existing products to new entrants and offer new products with less favorable benefits. Other insurers may attempt to skim cream through selective advertising, providing poor service to high-risk individuals, sharing risk with contracting providers to give the providers an incentive to cream skim, or simply bribing high-risk insureds to leave the plan. . . .

Insurers may not need even to take actions aimed at excluding particular individuals: Simply limiting choice of provider may be sufficient to exclude individuals who are currently high users of medical care because they may be reluctant to sever current ties with particular providers. One industry source . . . candidly stated that regulators "can't hold a candle" to the abilities of insurers to promote risk selection. Resources committed to cream skimming, however, result in a welfare loss for society, as cream skimming simply shifts risk to other parties, often to those least able to bear it, rather than providing a benefit to society.

Regulators may address the problem of subtle forms of cream skimming by attempting to alter the incentives faced by insurers. One approach is for regulators to use reinsurance or high-risk pool schemes to make higher-risk insureds more attractive to insurers and, conversely, to make cream skimming less attractive. Reinsurance or high-risk pool schemes indeed may be necessary to keep insurers with too many high-risk insureds from leaving the market altogether. . . . Alternatively, premiums paid to insurers can be risk adjusted through some kind of prepayment pooling mechanisms. . . . Operation of these pools, however, requires extensive and intrusive government involvement in private health insurance markets. There is also always the possibility that insurers may be able to predict risk better than the risk adjustment mechanism and use this information to cream skim low-risk patients or to dump high-risk patients.

Finally, as community rating and risk adjustment make the purchase of insurance less and less attractive to the young and healthy, a number of nations have chosen to subsidize the purchase of private insurance to make it more affordable to those who otherwise might not purchase it. Absent sizable subsidies, individual insurance remains unaffordable to many. . . . Australia recently adopted a policy of reimbursing privately insured individuals thirty percent of their health insurance premiums. . . . In the United States, current tax subsidies for employment-related insurance cost nearly $125 billion in 1998, over half the amount spent on the Medicare or Medicaid programs. The current tax credit and voucher proposals in the United States would serve the same end, though without supplemental regulation to improve access, they probably would do so poorly.

NOTES

1. *Why Employment-Based?* Professor Jost discusses some of the reasons health insurance in the United States is primarily employment-based. Groups identified by employment tend to be relatively neutral on risk (or even favorable since only people healthy enough to work are direct beneficiaries); they tend to disguise the cross-subsidization that occurs between high- and low-risk individuals within the group; and they are able to take advantage of tax subsidies targeted to insurance provided through employment.

But there are other reasons as well. A primary one is historical accident. The United States began financing health insurance through a private system during the first half of the 20th century and, once a basic system has matured, it is difficult to make dramatic changes. This is known as "path dependence" and it is also true for the health care systems in Canada and the United Kingdom, albeit with national, public health insurance systems instead of private ones. CAROLYN HUGHES TOUHY, ACCIDENTAL LOGICS: THE DYNAMICS OF CHANGE IN THE HEALTH CARE ARENA IN THE UNITED STATES, BRITAIN, AND CANADA (1999).

In addition, employment-based health insurance may be highly valued by both employers and employees. For employers, as indicated earlier, health insurance can be structured to help an employer select and retain a particular type of workforce, and to perform other functions. For employees, the employer may be a good agent for purchasing health insurance, better able to evaluate, price, and monitor the complex contractual arrangements between doctor (or other provider) and patient than the employees could do on their own. Pamela B. Peele et al., *Employer-Sponsored Health Insurance: Are Employers Good Agents for Their Employees*, 78 MILBANK Q. 5, 19 (2000) ("[Our empirical study demonstrates that employers] provide a valued service and contribute to individual employees' welfare by purchasing their health insurance").

2. Why Private? A private health insurance system has several potential advantages: the ability to provide differentiated products to respond to customer preferences, avoiding the deadweight losses from the taxes required to support a public system, flexibility and innovation in controlling costs and improving quality, and market pressures to hold costs down.

The problems identified by Professor Jost, however, inevitably lead to regulation which may limit the ability of a private system to provide these advantages. Consider:

- *Differentiated Products.* Congress requires all health insurance to provide certain benefits, such as guarantees of continued coverage, hospital stays after childbirth, and reconstruction surgery after mastectomies. Congress is commonly under pressure to guarantee other types of features, such as access to specialists and coverage for prescriptions. The states impose similar mandates on insured plans. On average, each state has 20 legislative mandates requiring features such as mammography screening and alcoholism treatment. These requirements tend to standardize policies and make it more difficult for insurers to tailor policies to customer preferences.

- *Deadweight Losses from Taxes.* The "private" system in the United States still provides very significant tax subsidies to attend to the undercoverage problem endemic in a purely private system. ANALYTICAL PERSPECTIVES, BUDGET OF THE UNITED STATES GOVERNMENT, FISCAL YEAR 2006, Table 19-1, 317-19 (2005) (in 2006, $126 billion in tax advantages for employer-provided health insurance).

- *Costs/Quality.* HMOs in the United States were a market innovation which turned out to be effective in controlling costs, with no measurable losses in health care outcomes. Yet it resulted in considerable pressure to regulate, and the regulation often undermines the cost-saving innovations.

- *Market Pressure to Limit Costs.* These pressures may be more than offset by the increased costs of a private system, such as marketing and underwriting costs. Overhead for private health insurance in the United States is 19% of overall revenue, compared to 3% for Medicare and 1% in the Canadian national health insurance program. David U. Himmelstein & Steffie Woolhandler, *Mayhem in the Medical Marketplace*, 56 MONTHLY REV. 26, 28 (2004).

3. The Convergence of Public and Private Systems. The "private" system in the United States has many public aspects, such as mandated benefits, large tax subsidies, and continuation coverage requirements. Conversely, in the "public" systems in other countries, private insurance almost always plays an important role. In some countries, such as Germany and the Netherlands, consumers can purchase private insurance and opt out of the public system completely; in other countries, such as France and Canada, private insurance is used to supplement the public system, for example, to cover nonessential services or to purchase greater-than-normal access or convenience. Jost, *supra*, at 429-30. Thus, discussing the relative merits of pure "public" and "private" systems is largely irrelevant; those systems simply do not exist. The health care debate, like most important debates, is complicated and cannot be resolved at a purely ideological level.

B.　ERISA PREEMPTION

ERISA has a very broad preemption provision. Section 514(a) provides that ERISA "supercede[s] any and all State laws insofar as they may now or hereafter relate to any [pension or welfare] plan." There are exceptions from preemption, but they are fairly narrow. The most important exceptions are for state insurance, banking, and securities laws; generally applicable criminal laws; and qualified domestic relations orders. ERISA § 514(b).

The legislative history is also clear that the preemption provision was intended to be broad. The original House and Senate bills would have preempted state laws only to the extent that they related to matters that were *actually regulated* by ERISA (for example, state laws relating to reporting and disclosure requirements and fiduciary standards). State laws on other matters, even though related to pension and welfare plans, would not have been preempted. In conference, however, the bill was changed to include the broad preemption language of section 514. This was emphasized by one of the major sponsors of the legislation, Representative John Dent: "[T]he crowning achievement of this legislation [is] the reservation to Federal authority of the sole power to regulate the field of [pension and welfare] plans. With the preemption of the field, we round out the protection afforded participants by eliminating the threat of conflicting and inconsistent State and local regulations. . . ." 120 Cong. Rec. 29,197 (1974).

Preemption issues are difficult throughout labor and employment law. They are no easier here. Preemption under ERISA, however, poses a special concern because it is combined with ERISA's very limited substantive regulation of welfare plans. The risk is that federal protection of employee interests is or will become inadequate, while at the same time state and local efforts to provide protection will be frustrated because of the broad preemption.

METROPOLITAN LIFE INSURANCE CO. v. MASSACHUSETTS
United States Supreme Court
471 U.S. 724 (1985)

JUSTICE BLACKMUN delivered the opinion of the Court.

A Massachusetts statute requires that specified minimum mental-health-care benefits be provided a Massachusetts resident who is insured under a general insurance policy, an accident or sickness insurance policy, or an employee health-care plan that covers hospital and surgical expenses. The . . . question before us in these cases is whether the state statute, as applied to insurance policies purchased by employee health-care plans regulated by the federal Employee Retirement Income Security Act of 1974, is pre-empted by that Act. . . .

I

General health insurance typically is sold as group insurance to an employer or other group. Group insurance presently is subject to extensive state regulation, including regulation of the carrier, regulation of the sale and advertising of the insurance, and regulation of the content of the contracts. Mandated-benefit laws, that require an insurer to provide a certain kind of benefit to cover a specified illness or procedure whenever someone purchases a certain kind of insurance, are a subclass of such content regulation. . . .

The substantive terms of group-health insurance contracts . . . have been extensively regulated by the States. For example, the majority of States currently require that coverage for dependents continue beyond any contractually imposed age limitation when the dependent is incapable of self-sustaining employment because of mental or physical handicap; such statutes date back to the early 1960's. And over the last 15 years all 50 States have required that coverage of infants begin at birth, rather than at some time shortly after birth, as had been the prior practice in the unregulated market. Many state statutes require that insurers offer on an optional basis particular kinds of coverage to purchasers. Others require insurers either to offer or mandate that insurance policies include coverage for services rendered by a particular type of health-care provider.

Mandated-benefit statutes, then, are only one variety of a matrix of state laws that regulate the substantive content of health-insurance policies to further state health policy. Massachusetts Gen. Laws Ann., ch. 175, § 47B (Supp. 1985), is typical of mandated-benefit laws currently in place in the majority of States.[10] With respect to a Massachusetts resident, it requires any general health-insurance policy that provides hospital and surgical coverage, or any benefit plan that has such coverage, to provide as well a certain minimum of mental-health protection. In particular, § 47B requires that a health-insurance policy provide 60 days of coverage for confinement in a mental hospital, coverage for confinement in a general hospital equal to that provided by the policy for nonmental illness, and certain minimum outpatient benefits.

Section 47B was designed to address problems encountered in treating mental illness in Massachusetts. The Commonwealth determined that its working people needed to be protected against the high cost of treatment for such illness. It also believed that, without insurance, mentally ill workers were often institutionalized in large state mental hospitals, and that mandatory insurance would lead to a higher incidence of more effective treatment in private community mental-health centers.

In addition, the Commonwealth concluded that the voluntary insurance market was not adequately providing mental-health coverage, because of "adverse selection" in mental-health insurance: good insurance risks were not

---

[10] According to the Health Insurance Association of America, 26 States have promulgated 69 mandated-benefit laws. Different States mandate a great variety of different kinds of insurance coverage. For example, many require alcoholism coverage, while others require certain birth-defect coverage, outpatient kidney-dialysis coverage, or reconstructive surgery for insured mastectomies.

purchasing coverage, and this drove up the price of coverage for those who otherwise might purchase mental-health insurance. The legislature believed that the public interest required that it correct the insurance market in the Commonwealth by mandating minimum-coverage levels, effectively forcing the good-risk individuals to become part of the risk pool, and enabling insurers to price the insurance at an average market rather than a market retracted due to adverse selection. Section 47B, then, was intended to help safeguard the public against the high costs of comprehensive inpatient and outpatient mental-health care, reduce nonpsychiatric medical-care expenditures for mentally related illness, shift the delivery of treatment from inpatient to outpatient services, and relieve the Commonwealth of some of the financial burden it otherwise would encounter with respect to mental-health problems.

It is our task in these cases to decide whether such insurance regulation violates or is inconsistent with federal law.

The federal Employee Retirement Income Security Act of 1974 (ERISA), comprehensively regulates employee pension and welfare plans. An employee welfare-benefit plan or welfare plan is defined as one which provides to employees "medical, surgical, or hospital care or benefits, or benefits in the event of sickness, accident, disability [or] death," whether these benefits are provided "through the purchase of insurance or otherwise." § 3(1). Plans may self-insure or they may purchase insurance for their participants. Plans that purchase insurance — so-called "insured plans" — are directly affected by state laws that regulate the insurance industry. . . .

ERISA . . . contains almost no federal regulation of the terms of benefit plans. It does, however, contain a broad pre-emption provision declaring that the statute shall "supersede any and all State laws insofar as they may now or hereafter relate to any employee benefit plan." § 514(a). Appellant Metropolitan . . . argues that ERISA pre-empts Massachusetts' mandated-benefit law insofar as § 47B restricts the kinds of insurance policies that benefit plans may purchase.

While § 514(a) of ERISA broadly pre-empts state laws that relate to an employee-benefit plan, that pre-emption is substantially qualified by an "insurance saving clause," § 514(b)(2)(A), which broadly states that, with one exception, nothing in ERISA "shall be construed to exempt or relieve any person from any law of any State which regulates insurance, banking, or securities." The specified exception to the saving clause is found in § 514(b)(2)(B), the so-called "deemer clause," which states that no employee-benefit plan, with certain exceptions not relevant here, "shall be deemed to be an insurance company or other insurer, bank, trust company, or investment company or to be engaged in the business of insurance or banking for purposes of any law of any State purporting to regulate insurance companies, insurance contracts, banks, trust companies, or investment companies." Massachusetts argues that its mandated-benefit law, as applied to insurance companies that sell insurance to benefit plans, is a "law which regulates insurance," and therefore is saved from the effect of the general pre-emption clause of ERISA. . . .

II

Appellants are Metropolitan Life Insurance Company and Travelers Insurance Company (insurers) who are located in New York and Connecticut respectively and who issue group-health policies providing hospital and surgical coverage to plans, or to employers or unions that employ or represent employees residing in Massachusetts. Under the terms of § 47B, both appellants are required to provide minimal mental-health benefits in policies issued to cover Commonwealth residents.

In 1979, the Attorney General of Massachusetts brought suit in Massachusetts Superior Court for declaratory and injunctive relief to enforce § 47B. The Commonwealth asserted that since January 1, 1976, the effective date of § 47B, the insurers had issued policies to group policyholders situated outside Massachusetts that provided for hospital and surgical coverage for certain residents of the Commonwealth. It further asserted that those policies failed to provide Massachusetts-resident beneficiaries the mental-health coverage mandated by § 47B, and that the insurers intended to issue more such policies, believing themselves not bound by § 47B for policies issued outside the Commonwealth. In their answer, the insurers admitted these allegations. . . .

III

In deciding whether a federal law pre-empts a state statute, our task is to ascertain Congress' intent in enacting the federal statute at issue. Pre-emption may be either express or implied, and is compelled whether Congress' command is explicitly stated in the statute's language or implicitly contained in its structure and purpose. The narrow statutory ERISA question presented is whether § 47B is a law "which regulates insurance" within the meaning of § 514(b)(2)(A) and so would not be pre-empted by § 514(a).

A

Section 47B clearly "relate[s] to" welfare plans governed by ERISA so as to fall within the reach of ERISA's pre-emption provision, § 514(a). . . . The phrase "relate to" [in § 514(a) is] given its broad common-sense meaning, such that a state law "relate[s] to" a benefit plan "in the normal sense of the phrase, if it has a connection with or reference to such a plan." The pre-emption provision was intended to displace all state laws that fall within its sphere, even including state laws that are consistent with ERISA's substantive requirements. "[E]ven indirect state action bearing on private pensions may encroach upon the area of exclusive federal concern."

Though § 47B is not denominated a benefit-plan law, it bears indirectly but substantially on all insured benefit plans, for it requires them to purchase the mental-health benefits specified in the statute when they purchase a certain kind of common insurance policy. . . . [T]he mandated-benefit law as applied relates to ERISA plans and thus is covered by ERISA's broad pre-emption provision set forth in § 514(a).

B

Nonetheless, the sphere in which § 514(a) operates was explicitly limited by § 514(b)(2). The insurance saving clause preserves any state law "which regulates insurance, banking, or securities." The two pre-emption sections, while clear enough on their faces, perhaps are not a model of legislative drafting, for while the general pre-emption clause broadly pre-empts state law, the saving clause appears broadly to preserve the States' lawmaking power over much of the same regulation. While Congress occasionally decides to return to the States what it has previously taken away, it does not normally do both at the same time.

Fully aware of this statutory complexity, we still have no choice but to "begin with the language employed by Congress and the assumption that the ordinary meaning of that language accurately expresses the legislative purpose." We also must presume that Congress did not intend to pre-empt areas of traditional state regulation.

To state the obvious, § 47B regulates the terms of certain insurance contracts, and so seems to be saved from pre-emption by the saving clause as a law "which regulates insurance." This common-sense view of the matter, moreover, is reinforced by the language of the subsequent subsection of ERISA, the "deemer clause," which states that an employee-benefit plan shall not be deemed to be an insurance company "for purposes of any law of any State purporting to regulate insurance companies, *insurance contracts,* banks, trust companies, or investment companies." § 514(b)(2)(B) (emphasis added). By exempting from the saving clause laws regulating insurance contracts that apply directly to benefit plans, the deemer clause makes explicit Congress' intention to include laws that regulate insurance contracts within the scope of the insurance laws preserved by the saving clause. Unless Congress intended to include laws regulating insurance contracts within the scope of the insurance saving clause, it would have been unnecessary for the deemer clause explicitly to exempt such laws from the saving clause when they are applied directly to benefit plans.

The insurers nonetheless argue that § 47B is in reality a health law that merely operates on insurance contracts to accomplish its end, and that it is not the kind of traditional insurance law intended to be saved by § 514(b)(2)(A). We find this argument unpersuasive.

Initially, nothing in § 514(b)(2)(A), or in the "deemer clause" which modifies it, purports to distinguish between traditional and innovative insurance laws. The presumption is against pre-emption, and we are not inclined to read limitations into federal statutes in order to enlarge their pre-emptive scope. Further, there is no indication in the legislative history that Congress had such a distinction in mind.

Appellants assert that state laws that directly regulate the insurer, and laws that regulate such matters as the way in which insurance may be sold, are traditional laws subject to the clause, while laws that regulate the substantive terms of insurance contracts are recent innovations more properly seen as health laws rather than as insurance laws, which § 514(b)(2)(A) does not save. This distinction reads the saving clause out of ERISA entirely, because laws that regulate only the insurer, or the way in which it may sell insurance, do not "relate to" benefit plans in the first instance. Because they would not be pre-empted by § 514(a), they do not need to be "saved" by § 514(b)(2)(A). There is no indication that Congress could have intended the saving clause to operate only to guard against too expansive readings of the general pre-emption clause that might have included laws wholly unrelated to plans. Appellants' construction, in our view, violates the plain meaning of the statutory language and renders redundant both the saving clause it is construing, as well as the deemer clause which it precedes, and accordingly has little to recommend it.

Moreover, it is both historically and conceptually inaccurate to assert that mandated-benefit laws are not traditional insurance laws. As we have indicated, state laws regulating the substantive terms of insurance contracts were commonplace well before the mid-70's, when Congress considered ERISA. The case law concerning the meaning of the phrase "business of insurance" in the McCarran-Ferguson Act, 15 U.S.C. § 1011 *et seq.,* also strongly supports the conclusion that regulation regarding the substantive terms of insurance contracts falls squarely within the saving clause as laws "which *regulate* insurance."

Cases interpreting the scope of the McCarran-Ferguson Act have identified three criteria relevant to determining whether a particular practice falls within that Act's reference to the "business of insurance": "*first,* whether the practice has the effect of transferring or spreading a policyholder's risk; *second,* whether the practice is an integral part of the policy relationship between the insurer and the insured; and *third,* whether the practice is limited to entities within the insurance industry." *Union Labor Life Ins. Co. v. Pireno,* 458 U.S. 119 (1982) (emphasis in original). Application of these principles suggests that mandated-benefit laws are state regulation of the "business of insurance."

Section 47B obviously regulates the spreading of risk: as we have indicated, it was intended to effectuate the legislative judgment that the risk of mental-health care should be shared. It is also evident that mandated-benefit laws directly regulate an integral part of the relationship between the insurer and the policyholder by limiting the type of insurance that an insurer may sell to the policyholder. Finally, the third criterion is present here, for mandated-benefit statutes impose requirements only on insurers, with the intent of affecting the relationship between the insurer and the policyholder. Section 47B, then, is the very kind of regulation that this Court has identified as a law that relates to the regulation of the business of insurance as defined in the McCarran-Ferguson Act. . . .

In short, the plain language of the saving clause, its relationship to the other ERISA pre-emption provisions, and the traditional understanding of insurance regulation, all lead us to the conclusion that mandated-benefit laws such as § 47B are saved from pre-emption by the operation of the saving clause.

Nothing in the legislative history of ERISA suggests a different result. There is no discussion in that history of the relationship between the general pre-emption clause and the saving clause, and indeed very little discussion of the saving clause at all. In the early versions of ERISA, the general pre-emption clause pre-empted only those state laws dealing with subjects regulated by ERISA. The clause was significantly broadened at the last minute, well after the saving clause was in its present form, to include all state laws that relate to benefit plans. The change was made with little explanation by the Conference Committee, and there is no indication in the legislative history that Congress was aware of the new prominence given the saving clause in light of the rewritten pre-emption clause, or was aware that the saving clause was in conflict with the general pre-emption provision.[23] There is a complete absence of evidence that Congress intended the narrow reading of the saving clause suggested by appellants here. Appellants do call to our attention a few passing references in the record of the floor debate to the "narrow" exceptions to the pre-emption clause, but these are far too frail a support on which to rest appellants' rather unnatural reading of the clause.

We therefore decline to impose any limitation on the saving clause beyond those Congress imposed in the clause itself and in the "deemer clause" which modifies it. If a state law "regulates insurance," as mandated-benefit laws do, it is not pre-empted. . . .

We are aware that our decision results in a distinction between insured and uninsured plans, leaving the former open to indirect regulation while the latter are not. By so doing we merely give life to a distinction created by Congress in the "deemer clause," a distinction Congress is aware of and one it has chosen not to alter. We also are aware that appellants' construction of the statute would eliminate some of the disuniformities currently facing national plans that enter into local markets to purchase insurance. Such disuniformities, however, are the inevitable result of the congressional decision to "save" local insurance regulation. Arguments as to the wisdom of these policy choices must be directed at Congress. . . .

We hold that Massachusetts' mandated-benefit law is a "law which regulates insurance" and so is not pre-empted by ERISA as it applies to insurance contracts purchased for plans subject to ERISA. . . .

---

[23] The insurance saving clause appeared in its present form in bills introduced in 1970 that led to ERISA. The pre-emption clause apparently was broadened out of a fear that "state professional associations" would otherwise hinder the development of such employee-benefit programs as "pre-paid legal service programs." *See* 120 Cong. Rec. 29197 (1974) (remarks of Rep. Dent); *id.*, at 29933 (remarks of Sen. Williams); *id.*, at 29949 (remarks of Sen. Javits). There is no suggestion that the pre-emption provision was broadened out of any concern about state regulation of insurance contracts, beyond a general concern about "potentially conflicting State laws."

The Conference Committee that was convened to work out differences between the Senate and House versions of ERISA broadened the general pre-emption provision from one that pre-empted state laws only insofar as they regulated the same areas explicitly regulated by ERISA, to one that pre-empts all state laws unless otherwise saved. The change gave the insurance saving clause a much more significant role, as a provision that saved an entire body of law from the sweeping general pre-emption clause. There were no comments on the floor of either Chamber specifically concerning the insurance saving clause, and hardly any concerning the exceptions to the pre-emption clause in general. The change in the pre-emption provision was not disclosed until the Report was filed with Congress 10 days before final action was taken on ERISA. The House conferees filed their Report on August 12, 1974, while the Senate conferees filed their report the following day. ERISA was passed by the House on August 20, and by the Senate on August 22.

NOTES

1. *The Escape Hatch of Self-Insurance.* Mandated benefits, such as those discussed in *Metropolitan Life*, are very common in the States. More than 1,000 separate mandates are currently in state law; some states have as many as 40 separate ones. State mandates commonly require covered plans to provide insurance for certain types of conditions (such as alcoholism), treatments (such as mammography screening), and service providers (such as nurse midwives).

Metropolitan Life permits employers to avoid state regulation by self-insuring, and employers in large numbers have taken advantage of the escape hatch. In 1975, only about 5% of employers self-insured for health insurance. In 2004, 58% of all employees were in self-insured plans, including 85% of those in large plans with 1,000 or more employees. U.S. DEP'T HEALTH & HUMAN SERVS., MEDICAL EXPENDITURE PANEL SURVEY, 2004 EMPLOYER-SPONSORED HEALTH INSURANCE DATA, Table 1.B.2.b.(1) (2006).

2. *The "Plan" Requirement.* ERISA only preempts state laws that relate to "employee benefit *plans*." ERISA § 514(a). In the leading case on the plan requirement, the Supreme Court held that a Maine statute requiring employers to make a one-time severance payment to employees after a plant closing was not preempted because it did not establish a plan or require employers to maintain one:

> The requirement of a one-time lump-sum payment triggered by a single event requires no administrative scheme whatsoever to meet the employer's obligation. The employer assumes no responsibility to pay benefits on a regular basis, and thus faces no periodic demands on its assets that create a need for financial coordination and control. Rather, the employer's obligation is predicated on the occurrence of a single contingency that may never materialize. The employer may well never have to pay the severance benefits. To the extent that the obligation to do so arises, satisfaction of that duty involves only making a single set of payments to employees at the time the plant closes. To do little more than write a check hardly constitutes the operation of a benefit plan.

Fort Halifax Packing Co. v. Coyne, 482 U.S. 1, 12 (1987).

In *Curtis v. Nevada Bonding Corp.*, 53 F.3d 1023 (9th Cir. 1995), the employer agreed to provide health insurance for an employee, but never did. The employer reimbursed the employee for some minor medical expenses, but stopped when the employee was diagnosed with cancer. The employee sued alleging breach of contract and fraudulent misrepresentation. The Ninth Circuit held that these state law claims were not preempted by ERISA because the plan requirement was not met. ERISA coverage, the Court said, extends only to arrangements that are sufficiently specific to enable a reasonable person to "ascertain the intended benefits, beneficiaries, source of financing, and procedures for receiving benefits." *Id.* at 1028, *quoting Donovan v. Dillingham*, 688 F.2d 1367, 1373 (11th Cir. 1982). The Court held that a bare promise to provide health insurance was not sufficient to create a "plan" and, hence, that the plaintiff's state law claims were not preempted. Do you think the Court would have interpreted the plan requirement in the same way if ERISA provided viable alternatives to the state law claims? *See Kenney v. Roland Parson Contr'g Corp.*, 28 F.3d 1254, 1258-59 (D.C. Cir. 1994) (plan requirement met where employer deducted money from employee's wages and promised to contribute them to a pension fund, but never did).

3. The "Relate to" Requirement. ERISA only preempts state laws that "relate to" employee benefit plans. ERISA § 514(a). The Supreme Court has not read this requirement as expansively as it could, thus reducing the potential scope of ERISA preemption. Nevertheless, as the next case illustrates, the requirement still has bite.

RETAIL INDUSTRY LEADERS ASSOCIATION v. FIELDER
United States District Court, District of Maryland
435 F. Supp. 2d 481 (2006)

J. FREDERICK MOTZ, DISTRICT JUDGE.

Retail Industry Leaders Association ("RILA"), a trade association of which Wal-Mart Stores, Inc. ("Wal-Mart") is a member, has brought this action for declaratory and injunctive relief against James Fielder, Jr., in his official capacity as Maryland Secretary of Labor, Licensing, and Regulation ("the Secretary"). RILA seeks a declaration that the Maryland Fair Share Health Care Fund Act ("the Act" or "the Fair Share Act"), Md. Code Ann., Lab. & Empl. § 8.5-101 *et seq.*, is preempted by the federal Employment Retirement Income Security Act of 1974, 29 U.S.C. § 1001 *et seq.* ("ERISA"), and that the Act violates the Equal Protection Clause of the U.S. Constitution.

RILA has filed a motion for summary judgment, and the Secretary has filed a motion to dismiss or for summary judgment. RILA's motion will be granted, and the Secretary's motion will be denied.

I.

On January 12, 2006, the Maryland General Assembly enacted the Fair Share Act, which is scheduled to become effective January 1, 2007. The Act applies only to non-governmental employers of 10,000 or more people in the State. It requires that a for-profit employer that "does not spend up to 8% of the total wages paid to employees in the State on health insurance costs shall pay to the Secretary an amount equal to the difference between what the employer spends for health insurance costs and an amount equal to 8% of the total wages paid to employees in the State." For non-profit employers, the benchmark is 6%. The Act also requires an employer to report annually its total number of employees in the state, the amount spent by the employer on health insurance costs, and the percentage of payroll spent by the employer on health insurance costs. The Act defines "health insurance costs" as "the amount paid by an employer to provide health care or health insurance to employees in the State to the extent the costs may be deductible by an employer under federal tax law."

There are four non-governmental employers of 10,000 or more people in Maryland: Johns Hopkins University ("Johns Hopkins"), Northrop Grumman

Corp. ("Northrop Grumman"), Giant Food Inc. ("Giant Food"), and Wal-Mart. When enacting the law, the Maryland General Assembly anticipated that only Wal-Mart would be affected by the Act's spending requirement.[3] Johns Hopkins is a non-profit institution that meets the lower 6% standard the legislature set for non-profits. Northrop Grumman successfully lobbied for a provision in the Act that permits employers to exclude, for purposes of calculating the percentage of payroll spent on health care, compensation paid to its employees above the median household income in Maryland. This exclusion permits Northrop Grumman to meet the requirement. Giant Food, which actively lobbied for enactment of the legislation, spends substantially in excess of 8% of the total wages it pays to employees in Maryland on health insurance costs. On the other hand, according to the declaration submitted by Gregory Goggans, Wal-Mart's Director of United States Benefits Design, "Wal-Mart has never [since July 2003] made contributions to the health care plans offered to its Maryland employees that were equal to or greater than 8% of the 'total compensation' (as that term is defined in the Act) paid to Maryland employees." . . .

V.

. . . .

Section 514(a) of ERISA preempts "any and all State laws insofar as they may now or hereafter relate to any employee benefit plan" covered by ERISA. ERISA § 514(a). The Supreme Court has observed repeatedly that ERISA's preemption provision is "clearly expansive." *Egelhoff v. Egelhoff*, 532 U.S. 141, 146 (2001). At the same time, the Court has recognized that the term "relate to" cannot be given its most expansive meaning, or else "for all practical purposes pre-emption would never run its course." *Id.* In order to provide discipline to the ERISA preemption inquiry, the Court has held that a law "relates to" an ERISA plan if it has either a "reference to" or "connection with" such a plan. *Shaw v. Delta Air Lines, Inc.*, 463 U.S. 85, 96-97 (1983). Because I find that the Fair Share Act has a "connection with" an ERISA plan and is preempted on that ground, I do not reach the "reference to" issue.[12]

---

[3] *See, e.g.,* Floor debate on Senate Bill 790, 2006 Leg., 421st Sess. (Md. Jan. 12, 2006) (statement of Sen. Miller, co-sponsor of the law) ("Is Wal-Mart afraid? You bet they are."); Floor debate on House Bill 1284, 2006 Leg., 421st Sess. (Md. Jan. 12, 2006) (statement of Del. Healey, co-sponsor of the law) ("We don't want to kill Wal-Mart. We don't want to kill this giant. We want this giant to behave itself."). . . .

[12] A state statute has a "reference to" ERISA where it "acts immediately and exclusively upon ERISA plans" or "where the existence of ERISA plans is essential to the law's operation." *Cal. Div. of Labor Standards Enforcement v. Dillingham Constr., N.A., Inc.*, 519 U.S. 316, 325 (1997). The reference in the Fair Share Act to ERISA plans is direct and express. The payment required by the Act is measured, in part, by the amount of an employer's "health insurance costs" which the Act defines as "the amount paid by an employer to provide health insurance to employees." Md. Code Ann., Lab. & Empl. §§ 8.5-104(b) & 101(d)(1). In *District of Columbia v. Greater Washington Board of Trade*, the Court found ERISA preemption on the basis of statutory language nearly identical to that used in the Fair Share Act. 506 U.S. 125, 130 (1992). However, *Greater Washington Board of Trade* involved a city ordinance requiring employers that provided health insurance coverage for their employees to provide equivalent health insurance coverage for injured employees eligible for workers' compensation benefits. Thus, the ordinance was a benefit-mandating statute that also had a "connection with" ERISA plans. It is not clear that if a statute

In determining whether a statute has a "connection with" an ERISA plan, a court must look to (1) "the objectives of the ERISA statute as a guide to the scope of the state law that Congress understood would survive"; and (2) "the nature of the effect of the state law on ERISA plans." *Egelhoff v. Egelhoff*, 532 U.S. 141, 147.

In regard to the first factor, the main objective of ERISA's preemption clause is "to avoid a multiplicity of regulation in order to permit the nationally uniform administration of employee benefit plans." *New York State Conference of Blue Cross & Blue Shield Plans v. Travelers Ins. Co.*, 514 U.S. 645, 657 (1995). "Uniformity is impossible, however, if plans are subject to different legal obligations in different States." *Egelhoff v. Egelhoff*, 532 U.S. 141, 148. The Fair Share Act creates health care spending requirements that are not applicable in most other jurisdictions. Moreover, its requirements directly conflict with the requirements of at least two other jurisdictions (New York City and Suffolk County, NY), N.Y.C. Admin. Code § 22-506(c)(2); Suffolk County, N.Y., Reg. Local Law § 335-3(A),[13] and conflict with similar pending legislation in many other states, *see, e.g.,* Oklahoma H.B. 2678, 50th Leg., 2d Sess. (2006) (requiring employee health care expenditures of 9% for for-profit employers); Minnesota H.F. 2573, 84th Legis. Sess. (2006) (10%). Further, as a consequence of the Act, a nationwide employer like Wal-Mart must segregate a separate pool of expenditures for its Maryland employees and structure its contributions — and employees' deductibles and co-pays — with an eye to how this will affect the Act's 8% spending requirement.

As to the second factor of the "connection with" test, the intended effect of the Act is to force Wal-Mart to increase its contribution to its health benefit plan, which is an ERISA plan, and the actual effect of the Act will be to coerce Wal-Mart into doing so. Therefore, this factor is fully satisfied.

My finding that the Act is preempted is in accordance with long established Supreme Court law that state laws which impose employee health or welfare mandates on employers are invalid under ERISA. *See, e.g., Greater Washington Bd. of Trade*, 506 U.S. 125; *Shaw*, 463 U.S. 85. The Secretary contends, however, that these authorities are not controlling because a trilogy of cases, *Travelers*, 514 U.S. 645, *Dillingham*, 519 U.S. 316, and *DeBuono v. NYSA-ILA Medical and Clinical Services Fund*, 520 U.S. 806 (1997), have "changed the landscape of ERISA preemption analysis." The short answer to this contention, of course, is that this court has no authority to disregard Supreme Court precedent on the basis of the prediction that the Court would overrule its decisions.

Moreover, the Secretary over-reads the cases upon which he relies. Although, as the Fourth Circuit noted in *Coyne & Delany Co. v. Selman*, 98 F.3d

---

did not mandate benefits or otherwise interfere with uniform funding and administration of ERISA plans, the Supreme Court would hold that literal application of the "reference to" language requires preemption.

[13] The fact that two local jurisdictions, New York City and Suffolk County, have enacted "fair share" legislation of their own highlights the uniformity problem. Unless such legislation is deemed to be preempted, nationwide employers potentially will face not only fifty different requirements imposed by the States, but also a virtually limitless number of requirements that local subdivisions in each State may enact.

1457, 1466-67, 1468 (4th Cir. 1996), the Supreme Court in *Travelers* "narrow[-ed]" its "interpretation of the scope of ERISA preemption" and "adopted a pragmatic approach" to determining whether a state law "relate[s] to" an employee benefit plan, nothing in *Travelers* or its progeny suggests that the Court would now uphold a state statute or local ordinance mandating that an employer provide a certain type or monetary level of welfare benefits in an ERISA plan. Indeed, in *Selman* itself, the Fourth Circuit recognized that "Congress intended ERISA to preempt at least three categories of state law that can be said to have a connection with an ERISA plan," including laws that "mandate employee benefit structures or their administration" and "laws that bind employers or plan administrators to particular choices or preclude uniform administrative practice." *Id.* at 1468.

A short description of the statutes involved in *Travelers, DeBuono,* and *Dillingham* is sufficient to demonstrate that they lie at the periphery of ERISA analysis, not (as does the Fair Share Act) at its core. At issue in *Travelers* was a New York statute that imposed a surcharge on hospital rates for patients who were covered by commercial insurers or who participated in HMOs (as distinct from Blue Cross/Blue Shield).[14] The surcharge was challenged by commercial insurers on the ground that it increased the cost paid by ERISA plans that contracted with the taxed entities. The Court rejected the challenge, finding that the law had only an incidental effect on ERISA plans and did not "frustrat[e] plan administrators' continuing obligation to calculate uniform benefit levels nationwide." *Travelers*, 514 U.S. at 658.

Dillingham involved a California wage law that permitted employers to pay a lower wage for apprentices only if the worker participated in a state-approved apprenticeship program. In California many (but not all) apprenticeship programs are ERISA plans, and the plaintiff contended that the California statute "related" to ERISA plans because it provided economic incentives for ERISA-covered apprenticeship programs to meet the requirements for approval under California law. The Court disagreed, finding, *inter alia,* that California's requirements were "substantively similar" to federal standards for apprenticeship programs, thereby reducing the possibility that "multi state apprentice programs . . . [would be] saddled with 'the administrative and financial burden of complying with conflicting directives among States or between States and the Federal Government.'" *Dillingham*, 519 U.S. at 333 n.10 (quoting *Ingersoll-Rand Co. v. McClendon*, 498 U.S. 133, 142 (1990)).

In *DeBuono,* an ERISA plan that owned and operated three medical centers challenged a New York tax "on gross receipts for patient services at hospitals, residential health care facilities, and diagnostic and treatment centers." *DeBuono*, 520 U.S. at 809-10. Because the New York tax "target[ed]" the "health care industry" as a whole and thus "clearly operat[ed] in a field that has been traditionally occupied by the States," *id.* at 814 & n.10, the Court found no preemption. As the Court further explained, the challenged law simply imposed "a tax on hospitals" and "[m]ost hospitals are not owned or operated by ERISA funds." *Id.* at 816.

---

[14] The surcharge was based upon the facts that Blue Cross/Blue Shield allegedly paid hospitals more promptly than other insurers and accepted subscribers whom other insurers rejected as unacceptable risks. *Travelers*, 514 U.S. at 658.

The Fair Share Act stands in stark contrast to the statutes challenged in *Travelers, Dillingham,* and *DeBuono.* The Act is not merely tangentially related to ERISA plans but is focused upon them. Indeed, as the legislative history makes clear, the Fair Share Act is targeted directly at the ERISA plan of a particular employer. Moreover, the economic effect of the Fair Share Act upon Wal-Mart's ERISA plan could not be more direct: it would require Wal-Mart to increase its health care benefits for Maryland employees and to administer its plan in such a fashion as to ensure that the statutory spending required by the Act is met. Thus, the Act violates ERISA's fundamental purpose of permitting multi-state employers to maintain nationwide health and welfare plans, providing uniform nationwide benefits and permitting uniform national administration.[15]

As an alternative defense to RILA's preemption claim, the Secretary argues that the Act does not "mandate" that an employer of 10,000 or more employees must contribute an amount equal to 8% or more of its payroll to its ERISA plan. According to the Secretary, there are three steps that an employer whose health care expenditures do not meet the statutory spending requirement could take instead of increasing its health care benefits.

First, the Secretary suggests that an employer could comply with the Act by contributing to Health Savings Accounts ("HSAs") for its employees. However, HSAs fall outside the definition of ERISA plans only if "the establishment of the HSAs is completely voluntary on the part of the employees." Employee Benefits Sec. Admin., U.S. Dep't of Labor, Field Assistance Bulletin 2004-1, Apr. 7, 2004. Therefore, an employer could not ensure its compliance with the Act by contributing to HSAs; whether or not it met the statutory expenditure threshold would depend upon whether the HSAs were its employees' preferred means of receiving health benefits.

Second, the Secretary contends that an employee could comply with the Act by spending an amount equal to the requisite percentage of its payroll on first aid facilities. This contention is based upon 29 C.F.R. § 2510.3-1(c)(2), which excepts from the definition of ERISA plans "[t]he maintenance on the premises of an employer of facilities for the treatment of minor injuries or illness or rendering first aid in case of accidents occurring during working hours." While the Secretary's argument may evidence the active imagination of his lawyers, it is utterly out of line with reality. It is through ERISA plans that health care is offered by all four of the employers subject to the Act's requirements, including Wal-Mart, at whom the Act is particularly directed. Moreover, it demeans the seriousness of purpose of the Maryland General Assembly to suggest that it would address health care delivery and cost issues by enacting legislation that could result in a major employer providing health benefits to

---

[15] Of course, I am expressing no opinion on whether legislative approaches taken by other States to the problems of health care delivery and its attendant costs would be preempted by ERISA. For example, the Commonwealth of Massachusetts has recently enacted legislation that addresses health care issues comprehensively and in a manner that arguably has only incidental effects upon ERISA plans. In light of what is generally perceived as a national health care crisis, it would seem that to the extent ERISA allows, it is strongly in the public interest to permit states to perform their traditional role of serving as laboratories for experiment in controlling the costs and increasing the quality of health care for all citizens.

its employees by constructing first aid facilities to minister to minor injuries they have suffered.

The Secretary's third argument is that the Act by its terms does not require an employer to spend a certain amount on health care costs but rather simply provides that if the employer does not do so, it shall pay to the Secretary an amount equal to the difference between its actual health care expenditures and the required amount. Again, while this is theoretically true, it does not even approximate reality. If employers are faced with the choice of paying a sum of money to the State or offering an equal sum of money to their employees in the form of health care, no rational employer would choose to pay the State. While repeatedly emphasizing that employers have a "choice," the Secretary does not offer a single reason why an employer would pay the State rather than generate good will with its work force by increasing its employees' benefits. The "choice" here is a Hobson's choice. *See Travelers*, 514 U.S. at 664 (noting that a Hobson's choice "would be treated as imposing a substantive mandate").

Not only is this proposition self-evident, it is supported by all of the evidence in the record. As previously stated, Wal-Mart, the only company that the Act's assessment provision would affect, has submitted an affidavit that it would increase its contribution to its employees' ERISA plans rather than pay the State. This common sense conclusion is conceded by one of the *amicus curiae* that has submitted a brief on behalf of the Secretary: "It makes better business sense to spend on benefits to one's own employees rather than to pay a tax into a general fund for low-income residents' health care." Moreover, that is precisely the result the General Assembly expected and intended. A statement made by Senator Miller, one of the Act's sponsors, makes clear that the purpose of the spending provision of the Act is to require increased payments for the provision of health benefits. Likewise, the testimony before the Senate Finance Committee of a representative of Giant Foods, which lobbied in favor of the bill confirms that any employer would give additional benefits to its own employees rather than paying money to the State.

VI.

The final question to be addressed is whether the Act violates the Equal Protection Clause. Because the Act relates to economic and social policy that does not create a suspect classification or infringe upon fundamental interests, it is presumed constitutional and "must be upheld against equal protection challenge if there is any reasonably conceivable state of facts that could provide a rational basis for the classification." *FCC v. Beach Communications*, 508 U.S. 307, 313 (1993) (citations omitted). . . .

The ostensible purpose of the Act upon which the Secretary relies in defending against RILA's equal protection challenge is that it requires employers whose health care expenditures fall below the statutory minimum to contribute to a fund that will help defray the State's ballooning Medicaid costs. RILA argues that given this purpose, the Act is irrationally underinclusive because fewer than 2% of Maryland employees work for employers with 10,000 or more employers. Moreover, according to the State's own estimate, even if Wal-Mart were to pay a penalty equal to 1% of its payroll, that would yield about $2.7 million in revenue, which is an insignificant fraction of the State's $4.3 billion Medicaid budget. . . . Thus, RILA contends that the Act exempts the "vast majority of Maryland employers who, when aggregated as a class, contribute to the problem" of the burgeoning Medicaid expenditures "on a far greater scale than the handful of covered employers." According to RILA, "[a] state that intends to address a serious state-wide problem does not enact a law that it knows will affect only one company."

RILA's contention is not without force. There is no data in the legislative record (or in the record before this court) concerning the number of employers in the State at various levels of employment, *e.g.*, 100, 250, 500, 1,000, 2,000, 5,000, or 9,000 employees. Likewise, there is no data to show the amount that the Medicaid budget would be reduced if employers at different levels of employment were covered by the Act.

Such information clearly was relevant to the asserted purpose of the Fair Share Act, and it would be entirely reasonable to say that it is inherently irrational for a legislature to make a classification (as the General Assembly did in adopting the 10,000 employee requirement) without any underlying data to support it. Moreover, although, as the Secretary contends, classifications between "large" and "small" are routinely made by legislatures and generally upheld by the courts, a classification between employers who employ 10,000 or more and those who employ 10,000 or less is an extraordinarily broad one. Certainly, a legislature might have a legitimate concern not to force a "small" employer out of business or, at least, to reduce its workforce, by subjecting it to a mandatory benefit regulation. However, that concern presumably would lead to a definition of "small" that would not encompass an employer of 9,999 persons — the definition implicitly contained in the Act. Likewise, although the law also generally permits classifications to be drawn between for-profit and non-profit entities, the rationality of permitting a giant non-profit institution to provide substantially less health care benefits to its employees than a comparably sized for-profit company is subject to question.[16]

That said, under existing law RILA's equal protection challenge is unavailing. The Supreme Court has made it clear that "equal protection is not a license for courts to judge the wisdom, fairness, or logic of legislative choices."

---

[16] In contrast, the provision that results in Northrop Grumman being exempted from the payment requirement under the Act is clearly rational. Md. Code Ann., Lab. & Empl. § 8.5-103(b). The effect of that provision is to exclude, for purposes of calculating the percentage of payroll spent on health care, compensation paid above the median household income in Maryland. To illustrate this by an easy example, assume that a for-profit employer has a total payroll of $200 million, $50 million of which is paid to persons who earn salaries above the median household income. Assume further that the employer contributes $14 million to employee health care benefits. If the portion of the payroll in excess of the median income is not excluded from the spending formula, the employer would not have met the minimum expenditure requirement of the Fair Share Act since $14 million is only 7% of $200 million. On the other hand, if the higher-than-median portion of the payroll is excluded from the spending formula, the employer does meet the Act's expenditure requirement since $14 million is 10.7% of $150 million. The latter calculation is rationally related to the ostensible purpose of the Act because, as RILA conceded at the hearing, employees' health care benefits do not generally increase with their salary or wages, and persons with a household income above the median in Maryland are, at least generally, not eligible for Medicaid benefits.

Beach Communications, 508 U.S. at 313. A necessary corollary of this principle is that legislatures are permitted the "leeway to approach a perceived problem incrementally." *Id*. at 316.

The cases RILA cites in support of its argument are not to the contrary. In *Smith v. Cahoon,* the Court struck down a state regulation that required transporters of certain food products to carry accident insurance. 283 U.S. 553, 565-66 (1931). As to the regulation's goal of protecting citizens who traveled on the highways with these transporters, the Court could discern no rational reason for "making a distinction between those who carry for hire farm products, or milk or butter, or fish or oysters, and those who carry for hire bread or sugar, or tea or coffee, or groceries in general, or other useful commodities." *Id*. at 567.

Likewise, in *Williams v. Vermont,* the Court invalidated an automobile use tax that exempted from payment those who, while residents of Vermont, had bought and paid sales taxes for their automobile outside of the state, but denied the exemption to persons who had done the same before moving to Vermont. 472 U.S. 14 (1985). Because such use taxes were "designed to protect a state's revenues by taking away the advantages to residents of traveling out of state to make untaxed purchases, and to protect local merchants from out-of-state competition which, because of its lower or nonexistent tax burdens, can offer lower prices," the Court held that it was irrational of the legislature to draw a line based on whether the purchaser lived in Vermont at the time of their purchase. So drawn, "there is no disincentive to the Vermont resident's purchasing outside the State, and there is a penalty on those who bought out-of-state but could not have been expected to do otherwise."

All that *Cahoon* and *Williams* stand for is the unremarkable proposition that legislatures cannot make distinctions that are *per se* irrational when considered in light of the purpose of the statute of which they are a part. In the present case, the distinctions drawn by the General Assembly are not necessarily irrational in and of themselves. What is lacking is any supporting information for the distinctions in the legislative record. Under current Supreme Court law, this difference is one of constitutional significance and undermines RILA's equal protection challenge.

RILA makes a secondary argument that the Act violates the Equal Protection Clause because it was intentionally targeted at Wal-Mart. In support of this argument, RILA cites Justice Jackson's eloquent statement in his concurring opinion in *Railway Express Agency Inc. v. New York*, 336 U.S. 106, 112-13 (1949), that "nothing opens the door to arbitrary action so effectively as to allow . . . officials to pick and choose only a few to whom they will apply legislation and thus to escape the political retribution that might be visited upon them if larger numbers were affected."

Here, the legislation enacted by the General Assembly may well have been more thoughtfully considered (and the members of the Assembly more politically accountable) if it had subjected more than a single employer to its spending requirement. However, unless there is a reason to "infer antipathy" from the targeting of a particular group or person, "[t]he Constitution presumes that . . . even improvident decisions will eventually be rectified by the democratic process and that judicial intervention is generally unwarranted no matter how unwisely we may think a political branch has acted." *Beach Communications*, 508 U.S. at 314. It is only in cases involving politically vulnerable groups that the Supreme Court has appeared to rely, at least in part, on legislative antipathy when invalidating a law under the rational basis test. *See Romer v. Evans*, 517 U.S. 620 (1996) (invalidating Colorado constitutional amendment that prohibited the state and local governments from passing laws to protect persons from discrimination based on their sexual orientation); *City of Cleburne v. Cleburne Living Center, Inc.*, 473 U.S. 432 (1985) (invalidating zoning ordinance that authorized a denial of a special use permit for mentally retarded persons to live together in a group home). Wal-Mart does not contend that it is similarly situated to the plaintiffs in *Romer* and *Cleburne,* and the fact that it is the only entity subject to the spending requirement of the Fair Share Act is not itself sufficient to make out a viable equal protection claim. . . .

It is declared and adjudged that the Maryland Fair Share Health Care Act is preempted by the Employment Retirement Income Security Act of 1974.

NOTES

1. ***Preemption Predictions.*** One of the country's leading ERISA practitioners issued an opinion letter prior to the principal case in which she concluded not only that ERISA did not preempt the Maryland Fair Share Health Care Fund Act, but that it could not even be reasonably argued that the law was preempted. The former may still be true as the case is on appeal, but *RILA* demonstrates that the latter certainly was not true.

The basic tension here is between ERISA's central policy of uniformity and the conflicting value of state experimentation. As Judge Motz said in *RILA*, "it is strongly in the public interest to permit states to perform their traditional role of serving as laboratories for experiment in controlling the costs and increasing the quality of health care for all citizens." *RILA, supra*, at note 15. The complexity of ERISA preemption and the difficulty even experts have in predicting results cuts in a particular direction on this balance. State legislatures are less likely to invest time and political capital on major health care reform when there is great uncertainty about whether their efforts will survive.

2. *Meanwhile in Massachusetts.* Massachusetts recently enacted a more comprehensive approach to health care. MASS. GEN. LAWS ANN. ch. 58 (2006). Parts of the law present significant ERISA preemption issues. The law requires employers with more than 10 employees to offer a "cafeteria" plan to their employees. A cafeteria plan is one which permits employees to choose between two or more types of benefits (such as cash, life insurance, and health insurance). I.R.C. § 125. The plan could be entirely employee funded, but establishing a cafeteria plan would permit employees to pay for benefits with pre-tax dollars. In addition, if an employer with 11 or more employees does not make a "fair and reasonable premium contribution" to an employee health plan, it must pay a "fair share employer contribution" to the Commonwealth for each full-time equivalent employee. The amount of the "fair share" is

capped at $295 per employee, but employers who do not provide insurance *and* who have employees who use free medical services provided by the Commonwealth must also pay a "free rider surcharge." The surcharge ranges from 10% to 100% of the Commonwealth's costs for services to those employees, with the first $50,000 per employer exempted.

Given the recent track record of more experienced ERISA practitioners, we will refrain from predicting whether the Massachusetts law will survive a preemption challenge. But we will predict that if the law is found to be preempted, the decision will chill state efforts to address problems with the health care system.

C. PROBLEMS WITH ENFORCEMENT

ERISA contains its own comprehensive enforcement provisions. ERISA §§ 501-503. But they are limited in a number of ways. For example, compensatory and punitive damages are not available and there is no right to a jury trial in suits to recover benefits. For years, the combination of these limits on remedies under ERISA and its broad preemption of state law remedies has produced troubling outcomes for injured patients, and worrisome incentives for employers. Periodically, pressure builds on Congress to address these problems but, to date, the status quo has proven too powerful to overcome.

CORCORAN v. UNITED HEALTHCARE, INC.
United States Court of Appeals, Fifth Circuit
965 F.2d 1321, *cert. denied*, 506 U.S. 1033 (1992)

KING, CIRCUIT JUDGE:

I. *Background*

. . . .

Florence Corcoran, a long-time employee of South Central Bell Telephone Company (Bell), became pregnant in early 1989. In July, her obstetrician, Dr. Jason Collins, recommended that she have complete bed rest during the final months of her pregnancy. Mrs. Corcoran applied to Bell for temporary disability benefits for the remainder of her pregnancy, but the benefits were denied. This prompted Dr. Collins to write to Dr. Theodore J. Borgman, medical consultant for Bell, and explain that Mrs. Corcoran had several medical problems which placed her "in a category of high risk pregnancy." Bell again denied disability benefits. . . . As Mrs. Corcoran neared her delivery date, Dr. Collins ordered her hospitalized so that he could monitor the fetus around the clock.[1]

Mrs. Corcoran was a member of Bell's Medical Assistance Plan (MAP or "the Plan"). MAP is a self-funded welfare benefit plan which provides medical benefits to eligible Bell employees. It is administered by defendant Blue Cross

---

[1] This was the same course of action Dr. Collins had ordered during Mrs. Corcoran's 1988 pregnancy. In that pregnancy, Dr. Collins intervened and performed a successful Caesarean section in the 36th week when the fetus went into distress.

and Blue Shield of Alabama (Blue Cross) pursuant to an Administrative Services Agreement between Bell and Blue Cross. The parties agree that it is governed by ERISA. Under a portion of the Plan known as the "Quality Care Program" (QCP), participants must obtain advance approval for overnight hospital admissions and certain medical procedures ("pre-certification"), and must obtain approval on a continuing basis once they are admitted to a hospital ("concurrent review"), or plan benefits to which they otherwise would be entitled are reduced.

QCP is administered by defendant United HealthCare (United) pursuant to an agreement with Bell. United performs a form of cost-containment service that has commonly become known as "utilization review." The Summary Plan Description (SPD) explains QCP as follows:

> The Quality Care Program (QCP) . . . assists you and your covered dependents in securing quality medical care according to the provisions of the Plan while helping reduce risk and expense due to unnecessary hospitalization and surgery. They do this by providing you with information which will permit you (in consultation with your doctor) to evaluate alternatives to surgery and hospitalization when those alternatives are medically appropriate. In addition, QCP will monitor any certified hospital confinement to keep you informed as to whether or not the stay is covered by the Plan.

Two paragraphs below, the SPD contains this statement: *When reading this booklet, remember that all decisions regarding your medical care are up to you and your doctor.* It goes on to explain that when a beneficiary does not contact United or follow its pre-certification decision, a "QCP Penalty" is applied. The penalty involves reduction of benefits by 20 percent for the remainder of the calendar year or until the annual out-of-pocket limit is reached. Moreover, the annual out-of-pocket limit is increased from $1,000 to $1,250 in covered expenses, not including any applicable deductible. According to the QCP Administrative Manual, the QCP penalty is automatically applied when a participant fails to contact United. However, if a participant complies with QCP by contacting United, but does not follow its decision, the penalty may be waived following an internal appeal if the medical facts show that the treatment chosen was appropriate. . . .

In accordance with the QCP portion of the plan, Dr. Collins sought pre-certification from United for Mrs. Corcoran's hospital stay. Despite Dr. Collins's recommendation, United determined that hospitalization was not necessary, and instead authorized 10 hours per day of home nursing care. Mrs. Corcoran entered the hospital on October 3, 1989, but, because United had not pre-certified her stay, she returned home on October 12. On October 25, during a period of time when no nurse was on duty, the fetus went into distress and died.

Mrs. Corcoran and her husband, Wayne, filed a wrongful death action in Louisiana state court alleging that their unborn child died as a result of various acts of negligence committed by Blue Cross and United. Both sought damages for the lost love, society and affection of their unborn child. In addition, Mrs. Corcoran sought damages for the aggravation of a pre-existing depressive condition and the loss of consortium caused by such aggravation, and Mr. Corcoran sought damages for loss of consortium. The defendants removed the action to federal court on grounds that it was pre-empted by ERISA and that there was complete diversity among the parties. [The District Court held that the Corcoran's claims were preempted by ERISA and granted summary judgment for the defendants.]

III. *Pre-Emption of the State Law Cause of Action*

A. *The Nature of the Corcorans' State Law Claims*

The Corcorans' original petition in state court alleged that acts of negligence committed by Blue Cross and United caused the death of their unborn child. Specifically, they alleged that Blue Cross wrongfully denied appropriate medical care, failed adequately to oversee the medical decisions of United, and failed to provide United with Mrs. Corcoran's complete medical background. They alleged that United wrongfully denied the medical care recommended by Dr. Collins and wrongfully determined that home nursing care was adequate for her condition. It is evident that the Corcorans no longer pursue any theory of recovery against Blue Cross. . . . We, therefore, analyze solely the question of pre-emption of the claims against United. . . .

The Corcorans based their action against United on [Lousiana malpractice law. Although that law is unclear, we assume the Corcorans can state a cause of action. Our] task now is to determine whether such a cause of action is pre-empted by ERISA.

B. *Principles of ERISA Pre-emption*

. . . .

ERISA contains an explicit pre-emption clause, which provides, in relevant part:

> Except as provided in subsection (b) of this section, the provisions of this subchapter and subchapter III of this chapter shall supersede any and all State laws insofar as they may now or hereafter relate to any employee benefit plan described in [ERISA § 4(a)]. . . .

ERISA § 514(a).[10] It is by now well-established that the "deliberately expansive" language of this clause is a signal that it is [to] be construed extremely broadly. *See FMC Corp. [v. Holliday]*, 498 U.S. [52,] 58 (1990) ("[t]he pre-emption clause is conspicuous for its breadth"). The key words "relate to" are used in such a way as to expand pre-emption beyond state laws that relate to the specific subjects covered by ERISA, such as reporting, disclosure and fiduciary obligations. Thus, state laws "relate to" employee benefit plans in a much broader sense — whenever they have "a connection with or reference to such a plan." *Shaw v. Delta Air Lines, Inc.*, 463 U.S. 85, 96-97 (1983). This sweeping pre-emption of state law is consistent with Congress's decision to

---

[10] Statutory, decisional and all other forms of state law are included within the scope of the preemption clause. ERISA § 514(c)(1) ("The term 'State law' includes all laws, decisions, rules, regulations, or other State action having the effect of law, of any State"). Section 514(b)(2)(A) exempts certain state laws from pre-emption, but none of these exemptions is applicable here.

create a comprehensive, uniform federal scheme for the regulation of employee benefit plans.

The most obvious class of pre-empted state laws are those that are specifically designed to affect ERISA-governed employee benefit plans. *See Mackey v. Lanier Collection Agency & Serv., Inc.*, 486 U.S. 825, 829-30 (1988) (statute explicitly barring garnishment of ERISA plan funds is pre-empted); *Ingersoll-Rand v. McClendon*, 498 U.S. 133, 138-45 (cause of action allowing recovery from employer when discharge is premised upon attempt to avoid contributing to pension plan is pre-empted). But a law is not saved from pre-emption merely because it does not target employee benefit plans. Indeed, much pre-emption litigation involves laws of general application which, when applied in particular settings, can be said to have a connection with or a reference to an ERISA plan. *See Pilot Life [Ins. Co. v. Dedeaux]*, 481 U.S. 41, 47-48 (common law tort and contract causes of action seeking damages for improper processing of a claim for benefits under a disability plan are pre-empted); *Shaw*, 463 U.S. at 95-100 (statute interpreted by state court as prohibiting plans from discriminating on the basis of pregnancy is pre-empted). On the other hand, the Court has recognized that not every conceivable cause of action that may be brought against an ERISA-covered plan is pre-empted. "Some state actions may affect employee benefit plans in too tenuous, remote or peripheral a manner to warrant a finding that the law 'relates to' the plan." *Shaw*, 463 U.S. at 100 n. 21. Thus, "run-of-the-mill state-law claims such as unpaid rent, failure to pay creditors, or even torts committed by an ERISA plan" are not pre-empted. *Mackey*, 486 U.S. at 833 (discussing these types of claims in dicta).

C. Pre-emption of the Corcorans' Claims

Initially, we observe that the common law causes of action advanced by the Corcorans are not that species of law "specifically designed" to affect ERISA plans, for the liability rules they seek to invoke neither make explicit reference to nor are premised on the existence of an ERISA plan. Rather, applied in this case against a defendant that provides benefit-related services to an ERISA plan, the generally applicable negligence-based causes of action may have an effect on an ERISA-governed plan. In our view, the pre-emption question devolves into an assessment of the significance of these effects.

1. United's position — it makes benefit determinations, not medical decisions

United's argument in favor of pre-emption is grounded in the notion that the decision it made concerning Mrs. Corcoran was not primarily a medical decision, but instead was a decision made in its capacity as a plan fiduciary about what benefits were authorized under the Plan. All it did, it argues, was determine whether Mrs. Corcoran qualified for the benefits provided by the plan by applying previously established eligibility criteria. The argument's coup de grace is that under well-established precedent, participants may not sue in tort to redress injuries flowing from decisions about what benefits are to be paid under a plan. . . .

In support of its argument, United points to its explanatory booklet and its language stating that the company advises the patient's doctor "what the medical plan will pay for, based on a review of [the patient's] clinical information and nationally accepted medical guidelines for the treatment of [the patient's] condition." It also relies on statements to the effect that the ultimate medical decisions are up to the beneficiary's doctor. It acknowledges at various points that its decision about what benefits would be paid was based on a consideration of medical information, but the thrust of the argument is that it was simply performing commonplace administrative duties akin to claims handling.

Because it was merely performing claims handling functions when it rejected Dr. Collins's request to approve Mrs. Corcoran's hospitalization, United contends, the principles of *Pilot Life* and its progeny squarely foreclose this lawsuit. In *Pilot Life*, a beneficiary sought damages under various state-law tort and contract theories from the insurance company that determined eligibility for the employer's long term disability benefit plan. The company had paid benefits for two years, but there followed a period during which the company terminated and reinstated the beneficiary several times. The Court made clear, however, that ERISA pre-empts state-law tort and contract actions in which a beneficiary seeks to recover damages for improper processing of a claim for benefits. United suggests that its actions here were analogous to those of the insurance company in *Pilot Life*, and therefore urges us to apply that decision.

2. *The Corcorans' position — United makes medical decisions, not benefit determinations*

The Corcorans assert that *Pilot Life* and its progeny are inapposite because they are not advancing a claim for improper processing of benefits. Rather, they say, they seek to recover solely for United's erroneous medical decision that Mrs. Corcoran did not require hospitalization during the last month of her pregnancy. This argument, of course, depends on viewing United's action in this case as a medical decision, and not merely an administrative determination about benefit entitlements. Accordingly, the Corcorans, pointing to the statements United makes in the QCP booklet concerning its medical expertise, contend that United exercised medical judgment which is outside the purview of ERISA pre-emption.

The Corcorans suggest that a medical negligence claim is permitted . . . because it (1) involves the exercise of traditional state authority and (2) is a law of general application which, although it affects relations between principal ERISA entities in this case, is not designed to affect the ERISA relationship.

3. *Our view — United makes medical decisions incident to benefit determinations*

We cannot fully agree with either United or the Corcorans. Ultimately, we conclude that United makes medical decisions — indeed, United gives medical advice — but it does so in the context of making a determination about the availability of benefits under the plan. Accordingly, we hold that the Louisiana tort action asserted by the Corcorans for the wrongful death of their child allegedly resulting from United's erroneous medical decision is pre-empted by ERISA.

Turning first to the question of the characterization of United's actions, we note that the QCP booklet and the SPD lend substantial support to the Corcorans' argument that United makes medical decisions. United's own booklet tells beneficiaries that it "assess[es] the need for surgery or hospitalization and . . . determine[s] the appropriate length of stay for a hospitalization, based on nationally accepted medical guidelines." United "will discuss with your doctor the appropriateness of the treatments recommended and the availability of alternative types of treatments." Further, "United's staff includes doctors, nurses, and other medical professionals knowledgeable about the health care delivery system. Together with your doctor, they work to assure that you and your covered family members receive the most appropriate medical care." According to the SPD, United will "provid[e] you with information which will permit you (in consultation with your doctor) to evaluate alternatives to surgery and hospitalization when those alternatives are medically appropriate."

United makes much of the disclaimer that decisions about medical care are up to the beneficiary and his or her doctor. While that may be so, and while the disclaimer may support the conclusion that the relationship between United and the beneficiary is not that of doctor-patient, it does not mean that United does not make medical decisions or dispense medical advice. In response, United argues that any such medical determination or advice is made or given in the context of administering the benefits available under the Bell plan. Supporting United's position is the contract between United and Bell, which provides that "[United] shall contact the Participant's physician and based upon the medical evidence and normative data determine whether the Participant should be eligible to receive full plan benefits for the recommended hospitalization and the duration of benefits."

United argues that the decision it makes in this, the prospective context, is no different than the decision an insurer makes in the traditional retrospective context. The question in each case is "what the medical plan will pay for, based on a review of [the beneficiary's] clinical information and nationally accepted medical guidelines for the treatment of [the beneficiary's] condition." A prospective decision is, however, different in its impact on the beneficiary than a retrospective decision. In both systems, the beneficiary theoretically knows in advance what treatments the plan will pay for because coverage is spelled out in the plan documents. But in the retrospective system, a beneficiary who embarks on the course of treatment recommended by his or her physician has only a potential risk of disallowance of all or a part of the cost of that treatment, and then only after treatment has been rendered. In contrast, in a prospective system a beneficiary may be squarely presented in advance of treatment with a statement that the insurer will not pay for the proposed course of treatment recommended by his or her doctor and the beneficiary has the potential of recovering the cost of that treatment only if he or she can prevail in a challenge to the insurer's decision. A beneficiary in the latter system would likely be far less inclined to undertake the course of treatment that the insurer has at least preliminarily rejected.

By its very nature, a system of prospective decisionmaking influences the beneficiary's choice among treatment options to a far greater degree than does the theoretical risk of disallowance of a claim facing a beneficiary in a retrospective system. Indeed, the perception among insurers that prospective determinations result in lower health care costs is premised on the likelihood that a beneficiary, faced with the knowledge of specifically what the plan will and will not pay for, will choose the treatment option recommended by the plan in order to avoid risking total or partial disallowance of benefits. When United makes a decision pursuant to QCP, it is making a medical recommendation which — because of the financial ramifications — is more likely to be followed.

Although we disagree with United's position that no part of its actions involves medical decisions, we cannot agree with the Corcorans that no part of United's actions involves benefit determinations. In our view, United makes medical decisions as part and parcel of its mandate to decide what benefits are available under the Bell plan. As the QCP Booklet concisely puts it, United decides "what the medical plan will pay for." When United's actions are viewed from this perspective, it becomes apparent that the Corcorans are attempting to recover for a tort allegedly committed in the course of handling a benefit determination. The nature of the benefit determination is different than the type of decision that was at issue in *Pilot Life*, but it is a benefit determination nonetheless. The principle of *Pilot Life* that ERISA pre-empts state-law claims alleging improper handling of benefit claims is broad enough to cover the cause of action asserted here.

Moreover, allowing the Corcorans' suit to go forward would contravene Congress's goals of "ensur[ing] that plans and plan sponsors would be subject to a uniform body of benefit law" and "minimiz[ing] the administrative and financial burdens of complying with conflicting directives among States or between States and the Federal Government." *Ingersoll-Rand Co.*, 498 U.S. at 142. Thus, statutes that subject plans to inconsistent regulatory schemes in different states, thereby increasing inefficiency and potentially causing the plan to respond by reducing benefit levels, are consistently held pre-empted. *See Alessi v. Raybestos-Manhattan, Inc.*, 451 U.S. 504, 524 (1981) (striking down law which prohibited plans from offsetting benefits by amount of worker compensation payments); *Shaw*, 463 U.S. at 105 n. 25 (striking down law which prohibited plans from discriminating on basis of pregnancy); *FMC Corp.*, 498 U.S. at 60 (striking down law which eliminated plans' right of subrogation from claimant's tort recovery). But in *Ingersoll-Rand*, the Court, in holding pre-empted the Texas common law of wrongful discharge, when applied against an employer who allegedly discharged an employee to avoid contributing to the employee's pension plan, made clear that a state common law cause of action is equally capable of leading to the kind of patchwork scheme of regulation Congress sought to avoid:

> It is foreseeable that state courts, exercising their common law powers, might develop different substantive standards applicable to the same employer conduct, requiring the tailoring of plans and employer

conduct to the peculiarities of the law of each jurisdiction. Such an outcome is fundamentally at odds with the goal of uniformity that Congress sought to implement.

498 U.S. at 142. Similarly, although imposing liability on United might have the salutary effect of deterring poor quality medical decisions, there is a significant risk that state liability rules would be applied differently to the conduct of utilization review companies in different states. The cost of complying with varying substantive standards would increase the cost of providing utilization review services, thereby increasing the cost to health benefit plans of including cost containment features such as the Quality Care Program (or causing them to eliminate this sort of cost containment program altogether) and ultimately decreasing the pool of plan funds available to reimburse participants.[16] . . .

The acknowledged absence of a remedy under ERISA's civil enforcement scheme for medical malpractice committed in connection with a plan benefit determination does not alter our conclusion. While we are not unmindful of the fact that our interpretation of the pre-emption clause leaves a gap in remedies within a statute intended to protect participants in employee benefit plans, the lack of an ERISA remedy does not affect a pre-emption analysis. Congress perhaps could not have predicted the interjection into the ERISA "system" of the medical utilization review process, but it enacted a pre-emption clause so broad and a statute so comprehensive that it would be incompatible with the language, structure and purpose of the statute to allow tort suits against entities so integrally connected with a plan.

IV. *Extracontractual Damages*

The Corcorans argue in the alternative that the damages they seek are available as "other appropriate equitable relief" under ERISA § 502(a)(3). That section provides:

> (a) A civil action may be brought —
>
>   . . . .
>
> (3) by a participant, beneficiary, or fiduciary (A) to enjoin any act or practice which violates any provision of this subchapter or the terms of the plan, or (B) to obtain other appropriate equitable relief (i) to

---

[16] We find *Independence HMO, Inc. v. Smith*, 733 F. Supp. 983 (E.D. Pa. 1990), cited by the Corcorans, distinguishable on its facts. In *Smith*, the district court did not find pre-empted a state court malpractice action brought against an HMO by one of its members. The plaintiff sought to hold the HMO liable, under a state-law agency theory, for the alleged negligence of a surgeon associated with the HMO. The case appears to support the Corcorans because the plaintiff was attempting to hold an ERISA entity liable for medical decisions. However, the medical decisions at issue do not appear to have been made in connection with a cost containment feature of the plan or any other aspect of the plan which implicated the management of plan assets, but were instead made by a doctor in the course of treatment. We also find *Eurine v. Wyatt Cafeterias*, 1991 WL 207468 (N.D. Tex. 1991), cited in the Corcorans' reply brief, irrelevant to this case. In *Eurine*, an employee of Wyatt Cafeterias sued after she slipped and fell at work. Wyatt had opted out of Texas's workers' compensation scheme, but provided benefits for injured employees pursuant to an ERISA plan. The court held that a tort suit against the employer for its negligence in failing to maintain the floor in a safe condition had nothing to do with the ERISA relationship between the parties, but instead arose from their distinct employer-employee relationship.

redress such violations or (ii) to enforce any provisions of this subchapter or the terms of the plan; . . .

Section 502(a)(3) provides for relief apart from an award of benefits due under the terms of a plan. When a beneficiary simply wants what was supposed to have been distributed under the plan, the appropriate remedy is § 502(a)(1)(B). Damages that would give a beneficiary more than he or she is entitled to receive under the strict terms of the plan are typically termed "extracontractual." Section 502(a)(3) by its terms permits beneficiaries to obtain "other appropriate equitable relief" to redress (1) a violation of the substantive provisions of ERISA or (2) a violation of the terms of the plan. Although the Corcorans have neither identified which of these two types of violations they seek to redress nor directed us to the particular section of the Plan or ERISA which they claim was violated, we need not determine this in order to resolve the issue before us. As outlined below, we find that the particular damages the Corcorans seek — money for emotional injuries — would not be an available form of damages under the trust and contract law principles which, the Corcorans urge, should guide our interpretation of ERISA's remedial scheme. Thus, we hold that even under the interpretation of § 502(a)(3) urged by the Corcorans, they may not recover.

[The Court held that the damages sought by the Corcorans — emotional distress damages — were not available as "other appropriate equitable relief" under § 502(a)(3). The Court's rationale was that only trust and contract doctrines were incorporated into ERISA and that neither doctrine permits the kind of emotional distress damages claimed by the Corcorans. Later, the United States Supreme Court agreed with that conclusion, but based its decision on the meaning of the word "equitable" in § 502(a)(3). The limitation to "equitable" relief, the Court held, limits the available relief to that traditionally viewed as equitable, such as an injunction or restitution, and precludes relief traditionally viewed as legal, such as compensatory or punitive damages. *Mertens v. Hewitt Assocs.*, 508 U.S. 248 (1993).]

The result ERISA compels us to reach means that the Corcorans have no remedy, state or federal, for what may have been a serious mistake. This is troubling for several reasons. First, it eliminates an important check on the thousands of medical decisions routinely made in the burgeoning utilization review system. With liability rules generally inapplicable, there is theoretically less deterrence of substandard medical decisionmaking. Moreover, if the cost of compliance with a standard of care (reflected either in the cost of prevention or the cost of paying judgments) need not be factored into utilization review companies' cost of doing business, bad medical judgments will end up being cost-free to the plans that rely on these companies to contain medical costs.[20] ERISA plans, in turn, will have one less incentive to seek out the companies that can deliver both high quality services and reasonable prices.

Second, in any plan benefit determination, there is always some tension between the interest of the beneficiary in obtaining quality medical care and

---

[20] We note that, were the Corcorans able to recover against United under state law, the contract between Bell and United indicates that United would bear the cost. However, the general application of a liability system to utilization review companies would ultimately result in increased costs to plans such as the Bell plan as it became more expensive for companies such as United to do business.

the interest of the plan in preserving the pool of funds available to compensate all beneficiaries. In a prospective review context, with its greatly increased ability to deter the beneficiary (correctly or not) from embarking on a course of treatment recommended by the beneficiary's physician, the tension between interest of the beneficiary and that of the plan is exacerbated. A system which would, at least in some circumstances, compensate the beneficiary who changes course based upon a wrong call for the costs of that call might ease the tension between the conflicting interests of the beneficiary and the plan.

Finally, cost containment features such as the one at issue in this case did not exist when Congress passed ERISA. While we are confident that the result we have reached is faithful to Congress's intent neither to allow state-law causes of action that relate to employee benefit plans nor to provide beneficiaries in the Corcorans' position with a remedy under ERISA, the world of employee benefit plans has hardly remained static since 1974. Fundamental changes such as the widespread institution of utilization review would seem to warrant a reevaluation of ERISA so that it can continue to serve its noble purpose of safeguarding the interests of employees. Our system, of course, allocates this task to Congress, not the courts, and we acknowledge our role today by interpreting ERISA in a manner consistent with the expressed intentions of its creators.

NOTES

1. *Avoiding Preemption.* Plaintiffs have been creative in attempting to avoid the consequences of cases like *Corcoran*, with mixed results. They argued, for example, that:

- Even if a decision is made by an ERISA plan, they should be able to rely on state law to challenge decisions on the *quality* of the care provided, in contrast to *Corcoran* which challenged a decision to deny benefits. *See Dukes v. U.S. Healthcare, Inc.*, 57 F.3d 350 (3d Cir. 1995) (recognizing state claims challenging quality decisions, distinguishing *Corcoran*).

- Decisions to deny care by an ERISA-covered HMO, acting through its physicians, are *fiduciary* decisions and, hence, subject to the broad remedies available under ERISA's fiduciary sections, in contrast to the narrower remedies available under ERISA's benefit enforcement sections considered in *Corcoran*. *See Pegram v. Herdrich*, 530 U.S. 211 (2000) (holding that mixed eligibility and medical decisions are not fiduciary decisions under ERISA).

- Even if the medical and eligibility decisions themselves are shielded, a plan violates its fiduciary duties if it fails to *disclose* to participants compensation arrangements with physicians which encourage them to deny care. *Compare Shea v. Esensten*, 107 F.3d 625 (8th Cir. 1997) (plans must disclose), *with Weiss v. CIGNA Healthcare, Inc.*, 972 F. Supp. 748 (S.D.N.Y. 1997) (no duty to disclose).

Employers have also been creative in attempting to take advantage of ERISA's barriers to liability. Technically, the limits on liability are available only to self-funded ERISA plans themselves and only for benefit, not medical, decisions. But, to the extent employers could extend the shield of ERISA to service providers, employers would be able to share in the savings by paying lower rates for health care services provided to employees. At the extreme, a large employer could provide health care services, not by contract with independent service providers (such as individual physicians or an HMO), but through an HMO which is wholly owned and funded by the employer. Theoretically, every decision would then be subject to ERISA's remedial limitations. *But cf. De Buono v. NYSA-ILA Med. & Clinical Servs. Fund*, 520 U.S. 806 (1997) (state tax on medical services not preempted even when applied to medical centers owned and operated by ERISA plan).

2. *Issues in ERISA Enforcement*. Congress regularly considers problems with ERISA enforcement. But ERISA has proven to be extraordinarily stable considering the rapidly changing environment within which it operates. In large part, this is a testament to the difficulty of the issues that are presented when change is considered:

- *Federalism*. Should Congress provide its own set of federal regulations or simply ease ERISA's broad preemption and permit the States to begin regulating? Easing preemption would infringe on ERISA's long-standing and strong policy favoring uniform rules to minimize costs, avoid forum shopping, and prevent potentially conflicting State regulations. On the other hand, enacting uniform federal regulations would require a long and complicated federal statute and prevent State experimentation and innovation.

- *Mandated Benefits*. Should Congress require plans to include certain types of benefits, such as broad access to emergency care, to obstetrical and gynecological care, and to specialists? These benefits have broad popular support and seem central to an adequate package of health insurance. On the other hand, every mandated benefit imposes some extra costs and employers are not required to provide health insurance; mandated benefits may aggravate the undercoverage problem.

- *Independent Review*. Should Congress require review of benefit denials by review panels independent of the plan and employer? These reviews would avoid the conflict of interest present when plans deny claims; they may lead to fewer improper denials. On the other hand, the plans will need to pay for this extra layer of review which, once again, may aggravate the undercoverage problem.

- *Caps on Liability*. Should Congress impose caps on compensatory and punitive damages? Because the outcomes in these cases can be so horrendous, the possibility of extremely large awards is very real. Caps on the more discretionary types of liability is a possible approach to this problem. On the other hand, caps tend to shield only the most flagrant and unsympathetic offenders.

- *Employer Liability*. Should Congress permit liability only against health care plans, such as HMOs, and prohibit direct employer liability? Since employers make the decision whether to offer health insurance, a shield against liability may ameliorate the undercoverage problem. On the other hand, no matter where the initial liability falls, most economists believe that the costs ultimately will fall on employers (through increased premiums) and, ultimately, employees themselves (through lower wage increases). Mark V. Pauly, *Taxation, Health Insurance and Market Failure in the Medical Economy*, 24 J. ECON. LIT. 629 (1986). If this is true, no law can shield employers or employees from higher costs resulting from increased legal liability.

D. PORTABILITY

A major problem with employment-based health insurance occurs when workers leave their jobs.[*] In the absence of legal regulation, these workers and their dependents may be ineligible for their old employer's plan and they may not be able to obtain new coverage immediately. A new employer may have a waiting period and, in addition, may exclude pre-existing medical conditions from coverage. Individual health-insurance policies may be available, but they also may exclude pre-existing conditions and, in additon, tend to be expensive because of adverse selection problems and high administrative costs. Health insurers naturally are suspicious that an individual seeking health coverage is anticipating major health expenses. As a result, premiums for individual polcies tend to be high.

This problem with the "portability" of employer-based health insurance is significant. In a recent year, about 700,000 Americans lost their health insurance each month because they, or a spouse or parent, lost their job. The median length of a lapse in coverage was about seven months. Problems with portability, then, contribute to the more general problem: millions of Americans do not have health insurance. In 2004, about 18 percent of the nonelderly population (or 45 million people) did not have health insurance. Paul Fronstin, *Sources of Health Insurance & Characteristics of the Uninsured*, EBRI ISSUE BRIEF NO. 287, Nov. 2005, at 4. Lack of portability is also a concern because it may interfere with the ability of workers to move to more productive jobs. If workers fear problems with their health insurance coverage (for example, because they or their dependents have pre-existing conditions), they may be locked into their current jobs. *See* Jonathan Gruber & Brigitte C. Madrian, *Health Insurance, Labor Supply, and Job Mobility: A Critical Review of the Literature*, *in* HEALTH POLICY & THE UNINSURED 97 (Catherine G. McLaughlin, ed., 2004) (problems with health insurance reduce job mobility by 10-35%).

Congress has responded to the portability problem twice. In 1986, Congress required employers who offer group health insurance to continue to provide coverage for eighteen to thirty-six months from the time of an event (such as a death or job termination) that might otherwise result in loss of coverage.

---

[*] More generally, these types of problems arise whenever a covered worker or a beneficiary is no longer eligible for coverage under the employer's plan. This may occur for a variety of reasons in addition to leaving a job. Coverage may be lost, for example, if the covered worker suffers a reduction in hours, upon divorce, or when a dependent child is no longer eligible for coverage. *See* ERISA § 603.

ERISA §§ 601-608. This type of coverage is called "COBRA" continuation coverage because it was initially enacted as part of the Consolidated Omnibus Budget Reconciliation Amendment Act of 1986. The basic approach of COBRA is to require continued coverage with the "old" employer to give the employee (or spouse or dependent) time to find new health insurance coverage.

COBRA requires employers with twenty or more employees to provide continuation coverage to "covered employees" and "qualified beneficiaries" after "qualifying events." Qualified beneficiaries include the spouse and dependent children of an employee who is covered by the plan. ERISA § 607(3). The qualifying event for an employee is generally termination (although continuation coverage is not required for terminations for "gross misconduct"); for spouses, the qualifying event is usually death of the employee, divorce, or legal separation; and for dependents, the qualifying event is generally loss of dependency status under the terms of the health plan, for example, by becoming too old to be covered as a dependent child. § 603. Employers are required to notify each covered employee and spouse of their COBRA rights at the commencement of coverage under the plan and when a qualifying event occurs. § 606. The employee or qualifying beneficiary has sixty days after the qualifying event to decide whether to accept COBRA coverage. § 605(1). The plan may require those accepting COBRA coverage to pay a premium, but it may not exceed 102 percent of the premium for active employees for the first 18 months of coverage or 150 percent later. § 602(3).

In 1996, Congress reacted to the portability problem again. This time it enacted the Health Insurance Portability and Accountability Act ("HIPAA"). While COBRA looked to the old employer as the primary source of insurance to bridge the gap during transition periods, HIPAA looks instead to new employers and the private insurance market. HIPAA limits the ability of new employers and private insurers to deny health insurance coverage to new applicants. For example, it limits the ability to deny coverage because of pre-existing conditions or through waiting periods. Hence, HIPAA deals with the portability problem by making it easier for employees and their dependents to get health insurance from their new employers or from insurance companies.

HIPAA imposes requirements on group health plans offered by employers (regardless of whether they are insured or self-insured), on insurers who offer group insurance, and on insurers who offer health insurance policies to individuals:

- For group health plans, HIPAA has two principal requirements. First, group health plans cannot limit coverage for pre-existing conditions for more than 12 months and even that period must be reduced by periods of "creditable coverage" under other health plans. "Creditable coverage" includes most kinds of health insurance, but excludes any coverage occurring before a break in coverage of 63 days or more. ERISA § 701. Thus, a new employee who was covered under her immediately preceding employer's health plan for eight months would need to satisfy only a four-month limit on coverage with a new employer. However, if she had been without health insurance for 63 or more days (perhaps because she declined to purchase COBRA continuation coverage from her old employer's plan and took more than 62 days to find the new job), the new employer could impose a 12-month waiting period. One implication of this requirement is that "old" employers must provide employees with certifications of their prior health insurance coverage. ERISA § 701(e).

Second, HIPAA provides that group health plans cannot have eligibility rules (such as waiting periods or requirements for continued eligibility) based on health-related factors, such as physical or mental condition, disability, or medical history. § 702(a). Similarly, a group health plan may not require any individual to pay higher premiums because of any of these health-related factors. § 702(b).

- For insurers who offer group insurance, HIPAA requires insurers operating in the small group market to issue health insurance to all small employers and to accept every eligible individual of those employers. 42 U.S.C. § 300gg-11(a). The small group market covers employers with 2 to 50 employees. § 300gg-91(e)(4). Insurers may deny coverage to small employers only for specified reasons, such as inadequate financial reserves to underwrite additional insurance. § 300gg-11(d)-(f). HIPAA also requires insurers in the large and small group markets to renew policies except for specified reasons, such as nonpayment of premiums or fraud. § 300gg-12.

- For insurers who offer health insurance to individuals, HIPAA requires insurers to issue policies to "eligible individuals" and to renew them. 42 U.S.C. § 300gg-41. "Eligible individuals" are people who have been covered for at least 18 months under a group health plan, who are not eligible for any other group health insurance, and who do not have health insurance. § 300gg-41(b). The policies made available to eligible individuals must be either the two highest-volume individual policies offered by the insurer or two policies that are representative of the policies issued by the insurer. § 300gg-41(c). As with group health plans, HIPAA imposes restrictions on the ability of insurers to limit coverage because of pre-existing conditions. § 300gg-41(a)(1)(B).

COBRA and HIPAA have spawned a veritable snakepit of complicated regulations. One set of issues concerns the terminating employer's responsibilities under COBRA when the worker is covered by a spouse's health insurance plan as well. The following case deals with this issue.

GEISSAL v. MOORE MEDICAL CORP.
United States Supreme Court
524 U.S. 74 (1998)

JUSTICE SOUTER delivered the opinion of the Court.

The Employee Retirement Income Security Act of 1974 (ERISA), as amended by the Consolidated Omnibus Budget Reconciliation Act of 1985 (COBRA), authorizes a qualified beneficiary of an employer's group health plan to obtain continued coverage under the plan when he might otherwise lose that benefit for certain reasons, such as the termination of employment. The issue in this case is whether [ERISA] allows an employer to deny COBRA continuation coverage to a qualified beneficiary who is covered under another group health plan at the time he makes his COBRA election. We hold that it does not.

I

On July 16, 1993, the respondent Moore Medical Corporation fired James Geissal, who was suffering from cancer. While employed, Geissal was covered under Moore's group health plan as well as the health plan provided by his wife's employer, Trans World Airlines (TWA), through Aetna Life Insurance Company.

According to Geissal, soon after he lost his job, Moore told him that he had a right under COBRA to elect to continue coverage under Moore's plan. Geissal so elected, and made the necessary premium payments for six months. On January 27, 1994, however, Moore informed Geissal it had been mistaken: he was not actually entitled to COBRA benefits because on the date of his election he was already covered by another group health plan, through his wife's employer.

Geissal then brought this suit against Moore. . . . Geissal charged Moore with violating COBRA by renouncing an obligation to provide continuing health benefits coverage. . . .

After limited discovery, Geissal moved for partial summary judgment. . . . While the summary judgment motion was pending, Geissal died of cancer, and petitioner Bonnie Geissal, his wife and personal representative of his estate, replaced him as plaintiff.

The Magistrate Judge hearing the case . . . granted partial summary judgment . . . in favor of Moore. . . .

The Court of Appeals for the Eighth Circuit affirmed and we granted certiorari to resolve a conflict among the Circuits on whether an employer may deny COBRA continuation coverage under its health plan to an otherwise eligible beneficiary covered under another group health plan at the time he elects coverage under COBRA.

II

A

The Consolidated Omnibus Budget Reconciliation Act of 1985 amended the Employee Retirement Income Security Act [to] require an employer who sponsors a group health plan to give the plan's "qualified beneficiaries" the opportunity to elect "continuation coverage" under the plan when the beneficiaries might otherwise lose coverage upon the occurrence of certain "qualifying events," including the death of the covered employee, the termination of the covered employee's employment (except in cases of gross misconduct), and divorce or legal separation from the covered employee. [ERISA § 603]. Thus, a "qualified beneficiary" entitled to make a COBRA election may be a "covered employee," (someone covered by the employer's plan because of his own employment), or a covered employee's spouse or dependent child who was covered by the plan prior to the occurrence of the "qualifying event." [§ 607(3)].

COBRA demands that the continuation coverage offered to qualified beneficiaries be identical to what the plan provides to plan beneficiaries who have not suffered a qualifying event. [§ 602(1)]. The statute requires plans to advise beneficiaries of their rights under COBRA both at the commencement of coverage and within 14 days of learning of a qualifying event, [§ 606(a)], after which qualified beneficiaries have 60 days to elect continuation coverage, [§ 605(1)]. If a qualified beneficiary makes a COBRA election, continuation coverage dates from the qualifying event, and when the event is termination or reduced hours, the maximum period of coverage is generally 18 months; in other cases, it is generally 36. [§ 602(2)(A)]. The beneficiary who makes the election must pay for what he gets, however, up to 102 percent of the "applicable premium" for the first 18 months of continuation coverage, and up to 150 percent thereafter. [§ 602(3)]. The "applicable premium" is usually the cost to the plan of providing continuation coverage, regardless of who usually pays for the insurance benefit. [§ 604]. Benefits may cease if the qualified beneficiary fails to pay the premiums, [§ 602(2)(C)], and an employer may terminate it for certain other reasons, such as discontinuance of the group health plan entirely, [§ 602(2)(B)]. COBRA coverage may also cease on

"[t]he date on which the qualified beneficiary first becomes, after the date of the election —

"(i) covered under any other group health plan (as an employee or otherwise), which does not contain any exclusion or limitation with respect to any preexisting condition of such beneficiary, or

"(ii) entitled to benefits under title XVIII of the Social Security Act."

[§ 602(2)(D)].

B

Moore . . . believes that James Geissal's coverage under the TWA plan defeats the claim for COBRA coverage after his election to receive it. As Moore reads [§ 602(2)(D)(i)], it is not relevant when a qualified beneficiary first obtains other health insurance coverage; instead, Moore submits, all that matters is whether, at any time after the date of election, the beneficiary is covered by another group health plan. In any event, Moore claims, James Geissal first became covered under the TWA plan only after his COBRA election, because it was only at that moment that his TWA coverage became primary.

Moore's reading, however, will not square with the text. Subsection [602(2)(D)(i)] does not provide that the employer is excused if the beneficiary "is" covered or "remains" covered on or after the date of the election. Nothing in [§ 602(2)(D)(i)] says anything about the hierarchy of policy obligations, or otherwise suggests that it might matter whether the coverage of another group health plan is primary. So far as this case is concerned, what is crucial is that [§ 602(2)(D)(i)] does not speak in terms of "coverage" that might exist or continue; it speaks in terms of an event, the event of "becom[ing] covered." This event is significant only if it occurs, and "first" occurs, at a time "after the date of the election." It is undisputed that both before and after James Geissal elected COBRA continuation coverage he was continuously a beneficiary of TWA's group health plan. Because he was thus covered before he made his COBRA election, and so did not "first become" covered under the TWA plan after the date of election, Moore could not cut off his COBRA coverage under the plain meaning of [§ 602(2)(D)(i)].

Moore argues, to the contrary, that there is a reasonable sense in which a beneficiary does "first becom[e]" covered under a pre-existing plan "after the date of the election," even when prior coverage can be said to persist after the election date: the first moment of coverage on the day following the election is the moment of first being covered after the date of the election. *See National Cos. Health Benefit Plan v. St. Joseph's Hosp., Inc.*, 929 F.2d 1558, 1570 (11th Cir. 1991) ("[I]t is immaterial when the employee acquires other group health coverage; the only relevant question is when, after the election date, does that other coverage take effect. In the case of an employee covered by preexisting group health coverage, . . . the first time after the election date that the employee becomes covered by a group health plan other than the employer's plan is the moment after the election date"). But that reading ignores the condition that the beneficiary must "first becom[e]" covered after election, robbing the modifier "first" of any consequence, thereby equating "first becomes . . . covered" with "remains covered." It transforms the novelty of becoming covered for the first time into the continuity of remaining covered over time.

Moore argues, further, that even if our reading of the statute is more faithful to its plain language, Congress could not have meant to give a qualified beneficiary something more than the right to preserve the status quo as of the date of the qualifying event.[2] Moore points out that if the phrase "first becomes covered . . . after" the date of election does not apply to any coverage predating election, then the beneficiary is quite free to claim continuation coverage even if he has obtained entirely new group coverage between the qualifying event and the election; in that case, on our reading, COBRA would not be preserving the circumstances as of the date of the qualifying event.

That the plain reading does not confine COBRA strictly to guardianship of the status quo is, of course, perfectly true, though it is much less certain whether this fact should count against the plain reading (even assuming that the obvious reading would be vulnerable to such an objection). The statute is neither cast expressly in terms of the status quo, nor does it speak to the status quo on the date of the qualifying event except with reference to the

---

[2] Moore also argues that Congress could not have intended to render COBRA-eligible those individuals with pre-existing coverage under another health plan at the time of election, because such individuals who in fact elect COBRA coverage are typically high-risk. As a result, Moore contends, covering them under COBRA tends to increase an employer's overall cost of providing a group health plan, and may cause some employers to cease offering a group health plan entirely. This may or may not be true. If substantiated, the argument would be considered in construing the scope of a vague provision; [§ 602(2)(D)(i)], however, is not vague.

coverage subject to election. Nor does a beneficiary's decision to take advantage of another group policy not previously in effect carry any indicia of the sort of windfall Congress presumably would have disapproved. Since the beneficiary has to pay for whatever COBRA coverage he obtains, there is no reason to assume that he will make an election for coverage he does not need, whether he is covered by another policy in place before the qualifying event or one obtained after it but before his election.

Still, it is true that if during the interim between the qualifying event and election a beneficiary gets a new job, say, with health coverage (having no exclusion or limitation for his condition), he will have the benefit of COBRA, whereas he will not have it if his new job and coverage come after the election date. Do we classify this as an anomaly or merely a necessary consequence of the need to draw a line somewhere? For the sake of argument we might call it an anomaly, but that would only balance it against the anomaly of Moore's own position, which defies not only normal language usage but the expectations of common sense: since an election to continue coverage is retroactive to the date of the qualifying event, under Moore's reading of [§ 602(2)(D)(i)], an election that is ineffective to bring about continuation coverage for the roughly 18 (or 36) month statutory period would nonetheless have the surprising effect of providing continuation coverage for the period of weeks, or even days, between the event and the election. One wonders why Congress would have wanted to create such a strange scheme. Thus, assuming that our reading of [§ 602(2)(D)(i)] produces an anomaly, so does Moore's.

But this is not all, for the anomalous consequences of Moore's position are not exhausted without a look at the interpretative morass to which it has led in practice. To support its thesis that Congress meant individuals situated like James Geissal to be ineligible for COBRA benefits, Moore points to a statement in the House Reports on the original COBRA bill, that "[t]he Committee [on Ways and Means] is concerned with reports of the growing number of Americans without any health insurance coverage and the decreasing willingness of our Nation's hospitals to provide care to those who cannot afford to pay." H.R. Rep. No. 99-241, pt. 1, p. 44 (1985). Of course, if this concern (expressed in one House committee report) were thought to be a legitimate limit on the meaning of the statute as enacted, there would be no COBRA coverage for any beneficiary who had "any health insurance" on the date of election, or obtained "any" thereafter. But neither Moore nor any court rejecting the plain reading has gone quite so far. Instead, that draconian alternative has been averted by a nontextual compromise.

The compromise apparently alludes to the proviso that [§ 602(2)(D)(i)] applies so as to authorize termination of COBRA coverage only if the coverage provided by the other group health plan "does not contain any exclusion or limitation with respect to any preexisting condition of such beneficiary." Moore urges us to hold, as some Courts of Appeals have done, that although Congress generally intended to deny COBRA coverage to individuals with other group insurance on the election date, there will still be COBRA eligibility in such cases if there is a "significant gap" between the coverage offered by the employer's plan and that offered by the beneficiary's other group health plan.[3] When there is such a gap, some courts have explained, it cannot be said that the employee is truly "covered" by his pre-existing insurance coverage.

This "significant gap" approach to [§ 602(2)(D)(i)] is plagued with difficulties, however, beginning with the sheer absence of any statutory support for it. Subsection [602(2)(D)(i)] makes no mention of what to do when a person's other coverage is generally inadequate or inferior; instead, it provides merely that coverage under a later-acquired group health plan will not terminate COBRA rights when that plan limits or excludes coverage for a pre-existing condition of the beneficiary. The proviso applies not when there is a "gap" or difference between the respective coverages of the two policies, but when the later-acquired group coverage excludes or limits coverage specific to the beneficiary's pre-existing condition. It is this "gap" between different coverage provisions of the non-COBRA plan, not a gap between the coverage provisions of the COBRA plan and the non-COBRA plan, that Congress was legislating about.

But even leaving textual inadequacy aside, there is further trouble under the "significant gap" approach. Needless to say, when the proviso (as written) arguably does apply, its applicability is easy to determine. Once the beneficiary's pre-existing condition is identified, a court need only look among the terms of the later policy for an exclusion or limitation peculiar to that condition. If either is found, COBRA continuation coverage is left undisturbed; if neither is found, the consequence of obtaining this later insurance is automatic. Applying the significant gap rule, on the other hand, requires a very different kind of determination, essentially one of social policy. Once a gap is found, the court must then make a judgment about the adequacy of medical insurance under the later group policy, for this is the essence of any decision about whether the gap between the two regimes of coverage is "significant" enough. This is a powerful point against the gap interpretation for two reasons. First, the required judgment is so far unsuitable for courts that we would expect a clear mandate before inferring that Congress meant to foist it on the judiciary.[4] What is even more strange, however, is that Congress would have meant to inject the courts into the policy arena, evaluating the adequacy of non-COBRA coverage that happened to be in place prior to the COBRA election, while at the same time intending to limit the judicial intrusion, and leave the beneficiary to the unmediated legal consequences of the terms of the non-COBRA coverage that happened to become effective after the election. One just cannot credibly attribute such oddity to congressional intent.

---

[3] The lower courts have disagreed about whether this "significant gap" interpretation should be made by evaluating the actual expenses an employee incurs as a result of COBRA cancellation, or by comparing the policies' provisions in light of the information available to the employer on the day of the COBRA election.

[4] The unlikelihood, indeed, appears overwhelming when one considers that the same comparison would have to be made when the beneficiary was covered under Medicare, which is treated like a separate group plan for present purposes, see [§ 602(2)(D)(ii)].

In sum, there is no justification for disparaging the clarity of [§ 602(2)(D)(i)]. The judgment of the Court of Appeals is vacated, and the case is remanded for further proceedings consistent with this opinion.

It is so ordered.

NOTES

1. *Adverse Selection and the Cost of COBRA premiums.* Justice Souter errs in describing the premium charged to persons electing COBRA continuation coverage as "the cost to the plan of providing continuation coverage," implying that COBRA participants pay their own way. In fact, the premium for continuation coverage cannot be more than 102% of the cost to the plan of covering other employees. ERISA § 604(1).

This limitation on premiums combines with adverse selection to make COBRA an expensive mandatory feature for employers. Since healthy persons faced with the sudden loss of income from losing their job tend to forego COBRA coverage, the persons selecting coverage tend to be more high risk on average than the normal employee. Additionally, the stress caused by the loss of employment adds to the likelihood that terminated employees will have health problems. This adverse selection results in insurance claims from COBRA recipients far exceeding their premium payments. One study found that COBRA recipients receive about $350 in benefits for every $100 in premiums paid. Employers and other employees must make up the difference. At the margin, some employers may not offer health insurance at all because of the extra costs.

These adverse selection concerns are also present for the "guaranteed issue" portions of HIPAA. Insurers must issue policies to small employers and to individuals, under certain conditions. Consider HIPAA's guarantee of an individual health insurance policy. Individuals who expect high medical costs will be more likely to seek these policies. If that occurs, the pool of people covered by individual policies will become less healthy overall and, hence, the amount of benefits that must be paid will increase. Insurance companies would then charge more for all individual policies to cover the extra costs, which may mean that some "healthy" individuals decide to drop their policies. (HIPAA does not regulate how much insurers can charge for individual policies.) The magnitude of the adverse selection effect, and the extent to which it might increase costs and the number of "voluntarily" uninsured persons, was a major part of the debate on HIPAA.

2. *Adverse Selection Aggravated.* COBRA's adverse selection problem is aggravated because the terminated employee can elect coverage retroactively to the date of the qualifying event. In *Schlett v. Avco Financial Services, Inc.,* 950 F. Supp. 823 (N.D. Ohio 1996), for example, a pregnant employee was reduced to part-time status on January 1, which made her ineligible for the employer's insurance plan and thus eligible for COBRA continuation coverage. She gave birth prematurely on February 17, and elected COBRA continuation coverage on February 24. All but $12,500 of the $130,000 in medical bills were covered under her husband's policy, but the remainder made COBRA coverage a good deal. Today, the employer's plan would have to pay: the election was proper (it must be made within 60 days of the qualifying event) and the employer, after *Geissal*, would not have been permitted to deny COBRA coverage because of the pre-existing coverage under her husband's policy. (*Schlett* was a pre-*Geissal* case which denied COBRA coverage because of the pre-existing policy.)

3. *Help from HIPAA?* *Geissal* arose before HIPAA became effective. If COBRA had been unavailable, would HIPAA have helped? HIPAA facilitates transitions from one employer to another by limiting the ability of the new employer to impose waiting periods and pre-existing condition limitations. But Geissal did not have a new job and was not in a position to seek one. HIPAA also deals with the problems of small employers in getting and keeping health insurance for their employees, but that was not at issue here. Finally, HIPAA attempts to facilitate movement from employers to the private insurance market by requiring insurers to offer individual policies to eligible individuals. Geissal, however, was not an "eligible individual" because he had other health insurance coverage. 42 U.S.C. § 300gg-41(b)(2). Can you think of any reason that HIPAA permits an insurer to deny coverage if an individual has *any* other health insurance coverage, while COBRA only permits an employer to deny coverage because of other insurance obtained after the COBRA election?

4. *More Soup.* OBRA is a related alphabet-soup requirement. Enacted as part of the Omnibus Budget Reconciliation Act of 1993, OBRA's principal requirement makes possible qualified medical child support orders (QMCSO). A QMCSO is an order or agreement made pursuant to a state domestic relations law which requires a group health plan to provide coverage to the child of a plan participant. The typical situation would be one where the custodial parent in a divorce obtains an order or agreement requiring the non-custodial parent to enroll a child in the latter's health care plan at his/her expense. A QMCSO cannot require a plan to provide a new or different type of benefit, but the plan must enroll the dependent child in the plan if presented with a valid QMCSO. ERISA § 609. *See also* ERISA § 514(b)(7) (state law is not preempted with regard to QMCSOs). If this all sounds familiar, it should. QMCSOs are often called "kiddie QDROs" because they are modeled after qualified domestic relations orders designed to protect the pension interests of spouses upon divorce, which we discussed in the prior chapter.

E.   HEALTH-CARE COVERAGE FOR INDIVIDUALS WITH DISABILITIES

McGANN v. H & H MUSIC CO.
United States Court of Appeals, Fifth Circuit
946 F.2d 401 (1991)

Garwood, Circuit Judge:

Plaintiff-appellant John McGann (McGann) filed this suit under section 510 of the Employee Retirement Income Security Act of 1974 (ERISA), against defendants-appellees H & H Music Company (H & H Music) . . . and General American Life Insurance Company (General American) claiming that they discriminated against McGann, an employee of H & H Music, by reducing benefits available to H & H Music's group medical plan beneficiaries for treatment for acquired immune deficiency syndrome (AIDS) and related illnesses. The district court granted defendants' motion for summary judgment on the ground that an employer has an absolute right to alter the terms of medical coverage available to plan beneficiaries. We affirm.

McGann, an employee of H & H Music, discovered that he was afflicted with AIDS in December 1987. Soon thereafter, McGann submitted his first claims for reimbursement under H & H Music's group medical plan . . . issued by General American, the plan insurer, and informed his employer that he had AIDS. McGann met with officials of H & H Music in March 1988, at which time they discussed McGann's illness. Before the change in the terms of the plan, it provided for lifetime medical benefits of up to $1,000,000 to all employees.

In July 1988, H & H Music informed its employees that, effective August 1, 1988, changes would be made in their medical coverage. These changes included, but were not limited to, limitation of benefits payable for AIDS-related claims to a lifetime maximum of $5,000.[1] No limitation was placed on any other catastrophic illness. H & H Music became self-insured under the new plan and General American became the plan's administrator. By January 1990, McGann had exhausted the $5,000 limit on coverage for his illness.

In August 1989, McGann sued H & H Music . . . and General American under section 510 of ERISA, which provides, in part, as follows:

> It shall be unlawful for any person to discharge, fine, suspend, expel, discipline, or discriminate against a participant or beneficiary for exercising any right to which he is entitled under the provisions of an employee benefit plan, . . . or for the purpose of interfering with the attainment of any right to which such participant may become entitled under the plan. . . .

McGann claimed that defendants discriminated against him in violation of both prohibitions of section 510. He claimed that the provision limiting coverage for AIDS-related expenses was directed specifically at him in retaliation for exercising his rights under the medical plan and for the purpose of interfering with his attainment of a right to which he may become entitled under the plan.

Defendants, conceding the factual allegations of McGann's complaint, moved for summary judgment. These factual allegations include no assertion that the reduction of AIDS benefits was intended to deny benefits to McGann for any reason which would not be applicable to other beneficiaries who might then or thereafter have AIDS, but rather that the reduction was prompted by the knowledge of McGann's illness, and that McGann was the only

---

[1] Other changes included increased individual and family deductibles, elimination of coverage for chemical dependency treatment, adoption of a preferred provider plan, and increased contribution requirements.

beneficiary then known to have AIDS.[4] On June 26, 1990, the district court granted defendants' motion. . . .

McGann contends that defendants violated both clauses of section 510 by discriminating against him for two purposes: (1) "for exercising any right to which [the beneficiary] is entitled," and (2) "for the purpose of interfering with the attainment of any right to which such participant may become entitled." In order to preclude summary judgment in defendants' favor, McGann must make a showing sufficient to establish the existence of a genuine issue of material fact with respect to each material element on which he would carry the burden of proof at trial.

At trial, McGann would bear the burden of proving the existence of defendants' specific discriminatory intent as an essential element of either of his claims. Thus, in order to survive summary judgment McGann must make a showing sufficient to establish that a genuine issue exists as to defendants' specific intent to retaliate against McGann for filing claims for AIDS-related treatment or to interfere with McGann's attainment of any right to which he may have become entitled.

Although we assume there was a connection between the benefits reduction and either McGann's filing of claims or his revelations about his illness, there is nothing in the record to suggest that defendants' motivation was other than as they asserted, namely to avoid the expense of paying for AIDS treatment (if not, indeed, also for other treatment), no more for McGann than for any other present or future plan beneficiary who might suffer from AIDS. McGann concedes that the reduction in AIDS benefits will apply equally to all employees filing AIDS-related claims and that the effect of the reduction will not necessarily be felt only by him. He fails to allege that the coverage reduction was otherwise specifically intended to deny him particular medical coverage except "in effect." He does not challenge defendants' assertion that their purpose in reducing AIDS benefits was to reduce costs.

Furthermore, McGann has failed to adduce evidence of the existence of "any right to which [he] may become entitled under the plan." The right referred to in the second clause of section 510 is not simply any right to which an employee may conceivably become entitled, but rather any right to which an employee may become entitled pursuant to an existing, enforceable obligation assumed by the employer. "Congress viewed [section 510] as a crucial part of ERISA because, without it, employers would be able to circumvent the provision of *promised* benefits." *Ingersoll-Rand Co. v. McClendon,* 498 U.S. 133, 143 (1990) (emphasis added).

McGann's allegations show no *promised* benefit, for there is nothing to indicate that defendants ever promised that the $1,000,000 coverage limit was permanent. The H & H Music plan expressly provides: "Termination or Amendment of Plan: The Plan Sponsor may terminate or amend the Plan at any time or terminate any benefit under the Plan at any time." There is no allegation or evidence that any oral or written representations were made to

---

[4] We assume, for purposes of this appeal that the defendants' knowledge of McGann's illness was a motivating factor in their decision to reduce coverage for AIDS-related expenses, that this knowledge was obtained either through McGann's filing of claims or his meetings with defendants, and that McGann was the only plan beneficiary then known to have AIDS.

McGann that the $1,000,000 coverage limit would never be lowered. Defendants broke no promise to McGann. The continued availability of the $1,000,000 limit was not a right to which McGann may have become entitled for the purposes of section 510.

To adopt McGann's contrary construction of this portion of section 510 would mean that an employer could not effectively reserve the right to amend a medical plan to reduce benefits respecting subsequently incurred medical expenses, as H & H Music did here, because such an amendment would obviously have as a purpose preventing participants from attaining the right to such future benefits as they otherwise might do under the existing plan absent the amendment. But this is plainly not the law, and ERISA does not require such "vesting" of the right to a continued level of the same medical benefits once those are ever included in a welfare plan.

McGann appears to contend that the reduction in AIDS benefits alone supports an inference of specific intent to retaliate against him or to interfere with his future exercise of rights under the plan. McGann characterizes as evidence of an individualized intent to discriminate the fact that AIDS was the only catastrophic illness to which the $5,000 limit was applied and the fact that McGann was the only employee known to have AIDS. He contends that if defendants reduced AIDS coverage because they learned of McGann's illness through his exercising of his rights under the plan by filing claims, the coverage reduction therefore could be "retaliation" for McGann's filing of the claims.[6] Under McGann's theory, any reduction in employee benefits would be impermissibly discriminatory if motivated by a desire to avoid the anticipated costs of continuing to provide coverage for a particular beneficiary. McGann would find an implied promise not to discriminate for this purpose; it is the breaking of this promise that McGann appears to contend constitutes interference with a future entitlement.

McGann cites only one case in which a court has ruled that a change in the terms and conditions of an employee-benefits plan could constitute illegal discrimination under section 510.[7] *Vogel v. Independence Federal Sav. Bank,* 728 F. Supp. 1210 (D. Md. 1990). In *Vogel,* however, the plan change at issue resulted in the plaintiff and only the plaintiff being excluded from coverage. McGann asserts that the *Vogel* court rejected the defendant's contention that mere termination of benefits could not constitute unlawful discrimination under section 510, but in fact the court rejected this claim not because it found that mere termination of coverage could constitute discrimination under section 510, but rather because the termination at issue affected only the beneficiary. Nothing in *Vogel* suggests that the change there had the potential to then or thereafter exclude any present or possible future plan beneficiary

---

[6] We assume that discovery of McGann's condition — and realization of the attendant, long-term costs of caring for McGann — did in fact prompt defendants to reconsider the $1,000,000 limit with respect to AIDS-related expenses and to reduce the limit for future such expenses to $5,000.

[7] Additionally, McGann relies on three cases involving wrongful termination claims brought under section 510. *Fitzgerald v. Codex Corp.,* 882 F.2d 586 (1st Cir. 1989); *Kross v. Western Electric Co.,* 701 F.2d 1238 (7th Cir. 1983); *Folz v. Marriott Corp.,* 594 F. Supp. 1007 (W.D. Mo. 1984). In none of these cases, however, did the employer alter the terms or conditions of the plan at issue. Nor did any one of the three suggest that the changing of the terms of the plan might constitute a violation of section 510.

other than the plaintiff. *Vogel* therefore provides no support for the proposition that the alteration or termination of a medical plan could alone sustain a section 510 claim. Without necessarily approving of the holding in *Vogel*, we note that it is inapplicable to the instant case. The post-August 1, 1988 $5,000 AIDS coverage limit applies to any and all employees.[8] . . .

McGann's claim cannot be reconciled with the well-settled principle that Congress did not intend that ERISA circumscribe employers' control over the content of benefits plans they offered to their employees. McGann interprets section 510 to prevent an employer from reducing or eliminating coverage for a particular illness in response to the escalating costs of covering an employee suffering from that illness. Such an interpretation would, in effect, change the terms of H & H Music's plan. Instead of making the $1,000,000 limit available for medical expenses on an as-incurred basis only as long as the limit remained in effect, the policy would make the limit *permanently* available for all medical expenses as they might thereafter be incurred because of a single event, such as the contracting of AIDS. Under McGann's theory, defendants would be effectively proscribed from reducing coverage for AIDS once McGann had contracted that illness and filed claims for AIDS-related expenses. If a federal court could prevent an employer from reducing an employee's coverage limits for AIDS treatment once that employee contracted AIDS, the boundaries of judicial involvement in the creation, alteration or termination of ERISA plans would be sorely tested. . . .

Proof of defendants' specific intent to discriminate among plan beneficiaries on grounds not proscribed by section 510 does not enable McGann to avoid summary judgment. ERISA does not broadly prevent an employer from "discriminating" in the creation, alteration or termination of employee benefits plans; thus, evidence of such intentional discrimination cannot alone sustain a claim under section 510. That section does not prohibit welfare plan discrimination between or among categories of diseases. Section 510 does not mandate that if some, or most, or virtually all catastrophic illnesses are covered, AIDS (or any other particular catastrophic illness) must be among them. It does not prohibit an employer from electing not to cover or continue to cover AIDS, while covering or continuing to cover other catastrophic illnesses, even though the employer's decision in this respect may stem from some "prejudice" against AIDS or its victims generally. The same, of course, is true of any other disease and its victims. That sort of "discrimination" is simply not addressed by section 510. Under section 510, the asserted discrimination is illegal only if it is motivated by a desire to retaliate against an

---

[8] [T]he district court stated as one ground for its decision that an employer has an absolute right to alter the terms of an employee benefits plan, barring contractual provisions to the contrary. *See Deeming v. American Standard, Inc.,* 905 F.2d 1124, 1127 (7th Cir. 1990) ("allegation that the employer-employee relationship, and not merely the pension plan, was changed in some discriminatory or wrongful way" is "a fundamental prerequisite to a § 510 action"); *Owens v. Storehouse, Inc.,* 773 F. Supp. 416, 418 (N.D. Ga. 1991) (relying on *Deeming* in rejecting claim that employer violated section 510 by reducing AIDS benefits from $1,000,000 to $25,000 under employee health plan on ground that "§ 510 was designed to protect the 'employment relationship,' not the integrity of specific plans.") We do not find it necessary to decide this question.

employee or to deprive an employee of an existing right to which he may become entitled. The district court's decision to grant summary judgment to defendants therefore was proper.

Its judgment is accordingly affirmed.

NOTES

1. ***The Attractions of Self-Insurance.*** Subsequent to *McGann,* the state in which the case arose enacted a statute that prohibits insurers from canceling health insurance policies because an insured has been diagnosed as having the HIV virus or AIDS. Tex. Ins. Code Ann. § 3.70-3A. Even if the statute had been in force at the time, however, it would not have helped McGann. When H & H Music learned of McGann's illness, one of its first steps was to self-insure. This ensured that its actions could not be challenged under state laws regulating insurance companies.

2. ***What About HIPAA?*** HIPAA prohibits group health plans, whether insured or self-insured, from discriminating against individual participants and beneficiaries based on health status. ERISA § 702. Would HIPAA have helped McGann? Probably not. Section 702 prohibits health-status discrimination only with respect to eligibility rules, such as waiting periods before one can join a plan. § 702(a)(1). The Section specifically denies any intent to infringe on an employer's ability to "establish[] limitations or restrictions on the amount, level, extent, or nature of the benefits or coverage for similarly situated individuals enrolled in the plan." § 702(a)(2)(B). *See* House Conf. Rep. No. 104-736, 104th Cong., 2d Sess. 186-87, *reprinted in* 1996 U.S.C.C.A.N. 1990, 1999-2000 (under provision, employer cannot deny benefits to an individual beneficiary if they are available to others, but it can deny benefits to all beneficiaries even if denial has disparate impact on certain individuals).

3. ***What About the ADA?*** *McGann* also arose before the effective date of the Americans With Disabilities Act. Would it have helped McGann?

The EEOC's position is that separate and lower caps on coverage for HIV/AIDS generally violate the ADA. Caps are permissible only if the employer can demonstrate that the cap was justified actuarially in the same way as other benefit limitations; that coverage would undermine the solvency of the plan; that coverage would require unacceptable changes in coverage or premiums; or that the excluded benefits have no medical value. EEOC, Compliance Manual, Chap. 3 (2000). Although the burden is heavy, H & H Music may have been able to justify its cap. H & H Music was a small employer, so continued coverage may have threatened the solvency of the plan or produced "unacceptable" increases in premiums.

The leading court case on the issue denies that a cap on HIV/AIDS is cognizable discrimination at all. In *Doe v. Mutual of Omaha Insurance Co.,* 179 F.3d 557 (7th Cir. 1999), plaintiffs challenged a $25,000 lifetime cap on AIDS coverage in policies offered by an insurance company. The Court held that the cap was not discrimination:

> The common sense of the [ADA] is that the content of the goods or services offered . . . is not regulated. A camera store may not [bar the

door or] refuse to sell cameras to a disabled person, but it is not required to stock cameras specially designed for such persons. . . . It is hardly a feasible judicial function to decide whether shoestores should sell single shoes to one-legged persons and if so at what price, or how many Braille books the Borders or Barnes and Nobles bookstore chains should stock in each of their stores.

Id. at 560. This interpretation was challenged by the dissent:

The majority believes we are being asked to regulate the content of insurance policies — something we should not do under the ADA. But as I see it we are not being asked to regulate content; we are being asked to decide whether an insurer can discriminate against people with AIDS, refusing to pay for them the same expenses it would pay if they did not have AIDS. The ADA assigns to courts the task of passing judgment on such conduct. And to me the Mutual of Omaha policies at issue violate the Act.

[The majority's] opinion likens the insurance company here to a camera store forced to stock cameras specially designed for disabled persons. . . . I think the analogy misses the mark. The better analogy would be that of a store which lets disabled customers in the door, but then refuses to sell them anything but inferior cameras.

Id. at 565. *Doe* was a public accommodations case under Title III of the ADA rather than an employment case under Title I, but the basic meaning of discrimination under the statute should be the same for both Titles.

4. *How About Some Soup?* If denying coverage for HIV and AIDS is a problem, a more direct and sure-fire solution would be a federal statute requiring plans to provide coverage. Congress has not seen fit to enact such a statute in response to *McGann*. But the approach has been used to require coverage in other situations. ERISA's alphabet-soup provisions require:

- Plans that provide coverage for hospital stays in connection with childbirth to guarantee at least a 48-hour hospital stay for normal childbirth and at least a 96-hour stay for birth by caesarean section. ERISA § 711.

- Plans that provide mental health benefits to have the same or greater lifetime and annual limits for mental health benefits as for medical or surgical care benefits. ERISA § 712.

- Plans that provide medical and surgical benefits for mastectomies to provide coverage for reconstruction and prostheses. ERISA § 713.

While these requirements seem fair and sensible, the basic tension here is that nothing in ERISA or elsewhere requires employers to provide health insurance. Thus, adding requirements like these may, at the margin, result in fewer employers providing health insurance at all. Ultimately, it is this balance between better coverage versus no coverage that will determine whether alphabet-soup requirements are viewed as ill-advised "ad hoc" approaches or as prudential "incremental reform." Colleen E. Medill, *HIPAA and Its Related Legislation: A New Role for ERISA in the Regulation of Private Health Care Plans?*, 65 TENN. L. REV. 485, 508 (1998).

F. RETIREE HEALTH CARE

Employers often promise health insurance for employees who retire. This is a benefit that can help employers retain employees who value this future benefit while, ironically, also helping them to ease older, less productive employees into retirement by addressing one of their principal concerns.

But, for a number of reasons, employers have been paying extra attention to health benefits for retirees in recent years. The cost of retiree health benefits has increased faster than the cost of health benefits generally; changes in Medicare have shifted costs to corporate plans; changes in accounting rules have increased both employer awareness and the market saliency of these costs; and the trend towards early retirement has increased the proportion of retired employees who are not covered by Medicare and the proportion of retired to active employees.

One option for employers worried about these trends is to stop promising this benefit for future retirees, and employers have increasingly been pursuing that option. In 1988, 66 percent of large employers provided retiree health benefits. By 2002, the percentage had declined to just 34 percent. H.R. Conf. Rep. No. 108-391, at 484 (2003). But that still leaves a very substantial tail of costs from promises made to employees who have already retired. Employers have also attempted to reduce these costs. Those attempts have not gone unchallenged.

SPRAGUE v. GENERAL MOTORS CORP.
United States Court of Appeals, Sixth Circuit (en banc)
133 F.3d 388, *cert. denied*, 524 U.S. 923 (1998)

David A. Nelson, Circuit Judge.

In 1961 General Motors began paying part of the cost of health insurance for its salaried retirees and their surviving spouses. Three years later GM assumed the full cost of basic health insurance for its salaried retirees, and in 1968 it extended this benefit to surviving spouses as well. (In the interest of simplicity, further reference to surviving spouses will generally be omitted.)

. . .

Prior to 1985 the health care benefits were provided through arrangements with private insurers. The insurers issued each covered person a certificate of insurance describing the terms and conditions of the underlying policy.

GM became fully self-insured in 1985. At that time the company prepared a document, entitled "The General Motors Health Care Insurance Program for Salaried Employees," that set forth the terms and conditions of GM's self-insured health care program. The district court found that this document, together with subsequent documents announcing changes in coverage, comprised GM's health care benefits plan from and after 1985. . . .

GM has long made it a practice to inform its salaried employees and retirees of their health care coverage by providing them booklets containing summaries of the company's health insurance policies and programs. Prior to 1974 GM put out a booklet entitled "The GM Insurance Program for Salaried Employees." After ERISA took effect in 1974 the booklet became "Highlights of Your GM Benefits." Beginning in 1977 GM also issued a booklet called "Your Benefits in Retirement." Each of these publications went through a series of different editions.

A number of the booklets contained language informing plan participants that the health care plan called for GM to pay health insurance costs during retirement: . . .

- "Hospital-Medical Coverages: Your basic coverages will be provided at Corporation expense for your lifetime. . . ." Highlights of Your GM Benefits (1974).

- "Your basic health care coverages will be provided at GM's expense for your lifetime. . . ." Your Benefits in Retirement (1977). . . .

However, most of the booklets also put plan participants on notice of GM's right to change or terminate the health care plan at any time: . . .

- "General Motors believes wholeheartedly in this Insurance Program for GM men and women, and expects to continue the Program indefinitely. However, GM reserves the right to modify, revoke, suspend, terminate, or change the Program, in whole or in part, at any time. . . ." The General Motors Insurance Program for Salaried Employees (1965, 1968, and 1971).

For more than two decades GM has engaged in systematic reductions in the size of its salaried workforce. In this connection the company has launched special early retirement programs designed to induce salaried workers to retire before reaching normal retirement age. The inducements have included, among other things, offers to provide pension benefits to early retirees at levels not reduced to reflect the longer periods over which such benefits can be expected to accrue. Some of the early retirement programs were company-wide initiatives, while others applied to a particular plant, division, or group of plants or divisions.

Salaried employees who accepted early retirement were often asked to sign documents evincing their acceptance of the terms of the particular program under which they were retiring. From 1974 until 1984 GM utilized a so-called "short form" statement of acceptance. . . . In 1984, GM adopted the "long form" statement of acceptance. . . . Both forms had numerous variants, but all stated in essence that the early retiree had "reviewed the benefits applicable" and "accept[ed] them." In return for such benefits, the early retirees agreed to waive certain causes of action they might have had against GM.

Not all early retirees signed a statement of acceptance. Some merely signed a "statement of intent" to retire, while others apparently signed nothing. . . .

Many of the early retirees also received documents summarizing applicable retirement benefits. These summaries often informed retirees that their health insurance would be paid by GM for life. Again, however, such documents sometimes put the retirees on notice of GM's right to change benefits. . . .

Late in 1987 GM announced that early in the following year significant changes would become effective in health care coverage for both salaried employees and retirees. In the case of plan participants who elected traditional fee-for-service coverage, the changes included an annual deductible of $200 for individuals and $250 for families. Fee-for-service participants were required to make 20% co-payments on medical services, up to an annual maximum co-payment of $500. By reason of these two changes, fee-for-service plan participants could find themselves responsible for paying as much as $700 a year (with individual coverage) or $750 (with family coverage) that would previously have been paid by GM. . . .

The present lawsuit was commenced in August of 1989 by 114 salaried retirees who challenged the legality of the changes to the health care plan that took effect in 1988. The main thrust of the plaintiffs' complaint was that GM had bound itself to provide salaried retirees and their spouses basic health coverage for life, entirely at GM's expense. The right to such coverage vested upon retirement, according to the plaintiffs, so the coverage could never be changed or revoked.

Seven separate causes of action were pleaded: (1) failure to maintain the written plan documentation required by ERISA; (2) violation of the health care plan; (3) breach of fiduciary duty; (4) breach of contract; (5) equitable or promissory estoppel; (6) failure to supply requested information; and (7) failure to comply with the requirements for summary plan descriptions. The named plaintiffs purported to represent a class of some 84,000 similarly-situated individuals, about 50,000 of whom were early retirees and 34,000 of whom were general retirees.[5]

The district court entered partial summary judgment in favor of GM after making the following rulings:

- the plaintiffs' benefits did not vest under the terms of the welfare plan;

- the summary plan descriptions generally put the plaintiffs on notice of GM's right to amend or terminate the plan; and

- the plaintiffs had no claim for breach of fiduciary duty, GM not having acted in a fiduciary capacity when amending the plan. . . .

Following a lengthy bench trial, the district court made these rulings on the merits:

- GM was found to have made a bilateral contract with each early retiree to vest health care benefits at retirement;

- these bilateral contracts were held to be enforceable as ERISA plans or as modifications to the general plan;

- GM was held not to be estopped from changing the health care benefits of the general retirees, to whom it made no promises to vest benefits;

- GM was held to be estopped from changing the health care benefits of the early retirees based on the oral and written representations it made to them; and

---

[5] The term "early retirees" refers to salaried, non-union employees who agreed to retire between 1974 and 1988 under one of GM's special early retirement programs. The term "general retirees" refers to salaried, non-union employees who "voluntarily retired, either at age 65 or before, and were able to do so without GM's consent, pursuant to the terms of the General Motors Retirement Program for Salaried Employees."

- GM was enjoined during this appeal from making further adverse changes to the health care benefits of the prevailing plaintiffs. . . .

III

A

The plaintiffs' first theory of recovery is that GM committed a breach of the terms of the plan documents when it implemented the changes in 1988. Under the plan documents, according to the plaintiffs, their health care benefits were vested — and having vested, the benefits could not be altered without the plaintiffs' consent. . . .

ERISA distinguishes between pension plans and welfare plans. . . . Because the plan in question here provided health insurance to its participants, it was a welfare plan.

Welfare plans are specifically exempted from vesting requirements to which pension plans are subject. ERISA § 201(1). Therefore, employers "are generally free under ERISA, for any reason at any time, to adopt, modify, or terminate welfare plans." *Curtiss-Wright Corp. v. Schoonejongen*, 514 U.S. 73, 78 (1995). Employers may vest welfare benefits if they choose to do so, however. *See Inter-Modal Rail Employees Ass'n v. Atchison, Topeka & Santa Fe Ry.*, 520 U.S. 510, 515 (1997) (an employer may "contractually cede[] its freedom" not to vest benefits).

To vest benefits is to render them forever unalterable. Because vesting of welfare plan benefits is not required by law, an employer's commitment to vest such benefits is not to be inferred lightly; the intent to vest "must be found in the plan documents and must be stated in clear and express language." *Wise v. El Paso Natural Gas Co.*, 986 F.2d 929, 937 (5th Cir. 1993). It is the plaintiffs' burden to prove GM's intent to vest.

The plaintiffs have not seriously disputed that the plan itself permitted GM to amend or terminate benefits. Instead the plaintiffs focus on the plan summaries, which must "be written in a manner calculated to be understood by the average plan participant, and shall be sufficiently accurate and comprehensive to reasonably apprise such participants and beneficiaries of their rights and obligations under the plan." ERISA § 102(a)(1).

In *Edwards v. State Farm Mut. Auto. Ins. Co.*, 851 F.2d 134, 136 (6th Cir. 1988), we held that "statements in a summary plan are binding and if such statements conflict with those in the plan itself, the summary shall govern." Application of the *Edwards* principle, the plaintiffs say, compels a judgment in their favor. We disagree.

The principle announced in *Edwards* was based on ERISA's directive that plan administrators furnish summary plan descriptions to participants and beneficiaries. This requirement did not become generally effective until 1977. We could not hold GM liable for violations of a statutory requirement based on actions taken prior to the effective date of that requirement. If the plaintiffs have any cause of action based on GM's pre-1977 summaries, it is probably not one based on ERISA. It appears likely that only the booklets issued in

1977 and thereafter are relevant to the inquiry. We shall assume that all of the booklets issued in 1977 or later were intended to serve as summary plan descriptions.

Most of the summary plan descriptions unambiguously reserved GM's right to amend or terminate the plan. For example:

- "General Motors Corporation reserves the right to amend, change or terminate the Plans and Programs described in this booklet." Your GM Benefits (1984).

- "The Corporation reserves the right to amend, modify, suspend, or terminate its benefit Plans or Programs by action of its Board of Directors." Your Benefits in Retirement (1985).

The plaintiffs counter by pointing out that these summaries also told them that their health coverage would be paid "at no cost to" them and "for [their] lifetime[s]." Such language, they argue, created an ambiguity within the summaries that must be resolved by extrinsic evidence. . . .

We see no ambiguity in a summary plan description that tells participants both that the terms of the current plan entitle them to health insurance at no cost throughout retirement and that the terms of the current plan are subject to change.

> "To read this summary as saying that the plan can never be changed in such a way as to mandate retiree contributions for continued medical coverage is to read into the summary something its authors did not put there (a promise to provide lifetime 'paid up' medical insurance), while reading out of the summary something that clearly was put there (an express reservation of right to change the plan)." *Musto [v. American Gen. Corp.]*, 861 F.2d [897,] 906 [(6th Cir. 1988)].

As the Third Circuit explained in a similar case, "the promise made to retirees was a qualified one: the promise was that retiree medical benefits were for life provided the company chose not to terminate the plans, pursuant to clauses that preserved the company's right to terminate the plan under which those benefits are provided." *Unisys Corp. [Retiree Med. Benefits ERISA Litig.]*, 58 F.3d [896,] 904 n.12 [(3rd Cir. 1995)].

Not all of the summaries clearly stated that GM could amend or terminate the plan. But the failure to allude to this power in some of the booklets did not prejudice GM's right, clearly stated in the plan itself, to change the plan's terms.

In the first place, the principle announced in *Edwards* does not apply to silence. An omission from the summary plan description does not, by negative implication, alter the terms of the plan itself. The reason is obvious: by definition, a summary will not include every detail of the thing it summarizes. GM's failure to include in some summaries a notice of its right to change the plan does not trump the clearly-stated right to do so in the plan itself.

In the second place, GM was not required to disclose in the summary plan descriptions that the plaintiffs' benefits were not vested.

ERISA specifies in detail the information that every summary plan description "shall contain." *See* ERISA § 102(b). Among the items a summary must include is "a description of the provisions providing for nonforfeitable pension benefits." Despite having required that summaries inform plan participants about the vesting of benefits under pension plans, Congress did not require such information for welfare plans; neither did the Department of Labor in its ERISA reporting and disclosure regulations. *See* 29 C.F.R. § 2520.102-3(n) (summary plan descriptions shall contain, "*[i]n the case of an employee pension benefit plan*, a description and explanation of the plan provisions for . . . vesting") (emphasis added). The absence of a similar requirement for welfare plans was no mistake. ERISA, after all, is a "comprehensive and reticulated statute," and the reporting and disclosure requirements are themselves "comprehensive." *Curtiss-Wright*, 514 U.S. at 83. We decline to apply the judge-made rule of *Edwards* in such a way as to augment the detailed disclosure provisions of the statute.

Neither the GM plan itself nor any of the various summaries of the plan states or even implies that the plaintiffs' benefits were vested. Accordingly, we conclude that the district court acted correctly in granting summary judgment to GM on the plaintiffs' claim that the company violated the terms of its plan.

B

We turn next to the theory that GM bilaterally contracted with each early retiree to vest benefits. All of the early retirees took retirement under one of the special early retirement programs offered by GM between 1974 and 1988. The early retirees argue that, as the district court held, the statements, promises, and representations GM made to them in connection with these programs, and the documents that they signed, created binding bilateral contracts. The alleged contracts, which supposedly provided for vesting of the early retirees' health care benefits, are said to be enforceable either as modifications to the general plan, or as ERISA plans themselves, or as a matter of federal common law.

ERISA requires that every plan "shall be established and maintained pursuant to a written instrument." ERISA § 402(a)(1). ERISA also requires, as we have said, a written summary plan description that will "reasonably apprise . . . participants and beneficiaries of their rights and obligations under the plan." ERISA § 102(a).

The writing requirement ensures that "every employee may, on examining the plan documents, determine exactly what his rights and obligations are under the plan." *Curtiss-Wright*, 514 U.S. at 83. And the requirement lends predictability and certainty to employee benefit plans. This serves the interests of both employers and employees.

Our court has consistently refused to recognize oral modifications to written plan documents. "[W]e are quite certain," we have explained, "that Congress, in passing ERISA, did not intend that participants in employee benefit plans should be left to the uncertainties of oral communications in finding out precisely what rights they were given under their plan." *Musto*, 861 F.2d at 909-10. Therefore, the "clear terms of a written employee benefit plan may not be modified or superseded by oral undertakings on the part of the employer." *Id.* at 910. The plaintiffs may not invoke oral statements by GM personnel in order to modify the terms of the written plan.

Neither can we accept the argument that the plan was modified or superseded either by the written "statements of acceptance" signed by some of the named plaintiffs or by the written representations received by some from GM. . . . None of GM's representations suggested that the plan was being modified. The statements of acceptance, moreover, merely said that the employee "ha[d] reviewed the benefits applicable to [him]" and "accept[ed] them." Far from modifying the terms of the welfare plan, it seems to us, this language incorporated the plan's terms.

The statements of acceptance were not ERISA plans themselves. Every ERISA plan must specify a funding mechanism, must allocate operational and administrative responsibilities, and must state how payments are made to and from the plan. ERISA § 102(b)(1)-(2), (4). While it is at least conceivable that an enforceable ERISA plan might not meet all of these requirements, the alleged bilateral contracts at issue here met none of them. The "statements of acceptance" simply did not purport to be ERISA plans, and we decline to treat them as such.

For us to sanction informal "plans" or plan "amendments" — whether oral or written — would leave the law of employee benefits in a state of uncertainty and would create disincentives for employers to offer benefits in the first place. Such a result is not in the interests of employees generally, and it is certainly not compatible with the goals of ERISA. "Altering a welfare plan on the basis of non-plan documents and communications, absent a particularized showing of conduct tantamount to fraud, would undermine ERISA."

IV

The plaintiffs argue that GM is estopped from enforcing the terms of the written plan against them. After the bench trial, the district court found that GM made no misleading representations to the general retirees. That finding appears unassailable. As to the early retirees, however, the district court ruled that GM was estopped from enforcing the plan because it misrepresented the plan's terms. In this, we believe, the court erred as a matter of law.

[Although] equitable estoppel may be a viable theory in ERISA cases, [it] cannot be applied to vary the terms of unambiguous plan documents; estoppel can only be invoked in the context of ambiguous plan provisions. There are at least two reasons for this. First, as we have seen, estoppel requires reasonable or justifiable reliance by the party asserting the estoppel. That party's reliance can seldom, if ever, be reasonable or justifiable if it is inconsistent with the clear and unambiguous terms of plan documents available to or furnished to the party. Second, to allow estoppel to override the clear terms of plan documents would be to enforce something other than the plan documents themselves. That would not be consistent with ERISA.

In the case at bar, we conclude that the plaintiffs' estoppel claims fail as a matter of law. As we have said, GM's plan and most of the summary plan descriptions issued to the plaintiffs over the years unambiguously reserved to GM the right to amend or terminate the plan. In the face of GM's clearly-stated right to amend — a right contained in the plan to which the plaintiffs had access and in many of the summaries they were given — reliance on statements allegedly suggesting the contrary was not, and could not be, reasonable or justifiable, especially when GM never told the plaintiffs that their benefits were vested or fully paid-up.

V

The last theory of recovery, applicable only to the early retirees, is that GM was in breach of the fiduciary duty it owed such retirees as administrator of their welfare plan. The district court dismissed this claim in its entirety, holding that an employer is not a fiduciary when it amends or terminates a plan.

The court's holding was correct as far as it went. GM did not act as a fiduciary in deciding to change its health insurance policies. The plaintiffs argue, however, that the district court misconstrued the breadth of their fiduciary duty claim. The claim, they say, encompassed all of GM's oral and written representations to them in connection with the special early retirement programs. We agree with this interpretation of the complaint. . . .

In *Varity Corp. v. Howe*, 516 U.S. 489 (1996), the Supreme Court held that an employer acted in a fiduciary capacity when making misrepresentations to its employees about their benefit plan. The employer in that case created a new subsidiary to enable the parent to shed some of its debt, knowing that the subsidiary might well fail. The employer induced employees to transfer to the new subsidiary with deliberately misleading assurances that the new subsidiary would be financially successful and that employee benefits plan would be financially sound and would not change.

The Court held that the employer, in making these misrepresentations about the status of the plan, was exercising "discretionary authority" in connection with the plan's "management" or "administration," as those terms are used in § 3(21)(A). Applying the law of trusts, which it said would inform the fiduciary inquiry, the Court stated that "conveying information about the likely future of plan benefits" was a discretionary act of plan administration. The employer therefore acted in a fiduciary capacity when it misled its employees, and its misrepresentations amounted to a breach of fiduciary duty.

Varity Corp. teaches that GM may have acted in a fiduciary capacity when it explained its retirement program to the early retirees. As a matter of law, however, we do not believe that GM committed a breach of any applicable fiduciary duty. In the first place, GM never told the early retirees that their health care benefits would be fully paid up or vested upon retirement. What GM told many of them, rather, was that their coverage was to be paid by GM for their lifetimes. This was undeniably true under the terms of GM's then-existing plan. . . .

GM's failure, if it may properly be called such, amounted to this: the company did not tell the early retirees at every possible opportunity that which it had told them many times before — namely, that the terms of the plan were subject to change. There is, in our view, a world of difference between the employer's deliberate misleading of employees in *Varity Corp.* and GM's failure to begin every communication to plan participants with a caveat.

In the second place, as we have said, GM was not required to disclose in its summary plan descriptions that the plan was subject to amendment or termination. *See* ERISA § 102(b); 29 C.F.R. § 2520.102-3. It would be strange indeed if ERISA's fiduciary standards could be used to imply a duty to disclose information that ERISA's detailed disclosure provisions do not require to be disclosed. As a matter of statutory construction, a specific statutory provision governs a general one — and here the "comprehensive" disclosure provisions control the broad fiduciary duty standard. . . .

Had an early retiree asked about the possibility of the plan changing, and had he received a misleading answer, or had GM on its own initiative provided misleading information about the future of the plan, or had GM been required by ERISA or its implementing regulations to forecast the future, a different case would have been presented. But we do not think that GM's accurate representations of its current program can reasonably be deemed misleading. GM having given out no inaccurate information, there was no breach of fiduciary duty. . . .

[LIVELY and MERRITT delivered separate opinions concurring in part and dissenting in part.]

BOYCE F. MARTIN, JR., CHIEF JUDGE, with whom JUDGES MOORE and COLE join, dissenting. . . .

There are several issues in this case — vested rights, estoppel, class certification, fiduciary duty — but the underlying question is clear: Do the retirees have a right to the lifetime free health care General Motors promised them or can General Motors renege on its promise? In finding for General Motors, the *en banc* majority determined that General Motors was not legally bound by its promise. General Motors has profited from distributing a welter of contradictory materials on its health coverage. In light of General Motors's obscurantism, though, it seems paradoxical that General Motors would have some claims dismissed and win others at the summary judgment stage. At the very least, plaintiffs should have the benefit of a trial on some issues to unravel the web of misinformation General Motors has woven. Instead, General Motors profits from having a salaried workforce that operated under the assumption it would receive lifetime health care. When the bill came due, though, General Motors was allowed to walk away.

To follow the *en banc* majority's decision, it is heads, General Motors wins; tails, the employees lose. I disagree with this outcome, and believe the district court's final judgment should be affirmed in part and reversed and remanded in part. . . .

I. *Vested Rights*

A. *General Retirees*

General Motors's summary plan descriptions suffer from either the internal inconsistency of contradictory terms or the external inconsistency of conflict with underlying formal plan documents. In some of the summary plan descriptions there is no internal ambiguity — the plan guarantees lifetime health care with no disclaimer. This is true of the 1974, 1977, and 1980 "Your GM Benefits" brochures. These summary plan descriptions, however, are at odds with the underlying plan documents, which do include a reservation of rights. In *Edwards v. State Farm Mut. Auto. Ins. Co.*, 851 F.2d 134 (6th Cir. 1988), this Court enunciated a principle for dealing with such discrepancies: "This Circuit has decided that statements in a summary plan are binding and if such statements conflict with those in the plan itself, the summary shall govern." *Id.* at 136. The *Edwards* principle governs pension plans and welfare plans.

From 1974 to 1985 the summary plan descriptions contained no reservation of rights and did carry a guarantee of lifetime health care. The *en banc* majority notes that "*Edwards* does not apply to silence," and argues that the summaries were silent on General Motors's right to change the plan. This ignores, however, the plain import of statements such as "at GM's expense for your lifetime." Just because the summary does not speak to General Motors's rights in the same language used in the plan does not mean the summaries are silent on the issue. Noting that benefits are "for your lifetime" is tantamount to saying that General Motors cannot change the plan.

. . . .

In sum, the district court should have had an opportunity on remand to determine whether the 1974 "Your GM Benefits" booklet was a summary plan document and whether the "Your Benefits in Retirement," in particular the 1980 edition, were distributed only to retirees. If those questions were answered affirmatively, there would be an eleven-year window from 1974 to 1985 in which the summary plan documents, which govern under *Edwards*, contained an unambiguous promise of lifetime health care. For general retirees who retired while these summary plan descriptions were in effect, this uncontradicted promise would be sufficient to vest their rights to lifetime health care. They deserved a chance to prove that in the district court.

B. *Early Retirees*

The early retirees base their claims for vested rights to health care on the bilateral contracts they signed with General Motors. The *en banc* majority determined that such extra-plan documents carried no weight under ERISA. [I disagree.]

The early retirees' claims are founded on the early retirement agreements they signed and other representations General Motors made to them at retirement. These agreements, they argue, constitute binding, bilateral contracts with General Motors for lifetime health care — a bargained-for agreement. The early retirees not only gave up their jobs, but some also surrendered the right to bring causes of action, including civil rights and age discrimination claims, against the company. They argue that this mutual consideration entitles them to bring a breach of bilateral contract claim. Typically a breach of contract claim falls under state law, and ERISA preempts state law. ERISA § 514(a). Preemption need not sound the death knell for a contract-based claim, though. . . .

" 'The legislative history demonstrates that Congress intended federal courts to develop federal common law in fashioning' relief under ERISA." *Massachusetts Mut. Life Ins. Co. v. Russell*, 473 U.S. 134, 156 (1985) (Brennan, J., concurring). These contracts are best enforced under federal common law.

Given that the contracts are enforceable under federal common law, the focus then turns to divining the contracts' terms. The district court . . . argued that the agreements were not fully integrated, which opens the door to extrinsic evidence. This extrinsic evidence, as discussed above, includes written materials showing that General Motors personnel used almost virtually every possible permutation of the words "free lifetime health care" when presenting future benefits to employees. The district court . . . found enforceable contracts for [some of the] early retirees. . . . That judgment should have been affirmed.

II. *Estoppel*

The General Motors retirees are prime candidates for bringing an estoppel claim. General Motors clearly wanted employees, potential employees, retirees, and potential retirees to rely on its boastful presentations of its benefit programs. . . . The brochures in question here undoubtedly were helpful in the recruitment and retention of personnel, and, when the time came, the inducement of certain employees to take early retirement. Yet, when retirees claim that they relied on these representations, General Motors calls such reliance unjustifiable.

The *en banc* majority acknowledges that estoppel can be a viable theory in ERISA cases but makes a misstep in dismissing the early retirees' estoppel claim because there was no reasonable reliance. . . . Reliance on repeated assurances of free lifetime health care, sometimes couched with timid caveats, from one of the largest corporations in the world was not justifiable in the *en banc* majority's view. The *en banc* majority erred in this determination. . . .

Why could the general retirees not reasonably rely on materials that repeatedly promised them lifetime health care and only occasionally included a reservation of rights? . . .

IV. *Fiduciary Duty*

[B]oth general and early retirees, should have a chance to argue their breach of fiduciary duty claims. It is true that "a company does not act in a fiduciary capacity when deciding to amend or terminate a welfare benefits plan." It is also true, however, that "a fiduciary may not materially mislead those to whom the duties of loyalty and prudence . . . are owed." Had General Motors never created a right to free lifetime health care, it would be free to amend or even terminate the insurance for retirees. When an employer establishes a right to lifetime health care benefits through vesting, as General Motors has done, the employer loses the unfettered freedom to amend or terminate the plan. General Motors has violated its fiduciary duty, and the district court . . . erred in dismissing plaintiffs' fiduciary duty claim.

Conclusion

This is a classic case of corporate shortsightedness. When General Motors was flush with cash and health care costs were low, it was easy to promise employees and retirees lifetime health care. Later, when General Motors was trying to sweeten the pot for early retirees, health care was another incentive to get employees off General Motors's groaning payroll. Of course, many of the executives who promised lifetime health care to early and general retirees are probably long since gone themselves. Rather than pay off those perhaps ill-considered promises, it is easier for the current regime to say those promises never were made. There is the tricky little matter of the paper trail of written assurances of lifetime health care, but General Motors, with the *en banc* majority's assistance, has managed to escape the ramifications of its now-regretted largesse. . . .

NOTES

1. *Reconciling the Irreconcilable.* The conflict in *Sprague* was between language providing for lifetime benefits paid by GM and language permitting the plan to be amended at any time. The Court followed *Musto* in holding that the latter took precedence over the former. In *Musto,* however, the language granting the benefits did not say that the employer would provide them for the life of the employee.

Is there any way to reconcile the two types of provisions in *Sprague?* One possibility would be to argue that because employees forego current wages in return for the promise of lifetime health benefits, employers should not be permitted to renege on the promise after retirement. Prior to retirement, however, when employees can still react to an employer's change in promised retiree health benefits by increasing their wage demands, employers may amend their plans. *Cf. UAW v. Yard-Man, Inc.,* 716 F.2d 1476, 1482 (6th Cir. 1983). But that solution has its own problems. One problem relates to the bright line between retired and active workers. If an employer amended its plan today to exclude lifetime health benefits, the suggested rule would guarantee benefits for a thirty-year employee who retired yesterday, but deny benefits to a thirty-year employee due to retire tomorrow. More fundamentally, the suggested analysis assumes that employees rely on the promise of lifetime benefits and accept the corresponding wage reduction. Employees instead may very well discount the promise and rely instead on the provision permitting amendments; if employees did that, they would not accept wage reductions in return for the promise, and the basis for requiring employers to provide the lifetime benefits would disappear.

2. *Mixed Results.* *Sprague* is a leading case in the area, but the results in retiree benefit cases have been mixed. Indeed, another panel in the Sixth Circuit relied on language in *Sprague* to find *for* plaintiffs in a retiree health case. In *Sprague,* the court said that a different case would have been presented "[h]ad an early retiree asked about the possibility of the plan changing, and had he received a misleading answer, or had GM on its own initiative provided misleading information about the future of the plan." In *James v. Pirelli Armstrong Tire Corp.,* 305 F.3d 439 (6th Cir. 2002), *cert.*

denied, 538 U.S. 1033 (2003), the Court found for plaintiffs on both counts. On its own initiative, the company had provided misleading and inaccurate information in group meetings and exit interviews. It had also provided misleading, inaccurate or incomplete answers in response to questions by individual employees. If this reminds you of the *Beach* case in the preceding chapter, it should; the same fiduciary provisions of ERISA apply to both pension and welfare plans. For other cases finding for plaintiffs, see *Rosetto v. Pabst Brewing Co.*, 217 F.3d 539 (7th Cir. 2000), *cert. denied*, 531 U.S. 1192 (2001) (agreeing with *Sprague* presumption against vesting, but holding that ambiguity in documents required trial); *Maurer v. Joy Tech., Inc.*, 212 F.3d 907 (6th Cir. 2000) (holding that presumption against vesting is eased when benefits granted through a collective bargaining agreement; some employees entitled to vested benefits).

3. *Corporate Desperation*. *Sprague* refers to *Varity Corp. v. Howe*, 516 U.S. 489 (1996), a case in which the corporate strategy was to shed employee benefit liabilities by encouraging employees to transfer to a business unit destined to fail. The unit did fail and the employees lost their health care and other non-pension benefits, but they ultimately prevailed in their claim that Varity had violated its fiduciary duties by misleading them into transferring.

Later, a series of memos were uncovered illustrating the lengths to which Varity was willing to go to deal with its retiree health care costs. One benefits manager wrote "You have asked that I be inventive in coming up with a solution [to the problem of retiree health care costs.] As far as I can determine there is only one solution [that doesn't involve the risk of paying benefits in the end] and that would be the death of all existing retirees and survivors." Ellen E. Schultz, *Retirees Found Varity Untruthful*, WALL ST. J., Nov. 6, 2000, at C1. Unable to pursue that strategy and fully recognizing that it had promised lifetime benefits, the company nevertheless did its best to get out of the commitments through the transfer strategy and simply by cutting benefits. Ultimately, however, the attempt was unsuccessful.

4. *ERISA's Reporting and Disclosure Requirements*. ERISA's reporting and disclosure requirements apply to both pension and welfare plans. In addition to summary plan descriptions, § 102, plan administrators are required to provide each participant with a summary annual report, § 104(b)(3), and, for pension plans and upon written request, a statement of the participant's accrued benefits and nonforfeitable benefits. § 105(a). Plan administrators must also file summary plan descriptions, plan descriptions, and annual and terminal reports with the Secretary of Labor. § 101(b). The requirements can be enforced through a civil suit under § 502. The suit can seek actual damages, up to $100/day for failing to provide required information to a participant, and up to $1,000/day for failing to file an annual report with the Secretary of Labor. § 502(c). In addition, criminal sanctions are available for willful violations. § 501.

Sprague provides an introduction to the types of issues that arise under ERISA's reporting and disclosure provisions:

(a) *Which document controls in the event of a conflict: the plan itself or the summary plan description? Sprague* indicates, as have other courts, that the summary should control, because that is the document employees receive and rely on. *See Pierce v. Security Trust Life Ins. Co.*, 979 F.2d 23 (4th Cir. 1992); *Heidgerd v. Olin Corp.*, 906 F.2d 903 (2d Cir. 1990). The courts, however, have been unwilling to extend the employee notice rationale to documents other than the plan summary. *See, e.g., Alday v. Container Corp. of America*, 906 F.2d 660 (11th Cir. 1990) (increase in retiree contribution for health plan permissible because permitted by summary plan description even though other distributed documents — an employee handbook, letters sent to employees when they neared retirement age, and documents distributed at retirement seminars — did not inform employees of the company's ability to change the retiree health plan); *Hicks v. Fleming Co.*, 961 F.2d 537 (5th Cir. 1992) (employee could not rely on document he thought was a summary plan description; "looks like a duck, quacks like a duck" test would discourage employers from providing information to employees).

(b) *How specific does the summary plan description need to be?* Some courts have held that the summary must notify participants of their rights with a high degree of specificity. *See Ruotolo v. Sherwin-Williams Co.*, 622 F. Supp. 546 (D. Conn. 1985) (requirements violated where summary indicates all benefits may be lost by working when in fact the plan provided that only 70% of benefits would be lost); *Zittrouer v. Uarco Inc. Group Benefit Plan*, 582 F. Supp. 1471 (N.D. Ga. 1984) (requirements violated where summary failed to disclose one of many exclusions from coverage under a welfare plan providing benefits for stays in extended care facilities). *But see Dzinglski v. Weirton Steel Corp.*, 875 F.2d 1075 (4th Cir. 1989) (employer consent required for eligibility for early retirement; summary acceptable even though it did not specify reasons employer might grant or withhold consent).

(c) *Is reliance required before an employee can recover for a violation of the disclosure requirements?* Some circuits do not require any reliance to make out a violation, because such a requirement would "undermine the legislative command by imposing technical requirements upon the employee." *Edwards v. State Farm Mut. Auto. Ins. Co.*, 851 F.2d 134, 137 (6th Cir. 1988). *See also Hansen v. Continental Ins. Co.*, 940 F.2d 971 (5th Cir. 1991). Other circuits require plaintiffs to demonstrate some reliance on the SPD before they can recover. *See Branch v. G. Bernd Co.*, 955 F.2d 1574 (11th Cir. 1992); *Maxa v. John Alden Life Ins. Co.*, 972 F.2d 980 (8th Cir. 1992), *cert. denied*, 506 U.S. 1080 (1993).

G. PUBLIC POLICY INITIATIVES

Providing health care at a reasonable cost has proven to be a very difficult task in the United States. We spend a significantly higher proportion of our income on the health care system than our industrial competitors. In 2003, for example, we spent 15% of our gross domestic product on health care or $5,635 per person. By comparison, Germany spent 11% of its gross domestic product on health care ($2,996 per person); Canada 10% ($3,001); Japan 8%

($2,139), and the United Kingdom 7% ($2,231). OECD Factbook: Economic, Environmental & Social Statistics 34, 208 (2006). Our health outcomes, however, are generally no better than those in other countries. *Id.* at 200-06 (U.S. is below OECD average in life expectancy, infant mortality, and obesity). In part, this is because a high proportion of the United States population does not have any health insurance and, hence, does not enjoy easy access to the health care system. In 2004, about 45.5 million Americans did not have health insurance. Paul Fronstin, *Sources of Health Insurance & Characteristics of the Uninsured*, EBRI Issue Brief No. 287, Nov. 2005, at 4.

Many of the problems with the health care system, of course, are beyond the scope of a textbook on employment law. At the same time, however, most Americans obtain their health insurance through their employment and most of the initiatives designed to deal with the problems have direct relevance in the workplace. This section will not attempt to provide an overview of health care initiatives. It will, however, provide some ways of thinking about them.

Until recently, employer-provided health care was relatively unregulated. ERISA itself did not provide much substantive regulation and its broad preemption provision provided a broad shield from state laws attempting to regulate employee welfare plans. Two current trends are increasing the level of regulation. First, Congress has become increasingly interested in the area. Some of that interest has already resulted in substantive regulation, such as the alphabet-soup requirements discussed earlier. In addition, Congress regularly considers other, and often much more broad-ranging regulation. Second, the states have been re-invigorated in their attempts to regulate health care. The "Wal-Mart" law discussed in the *Retail Industry Leaders Ass'n* case is only one of many state initiatives since the Supreme Court signaled that ERISA preemption may not be as broad as previously thought. *New York State Conference of Blue Cross & Blue Shield Plans v. Travelers Ins. Co.*, 514 U.S. 645 (1995).

The general issue raised by these types of initiatives is: What is the appropriate role for government in regulating employer-provided health care?

LAWRENCE H. SUMMERS, SOME SIMPLE ECONOMICS OF MANDATED BENEFITS, 79 AEA Papers & Proceedings 177, 178-82 (1989) *

[The standard efficiency argument militates against requiring employers to provide any type of health insurance benefits,] just as it militates against other government interventions. Imagine that employers can compensate their workers in different ways: with cash, by providing them with insurance, or by giving them consumption goods directly. If employers and employees can negotiate freely over the terms of the compensation package, they will reach a mutually efficient outcome. If a health benefit that would cost an employer $20 to provide is worth $30 to prospective employees, employers could provide the benefit and reduce the employee's salary by between $20 and $30, leaving both better off. Reasoning of this sort demonstrates that

---

* Reprinted with permission of the author and the American Economic Association.

benefits will be provided up to the point where an extra $1 spent by employers on benefits is valued by employees at $1.

When is there ever a case for mandating benefits or publicly providing goods that employers could provide their workers? Most obviously, there is the paternalism, or "merit goods," argument that individuals value certain services too little. They may irrationally underestimate the probability of catastrophic health expenses, or of a child's illness that would require a sustained leave. In the pension context, this argument may be especially persuasive since individuals are likely to be especially inept at making intertemporal decisions. A closely related argument involves the idea that society cares more about equal consumption of some merit good commodities than about others.

There are at least two further rationales for mandating benefits that do not assume individual irrationality. First, there may be positive externalities associated with the good — externalities that cannot be captured by either the provider or the recipient. The most obvious example is health insurance. Society cares about preventing the spread of contagious diseases more than any individual does or would take account of. . . .

Much more important is the externality that arises from society's unwillingness or inability to deny care completely to those in desperate need, even if they cannot pay. The Congressional Budget Office estimates that there are 23 million American employees without health insurance. Health insurance for this group would cost about $25 billion. Currently, these uninsured employees incur $15 billion in health care costs for which they do not pay. The costs are borne in part by physicians and other providers of health care, but most of the cost is passed on to other consumers in the form of higher insurance and medical costs.

The externality here is quite large. About 60 percent of the benefit of employer-provided health insurance accrues ultimately to neither employer nor employee. Even with the current tax subsidy to employer-provided health insurance, there might be a further case for government action. . . .

There is a second, perhaps stronger, argument for government intervention in the market for fringe benefits based on adverse selection considerations. . . . If employees have more information about whether they will need parental leave or face high medical bills than their employers do, then employers that provide these benefits will receive disproportionately more applications from employees who require benefits and so will lose money. The market thus discourages provision of any fringe benefits.

Suppose, for example, that for the 10 percent of the population that knows it has health problems, health insurance is worth $300 and costs $270 to provide, and for the 90 percent of the population without preexisting conditions, health insurance is worth $100 and costs $90 to provide. Assume that individuals know whether they have problems or not, but employers cannot tell healthy from unhealthy individuals. Now consider what happens if employers do not offer health insurance. Any employer offering health insurance and a salary reduction of less than $100 would attract both classes of workers and would lose money, since the average cost of insurance would be $.9 \times \$90 + .1 \times \$270 = \$108$. Firms could offer insurance and reduce wages by between $270 and $300. This would attract only unhealthy individuals. Even leaving aside the consideration that for productivity reasons, firms might not prefer a personnel policy that was most likely to attract unhealthy workers, it is clear that the market solution will not provide universal insurance even though all individuals are willing to pay more than it costs to insure themselves.

The same argument holds in the case of other employee benefits. Workers know much better than their employers whether they are likely to go on parental leave or become disabled. They probably also know something about whether they are likely to become enmeshed in employment disputes. This suggests that there are efficiency arguments for limiting employers' ability to fire workers at will.

These two considerations suggest that it may be optimal for the government to intervene in the provision of goods that some employers provide their workers. [The question remains, however, whether goods such as health insurance should be provided directly by the government or whether the government should require employers to provide them.]

[A]t least some presumption should exist in favor of mandated benefits [over public provision]. Mandated benefits preserve employers' ability to tailor arrangements to their workers and to offer more than minimum packages. This avoids what might be called the "government provision trap." . . . Suppose that the government provides universal free health care of modest quality. This will be more attractive to many than paying the costs of high-quality care themselves, even though if they had to pay for all their care they would have selected high- rather than low-quality care.

Another argument in favor of mandated benefits [is that they] do not give rise to deadweight losses as large as those that arise from government tax collections. Suppose that the government required that all employers provide a certain benefit, say a leave policy, that cost employers $.10 per employee hour to provide. What would happen? Consider first employers whose employees previously valued the benefit at more than $.10 per hour and so had a leave package greater than $.10 per hour. They would not be affected at all by the government mandate, since they were previously in compliance with the law. For employees who valued the benefit at less than $.10 an hour, they would then receive the plan, at the cost of $.10.

What would happen to the wages of those receiving the benefit? . . . Two special cases are instructive. First, suppose that the mandated benefit is worthless to employees. In this very special case, the change in employment and wages corresponds exactly to what would be expected from a $.10 tax on employers. Since the mandated benefit is worthless to employees, it is just like a tax from the point of view of both employers and employees. Second, consider the case where employees valuation of the policy is arbitrarily close to $.10. In this case, the mandated benefit does not affect the level of employment, the employer's total employee costs, or the employee's utility.

The general point should be clear from this example. In terms of their allocational effects on employment, mandated benefits represent a tax at a rate equal to the *difference* between the employer's cost of providing the benefit and the employee's valuation of it, *not* at a rate equal to the cost to the employer of providing the benefit.

With this in mind, contrast the effects of mandating benefits with the effects of taxing all employers and using the proceeds to finance a public parental leave program. In the latter case, employers would abandon their plans, and the government would end up paying for all parental leave. This would mean far more tax distortions than in the mandated benefits case for two reasons. First, employers and employees who were unaffected by the mandated benefit program would be taxed for the parental leave program. This creates a larger deadweight loss. Second, for those employers and employees who are affected, the tax levied is equal to the full cost of parental leave, not the difference between the employers' cost and the workers' benefit. . . .

This analysis suggests at least two possible advantages of mandated benefits over public provision of benefits. First, mandated benefits are likely to afford workers more choice. Second, they are likely to involve fewer distortions of economic activity. Why then should not all social objectives be sought through mandated benefits? . . .

The most obvious problem with mandated benefits is that they only help those with jobs. Beyond the 25 million employed Americans without health insurance, another 13 million nonemployed Americans do not have health insurance. Mandated benefit programs obviously do not reach these people. There is certainly a case for public provision in situations where there is no employer who can be required to provide benefits.

A more fundamental problem comes when there are wage rigidities. Suppose, for example, that there is a binding minimum wage. In this case, wages cannot fall to offset employers' cost of providing a mandated benefit, so it is likely to create unemployment. This is a common objection to proposals for mandated health insurance, given that a large fraction of employees who are without health insurance are paid low wages. It is not clear whether this should be regarded as a problem with mandated benefits or minimum wages. Note that a payroll tax on employers directed at financing health insurance benefits publicly would have exactly the same employment displacement effects as a mandated health insurance program.

A different type of wage rigidity involves a requirement that firms pay different workers the same wage even though the cost of providing benefits differs. For example, the cost of health insurance is greater for older than for younger workers and the expected cost of parental leave is greater for women than men. If wages could freely adjust, these differences in expected benefit costs would be offset by differences in wages. If such differences are precluded, however, there will be efficiency consequences as employers seek to hire workers with lower benefit costs. It is thus possible that mandated benefit programs can work against the interest of those who most require the benefit being offered. Publicly provided benefits do not drive a wedge between the marginal costs of hiring different workers and so do not give rise to a distortion of this kind.

Another objection to mandated benefits is that they reduce the scope for government redistribution. Consider the example of old-age benefits. Many of the arguments I have discussed could be used to support a proposal to privatize Social Security. The principal problem with this proposal is that it would make the redistribution of lifetime income that is inherent in the operation of the current Social Security system impossible. Assuming perfectly flexible markets, wages for each type of worker would fall by the amount of benefits they could expect to receive from a mandated pension; there would be no transfer from [rich to poor]. If the government sought to prevent redistribution by preventing wage adjustments, unemployment among those most in need would result. The nonredistributive character of mandated benefit programs is a direct consequence of the fact that, as with benefit taxes, workers pay directly for the benefits they receive.

A different sort of objection to mandated benefits as a tool of social policy follows along the lines of the traditional conservative position that "the only good tax is a bad tax." If policymakers fail to recognize the costs of mandated benefits because they do not appear in the government budget, then mandated benefit programs could lead to excessive spending on social programs. There is no sense in which benefits become "free" just because the government mandates that employers offer them to workers. As with value-added taxes, it can plausibly be argued that mandated benefits fuel the growth of government because their costs are relatively invisible and their distortionary effects are relatively minor.

NOTES

1. *Who Are the Uninsured?* On average, the uninsured tend to match our preconceptions: they are likely to be part-time workers, with low incomes, young, single, less educated, minorities, non-citizens, and work for smaller firms. Stephen Blakely, *The Economic Costs of the Uninsured*, EBRI NOTES, Aug. 2000, at 1, 2. At the same time, however, people without health insurance can be found in virtually every segment of American society, except the elderly and seriously disabled (who are covered by Medicare). For example, five million of the uninsured have family incomes above $75,000 annually; 76% of the uninsured have jobs; many of the uninsured work full-time.

2. *The Employer's Interest.* Most economists believe that employers do not pay directly for increases in health insurance costs. Instead, those costs are passed on to workers in lower wages, often in the form of lower *increases* in wages than employees would otherwise receive. Mark V. Pauly, *Taxation, Health Insurance and Market Failure in the Medical Economy*, 24 J. ECON. LIT. 629 (1986). In this view, employers have two primary interests in health care costs. First, employers are interested in avoiding unexpected shocks that cannot be smoothly passed on to workers. The *McGann* case can be viewed as an example of an employer avoiding a shock by passing it on to workers (although the transfer was not exactly smooth). This interest also explains heightened employer concern in years when health care inflation is especially high; employers are especially concerned then because when increases in costs are large and sudden, it is difficult to pass them on to employees in the form of lower wages. Second, employers are interested in formulating a wage/health insurance package that will attract and retain a desirable workforce. An employer that offers a lower wage and better health insurance than its competitors might find that it attracts a workforce that tends to be unhealthy. An employer that offers a high wage and no health insurance benefits is sacrificing tax benefits that, in effect, subsidize its compensation package.

3. *Health Savings Accounts (HSAs).* HSAs are the latest big idea in health insurance. Under this arrangement, employees have individual tax-favored accounts out of which they pay most medical expenses backed up by a high-deductible insurance policy. If employees do not spend the entire amount in their accounts, they can carry over savings from year-to-year. I.R.C. § 223. Since they were first authorized in 2004, they have grown quickly. Today, more than three million individuals have invested more than $1 billion in HSAs.

HSAs are the main exhibit in a movement designed to encourage individuals to pay more attention to health care costs and become better consumers. But they are highly controversial. Among other things, critics worry that high out-of-pocket costs will discourage employees from getting needed care, especially preventative care. They also worry about adverse selection. If healthier employees opt for HSAs, it could lead to higher premiums for those left in traditional plans and, potentially, a death spiral for those plans. For conflicting views, compare Richard L. Kaplan, *Who's Afraid of Personal Responsibility? Health Savings Accounts and the Future of American Health Care,* 36 McGeorge L. Rev. 535 (2005) (HSAs empower consumers to decide for themselves how to spend their health care dollars, while protecting them against major calamities), with Paul Fronstin, *Early Experience with High-Deductible and Consumer-Driven Health Plans,* EBRI Issue Brief No. 288 (Dec. 2005) (people with HSAs are less satisfied with their health insurance, have higher out-of-pocket costs, and are more likely to skip or delay health care).

4. *Health Insurance and International Competitiveness.* Employers are often heard to complain that increases in the cost of health insurance will make them less able to compete internationally. In a recent year, for example, Chrysler spent $700 per vehicle on employee health care, twice as much as German automakers and three times as much as the Japanese. Similarly, Canada has a nationalized health care system that is funded predominantly by general tax revenues (so the burdens on employers are less direct) and that controls costs better (so overall health care expenditures are considerably lower than in the United States).

The claim that health care costs in the United States have adverse effects on international competitiveness, however, is difficult to resolve. Those making the claim generally assume that increases in the costs of health care will increase the overall cost of labor for employers. But employers are able to shift some portion of the increase in costs to employees. If employers were able to shift all of the increase in health care costs to employees (for example, by lowering wages), total labor costs and American competitiveness would remain constant. Thus, the competitiveness claim requires difficult empirical assessments of the increase in health care costs both in the United States and elsewhere, and of the ultimate incidence of those costs in each country. *See* CBO, Economic Implications of Rising Health Care Costs (1992) (international competitiveness not hurt because employers have been able to shift

higher health care costs to workers in the form of lower wages and less generous nonmedical benefits).

Part VIII

WORKPLACE INJURIES AND DISEASES

The forty-six men who were killed last year [1906] in the South Chicago plant of the United States Steel Corporation went to their deaths by a large number of different and divergent routes. Twelve of them were killed in the neighborhood of blast furnaces. . . . Three of them were electrocuted. Three of them were killed by falls from high places. . . . Four of them were burned to death by hot metal. . . . And ten of them were killed by railroad cars or by railroad locomotives. . . . The operating men who manage the Illinois Steel Company are human beings. They do not wish to commit either murder or suicide. But Steel is War. And it is also Dividends. . . . The figures that indicate production and profits are the only figures handled and scrutinized by the members of the board of directors. . . .

—William Hard, *Making Steel and Killing Men,* Everybody's Magazine, Nov. 1907, *reprinted in* The Muckrakers 342, 347-48, 354 (Arthur & Lila Weinberg eds., 1961).

Government regulations often have significant impact on the income and wealth of workers. To the extent that firms cannot pass on regulatory compliance cost increases to consumers, firms will absorb these costs by cutting wages, and by reducing employment. . . . If government regulations force firms out of business or into overseas production, employment of American workers will be reduced, making workers less healthy by reducing their incomes. OSHA should estimate whether the possible effect of compliance costs on workers' health will outweigh the health improvements that may result from decreased exposure to the regulated substances.

—James B. MacRae, Jr., of the Office of Management and Budget, in a March 1992 letter to the Labor Department suspending the proposed OSHA Air Contaminants Standard.

The issue of workplace safety and health is important and difficult. The stakes are high in terms of the human suffering and of the economic costs to workers, employers, and society.

What Has Happened to Workplace Safety and Health?

The peak in the number of fatalities resulting from workplace accidents was reached in 1907, the year Hard's article was published, when more than 7,000 workers were killed in just two industries: railroading and bituminous mines. Fortunately, the fatality rate resulting from accidents has significantly declined in the last 100 years. The Bureau of Labor Statistics (BLS) began a comprehensive Census of Fatal Occupational Injuries in 1992 and since then the annual number of workplace fatalities has varied between 6,632 and 5,534. The number of fatalities was 5,764 in 2004, which was 4.1 fatal occupational injuries per 100,000 workers.

The workplace injury rate also generally declined during the last 100 years but in an irregular pattern. A substantial overall decline in injury rates occurred between 1926 and 1958, but then the rate increased in a period that lasted until 1970. This deterioration in injury rates was one reason why the Occupational Safety and Health Act of 1970 was enacted. Since 1972, when the Bureau of Labor Statistics (BLS) introduced new measures of workplace safety, the injury rate has fluctuated. The annual number of injuries resulting in lost workdays (including days with job transfer or work restrictions) per 100 workers increased from 1972 to 1980, declined until 1986, increased until 1990, and then declined substantially in subsequent years, reaching 2.5 cases per 100 full-time workers in 2004.

The accuracy of the data on the frequency and severity of workplace injuries has been challenged. For example, BLS reported 6.3 million job-related injuries in 1992, while Paul Leigh reported 13.3 million injuries in the entire workforce that year. J. PAUL LEIGH ET AL., COSTS OF OCCUPATIONAL INJURIES AND ILLNESSES (2000). An even greater shortfall was found by Kenneth D. Rosenman et al., *How Much Work-Related Injury and Illness is Missed By the Current National Surveillance System?*, 48 J. OCCUPATIONAL & ENVTL. MED. 357 (2006), who estimated that the BLS data did not include 60 to 67 percent of the workplace injuries in Michigan in 1999, 2000, and 2001.

The data on workplace diseases are also problematic. The BLS reported about 457,500 workplace illnesses in 1992, but Steven Markowitz, *Number of Illnesses, in* J. PAUL LEIGH ET AL., *supra*, estimated there were about 1.2 million cases of occupational diseases that year, while Rosenman reported that the BLS data did not capture 66 to 69 percent of the workplace diseases in Michigan in 1999 to 2001. The problems with workplace diseases are not limited to deficiencies in the BLS data. J. Paul Leigh & John A. Robbins, *Occupational Disease and Workers' Compensation: Coverage, Costs, and Consequences*, 82 MILLBANK Q. 689 (2004), estimate that nationally workers' compensation programs did not compensate 98.9 percent of the deaths due to occupational diseases in 1999.

The essence of this review is that workplace fatalities from accidents have substantially declined in the last 100 years. The long-term trend for workplace injuries also shows improvement, although there have been periods when workplace safety deteriorated and the data for injuries are less reliable than for workplace deaths. The evidence on the number of occupational diseases indicates there is a serious undercounting problem, which complicates an overall assessment of the magnitude of and trends for occupational diseases. There appears to have been a modest improvement in workplace safety and health in the last thirty-five years, but that conclusion must be qualified because of the studies challenging the accuracy of BLS data.

The Costs of Workplace Injuries and Diseases

The national costs of the workers' compensation program, which provides medical care, cash benefits, and rehabilitation services to workers disabled by work-related injuries or diseases, have increased substantially since 1960. The employers' costs of workers' compensation increased from 0.93% of payroll in 1960 to 2.18% of payroll in 1990 and then declined to 1.76% of payroll in 2004, when the total costs for employers were $87.4 billion.

There are other significant costs associated with workplace injuries and diseases in addition to the expenses of the workers' compensation program. Leigh and his co-authors estimate that the indirect costs, including lost wages and the expenses that employers incur for retraining replacement workers, were $104 billion in 1992. These indirect costs plus direct costs (such as medical benefits provided by the workers' compensation program) resulted in total costs for workplace injuries and diseases of $156 billion in that year, which were far more than the combined costs for AIDS ($30 billion) and Alzheimer's disease ($67 billion). This emphasizes the importance of the topics examined in this Part.

The Goals of Health and Safety Programs

The basic goals of government health and safety programs are clear, at least if presented only in broad outline. The goals are, first, the *prevention* of workplace injuries and illnesses and, second, the *compensation* of workers when they do become injured or ill, including the provision of cash benefits, medical care, and rehabilitation services. The goals become less clear, however, as one begins to flesh them out: At what price, for example, should the prevention goal be pursued? What if eliminating a certain class of workplace injuries is so expensive it will mean the loss of significant numbers of jobs? Are slightly more dangerous jobs better than no jobs at all? Is government in a better position to make this kind of trade-off than workers and employers?

This Part considers four principal approaches that seek to achieve the basic goals:

(1) *The Labor Market.* Workers will require a risk premium to induce them to accept a job that is likely to result in a workplace injury. The risk premium represents ex ante compensation for any injury that occurs. The employer has an incentive to improve workplace safety in order to reduce the risk premium. Thus, the labor market serves both the prevention and compensation goals.

(2) *Tort Suits.* A worker who is injured on the job can bring a tort suit against the employer or other party responsible for the injury. The recovery

from the suit provides ex post compensation for the injury. The employer has an incentive to improve safety in the workplace to avoid liability in a tort suit. Thus, tort suits also serve both the prevention and compensation goals.

(3) *Workers' Compensation.* A worker who is injured on the job receives cash benefits, rehabilitation services, and medical care, which represent ex post compensation. The program is financed by premiums paid by employers that are experience rated, that is, an employer's premiums decrease if the program provides compensation for fewer work injuries. Thus, workers' compensation also serves both the compensation and prevention goals.

(4) *Safety and Health Laws.* The employer is required to provide a safe and healthy workplace. The immediate purpose of the program is prevention, although to the extent that workplace injuries and diseases are prevented, fewer workers will require compensation.

Several criteria are useful for comparing the principal approaches for addressing workplace safety and health concerns. First, is the approach *adequate?* That is, does it provide sufficient resources and incentives to achieve the compensation and prevention goals? Second, is the approach *equitable?* Are various classes of workers (such as unionized and non-unionized workers) and employers (such as large and small employers) treated fairly under the approach? Third, does the approach provide *delivery system efficiency?* The delivery system is comprised of employers, insurance carriers, state and federal agencies, attorneys, doctors, and others who provide the benefits and services in the approach. Is the approach administratively efficient, in the sense that it achieves the desirable levels of adequacy and equity with the least use of delivery system resources?

The four approaches to prevention and compensation do not have a clear chronological order. Indeed, all but the workers' compensation program were used in some form in the nineteenth century, and all four approaches have been used throughout most of the twentieth century. The order in which the approaches are treated in this Part differentiates between the "prestatutory approaches" — namely the labor market and tort suits (discussed in Chapter 21) — and the statutory approaches exemplified by workers' compensation, with most state statutes enacted between 1910 and 1920 (discussed in Chapter 22), and by safety and health acts, notably the Occupational Safety and Health Act (OSHAct), enacted in 1970 (discussed in Chapter 23). (Some states had enacted safety statutes in the nineteenth century, but the OSHAct is the major safety and health law.) This Part also examines the interrelationships between the four approaches at several places, most notably in Chapter 24, which also assesses the four approaches using the adequacy, equity, and efficiency criteria.

Chapter 21

THE PRESTATUTORY APPROACHES

A. THE LABOR MARKET

RONALD G. EHRENBERG, WORKERS' COMPENSATION, WAGES, AND THE RISK OF INJURY, in NEW PERSPECTIVES IN WORKERS' COMPENSATION 71, 74-81 (John F. Burton, Jr. ed., 1988)[*]

Consider a simplified world in which the labor market is competitive, workers have perfect information about the risks of injury associated with each job, and there are no barriers to mobility between jobs. Suppose also that firms differ in their production technology; that each technology has certain inherent risks of injury associated with it, which can be reduced if firms expend resources to do so; and that the marginal cost (to the employer) of reducing risks varies across firms.

Assume also, initially, that workers value positively their expected earnings per period (earnings times the probability of not being injured) and value negatively the probability of being injured. Workers will move to firms whose wage rates-risk of injury combination maximizes their well-being and, if all workers have identical preferences, firms with higher risks of injury would have to pay higher wages to attract workers. The mobility of workers would thus lead to *fully compensating* wage differentials, or wage differentials that compensate workers for the disutility they would suffer from risk of injury.

In such a world, firms would offer the wage rates-risk of injury combination so that their marginal cost for injury reduction would equal their marginal benefits from injury reduction. The former includes the costs of resources devoted to preventing accidents, while the latter includes the lower bill for wages associated with the lower accident rate, less downtime in production, and reduced hiring and training costs of replacements for injured workers. If the marginal cost of preventing accidents varied across firms, different firms would offer different "wage-injury rate packages." . . .

Compensating Wage Differentials

The first issue is whether markets "work" in the sense that wage differentials arise to compensate workers for exposure to risk of injury. Numerous studies have . . . attempted to ascertain if wage rates are positively associated with various measures of injury risk (fatal accident rates, nonfatal accident rates, work-days lost as a result of accident rates, and so on), after other

[*] Reprinted from *New Perspectives in Workers' Compensation,* edited by John F. Burton, Jr. Used with permission of the publisher: ILR Press, School of Industrial and Labor Relations, Cornell University, Ithaca, NY 14853-3901. Copyright 1988 by Cornell University.

personal characteristics that should influence wages (e.g., education, experience) are controlled for.

These studies uniformly tend to find that there is a positive association between fatal accident rates and wages. The relationship between nonfatal accident rates and wages is less well established, however; it appears in some studies but not in others. Most studies indicate that the magnitude of compensating wage differentials is larger in the union sector than in the nonunion sector, an expected result given that accident rates tend to be higher in the union sector and that unions may serve the role of winning wage differentials at the bargaining table to compensate their members for unfavorable job characteristics when "the market" fails to produce such differentials. . . .

Unfortunately, this voluminous literature provides very little that is of use for public policy. Presumably one wants to know if (1) the market is providing appropriate incentives for employers to take actions to reduce injury rates and (2) the market is *fully* compensating workers for risk of injury. As discussed below, no answer to either of these questions is provided by these studies.

With respect to the first question, the issue is really whether the positive association between wages and risk-of-injury measures reflects a compensating wage differential for risk of injury. Jobs may offer a variety of undesirable working conditions in addition to risk of injury; these may include having to work in a noisy environment, having to do repetitive tasks, being required to do heavy lifting, and lacking the opportunity to make independent judgments. Many of these job characteristics are probably highly correlated with risk of injury on the job, and workers may demand wage premiums to accept them. As a result, when one omits these other job characteristics from the analysis, any effect they have on wages is captured by the risk-of-injury variable. Thus one may well overstate the true magnitude of the compensating wage differentials for risk of injury. When a few investigators have included other working conditions along with risk of injury in wage equations, the risk-of-injury variables tended not to be significantly associated with wages. Whether this is due to the high collinearity of the working conditions variables (which makes estimates imprecise) or to the nonexistence of a true wage-risk of injury differential cannot be determined. In either case, the evidence on the existence of compensating wage differentials *for* risk of injury is not as well established as the various studies would have us believe.

Suppose we ignore this problem and assume that wage differentials for risk of injury do exist. How could one hope to decide that their magnitudes are sufficiently large to permit one to conclude that they *fully* compensate workers for the disutility associated with risk of injury? Only if they are, as is implicitly assumed in a discussion of the subject in chapter 6 of the 1987 *Economic Report of the President*,* is the case for government intervention to improve occupational safety weakened. . . .

Now, if one truly believes that all labor markets are competitive, it is a tautology that whatever wage differentials are generated by these markets

---

* Portions of Chapter 6 of the 1987 *Economic Report of the President* are included in Chapter 24 of this volume.

will be "fully compensating" ones. Once one allows for market imperfections, however, the question becomes an empirical one. The mere existence of *some* wage differential does *not* imply that it is a fully compensating one.

Estimates of the compensating wage differentials associated with the risk of fatal injury at the workplace suggest that individuals are paid a premium of 1 to 4 percent of their wages to compensate them for existing risks of fatal injury; this leads (given the magnitude of fatal injury rates) to imputed values of lives in the range of $200,000 to $3,500,000. Researchers have no way of evaluating (nor have they even tended to consider) whether differentials in this range truly fully compensate workers for risk of fatal injury.

As a result, the potential usefulness for public policy in occupational safety of estimates of compensating wage differentials for injury risk is limited. On the one hand, if these estimates truly reflect differentials paid for risk of injury, they may provide only lower-bound estimates of the value of life. On the other hand, if they also reflect a premium paid for other unmeasured unfavorable job characteristics that are correlated with job risk, they may lead one to overstate the true value of life.

NOTES

1. *Insufficient Wage Premiums for Dangerous Work?* For a number of reasons, workers may not ask for a wage premium that is high enough to offset their risk of injury. Consider the arguments of Professor Rose-Ackerman:

> The market will then work efficiently only if potential new employees can observe the riskiness of jobs. . . . One way such information might be provided is through a learning process. The first round of employees are uninformed of the risks, but after they are injured, other members of the labor force observe their injuries and illnesses and infer that the company should pay a wage premium or reduce workplace hazards.
>
> There are several reasons why this feedback process will work poorly. First, many hazards take a long time to produce injuries. Second, even if they happen quickly, potential employees will not observe many of the injured in a large labor market. . . . Third, the level of hazard depends on workers as well as workplaces. Some workers are more susceptible to hazards because of their genetic characteristics or their life style — for example, whether or not they are smokers. Thus, it may be difficult to infer one's own risk by observing the harm suffered by others. Fourth, workplace conditions change with technology and chemical processes so the past may be a poor guide to the future. For all these reasons, regulations that require employers to inform employees of hazards are easy to justify. . . .
>
> But the mere provision of information may not be sufficient for several different reasons. The first turns on the limited information-processing capacities of people, especially when it comes to probabilistic information. Rather than engage in a massive educational campaign, it may be more efficient to regulate employers directly through administrative orders or incentive schemes. . . . The second has to

do with monopsony power. Some employers operate in labor markets where employees have very poor options. Then the employers can make take-it-or-leave-it offers to workers, which include worker acceptance of unhealthy and unsafe working conditions. . . .

A third justification concerns the production function for health and safety. Many actions an employer can take are "local public goods" so far as workers are concerned. If dust collectors are installed, they will benefit all employees on a shop floor. . . . However, if the employees are not organized into a union, individual workers may be unwilling to modify their wage demands enough to make the health and safety investment worthwhile. If employers do not know the value workers place on safety, they may be unwilling to experiment with costly changes that may not pay off in lower wage increases or improved productivity. . . .

Finally . . . [g]iven the widespread existence of health insurance, welfare, and publicly subsidized health care for the poor and old, individuals do not bear all of the costs of their illnesses and injuries. Furthermore, individuals may not properly weigh the pain and suffering of their relatives and friends. [Hence,] individuals may fail to take into account all the social costs of their risky employment decisions. Individuals, but not society as a whole, are insulated from some of the costs of workplace accidents and illness. This insulation provides a final public policy justification for public regulation of these risks.

SUSAN ROSE-ACKERMAN, RETHINKING THE PROGRESSIVE AGENDA: THE REFORM OF THE AMERICAN REGULATORY STATE 86-88 (1992). *

2. *Appropriate or Too High Wage Premiums for Dangerous Work?*
Reason and evidence suggest that workers may ask for an appropriate wage premium or even a premium that more than offsets the risk of injury:

The available evidence suggests that workers utilize diverse forms of information in a reasonable fashion to form their risk judgments. Although there are not available data on workers' perceptions of fatality risks, overall assessments of nonfatal risk levels follow expected patterns. In particular, workers' risk perceptions are strongly correlated with [the U.S. Bureau of Labor Statistics] nonfatal injury risk measures and are influenced in the expected manner by opportunities for learning on the job. These influences include experiencing an injury oneself, hearing of injuries to other workers, seeing hazard warning signs, and observing whether the physical conditions at the workplace are pleasant.

Comparable data are not available to assess the extent of the correspondence between subjective risk perceptions and actual fatality risk levels. It is, however, noteworthy that fatality risks are several orders of magnitude smaller than nonfatal risks. To the extent that any systematic bias arises in risk perceptions, it is that individuals

---

* Reprinted by permission of Susan Rose-Ackerman.

generally display a tendency to overestimate small probabilities and underestimate large probabilities.

MICHAEL J. MOORE & W. KIP VISCUSI, COMPENSATION MECHANISMS FOR JOB RISKS 74-75 (1990).

3. *Further Evidence on Compensating Differentials.* There is a burgeoning literature on compensating wage differentials for the risks of workplace death and injury. Recent estimates for the United States suggest that wages increase about one percent for workers who face twice the average risk of a fatality on the job (the average is about one death per 25,000 workers per year). RONALD G. EHRENBERG & ROBERT S. SMITH, MODERN LABOR ECONOMICS 245 (9th ed. 2006). The data on wage premiums received by workers to accept risk can be used to calculate the implicit value workers place on their lives. A 2003 survey of more than 30 labor market studies found that the median estimate of the implicit value of life was about $7 million in 2000 dollars, with most estimates in the $3.8 million to $9 million range. W. Kip Viscusi & Joseph E. Aldy, *The Value of a Statistical Life: A Critical Review of Market Estimates Throughout the World*, 27 J. RISK & UNCERTAINTY 5, 18 (2003). *See generally* John F. Burton, Jr. & James R. Chelius, *Workplace Safety and Health Regulations: Rationale and Results, in* GOVERNMENT REGULATION OF THE EMPLOYMENT RELATIONSHIP 253-93 (Bruce E. Kaufman ed., 1997).

B. TORT SUITS

FARWELL v. BOSTON & WORCESTER RAIL ROAD CORP.
Supreme Judicial Court of Massachusetts
45 Mass. (4 Met.) 49 (1842)

SHAW, C. J. This is an action of new impression in our courts, and involves a principle of great importance. It presents a case, where two persons are in the service and employment of one company, whose business it is to construct and maintain a rail road, and to employ their trains of cars to carry persons and merchandize for hire. They are appointed and employed by the same company to perform separate duties and services, all tending to the accomplishment of one and the same purpose — that of the safe and rapid transmission of the trains; and they are paid for their respective services according to the nature of their respective duties, and the labor and skill required for their proper performance. The question is, whether, for damages sustained by one of the persons so employed, by means of the carelessness and negligence of another, the party injured has a remedy against the common employer. It is an argument against such an action, though certainly not a decisive one, that no such action has before been maintained.

It is laid down by Blackstone, that if a servant, by his negligence, does any damage to a stranger, the master shall be answerable for his neglect. But the damage must be done while he is actually employed in the master's service; otherwise, the servant shall answer for his own misbehavior. This rule is obviously founded on the great principle of social duty, that every man, in the management of his own affairs, whether by himself or by his agents or servants, shall so conduct them as not to injure another; and if he does not, and another thereby sustains damage, he shall answer for it. If done by a servant, in the course of his employment, and acting within the scope of his authority, it is considered, in contemplation of law, so far the act of the master, that the latter shall be answerable *civiliter*. But this presupposes that the parties stand to each other in the relation of strangers, between whom there is no privity; and the action, in such case, is an action sounding in tort. The form is trespass on the case, for the consequential damage. The maxim *respondeat superior* is adopted in that case, from general considerations of policy and security.

But this does not apply to the case of a servant bringing his action against his own employer to recover damages for an injury arising in the course of that employment, where all such risks and perils as the employer and the servant respectively intend to assume and bear may be regulated by the express or implied contract between them, and which, in contemplation of law, must be presumed to be thus regulated.

The same view seems to have been taken by the learned counsel for the plaintiff in the argument; and it was conceded, that the claim could not be placed on the principle indicated by the maxim *respondeat superior,* which binds the master to indemnify a stranger for the damage caused by the careless, negligent or unskillful act of his servant in the conduct of his affairs. The claim, therefore, is placed, and must be maintained, if maintained at all, on the ground of contract. As there is no express contract between the parties, applicable to this point, it is placed on the footing of an implied contract of indemnity, arising out of the relation of master and servant. It would be an implied promise, arising from the duty of the master to be responsible to each person employed by him, in the conduct of every branch of business, where two or more persons are employed, to pay for all damage occasioned by the negligence of every other person employed in the same service. If such a duty were established by law — like that of a common carrier, to stand to all losses of goods not caused by the act of God or of a public enemy — or that of an innkeeper, to be responsible, in like manner, for the baggage of his guest; it would be a rule of frequent and familiar occurrence, and its existence and application, with all its qualifications and restrictions, would be settled by judicial precedents. But we are of opinion that no such rule has been established, and the authorities, as far as they go, are opposed to the principle.

The general rule, resulting from considerations as well of justice as of policy, is, that he who engages in the employment of another for the performance of specified duties and services, for compensation, takes upon himself the natural and ordinary risks and perils incident to the performance of such services, and in legal presumption, the compensation is adjusted accordingly. And we are not aware of any principle which should except the perils arising from the carelessness and negligence of those who are in the same employment. These are perils which the servant is as likely to know, and against which he can effectually guard, as the master. They are perils incident to the service, and which can be as distinctly foreseen and provided for in the rate of compensation as any others. To say that the master shall be responsible because the damage is caused by his agents, is assuming the very point which remains to be proved. They are his agents to some extent, and for some purposes; but whether he is responsible, in a particular case, for their negligence, is not decided by the single fact that they are, for some purposes, his agents. It seems to be now well settled, what ever might have been thought formerly, that underwriters cannot excuse themselves from payment of a loss by one of the perils insured against, on the ground that the loss was caused by the negligence or unskillfulness of the officers or crew of the vessel, in the performance of their various duties as navigators, although employed and paid by the owners, and, in the navigation of the vessel, their agents. I am aware that the maritime law has its own rules and analogies, and that we cannot always safely rely upon them in applying them to other branches of law. But the rule in question seems to be a good authority for the point, that persons are not to be responsible, in all cases, for the negligence of those employed by them.

If we look from considerations of justice to those of policy, they will strongly lead to the same conclusion. In considering the rights and obligations arising out of particular relations, it is competent for courts of justice to regard considerations of policy and general convenience, and to draw from them such rules as will, in their practical application, best promote the safety and security of all parties concerned. This is, in truth, the basis on which implied promises are raised, being duties legally inferred from a consideration of what is best adapted to promote the benefit of all persons concerned, under given circumstances. To take the well known and familiar cases already cited; a common carrier, without regard to actual fault or neglect in himself or his servants, is made liable for all losses of goods confided to him for carriage except those caused by the act of God or of public enemy, because he can best guard them against all minor dangers, and because, in the case of actual loss, it would be extremely difficult for the owner to adduce proof of embezzlement, or other actual fault or neglect on the part of the carrier, although it may have been the real cause of the loss. The risk is therefore thrown upon the carrier, and he receives, in the form of payment for the carriage, a premium for the risk which he thus assumes. . . .

We are of opinion that these considerations apply strongly to the case in question. Where several persons are employed in the conduct of one common enterprise or undertaking, and the safety of each depends much on the care and skill with which each other shall perform his appropriate duty, each is an observer of the conduct of the others, can give notice of any misconduct, incapacity or neglect of duty, and leave the service, if the common employer will not take such precautions, and employ such agents as the safety of the whole party may require. By these means, the safety of each will be much more effectually secured, than could be done by a resort to the common employer for indemnity in case of loss by the negligence of each other. Regarding it in this light, it is the ordinary case of one sustaining an injury in the course of his own employment, in which he must bear the loss himself, or seek his remedy, if he have any, against the actual wrong-doer.

In applying these principles to the present case, it appears that the plaintiff was employed by the defendants as an engineer, at the rate of wages usually paid in that employment, being a higher rate than the plaintiff had before received as a machinist. It was a voluntary undertaking on his part, with a full knowledge of the risk incident to the employment; and the loss was sustained by means of an ordinary casualty, caused by the negligence of another servant of the company. Under these circumstances, the loss must be deemed to be the result of a pure accident, like those to which all men, in all employments, and at all times, are more or less exposed; and like similar losses from accidental causes, it must rest where it first fell, unless the plaintiff has a remedy against the person actually in default; of which we give no opinion.

It was strongly pressed in the argument, that although this might be so, where two or more servants are employed in the same department of duty, where each can exert some influence over the conduct of the other, and thus to some extent provide for his own security; yet that it could not apply where two or more are employed in different departments of duty, at a distance from each other, and where one can in no degree control or influence the conduct of another. But we think this is founded upon a supposed distinction, on which it would be extremely difficult to establish a practical rule. When the object to be accomplished is one and the same, when the employers are the same, and the several persons employed derive their authority and their compensation from the same source, it would be extremely difficult to distinguish, what constitutes one department and what a distinct department of duty. It would vary with the circumstances of every case. If it were made to depend upon the nearness or distance of the persons from each other, the question would immediately arise, how near or how distant must they be, to be in the same or different departments. In a blacksmith's shop, persons working in the same building, at different fires, may be quite independent of each other, though only a few feet distant. In a ropewalk, several may be at work on the same piece of cordage, at the same time, at many hundred feet distant from each other, and beyond the reach of sight and voice, and yet acting together. . . .

Plaintiff nonsuit.

NOTES

1. *Economics and Irrelevance.* The court says the "legal presumption" is that the pay of workers is adjusted to compensate them for the risk that they will be injured by the negligence of a co-worker. If wages do adjust this way, then changing the legal rule is irrelevant as to whether employers receive adequate economic incentives to prevent workplace injuries and is also irrelevant as to whether on average workers receive adequate compensation. Either way, the employer pays and workers are compensated. With the fellow servant rule, workers are paid through an increase in their wages that compensates them for the risk of injury. Alternatively, if the employer is liable, the worker receives lower wages (because she no longer receives compensation for the risk of injury from the negligence of fellow servants), but is compensated after the injury occurs by the tort suit recovery.

2. *Winners and Losers: The Tort System as Insurance.* Assuming that the "legal presumption" describes reality, workers as a group are neither helped nor hurt by the fellow servant rule: workers receive compensation for injuries caused by fellow servants either *ex ante* if the fellow servant rule applies or *ex post* if it does not. Thus workers can in principle receive adequate protection regardless of the operation of the fellow servant rule. But *individual* workers can be either winners or losers, so an equity problem occurs. With the fellow servant rule limiting recovery, workers who accept the wage premium for absorbing the risk of injury, but who are not injured, are winners; workers who are injured are losers. One way of viewing abrogation of the fellow servant rule, then, is as employer-provided insurance designed to improve equity. Workers who are not injured are not winners because they did not receive a wage premium for accepting the risk of injury; workers who are injured are not losers because they are fully compensated for their injuries *ex post*.

3. *The Unholy Trinity.* The fellow servant rule was one of three common law doctrines that severely limited the ability of workers at the turn of the century to recover from their employers for workplace injuries. The other two were contributory negligence and assumption of the risk.

The doctrine of contributory negligence barred recovery if the injured worker's negligence contributed at all to her injuries. Although a general defense in tort cases at the time, the doctrine was applied with special vigor in cases brought by injured workers. If the worker's negligence was 1% responsible for her injuries and the employer's negligence was 99% responsible, the worker could not recover.

The assumption of the risk doctrine barred recovery for the ordinary risks of employment; the extraordinary risks of employment, if the worker knew of them or might reasonably have been expected to know of them; and the risks arising from the carelessness, ignorance, or incompetency of fellow servants.

4. *Workers' Chances for Recovery.* A critical assessment of the reliance on tort suits to deal with workplace injuries was provided in C. Arthur Williams, Jr. & Peter S. Barth, Compendium on Workmen's Compensation 11 (1973):

> Before 1910, in almost every State the laws determining employers' responsibility for industrial injuries had been handed down from the pre-industrial period in England and the United States. Under these laws an injured worker's only recourse was through the courts and his chances of recovery were slight. It has been estimated that not more than 13 percent of injured employees ever recovered damages under the common law, even though 70 percent of the injuries were estimated to have been related to working conditions or employer's negligence. This inability to recover damages was due to the changes "wrought by the factory system and modern industry which had strained, beyond their capacity for adoption, common law doctrines developed to meet the needs of a simple economy."

Chapter 22

WORKERS' COMPENSATION

A. THE ORIGINS OF WORKERS' COMPENSATION

C. ARTHUR WILLIAMS, JR. & PETER S. BARTH, COMPENDIUM ON WORKMEN'S COMPENSATION 13-18 (1973)

Employers' Liability Statutes

[Dissatisfaction with the labor market and tort suits as solutions to the problem of workplace safety and health resulted, first, in the enactment of employers' liability statutes, and only later in enactment of workers' compensation laws.]

The employer liability acts did not attempt to create a new system of liability in the industrial relationship. They were based on the theory that the employee must bear the economic loss of an industrial injury unless he could show that some other person was directly responsible, through a negligent act or omission, for the occurrence of the accident. The employer was liable only for his own negligence, or at most for the liability of someone for whom he was directly responsible under the doctrine of *respondeat superior*. These statutes were merely intended to restore the worker to a position no worse than that of a stranger injured by the negligence of an employer or his employees.

Effects on Employer Defenses

Many of these employer liability statutes were extremely narrow in scope, confining their modifications to a specific industry or a particular defense. For example, the Georgia Act of 1855, the first such statute enacted, abolished the fellow servant rule for railroad companies only. While later enactments were often broader than the Georgia statute, none attempted to abrogate all three of the employer defenses for every employer-employee relationship. By 1907, 26 States had enacted employer liability acts, with most of these abolishing the fellow-servant rule while a few limited the assumption of risk and contributory negligence doctrines as well. . . .

Deficiencies of Employers' Liability Statutes

Employers' liability statutes did not provide an adequate solution for the problems arising from industrial accidents. They were, in fact, a tremendous source of worry, dissatisfaction, and friction to the employers and workers. As accidents frequently arise from the methods of carrying on a business, the responsibility for the resulting injuries must be assigned to conditions rather than persons. In contrast, under these statutes, liability was based on personal fault. Thus the economic loss for accidents of this nature had to be borne by the injured worker. These uncompensated accidents often gave rise to dependency and destitution, with the worker and his family forced to seek relief through various charitable organizations. This resulting status of enforced pauperization had a dehumanizing effect upon the injured worker.

Another source of criticism of this system stemmed from the fact that liability could be established only by a suit at law. . . .

Workmen's Compensation in the United States

In the United States, efforts to implement a system of compensation for industrial injuries lagged far behind the countries of Europe. As work-related injuries and diseases and their sequellae grew less and less tolerable towards the end of the 19th century, the situation became ripe for a radical change. The first evidence of interest in workmen's compensation was seen in 1893 when legislators seized upon John Graham Brooks' account of the German system as a clue to the direction of efforts at reform. This interest was further stimulated by the passage of the British Compensation Act of 1897.

Early Labor and Management Positions

In 1898 the Social Reform Club of New York drafted a bill proposing automatic compensation for some types of industrial accidents. This bill was opposed by various labor organizations who did not accept the concept of compensation at this time. They were fearful that State development of guildlike provisions for pensions and other welfare benefits would reduce the workers' loyalty to the unions. They supported legislation modifying the employers' common law defenses which they believed would produce court awards much higher than automatic compensation. Agitation along these lines resulted in the Reform Club's compensation bill "dying on the drawing board" and ultimately led to the passage of employer liability statutes.

In contrast to this opposition by labor leaders, many private corporations, particularly the railroads, had come to favor such plans. . . .

By 1910 labor had shifted its position because of the failure of liability statutes to provide a remedy, and began to work actively for compensation legislation. The National Civic Federation, which claimed to represent business, labor, and the public, managed to unify the various labor organizations and gain the attention of the State legislatures. With labor and industry lobbying for effective compensation legislation, the movement toward reform was in full swing.

The First Laws

. . . .

By 1908, there was still no workmen's compensation act in the United States. President Theodore Roosevelt, realizing the injustice, urged the passage of an act for Federal employees in a message to Congress in January. He pointed out that the burden of an accident fell upon the helpless man, his wife, and children. The President declared that this was "an outrage." Later in 1908 Congress passed a compensation act covering certain Federal employees. Though utterly inadequate, it was the first real compensation act passed in the United States. . . .

In 1910 New York became the first State to adopt a workmen's compensation act of general application which was compulsory for certain especially hazardous jobs and optional for others. "Although most corporate leaders and politicians of prominence, such as Theodore Roosevelt and President Taft, had publicly endorsed workmen's compensation, there was a residue of conservative opposition to such 'radical' social legislation." This conservative view was expressed by the courts who felt that these acts were plainly revolutionary by common law standards. Thus, in 1911 in *Ives v. South Buffalo Railway Company*[, 94 N.E. 431 (N.Y. 1911),] the Court of Appeals of New York held the New York act unconstitutional on the grounds of deprivation of property without due process of law. This decision was met with an explosion of criticism from all sides. Theodore Roosevelt was so angry that he openly advocated the passage of laws which would permit the recall of judicial decisions. While even the supporters of compensation legislation considered this measure too extreme, fear of its passage prompted many conservatives to support compensation legislation by more traditional means.

Following the *Ives* decision many State courts adopted a more liberal attitude toward compensation. Unfortunately, this decision had residual effects on the system. The "fear of unconstitutionality impelled the legislatures to pass over the ideal type of coverage, which would be both comprehensive and compulsory, in favor of more awkward and fragmentary plans . . . [to] ensure [their] constitutional validity." Elective or optional statutes became the rule, and several States limited their coverage to hazardous employment. By the time the U.S. Supreme Court held in 1917 that compulsory compensation laws were constitutional, the pattern of elective statutes had been set. . . .

The 1911 Wisconsin workmen's compensation act was the first law to become and remain effective. The laws of four other States (Nevada, New Jersey, California, and Washington) also became effective that year. Although 24 jurisdictions had enacted such legislation by 1925, workmen's compensation was not provided in every State until Mississippi enacted its law in 1948.

NEW YORK CENTRAL RAILROAD CO. v. WHITE
United States Supreme Court
243 U.S. 188 (1917)

Mr. Justice Pitney delivered the opinion of the court.

A proceeding was commenced by defendant in error before the Workmen's Compensation Commission of the State of New York, established by the Workmen's Compensation Law of that State, to recover compensation from the New York Central & Hudson River Railroad Company for the death of her husband, Jacob White, who lost his life September 2, 1914, through an accidental injury arising out of and in the course of his employment under that company. The Commission awarded compensation in accordance with the terms of the law; its award was affirmed [by the state courts]. Federal questions having been saved, the present writ of error was sued out by the New York Central Railroad Company. . . .

We turn to the constitutional question. . . .

In a previous year, the legislature enacted a compulsory compensation law applicable to a limited number of specially hazardous employments, and requiring the employer to pay compensation without regard to fault. Laws 1910, Chap. 674. This was held by the Court of Appeals in *Ives v. South Buffalo Ry. Co.*, 201 N.Y. 271, to be invalid because in conflict with the due process of law provisions of the state constitution and of the Fourteenth Amendment. Thereafter, and in the year 1913, a constitutional amendment was adopted, effective January 1, 1914, declaring:

> Nothing contained in this constitution shall be construed to limit the power of the legislature to enact laws for the protection of the lives, health, or safety of employees. . . .

In December, 1913, the legislature enacted the law now under consideration. . . . The act was sustained by the Court of Appeals as not inconsistent with the Fourteenth Amendment and that decision was followed in the case at bar.

The scheme of the act is so wide a departure from common-law standards respecting the responsibility of employer to employee that doubts naturally have been raised respecting its constitutional validity. The adverse considerations urged or suggested in this case and in kindred cases submitted at the same time are: (a) that the employer's property is taken without due process of law, because he is subjected to a liability for compensation without regard to any neglect or default on his part or on the part of any other person for whom he is responsible, and in spite of the fact that the injury may be solely attributable to the fault of the employee; (b) that the employee's rights are interfered with, in that he is prevented from having compensation for injuries arising from the employer's fault commensurate with the damages actually sustained, and is limited to the measure of compensation prescribed by the act; and (c) that both employer and employee are deprived of their liberty to acquire property by being prevented from making such agreement as they choose respecting the terms of the employment. . . .

In considering the constitutional question, it is necessary to view the matter from the standpoint of the employee as well as from that of the employer. For, while plaintiff in error is an employer, and cannot succeed without showing that its rights as such are infringed yet . . . the exemption from further liability is an essential part of the scheme, so that the statute if invalid as against the employee is invalid as against the employer.

The close relation of the rules governing responsibility as between employer and employee to the fundamental rights of liberty and property is of course recognized. But those rules, as guides of conduct, are not beyond alteration by legislation in the public interest. No person has a vested interest in any rule of law entitling him to insist that it shall remain unchanged for his benefit. The common law bases the employer's liability for injuries to the employee upon the ground of negligence; but negligence is merely the disregard of some duty imposed by law; and the nature and extent of the duty may be modified by legislation, with corresponding change in the test of negligence. Indeed, liability may be imposed for the consequences of a failure to comply with a statutory duty, irrespective of negligence in the ordinary sense; safety appliance acts being a familiar instance. . . .

But it is not necessary to extend the discussion. This court repeatedly has upheld the authority of the States to establish by legislation departures from the fellow-servant rule and other common-law rules affecting the employer's liability for personal injuries to the employee. . . .

It is true that in the case of the statutes thus sustained there were reasons rendering the particular departures appropriate. Nor is it necessary, for the purposes of the present case, to say that a State might, without violence to the constitutional guaranty of "due process of law," suddenly set aside all common-law rules respecting liability as between employer and employee, without providing a reasonably just substitute. . . . The statute under consideration sets aside one body of rules only to establish another system in its place. If the employee is no longer able to recover as much as before in case of being injured through the employer's negligence, he is entitled to moderate compensation in all cases of injury, and has a certain and speedy remedy without the difficulty and expense of establishing negligence or proving the amount of the damages. Instead of assuming the entire consequences of all ordinary risks of the occupation, he assumes the consequences, in excess of the scheduled compensation, of risks ordinary and extraordinary. On the other hand, if the employer is left without defense respecting the question of fault, he at the same time is assured that the recovery is limited, and that it goes directly to the relief of the designated beneficiary. And just as the employee's assumption of ordinary risks at common law presumably was taken into account in fixing the rate of wages, so the fixed responsibility of the employer, and the modified assumption of risk by the employee under the new system, presumably will be reflected in the wage scale. The act evidently is intended as a just settlement of a difficult problem, affecting one of the most important of social relations, and it is to be judged in its entirety. We have said enough to demonstrate that, in such an adjustment, the particular rules of the common law affecting the subject-matter are not placed by the Fourteenth Amendment beyond the reach of the law making power of the State; and thus we are brought to the question whether the method of compensation that is established as a substitute transcends the limits of permissible state action.

We will consider, first, the scheme of compensation, deferring for the present the question of the manner in which the employer is required to secure payment.

Briefly, the statute imposes liability upon the employer to make compensation for disability or death of the employee resulting from accidental personal injury arising out of and in the course of the employment, without regard to fault as a cause except where the injury or death is occasioned by the employee's willful intention to produce it, or where the injury results solely from his intoxication while on duty; it graduates the compensation for disability according to a prescribed scale based upon the loss of earning power, having regard to the previous wage and the character and duration of the disability; and measures the death benefits according to the dependency of the surviving wife, husband, or infant children. . . .

Of course, we cannot ignore the question whether the new arrangement is arbitrary and unreasonable, from the standpoint of natural justice. . . . It is plain that, on grounds of natural justice, it is not unreasonable for the State, while relieving the employer from responsibility for damages measured by common-law standards and payable in cases where he or those for whose conduct he is answerable are found to be at fault, to require him to contribute a reasonable amount, and according to a reasonable and definite scale, by way of compensation for the loss of earning power incurred in the common enterprise, irrespective of the question of negligence, instead of leaving the entire loss to rest where it may chance to fall — that is, upon the injured employee or his dependents. Nor can it be deemed arbitrary and unreasonable, from the standpoint of the employee's interest, to supplant a system under which he assumed the entire risk of injury in ordinary cases, and in others had a right to recover an amount more or less speculative upon proving facts of negligence that often were difficult to prove, and substitute a system under which in all ordinary cases of accidental injury he is sure of a definite and easily ascertained compensation, not being obliged to assume the entire loss in any case but in all cases assuming any loss beyond the prescribed scale.

Much emphasis is laid upon the criticism that the act creates liability without fault. This is sufficiently answered by what has been said, but we may add that liability without fault is not a novelty in the law. The common-law liability of the carrier, of the inn-keeper, of him who employed fire or other dangerous agency or harbored a mischievous animal, was not dependent altogether upon questions of fault or negligence. Statutes imposing liability without fault have been sustained. . . .

Viewing the entire matter, it cannot be pronounced arbitrary and unreasonable for the State to impose upon the employer the absolute duty of making a moderate and definite compensation in money to every disabled employee, or in case of his death to those who were entitled to look to him for support, in lieu of the common-law liability confined to cases of negligence.

This, of course, is not to say that any scale of compensation, however insignificant on the one hand or onerous on the other, would be supportable. In this case, no criticism is made on the ground that the compensation prescribed by the statute in question is unreasonable in amount, either in general or in the particular case. Any question of that kind may be met when it arises.

But, it is said, the statute strikes at the fundamentals of constitutional freedom of contract; and we are referred to two recent declarations by this court. The first is this: "Included in the right of personal liberty and the right of private property — partaking of the nature of each — is the right to make contracts for the acquisition of property. Chief among such contracts is that of personal employment, by which labor and other services are exchanged for money or other forms of property. If this right be struck down or arbitrarily interfered with, there is a substantial impairment of liberty in the long-established constitutional sense." *Coppage v. Kansas*, 236 U.S. 1, 14 (1915). And this is the other: "It requires no argument to show that the right to work for a living in the common occupations of the community is of the very essence of the personal freedom and opportunity that it was the purpose of the [Fourteenth] Amendment to secure." *Truax v. Raich*, 239 U.S. 33, 41 (1915).

It is not our purpose to qualify or weaken either of these declarations in the least. And we recognize that the legislation under review does measurably limit the freedom of employer and employee to agree respecting the terms of employment, and that it cannot be supported except on the ground that it is a reasonable exercise of the police power of the State. In our opinion it is fairly supportable upon that ground. And for this reason: The subject matter in respect of which freedom of contract is restricted is the matter of compensation for human life or limb lost or disability incurred in the course of hazardous employment, and the public has a direct interest in this as affecting the common welfare. . . .

Judgment affirmed.

NOTES

1. *Early Statutes.* The New York workers' compensation statute described in *New York Central Railroad v. White* was typical of the original workers' compensation laws enacted in most states.

> Coverage of the early laws was limited: even when elective, most acts applied only to specified hazardous industries. None covered all classes of employees. Agricultural workers, domestic help, and casual workers were most commonly excluded. Only a few acts applied to public employment. In general, compensation laws limited indemnity benefits to maximum total amounts, even for permanent disability or death. Cash benefits were usually stated as a percent of wages at the time of injury, 50 percent being the most common, although a few acts provided for about two-thirds of wages, subject to statutory maximum compensation ranging from $10 weekly in several states up to $15. Several states made no provision at all for medical benefits. Where provided they were limited in duration or amount or both.

> None of the early State compensation acts expressly covered occupational diseases. Statutes which provided compensation for "injury" were frequently interpreted to include disability from disease, but those acts which limited compensability to "injury by accident" excluded occupational disease. All except Oregon's act required uncompensated waiting periods of one to nine weeks, with several providing retroactive payments after a prescribed period.

C. Arthur Williams, Jr. & Peter S. Barth, Compendium on Workmen's Compensation 18 (1973).

2. *The Workers' Compensation Principle.* The workers' compensation principle has two elements. Workers benefit from a no-fault system, which enables them to recover in many situations in which tort suits would be unsuccessful. Employers benefit from limited liability, which means that the limited benefits provided in the workers' compensation statute are the only liability of the employer to its employees. Professor Epstein has restated the trade-off that is the essence of the workers' compensation principle:

> [T]he basic structure of the bargain was well understood with passage of the Act. The broad coverage formula eliminated the need to determine negligence on both sides and assumption of the risk — all inquiries with a high degree of uncertainty. In exchange for the broad coverage formula, the workman received a level of compensation that, by design left him *worse off* than if the injury itself had never taken place. The low levels of the benefits doubtless proved nettlesome to workers *after* injuries. But to concentrate on that point is to miss the central role. First, low damages help keep down the overall costs of the plan, which will induce employers to continue to hire labor. Second, low benefits help prevent fraud against the plan, as there is less to gain by pretending that an injury, or its consequences, is work-related. Third, the low awards create additional incentives upon the worker for self-protection and therefore act as an implicit substitute for assumption of risk and contributory negligence.

Richard A. Epstein, *The Historical Origins and Economic Structure of Workers' Compensation Law,* 16 GA. L. REV. 775, 800 (1982).

3. *Constitutional Limits at the Origins of Workers' Compensation.* The Fourteenth Amendment to the U.S. Constitution was the basis for the challenge to the New York law. Another significant constitutional limitation on federal involvement in workers' compensation statutes was the Supreme Court's interpretation of the Commerce Clause of the U.S. Constitution. U.S. Const. art. I, § 8, cl. 3. The interpretation of this clause by the Supreme Court prior to the 1930s meant that the authority of Congress to deal with this issue was quite limited, and hence that workers' compensation statutes dealing with most private-sector employees had to be enacted at the state level.

4. *Current Constitutional Limits on Workers' Compensation.* Later in this chapter, we examine constitutional challenges to statutes that eliminate both workers' compensation *and* tort remedies for workplace injuries. Other constitutional issues also occasionally arise in workers' compensation cases. *See, e.g., Breen v. Carlsbad,* 120 P.3d 413 (N.M. 2005) (statute limiting compensation for mental disabilities to 100 weeks while compensation for physical impairments could last up to 700 weeks held to violate the equal protection guarantees of the New Mexico Constitution); *Stavenjord v. Montana,* 67 P.3d 229 (Mont. 2003) (statute that limited a claimant to $10,000 because her disability resulted from a disease, while her benefits would have been $27,027 if the cause had been an injury, held to violate the equal protection provision in the Montana constitution); *Whiteside v. Smith,* 67 P.3d 1240 (Colo. 2003) (Colorado statute requiring an injured worker to pay $675 for an independent medical exam if the employer-selected physician makes an initial decision to terminate benefits held to violate the due process guarantee of the U.S. Constitution as applied to indigent workers). However, a $12,500 limit on attorney fees, which the Workers' Compensation Judge described as "miserly," was held not to violate state constitutional rights to equal protection and due process in *Wagner v. AGW Consultants*, 114 P.3d 1050 (N.M. 2005). The Arizona constitution mandates that an employee receive workers' compensation if the workplace injury [interpreted as including occupational diseases] "is caused in whole, or in part, or contributed to, by a necessary risk or danger of such employment . . . ." Grammatico admitted he had smoked marijuana and ingested methamphetamine in the two days prior to his workplace injury and his post-accident urine test showed positive results for these substances plus amphetamine. He was denied benefits under a statute that disqualifies a worker who fails to pass a drug test unless the employee proves the use of the unlawful substance "was not a contributing cause of the employee's injury." The Arizona Supreme Court, in *Grammatico v. Industrial Commission*, 117 P.3d 786, 791 (Ariz. 2005) held the statute "cannot be constitutionally interpreted to require proof that the disease was *solely* or *exclusively* caused by the industrial exposure."

5. Who Pays for Workers' Compensation? The national costs of the workers' compensation program were $87.4 billion in 2004. But who pays for the program? The dominant view among lawyers is found in the first paragraph of the leading legal treatise.

> Workers' compensation is a mechanism for providing cash-wage benefits and medical care to victims of work-connected injuries, and for placing the cost of these injuries ultimately on the consumer, through the medium of insurance, whose premiums are passed on in the cost of the product.

Arthur Larson & Lex K. Larson, Larson's Worker's Compensation 1-1 (Desk ed., 2006).

An alternative view — suggesting that employers bear at least a portion of the costs of the workers' compensation program — is found in Justice Pitney's 1917 opinion:

> Who is to bear the charge? It is plain that, on grounds of natural justice, it is not unreasonable for the State, while relieving the employer from responsibility for damages measured by common-law standards and payable in cases where he or those for whose conduct he is answerable are found to be at fault, to require him to contribute a reasonable amount, and according to a reasonable and definite scale, by way of compensation for the loss of earning power incurred in the common enterprise, irrespective of the question of negligence, instead of leaving the entire loss to rest where it may chance to fall — that is, upon the injured employee or his dependents.

New York Central Railroad Co. v. White, 243 U.S. 188, 203-04 (1917).

There is yet another view about who pays for workers' compensation. This position, largely espoused by economists, is that workers pay for much of the workers' compensation program. The mechanism is that workers are paid lower wages than they would have received in the absence of workers' compensation. The essence of the modern economists' position about who pays for workers' compensation was also anticipated by Justice Pitney:

> And just as the employee's assumption of ordinary risks at common
> law presumably was taken into account in fixing the rate of wages,
> so the fixed responsibility of the employer, and the modified assump-
> tion of risk by the employee under the new system, presumably will
> be reflected in the wage scale.

Id. at 201-02.

There is some disagreement among economists, but one analysis suggests
that employers bear 40 percent of the costs of workers' compensation, consumers bear 20 percent, and workers bear the remaining 40 percent. J. PAUL
LEIGH ET AL., COSTS OF OCCUPATIONAL INJURIES AND ILLNESSES 177-79 (2000).

6. *The National Commission.* The initial workers' compensation statutes,
whatever their limits, nonetheless represented the first social insurance
program in the United States and thus meant that for the first two decades
of the program (until the mid-1930s) the government was doing more for
injured workers than for unemployed or retired workers. With the enactment
of the unemployment insurance and Social Security programs in the 1930s
and the expansion of those programs in subsequent decades, the "luster" of
workers' compensation faded. By the 1960s, the proportion of the workforce
covered by workers' compensation was less than the coverage of Social
Security and unemployment insurance. Moreover, workers' compensation cash
benefit increases lagged behind increases in wages in the period between 1940
and the 1960s.

One result of these developments was increasing criticism of the workers'
compensation program during the 1960s that in turn led to the creation of
the National Commission on State Workmen's Compensation Laws by the
Occupational Safety and Health Act of 1970. Despite the membership of the
Commission (most were Republicans appointed by President Nixon), *The
Report of the National Commission on State Workmen's Compensation Laws*
was critical of state workers' compensation laws:

> The inescapable conclusion is that State workmen's compensation
> laws in general are inadequate and inequitable. While several States
> have good programs, and while medical care and some other aspects
> of workmen's compensation are commendable in most States, the
> strong points are too often matched by weak.

Id. at 119.

The National Commission identified five objectives for a modern workers'
compensation program: (1) broad coverage of employees and work-related injuries and diseases; (2) substantial protection against interruption of income;
(3) sufficient medical care and rehabilitation services; (4) promotion of safety;
and (5) an effective delivery system. The National Commission made eighty-
four specific recommendations for state workers' compensation programs,
several of which will be discussed in this chapter. The Commission also
identified nineteen recommendations as essential, and called for a significant
improvement in state laws, compelled by federal workers' compensation
standards if necessary to achieve these nineteen essential recommendations.
Federal standards have not been enacted, but many states improved their
laws in response to the recommendations of the National Commission.

The impact of the National Commission on state workers' compensation laws, and the relevance and limitations of the Commission's analysis for workers' compensation in the 21st Century are examined in John F. Burton, Jr., *The National Commission on State Workmen's Compensation Laws*, and Peter S. Barth, *Some Reflections on the National Commission and its Legacy*, *in* WORKERS' COMPENSATION COMPENDIUM 2005-06, VOLUME ONE 347-61 (John F. Burton, Jr. et al., eds., 2005).

B. AN OVERVIEW OF CURRENT WORKERS' COMPENSATION PROGRAMS

1. COVERAGE OF EMPLOYEES AND EMPLOYERS

Not all employees and employers are covered by workers' compensation. Recent estimates indicate that nationally about 96% of workers are covered. Some states cover virtually all employees, while only about 75% of workers are covered in Texas, which is the only state in which workers' compensation coverage is elective for employers. The other gaps in coverage occur because some states exempt: (1) employers with a limited number of employees (e.g. three or less); (2) certain industries, such as state and local government and agriculture; and (3) certain occupations, such as household workers.

In addition, the laws are designed to cover employees, which means that workers who are independent contractors normally are not covered. Moreover, certain employees — those who are casual workers or workers not engaged in the normal trade or business of the employer — may not be protected by the act even when their employers are within the scope of the act.

2. COVERAGE OF INJURIES AND DISEASES

Even workers who are covered by workers' compensation statutes must meet certain legal tests in order to receive benefits. There is a four-step test found in most state workers' compensation laws: (1) there must be a *personal injury*, which in some jurisdictions is interpreted to exclude mental illness; (2) that results from an *accident*, which is interpreted in some states to exclude injuries that develop over a long period of time, as opposed to those injuries resulting from a traumatic incident; (3) that must *arise out of employment*, which means that the source of the injury must be related to the job; and (4) that must occur during the *course of employment*, which normally requires that the injury occur on the employer's premises and during working hours. Most work-related injuries can meet these four tests, although there are thousands of cases testing the exact meaning of each of these four steps.

The coverage of diseases is a problem in workers' compensation. Many diseases could not meet the accident test because they develop over a prolonged period. In addition the statutes used to contain limited lists of diseases that were compensable. Fortunately, the restricted lists of diseases have now been abandoned in all jurisdictions. Now, typically, there is a list of specified occupational diseases followed by a general category permitting the compensation of other occupational diseases.

Nonetheless, there are restrictions in language pertaining to work-related diseases still found in many laws, such as statutes of limitations that require the claim to be filed within a limited period after the last exposure to the substance causing the disease, even if the disease does not manifest itself for a prolonged period. Also, some state courts have interpreted the general category of occupational diseases to only cover those diseases that are peculiar to or characteristic of the occupation of the employee seeking coverage.

3. MEDICAL CARE AND REHABILITATION SERVICES

Most state workers' compensation laws require the employer to provide full medical benefits without cost to the worker. This portion of the workers' compensation program has become increasingly expensive in the last decade, with medical benefits now accounting for about 48% of all benefit payments by state workers' compensation programs, up from one-third in the early 1980s. Unlike most health care plans, there are usually no deductibles or co-insurance provisions that require employees to share the expense of medical care.

Fee schedules have been issued by many state workers' compensation agencies that limit medical charges, which have made some medical care providers reluctant or unwilling to provide services to injured workers. Other providers appear to react to fee schedules by increasing the quantity of health care services provided. There is disagreement about whether the fee schedules are effective in reducing expenditures on medical care.

Another approach to reducing workers' compensation health care expenditures used in a number of states is to allow the insurance carrier or employer (rather than the employee) to choose the treating physician. Again, there is disagreement about the effect of such limits on employee choice on the quality and cost of health care. In recent years, there has also been a rapid increase in the use of managed health care in the workers' compensation programs in a number of states, including such techniques as HMOs, PPOs, and utilization review. There is limited evidence about the effect of these cost containment efforts on medical costs and quality in the workers' compensation system.

Medical rehabilitation, such as physical therapy, is likely to be provided by the workers' compensation laws. However, many states do not provide vocational rehabilitation services that may be necessary to prepare the injured worker for a new job.

4. CASH BENEFITS

Cash benefits vary substantially among the states, with wide variations in maximum weekly benefits and maximum durations of benefits. Each state also provides a variety of types of cash benefits. A general characteristic of the cash benefits is that they are not subject to state or federal income taxes.

a. Temporary Total Disability Benefits

These benefits are paid to someone who is completely unable to work but whose injury is of a temporary nature. The weekly benefit in most jurisdictions is two-thirds of the worker's preinjury wage, subject to maximum and minimum amounts as prescribed by state law. There is also a waiting period during which the worker receives no benefits. However, if the worker is still disabled beyond a specified date, known as the retroactive date, then the benefits for the waiting period are paid on a retroactive basis.

b. Temporary Partial Disability Benefits

These benefits are paid to someone who is still recovering from a workplace injury or disease and who is able to return to work but has limitations on the amount or intensity of work that can be provided during the healing period. The weekly benefit in most jurisdictions is two-thirds of the difference between the worker's preinjury wage and the worker's current earnings, subject to a maximum amount as prescribed by state law.

c. Permanent Partial Disability (PPD) Benefits

PPD benefits are the most complicated, controversial, and expensive type of workers' compensation benefit. They are paid to a worker who has a permanent consequence of his or her work-related injury or disease that is not totally disabling. An example would be someone who has lost a hand in an accident.

There are two general approaches to permanent partial disability benefits. *Scheduled PPD benefits* are paid for those injuries that are included in a list found in the workers' compensation statute. In New York, for example, 100% loss of an arm entitles the worker to 312 weeks of benefits. The schedules are also applied to partial loss of the arm, so that a 50% loss of an arm in New York is worth 156 weeks of benefits. The schedules in most jurisdictions provide benefits whether the injury results in amputation or a loss of use of the body part. Normally the schedule is limited to the body extremities such as arms, legs, hand and feet, plus eyes and ears. (These schedules are sometimes referred to as "Meat Charts." In Australia, the schedules are known as "The Table of Maims.")

Nonscheduled PPD benefits are paid for those permanent injuries that are not on the schedule, such as back cases. The basis for these benefits depends on the jurisdiction. In states like New Jersey that use the "impairment approach," the back injury is rated in terms of the seriousness of the medical consequences. (In New Jersey, 25% of loss of the whole person in a medical sense translates into 25% of 600 weeks or 150 weeks of benefits). In states like Wisconsin that use the "loss of earning capacity approach," the back injury is rated considering the medical consequences as well as factors, such as age, education, and job experience, that affect the worker's earning capacity. (In Wisconsin, 25% of loss of earning capacity translates into 25% of 1000 weeks or 250 weeks of benefits).

These benefit durations for scheduled PPD benefits and for nonscheduled permanent partial benefits in those jurisdictions relying on the impairment approach or on the loss of earning capacity approach are fixed in the sense that the worker receives that duration of benefits whether or not she has actual wage loss for that period. During the period that these types of permanent partial benefits are being paid, the weekly benefit is normally calculated as two-thirds of preinjury wages, subject to maximum and minimum weekly benefit amounts.

The nonscheduled permanent partial disability benefits in New York rely on a fundamentally different approach, usually referred to as the "wage-loss approach." The worker only receives benefits if, in addition to having an injury with permanent consequences, the worker also has actual wage loss due to the work-injury. The weekly nonscheduled permanent partial disability benefit in New York is two-thirds of the difference between the worker's earnings prior to the injury and the worker's earnings after the healing period is over, subject to a maximum weekly amount. In New York, these nonscheduled permanent partial disability benefits can continue for as long as the worker has earnings losses due to the work-related injury, which can be for the rest of the worker's life.

d. Permanent Total Disability Benefits

Permanent total disability benefits are paid to someone who is completely unable to work for an indefinite period. Permanent total status is assigned if the worker has specified types of injuries, such as the loss of two arms, or more generally if the facts in the case warrant an evaluation as a permanent total disability. This is a relatively uncommon type of case in workers' compensation. The weekly benefit for a permanent total disability is normally two-thirds of the preinjury wage, subject to maximum and minimum amounts as prescribed by state law. In most states, the permanent total disability benefits are paid for the duration of total disability or for life. In a number of states, however, there are arbitrary limits on total dollar amounts or duration of these benefits.

e. Death Benefits

Death benefits are paid to the survivor of a worker who was killed on the job. In many jurisdictions the weekly benefit depends on the number of survivors. For example, a widow or widower might receive a benefit that is 50% of the deceased worker's wage, while a widow or widower with a child might receive a weekly benefit that is 66⅔% of the deceased worker's wage. These benefits are subject to minimum and maximum weekly amounts. Most states provide the benefits for the duration of the survivor's lifetime if the survivor is a widow or widower and for children's benefits at least until age eighteen, but there are a number of states that have limits on the dollar amounts or on the durations of survivors' benefits.

5. FINANCING OF BENEFITS

Workers' compensation benefits are prescribed by state laws, but these laws assign the responsibility for the provision of the benefits to the employer. The employer in turn provides the benefits by one of three mechanisms: (i) by purchasing insurance from a private insurance carrier; (ii) by purchasing insurance from a state workers' compensation fund; or (iii) by qualifying as a self-insurer and paying its own employees directly. Some states, such as New

York, have all three options available. (This is known as the three-way system.) Other states, such as Ohio, restrict the choices to the state fund (known as an exclusive or monopolistic state fund) or self-insurance. Federal government employees are all covered by a government fund. Still other jurisdictions, such as Nebraska, New Jersey, and Wisconsin, restrict the choices to private insurance carriers or self-insurance. Nationally, about 55% of all benefits are paid by private insurance carriers, about 25% by state and federal funds, and about 20% by self-insuring employers.

The workers' compensation insurance premiums are experience rated. There are several steps in the experience rating process. Every employer who purchases insurance is assigned to a particular insurance classification (*e.g.* a lumber yard is assigned to class 8232); then the initial insurance rate can be determined by looking in an insurance manual that specifies the "manual rate" for each insurance classification. These manual rates are in terms of so many dollars per hundred dollars of payroll. (For example, a manual rate of $2.00 means that an employer who has a worker paid $300 a week must pay a $6.00 per week insurance premium for that worker.) The manual rates vary substantially within each state, reflecting the previous experience with benefit payments for all the employers in that classification. Manual rates in a particular state might range from $40 per $100 of payroll for logging to $.75 per $100 of payroll for clerical workers.

Those employers who are of medium or large size are eligible for firm-level experience rating. This means that they will pay more or less than the premiums suggested by the manual rates, depending on their own experience relative to other firms in the same insurance classification. For example, a lumber yard with a particularly adverse record of benefit payments might end up paying $6 per $100 of payroll even though the manual rate is $2 per $100 of payroll.

Employers that self-insure — that is, pay benefits to their own employees without use of an insurance carrier — represent an ultimate form of experience rating, although self-insuring employers generally purchase excess risk policies that protect them against unusually adverse experience.

6. ADMINISTRATION OF WORKERS' COMPENSATION

There are wide variations among the states in how the workers' compensation programs are administered. There are several dimensions of the differences among states.

a. The Initial Responsibility for Payment

Most states use what is known as the direct payment system, in which employers are obligated to begin payment as soon as the worker is injured and the employer accepts liability. Other states use the agreement system, where the employers have no obligation to begin payments until an agreement is reached with the employee concerning the amount due. The agreement system is likely to involve delays in many cases.

b.   The Functions of the Administrative Agency

Most states have a workers' compensation agency that is responsible for administering the program. One function of the agency is adjudication of disputes between workers and employers or insurance carriers. In most agencies, the initial level of decision is made by an administrative law judge (ALJ) or an official with similar duties, such as a hearing examiner. The decisions of the ALJ normally can be appealed to an appeals board (or commission) within the workers' compensation agency. Then, appeals from the workers' compensation board typically enter the state court system at the appellate court level.

The state workers' compensation agencies vary considerably in their administrative styles. At one extreme are agencies, such as those in New Jersey, that are passive. They essentially do nothing but wait for problems to arise and then perform the adjudication function. The other extreme is Wisconsin, where the agency can be characterized as active because it performs three functions in addition to adjudication. The Wisconsin agency engages in extensive record keeping, monitors the performance of carriers and employers, and provides evaluations (e.g., of the extent of permanent disability) that help the parties resolve disputes without resorting to litigation.

c.   Closing of Cases

In many states, cases are closed by agreement of the parties (subject to approval of the workers' compensation agency in some states). These are generally known as compromise and release agreements, because a compromise is reached on the amount of benefits paid and the employer is released from any further obligations. Normally the benefits are paid in a lump sum. These compromise and release agreements are often criticized, because they mean that workers who subsequently have additional need for medical care or income benefits cannot obtain them from the employer.

d.   Extent of Litigation

States vary widely in the extent of litigation (including any use of an attorney by the worker to help receive benefits). Wisconsin is an extreme example of a state where lawyers are involved in only a minority of cases. At the other extreme, states such as California and Illinois have lawyers involved in the great majority of cases, especially those that involve anything other than a relatively short period of temporary total benefits. The worker's attorney's fee is almost always deducted from the cash benefit.

C.   THE EXCLUSIVITY OF WORKERS' COMPENSATION

Exclusivity is one of the founding principles of workers' compensation. In exchange for a no-fault system (which benefited workers), workers' compensation became the exclusive remedy against the employer for a worker injured on the job (which benefited employers). There are, however, several exceptions to the exclusive remedy doctrine that allow an injured employee to bring a tort suit against the employer or another party.

1. TORT SUITS AND OTHER LEGAL ACTIONS AGAINST THE EMPLOYER

MILLISON v. E.I. DU PONT DE NEMOURS & CO.
Supreme Court of New Jersey
501 A.2d 505 (1985)

CLIFFORD, J.

The New Jersey Workers' Compensation Act, *N.J.S.A.* 34:15-1 to -128 (Compensation Act), contains an exclusive-remedy provision in *N.J.S.A.* 34:15-8. The issue in these consolidated cases is whether that provision precludes employees who have suffered occupational diseases from maintaining a separate tort action against their employer and against company physicians. The employees charge the employer and physicians with intentionally exposing the employees to asbestos in the workplace, deliberately concealing from employees the risks of exposure to asbestos, and fraudulently concealing specific medical information obtained during employee physical examinations that reveal diseases already contracted by workmen. We hold that although the employees are limited to workers' compensation benefits for any initial occupational-disease disabilities related to the hazards of their employment experience, the Compensation Act does not bar plaintiffs' cause of action for aggravation of those illnesses resulting from defendants' fraudulent concealment of already-discovered disabilities. . . .

II

. . . .

The thrust of plaintiffs' allegations is that there was something akin to a conspiratorial agreement between du Pont and its medical staff that resulted in harm to plaintiffs. They assert generally that defendants, with knowledge of the adverse health consequences of asbestos use and exposure, and as part of a concerted plan for profit, deliberately exposed the plaintiffs to a dangerous work environment. Their claims focus on two separate situations, however.

The first count of the complaint avers that defendants knew or should have known of the dangers associated with asbestos exposure, that they therefore had a duty to inform plaintiffs and to protect them from those dangers, but that they nonetheless acted intentionally to conceal from plaintiffs all information regarding the health hazards of asbestos. In count two of their complaint, plaintiffs allege that du Pont and the company physicians fraudulently concealed from plaintiffs the fact that company medical examinations had revealed that certain plaintiffs-employees had contracted asbestos-related diseases. They assert that each year the du Pont doctors would give employees complete physical examinations, including chest x-rays, pulmonary function tests, electrocardiograms, urine analyses, and blood tests. Plaintiffs contend that the results of these physical exams indicated that plaintiffs-employees had contracted serious pulmonary and respiratory abnormalities associated with exposure to asbestos. They further maintain that rather than provide medical treatment for these ailing employees, defendants fraudulently concealed plaintiffs' asbestos-related diseases and sent them back into the workplace, where their initial infirmities were aggravated by additional exposure to asbestos. Plaintiffs claim that the time from defendants' first knowledge of the employee's condition to the time when the employee was told of the danger was as long as eight years.

III

It is undisputed that plaintiffs' injuries, if proven, are compensable under the Compensation Act. The controversy presented, however, calls for a determination of whether the legislature intended that the Compensation Act should serve as a worker's sole and exclusive remedy under circumstances such as those alleged. The pertinent statute, N.J.S.A. 34:15-8, declares that when, by express or implied agreement, the parties have accepted the provisions of the Compensation Act and the employee qualifies for benefits under the conditions of the Act, the employee shall ordinarily be barred from the pursuit of other remedies.[2] As the statute expressly indicates, however, an exception to the exclusivity provision is available when plaintiffs can prove an "intentional wrong." . . .

Plaintiffs argue that their charges that defendants knowingly and deliberately exposed employees to a hazardous work environment and fraudulently concealed existing occupational diseases are sufficient to fall within the Act's limited "intentional wrong" exception and to take their injuries outside the intended scope of the Compensation Act. However, as noted by the Appellate Division in granting defendants' motions to dismiss, in order to satisfy the Compensation Act's definition of "intentional wrong," claimants have heretofore been required to show a deliberate intention to injure. . . . This requirement of proving actual intent to injure in order to avoid the exclusivity of a workers' compensation act is the subject of comment by Professor Larson in his multivolume treatise on Workers' Compensation Law:

> Even if the alleged conduct goes beyond aggravated negligence, and includes such elements as knowingly permitting a hazardous work condition to exist, knowingly ordering claimant to perform an extremely dangerous job, willfully failing to furnish a safe place to work, or even willfully and unlawfully violating a safety statute, this still falls short of the kind of actual intention to injure that robs the injury of accidental character. . . .
>
> If these decisions seem rather strict, one must remind oneself that what is being tested here is not the degree of gravity or depravity of the employer's conduct, but rather the narrow issue of intentional versus accidental quality of the precise event producing injury. The intentional removal of a safety device or toleration of a dangerous condition may or may not set the stage for an accidental injury later. But in any normal use of the words, it cannot be said, if such an injury does happen, that this was deliberate infliction of harm comparable to an intentional left jab to the chin.

---

[2] Absent an express written statement to the contrary, N.J.S.A. 34:15-9 creates a presumption that the parties to every employment contract have agreed to be governed by the provisions of the Compensation Act.

[2A A. LARSON, THE LAW OF WORKMEN'S COMPENSATION, § 68.13 at 13-22 to 13-27 (1983) (footnotes omitted).]

The approach explicated by Professor Larson emphasizes the narrow or limited character of the exception. . . . The approach of construing and applying the exception in the most limited fashion consistent with the purpose of the law is followed by the vast majority of jurisdictions that have considered whether allegedly egregious employer conduct warrants the recognition of a separate cause of action outside the compensation system. . . .

V

Mindful of the origins of the Compensation Act and its subsequent development, we turn to the precise legal issue posed by this appeal: what categories of employer conduct will be sufficiently flagrant so as to constitute an "intentional wrong," thereby entitling a plaintiff to avoid the "exclusivity" bar of N.J.S.A. 34:15-8? Plaintiffs contend that du Pont and the doctors, in exposing the employees to asbestos and concealing medical information, acted knowingly and deliberately, not accidentally or negligently, so that defendants' conduct must be considered an "intentional wrong" within the meaning of the statute. Defendants, relying on the bulk of the authority on this topic, conversely assert that only conduct amounting to actual intent to injure employees will be sufficient to qualify as an "intentional wrong" in the context of a workers' compensation statute, and that the plaintiffs' complaints fall short of alleging "deliberate infliction of harm comparable to an intentional left jab to the chin." 2A A. LARSON, *supra,* § 68.13 at 13-27.

Although we are certain that the legislature could not have intended that the system of workers' compensation would insulate actors from liability outside the boundaries of the Act for all willful and flagrant misconduct short of deliberate assault and battery, we are equally sure that the statutory scheme contemplates that as many work-related disability claims as possible be processed exclusively within the Act. Moreover, if "intentional wrong" is interpreted too broadly, this single exception would swallow up the entire "exclusivity" provision of the Act, since virtually all employee accidents, injuries, and sicknesses are a result of the employer or a co-employee intentionally acting to do whatever it is that may or may not lead to eventual injury or disease. Thus in setting an appropriate standard by which to measure an "intentional wrong," we are careful to keep an eye fixed on the obvious: the system of workers' compensation confronts head-on the unpleasant, even harsh, reality — but a reality nevertheless — that industry knowingly exposes workers to the risks of injury and disease.

The essential question therefore becomes what level of risk-exposure is so egregious as to constitute an "intentional wrong." We are confident that the *quid pro quo* of workers' compensation — employer makes swift and certain payment without regard to his own fault in exchange for immunity from liability at law — can best be preserved by applying the "intent" analysis of Dean Prosser to determine what is an "intentional wrong" within the meaning of the Act. According to Prosser, the mere knowledge and appreciation of a risk — something short of substantial certainty — is not intent. The defendant who acts in the belief or consciousness that the act is causing an appreciable risk of harm to another may be negligent, and if the risk is great the conduct may be characterized as reckless or wanton, but it is not an intentional wrong. . . .

In adopting a "substantial certainty" standard, we acknowledge that every undertaking, particularly certain business judgments, involve some risk, but that willful employer misconduct was not meant to go undeterred. The distinctions between negligence, recklessness, and intent are obviously matters of degree, albeit subtle ones, as the thoughtful dissent so powerfully points out. In light of the legislative inclusion of occupational diseases within the coverage of the Compensation Act, however, the dividing line between negligent or reckless conduct on the one hand and intentional wrong on the other must be drawn with caution, so that the statutory framework of the Act is not circumvented simply because a known risk later blossoms into reality. We must demand a virtual certainty. . . .

There is another significant component to the level of risk exposure that will satisfy the "intentional wrong" exception. Courts must examine not only the conduct of the employer, but also the context in which that conduct takes place: may the resulting injury or disease, and the circumstances in which it is inflicted on the worker, fairly be viewed as a fact of life of industrial employment, or is it rather plainly beyond anything the legislature could have contemplated as entitling the employee to recover *only* under the Compensation Act?

Examining the allegations in these cases in light of the foregoing principles, we conclude that count one of plaintiffs' complaints seeking damages beyond those available through workers' compensation for their initial work-related occupational diseases must fall. Although defendants' conduct in knowingly exposing plaintiffs to asbestos clearly amounts to deliberately taking risks with employees' health, as we have observed heretofore the mere knowledge and appreciation of a risk — even the strong probability of a risk — will come up short of the "substantial certainty" needed to find an intentional wrong resulting in avoidance of the exclusive-remedy bar of the compensation statute. In the face of the legislature's awareness of occupational diseases as a fact of industrial employment, we are constrained to conclude that plaintiffs-employees' initial resulting occupational diseases must be considered the type of hazard of employment that the legislature anticipated would be compensable under the terms of the Compensation Act and not actionable in an additional civil suit.

We acknowledge a certain anomaly in the notion that employees who are severely ill as a result of their exposure to asbestos in their place of employment are forced to accept the limited benefits available to them through the Compensation Act. Despite the fact that the current system sometimes provides what seems to be, and at times doubtless is, a less-than-adequate remedy to those who have been disabled on the job, all policy arguments regarding any ineffectiveness in the current compensation system as a way to address the problems of industrial diseases and accidents are within the exclusive province of the legislature. . . .

Plaintiffs have, however, pleaded a valid cause of action for aggravation of their initial occupational diseases under the second count of their complaints. Count two alleges that in order to prevent employees from leaving the workforce, defendants fraudulently concealed from plaintiffs the fact that they were suffering from asbestos-related diseases, thereby delaying their treatment and aggravating their existing illnesses. As noted earlier, du Pont's medical staff provides company employees with physical examinations as part of its package of medical services. Plaintiffs contend that although plaintiffs' physical examinations revealed changes in chest x-rays indicating asbestos-related injuries, du Pont's doctors did not inform plaintiffs of their sicknesses, but instead told them that their health was fine and sent them back to work under the same hazardous conditions that had caused the initial injuries.

These allegations go well beyond failing to warn of potentially-dangerous conditions or intentionally exposing workers to the risks of disease. There is a difference between, on the one hand, tolerating in the workplace conditions that will result in a certain number of injuries or illnesses, and, on the other, actively misleading the employees who have already fallen victim to those risks of the workplace. An employer's fraudulent concealment of diseases already developed is not one of the risks an employee should have to assume. Such intentionally-deceitful action goes beyond the bargain struck by the Compensation Act. But for defendants' corporate strategy of concealing diseases discovered in company physical examinations, plaintiffs would have minimized the dangers to their health. Instead, plaintiffs were deceived — or so they charge — by corporate doctors who held themselves out as acting in plaintiffs' best interests. The legislature, in passing the Compensation Act, could not have intended to insulate such conduct from tort liability. We therefore conclude that plaintiffs' allegations that defendants fraudulently concealed knowledge of already-contracted diseases are sufficient to state a cause of action for aggravation of plaintiffs' illnesses, as distinct from any claim for the existence of the initial disease, which is cognizable only under the Compensation Act. . . .

Those corporate medical departments that do their best to provide legitimate medical services to their workers, yet commit a negligent error along the way, have no reason to fear increased liability as a result of our holding. On the other hand, those corporations that would use their medical departments as a tool to prevent employees from learning of known injuries that are substantially certain to be aggravated by lack of disclosure must be deterred from embarking on such a course of conduct. . . .

VIII

As to so much of plaintiffs' complaints as seek damages for deliberate exposure to asbestos and to the risks associated with that exposure, we hold that those claims are compensable exclusively under the Compensation Act. They were dismissed by the trial court and the judgment of dismissal was affirmed by the Appellate Division. So much of the Appellate Division's judgment as embraces dismissal of the first count of the complaint is affirmed.

Plaintiffs have pleaded a valid cause of action in their second count as against du Pont and its physicians, based on an intentional wrong.

Handler, J., concurring in part and dissenting. . . .

The Court today recognizes that in order for an injured worker suffering from an occupation-related disease to bring a common-law action against his employer based upon "intentional wrong," thereby escaping the exclusivity provision of the Workers' Compensation Act under N.J.S.A. 34:15-8, the worker must prove that the employer's actions were "substantially certain" to cause the resultant disease. The Court also interprets the "intentional wrong" exception to the exclusive remedy of the Compensation Act as encompassing intentional wrongs committed by employers as well as a worker's co-employees.

I agree with these propositions of law. However, I think that the Court errs in applying its standard to the facts of this case. While the Court professes to endorse the "substantially certain" standard in construing the "intentional wrong" exception, its rejection of plaintiffs' common-law cause of action in the context of this case in effect requires that an employee demonstrate a much higher degree of knowledge on the part of the employer than "substantial certainty." The effect of the Court's decision is to impose a level of knowledge of resultant harm that is virtually akin to a showing of subjective intent or actual purpose to inflict injury. I take issue with the Court's application because, as I view the record, plaintiffs have presented a cause of action that genuinely and fairly raises the issue of whether or not defendants in this case possessed and concealed information indicating that exposure to asbestos was "substantially certain" to cause the occupational diseases that have debilitated the plaintiffs. I would thus reverse the lower court's disposition of plaintiffs' "initial intentional concealment and exposure" claims and permit that cause of action to proceed to a plenary trial.

The Court also upholds plaintiffs' claims against du Pont and its physicians for fraudulent failure to disclose the plaintiffs' contraction of asbestos engendered diseases and consequent aggravation of those diseases. I concur in the majority's disposition of this claim. . . .

NOTES

1. *New Jersey Cases Involving the Intentional Injury Exception.* The New Jersey Supreme Court revisited the intentional injury exception to the exclusive remedy provision in *Laidlow v. Hariton Machinery Co.*, 790 A.2d 884 (N.J. 2002). Laidlow was injured when his hand was pulled into a rolling mill. The company installed a safety guard on the rolling mill, but from 1979 until Laidlow's accident in 1992, the guard was always "tied up" and inoperative. The only exception was during OSHA inspections, when the wire holding up the safety guard was released. The employer conceded the guard was usually removed for speed and convenience.

Although there were no accidents before 1992, both Laidlow and a fellow worker had close calls when they were able to pull their hands out of the machine just in time to escape injury. Those incidents were reported to the employer. Moreover, prior to his accident, Laidlow spoke to Portman, his supervisor, three times about the safety guard and a professional engineer certified that the employer knew there was a "'virtual' certainty of injury" from operation of the mill without a guard.

The trial court concluded the facts alleged by Laidlow did not demonstrate an intentional wrong and granted the employer's and Portman's motions for summary judgment. The Appellate Division affirmed the dismissals. The New Jersey Supreme Court reversed the judgment of the Appellate Division, remanded the case for trial, and clarified its holding in the 1985 *Millison* case.

> What is critical, and what often has been misunderstood, is that we cited Professor Larson and the cases relying on his approach for informational, not precedential, purposes. *Millison*, in fact, specifically rejected Professor Larson's thesis that in order to obtain redress outside the Workers' Compensation Act an employee must prove that the employer subjectively desired to harm him. In place of Larson's theory, we adopted Dean Prosser's broader approach to the concept of intentional wrong.

> Under Prosser's approach, an intentional wrong is not limited to action taken with a subjective desire to harm, but also includes instances where an employer knows that the consequences of those acts are substantially certain to result in such harm.

Id. at 891.

The New Jersey Supreme Court also clarified the additional requirements for the intentional wrong exception.

> In addition to adopting Prosser's "substantial certainty" test relative to conduct, in *Millison* we added a crucial second prong to the test:

> Courts must examine not only the conduct of the employer, but also the context in which that conduct takes place: may the resulting injury or disease, and the circumstances in which it is inflicted on the worker, fairly be viewed as a fact of life of industrial employment, or is it rather plainly beyond anything the legislature could have contemplated as entitling the employee to recover *only* under the Compensation Act? . . .

Id. at 892.

The court concluded that a directed verdict was inappropriate because the facts could have led a jury to conclude that the employer was aware of the virtual certainty of injury from the unguarded rolling mill and that if Laidlow's allegations were proven, the context prong could also be met.

Would you allow the plaintiff to proceed with a tort suit in New Jersey in these situations? (1) A worker was killed when he fell into a sand hopper. OSHA had previously cited the employer for *inter alia* failing to identify permit-required confined spaces, to implement lockout procedures, and to train employees in safety matters. A professional engineer contended the employer deliberately provided information to OSHA indicating it was addressing each of the violations but did not follow through. *Crippen v. Central Jersey Concrete Pipe Co.*, 823 A.2d 789 (N.J. 2003) (yes). (2) A worker, who normally installed sprinkler systems, was asked to assist with snow removal. A safety lever that normally stops the blades on a snow blower when the operator takes his or her hands off the handle bar was taped by someone unknown to allow the blades to spin continuously. The worker pushed some snow down a clogged chute and injured his fingers. *Tomeo v. Thomas Whitesell Constr. Co., Inc.*, 823 A.2d 64 (N.J. 2002) (no). The court drew a distinction between industrial machinery and a consumer product, for which there is a presumption that users will heed the warnings about inherent dangers.

2. *The Intentional Injury Exception in Michigan.* The ability of injured workers to use the intentional injury exception depends in part on the language in the state's workers' compensation statute. Michigan provides a good example of how that language can change over time. The Michigan Supreme Court in *Beauchamp v. Dow Chemical Co.*, 398 N.W.2d 882 (Mich. 1986), held that an intentional tort provided an exception to the exclusive remedy doctrine, and that "intention" included any injury in which the employer intended an act and believed that the injurious consequence was "substantially certain" to occur.

The Michigan legislature reacted in 1987 by amending the workers' compensation statute to provide that an intentional injury occurs only when "the employer had actual knowledge that an injury was certain to occur and willfully disregarded that knowledge." MICH. COMP. LAWS § 418.131(1). The Michigan Supreme Court interpreted this language in *Travis v. Dreis & Krump Mfg. Co.*, 551 N.W.2d 132 (Mich. 1996). Travis had been assigned to work on an unfamiliar machine that her supervisor knew (but did not tell her) had a history of unpredictable malfunctions. The tool room supervisor told the supervisor that the machine needed to be shut down and fixed or rebuilt, or that someone would be hurt. After this conversation, some repairs were made on the machine and the supervisor believed it was functioning properly. However, the machine malfunctioned and Travis suffered amputation of two fingers and multiple crushing injuries to both hands. The trial court granted summary judgment to the employer because it could not find that the facts constituted an intentional injury, and the Michigan Supreme Court agreed because the 1987 legislation requires an "extremely high standard" of showing that an injury was "certain" to occur. *Id.* at 143.

Consider an alternative set of facts. An employee's job includes pouring wet scrap metal objects into a furnace containing molten aluminum. The employee warned the employer about the dangerous circumstances under which he was required to work and the lack of protective devices. He suffers minor burns from this task and is sent home. He is then called back the same day to perform the same job function, and is severely burned this time. Would this constitute an intentional injury under the 1987 Michigan legislation? *See Golec v. Metal Exch. Corp.*, 551 N.W.2d 132 (Mich. 1996) (yes, because of actual knowledge of specific injury which had already been proven "certain" to occur).

3. *A Taxonomy of Approaches to the Intentional Injury Exception.* When will an employee be able to bring a tort suit against the employer because the employer engaged in activity that represented an intentional injury to the employee? There are at least five possible answers to this question.

(i) *There is no intentional injury exception.* ARTHUR LARSON & LEX K. LARSON, LARSON'S WORKERS' COMPENSATION § 103.01 (Desk ed., 2006), identify several states that do not recognize the intentional injury exception to the exclusivity of the workers' compensation remedy, including Alabama, Indiana, and Pennsylvania.

(ii) *The exception requires an actual intent to injure.* The "almost unanimous rule" is that the intentional injury exception requires misconduct of the employer that represents "a conscious and deliberate intent directed to the purpose of inflicting an injury." LARSON & LARSON § 103.03. Thus "accidental injuries caused by the gross, wanton, willful, deliberate, intentional, reckless, culpable, or malicious negligence, [or] breach of statute" are not sufficient to satisfy the intentional injury exception. Since there appears to be some overlap in these excerpts from the same sentence in the Larsons' treatise of what would constitute an exception based on actual intent, the authors provide further clarification: the actual intent to injure exception only applies when there was "deliberate infliction of harm comparable to an intentional left jab to the chin." Cases illustrating conduct that does not represent an actual intention to injure include knowingly permitting a hazardous work condition to exist; knowingly ordering an employee to perform an extremely dangerous job; willfully violating a safety statute; refusing to respond to an employees' medical needs and restrictions; and withholding information about worksite hazards.

(iii) *The exception requires employer conduct that is substantially certain to cause injury or death.* Almost a dozen jurisdictions, including Michigan, New Jersey, and West Virginia, allow injured employees to bring tort suits against employers when the employers' conduct was substantially certain to cause the injury. LARSON & LARSON § 103.04.

Although the Larsons suggest that this standard subjects employers to common law suits for actions that "might under ordinary circumstances be viewed as gross negligence," the states listed by the authors involve decisions that appear to require more than gross negligence. Thus, the West Virginia decision cited by the Larsons as the first decision to depart from what they characterized as the "pure intent" standard, *Mandolidis v. Elkins Indus., Inc.*, 246 S.E.2d 907 (1978), allowed tort suits for employer behavior that involved "willful, wanton, and reckless behavior."

(iv) *The exception requires employer conduct that is willful.* A unique approach was adopted by the New Mexico Supreme Court in *Delgado v. Phelps Dodge Chino, Inc.*, 34 P.3d 1148 (N.M. 2001), which was analyzed by Robert Aurbach, *Delgado v. Phelps Dodge Chino, Inc.: A Case Study in Judicial Legislation, in* WORKERS' COMPENSATION COMPENDIUM 2005-06, VOLUME ONE 252-55 (John F. Burton, Jr. et al., eds., 2005):

> The facts alleged by the plaintiff were truly horrific. The worker [was ordered to remove a ladle overfilled with molten material]. The worker complied, despite protesting that he was unqualified to deal with the emergency. The worker's efforts failed catastrophically, resulting in severe burns over virtually his entire body, causing his death a few weeks later. . . . The court went on to criticize the actual intent to injure rule, saying that it unbalanced the Workers' Compensation Act in favor of employers. The court noted that statutory language denied compensation to workers when they were intoxicated, when they engaged in willful conduct resulting in their injury, and

when they intentionally self-inflicted injury. The actual intent to injure standard absolved the employer of tort liability for "willful" behavior resulting in injury to the worker, while the worker was denied a workers' compensation remedy if they engaged in "willful" behavior resulting in their injury. . . .

The court established a three-prong test for determination of "will-ful" conduct by the employer that would deprive him of exclusive rem-edy protection for injuries to a worker, holding that:

> . . . willfulness renders a worker's injury non-accidental, and therefore outside the scope of the Act, when: (1) the worker or employer engages in an intentional act or omission, without just cause or excuse, that is reasonably expected to result in the injury suffered by the worker; (2) the worker or employer expects the intentional act or omission to result in the injury, or has utterly disregarded the consequences; and (3) the intentional act or omis-sion proximately causes the injury.

(v) *The exception requires employer conduct that is negligent, wanton, reckless, or (arguably, even) grossly negligent.* We are unaware of any jurisdic-tion that allows an employee to bring a tort suit against an employer because the employer engaged in conduct that was merely negligent, wanton, or reckless. Moreover, despite the assertion by the Larsons to the contrary, we are unaware of cases in which gross negligence made an employer subject to a tort suit (short of facts that indicated the employer was actually aware the employee was exposed to conditions that made it substantially certain the employee was going to be injured, which we consider involving more than gross negligence).

4. Fraud by Employer in Defending Claim. Suppose a worker files a workers' compensation claim and the employer challenges the claim by filing false documents. Because of the employer's fraud, the Workers' Compensation Board initially denies the claim, requiring the worker to hire a lawyer to uncover the fraud and appeal the Board's ruling. Eventually the employee receives his workers' compensation award. Should the employee be allowed to bring a fraudulent misrepresentation action and, if so, what are the appropriate damages? The danger of such an action is that employers will be chilled from vigorously defending against compensation claims. *See Persinger v. Peabody Coal Co.,* 474 S.E.2d 887 (W. Va. 1996) (allowing action for full compensatory damages, including annoyance and inconvenience, plus punitive damages and attorney's fees).

5. Sexual Harassment as a Basis for Tort Recovery. Cathy Jean Coates and Madeline Duran were employees at Sam's Club, a unit of Wal-Mart. Toby Alire was a fellow employee who eventually became a supervisor. Coats and Duran claimed that Alire physically and verbally sexually harassed them and other employees, including grabbing Duran's breasts and pulling open another employee's blouse to look at her breasts. Although Coats and Duran reported these incidents to management and the store manager personally witnessed one incidence of Alire's sexual harassment, he was not disciplined. Wal-Mart continued to employ Alire even after he was convicted of the assault, kidnapping, and rape of his girlfriend. Wal-Mart did terminate Alire while he was in jail because his absence violated the company's leave policies.

Coates and Duran filed a tort suit against Wal-Mart alleging negligent supervision and intentional infliction of emotional distress. The jury found in their favor and *inter alia* awarded Duran $1,200,000 and Coates $555,000 in punitive damages. Wal-Mart appealed the award on several grounds, including a contention that Coates and Duran were barred from raising a tort claim because the workers' compensation act provides the exclusive remedy for work-related injuries. The New Mexico Supreme Court scrutinized this argument:

> While it is true that the basic essence of the exclusivity provisions is that the WCA's [workers' compensation act's] remedy is exclusive to all other remedies against the employer for the same injury, the exclusivity provision is not an absolute bar. . . . [T]he WCA will preclude other claims only if the injury falls within the scope of the WCA. . . . A claim falls outside the WCA for work-related injuries if: 1) the injuries do not arise out of employment; 2) substantial evidence exists that the employer intended to injure the employee; or 3) the injuries are not those compensable under the WCA. Although any one of the preceding exceptions removes the claim from the coverage of the WCA, all three exceptions exist here.

Coates v. Wal-Mart Stores, Inc., 976 P.2d 999, 1004 (N.M. 1999).

When female employees alleged that male employees repeatedly touched them and made verbal sexual advances, a suit was allowed to proceed to trial. The Florida Supreme Court offered this rationale:

> Workers' compensation is directed essentially at compensating a worker for lost resources and earnings. This is a vastly different concern than is addressed by the sexual harassment laws. While workplace injuries rob a person of resources, sexual harassment robs the person of dignity and self esteem.

Byrd v. Richardson-Greenshields Sec., Inc., 552 So. 2d 1099, 1104 (Fla. 1989).

Several cases have barred tort claims for intentional infliction of emotional distress because of the exclusive remedy provision of workers' compensation statutes. In *Konstantopoulos v. Westvaco Corp.*, 112 F.3d 710 (3rd Cir. 1997), *cert. denied*, 522 U.S. 1128 (1998), the Court of Appeals affirmed dismissal of a claim for intentional infliction of emotional distress as well as a claim for sexual assault and battery based in part on a certification from the Supreme Court of Delaware that "an employee's claim against her employer for personal injuries sustained during the course of employment, even if the offending conduct was of a sexual nature, is limited to the compensation provided by the [Workers' Compensation] Act." The offensive conduct included sexually suggestive behavior directed towards Konstantopoulos and a request to her from a fellow employee with "his pants' flap open" to "look at this." In *DeFronzo v. Conopco, Inc.*, 357 F. Supp. 2d 1062 (N.D. Ill. 2005), the Court barred an intentional infliction of emotional distress claim based on sexual harassment because of the exclusivity provisions of the Illinois workers' compensation statute. DeFronzo alleged that a female co-worker repeatedly kicked and grabbed his genitals and otherwise harassed him.

Some states decide whether the exclusive remedy provision protects the employer against tort suits resulting from sexual harassment by examining the type of injury sustained by the worker. LARSON & LARSON § 104.05[4] (Desk ed., 2006) explains this approach.

> Usually, an exclusivity challenge will hinge upon the type of injury sustained. Thus, if the gravamen of the complaint is humiliation, mental distress, indignity, embarrassment or such typical job discrimination items as lost wages or loss of promotion, the exclusiveness clause does not apply. However, if a substantial portion of the complaint involves physical injury, *or the kind of mental or nervous injury or emotional distress compensable under the Act*, most states will hold the action to that extent banned. An important corollary of this rule is that the more liberal a jurisdiction is in compensating for mental-mental injuries, the more the range of possible tort suits is reduced.

6. *Other Remedies for Sexual Harassment.* While a worker may not be able to recover in a tort suit against the employer because of the workers' compensation exclusivity principle, recovery may be possible under Title VII or under a state fair employment statute. One reason exclusivity was so important in sexual harassment cases was that until the enactment of the Civil Rights Act of 1991, Title VII did not permit compensatory damages for sexual harassment. Workers thus attempted tort suits instead of bringing Title VII suits in order to receive adequate relief.

2. NO REMEDY AGAINST THE EMPLOYER?

LIVITSANOS v. SUPERIOR COURT
Supreme Court of California
828 P.2d 1195 (1992)

ARABIAN, J.

We granted review to consider whether the exclusive remedy provisions of the Workers' Compensation Act apply to bar an employee's claims for intentional and negligent infliction of emotional distress, where no physical injury or disability is alleged. We hold that claims for intentional or negligent infliction of emotional distress are preempted by the exclusivity provisions of the workers' compensation law, notwithstanding the absence of any compensable physical disability. We further conclude that, for unrelated reasons, the case must be remanded to the Court of Appeal for further proceedings consistent with the views set herein.

Facts

. . . .

Plaintiff Apostol Livitsanos began his employment at Continental Culture Specialists, Inc. (Continental), a yogurt manufacturing company owned by

Vasa Cubaleski (Cubaleski), in 1976 in the shipping department. Two years later, plaintiff was promoted to supervisor of the department and in 1980 he was made manager, with attendant salary increases. . . .

In 1984, Continental's regular distributor went out of business, leaving Continental without a distributor. Plaintiff and another Continental employee, Andy Stylianou, formed a company, known as ABA, exclusively to distribute Continental's products. Plaintiff and Stylianou operated the distributorship with full knowledge and approval of defendants Continental and Cubaleski.

Throughout plaintiff's term of employment, defendant Cubaleski praised plaintiff's performance, telling him that he had "saved the company," and that he would "someday own Continental."

In late 1988 or early 1989, for no apparent reason, Cubaleski began a campaign of harassment against plaintiff. This campaign took several forms. Cubaleski falsely accused plaintiff, along with Continental's office manager, of writing fraudulent checks to an outside contractor as part of a scheme to siphon funds away from Continental. Cubaleski communicated this charge to other Continental employees, as well as to an employee of an outside accounting firm. In addition, Cubaleski told Continental employees and others that $800,000 was "missing" from Continental, implying that plaintiff had stolen the money. Cubaleski threatened to have plaintiff "put in jail" because of the "missing" money.

. . . .

In August 1989, Cubaleski insisted that plaintiff and Stylianou sell their distributorship company, ABA, to another distributor that Continental wished to employ. At the time, one of the clients of ABA was indebted to the company because Continental had asked ABA to extend $100,000 credit to this customer. Cubaleski promised that, if plaintiff sold ABA, Continental would assume responsibility for the $100,000 credit. After plaintiff agreed to sell ABA, Cubaleski demanded that plaintiff sign a promissory note for the $100,000 credit and agree to personal liability or he would "be in trouble." Plaintiff signed the note. Approximately two weeks later, plaintiff was terminated.

Plaintiff was discharged with no warning, no explanation and no severance pay. After the termination, Cubaleski told other Continental employees that plaintiff's company had been improperly buying fruit toppings to resell, using Continental's money. The accusations were false. After the termination, Cubaleski also told other Continental employees that plaintiff had stolen $800,000 from Continental and that plaintiff was blackmailing Cubaleski.

Plaintiff filed suit against Continental and Cubaleski for breach of contract, defamation, intentional infliction of emotional distress, negligent infliction of emotional distress, and money lent. He alleged that defendants engaged in a campaign of harassment resulting in the wrongful termination of his employment. Defendants demurred to the causes of action for defamation and negligent and intentional infliction of emotional distress. The trial court sustained Continental's demurrers without leave to amend, apparently on the ground that the employer's conduct was "a normal part of the employment relationship" and therefore barred by the Workers' Compensation Act (*Cole v. Fair Oaks Fire Protection Dist.* (1987) 43 Cal. 3d 148, 160 (hereafter *Cole*)). Cubaleski's demurrers were also sustained, but leave to amend was granted as to limited issues. The Court of Appeal, citing *Cole,* summarily denied plaintiff's petition for writ of mandate.

Discussion

1. *Intentional Infliction of Emotional Distress*

Plaintiff contends that because he did not allege any physical injury or disability resulting from defendants' conduct, his cause of action for intentional infliction of emotional distress is outside the scope of the workers' compensation law, and thus not governed by *Cole.* He relies principally on *Renteria v. County of Orange* (1978) 82 Cal. App. 3d 833, 838 (hereafter *Renteria*), which held that a cause of action for intentional infliction of emotional distress is outside the scope of the workers' compensation scheme where the injury is purely "emotional," and no "physical" disability is alleged.

We have not heretofore been called upon to reconcile the principles of *Cole* and *Renteria.* In *Cole,* the employer engaged in a campaign of harassment which caused the plaintiff severe physical injury and disability. We held that the injuries were compensable under workers' compensation notwithstanding the egregious nature of the employer's misconduct, because such actions "are a normal part of the employment relationship." There was no allegation, however, that the plaintiff had suffered a "purely emotional" injury. . . . Here, plaintiff has not alleged any physical injury or disability resulting from the employer's conduct.[4] Thus . . . we are called upon to construe the principles we adduced in *Cole* in the context of a case of purely emotional injury.

We begin with a review of *Renteria.* The plaintiff filed a civil action against his employer and fellow employees alleging numerous acts of harassment designed to discriminate against him because of his Mexican-American ancestry. The defendants successfully demurred on the ground the action was barred by the exclusive remedy provisions of the workers' compensation law. The Court of Appeal reversed, holding that the cause of action for intentional infliction of emotional distress was not barred.

The court first rejected the defendants' claim that emotional distress damages are generally recoverable in a workers' compensation proceeding. Although physical injury (e.g., a heart condition) caused by mental and emotional stress, or disabling mental illness caused by job pressures are compensable, the court held that "mental suffering, *as such,*" without accompanying physical injury or disability, was not a compensable injury. (*Renteria, supra,* 82 Cal. App. 3d 833, 839; italics in original.) The court noted that the fact that an injury was noncompensable did not, "by itself, abrogate the exclusive remedy provisions of the Workers' Compensation Act." It determined, however, that the plaintiff's action was "not an isolated instance of a physical

---

[4] We reject defendants' suggestion that allegations plaintiff suffered "nervousness" necessarily constitute physical injury. Terms such as nervousness, anxiety, worry, humiliation, embarrassment, apprehension, and others, refer to subjective emotional states.

injury which is noncompensable, but an entire class of civil wrongs outside the contemplation of the workers' compensation system."

It reached this conclusion, evidently, in large part because the alleged wrong involved intentional injury. As the court stated: "While it is possible to believe that the Legislature intended that employees lose their right to compensation for certain forms of negligently or accidentally inflicted physical injuries in exchange for a system of workers' compensation featuring liability without fault, compulsory insurance, and prompt medical care, it is much more difficult to believe that the Legislature intended the employee to surrender all right to any form of compensation for mental suffering caused by extreme and outrageous misconduct by an employer." The *Renteria* court therefore concluded that the cause of action for intentional infliction of emotional distress constituted an implied exception to workers' compensation exclusivity under conditions where the " 'essence of the tort, in law, [was] non-physical. . . .' "

. . . .

[T]he proposition that intentional or egregious employer conduct is necessarily outside the scope of the worker's compensation scheme is erroneous. This was the precise problem which we addressed in *Cole*, where we noted that many intentional acts by an employer could be expected to cause emotional distress and yet do not lie outside the proper scope of workers' compensation. Even intentional "misconduct" may constitute a "normal part of the employment relationship." . . .

Furthermore, as we observed in *Cole*, the *Renteria* court's distinction between "physical" and "emotional" injury presents a glaring anomaly: If the employer's misconduct causes "purely emotional" distress, then the employee may maintain a civil action with full tort remedies; if the employer's conduct is so outrageous as to cause actual physical disability, however, the employee is limited to the recovery of workers' compensation. Thus, the more reprehensible the employer's conduct, the more likely that such conduct would be shielded by the workers' compensation exclusivity rule. It would then be in the employer's best interest to make conditions so intolerable for an employee and to cause such a level of emotional distress that the employee could not work as a result. Thus, the employer could avoid civil liability for the most egregious misconduct.

Clearly, the law should not, and need not, countenance such paradoxical results. The "physical" versus "emotional" dichotomy is logically insupportable. More importantly, it is contrary to the text and purposes of the workers' compensation law.

The touchstone of the workers' compensation system is industrial injury which results in *occupational disability* or death. Labor Code section 3208 defines "injury" as "*any* injury or disease arising out of the employment . . . ." (Italics added.) Labor Code section 3208.1 describes "specific" injuries "occurring as the result of one incident or exposure *which causes disability or need for medical treatment*" and "cumulative" injury as "occurring as repetitive mentally or physically traumatic activities extending over a period of time, the combined effect of *which causes any disability or need for medical treatment.*" (Italics added.) Thus, as the court in *Coca-Cola Bottling Co. v. Superior Court* (1991) 233 Cal. App. 3d 1273, observed, "a compensable injury is one which causes disability or need for medical treatments." (*Id.* at p. 1284.)

Moreover, the workers' compensation system is designed to compensate only for such disability or need for treatment as is occupationally related. "Temporary disability" benefits are a substitute for lost wages during a period of temporary incapacity from working; "permanent disability" payments are provided for permanent bodily impairment, to indemnify for impaired future earning capacity or decreased ability to compete in an open labor market. The basic purpose of the Workers' Compensation Act is to compensate for the disabled worker's diminished ability to compete in the open labor market, not to compensate every work-related injury.

Thus, compensable injuries may be physical, emotional or both, so long as they are disabling. . . .

Compensation for psychiatric injury is not new. . . . An employee who suffers a disabling emotional injury caused by the employment is entitled, upon appropriate proof, to workers' compensation benefits, including any necessary disability compensation or medical or hospital benefits.

Thus, the *Renteria* court plainly erred in suggesting that emotional injury which results in an industrial disability is not compensable under the Workers' Compensation Act. So long as the basic conditions of compensation are otherwise satisfied, and the employer's conduct neither contravenes fundamental public policy (*Tameny v. Atlantic Richfield Co., supra,* 27 Cal. 3d 167) nor exceeds the risks inherent in the employment relationship (*Cole, supra,* 43 Cal. 3d 148), an employee's emotional distress injuries are subsumed under the exclusive remedy provisions of workers' compensation.

The conclusion that emotional injury lies within the scope of the workers' compensation law does not complete the analysis, however. For injury must also result in an industrial *disability* compensable under workers' compensation. It is theoretically possible to incur a work-related injury that results in no compensable industrial disability. Indeed, this was one of the concerns originally addressed in *Renteria.* And *Renteria* itself contains the answer: "The existence of a noncompensable injury does not, by itself, abrogate the exclusive remedy provisions of the Workers' Compensation Act."

This proposition was more fully explained by the court in *Williams v. State Compensation Ins. Fund* (1975) 50 Cal. App. 3d 116, where an employee who allegedly suffered a loss of sexual function as the result of an industrial injury asserted that his civil claim should go forward because such losses were not compensable under workers' compensation. The court rejected the argument, explaining as follows: "Plaintiff is correct in arguing that the statutory emphasis on *occupational* disability as a rating factor denigrates the compensability of nonoccupational handicaps. Decisions in other states hold that the workers' compensation law provides the exclusive remedy for industrial injury even though the resulting disability — for example, sexual impotence — is noncompensable. The theory underlying the out-of-state decisions is that the workers' compensation plan imposes reciprocal concessions upon employer and employee alike, withdrawing from each certain rights and defenses available at common law; the employer assumes liability without fault, receiving relief from some elements of damage available at common law; the employee gains relatively unconditional protection for impairment of his earning capacity, surrendering his common law right to elements of damage unrelated to earning capacity; the work-connected injury engenders a single remedy against the employer, exclusively cognizable by the compensation agency and not divisible into separate elements of damage available from separate tribunals; *a failure of the compensation law to include some elements of damage recoverable at common law is a legislative and not a judicial problem.* (*Id.* at 122, italics added.)[6]

In sum, where the employee suffers annoyance or upset on account of the employer's conduct but is not disabled, does not require medical care, and the employer's conduct neither contravenes fundamental public policy nor exceeds the inherent risks of the employment, the injury will simply not have resulted in any occupational impairment compensable under the workers' compensation law or remediable by way of a civil action. To be sure, the theoretical class of cases which fit these criteria, in which there will be *no* remedy, would appear to be rather limited. Nevertheless, the possibility of a lack of a remedy in a few cases does not abrogate workers' compensation exclusivity. Not every aggravation in normal employment life is compensable.[7]

The question remains whether, in light of the foregoing principles, the demurrers to plaintiff's causes of action for intentional and negligent infliction of emotional distress were properly sustained. As discussed above, there is no merit to plaintiff's assertion that purely emotional injuries lie outside the scope of the workers' compensation system. The mere failure to allege physical disability will not entitle the injured employee to a civil action. To this extent, the demurrers were properly sustained.

Plaintiff's contention that defendants' misconduct exceeded the normal risks of the employment relationship is another matter. Plaintiff has alleged that defendants engaged in a campaign of outrageous and harassing conduct, which included falsely claiming that plaintiff embezzled money from Continental and tried to sabotage the company's product; compelling plaintiff to sell his independent distribution company, ABA, and demanding possession

---

[6] It should be noted that the portion of *Williams v. State Compensation Ins. Fund,* discussed in *Renteria,* apparently dealt with the question of rating factors with respect to an award of *permanent* disability benefits. An employee who suffered injury to the groin and thigh area from a machine used at work might well require medical treatment for the injuries and temporary disability benefits while off work. The employee would of course be entitled to such benefits, whether or not there was ultimately any residual ratable "permanent" disability. In addition, as the *Williams* court noted, Labor Code section 4660 provides that disfigurement, as well as occupational handicap, is a basis for an award of permanent disability. The court stated that "Whether disfigurement in the statutory sense requires visible mutilation or, on the contrary, comprehends a functional impairment without external manifestations, is an open question in California." (50 Cal. App. 3d at 123, fn. 3.) In *Williams,* the plaintiff did not urge that the injury to his genital organs constituted a disfigurement within the meaning of Labor Code section 4660, apparently because such a claim would have defeated his contention that his injury was not covered by workers' compensation and supported an independent action. The court accordingly did not address the disfigurement question.

[7] *Renteria* does not fall in this category. In that case, racial discrimination appears to have been the motivating force behind the employer's misconduct. Thus, the plaintiffs could have filed a civil suit based on a violation of fundamental public policy under principles set forth in *Tameny v. Atlantic Richfield Co., supra,* 27 Cal. 3d 167.

of its books and records; and forcing plaintiff to sign a $100,000 promissory note for a debt owed to ABA under threat of retaliation if he refused. The circumstances of the discharge were further complicated by the fact that plaintiff apparently occupied a dual status in his relationship with defendants: as employee, and as independent distributor of Continental's product.

In summarily denying plaintiff's petition for writ of mandate, the Court of Appeal cited *Cole.* In so doing, however, it is unclear whether the court was concerned with the *Renteria* issue or the nature of defendants' alleged misconduct. *Cole,* of course, addressed both issues. Its central holding that workers' compensation provides the exclusive remedy for torts that comprise "a normal part of the employment relationship" has been discussed. However, as also noted, while *Cole* did not resolve the *Renteria* issue it acknowledged the "anomaly" which that decision had engendered.

Whatever the Court of Appeal's intentions in issuing a summary denial, it plainly failed to render a decision on the merits. In light of the serious allegations set forth in plaintiff's complaint, however, we conclude that the issue is an important one which should be addressed in a written opinion by the Court of Appeal. Accordingly, we shall remand the matter to the Court of Appeal with directions to consider whether, in this regard, the demurrers to the causes of action for negligent and intentional infliction of emotional distress were properly sustained.

2. *Defamation*

In addition to his claims of intentional and negligent infliction of emotional distress, plaintiff asserted a cause of action for defamation based on defendants' allegedly false statements accusing plaintiff of embezzlement and other misconduct against the company. Plaintiff claimed that the statements were slanderous per se, that he was "shocked and humiliated" by their publication, and that he suffered general damages to his reputation of $1 million.

The trial court ruled that the defamation claim was barred by the exclusive remedy provisions of the Workers' Compensation Act; the Court of Appeal denied plaintiff's petition for writ of mandate, citing *Cole.*

We have not heretofore ruled on the question whether defamation claims arising out of the course and scope of employment are barred by the exclusive remedy provisions of the Workers' Compensation Act.[9] We need not do so here. For even assuming, without deciding, that certain defamatory remarks in the employment context may be subject to workers' compensation, as we noted in the previous section the seriousness of the allegations in plaintiff's complaint and the hybrid nature of the relationship between plaintiff and defendants raise the further issue whether defendants' conduct was outside the scope and normal risks of employment. Therefore, on remand the Court of Appeal is directed to address these issues.

---

[9] A number of courts have apparently determined that the gravamen of an action for libel or slander is damage to "reputation," a "proprietary" as distinct from a physical or mental injury, and therefore have concluded that defamation does not lie within the purview of the workers' compensation law. . . . Other states have apparently concluded otherwise. Although the issue is an interesting and unsettled one, as explained above it is not one which necessarily requires resolution here.

Disposition

Plaintiff's contention that *Renteria* compels reversal of the order of the superior court sustaining the demurrer to his causes of action for negligent and intentional infliction of emotional distress is without merit. Nevertheless, the judgment of the Court of Appeal summarily denying plaintiff's petition for writ of mandate for relief from that order is reversed, and the case is remanded to the Court of Appeal to consider on the merits the remaining issues identified herein.

NOTES

1. *No Remedy Anywhere I? Injuries or Diseases Covered but Not the Consequences.* Normally, an employee injured at work will receive workers' compensation benefits and, because of the exclusive remedy principle, will be barred from a tort suit against the employer. There are, however, two situations in which an employee may not qualify for workers' compensation benefits and may also not be able to bring a tort suit against the employer. In the first situation, the worker meets all of the legal tests for workers' compensation coverage, but the workers' compensation statute does not provide benefits for the adverse consequences of the injury or disease experienced by the worker. In *Livitsanos*, the California Supreme Court held that claims for intentional or negligent infliction of emotional distress at the workplace are preempted by the exclusivity provisions of the workers' compensation law so long as "the employer's conduct neither contravenes fundamental public policy nor exceeds the risks inherent in the employment relationship." The general rule is that "if the injury itself comes within the coverage formula, an action for damages is barred although the particular element of damage is not compensated for, as in the case of disfigurement in some states, impotency, or pain and suffering." ARTHUR LARSON & LEX K. LARSON, LARSON'S WORKERS' COMPENSATION 100-1 (Desk ed., 2006).

2. *No Remedy Anywhere IIA? Injuries or Diseases Not Covered: Statutory Challenges.* The second situation where there may be no remedy is when the injury or disease is not covered by the workers' compensation statute, and the worker may also be precluded from bringing a tort suit. Kleinhesselink, who was a safety coordinator, experienced mental and physical conditions resulting from mental stress at the workplace because his safety recommendations were ignored, resulting in deaths and injuries. The case arose in a state that (1) made workers' compensation the exclusive remedy for work-related injuries and diseases, and (2) excluded the type of conditions Kleinhesselink experienced from coverage because their cause was mental rather than physical. The employee filed a tort suit alleging two counts of negligence against the employer. Can the employer have the counts dismissed because of the exclusive remedy provision? *Kleinhesselink v. Chevron*, 920 P.2d 108 (Mont. 1996) (no, because the trade-off of no-fault recovery for employees in return for protection from large damage awards for employers means that "it is axiomatic that there must be some possibility of recovery by the employee for the compromise to hold"). A contrasting decision is *Bias v. Eastern Associated Coal Corp.*, 2006 W. Va. LEXIS 43 (W. Va. 2006). The workers' compensation statute excludes mental injuries with a non-physical cause ("mental-mental injuries"), which precluded Bias from bringing a workers' compensation suit. The statute also provided immunity to employers from damage suits for work-related injuries unless the employer (1) defaulted on payment of workers' compensation premiums or (2) deliberately intended to produce injury or death to the employee, or (3) the legislature expressly provides an employee a private remedy outside the workers' compensation system. Since none of these exceptions was applicable, Bias had no remedy.

3. *No Remedy Anywhere IIB? Injuries or Diseases Not Covered: Constitutional Challenges.* *Smothers v. Gresham Transfer, Inc.*, 23 P.3d 333 (Or. 2001), is an example of a successful constitutional challenge to the exclusivity doctrine. The Oregon legislature passed legislation in 1993 denying workers' compensation benefits unless the worker could prove that work exposure was the major contributing cause of an occupational disease. In 1995, the workers' compensation statute was amended to provide that workers' compensation was the exclusive remedy for work-related injuries and diseases, even if the condition was not compensable because the work condition was not the major contributing cause. The court ruled that the Oregon constitution did not allow the legislature to eliminate both workers' compensation and tort remedies. Another example is *Automated Conveyor Systems v. Hill*, 362 Ark. 215 (2005), in which the Arkansas Supreme Court held that disallowing a tort suit for injuries not expressly covered by the workers' compensation act "is not in line with its stated purpose and, in addition, would contravene . . . the Arkansas Constitution." Such examples are rare, however. Indeed, ARTHUR LARSON & LEX K. LARSON, LARSON'S WORKERS' COMPENSATION § 100.02 (Desk ed., 2006), state that "Exclusiveness clauses have consistently been held to be constitutional, under the equal protection and due process clauses of both federal and state constitutions. Attacks based on specific state constitutional provisions, such as those creating a right of action for wrongful death, have fared no better."

An example of an unsuccessful constitutional challenge is *Shamrock Coal v. Maricle*, 5 S.W.3d 130 (Ky. 1999). The Kentucky legislature amended the law to eliminate workers' compensation benefits for workers who had less than a 20 percent respiratory impairment as a result of black lung disease. The employer subsequently laid off nineteen workers who would have been entitled to workers' compensation benefits under the prior law but who were not entitled to benefits because of the new impairment threshold. The Kentucky Supreme Court in a 4-3 decision held that the employer could rely on the exclusive remedy provision even though the workers had no remedy.

4. *Challenges to the Exclusivity Doctrine Based on the U.S. Constitution.* Section A of this chapter includes the seminal case upholding the constitutionality of the New York workers' compensation statute. One part of the Supreme Court's rationale was as follows:

> Viewing the entire matter, it cannot be pronounced arbitrary and unreasonable for the State to impose upon the employer the absolute duty of making a moderate and definite compensation in money to every disabled employee, or in case of his death to those who were

entitled to look to him for support, in lieu of the common-law liability to cases of negligence.

This, of course is not to say that any scale of compensation, however, insignificant on the one hand or onerous on the other, would be supportable.

New York Central Railroad Co. v. White, 243 U.S. 188, 205-06 (1917).

Does this "ancient" pronouncement of a constitutional principle have any continuing validity as the basis for a challenge to the exclusivity doctrine in a state workers' compensation statute when, as in Kentucky, the state provides no remedy for a workplace injury or disease?

3. TO WHOM DOES THE EXCLUSIVE REMEDY PROVISION APPLY?

The exclusive remedy principle means that the only recovery of the injured worker against his or her employer is workers' compensation benefits, unless the worker can take advantage of one of the exceptions to exclusivity discussed in the previous subsections. The injured worker may, however, be able to bring a tort suit against a third party who was at least partially responsible for the injury. Since that third party did not participate in the exchange that established workers' compensation, which provided a no-fault program for employees in exchange for limited liability for the employer, the third party cannot claim immunity from a tort suit by invoking the exclusive remedy principle.

The claim against a third party can arise in a wide variety of circumstances. The third party, for example, may be the manufacturer of machinery that was defective in design and sold to the employer of the injured worker. In recent years, a number of third party suits have involved workers who contracted cancer or other diseases as a result of working with asbestos. Many of these workers have successfully sued manufacturers of asbestos, such as Johns-Manville, which did not provide adequate warnings about the danger of working with asbestos. An interesting recent example involves workers at a microwave popcorn factory who developed severe respiratory problems from exposure to butter-flavoring fumes. After receiving workers' compensation benefits from the employer, the workers sued International Flavors & Fragrances, the maker of the flavoring, and the workers whose cases were resolved received more than $50 million in awards. *Jury Awards Worker From Popcorn Plant*, AKRON BEACON JOURNAL (Ohio), Sept. 3, 2005, at D2.

In general, the third party is liable for the entire amount of the damages experienced by the worker, including loss of wages, medical expenses, pain and suffering, and, where appropriate, punitive damages. In most states, the third party cannot require the employer to pay a portion of the damages, even when the employer is partially responsible for the damages to the employee. There might be, for example, joint negligence of the third party, who improperly designed a machine, and the employer, who removed a safety guard from the machine in order to speed production. Despite the joint negligence, in most jurisdictions the third party is liable for the entire amount of damages. The courts have reasoned that the exclusivity principle of workers' compensation would be jeopardized if the third party were allowed to require the employer to pay for part of the damages.

The employer is not only usually excused from responsibility for any portion of the damages when a third party is successfully sued by the employee, in most jurisdictions the employer can recover an amount from the award to reimburse the employer for any workers' compensation benefits that have been provided to the employee. Thus, if the employee sues the machine tool manufacturer whose negligence was partially responsible for the injury and recovers $100,000, the employer who has expended $40,000 on workers' compensation benefits can recoup those expenditures from the damage award in a subrogation action. This avoids a double recovery, since presumably the damages in the tort suit include payment for medical care and lost wages that were compensated for by the workers' compensation program.

The general principles involving the relationships among workers, third parties, and employers are not followed in every jurisdiction. A few jurisdictions, for example, require the injured worker to elect either workers' compensation or a tort suit. States vary about whether only the employee can bring the suit against the third party, or whether the employer also has this right, or whether both the employee and employer have the right.

In most jurisdictions, the comparative negligence of the employee but not the employer is used to establish the maximum liability of the third party in a suit brought by the employee. Thus, if the total damages were $1,000,000 and the third party was 50% responsible, while the employer and employee were each 25% responsible, then the employee could recover $750,000 in damages from the third party. In most jurisdictions, the employer would still be able to recover any workers' compensation benefits paid from this award in a subrogation action.

NOTES

1. *Insurer as Third Party.* A few states allow employees to sue the employer's insurance carrier for negligent inspection of the workplace or negligent medical care. *See Nelson v. Union Wire Rope Corp.*, 199 N.E.2d 769 (Ill. 1964) (interpreting Florida law to allow a carrier to be sued for negligence in its voluntary inspection of employer's elevator cable). The large majority of jurisdictions, however, immunize insurance companies from such suits under the exclusive remedy principle. *See, e.g., Sims v. United States Fidelity & Guaranty Co.*, 782 N.E.2d 345 (Ind. 2003).

2. *Emotional Distress Caused by Insurance Carriers.* Employees sometimes sue insurance carriers for emotional distress caused by overly vigorous investigation of claims.

A case whose melodramatic facts helped to popularize this cause of action was *Unruh v. Truck Insurance Exchange*, 498 P.2d 1063 (Cal. 1972). The carrier, suspecting employees of malingering, sent a team of two investigators to get evidence for its suspicions. One got the female plaintiff emotionally involved with him. The other clandestinely photographed their activities, including her negotiating barrel bridges and the like at Disneyland in a fashion inconsistent with continued back disability. The shock of this revelation in the hearing room caused the plaintiff to suffer a violent emotional collapse, leading to protracted hospitalization. A cause of action was held to lie against the carrier, free of the exclusiveness bar.

In that picturesque situations like this are not very common, this category would perhaps deserve little attention were it confined to comparable acts of treachery by insurance carriers. But when the underlying principle is extended to deliberate delay or terminations of payments by carriers, the potential importance of the principle becomes painfully clear. The first major case to make this extension was *Stafford v. Westchester Fire Insurance Co.*, 526 P.2d 37 (Alaska 1974), involving an aggravated set of facts showing deliberate delay and harassment by the carrier. An action was held to lie. A rash of similar attempts followed. In several extreme cases, *Stafford* was followed. But the significant fact for these purposes is that in most subsequent cases the courts rejected the cause of action, seeing the danger of this development as an open-ended invitation to sue in tort for any delay in payment, merely by calling it intentional infliction of emotional distress, or "outrage," or some such term.

Arthur Larson, *Tensions of the Next Decade, in* New Perspectives in Workers' Compensation 21, 25-26 (John F. Burton, Jr. ed., 1988).

An example of the courts' resistance to broach the exclusive remedy provision because of alleged intentionally inflicted emotional distress is *Winterberg v. Transportation Insurance Co.*, 72 F.3d 318 (3d Cir. 1995) (applying Pennsylvania law). The court affirmed dismissal of the tort suit because of the exclusive remedy doctrine even if the insurance carrier behaved egregiously in handling the workers' compensation claim. The carrier allegedly improperly terminated medical services and cash benefits, and sent the worker to a physician for a medical examination in which she was emotionally and physically abused. Winterberg asserted that she fell during the exam after the doctor roughly grabbed her foot, and that he refused to assist her even though she further injured herself because of the fall.

3. Fellow Employee as Third Party. In most, but not all, states, employees as well as the employer are immune from suits for workplace injuries they inflict upon fellow employees. The protection for the fellow employee is provided by statutory language, such as that found in the New Jersey workers' compensation statute that provides immunity for "an act or omission occurring while such person was in the same employ as the person injured . . . ." N.J. Rev. Stat. § 34:15-8. Suppose Cadorette, a supervisor at Acme, improperly removes the safety tape from a computerized saw some time before he leaves the firm in November 1988. Suppose Estrada is hired in March 1989 and is injured in May 1989 because of Cadorette's removal of the safety tape. Can Estrada bring a tort suit against former employee Cadorette? *Estrada v. Hendricksaw Corp.*, 695 A.2d 323 (N.J. Super. Ct. App. Div. 1997) (no, because the fellow-employee immunity applies to former as well as current employees).

4. Physician as a Third Party. Westinghouse had an agreement with Doctors Care to perform physical exams for Westinghouse employees. Dr. Blanchard, an employee of Doctors Care, examined Fuller, a Westinghouse employee and apparently failed to inform him in 1996 of his elevated PSA level. In 1997, Dr. Blanchard retested Fuller and informed him of his abnormal PSA level. Fuller saw a urologist, who diagnosed him with prostate cancer and informed him that treatment options were limited because of the progression of the cancer. Fuller died in 1998 and his wife sued Dr. Blanchard. The court affirmed the lower court in finding that Dr. Blanchard was an independent contractor and not a co-employee of Fuller, and therefore the widow's malpractice claim was not barred by the exclusive remedy provision of the workers' compensation act. *Fuller v. Blanchard*, 595 S.E.2d 831 (S.C. Ct. App. 2004).

5. ***The Employer as a Third Party: The Dual Capacity Doctrine.*** Some employees have attempted to sue their employers by characterizing them as something else, for example, as a supplier of goods or medical services. Occasionally, courts accept the dual characterization and allow the tort claim. For example, in *Mercer v. Uniroyal, Inc.*, 361 N.E.2d 492 (Ohio Ct. App. 1976), a truck driver employed by Uniroyal was injured when a Uniroyal tire blew out. The Ohio Appellate Court allowed his product liability suit against Uniroyal.

Dual capacity suits are rarely successful. In *McCormick v. Caterpillar Tractor Co.*, 423 N.E.2d 876 (Ill. 1981), for example, an employee sued the employer for malpractice by the company doctor. The Illinois Supreme Court held the claim barred by the exclusive remedy provision of workers' compensation, reasoning that state law required the employer to provide medical services to the employee. The Illinois Court of Appeals did allow one count of a tort suit to proceed by relying on the dual capacity doctrine in *Goins v. Mercy Center for Health Care Services*, 667 N.E.2d 652 (Ill. Ct. App. 1996). Scott Goins, a hospital security officer, became infected with the HIV virus in the process of restraining a patient with AIDS. Goins alleged that Mercy Center violated the AIDS Confidentiality Act by disclosing his condition to other employees. The court allowed the cause of action, reasoning that at the time of the alleged violations of the Confidentiality Act, "Mercy Center's role had changed from that of an employer providing statutorily-required medical treatment to that of a medical provider which owed Scott the same duty that it owed to all other patients similarly situated, namely confidentiality regarding his AIDS test. Accordingly . . . we find that Scott's claims for violations of the Confidentiality Act were not barred by the Workers' Compensation Act's exclusive remedy provisions." *Id.* at 657.

6. ***Exclusive Remedies and Family Members.*** The exclusive remedy doctrine generally protects employers from suits by the worker's spouse, parents, or children for harm resulting from workplace incidents. However, the results depend in part on the language of the jurisdiction's exclusive remedy provision. In general, there are two types of clauses: (1) the narrowest limitation on suits by other family members, exemplified by the Rhode Island statute, which only says that the employee waives "his" common law rights by coming under workers' compensation; and (2) the significant limitation by detailed specification, typified by the New York workers' compensation act, which states that the excluded suits include those by "such employee, his or her personal representatives, spouse, parents, dependents, distributees, or any person otherwise entitled to recover damages, contribution or indemnity, at common law or otherwise, on account of such injury or death . . . ." ARTHUR LARSON & LEX K. LARSON, LARSON'S WORKERS' COMPENSATION § 101.01 (Desk ed., 2006).

7. *Exclusive Remedies and Independent Contractors.* General issues relating to the distinction between employees and independent contractors were considered in Chapter 2. The distinction is important in workers' compensation because only an employee is entitled to the protection of the program. A classic workers' compensation case that illustrates the application of the tests used to decide whether a worker is an employee or independent contractor is *Marcum v. State Accident Insurance Fund*, 565 P.2d 399 (Or. Ct. App. 1977).

Generally in cases of this type, the individual is attempting to demonstrate that he or she is an employee in order to receive benefits. Hoste was a member of the National Ski Patrol who was asked by the ski school director to forerun the course to assure it was safe, during which demonstration he fell and fractured his vertebra causing paralysis from which he is unlikely to recover. Hoste did not receive any wages, but did receive a ski pass, complimentary hot beverages, and discounts on food and purchases at the resort's stores. The Michigan Supreme Court reversed the magistrate who made the initial decision and the Court of Appeals, holding that the benefits did not represent payments intended as wages. The Supreme Court described Hoste as a "'gratuitous worker,' who was not an 'employee,' but rather an individual assisting another with a view toward furthering his own interests." *Hoste v. Shanty Creek Mgmt., Inc.*, 592 N.W.2d 360 (Mich. 1999).

The interesting twist in workers' compensation is that sometimes the injured individual is attempting to convince the court that he is *not* an employee, so the exclusive remedy provision barring tort suits can be avoided. Consider the plight of Keith Hallal, who, as a full-time student pursuing a degree in sports management, received an internship with the Orlando Magic basketball team. He injured his ear when his head struck an antenna protruding from the wall of the supply room. Hallal claimed he was a volunteer because he did not receive monetary remuneration for his services. In Florida, a "volunteer" is specifically excluded from the definition of "employee" in the workers' compensation statute, and so Hallal appeared well down the road to a tort suit recovery. However, interns with the Magic are required to attend all home games for which they are paid $25 per game. The court trenchantly disposed of the suit. "Such payment constitutes monetary remuneration. Therefore, Mr. Hallal was not a 'volunteer.' On this basis, final summary judgment was properly entered in favor of the Magic." *Hallal v. RDV Sports, Inc.*, 682 So. 2d 1235, 1237 (Fla. Dist. Ct. App. 1996).

8. *Exclusive Remedies and Non-Covered Employees.* Some employees are not covered by a workers' compensation statute and therefore, in general, their employers are not protected by the exclusive remedy provisions. Most workers' compensation statutes exclude certain industries (e.g., state and local government), or occupations (household workers), or small employers (e.g., those with three or fewer employees), or make the laws elective for employers (most notably in Texas). In addition, employees may not be covered if they are casual workers or do not work in the regular business of the employer.

Larson's treatise catalogs several approaches found in state workers' compensation statutes in dealing with casual employment and employment outside of the business of the employer:

(i)   Four states exclude all casual employment;

(ii)   Twenty-seven states (plus the District of Columbia) exclude employments that are both casual and not in the course of the employer's trade, business, or profession;

(iii)   Eight states exclude all employments not in the course of the employer's trade, business, or profession; and

(iv)   Several states apparently cover all employees (not otherwise excluded) regardless of whether they are casual or not working in the course of the employer's trade, business, or profession.

ARTHUR LARSON & LEX K. LARSON, LARSON'S WORKERS' COMPENSATION § 72.01 (Desk ed., 2006).

D.   WHICH INJURIES ARE COMPENSABLE?

Even a worker who has established that his employment is covered by the state workers' compensation statute will not receive workers' compensation benefits for every injury that affects the worker. The worker must establish that the injury was work-related. With only minor variations, almost all workers' compensation statutes provide the following definition of "work-related":

> "Injury" and "personal injury" means only accidental injuries arising out of and in the course of employment.

This language has been interpreted to encompass four legal tests, all of which must be met for the worker's injury to be compensable:

(i)   an injury

(ii)   resulting from an accident that

(iii)   arose out of employment (the "AOE test") and

(iv)   in the course of employment (the "COE test").

1.   TEST ONE: IN THE COURSE OF EMPLOYMENT

a.   Activity: Mixed Social and Business Activities

EZZY v. WORKERS' COMPENSATION APPEALS BOARD
California Court of Appeals
194 Cal. Rptr. 90 (1983)

SMITH, ASSOCIATE JUDGE:

Petitioner, Marilyn Ezzy, sought and was granted a writ of review after the Workers' Compensation Appeals Board [hereafter WCAB] denied Ezzy's petition for reconsideration and affirmed the decision of the workers' compensation judge who found that petitioner's injury did not arise out of and in the course of her employment.

The sole issue before us is whether the injury to petitioner's finger, which occurred during a company-sponsored softball game, arises out of and in the course of her employment, and is therefore compensable.

Marilyn Ezzy (hereafter "Ezzy") at all relevant times was employed by the law firm of Gassett, Perry & Frank (hereafter "GPF") as a law clerk. On or about August 15, 1980, Ezzy participated in an employer-sponsored softball game, during which she injured the little finger on her right hand as she attempted to catch a fly ball.

The record of the WCAB hearing discloses that GPF participated in a softball league composed primarily of civil defense law firms. The rules of the league required that the teams be composed of both men and women, and required forfeiture if less than four women were present on each team.

John Burton (hereafter "Burton") is a partner in GPF, and was the team coach. Burton stated that he did not have to recruit players; a sign up was conducted of all those who wanted to play. Burton testified that it was not a requirement that everyone will play. Some of the older and less athletically inclined members of the firm did not play. Some, but not all, of the secretaries participated. Everyone in the GPF firm, player and non-player alike, was provided at the firm's expense a special teeshirt emblazoned with his or her GPF billing number. Burton testified that GPF paid for the balls, bats and post-game refreshments. A postseason awards banquet was provided by GPF to which all employees were invited. Burton stated that no one was ever reprimanded or fired for not playing.

Burton further testified that his secretary sent around memos reminding office personnel of games or practice. Burton stated that Administrative Director's Rule 9883, regarding off-duty recreational activities, was neither posted nor read to employees. Burton testified that "the better players were more encouraged to be present than some of the ones that were not so good. That would also depend on how many men we had and how many women we had." Burton stated that his team had never forfeited a game, and that he always had the correct number of female players there. He further testified that he did have one or two problems making sure one of their key women would be present at the games. Burton admitted that, although no business was derived from the games, they were very good for office spirit.

Ezzy testified that she did not volunteer but was "drafted" to join the team. On the first day after she returned from vacation, Burton approached Ezzy, handed her a teeshirt, a schedule of games and practices, and said, "At the next one we'll see you there." Ezzy understood there was a coed requirement, and when there appeared to be a shortage of women, the female members were urged to get out and play. Ezzy felt there was a spirit of camaraderie that the firm was trying to create, and that the strong urgings to play and the concern over having an adequate number of females led her to believe that she should play softball. Ezzy stated that the firm paid for post-game pizza and other refreshments. Ezzy testified that on one occasion home movies of a softball game were shown in the conference room of GPF offices during working hours, and that she and others were called in to watch. At the awards banquet, Burton received a whip as a gag-gift because he was such a "hard driver."

In his "Opinion On Decision," the workers' compensation judge stated that participation in the softball game, while encouraged, was not a requirement or a reasonable expectancy of petitioner's job. Petitioner contends that the workers' compensation judge erred in concluding that petitioner's injury did not occur in the course of employment. We agree.

Discussion

I

. . . .

Before examining the evidence as reflected by the record, we must consider the applicable statute, section 3600, subdivision (a)(8), which reads, in pertinent part, as follows:

> (a) Liability for the compensation provided by this division . . . shall, without regard to negligence, exist against an employer for any injury sustained by his or her employees arising out of and in the course of the employment and for the death of any employee if the injury proximately causes death, in those cases where the following conditions of compensation concur: . . .

> (8) Where the injury does not arise out of voluntary participation in any off-duty recreational, social, or athletic activity not constituting part of the employee's work-related duties, *except where these activities are a reasonable expectancy of, or are expressly or impliedly required by, the employment.* The administrative director shall promulgate reasonable rules and regulations requiring employers to post and keep posted in a conspicuous place or places a notice advising employees of the provisions of this subdivision. Failure of the employer to post such a notice shall not constitute an expression of intent to waive the provisions of this subdivision. (Emphasis added.)

The clear language of section 3600, subdivision (a)(8) first states the rule — recovery may be had for injuries arising out of and in the course of employment if those injuries do *not* arise out of voluntary participation in athletic activities. Stated conversely, no recovery may be had where the injury arises from voluntary participation in athletic activities. The section then states exceptions to the rule of non-compensability. Where athletic activities are either a "reasonable expectancy of, or are expressly or impliedly required by, the employment" injuries arising therefrom *are compensable.*

The key legal question to be decided here is whether Ezzy's participation was a reasonable expectancy of her employment at GPF.

Respondent erroneously assumes that the question of "reasonable expectancy" is one of fact. While factual findings form the foundation upon which a court bases its determination that a "reasonable expectancy" exists, the question requires a conclusion derived from those facts which is itself *legal* in nature. Furthermore, the question of "reasonable expectancy" is but a subset of the ultimate issue — whether the applicant's injury arose out of and in the course of her employment.

With respect to the ultimate issue, the scope of our review is clear: "Where . . . there is no real dispute as to the facts, the question of whether an injury was suffered in the course of employment is one of law and a purported finding of fact on that question is not binding on an appellate court."

Other areas of the law have attempted to give a specific meaning to this phrase. In connection with insurance law, the "doctrine of reasonable expectations" has been applied so that ambiguities in an insurance policy are to be resolved in accordance with *the reasonable expectations of the insured.* With respect to Fourth Amendment law, a person's "reasonable expectation of privacy" is one which is *subjectively* held by the person searched, and which society recognizes as *objectively* reasonable. In the context of labor law, for purposes of establishing whether a person is an employee when determining whether a majority of employees have agreed to union representation, the determination is based upon *the employee's reasonable expectation* of future or continued employment.

In each of the situations mentioned above, the law looks to the expectations of the person who is being protected and measures his subjective understanding against a neutral and unbiased standard. It is our view that the test of "reasonable expectancy of employment" in the context of the case at bar consists of two elements: (1) whether the employee subjectively believes his or her participation in an activity is expected by the employer, and (2) whether that belief is objectively reasonable.

The effect of this test is to recognize *only* expectations which are objectively reasonable. Stated another way, the employer is protected from liability for injuries where an employee's belief that he or she is expected to participate in an activity is unreasonable. The burden rests upon an employer to insure that no subtle or indirect pressure or coercion is applied to induce involuntary participation by an employee. We do not find this burden to be an onerous one, for the employer's means of protecting himself are peculiarly within his own control.

We turn next to legislative intent. . . . The bill analysis prepared by the Assembly Committee on Finance, Insurance, and Commerce . . . stated "[t]he thrust of [the proposed legislation] appears to overrule . . . *Goodman v. Fireman's Fund American Insurance Co.* (1974) 74 OAK 49472, [which] found that a water skiing injury to an airline stewardess during a four-day layover in Tahiti was an employment-related injury" and therefore compensable. According to the bill analysis, the legislation was also intended to overrule *Lizama v. Workmen's Comp. Appeals Bd.* (1974) 40 Cal. App. 3d 363, which held compensable an injury to a janitor, who, after receiving permission from his employer, used a company power saw after work hours. The committee report emphasized that the activities were held compensable because they were reasonably foreseeable or expectable in the work setting.

Section 3600, subdivision (a)(8) was therefore intended to draw a brighter line delimiting compensability by replacing the general foreseeability test with one of "reasonable expectancy" of employment.

At the time Assembly Bill No. 2555 was under consideration, two cases adjudicated by the WCAB in 1976 and 1977 were presumptively known to the Legislature, yet there is no hint in the committee analysis that the Legislature was displeased with those results.

In *Pacific Tel. & Tel. Co. v. Workers' Comp. Appeals Bd. (Brady)* (1976) 41 Cal. Comp. Cases 771, Ms. Brady, an employee of the phone company, was injured while playing softball on a team made up wholly of Pacific Telephone Company employees. The team played other phone company teams comprising the league. The games were played off the employer's premises after working hours. Ms. Brady was not a regular team member, but participated on this occasion because the team would otherwise have had to forfeit for lack of sufficient players. Ms. Brady felt job pressure to play when asked to do so by team members who included Ms. Brady's supervisor. The management of the telephone company permitted league formation meetings to be conducted on the premises, and promulgated safety rules. The company photocopy machine was used in the dissemination of league and team information. Also, raffles to benefit the league were conducted on company premises during working hours. The WCAB judge relied upon (1) substantial employment involvement in creation and operation of the league, (2) benefit to the employer of improved employee morale, and (3) the job-related pressure upon Ms. Brady which led to her participation. The Court of Appeal denied a petition for writ of review.

In *California Highway Patrol v. Workers' Comp. Appeals Bd. (Loveless)* (1977) 42 Cal. Comp. Cases 264, the WCAB found that a highway patrol officer's injury was compensable. Officer Loveless played on a softball team representing the Monterey area office of the CHP which participated in the Central Coast Counties Police League. Notices of games were posted in the locker room, play was encouraged by state and local CHP management. The WCAB judge concluded the softball activity was part and parcel of Loveless' job. The Court of Appeal denied CHP's petition for a writ of review.

Both the *Pacific Tel. & Tel.* and *California Highway Patrol* cases, in finding athletic injuries compensable, go beyond the broad "foreseeability" test of *Goodman* and *Lizama*. Rather these cases rely upon the more specific factors of employer involvement, benefit to employer, and job-related pressure to participate to find an activity within the course of employment. . . .

We conclude that it was the Legislature's intent to eliminate from the workers' compensation scheme *only* those injuries which were remotely work-connected. The use of such terms as "reasonable expectancy" and "impliedly required" in section 3600, subdivision (a)(8) is evidence that the Legislature recognized the potential use by employers of indirect means to encourage participation in an activity, and that such indirect encouragement changes the voluntary character of such participation. The Legislature intended that injuries occurring under such circumstances should be considered work-connected, and must fall within the coverage of the workers' compensation scheme.

II

In the case at bar we conclude that facts evident from the record establish that petitioner's injury resulted from participation in an activity which was a "reasonable expectancy" of her employment, and therefore occurred in the course of her employment.

Petitioner was a part-time law clerk in her second year of law school, a position which is low in the legal profession's hierarchy. As such, petitioner was more than usually vulnerable to pressure or suggestion that she join the law firm's softball team. Thus, when she was urged to play by one of the firm's partners, who was also the team coach, it was reasonable for petitioner to feel that she was expected to participate.

There was relatively more pressure on female employees to participate because of the league's requirement that four women be present on the field at all times.

A substantial benefit to the firm was generated by participation in the softball team by virtue of improved office cooperation, spirit, morale and camaraderie.

The law firm paid for all equipment, for teeshirts for team members and other employees of the firm, as well as for post-game refreshments. The firm sponsored an awards banquet to which team members and other employees were invited.

It is also undisputed that the law-firm employer had neither posted nor read to its employees the contents of Administrative Director's Rule 9883, which reads as follows:

> *Notice to Employee Concerning Off-Duty Recreational Social, or Athletic Activity.* Every employer shall post and keep posted in a conspicuous place or places, the following notice:

> Your employer or its insurance carrier may not be liable for the payment of workers' compensation benefits for any injury which arises out of an employee's voluntary participation in any off-duty recreational, social, or athletic activity which is not a part of the employee's work-related duties.

Section 3600, subdivision (a)(8) states that "[f]ailure of the employer to post such a notice shall not constitute an expression of intent to waive the provisions of this subdivision." Nonetheless, in the case at bar, employer's failure to post the required notice was contrary to a statutory directive which was intended to inform an employee of the jeopardy of non-coverage by workers' compensation insurance when voluntarily involved in athletic events. While not a waiver of the subdivision's provisions, an employer's failure to post the required notice makes any action by the employer which tends to encourage participation in athletic events appear more coercive in effect.

The facts present a close case. We are, however, mindful of Labor Code section 3202 which mandates: "The provisions of Division 4 and Division 5 of this code shall be liberally construed by the courts with the purpose of extending their benefits for the protection of persons injured in the course of their employment."

In the case at bar, the record shows that petitioner subjectively believed that her employer expected her to participate in the company sponsored baseball activities. Petitioner so stated under oath. We have determined that her subjective belief was objectively reasonable, and, therefore, conclude that petitioner's injury arose out of and in the course of her employment.

The decision of the Workers' Compensation Appeals Board is annulled and the cause is remanded to that board for proceedings consistent with the views expressed herein.

MILLER, J., concurs.

ROUSE, ASSOCIATE JUSTICE, concurring:

I concur, but not without comment.

Admittedly, the question of whether this particular activity was a reasonable expectancy of petitioner's employment is a legal issue which this court may properly redetermine, based upon facts set forth in the record. Nevertheless, I am reluctant to "second guess" the workers' compensation judge (a specialist in that field) whose adjudication has been reviewed and endorsed by the Workers' Compensation Board, in what, in my perception, is a close case. Since substantial evidence supports that judge's conclusion I would hold that his determination of the matter must prevail were it not for those cases cited wherein awards of compensation were made in situations which are, in my judgment, factually indistinguishable from petitioner's case.

One of the functions of an appellate court in announcing its decision is to ensure uniformity and consistency in the rules applied by various inferior tribunals. I believe that is what the decision in this case seeks to accomplish, and it is for this limited reason that I concur in the opinion.

NOTE

Is Softball More Reasonable than Basketball? A police officer injured his leg while off duty playing in a pickup game of basketball at a private facility. The employer did not sponsor or encourage the employee to participate in the game. The police department has a regulation stating that officers shall maintain good physical condition, and the officer argued that the department expected him to engage in occasional pickup games of basketball in order to stay in shape. The court concluded that the evidence did not support a finding that the officer subjectively believed that his employer expected him to engage in an occasional pickup basketball game and that, in any event, such a subjective belief would have been objectively unreasonable. "Thus, it cannot be said that the specific activity during which he was injured was a reasonable expectancy of, or was expressly or impliedly required by, his employment." *City of Stockton v. Jenneiahn*, 125 Cal. App. 4th 1513, 1516 (Cal. Ct. App. 2006).

b. Activity: Horseplay

PROWS v. INDUSTRIAL COMMISSION
Supreme Court of Utah
610 P.2d 1362 (1980)

WILKINS, JUSTICE:

This is an appeal from an Order of the Industrial Commission (hereafter "Commission") denying the application for Workmen's Compensation benefits by Michael Prows (hereinafter "Petitioner").

The facts of this case are essentially undisputed. Petitioner was employed as a truck driver by Respondent Bergin Brunswig Company (hereafter "Bergin"). His duties included loading medical supplies onto his delivery truck and making deliveries to doctors, hospitals, and clinics.

The boxes containing the medical supplies measured approximately eleven and one-half by twenty-four inches, and each box was secured by elastic bands (also described as "rubber bands"). Each rubber band was approximately twelve inches long by three-eighths inch wide.

Testimony before the administrative law judge established that the rubber bands were used by some of Bergin's employees for "rubber bands fights." Petitioner and one of his co-employees testified that the "fights" were an almost daily occurrence. One of Bergin's supervisors testified that he observed such "fights" perhaps two or three times a month, and that when he observed one he discouraged its continuation.

On March 3, 1978, Petitioner was engaged in his usual assigned duties and was loading supplies on his delivery truck. As he was unloading boxes of supplies from a hand truck and onto his delivery truck, he was hit by one or two rubber bands which were flipped at him by two co-employees standing nearby. Petitioner thereupon flipped a rubber band back at his "attackers." One of the co-employees then ripped an approximately eighteen inch long piece of wood off a nearby pallet and came toward Petitioner brandishing the wood like a sword. Petitioner took the wood from his co-employee, placed a rubber band between the handles of his hand truck and attempted to shoot the wood into the air in a slingshot fashion. The piece of wood, instead of sailing into the air, struck Petitioner in the right eye, severely injuring him.

In denying compensation the administrative law judge found, *inter alia,* that there had been numerous incidents of "horseplay" indulged in by Bergin's employees, including flipping rubber bands, and that this type of activity had been discouraged and was not condoned by Bergin; that the horseplay represented a "complete abandonment of the employee's duties"; and that the petitioner had "failed to prove that his accident arose out of or was in the scope of his employment."

In denying Petitioner's Motion for Review, the Commission adopted the administrative law judge's Findings of Fact, Conclusions of Law, and Order.

Section 35-1-45 of Utah's Workmen's Compensation Act provides in pertinent part:

> Every employee . . . who is injured by accident arising out of or in
> the course of his employment, wheresoever such injury occurred,
> provided the same was not purposely self-inflicted, shall be entitled
> to receive, and shall be paid such compensation for loss sustained on
> account of such injury . . . as herein provided. . . .

This Court, along with the courts of other jurisdictions, has recognized that
concepts of negligence, contributory negligence, fault, and similar tort concepts have no place within the remedial framework of the compensation act.
In *Twin Peaks Canning Co. v. Industrial Commission,* [196 P. 853 (Utah
1921)] this Court stated:

> Our statute only excluded those injuries which are "purposely self-
> inflicted." As we read the statute, therefore, it is not enough that the
> employé merely disregards some rule, regulation, or order of the
> master, since such conduct may constitute nothing more than ordinary
> negligence on the part of the employé, and mere negligence does not
> destroy the right to compensation.

. . . With these basic principles in mind, we turn now to an analysis of
whether and under what circumstances injuries sustained as a result of
"horseplay" on the part of an employee may not be compensated under the
act.

In his treatise, THE LAW OF WORKMEN'S COMPENSATION (1979), Professor
Arthur Larson (hereafter "Larson") lists four "actual or suggested treatments
of the problem" of participants in horseplay:

> 1. The "aggressor defense" which results in the denial of compensa-
> tion in any case where the injured employee instigated or participated
> in the horseplay. It is reasoned that by instigating the horseplay the
> employee has voluntarily stepped aside from his employment.

> 2. The New York Rule which permits even an instigator of or
> participant in horseplay to recover if the horseplay was a regular
> incident of the employment as distinguished from an isolated act.

> 3. The view that an instigator or participant should be treated the
> same as a non-participant since it is the conditions of the employment
> that induce the horseplay.

> 4. The rule proposed by Larson that an instigator or participant
> should recover if, by ordinary "course of employment" standards, his
> indulgence in horseplay does not amount to a *substantial deviation*
> from the employment.

As the basis for the fourth approach above, Larson proposes a four-part test
to analyze any particular act of horseplay to determine whether the horseplay
constitutes such a substantial deviation as to justify denying compensation
to a participant therein. Whether initiation of or participation in horseplay
is a deviation from course of employment depends on (1) the extent and seriousness of the deviation, (2) the completeness of the deviation (i.e., whether
it was commingled with the performance of duty or involved an abandonment
of duty), (3) the extent to which the practice of horseplay had become an
accepted part of the employment, and (4) the extent to which the nature of
the employment may be expected to include some such horseplay.

This Court has heretofore had only one occasion to examine the issue of horseplay in the workmen's compensation setting. In *Twin Peaks Canning Company v. Industrial Commission, supra,* an award of compensation to the dependents of a worker who was killed as a result of horseplay in which "the deceased was the instigator and the principal, if not the sole actor" was affirmed by this Court. The analysis in *Twin Peaks* turned on whether the deceased employee could be said to have been killed while "in the course of" his employment in light of his activities in using an elevator located on the premises of his employer, the use of which elevator by the deceased was allegedly forbidden by the employer. Although the words "deviation from employment" are nowhere found in the *Twin Peaks* opinion, it is clear that the Court was wrestling with the question of when a deviation from the assigned duties of an employee was sufficient to take that employee out of the course of his employment. In our view, the analysis in *Twin Peaks* though lacking the formal structure of the test proposed by Larson, is founded on the same general principles.[15] We therefore adopt Larson's four-part test to determine whether a particular act of horseplay constitutes such a deviation that it can be said that the resulting injury did not arise in the course of the employment and hence is not compensable.

(1) *Extent and seriousness of the deviation.*

In *Twin Peaks* the Court observed:

> A careful reading of the decided cases will, however, disclose that the mere fact that the injured employe, at the time of the accident, was not in the discharge of his usual duties or was not directly engaged in anything connected with those duties, does not necessarily prevent him from recovering compensation in case of accidental injury. In that connection it must be remembered that, while a human being may do no more than what a machine might do, yet he can not be classed as a machine merely.

Recognizing that "a little nonsense now and then is relished by the best of [workers]," it is clear that the better reasoned decisions make allowances for the fact that workers cannot be expected to attend strictly to their assigned duties every minute they are on the job. That is not to say that substantial excursions from job assignments need be tolerated or if injury occurs during such excursions, compensation need be paid. In the case at bar, Petitioner was engaged in the performance of his assigned duties when he was playfully "attacked" by co-workers flipping rubber bands. Petitioner then momentarily set aside his duties and took up the challenge. In an exchange lasting a matter of minutes, Petitioner was injured. As Larson points out:

---

[15] Mr. Justice Hall in his dissenting opinion distinguishes *Twin Peaks* from the case at bar and emphasizes that the Court there considered the case borderline. The dissent focuses particularly on the fact that *Twin Peaks* involved a 14-year old boy while Petitioner here was almost 22 years old at the time he was injured. A close reading of *Twin Peaks* reveals that the dicta concerning the worker's age were part of an analysis of the effect of the violation of a rule of the employer and whether the worker's death could be considered to have been "purposely self-inflicted."

The substantial character of a horseplay deviation should not be judged by the seriousness of its consequences in the light of hindsight, but by the extent of the work-departure in itself. This is not always easy to do, especially when a trifling incident escalates or explodes into a major tragedy.

We think the converse of this principle is likewise true; the fact that a major tragedy has occurred should not dictate an award of compensation when that tragedy resulted from a deviation so extensive and serious that the employment can be said to have been abandoned. However, it is our opinion that the deviation involved in the case at bar was short in duration and when disassociated from the serious consequences which resulted, relatively trivial.

(2) *Completeness of the deviation.*

Petitioner was, at the time he was "attacked" by his co-employees, engaged in the discharge of his duties. Had he not been injured, he would presumably have completed loading the truck and carried on with his deliveries. The horseplay he engaged in was clearly "commingled with the performance of duty" and hence did not constitute an "abandonment of duty." Larson points out:

> . . . [T]he particular act of horseplay is entitled to be judged according to the same standards of [extent] and duration of deviation that are accepted in other [fields,] such as resting, seeking personal comfort, or indulging in incidental personal errands. If an employee momentarily walks over to a co-employee to engage in a friendly word or two, this would nowadays be called an insubstantial deviation. If he accompanies this friendly word with a playful jab in the ribs, surely it cannot be said that an entirely new set of principles has come into play. The incident remains a simple human diversion subject to the same tests of extent of departure from the employment as if the playful gesture had been omitted.

> At the other extreme, there are cases in which the prankster undertakes a practical joke which necessitates the complete abandonment of the employment and the concentration of all his energies for a substantial part of his working time on the horseplay enterprise. When this abandonment is sufficiently complete and extensive, it can only be treated the same as abandonment of the employment for any other personal purpose, such as an extended personal errand or an intentional four-hour nap.

(3) *Extent to which horseplay has become a part of the employment.*

The evidence adduced at the hearing before the administrative law judge was conflicting on the frequency of "rubber band fights," but clearly such "fights" had become a part of the employment, whether the "fights" occurred "daily" or "two or three times a month." As Larson points out:

> The controlling issue is whether the custom had *in fact* become a part of the employment; the employer's knowledge of it can make it neither more nor less a part of the employment — at most it is evidence of incorporation of the practice into the employment. (Italics in original.)

We do not consider the fact that apparently no employee of Bergin had ever attempted before to flip a piece of wood with a rubber band as indicating that such a practice could not be considered a part of the employment. The elements of the practice, which must be conceded to have been part of the employment, were not significantly enlarged or so modified so as to no longer constitute a part of the employment.

(4) *Extent to which nature of employment may be expected to include some such horseplay.*

This element of Larson's approach focuses on the foreseeability of horseplay in any given employment environment and on the particular act of horseplay involved. Considerations which may enter into the analysis of this point include whether the work involves lulls in employment activity or is essentially continuous, and the existence of instrumentalities which are part of the work environment and which are readily usable in horseplay situations. This list is not intended to be exhaustive but rather illustrative of the possibilities. In the present case all of the elements which joined to result in Petitioner's injury — the hand truck, the rubber bands, and the piece of wood — were part and parcel of the work environment. It therefore is not difficult to foresee that horseplay of the type engaged in by Petitioner was to be expected.

By adopting the approach suggested by Larson, this Court does not intend the adoption of a test which by mechanical application will in cases involving horseplay dictate a "correct result." Indeed this approach is not susceptible of mechanical application but rather is intended as a method of analysis to assist the Industrial Commission in consideration of future cases coming before it involving horseplay. It is this Court's view that when the underlying policy of the compensation act is effectuated in the light of the analysis suggested herein, a rational result can be expected.

While we remain committed to the proposition that this Court will examine the evidence in a compensation case only to ascertain whether there is any substantial evidence in support of the findings of the Commission and whether the Commission has acted without or in excess of its jurisdiction, under the facts of this case we believe as a matter of law that there was not a substantial deviation such that it can be said that the resulting injury did not arise in the course of the employment and hence is not compensable. The record herein reveals no substantial evidence supporting the finding of the Commission that by engaging in horseplay, Petitioner "completely abandoned" his duties and hence was not injured in the course of his employment. Therefore the Order of the Commission is reversed. Costs to Petitioner and against Bergin.

MAUGHAN and STEWART, JJ., concur.

HALL, JUSTICE, dissenting:

I respectfully dissent.

In reversing the order of the Commission, the majority opinion rules "*as a matter of law* that there was not a substantial deviation" from petitioner's course of employment (emphasis added). My primary concern with such a ruling is that a decision as to whether one is injured by accident arising out of or in the course of his employment is not a law matter, but a factual one. Once the Commission has found the facts, this Court has traditionally refrained from disturbing such findings whenever there is substantial evidence to support them.

The majority relies upon the case of *Twin Peaks Canning Company v. Industrial Commission* as being consistent with its holding. On the contrary, in *Twin Peaks* the Court affirmed the findings of the Commission and acknowledged the standard of review referred to *supra*. Furthermore, the facts in *Twin Peaks* are readily distinguishable in several particulars. For example, in *Twin Peaks,* the fatal injury occurred during a lull in the work, at a time when there was no work to perform; in the instant case, petitioner was actively engaged in his work when he abandoned it for the purpose of "horseplay." Also, at the time of the accident in *Twin Peaks* the injured party was a minor (14 years of age) whereas in the instant case, petitioner was 22 years of age. The Court specifically acknowledged that *Twin Peaks* was a borderline case (which further suggests the importance of the *factual* determination) and that "if the deceased had been a man of mature years and experience, we might have reached a different conclusion."

The approach suggested by Professor Larson may well assist in determining whether the accident arises out of or in the course of one's employment. However, even if this four-step analysis is applied, it is the fact-finder (not this Court) which must evaluate and weigh each element individually and collectively. This includes the element the majority treats as a law matter, that of substantial deviation from petitioner's course of employment.

. . . .

CROCKETT, CHIEF JUSTICE, concurs in the dissent of HALL, J.

NOTE

Workplace Courtesy in the Heartland. As Farmer started to clock out, he brushed his time card across Swindel's midsection. Farmer denied Swindel's allegation that Farmer also gave him a "titty twister." The hearing judge found that Farmer did not provoke the ensuing injury to his back, which resulted when Swindel, who weighed approximately 470 pounds, bent Farmer backwards over a machine. The court affirmed an earlier decision that a participant in horseplay is not entitled to workers' compensation benefits, but that an innocent victim of horseplay by others is entitled to benefits. The court also found that "the incident was within the scope of employment as ordinary courtesies to a fellow employee, and Farmer's injuries 'arose out of' his employment." *Depuy v Farmer*, 847 N.E.2d 160, 165 (Ind. 2006).

c. Time and Place: Going and Coming Rule

SANTA ROSA JUNIOR COLLEGE v. WORKERS' COMPENSATION APPEALS BOARD
Supreme Court of California
708 P.2d 673 (1985)

KAUS, JUSTICE:

The Workers' Compensation Act (Lab. Code, § 3201 et seq.) establishes the liability of an employer "for any injury sustained by his or her employees arising out of and in the course of the employment." Almost 70 years ago, we adopted the "going and coming rule" as an aid in determining whether an injury occurred in the course of the employment. Generally prohibiting compensation for injuries suffered by an employee while commuting to and from work, the going and coming rule has been criticized by courts and commentators alike as being arbitrary and harsh. It has generated a multitude of exceptions which threaten, at times, to defeat the rule entirely. This appeal confronts us with the question of whether one such exception should be dramatically expanded to create, in effect, a "white-collar" nullification of the rule.

Santa Rosa Junior College (college) challenges a decision of the Workers' Compensation Appeals Board (board) awarding death benefits to JoAnne Smyth, widow of a community college instructor who was killed in an automobile accident on his way home from the campus. At issue is the applicability of the going and coming rule to school teachers who regularly take work home. If, in such cases, the home may be fairly regarded as a "second jobsite," the rule does not apply and injuries sustained en route are compensable. If the fact that the employee regularly takes work home does not establish the home as a second jobsite, compensation is barred.

We conclude that — unless the employer requires the employee to labor at home as a condition of the employment — the fact that an employee regularly works there does not transform the home into a second jobsite for purposes of the going and coming rule.

Facts

Joseph Smyth was a mathematics instructor and head of the mathematics department at the college. About 6 p.m. on March 16, 1982, he was killed in an accident while driving his personal automobile home from work. His home was located in Ukiah, about 60 miles from the Santa Rosa campus. The family had moved to Ukiah six years earlier for their own convenience. . . .

It is undisputed that at the time of the accident Smyth had with him some student papers he intended to grade that evening. Indeed, Smyth regularly worked at home in the evenings. . . . At home, he worked in a section of the living room reserved for that purpose, where he kept duplicate copies of necessary books. The work usually consisted of grading papers or exams; occasionally, he would also prepare lesson plans or future class schedules at home. Mrs. Smyth testified that her husband worked at home rather than on campus because on campus, he was subject to interruption by students or other business, and, in addition, he wished to spend time with his family.

Smyth's habit of working at home in the evenings was not unusual for members of the college's faculty; working at home appears to have been the rule, not the exception. Patrick Boyle, one of Smyth's colleagues and a former department head, testified that he and many other instructors regularly took work home. In his opinion, the work could not be completed during normal working hours because teachers were subject to interruption in their offices by students (both during the day and at night) and no suitable alternatives for uninterrupted work existed on campus. . . .

Edmund Buckley, associate dean of instruction at the college, testified that the administration neither encouraged nor discouraged working at home. Noting that "it's common for many, many instructors to take work home," he stated that during his own four-year tenure as a departmental head he had been able to avoid interruptions in his office "to some degree — not to a great degree." Buckley had occasionally worked in the library grading papers, a solution he considered "satisfactory" because he found "study carrels that nobody else knew about." He had never received any complaints from instructors to the effect that their working facilities on campus were inadequate. . . .

An office was provided for each instructor at the college. Undisputed evidence shows that Smyth could have eliminated or reduced student interruptions by posting office hours. Moreover, the record shows — not surprisingly — that Smyth was also subject to interruption while working at home.

The workers' compensation judge concluded that Smyth's death did not occur in the course of employment. He found that Smyth had adequate facilities and sufficient time to complete his work on campus and that it was Smyth's choice to work at home.

Acting on a petition for reconsideration, a three-member board panel, by a two-to-one vote, held that the death arose out of and occurred during the course of employment. The board concluded that because of the nature of the work and the frequent interruptions from students and phone calls, Smyth was "essentially required to maintain a second worksite in his home." It reasoned that in this case "[the] work at home was more a matter of business necessity than of personal convenience." Accordingly, the board awarded death benefits to Mrs. Smyth.

The college seeks review of the board's decision.

Discussion

As the employer, the college is liable for the death benefits provided under the act only if Smyth's accident arose "out of and in the course of the employment" and if certain "conditions of compensation" were present. (Lab. Code, § 3600.) We note at the outset that where, as here, there is no real dispute as to the facts, "the question of whether an injury was suffered in the course of employment is one of law and a purported finding of fact on that question is not binding on an appellate court."

We originally adopted the going and coming rule as one means of determining when an accident should be treated as an "accident arising out of and in the course of the employment." In *Ocean Accident & Guar. Co. v. Industrial Acc. Com.* (1916) 159 P. 1041, the issue was whether a fatal accident suffered by a seaman as he attempted to reboard his ship after going ashore for personal reasons arose out of and occurred within the scope of his employment. Observing that the language of the act was identical to that of the English Workmen's Compensation Act (enacted in 1897), we looked to English case law for guidance. We concluded that "there are excluded from the benefits of the act all those accidental injuries which occur while the employee is going to or returning from his work . . . ."

Of course, we recognized that in the broadest sense an injury occurring on the way to one's place of employment is an injury "growing out of and incident to his employment," since "a necessary part of the employment is that the employee shall go to and return from his place of labor." However, the right to an award is founded not "upon the fact that the injury grows out of and is incidental to his employment," but, rather, "upon the fact that the *service* he is rendering at the time of the injury grows out of and is incidental to the employment." (Emphasis original.) Therefore, we reasoned, "an employee going to and from his place of employment is not rendering any service, and begins to render such service only when [arriving at the place of employment]."

The going and coming rule resulted from the type of judicial line-drawing frequently required when construing and applying vague or open-ended statutory provisions. With its genesis in the practical need of drawing a "line" delineating an employee's "scope of employment," the rule was necessarily arbitrary, later explanations of its underlying rationale notwithstanding. California courts — manifesting much unease both in applying as well as in refusing to apply the rule — have recognized this essential arbitrariness and its potential harshness.

Indeed, it has become customary for courts to introduce each new discussion of the rule with a litany of reservations and qualifications: the rule is a "slippery concept" which is "riddled with exceptions"; "[much] criticized and subject to numerous exceptions, the rule is difficult to apply uniformly"; it has had a "tortuous history"; neither the rule nor its exceptions are susceptible to "automatic application"; each case "must be adjudged by the facts which are peculiarly its own"; "application of the rule has been especially difficult in 'borderline cases' . . . ." Finally, most attempts to exorcise or anesthetize the rule depart from or culminate in an invocation of Labor Code section 3202, which provides that the act "shall be liberally construed by the courts with the purpose of extending [its] benefits for the protection of persons injured in the course of their employment." Having shown that years of case law have properly eviscerated the going and coming rule, courts then go on to explain why the particular facts of the case fall into one of the many established exceptions to the rule.

The trouble is that the facts in this case do not fit convincingly into any of the established limitations or exceptions. Because Smyth's accident occurred miles away from the Santa Rosa campus, exceptions to the "premises line" doctrine[11] cannot reasonably be invoked to render the going and coming rule inapplicable. Smyth received no special or additional compensation for his commute; therefore, the "wage payment or travel expense" exception cannot apply.[12] The college did not require Smyth to furnish his own vehicle on the job. If it had, the "required transportation" exception would have curtailed application of the going and coming rule.

Smyth's employment at the college in no way created a "special risk." Under that exception, an injury is compensable if, before entry upon the premises, an employee suffers injury from a special risk causally related to employment. (*Gen. Ins. Co. v. Workmen's Comp. App. Bd. (Chairez)* (1976) 16 Cal. 3d 595, 600.) "The facts that an accident happens upon a public road and that the danger is one to which the general public is likewise exposed, however, do not preclude the existence of a causal relationship between the accident and the employment if the danger is one to which the employee, by reason of and in connection with his employment, is subjected peculiarly or to an abnormal degree." (*Freire v. Matson Nav. Co.* (1941) 19 Cal. 2d 8, 12.) In *Chairez,* we devised a two-prong test to determine applicability of the special risk exception: the exception will apply (1) if "but for" the employment the employee would not have been at the location where the injury occurred and (2) if "the risk is distinctive in nature or quantitatively greater than risks common to the public." While the circumstances of Smyth's accident certainly meet the first requirement (i.e., the accident would not have occurred "but for" the employment), his employment at the college did not subject him to a risk which was distinct or quantitatively greater than that common to the public generally.

We also find no merit in the suggestion that Smyth's accident occurred while he was on "special mission" or "errand" which was reasonably undertaken at the request or invitation of his employer.[13] In relation to his routine duties,

---

[11] For purposes of applying the going and coming rule, the employment relationship begins when the employee enters the employer's premises. We have reaffirmed the "premises line" rule, stating that it "has the advantage of enabling courts to ascertain the point at which employment begins — objectively and fairly." However, injuries sustained in close proximity to the employer's premises may, in fact arise out of the employment, especially when the accident occurs in the parking lot used by employees or on public property immediately adjacent to the workplace. Recognizing this, we have defined the course of employment to include a "reasonable margin of time and space necessary to be used in passing to and from the place where the work is to be done." Where the employment itself creates a danger to employees entering or leaving the premises, we have posited a "field of risk" or "zone of danger," the extent of which varies from case to case, depending on the degree to which the employer's conduct contributes directly as a proximate cause of the employee's injuries. This line of cases stems from one of the earliest attempts to circumvent or soften *Ocean Accident.* (See *Judson Mfg. Co. v. Ind. Acc. Com.* (1919) 181 Cal. 300, 302 ["It would be a harsh and indefensible rule that would withhold compensation from an employee engaged in traversing a dangerous pathway in his employer's building on his way to his own particular place of work therein, on the ground that he had not yet entered upon the real work of his employment"].)

[12] The fact that an employer compensates an employee for the commuting time implies an agreement that the employment relationship shall continue during the period of going and coming.

[13] "An injury suffered by an employee during his regular commute is compensable if he was also performing a special mission for his employer." (*Chairez, supra,* 16 Cal. 3d at p. 601.) The employee's conduct is "special" if it is "extraordinary in relation to routine duties, not outside the scope of employment." The closely related "dual purpose" rule also appears inapplicable. In *Lockheed Aircraft Corp. v. Ind. Acc. Com.* (1946) 28 Cal. 2d 756, we held that "where the employee

there was nothing "extraordinary" about his commute on March 16, 1982. The accident occurred, quite simply, during his regular commute between the college and his home in Ukiah. Smyth's practice of taking work home with him in the evenings cannot convert a routine commute into a "special mission."

Finally, we have recognized a "home as a second jobsite" exception to the going and coming rule. It is this exception — or an extension of it — which the board used in concluding that the rule does not preclude compensation in this case. Generally, "[work] done at home may exempt an injury occurring during a regular commute from the going and coming rule if circumstances of the employment — and not mere dictates of convenience to the employee — make the home a second jobsite. If the home becomes a second business situs, the familiar rule applies that injury sustained while traveling between jobsites is compensable." (*Wilson v. Workmen's Comp. App. Bd.* (1976) 16 Cal. 3d 181, 184) We noted that the commute does not constitute a business trip if the employees work at home for their own convenience "serving the employee's own convenience in selecting an off-premise place to work is a personal and not a business purpose."

The facts underlying Smyth's claim to a "home as a second jobsite" exception closely resemble those advanced by the applicant in *Wilson.* Like Smyth, Wilson was a teacher. She was injured in an automobile accident while driving to her school. Instructors at her school commonly graded papers and planned lessons outside class periods or at home in the evening, as the class schedule did not set aside a specific period for these activities. Although teachers could complete class preparation at school, they usually chose to work at home for their own convenience. At the time of the accident, Wilson's car contained miscellaneous supplies for use in her art class, materials graded at home the previous evening, and her teaching manual and other books.

In *Wilson,* we affirmed the board's determination that the applicant's home did not constitute a second jobsite warranting exemption from the going and coming rule. Her explicit job requirements demanded only that she report to the school premises, and "[her] employer's implicit requirement to work beyond classroom hours did not require labor at home."

Applicant in the present case contends that the board properly concluded that it was an implied term or condition of Smyth's employment contract that he take work home in the evenings — that it was "more a matter of business necessity than of personal convenience." On this basis, the board distinguished *Wilson,* wherein there was no claim that school facilities were not sufficient to allow completion of the required work.

It is not entirely clear whether the board's determination that Smyth was "implicitly required" to use his home as a second jobsite represents a conclusion of law or a finding of fact. Much of the language used by the board suggests that it was a legal conclusion which the board drew from the uncontradicted evidence in the record: *"The picture that emerges from the*

---

is combining his own business with that of his employer, or attending to both at substantially the same time, no nice inquiry will be made as to which business he was actually engaged in at the time of injury, unless it clearly appears that neither directly or indirectly could he have been serving his employer." The dual purpose situation usually arises when the employees combine their personal business with a "special errand" or "mission."

testimony of the various witnesses is that the decedent was essentially required to maintain a second worksite in his home"; ". . . *we conclude that the decedent was implicitly authorized* to perform part of his duties at home . . ."; "clearly this was an accepted practice. *It appears* moreover, *that this was in effect an implied term or condition* of the employment contract"; "his home was *in effect a second worksite* due to the fact that he was *implicitly required* to work at home". (Italics added.)

These passages suggest that the board concluded that where an employee works long hours and is subject to interruption at the workplace and where fellow employees commonly take work home with the knowledge and implicit permission of the employer, general principles of workers' compensation law establish that the employee is, as a matter of law, "implicitly required" to use his home as a second jobsite. There is no authority, however, to support such a proposition. *Wilson* makes quite clear that a home does not become a second jobsite simply because one's employment requires long working hours and the employer knows that the employee frequently brings work home. As we observed in *Wilson*, "[the] contemporary professional frequently takes work home. There, the draftsman designs on a napkin, the businessman plans at breakfast, the lawyer labors in the evening. But this hearthside activity — while commendable — does not create a white collar exception to the going and coming rule." Thus, to the extent that the board's "implicit requirement" determination amounts to a legal conclusion, it cannot be reconciled with *Wilson*.

Furthermore, we find little to commend the white-collar exception which we refused to establish in *Wilson*. It would, *a fortiori*, extend workers' compensation benefits to workers injured in the homes themselves, as well as en route to and from their regular work places. Ironically, a white collar exception would probably not diminish the controversy surrounding the going and coming rule; it would merely shift it to a new and equally arbitrary "line" defining the "course of employment."[16] Would the fact that an employee regularly took work-related materials home suffice to create a second jobsite, or would the employee have to show that he *actually* worked at home? How would we treat employees who work at home on some evenings but not on

---

[16] The going and coming rule and its many exceptions are all "arbitrary" — judicial responses to the practical necessity of establishing guidelines for use in determining whether a worker's injury arose out of and in the course of employment. Like all arbitrary rules, they are, in borderline cases, widely perceived as unfair. . . . As one commentator observed, "[it] is a familiar problem in law, when a sharp, objective, and perhaps somewhat arbitrary line has been drawn . . . to encounter demands that the line be blurred a little to take care of the closest cases. For example, one writer says that there is no reason in principle why states should not protect employees 'for a reasonable distance' before reaching or after leaving the employer's premises. This, however, only raises a new problem because it provides no standard by which the reasonableness of the distance can be judged. It substitutes the widely varying subjective interpretation of 'reasonable distance' by different administrators and judges for the physical fact of a boundary line. At the same time, it does not solve the original problem, because each time the premises are extended a 'reasonable distance,' there will inevitably arise new cases only slightly beyond that point — and the cry of unfairness of drawing distinctions based on only a few feet of distance will once more be heard." (1 LARSON, WORKMEN'S COMPENSATION LAW, § 15.12(a).) While the going and coming rule (and its exceptions) can hardly be considered to be as "sharp" and "objective" as the premises-line doctrine which Larson was defending, we believe that his reasoning is applicable to the issues in this case.

others, depending on their personal inclinations? And, of course, new problems of the "frolics and detours" variety would plague the new exception.

On the other hand, insofar as the board's determination that the employee was "implicitly required" to maintain his home as a second jobsite was intended as a finding of fact, it is simply not supported by substantial evidence in the record. Although the evidence shows that most faculty members took work home and that the employer was well aware of this practice, there is nothing in the record which indicates that faculty members were *required* — implicitly or otherwise — to work at home rather than on campus. Rather, the evidence reveals that professors worked at home by choice, not because of the dictates of their employer. On this record, there is no room for a factual finding that working at home was a condition of Smyth's employment.

Therefore, applying established "going and coming rule" principles and precedents, we conclude that the board erred in awarding compensation. We could, of course, abrogate the rule or expand any of its exceptions, for they have evolved simply as "the product of judicial gloss on the statutory conditions of compensability." However, they have become an important part of our workers' compensation law. Although the Legislature has enacted significant changes in the Workers' Compensation Act during the last 70 years, it has not disturbed the going and coming rule or its judicially created exceptions. Unless the judiciary can devise rules which are fairer, less arbitrary, less problematic in application, and more clearly consistent with the public policies underlying the act, it should leave to the Legislature the major task of restructuring the rules governing employer liability.

Smyth's accident occurred during a routine commute from college to home. We conclude that the facts of this case are essentially indistinguishable from those of *Wilson v. Workmen's Comp. App. Bd.* and that our holding in *Wilson* should govern here.

The decision of the board is annulled.

REYNOSO, JUSTICE, dissenting:

I respectfully dissent. Courts have fashioned the "going and coming" rule to aid in determining whether an injury occurred "in the course of the employment." In applying this rule, courts have held "non-compensable the injury that occurs during a local commute en route to a fixed place of business at fixed hours in the absence of special or extraordinary circumstances." By narrowly focusing on the rule and its numerous exceptions, however, the majority in this case has lost sight of the primary statutory test. Since Smyth's accident clearly occurred in the course of his employment, it should be compensable.

. . . .

Smyth's accident during his Ukiah commute should be compensable because it was a dual purpose trip, serving both his personal purpose of making a trip home and the business purpose of reaching a second jobsite. In such a situation, the court should look for three principal indicia to establish a compensable injury: "the quantity and regularity of work performed at home; the continuing presence of work equipment at home; and special circumstances of the particular employment that make it necessary and not merely person-ally convenient to work at home." (1 LARSON, THE LAW OF WORKMEN'S COMPENSATION (1985) § 18.32 at p. 4-309.)

Here, testimony demonstrated that Smyth brought home one or two hours of work almost every night. In addition, part of the Smyths' living room was reserved as his work place, in which he kept duplicate copies of his books. Finally, it was more than a matter of personal convenience to work at home. To be an effective teacher, Smyth needed to be accessible to students while in his office. Frequent interruptions by students, however, made it impossible for him to complete his preparatory work on campus. Furthermore, Smyth served as head of the mathematics department. In this capacity, he assumed the responsibility of supervising and evaluating the night instructors as well as the burden of administrative work, which included receiving all telephone calls for the department. This evidence supports the board's finding that Smyth's home was a second jobsite.

. . . .

NOTES

1. The "Gray Area" Exception. Tompkins emerged from the subway two blocks from Two World Trade Center, where he worked, and was injured by flying debris when the building exploded on September 11, 2001. The court upheld the finding that his injury was compensable. While generally an employee is not considered within the scope of employment while traveling to and from work, "certain exceptions to this rule exist and are enhanced as the employee draws physically nearer to the workplace until he or she has entered a 'gray area' where the risks of travel to or from work may be said to merge with the risks of employment." *Tompkins v. Morgan Stanley*, 1 A.D.3d 695 (N.Y. App. Div. 2003).

2. Traveling to a Convention. Ehrgott brought a tort suit against the estate of a fellow employee, Jones, as a result of an accident that occurred while Jones was driving them to the Newark Airport. Jones and another passenger in the car were killed and Ehrgott was seriously and permanently disabled. Both Ehrgott and Jones were employees of Hoechst-Roussel Pharma-ceuticals, and were on the way to an annual meeting of the American Chemical Society in Las Vegas. Ehrgott and Jones would have been covered by workers' compensation while attending the meeting. The issue in the case was whether the trip to the airport fell within the definition of the "going and coming" rule (in which case workers' compensation coverage was not legally required) or whether this trip fell within the "special-mission provision" of the New Jersey statute (in which case Ehrgott was covered by workers' compensation and Jones was protected from a tort suit because the exclusive remedy provision in the New Jersey workers' compensation statute extends to fellow employees). The special-mission provision provides that the employee is deemed to be in the course of employment when he is both required by the employer to be away from his place of employment and is then actually engaged in the direct performance of duties assigned or directed by the employer. The court held that Ehrgott's trip fell within the special-mission provision and therefore the proper remedy was workers' compensation and not a tort suit. Note the irony of the case: Ehrgott was arguing that he did *not* have workers' compensation coverage in order to be able to bring a tort suit against the estate of a fellow employee. *Ehrgott v. Jones*, 506 A.2d 40 (N.J. Super. Ct. App. Div. 1986).

2. TEST TWO: ARISING OUT OF EMPLOYMENT

The second test that a worker must meet in order to receive workers' compensation benefits is that there be an injury "arising out of employment." This test is used to distinguish among three types of risk that are associated with any workplace: (1) occupational risks, such as machinery breaking, that are universally compensable because they are associated with the employment; (2) personal risks, which are universally noncompensable since they are personal to the claimant, such as a heart seizure resulting from a drug overdose; and (3) "neutral" risks, where the cause of the injury is neither distinctly occupational nor distinctly personal in character or where the cause is unknown. *See* Figure 22-1. Neutral risks may or may not be compensable depending on the legal doctrine used in a particular state and on the specific facts of the case.

Figure 22-1
Three Categories of Risk

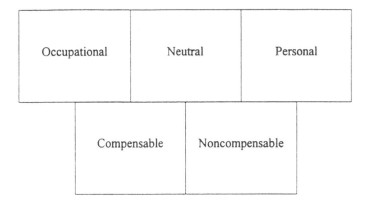

The first step in deciding whether a particular case meets the arising out of employment (AOE) test is to decide the category of risk involved in the case. Most cases will involve either occupational or personal risks, and therefore whether the case meets the AOE test is easily resolved and the AOE inquiry ends. If, however, the case is one of the unusual variety that involves a neutral risk, the legal inquiry becomes more complicated and two more steps are necessary.

The second step is to determine the type of neutral risk. This may affect the resolution of the case because some states use different legal tests for different types of neutral risks. (As will be discussed later in this section, more states used to differentiate among types of neutral risks than currently do, but the distinctions are still relevant in many jurisdictions.) Among the types of neutral risks are (1) an "Act of God" or (depending on your philosophical view) an "Act of Nature," such as a worker injured by lightning, a wild animal bite, an earthquake, a windstorm, a sunstroke, or a similar calamity of nature; (2) assault by a stranger; (3) "street risks," which are harms such as dog bites, police bullets, or other maladies associated with being on a public street; and (4) unexplained death.

The legal doctrine used in a jurisdiction to deal with a particular type of neutral risk (or used to decide all neutral risks in the state) is the third step that is crucial to the outcome of the case. Larson has identified five lines of interpretation of the "arising out of employment" test. In increasing liberality these are:

(1) *The Proximate Cause Doctrine.* This rule, now obsolete, required that the harm be foreseeable as a hazard of this kind of employment and that an unbroken chain of causation connect the hazard and the injury without any intervening cause. This test would make all neutral risks (and even some occupational risks) noncompensable.

(2) *The Peculiar Risk Doctrine.* The rule used by most states in the past, but now largely abandoned, which requires that the hazard be peculiar to (and increased by) the employment.

(3) *The Increased Risk Doctrine.* The rule still used in many if not most states, which requires that the job increase the quantity of the risk, even if the risk is not peculiar to the occupation. A park ranger mauled by a bear would satisfy this test (although not the two previous tests).

(4) *The Actual Risk Doctrine.* The position of a substantial number of states, which allows compensation even if the risk that caused the injury was common to the public, as long as it was an actual risk of this employment. An alternative term for this test (and one that helps clarify the meaning) is the normal risk doctrine: the risk may be no greater than the risks faced by the public, but is compensable if it is a normal risk of this job. A worker in a 24-hour convenience store in a dangerous neighborhood may not face greater risk of assault by a stranger than anyone else in the area (which means that the increased risk doctrine would not be satisfied), but such an assault is an actual (or normal) risk of being a clerk in such a store, and thus would meet the actual risk doctrine.

(5) *The Positional Risk Doctrine.* The position of a growing minority of states, which allows compensation for all injuries that would not have occurred but for the fact that the conditions of the employment placed the claimant in the position where he or she was injured. A worker in a 24-hour convenience store who is in the back room sorting bottles and who is killed by a freak lightning bolt that ricochets through the store could meet this doctrine, but not the other four tests.

These tests are explicated in the succeeding cases, which were selected in part to illustrate the historical evolution of the legal approaches to deciding which neutral risks are compensable.

DONAHUE v. MARYLAND CASUALTY CO.

Supreme Judicial Court of Massachusetts

116 N.E. 226 (1917)

CROSBY, J.:

The evidence presented to the committee of arbitration was in substance as follows: The claimant, who was employed by the insured in the sale of church goods, on February 21, 1916, left his employer's place of business in Boston, and proceeded by train to Lowell and thence by electric cars to the village of Collinsville in Lowell. Upon leaving the electric cars, he went to the house of a clergyman, which was distant about ten minutes' walk from the car line, and after completing his business there left and started to walk back. He had proceeded about thirty-five or forty feet when he slipped on the ice and fell, sustaining a broken ankle. When injured he was walking in the middle of the street, the sidewalk being impassable on account of ice. He was employed principally as a traveling salesman, but worked in the store during the Christmas and Easter seasons. More than half of the time he was outside his employer's store visiting different places throughout New England for the purpose of selling church goods. He traveled by steam railroads, electric cars, and on foot — using cars when available. When he left the house of the clergyman he intended to take a car to Lexington to sell some goods there. The committee found that the employee received an injury in the course of and arising out of his employment.

At the hearing before the Industrial Accident Board in addition to the evidence before the committee above recited, the employee testified:

> I was going to get a car to Lexington when I fell. The street was a mass of ice. I never saw anything like it before or since.

The finding that the injury was received in the course of the employment was warranted. The question remains whether there was any evidence that the injury arose out of the employment. An injury arises out of the employment when there is a causal connection between the conditions under which the work is to be performed and the resulting injury. An injury cannot be found to have arisen out of the employment unless the employment was a contributing, proximate cause. If the risk of injury to the employee was one to which he would have been equally exposed apart from his employment, then the injury does not arise out of it. As was said by this court in *McNicols' Case*[, 102 N.E. 697 (Mass. 1913)]:

> The causative danger must be peculiar to the work and not common to the neighborhood. It must be incidental to the character of the business and not independent of the relation of master and servant.

The undisputed evidence shows that while the employee was walking along the street in the course of his employment on his way to the electric car line, he slipped upon the ice and received the injury for which he seeks compensation. Manifestly the injury so received did not result in any proper sense from a risk incidental to the employment. It seems plain that the danger of the employee's slipping upon the ice in a public street was not peculiar to his work, but was a hazard common to persons engaged in any employment who had occasion to travel along the streets. The risk of slipping upon the icy pavement was common to the public who had occasion to pass over it on foot. It was a danger due to climatic conditions to which persons in that locality, however employed or if not employed at all, were equally exposed.

As the hazard of slipping on the ice in the street was not a causative danger peculiar to the claimant's employment, the injury received could not properly be found to have arisen out of the employment.

The decree of the superior court must be reversed, and a decree entered in favor of the insurer.

So ordered.

KATZ v. A. KADANS & CO.
New York Court of Appeals
134 N.E. 330 (1922)

POUND, J.

This is a workmen's compensation case. Louis Katz, the claimant, was a dairyman's chauffeur. On May 7, 1920, when he was driving his employer's car west on Canal Street after delivering some cheese, an insane man stabbed him. A lot of people were running after the insane man and he stabbed any one near him. The question is whether claimant's injuries arose out of his employment.

If the work itself involves exposure to perils of the street, strange, unanticipated, and infrequent though they may be, the employee passes along the streets when on his master's occasions under the protection of the statute. This is the rule unequivocally laid down by the House of Lords in England:

> "When a workman is sent into the street on his master's business . . . his employment necessarily involves exposure to the risks of the streets and injury from such a cause [necessarily] arises out of his employment."

Dennis v. White, [1917] L.R. App. Cas. 479.

So we have to concern ourselves only with the question whether claimant's accident arose out of a street risk.

Cases may arise where one is hurt in the street, but where the risk is of a general nature, not peculiar to the street. Lightning strikes fortuitously in the street; bombs dropped by enemy aircraft do not expose to special danger persons in a street as distinguished from those in houses. The danger must result from the place to make it a street risk, but that is enough if the workman is in the place by reason of his employment, and in the discharge of his duty to his employer. The street becomes a dangerous place when street brawlers, highwaymen, escaping criminals, or violent madmen are afoot therein as they sometimes are. The danger of being struck by them by accident is a street risk because it is incident to passing through or being on the street when dangerous characters are abroad.

Particularly on the crowded streets of a great city, not only do vehicles collide, pavements become out of repair, and crowds jostle, but mad or biting dogs may run wild, gunmen may discharge their weapons, police officers may shoot at fugitives fleeing from justice, or other things may happen from which accidental injuries result to people on the streets which are peculiar to the use of the streets and do not commonly happen indoors.

The risk of being stabbed by an insane man running amuck seems in a peculiar sense a risk incidental to the streets to which claimant was exposed by his employment. *Matter of Heidemann v. Am. Dist. Tel. Co.,* 130 N.E. 302 [(N.Y. 1921)], does not hold that where the street risk is one shared equally by all who pass or repass, whether in or out of employment, it should be shown that the employment involves some special exposure; that the night watchman is exposed by his employment to the risk of being shot by accident as he nears a sudden brawl which it is his duty to investigate, while the night clerk whose business brings him on the street, but whose duty is not to seek danger, is not so exposed. We decided the case before us and no other, dwelling naturally upon those features of the situation which emphasized the connection between the risk and the employment. But the fact that the risk is one to which every one on the street is exposed does not itself defeat compensation. Members of the public may face the same risk every day. The question is whether the employment exposed the workman to the risks by sending him on to the street, common though such risks were to all on the street.

The order should be affirmed, with costs.

HOGAN, CARDOZO, and CRANE, JJ., concur.

HISCOCK, C. J., and MCLAUGHLIN and ANDREWS, JJ., dissent.

NOTES

1. *Evolution of the Street Risk Doctrine.* The *Donahue* and *Katz* cases present in a capsule view the evolution of the street risk doctrine. In *Donahue,* decided in 1917, street risks were treated like all other forms of neutral risks (and the peculiar risk test was used). In *Katz,* decided in New York in 1922 and still the approach used in some jurisdictions today (although not New York), the court differentiated street risks from other types of neutral risks and then used a more liberal doctrine for street risks than was being used contemporaneously for other neutral risks. The pattern now in such states is to use the increased risk doctrine for most neutral risks, but a more liberal doctrine (typically the actual risk test) for street risks.

2. *The Street Risk Sequence.* In those states which use a different doctrine for street risks than for other types of neutral risks, the logical sequence in applying the AOE test is first to decide which of the three categories of risk is involved; then (assuming the risk is a neutral risk), decide which type of neutral risk is involved; and then decide which legal doctrine is applicable.

HANSON v. REICHELT

Supreme Court of Iowa

452 N.W.2d 164 (1990)

LAVORATO, JUSTICE.

This appeal arises out of the death of a farm employee who suffered a heatstroke while working. The Iowa industrial commissioner denied benefits, finding that the employee's injury did not arise out of his employment. In making this finding, the commissioner applied the general public-increased risk rule, a rule this court first approved in a workers' compensation case involving heatstroke more than fifty years ago.

. . . .

We now adopt the actual risk rule in workers' compensation cases involving injuries from exposure to the elements. We think here, however, that the agency should be allowed to decide the liability issue in light of the rule we adopt today. So we affirm in part and vacate in part the decision of the court of appeals. We reverse the judgment of the district court and remand for further proceedings consistent with this opinion.

On June 24, 1983, D. Van Maanen agreed to buy some hay from Sherman Reichelt. Reichelt had already baled some of the hay. The remainder of the hay sold to Van Maanen had to be baled, and all of the hay had to be stacked on a hayrack and transported from Riechelt's field.

Reichelt hired Dennis L. Hanson to help with the baling. When the baling operation began, the weather was very hot; the recorded temperature that day reached a high of 95 degrees.

At about 2:30 p.m. on June 24, Van Maanen's wife, Van Maanen, Reichelt, and Hanson began working in the field. Hanson's job was twofold: he stacked bales and drove empty and full hayracks to and from the field. Each bale weighed about sixty pounds. Hanson did this for about an hour and a half. But at no time did he work more than twenty-five minutes without a break.

At some point Hanson quit and sat down in the field. About thirty minutes later, Reichelt drove up in his pickup and found Hanson passed out.

Reichelt called for medical assistance; an ambulance arrived about 5:00 p.m. and took Hanson to a hospital in Newton. The doctors there determined that Hanson had suffered a heatstroke. Later Hanson was transferred to Iowa Methodist Medical Center in Des Moines where he underwent extensive treatment and finally died on July 18, 1983.

Hanson's father and mother were appointed administrators of their son's estate. As such the parents filed a petition with the Iowa Industrial Commission in June 1984. They sought medical and death benefits from Reichelt and Reichelt's insurance carrier.

A deputy industrial commissioner in an arbitration decision found that Hanson's death did not arise out of his employment and denied benefits. The administrators appealed to the commissioner who affirmed.

The administrators then filed in the district court a petition for judicial review of the commissioner's decision. The district court affirmed.

The administrators appealed from the district court's decision, and we transferred the case to the court of appeals. The court of appeals found that Hanson's death did arise out of his employment. So it reversed the judgment of the district court.

. . . .

Reichelt and his carrier sought further review of the court of appeals decision, which we granted. The narrow issue we must decide is whether the agency properly applied the law when it found that Hanson's death did not arise out of his employment.

I

When we review a district court decision on the validity of agency action, we ask only whether the district court has correctly applied the law. The district court is itself acting in an appellate capacity to correct errors of law made by the agency. In our review of the district court's action in such capacity, we merely apply the standards of Iowa Code section 17A.19(8) to the agency action to determine whether our conclusions are the same as those of the district court. If our conclusions are the same, we must affirm. Likewise, if our conclusions differ, we must reverse.

II

In these proceedings the administrators had the burden to prove by a preponderance of the evidence that Hanson had suffered an injury that arose out of and in the course of his employment. . . .

Both sides agree that Hanson's injury — the heatstroke — arose during the course of his employment. So, as we said, our sole issue is whether Hanson's injury arose out of his employment.

III

In the past this court addressed the issue whether a heatstroke is compensable in workers' compensation cases. *See, e.g., Wax v. Des Moines Asphalt Paving Corp.,* 263 N.W. 333 (Iowa 1935); *West v. Phillips,* 288 N.W. 625 (Iowa 1939). In *Wax* an employee suffered a heatstroke while digging a trench in 100+ degree temperatures. The industrial commissioner allowed benefits, and the district court affirmed. Viewing the same facts, we held as a matter of law that the heatstroke did not arise out of the employment. In other words, there was no causal connection between the employment and the injury.

In reaching this conclusion, we adopted and applied the general public-increased risk rule which provides that

> [i]f the employment brings with it no greater exposure to injurious results from natural causes, and neither contributes to produce these nor to aggravate their effect, as from lightning, severe heat or cold, than those to which persons generally in that locality, whether so employed or not, are equally exposed there is no causal connection between the employment and the injury. But where the employment

brings a greater exposure and injury results, the injury does arise out of the employment.

Simply put, the rule permits recovery "only in cases where the [employee] is exposed to conditions of temperature unusual or more intense than those experienced by [employees] of the community in general."

Relying on the same rule, we reached an opposite result in *West v. Phillips*. There a bakery employee became ill while working the night shift. The employee died the next day. His doctor testified that the employee showed substantially all the symptoms of heat exhaustion. The doctor performed an autopsy. He found that the employee had severe heart trouble and that the heat exhaustion had hastened the employee's death.

In *West* experts testified that heat infiltration from the tar roof, an inefficient fan inside, and artificial heat from the oven combined to make it 10 to 12 degrees hotter inside. During the day, the temperatures outside had reached 108.

We thought that the testimony of the experts was sufficient to sustain a finding "that there was excessive heat in the bakeshop caused by artificial heat." Such a finding, of course, met the recovery requirement of the general public-increased risk rule: the employee must be exposed to conditions of temperature unusual or more intense than those experienced by employees of the community in general. In addition, we thought the doctor's testimony was sufficient to establish the necessary causal connection between the employee's death and the heat exhaustion.

The facts here are on all fours with the facts in *Wax*. So it is not surprising that the deputy reached the same conclusion as we did in *Wax*: no causal connection between the death and the injury.

One noted authority criticizes the general public-increased risk rule because of the way courts define the general public:

> The heart of the difficulty is almost entirely in defining the general public with which the comparison is made. It is here that many of the negative cases have gone wide of the mark. Clearly, since the object of the comparison between the exposure of this employee and the exposure of the public is to isolate and identify the distinctive characteristics of this employment, the comparison should be made with a broad cross section of the public having no characteristics specially selected because they resemble those of the employment. Because most of these cases arise during extreme hot, cold, rainy, or stormy weather, the most direct way to approach a working rule is to ask: What does the average man, free of the obligation of any particular employment, do when it is twenty below, or a hundred in the shade, or raining, sleeting or snowing violently? There may be various answers as to what he does, but there is one clear answer as to what he does not do. He does not stay outdoors all day.

1 LARSON, WORKMEN'S COMPENSATION LAW, § 8.42 (1984).

Larson gives an example of the proper application of the general public-increased risk rule from a Texas sunstroke case in which the court succinctly and clearly summed up the rule:

In the case before us the very work which the decedent was doing for his employer exposed him to a greater hazard from heatstroke than the general public was exposed to for the simple reason that the general public were not pushing wheelbarrow loads of sand in the hot sun on that day.

Several jurisdictions have discarded the general public-increased risk rule in cases involving effects of exposure to the elements. In its place, these courts have adopted the actual risk rule.

In *Hughes* [*v. St. Patrick's Cathedral*, 156 N.E. 665 (N.Y. 1927)], the employee suffered heat prostration while working outdoors. In holding for the employee, the court summed up the actual risk rule in two sentences:

Heat prostration is an accidental injury arising out of and during the course of the employment, if the nature of the employment exposes the workman to risk of such injury. Although the risk may be common to all who are exposed to the suns [*sic*] rays on a hot day, the question is whether the employment exposes the employee to the risk.

Reaching the same result on similar reasoning in an accidental freezing case, the Wisconsin Supreme Court said:

The injury in the instant case clearly grew out of and was incidental to the employment. It makes no difference that the exposure was common to all out of door employments in that locality in that kind of weather. The injury grew out of that employment and was incidental to it. It was a hazard of the industry.

Eagle River Bldg. & Supply Co. v. Peck, 225 N.W. 690, 691 (1929).

We think the actual risk rule is the better rule and more in line with how we construe our Workers' Compensation Act. We construe the Act liberally in favor of the employee; we resolve all doubts in favor of the employee.

Moreover, the actual risk rule makes no comparison between risks found by the employee and those found by the general public. So the rule is not subject to the same criticisms that have been voiced against the general public-increased risk rule.

We adopt the actual risk rule in cases involving injuries from exposure to the elements. If the nature of the employment exposes the employee to the risk of such an injury, the employee suffers an accidental injury arising out of and during the course of the employment. And it makes no difference that the risk was common to the general public on the day of the injury.

IV

Because the district court's judgment is based on a rule of law we now renounce, we must reverse. But we think the agency should be allowed to decide the liability issue in light of the actual risk rule. So we affirm that part of the court of appeals decision which reversed the judgment of the district court. We vacate that part of the court of appeals decision which held that Hanson's injury arose out of his employment. We reverse the judgment of the district court and remand for further proceedings consistent with this opinion.

NOTES

1. *Evolution of the AOE Test in Iowa.* James Miedema was a laborer at the Dial Corporation. He clocked in for his shift and then went to the restroom while getting ready to work. After turning to flush the toilet, he experienced severe pain in his lower back, was taken to the emergency room at the local hospital, and was out of work for a month. The injury occurred in the course of employment, but did it meet the arising out of the employment test? The Iowa Supreme Court, in *Miedema v. Dial Corp.*, 551 N.W.2d 309 (Iowa 1996), indicated that it had adopted the actual risk rule in *Hanson v. Reichelt* and that its analysis applies here. However, consider this language from the decision: "Miedema fails to establish that use of Dial's restroom exposed him to any increased risk of injury." *Id.* at 311. Does the Iowa Supreme Court understand the distinction between the increased risk doctrine and the actual risk doctrine?

2. *The AOE Test in Virginia.* Joanne Lucas was a driver for Federal Express. Following a package pickup, she placed the key in the ignition and the truck was struck by lightning. She was taken to the hospital and subsequently experienced various physical maladies, such as her feet turning bright yellow and then displaying black dots. As a result of the incident, Lucas was diagnosed with post-traumatic stress disorder and was unable to return to work. The court quoted an earlier case: "In Virginia, we have adopted the 'actual risk test,' which requires only that the employment expose the workman to the particular danger from which he was injured, notwithstanding the exposure of the public generally to like risks." The court also opined that "she must prove that the employment activity in which she was engaged exposed her to the injurious risk to an extent to which people were not ordinarily exposed, and thus caused her injuries." In addition, the court explained that if an employee is injured by some natural force such as being struck by lightning, "when the nature of the employment, or some condition, or environment therein brings into existence a special or peculiar risk to the disastrous forces of nature, the injury or death of a employee may be compensated as a risk of the employment." Lucas presented evidence on the truck's electrical and structural characteristics, including an antenna. Nonetheless, the court denied compensation because "there is no competent evidence relating how these characteristics caused her injury by exposing her to a particular risk of injury from lightning not otherwise experienced by any other person in the same vicinity." *Lucas v. Federal Express*, 583 S.E.2d 56, 59-60 (Va. Ct. App. 2003). Does the Court of Appeals of Virginia understand the distinctions among the peculiar risk doctrine, the increased risk doctrine, the actual risk doctrine, and the positional risk doctrine?

NIPPERT v. SHINN FARM CONSTRUCTION CO.
Supreme Court of Nebraska
388 N.W.2d 820 (1986)

Per Curiam.

Dennis W. Nippert appeals the dismissal of a suit filed against his employer, Shinn Farm Construction Company, in the Nebraska Workers' Compensation

Court. Nippert seeks compensation for total temporary disability and permanent partial disability suffered as a result of injuries sustained in a tornado on October 18, 1979.

A single judge of the compensation court found, under the "act of nature" doctrine, that the accident which caused Nippert's injury did not "arise out of" his employment as required for recovery under the Workers' Compensation Act. . . . On rehearing, a three-judge panel affirmed the order of dismissal. We reverse.

Nippert was employed by Shinn Farm Construction Company on October 18, 1979. On this date he and other workers were erecting a hog shed on a farm near Wamego, Kansas. The workers were inside the nearly completed building, preparing to leave the jobsite for the day, when a tornado approached the area at approximately 6 p.m. The weather service had issued tornado warnings, but the construction workers had received no such information. The wind force inside the building was so strong that the workers were unable to move, a phenomenon apparently resulting from the fact that the doors on the southeast and northeast corners of the building had not yet been installed.

At some point the walls of the 40- by 60-foot building collapsed, and the roof fell to the ground intact. Miraculously, no one was injured when the building fell. The wind then subsided for a few moments, but about a minute later the tornado picked Nippert up and hurled him to the ground some 30 feet away. Nippert's leg was fractured, and he later developed back problems.

The storm system that hit the jobsite injured 11 people and caused extensive property damage throughout northeast Kansas. On the farm where the company was erecting the hog shed, Roger Shinn observed extensive damage to two silos, the destruction of a large machine shed and barn, and damaged machinery and equipment, including a truck which was thrown into a feedlot. The storm had also destroyed or damaged buildings on two adjacent farms. The tornado's path was 2 to 12 miles wide, and it traveled approximately 58 miles.

Nippert was treated for his injuries, but he was unable to return to work until November 1980. Shinn Construction Company voluntarily paid Nippert's medical expenses as well as temporary total disability benefits and permanent partial disability benefits based on a 20-percent permanent disability of his left leg. It was not until Nippert filed a petition seeking additional benefits that the company raised a question of liability.

Based upon the increased risk doctrine, the Nebraska Workers' Compensation Court rejected Nippert's claim for benefits. We recently reviewed this doctrine in *McGinn v. Douglas County Social Services Admin.,* 317 N.W.2d 764 (Neb. 1982). In a 4-to-3 opinion, the majority held that an employee is entitled to benefits under the provisions of the Nebraska Workers' Compensation Act only when an accident arises both out of and in the course of employment: "The term 'arising out of' describes the accident and its origin, cause, and character, i.e., whether it resulted from the risks arising from within the scope or sphere of the employee's job." An injury caused by the elements arises out of employment only if the employee is exposed to a different hazard than others generally in the area where the injury occurred.

Nippert's theory on appeal is twofold. First, he asks this court to overrule the increased risk test and adopt the positional risk test. Second, if the court continues to apply the increased risk test, Nippert asks for reversal on the grounds that the dismissal was against the great weight of evidence that he was exposed to an increased risk of injury in his work environment and, therefore, that his injuries arose out of his employment.

We agree with Nippert's first theory, and to the extent that *McGinn* and earlier cases are inconsistent with it, they are overruled. In *McGinn* we were asked to adopt the positional risk test, the rationale being that an accident arises out of employment when an employee is where he is required to be at the time the act of nature occurs and causes the employee's injury. We rejected the argument and affirmed the increased risk doctrine as the law in this state. The increased risk doctrine requires an employee to demonstrate that his employment duties expose him to a greater risk or hazard than that to which the general public in the area is exposed.

After careful consideration we have concluded that the better rule is the positional risk test espoused by the dissent in *McGinn*. Under this theory an employee's injuries are compensable as long as his employment duties put him in a position that he might not otherwise be in which exposes him to a risk, even though the risk is not greater than that of the general public. In 1 A. LARSON, THE LAW OF WORKMEN'S COMPENSATION § 8.12 at 3-23 (1985), the positional risk test is stated as follows: "[W]hen one in the course of his employment is reasonably required to be at a particular place at a particular time and there meets with an accident, although one which any other person then and there present would have met with irrespective of his employment, that accident is one 'arising out of' the employment of the person so injured."

The record shows that Nippert's employment required him to be in the area where the tornado struck. The record also reflects that the storm caused Nippert's injuries. The judgment of the Workers' Compensation Court is reversed.

WHITE, J., participating on briefs.

CAPORALE, JUSTICE, dissenting.

I dissent and lament the wound inflicted by the majority upon a venerable but endangered friend: The Rule of Law.

Reasonable minds schooled in the law are certainly entitled to differ as to whether the "increased risk" or the "positional risk" rule is the better reasoned one. Thus, were this a case of first impression, a majority of this court would have both the right as well as the duty to choose one rule over the other. But this is not a case of first impression. Nor is it a case dealing with a nonstatutory principle of common law.

The Legislature enacted the compensation act 73 years ago. Thirteen years later, this court interpreted the "arising out of and in the course of" language of the act for the first time. *Gale v. Krug Park Amusement Co.*, 208 N.W. 739, 741 (Neb. 1926), determined that to be compensable an injury caused by the elements must result from a hazard "greater than that to which the public generally is subjected." During the intervening 60 years, the Legislature has seen fit to let that consistently applied judicial interpretation of its enactment stand. The most recent application was in *McGinn v. Douglas County Social Services Admin.* . . .

The controlling rule of law is that where a judicial interpretation of a statute has not evoked a legislative amendment, it is to be presumed that the Legislature has acquiesced in the court's determination of the legislative intent. . . .

It seems to me we are not free to ignore the legislative acquiescence rule at our whim. Such a selective application of any rule is arbitrary and capricious and robs the law of the predictability it needs. . . .

The only significant thing which has changed since this court's first interpretation of the "arising out of and in the course of" language of the compensation act is the composition of this court. I respectfully submit that if the law depends upon nothing more than the predilections of those who happen to sit on this tribunal at any given time, there is no law.

The only mistake the compensation court made was to apply the law as this court had declared it to be. I would affirm.

BOSLAUGH and HASTINGS, JJ., join in this dissent.

NOTE

Is the AOE Test a Relic? A growing number of states have adopted the positional risk test. Does this mean that every injury meeting the other three tests (course of employment, injury, and accident) is compensable? Bruce Money was employed by Coin Depot Corporation as an armored truck security guard. He was required to carry a gun, with which he had a propensity to play Russian Roulette. On his last day at work, he "pulled out his gun, put a bullet in the cylinder, spun the cylinder, placed the gun against his chin, and pulled the trigger." On his second try, the gun fired and killed him instantly. The Judge of Compensation held the death was work-related, and compared the circumstances to "horseplay" cases in which the deviation from the normal course of employment can be considered minor. The appeals court in New Jersey reversed the decision. The court relied on the distinction among three categories of risk that may result in an accident arising out of employment: risks "distinctly associated" with the employment; "neutral" risks; and "personal" risks. In New Jersey, the first two types of risks are compensable, but personal risks are not. The court felt that a game of Russian Roulette represented a major deviation from the normal course of employment and thus constituted a personal risk. *Money v. Coin Depot Corp.*, 672 A.2d 751 (N.J. Super. Ct. App. Div. 1997). Under what circumstances would an accidental discharge of a gun by a guard or police officer be compensable?

3. TRADEOFFS BETWEEN TESTS ONE AND TWO

TECHNICAL TAPE CORP. v. INDUSTRIAL COMMISSION
Supreme Court of Illinois
317 N.E.2d 515 (1974)

WARD, JUSTICE:

This is a direct appeal . . . by the employer-respondent, Technical Tape Corporation, from a judgment of the circuit court of Jackson County, which affirmed an award of the Industrial Commission in favor of the employee-claimant, Terry Crain, for temporary disability, partial incapacity and permanent disfigurement under the Workmen's Compensation Act.

On January 31, 1969, Terry Crain, who was working on the three-to-eleven p.m. shift at the Technical Tape Corporation, was told to clean the residue from a glue churn. The churn was five feet long, five feet wide, and three feet deep. It had a capacity of approximately 200 gallons and was completely enclosed except for a small opening on the top. The ingredients of the glue included toluene, which is a solvent, resins, and rubber.

When the claimant came out of the churn at 10:45 p.m., after working in it for over a half hour, he testified he felt a burning sensation in his feet and legs. He also felt nauseated. The record shows that after leaving the plant at the completion of his shift the claimant drove his car erratically for about five miles and then ran a stop sign and collided with another car. He suffered a disfigurement of his left ear, a fractured skull, and a partial loss of the use of his right foot.

The only witnesses at the hearing before the arbitrator were the claimant and his father, George Crain, who also was employed at the Technical Tape Corporation. The father testified he saw Terry as he was coming out of the churn after cleaning it. He noticed that there were "two big red streaks on both sides of Terry's neck." He said that he admonished Terry for doing that work because it was his experience that employees who worked in such churns would "get so drunk [they could] hardly get out of them." He testified that at that time Terry told him that he was dizzy and felt ill.

Because he was concerned about his son's condition, George Crain attempted to see Terry again before he left for home. However, upon reaching the parking lot he heard the motor of Terry's auto roar "as loud as it would go" and saw him speed out of the parking lot. He got into his car and began to follow Terry. He said Terry drove through a four-way stop intersection without stopping and minutes later narrowly missed hitting a railroad-crossing gate that was being lowered. Terry's car would have struck the gate if the crossing guard had not quickly raised it. The gate was re-lowered and the father had to wait for a crossing train to pass. When it did he continued his pursuit of Terry. He drove about five miles and came upon the scene of the collision.

Terry Crain testified that he hardly remembered climbing from the churn. He testified that the last thing he recalled the night of the accident was "clocking out of the plant" shortly after 11 p.m. He said he did not recall anything until he awakened in a hospital two weeks later. The employer did not offer any evidence at the hearing before the arbitrator. The arbitrator found in favor of the claimant and entered an award for 20 3/7 weeks of temporary total compensation, 6 weeks of compensation for the permanent disfigurement of the left ear, 60 weeks of compensation for a fracture of the skull and 85 1/4 weeks of compensation representing 55% permanent loss of the use of the right foot.

Upon the filing of a petition for review by the employer with the Industrial Commission, the deposition of Dr. Host von Paleske, who specializes in orthopedic surgery, was admitted into evidence in behalf of the claimant. Dr. Von Paleske stated that when he examined the claimant shortly before midnight on the night of the accident it was obvious that the claimant had been exposed to a large amount of toluene, because the odor of toluene came not only from his nostrils and mouth but from his skin and hair as well. He said that exposure to toluene for a long period of time could cause dizziness and "almost a drunken-type feeling." Dr. Von Paleske said that toluene produced an effect similar to that caused by alcohol. The respondent did not offer evidence before the Commission. . . .

An injury must "arise out of" and "in the course of" employment to be compensable under the Workmen's Compensation Act.

"While the phrase 'in the course of employment' relates to the time, place and circumstances of the injury, the phrase 'arising out of the employment' refers to the requisite causal connection between the injury and the employment." In order for an injury to "arise out of" employment it must have had its origin in some risk connected with, or incidental to, the employment, so that there is a causal connection between the employment and the injury.

Professor Larson, in The Law of Workmen's Compensation, has observations which have relevance to this case. He comments:

> . . . [I]n Workmen's Compensation the controlling event is something done *to*, not *by*, the employee, and since the real question is whether this something was an industrial accident, the *origin* of the accident is crucial, and the moment of manifestation should be immaterial . . . .

> . . . [The Act] does not say that the injury must "occur" or "be manifested" or "be consummated" [*sic*] in the course of employment. It merely says that it must "arise . . . in the course of employment." "Arising" connotes origin, not completion or manifestation. If a strain occurs during employment hours which produces no symptoms, and claimant suffers a heart attack as a result sometime after working hours, the injury is compensable.

1 A. Larson, The Law of Workmen's Compensation, sec. 29.22.

Dr. Von Paleske testified here that if a person were exposed to toluene for any length of time, it would be absorbed into the blood stream, the lungs and eventually into the fatty tissues, which could "cause a feeling of dizziness, almost a drunken-type feeling." He further testified that it was obvious that the claimant had been exposed to and had absorbed a high concentration of toluene. There was uncontradicted evidence that when the claimant had finished cleaning the churn he was dizzy and sick to his stomach. He behaved erratically and then drove his car bizarrely and recklessly before he was involved in the collision.

The evidence showed that the claimant's intoxication was a result of his cleaning the churn and that the injuries sustained in the collision had their origin in the intoxication. It cannot be reasonably said that the Commission's finding that the claimant's injuries arose out of and in the course of his employment was contrary to the manifest weight of the evidence. . . .

Judgment affirmed.

NOTES

1. *Asleep at the Wheel: Variant I.* Snowbarger was required to work 86 out of a 100 hour period during an emergency created by an ice storm. He performed such tasks as cutting up trees and digging holes by hand. While driving home after leaving work at 1:00 a.m., he fell asleep. His car went over the centerline of the highway and crashed head-on into another vehicle, and he died as a result of the accident. The scene of the crash was 22 miles from his place of employment. The Supreme Court of Missouri awarded benefits to his dependents. The court held there was an exception to the statutory language narrowly defining the course of employment because the deceased "encountered an abnormal exposure to an employment related peril" as a result of the unusually long overtime hours he had worked. *Snowbarger v. Tri-County Electric Cooperative*, 793 S.W.2d 348 (Mo. 1990).

2. *Asleep at the Wheel: Variant II.* Theurer worked his normal shift from 3:30 to 8:00 p.m. Then, in order to make some extra money, he voluntarily worked from midnight until 8:21 a.m. While driving home after leaving work, he fell asleep. His car went over the centerline of the highway and crashed head-on into another vehicle, and he died as a result of the accident. The plaintiff, who was Theurer's mother, filed a wrongful death action alleging that the defendant negligently caused Theurer's death. The defendant argued that Theurer's injury and resulting death were compensable under the workers' compensation law, and therefore the negligence suit was barred by the exclusive remedy provision. The defendant argued that an injury does not have to satisfy both traditional requirements of "arising out of" and "in the course of" in order to be compensable. Instead, the defendant argued, the AOE and COE requirements are merged into a single concept of "work-connection" and, if a sufficient nexus exists between the accident and the employment, any resulting injury is "work-connected," and therefore is compensable. The Supreme Court of Oregon rejected the argument. The court stated that, even though it had adopted the work-connected test, nonetheless both the AOE and COE elements of the compensability test must be satisfied to some degree. In this case, the factors supporting the AOE requirement were strong, but the court found that the COE requirement was not satisfied at all because Theurer had completed his work and was returning home at the time of his death, bringing his commute squarely within the going and coming rule. Since the COE test was not met, his mother was not entitled to workers' compensation benefits, and therefore the exclusivity provisions of the workers' compensation law did not bar her wrongful death action. *Krushwitz v. McDonald's Restaurants, Inc.*, 919 P.2d 465 (Or. 1996).

3. *Is Fungibility a Virtue?* One interpretation of *Technical Tape*, *Snowbarger*, and *Krushwitz* is that a "strong" case for the AOE test will offset a "weak" case for the COE test. Presumably the converse could also be true: a compelling COE case could offset a questionable AOE case. Such flexibility will allow some workers to receive workers' compensation benefits when their disabilities are evidently caused by the workplace, but the facts do not satisfy the normal requirements for one of the tests for compensability. But such flexibility may lead to greater uncertainty and more litigation if — instead of two independent tests with reasonably well-defined legal doctrines — there are now two tests that relate to each other in an unpredictable way.

4. TEST THREE: ACCIDENT

MATTHEWS v. R.T. ALLEN & SONS
Supreme Judicial Court of Maine
266 A.2d 240 (1970)

WEATHERBEE, JUSTICE.

The Petitioner, a 43 year old woods-worker, testified that on November 13, 1967 he was employed loading pulpwood onto trucks by hand. He had worked at this since 7:00 A.M. and the lifting evidently involved bending and straightening the back. The sticks were four feet long and from four inches to two feet in diameter. At about 10:30 or 11:00 A.M. he felt pain in his back but he continued to work. During his noon lunch period while he ate his lunch in the truck, the pain became worse. He worked one to one and a half hours after lunch at which time the pain was so great that he reported to his employer that he was unable to continue and went home. During the next four days the back pain continued to increase in severity and he could not go to work. On November 18 he was admitted to the Maine Coast Memorial Hospital in Ellsworth and on December 10 he was transferred to the Maine Medical Center in Portland where a herniated disc was removed. He returned to work the first of May, 1968.

On cross-examination he testified that the pain began that morning gradually and was not associated with any "specific lifting, slipping or tripping." He admitted he had told an insurance company investigator that the pain came on while he was sitting in the truck at noon but he testified that he had noticed the pain while working that morning. ". . . [B]ut when I first noticed it why it didn't bother me to lift or anything. It was after when I started to straighten up to pull myself back." At noon it had become worse. He agreed that he told the doctors that the pain came on gradually and "got worse and worse and worse" as he worked. He also said that on previous occasions while doing woods work he had had low back pains but they were never disabling.

The doctors' reports and hospital discharge summaries add only that the Petitioner had been admitted to the Ellsworth hospital suffering such severe pain that he "could hardly move." During the next four days the pain increased in severity and also radiated down into his left leg and foot. After two weeks of conservative treatment his condition had only worsened. A myelogram showed a defect in the L4-5 interspace on the left and surgery disclosed an acutely herniated disc in that area, which was removed.

The doctors' reports expressed no opinion as to the precipitating cause of the injury, whether it may have developed prior to November 13, 1967 or, if so, whether the exertion of November 13 may have aggravated the condition except for one significant comment to be discussed later.

The Commissioner found:

> The evidence, we find, is insufficient to support a finding that Mr. Matthews sustained a personal injury by accident arising out of and in the course of his employment. We cannot conclude from the testimony that the disc condition which disabled him on November 13, 1967, resulted from any single episode, or traumatic incident. The medical history given by Mr. Matthews and his testimony on cross examination, indicate that the symptoms of the underlying disc condition became disabling on November 13, 1967, but that the herniated disc had developed prior to that time — probably gradually. It is our decision that the petition must be dismissed.

Our own findings lead us to an opposite conclusion.

The Petitioner has the burden of proving that he suffered a personal injury by accident arising out of and in the course of his employment.

The Workmen's Compensation Law represents a relatively recent concept of responsibility without negligence. While the early cases usually concerned accidental injuries where an external force was applied to an external portion of the body, our own Court decided early in the development of our law that the term injury by accident includes incidents where internal parts of the physical structure break down under external force, including the stress of labor. While this may more dramatically occur as a result of a slip, a fall or a single unusual strained effort, we have found other such internal break-downs to have resulted from the usual work which the workman was performing in his usual, normal way. In short, we have construed the term "accident" to include not only injuries which are the results of accidents but also injuries which are themselves accidents. In *Brown's Case*, 123 A. 421 (Me. 1924) a fatal heart dilation resulted from the exertion of shoveling snow. In *Patrick v. J.B. Ham Co.*, 111 A. 912 (Me. 1921) the Petitioner's husband suffered a cerebral hemorrhage while performing his regular duties of lifting sacks of grain. In *Taylor's Case*, 142 A. 730 (Me. 1928) the Petitioner's husband had been lifting heavy objects in the course of his usual work and a particularly vigorous straining caused a pulmonary embolism.

This position is in agreement with that taken by the great majority of American jurisdictions and follows the rule recognized in England which in many respects furnished the model for our own Act. In England the Courts soon came to hold that an unexpected, unforeseen or unintended result from usual or customary exertion constitutes an injury by accident even though there is no unexpected or fortuitous cause.

In some of the earlier decisions holding that the breaking down of internal parts might be accidents under the statute, the death or incapacity occurred suddenly as the internal part dramatically gave way. This furnished another similarity to the usual concept of accident occurring when an external force is applied violently to an external part and assisted this Court in arriving at its conclusion that the Legislature intended both situations to be considered industrial accidents. "If a laborer performing his usual task, in his wonted way, by reason of strain, breaks his wrist, nobody would question the accidental nature of the injury. If instead of the wrist it is an artery that breaks, the occurrence is just as clearly an accident." Certainly the sudden quality of a mishap often makes it more clearly distinguishable from the mere malfunctioning of an organ which develops through natural progression, unrelated to the employment.

This thinking led our Court in early decisions to describe an accidental injury as being "unusual, undesigned, unexpected, sudden" (*Brown's Case, supra,* where the employee "suddenly became dizzy, faint and short of breath" while shoveling snow). As recently as in *Bernier v. Cola-Cola Bottling Plants, Inc.,* 250 A.2d 820 (Me. 1969) in pointing out that the Petitioner need not prove that his back strain resulted from "any unusual slip, fall, etc., in other words, external injury" we quoted *Brown's Case* to hold that "an internal injury that is itself sudden, unusual, and unexpected is none the less accidental because its external cause is a part of the victim's ordinary work."

This is not to say, however, that the internal accident must have demonstrated itself by a sudden, dramatic effect upon the victim.

In *Taylor's Case* the victim continued work until noontime when for the first time he complained of pain in his chest. He continued to work, although with difficulty, that afternoon but his condition worsened and he died some ten days later. It will be noted that this Court then stated the rule to be that

> . . . [I]f the strain were not accidental, it is the unusual, undesigned, unexpected *or* sudden results of the strain, not necessarily the strain itself, which make the accidental injury necessary under the law. (Emphasis added.)

We concur in the statement found in 58 Am. Jur., Workmen's Compensation § 196:

> While the concept of accident is ordinarily understood as embodying a certain degree of element of suddenness in the occurrence of the event, and is frequently so defined, it is not always required that the occurrence be instantaneous.

In our present case there is a dearth of medical opinion that might assist us regarding the probable onset of the Petitioner's disabling condition. We are not told how soon pain and disability would be expected to follow the herniation of an intervertebral disc. However, as valuable as medical opinion is, it is not always essential, and sound and rational conclusions in Workmen's Compensation matters may often be drawn from facts proven and inferences to be logically drawn therefrom although lacking the support of expert opinion. . . .

We find no significant dispute in the testimony. It reveals a 43 year old woods-worker who had had low back pains in the past, usually associated with his work, but never to the extent of being disabling. On this occasion the pain began while he was loading sticks of pulpwood, some very heavy. He continued to work several hours while the pain got "worse and worse and worse." After he stopped working the pain continued to increase in severity and to extend in area until relieved by surgery. Surgery disclosed that an extruding mass from the ruptured disc was pressing against the nerve and obviously bowing it outward and upward. . . .

We are called upon to decide whether Petitioner's disability, hospitalization and surgery were casually connected with his activities while loading pulpwood that November 13. Whether Petitioner's disc ruptured abruptly the morning of November 13 or whether the defective condition developed gradually during his previous episodes of low back pain is not controlling here. The scanty facts presented to us lead us to the conclusion that in either case the heavy labor of November 13 constituted the critical episode which completely incapacitated the man with increasing and unrelieved crippling pain until surgery removed the ruptured part.

While we do not know the moment when the actual herniation occurred its causal connection with the labor of November 13 seems apparent. In other words the personal injury appears either to have been caused by the exertions of November 13 or aggravated by them. We have repeatedly held that if stress of labor aggravates or accelerates the development of a preexisting infirmity causing an internal breakdown of that part of the structure a personal injury by accident occurs. The point is dramatized by the language of the Court in *Lachance's Case*, 118 A. 370, 372 (Me. 1922):

> If Lachance, but for the hurt, would not have died at the time at which, and in the way in which, he did die, then, within the meaning of the Workmen's Act, the unfortunate occurrence, though it merely hastened a deep-seated disorder to destiny, must be held to have resulted in an injury causing death.

Although neither the Ellsworth orthopedic surgeon who originally treated Petitioner nor the Portland neuro-surgeon who performed the surgery was called to testify, the orthopedic surgeon (who also assisted in the operation) commented tersely in his written report:

> Unfortunately, after the pain had developed he continued to work until the job was completed.

We infer from this that it was his opinion that Petitioner's exertion in loading the trucks at least contributed to his disability and to his need for surgery.

We find that Petitioner sustained a personal injury by accident arising out of and in the course of his employment on November 13, 1967.

Appeal sustained.

NOTES

1. *Accident Test Expanded.* Analytically, the "accident" test consists of four components:

    I. Unexpectedness

        A. Of Cause

        B. Of Result

    II. Definite Time

        A. Of Cause

        B. Of Result

To illustrate the meaning of these tests, if a court requires the unexpectedness to apply to the cause of the injury, then a worker who is injured because a machine falls on him can receive compensation, while compensation will be denied to a worker who is performing her normal duties of carrying heavy wheat sacks and suffers a heart attack, even though medical evidence confirms the attack was caused by heavy lifting. However, if the court says that the unexpected aspect of the accident requirement can be met by the nature of the result, then the heart attack caused by the normal but strenuous lifting would be compensable.

A similar two-way distinction applies to the requirement of a definite time or event. The cause may be gradual and the result precisely distinguishable, such as dust poisoning that causes a sudden collapse of a lung. Or the etiology may be easily specified, such as a fall into the river, while the pathology may intermittently progress to pneumonia. Again, the compensability of the lung collapse or the pneumonia depends on whether the court is looking for a definite time that can be assigned to the cause, the result, or both.

If both aspects of both the unexpectedness and the definite time requirements are met, such as might occur in an explosion, then the case for compensability is the clearest. The opposite extreme is the typical occupational disease, where all the elements are lacking. The problems posed by occupational diseases are examined in more detail in a later section.

2. *A Jaundiced View of the Accident Test.* THE REPORT OF THE NATIONAL COMMISSION ON STATE WORKMEN'S COMPENSATION LAWS 49 (1972) provided this analysis of the accident test:

> An "accident" has frequently been defined as a sudden unexpected event, determinate as to time and place. The "accident" requirement has been a bar to compensability, especially in the past, because of failure in a particular case to meet one or more requirements in this definition. Compensation, for example, has been denied when nothing unexpected or unusual occurred. If a man strained his back while doing regular work in the usual fashion, it was to be expected.

> This narrow interpretation of "accident" has to a large extent been discarded. Where it persists, it is undesirable as it serves to bar compensation for injuries that are clearly work-related.

> There should be no legal impediments to full coverage of all injuries which are work related.

We recommend that the "accident" requirement be dropped as a test for compensability.

5. TEST FOUR: PERSONAL INJURY

The injury test can be conceptualized as the two-by-two matrix shown in Figure 22-2:

Figure 22-2
The Injury Test Matrix

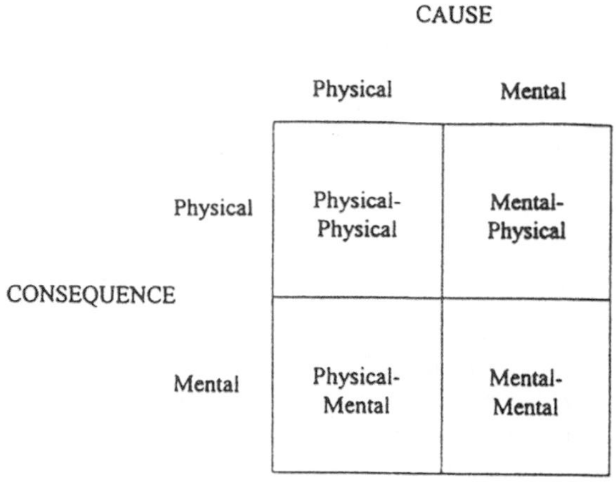

CAUSE

	Physical	Mental
Physical	Physical-Physical	Mental-Physical
Mental	Physical-Mental	Mental-Mental

CONSEQUENCE

The injury test will be met when both the cause and the effect of the personal harm are physical: the "physical-physical" case. (The ballerina loses her toe because the theater scaffolding collapses.) Likewise, the injury test will be satisfied in almost all jurisdictions when the cause is physical and the result is both physical and mental: the "physical-mental" case. (The ballerina injures her toe when the scaffolding collapses and suffers a mental breakdown when she realizes that her career is over.) Similarly, most states hold the injury test to be satisfied when the mental cause leads to a physical consequence: the "mental-physical" case. (The ballerina is humiliated by the dance company director and slashes off her toes in a rage.) The most problematic cases are those that involve both a mental cause and a mental consequence: the "mental-mental" case. (The ballerina is humiliated by the dance company director and thinks about slashing off her toes, but instead suffers a mental collapse.) Some states deal with such cases as injuries and some as diseases: we return to these mental-mental cases in a later section after we introduce the complications of compensating work-related diseases.

NOTE

Cause and Consequence for Whom? Ohio will compensate stress or other mental disorders so long as there is a physical cause or a physical consequence of the mental condition, but will not provide compensation when the claim involves both a mental cause and a mental consequence. Bailey accidentally ran over and killed a co-worker and as a result was severely depressed. The Industrial Commission denied benefits because Bailey had not experienced a physical injury that led to his depression. On appeal, the Ohio Supreme Court said that the legislature had limited claims for psychiatric conditions to situations resulting from an injury or disease, but the legislature had never said that the injury had to involve the same person who was affected by the mental disorder. Under the circumstances, the court concluded that the legislature intended to allow compensation for the mental condition. *Bailey v. Republic Eng'g Steels, Inc.*, 741 N.E.2d 121 (Ohio 2001).

E.   WHICH DISEASES ARE COMPENSABLE?

TISCO INTERMOUNTAIN v. INDUSTRIAL COMMISSION
Supreme Court of Utah
744 P.2d 1340 (1987)

HALL, CHIEF JUSTICE:

Plaintiffs challenge the award of death benefits made to defendant Jean B. Werner under the provisions of the Utah Occupational Disease Disability Law.

Defendant Jean B. Werner is the widow of George Jakob Werner. Mr. Werner had been employed since 1947 as an insulation mechanic. Most insulation was asbestos-based until 1971, when the federal government banned the use of asbestos in insulation. Thus, Mr. Werner was continuously exposed to asbestos from 1947 until at least 1971. In 1977, Mr. Werner formed his own insulation company, Tisco Intermountain ("Tisco").

In December 1981, Mr. Werner noticed that his stomach was distended, his navel was red, and he was very tired. In February or March 1982, he sought medical treatment. In June 1982, he underwent surgery on his stomach, at which time a malignant tumor was found. Thereafter, he underwent chemotherapy, but died in January 1983 from complications attendant to peritoneal mesothelioma.

Mrs. Werner made a claim for death benefits under the Occupational Disease Disability Law, alleging that Mr. Werner developed cancer and died as a result of exposure to asbestos during the course of his employment with Tisco. The administrative law judge found that Mr. Werner was injuriously exposed to asbestos during the course of his employment with Tisco and that Mrs. Werner was therefore entitled to death benefits.

Plaintiffs filed a motion for review of the administrative law judge's order. The motion was denied by the Industrial Commission, and a final order was entered.

Plaintiffs' first point on appeal is that the Commission abused its discretion in awarding death benefits under the Occupational Disease Disability Law because there was no substantial credible evidence of exposure to asbestos during the deceased employee's period of employment with the employer against whom the award was made. It was undisputed that Mr. Werner was exposed to asbestos from 1947 until 1971. However, any claim against Mr. Werner's employers during that period was barred by the statute of limitations set forth in Utah Code Ann. § 35-2-13(b)(4) (1974). Furthermore, Utah Code Ann. § 35-2-14 (1974) states: "The only employer liable shall be the employer in whose employment the employee was last injuriously exposed to the hazards of such disease . . . ."

The record, viewed in its entirety, does not contain sufficient evidence to support the conclusion that Mr. Werner was "last injuriously exposed" to asbestos while at Tisco. Only three witnesses were called, Mrs. Werner, Joseph Collins, and Darrell Kinder. Each witness recounted the many years Mr. Werner was employed as a mechanic by various insulation contractors and the frequent exposure he had to asbestos products prior to 1968 or 1969, when he accepted an office position with Mountain States Insulation. None of the witnesses related any specific exposure that Mr. Werner had to asbestos products from 1971 until his death. Rather, they spoke only in very general terms.

When asked if she had any knowledge of the insulation products used by Tisco, Mrs. Werner responded: "Not an awfully lot. I know that it was the kind they had — it was not the kind that they had used prior or previously because it had been outlawed, more or less, and so you had to go into new forms . . . ." In response to the next question, whether the insulation material used by Tisco had an asbestos base, Mrs. Werner unequivocally stated that it did not.

Collins testified that transite pipe composed of one-half cement and one-half asbestos was utilized in the industry as a substitute for asbestos-based insulation used prior to 1971. When asked whether Mr. Werner ever engaged in an operation that included the cutting of transite pipe or sheets, his response was: "I personally never seen him, but knowing it was part of the trade and we all did it at one time or another, I'd have to say yes." When asked if he knew whether Mr. Werner used transite material in his business at Tisco, Collins responded that he did not.

Kinder's testimony reiterated the exposure Mr. Werner had to asbestos on various jobs through 1970. However, he expressed no knowledge of any such exposure at Tisco. He simply stated that he was aware that Tisco was engaged in the insulation business. . . .

The medical issues were submitted to a medical panel, which concluded that the delay between first exposure to asbestos and the development of malignant mesothelioma can range from fifteen to twenty years. Any latency period less than fifteen years would cast doubt on the relationship of the disease to a particular occupational or environmental exposure. If fifteen years is accepted as the minimal latency period prior to development of malignant mesothelioma, Mr. Werner's exposures prior to 1968 were the main cause for his terminal condition. In theory, a cessation of exposure in 1968 may have decreased the risk for his development of the malignant mesothelioma. . . .

The administrative law judge acknowledged in his findings that in the absence of evidence that Mr. Werner was injuriously exposed to asbestos at Tisco, Mrs. Werner's claim would fail since section 35-2-13 of the Occupational

Disease Disability Law requires in subsection (b)(4) that in the absence of exceptions not relevant here, death from an occupational disease must result within three years from the last date on which the employee actually worked for the employer against whom benefits are claimed. Application of section 35-2-14 in this case would require that a claim be made against Mountain States Insulation, which claim would be barred since Mr. Werner last worked there in 1976.

Faced with such harsh circumstances, the administrative law judge strained to fashion a remedy. The following passage is extracted from his findings:

> Recognizing this insufficiency of remedy with respect to asbestos cases, and resolving the doubt in favor of the applicant and in favor of coverage, I find that George Jakob Werner was injuriously exposed to the hazards of asbestos while employed by the defendant Tisco Intermountain, Inc.

Policy considerations in workers' compensation cases dictate that statutes should be liberally construed in favor of an award. However, policy considerations have no application in the absence of any evidence to support an award, nor can they be used to controvert the clear meaning of the statutory requirements upon which an award must be based.

In the instant case, it clearly appears that the award of benefits is unsupported by substantial credible evidence, and that is the standard this court must apply. In awarding benefits, the administrative law judge also ignored competent medical evidence that negatives a finding of medical causation. . . .

The award of benefits is vacated and set aside. No costs awarded.

STEWART, ASSOCIATE C.J., and DURHAM and ZIMMERMAN, JJ., concur.

HOWE, J., dissents.

NOTES

1. *The Continuing Vitality of the Statute of Limitations.* During his employment with Gulf Oil, Kenneth Cable was periodically exposed to the carcinogens coumene and benzene, most recently in July 1981. He was no longer employed by Gulf Oil after March 1983. In July 1988, he was diagnosed with bladder cancer and was advised that the cause was his exposure to coumene and benzene. The manifestation of the cancer occurred less than 300 weeks after he ended his employment with Gulf, but more than 300 weeks after his last exposure to the carcinogens. The Pennsylvania workers' compensation act provides, in part, that "whenever occupational disease is the basis for compensation, for disability or death under this act, it shall apply only to disability or death resulting from such disease and occurring within three hundred weeks after the last date of employment in an occupation or industry to [sic] which he was exposed to hazards of such disease . . . ." 77 PA. CONS. STAT. § 411(2). The Supreme Court of Pennsylvania held the cancer was not compensable because the relevant employment for the statute of limitations is the employment in which the employee was exposed to the coumene and benzene, not the subsequent employment with the employer in which he was not exposed to the carcinogens. *Cable v. Workmen's Comp. Appeal Bd.*, 664 A.2d 1349 (Pa. 1995).

The statue of limitations also adversely affected construction workers in Connecticut, who were exposed to toxic chemicals, including benzene, while building a plant in 1999 but who did not become ill or die until 2004. Ronald Nobili, president of the union local, said "The statute says that a person has one year from the date of the incident to file a claim. The problem is that this kind of cancer has a five-year latency period." Frank Juliano, *Workers' Comp Claims Being Rejected — Chemical Exposure Claims Lead to Rejections — Workers Had 1 Year to File*, CONN. POST, Dec. 13, 2004.

2. *A Humane Alternative.* The *Cable* and *Tisco Intermountain* cases and the Connecticut news account provide examples of how a long latency period for a work-related disease can interact with a restrictive statute of limitations to defeat a claim for workers' compensation benefits. Workers in Connecticut, Utah, and Pennsylvania who are exposed to toxic substances should be advised to die quickly. A more humane alternative would be for these states to adopt statutes of limitations that run from the date of impairment or disability rather than from the date of last exposure.

3. *Scheduled Diseases.* The accident test served to bar compensation for many work-related diseases. Although many diseases contracted as a result of sudden unexpected exposure were held to be compensable, e.g., pneumonia contracted while working in a sudden storm, compensation sometimes was denied for diseases associated with chronic exposure to adverse agents at the workplace. An example where benefits were denied because the worker did not meet the accident test is *Combes v. Industrial Special Indemnity*, 20 P.3d 689 (Idaho 2000). Combes aggravated a preexisting but non-disabling condition of asthma by gradual exposure to dust, pollen, and animal dander over a three- to six-month period. As result, Combes was permanently and totally disabled. The court ruled that Combes did not meet the accident requirement for occupational diseases because there was no single traumatic event that led to his disability.

Many states responded to the problems caused by use of the accident test by adding to their statutes a list or schedule of compensable occupational diseases resulting from exposures to toxic substances. An example of such a schedule is Section 3(2) of the New York workers' compensation law, which is included in the Statutory Supplement. There are 29 specific diseases with associated processes, ranging from Anthrax resulting from handling of wool, hair, bristles, hides, or skins to Silicosis or other dust diseases resulting from any process involving exposure to silica or other harmful dust. While the schedules of compensable diseases help those workers whose diseases are included, the schedules in most workers' compensation statutes are typically obsolete in terms of current medical knowledge.

4. *Other Occupational Diseases.* All state workers' compensation laws that contain a schedule of occupation diseases now contain a residual category providing for coverage of other occupational diseases. For example, Section 3(2) of the New York workers' compensation statute provides as a 30th category of coverage: "Any and all occupational diseases." In addition, Section 48 of the New York statute (also included in the Statutory Supplement) in effect provides that a disease not covered by Section 3(2) is compensable if the disease meets the statutory definition of an accidental personal injury. Among the 29 diseases specifically enumerated in the statute, the residual category covering all occupational diseases, and the Section 48 safeguard for other diseases, universal coverage of work-related diseases might be expected in New York. However, the "any and all occupational diseases" category has been interpreted by the New York courts to only apply to diseases that result from some unusual aspect of the job. Thus a moderate amount of temperature change commonly found outside work or in other jobs that nonetheless led to splotches on the legs of a theatre ticket seller was held not to be compensable in *Goldberg v. 954 March Corp.*, 276 N.Y. 313 (1938).

5. *The New York Tangle.* The effect of the restrictive interpretation of "any and all occupational diseases" in New York is not a historical curiosity. Rudy Washington, Deputy Mayor of New York City on September 11, 2001, rushed to the World Trade Center after the planes struck the building and spent considerable time at the site for weeks afterwards. He subsequently developed severe respiratory ailments and filed a claim for workers' compensation benefits in December 2004. In March 2006, a workers' compensation ALJ ruled that Washington was entitled to health care benefits because he had been injured on the job. The next month, however, lawyers for the city appealed, arguing that he was not entitled to benefits because he did not file his claim within two years of the injury. After a spate of news accounts, Mayor Michael Bloomberg intervened on Washington's behalf and the appeal was withdrawn. Sewell Chan, *City Workers' 9/11 Claims Meet Obstacles*, N.Y. TIMES, May 22, 2006, at B1. Legislation was subsequently enacted in New York applicable to "a participant in World Trade Center rescue, recovery or clean-up operations" that extended the statute of limitations to allow claims filed within two years after (1) the participant was disabled from a qualifying condition or (2) the participant knew or should have know that the qualifying condition was causally related to his or her participation in the rescue, recovery, and clean-up operations, whichever is the later date.

The Rudy Washington case was caused by several features of the New York workers' compensation statute. (1) The list of 29 occupational diseases specifically enumerated in § 3(2) of the workers' compensation statute is quite restrictive (e.g., byssinoises caused by any process involving exposure to raw cotton). (2) The residual category of "any and all occupational diseases" has been interpreted to require the disease to be produced as "the natural incident of a particular occupation." Washington did not meet this test because a respiratory disease is not a natural consequence of being a Deputy Mayor. (3) Since Washington did not have a compensable disease, he was required to establish his eligibility for workers' compensation benefits by demonstrating that his disability resulted from an accidental injury, which he was able to do. (4) The statute of limitations for an occupational disease is two years from disablement or after the claimant knew or should have known that disease is due to the nature of the employment. However, Washington did not have an occupational disease as defined in the New York statute, so he could not use this statute of limitation. (5) The statute of limitation for injury is two years from the date of the injury. Since more than two years passed between September

11, 2001 and December, 2004, when Washington filed his claim, he did not qualify for benefits.

Rudy Washington was rescued from this tangle of requirements by the intervention of a benevolent Mayor. Other participants in the rescue, recover, and clean-up operations from 9/11 were rescued by the special legislation. Should this legislation have been confined to these participants, or should all New York workers who experience work-related diseases that do not meet the state's definition of occupational disease have been included in the legislation?

6. *How Inclusive of Occupational Diseases Are Workers' Compensation Programs?* A 2004 study used a three-stage process to estimate the coverage of occupational diseases by workers' compensation programs. J. Paul Leigh & John A. Robbins, *Occupational Disease and Workers' Compensation: Coverage, Costs, and Consequences*, 82 MILLBANK Q. 689 (2004). First, they used epidemiological data from the medical literature to estimate the deaths and medical costs associated with occupational diseases. Second, they used data from state workers' compensation agencies to estimate the number of cases and deaths attributed to occupational diseases covered by the program and the costs of those diseases. Third, the results of the first two stages were compared to estimate the amount workers' compensation under-compensated occupational diseases and the extent of the costs shifted from workers' compensation to other sources of support.

The comparison indicated that workers' compensation programs did not compensate 98.9 percent of the deaths due to occupational diseases in 1999, with a range of estimates from 91.9 percent to 99.9 percent. They also concluded that workers and their families probably bear the greatest share of the direct costs of occupational diseases. Other bearers of the medical costs not paid for by workers' compensation include private health insurance, Medicaid, and Medicare.

F. INJURIES AND DISEASES FOR WHICH COMPENSABILITY IS PROBLEMATIC

Workplace stress, which is examined in this section, is an example of a condition for which the determination of compensability is most vexing. Other similar conditions not examined here include cumulative trauma (including carpel tunnel syndrome), back disorders, respiratory diseases, heart disease, and many types of cancers.

There are several common characteristics of these maladies. First, workers' compensation law sometimes treats these conditions as injuries, sometimes as diseases, and sometimes as both. Second, the troublesome cases typically involve injuries or diseases resulting from an interaction of congenital, degenerative, work-related, and/or personal lifestyle factors. Third, the symptoms may include subjective complaints ("my back hurts") in addition to (or instead of) "objective" medical evidence (the MRI reveals a physical abnormality in the back). Fourth, there often are competing medical theories (and almost always competing medical testimony in serious cases) about the cause of the worker's disorder. Fifth, the legal rules used to decide whether a condition is work-related often are inconsistent with prevailing medical opinions about causation.

A sixth common characteristic of these conditions pertains to disabilities that result from the interaction of old (or underlying) medical problems and a new work-related accident or exposure. The traditional legal doctrine pertaining to disability resulting from a workplace accident or exposure interacting with a preexisting medical problem that has not previously limited the worker's performance at work is that the employer is responsible for the entire resulting disability. The doctrine is often summarized as: "the employer takes the worker as it finds her."

A seventh characteristic is that many states amended their workers' compensation laws in the 1990s to make it more difficult for workers with these conditions to satisfy the legal requirements for compensability. Several approaches to constricting compensability are examined in this section.

1. WORKPLACE STRESS

CHICAGO BOARD OF EDUCATION v. INDUSTRIAL COMMISSION
Appellate Court of Illinois
523 N.E.2d 912, *appeal denied*, 530 N.E.2d 241 (Ill. 1988)

JUSTICE MCCULLOUGH delivered the opinion of the court:

. . . .

Claimant, a 56-year-old school teacher, was employed by respondent from June 1967 to June 1978 and was assigned exclusively to the Hefferen Elementary School where he taught a variety of subjects. In September 1978, instead of returning to his teaching duties after the summer recess, claimant sought treatment at the Portage-Cragin Mental Health Center where he was counseled on a weekly basis by Deborah Gessner, a psychiatric social worker. Claimant took a 25-month leave of absence from the Chicago Board of Education (Board) and except for tutoring a blind student and selling hot dogs for a short time was not gainfully employed during that period. He applied for reinstatement to his teaching position in January 1981 but was rejected because he failed a psychiatric evaluation conducted by respondent's psychiatrist.

At the hearing before the arbitrator, Deborah Gessner testified she counseled claimant for a "great psychological debilitation" which she stated was caused by the gradual deterioration of claimant's work environment, chaos in the classroom, lack of support from the administration, physical assault by students, inability to comply with school regulations, unmanageable students, inability to control the classroom, and physical isolation in a mobile classroom detached from the main school facility. Gessner testified claimant's condition was a reactive depression characterized by feelings of hopelessness, failure and inadequacy emanating from claimant's work environment.

On cross-examination, Gessner discounted claimant's childhood experiences and the fact he had been hospitalized for psychiatric care while in the Army in 1944 as factors in claimant's present condition of ill-being. Gessner also believed claimant had a stable marital and family relationship with his wife and children which was not a source of claimant's depression. . . .

Petitioner testified extensively concerning incidents of stress, assaults, and injuries he received in the course of his teaching duties. On March 4, 1974, while unloading teaching materials from his car, which he was forced to remove from a mobile classroom each evening because of vandalism, claimant was struck on his right shoulder by a piece of concrete.

On March 18, 1974, while performing the same task, he was robbed at knife point by three men. While cooperating with police in the investigation of this crime, he received an anonymous phone call directing him to drop the investigation.

On April 3, 1974, a female student engaged in a fight with another student, kicked and scratched him when he attempted to intervene.

On May 9, 1974, he was kicked and bitten by a student who was engaged in a fistfight.

On the last day of school in 1973 claimant was chased from the school yard by 12 to 15 students and was struck in the back with a rock. . . .

On January 5, 1976, while in the main school building, after school hours, claimant saw a boy lying on the floor and went to his aid. Claimant testified the child was faking injury and pushed claimant causing him to fall and injure his back.

On January 5, 1978, a violent fight broke out between two boys in the classroom. While intervening, one child grabbed claimant's arm and struck it on a table. His right elbow was injured requiring medical attention, including a brace and sling. Claimant is still treated for the injury to his elbow and his back which he reinjured on October 25, 1977, while moving books at the direction of the principal.

Claimant also testified to a variety of working conditions which exacerbated his problems. In 1976 the school board made a change in the duties of teachers requiring more paperwork. Claimant maintained he spent two to four hours each night keeping up with the additional reports he was required to prepare. He had continuous difficulty keeping discipline in the classroom because of the nature of the students being taught and although unruly children were sent to the principal's office, they were often returned to the classroom without being disciplined or counseled. Claimant maintained this was a violation of the union contract.

Claimant was also a member of the teacher professional and problem committee, a group of faculty members who submitted problems to the principal. Claimant testified the principal did not resolve faculty complaints about increased paperwork and discipline.

Claimant also maintained the principal was abusive to him, citing a September 1976 incident when the principal yelled at him and cursed him for being late and leaving his class unattended for several minutes while the class went to recess. This incident occurred on the playground in full view of the entire school and claimant stated he felt humiliated.

In May 1978, claimant testified a female student was brought to his classroom and placed there for the remainder of the school year. The student had just broken the leg of another teacher by striking her with a chair. Although claimant objected to the inclusion of the student in his class, he was told there was nothing he could do about it. The child was violent and refused to do any work for the remainder of the school year.

Claimant testified he could not return to teaching in the fall of 1978 because he could not face the assignment citing, in particular, the incident in which his arm was injured which affected his ability to do his job because he was right-handed. He also found stressful the 1978 incident in which the female student was assigned to his class.

On cross-examination, claimant stated he grew up in a poor family and was raised by his mother after his father disappeared. He admitted being discharged from the Army because of psychiatric problems manifesting themselves in outbursts of crying and tremors. . . .

Claimant admitted he did not have many friends and separated from his family in April 1979 because he was continually fighting with his wife and children. He denied any physical altercations occurred, however. He stated he moved out of the house to find a calmer atmosphere at the suggestion of one of his psychologists. He became upset when his teenage daughter brought friends to the house and caused a commotion. He was also disturbed by his adult son who lived at home and made noise playing the stereo. He denied telling a psychiatrist he and his wife engaged in physical fights. He also admitted that from 1970 through 1977 he received excellent ratings on his teacher evaluations, the second highest rating a teacher could achieve. . . .

As we have indicated, the arbitrator and Commission awarded benefits under the Occupational Diseases Act.

On appeal, the issue is whether claimant established he was exposed to the hazards of or sustained an injury from an occupational disease. Section 1(d) of the Occupational Diseases Act states in pertinent part:

> In this Act the term "Occupational Disease" means a disease arising out of and in the course of the employment or which has become aggravated and rendered disabling as a result of the exposure of the employment. Such aggravation shall arise out of a risk peculiar to or increased by the employment and not common to the general public. A disease shall be deemed to arise out of the employment if there is apparent to the rational mind, upon consideration of all the circumstances, a causal connection between the conditions under which the work is performed and the occupational disease. The disease need not to have been foreseen or expected but after its contraction it must appear to have had its origin or aggravation in a risk connected with the employment and to have flowed from that source as a rational consequence.

On appeal, respondent argues claimant has not established he suffers from an occupational disease within the meaning of the act and, alternatively, the Commission's decision to award compensation is against the manifest weight of the evidence. Relying upon *Pathfinder Co. v. Industrial Comm'n* (1976), 343

N.E.2d 913, and *Peoria County Belwood Nursing Home v. Industrial Comm'n* (1987), 505 N.E.2d 1026, claimant maintains compensation is available under the Occupational Diseases Act for mental disorders suffered in the absence of physical trauma or injury which develop gradually over a period of time without the necessity of finding that the injury occurred as a result of specific incidents traceable to a definite time, place, and cause.

The first issue we must resolve is whether on-the-job mental stress which results in emotional illness in the absence of physical trauma and sudden disablement traceable to a definite time, place, or cause is compensable under the Occupational Diseases Act. The language employed in the opening paragraph of section 1(d) of our Occupational Diseases Act speaks of diseases a worker is exposed to on the job causing disability as a result of that exposure. On-the-job stress, of itself, is not a disease. Events and conditions capable of producing stress exist in every employment environment. Stress occasioned in reaction to employment demands may, in turn, cause mental disorders. Whether mental illness qualifies as an occupational disease depends upon whether the employee can establish the risk to which he was exposed arose out of and in the course of his employment and has a clear causal relationship to the disability suffered. Under our diseases act the disease must flow from that risk as a rational consequence.

The causal connection between claimant's mental disability and the gradual mental stimuli which allegedly produced the disease is not readily apparent. Whereas the rational mind can perceive a clear connection between exposure to asbestos and the subsequent contraction of asbestosis, for instance, there is a much more tenuous link in a situation where a person suffers a gradually developing mental disability which, in retrospect, is attributed to factors such as worry, anxiety, tension, pressure, and overwork without proof of a specific time, place, and event producing the disability.

To recognize that our occupational disease law would allow compensation for any mental diseases and disorders caused by on-the-job stressful events or conditions would, in the words of one court, open a floodgate for workers who succumb to the everyday pressures of life. We reject claimant's argument the supreme court opinion in *Pathfinder* supports such a result. There, the supreme court, mindful of the potential for abuse in cases of alleged psychological injury through fabrication, allowed recovery on the basis the nonphysical traumatic events triggering the mental disability were uncommonly gruesome and the disability immediate and sudden. *Pathfinder* does not authorize compensation under the Workers' Compensation Act for anxiety, emotional stress or depression which develop over time in the normal course of an employment relationship. . . .

The issue then is under what circumstances our occupational disease statute provides compensation for mental disorders emanating from on-the-job stressful conditions. Section 1(d) of our Act requires that the disease must appear to have had its origin in a "risk connected with the employment and to have flowed from that source as a rational consequence." Many courts have considered this issue with varying results. (*See generally* 1B A. LARSON, WORKMEN'S COMPENSATION LAW § 42.23(b).) We conclude, upon examination of the several lines of precedent that if nontraumatically induced mental disorders due to a gradual deterioration of mental processes are compensable under our Occupational Diseases Act, a causal connection between the employment and the disability must be established by showing that the employment exposed the employee to an identifiable condition of the employment that is not common and necessary to all or to a great many occupations. Stated differently, mental disorders not resulting from trauma must arise from a situation of greater dimensions than the day to day emotional strain and tension which all employees must experience. As the Supreme Judicial Court of Maine reasoned in *Townsend v. Maine Bureau of Public Safety* (Me. 1979), 404 A.2d 1014: "[A] higher threshold level than simply the usual and ordinary pressures that exist in any working situation would erect an appropriate buffer between the employer and a host of malingering claims." Making this a requirement in an occupational disease claim is consistent with the ruling in *Pathfinder,* a compensation case which predicated recovery upon substantial evidence of a sudden, severe emotional shock precipitated by an uncommonly frightening event well beyond that to which the employee would otherwise be exposed in the normal employment environment.

It follows that if the conditions producing disability must be extraordinary, they must also, from an objective standpoint, exist in reality. The employee must establish that the stressful conditions actually exist on the job. It is not sufficient that the employee believe, although mistakenly, the conditions exist. . . .

Applying this test to the facts of this case, we conclude claimant has not established he suffers an occupational disease within the meaning of the act. The conditions allegedly producing the injury are no greater than those any teacher might face in an educational setting. Unruly students, an unresponsive administration, and the burdens of paperwork and record keeping are not unusual. Although claimant expressed fear for his safety, we find it significant that none of the events he described occurring over an extended period of years produced any demonstrable symptoms of mental disturbance coextensive with the events allegedly precipitating the fear. In fact, claimant's breakdown did not occur while in the course of employment with the Board. Rather, the first evidence of mental disability surfaced at the conclusion of summer vacation prior to the start of a new school year.

We also discount the testimony of the psychiatric social worker that claimant's problem emanated solely from his work environment. Her opinion was rendered without benefit of all the facts and was based, in part, on faulty information. The social worker, for instance, minimized claimant's relationship with his family, believing it was harmonious, when in fact, claimant was having severe marital difficulties. The social worker also based her opinion, in part, on claimant's perception that the principal was demeaning to claimant when there is no objective evidence, other than claimant's perception, to support this claim and testimony was presented directly refuting it by other faculty members. Under these circumstances, we do not believe claimant established that the events giving rise to the disability were out of the ordinary in relation to the normal workplace environment or that some objectively existed in reality or that they were the predominating cause of his illness. Accordingly, we do not believe claimant has proved his depressive disorder arose out of and in the course of his employment or was the consequence of an accidental injury.

For the foregoing reasons, the judgment of the circuit court and the decision of the Industrial Commission are reversed.

BARRY, P.J., and MCNAMARA, WOODWARD and CALVO, JJ., concur.

NOTES

1. *Approaches to Stress Claims.* Stress claims are a subcategory of the mental cause and mental consequence (or mental stimulus-mental injury) cases, which are shown in Figure 22-2 and which are generally referred to as "mental-mental" cases. Larson's treatise identifies four approaches that states use to analyze stress claims. The eight states in Group One find mental injury produced by mental stimulus compensable even if the stress is gradual and not unusual by comparison with that of ordinary life or employment. There are about a dozen states in Group Two that hold "mental-mental" cases compensable even if the stimulus is gradual, but only if the stress is unusual. Over half a dozen states in Group Three find "mental-mental" cases compensable, but only if the stimulus is sudden. In Group Four there are over a dozen states that never compensate "mental-mental" cases; there must be some physical component in the injury. A number of states have yet to decide the compensability of mental-mental cases. ARTHUR LARSON & LEX K. LARSON, LARSON'S WORKERS' COMPENSATION § 56.06 (Desk ed., 2006).

2. *Stress from Personnel Decisions.* Many workers' compensation stress claims arise from personnel decisions, such as layoffs or transfers. Most jurisdictions are unwilling to compensate for such mental injuries, for fear of an avalanche of claims.

A typical case arose in Arizona. Lapare was a Trailways bus driver for over twenty years. In 1984, the drivers were informed that the company was in financial difficulty and wanted to reduce their pay. Rumors spread concerning pay cuts, layoffs, and the insolvency of the pension plan. During a stopover, Lapare attended an impromptu union meeting, where several drivers concluded they were about to lose their jobs. When Lapare resumed driving after the meeting, he became disoriented and considered crashing the bus. After reaching the next stop, he had to be replaced by another driver. Lapare later consulted two psychiatrists, who agreed that he had suffered a mental breakdown from the anxiety of job loss. The court upheld the denial of benefits, declining "to hold that notice of a possible job loss or reduction in pay is sufficiently unexpected, unusual or extraordinary in modern society to justify compensation benefits for a worker's resulting emotional injury." *Lapare v. Indus. Comm.*, 742 P.2d 819 (Ariz. Ct. App. 1987).

Arizona is listed in Larson's Group Two category of states, which find mental-mental cases compensable only if caused by an unusual stimulus. In Arizona, impending loss of your job after twenty years with the same employer apparently is not considered unusual.

An outlying decision in Massachusetts allowed compensation for being laid off or transferred. Kelly had worked twenty-two years for her firm when she was told she would be laid off due to company cutbacks in the department. Kelly became upset, departed from work early, and remained upset over the weekend. Upon returning to work on Monday, she was informed that she could transfer to the cable department. Kelly was not satisfied with that proposal, and the same day became depressed, developed chest pains, and was transported to a hospital where she was placed on medication. She did not return to work for six weeks. Nine days after beginning work in the cable department, she experienced chest pains and was again taken to the hospital. She subsequently lost weight, had problems sleeping, and underwent psychiatric treatment for depression.

The Massachusetts Supreme Judicial Court held that Kelly could receive compensation, because her disability arose out of and in the course of employment. The court then rejected the argument that Kelly's emotional disability needs to result from an "unusual and objectively stressful or traumatic event" in order to be entitled to workers' compensation. Regardless of the particular vulnerabilities to injury a worker may have, the employer takes that individual "as is."

The court concluded that stress from layoffs should be viewed as a cost of doing business:

> We recognize that layoffs and job transfers are frequent events, and that emotional injuries are more prone to fabrication and less susceptible to substantiation than are physical injuries. Nevertheless, it is within the Legislature's prerogative to determine, as a matter of public policy, whether one of the costs of doing business in this Commonwealth shall be the compensation of those few employees who do suffer emotional disability as a result of being laid off or transferred, and it is also the Legislature's prerogative to say whether determination of the existence of such a disability is appropriately left to the expertise of the Industrial Accident Board.

Kelly's Case, 477 N.E.2d 582, 585 (Mass. 1985).

The Massachusetts legislature responded by enacting legislation in 1985 that precluded workers' compensation benefits for personnel actions:

> No mental or emotional disability arising principally out of a bona fide, personnel action including a transfer, promotion, demotion, or termination except such action which is the intentional infliction of emotional harm shall be deemed to be a personal injury within the meaning of this chapter.

Mass. Gen. Laws ch. 152, § 29.

Several other states have adopted the Massachusetts approach of precluding claims for work-related stress that results from bona fide personnel decisions by management. Thus, in New York an employee was denied benefits for post-traumatic stress disorder and depression she alleged were caused by her transfer from a position as customer service representative to a position in sales because the transfer was considered a bona fide personnel decision. *Spencer v. Time Warner Cable*, 717 N.Y.S.2d 711 (N.Y. App. Div. 2000), *appeal denied*, 748 N.E.2d 1074 (2001).

3. *Compensable Stress From a Single Incident.* Mental stress is most likely to be compensable when caused by a single workplace incident other than notice of firing or layoff. For example, Jones, a home health care nurse, went to a housing project to see a patient. Upon arriving there she was told to call her supervisor, who told her that an anonymous phone call had threatened her safety. The police then escorted the nurse from the housing project. This incident greatly disturbed her, and she awoke that night in hysterics. She became frightened and paranoid, and did not return to work the next day. When notifying his wife's employer, Jones' husband learned that a man on a roof of the housing project had been using binoculars to watch his wife. Jones became frightened and withdrawn, and was not able to leave her house unless accompanied. She experienced recurrent nightmares about armed men, and had flashbacks about another nurse who had been killed in the housing project. Her family physician referred her to a psychiatrist, and she was diagnosed as suffering from Post Traumatic Stress Disorder resulting from the housing project incident.

Louisiana was a Group Four state that according to Larson never found mental-mental cases compensable. Nevertheless, the court upheld an award of benefits, reasoning that the nurse had been subjected to an "unforeseen event" and noting "the scientific fact that mental disorders constitute an injury to the physical capabilities of a worker." *Jones v. City of New Orleans*, 514 So. 2d 611, 613 (La. Ct. App. 1987).

4. *The Recent Trend to Limit Compensability of Stress Claims.* A number of jurisdictions enacted legislation in the 1990s limiting the number of stress claims that qualify for workers' compensation benefits. Montana appears to have undertaken the most extreme reform since it now denies coverage for a mental injury even accompanied by a disabling physical injury (the physical-mental category identified in Figure 22-2), which is probably compensable in all other jurisdictions. Thus a firefighter was denied compensation for his post-traumatic stress disorder after he was struck by an exploding ball of fire in a burning home that caused first and second degree burns on his hands and face. *Yarborough v. Montana Mun. Ins. Auth.*, 938 P.2d 679 (Mont. 1997).

Most states have confined themselves to tightening the standards for mental-mental injuries. These claims have been totally eliminated by statutory amendments in states such as Kentucky, Florida, Oklahoma, Wyoming, and West Virginia, several of which previously compensated stress claims under some circumstances. Other states have not totally eliminated stress claims, but have enacted a variety of limitations that Lex Larson, 2 LARSON'S WORKERS' COMP. NEWS 120 (1996), places in five categories: (1) requiring a set amount or type of stress, such as the Arkansas requirement that the claimant be the victim of a crime of violence, ARK. CODE ANN. § 11-9-113; (2) raising the standard of causation, such as the Colorado requirement that the stress be "proximately caused solely by hazards to which the worker would not have been equally exposed outside the employment," COLO. REV. STAT. ANN. § 8-41-302; (3) increasing the burden of proof, such as the Maine requirement that the stress claims must be shown by clear and convincing evidence, ME. REV. STAT. ANN. tit. 39A, pt. 1, ch. 5 § 201(3); (4) imposing specific diagnostic guidelines; and (5) limiting benefits, such as the twenty-six weeks limit in Arkansas, ARK. CODE ANN. § 11-9-113(b)(1). A number of states, such as Arkansas, California, and Oregon have incorporated more than one of these restrictions.

2. RECENT TRENDS IN COMPENSABILITY

EMILY A. SPIELER & JOHN F. BURTON, JR., COMPENSATION FOR DISABLED WORKERS: WORKERS' COMPENSATION in NEW APPROACHES TO DISABIILTY IN THE WORKPLACE 205, 220-24 (Terry Thomason et al., eds., 1998) [*]

More restrictive rules governing benefit eligibility have played a critical role in the declining workers' compensation cost in the 1990s. Since each state's program is an interdependent system with its own history of tradeoffs among key provisions, it is important to be careful in making generalizations in trends. Some of the more common types of changes in the availability of benefits are, however, apparent.

Changes in compensability of particular conditions

One of the most obvious constraints on benefit availability involves statutory or regulatory changes that explicitly limit the compensability of claims involving particular medical diagnoses. Not surprisingly, the focus has been on health conditions that are potentially most costly to a compensation program.

For example, many states substantially restricted the right of workers to make claims for psychological injuries resulting from a mental stimulus in the absence of a physical injury (so-called "mental-mental" claims). . . .

Injuries caused by repetitive trauma, such as carpal tunnel syndrome and noise induced hearing loss present a similar picture. As the incidence of these claims sky-rocketed, state legislatures responded by tightening eligibility standards, using the same mechanisms used to limit compensability of stress claims. In Virginia, the state's supreme court ruled that repetitive injury claims were non-compensable under the language of the state statute. In response to the criticism of these decisions, the Virginia legislature amended the workers' compensation statute to provide nominal, but very narrow, coverage for these conditions.

Limitations on coverage when the injury involves aggravation of a pre-existing condition

Other changes are subtler than explicit restrictions on the compensability of specific conditions. Traditionally, employers were said to "take workers as they found them." This meant that workers with preexisting conditions were not barred from coverage for work injuries, even if the underlying condition

---

[*] Copyright © 1998 by the Industrial Relations Research Association. Reprinted by permission.

contributed to the occurrence of the injury or to the extent of the resulting disability. Through a variety of legislative and judicial changes, rules governing compensation for preexisting conditions or aggravation have been tightened in many jurisdictions.

For example . . . both state courts and legislatures have moved to restrict compensation of injuries involving aggravation of preexisting conditions. Most significantly, several states now limit compensation when the current injury is not the sole or major cause of disability. These limitations come in a variety of forms: excluding injuries or resulting disabilities if they are the effects of "the natural aging process"; requiring that work be the "major" or "predominant" cause or "the major contributing factor" of any disability; and excluding injuries for which current work is merely the triggering factor. These changes are reinforced by heightened evidentiary standards for claimants, including requirements of "objective medical evidence" (discussed below), and by stricter rules and shorter time limits for reopening prior claims when progression of a condition occurs.

Judicial application of these statutory developments illustrates their effects on workers. For example, the Oregon rule requiring that work be the predominant cause of the injury resulted in a finding that when a preexisting condition predisposed a worker to airway irritation, the resulting, occupationally-caused, lung disease was not compensable. In Illinois, a reviewing court denied benefits for occupational lung disease to a coal miner who presented medical evidence of occupational lung disease and who had worked for 25 years in underground mines where he was "continually exposed to coal dust"; the court nevertheless found, despite a statutory presumption of causation in cases involving miners' lung diseases, that his claim was appropriately denied, based upon the claimant's smoking history and conflicting medical testimony. . . .

Procedural and evidentiary changes in claims processing that restrict compensability

Finally, statutory and administrative changes in procedural rules and evidentiary standards are resulting in restrictions on the number of compensable claims in many programs. For example, statutory changes in a number of states now require a claimant to prove both that the injury was primarily work-related and that the resulting medical condition can be documented by "objective medical" evidence. The requirement for objective evidence excludes claims based upon subjective reports of patients that cannot be substantiated by objective evidence, including debilitating musculoskeletal injuries that involve soft tissue damage and reports of pain and psychological impairment. These heightened requirements appear to be rooted both in a desire to save money and in a distrust of subjective injury reports.

In addition, claimants are sometimes asked to meet increasingly strict burdens of proof. In a landmark case under the federal black lung compensation law, the U.S. Supreme Court . . . ruled that, due to requirements in the Administrative Procedures Act, claimants must prove their cases by a "preponderance of the evidence." The result was a reduction in the number of approved claims. Amendments to some state statutes now require, either in all claims or for specifically delineated ones, that claimants meet this "preponderance" standard or, for some injuries or diseases, the even more difficult standard of "clear and convincing evidence." Because many workers' compensation programs gave claimants the benefit of the doubt in close cases in the past, these changes are significant.

NOTES

1. *Arkansas Travelers*. The Arkansas workers' compensation law was amended in 1993 to eliminate the requirement that the act should be applied liberally and that all doubts should be resolved in favor of the worker. The amendment also requires evidence to be weighed impartially, without giving the benefit of the doubt to either party, and requires the courts to construe the provisions of the Act strictly. The Act also added a new definition: Compensable injury does not include an injury that was inflicted upon the employee at a time when employment services were not being performed. ARK. CODE ANN. § 11-9-102.

Leah Hightower, a teacher at a day-care center was ordered to report to work despite the encasement of the employer's parking lot in a sheet of ice. She slipped and fell, hurt her back, and missed two weeks of work. The Court of Appeals indicated that under the law prior to 1993, her injury would have been compensable because there was an exception to the going-and-coming rule for injuries that occurred on the employer's premises. However, the court said that the 1993 definition of compensable injury seemed clearly aimed at eliminating the premises exception to the going-and-coming rule. Under a strict construction of the law, "merely walking to and from one's car, even on the employer's premises, does not qualify as performing 'employment services.'" *Hightower v. Newark Pub. Sch. Sys.*, 943 S.W.2d 608 (Ark. Ct. App. 1997).

Cheri Pettey was also injured in Arkansas after the 1993 amendments. She was a nursing assistant who traveled to patients' homes to provide nursing service. She was compensated according to the time spent at each patient's home. She did not receive compensation for travel expenses or for travel time, and used her own vehicle to travel to the patients' homes. Pettey had reported to the employer's office to pick up supplies and was on the way to her first patient of the day when she lost control of her auto and was injured. Is the injury compensable? The Arkansas Supreme Court said yes. The court recognized that an employee generally does not meet the course of employment test when traveling to and from the workplace. However, there are traditional exceptions to the going-and-coming rule, such as situations when the travel is an integral part of the job because the employee must travel from job site to job site. The court was not persuaded that the fact the employee was not paid for the travel time meant the trip was not in the course of employment (really, the triple negative was in the court's opinion!), in part because the employee was required to furnish her own conveyance and in part because the facts "clearly demonstrate that travel was a necessary part of her employment." *Olsten Kimberly Quality Care v. Pettey*, 944 S.W.2d 524, 527 (Ark. 1997).

2. *The Effects of Statutory Changes in Oregon.* Between 1987 and 1995, the Oregon legislature passed several amendments to the workers' compensation statute that made it harder for workers to qualify for benefits. These changes *inter alia* provided that claims were compensable only if work was the "major cause" of the permanent disability and that medical evidence must be based on "objective findings." "Our judgment . . . is that by the mid-1990s the Oregon legislation had reduced costs and benefits by about 20% to 25% below what the amounts would have been if [the amendments] had not been enacted." Terry Thomason & John F. Burton, Jr., *The Effects of Changes in the Oregon Workers' Compensation Program on Employees' Benefits and Employers' Costs, in* Workers' Compensation Compendium 2005-06, Volume One 387-405, 403 (John F. Burton, Jr. et al., ed., 2005).

3. *The Daubert Rule and Workers' Compensation.* Several Supreme Court decisions, beginning with *Daubert v. Merrell Dow Pharmaceuticals, Inc.*, 509 U.S. 579 (1993), interpreted Federal Rule of Evidence 702 and established the *Daubert* rule, which controls the admission of expert testimony in the Federal Courts. Oklahoma provides a case study of the potential impact of the *Daubert* rule on workers' compensation programs:

> On July 1, 2005, the Oklahoma Legislature amended certain definitions in the workers' compensation scheme. Specifically, a definition was added defining objective medical evidence as follows:

> 17. "Objective medical evidence" means evidence which meets the criteria of Federal Rule of Evidence 702 and all U.S. Supreme Court case law applicable thereto. . . .

> [I]t appears that Title 85 O.S. §§ 3(17) and 17(A)(1), applying the *Daubert* standard, constitute a procedural rule and must be given retroactive effect in Oklahoma's Workers (sic) Compensation Court. The ramifications of such a rule are wide-ranging. The thousands of pending workers' compensation claims are all implicated. . . . A *Daubert* challenge would not be warranted in every workers' compensation case. A medical doctor is probably still competent to render an opinion as to impairment resulting from a back strain. However, any injury claim where the reliability of an expert's opinion is called into question, either because of a flawed methodology or issues pertaining to the expert's qualifications, necessitates the application of the standards of *Daubert* and its progeny in testing the admissibility of the expert's opinions. . . .

> The Workers' Compensation Court . . . must assess the reliability and the relevance of the proffered expert testimony by determining: (1) whether the expert has the requisite qualifications to render an opinion, (2) whether the expert used appropriate methodology or testing in arriving at his or her opinions, (3) whether the testimony is relevant, that is, whether it "fits" the facts of the case, and (4) whether the expert relied on facts or data of a type reasonably relied upon by experts in the particular field. . . .

> [T]he *Daubert* Court listed several . . . factors that a trial judge should take into account in determining the admissibility of expert scientific testimony:

- Whether the scientific theory or technique at issue can be and has been tested. . . .

- Whether the scientific theory or technique at issue has been subjected to peer review and publication. . . .

- Whether the scientific theory or technique at issue has attracted widespread acceptance or only minimal support within the relevant scientific community. . . .

- Was the expert's opinion developed solely for litigation purposes. . . .

Courts have repeatedly excluded testimony where the expert has developed his opinion "expressly for the purpose of testifying" and has not "done any research on his theories out the context of [this and other] lawsuits."

Andrew D. Downing, *Daubert and Exposure Cases in Oklahoma*, Workers' Compensation & Employers' Liability Law Committee Newsletter (A.B.A., Chicago, IL.) Spring 2006, at 8, 23, 26, 27.[*]

G. CASH BENEFITS

The workers' compensation program in each jurisdiction provides several types of cash benefits, depending on the extent and duration of the worker's disability, or whether the worker is killed.

Three distinct time periods are pertinent in determining the amount and type of cash benefits that will be paid to a worker with a compensable injury or disease. The employee's average wage in the *preinjury period* is used in calculating the cash benefits paid by the workers' compensation program. The consequences of a work-related injury or disease can be categorized as temporary or permanent, a distinction that has an important bearing on the types of cash benefits that are provided.

The *temporary disability period* refers to the time from the occurrence of the injury until the date of maximum medical improvement (MMI). During this period, which is often referred to as the healing period, the worker will receive temporary total disability or temporary partial disability benefits.

Most workers completely recover by the end of the healing period, and so only qualify for temporary disability benefits. A substantial minority of workers have permanent consequences of their injury or disease that persist after the date of MMI. For such a worker, there is a period following MMI that is referred to as the *permanent disability period*. During this period, the worker will receive permanent partial disability (PPD) or permanent total disability benefits.

The distinction between the temporary disability period and the permanent disability period can be significant for workers with permanent consequences of the injury or disease. A number of states, for example, have lower maximum weekly benefits for PPD benefits than for temporary total disability benefits. Also, as will be examined later in this section, once a worker qualifies for PPD

---

benefits, the benefits may terminate even if the worker continues to experience loss of earnings due to the work-related injury or disease.

Many states do not use the term "maximum medical improvement." Most states, however, either use similar terms that denote the existence of MMI (such as the injury is "permanent and stationary") or have practices that indicate that the healing period is over (e.g., the date when the case is considered ready to schedule for a hearing to determine the amount of PPD benefits).

1. TEMPORARY DISABILITY BENEFITS

a. Temporary Total Disability Benefits

TOBIN v. SHORE ALL STAR
Superior Court of New Jersey, Appellate Division
876 A.2d 326 (2005)

STERN, P.J.A.D.

The respondent-employer, All Shore All Star Cheerleading & Gymnastics, appeals from a judgment awarding $11,748 in temporary disability benefits for eighteen and 6/7 weeks from August 5, 2003 to December 15, 2003, after petitioner resumed her duties as owner of All Shore but was not paid as an instructor. All Shore argues that "petitioner was not entitled to temporary disability benefits" for that period as she "was not totally disabled on a temporary basis and unable to work as a result of a work-related injury" because she had resumed "performing light duty." . . .

Petitioner is "the owner and chief gymnastics instructor at All Shore. . . ." She suffered an injury to her right shoulder as a result of an assault incident to her work on May 1, 2003, and on August 5, 2003 was "released" by her doctor to do "lite duty with no use of [her] right arm or shoulder."

. . . .

At the time she sought the temporary disability benefits, All Shore had approximately ten employees all of whom, with the exception of one individual who serves as "full-time" bookkeeper and office manager, are instructors who are paid at an "hourly" rate. The rate is based on the instructor's experience, and petitioner was paid $15.00 an hour as "the most experience[d] and valuable gymnastics instructor."

Petitioner further testified that before her injury on May 1, petitioner worked between twelve and thirteen hours each day in the summer, instructing day camp classes as well as evening classes. During the remainder of the year, petitioner worked five to six hours a night. Petitioner also provided private instruction for which she was paid $30.00 for a half-hour. Petitioner testified that she generally collected a net income of about $620 to $650 per week for her work as an instructor. The parties stipulated that "her gross weekly wage" was $890 per week before the accident.

In addition to providing instruction, petitioner also had other responsibilities as the owner of the facility. These duties included unlocking the facility, general supervision of the business, and handling injured students. Prior to her injury, petitioner did not collect a salary for the duties associated with ownership of the business, but was paid only for performing her duties as an instructor.

After petitioner was injured, she worked for a couple of weeks, "trying to tolerate the pain." She testified that "[t]he pain just got too intense and I couldn't take the pain." She explained that she stopped instructing because she had a "safety concern" for the students she needed to spot and catch because she felt like she "physically couldn't do it." Because of her inability to use her right arm and to spot, she was required to hire "an additional instructor to perform [her] duties," and returned to work as an instructor for "two or three" hours a day in "mid December" 2003.

The judge of compensation ruled for petitioner. He found:

> Petitioner's testimony, and certification, were consistent and totally credible. The factual situation is quite simple as outlined above. The statute which controls (N.J.S.A. 34:15-38) provides that temporary disability is to be paid if the petitioner is "unable to continue to work by reason of the accident", and that the temporary disability continues until the petitioner is so far restored as the "permanent character of the injury will [permit]". Case law is clear that respondent is required to offer light duty, but if there is no light duty available, respondent is under the obligation to provide temporary disability.
>
> The court finds based on the facts . . . that petitioner during the time period in question was not able to perform her duties as a gymnastics instructor and that no light duty was available to her. Accordingly, she is entitled to temporary disability payments at $623 a week for 18 6/7 weeks (August 5-December 15, 2003) equaling $11,748.

All Shore argues that because petitioner was able to do light work during the period in dispute, she was not entitled to temporary disability benefits under the workers' compensation statute. However, because the decision of the judge of compensation is supported by "sufficient credible evidence" on the record, we affirm the judgment. . . . An employee's ability to do some light work is not a basis for denying benefits when the employee is trained in a skill which she cannot perform because of her injury or when her employer has no light work available.

In *Harbatuk v. S & S Furniture Systems Insulation,* 512 A.2d 537 (N.J. App. Div. 1986), we reversed the denial of temporary disability benefits although the employee was capable of doing light work, such as painting toys and repairing bicycles, while he was awaiting surgery for his occupational injury. We noted that the petitioner had been trained as a carpenter, that this was the only vocational skill he had, and that the employer had no light duty work available for him. . . .

Similarly, in *Cleland v. Verona Radio,* 33 A.2d 712 (N.J. 1943) discussed in *Harbatuk,* the former Supreme Court sustained a grant of continued disability payments to a salesman who subsequently purchased and managed his own chicken farm. While the petitioner was able to feed the chickens and clean the eggs, he was forced to hire an employee to do the work petitioner could not perform even though, as in this case, he was able to manage the business. The court observed that the ability to do light or intermittent work "is not inconsistent with total incapacity."

. . . .

It may be that petitioner was able to perform, and actually performed, light duty but it was the type for which she was not paid as a salaried employee. As in *Harbatuk* and *Cleland* here "[t]he ability for light and intermittent or sedentary work is not inconsistent *per se* with total disability," and "the fact that an individual is capable of working a few hours at a time at light work does not affect the right to temporary total disability payments." Although owner and president of All Shore, petitioner has been employed as a gymnastics instructor and was its most skilled and experienced instructor. While she was capable of doing work as president, she was paid only as instructor and was not paid for the period during which she could not perform her duties as an instructor. In essence, petitioner's specialized training and experience as an instructor established her value to the company and provided the justification for her pay. Moreover, another instructor was paid to replace her. As the judge of compensation found her credible, his findings support his conclusion that she was entitled to temporary benefits during the period in question.

. . . .

The judgment of the Division of Workers' Compensation is affirmed.

NOTE

Temporary Total Disability (TTD) Benefits. TTD benefits normally are paid to an injured worker who is completely unable to work during the period between the date of injury and the date of maximum medical improvement, although *Tobin* provides an example of an exception to that rule. There is a waiting period before the temporary total disability benefits begin. However, if the worker is still disabled beyond a specified date, known as the retroactive date, then the benefits for the waiting period are paid on a retroactive basis. In insurance terminology, the waiting period is a form of deductible during which time the worker bears the loss of wages resulting from the injury.

In most states, after the waiting period for benefits is satisfied, the weekly benefit is two-thirds of the preinjury wage, subject to maximum and minimum amounts. The worker will receive two-thirds of his or her preinjury wage or the state maximum weekly benefit, whichever is less. Or, for a low-wage worker, the worker will receive two-thirds of his or her preinjury wage, or the state minimum benefit, whichever is more. In insurance terminology, the one-third share of lost wages borne by the worker is a form of coinsurance.

Workers' compensation benefits are not subject to income tax. Because of the progressive federal income tax plus the income tax imposed by many states, the temporary total disability benefits, if calculated as two-thirds of gross wages, can represent a higher proportion of take-home pay. In some instances, the workers' compensation benefits can represent more than 100%

of lost take-home pay. In recognition of the work disincentives that such high replacement rates may cause for some workers, some states calculate temporary total disability benefits as a percentage (for example, 80%) of a worker's spendable weekly earnings. Spendable earnings are defined as gross wages minus the deductions for the federal and state income taxes and the federal Social Security tax (FICA).

b. Temporary Partial Disability Benefits

CARR v. VIRGINIA ELECTRIC & POWER CO.
Court of Appeals of Virginia
487 S.E.2d 878 (1997)

FITZPATRICK, J.:

Dennis L. Carr (claimant) appeals a decision of the Workers' Compensation Commission denying him an award of temporary partial disability benefits. He contends that the commission erred in failing to award him benefits for the time periods during which he performed light duty work but received no opportunities for overtime. For the reasons that follow, we reverse the decision of the commission.

I. *Background*

Claimant was employed with Virginia Power (employer) as a lineman for approximately twenty-three years. During his employment as a lineman, claimant's duties included "climb[ing] poles," "work[ing] out of a bucket truck," trouble shooting, building lines, and "restor[ing] service customers when they're out of lights." Claimant typically worked more than forty hours per week and regularly received overtime compensation. Additionally, claimant received bonus or incentive pay when he "filled other shifts" or worked "outside of his department of geographic area." On July 5, 1995, claimant, who is left-handed, suffered a compensable injury resulting in the amputation of his left ring finger.

Subsequently, claimant was paid wages in lieu of compensation for periods of total incapacitation from July 6, 1995 through August 5, 1995, and from September 26, 1995 through October 15, 1995. Claimant performed light duty work from August 6, 1995 through September 25, 1995, and from October 16, 1995 and continuing. Claimant testified that he returned only to light duty work "because my doctor says I can't do line work anymore." A letter from one of claimant's doctors states that claimant's injury "precludes him from performing all of his regular duties as an electrician." Claimant's light duty work included the following responsibilities: "some inspection work on [the] equipment, visual, just visual inspections, and . . . reading some meters from time to time." During the light duty work, claimant worked "eight hours a day, 40-hour week." He received, during his light duty work, approximately $114.16 less per week than he received at his pre-injury work. However, during his light duty work, he was neither offered overtime work, nor paid additional wages; nor did he receive any "shift differential."

At the hearing on April 12, 1996 before the deputy commissioner, claimant admitted that he sometimes declined or was unavailable to work overtime, that he had been disciplined for having low acceptance rates for overtime, and that he did not know exactly how much overtime he would have been offered. Finally, claimant testified that he knew that overtime had been offered to other linemen during the time period in question, and stated that he would have accepted such an opportunity if it had been offered.

David H. Driggs (Driggs), the construction superintendent, testified that there was no way to predict how much overtime would be available to any given employee from year to year, and that, in the past, claimant failed to maintain the amount of overtime required by the company. However, Driggs also testified that, during the past ten years, overtime had always been offered to linemen.

Following the hearing, the deputy commissioner denied claimant's request for temporary partial disability benefits for the wage loss allegedly resulting from his lack of overtime work, and found that "the reduction in earnings stems from purely economic factors unrelated to the accident. Therefore, the claimant has failed to prove a causal nexus between the accident and his loss of earnings."

. . . [T]he full commission reviewed the record and . . . affirmed the decision of the deputy commissioner that denied claimant temporary partial benefits for wages lost due to a lack of overtime work or shift differential.

II. *Wage Loss*

Claimant contends that because he was offered light duty work without the opportunity to work overtime, shift differential, or out-of-business-area pay, he suffered a wage loss below his pre-injury wage. Additionally, claimant argues that his wage loss is properly attributable to his occupational injury, as medically imposed restrictions prevented him from performing his pre-injury job and receiving extra earnings, and it is therefore compensable under Code § 65.2-502.[2]

We recently addressed the issue of the impact of economic or business conditions on a partially disabled claimant's right to compensation. *See Consolidated Stores Corporation v. Graham*, 486 S.E.2d 576 (Va. App. 1997). In that case, some time after her injury, claimant was authorized to perform light duty work. She was offered and she accepted a position as a sales clerk in which she made the same hourly wage as her pre-injury position as a "stocker." However, "due to economic conditions, [employer] assigned [claimant] a reduced number of hours, resulting in an average weekly wage of less

---

[2] Code § 65.2-502, Compensation for partial incapacity, provides as follows:

> Except as otherwise provided in § 65.2-503 or § 65.2-510, when the incapacity for work resulting from the injury is partial, the employer shall pay, or cause to be paid, as hereinafter provided, to the injured employee during such incapacity a weekly compensation equal to 66⅔ percent of the difference between his average weekly wages before the injury and the average weekly wages which he is able to earn thereafter, but not more than 100 percent of the average weekly wage of the Commonwealth as defined in § 65.2-500. In no case shall the period covered by such compensation be greater than 500 weeks.

than $108." *Id.* at 577. Although the deputy commissioner found that "any diminution in hours worked was a product of the down turn in business," the full commission reversed and found that the claimant had not been "released to her pre-injury job and that she was not performing all her pre-injury duties" and that the "fact that the availability of light duty work is limited due to economic conditions does not diminish the claimant's right to compensation when the injury prevents her from performing her regular job." *Id.* at 577.

Finding that claimant was not released to her pre-injury employment and that her light duty responsibilities as a store clerk were not commensurate with her pre-injury position of a stocker, we held that "the employer's financial condition and the availability of alternative work do not affect *the claimant's right to compensation due to an impaired capacity to perform his pre-injury duties.*" *Id.* at 578 (emphasis added). In reaching this decision, we relied on Code § 65.2-502:

> During a period of partial incapacity, a claimant performing work remains entitled to compensation benefits, determined in part by calculating the difference between the claimant's average weekly wage before and after the injury. Thus, by providing suitable alternative employment to a claimant, an employer may avoid paying compensation benefits.

Id. Accordingly, we held that because claimant was neither released to return to her pre-injury duties, nor restored to her pre-injury capacity by the employer's offered alternative light duty work, the employer remained liable to fulfill its duty to compensate claimant.

The circumstances in *Consolidated* are remarkably similar to those of the instant case. Here, employer offered claimant light duty work similar in pay to his pre-injury employment as a lineman. As in *Consolidated*, however, claimant suffered a wage loss at the light duty position that he would not have incurred at his pre-injury placement. "The threshold test for compensability is whether the employee is 'able fully to perform the duties of his pre[-]injury employment.'" . . . Under the holding in *Consolidated*, the employer is relieved of its duty to compensate the claimant only if it offers the claimant employment in his or her "pre-injury capacity" and the claimant has been released to perform the work. In both *Consolidated* and this case, the employer failed to make this offer. Claimant, who made at least some overtime in his previous position, now makes none. The evidence demonstrated that other linemen continue to receive overtime and that claimant's range of duties in his light duty work is not equivalent to his pre-injury duties as a lineman. Thus, claimant has not been released to his pre-injury capacity as a lineman. Accordingly, employer's inability to predict the available overtime to the linemen during the period in question does not diminish claimant's right to compensation, as his work-related injury prevents him from performing lineman duties, and employer remains liable for the wage loss suffered by claimant. . . .

For the foregoing reasons, the decision of the commission is reversed and the case remanded for the commission to enter an order consistent with this opinion.

Reversed and remanded.

2. PERMANENT PARTIAL DISABILITY BENEFITS

a. Introduction

Permanent partial disability (PPD) benefits are paid to those workers who have injuries that are serious enough to have permanent consequences but not serious enough to be totally disabling. One observer has identified PPD cash benefits as "the most expensive and complex type of benefit provided by workers' programs." John F. Burton, Jr., *Permanent Partial Disability Benefits in* WORKPLACE INJURIES AND DISEASES: PREVENTION AND COMPENSATION (Karen Roberts et al., eds., 2005).

For those workers with relatively serious injuries, several permanent consequences are possible. There may be a persistence of pain and suffering and a continuing need for medical care and rehabilitation. Of particular interest are the other permanent consequences shown in Figure 22-3 because they are the focus of most of the debate concerning the design of permanent disability benefits in a workers' compensation program.

Figure 22-3
Permanent Consequences of an Injury or Disease

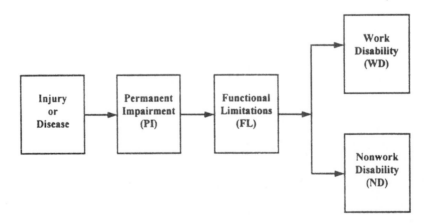

A permanent impairment (PI) is any anatomic or functional abnormality or loss that remains after maximum medical improvement has been achieved. Examples of permanent impairments are an amputated limb or an enervated muscle. The impairment probably causes the worker to experience functional limitations (FL). Physical performance may be limited in such activities as walking, climbing, reaching, and hearing, and, in addition, the worker's emotional and mental performance may be limited. Functional limitations, in turn, are likely to result in disability, of which two types should be recognized. Work disability (WD) refers to the loss of earning capacity or loss of actual earnings that result from the functional limitations, while nonwork disability (ND) includes the loss of the capacities for other aspects of life, including recreation and the performance of household tasks.

Work disability can be conceptualized as having the two phases shown in Figure 22-4: the loss of earning capacity (LEC) that results in actual wage loss (AWL). In a strict sense, these two aspects of work disability must accompany one another. An actual loss of earnings only occurs if there is loss of earning capacity. Nevertheless, the distinction is important because (as discussed later in this subsection) some types of workers' compensation benefits are based solely on a determination of a *presumed* loss of earning capacity.

Figure 22-4
Two Phases of Work Disability

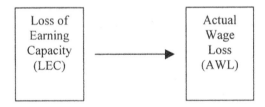

States use several different operational approaches for permanent disability benefits depending on which of the permanent consequences shown in Figure 22-3 and Figure 22-4 is used as a proxy for or measure of work disability. In most jurisdictions, the choice of an operational approach for PPD benefits first depends on whether the worker's injury is a scheduled or nonscheduled injury.

Scheduled v. Nonscheduled Injuries

The workers' compensation statutes in most states contain a schedule that lists the number of weeks or the dollar amounts of compensation benefits to be paid for the physical loss or (in most jurisdictions) the loss of use of specified parts of the body. A scheduled injury is any injury that is specifically enumerated in the workers' compensation statute. In addition to listing the upper and lower extremities (the arm, leg, hand, foot, fingers, and toes), states commonly schedule benefits for the loss of an eye and for hearing and vision loss.

Injuries to the trunk, internal organs, nervous system, and other body systems usually are not included in the list of injuries found in the statutes; these are nonscheduled injuries. In some states, they are referred to as "unscheduled" injuries.

In the next subsection, we examine the handling of scheduled injuries. The following three subsections then examine three different ways that states handle nonscheduled injuries.

b. Scheduled Permanent Partial Disability Benefits

A worker who suffers the physical loss of a part of the body included in a schedule is evaluated in terms of the seriousness of the impairment. In New Jersey, an injury that leads to the loss of use of a body part found in the schedule is evaluated in terms of the extent of loss of functional limitations. Thus in New Jersey — which equates the loss of a hand with 245 weeks of benefits — a worker with an injury that causes a 20% loss of the use of a hand will receive forty-nine weeks of benefits. (Loss of a body part by amputation results in an additional 10% award.) Most states (including New Jersey) pay scheduled benefits if the worker experiences either a physical loss or a loss of use of the body part found in the schedule, but there are some states that confine scheduled benefits to amputations. Also, in most jurisdictions, the worker is not entitled to benefits after the scheduled duration expires even if the worker continues to experience actual wage loss because of the work-related injury. In some states, such as Michigan, there are exceptions to this generalization. *See Van Dorpel v. Haven-Busch Co.*, 85 N.W.2d 97 (Mich. 1957), which allowed additional benefits to a workers who was unable to work after his scheduled benefits expired.

c. Category I: Nonscheduled PPD Benefits Based on Impairment

Three categories of operational approaches for nonscheduled permanent partial disability benefits can be identified. The Category I approach is represented by New Jersey, although some aspects of the state's program make the designation less than perfect.

In the Category I approach, an injury with permanent consequences must first be classified as scheduled or nonscheduled. The New Jersey provisions for scheduled PPD benefits were discussed in the previous subsection. If the injury is nonscheduled, the Category I approach evaluates them in terms of the resulting permanent impairments (PI) or functional limitations (FL). For example, a worker may experience structural damage to a vertebra and the spinal column, which are injuries not found on the schedule. The impairment itself may be evaluated (the disc is herniated) or the consequent functional limitation may be assessed (the worker is restricted in his ability to lift, stoop, or perform certain motions that he was able to make before the injury). This approach to nonscheduled injuries usually produces a percentage rating that relates the worker's condition to that of a whole person (or to a "totally disabled" person). Thus, in New Jersey the statute equates a whole person to 600 weeks, and a worker with an impairment rating of 25% would receive 150 weeks of permanent partial disability benefits.

d. Category II: Nonscheduled PPD Benefits Based on Loss of Earning Capacity

The second general approach to nonscheduled permanent partial disability benefits is exemplified by Iowa. As in the first approach, an injury with permanent consequences must first be classified as scheduled or nonscheduled in the Category II approach. The initial choice in Iowa is similar to that in New Jersey, with arms, legs, hands, etc., in the statutory schedule, while backs and internal organs are nonscheduled injuries.

The distinctive attribute of the Category II approach to permanent partial disability benefits concerns the treatment of nonscheduled benefits. In states using this approach, an assessment is made of the worker's loss of earning capacity resulting from the work-related injury or disease. This evaluation takes into account the seriousness of the worker's permanent impairments and functional limitations (as in the Category I approach) but also considers such factors as the worker's age, education, and prior work experience. This approach to nonscheduled injuries usually produces a rating indicating the percentage loss in earning capacity due to the injury. The statute equates full earning capacity to a specified duration, which in Iowa is 500 weeks. Thus, an Iowa worker with a 25% loss of earning capacity would receive 125 weeks of permanent partial disability benefits.

SJOBERG'S CASE
Appeals Court of Massachusetts
462 N.E.2d 353 (1984), *aff'd*, 476 N.E.2d 196 (Mass. 1985)

DREBEN, JUSTICE.

The insurer appeals from a judgment in favor of the employee affirming a decision of the Industrial Accident Board (board) which awarded the employee forty dollars a week partial compensation. . . . At issue is whether an employee whose earning capacity is impaired by industrial injuries is precluded, as matter of law, from obtaining benefits because, by working more than fifty hours a week, his average post-injury earnings exceed his average pre-injury weekly wage. We hold that he is not so precluded.

On October 22, 1977, and again on June 12, 1978, the employee suffered severe back pain while performing work as a pressman and molder. The board . . . found that as a result of his injuries, the employee could not perform any work which made heavy physical demands on his back and that, prior to these injuries, he had had no such limitation. The board also found that the various jobs held by the employee since leaving his employer each paid a significantly lower hourly wage than his former job. It was only by working more than fifty hours a week, including overtime, that the employee could match, and even slightly exceed, his former earnings. While considering the weekly wages before and after the injury "as important pieces of evidence" . . . the reviewing board viewed the post-injury earnings of the employee as "not conclusive on the issue of loss of earning capacity" and awarded him forty dollars a week for such loss.

We think the board's decision comports with the statute and its purpose. The award under G.L. c. 152, § 35, is for impairment of earning capacity, and is measured with certain upper limits not now relevant, as follows: "While the incapacity for work resulting from the injury is partial, the insurer shall pay the injured employee a weekly compensation equal to the entire difference between his average weekly wage before the injury and the average weekly wage he is able to earn thereafter . . . ."

The dollar amount actually received is not conclusive in determining the average weekly wage. In some cases this is true even for pre-injury wages. Thus, in *Shaw's Case,* 141 N.E. 858 (Mass. 1923), the court, albeit without discussion, excluded overtime in computing the employee's average weekly wage before the injury. The cases concerning post-injury earnings emphasize that compensation "is to be measured by the amount the employee was capable of earning and not necessarily by what he actually earned." The employee is to be paid "for the loss of earnings caused by the injury" and not for a loss of earnings caused by other factors. Thus, if an employee's earnings are reduced because he works less than a normal work week, he is entitled to partial compensation only if the diminution is due to his injuries and not because of a lack of demand for his labor.

Similarly, if an employee's income is higher because of factors other than his earning capacity, the income due to these factors is not to be taken into account. In *Shaw's Case,* it was held that even though an employee's wages were elevated to the same level as before by reason of a gratuity from his employer, the employee could still recover for his impaired earning capacity. Although he received full wages, he was not able to earn them, and the gratuity was irrelevant. . . .

Where, as here, the board found an impairment of earning capacity and a reduced per hour wage, we see no reason to deny compensation because the diminution of earning capacity is concealed by the longer hours worked . . . . The statute bids comparison of pre- and post-injury weekly wages. A fair comparison is possible only if like factors are considered. "[O]nly by the elimination of all variables except the injury itself" can "a reasonably accurate estimate . . . be made of the impairment of earning capacity attributable to the injury." *Arizona Pub. Serv. Co. v. Industrial Comm'n,* 492 P.2d 1212 (Ariz. 1972).

Inflation of post-injury earnings by reason of longer working hours interjects, in our opinion, an extraneous factor. *See* 2A Larson, Workmen's Compensation § 57.33 (1982).[4] . . . Accordingly, we hold the award for impaired earning capacity under G.L. c. 152, § 35, was not "tainted by error of law."

NOTES

1. ***Loss of Earning Capacity versus Actual Earnings.*** In *Carr v. Virginia Electric & Power Co.,* 487 S.E.2d 878 (Va. 1997), which involved

---

[4] Larson states (footnotes omitted), "Most obviously of all, although the wage comparison is usually on a weekly or monthly basis, it would not be fair to offset loss due to physical impairment by earnings attributable solely to claimant's having worked more hours per week. Overtime worked after the injury should be omitted from consideration if overtime was not included in the calculation of the preinjury wage basis. Similarly, if claimant's hourly wage has fallen, he is entitled to a partial award even if the reduction has been offset by his working longer hours."

temporary partial disability benefits, the court held that benefits should be based on the difference between the workers' actual earnings during the healing period and the earning capacity (including overtime payments) the worker would have had during the healing period if the worker had not been injured. In *Sjoberg's Case*, which involved permanent partial disability benefits, the court held that the benefits should be based on the difference between the workers' actual earnings prior to the injury (which was, in effect, being used as a proxy for the earning capacity that Sjoberg would have had in the permanent disability period if he had not been injured) and the diminished earning capacity (excluding overtime) the worker had during the permanent disability period (which had been reduced as a result of the injury).

2. *The Prospective Benefit Approach.* Both the scheduled and nonscheduled benefits in the Category I and II approaches rely on the *ex ante* or prospective benefit approach. There are distinctive features of the *ex ante* approach. First, although the presumed rationale for the permanent disability benefits is the actual loss of wages resulting from the work-related injury or disease, all of these benefits rely on proxies for that actual wage loss. As suggested by the chain of causation shown in Figures 22-3 and 22-4, such a use of proxies is not logically flawed since presumably the actual wage loss will result from the other permanent consequences.

The second feature of the *ex ante* approach is that the decision about the amount of the benefits is made after the medical condition has stabilized but before most or all of the actual wage loss occurs for which benefits are intended. That is, the amount of the permanent disability benefits is determined near the beginning of the period of permanent disability and once the determination is made, the amount is seldom adjusted. Thus the permanent disability benefits are paid for expected wage loss during the period of permanent disability on a prospective (or *ex ante*) basis.

A Supreme Court decision provides a qualification to this characterization of the nature of the *ex ante* approach. Under the Longshore and Harbor Workers' Compensation Act, adjustments in the extent of loss of earning capacity can be made over time in response to factors such as the worker's experience in the labor market. The decision indicates that the line between the Category II and Category III approaches to PPD benefits is somewhat blurry rather than perfectly bright. *See Metropolitan Stevedore Co. v. Rambo*, 521 U.S. 121 (1997).

e. Category III: Nonscheduled PPD Benefits Based on Actual Wage Loss

The third approach to permanent partial disability benefits is represented by New York. However, the distinctive feature of the New York approach for nonscheduled permanent partial disability benefits — the use of the wage-loss approach — is found in a somewhat different guise in several other jurisdictions, including Michigan and several of the Canadian provinces.

In New York, the first step in determining the applicable benefits for an injury with permanent consequences is to determine whether the injury is scheduled or nonscheduled. The distinction is similar to that used in New

Jersey and Iowa, with arms, legs, and other bodily extremities scheduled and internal organs and the back nonscheduled. The scheduled durations are, to be sure, different among the states, with the New York arm worth only 312 weeks.

The major differences among the states pertain to the nonscheduled permanent partial disability benefits. The Category III states rely on the wage-loss approach, which requires the worker to demonstrate that he or she has experienced an actual loss of earnings because of the work-related injury or disease. One of the challenges of the wage-loss approach is determining when actual losses of earnings are due to the work-related injury disease or to other factors.

LEEBER v. LILCO

Supreme Court of New York, Appellate Division, Third Department
816 N.Y.S.2d 205 (2006)

MUGGLIN, J.

Appeal from a decision of the Workers' Compensation Board, filed January 21, 2005, which ruled that claimant was not entitled to workers' compensation benefits subsequent to December 11, 2002.

During claimant's many years as a maintenance supervisor employed by LILCO and its successor, he suffered exposure to asbestos. A Workers' Compensation Law Judge (hereinafter WCLJ) found that claimant suffered from occupational asbestosis and asbestosis-related pleural disease, and that the date of disablement was November 30, 1998, the date upon which he retired at the age of 55, findings which are not in dispute in this appeal. While claimant accepted an incentive package to retire, there was evidence that his decision to retire was related to his occupational disease. Claimant has not sought work since his retirement, although the record bears evidence that he could perform sedentary work in an environment free of contaminants. The WCLJ found that claimant has a permanent partial disability, that his decision to retire was based in part on his disability, and thus, he did not voluntarily withdraw from the labor market, findings which are not challenged in this appeal. Upon LILCO's administrative appeal, the Workers' Compensation Board affirmed the decision of the WCLJ, but held that claimant would not be entitled to awards of compensation subsequent to the date on which he first testified that he had not sought any work after his retirement. Claimant appeals.

When presented with a case of this nature, the Board must engage in a three-step analysis. First, the Board must determine whether claimant's permanent partial disability caused or contributed to his decision to retire. If it did not, the Board may then conclude that claimant voluntarily withdrew from the labor market and is not entitled to continued compensation. Next, however, if claimant's permanent partial disability caused or contributed to his decision to retire, an inference arises that his earning capacity is reduced by the disability and claimant is entitled to compensation until the inference is removed from the case. The third step involves removal of the inference. That occurs only when the employer or workers' compensation carrier submits "direct and positive proof that something other than the disability was the sole cause of claimant's reduced earning capacity after retirement." Proof that the claimant has not sought work postretirement, by itself, does not defeat the inference or shift the burden to claimant to show that the disability was a cause of the reduction. Thus, the Board erred in disallowing awards to claimant on the ground that he had not sought employment within his physical limitations postretirement.

NOTES

1. _Leeber in New York._ If Leeber had been disabled in New Jersey (our example of the Category I approach), the extent of his impairment would have been rated at the hearing. If, for example, the condition was rated at 30 percent, he would have received 180 weeks of PPD benefits (600 weeks times 30%) regardless of his subsequent experience in the labor market, including whether he had retired. If Leeber had been disabled in Iowa (our example of the Category II approach), the extent of his loss of earning capacity would have been rated at the hearing. If, for example, Leeber's impairment plus his age and other factors resulted in a assessment that he had lost 40 percent of his earning capacity, he would have received 200 weeks of PPD benefits (500 weeks times 40%), regardless of his subsequent experience in the labor market, including whether he had retired. However, since Leeber was disabled in New York (our example of the Category III approach), the duration of the PPD benefits was not determined by the extent of his impairment or his age, etc. Rather, the duration of Leeber's benefits depended on his establishing that his lack of actual earnings was due to the permanent consequences of his workplace injury. The fact that he had retired did not necessarily make him ineligible for PPD benefits.

2. _Traits of the Wage-Loss Approach._ Several of the traits of a "pure" wage-loss approach are worth emphasizing. One trait is that, unless the worker has actual earnings after the date of MMI that are less than the worker's preinjury earnings, no benefits are paid even if the work injury has resulted in an impairment, functional limitation, or loss of earning capacity. This is a crucial difference between the true wage-loss approach (Category III) and the loss of earning capacity approach (Category II); a worker who experiences a loss of earning capacity but no actual loss of earnings is precluded from benefits in the wage-loss approach but is not precluded in the loss of earning capacity approach. The "no present wage loss/no benefits" outcome is not a mere hypothetical result: in one year, almost 10% of all nonscheduled cases in New York were closed with no permanent disability benefits because the workers were experiencing no actual loss of earnings at the date of the hearing, even though they had other permanent consequences of their injuries.

Another characteristic of the wage-loss approach is that the total duration of the permanent disability benefits is _not_ determined shortly after the date of MMI, as in Categories I and II. Instead, the duration of benefits depends on the length of time the worker experiences actual losses of earnings due to the work injury. In New York, this duration can range from zero weeks (for those cases closed with no present wage loss) to the balance of the worker's life. If at the time the case is initially classified as a nonscheduled permanent partial disability in New York, the worker experiences a wage loss, benefits commence under the option entitled "wage loss — benefits continue for duration of wage loss." The length of time these benefits will continue is unknown because the duration of subsequent wage loss is unknown. Furthermore, the worker's eligibility for nonscheduled benefits can change through time. For example, a worker whose case is initially closed with no benefits because of no present wage loss can reopen the case for up to eighteen years after the date of injury or eight years after the last benefit payment. Permanent partial benefits can commence after the reopening if the work injury is then causing lost earnings. This approach can be described as a retrospective or *ex post* approach to permanent disability benefits because the amount and duration of permanent disability benefits are not known until the period of permanent disability is over (or the period for reopening has expired).

There is a third outcome for a nonscheduled permanent partial disability case in New York, namely the lump sum settlement. The lump sum settlement in New York is essentially a compromise and release (C & R) agreement, in which the parties reach a compromise concerning the amount of benefits to be paid, the worker receives a lump-sum payment, and the employer is released from any further liability for the particular injury. The use of a C & R agreement or a lump-sum settlement basically transforms a case from one relying on a Category III approach (where the amount of permanent disability benefits in a case is unknown until the end of the period of permanent disability or the period for reopening has expired) into a Category II approach (where the amount of permanent disability benefits is determined near the beginning of the period of permanent disability based on an assessment of the extent of loss of earning capacity).

3. PERMANENT TOTAL DISABILITY BENEFITS

Permanent total disability benefits are paid to an injured worker who is considered completely unable to work after the date of maximum medical improvement. In most states, the weekly benefit is two-thirds of the preinjury wage, subject to maximum and minimum weekly benefits as prescribed by state law. Most workers' compensation statutes also provide that a worker will be classified as permanently and totally disabled if specified losses occur, which can be considered a form of "scheduled" permanent total disability benefits because the worker does not need to demonstrate he has no actual earnings. Thus, the Ohio workers' compensation statute provides that "The loss or loss of use of both hands or both arms, or both feet or both legs, or both eyes, or any two thereof shall constitute total and permanent disability . . . ." OHIO REV. CODE ANN. § 4123.58(C). Suppose a worker is injured at work and his left leg is amputated above the knee. Suppose the worker resumes employment after receiving his artificial leg. Does he meet the statutory definition of permanent total disability since he lost two body parts (his left foot and his left leg)? Yes, according to the Ohio Supreme Court. *International Paper v. Trucinski*, 833 N.E.2d 728 (Ohio 2004). Not any more, according to the Ohio Legislature, which enacted legislation in 2006 that clarified the loss of one limb does not constitute the loss of two body parts.

A worker can also be classified as permanently and totally disabled based on the facts in the case. This might be done by using the "odd-lot" doctrine, which is examined in the *Guyton* case below.

GUYTON v. IRVING JENSEN CO.
Supreme Court of Iowa
373 N.W.2d 101 (1985)

McCORMICK, JUSTICE.

In this case of first impression we adopt the "odd-lot doctrine" in workers' compensation cases. . . .

Petitioner Frank Guyton, Jr . . . hurt his back on May 5, 1978, while working for respondent Irving Jensen Company in Sioux City, when he was struck in the left hip by a cement truck. Workers' compensation benefits were paid during three months in 1978. In the review-reopening proceeding, he sought benefits for permanent disability, and the dispute concerns the extent of his compensable disability.

The industrial commissioner . . . determined Guyton's disability to be twenty percent. In accordance with these findings, the commissioner awarded Guyton benefits based on a twenty percent industrial disability.

Thus the commissioner equated Guyton's ability to obtain employment with his ability to perform physical activity in "junking." In this context, Guyton's industrial disability was determined to be approximately the same as his fifteen to twenty percent functional disability. The availability of suitable employment was not discussed.

The commissioner did not in his analysis address any of the other factors to be considered in determining industrial disability. Industrial disability means reduced earning capacity. Bodily impairment is merely one factor in gauging industrial disability. Other factors include the worker's age, intelligence, education, qualifications, experience, and the effect of the injury on the worker's ability to obtain suitable work. When the combination of factors precludes the worker from obtaining regular employment to earn a living, the worker with only a partial functional disability has a total industrial disability.

Abundant evidence concerning the other factors was adduced in this case. Guyton is a black man approximately 40 years old who does not know his age. He grew up in Mississippi where he had about one month of formal education. He cannot read or write or make change. The evidence included results of psychological tests administered for social security disability purposes. The tests showed Guyton to be mildly retarded. Considering his retardation with his lack of education and illiteracy, the examiner concluded Guyton "will be limited in competitive employment to jobs of an unskilled, repetitive nature requiring no literacy."

Guyton's employment history before his injury included work as a farm hand in Mississippi, fertilizer bagger in Waterloo, laborer in a Waterloo bottling plant for six years, city garbage man, and janitor at the Waterloo sewage plant. He was working as a laborer on highway construction when he was injured.

The uncontroverted medical evidence was that Guyton received a lower back sprain in the truck mishap, resulting in some percentage of permanent physical impairment due to recurrent pain. Substantial evidence supports the commissioner's finding that this impairment is fifteen to twenty percent of the body. Guyton's physician testified that he would have good days and bad days but could not do any job on a regular basis that involved bending, prolonged sitting, or even lifting as little as ten or fifteen pounds. He believed Guyton could not perform the work in the kind of jobs he previously had.

Testimony was received from a vocational counselor. Based on the medical and psychological data and her study of the job market, she said that before his injury Guyton could expect to obtain elemental employment in the bottom ten percent of the job market. After his injury she did not believe he could even obtain jobs of that type. She said Guyton might find work in a sheltered workshop that would pay approximately $1430 a year. In a normal economic climate, she believed most employers would eliminate him as a job applicant. If he were hired, she thought he would be put in a "last hired, first fired" category. His physical and mental limitations would combine to screen him out of job opportunities. She concluded that Guyton had "little, if any, possibility of job placement in substantial gainful activity." As a result, she said she considered him to be 100 percent vocationally disabled.

The record contains substantial evidence of Guyton's efforts since his injury to find employment. He applied for work with the assistance of a friend at numerous places in the Waterloo area and up to 150 miles away. He had not found employment in this period of more than four years. He subsisted by earning small amounts through his junking activities and through social security disability compensation. There was no evidence that jobs were available to persons with his combination of impairments. . . .

In determining the correct rule of law to be applied to this record we must address Guyton's contention that Iowa recognizes the "odd-lot doctrine." He argued this contention before the commissioner and in district court. The commissioner believed that doctrine is implicit in the industrial disability standard enunciated in our cases, and we agree. We now formally adopt the doctrine.

Under that doctrine a worker becomes an odd-lot employee when an injury makes the worker incapable of obtaining employment in any well-known branch of the labor market. An odd-lot worker is thus totally disabled if the only services the worker can perform are "so limited in quality, dependability, or quantity that a reasonably stable market for them does not exist . . . ." *Lee v. Minneapolis Street Railway Co.,* 41 N.W.2d 433, 436 (Minn. 1950). A person who has no reasonable prospect of steady employment has no material earning capacity. This concept . . . is recognized in virtually every jurisdiction. *See* 2 A. Larson, THE LAW OF [WORKERS'] COMPENSATION, § 57.51 at 10-164.24 (1983). The evidence in the present case would permit the finder of fact to find Guyton is an odd-lot employee.

In most jurisdictions, the odd-lot doctrine involves an allocation of the burden of production of evidence that has not been addressed in our prior cases. Professor Larson states the general rule as follows:

A suggested general-purpose principle on burden of proof in this class of cases would run as follows: If the evidence of degree of obvious physical impairment, coupled with other facts such as claimant's mental capacity, education, training, or age, places claimant prima facie in the odd-lot category, the burden should be on the employer to show that some kind of suitable work is regularly and continuously available to the claimant. Certainly in such a case it should not be enough to show that claimant is physically capable of performing light work, and then round out the case for non-compensability by adding a presumption that light work is available. It is a well-known fact of modern economic life that the demand for unskilled and semiskilled labor has been rapidly declining with the advent of the age of mechanization and automation, and that the great bulk of the persistent hard-core unemployment of the United States is in these categories.

2 A. Larson, *supra,* at 10-164.95 to 10-164.113. Our cases make it clear that the burden of persuasion on the issue of industrial disability always remains with the worker. The cases, however, have distinguished between burden of persuasion and burden of production in other workers' compensation situations. Before today we were not required to decide whether a presumption exists that suitable work is available to an odd-lot employee or whether evidence must be adduced on that subject.

We adopt the burden of proof allocation enunciated in Professor Larson's statement of the general rule. We emphasize that this rule merely allocates the burden of production of evidence. It is triggered only when the worker makes a prima facie case for inclusion in the odd-lot category. . . .

We therefore hold that when a worker makes a prima facie case of total disability by producing substantial evidence that the worker is not employable in the competitive labor market, the burden to produce evidence of suitable employment shifts to the employer. If the employer fails to produce such evidence and the trier of fact finds the worker does fall in the odd-lot category, the worker is entitled to a finding of total disability.

The court of appeals, without using the burden-shifting aspect of the odd-lot employee doctrine, nevertheless found Guyton carried his burden to prove total disability as a matter of law. We do not agree. Even under the odd-lot doctrine that we adopt today the trier of fact is free to determine the weight and credibility of the evidence in determining whether the worker's burden of persuasion has been carried. Only in an exceptional case would evidence be sufficiently strong to compel a finding of total disability as a matter of law. The evidence in the present case is not that strong. As demonstrated in the analysis of the commissioner, a dispute existed in the evidence concerning the effect of Guyton's injury on his ability to hold and keep a job. Although Guyton clearly made a prima facie case that he is totally disabled, the evidence was not strong enough to compel that holding as a matter of law. The evidence would permit a finding that his inability to obtain employment was attributable to unsatisfactory work history unrelated to his injury.

Upon remand, in view of the burden-shifting aspect of the odd-lot doctrine we adopt today, the commissioner shall give the parties an opportunity to offer such additional evidence as they wish on the issue of availability of suitable employment for Guyton. The commissioner shall make new findings of fact and conclusions of law in accordance with today's holding.

Decision of court of appeals vacated; judgment of district court reversed and remanded.

All Justices concur except WOLLE, J., who takes no part.

4. DEATH BENEFITS

Death benefits are paid to the survivor or survivors of a worker killed on the job. In some jurisdictions, the weekly benefit depends on the number of survivors. For example, a widow or widower might receive a benefit that is 50% of the deceased worker's wage, while a widow or widower with a child might receive a weekly benefit that is 66⅔% of the deceased worker's wage. The death benefits are subject to minimum and maximum weekly amounts.

H. MEDICAL AND REHABILITATION BENEFITS

Most state workers' compensation laws require the employer to provide medical benefits without cost to the workers. Unlike many health care plans (and unlike workers' compensation cash benefits), there are no deductibles or co-insurance provisions that require employees to share the expenses of medical benefits. Fee schedules have been issued by many state workers' compensation agencies that limit medical charges, which have made some medical care providers reluctant or unwilling to provide services to injured workers. During the 1990s, managed care was introduced into the workers' compensation health care delivery systems in many states.

Medical rehabilitation, such as physical therapy, is provided in most states by the workers' compensation program. However, many states do not provide vocational rehabilitation services that may be necessary to equip the injured worker to return to the former job or, where necessary, to handle a new job.

While in general medical care and medical rehabilitation are provided to injured workers in all states, there are limits to what the workers' compensation programs will cover.

PETRILLA v. WORKMEN'S COMPENSATION APPEAL BOARD
Commonwealth Court of Pennsylvania
692 A.2d 623 (1997)

Opinion by JUDGE DOYLE

Robert J. Petrilla (Claimant) appeals from an order of the Workmen's Compensation Appeal Board (Board) which affirmed the referee's decision denying his petition for review. The issues raised on appeal are: (1) whether under Section 306(f) of the Workers' Compensation Act (Act), Claimant is entitled to reimbursement for home nursing care provided by his wife; and (2) whether a van equipped with special devices designed to enable Claimant to travel in his wheelchair constitutes "orthopedic appliances" under Section 306(f) of the Act. Claimant, while employed by People's Natural Gas Company

(Employer), sustained a work-related injury on January 23, 1979 and began receiving total disability benefits pursuant to a notice of compensation payable. Due to the work injury, Claimant became a paraplegic, and he is currently confined to a wheelchair.

On December 11, 1991, Claimant filed a petition for review, alleging that Employer refused to provide medically necessary transportation and pay for reasonably incurred medical expenses for home nursing care provided by his wife. In its answer, Employer alleged that it had offered to retrofit Claimant's vehicle with hand controls or other modifications to enable him to drive, that it had no obligation to provide the vehicle itself, and that it had no obligation to pay for the services provided by Claimant's wife, who was not a duly licensed practitioner of the healing arts.

To support the petition, Claimant and his wife testified at the hearing. Claimant also presented the deposition testimony of his treating physician, Gilbert Brenes, M.D. The following facts found by the referee are undisputed. Claimant needs home nursing care for regular catheterization, daily bowel training and assistance in getting in and out of bed, getting dressed and his daily exercises. In addition, Claimant must be turned in his bed every two hours to avoid skin problems. Claimant's wife received training for home nursing care at the Harmarville Center where Claimant was treated. She provided home care for Claimant until she left him in April 1990. Employer thereafter provided nursing care until Claimant was discharged from the Harmarville Center on August 16, 1990 upon his wife's return. Claimant's wife again left Claimant in August 1991, and Employer has since provided nursing care for Claimant. Claimant requested reimbursement for the services provided by his wife in the amount of $100 per day.

The Harmarville Center prescribed a specially equipped van for Claimant because he could no longer transport himself in a standard size car with modified controls due to his medical conditions. Claimant requested $37,940 for such a van.

The referee denied Claimant's petition, concluding that the services provided by Claimant's wife did not fall within "services rendered by duly licensed practitioners of the healing arts" under Section 306(f)(1) of the Act, and further, that the requested van similarly did not fall within "orthopedic appliances" under Section 306(f)(4). On appeal, the Board affirmed the referee's decision.

Claimant first contends that the home nursing care provided by his wife is recoverable under Section 306(f)(1) of the Act in effect when Claimant filed the petition. Section 306(f)(1) provided that "[t]he employer shall provide payment for reasonable surgical and medical services, services rendered by duly licensed practitioners of the healing arts, medicines, and supplies, as and when needed . . . ." Services provided to a claimant by someone who is not a licensed practitioner of the healing arts, to be recoverable under Section 306(f)(1), must be provided under the supervision of a practitioner, or at a minimum, by a referral from the practitioner. . . .

In this matter, it is undisputed that Claimant's wife provided the care without any supervision of Dr. Brenes or any other licensed practitioner.

Moreover, the mere fact that Claimant's wife received training for the home nursing care of her husband at the Harmarville Center does not make her services compensable under Section 306(f)(1).

In *Linko v. Workmen's Compensation Appeal Board (Roadway Express, Inc.)*, 621 A.2d 1188 (Pa. Cmwlth. 1993), after the claimant sustained the work injury, his wife left her job as a nurse's aide to care for the claimant. The claimant later sought reimbursement for the services provided by his wife during his convalescence. This Court held that the claimant was not entitled to reimbursement, noting, *inter alia*, that the claimant did not actually pay for the services rendered by his wife, and that her care for her husband was not different from that which husband or wife would perform for an injured spouse.

As in *Linko*, Claimant did not hire his wife for the home nursing care, nor did he pay for her services. Rather, she voluntarily provided the care to her injured husband. As the Supreme Court observed, "[t]he plaintiff cannot recover for the nursing and attendance of the members of his own household, unless they are hired servants" because such care by family members "involves the performance of the ordinary offices of affection, which is their duty . . . ." *Goodhart v. Pennsylvania Railroad Co.*, 35 A. 191, 192 (Pa. 1896). Hence, the referee and the Board properly concluded that Claimant is not entitled to reimbursement for the services provided by his wife under Section 306(f) of the Act.

Claimant next contends that Employer must provide a specially equipped van to enable him to travel in his wheelchair. Section 306(f)(4) provides that the employer must pay for "medicines and supplies, hospital treatment, services and supplies *and orthopedic appliances*, and prostheses." 77 P.S. § 531(4) (emphasis added). Employer is willing to provide the necessary modifications to a van, but refuses to provide a van itself. Employer contends that the van requested by Claimant does not fall within "orthopedic appliances" under Section 306(f)(4).

In *Rieger v. Workmen's Compensation Appeal Board (Barnes & Tucker Co.)*, 521 A.2d 84 (Pa. Commw. Ct. 1987), this Court held that a wheelchair is an "orthopedic appliance," and that devices which will aid the claimant in the use of his wheelchair, such as the bars placed in a bathroom, ramps leading to and from his home, as well as retrofitting of claimant's automobile with hand controls, also fall within the definition of "orthopedic appliances" under Section 306(f)(4). The Court reasoned:

> [A] wheelchair was in fact a necessity for the claimant, and if a wheelchair is necessary, then it logically follows that minor modifications needed to facilitate the use of the appliance must also be considered a necessity. . . .

> [T]he intent of the Act is not that a claimant be forced either to rely upon the charity of his family and friends or to rely upon hired assistance in order to perform those daily tasks, duties and business that he was previously able to perform, when a simple, inexpensive remedy is available at hand. If the claimant's injuries make it impossible to leave his home, the remedial nature of the Act would be frustrated by a failure to provide a one-time expenditure.

521 A.2d at 87.

In the matter *sub judice*, the referee accepted Dr. Brenes' testimony and found that due to his conditions of bilateral carpal tunnel syndrome and rotator cuff syndrome in his right shoulder, which are related to the 1979 work injury, Claimant was no longer able to transport himself in a standard size automobile with modified controls, and that he therefore needed a van with various modifications. Dr. Brenes stated in his July 21, 1992 medical report:

> I have, therefore, prepared a prescription for the type of vehicle that will be necessary to allow Mr. Petrilla to transport himself from place to place. I believe that such a vehicle is a medical necessity as it will enable him to obtain treatment without assistance and possibly alleviate the existing home care needs.

Employer has acknowledged and agreed that it is responsible for the necessary modifications to a motor vehicle, including a van, which would be necessary because of Claimant's handicaps. However, Employer argues that it should not have to pay for the cost of the van itself. The WCJ agreed and reached the conclusion that the issue was one of pure law and statutory interpretation and that a van was not an "orthopedic appliance" within the meaning of Section 306(f)(4) of the Act. The Board affirmed and the issue now presented on appeal is a further extension of this Court's holding in *Rieger*; one which has not been squarely addressed in this Commonwealth, but has recently been addressed in our sister state of Maryland.

In *R & T Construction Co. v. Judge*, 594 A.2d 99 (Md. 1991), a quadriplegic injured worker filed a workers' compensation claim for a specially equipped van and, *inter alia*, the cost of enlarging and remodeling his home to accommodate his "sip and puff" controlled wheelchair. In an extensive and wide-ranging opinion which considered the case law and similar compensation statutes in a number of other states, including this Court's decisions in *Rieger* and *Bomboy*, the Maryland Court of Appeals held that a specially equipped van is not compensable "medical equipment or apparatus" under Article 101, § 37(a) of the Maryland Code (1957, 1985 Repl. Vol.), which is Maryland's equivalent of our Workers' Compensation Act provision. The *R & T* Court went further and, quoting A. Larson, 2 *The Law of Workmen's Compensation* § 61.13(a), at 10-863 (1989), summarized the case law on the issue by stating that "as to specially-equipped automobiles for paraplegics, the cases have uniformly denied reimbursement, on the ground that an automobile is simply not a medical apparatus or device." 594 A.2d at 108 (footnote omitted).

While not controlling the resolution of the issue in this Commonwealth, of course, the statutory language in Maryland's statue is strikingly similar to ours and compels the same logical analysis. First, "medical apparatus or prosthetic appliance" (Md.) and an "orthopedic appliance" (Pa.) have, for our purposes, almost identical definitions and are thus very similar in scope. Obviously, neither the phrase "*medical* apparatus or prosthetic *appliance*" nor the term "orthopedic *appliance*," in this context, refers to a motor vehicle for general transportation use. The general use of a vehicle must, of course, be distinguished from the retrofitting of that vehicle, without which the vehicle could not be operated by the claimant. It is the modifications and additional "appliances," not the vehicle itself, which are necessary to accommodate the claimant's work-related injury. Thus, the special retrofitting is an "orthopedic appliance," *Rieger*, while a van itself is not.

Second, by analogy, while the special remodeling of an injured worker's home to make it wheelchair accessible might be analogous to the cost of retrofitting a motor vehicle so that the vehicle is accessible to a paraplegic, the cost of the van itself might also be analogized to the cost of purchasing the home itself, which is noncompensable; to argue that these latter costs should be compensable is simply untenable.

Finally, considering only the cost of the van in this case, i.e., $37,940, which would have a limited life expectancy, we would have to further conclude that the expenditure would be prohibitive under *Bomboy*, where the Court found that a cost of $30,000 to $35,000 for additional modifications in the home to accommodate the claimant's wheelchair were unreasonable after the employer had already spent $5,000 to convert the claimant's basement into living quarters. The *Bomboy* Court opined:

> Moreover, in *Rieger*, the employer modified the claimant's home at a cost of $433.02. In this case, the employer had already provided approximately $5,000.00 in modifications, and the claimant now seeks additional modifications, at a cost of approximately $30,000.00 to $35,000.00
>
> Because additional home modifications would result in a substantial cost burden on the employer, and because the claimant proposed no alternatives, we conclude that *Rieger* does not support the claimant's request for an attached garage and a wheelchair lift.

572 A.2d at 250. The cost of providing a $37,940 vehicle would be equally as burdensome.

Accordingly, we affirm the determination of the Board.

Dissenting Opinion by SENIOR JUDGE MIRARCHI [omitted].

NOTES

1. *Limits on Van Modifications.* The holding in *Petrilla* that the employer is only responsible for the cost of modifying a van for a disabled worker, but not for the cost of the van itself, is in agreement with decisions in most jurisdictions. The rule was applied in a different context in *Strickland v. Bowater, Inc.*, 472 S.E.2d 635 (S.C. Ct. App. 1996). Strickland sustained an accident to his head and neck. He was not initially disabled, but underwent surgery to remove a herniated disc. As a result of complications during the surgery, he was rendered a quadriplegic and was awarded permanent total disability benefits. Bowater agreed to pay for the cost of modifying a van for Strickland's use and for the difference in cost between an average mid-sized automobile and an unmodified van. The court decided that Bowater was not required to pay the full cost of the unmodified van.

2. *Limits on Spousal Reimbursement.* The other holding in *Petrilla*, that the employer was not entitled to reimbursement for home nursing care provided by his wife, is not as consistently followed in other jurisdictions. The differences in statutes and facts among cases are important. The Supreme

Court of Vermont affirmed an order of the Commissioner of the Vermont Department of Labor and Industry requiring the employer to pay the worker $207,312 for nursing services provided by his spouse. Close suffered a severe head injury and was subject to seizures, severe disorientation, and memory loss. As a result, he required supervision twenty-four hours a day, as well as assistance in dressing, eating, and taking his medication. Close's wife was assigned a number of tasks by his physician, which she provided between March 1989, when he was discharged from the hospital, and March 1995, when he was admitted to an assisted-living facility. The court indicated that this was the first case that required an interpretation of the Vermont workers' compensation statute requiring an employer to "furnish reasonable surgical, medical and nursing services." The court reviewed a number of decisions in other states, and found that they reflected a flexible approach, considering such factors as the nature of the services provided, the need for continuous care, the medical condition of the injured worker, and whether a reasonable value can be assigned to the services provided. Using these factors for guidance, the court concluded that the facts in this case justified the payment to the spouse. *Close v. Superior Excavating Co.*, 693 A.2d 729 (Vt. 1997).

SHAWNEE MANAGEMENT CORP. v. HAMILTON
Court of Appeals of Virginia
480 S.E.2d 773, *aff'd en banc,* 492 S.E.2d 456 (Va. 1997)

Opinion by CHIEF JUDGE NORMAN K. MOON

Shawnee Management Corporation appeals the decision of the commission awarding Rhonda C. Hamilton benefits. The dispositive question is whether Shawnee must continue paying disability benefits to Hamilton who did not stop smoking cigarettes and/or lose weight as required by her treating physician in order to undergo surgery. We find that because Hamilton's failure to quit smoking renders her unable to receive medical treatment for her compensable injury, her refusal to stop smoking constitutes refusal of medical treatment, and therefore precludes her right to compensation until she complies.

On October 25, 1991, Hamilton, a resident of Winchester Virginia, slipped on a wet floor at her place of employment and injured her back. By agreement, an award was entered for temporary total disability benefits beginning November 2, 1991.

On January 25, 1993, Hamilton underwent back surgery to correct her injuries. About early April she moved from Winchester, Virginia, to Manassas, Virginia, but continued to travel back and forth to Winchester for treatment by Dr. Zoller. On July 20, 1993 Dr. Zoller released her to return to light work with several restrictions. In August, 1993, Shawnee sent a job description to Dr. Zoller, describing a cashier position at a Winchester Hardees. Shawnee intended to offer Hamilton the position pending Dr. Zoller's approval of the job. Dr. Zoller noted in Hamilton's medical records that:

> I got a job description from Shawnee Corporation and I read it to [Hamilton] and I said that there was no way I could legitimately say no to this offer. They are bending over backwards to accommodate her

and it certainly seems like it would be doable by anybody other than possibly a quadriplegic.

Hamilton testified that in late August Shawnee offered her the cashier position. She testified that she declined to take the position because her back still hurt and the hour and one-half commute each direction was excessive given that she would only work two or three hours each day. She testified, "I told [Dr. Zoller], you know, since I was so far away that I was going to try to babysit my daughter's kids. I didn't really look at as [*sic*] refusing, I just — it would have been too far to have drove [*sic*]." Hamilton also testified that she had looked for work within her capabilities. She testified: "I've applied for jobs. But . . . they don't really want someone that they have to limit. So, I didn't — I wasn't accepted." She also testified that during the two year period in which she could have returned to work, she did not register with the Virginia Employment Commission and applied for work with only three stores.

On September 14, 1993, Shawnee filed an application to suspend Hamilton's benefits on the basis that she had refused selective employment within her residual capacity. Hamilton's benefits were suspended as of September 13, 1993, not on the basis of Shawnee's application, but because Hamilton had failed to keep the commission informed of her mailing address. In December, 1993, Hamilton moved back to Winchester, Virginia.

In August, 1994, Dr. Zoller referred Hamilton to Dr. John P. Kostuik at Johns Hopkins for a second opinion. Dr. Kostuik determined that additional surgery was needed. Both doctors agreed that the procedure should not be undertaken until Hamilton stopped smoking and lost some weight. On or about August 25, 1994, Dr. Zoller wrote to Shawnee's insurance carrier and reiterated that Hamilton could return to work and that she was once again living in Winchester. Dr. Zoller noted that the restrictions for work remained "totally unchanged" from July, 1993.

Hamilton testified that she had previously quit smoking in order to undergo the original back surgery in January, 1993. She stated that she refrained from smoking for sixteen to eighteen months, but explained that "my son got in trouble and my sister kept on, here take a drag and calm your nerves, calm your nerves. So I started up again." Hamilton testified that she smoked two packs of cigarettes a day at the time. Drs. Zoller and Kostuik instructed her to stop in order to undergo the additional surgery. Since that time, Hamilton testified, she has reduced her smoking to five or so cigarettes a day. She has also gained approximately sixty pounds.

On January 3, 1995, Dr. Zoller wrote to Shawnee's insurer explaining that he had changed his mind regarding Hamilton's ability to return to work, stating that "it probably would have been more worthwhile to keep her on with off-work from that time [July 20, 1993] until the present time. . . . I feel that [Hamilton] should be considered off work the entire period of time, never having been allowed to go back to work." Dr. Zoller noted on February 22, 1995 that Hamilton had not stopped smoking and that they could not proceed with surgery until she stopped.

On January 31, 1995, Hamilton filed a change in condition application seeking temporary total disability benefits beginning September 14, 1993. The deputy commissioner considered Hamilton's application and Shawnee's application still pending from September 14, 1993. The deputy commissioner found Hamilton's failure to stop smoking warranted continued suspension of her benefits until such time as she stopped in order to undergo the corrective surgery. The deputy commissioner specifically declined to reach the other defenses raised by Shawnee or Shawnee's application, although evidence was presented by the parties on these issues.

On Hamilton's appeal, the full commission reversed the deputy commissioner's ruling and summarily disposed of every defense raised by Shawnee and Shawnee's application.

Smoking as Refusal of Medical Care

Workers' compensation benefits may be suspended where a claimant refuses medical treatment. *Davis v. Brown & Williamson Tobacco Co.*, 348 S.E.2d 420, 422 (Va. App. 1986).

Here, Hamilton's continued smoking completely prohibits her from receiving treatment. Hamilton was informed unequivocally that before she could have surgery she must "quit [smoking] altogether." Her doctor explained to her that the surgery she required could not be performed while she continued to smoke and to suffer the effects of routine cigarette use. Until she quits smoking, she will remain totally disabled because of her injury and consequently unable to work. Hamilton's continued smoking constitutes a complete and total bar to her treatment and therefore bars her ability to reenter the work force.

Hamilton is faced with the choice of having to quit smoking entirely or to continue her current condition without treatment. No evidence in the record proved that Hamilton is so addicted to tobacco that she cannot stop smoking. To the contrary, Hamilton testified that she had, on her doctor's order, previously stopped smoking for a period of sixteen to eighteen months. Further, Hamilton testified that she had reduced her smoking from two packs a day to five cigarettes a day. This record does not support a finding that Hamilton should be entitled to continue drawing benefits while she chooses to forgo the medical treatment determined by her doctor. Hamilton's decision to keep smoking, knowing it prevents her from having surgery, is no more or less than a decision not to undergo the medical treatment proscribed by her treating physician. Therefore, her benefits should be suspended.

Holding that Hamilton's claim for compensation was properly denied, we need not reach the additional issue raised by Shawnee concerning whether Hamilton may refuse selective employment because she has moved away from her original job location.

Reversed.

NOTE

When Is an Injured Worker Required to Accept Medical Care and Rehabilitation Services? A worker recovered to the extent possible through medical treatment. His further recovery would have required exercise or use of the injured shoulder, which he refused to do. The court refused his claim for temporary total disability benefits because "to allow him three or four hundred weeks compensation will destroy all incentive to rehabilitate his arm by exercise." *Turner v. Neeb Kearney & Co.*, 139 So. 2d 3 (La. Ct. App. 1962).

Chapter 23

THE OCCUPATIONAL SAFETY AND HEALTH ACT

Statutes regulating workplace safety were (along with laws dealing with child labor) the earliest types of protective labor legislation enacted by the states, with many of the statutes dating to the nineteenth century. Workplace safety legislation did not receive significant attention through the first half of the twentieth century, however. This lack of attention was in part due to the generally improving safety statistics for several decades after most states enacted workers' compensation statutes between 1910 and 1920. In addition, with the onset of the depression in the 1930s, other aspects of the labor market received primary attention. Thus the 1930s and the immediate postwar period of the 1940s saw significant legislation enacted dealing with areas such as labor-management relations, wages and work hours, unemployment, and retirement income.

Attention shifted to workplace safety and health in the 1960s in part because other areas of the workplace had been dealt with by federal legislation. An even more important explanation for the new focus on safety was the increase in the injury rate in the manufacturing sector during the 1960s. Although it was not entirely clear what caused the deterioration in workplace safety, a virtual consensus was reached at the federal level that some action was necessary to reverse the trend and that states were unable or unwilling to enact the strict regulations necessary to improve workplace safety and health.

Numerous bills were introduced in Congress in the late 1960s. The ultimate result was the Occupational Safety and Health Act of 1970 (OSHAct, or the Act), which was passed with large majorities in both the House and Senate and signed with a strong endorsement by President Nixon on December 29, 1970. The Act became effective 120 days later and soon became one of the most controversial pieces of federal legislation dealing with the workplace. Yet, despite more than three decades of criticism from virtually every interest group concerned about workplace safety and health, the Act has not been significantly amended — in part because the criticisms from parties such as organized labor about lack of vigor in enforcement have been countered by charges from participants such as employer groups about excessive stringency of regulation.

A. AN OVERVIEW OF THE ACT

1. COVERAGE

The OSHAct covers virtually all private sector workers. *See* OSHAct § 4. The primary exceptions are workers covered by other federal safety legislation, such as railroad workers. Federal employees are not covered, although § 19(a) requires the head of each federal agency to establish and maintain a comprehensive safety and health program consistent with the standards promulgated under the Act. In 1998, § 3(5) was amended to treat the U.S. Postal Service as if it were a private-sector employer. State and local government employees are not covered; however, if a state has an approved plan (as described below), state and local employees must be covered. In addition, since 1977, Congress has limited or eliminated some aspects of normal enforcement activities for certain employers. Examples are small employers (those with ten or fewer employees) with good safety records, who are exempt from regular inspections, and small farms, which are entirely exempt from the Act.

2. OSHA'S ADMINISTRATIVE STRUCTURE

The OSHAct created three major federal agencies to implement federal policy in occupational safety and health.

First, it created the Occupational Safety and Health Administration (OSHA) within the Department of Labor. OSHA is responsible for promulgating standards, inspecting workplaces for compliance, and prosecuting violations.

Second, it created the National Institute for Occupation Safety and Health (NIOSH) as part of the Department of Health and Human Services (known in 1970 as the Department of Health, Education and Welfare). *See* OSHAct § 22. NIOSH conducts research and makes proposals for new health and safety standards.

Third, it established a new independent agency, the Occupational Safety and Health Review Commission (OSHRC or the Commission). *See* OSHAct § 12. Administrative law judges are responsible for the initial level of dispute adjudication between OSHA and a party charged with a violation of the Act. Appeals are made to the Commission, which has three members appointed by the President.

In addition, the Act established the National Advisory Committee on Occupation Safety and Health (NACOSH), a permanent committee of twelve members who represent management, labor, safety and health professionals, and the public. *See* OSHAct § 7(a). The NACOSH advises the Secretaries of Labor and of Health and Human Services on matters relating to the Act. Finally, there are Advisory Committees that assist the Secretary of Labor in evaluating specific proposed health or safety standards.

This separation of functions among agencies differs from the usual agency model. Congress hoped to assure employers that the separation of functions would prevent any one agency from wielding too much power.

3. PROMULGATION OF STANDARDS

Congress, in enacting the OSHAct, did not directly prohibit or require specific actions by employers. Instead, § 5(a)(1) subjects the employer to a general duty to "furnish to each of his employees employment and a place of employment which are free from recognized hazards that are causing or are likely to cause death or serious physical harm. . . ." In addition, § 5(a)(2) requires each employer to "comply with occupational safety and health standards promulgated under this Act." The Act requires that the Secretary of Labor (acting through OSHA) promulgate standards under the administrative procedures specified in the Act, and the Secretary has issued several thousand such occupational safety and health standards.

The OSHAct approach to standards stands in contrast to some other legislation dealing with the workplace. For example, the National Labor Relations Act (NLRA) contains standards for employer and union behavior in the text of the law, such as the detailed specification in § 8(d) of what the "duty to bargain" entails. The OSHAct text has no equivalent detailed standard, only the vague general duty clause and the requirement to comply with OSHA-promulgated standards. OSHA standards consist of three types: interim standards, emergency temporary standards, and permanent standards.

4. INTERIM STANDARDS

Section 6(a) of the OSHAct authorized the Secretary of Labor to issue interim standards during the first two years of the Act without adhering to the formal rule-making procedure required for new permanent standards. Sometimes referred to as start-up standards, the interim standards were to be derived from either "established Federal standards," which were those already issued by the Federal government under other laws, or from "national consensus standards," which were those already issued by a nationally recognized standards-producing organization. Once promulgated, interim standards remain in effect until revoked or revised using the procedure for new permanent standards.

The Act became effective in April 1971. In May 1971, the Secretary of Labor promulgated all 4,400 established federal standards and national consensus standards, twenty-three months before the deadline for the promulgation of interim standards. Although it is doubtful the Secretary could have carefully scrutinized that many standards even if he had taken the full two years, the immediate adoption of all the potential interim standards caused great controversy.

One source of the controversy was the overwhelming complexity of the rules that were suddenly imposed on employers. The interim standards required over 300 pages in the Federal Register, not including some standards that were incorporated by reference. Some of the interim standards were criticized as too vague, while others were attacked as unnecessarily specific and even meddlesome.

In response to the widespread criticism of the interim standards, OSHA deleted approximately 600 safety standards in 1978 on the grounds that the standards were either obsolete, directed to comfort rather than safety, directed to the public rather than to employees, enforced by other agencies, contingent on manufacturer approval, too detailed, or covered by other standards.

Another problem was that many of the consensus standards from which the interim standards were derived contained advisory rather than mandatory language. For example, the American National Standards Institute (ANSI) scaffolding standard suggested that "[g]uardrails and toeboards *should* be installed on all open sides and ends of platforms more than 10 feet above the ground or floor." In promulgating the interim scaffolding standard, the Secretary of Labor altered the ANSI standard to read: "Guardrails and toeboards *shall* be installed on all open sides and ends of platforms more than 10 feet above the ground or floor" (emphasis added). The standard was struck down because of the alteration of "should" to "shall." *See Usery v. Kennecott Copper Corp.*, 577 F.2d 1113 (10th Cir. 1977).

The problems resulting from unenforceable interim standards were compounded by a subsequent decision. Most courts have held that the general duty clause cannot be used as a basis for a citation against an employer when there is a specific standard applicable to the hazard. The Commission held that use of the general duty clause was blocked even if the standard itself was unenforceable because the Secretary had converted a "should" in the consensus standard into a "shall" in the interim standard. *See A. Prokosch & Sons Sheet Metal*, 8 O.S.H. Cas. (BNA) 2077 (1980). In response to this decision, in 1984 OSHA formally removed 153 provisions of the general industry standards that had adapted advisory standards from ANSI. Rather than promulgate permanent standards in their place, OSHA decided to rely on other general industry standards with mandatory language, or upon the general duty clause, to enforce the Act in these areas.

Despite these deletions, the remaining interim standards adopted in 1971 constitute the bulk of the OSHA standards that are currently in effect.

5. EMERGENCY TEMPORARY STANDARDS

Section 6(c) of the OSHAct authorizes the Secretary to issue an emergency temporary standard (ETS) after a relatively simple procedure. For an ETS, OSHA need not conduct hearings or use advisory committees. The ETS is effective immediately upon publication in the Federal Register. It can remain in effect for six months (unless replaced earlier by a permanent standard).

To promulgate an ETS, the Secretary must determine "(A) that employees are exposed to grave danger from exposure to substances or agents determined to be toxic or physically harmful or from new hazards, and (B) that such emergency standard is necessary to protect employees from such danger."

OSHA has issued only nine emergency temporary standards in the history of the Act. Of these, only three were not challenged in court and went into effect. One ETS — for acrylonitrile, a chemical used in textile production — was challenged but went into effect when the Sixth Circuit denied a stay. The other five ETSs were vacated or stayed by the courts.

The experience with the 1983 ETS for asbestos indicates the extreme difficulty that OSHA has experienced with the courts in issuing emergency temporary standards. OSHA issued the original asbestos standard in 1971 as an interim standard under § 6(a). In 1983, OSHA revisited the asbestos health issue and issued an emergency temporary standard, which lowered the permissible exposure level (PEL) for asbestos. OSHA wrote a preamble to the proposed ETS indicating that the standard was based on information that postdated the 1975 proposal and therefore was a "new regulatory initiative." OSHA concluded that eighty lives could be saved by the more stringent ETS.

The Fifth Circuit scrutinized the 1983 ETS for asbestos. The court indicated that the ETS provision is "an extraordinary power to be used only in 'limited situations' in which a grave danger exists, and then, to be 'delicately exercised.' The Agency cannot use its ETS powers as a stop-gap measure." The court agreed with OSHA that new awareness of the danger of asbestos could justify the Secretary's action to issue an ETS. Nevertheless, the court was not persuaded that OSHA had demonstrated that the asbestos ETS would save eighty lives. The court also found uncertainty concerning the beneficial effect of the ETS from the fact that OSHA was not fully enforcing the current asbestos standard. Because of these various uncertainties concerning the benefits that would result from the proposed ETS, the court held that "an ETS that lacks support in the record for the basis OSHA has articulated must be declared invalid." *Asbestos Information Ass'n/N.A. v. OSHA*, 727 F.2d 415, 425-26 (5th Cir. 1984).

As a practical matter, the ETS provision in the OSHAct is probably moribund. The challenge of convincing the courts that employees are exposed to a grave danger and that the emergency temporary standard is necessary to protect the employees from the danger is formidable. Moreover, the ETS expires no later than six months after publication, and given the long delays in issuing permanent standards, the ETS would probably lapse long before a new permanent standard could take effect.

6. PERMANENT STANDARDS

Permanent standards (including revisions or revocations of interim standards) are covered by § 6(b) of the OSHAct. The procedure for promulgating a permanent standard consists of several steps:

(i) A standard can be proposed by the Secretary or by any interested party. NIOSH, for example, may conduct research that leads to a proposed standard that is forwarded to the Secretary, who will review and may publish the proposed standard.

(ii) (Optional) An Advisory Committee can assess the proposed standard and provide recommendations to the Secretary.

(iii) The Secretary announces the proposed standard in the Federal Register.

(iv) Any interested party may submit written data or comments on the proposed standard.

(v) Any interested party can file written objections to the proposed rule and request a public hearing, which must be held by the Secretary.

(vi) The Office of Management and Budget, another Executive agency, generally reviews the proposed standard. This step, while not enumerated in the Act, has nonetheless occurred for a number of proposed standards.

(vii) The Secretary shall either issue the proposed standard or a modified standard, or shall make a determination that a standard should not be issued.

(viii) If a standard is promulgated, any person who may be adversely affected may obtain a pre-enforcement review of the standard by filing a petition challenging its validity with an appropriate court of appeals.

(ix) The court of appeals is to uphold the determinations of the Secretary that resulted in the standard "if supported by substantial evidence in the record considered as a whole."

(x) The Supreme Court, at its discretion, may review the decision of courts of appeal.

The development and promulgation of new standards was to be at the heart of the OSHAct. After thirty-five years, however, OSHA has promulgated only about fifty permanent health and safety standards under § 6(b). One particularly significant reason for the slow pace is the amount of effort that OSHA has devoted to defending the standards in court. As indicated, after the Secretary has promulgated the standard, any person who may be adversely affected may obtain a pre-enforcement review.

Section 6(f) of the OSHAct instructs the reviewing court to uphold the Secretary's determinations "if supported by substantial evidence in the record considered as a whole." The congressional command to use "substantial evidence" review is unusual for agency rule-making proceedings. Normally, courts review for substantial evidence when agencies have made determinations of fact in the course of formal, trial-like proceedings. It is unclear how courts should review for substantial evidence when the agency decision is based on a policy preference. The more common standard for courts in reviewing informal rulemaking is to uphold the agency decision unless it is "arbitrary and capricious." *See* Administrative Procedure Act § 706(2).

The landmark OSHA case concerning the standard of review is *Industrial Union Department v. Hodgson*, 499 F.2d 467 (D.C. Cir. 1974). In reviewing an OSHA standard for asbestos, the court noted that the administrative record differed from one "customarily conceived of as appropriate for substantial evidence review," and emphasized that the Secretary's determinations "are on the frontiers of scientific knowledge, and consequently . . . depend to a greater extent upon policy judgments and less upon purely factual analysis." The court declared that it would use the substantial evidence standard to review the facts underlying the Secretary's determinations. But when reviewing policy judgments, it would "approach our reviewing task with a flexibility informed and shaped by sensitivity to the diverse origins of the determinations that enter into a legislative judgment."

At the opposite extreme, the Fifth Circuit has been unwilling to disavow the substantial evidence formulation. The court applies the substantial evidence test to OSHA's legislative policy decisions as well as to its factual findings. *See National Grain & Feed Ass'n v. OSHA*, 866 F.2d 717 (5th Cir. 1989).

7. VARIANCES

An employer can request variances to standards by filing an application with the Secretary of Labor. There are two types of variances.

Temporary variances are granted for a maximum of two years. The employer must satisfy several requirements: (1) the employer cannot meet the standard by its effective date because of a shortage of technical or professional personnel or because construction cannot be completed on time; (2) employees are being protected in the interim; and (3) the standard will be complied with as soon as possible. *See* OSHAct § 6(b)(6)(A).

Permanent variances can be granted if the Secretary determines that the employer has provided alternative means to provide a workplace that is as safe and healthful as it would be if the employer had complied with the standard. *See* OSHAct § 6(d).

8. THE GENERAL DUTY CLAUSE

As previously discussed, § 5(a)(2) requires each employer to comply with the interim, emergency temporary, and permanent standards promulgated under § 6 of the OSHAct. In addition, § 5(a)(1) subjects the employer to a general duty to "furnish to each of his employees employment and a place of employment which are free from recognized hazards that are causing or are likely to cause death or serious physical harm. . . ." In general, a citation under § 5(a)(1) is only permitted if no specific standard promulgated under § (6) applies.

There are four elements of a general duty violation:

(1) The employer failed to keep the workplace free of a hazard to which employees of that employer were exposed;

(2) The hazard was recognized;

(3) The hazard was causing or was likely to cause death or serious physical harm; and

(4) There was a feasible method to correct the hazard.

9. ENFORCEMENT

The Secretary may issue regulations requiring employers to maintain accurate records of work-related injuries and diseases. *See* OSHAct § 8(c). There are some exceptions to this requirement, including (since 1983) the virtual elimination of record keeping responsibilities for employers in the retail trade, finance, insurance, real estate, and services sectors.

The Secretary of Labor has broad powers to inspect workplaces. *See* OSHAct § 8(a). OSHA has developed a regular inspection program, and will also inspect a particular employer on the basis of an employee complaint. The inspection process is governed by a series of rules, such as the prohibition on advance notice to an employer of an impending inspection, the requirement for OSHA to obtain a warrant, and the right of an employee to participate in the inspection.

If an OSHA compliance officer finds a violation of the Act, the Secretary is required to issue a citation to the employer that describes the nature of the violation and fixes a reasonable time for abatement. OSHAct § 9(a). The employer has fifteen working days after receipt of the citation to notify the Secretary that he intends to contest the citation. OSHAct § 10(a). Any employee or representative of employees also has fifteen working days after the employer receives the citation to file a notice with the Secretary alleging that the period of time fixed in the citation for the abatement of the violation is unreasonable. OSHAct § (10)(c).

If a citation is issued, § 10(a) requires the Secretary to notify the employer of any proposed penalty and allows the employer fifteen working days to notify the Secretary that he intends to contest the proposed penalty.

Penalties for employers vary depending on the severity of the offense. *See* OSHAct § 17. For a nonserious violation, the fine is $0 to $7,000; for a serious violation, the fine is $100 to $7,000; for a repeat violation, the fine is $0 to $70,000; for a willful violation, the fine is $5,000 to $70,000; and for a failure to abate, the fine is $0 to $7,000 per day. There are three criminal penalties under the OSHAct: for a willful violation that results in death, § 17(e) provides for a fine up to $10,000 plus a jail sentence up to six months for the first conviction; for giving advance notice of an inspection, §17(f) imposes a fine up to $1,000 and imprisonment up to six months; and for knowingly making a false statement, representation, or certification, § 17(g) provides for a fine up to $10,000 and imprisonment up to six months. Individuals and corporations may also be prosecuted under the Criminal Fine Endorsement Act, 18 U.S.C. § 3571, which includes substantial penalties.

There were two amendments to the Act pertaining to enforcement in 1998. Section 8(h) was added to prohibit the Secretary from using the results of enforcement activities, such as the number of citations issued or penalties assessed, to evaluate employees involved in the enforcement of the Act. Also, § 21(d) was added to codify OSHA's consultation program.

10. PROCEDURE IN CONTESTED CASES

The employer may file a notice of contest within fifteen working days of receipt of the citation. The employer may contest the citation, the penalty, or the abatement period. OSHAct § 10(a). The case will be assigned to an Administrative Law Judge appointed by the Commission. A representative of the Secretary of Labor will prosecute the case. Most contested cases are settled without a hearing. If the case does result in a hearing, the ALJ will issue a decision.

The Commission may review the ALJ's decision on the basis of a petition for a discretionary review filed by any aggrieved party or because a Commission member directs a review of the ALJ's decision. The Commission has ultimate responsibility for making findings of fact, but will normally defer to the ALJ's findings of fact. If the employer contests the citation, the abatement requirement is tolled until the Commission issues a final order.

The decision of the Commission may in turn be appealed to a United States court of appeals. OSHAct § 11. Any person adversely affected or aggrieved by a final order of the Commission may file a petition for review in the circuit in which the alleged violation occurred, where the employer has its principal office, or in the District of Columbia. The Secretary may seek review only in the first two of these choices. The filing of a petition with the court of appeals does not automatically operate as a stay on the Commission's order, but the employer can request such a postponement from the court. After the court of appeals issues its decision, the losing party can seek discretionary review from the Supreme Court by filing a petition for a writ of certiorari.

11. IMMINENT DANGER

A danger is imminent if it "could reasonably be expected to cause death or serious physical harm immediately or before the imminence of such danger can be eliminated through the enforcement procedures otherwise provided by this Act." OSHAct § 13(a). When there is an imminent danger and the employer will not eliminate the danger immediately or remove the employees from the location of the imminent risk, the Secretary of Labor can seek a temporary restraining order for a period of up to five days from a U.S. district court *ex parte* (i.e., the employer need not be involved).

12. STATE PLANS

The OSHAct preempts most state safety and health activities, subject to certain exceptions examined in later sections. Even in those areas where federal preemption operates, however, states can run their own safety and health program if:

(i) a state agency is designated to run the program;

(ii) the state agency has sufficient funds and legal authority to conduct the program; and

(iii) the state health and safety standards are at least as effective as the Federal standards.

See OSHAct § 18(c).

13. OTHER PROVISIONS OF THE ACT

The OSHAct has numerous other provisions. The Secretary of Labor and the Secretary of Health and Human Services are authorized by § 8(g) to prescribe rules and regulations deemed necessary to carry out their responsibilities under the OSHAct. Rules and regulations are not subject to the procedural requirements specified for the promulgation of permanent standards, but rules and regulations that create new rights and duties must be promulgated in accordance with the Administrative Procedure Act and can be challenged in Federal district courts. Other sections of the Act are less relevant for workplace safety and health, such as the provision in § 31 dealing with emergency locator beacons for fixed-wing, powered aircraft.

14. THE SMALL BUSINESS REGULATORY ENFORCEMENT FAIRNESS ACT

Separate from the OSHAct itself, the Small Business Regulatory Enforcement Fairness Act of 1996 (SBREFA) has had a major impact on the promulgation of standards under the OSHAct and on the Act's enforcement.

Subtitle A requires OSHA to develop "small entity compliance guides" for essentially all standards.

Subtitle B requires the SBA to establish an Ombudsman who will act as an advocate for small business in their dealings with OSHA and other regulatory agencies. OSHA was also required to establish a program to provide reductions in, and even waivers of, penalties for small businesses.

Subtitle C requires OSHA to reimburse small businesses for fees and expenses incurred during agency enforcement actions when a court finds that OSHA actions are unreasonable.

Subtitle D expands the provisions of the Regulatory Flexibility Act (RFA) which had been enacted in 1980. The RFA required agencies, such as OSHA, to prepare a regulatory flexibility analysis ("reg-flex") to accompany any notice of a rule that affects small businesses. The reg-flex analysis is required *inter alia* to describe the impact of the rule on small businesses, the objectives and legal basis for the rule, and significant alternatives to the rule that could accomplish the stated objectives while minimizing significant economic impacts on small businesses. Subtitle D also significantly expands the opportunities for judicial review of rules affecting small businesses.

Subtitle E of the SBREFA, generally referred to as the "Congressional Review Act of 1996" or the "CRA", requires OSHA to send a report containing any new standard to the House, Senate, and the General Accounting Office (GAO). Within fifteen days, the GAO must report to Congress whether OSHA has properly followed all procedures in developing the rule. Congress then has sixty session days to review the rule. Senate filibusters are not permitted. Congress can pass a joint resolution of disapproval and a rejected rule cannot take effect or be reissued in substantially the same form except by an Act of Congress or a determination by the President that the rule is in the public interest. The CRA was used for the first time in March 2001 to overturn the ergonomics standard issued during the last days of the Clinton administration.

B. SUBSTANTIVE CRITERIA FOR OSHA STANDARDS

The Act does not clearly enunciate the substantive criteria to be used by OSHA in setting standards. Section 6(b)(5) provides in part that:

> The Secretary, in promulgating standards dealing with toxic material or harmful physical agents under this subsection, shall set the standard which most adequately assures, to the extent feasible, on the basis of the best available evidence, that no employee will suffer material impairment of health or functional capacity even if such employee has regular exposure to the hazard dealt with by such standard for the period of his working life. . . . In addition to the attainment

of the highest degree of health and safety protection for the employee, other considerations shall be the latest available scientific data in the field, the feasibility of the standards, and experience gained under this and other health and safety laws. Whenever practicable, the standard promulgated shall be expressed in terms of objective criteria and of the performance desired.

The definitions section for the Act provides only limited assistance to assessing the validity of a standard:

The term "occupational safety and health standard" means a standard which requires conditions, or the adoption or use of one or more practices, means, methods, operations or processes, reasonably necessary or appropriate to provide safe or healthful employment and places of employment.

OSHAct § 3(8). A recurring issue under the OSHAct is what criteria OSHA should use when creating standards. The most prominent substantive criteria that have been proposed are (1) technological feasibility, (2) economic feasibility, (3) benefits to workers' health or safety, and (4) cost-benefit analysis.

These four substantive criteria are usually considered in the context of permanent standards issued under § 6(b), but they also apply to some degree to the interim standards under § 6(a), the emergency temporary standards under § 6(c), and the application of the § 5(a) general duty clause. After we introduce the criteria in this section, we will examine their use for permanent standards and the general duty clause in subsequent sections.

1. THE FIRST AND SECOND CRITERIA: TECHNOLOGICAL AND ECONOMIC FEASIBILITY

AFL-CIO v. BRENNAN
United States Court of Appeals, Third Circuit
530 F.2d 109 (1975)

Gibbons, Circuit Judge:

The American Federation of Labor and Congress of Industrial Organizations and the Industrial Union Department, AFL-CIO (Petitioners), by a petition filed pursuant to § 6(f) of the Occupational Safety and Health Act (OSHA), challenge . . . a revision of the safety standards applicable to mechanical power presses. . . . At issue is the Secretary's decision to eliminate the "no hands in dies" standard for mechanical power presses, adopted in 1971. . . .

We conclude that each of the Secretary's reasons for his departure from the no hands in dies standard, whatever its legal merit may be, is supported by substantial evidence in the record as a whole. Thus we now address petitioner's legal challenges.

B. *Relevancy of the Secretary's Reasons*

Petitioner contends that the Secretary's reliance on technological and economic infeasibility, even though his findings to that effect are supported by substantial evidence, was impermissible in standard setting proceedings under OSHA.

(1) *Technological Infeasibility*

Acknowledging that for many applications the no hands in dies standard is technologically infeasible, and that the result of its universal application will be the elimination of some businesses and some jobs, petitioner urges that this is exactly the result that Congress sought to accomplish. Neither this court nor, so far as our research discloses any other court, has construed OSHA in so Procrustean a fashion. Undoubtedly the most certain way to eliminate industrial hazards is to eliminate industry. But the congressional statement of findings and declaration of purpose and policy in § 2 of the Act shows that the upgrading of working conditions, not the complete elimination of hazardous occupations, was the dominant intention. In an enforcement context we have noted that while Congress in enacting OSHA intended to reduce the number of workplace injuries, it did not intend to impose strict liability on employers for unavoidable occupational hazards. *Brennan v. OSHRC,* 502 F.2d 946, 951 (3d Cir. 1974). We do not question that there are industrial activities involving hazards so great and of such little social utility that the Secretary would be justified in concluding that their total prohibition is proper if there is no technologically feasible method of eliminating the operational hazard. But while Congress gave the Secretary license to make such a determination in specific instances, it did not direct him to do so in every instance where total elimination of risk is beyond the reach of present technology. Section 6(b)(5) of the Act, dealing with standards for toxic materials, explicitly confines the Secretary's rule-making authority within technologically feasible boundaries. If the Secretary may consider technological feasibility with respect to the elimination of hazards from toxic materials, then *a fortiori* he must be permitted to do so with respect to other hazards under the more general language of § 6(a).

Although we hold that the Secretary may, consistent with the statute, consider the technological feasibility of a proposed occupational health and safety standard promulgated pursuant to § 6(a), we agree with the Second Circuit in *Society of Plastics Industry, Inc. v. OSHA,* 509 F.2d 1301, 1308 (2d Cir. 1975), that, at least to a limited extent, OSHA is to be viewed as a technology-forcing piece of legislation. Thus the Secretary would not be justified in dismissing an alternative to a proposed health and safety standard as infeasible when the necessary technology looms on today's horizon. Nevertheless, we are satisfied that the Secretary in this case has placed this factor in its proper perspective. The Secretary found, and we believe there is substantial evidence to support such a finding, that compliance with no hands in dies is not technologically feasible in the "near future." This finding necessarily implies consideration both of existing technological capabilities and imminent advances in the art. We do not believe that the Act imposes any heavier obligation.

(2) *Economic Infeasibility*

This court has not yet considered whether OSHA permits the Secretary, in adopting standards, to take into account the likely economic impact of those standards. The text of the statute does not address the point specifically, and the legislative history is at best cloudy. In *Industrial Union Department, AFL-CIO v. Hodgson,* [499 F.2d 467 (D.C. Cir. 1974)], Judge McGowan addresses the issue:

> There can be no question that OSHA represents a decision to require safeguards for the health of employees even if such measures substantially increase production costs. This it not, however, the same thing as saying that Congress intended to require immediate implementation of all protective measures technologically achievable without regard for their economic impact. To the contrary, it would comport with common usage to say that a standard that is prohibitively expensive is not "feasible." Senator Javits, author of the amendment that added the phrase in question to the Act, explained it in these terms:
>
> > As a result of this amendment the Secretary, in setting standards, is expressly required to consider feasibility of proposed standards. This is an improvement over the Daniels bill, which might be interpreted to require absolute health and safety in all cases, regardless of feasibility, and the Administration bill, which contains no criteria for standards at all.
>
> The thrust of these remarks would seem to be that practical considerations can temper protective requirements. Congress does not appear to have intended to protect employees by putting their employers out of business — either by requiring protective devices unavailable under existing technology or by making financial viability generally impossible.
>
> This qualification is not intended to provide a route by which recalcitrant employers or industries may avoid the reforms contemplated by the Act. Standards may be economically feasible even though, from the standpoint of employers, they are financially burdensome and affect profit margins adversely. Nor does the concept of economic feasibility necessarily guarantee the continued existence of individual employers. It would appear to be consistent with the purposes of the Act to envisage the economic demise of an employer who has lagged behind the rest of the industry in protecting the health and safety of employees and is consequently financially unable to comply with new standards as quickly as other employers. As the effect becomes more widespread within an industry, the problem of economic feasibility becomes more pressing. For example, if the standard requires changes that only a few leading firms could quickly achieve, delay might be necessary to avoid increasing the concentration of that industry. Similarly, if the competitive structure or posture of the industry would be otherwise adversely affected — perhaps rendered unable to compete with imports or with substitute products — the Secretary could properly consider that factor. These tentative examples are offered not to illustrate concrete instances of economic unfeasibility but rather to suggest the complex elements that may be relevant to such a determination.

Judge McGowan has, we believe, arrived at a proper construction of the statute. Congress did contemplate that the Secretary's rulemaking would put out of business some businesses so marginally efficient or productive as to be unable to follow standards otherwise universally feasible. But we will not impute to congressional silence a direction to the Secretary to disregard the possibility of massive economic dislocation caused by an unreasonable standard. An economically impossible standard would in all likelihood prove unenforceable, inducing employers faced with going out of business to evade rather than comply with the regulation. The Act does vest the Secretary with authority to enforce his regulations, but the burden of enforcing a regulation uniformly ignored by a majority of industry members would prove overwhelming. We therefore conclude that the Secretary may in the weighing process consider the economic consequences of his quasi-legislative standard-setting. We reject the petitioner's contrary contention. . . .

III. *Conclusion*

We conclude that the Secretary's statement of reasons does not adequately disclose why the rule he adopted will better effectuate the purposes of OSHA than would the national consensus standard which it supplants. The cause will be remanded to the Occupational Safety and Health Administration of the Department of Labor for the preparation of a more complete statement of reasons in accordance with this opinion.

NOTE

Regulatory Winners and Losers. In the *Hodgson* case, Judge McGowan argued that OSHA standards may be appropriate even if they drive some employers out of business. He speculated that one concern with such an OSHA standard would be the increased concentration in the industry, which might lead to monopoly pricing. This leads to the more general question: do OSHA standards harm all firms in an industry, or might some firms actually benefit because they incur relatively low compliance costs?

Professors Bartel and Thomas have explained the competing influences this way:

> A common error in popular expressions of political economy is the presumption that all firms oppose environmental and safety regulations because these edicts raise business costs. The flaw in this presumption arises from an exclusive focus on what we will call the "direct effects" of regulation — the . . . effects of regulation on single firms or individuals. Examples of the direct effects of environmental and safety regulations include increased safety of products and workplaces, decreased emissions of pollutants, and increased manufacturing costs. While direct effects dominate popular perceptions of regulation, the often pronounced heterogeneity among firms gives rise to additional . . . effects that we will call "indirect effects" — the competitive advantages that arise from the asymmetrical distributions of regulatory effect among different groups of firms and workers. For example, if the cost burden of certain regulations falls heavily on one

group of firms and lightly on a second group, then an indirect effect of these regulations is to provide cost advantage to the second group of firms. It is extremely important to recognize that, for many firms and workers, the indirect effects of regulation can outweigh (in terms of economic importance) the direct effects. If the competitive advantage gained through indirect effects is sufficiently large, it can more than offset any direct costs, producing a net benefit for the regulated firm and its workers. . . . [T]he Occupational Safety and Health Administration (OSHA) cotton dust standard [is] among the many regulations where indirect effects have been shown to predominate.

Ann P. Bartel & Lacy Glenn Thomas, *Predation Through Regulation: The Wage and Profit Effects of the Occupational Safety and Health Administration and the Environmental Protection Agency*, 30 J.L. & ECON. 239, 239-40 (1987).

Bartel and Thomas divide indirect effects of OSHA regulation into two types. First is the compliance asymmetry whereby some firms suffer a greater cost burden per unit of output. Generally, firms experience large economies of scale in complying with OSHA regulations, so that the compliance burden falls hardest on smaller firms. Second are enforcement asymmetries. Bartel and Thomas found that the OSHAct was enforced more intensely (per worker) against small, nonunion, and Sun Belt firms.

2. THE THIRD CRITERION: BENEFITS TO WORKERS' HEALTH OR SAFETY

The Secretary must demonstrate through scientific evidence the benefits to workers' health or safety from a proposed standard under § 6 or an enforcement action under the § 5(a) general duty clause. If, for example, a proposed standard deals with a substance that is alleged to be carcinogenic, then the evidence must demonstrate the medical risks associated with current exposure levels and the benefits to health that will result from reduced exposure to the substance.

The scientific evidence can be produced in an epidemiological study, which examines the effect of exposure to the substance on humans, or in animal experiments, which are used to project the likely effect of exposure on humans. Each approach has advantages and disadvantages.

Epidemiological studies have the obvious advantage of relying on direct evidence of the effect on humans of exposure to the substance. There are several disadvantages, however. Historical exposure levels are likely to be high relative to current exposure levels or, more likely, to the levels proposed in a new standard, and so direct evidence on the health benefits of the proposal are unavailable. In addition, many workers have been exposed to a variety of potential carcinogens, and separating the effects of the substance being considered for regulation from the effects of other substances is difficult. The problem is compounded because the data are likely to be incomplete on exposure levels that workers were subjected to in an earlier period, perhaps decades ago — especially if the substance was not a suspected carcinogen at that time.

Another disadvantage of epidemiological studies is that creating a large enough sample of workers to derive statistically reliable results may be difficult, especially if the substance did not have widespread use or if the workers were in an industry with high labor turnover. Overcoming these factors in combination also means that epidemiological studies are likely to be expensive. Finally, but of great significance, it would be unethical for scientists to expose different groups of workers to different levels of exposure to a suspected carcinogen deliberately in order to produce compelling evidence about the benefits of reduced exposure that could result from a proposed health standard.

Animal studies allow scientists to overcome some of these difficulties. Animals such as rats or mice are relatively inexpensive and so relatively large numbers can be used to ferret out the differential effects of various exposure levels. Moreover, scientists can restrict exposure to other known carcinogens so the contribution to cancer of the substance of particular interest can be isolated.

One typical characteristic of animal studies does cause a problem: exposing animals to relatively high levels of the suspected substance to increase the likelihood that some of the animals in the sample will develop cancer. The projection of the results to lower exposure levels is controversial. An even more serious extrapolation is from animals to humans: mice, rats, and rabbits may be more (or less) susceptible to cancer from a particular substance than humans. Primates, such as monkeys or baboons, may be better sources of data that can be extrapolated to humans, but these animals are more expensive than rodents and thus sample sizes are likely to be smaller. Finally, all animal studies inevitably involve sacrifices of life, and animal rights advocates may object to the studies, even when they may save human lives.

"Quantitative risk assessment" and "risk analysis" are the terms commonly used in the occupational safety and health area to describe the procedure to establish the benefits to workers of a proposed OSHA standard. Broadly defined, quantitative risk assessment is a method to estimate the likelihood that a particular amount of exposure to a substance will cause cancer.

Quantitative risk assessment usually involves two extrapolations: (1) from animals to humans (because most data are from animal studies), and (2) from high doses (exposure levels) to low doses (because most studies involve high levels of exposure). The controversies involving the second extrapolation are represented in Figure 23-1, which involves a hypothetical substance, an industrial soap sold under the trade name of "Grimeoff." The horizontal axis represents the dose levels (in annual washings per worker (wpw)), with greater exposure levels to the suspected carcinogen shown as further to the right on the graph. The vertical axis represents the excess mortality rates (in excess deaths per year per 100,000 workers), with higher death rates shown as further up on the graph.

The solid line XY is a dose-response curve, which shows the relationship between exposure levels to Grimeoff and excess deaths derived from actual data (which may involve animals or possibly humans). The line XY shows that there is a positive relationship between dose levels of 100 wpw to 300 wpw. But what about the relationship between exposure to Grimeoff of less than

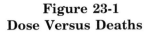

Figure 23-1
Dose Versus Deaths

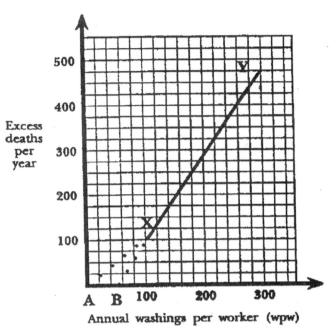

Annual washings per worker (wpw)

100 wpw? This may be relevant if there is a proposal to adopt an OSHA standard that would reduce the exposure level to 10 wpw. Can such a low exposure level be justified on the basis of quantitative risk assessment?

The answer depends on one's choice of two scientifically competing views. One view is that once a substance has been established as carcinogenic, there is no safe level of exposure to that substance. This view appears to be appropriate for some carcinogens, such as asbestos, for which even a minuscule level of exposure poses some risk of cancer. In terms of Figure 23-1, this view is represented by line AX, which represents a projection of the dose-response curve from the lowest value on line XY (that is, the lowest value for which actual data exist concerning the relationship between exposure to Grimeoff and cancer) through the origin.

A competing view is that even for a substance that is known to be carcinogenic in substantial amounts, there may be a lower threshold below which exposure does not pose a risk of cancer. This is, we hope, an accurate description of sunlight, which is known to produce excess skin cancer in those who have had incidents of sunburn. In terms of Figure 23-1, this view is represented by line BX, which represents a straight-line extrapolation from the lowest value on line XY through the horizontal axis at a value of 50 wpw. This extrapolation suggests that there is no risk of cancer associated with 50 or fewer washings per year using Grimeoff.

Alternatively stated, quantitative risk assessment would suggest that a proposed health standard of 10 wpw has a beneficial effect on workers' health if Grimeoff has no safe level of exposure, while the proposed standard is unnecessarily stringent if Grimeoff has a safe threshold of exposure of 50 wpw.

3. THE FOURTH CRITERION: COST-BENEFIT ANALYSIS

Another possible criterion for evaluating a proposed health or safety standard is cost-benefit analysis. A standard would be considered desirable or valid if the benefits of the standard equal or exceed its cost. At a certain level of abstraction, it would be hard to argue with the proposition that benefits should equal or exceed costs. As the approach is used by economists, however, there are skeptics.

One controversial aspect is that a monetary value must be assigned to the possible advantages and disadvantages of a proposed activity. In theory, the proper way to measure the benefits of a proposed government program is to determine the maximum amount that beneficiaries are willing to pay for the program. But determining the value that citizens receive from a government program is not easy. If, for example, a pollution control is installed in a plant that reduces emissions, it is difficult to exclude any individual worker from its benefits. However, a particular worker who actually prefers the lower risks of respiratory disease may claim the lower emissions are of no value to her if she thinks the costs of the pollution control may be reflected in a lower wage. This is known as the "free rider" problem. Another problem of determining the monetary benefits of a proposed health or safety standard is that most workers are likely to have a hard time answering a question such as: "How much would you be willing to pay for a safety guard on your machine that will reduce the probability of your being killed this year by one chance in ten thousand?"

The economist's solution to the problems of obtaining information from workers about the value they place on safety and health is to rely on information from the labor market. After taking into account all other factors that should affect wages (such as skill levels, education, experience, job stability, working conditions), the economist compares the wages of jobs that differ in their rate of workplace injuries or fatalities. If higher risk jobs pay higher wages, *ceteris paribus,* then the risk premium provides an indirect measure of the value that workers place on their own lives and by inference the amount they are willing to pay for health and safety standards that reduce the chance of losing one's life by a certain probability. Thus, if a wage premium of $300 is typically paid for each increase in the yearly death rate of 1 in 10,000, then a proposed health standard that would reduce the probabilities of death by 2 in 10,000 annually would be worth $600 per year per worker.

The total dollar figure for the expected annual benefits of a standard is calculated as the benefits per worker times the number of affected workers. Figure 23-2 plots the total benefits from OSHA standards of different levels of effectiveness. The vertical axis measures total annual benefits (or costs) in dollars, while the horizontal axis measures the size of the OSHA program (with increasingly stringent standards further to the right). The marginal benefits (or costs) are measured by the slope of the total benefits (or total costs) lines.

Figure 23-2
Costs and Benefits of an OSHA Program

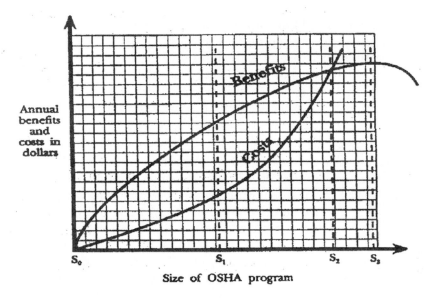

Size of OSHA program

Cost-benefit analysis also requires that costs of the government programs be measured. The costs represent a measure of all the resources used to provide the program, which in the case of an OSHA standard would include matters such as wages of personnel involved in administering or supervising the standard, capital expenditures for safety equipment or for pollution control devices, and costs of training workers. The annual costs of the various size government programs are also plotted in Figure 23-2.

The final step in cost-benefit analysis is to determine the appropriate size of the program (which in the context of OSHA can be understood as the stringency of the standard). Three solutions can be contrasted: (1) the economist's solution, (2) the nontransferable resources solution, and (3) the maximum-safety-at-all-costs solution.

The economist's solution would choose the size of the OSHA program for which the marginal benefit of the program is equal to the marginal cost. In terms of the graph, this occurs where the slopes of the total benefit and cost curves are equal (which is also where the vertical distance between the two programs is greatest). In Figure 23-2, the optimal size of the program is S_1.

The reason why S_1 is the optimal size and not a larger program (such as S_2, where the benefit and cost curves intersect) goes to the essence of the rationale for cost-benefit analysis. Economists argue that the costs are opportunity costs — that is, the resources used for this particular program have alternative uses in the economy. For example, if OSHA did not promulgate a particular standard, the resources thus released could be used elsewhere in the economy to improve highway safety, or support medical research or law school scholarships, or implement an OSHA standard for some other substance. The increase in the OSHA program shown in Figure 23-2 between

S_0 and S_1 is pulling resources from elsewhere in the economy at a cost that is less than the benefit of this program: i.e., the marginal benefit of increasing the program exceeds the marginal cost until the program reaches size S_1. Beyond that point, the additional benefits on a larger program are less than the costs of the expanded program: the alternative uses of the resources have greater value than their use in expanding this OSHA program beyond S_1. Conversely, an OSHA standard should not be less stringent than the standard represented by S_1 because the additional resources needed to expand this OSHA program to S_1 have lower value in some alternative use.

The nontransferable resources solution rejects the assumption used by economists that resources used for a particular OSHA standard have an opportunity cost. The rejection could be based on a view that society often has unused resources in the form of unemployed workers or idle plant and equipment (or perhaps uninvested savings) that could be used to expand the OSHA program without reducing the size of any other program. An alternative justification for rejecting the opportunity costs approach is a perception that the amount of resources devoted to uses other than OSHA is determined by political factors, and that expanding (or contracting) OSHA will not affect the sizes of these other programs. In this nontransferable resources solution approach, the size of the OSHA program should be expanded until the total costs of the program equal the total benefits, which occurs at size S_2 in Figure 23-2. Between S_1 and S_2, increasing the size of the OSHA program makes the workplace safer. So long as the total costs of OSHA do not exceed the total benefits of the program, supporters of this approach would advocate expanding the program.

The maximum-safety-at-all-costs solution would increase the size of the OSHA program until additional resources devoted to expanding the program would lead to a reduction in safety. This would represent size S_3 in Figure 23-2, where the total benefits curve peaks. The downturn in benefits of an expanded OSHA program beyond S_3 might occur if, for example, regulations became so complex that employers began a campaign of massive evasion of the program rather than even trying to comply. Between S_2 and S_3 the excess of the total costs of the OSHA program over the total benefits continues to grow. One possible justification for expanding the program beyond S_2 is that the procedure used to derive the benefits of the OSHA program shown in the graph assumes that the value of life is finite. If, to the contrary, the value of human life is assumed to be infinite, then there is ample justification for expanding the size of the OSHA program so long as one additional life is saved.

Despite the compelling logic (!) that justifies the use of the economist's solution to cost-benefit analysis, the approach is controversial, especially in the context of occupational safety and health. Some persons object to the notion that a monetary value can be placed on life, which is a necessary assumption of this approach. In addition, many object to the validity and usefulness of the research results concerning compensating wage differentials. (An alternative source of the value of human life is the monetary damages found by juries in wrongful death suits.) A number of technical problems associated with cost-benefit analysis makes the approach complicated in practice.* Last, but not least, is the issue of the legal status of cost-benefit analysis under the OSHAct.

C. LEGAL CHALLENGES TO PERMANENT STANDARDS

Technological feasibility and economic feasibility were established as legal requirements soon after the OSHAct was enacted. The greatest controversies involve the meaning of benefits to workers' health or safety, and the permissibility of cost-benefit analysis.

Industrial Union Dep't v. American Petroleum Inst. (The Benzene Case), 448 U.S. 607 (1980). The Supreme Court's first attempt at these issues arose in its review of OSHA's benzene standard, a substance known (at least at high dosages) to cause leukemia. Promulgated in 1978, that standard revised an interim standard, reducing the maximum permissible exposure level (PEL) for benzene from 10 parts per million (ppm) averaged over 8 hours to 1 ppm averaged over 8 hours. The new standard also reduced the short-term exposure level to a maximum of 5 ppm over any 5 minutes. OSHA had no animal data on benzene and the epidemiological data primarily involved human exposures at concentrations well above the previous standard's level of 10 ppm. In the absence of data concerning the excess risk of leukemia at exposure levels below 10 ppm, OSHA assumed a positive dose-response relationship between exposure to benzene and excess mortality and also assumed that there was no safe level of benzene. In essence, OSHA argued that the only limits on the degree of stringency of the standard were technological and economic feasibility.

The Court of Appeals for the Fifth Circuit vacated the benzene standard on two grounds: (1) OSHA had failed to provide evidence concerning the expected benefits that would result from reducing the PEL, and (2) OSHA had failed to compare the benefits and costs of the proposed standard.

The Supreme Court affirmed the judgment of the Court of Appeals, but without a majority opinion. In the plurality opinion, Justice Stevens finessed the cost-benefit issue by finding that § 3(8) imposes a threshold burden upon OSHA to show that the new benzene standard would benefit the health of workers by alleviating a significant risk, a burden that OSHA did not carry.

> Our resolution of the issues in these cases turns, to a large extent, on the meaning of the relationship between § 3(8), which defines a health and safety standard as a standard that is "reasonably necessary and appropriate to provide safe or healthful employment," and § 6(b)(5), which directs the Secretary in promulgating a health and safety standard for toxic materials to "set the standard which most adequately assures, to the extent feasible, on the basis of the best

---

* One example is the treatment of multi-year projects. If, for example, the costs of a new health standard will largely occur in the first five years (while capital equipment is installed and new processes installed) while the benefits may accrue more evenly over twenty years, then deciding the appropriate size of the project is contingent on the size of the discount rate used to determine the present value of the benefits and the costs. With costs concentrated in early years and benefits distributed evenly over the life of the project, the higher the discount rate used to calculate present values, the lower is the ratio of benefits to costs.

available evidence, that no employee will suffer material impairment of health or functional capacity. . . ."

By empowering the Secretary to promulgate standards that are "reasonably necessary or appropriate to provide safe or healthful employment and places of employment," the Act implies that, before promulgating any standard, the Secretary must make a finding that the workplaces in question are not safe. But "safe" is not the equivalent of "risk-free." There are many activities that we engage in every day — such as driving a car or even breathing city air — that entail some risk of accident or material health impairment; nevertheless, few people would consider these activities "unsafe." Similarly, a workplace can hardly be considered "unsafe" unless it threatens the workers with a significant risk of harm.

Therefore, before he can promulgate *any* permanent health or safety standard, the Secretary is required to make a threshold finding that a place of employment is unsafe — in the sense that significant risks are present and can be eliminated or lessened by a change in practices. This requirement applies to permanent standards promulgated pursuant to § 6(b)(5), as well as to other types of permanent standards.

Id. at 639, 642.

In applying this threshold test to the benzene standard, Justice Stevens first rejected OSHA's carcinogen policy. OSHA's carcinogen policy, never formally promulgated as a standard, states that whenever a carcinogen is involved, in the absence of definitive proof of a safe level, OSHA will assume that any level above zero presents some increased risk of cancer. In rejecting the carcinogen policy, Justice Stevens pointed out "there are literally thousands of substances used in the workplace that have been identified as carcinogens or suspect carcinogens, [and] the Government's theory would give OSHA power to impose enormous costs that might produce little, if any, discernible benefit." *Id.* at 645.

Justice Stevens also rejected OSHA's contention that even if its carcinogen policy was found to be invalid, the benzene standard was still valid under OSHA's mandate to regulate hazardous materials. Even though OSHA's written explanation of the standard was 184 pages long, Stevens found it "noteworthy" that at no point in its explanation did OSHA quote or cite § 3(8) of the Act, and OSHA never made a finding that the new standard was reasonably necessary or appropriate to provide safe or healthful employment.

Justice Powell, concurring in part, was the only Justice expressly reaching the cost-benefit question. Justice Powell agreed with the plurality that OSHA had not met the threshold requirement of § 3(8). But even if OSHA had properly met this burden, Justice Powell argued, the statute also requires OSHA to determine that "the economic effects of its standard bear a reasonable relationship to the expected benefits." *Id.* at 667. Justice Powell found this type of cost-benefit analysis necessary since "an occupational standard is neither 'reasonably necessary' nor 'feasible' . . . if it calls for expenditures wholly disproportionate to the expected health and safety benefits." *Id.*

Justice Rehnquist provided the fifth vote to strike down the benzene standard, but he refused to join Justice Stevens' analysis. Instead, he would have struck down OSHA's authority to promulgate standards under § 6(b)(5) as an unconstitutional delegation of Congress's authority to legislate, a position he repeated the following year in the *Cotton Dust* case.

Justice Marshall, on behalf of four Justices, dissented in the case. He would have upheld the benzene standard as being properly based on "feasibility analysis."

NOTES

1. *Significant Risk Test.* Justice Stevens' threshold test, in essence, demands that the proposed OSHA standard must benefit workers' health. This test, usually referred to as the significant risk test, requires that OSHA (1) show that the current exposure level for a substance (such as benzene) represents a significant risk to workers, and (2) demonstrate by substantial evidence that the new standard would eliminate or reduce the risk. This evidence cannot rely on extrapolations of the type represented by line AX in Figure 23-1, which, as you will recall, ultimately rested on an assumption that there is no safe exposure level to a carcinogen.

OSHA soon adapted to the requirements imposed by the *Benzene* decision. Within months after the *Benzene* decision, the Court of Appeals for the District of Columbia, in *United Steelworkers v. Marshall*, 647 F.2d 1189 (D.C. Cir. 1980), *cert. denied*, 453 U.S. 913 (1981), upheld OSHA's 50-microgram standard for lead exposures and indicated that OSHA clearly met the significant risk test by providing substantial evidence that the previous exposure level to lead posed a significant risk to workers and that the proposed standard would reduce this risk.

2. *What Constitutes a Significant Risk?* The plurality opinion by Justice Stevens in the *Benzene* case contains this passage:

> It is the Agency's responsibility to determine, in the first instance, what it considers to be a "significant" risk. Some risks are plainly acceptable and others are plainly unacceptable. If, for example, the odds are one in a billion that a person will die from cancer by taking a drink of chlorinated water, the risk clearly could not be considered significant. On the other hand, if the odds are one in a thousand that regular inhalation of gasoline vapors that are 2% benzene will be fatal, a reasonable person might well consider the risk significant and take appropriate steps to decrease or eliminate it. Although the Agency has no duty to calculate the exact probability of harm, it does have an obligation to find that a significant risk is present before it can characterize a place of employment as "unsafe."

Industrial Union Dep't v. American Petroleum Inst., 448 U.S. at 607, 655 (1980).

The courts and OSHA have used this language as a starting point for defining the meaning of significant risk. The Supreme Court's formulation is ambiguous concerning the period during which the exposure is to be measured. The chlorinated water example ("taking a drink") sounds as if the risk is to be determined for a single exposure to the carcinogen, while the gasoline vapors example ("regular inhalation") indicates that the risk is to be measured over an extended time period. The Court's formulation is also unclear about the time period during which the cancer is supposed to occur. Does the "one in a thousand" refer to the odds of developing cancer in a short period, such as a month or a year, or to the odds of developing cancer over a longer period, such as a lifetime?

The District of Columbia Court helped answer these questions. The case involved new standards for formaldehyde, which reduced the permissible exposure limit ("PEL") to one part per million ("ppm") as an 8-hour time-weighted average and the short-term exposure limit ("STEL") to 2 ppm. The court remanded the case to OSHA for reconsideration of its calculation of the risk of cancer from formaldehyde at 1 ppm. OSHA had failed to explain its finding that the 1 ppm level of exposure resulted in an insignificant risk. The opinion indicated that a significant risk exists if (1) there is a one in a thousand chance that a worker will develop cancer during the worker's life-time, and (2) that risk results from exposure during a working career to formaldehyde at the PEL of 1 ppm. *United Auto Workers v. Pendergrass*, 878 F.2d 389 (D.C. Cir. 1989). The issue of what constitutes a significant risk is examined further in the next case.

AMERICAN TEXTILE MANUFACTURERS INSTITUTE v. DONOVAN
United States Supreme Court
452 U.S. 490 (1981)

Justice Brennan delivered the opinion of the Court.

In 1978, the Secretary, acting through the Occupational Safety and Health Administration (OSHA), promulgated a standard limiting occupational exposure to cotton dust, an airborne particle byproduct of the preparation and manufacture of cotton products, exposure to which induces a "constellation of respiratory effects" known as "byssinosis." . . .

Petitioners in these consolidated cases, representing the interests of the cotton industry, challenged the validity of the "Cotton Dust Standard" in the Court of Appeals for the District of Columbia Circuit pursuant to § 6(f) of the Act. They contend in this Court, as they did below, that the Act requires OSHA to demonstrate that its Standard reflects a reasonable relationship between the costs and benefits associated with the Standard. Respondents, the Secretary of Labor and two labor organizations, counter that Congress balanced the costs and benefits in the Act itself, and that the Act should therefore be construed not to require OSHA to do so. They interpret the Act as mandating that OSHA enact the most protective standard possible to eliminate a significant risk of material health impairment, subject to the constraints of economic and technological feasibility. The Court of Appeals held that the Act did not require OSHA to compare costs and benefits. *AFL-CIO v. Marshall*, 617 F.2d 636 (1979). We granted certiorari to resolve this important question, which was presented but not decided in last Term's *Industrial Union Dep't v. American Petroleum Inst.*, 448 U.S. 607 (1980), and to decide other issues related to the Cotton Dust Standard.

I

Byssinosis, known in its more severe manifestations as "brown lung" disease, is a serious and potentially disabling respiratory disease primarily caused by the inhalation of cotton dust. . . .

The Cotton Dust Standard promulgated by OSHA establishes mandatory PEL's [Permissible Exposure Limit] over an 8-hour period of 200 μg/m^3 [micrograms per cubic meter of air] for yarn manufacturing, 750 μg/m^3 for slashing and weaving operations, and 500 μg/m^3 for all other processes in the cotton industry. These levels represent a relaxation of the proposed PEL of 200 μg/m^3 for all segments of the cotton industry.

OSHA chose an implementation strategy for the Standard that depended primarily on a mix of engineering controls, such as installation of ventilation systems, and work practice controls, such as special floor-sweeping procedures. Full compliance with the PEL's is required within four years, except to the extent that employers can establish that the engineering and work practice controls are infeasible. During this compliance period, and at certain other times, the Standard requires employers to provide respirators to employees. Other requirements include monitoring of cotton dust exposure, medical surveillance of all employees, annual medical examinations, employee education and training programs, and the posting of warning signs. A specific provision also under challenge in the instant case requires employers to transfer employees unable to wear respirators to another position, if available, having a dust level at or below the Standard's PEL's, with "no loss of earnings or other employment rights or benefits as a result of the transfer."

On the basis of the evidence in the record as a whole, the Secretary determined that exposure to cotton dust represents a "significant health hazard to employees," and that "the prevalence of byssinosis should be significantly reduced" by the adoption of the Standard's PEL's. In assessing the health risks from cotton dust and the risk reduction obtained from lowered exposure, OSHA relied particularly on data showing a strong linear relationship between the prevalence of byssinosis and the concentration of lint-free respirable cotton dust. Even at the 200 μg/m^3 PEL, OSHA found that the prevalence of at least Grade 2 byssinosis would be 13% of all employees in the yarn manufacturing sector.

In promulgating the Cotton Dust Standard, OSHA interpreted the Act to require adoption of the most stringent standard to protect against material health impairment, bounded only by technological and economic feasibility. OSHA therefore rejected the industry's alternative proposal for a PEL of 500 μg/m^3 in yarn manufacturing, a proposal which would produce a 25% prevalence of at least Grade 2 byssinosis. The agency expressly found the Standard to be both technologically and economically feasible based on the evidence in the record as a whole. Although recognizing that permitted levels of exposure to cotton dust would still cause some byssinosis, OSHA nevertheless rejected the union proposal for a 100 μg/m^3 PEL because it was not within the "technological capabilities of the industry." Similarly, OSHA set PEL's for some segments of the cotton industry at 500 μg/m^3 in part because of limitations of technological feasibility. Finally, the Secretary found that "engineering dust controls in weaving may not be feasible even with massive expenditures by the industry," and for that and other reasons adopted a less stringent PEL of 750 µg/m^3 for weaving and slashing.

The Court of Appeals upheld the Standard in all major respects. The court rejected the industry's claim that OSHA failed to consider its proposed alternative or give sufficient reasons for failing to adopt it. The court also held that the Standard was "reasonably necessary and appropriate" within the meaning of § 3(8) of the Act, because of the risk of material health impairment caused by exposure to cotton dust. Rejecting the industry position that OSHA must demonstrate that the benefits of the Standard are proportionate to its costs, the court instead agreed with OSHA's interpretation that the Standard must protect employees against material health impairment subject only to the limits of technological and economic feasibility. The court held that "Congress itself struck the balance between costs and benefits in the mandate to the agency" under § 6(b)(5) of the Act, and that OSHA is powerless to circumvent that judgment by adopting less than the most protective feasible standard. Finally, the court held that the agency's determination of technological and economic feasibility was supported by substantial evidence in the record as a whole.

We affirm in part, and vacate in part.[25]

___

[25] The postargument motions of the several parties for leave to file supplemental memoranda are granted. We decline to adopt the suggestion of the Secretary of Labor that we should "vacate the judgment of the court of appeals and remand the case so that the record may be returned to the Secretary for further consideration and development." We also decline to adopt the suggestion of petitioners that we should "hold these cases in abeyance and . . . remand the record to the court of appeals with an instruction that the record be remanded to the agency for further proceedings."

At oral argument, and in a letter addressed to the Court after oral argument, petitioners contended that the Secretary's recent amendment of OSHA's so-called "Cancer Policy" in light of this Court's decision in *Industrial Union Dept. v. American Petroleum Institute,* 448 U.S. 607 (1980), was relevant to the issues in the present cases. We disagree.

OSHA amended its Cancer Policy to "carry out the Court's interpretation of the Occupational Safety and Health Act of 1970 that consideration must be given to the significance of the risk in the issuance of a carcinogen standard and that OSHA must consider all relevant evidence in making these determinations." 46 Fed. Reg. 4889, col. 3 (1981). Previously, although lacking such evidence as dose-response data, the Secretary presumed that no safe exposure level existed for carcinogenic substances. Following this Court's decision, OSHA deleted those provisions of the Cancer Policy which required the "automatic setting of the lowest feasible level" without regard to determinations of risk significance. 46 Fed. Reg. 4890, col. 1 (1981).

In distinct contrast with its Cancer Policy, OSHA expressly found that "exposure to cotton dust presents a significant health hazard to employees," 43 Fed. Reg. 27350, col. 1 (1978), and that "cotton dust produced significant health effects at low levels of exposure," *id.,* at 27358, col. 2. In addition, the agency noted that "grade ½ byssinosis and associated pulmonary function decrements are significant health effects in themselves and should be prevented in so far as possible." *Id.,* at 27354, col. 2. In making its assessment of significant risk, OSHA relied on dose-response curve data (the Merchant Study) showing that 25% of employees suffered at least grade ½ byssinosis at a 500 µg/m^3 PEL, and that 12.7% of all employees would suffer byssinosis at the 200 µg/m^3 PEL standard. *Id.,* at 27358, cols. 2 and 3. Examining the Merchant Study in light of other studies in the record, the agency found that "the Merchant study provides a reliable assessment of health risk to cotton textile workers from cotton dust." *Id.,* at 27357, col. 3. OSHA concluded that the "prevalence of byssinosis should be significantly reduced" by the 200 µg/m^3 PEL. *Id.,* at 27359, col. 3; *see id.,* at 27359, col. 1 ("200 µg/m^3 represents a significant reduction in the number of affected workers"). It is difficult to imagine what else the agency could do to comply with this Court's decision in *Industrial Union Dept. v. American Petroleum Institute.*

II

The principal question presented in these cases is whether the Occupational Safety and Health Act requires the Secretary, in promulgating a standard pursuant to § 6(b)(5) of the Act, to determine that the costs of the standard bear a reasonable relationship to its benefits. Relying on §§ 6(b)(5) and 3(8) of the Act, petitioners urge not only that OSHA must show that a standard addresses a significant risk of material health impairment, see *Industrial Union Dept. v. American Petroleum Institute,* 448 U.S., at 639 (plurality opinion), but also that OSHA must demonstrate that the reduction in risk of material health impairment is significant in light of the costs of attaining that reduction.[26] Respondents on the other hand contend that the Act requires OSHA to promulgate standards that eliminate or reduce such risks "to the extent such protection is technologically and economically feasible."[27] To resolve this debate, we must turn to the language, structure, and legislative history of the Act.

A

The starting point of our analysis is the language of the statute itself. Section 6(b)(5) of the Act (emphasis added), provides:

> The Secretary, in promulgating standards dealing with toxic materials or harmful physical agents under this subsection, shall set the standard which most adequately assures, *to the extent feasible,* on the basis of the best available evidence, that no employee will suffer material impairment of health or functional capacity even if such

---

[26] Petitioners ATMI et al. express their position in several ways. They maintain that OSHA "is required to show that a reasonable relationship exists between the risk reduction benefits and the costs of its standards." Petitioners also suggest that OSHA must show that "the standard is expected to achieve a *significant reduction in* [the significant risk of material health impairment]" based on "an assessment of the costs of achieving it." Allowing that "[this] does not mean that OSHA must engage in a rigidly formal cost-benefit calculation that places a dollar value on employee lives or health," petitioners describe the required exercise as follows:

> First, OSHA must make a responsible determination of the costs and risk reduction benefits of its standard. Pursuant to the requirement of Section 6(f) of the Act, this determination must be factually supported by substantial evidence in the record. The subsequent determination whether the reduction in health risk is "significant" (based upon the factual assessment of costs and benefits) is a judgment to be made by the agency in the first instance.

Respondent Secretary disputes petitioners' description of the exercise, claiming that any meaningful balancing must involve "placing a [dollar] value on human life and freedom from suffering," and that there is no other way but through formal cost-benefit analysis to accomplish petitioners' desired balancing. . . . Whether petitioners' or respondent's characterization is correct, we will sometimes refer to petitioners' proposed exercise as "cost-benefit analysis."

[27] As described by the union respondents, the test for determining whether a standard promulgated to regulate a "toxic material or harmful physical agent" satisfies the Act has three parts:

> First, whether the "place of employment is unsafe — in the sense that significant risks are present and can be eliminated or lessened by a change in practices." Second, whether of the possible available correctives the Secretary has selected "*the* standard . . . that is most protective." Third, whether that standard is "feasible."

We will sometimes refer to this test as "feasibility analysis."

employee has regular exposure to the hazard dealt with by such standard for the period of his working life.

Although their interpretations differ, all parties agree that the phrase "to the extent feasible" contains the critical language in § 6(b)(5) for purposes of these cases.

The plain meaning of the word "feasible" supports respondents' interpretation of the statute. According to Webster's Third New International Dictionary of the English Language 831 (1976), "feasible" means "capable of being done, executed, or effected." . . . Thus, § 6(b)(5) directs the Secretary to issue the standard that "most adequately assures . . . that no employee will suffer material impairment of health," limited only by the extent to which this is "capable of being done." In effect then . . . Congress itself defined the basic relationship between costs and benefits, by placing the "benefit" of worker health above all other considerations save those making attainment of this "benefit" unachievable. Any standard based on a balancing of costs and benefits by the Secretary that strikes a different balance than that struck by Congress would be inconsistent with the command set forth in § 6(b)(5). Thus, cost-benefit analysis by OSHA is not required by the statute because feasibility analysis is.[29] *See Industrial Union Dept. v. American Petroleum Institute,* 448 U.S., at 718-719 (MARSHALL, J., dissenting).

When Congress has intended that an agency engage in cost-benefit analysis, it has clearly indicated such intent on the face of the statute. [The Court then discusses several other statutes, including the Flood Control Act of 1936 and the Outer Continental Shelf Lands Act Amendments of 1978.] These and other statutes demonstrate that Congress uses specific language when intending that an agency engage in cost-benefit analysis. Certainly in light of its ordinary meaning, the word "feasible" cannot be construed to articulate such congressional intent. We therefore reject the argument that Congress required cost-benefit analysis in § 6(b)(5).

B

Even though the plain language of § 6(b)(5) supports this construction, we must still decide whether § 3(8), the general definition of an occupational safety and health standard, either alone or in tandem with § 6(b)(5), incorporates a cost-benefit requirement for standards dealing with toxic materials or harmful physical agents. Section 3(8) of the Act (emphasis added) provides:

> The term "occupational safety and health standard" means a standard which requires conditions, or the adoption or use of one or more

---

[29] In these cases we are faced with the issue whether the Act requires OSHA to balance costs and benefits in promulgating a *single* toxic material and harmful physical agent standard under § 6(b)(5). Petitioners argue that without cost-benefit balancing, the issuance of a single standard might result in a "serious [misallocation] of the finite resources that are available for the protection of worker safety and health," given the other health hazards in the workplace. This argument is more properly addressed to other provisions of the Act which may authorize OSHA to explore costs and benefits for deciding between issuance of several standards regulating different varieties of health and safety hazards, *e.g.,* § 6(g) of the Act, 29 U.S.C. § 655(g); or for promulgating other types of standards not issued under § 6(b)(5). We express no view on these questions.

practices, means, methods, operations, or processes, *reasonably neces-sary or appropriate* to provide safe or healthful employment and places of employment.

Taken alone, the phrase "reasonably necessary or appropriate" might be construed to contemplate some balancing of the costs and benefits of a standard. Petitioners urge that, so construed, § 3(8) engrafts a cost-benefit analysis requirement on the issuance of § 6(b)(5) standards, even if § 6(b)(5) itself does not authorize such analysis. We need not decide whether § 3(8), standing alone, would contemplate some form of cost-benefit analysis. For even if it does, Congress specifically chose in § 6(b)(5) to impose separate and additional requirements for issuance of a subcategory of occupational safety and health standards dealing with toxic materials and harmful physical agents: it required that those standards be issued to prevent material impairment of health *to the extent feasible*. Congress could reasonably have concluded that *health* standards should be subject to different criteria than *safety* standards because of the special problems presented in regulating them.

Agreement with petitioners' argument that § 3(8) imposes an additional and overriding requirement of cost-benefit analysis on the issuance of § 6(b)(5) standards would eviscerate the "to the extent feasible" requirement. Standards would inevitably be set at the level indicated by cost-benefit analysis, and not at the level specified by § 6(b)(5). For example, if cost-benefit analysis indicated a protective standard of 1,000 μg/m³ PEL, while feasibility analysis indicated a 500 μg/m³ PEL, the agency would be forced by the cost-benefit requirement to choose the less stringent point. We cannot believe that Congress intended the general terms of § 3(8) to countermand the specific feasibility requirement of § 6(b)(5). Adoption of petitioners' interpretation would effectively write § 6(b)(5) out of the Act. We decline to render Congress' decision to include a feasibility requirement nugatory, thereby offending the well-settled rule that all parts of a statute, if possible, are to be given effect. Congress did not contemplate any further balancing by the agency for toxic material and harmful physical agents standards, and we should not " 'impute to Congress a purpose to paralyze with one hand what it sought to promote with the other.' "[32]

---

[32] This is not to say that § 3(8) might not require the balancing of costs and benefits for standards promulgated under provisions other than § 6(b)(5) of the Act. As a plurality of this Court noted in *Industrial Union Dept.,* if § 3(8) had no substantive content, "there would be no statutory criteria at all to guide the Secretary in promulgating either national consensus standards or permanent standards other than those dealing with toxic materials and harmful physical agents." Furthermore, the mere fact that a § 6(b)(5) standard is "feasible" does not mean that § 3(8)'s "reasonably necessary or appropriate" language might not impose additional restraints on OSHA. For example, all § 6(b)(5) standards must be addressed to "significant risks" of material health impairment. In addition, if the use of one respirator would achieve the same reduction in health risk as the use of five, the use of five respirators was "technologically and economically feasible," and OSHA thus insisted on the use of five, then the "reasonably necessary or appropriate" limitation might come into play as an additional restriction on OSHA to choose the one-respirator standard. In this case we need not decide all the applications that § 3(8) might have, either alone or together with § 6(b)(5).

C

The legislative history of the Act, while concededly not crystal clear, provides general support for respondents' interpretation of the Act. . . .

III

Section 6(f) of the Act provides that "[the] determinations of the Secretary shall be conclusive if supported by substantial evidence in the record considered as a whole." Petitioners contend that the Secretary's determination that the Cotton Dust Standard is "economically feasible" is not supported by substantial evidence in the record considered as a whole. In particular, they claim (1) that OSHA underestimated the financial costs necessary to meet the Standard's requirements; and (2) that OSHA incorrectly found that the Standard would not threaten the economic viability of the cotton industry.

In statutes with provisions virtually identical to § 6(f) of the Act, we have defined substantial evidence as "such relevant evidence as a reasonable mind might accept as adequate to support a conclusion." *Universal Camera Corp. v. NLRB*, 340 U.S. 474, 477 (1951). The reviewing court must take into account contradictory evidence in the record, but "the possibility of drawing two inconsistent conclusions from the evidence does not prevent an administrative agency's finding from being supported by substantial evidence," *Consolo v. FMC*, 383 U.S. 607, 620 (1966). Since the Act places responsibility for determining substantial evidence questions in the courts of appeals, we apply the familiar rule that "[this] Court will intervene only in what ought to be the rare instance when the [substantial evidence] standard appears to have been misapprehended or grossly misapplied" by the court below. Therefore, our inquiry is not to determine whether we, in the first instance, would find OSHA's findings supported by substantial evidence. Instead we turn to OSHA's findings and the record upon which they were based to decide whether the Court of Appeals "misapprehended or grossly misapplied" the substantial evidence test.

. . . On the basis of the whole record, we cannot conclude that the Court of Appeals "misapprehended or grossly misapplied" the substantial evidence test.

IV

The final Cotton Dust Standard places heavy reliance on the use of respirators to protect employees from exposure to cotton dust, particularly during the 4-year interim period necessary to install and implement feasible engineering controls. One part of the respirator provision requires the employer to give employees unable to wear a respirator the opportunity to transfer to another position, if available, where the dust level meets the Standard's PEL. When such a transfer occurs, the employer must guarantee that the employee suffers no loss of earnings or other employment rights or benefits. Petitioners do not object to the transfer provision, but challenge OSHA's authority under the Act to require employers to guarantee employees' wage and employment benefits following the transfer. The Court of Appeals held that OSHA has such authority. We hold that, whether or not OSHA has this underlying authority, the agency has failed to make the necessary determination or statement of reasons that its wage guarantee requirement is related to the achievement of a safe and healthful work environment. . . .

V

When Congress passed the Occupational Safety and Health Act in 1970, it chose to place pre-eminent value on assuring employees a safe and healthful working environment, limited only by the feasibility of achieving such an environment. We must measure the validity of the Secretary's actions against the requirements of that Act. For "[the] judicial function does not extend to substantive revision of regulatory policy. That function lies elsewhere — in Congressional and Executive oversight or amendatory legislation." *Industrial Union Dept. v. American Petroleum Institute,* 448 U.S., at 663 (BURGER, C.J., concurring).

Accordingly, the judgment of the Court of Appeals is affirmed in all respects except to the extent of its approval of the Secretary's application of the wage guarantee provision of the Cotton Dust Standard at 29 CFR § 1910.1043(f)(2)(v) (1980). To that extent, the judgment of the Court of Appeals is vacated and the case remanded with directions to remand to the Secretary for further proceedings consistent with this opinion.

It is so ordered.

JUSTICE POWELL took no part in the decision of these cases.

JUSTICE STEWART, dissenting.

. . . Everybody agrees that under [§ 6(b)(5)] the Cotton Dust Standard must at least be *economically* feasible, and everybody would also agree, I suppose, that in order to determine whether or not something is economically feasible, one must have a fairly clear idea of how much it is going to cost. Because I believe that OSHA failed to justify its estimate of the cost of the Cotton Dust Standard on the basis of substantial evidence, I would reverse the judgment before us without reaching the question whether the Act requires that a standard, beyond being economically feasible, must meet the demands of a cost-benefit examination.

The simple truth about OSHA's assessment of the cost of the Cotton Dust Standard is that the agency never relied on any study or report purporting to predict the cost to industry of the Standard finally adopted by the agency. . . .

Of course, as the Court notes, this Court will re-examine a court of appeals' review of a question of substantial evidence "only in what ought to be the rare instance when the standard appears to have been misapprehended or grossly misapplied." But I think this is one of those rare instances where an agency has categorically misconceived the nature of the evidence necessary to support a regulation, and where the Court of Appeals has failed to correct the agency's error. . . .

Unlike the Court, I think it clear to the point of being obvious that, as a matter of law, OSHA's prediction of the cost of the Cotton Dust Standard lacks a basis in substantial evidence, since the agency did not rely on even a single estimate of the cost of the actual Standard it promulgated. Accordingly, I respectfully dissent.

JUSTICE REHNQUIST, with whom THE CHIEF JUSTICE joins, dissenting.

As the Court correctly observes, the phrase "to the extent feasible" contains the critical language for the purpose of these cases. We are presented with a remarkable range of interpretations of that language. Petitioners contend that the statute *requires* the Secretary to demonstrate that the benefits of its "Cotton Dust Standard," in terms of reducing health risks, bear a reasonable relationship to its costs. Respondents, including the Secretary of Labor at least until his post argument motion, counter that Congress itself balanced costs and benefits when it enacted the statute, and that the statute *prohibits* the Secretary from engaging in a cost-benefit type balancing. Their view is that the Act merely requires the Secretary to promulgate standards that eliminate or reduce such risks "to the extent . . . technologically or economically feasible." As I read the Court's opinion, it takes a different position. It concludes that, at least as to the "Cotton Dust Standard," the Act does not require the Secretary to engage in a cost-benefit analysis, which suggests of course that the Act *permits* the Secretary to undertake such an analysis if he so chooses. . . .

[In enacting § 6(b)(5)] Congress had at least three choices. It could have required the Secretary to engage in a cost-benefit analysis prior to the setting of exposure levels, it could have prohibited cost-benefit analysis, or it could have permitted the use of such an analysis. Rather than make that choice and resolve that difficult policy issue, however, Congress passed. Congress simply said that the Secretary should set standards "to the extent feasible." Last year, JUSTICE POWELL reflected that "one might wish that Congress had spoken with greater clarity." *American Petroleum Institute,* 448 U.S., at 668 (POWELL, J., concurring in part and in judgment). I am convinced that the reason that Congress did not speak with greater "clarity" was because it could not. The words "to the extent feasible" were used to mask a fundamental policy disagreement in Congress. I have no doubt that if Congress had been required to choose whether to mandate, permit, or prohibit the Secretary from engaging in a cost-benefit analysis, there would have been no bill for the President to sign.

The Court seems to argue that Congress *did* make a policy choice when it enacted the "feasibility" language. Its view is that Congress required the Secretary to engage in something called "feasibility analysis." But those words mean nothing at all. They are a "legislative mirage, appearing to some Members [of Congress] but not to others, and assuming any form desired by the beholder." . . .

In believing that § 6(b)(5) amounts to an unconstitutional delegation of legislative authority to the Executive Branch, I do not mean to suggest that Congress, in enacting a statute, must resolve all ambiguities or must "fill in all of the blanks." Even the neophyte student of government realizes that legislation is the art of compromise, and that an important, controversial bill is seldom enacted by Congress in the form in which it is first introduced. It is not unusual for the various factions supporting or opposing a proposal to accept some departure from the language they would prefer and to adopt substitute language agreeable to all. But that sort of compromise is a far cry from this case, where Congress simply abdicated its responsibility for the making of a fundamental and most difficult policy choice — whether and to what extent "the statistical possibility of future deaths should . . . be disregarded in light of the economic costs of preventing those deaths." That is a "quintessential legislative" choice and must be made by the elected representatives of the people, not by nonelected officials in the Executive Branch. . . .

In sum, the Court is quite correct in asserting that the phrase "to the extent feasible" is the critical language for the purposes of these cases. But that language is critical, not because it establishes a general standard by which those charged with administering the statute may be guided, but because it has precisely the opposite effect: in failing to agree on whether the Secretary should be either mandated, permitted, or prohibited from undertaking a cost-benefit analysis, Congress simply left the crucial policy choices in the hands of the Secretary of Labor. As I stated at greater length last Term, I believe that in so doing Congress unconstitutionally delegated its legislative responsibility to the Executive Branch.

NOTES

1. *Legality of Cost-Benefit Analysis.* Does the majority opinion in *Cotton Dust* prohibit OSHA from using cost-benefit analysis? Justice Rehnquist reads the court as permitting cost-benefit analysis.

In reading the Supreme Court tea leaves, it may help to consider the unusual briefing procedure in the case. The government submitted its briefs defending the cotton dust standard under the Carter Administration. Oral argument was held on January 21, 1981, the first day of the Reagan administration. President Reagan later issued an executive order requiring the use of cost-benefit analysis for any government regulation. OSHA then asked the Supreme Court to refrain from further consideration of the *Cotton Dust* case until the cost-benefit analysis was completed. The AFL-CIO and the Amalgamated Clothing and Textile Workers Unions, the union respondents in the case, opposed the OSHA request for a delay. The Supreme Court's response rejecting a delay appears in note 25, where the court declares it "difficult to imagine" what else the agency could do. Most commentators, albeit not Justice Rehnquist, interpret this note to mean that the Supreme Court rejected the claim that OSHA could engage in cost-benefit analysis.

2. *Cost-Effectiveness Principle.* As a result of the Supreme Court decision in the *Cotton Dust* case, OSHA announced that it would now rely on the principle of cost effectiveness to assess proposed OSHA standards. This principle requires OSHA to determine the level of protection from exposure to a particular substance by using criteria other than cost-benefit analysis. Once this level of desired protection has been reached, then OSHA is able to select the least expensive means of compliance that will achieve that level of protection. Thus, if OSHA decided that a PEL of 500 provides the desirable level of protection from substance X, and this PEL can be achieved either by redesigning the ventilation system or by encapsulating the oven that produces the emissions, then OSHA can choose the least expensive means to reach the PEL.

3. *Cost-Benefit Analysis in Other OSHA Areas.* Footnote 29 of the *Cotton Dust* opinion contemplates a greater role for cost-benefit analysis in areas other than § 6(b)(5) standards for toxic materials and harmful physical agents. In *National Grain & Feed Ass'n v. OSHA*, 866 F.2d 717 (5th Cir.), *cert. denied,* 490 U.S. 1065 (1989), the Fifth Circuit held that the Court would defer to the Secretary's position that the grain dust, which was covered by the grain handling standard, is not a "harmful physical agent" within the meaning of § 6(b)(5). The court therefore imposed a requirement that the grain handling standard must be "reasonably necessary or appropriate" to protect worker safety, using the language in § 3(8) of the Act. The court said that this requirement is intermediate between feasibility and a strict cost-benefit analysis. The intermediate requirement meant that costs must be "reasonably related" to benefits.

A similar result was reached in *UAW v. OSHA*, 37 F.3d 665 (D.C. Cir. 1994). This case involved the OSHA standard requiring employers to lockout or tagout machines being serviced so they cannot inadvertently be turned on. The court held that this standard was not covered by § 6(b)(5), since the lockout/tagout standard dealt with an immediately noticeable physical harm rather than toxic materials or harmful physical agents. OSHA found "that the relationship between the benefits secured by the lockout/tagout standard and the costs it imposes is reasonable." *Id.* at 670. While the court stated that "the current case does not require us to decide whether the statute requires a reasonable relationship between a rule's costs and its benefits," *id.*, the assurance by OSHA that the relationship between the benefits and costs for this standard was reasonable apparently was an important factor that persuaded the court to dismiss the petition for review of the OSHA lockout/tagout standard.

Generic Rulemaking

Almost all of the OSHA standards currently in effect are the interim standards that were issued in 1971, shortly after the OSHAct was effective. The new permanent standards issued under § 6(b) of the Act have been sparse: only about fifty have been issued in thirty-five years. The slow pace is at least partially explained by the considerable resources that OSHA had to devote to building a factual record supporting each standard so it would withstand the careful scrutiny of the courts.

Whatever the justification, the glacial pace of issuing new standards has led to criticisms of OSHA. One response has been the use of generic rulemaking. Most permanent OSHA standards deal with a single substance (such as cotton dust) that is used in a limited set of industries (such as cotton mills and yarn manufacturers). Generic rulemaking, in contrast, regulates a process that is common to many industries or regulates a broad range of substances.

There have been four efforts at generic rulemaking. According to Mintz, "A successful generic regulatory effort was OSHA's 1983 regulation on access to employee exposure and medical records, which requires that employers provide access to employees and to OSHA to existing employer-maintained exposure and medical records relevant to employees exposed to a broad range of toxic substances and harmful physical agents." BENJAMIN W. MINTZ, OSHA: HISTORY, LAW, AND POLICY 86 (1984).

Another apparent success was the Hazard Communications Standard (HCS), although employers might object to this assessment. OSHA promulgated the standard for the manufacturing sector in 1983, and then extended the HCS to nonmanufacturing employers in 1987. The standard requires, *inter alia,* that employers prepare lists of hazardous chemicals, that all hazardous chemicals leaving a chemical manufacturing plant be labeled, that material safety data sheets (MSDS) be provided to each customer of the chemical firm, that employers who use these chemicals make the MSDS available to employees, and that employees using the hazardous chemicals be trained about how to use the chemicals safely.

The Hazard Communication Standard is one of the most significant requirements the OSHAct has placed on employers. For example, the OSHA standard most frequency cited in OSHA inspections during fiscal year 2005 was the HCS requirement that employers have a written program. In order to determine which chemicals are hazardous, manufacturers must rely on several sources, including Threshold Limit Values (TLV) adopted by the American Conference of Governmental Industrial Hygienists (ACGIH). An argument that the HCS invalidly delegated legislative authority to the ACGIH by relying on that organization's determination that a chemical is hazardous was rejected in *Associated Builders & Contractors, Inc. v. OSHA*, 862 F.2d 63, 69 (3d Cir. 1988), *cert. denied*, 490 U.S. 1003 (1989). The ACGIH adopted new TLVs in 2006, which were challenged by several trade organizations asserting "the process used by ACGIH to produce TLVs involves secrecy, conflict of interest, and junk science." *Industry Attempts Under Way to Derail OSHA's Use of ACGIH Threshold Limit Values*, 36 O.S.H. Rep. (BNA) 483 (May 25, 2006). OSHA responded to the challenge by arguing: "Nothing in the HCS requires compliance with the TLVs; therefore the HCS does not incorporate the TLVs by reference, and it does not delegate regulatory authority to ACGIH." *NAM, Other Industry Groups Ask Court to Review Rule Incorporating ACGIH TLVs*, 36 O.S.H. Rep. (BNA) 358 (April 20, 2006). OSHA is distinguishing between the level of chemical exposure that must be communicated to workers and others as a result of the HCS and the level of exposure that will result in enforcement activities requiring the employer to reduce the level of exposure.

A less successful effort at generic rulemaking was the 1980 Carcinogens Policy (Cancer Policy), which provided procedures for the identification, classification, and regulation of potential carcinogens, and two "model standards" for emergency temporary and permanent standards for carcinogens. In addition to the beating by Justice Stevens in the *Benzene* case, the Carcinogens Policy suffered direct challenges in several courts and was never implemented in a rulemaking proceeding. *See* MINTZ, *supra,* at 86-88.

The latest effort at generic rulemaking by OSHA was the 1989 Air Contaminant Standard, which set permissible exposure limits for 428 toxic substances. OSHA described the standard as "its most significant workplace exposure action ever." 18 O.S.H. Rep. (BNA) 1475-76 (Jan. 18, 1989). Despite this accolade, the Air Contaminants Standard was challenged in 28 suits, a number which was eventually reduced by settlements to 11 cases. The Eleventh Circuit was picked by random selection to hear the consolidated cases.

AFL-CIO v. OSHA
United States Court of Appeals, Eleventh Circuit
965 F.2d 962 (1992)

FAY, CIRCUIT JUDGE:

In 1989, the Occupational Safety and Health Administration ("OSHA") . . . issued its Air Contaminants Standard, a set of permissible exposure limits for 428 toxic substances. In these consolidated appeals, petitioners representing various affected industries and the American Federation of Labor and Congress of Industrial Organizations ("AFL-CIO" or "the union") challenge both the procedure used by OSHA to generate this multi-substance standard and OSHA's findings on numerous specific substances included in the new standard. For the reasons that follow, we vacate the Air Contaminants Standard and remand to the agency.

I. *Background*

. . . Section 6(a) of the Act provided that in its first two years, OSHA should promulgate "start-up" standards, on an expedited basis and without public hearing or comment, based on "national consensus" or "established Federal standard[s]" that improve employee safety or health. *Id.* § 655(a). Pursuant to that authority, OSHA in 1971 promulgated approximately 425 permissible exposure limits ("PELs") for air contaminants, derived principally from federal standards applicable to government contractors under the Walsh-Healey Act, 41 U.S.C. § 35.

The Act then provides two mechanisms to update these standards. Most new standards or revised existing standards must be promulgated under the requirements of section 6(b) of the OSH Act. 29 U.S.C. § 655(b).

OSHA may also issue Emergency Temporary Standards under section 6(c) of the OSH Act, 29 U.S.C. § 655(c), when it "determines that employees are exposed to grave danger from exposure" to toxic substances. However, once OSHA has published an emergency standard, proceedings must commence for issuance of a regular standard under section 6(b).

On June 7, 1988, OSHA published a Notice of Proposed Rulemaking for its Air Contaminants Standard. In this single rulemaking, OSHA proposed to issue new or revised PELs for over 400 substances. OSHA limited the scope of this rulemaking to those substances for which the ACGIH [American Conference of Governmental Industrial Hygienists] recommended limits that were either new or more protective than the existing PELs. There was an initial comment period of forty-seven days, followed by a thirteen-day public hearing. Interested parties then had until October 7, 1988 to submit post-hearing evidence and until October 31, 1988 to submit post-hearing briefs.

OSHA then issued its revised Air Contaminants Standard for 428 toxic substances on January 19, 1989. This standard, which differs from the proposal in several respects, lowered the PELs for 212 substances, set new PELs for 164 previously unregulated substances, and left unchanged PELs for 52 substances for which lower limits had originally been proposed. The standard established an approximately four-year period for employers to come into compliance with the new standard using engineering and work practice controls. Until that time, employers may use respirators or any other reasonable methods to comply with the standards.

Various industry groups, the AFL-CIO, and specific individual companies filed challenges to the final standard in numerous United States Courts of Appeals. Pursuant to 28 U.S.C. § 2112(a), all petitions for review of the Air Contaminants Standard were transferred to this court, where they have been consolidated for disposition. . . .

III. *Discussion*

In challenging the procedure by which OSHA promulgated the Air Contaminants Standard, a group of industry petitioners complain that OSHA's use of generic findings, the lumping together of so many substances in one rulemaking, and the short time provided for comment by interested parties, combine to create a record inadequate to support this massive new set of PELs. The union also challenges the rulemaking procedure utilized by OSHA for the Air Contaminants Standard. Not surprisingly, however, the union claims that this procedure resulted in standards that are systematically underprotective of employee health. . . .

A. *"Generic" Rulemaking*

Unlike most of the OSHA standards previously reviewed by the courts, the Air Contaminants Standard regulates not a single toxic substance, but 428 different substances. The agency explained its decision to issue such an omnibus standard in its Notice of Proposed Rulemaking:

> OSHA has issued only 24 substance-specific health regulations since its creation. It has not been able to review the many thousands of currently unregulated chemicals in the workplace nor to keep up with reviewing the several thousand new chemicals introduced since its creation. It has not been able to fully review the literature to determine if lower limits are needed for many of the approximately 400 substances it now regulates.

> Using past approaches and practices, OSHA could continue to regulate a small number of the high priority substances and those of greatest public interest. However, it would take decades to review currently used chemicals and OSHA would never be able to keep up with the many chemicals which will be newly introduced in the future.

53 Fed. Reg. at 20963. For this reason, "OSHA determined that it was necessary to modify this approach through the use of *generic* rulemaking, which would simultaneously cover many substances." 54 Fed. Reg. at 2333 (emphasis added).

"Generic" means something "common to or characteristic of a whole group or class; typifying or subsuming; not specific or individual." WEBSTER'S THIRD NEW INTERNATIONAL DICTIONARY 945 (1966). Previous "generic" rulemakings by OSHA have all dealt with requirements that, once promulgated, could be applied to numerous different situations. . . .

By contrast, the new Air Contaminants Standard is an amalgamation of 428 unrelated substance exposure limits. There is little common to this group of diverse substances except the fact that OSHA considers them toxic and in need of regulation. In fact, this rulemaking is the antithesis of a "generic" rulemaking; it is a set of 428 specific and individual substance exposure limits. Therefore, OSHA's characterization of this as a "generic" rulemaking is somewhat misleading.

Nonetheless, we find nothing in the OSH Act that would prevent OSHA from addressing multiple substances in a single rulemaking. Moreover, because the statute leaves this point open and because OSHA's interpretation of the statute is reasonable, it is appropriate for us to defer to OSHA's interpretation. However, we believe the PEL for each substance must be able to stand independently, i.e., that each PEL must be supported by substantial evidence in the record considered as a whole and accompanied by adequate explanation. OSHA may not, by using such multi-substance rulemaking, ignore the requirements of the OSH Act. Both the industry petitioners and the union argue that such disregard was what in essence occurred. Regretfully, we agree.

B. *Significant Risk of Material Health Impairment*

Section 3(8) of the OSH Act defines "occupational health and safety standard" as "a standard which requires conditions, or the adoption or use of one or more practices, means, methods, operations, or processes, *reasonably necessary or appropriate* to provide safe or healthful employment and places of employment." 29 U.S.C. § 652(8) (emphasis added). The Supreme Court has interpreted this provision to require that, before the promulgation of any permanent health standard, OSHA make a threshold finding that a significant risk of material health impairment exists at the current levels of exposure to the toxic substance in question, "and that a new, lower standard is therefore 'reasonably necessary or appropriate to provide safe or healthful employment and places of employment.'" *Benzene,* 448 U.S. at 615. OSHA is not entitled to regulate *any* risk, only those which present a "significant" risk of "material" health impairment. OSHA must therefore determine: (1) what health impairments are "material," and (2) what constitutes a "significant" risk of such impairment. . . .

Once OSHA finds that a significant risk of material health impairment exists at current exposure levels for a given toxic substance, any standard promulgated to address that risk must comply with the requirements of section 6(b)(5) of the OSH Act, 29 U.S.C. § 655(b)(5). That section provides that the agency

> in promulgating standards dealing with toxic materials or harmful physical agents under this subsection, shall set the standard which *most adequately assures, to the extent feasible, on the basis of the best*

available evidence, that no employee will suffer material impairment of health or functional capacity even if such employee has regular exposure to the hazard dealt with by such standard for the period of his working life. . . .

Id. (emphasis added). In other words, section 6(b)(5) mandates that the standard adopted "prevent material impairment of health to the extent feasible." *ATMI,* 452 U.S. at 512 (emphasis omitted).

1. *Material Impairment*

In this rulemaking, OSHA grouped the 428 substances into eighteen categories by the primary health effects of those substances, for example, neuropathic effects, sensory irritation, and cancer. Industry petitioners charge that for several categories of substances OSHA failed to adequately justify its determination that the health effects caused by exposure to these substances are "material impairments." We disagree.

Petitioners cite the category of "sensory irritation" as a particularly egregious example. At the beginning of the discussion for each category, the agency summarized the types of health effects within that category, and discussed why those effects constituted "material impairments." . . .

In addition, in the more general discussion of OSHA's approach to this rulemaking, OSHA also recognized that

> irritation also covers a spectrum of effects, some serious and some trivial. Hence, complaints of minor irritation would not in and of itself constitute material impairment.
>
> In addition, OSHA would weigh irritation with physical manifestations more heavily than irritation with purely subjective responses. This does not mean that purely subjective responses would not constitute material impairment. That judgment would depend on the magnitude of the irritation.

Id. at 2362. We interpret this explanation as indicating that OSHA finds that although minor irritation may not be a material impairment, there is a level at which such irritation becomes so severe that employee health and job performance are seriously threatened, even though those effects may be transitory. We find this explanation adequate. OSHA is not required to state with scientific certainty or precision the exact point at which each type of sensory or physical irritation becomes a material impairment. Moreover, section 6(b)(5) of the Act charges OSHA with addressing all forms of "material impairment of health *or functional capacity,*" and not exclusively "death or serious physical harm" or "grave danger" from exposure to toxic substances. Overall, we find that OSHA's determinations of what constitute "material impairments" are adequately explained and supported in the record.

2. *Significant Risk*

However, the agency's determination of the extent of the risk posed by individual substances is more problematic. . . . OSHA has a responsibility to quantify or explain, at least to some reasonable degree, the risk posed by *each* toxic substance regulated. Otherwise, OSHA has not demonstrated, and this court cannot evaluate, how serious the risk is for any particular substance, or whether *any* workers will in fact benefit from the new standard for any particular substance. If each of these 428 toxic substances had been addressed in separate rulemakings, OSHA would clearly have been required to estimate in some fashion the risk of harm for each substance. OSHA is not entitled to take short-cuts with statutory requirements simply because it chose to combine multiple substances in a single rulemaking.

However, OSHA's discussions of individual substances generally contain no quantification or explanation of the risk from that individual substance. The discussions of individual substances contain summaries of various studies of that substance and the health effects found at various levels of exposure to that substance. However, OSHA made no attempt to estimate the risk of contracting those health effects. Instead, OSHA merely provided a conclusory statement that the new PEL will reduce the "significant" risk of material health effects shown to be caused by that substance, without any explanation of how the agency determined that the risk was significant. However, OSHA did make a generic finding that the Air Contaminants Standard as a whole would prevent 55,000 occupational illnesses and 683 deaths annually.

Moreover, a determination that the new standard is "reasonably necessary or appropriate," 29 U.S.C. § 652(8), and that it is the standard that "most adequately assures . . . that no employee will suffer material impairment of health or functional capacity," *id.* § 655(b)(5), necessarily requires some assessment of the level at which significant risk of harm is eliminated or substantially reduced. Yet, with rare exceptions, the individual substance discussions in the Air Contaminants Standard are virtually devoid of reasons for setting those individual standards. In most cases, OSHA cited a few studies and then established a PEL without explaining why the studies mandated the particular PEL chosen. For example, the PEL for bismuth telluride appears to be based on a single study that showed almost no effects of any kind in animals at several times that concentration. Similarly, the PEL for ferrovanadium dust was based on pulmonary changes at exposure levels many hundreds of times higher than OSHA's new standard. For some substances, OSHA merely repeated a boilerplate finding that the new limit would protect workers from significant risk of some material health impairment. For example, OSHA did not cite any studies whatsoever for its aluminum welding fume standard, or its vegetable oil mist standard. . . .

Mere conclusory statements, such as those made throughout the Air Contaminants Standard, are simply inadequate to support a finding of significant risk of material health impairment.

On the other hand, OSHA established PELs for carbon tetrachloride and vinyl bromide, both carcinogens, at levels where OSHA itself acknowledged that the risk of material health impairment remained significant. For carbon tetrachloride, OSHA stated that at the new level, "residual risk continues to be significant . . . 3.7 excess deaths per 1,000 workers exposed over their working lifetimes." For vinyl bromide, OSHA stated that the new PEL "will not eliminate this significant risk, because . . . residual risk [at the new level] is 40 excess deaths per 1,000 exposed workers . . . [and thus] is clearly significant." The only explanation given by OSHA in the final rule for setting its standard where a significant risk of material health impairment remains was that the time and resource constraints of attempting to promulgate an air contaminants standard of this magnitude prevented detailed analysis of these substances. OSHA did not claim in the final rule that the PELs for these two substances were necessary because of feasibility concern.

The agency's response to this criticism is unpersuasive. OSHA first contends that quantitative risk analysis using mathematical models like the ones developed for carcinogens was impossible for this rulemaking because no such models exist for noncarcinogens. . . .

Yet, in several previous rulemakings, OSHA apparently succeeded in determining how many workers were exposed to a particular substance or how much risk would be alleviated by a new standard, even though those particular substances were *not* carcinogens. *See United Steelworkers,* 647 F.2d at 1245-51 (lead poisoning); *AFL-CIO v. Marshall,* 617 F.2d at 646 (byssinosis caused by cotton dust); *see also Building & Constr.,* 838 F.2d at 1263 (asbestosis and cancer). It is therefore unclear whether the lack of a method to quantitatively assess the risk for noncarcinogens is a cause or a result of the agency's approach. . . .

The agency further claims that no quantification was required because OSHA's final standards " 'fall within a zone of reasonableness.' " However, without *any* quantification or any explanation, this court cannot determine what that "zone of reasonableness" is or if these standards fall within it.

OSHA also responds by noting that it incorporated "uncertainty" or "safety" factors into many PELs. However, OSHA did not use a uniform safety factor, but instead claims to have made a case-by-case assessment of the appropriate safety factor. . . . In this rulemaking, the difference between the level shown by the evidence and the final PEL is sometimes substantial. We assume, because it is not expressly stated, that for each of those substances OSHA applied a safety factor to arrive at the final standard. Nevertheless, the method by which the "appropriate" safety factor was determined for each of those substances is not explained in the final rule.

We find OSHA's use of safety factors in this rulemaking problematic. First, OSHA's use of safety factors in this rulemaking is very similar to the approach criticized by the Supreme Court in *Benzene.* Second, even assuming that the use of safety factors is permissible under the Act and *Benzene,* application of such factors without explaining the method by which they were determined, as was done in this case, is clearly not permitted.

From OSHA's description, safety factors are used to lower the standard below levels at which the available evidence shows no significant risk of material health impairment because of the *possibility* that the evidence is incorrect or incomplete; i.e., OSHA essentially makes an assumption that the existing evidence does not adequately show the extent of the risk. That may be a correct assumption, but beyond a general statement that the use of safety factors is common in the scientific community, OSHA did not indicate how the existing evidence for individual substances was inadequate to show the extent of the risk from those substances. . . .

The lesson of *Benzene* is clearly that OSHA may use assumptions, but only to the extent that those assumptions have some basis in reputable scientific evidence. If the agency is concerned that the standard should be more stringent than even a conservative interpretation of the existing evidence supports, monitoring and medical testing may be done to accumulate the additional evidence needed to support that more protective limit. *Benzene* does not provide support for setting standards below the level substantiated by the evidence. Nor may OSHA base a finding of significant risk at lower levels of exposure on unsupported assumptions using evidence of health impairments at significantly higher levels of exposure. Overall, OSHA's use of safety factors in this rulemaking was not adequately explained by this rulemaking record.

More generally, OSHA defends its failure to make more specific findings for each individual substance, as well as its decision to set the standards for several substances at levels where significant risks of material health impairment remain, by citing its authority to set priorities, 29 U.S.C. § 655(g), and the discretion permitted the agency in making policy decisions.

This implies that OSHA need no longer perform detailed analysis and explanation when promulgating PELs because the agency's analysis for other substances has been upheld in prior rulemakings. Besides displaying more than a touch of hubris, this passage reveals a fundamental misperception of the OSH Act and the caselaw interpreting that act.

While OSHA has probably established that most or all of the substances involved do pose a significant risk at some level, it has failed to establish that existing exposure levels in the workplace present a significant risk of material health impairment or that the new standards eliminate or substantially lessen the risk.

C. *Feasibility*

The Supreme Court has defined "feasibility" as " 'capable of being done, executed, or effected,' " *ATMI,* 452 U.S. at 508-09 (quoting Webster's Third New International Dictionary 831 (1976)), both technologically and economically. Again, the burden is on OSHA to show by substantial evidence the standard is feasible, although OSHA need not prove feasibility with scientific certainty. Despite OSHA's repeated claims that it made feasibility determinations on an industry-by-industry basis, it is clear that the agency again proceeded "generically."

1. *Technological Feasibility*

To show that a standard is technologically feasible, OSHA must demonstrate "that modern technology has at least conceived some industrial strategies or devices which are likely to be capable of meeting the PEL and which the industries are generally capable of adopting." *United Steelworkers,* 647 F.2d at 1266. Further, "the undisputed principle that feasibility is to be tested industry-by-industry demands that OSHA examine the technological feasibility of each industry individually." *Id.* at 1301. Courts have remanded OSHA determinations where the agency has not sufficiently analyzed the abilities of different industries to meet proposed standards.

In this rulemaking, OSHA first identified the primary air contaminant control methods. . . .

OSHA then organized its discussion of technological feasibility by industry sector using the Standard Industrial Classification (SIC) groupings. . . .

However, OSHA made no attempt to show the ability of technology to meet specific exposure standards in specific industries. Except for an occasional specific conclusion as to whether a particular process control could meet a particular PEL, OSHA merely presented general conclusions as to the availability of these controls in a particular industry.

OSHA correctly notes that all it need demonstrate is "a general *presumption* of feasibility for *an industry*." *United Steelworkers,* 647 F.2d at 1266 (second emphasis added); *see also ASARCO,* 746 F.2d at 496. However, as this quote indicates, "a general presumption of feasibility" refers to a specific industry-by-industry determination that a "typical firm will be able to develop and install engineering and work practice controls that can meet the PEL in most of its operations." *United Steelworkers,* 647 F.2d at 1272. OSHA can prove this "by pointing to technology that is either already in use or has been conceived and is reasonably capable of experimental refinement and distribution within the standard's deadlines." *Id.* Only when OSHA has provided such proof for a given industry does there arise "a presumption that industry can meet the PEL without relying on respirators, a presumption which firms will have to overcome to obtain relief in any secondary inquiry into feasibility."

. . . Thus, it is clear that the concept of "a general presumption of feasibility" does not grant OSHA a license to make overbroad generalities as to feasibility or to group large categories of industries together without some explanation of why findings for the group adequately represent the different industries in that group. We find that OSHA has not established the technological feasibility of the 428 PELs in its revised Air Contaminants Standard.

2. *Economic Feasibility*

Nor has OSHA adequately demonstrated that the standard is economically feasible. . . . The determination of economic feasibility is governed by the same principles as technological feasibility. It must be supported by substantial evidence and OSHA must demonstrate its applicability to the affected industries.

In this rulemaking, although OSHA ostensibly recognized its responsibility "to demonstrate economic feasibility for *an industry*," 54 Fed. Reg. at 2367 (emphasis added), the agency nevertheless determined feasibility for each industry *"sector"* . . . without explaining why such a broad grouping was appropriate. OSHA's economic feasibility determinations therefore suffer from the same faults as its technological feasibility findings. . . .

However, reliance on such tools as average estimates of cost can be extremely misleading in assessing the impact of particular standards on individual industries. Analyzing the economic impact for an entire sector could conceal particular industries laboring under special disabilities and likely to fail as a result of enforcement. Moreover, for some substances, OSHA failed even to analyze all the affected industry sectors. We find that OSHA has not met its burden of establishing that its 428 new PELs are either economically or technologically feasible. . . .

3. *Four-year Compliance Period*

The union also challenges OSHA's decision to allow four years, until December 31, 1992, for the implementation of engineering and work practice controls to bring industry into compliance with the new standards, while in the interim permitting compliance through the use of respirators. As a transitional provision, OSHA specified that employers must continue to achieve the 1971 PELs by adhering to the hierarchy of controls in 29 C.F.R. § 1910.1000(e), as they have been required to do since 1971. In adopting this four-year time period, OSHA stated that the agency's "experience is that for substances of normal difficulty, one to two years is sufficient," 54 Fed. Reg. at 2916, but that a four-year period "takes into account that some employers will have to control several substances and also considers those few substances where compliance may take greater efforts for some employers," *id.* That conclusory analysis falls short of justifying an across-the-board four-year period of delay, but is fully consistent with OSHA's treatment of this standard as a "generic" standard, without adequate consideration of individual substances or the effect of the new standards on individual industries.

This "generic" four-year compliance period is simply not adequately supported in the record. Unlike other standards where OSHA has exercised its "technology-forcing" authority and required that industries develop the technology to achieve the new standards, in this standard, "OSHA's feasibility analysis was based on what industry is already achieving or what could be achieved with standard 'off-the-shelf' technology, [and] there are few if any cases where OSHA is attempting to force technology." 54 Fed. Reg. at 2366. If the technology exists and is in many cases already being used, it is difficult to understand why four years is required for the implementation of this standard for all industries. If OSHA's concern was primarily economic feasibility, that too needed to be addressed for each industry or for each appropriate industrial grouping. . . .

IV. *Conclusion*

It is clear that the analytical approach used by OSHA in promulgating its revised Air Contaminants Standard is so flawed that it cannot stand. . . .

We have no doubt that the agency acted with the best of intentions. It may well be, as OSHA claims, that this was the only practical way of accomplishing a much needed revision of the existing standards and of making major strides towards improving worker health and safety. Given OSHA's history of slow progress in issuing standards, we can easily believe OSHA's claim that going through detailed analysis for each of the 428 different substances regulated was not possible given the time constraints set by the agency for this rulemaking. Unfortunately, OSHA's approach to this rulemaking is not consistent with the requirements of the OSH Act. Before OSHA uses such an approach, it must get authorization from Congress by way of amendment to the OSH Act. Legislative decisions on the federal level are to be made in the chambers of Congress. It is not for this court to undertake the substantial rewriting of the Act necessary to uphold OSHA's approach to this rulemaking.

Therefore, for the reasons stated above, we vacate the revised Air Contaminants Standard, and remand to the agency.

NOTES

1. *New Permanent Standards.* The *AFL-CIO v. OSHA* decision doomed efforts to expedite the process of promulgating generic standards that apply to a multiplicity of toxic substances. The alternative route is to issue a series of standards, each dealing with a particular toxic substance, harmful physical agent, or some other threat to workers' safety or health.

2. *The Ergonomics Standard.* The most noteworthy attempt to promulgate a permanent standard involved the ergonomics standard issued by OSHA in November 2000 in the waning months of the Clinton administration. The standard required employers to reduce the incidence of musculoskeletal disorders (MSDs) — including conditions such as carpal tunnel syndrome and back pain — resulting from lifting, assembly, and other cumulative or repetitive stresses. The ergonomics standard also provided for Work Restriction Protection (WRP) that required an injured worker who had work limitations placed on his or her current job or who was transferred to a temporary alterative job to be paid 100 percent of his or her earnings until the worker was able to return to the normal job, or was determined to be permanently unable to return to the normal job, or for 90 days, which ever comes first. The WRP also required that an injured worker who was unable to work would receive 90 percent of his or her normal earnings for a similar period of time.

OSHA estimated that 1.8 million workers have MSDs related to ergonomic factors each year and that the ergonomics standard would prevent 460,000 of these injures, which would reduce costs to employers by $9 billion a year. OSHA estimated that the ergonomics standard would cost employers about $4.5 billion a year to implement. *Work-Related Injury Rule Readied*, L.A. TIMES, Nov. 12, 2000, at A42.

Employers were not persuaded by the arguments presented by OSHA and other supporters of the ergonomics standard. One employer argument concerned costs: the Employment Policy Foundation, for example, argued that the actual cost of the ergonomics standard was as much as $99 billion a year. Another argument was that the Work Restriction Protection (WRP) provision inappropriately displaced state workers' compensation laws.

The Small Business Regulatory Enforcement Fairness Act of 1996 permits Congress and the President to review and reject permanent standards after they are promulgated by OSHA. The first use of the Act involved the ergonomics standard. The Senate and House voted to repeal the ergonomics standard, and President George W. Bush signed the congressional resolution of disapproval in March 2001.

OSHA subsequently issued ergonomics guidelines, which constituted advice rather than mandatory regulations, for nursing homes, poultry processing, and retail groceries, and OSHA is reviewing guidelines for shipyards. However, OSHA's ability to issue additional guidelines may be affected by a policy proposed by the Office of Management and Budget that would require Federal agencies to submit guidance documents for notice and public comments. *Outlook: OSHA in 2006*, 36 O.S.H. Rep. (BNA) S-5 (Jan. 12, 2006).

3. *The Steel Erection Standard.* Not every standard issued in the waning of the Clinton administration suffered the fate of the ergonomics standard. An example is the steel erection standard, which revised one of the interim standards issued in 1971. The new standard addresses hazards associated with steel erection, such as hoisting, decking, and placing steel joints. The steel erection standard was the first OSHA rule developed under the Negotiated Rulemaking Act of 1990. Despite the assistance provided by that act, the timetable for the adoption of the standard is indicative of the delays experienced in promulgating OSHA standards. The Steel Erection Negotiated Rulemaking Advisory Committee (SENRAC) was formed in 1994 to assist OSHA in developing the rule. SENRAC presented a consensus proposal to OSHA in July 1997. In September 1997, OSHA requested the Small Business Administration (SBA) to waive the review required for any federal regulation that will have a significant impact on small business. OSHA received the SBA waiver in January 1998 and then sent the proposal to the Office of Management and Budget (OMB) for review in May 1998. OMB completed its review in July 1998. OSHA subsequently made changes in the consensus proposal, which OMB approved on January 8, 2001. OSHA issued the standard on January 18, 2001, with a proposed effective date of July 18, 2001. On July 13, 2001 the Bush administration OSHA announced that the effective date for the steel erection standard would be postponed until January 18, 2002. A challenge by a coalition of steel and metal manufacturers to a portion of the standard dealing with bolting of joists rather than welding was denied in *Steel Joist Inst. v. OSHA*, 287 F.3d 1165 (D.C. Cir. 2002). Subsequently, OSHA revoked a portion of the standard dealing with slip resistance "because employers cannot comply with the provision." *OSHA Drops Slip Resistance Provision In Steel Rule Because of Inability to Comply*, 36. O.S.H. Rep. (BNA) 37 (Jan. 19, 2006).

4. *The Needlestick Standard.* Perhaps reflecting a frustration with the sluggish pace of the promulgation process by OSHA, in 2000 Congress enacted the Needlestick Safety and Prevention Act, P.L. 106-430, which directed OSHA to revise the bloodborne pathogen standard and exempted the agency from the normal procedures associated with issuing or amending permanent standards. OSHA estimated that 590,164 injuries occur each year in health care facilities involving contaminated needles or other sharp objects. Needlesticks and other cuts can expose workers to such pathogens as HIV, hepatitis B, and hepatitis C. OSHA responded to the Congressional directive and issued a revised standard in January 2001 that required employers to update their exposure control plans and to solicit input from employees concerning the selection of engineering and work-practice controls. The General Accounting Office estimated that the switch to safer devices would prevent about 69,000 needlestick injuries each year. The standard went into effect on April 18, 2001 as stipulated in the standard, although OSHA, under the new Bush administration, delayed enforcement for a 90-day outreach and education effort. *See Congressionally Mandated Rule Effective; OSHA Will Delay Enforcement for 90 Days*, 31 O.S.H. Rep. (BNA) 360 (April 19, 2001).

5. *The Hexavalent Chromium Standard.* OSHA issued a permanent standard establishing a permissible exposure limit (PEL) of 5 micrograms of hexavalent chromium per cubic meter of air in February 2006. Four lawsuits challenging the standard were quickly filed; two from industry groups asserting the PEL was too low and infeasible, and two from unions or advocacy groups arguing the PEL was too high to protect workers. The standard was issued in part because of an order from the Third Circuit Court of Appeals to expedite rulemaking on the compound. *Four Lawsuits Filed Challenging OSHA's Hexavalent Chromium Rule, Agency Says*, 36 O.S.H. Rep. (BNA) 423 (May 4, 2006).

D. THE GENERAL DUTY CLAUSE

NATIONAL REALTY & CONSTRUCTION CO. v. OSHRC
United States Court of Appeals, D.C. Circuit
489 F.2d 1257 (1973)

Before WRIGHT and ROBB, CIRCUIT JUDGES, and MATTHEWS, SENIOR DISTRICT JUDGE.

WRIGHT, CIRCUIT JUDGE.

We review here an order of the Occupational Safety and Health Review Commission which found National Realty and Construction Company, Inc. to have committed a "serious violation" of the "general duty clause" of the Occupational Safety and Health Act of 1970, for which a civil fine of $300 was imposed. Unable to locate substantial evidence in the record to support the Commission's finding of a violation, we reverse.

I. *The Proceedings and the Evidence*

. . . .

An employer's duties under the Act flow from two sources. First, by 29 U.S.C. § 654(a)(2) [§ 5(a)(2)], he must conform to the detailed health and safety standards promulgated by the Secretary of Labor under 29 U.S.C. § 655 [§ 6]. Second, where no promulgated standards apply, he is subject to the general duty to

> furnish to each of his employees employment and a place of employment which are free from recognized hazards that are causing or are likely to cause death or serious physical harm to his employees.

[§ 5(a)(1),] 29 U.S.C. § 654(a)(1). Breach of the general duty opens an employer to fines of up to $1,000 per violation, some fine in this range being mandatory if the violation is "serious," 29 U.S.C. § 666(b) and (c). Employer duties are enforced through citations and proposed penalties issued by the Secretary of Labor, contested matters being adjudicated by the Commission, an independent body of safety experts.

On September 24, 1971 the Secretary cited National Realty for serious breach of its general duty

> in that an employee was permitted to stand as a passenger on the running board of an Allis Chalmers 645 Front end loader while the loader was in motion.

After National Realty filed timely notice of contest, the Secretary entered a formal complaint charging that National Realty had

> permitted the existence of a condition which constituted a recognized hazard that was likely to cause death or serious physical harm to its employees. Said condition, which resulted in the death of foreman O. C. Smith, arose when Smith stood as a passenger on the running board of a piece of construction equipment which was in motion.

. . . .

On September 16, 1971, at a motel construction site operated by National Realty in Arlington, Virginia, O. C. Smith, a foreman with the company, rode the running board of a front-end loader driven by one of his subordinates, Clyde Williams. The loader suffered a stalled engine while going down an earthen ramp into an excavation and began to swerve off the ramp. Smith jumped from the loader, but was killed when it toppled off the ramp and fell on him. John Irwin, Smith's supervisor, testified that he had not seen the accident, that Smith's safety record had been very good, that the company had a "policy" against equipment riding, and that he — Irwin — had stopped the "4 or 5" employees he had seen taking rides in the past two years. The loader's driver testified that he did not order Smith off the vehicle because Smith was his foreman; he further testified that loader riding was extremely rare at National Realty. Another company employee testified that it was contrary to company policy to ride on heavy equipment. A company supervisor said he had reprimanded violators of this policy and would fire second offenders should the occasion arise. Simms, the inspector, testified from personal experience that the Army Corps of Engineers has a policy against equipment riding. He stated he was unaware of other instances of equipment riding at National Realty and that the company had "abated" its violation. Asked to define abatement, Simms said it would consist of orally instructing equipment drivers not to allow riding.

The hearing examiner dismissed the citation, finding that National Realty had not "permitted" O. C. Smith to ride the loader, as charged in the citation and complaint. . . . Upon reviewing the hearing record, the Commission reversed its examiner by a 2-1 vote, each commissioner writing separately. Ruling for the Secretary, Commissioners Burch and Van Namee found inadequate implementation of National Realty's safety "policy." Rejecting the hearing examiner's factual findings in part, Commissioner Burch stated that it was "incredible" that an oral safety policy could have reduced equipment riding to a rare occurrence. Commissioner Van Namee reasoned that the Smith incident and the "4 or 5" occurrences shown on the record "put respondent on notice that more was required of it to obtain effective implementation of its safety policy." The majority commissioners briefly suggested several improvements which National Realty might have effected in its safety policy: placing the policy in writing, posting no-riding signs, threatening riders with automatic discharge, and providing alternative means of transport at the construction site. In dissent, Commissioner Moran concluded that the Secretary had not proved his charge that National Realty had "permitted" either equipment riding in general or the particular incident which caused Smith's death.

II. *The Issues*

. . . Under the [general duty] clause, the Secretary must prove (1) that the employer failed to render its workplace "free" of a hazard which was (2) "recognized" and (3) "causing or likely to cause death or serious physical harm." The hazard here was the dangerous activity of riding heavy equipment. The record clearly contains substantial evidence to support the Commission's finding that this hazard was "recognized"[32] and "likely to cause death or serious physical harm."[33] The question then is whether National Realty rendered its construction site "free" of the hazard. In this case of first impression, the meaning of that statutory term must be settled before the sufficiency of the evidence can be assessed.

Construing the term in the present context presents a dilemma. On the one hand, the adjective is unqualified and absolute: A workplace cannot be just "reasonably free" of a hazard, or merely as free as the average workplace in the industry. On the other hand, Congress quite clearly did not intend the general duty clause to impose strict liability: The duty was to be an achievable one. Congress' language is consonant with its intent only where the "recognized" hazard in question *can be* totally eliminated from a workplace. A hazard consisting of conduct by employees, such as equipment riding, cannot, however, be totally eliminated. A demented, suicidal, or willfully reckless employee may on occasion circumvent the best conceived and most vigorously

---

[32] An activity may be a "recognized hazard" even if the defendant employer is ignorant of the activity's existence or its potential for harm. The term received a concise definition in a floor speech by Representative Daniels when he proposed an amendment which became the present version of the general duty clause:

> A recognized hazard is a condition that is known to be hazardous, and is known not necessarily by each and every individual employer but is known taking into account the standard of knowledge in the industry. In other words, whether or not a hazard is "recognized" is a matter for objective determination; it does not depend on whether the particular employer is aware of it.

116 Cong. Rec. (Part 28) 38377 (1970). The standard would be the common knowledge of safety experts who are familiar with the circumstances of the industry or activity in question. The evidence below showed that both National Realty and the Army Corps of Engineers took equipment riding seriously enough to prohibit it as a matter of policy. Absent contrary indications, this is at least substantial evidence that equipment riding is a "recognized hazard."

[33] Presumably, any given instance of equipment riding carries a less than 50% probability of serious mishap, but no such mathematical test would be proper in construing this element of the general duty clause. *See* Morey, *The General Duty Clause of the Occupational Safety and Health Act of 1970,* 86 HARV. L. REV. 988, 997-998 (1973). If evidence is presented that a practice could eventuate in serious physical harm upon other than a freakish or utterly implausible concurrence of circumstances, the Commission's expert determination of likelihood should be accorded considerable deference by the courts. For equipment riding, the potential for injury is indicated on the record by Smith's death and, of course, by common sense.

enforced safety regime. This seeming dilemma is, however, soluble within the literal structure of the general duty clause. Congress intended to require elimination only of preventable hazards. It follows, we think, that Congress did not intend unpreventable hazards to be considered "recognized" under the clause. Though a generic form of hazardous conduct, such as equipment riding, may be "recognized," unpreventable instances of it are not, and thus the possibility of their occurrence at a workplace is not inconsistent with the workplace being "free" of recognized hazards.

Though resistant to precise definition, the criterion of preventability draws content from the informed judgment of safety experts. Hazardous conduct is not preventable if it is so idiosyncratic and implausible in motive or means that conscientious experts, familiar with the industry, would not take it into account in prescribing a safety program. Nor is misconduct preventable if its elimination would require methods of hiring, training, monitoring, or sanctioning workers which are either so untested or so expensive that safety experts would substantially concur in thinking the methods infeasible. All preventable forms and instances of hazardous conduct must, however, be entirely excluded from the workplace. To establish a violation of the general duty clause, hazardous conduct need not actually have occurred, for a safety program's feasibly curable inadequacies may sometimes be demonstrated before employees have acted dangerously. At the same time, however, actual occurrence of hazardous conduct is not, by itself, sufficient evidence of a violation, even when the conduct has led to injury. The record must additionally indicate that demonstrably feasible measures would have materially reduced the likelihood that such misconduct would have occurred.

C. *Deficiencies in This Record*

The hearing record shows several incidents of equipment riding, including the Smith episode where a foreman broke a safety policy he was charged with enforcing. It seems quite unlikely that these were unpreventable instances of hazardous conduct. But the hearing record is barren of evidence describing, and demonstrating the feasibility and likely utility of, the particular measures which National Realty should have taken to improve its safety policy. Having the burden of proof, the Secretary must be charged with these evidentiary deficiencies.

The Commission sought to cure these deficiencies *sua sponte* by speculating about what National Realty could have done to upgrade its safety program. These suggestions, while not unattractive, came too late in the proceedings. An employer is unfairly deprived of an opportunity to cross-examine or to present rebuttal evidence and testimony when it learns the exact nature of its alleged violation only after the hearing. As noted above, the Secretary has considerable scope before and during a hearing to alter his pleadings and legal theories. But the Commission cannot make these alterations itself in the face of an empty record.[40] To merit judicial deference, the Commission's expertise must operate upon, not seek to replace, record evidence.

---

[40] It is patently unfair for an agency to decide a case on a legal theory or set of facts which was not presented at the hearing. The Commission suggested that National Realty should have

Only by requiring the Secretary, at the hearing, to formulate and defend *his own* theory of what a cited defendant should have done can the Commission and the courts assure even-handed enforcement of the general duty clause.[41] Because employers have a general duty to do virtually everything possible to prevent and repress hazardous conduct by employees, violations exist almost everywhere, and the Secretary has an awesomely broad discretion in selecting defendants and in proposing penalties. To assure that citations issue only upon careful deliberation, the Secretary must be constrained to specify the particular steps a cited employer should have taken to avoid citation, and to demonstrate the feasibility and likely utility of those measures.

Because the Secretary did not shoulder his burden of proof, the record lacks substantial evidence of a violation, and the Commission's decision and order are, therefore,

Reversed.

NOTES

1. *The Four Elements of a General Duty Violation.* *National Realty* articulated three elements that OSHA must prove to establish a general duty violation. Subsequent decisions by the Review Commission and the courts have established four elements of a general duty violation:

> (1) a condition or activity in the workplace presents a hazard to an employee;
>
> (2) the condition or activity is recognized as a hazard;
>
> (3) the hazard is causing or is likely to cause death or serious physical harm; and

---

posted "no-riding" signs or reduced its safety policy to writing, but the Secretary introduced no testimony indicating the value of such precautions relative to "orally" disseminated safety policies. The Commission [made several other suggestions, without the Secretary introducing evidence on point]. In short, the Commissioners attempted to serve as expert witnesses for the Secretary. This is not their role. The Secretary should have called his own expert or experts at the hearing.

[41] Such precautions will not, of course, make the broad commands of the general duty clause any more precise and clear to *prospective* violators of the clause. But any statute or rule of law imposing general obligations raises certain problems of fair notice. [T]he Commission can ameliorate the fair notice problem by attending carefully to the statutory definition of a "serious violation": . . . 29 U.S.C. § 666(j). Where the hazard involved is a form of hazardous conduct by employees, an employer's safety program is in "serious" violation of the general duty clause only if (1) the misconduct involves a substantial risk of harm and is substantially probable under the employer's regime of safety precautions, or (2) the employer, with the exercise of reasonable diligence, could have known that its safety program failed the standards of the clause by failing to preclude the occurrence of preventable misconduct. If either condition applies, it is hardly unfair for the Commission to assume that the defendant-employer had at least constructive notice that the law required more than was being done. Only if a violation is serious is a penalty necessarily imposed. *Compare* 29 U.S.C. § 666(b) *with* 29 U.S.C. § 666(c). While the Commission has the clear authority to impose a penalty even if the violation is not serious, a zero penalty, coupled with an abatement order, would obviously be the proper response where the Commission determined that the defendant-employer had no notice, *i.e.*, no duty to know, that its safety regime was defective. . . .

(4) a feasible means exists to eliminate or materially reduce the hazard.

RANDY S. RABINOWITZ, OCCUPATIONAL SAFETY AND HEALTH LAW 91 (2d ed. 2002).

2. *Element One: There Must Be A Workplace Hazard That Affects an Employee.* Several sub-elements can be identified. The person facing a hazard must be an employee of the cited employer and not, for example, an independent contractor. The requirement that the employer provide "a place of employment" which is free from hazards has been broadly construed; for example, a truck used to transport workers is within the scope of the general duty clause. In addition, there must be "a sufficient causal connection between the harm and the workplace." *Secretary of Labor v. Pepperidge Farm, Inc.*, 17 O.S.H. Cas. (BNA) 1993 (1997). *See generally* MARK ROTHSTEIN, OCCUPATIONAL SAFETY AND HEALTH LAW §§ 6.3-6.5 (2006).

Does an employer's policy that excludes women aged 16 to 50 from working in the lead pigments department unless they have been surgically sterilized constitute "a hazard" under section 5(a)(1)? As a result of this policy, five women were sterilized in order to retain their positions. A majority of the Review Commission held that "Congress did not intend the Act to apply to every conceivable aspect of employer-employee relations" and that the policy was not a hazard within the meaning of the general duty clause. A hazard was defined to include processes and materials that cause injury and disease by operating directly on employees as they engage in work-related activities. *See American Cyanamid Co.*, 9 O.S.H. Cas. (BNA) 1956 (1981), *aff'd*, 741 F.2d 444 (D.C. Cir. 1984).

3. *Element Two: The Hazard Must Be Recognized.* What is the meaning of a recognizable hazard? Suppose, for example, that the workers and the employer who manufacture Grimeoff, an industrial soap, do not realize that the odorless fumes that spew from the soap vat are carcinogenic, although epidemiologists know this fact. Is the hazard recognizable? In note 32 of the *National Realty* decision, Judge Wright stated that "an activity may be a 'recognized hazard' even if the defendant employer is ignorant of the activity's existence or its potential for harm." Contrast this view with that of Representative Steiger, one of the primary authors of the OSHAct. In explaining the Act on the House floor, he defined the term "recognized hazards" as hazards "that can readily be detected on the basis of the basic human senses. Hazards which require technical or testing devices to detect them are not intended to be within the scope of the general duty requirement." 116 CONG. REC. H42,206 (daily ed. Dec. 17, 1970).

Despite this warning that recognized hazards must be detectable by the human senses, OSHA has consistently treated section 5(a)(1) as also covering hazards whose detection requires monitoring devices. This policy was upheld in *American Smelting & Refining Co. v. OSHRC*, 501 F.2d 504 (8th Cir. 1974). *See generally* BENJAMIN W. MINTZ, OSHA: HISTORY, LAW, AND POLICY 446 (1984).

As a policy matter, do we want to hold employers responsible under the general duty clause for hazards that are not immediately obvious? Should not employer responsibility for these types of nonobvious hazards only result from the violation of a permanent standard issued under section 6(b), the promulgation of which will put the employer on notice of possible liability?

4. *Element Three: Likelihood of Death or Serious Harm.* The courts and the Commission have tried several approaches to defining a likelihood of death or serious injury, which can perhaps be better understood by distinguishing among three statistical measures. *Pe* is the probability of a harmful event occurring (e.g., an injury) per unit of exposure (e.g., per use of a machine or per year or per working career). *Pdsh* is the probability of death or serious harm occurring, assuming that a harmful event has occurred. *Pzap* is the product of *Pe* and *Pdsh* and represents the probability of death or serious harm occurring per unit of exposure.

The legal issue is: what values of *Pe, Pdsh,* or *Pzap* constitute a sufficient "likelihood of death or serious injury" that a violation of section 5(a)(1) has occurred? Note 33 of *National Realty* provides an admonition against a mathematical approach, but nonetheless offers some guidance about the level of *Pzap* necessary for a violation. That "a given instance of equipment riding carries a less than 50% probability of serious mishap" does not preclude a finding of a violation so long as serious physical harm (presumably this means *Pzap*) is not "freakish or utterly implausible." Does this mean that *Pzap* could be as low as .001? How about .0001?

While the court in *National Realty* thus appears to have framed the statistical test in terms of the necessary level of *Pzap,* the Commission thereafter began to examine the components *Pe* and *Pdsh.*

The current meaning of the likelihood of death or serious physical harm begins with *Secretary of Labor v. Kastalon, Inc.*, 12 O.S.H. Cas. (BNA) 1928 (1986), which embraced the "significant risk" test. The commission overturned Kastalon's OSHA citation by holding that "in order to establish a significant risk in a section 5(a)(1) case involving a carcinogen, the Secretary must show the probability that employees will contract cancer under the conditions present in the workplace. This is consistent with the Supreme Court decision in the *Benzene* Case." As discussed in note 2 after the *Benzene* case (*Industrial Union Dep't v. American Petroleum Inst.*, 448 U.S. 607 (1980)), the significant risk test may require at least a one in a thousand chance of developing cancer from exposure to a carcinogen during a working career. Thus, in terms of the statistical measures used in this note, the Commission in *Kastalon* appeared to be requiring a *Pzap* of at least .001 per working career in order to find a violation of the general duty clause.

This interpretation must be tempered by the Commission's explanation of the *Kastalon* decision in *Secretary of Labor v. Waldon Healthcare Center*, 16 O.S.H. Cas. (BNA) 1052 (1993). Waldon was issued a citation alleging a violation of the general duty clause because nurses and nursing assistants were exposed to Hepatitis B virus ("HBV") through possible direct contact with blood or other bodily fluids. The Commission concluded that "the evidence establishes that the risk of contacting blood during the various nursing home procedures is rather low . . . ." (Using our terminology, this could be interpreted as meaning that *Pe* was low.) The Commission also concluded that the "evidence amply demonstrates that a person who contracts the HBV virus is likely to suffer death or serious physical harm." (Using our terminology, this is equivalent to saying that *Pdsh* is high.)

The Commission stated that "[t]he essence of the *Kastalon* holding is that when citing a violation of the general duty clause, the Secretary must establish that the cited condition actually poses a hazard to employees. . . . Therefore, when the Secretary proceeds under the general duty clause, he must meet the same minimal criterion regarding the nature of the alleged hazards he does when promulgating a section 5(a)(2) standard." The Commission stated that those minimal criteria are provided in the *Benzene* case, and provided this guidance as to the meaning:

> Contrary to [the respondent's] argument, to be consistent with the Supreme Court decision in the "*Benzene* Case," there is no requirement that there be a "significant" risk of the hazard coming to fruition, only that if the hazardous event occurs, it would create a "significant risk" to employees.

This passage from *Waldon* appears to endorse the "possibility" test for determining whether element three of the general duty clause has been satisfied. And the required probability of *Pe* appears to be quite low, perhaps no more than one chance in ten thousand (.0001). One problem with this interpretation is that the Commission treats the holding in *Waldon* as if it were consistent with the *Benzene* case. However, while the Commission in *Waldon* interpreted the *Benzene* case as imposing "no requirement that there be a 'significant risk' of the hazard coming to fruition," the general interpretation of the significant risk test imposed by the *Benzene* case is that there must be at least a one in a thousand chance that the worker will develop cancer or some other serious harm during the worker's lifetime. *Pzap* cannot be at least one in a thousand unless *Pe* is at least one in a thousand since the value of *Pdsh* must be one or less. Thus the Commission now appears to be requiring a lower *Pe* for a general duty clause violation than the *Pe* that the federal courts require to meet the significant risk test for permanent standards.

This applicability of *Kastalon* was further limited by *Pepperidge Farm, Inc.*, 17 O.S.H. Cas. (BNA) 1993 (1997). The Commission noted that *Kastalon* involved a toxic substance for which no safe exposure level had been established and therefore the Secretary was required to show there was a significant risk. However, the risk at Pepperidge Farm involved ergonomics hazards that had already resulted in human injury and thus "neither precedent nor common sense require[s] that the finding of hazard be foresworn until there is determination of the threshold at which there occurs a substantial risk of injury". *Id.* at 2013. Does this mean that the existence of one actual injury (*Pe* > 0.0000) that results in a death or serious physical harm satisfies the significant risk test?

5. Element Four: A Feasible Method to Correct the Hazard. The Commission remanded the case to an ALJ in *Beverly Enterprises* with this admonition:

> The last remaining element of proof of a violation of section 5(a)(1) is the existence of feasible means of abating or correcting the recognized hazard. The Secretary must specify the proposed abatement

measures and demonstrate both that the measures are capable of being put into effect and that they would be effective in materially reducing the incidence of the hazard. The Secretary must also show that her proposed abatement measures are economically feasible.

What other limitations are there on the responsibilities of the employer to deal with recognized hazards at the worksite? For example, suppose that an employer operates in an area subject to earthquakes. Is an earthquake a hazard for which the employer is responsible under section 5(a)(1)? The *National Realty* decision suggests that "hazard" means "preventable hazard," which presumably would absolve an employer from liability for an injury resulting from an earthquake because there is no feasible method to correct the hazard.

But what about hazardous conduct by an employee? *National Realty* indicates that hazardous conduct "is not preventable if it so idiosyncratic and implausible in motive or means that conscientious experts, familiar with the industry, would not take it into account in prescribing a safety program." Did the conduct of the supervisor who was injured in the case meet this test? As a policy matter, should OSHA make employers responsible only for hazards that are preventable? If National Realty had been made responsible for the supervisor's injury, perhaps under a standard of absolute liability, the costs of the hazardous conduct would have been reflected in the price of the firm's product, which in turn would have resulted in less consumption of the product. Should the OSHAct be interpreted to encourage reduced consumption and production of products that involve hazards to workers, even when, from the standpoint of the employer, the hazard is not preventable? An absolute liability standard would also force employers to implement the latest technology and training methods in order to avoid injuries and fatalities.

The fourth element of a section 5(a)(1) violation also raises an equity issue. Suppose, for example, that the manufacturer of Grimeoff is in an industry that routinely allows impurities in the soap that are causing the health problem. Nonetheless, the engineers for the manufacturer of Grimeoff have identified a relatively expensive process that will remove the impurities. Is Grimeoff required to use this process when the industry practice is to leave the impurities in the soap? The *National Realty* decision represents the majority view, namely that an employer's obligations are not limited by industry practice. But is it appropriate to put an employer at a competitive disadvantage by imposing a higher standard of performance on the firm through the general duty clause?

6. The Relationship Between Section 5(a)(1) and Section 6 Standards. Suppose a permanent standard has been issued under section 6(b) that limits the use of Grimeoff to ten washes per week. NIOSH then develops evidence that any exposure greater than five washes per week causes an excess mortality rate. Can OSHA use the general duty clause to impose a more stringent exposure rule for Grimeoff than is provided in the permanent standard?

The general rule is that a citation under section 5(a)(1) is only proper if no specific standard applies. In *United Auto Workers v. General Dynamics Land Systems Division*, 815 F.2d 1570 (D.C. Cir. 1987), the court reviewed an order of the Commission that had vacated a citation for violation of the general duty clause for exposing workers to freon vapors in confined spaces. The employer had complied with the specific standard limiting the amount of exposure to freon, but there was evidence that the employer was aware that workers were still experiencing serious medical problems from freon. The court remanded the case to the Commission and directed it to address the merits of the section 5(a)(1) citation with this instruction:

> Therefore if (as is alleged in this case) an employer knows a particular safety standard is inadequate to protect his workers against the specific hazard it is intended to address, or that the conditions in his place of employment are such that the safety standard will not adequately deal with the hazards to which his employees are exposed, he has a duty under section 5(a)(1) to take whatever measures may be required by the Act, over and above those mandated by the safety standard, to safeguard his workers. In sum, if an employer knows a specific standard will not protect his workers against a particular hazard, his duty under section 5(a)(1) will not be discharged no matter how faithfully he observes that standard. Scienter is the key.

Id. at 1577.

E. ENFORCEMENT

OSHA enforces the Act through inspections conducted by a compliance officer. Section 9(a) of the OSHAct and OSHA regulations require that OSHA issue citations for all violations detected.[*] The citation must fix a reasonable time for the abatement of each violation. OSHA may also propose a penalty for each alleged violation. The employer can contest the proposed penalty, and the employer, any employee, or representative of the employee may contest the period for the abatement, in which case the case will be heard by the Occupational Safety and Health Review Commission. Commission decisions can be appealed to the Federal courts. OSHAct § 11(a). The Secretary of Labor can also obtain enforcement of Commission final orders by federal appellate courts under section 11(b) of the Act. The law requires the court to issue the order unless there is a procedural defect in the request. The measure was rarely used before 2003, but by early 2006 the Secretary had sought 21 enforcement orders and 19 had been enforced. *Section 11(b) Advantages Lauded As Enforcement Tool for Labor Secretary*, 36 O.S.H. Rep. (BNA) 256 (March 16, 2006).

Inspection Activity

The inspection task of OSHA is daunting. OSHA has jurisdiction over some seven million workplaces, and in recent years there have been only about 1,100 federal and probably fewer than 1,000 state safety inspectors. The number of inspections has varied considerably during the past thirty-five years. Inspection activity peaked at 91,516 inspections in fiscal year 1976, set a record

---

[*] OSHA funds on-site safety and health consultation visits under cooperative agreements with agencies in 48 states. One requirement of such consultations is that if an imminent danger is discovered, the employer must abate the hazard immediately.

low of 24,024 in fiscal year 1996, and averaged about 38,200 per year in fiscal years 2001-2005. The relatively low level of inspections has sparked criticism. An AFL-CIO study found that, on average, OSHA federal compliance officers inspect workplaces only once every 117 years. *Job Safety Commitment Lacking, Hazards Increasing, AFL-CIO Reports*, 36 O.S.H. Rep. (BNA) 385 (April 27, 2006). An inspection can, however, result in multiple citations.** In fiscal year 2005, 38,714 inspections resulted in 85,307 citations.

Penalties

As a result of an inspection, the employer can be cited and sent a notice of a proposed penalty. All willful violations are proposed either as serious (with penalties ranging from $25,000 to $70,000) or as other than serious (with a minimum penalty of $5,000). Since 1995, this policy has been adjusted for the benefit of small employers. For example, employers with fewer than fifty employees are no longer subject to the $25,000 minimum for serious violations.

The three criminal penalties under the Act are for a willful violation that results in death; for giving advance notice of an inspection; and for knowingly making a false statement, representation, or certification. OSHA FIELD INSPECTION REFERENCE MANUAL, Chap. IV, OSHA Instruction CPL 02-00-103 (Sept. 26, 1994).

OSHA as the Bad Cop

OSHA relies on a site-specific targeting (SST) plan to schedule unannounced comprehensive inspections for high hazard work sites. For fiscal year 2006, the annual survey of illnesses and injuries of some 80,000 employers was used to place approximately 4,250 workplaces on the primary list for unannounced comprehensive inspections. *4,250 Work Sites on 2006 Targeted List; High-Hazard, Lower-Rate Sites Dropped*, 36 O.S.H. Rep. (BNA) 493 (June 1, 2006).

In recent years, OSHA has used the enhanced enforcement program (EEP) to target recalcitrant employers for priority investigations. A firm can qualify for the EEP program by meeting specified criteria, such as a fatality inspection in which OSHA finds a high-gravity serious violation related to the death, or an inspection that results in two failure-to-abate notices where the underlying violations were classified as high gravity serious. OSHA recorded 593 EEP cases in fiscal year 2005, bringing the total to 906 EEP cases since the program began in October 2003. *EEP Cases in FY 2005 Nearly Double Over Previous Year's Tally, OSHA Figures Show*, 35 O.S.H. Rep. (BNA) 1117 (Dec. 8, 2005).

OSHA levied its largest penalty in its history in 2005 when it fined BP Products North America $21.4 million for safety and health violations associated with an explosion at the company's Texas City refinery that killed 15 and injured more than 170 workers. A subsequent inspection of the company's Oregon, Ohio refinery under OSHA's Enhanced Enforcement Program found

---

** An example of multiple citations involved the John J. Steuby Co., which received 12 willful, 37 serious, one repeat, and three other-than-serious citations for alleged violations. *Machine Injuries, Amputations at Company Result in $788,000 Fine*, 53 OSHA Citations, 36 O.S.H. Rep. (BNA) 37 (Jan. 19, 2006).

violations similar to those at the Texas City refinery and resulted in additional fines. *BP Products North America Fined $2.4 Million for Hazard at Ohio Refinery*, 36 O.S.H. Rep. (BNA) 381 (April 27, 2006).

OSHA as the Good Cop

While OSHA has been increasing its enforcement activity for recalcitrant employers, it has also been attempting to promote a less contentious relationship with the business community. OSHA Administrator Edwin Foulke said the agency "should be perceived as the good neighborhood cop on the corner, the one who provides directions and advice to people needing assistance." To be sure, he added a qualifier: "that 'good' cop will hand you a ticket if you run a red light." Sandy Smith, *ASSE: OSHA's Role is Good Cop, Says Foulke*, OCCUPATIONAL HAZARDS (June 12, 2006), *available at* http://www.occupationalhazards.com/articles/15283. A longstanding cooperative program established in 1982, the Voluntary Protection Program (VPP), is a recognition system for employers who exceed OSHA's requirements and who actively involve employees in dealing with specific hazards of the workplace. Qualifying sites are provided a one-year exemption from scheduled OSHA inspections, although OSHA may still inspect the firms in response to worker complaints or reports of fatalities or multiple injuries. During fiscal year 2005, OSHA added 276 participants to several variants of the VPP. "In addition, the agency entered into 56 strategic partnerships and 158 alliances. Another 273 participants were enrolled in the agency's Safety and Health Achievement Recognition Program (SHARPS)." *Outlook: OSHA in 2006*, 36 O.S.H. Rep. (BNA) S-5 (Jan. 12, 2006).

Types of Inspections

OSHA conducts two types of inspections: First are the programmed inspections of targeted high-hazard industries and workplaces. Second are unprogrammed inspections triggered by accident reports, employee complaints, referrals, or other publicity. The inspection is governed by a series of rules, such as the prohibition on advance notice to an employer of an impending inspection. The purpose of this requirement is to maximize the effectiveness of OSHA inspections, since most employers are unlikely to be inspected more than once a decade. But what happens if the employer who is surprised by a visit from the OSHA inspector refuses to allow entry to the plant?

MARSHALL v. BARLOW'S, INC.
United States Supreme Court
436 U.S. 307 (1978)

MR. JUSTICE WHITE delivered the opinion of the Court.

Section 8(a) of the Occupational Safety and Health Act of 1970 (OSHA or Act) empowers agents of the Secretary of Labor (Secretary) to search the work area of any employment facility within the Act's jurisdiction. The purpose of the search is to inspect for safety hazards and violations of OSHA regulations. No search warrant or other process is expressly required under the Act.

On the morning of September 11, 1975, an OSHA inspector entered the customer service area of Barlow's, Inc., an electrical and plumbing installation business located in Pocatello, Idaho. The president and general manager, Ferrol G. "Bill" Barlow, was on hand; and the OSHA inspector, after showing his credentials, informed Mr. Barlow that he wished to conduct a search of the working areas of the business. Mr. Barlow inquired whether any complaint had been received about his company. The inspector answered no, but that Barlow's, Inc., had simply turned up in the agency's selection process. The inspector again asked to enter the nonpublic area of the business; Mr. Barlow's response was to inquire whether the inspector had a search warrant. The inspector had none. Thereupon, Mr. Barlow refused the inspector admission to the employee area of his business. He said he was relying on his rights as guaranteed by the Fourth Amendment of the United States Constitution.

Three months later, the Secretary petitioned the United States District Court for the District of Idaho to issue an order compelling Mr. Barlow to admit the inspector. The requested order was issued on December 30, 1975, and was presented to Mr. Barlow on January 5, 1976. Mr. Barlow again refused admission, and he sought his own injunctive relief against the warrantless searches assertedly permitted by OSHA. A three-judge court was convened. On December 30, 1976, it ruled in Mr. Barlow's favor. Concluding that *Camara v. Municipal Court,* 387 U.S. 523, 528-529 (1967), and *See v. Seattle,* 387 U.S. 541, 543 (1967), controlled this case, the court held that the Fourth Amendment required a warrant for the type of search involved here and that the statutory authorization for warrantless inspections was unconstitutional. An injunction against searches or inspections pursuant to § 8(a) was entered. The Secretary appealed, challenging the judgment, and we noted probable jurisdiction.

I

The Secretary urges that warrantless inspections to enforce OSHA are reasonable within the meaning of the Fourth Amendment. Among other things, he relies on § 8(a) of the Act, which authorizes inspection of business premises without a warrant and which the Secretary urges represents a congressional construction of the Fourth Amendment that the courts should not reject. Regrettably, we are unable to agree.

The Warrant Clause of the Fourth Amendment protects commercial buildings as well as private homes. To hold otherwise would belie the origin of that Amendment, and the American colonial experience. An important forerunner of the first 10 Amendments to the United States Constitution, the Virginia Bill of Rights, specifically opposed "general warrants, whereby an officer or messenger may be commanded to search suspected places without evidence of a fact committed." The general warrant was a recurring point of contention in the Colonies immediately preceding the Revolution. The particular offensiveness it engendered was acutely felt by the merchants and businessmen whose premises and products were inspected for compliance with the several parliamentary revenue measures that most irritated the colonists. . . . Against this background, it is untenable that the ban on warrantless searches was not intended to shield places of business as well as of residence.

This Court has already held that warrantless searches are generally unreasonable, and that this rule applies to commercial premises as well as homes. In *Camara v. Municipal Court, supra,* at 528-529, we held:

> [Except] in certain carefully defined classes of cases, a search of private property without proper consent is "unreasonable" unless it has been authorized by a valid search warrant.

On the same day, we also ruled:

> As we explained in *Camara,* a search of private houses is presumptively unreasonable if conducted without a warrant. The businessman, like the occupant of a residence, has a constitutional right to go about his business free from unreasonable official entries upon his private commercial property. The businessman, too, has that right placed in jeopardy if the decision to enter and inspect for violation of regulatory laws can be made and enforced by the inspector in the field without official authority evidenced by a warrant.

See v. Seattle, supra, at 543.

These same cases also held that the Fourth Amendment prohibition against unreasonable searches protects against warrantless intrusions during civil as well as criminal investigations. The reason is found in the "basic purpose of this Amendment . . . [which] is to safeguard the privacy and security of individuals against arbitrary invasions by governmental officials." *Camara, supra,* at 528. If the government intrudes on a person's property, the privacy interest suffers whether the government's motivation is to investigate violations of criminal laws or breaches of other statutory or regulatory standards. It therefore appears that unless some recognized exception to the warrant requirement applies, *See v. Seattle* would require a warrant to conduct the inspection sought in this case.

The Secretary urges that an exception from the search warrant requirement has been recognized for "pervasively regulated [businesses]," *United States v. Biswell,* 406 U.S. 311, 316 (1972), and for "closely regulated" industries "long subject to close supervision and inspection." *Colonnade Catering Corp. v. United States,* 397 U.S. 72, 74, 77 (1970). These cases are indeed exceptions, but they represent responses to relatively unique circumstances. Certain industries have such a history of government oversight that no reasonable expectation of privacy, see *Katz v. United States,* 389 U.S. 347, 351-352 (1967), could exist for a proprietor over the stock of such an enterprise. Liquor (*Colonnade*) and firearms (*Biswell*) are industries of this type; when an entrepreneur embarks upon such a business, he has voluntarily chosen to subject himself to a full arsenal of governmental regulation.

Industries such as these fall within the "certain carefully defined classes of cases," referenced in *Camara,* 387 U.S., at 528. The element that distinguishes these enterprises from ordinary businesses is a long tradition of close government supervision, of which any person who chooses to enter such a business must already be aware. "A central difference between those cases [*Colonnade* and *Biswell*] and this one is that businessmen engaged in such federally licensed and regulated enterprises accept the burdens as well as the benefits of their trade, whereas the petitioner here was not engaged in any regulated or licensed business. The businessman in a regulated industry in effect consents to the restrictions placed upon him." *Almeida-Sanchez v. United States,* 413 U.S. 266, 271 (1973).

The clear import of our cases is that the closely regulated industry of the type involved in *Colonnade* and *Biswell* is the exception. The Secretary would make it the rule. Invoking the Walsh-Healey Act of 1936, 41 U.S.C. § 35 et seq., the Secretary attempts to support a conclusion that all businesses involved in interstate commerce have long been subjected to close supervision of employee safety and health conditions. But the degree of federal involvement in employee working circumstances has never been of the order of specificity and pervasiveness that OSHA mandates. It is quite unconvincing to argue that the imposition of minimum wages and maximum hours on employers who contracted with the Government under the Walsh-Healey Act prepared the entirety of American interstate commerce for regulation of working conditions to the minutest detail. Nor can any but the most fictional sense of voluntary consent to later searches be found in the single fact that one conducts a business affecting interstate commerce; under current practice and law, few businesses can be conducted without having some effect on interstate commerce.

The Secretary also attempts to derive support for a *Colonnade-Biswell*-type exception by drawing analogies from the field of labor law. In *Republic Aviation Corp. v. NLRB,* 324 U.S. 793 (1945), this Court upheld the rights of employees to solicit for a union during nonworking time where efficiency was not compromised. By opening up his property to employees, the employer had yielded so much of his private property rights as to allow those employees to exercise § 7 rights under the National Labor Relations Act. But this Court also held that the private property rights of an owner prevailed over the intrusion of nonemployee organizers, even in nonworking areas of the plant and during nonworking hours. *NLRB v. Babcock & Wilcox Co.,* 351 U.S. 105 (1956).

The critical fact in this case is that entry over Mr. Barlow's objection is being sought by a Government agent. Employees are not being prohibited from reporting OSHA violations. What they observe in their daily functions is undoubtedly beyond the employer's reasonable expectation of privacy. The Government inspector, however, is not an employee. Without a warrant he stands in no better position than a member of the public. What is observable by the public is observable, without a warrant, by the Government inspector as well. The owner of a business has not, by the necessary utilization of employees in his operation, thrown open the areas where employees alone are permitted to the warrantless scrutiny of Government agents. That an employee is free to report, and the Government is free to use, any evidence of noncompliance with OSHA that the employee observes furnishes no justification for federal agents to enter a place of business from which the public is restricted and to conduct their own warrantless search.

II

The Secretary nevertheless stoutly argues that the enforcement scheme of the Act requires warrantless searches, and that the restrictions on search discretion contained in the Act and its regulations already protect as much privacy as a warrant would. The Secretary thereby asserts the actual reasonableness of OSHA searches, whatever the general rule against warrantless searches might be. Because "reasonableness is still the ultimate standard," *Camara v. Municipal Court,* 387 U.S., at 539, the Secretary suggests that the Court decide whether a warrant is needed by arriving at a sensible balance between the administrative necessities of OSHA inspections and the incremental protection of privacy of business owners a warrant would afford. He suggests that only a decision exempting OSHA inspections from the Warrant Clause would give "full recognition to the competing public and private interests here at stake." *Ibid.*

The Secretary submits that warrantless inspections are essential to the proper enforcement of OSHA because they afford the opportunity to inspect without prior notice and hence to preserve the advantages of surprise. While the dangerous conditions outlawed by the Act include structural defects that cannot be quickly hidden or remedied, the Act also regulates a myriad of safety details that may be amenable to speedy alteration or disguise. The risk is that during the interval between an inspector's initial request to search a plant and his procuring a warrant following the owner's refusal of permission, violations of this latter type could be corrected and thus escape the inspector's notice. To the suggestion that warrants may be issued *ex parte* and executed without delay and without prior notice, thereby preserving the element of surprise, the Secretary expresses concern for the administrative strain that would be experienced by the inspection system, and by the courts, should *ex parte* warrants issued in advance become standard practice.

We are unconvinced, however, that requiring warrants to inspect will impose serious burdens on the inspection system or the courts, will prevent inspections necessary to enforce the statute, or will make them less effective. In the first place, the great majority of businessmen can be expected in normal course to consent to inspection without warrant; the Secretary has not brought to this Court's attention any widespread pattern of refusal.[11] In those cases where an owner does insist on a warrant, the Secretary argues that inspection efficiency will be impeded by the advance notice and delay. The Act's penalty provisions for giving advance notice of a search, Section 17(f), and the Secretary's own regulations, 29 CFR § 1903.6 (1977), indicate that surprise searches are indeed contemplated. However, the Secretary has also promulgated a regulation providing that upon refusal to permit an inspector to enter the property or to complete his inspection, the inspector shall attempt to ascertain the reasons for the refusal and report to his superior, who shall "promptly take appropriate action, including compulsory process, if necessary." 29 CFR § 1903.4 (1977). The regulation represents a choice to proceed by process where entry is refused; and on the basis of evidence available from present practice, the Act's effectiveness has not been crippled by providing those owners who wish to refuse an initial requested entry with a time lapse while the inspector obtains the necessary process. Indeed, the kind of process

---

[11] We recognize that today's holding itself might have an impact on whether owners choose to resist requested searches; we can only await the development of evidence not present on this record to determine how serious an impediment to effective enforcement this might be.

sought in this case and apparently anticipated by the regulation provides notice to the business operator. If this safeguard endangers the efficient administration of OSHA, the Secretary should never have adopted it, particularly when the Act does not require it. Nor is it immediately apparent why the advantages of surprise would be lost if, after being refused entry, procedures were available for the Secretary to seek an *ex parte* warrant and to reappear at the premises without further notice to the establishment being inspected.

Whether the Secretary proceeds to secure a warrant or other process, with or without prior notice, his entitlement to inspect will not depend on his demonstrating probable cause to believe that conditions in violation of OSHA exist on the premises. Probable cause in the criminal law sense is not required. For purposes of an administrative search such as this, probable cause justifying the issuance of a warrant may be based not only on specific evidence of an existing violation but also on a showing that "reasonable legislative or administrative standards for conducting an . . . inspection are satisfied with respect to a particular [establishment]." *Camara v. Municipal Court,* 387 U.S., at 538. A warrant showing that a specific business has been chosen for an OSHA search on the basis of a general administrative plan for the enforcement of the Act derived from neutral sources such as, for example, dispersion of employees in various types of industries across a given area, and the desired frequency of searches in any of the lesser divisions of the area, would protect an employer's Fourth Amendment rights. We doubt that the consumption of enforcement energies in the obtaining of such warrants will exceed manageable proportions. . . .

Nor do we agree that the incremental protections afforded the employer's privacy by a warrant are so marginal that they fail to justify the administrative burdens that may be entailed. The authority to make warrantless searches devolves almost unbridled discretion upon executive and administrative officers, particularly those in the field, as to when to search and whom to search. A warrant, by contrast, would provide assurances from a neutral officer that the inspection is reasonable under the Constitution, is authorized by statute, and is pursuant to an administrative plan containing specific neutral criteria. Also, a warrant would then and there advise the owner of the scope and objects of the search, beyond which limits the inspector is not expected to proceed. These are important functions for a warrant to perform, functions which underlie the Court's prior decisions that the Warrant Clause applies to inspections for compliance with regulatory statutes.[22] *Camara v.*

---

[22] Delineating the scope of a search with some care is particularly important where documents are involved. Section 8(c) of the Act provides that an employer must "make, keep and preserve, and make available to the Secretary [of Labor] or to the Secretary of Health, Education and Welfare" such records regarding his activities relating to OSHA as the Secretary of Labor may prescribe by regulation as necessary or appropriate for enforcement of the statute or for developing information regarding the causes and prevention of occupational accidents and illnesses. Regulations requiring employers to maintain records of and to make periodic reports on "work-related deaths, injuries and illnesses" are also contemplated, as are rules requiring accurate records of employee exposures to potential toxic materials and harmful physical agents.

In describing the scope of the warrantless inspection authorized by the statute, § 8(a) does not expressly include any records among those items or things that may be examined, and § 8(c)

Municipal Court, 387 U.S. 523 (1967); *See v. Seattle,* 387 U.S. 541 (1967). We conclude that the concerns expressed by the Secretary do not suffice to justify warrantless inspections under OSHA or vitiate the general constitutional requirement that for a search to be reasonable a warrant must be obtained.

III

We hold that Barlow's was entitled to a declaratory judgment that the Act is unconstitutional insofar as it purports to authorize inspections without warrant or its equivalent and to an injunction enjoining the Act's enforcement to that extent. The judgment of the District Court is therefore affirmed.

So ordered.

NOTES

1. ***Probable Cause for a Warrant.*** The Fourth Amendment to the U.S. Constitution provides that "The right of the people to be secure in their persons, houses, papers, and effects, against unreasonable searches and seizures, shall not be violated, and no Warrants shall issue but upon probable cause, supported by Oath or affirmation, and particularly describing the place to be searched, and the persons or things to be seized." The "probable cause" requirement is not a serious obstacle for OSHA when an employer is selected on the basis of a programmed inspection targeted at a high-hazard industry. OSHA has experienced more difficulty in satisfying the probable cause requirement for unprogrammed inspections that result from events such as accident reports and employee complaints. In *Donovan v. Federal Clearing Die Casting Co.,* 655 F.2d 793 (7th Cir. 1981), the court held that two newspaper articles describing an industrial accident, in which one of Federal's employees allegedly had his hands severed while operating a hydraulic punch press, did not satisfy the probable cause requirement for specific evidence of a violation of the Act. A subsequent case from the same circuit, *In re Establishment Inspection of Microcosm,* 951 F.2d 121 (7th Cir. 1991), provides an extreme contrast. OSHA received an anonymous complaint about the use of solvents at Microcosm in a letter purportedly written by a friend of an employee. OSHA obtained an inspection warrant based on the complaint,

---

merely provides that the employer is to "make available" his pertinent records and to make periodic reports.

The Secretary's regulation, 29 CFR § 1903.3 (1977), however, expressly includes among the inspector's powers the authority "to review records required by the Act and regulations published in this chapter, and other records which are directly related to the purpose of the inspection." Further, § 1903.7 requires inspectors to indicate generally "the records specified in § 1903.3 which they wish to review" but "such designations of records shall not preclude access to additional records specified in § 1903.3." It is the Secretary's position, which we reject, that an inspection of documents of this scope may be effected without a warrant.

The order that issued in this case included among the objects and things to be inspected "all other things therein (including but not limited to records, files, papers, processes, controls and facilities) bearing upon whether Barlow's, Inc. is furnishing to its employees employment and a place of employment that are free from recognized hazards that are causing or are likely to cause death or serious physical harm to its employees, and whether Barlow's, Inc. is complying with . . ." the OSHA regulations.

which the company refused to honor. The court found the warrant to be valid and found the company in contempt for refusing to honor the warrant. The Seventh Circuit also upheld the validity of a search warrant in a more recent case, *In re Establishment Inspection of Kelly-Springfield Tire Co.*, 13 F.3d 1160 (7th Cir. 1994), when OSHA based the warrant on three interviews with a complaining employee after receiving a two-sentence written complaint about working conditions in the plant.

2. The Scope of the Inspection. What portion of the employer's premises can OSHA inspect when entry is obtained? If the employer has been chosen on the basis of a programmed inspection, the OSHA compliance officer has access to the entire premises. If the employer was selected for an unprogrammed inspection, the Commission and circuit courts have taken several positions. In *Burkhart Randall Division of Textron, Inc. v. Marshall*, 625 F.2d 1313 (7th Cir. 1980), the Seventh Circuit allowed a general inspection of the whole plant in response to an employee complaint about a specific violation. The same circuit later adopted a more restrictive view in *Donovan v. Fall River Foundry Co.*, 712 F.2d 1103 (7th Cir. 1983), in which the court said that, when a complaint was received about an area separate from the rest of the building, a warrant to inspect the entire premises was not appropriate unless OSHA presented some evidence to show that hazardous conditions existed elsewhere in the plant. At one time, the Review Commission had adopted an even more restrictive position. In *Secretary of Labor v. Sarasota Concrete Co.*, 9 O.S.H. Cas. (BNA) 1608 (1981), *aff'd*, 693 F.2d 1061 (11th Cir. 1982), the Commission held that when probable cause for the warrant is based on a specific violation, OSHA must limit its inspection to an examination of the alleged violative condition. That decision must be read in light of a subsequent decision from the same court, *Reich v. Montana Sulphur & Chemical Co.*, 32 F.3d 440 (11th Cir. 1994). An individual complained that the company did not x-ray welds or certify its welders. The court approved a subpoena for information relating to a range of procedures for welding as well as more general information, such as minutes of safety and health meetings. The court indicated that OSHA was not confined to inquiries limited to violations of specific standards applicable to welding, but could rely on the general duty clause as a basis for its subpoena. The court also said that OSHA could expand its inquiry into welding activities beyond the specific allegations made by the informant.

The Sixth Circuit scrutinized a full-scope inspection that was triggered by an employee complaint of a specific problem in *Trinity Industries, Inc. v. OSHRC*, 16 F.3d 1455 (6th Cir. 1994). OSHA had established a plan that calls for a full-scope inspection if: (1) an employee complaint sets forth reasonable grounds to believe a violation or danger exists; (2) the establishment is in an industry with a high injury rate; (3) a complete inspection of the facility has not been conducted in the last two years; and (4) the facility has an injury rate at or above the national average. The court held that a full-scope inspection was not permitted. The search must be limited in scope to the employee complaint that triggered the inspection, plus a review of the employer's injury and illness records. If the limited search and the injury and illness rewards lead OSHA to suspect that a further inspection is necessary, then a second warrant authorizing a full-scope inspection must be obtained.

CHAO v. OSHRC
United States Court of Appeals, Fifth Circuit
401 F.3d 355 (2005)

DeMoss, Circuit Judge:

This appeal stems from a final order of Respondent Occupational Safety and Health Review Commission (the "Commission"), which vacated in part citations issued by . . . Elaine Chao, Secretary of Labor (the "Secretary"), against . . . Eric K. Ho ("Ho") *et al.* (together "Ho Respondents"). For the following reasons, we DENY the petitions for review and AFFIRM the decision of the Commission.

Background

The penalties assessed . . . against Ho . . . all concern his behavior as proprietor of a worksite where workers were exposed to asbestos in the course of a project to renovate a building. On October 27, 1997, Ho individually purchased a defunct hospital and medical office building in Houston to develop the property as residential housing. Ho knew there was asbestos onsite. He was also aware that any alteration to asbestos-containing materials was to be handled by personnel licensed and registered with the Texas Department of Health ("TDH"). Ho instead hired Manuel Escobedo ("Escobedo") and Corston Tate ("Tate"), whose work he had previously used, to do the renovations. Escobedo hired 11 Mexican nationals, who were illegal immigrants, to assist. Renovations, including the removal of asbestos, started in January 1998.

At most, the workers were occasionally given dust masks not suitable for protection against asbestos. They were not issued protective clothing. Ho also did not provide a respiratory protection program, conduct medical surveillance, conduct asbestos monitoring, implement adequate ventilation or debris removal, inform the workers of the presence and hazards of asbestos, or provide any training whatsoever. There is no dispute that Ho was aware of the worksite conditions; he visited almost every day.

On February 2, 1998, a city inspector visited the worksite. After observing the conditions, he issued a stop-work order citing the possibility of exposure to asbestos, requiring that city approval be given before work could resume. Ho then began negotiating with a licensed contractor, Alamo Environmental ("Alamo"), to remove the asbestos. Alamo prepared an abatement estimate in accordance with Occupational Safety and Health Administration ("OSHA"), amongst other federal, guidelines. On March 27, 1998, Ho notified Alamo by fax that he agreed to their proposal.

However, during this period of negotiation, Ho had resumed work at the site under the same conditions, except that he directed all work be performed at night. The workers ate, and some lived, at the site. The workers had no potable water and only one portable toilet. Tate sometimes allowed workers to leave the property to use the restroom at a nearby commercial establishment; and Tate would purchase and bring back food for the workers when they gave him money. Ho continued to visit the worksite and was aware of these conditions.

Asbestos removal continued in this fashion until March 10, 1998. On March 11, 1998, as Ho had directed, daytime work resumed at the site. Ho had been informed that either the sprinkler system or fire hydrant valves had not been turned off and thus remained available for use. To wash out the building, Ho directed Tate to tap into an unmarked valve believed to be a water line. It turned out to be a gas line. An explosion later occurred when Tate started his truck; it injured Tate and two workers. On March 12, 1998, workers were summoned to Ho's office where they were given releases to sign, acknowledging receipt of $1000 as full payment for their work, and acknowledging receipt of $100 to release Ho from any claims that might arise from the explosion and fire. The releases were written in English, but an interpreter translated them for the workers.

After the explosion, TDH conducted an investigation. Samples of debris and the ambient air at the worksite showed levels of asbestos in excess of federal and state standards. The state notified Ho that the site remained unsafe and needed to be sealed by qualified personnel. Again, Ho used the same workers to install plywood over the windows and did not give them any protective equipment.

OSHA also conducted an investigation. As a result, the Secretary issued a total of 10 serious and 29 willful violations against Ho Respondents; these charges included 11 willful violations of 29 C.F.R. § 1926.1101(h)(1)(i) for failing to provide respirators to 11 employees removing asbestos and 11 willful violations of 29 C.F.R. § 1926.1101(k)(9)(i) and (viii) for failing to train the 11 employees on the hazards of asbestos and safety precautions. The Secretary also charged Ho Respondents with willfully violating the OSH Act's general duty clause, 29 U.S.C. § 654(a)(1), by ordering Tate to tap into the unmarked pipeline. Ho was also convicted of criminal violations of the Clean Air Act ("CAA"). This Court upheld his conviction.

Ho conceded before the ALJ that he violated the asbestos respirator and training standards. Ho argued that he was not subject to the OSH Act's requirements because he was not engaged in a business affecting interstate commerce. . . . He also challenged the per-employee citations of the respirator and training violations. Finally, Ho contended he did not violate the general duty clause of the OSH Act, or if he had violated it, that such violation was not willful.

The ALJ ruled that Ho's construction activities affected interstate commerce and Ho was liable for the OSH Act violations. . . . The ALJ determined the respirator and training violations were willful and upheld all 22 violations. The ALJ found also that Ho had violated the general duty clause of the OSH Act but that it could not be characterized as a willful violation because the Secretary failed to show that Ho actually knew of the danger or had a heightened awareness of the illegality of his conduct.

On review, the Commission affirmed that Ho was subject to the OSH Act and that Ho's violations of the respirator and training standards were willful. A divided Commission ruled that such violations were to be cited on a per-instance, not a per-employee, basis because it felt that the regulations plainly imposed a duty on employers to have a single training program and to provide respirators to the employees as a group. It thus vacated all but two of those citations. . . . The Commission affirmed the ALJ's finding that the general duty violation committed by Ho was not willful. The Commission also increased all the citations affirmed to their maximum penalties because of Ho's lack of good faith. The Secretary timely filed her petition for review, and the Ho Respondents timely filed their cross-petition.

Discussion

. . . .

Whether the Commission's legal conclusion that Ho did not willfully violate the general duty clause, § 654(a)(1), of the OSH Act, was arbitrary, capricious, an abuse of discretion, or not in accordance with law.

Section 654(a)(1) of the OSH Act requires employers to free their workplaces of "recognized hazards that are causing or are likely to cause death or serious physical harm to . . . employees." The specific general duty citation here arose from the explosion of natural gas released by tapping an unmarked valve. A willful violation is one committed voluntarily, with either intentional disregard of, or plain indifference to, OSH Act requirements. "'Willful' means action taken knowledgeably by one subject to the statutory provisions in disregard of the action's legality." In contrast, "the gravamen of a serious violation is the presence of a 'substantial probability' that a particular violation could result in death or serious physical harm." The employer's intent to violate an OSH Act standard is irrelevant to find a serious violation. The Commission's legal conclusions can only be set aside if they are arbitrary, capricious, an abuse of discretion, or not in accordance with law.

The Secretary argues the Commission's finding that Ho's violation of § 654(a)(1) was not willful was based on an erroneous legal standard requiring direct evidence of Ho's state of mind. The Secretary contends Ho demonstrated plain indifference in directing Tate to tap into the unmarked pipeline in an attempt to procure water for washing the building. According to the Secretary, this was a clear violation of the stop-work order Ho received in February. Therefore, the Secretary maintains Ho knew tapping into the pipeline without approval was illegal, even if he may not have known of the specific explosion hazard or that it was a violation of the general duty clause of the OSH Act. The Secretary argues direct evidence of Ho's state of mind was not required because proof of Ho's plain indifference to legal requirements in general was clearly established.

Ho Respondents reply that the Commission was correct to find that the Secretary had not met her burden of proof in showing Ho's violation as rising to the intent of willful. Ho Respondents maintain the Commission applied the correct legal standard, and substantial evidence on the record supports its decision that the § 654(a)(1) violation was not willful. Ho Respondents argue the Commission's reference to direct evidence amounted to a recognition that the Secretary had not put forth any evidence relevant to the specific circumstances of the violation in question. Ho emphasize[s] that the Secretary did not put forth any evidence of Ho's state of mind to show that he had a heightened awareness that instructing Tate to open the valve might be hazardous or that Ho consciously disregarded a known safety hazard related to the valve — that is, for this action to meet a showing of either intentional disregard of the OSH Act or plain indifference to employee safety. Ho Respondents stress there was no evidence directed to the intent accompanying this particular incident.

The Secretary argues that Ho's action here was part of a consistent illegal and voluntary course of conduct; all his actions were plainly indifferent to employee safety. However, although there may be evidence of a conscious pattern of illegal work practices by Ho with regard to the asbestos abatement, the challenged violation of the general duty clause does not concern Ho's many asbestos transgressions covered specifically by OSH Act regulations. In particular, it related to an employee being required to open a pipe of unknown content. Here, the Secretary presented no evidence relevant to Ho's state of mind on, or recognition of the hazards of, this particular action to direct Tate to open the unmarked valve. We thus agree with the Commission that plain indifference as to this specific hazardous action cannot be inferred, even from Ho's several OSH Act violations concerning the asbestos removal project.

Though the evidence need not indicate "bad purpose" or "evil motive" to commit a particular act, there must be evidence of that "extra ingredient needed for willfulness, either the element of intentional disregard or plain indifference." None existed in this record. Though Ho's pattern of illegal work practices may have been conscious, and his asbestos-related OSH Act violations found to be willful, this does not compel a finding of willfulness as to his specific instruction to open the unmarked valve. Therefore, because the Commission's legal determination as to Ho's lack of willfulness under § 654(a)(1) was neither arbitrary, capricious, nor an abuse of discretion, and accords with law, we accept its conclusion.

Whether the citations against Ho should have been assessed on a per-employee or per-instance basis.

The Secretary's discretion to cite multiple violations of an OSH Act standard is restricted "to those standards which are capable of such interpretation." "The test of whether the [OSH] Act and the cited regulation permits multiple or single units of prosecution is whether they prohibit individual acts, or a single course of action." "With few exceptions, the Commission has not affirmed multiple violations for violations of the same standard, or affirmed separate violations or penalties on a per employee exposed basis." The Commission here determined that the plain language of the training and respirator subsections of the asbestos standard at issue prescribed a single work practice instead of conduct unique and specific to each employee. It thus only affirmed one training and one respirator citation against Ho.

The Secretary argues the per-employee citations for asbestos training and respirator violations, with which she charged Ho Respondents, should have been affirmed by the Commission. The Secretary maintains that each time an employer commits a prohibited act or allows a prohibited condition to exist, the employer violates the OSH Act. The Secretary contends the Commission's analysis ignores the standards' plain language and the established test for determining which conditions or actions constitute separate violations under the OSH Act, as enunciated in the Commission's own prior cases and in this Court's caselaw. The Secretary insists the Commission also ignored basic precepts of prosecutorial discretion.

The Secretary argues that if a standard prohibits individual acts or conditions, the standard is violated each time the prohibited act or condition occurs. . . .

The general construction training standard, 29 C.F.R. § 1926.21(b)(2), which requires employers to "instruct each employee in the recognition and avoidance of unsafe conditions," has been interpreted as being citable on a per-employee basis. Portions of the lead standard have also been interpreted as permitting per-employee citations because the standard's medical removal subsection, 29 C.F.R. § 1910.1025(k)(1)(i)(D), and respirator fit-test subsection, 29 C.F.R. § 1910.1025(f)(3)(ii), required evaluation of individual employees. *Sanders Lean Co.*, 17 O.S.H. Cas. (BNA) 1197 (1995). *But see Arcadian*, 111 F.3d at 1196-99 (finding general duty clause of OSH Act directed at hazardous conditions did not allow per-employee citations but noting that worker training or removal standards could count each employee as the unit of violation); *Hartford Roofing*, 17 O.S.H. Cas. (BNA) 1361 (1995) (finding one unguarded roof edge requiring warning was single violation of 29 C.F.R. § 1926.500(g)(1)(i) and § 1926.500(g)(4) no matter how many employees were exposed to a fall but noting that the respirator protection standard, 29 C.F.R. § 1910.134, could count a separate violation as to each employee not provided a respirator). Neither the Secretary nor Ho Respondents advance any Fifth Circuit or Commission precedent interpreting the asbestos standard.

As to training violations, the Secretary maintains that Ho violated § 1926.1101(k)(9)(i), and (viii) of the asbestos regulations each time he assigned a worker to remove asbestos without providing the worker with individual training about the hazards of asbestos removal and about the required safeguards against those hazards. . . .

As to respirator violations, the Secretary points again to the plain language of § 1926.1101(h)(1)(i): "the employer shall provide respirators, and ensure that they are used . . . during all Class I asbestos jobs." 29 C.F.R. § 1926.1101(h)(1)(i) (1997). The Secretary . . . argues each of Ho's 11 employees required a personally fitted respirator that the employee had chosen. Thus, Ho was required to take employee-specific actions. . . .

In addition, the Secretary maintains the Commission used a flawed analysis to interpret the training and respirator regulations. The Secretary argues a training program is meaningless unless implemented on an individual basis. Likewise, Ho was required to give each worker an individual respirator. This was not a single, discrete act, but rather required initial fitting and then periodic refitting for each worker. The Secretary suggests a nonsensical reading would ensue if an employer not providing any respirators, like Ho, resulted in only one violation, while an employer who provided them but did not fit-test them received per-employee citations.

Finally, the Secretary argues that even if the standards were ambiguous, the Secretary's per-employee construction was reasonable and entitled to deference. That is, it sensibly conformed to the purpose and wording of the regulations. *See Martin v. OSHRC*, 499 U.S. 144, 150-51 (1991). The Secretary contends the Commission incorrectly failed to defer to the reasonableness of the Secretary's interpretation. . . .

Ho Respondents contend it is violative employer conduct or a violative condition, as opposed to the number of employees, that is the proper unit of prosecution. Ho Respondents also argue the Secretary's position is not to be accorded deference because the regulations are unambiguous and thus applied not per employee, but rather per violation. . . .

After reviewing the arguments advanced by the parties, we agree with the Commission's result that the training and respirator citations cannot be imposed per employee here. As to the asbestos respirator standard, we fully agree with the Commission's reasoning. However, as to the asbestos training standard, we affirm the Commission's result for different reasoning.

Asbestos training standard,
29 C.F.R. § 1926.1101(k)(9)(i); and (viii).

To begin, we find this standard's language ambiguous. Thus, unlike the Commission, which found the standard to be stated solely in inclusive terms, we agree with the Secretary that the language of the asbestos training standard allows the Secretary, in her discretion, to reasonably assess penalties on a per-employee basis.

Subpart (i) expressly refers to "a training program for all employees" performing Class I asbestos work and also speaks to the employer's requirement to "ensure their participation in the program," which language tends to indicate that one training program is to be provided for all employees as a unit and does not appear to make allowance for a per-employee assessment. 29 C.F.R. § 1926.1101(k)(9)(i) (1997). However, although subpart (viii) again refers to the singular "training program," it also goes on to state that the program "shall be conducted in a manner the employee is able to understand" and that the employer "shall ensure that each such employee is informed of the following." *Id.* § 1926.1101(k)(9)(viii).

These express references to the ability of the employee to understand and to "each such employee" being informed implicate the possibility that on an individual basis, employees may need distinct, discrete information not provided to "each such" other employee, perhaps due to differences in experience, language, and job skills. Although this Court has treated the reference to "each of his employees" in the general duty clause of the OSH Act to be entirely inclusive, this reading was made in the context of § 654(a)(1) being a "catchall provision" governing any recognized hazards of the workplace *not* covered by a specific regulation. There is a distinction when reading the specific asbestos training regulation, which does not have a "principal focus on hazardous conditions" such that "each" is only used to clarify that the employer's duty runs to all employees, "regardless of their individual susceptibilities (i.e., age or pregnancy)."

In contrast, subpart (viii) of the asbestos training standard instructs employers that the training program must be conducted in such a way that the employees understand and are informed of various asbestos-related hazards. *See* 29 C.F.R. § 1926.1101(k)(9)(viii) (1997). Whether an employee understands and is informed by a training program, as the regulation requires, may depend on his "individual susceptibilities." Thus, considering the interaction of the two subparts (i) and (viii) of the asbestos training standard together, we agree with the Secretary that § 1926.1101(k)(9) is ambiguous and therefore can be interpreted to allow for citation on a per-employee basis.

However, we find the Secretary's discretionary decision to cite Ho on a per-employee basis on these facts was unreasonable. In *Martin*, the Supreme Court explained the division of powers between the Secretary and the Commission under the OSH Act. 499 U.S. at 157-58. As a reviewing court, we "should defer to the Secretary only if the Secretary's interpretation *is* reasonable . . . ." That is, the Secretary's interpretation is not reasonable, and this Court can hold it unlawful and set it aside, if we find such interpretation to be "arbitrary, capricious, an abuse of discretion, or otherwise not in accordance with law . . . ."

Nothing in this record indicates that one training program regarding this Class I asbestos removal at the hospital site would not have abated the violation of both subparts (i) and (viii), nor that unique individual training sessions, or even more than one session, would have been necessary to abate the violation. The ALJ indicated that one training session, if all 11 workers had attended, would have been sufficient to meet the training standard here. The citations and evidence support that this was one Class I asbestos removal job on a single site at one address, performed by all the same 11 untrained workers, from the beginning to the end. Thus, although we acknowledge that there may be cases where per-employee citations of § 1926.1101(k)(9) based on unique circumstances of the employees might be considered reasonable, here we do not defer to the Secretary's unreasonable interpretation of the asbestos training regulation as applied to Ho. As the Commission's interpretation of the standard here was reasonable as applied to Ho's case, we affirm its assessment of one citation instead of 11 individual citations.

Asbestos respirator standard, 29 C.F.R. § 1926.1101(h)(1)(i).

Unlike the asbestos training standard, we read the plain language of the portion of the respirator standard for which Ho was cited as not allowing the Secretary the discretion to charge employers with per-employee citations. The regulation states: "The employer shall provide respirators, and ensure that they are used . . . during all Class I asbestos jobs." 29 C.F.R. § 1926.1101(h)(1)(i) (1997). The Secretary makes the seemingly logical argument that it makes little sense for a malicious employer who provides no respirators at all to be eligible for fewer violations than an employer who in good faith provides respirators but fails to comply with other subparts of the asbestos respirator standard governing the employee's ability to choose his type of respirator and periodic fit-testing requirements. However, there is simply no language in the general respiratory protection section that suggests the unit of prosecution could be based on each individual employee not receiving a respirator versus the employer's course of action in failing to provide respirators to his employees as a whole for the Class I asbestos job. Instead, we read the unit of prosecution for violating this standard as applying per Class I asbestos job. Here, the evidence indicates that Ho engaged in one Class I asbestos removal job at one hospital site for one sustained period of time.

In contrast, language in other parts of the asbestos respirator standard suggests citation on a per-employee basis might be appropriate. Subsection (h)(2)(iii) of the asbestos respirator standard contains language directing employers to provide an air-purifying respirator instead of a negative-pressure respirator to employees, but only when "an employee chooses to use this type of respirator." 29 C.F.R. § 1926.1101(h)(2)(iii)(A)(1). A violation could be counted each time the employer did not provide the chosen type of respirator to the individual employee who requested it. . . .

After considering the plain language of subsection (h)(1)(i) of the asbestos respirator standard, we agree with the Commission and find that the regulation does not provide for the assessment of citations on a per-employee basis, but rather on the basis of an employer's course of conduct in failing to provide respirators to his employees during a Class I asbestos job. Thus, Ho's failure to provide respirators to all 11 workers at the hospital site for the single Class I asbestos removal project was a single violation of the respirator regulation. Therefore, we affirm the Commission's assessment of one violation of § 1926.1101(h)(1)(i).

Whether the Commission abused its discretion in imposing the maximum penalties for Ho's OSH Act violations.

The Commission has the exclusive authority to assess penalties once a proposed penalty is contested. Section 17(j) of the OSH Act, 29 U.S.C. § 666(j), guides the Commission's assessment of a penalty. The Commission is to "give due consideration to the appropriateness of the penalty with respect to [1] the size of the business of the employer being charged, [2] the gravity of the violation, [3] the good faith of the employer, and [4] the history of previous violations." 29 U.S.C. § 666(j) (1990). "These factors are not necessarily accorded equal weight . . . ." Gravity of violation is the key factor. The Commission can, when appropriate, consider the number of employees exposed to the condition when analyzing gravity. This Court reviews the Commission's determination of the amount of an OSH Act penalty for abuse of discretion.

Ho Respondents argue that the Commission abused its discretion in failing to consider each of the four elements set forth in § 666(j) in its determination of the amounts of penalties to assess. Ho Respondents maintain it was an abuse of discretion to consider Ho's bad faith alone because all four factors are equally important.

The Secretary responds that the Commission did not err in assessing the maximum penalty for the two violations of the asbestos training and respirator standards it affirmed. The Secretary argues the Commission gave proper consideration to the statutory penalty criteria but concluded that Ho's extreme and appalling disregard for employee safety — his lack of good faith — outweighed other considerations in the context of this case.

After vacating 20 of the 22 asbestos training and respirator standard citations, the Commission increased the remaining willful penalties to the maximum $70,000 each and the serious penalties to the maximum $7,000 each to make a strong statement about Ho's illegal behavior. To be sure, the Commission rested much of its decision on Ho's lack of good faith. The Commission also, however, addressed the gravity of Ho's violations; it considered the number of employees he exposed to the cited conditions to be a significant indication of gravity. While this inquiry is a factor-based balancing test, there is no requirement of equal consideration of all factors. The Commission expressly considered and weighed Ho's lack of good faith and the gravity of the violations. Based on the circumstances present in Ho's particular case, we find the Commission did not abuse its discretion in assessing the maximum penalty amounts.

Conclusion

Having carefully considered the record of the case and the parties' respective briefing and arguments, for the reasons set forth above, we AFFIRM the Commission's decision.

EMILIO M. GARZA, CIRCUIT JUDGE, dissenting:

. . . .

The majority opinion holds that the language of 29 C.F.R. § 1926.1101(h)(1) *unambiguously* precludes per-employee citations and, thus, affirmed the Commission's ruling that the regulation does not require an individualized duty but instead applies to a single course of conduct. The majority opinion also finds that the language of 29 C.F.R. § 1926.1101(k)(9) — which the Commission determined addresses a single course of conduct, prohibiting per-employee citations — is ambiguous; however, it holds that the Secretary's interpretation is unreasonable and, hence, that the per-employee citations are prohibited. I disagree. The language of both provisions is ambiguous, and the majority opinion fails to defer to the Secretary's reasonable interpretation allowing per-employee citations. . . .

When the statutory language is not clear, "the Secretary's interpretation would be entitled to deference given her official duty, specialized expertise, investigatory knowledge and other experience relevant to carrying out the purposes of the Act." "In situations in which the meaning of [regulatory] language is not free from doubt, the reviewing court should give effect to the [Secretary's] interpretation so long as it is reasonable, that is, so long as the interpretation sensibly conforms to the purpose and wording of the regulations." This deference is given to the Secretary, not the Commission. . . . Thus, the inquiry is in two parts: (1) whether the language is ambiguous; and (2) whether the Secretary's interpretation is reasonable. If so, we *must* defer to that interpretation. . . .

[T]he majority has failed to show how the Secretary's interpretation is unreasonable. Accordingly, I would reverse the Commission's determination that per-employee citations are prohibited. . . .

The majority opinion affirmed the Commission's finding that the violation of the General Duty Clause was "serious" instead of "willful," reasoning that there was no evidence compelling a willful finding for the *specific* instruction to tap the unmarked valve. The Commission's legal conclusions may be set aside if they are arbitrary, capricious, an abuse of discretion, or otherwise not in accordance with law. The General Duty Clause of the OSH Act requires an employer to provide "each of his employees employment and a place of employment which are free from recognized hazards that are causing or are likely to cause death or serious physical harm to his employees." 29 U.S.C. § 654(a)(1).

"A violation is willful if it is committed with intentional, knowing or voluntary disregard for the requirements of the Occupational Safety and Health Act." Ho conceded that tapping into an unmarked pipe at a demolition site was a "recognized hazard." Instructing his employees to tap an unmarked pipe — a "recognized hazard" — evidences a plain indifference to the General Duty Clause. Even without the benefit of hindsight, it is self-evident that tapping an unmarked pipe is "likely to cause death or serious physical harm." Therefore, the Commission abused its discretion by finding Ho's violation of the General Duty Clause "serious" instead of "willful." Accordingly, I would vacate the Commission's order reducing the General Duty Clause violation to serious from willful.

For the above stated reasons, I respectfully dissent.

NOTE

Challenging OSHA Standards in Enforcement Actions. Employers can seek pre-enforcement judicial review of an OSHA standard under section 6(f). In addition, an employer cited for violating a standard can challenge its validity before the Commission under section 10(c), and on judicial review of the Commission's decision under section 11(a). The courts of appeal have split on whether an employer can challenge procedural defects in the underlying OSHA standard. *Compare National Indus. Constr., Inc. v. OSHRC*, 583 F.2d 1048 (8th Cir. 1978) (procedural attacks on newly promulgated standards must be raised in section 6(f) review or are deemed waived), *with Marshall v. Union Oil Co.*, 616 F.2d 1113 (1980) (procedural validity of OSHA regulation can be challenged in section 10(c) proceeding). More important is the possibility of challenging the substance of the OSHA standard in an enforcement action, particularly on the issue of whether compliance with the standard is feasible. Here, some courts have placed a greater burden on the Secretary in enforcing a standard against a particular employer than in defending the whole standard in a section 6(f) review. For example, in *Boise Cascade Corp. v. Secretary of Labor*, 694 F.2d 584 (9th Cir. 1982), the court noted that in promulgating a standard, the Secretary can satisfy the technological feasibility requirement by adopting a technology that is merely "looming on today's horizon." In an enforcement proceeding, however, the Secretary must show that "specific, technically feasible controls exist to abate the violation."

F. EMPLOYEE RIGHTS AND RESPONSIBILITIES

ATLANTIC & GULF STEVEDORES, INC. v. OSHA
United States Court of Appeals, Third Circuit
534 F.2d 541 (1976)

GIBBONS, CIRCUIT JUDGE.

The petitioners are stevedoring companies operating in the Port of Philadelphia. They employ longshoremen. The Secretary of Labor, pursuant to statutory authority, has adopted safety and health regulations for longshoring. Among those regulations is the so called "longshoring hardhat" standard:

> Employees shall be protected by protective hats meeting the specifications contained in the American National Standard Safety Requirements for Industrial Head Protection, Z89.1 (1969).

29 C.F.R. § 1918.105(a) (1975).

On April 10-11, 1973 an OSHA compliance officer inspected the Camden, New Jersey docks and discovered that nearly all of petitioners' longshoremen were working without hardhats. The Secretary cited petitioners for violation of § 5(a)(2) of OSHA, and proposed that civil penalties aggregating $455 be levied against the petitioners. Each citation also ordered immediate abatement of violations. Petitioners filed notices of contest, which resulted in a hearing before the Commission's Administrative Law Judge.

At the hearing the OSHA compliance officer testified that on the dates of his inspections, only a very small proportion of the longshoremen were wearing hardhats, that none of the petitioners had previously been cited for a violation of the hardhat standard, and that no injuries were involved. He also testified that between 1971, when the standard was adopted, and April 1973 there had been a moratorium in the Secretary's enforcement of it, because the longshoremen's unions opposed it and the rank-and-file preferred not to wear hardhats. . . .

Witnesses for the petitioners testified that stevedores in the Port of Philadelphia had, beginning in 1971, undertaken strenuous but unsuccessful efforts to obtain compliance with the standard by their longshoring employees; had furnished the required hardhats; had encouraged use of the headgear at regular safety meetings; had posted hardhat signs on their working premises; had used payroll envelope stuffers advocating hardhat wearing; and had placed hardhat safety messages on the hiring tapes. All this was to little avail, and each employer witness testified to a firm belief that wildcat strikes or walkouts would attend attempts to enforce the standard by firing employees who refused to comply. There is undisputed testimony that in another port a strike over that issue did occur. [4] There is, however, no testimony that these petitioners ever denied work to a longshoreman for his refusal to wear a hardhat.

---

[4] This strike occurred in the Port of New York in 1970, prior to the enactment of OSHA. The record also disclosed that stevedoring companies have successfully enforced the mandatory use regulation in the Port of Norfolk, but that longshoremen in the Port of San Francisco have resisted the use of hardhats.

The petitioners urged that the Secretary's citations and proposed penalties should be vacated because in view of the longshoremen's intransigent opposition to and their union's lukewarm support for the standard, compliance *by them* with the hardhat standard was not achievable. The Administrative Law Judge found the three employers in violation of 29 C.F.R. § 1918.105(a), but vacated the Secretary's proposed penalties. . . .

[On review, t]he Commission voted 2-1 to affirm the Administrative Law Judge's decision finding violations and vacating proposed penalties, but each Commissioner filed a separate opinion. Commissioner Cleary announced the decision of the Commission. He rejected as "largely speculative" the petitioners' contention that they had done all they could do without causing labor strife. In addition, he concluded that, at least when non-compliance by employees was neither unpredictable nor idiosyncratic, final responsibility for compliance with the Act's requirements rested with the employers.

Commissioner Van Namee, concurring, did not agree that the evidence of potential labor unrest was speculative. Nor did he agree that employers could under the Act be held strictly liable in all instances of technical non-compliance. Yet he concluded that in this instance the employers would, because of the terms of their collective bargaining agreements, have a remedy under § 301 of the Labor Management Relations Act, 29 U.S.C. § 185, against a wildcat strike. Commissioner Van Namee surmised that the availability of such a remedy made the fear of a strike, or at least an effective one, "nothing more than an illusion."[6] He recognized, however, that the applicability of a particular safety and health standard should not turn on whether the parties to the collective bargaining agreement agreed upon a grievance-arbitration procedure that was broad enough to permit a *Boys Markets* injunction. Such an approach would admit of selective enforcement of OSHA safety standards. To meet this objection Commissioner Van Namee said that irrespective of the existence of a *Boys Markets* remedy, the Commission itself had the statutory authority to issue cease and desist orders running against employees. These orders could be enforced by injunction in the Courts of Appeals pursuant to §§ 11(a) and (b) of the Act.

Chairman Moran dissented. Like Commissioner Van Namee, he rejected Commissioner Cleary's assessment of the evidence concerning the likelihood of walkouts over attempts to enforce the hardhat requirement. He concluded that the employers had taken all steps required of them under the Act. He also expressed doubt as to the availability of § 301 injunctive relief.

---

[6] That a *Boys Markets, Inc. v. Retail Clerks, Local 770,* 398 U.S. 235 (1970) remedy is available does not, of course, by itself conclusively answer petitioners' objection that employee recalcitrance makes compliance with the longshoring hardhat safety standard impossible. The stevedores could obtain a § 301 injunction only if they agreed to submit the hardhat dispute to arbitration. There can be no assurance, for example, that an arbitrator would decide that an employee who defied an express directive of his employer and ignored validly promulgated federal regulations could be discharged or otherwise disciplined for such conduct. We assume, however, that arbitration would most often sustain the employer prerogative in this regard. Where the collective bargaining agreement empowers the employer to seek § 301 relief, therefore, that remedy is likely to prove adequate. In those instances where it is demonstrably inadequate, the employers may nevertheless seek relief from liability by petitioning for a variance from the standard, 29 U.S.C. § 655(d), or for an extension of time in which to abate a cited violation 29 U.S.C. § 659(c). *See Part IIIB, infra.*

In summary, although the Commission order affirmed the citations, there is no opinion which can be said to represent a consensus. Two Commissioners, Moran and Van Namee, agree that the record contains substantial evidence tending to show that a work stoppage will occur if the petitioners take additional steps to enforce the hardhat requirement. Commissioner Van Namee concludes, however, that the availability of relief before the Commission against spontaneous employee obduracy renders this body of evidence irrelevant. Chairman Moran evidently does not share Commissioner Van Namee's expansive view of the Commission's powers, although he did not in this case address the issue. Commissioner Cleary flatly rejects any interpretation of OSHA that would permit the Commission to issue cease and desist orders against employees. Nevertheless, he regards the threat of work stoppages posed in this instance as largely speculative. In any event, Commissioner Cleary suggests that where, as here, employee non-compliance is neither unpredictable nor idiosyncratic, the employer has an absolute statutory duty to enforce the terms of the Act.

II

Section 11(a) of the Act directs the reviewing court to accept "[t]he findings of the Commission with respect to questions of fact, if supported by substantial evidence on the record considered as a whole. . . ." Because there is no opinion in which a majority of the Commission joined, there is no Commission finding of fact with respect to the likelihood that enforcement of the hardhat standard would provoke a work stoppage. But two Commissioners appear to have credited the testimony of the petitioners' witnesses that such a work stoppage was likely if not inevitable. We believe that such a finding would be supported by substantial evidence on the record as a whole.[7] Indeed, Commissioner Cleary's rejection of the evidence as "largely speculative," if it represented a finding of the Commission, probably would have to be dismissed as unsupported by substantial record evidence. Thus we assume, for purposes of this petition for review, that the longshoremen in the Port of Philadelphia are intransigent on the hardhat issue and are likely to strike if more vigorous enforcement efforts are undertaken.

This assumption serves to focus the specific and relatively narrow issue presented by this petition, viz., whether when employee non-compliance with an occupational safety or health standard is both predictable and virtually uniform, the employer must nevertheless enforce compliance even at the risk of concerted employee work stoppages. Because any answer to this inquiry is an adjudicatory conclusion, the scope of our review is less narrowly jacketed

---

[7] In addition to the evidence of the employers' futile attempts at friendly persuasion, and of the longshoremen's resistance in the Port of Philadelphia and elsewhere, the evidence showed that while initial compliance in 1971 with the regulation was good (about 80%), the rate of compliance quickly deteriorated. Apparently many workers tried the hats, found them uncomfortable or cumbersome, and discontinued their use.

The evidence also showed that although the stevedores had never actually denied employment to a longshoreman who refused to wear a hardhat, a 1971 threat of such action triggered an angry demonstration of longshoring foremen. Statistics showing that head injuries comprised only a small fraction (perhaps 1%) of total longshoring injuries fueled employee sentiment that hardhats did not protect against a significant occupational hazard and hence were unnecessary.

than with factual determinations. The law of this circuit is that we may set aside such conclusions if we find them to be arbitrary, capricious, an abuse of discretion or otherwise not in accordance with law.

A

In urging us to vacate the citations, petitioners place principal reliance on our decision in the *Hanovia Lamp* case. There we followed the holding of the District of Columbia Circuit in *National Realty & Construction Co. v. OSHRC*, rejecting a construction of the Act which would effectively make employers strictly liable for violations arising from employee misconduct. In *Hanovia Lamp* we held that an employer could be held answerable for a violation resulting from such misconduct only when "demonstrably feasible measures" existed for materially reducing its incidence. In reply the Secretary correctly points out that both *National Realty Construction* and *Hanovia Lamp* involved citations for violation of the Act's general duty clause, while this case involves a citation for violation of a specific safety standard. It seems to be the Secretary's position that employers are to be held to a higher standard of care under specific regulations than under the general duty clause. We decline to bifurcate the statute in such a manner, and attach no significance to the proffered distinction. . . . [T]he employer's task of guarding against the aberrational action of specific employees who violate specific safety standards is essentially no less difficult than under the general duty clause. Thus the *Hanovia Lamp* standard governing employer responsibility applies, in our view, to 29 C.F.R. § 1918.105(a) to the same extent as to the general duty clause.

But while *Hanovia Lamp* [and] *National Realty Construction* . . . supply us with the standard of liability to be applied to the facts of this case, they offer precious little insight into the question whether the petitioner stevedoring companies have breached their statutory duty of care. Those cases involved the unpredictable and unforeseeable actions of individual employees. This case involves the predictable, nearly universal actions of all the longshoremen. There is a demonstrably feasible measure which can be taken to prevent such concerted disobedience: the employer can refuse employment to those who insist on violating the standard. The discussions of strict liability in the cases referred to have no application to the instant situation, except to the extent that they are authority for the proposition that we will not construe OSHA to impose completely unreasonable burdens on employers within the Act's coverage.

We find guidance on this difficult question in our recent decision in *AFL-CIO v. Brennan*. In that case we reviewed action of the Secretary adopting a "no hands in dies" standard for the mechanical power press industry. We recognized that the economic feasibility of an occupational safety and health standard was relevant to our assessment of its statutory validity. We pointed out that an economically impossible standard would in all likelihood prove unenforceable, and that the burden of policing a regulation uniformly ignored by a majority of industry members would prove to be overwhelming. Thus we held that in promulgating regulations the Secretary could take into account the economic impact of a proposed standard. . . .

III

In this case the petitioners contend that the longshoring hardhat safety standard, insofar as it is applied to them, is invalid because attempts at enforcement would provoke a wildcat strike by their employees. The standard is, in their view, economically infeasible. They produced evidence tending to support this position in the proceeding before the Administrative Law Judge. We believe that petitioners have carried their burden of proof on the issue. The remaining question is the legal sufficiency of the defense. We turn, then, to the several grounds relied upon by the Commission in rejecting petitioners' challenge to the hardhat safety standard.

A

If Commissioner Van Namee is correct that the Commission has the power to issue cease and desist orders against employees as well as employers, then the economic infeasibility argument against the standard disappears from this case. Unlike the no hands in dies standard which we reviewed in *AFL-CIO v. Brennan*, the infeasibility claim in this case is bottomed not on the cost of forcing the technological change, but on the cost of a work stoppage caused by employee discontent with a simple, inexpensive and facially reasonable safety standard. If the Commission, and in turn this court, can issue coercive process against employees directly, the threat is eliminated and the defense overcome. It is far from clear, however, that the Commission enjoys the power for which Commissioner Van Namee argues.

Commissioner Van Namee finds the source of such coercive authority in a combination of § 2(b)(2) of the Act, § 5(b), and § 10(c). The latter provision authorizes the Commission to issue orders "affirming, modifying, or vacating the Secretary's citation . . . or directing other appropriate relief. . . ." Section 2(b)(2), in the section of the Act setting forth congressional findings and a declaration of policy, provides:

> (b) The Congress declares it to be its purpose and policy . . . to assure so far as possible every working man and woman in the Nation safe and healthful working conditions and to preserve our human resources —
>
>   . . . .
>
> (2) by providing that employers and employees have separate but dependent responsibilities and rights with respect to achieving safe and healthful working conditions. . . .

Section 5(b) provides that

> [e]ach employee shall comply with occupational safety and health standards and all rules, regulations, and orders issued pursuant to this chapter which are applicable to his own actions and conduct.

According to Commissioner Van Namee the employees' separate responsibilities under § 5(b) would be "meaningless and a nullity" if the Commission and this court, in an enforcement proceeding, were powerless to sanction employee disregard of safety standards and commission orders. . . .

With considerable misgivings, we conclude that Congress did not intend to confer on the Secretary or the Commission the power to sanction employees. Sections 2(b)(2) and 5(b) cannot be read apart from the detailed scheme of enforcement set out in §§ 9, 10 and 17 of the Act. It seems clear that this enforcement scheme is directed only against employers. Sections 9(a) and 10(a) provide for the issuance of citations and notifications of proposed penalties only to employers. Section 10(a) refers only to an employer's opportunity to contest a citation and notification of proposed penalty. Only after an employer has filed a notice of contest does the Commission obtain general jurisdiction. Employees and their representatives may then elect to intervene under § 10(c). The only independent right granted employees by § 10(c) is to contest before the Commission the reasonableness of any time period fixed by the Secretary in a citation for the abatement of a violation. Section 17 provides for the assessment of civil monetary penalties only against employers. That the Act's use of the term "employer" is truly generic is made plain in § 3, the definitional section, where "employer" and "employee" are separately defined. We find no room for loose construction of the term of art.

We are likewise unable to find support in § 5(b) for the proposition that the Act's sanctions can be directed at employees. Although this provision's injunction to employees is essentially devoid of content if not enforceable, we reluctantly conclude that this result precisely coincides with the congressional intent. . . . The Senate Report on the employee duty section . . . says:

> The committee recognizes that accomplishment of the purposes of this bill cannot be totally achieved without the fullest cooperation of affected employees. In this connection, Section 5(b) expressly places upon each employee the obligation to comply with standards and other applicable requirements under the act. . . .

> The committee does not intend the employee-duty provided in section 5(b) to diminish in any way the employer's compliance responsibilities or his responsibility to assure compliance by his own employees. Final responsibility for compliance with the requirements of this act remains with the employer.

We simply cannot accept the argument that a remedy for violations of § 5(b) can be implied from its terms. All the evidence points in the other direction.[18]

---

[18] Our conclusion is fortified by reference to the following post-enactment colloquy between Representative Steiger, a co-sponsor of OSHA, and Representative Hungate:

> MR. HUNGATE: Now, employer-employee. We have had a line of testimony about, tell this guy to wear a hardhat, or there are six guys on the job and five of them do and the other guy tosses it out, it is a hot day. And they come through and the employer gets fined and the employee does not. What can we do about that?

> MR. STEIGER: Well, Mr. Chairman when this bill was being considered, that was a question on which we spent a considerable amount of time. I would have to say the business community, at the time the bill was under consideration, took a very hard line that they did not want the Federal government to be in the business of disciplining their employees. . . . But on balance, Mr. Chairman, I would not want to see us amend the law to impose Federal government discipline on employees. I think that is something left between management and labor. . . .

Hearings before the Subcomm. on Environmental Problems Affecting Small Business of the Select Comm. on Small Business, 92d Cong., 2d Sess. 490-91 (1972).

Nor do we believe that the language in § 10(c) authorizing the Commission to issue orders "directing other appropriate relief" can be stretched to the point that it includes relief against employees. Rather, the generality of that language must be deemed limited by its context — relief in connection with the Secretary's citation. The Secretary appears not to have authority to issue a citation against an employee, and the Commission's powers cannot be any broader. "Other appropriate relief" refers to other appropriate relief against an employer.

This court's power under § 11(a) of the Act is framed in somewhat broader terms:

> Upon [the filing of a petition for review], the court shall have jurisdiction of the proceeding and of the question determined therein, and shall have power to grant such temporary relief or restraining order as it deems just and proper, and to make and enter upon the pleadings, testimony, and proceedings set forth in such record a decree affirming, modifying, or setting aside in whole or in part, the order of the Commission and enforcing the same to the extent that such order is affirmed or modified.

Clearly we can, in deciding whether and to what extent we will enforce a Commission order affirming a Secretary's citation, take into account the fact that employee intransigence in spite of employer best efforts would make enforcement inequitable. In such a case we could deny or limit enforcement. But § 11(a) does not grant to this court any independent authority to sanction employees.

B

We hold, then, that Commissioner Van Namee's reason for rejecting the petitioners' economic infeasibility defense cannot withstand analysis. We must face squarely the issue whether the Secretary can announce, and insist on employer compliance with a standard which employees are likely to resist to the point of concerted work stoppages. To frame the issue in slightly different terms, can the Secretary insist that an employer in the collective bargaining process bargain to retain the right to discipline employees for violation of safety standards which are patently reasonable, and are economically feasible except for employee resistance?

We hold that the Secretary has such power. As Part IIIA of this opinion has indicated, the entire thrust of the Act is to place primary responsibility for safety in the work place upon the employer. That, certainly, is a decision within the legislative competence of Congress. In some cases, undoubtedly, such a policy will result in work stoppages. But as we observed in *AFL-CIO v. Brennan*, the task of weighing the economic feasibility of a regulation is conferred upon the Secretary. He has concluded that stevedores must take all available legal steps to secure compliance by the longshoremen with the hardhat standard.

We can perceive several legal remedies which employers in petitioners' shoes might find availing. An employer can bargain in good faith with the representatives of its employees for the right to discharge or discipline any employee who disobeys an OSHA standard. Because occupational safety and health would seem to be subsumed within the subjects of mandatory collective bargaining — wages, hours and conditions of employment — the employer can, consistent with its duty to bargain in good faith, insist to the point of impasse upon the right to discharge or discipline disobedient employees. Where the employer's prerogative in such matters is established, that right can be enforced under § 301. Should discipline or discharge nevertheless provoke a work stoppage, *Boys Markets* injunctive relief would be available if the parties have agreed upon a no-strike or grievance and arbitration provision. And even in those cases in which an injunction cannot be obtained, or where arbitration fails to vindicate the employer's action, the employer can still apply to the Secretary pursuant to § 6(d) of the Act, for a variance from a promulgated standard, on a showing that alternative methods for protecting employees would be equally effective. Moreover, under § 10(c) the Secretary has authority to extend the time within which a violation of a standard must be abated.

In this case petitioners have produced no evidence demonstrating that they have bargained for a unilateral privilege of discharge or discipline, that they have actually discharged or disciplined, or threatened to discharge or discipline, any employee who defied the hardhat standard, or that they have petitioned the Secretary for a variance or an extension of the time within which compliance is to be achieved. We conclude that as a matter of law petitioners have failed to establish the infeasibility of the challenged regulation.

The order of the Commission enforcing the Secretary's citations will be affirmed. The petition for review will be denied.

WHIRLPOOL CORP. v. MARSHALL
United States Supreme Court
445 U.S. 1 (1980)

Mr. Justice Stewart delivered the opinion of the Court.

The Occupational Safety and Health Act of 1970 (Act) prohibits an employer from discharging or discriminating against any employee who exercises "any right afforded by" the Act.[2] The Secretary of Labor (Secretary) has promulgated a regulation providing that, among the rights that the Act so protects, is the right of an employee to choose not to perform his assigned task because of a reasonable apprehension of death or serious injury coupled with a reasonable belief that no less drastic alternative is available.[3] The question

---

[2] Section 11(c)(1), 29 U.S.C. § 660(c)(1).

[3] The regulation, 29 CFR § 1977.12 (1979), provides in full:

(a) In addition to protecting employees who file complaints, institute proceedings, or testify in proceedings under or related to the Act, section 11(c) also protects employees from discrimination occurring because of the exercise "of any right afforded by this Act." Certain rights are explicitly provided in the Act; for example, there is a right to participate as a party in enforcement proceedings (sec. 10). Certain other rights exist by necessary implication. For example, employees may request information from the Occupational Safety and Health Administration; such requests would constitute the exercise of a right afforded by the Act. Likewise, employees interviewed by agents of

presented in the case before us is whether this regulation is consistent with the Act.

I

The petitioner company maintains a manufacturing plant in Marion, Ohio, for the production of household appliances. Overhead conveyors transport appliance components throughout the plant. To protect employees from objects that occasionally fall from these conveyors, the petitioner has installed a horizontal wire-mesh guard screen approximately 20 feet above the plant floor. This mesh screen is welded to angle-iron frames suspended from the building's structural steel skeleton.

Maintenance employees of the petitioner spend several hours each week removing objects from the screen, replacing paper spread on the screen to catch grease drippings from the material on the conveyors, and performing occasional maintenance work on the conveyors themselves. To perform these duties, maintenance employees usually are able to stand on the iron frames, but sometimes find it necessary to step onto the steel mesh screen itself.

In 1973, the company began to install heavier wire in the screen because its safety had been drawn into question. Several employees had fallen partly through the old screen, and on one occasion an employee had fallen completely through to the plant floor below but had survived. A number of maintenance employees had reacted to these incidents by bringing the unsafe screen conditions to the attention of their foremen. The petitioner company's contemporaneous safety instructions admonished employees to step only on the angle-iron frames.

---

the Secretary in the course of inspections or investigations could not subsequently be discriminated against because of their cooperation.

(b)(1) On the other hand, review of the Act and examination of the legislative history discloses that, as a general matter, there is no right afforded by the Act which would entitle employees to walk off the job because of potential unsafe conditions at the workplace. Hazardous conditions which may be violative of the Act will ordinarily be corrected by the employer, once brought to his attention. If corrections are not accomplished, or if there is dispute about the existence of a hazard, the employee will normally have opportunity to request inspection of the workplace pursuant to section 8(f) of the Act, or to seek the assistance of other public agencies which have responsibility in the field of safety and health. Under such circumstances, therefore, an employer would not ordinarily be in violation of section 11(c) by taking action to discipline an employee for refusing to perform normal job activities because of alleged safety or health hazards.

(2) However, occasions might arise when an employee is confronted with a choice between not performing assigned tasks or subjecting himself to serious injury or death arising from a hazardous condition at the workplace. If the employee, with no reasonable alternative, refuses in good faith to expose himself to the dangerous condition, he would be protected against subsequent discrimination. The condition causing the employee's apprehension of death or injury must be of such a nature that a reasonable person, under the circumstances then confronting the employee, would conclude that there is a real danger of death or serious injury and that there is insufficient time due to the urgency of the situation, to eliminate the danger through resort to regular statutory enforcement channels. In addition, in such circumstances, the employee, where possible, must also have sought from his employer, and been unable to obtain, a correction of the dangerous condition.

On June 28, 1974, a maintenance employee fell to his death through the guard screen in an area where the newer, stronger mesh had not yet been installed.[4] Following this incident, the petitioner effectuated some repairs and issued an order strictly forbidding maintenance employees from stepping on either the screens or the angle-iron supporting structure. An alternative but somewhat more cumbersome and less satisfactory method was developed for removing objects from the screen. This procedure required employees to stand on power-raised mobile platforms and use hooks to recover the material.

On July 7, 1974, two of the petitioner's maintenance employees, Virgil Deemer and Thomas Cornwell, met with the plant maintenance superintendent to voice their concern about the safety of the screen. The superintendent disagreed with their view, but permitted the two men to inspect the screen with their foreman and to point out dangerous areas needing repair. Unsatisfied with the petitioner's response to the results of this inspection, Deemer and Cornwell met on July 9 with the plant safety director. At that meeting, they requested the name, address, and telephone number of a representative of the local office of the Occupational Safety and Health Administration (OSHA). Although the safety director told the men that they "had better stop and think about what [they] were doing," he furnished the men with the information they requested. Later that same day, Deemer contacted an official of the regional OSHA office and discussed the guard screen.

The next day, Deemer and Cornwell reported for the night shift at 10:45 p.m. Their foreman, after himself walking on some of the angle-iron frames, directed the two men to perform their usual maintenance duties on a section of the old screen.[6] Claiming that the screen was unsafe, they refused to carry out this directive. The foreman then sent them to the personnel office, where they were ordered to punch out without working or being paid for the remaining six hours of the shift.[7] The two men subsequently received written reprimands, which were placed in their employment files.

A little over a month later, the Secretary filed suit in the United States District Court for the Northern District of Ohio, alleging that the petitioner's actions against Deemer and Cornwell constituted discrimination in violation of § 11(c)(1) of the Act. [The District Court held that the employees met the requirements of the regulation, but denied relief holding that the regulation was inconsistent with the Act. The Court of Appeals for the Sixth Circuit reversed, holding that the regulation was valid and that the actions of Deemer and Cornwell were justified under it.]

---

[4] As a result of this fatality, the Secretary conducted an investigation that led to the issuance of a citation charging the company with maintaining an unsafe walking and working surface in violation of 29 U.S.C. § 654(a)(1). The citation required immediate abatement of the hazard and proposed a $600 penalty. Nearly five years following the accident, the Occupational Safety and Health Review Commission affirmed the citation, but decided to permit the petitioner six months in which to correct the unsafe condition. A petition to review that decision is pending in the United States Court of Appeals for the District of Columbia Circuit.

[6] This order appears to have been in direct violation of the outstanding company directive that maintenance work was to be accomplished without stepping on the screen apparatus.

[7] Both employees apparently returned to work the following day without further incident.

II

The Act itself creates an express mechanism for protecting workers from employment conditions believed to pose an emergent threat of death or serious injury. Upon receipt of an employee inspection request stating reasonable grounds to believe that an imminent danger is present in a workplace, OSHA must conduct an inspection. 29 U.S.C. § 657(f)(1). In the event this inspection reveals workplace conditions or practices that "could reasonably be expected to cause death or serious physical harm immediately or before the imminence of such danger can be eliminated through the enforcement procedures otherwise provided by" the Act, 29 U.S.C. § 662(a), the OSHA inspector must inform the affected employees and the employer of the danger and notify them that he is recommending to the Secretary that injunctive relief be sought. § 662(c). At this juncture, the Secretary can petition a federal court to restrain the conditions or practices giving rise to the imminent danger. By means of a temporary restraining order or preliminary injunction, the court may then require the employer to avoid, correct, or remove the danger or to prohibit employees from working in the area. § 662(a).

To ensure that this process functions effectively, the Act expressly accords to every employee several rights, the exercise of which may not subject him to discharge or discrimination. An employee is given the right to inform OSHA of an imminently dangerous workplace condition or practice and request that OSHA inspect that condition or practice. 29 U.S.C. § 657(f)(1). He is given a limited right to assist the OSHA inspector in inspecting the workplace, §§ 657(a)(2), (e), and (f)(2), and the right to aid a court in determining whether or not a risk of imminent danger in fact exists. *See* § 660(c)(1). Finally, an affected employee is given the right to bring an action to compel the Secretary to seek injunctive relief if he believes the Secretary has wrongfully declined to do so. § 662(d).

In the light of this detailed statutory scheme, the Secretary is obviously correct when he acknowledges in his regulation that, "as a general matter, there is no right afforded by the Act which would entitle employees to walk off the job because of potential unsafe conditions at the workplace." By providing for prompt notice to the employer of an inspector's intention to seek an injunction against an imminently dangerous condition, the legislation obviously contemplates that the employer will normally respond by voluntarily and speedily eliminating the danger. And in the few instances where this does not occur, the legislative provisions authorizing prompt judicial action are designed to give employees full protection in most situations from the risk of injury or death resulting from an imminently dangerous condition at the worksite.

As this case illustrates, however, circumstances may sometimes exist in which the employee justifiably believes that the express statutory arrangement does not sufficiently protect him from death or serious injury. Such circumstances will probably not often occur, but such a situation may arise when (1) the employee is ordered by his employer to work under conditions that the employee reasonably believes pose an imminent risk of death or serious bodily injury, and (2) the employee has reason to believe that there is not sufficient time or opportunity either to seek effective redress from his employer or to apprise OSHA of the danger.

Nothing in the Act suggests that those few employees who have to face this dilemma must rely exclusively on the remedies expressly set forth in the Act at the risk of their own safety. But nothing in the Act explicitly provides otherwise. Against this background of legislative silence, the Secretary has exercised his rulemaking power under 29 U.S.C. § 657(g)(2) and has determined that, when an employee in good faith finds himself in such a predicament, he may refuse to expose himself to the dangerous condition, without being subjected to "subsequent discrimination" by the employer.

The question before us is whether this interpretative regulation constitutes a permissible gloss on the Act by the Secretary, in light of the Act's language, structure, and legislative history. Our inquiry is informed by an awareness that the regulation is entitled to deference unless it can be said not to be a reasoned and supportable interpretation of the Act.

A

The regulation clearly conforms to the fundamental objective of the Act — to prevent occupational deaths and serious injuries. The Act, in its preamble, declares that its purpose and policy is "to assure so far as possible every working man and woman in the Nation safe and healthful working conditions and to *preserve* our human resources. . . ." 29 U.S.C. § 651(b). (Emphasis added.)

To accomplish this basic purpose, the legislation's remedial orientation is prophylactic in nature. The Act does not wait for an employee to die or become injured. It authorizes the promulgation of health and safety standards and the issuance of citations in the hope that these will act to prevent deaths or injuries from ever occurring. It would seem anomalous to construe an Act so directed and constructed as prohibiting an employee, with no other reasonable alternative, the freedom to withdraw from a workplace environment that he reasonably believes is highly dangerous.

Moreover, the Secretary's regulation can be viewed as an appropriate aid to the full effectuation of the Act's "general duty" clause. That clause provides that "[e]ach employer . . . shall furnish to each of his employees employment and a place of employment which are free from recognized hazards that are causing or are likely to cause death or serious physical harm to his employees." 29 U.S.C. § 654(a)(1). As the legislative history of this provision reflects, it was intended itself to deter the occurrence of occupational deaths and serious injuries by placing on employers a mandatory obligation independent of the specific health and safety standards to be promulgated by the Secretary. Since OSHA inspectors cannot be present around the clock in every workplace, the Secretary's regulation ensures that employees will in all circumstances enjoy the rights afforded them by the "general duty" clause.

The regulation thus on its face appears to further the overriding purpose of the Act, and rationally to complement its remedial scheme. In the absence of some contrary indication in the legislative history, the Secretary's regulation must, therefore, be upheld, particularly when it is remembered that safety legislation is to be liberally construed to effectuate the congressional purpose.

B

In urging reversal of the judgment before us, the petitioner relies primarily on two aspects of the Act's legislative history.

1

Representative Daniels of New Jersey sponsored one of several House bills that led ultimately to the passage of the Act. As reported to the House by the Committee on Education and Labor, the Daniels bill contained a section that was soon dubbed the "strike with pay" provision. This section provided that employees could request an examination by the Department of Health, Education, and Welfare (HEW) of the toxicity of any materials in their workplace. If that examination revealed a workplace substance that had "potentially toxic or harmful effects in such concentration as used or found," the employer was given 60 days to correct the potentially dangerous condition. Following the expiration of that period, the employer could not require that an employee be exposed to toxic concentrations of the substance unless the employee was informed of the hazards and symptoms associated with the substance, the employee was instructed in the proper precautions for dealing with the substance, and the employee was furnished with personal protective equipment. If these conditions were not met, an employee could "absent himself from such risk of harm for the period necessary to avoid such danger without loss of regular compensation for such period."

This provision encountered stiff opposition in the House. Representative Steiger of Wisconsin introduced a substitute bill containing no "strike with pay" provision. In response, Representative Daniels offered a floor amendment that, among other things, deleted his bill's "strike with pay" provision. He suggested that employees instead be afforded the right to request an immediate OSHA inspection of the premises, a right which the Steiger bill did not provide. The House ultimately adopted the Steiger bill.

The bill that was reported to and, with a few amendments, passed by the Senate never contained a "strike with pay" provision. It did, however, give employees the means by which they could request immediate Labor Department inspections. . . .

The petitioner reads into this legislative history a congressional intent incompatible with an administrative interpretation of the Act such as is embodied in the regulation at issue in this case. The petitioner argues that Congress' overriding concern in rejecting the "strike with pay" provision was to avoid giving employees a unilateral authority to walk off the job which they might abuse in order to intimidate or harass their employer. Congress deliberately chose instead, the petitioner maintains, to grant employees the power to request immediate administrative inspections of the workplace which could in appropriate cases lead to coercive judicial remedies. As the petitioner views the regulation, therefore, it gives to workers precisely what Congress determined to withhold from them.

We read the legislative history differently. Congress rejected a provision that did not concern itself at all with conditions posing real and immediate threats of death or severe injury. The remedy which the rejected provision furnished employees could have been invoked only after 60 days had passed following HEW's inspection and notification that improperly high levels of toxic substances were present in the workplace. Had that inspection revealed employment conditions posing a threat of imminent and grave harm, the Secretary of Labor would presumably have requested, long before expiration of the 60-day period, a court injunction pursuant to other provisions of the Daniels bill. Consequently, in rejecting the Daniels bill's "strike with pay" provision, Congress was not rejecting a legislative provision dealing with the highly perilous and fast-moving situations covered by the regulation now before us.

It is also important to emphasize that what primarily troubled Congress about the Daniels bill's "strike with pay" provision was its requirement that employees be paid their regular salary after having properly invoked their right to refuse to work under the section.[29] It is instructive that virtually every time the issue of an employee's right to absent himself from hazardous work was discussed in the legislative debates, it was in the context of the employee's right to continue to receive his usual compensation.

When it rejected the "strike with pay" concept, therefore, Congress very clearly meant to reject a law unconditionally imposing upon employers an obligation to continue to pay their employees their regular paychecks when they absented themselves from work for reasons of safety. But the regulation at issue here does not require employers to pay workers who refuse to perform their assigned tasks in the face of imminent danger. It simply provides that in such cases the employer may not "discriminate" against the employees involved. An employer "discriminates" against an employee only when he treats that employee less favorably than he treats others similarly situated.[31]

---

[29] Congress' concern necessarily was with the provision's compensation requirement. The law then, as it does today, already afforded workers a right, under certain circumstances, to walk off their jobs when faced with hazardous conditions. Under Section 7 of the National Labor Relations Act, 29 U.S.C. § 157, employees have a protected right to strike over safety issues. *See NLRB v. Washington Aluminum Co.,* 370 U.S. 9. Similarly, Section 502 of the Labor Management Relations Act, 29 U.S.C. § 143, provides that "the quitting of labor by an employee or employees in good faith because of abnormally dangerous conditions for work at the place of employment of such employee or employees [shall not] be deemed a strike." The effect of this section is to create an exception to a no-strike obligation in a collective-bargaining agreement. *Gateway Coal Co. v. Mine Workers,* 414 U.S. 368. The existence of these statutory rights also makes clear that the Secretary's regulation does not conflict with the general pattern of federal labor legislation in the area of occupational safety and health.

[31] Deemer and Cornwell were clearly subjected to "discrimination" when the petitioner placed reprimands in their respective employment files. Whether the two employees were also discriminated against when they were denied pay for the approximately six hours they did not work on July 10, 1974, is a question not now before us. The District Court dismissed the complaint without indicating what relief it thought would have been appropriate had it upheld the Secretary's regulation. The Court of Appeals expressed no view concerning the limits of the relief to which the Secretary might ultimately be entitled. On remand, the District Court will reach this issue.

2

The second aspect of the Act's legislative history upon which the petitioner relies is the rejection by Congress of provisions contained in both the Daniels and the Williams bills that would have given Labor Department officials, in imminent-danger situations, the power temporarily to shut down all or part of an employer's plant. These provisions aroused considerable opposition in both Houses of Congress. The hostility engendered in the House of Representatives led Representative Daniels to delete his version of the provision in proposing amendments to his original bill. The Steiger bill that ultimately passed the House gave the Labor Department no such authority. The Williams bill, as approved by the Senate, did contain an administrative shutdown provision, but the Conference Committee rejected this aspect of the Senate bill.

The petitioner infers from these events a congressional will hostile to the regulation in question here. The regulation, the petitioner argues, provides employees with the very authority to shut down an employer's plant that was expressly denied a more expert and objective United States Department of Labor.

As we read the pertinent legislative history, however, the petitioner misconceives the thrust of Congress' concern. Those in Congress who prevented passage of the administrative shutdown provisions in the Daniels and Williams bills were opposed to the unilateral authority those provisions gave to federal officials, without any judicial safeguards, drastically to impair the operation of an employer's business. Congressional opponents also feared that the provisions might jeopardize the Government's otherwise neutral role in labor-management relations.

Neither of these congressional concerns is implicated by the regulation before us. The regulation accords no authority to Government officials. It simply permits private employees of a private employer to avoid workplace conditions that they believe pose grave dangers to their own safety. The employees have no power under the regulation to order their employer to correct the hazardous condition or to clear the dangerous workplace of others. Moreover, any employee who acts in reliance on the regulation runs the risk of discharge or reprimand in the event a court subsequently finds that he acted unreasonably or in bad faith. The regulation, therefore, does not remotely resemble the legislation that Congress rejected.

C

For these reasons we conclude that 29 CFR § 1977.12(b)(2) (1979) was promulgated by the Secretary in the valid exercise of his authority under the Act. Accordingly, the judgment of the Court of Appeals is affirmed.

NOTES

1. *Back Pay for Whirlpool Employees.* On remand, the District Court held that Deemer and Cornwell were entitled to expungement of the written reprimands in their employment files. The court also awarded six hours of back pay because they were not given an opportunity to perform safe alternative work, rejecting the employer's argument that this would allow employees to strike with pay. *Marshall v. Whirlpool Corp.*, 9 O.S.H. Cas. (BNA) 1038 (N.D. Ohio 1980).

2. *The Limits of the Antidiscrimination Procedure.* Section 11(c) protects an employee from discharge or any manner of discrimination because the employee files a complaint, institutes any procedure, testifies in a proceeding, or exercises any right afforded by the Act. Despite the breadth of this language, there are limits to the antidiscrimination procedure. An employee has only 30 days after the occurrence of the discrimination to file a complaint with the Secretary of Labor. The Secretary is neither required to investigate the allegation nor to file an action on behalf of the complainant. There is no private right of action under § 11(c) and therefore an employee may not bring an action if the Secretary declines to pursue the complaint. The Secretary has also adopted a policy of deferring to other proceedings, such as arbitration, and deferring to the results of these other proceedings if certain criteria are met, such as the outcome not being clearly repugnant to the policy of the OSHAct.

If the Secretary does take action on behalf of the employee and prevails, Section 11(c)(2) provides that district courts can order "all appropriate relief," including reinstatement of the employee to his former position with back pay. Compensatory as well as exemplary damages may also be awarded under appropriate circumstances, such as when an employer consistently engaged in brash conduct, both in and out of court, and offered the Labor Department investigator a case of wine, "possibly in an attempt to influence the investigation." *Reich v. Cambridgeport Air Sys., Inc.*, 26 F.3d 1187 (1st Cir. 1994).

3. *Tort Suits for Employer Retaliation.* Common law actions have been brought by employees who were discharged for refusing to work under hazardous conditions or for reporting safety or health hazards to the government. Some courts have held that such employer retaliation against an employee who files an OSHA complaint constitutes a public policy exception to the employment-at-will doctrine and have approved such suits. *See Kulch v. Structural Fibers, Inc.*, 677 N.E.2d 308 (Ohio 1997). Another decision identified the inadequate OSHA remedies as a reason for holding that a common law wrongful-discharge action was not barred. *Flenker v. Willamette Indus.*, 967 P.2d 295 (Kan. 1998). Other courts have held that the remedy for retaliatory discharge provided by § 11(c) of the OSHAct (or similar state statutory protection) precludes the discharged worker from bringing a common-law wrongful-discharge action. *See, e.g., Burnham v. Karl & Gelb, P.C.*, 745 A.2d 178 (Conn. 2000).

G.   FEDERAL VERSUS STATE AUTHORITY FOR WORKPLACE SAFETY AND HEALTH

1.   STATE AUTHORITY CEDED UNDER OSHA

The OSHAct preempts state safety and health activities, although, as later subsections indicate, there are controversies about the limits of federal preemption of certain areas of state responsibility, such as criminal laws, that have an indirect effect on workplace safety and health. However, even in those areas where federal preemption clearly operates, namely the promulgation and enforcement of occupational health and safety standards, states can run their own safety and health programs if certain conditions are met. Section 18(c) of the Act provides that the Secretary of Labor may approve a state plan for the development and enforcement of occupational safety and health standards if, in the judgment of the Secretary, the state plan meets a number of conditions, including:

(i) a state agency is designated to run the program;

(ii) the state agency has sufficient funds and legal authority to conduct the program; and

(iii) the state health and safety standards are at least as effective as the federal standards.

The Secretary of Labor has the authority to decide whether to accept a state's plan, to monitor the state's performance, or to revoke a state's authority to operate its own plan.

As of 2006, there were twenty-three approved state plans (including "state" plans in the Virgin Islands and Puerto Rico) covering private sector and state and local government employees. In addition, New York, New Jersey, and Connecticut had approved plans for state employees only. Federal funds reimburse states for up to 50% of the operating costs of approved state plans. If a state does not have an approved state plan, then OSHA is responsible for enforcing all health and safety standards for private sector employers in the state at no cost to the state's taxpayers. Among those states without an approved state plan, all but three (Alabama, Delaware, and Florida) have safety and health programs applicable to public sector workers.

The status of the state plans received considerable attention in the aftermath of the September 1991 fire at the Imperial Food Products' poultry processing plant in Hamlet, North Carolina. That disaster killed twenty-five workers who were trapped behind exit doors that were locked in violation of a safety standard. North Carolina, one of the twenty-three jurisdictions that run their own safety and health programs, had never inspected the Imperial Food Products' plant. In April 1992, OSHA announced it was taking preliminary steps to withdraw approval of North Carolina's state plan. Then in July 1992, OSHA relented and indicated that enough improvements had been made in North Carolina to warrant the state's continued operation of the plan.

State plans vary in terms of how aggressively they adopt their own standards. California has been relatively active and recently adopted workplace exposure limits for 18 substances more stringent than the Federal standards. *California Standards Board Adopts Tighter Exposure Limits for 18 Substances*, 36 O.S.H. Rep. (BNA) 439 (May 11, 2006). States also differ in the extent of their enforcement activities. A report on selected jurisdictions found a range of 1 inspector for every 18,258 workers in North Carolina to 1 inspector for every 106,178 workers in California, compared to 1 inspector for every 58,565 workers for the Federal OSHA program. *California Union Submits Budget Proposal to increase Number of State Safety Inspectors by 100*, 36 O.S.H. Rep. (BNA) 270 (March 23, 2006).

2. OTHER SOURCES OF STATE AUTHORITY

The OSHAct preempts state health and safety plans that directly compete with OSHA standards unless, as discussed in the previous subsection, the Secretary of Labor has approved a state plan that meets certain conditions spelled out in section 18 of the Act. But what about state laws with "dual impacts," one of which involves regulation of workplace safety and health? Two examples of such state laws are "right-to-know" acts and occupational licensing acts, which protect both workers and the general public.

"Right-to-know" laws were enacted in about thirty states during the 1980s to provide information about hazardous substances in the workplace. An example is the New Jersey Worker and Community Right to Know Act, N.J. STAT. ANN. § 34:5A14, which required employers to disclose information about toxic chemicals to public safety officers, workers, and environmental control officials. One rationale for such disclosure to nonworkers is that police or firefighters who are summoned to a plant need to know what chemicals are present in order to decide if fumes are life-threatening and to know what firefighting techniques are appropriate.

OSHA promulgated the Hazard Communication Standard (HCS) for the manufacturing sector in 1983. (The content of the standard is discussed in Section C of this chapter.) One of the reasons why OSHA issued the HCS was to preempt state right-to-know laws and thus reduce burdens for employers.

The Hazard Communication Standard is one of the most significant requirements that the OSHAct has placed on employers. For example, the OSHA standard most frequency cited in OSHA violations during fiscal year 2005 was the HCS requirement that employers have a written program. Despite this intensive use, one of the reasons why OSHA issued the HCS was to preempt state right-to-know laws and thus reduce burdens for employers.

A series of decisions by the Third Circuit drew distinctions between those portions of the right-to-know laws that were preempted by OSHA and those portions that could remain operative. In *New Jersey State Chamber of Commerce v. Hughey (Hughey I)*, 774 F.2d 587 (3d Cir. 1985), for example, the court held that the provision requiring manufacturing employers to complete workplace surveys was preempted, but that the provisions requiring reports of environmental hazards to agencies concerned with public health were not preempted. The Pennsylvania Right to Know Law was challenged in *Manufacturers Ass'n of Tri-County v. Knepper*, 801 F.2d 130 (3d Cir. 1986). In this decision, the Third Circuit again distinguished between certain provisions that were preempted (such as education and training requirements for employees in manufacturing) and other provisions that were not (such as a hazard survey that was more inclusive than the HCS list of hazardous chemicals).

OSHA amended the Hazard Communication Standard in 1987. In addition to expanding coverage to nonmanufacturing employers, the preemption language was strengthened: thus state provisions concerning material safety data sheets (MSDSs), labeling of chemicals, and training programs "for the primary purpose" of assuring worker safety and health were explicitly preempted. The Third Circuit considered this language in *New Jersey Chamber of Commerce v. Hughey (Hughey II)*, 868 F.2d 621 (3d Cir. 1989), and decided that the container-labeling provision of the New Jersey right-to-know law would not be preempted because the state law would not serve as an obstacle to the accomplishment of the federal standard. The efforts of the Third Circuit to distinguish between those portions of a state's right-to-know law that are preempted by OSHA and those portions that are not preempted serve as a backdrop to the next case.

GADE v. NATIONAL SOLID WASTES MANAGEMENT ASSOCIATION
United States Supreme Court
505 U.S. 88 (1992)

JUSTICE O'CONNOR announced the judgment of the Court and delivered an opinion, Parts I, III, and IV of which represent the views of the Court, and Part II of which is joined by THE CHIEF JUSTICE, JUSTICE WHITE, and JUSTICE SCALIA.

In 1988, the Illinois General Assembly enacted the Hazardous Waste Crane and Hoisting Equipment Operators Licensing Act and the Hazardous Waste Laborers Licensing Act (together, licensing acts). The stated purpose of the acts is both "to promote job safety" and "to protect life, limb and property." In this case, we consider whether these "dual impact" statutes, which protect both workers and the general public, are pre-empted by the federal Occupational Safety and Health Act of 1970 (OSH Act), and the standards promulgated thereunder by the Occupational Safety and Health Administration (OSHA).

I

The OSH Act authorizes the Secretary of Labor to promulgate federal occupational safety and health standards. In the Superfund Amendments and Reauthorization Act of 1986 (SARA), Congress directed the Secretary of Labor to "promulgate standards for the health and safety protection of employees engaged in hazardous waste operations" pursuant to her authority under the OSH Act. In relevant part, SARA requires the Secretary to establish standards for the initial and routine training of workers who handle hazardous wastes.

In response to this congressional directive, OSHA, to which the Secretary has delegated certain of her statutory responsibilities, promulgated regulations on "Hazardous Waste Operations and Emergency Response," including detailed regulations on worker training requirements. The OSHA regulations require, among other things, that workers engaged in an activity that may expose them to hazardous wastes receive a minimum of 40 hours of instruction off the site, and a minimum of three days actual field experience under the supervision of a trained supervisor. . . .

In 1988, while OSHA's interim hazardous waste regulations were in effect, the State of Illinois enacted the licensing acts at issue here. The laws are designated as acts "in relation to environmental protection," and their stated aim is to protect both employees and the general public by licensing hazardous waste equipment operators and laborers working at certain facilities. Both acts require a license applicant to provide a certified record of at least 40 hours of training under an approved program conducted within Illinois, to pass a written examination, and to complete an annual refresher course of at least eight hours of instruction. In addition, applicants for a hazardous waste crane operator's license must submit "a certified record showing operation of equipment used in hazardous waste handling for a minimum of 4,000 hours." Employees who work without the proper license, and employers who knowingly permit an unlicensed employee to work, are subject to escalating fines for each offense. . . .

Shortly before the state licensing acts were due to go into effect, the [National Solid Waste Management Association (the Association)] brought a declaratory judgment action in United States District Court against [The Director] of the Illinois Environmental Protection Agency (IEPA). The Association sought to enjoin IEPA from enforcing the Illinois licensing acts, claiming that the acts were pre-empted by the OSH Act and OSHA regulations and that they violated the Commerce Clause of the United States Constitution. The District Court held [that the Illinois acts were not preempted. The Seventh Circuit reversed in part, and remanded for further consideration.]

We granted certiorari to resolve a conflict between the decision below and decisions in which other Courts of Appeals have found the OSH Act to have a much narrower pre-emptive effect on "dual impact" state regulations.

II

Before addressing the scope of the OSH Act's pre-emption of dual impact state regulations, we consider petitioner's threshold argument . . . that the Act does not pre-empt nonconflicting state regulations at all. . . .

In the OSH Act, Congress endeavored "to assure so far as possible every working man and woman in the Nation safe and healthful working conditions." 29 U.S.C. § 651(b). To that end, Congress authorized the Secretary of Labor to set mandatory occupational safety and health standards applicable to all businesses affecting interstate commerce, and thereby brought the Federal Government into a field that traditionally had been occupied by the States. Federal regulation of the workplace was not intended to be all-encompassing, however. First, Congress expressly saved two areas from federal pre-emption. Section 4(b)(4) of the OSH Act states that the Act does not "supersede or in any manner affect any workmen's compensation law or . . . enlarge or diminish or affect in any other manner the common law or statutory rights, duties, or liabilities of employers and employees under any law with respect to injuries, diseases, or death of employees arising out of, or in the course of, employment." Section 18(a) provides that the Act does not "prevent any State agency or court from asserting jurisdiction under State law over any occupational safety or health issue with respect to which no [federal] standard is in effect."

Congress not only reserved certain areas to state regulation, but it also, in § 18(b) of the Act, gave the States the option of pre-empting federal regulation entirely. That section provides:

Submission of State plan for development and enforcement of State standards to preempt applicable Federal standards.

Any State which, at any time, desires to assume responsibility for development and enforcement therein of occupational safety and health standards relating to any occupational safety or health issue with respect to which a Federal standard has been promulgated [by the Secretary under the OSH Act] shall submit a State plan for the development of such standards and their enforcement.

About half the States have received the Secretary's approval for their own state plans as described in this provision. Illinois is not among them.

In the decision below, the Court of Appeals held that § 18(b) "unquestionably" pre-empts any state law or regulation that establishes an occupational health and safety standard on an issue for which OSHA has already promulgated a standard, unless the State has obtained the Secretary's approval for its own plan. Every other federal and state court confronted with an OSH Act pre-emption challenge has reached the same conclusion, and so do we.

Pre-emption may be either expressed or implied, and "is compelled whether Congress' command is explicitly stated in the statute's language or implicitly contained in its structure and purpose." Absent explicit pre-emptive language, we have recognized at least two types of implied pre-emption: field pre-emption, where the scheme of federal regulation is " 'so pervasive as to make reasonable the inference that Congress left no room for the States to supplement it,' " and conflict pre-emption, where "compliance with both federal and state regulations is a physical impossibility," or where state law "stands as an obstacle to the accomplishment and execution of the full purposes and objectives of Congress."

Our ultimate task in any pre-emption case is to determine whether state regulation is consistent with the structure and purpose of the statute as a whole. Looking to "the provisions of the whole law, and to its object and policy," we hold that nonapproved state regulation of occupational safety and health issues for which a federal standard is in effect is impliedly pre-empted as in conflict with the full purposes and objectives of the OSH Act. The design of the statute persuades us that Congress intended to subject employers and employees to only one set of regulations, be it federal or state, and that the only way a State may regulate an OSHA-regulated occupational safety and health issue is pursuant to an approved state plan that displaces the federal standards. The principal indication that Congress intended to pre-empt state law is § 18(b)'s statement that a State "shall" submit a plan if it wishes to "assume responsibility" for "development and enforcement . . . of occupational safety and health standards relating to any occupational safety or health issue with respect to which a Federal standard has been promulgated." The unavoidable implication of this provision is that a State may not enforce its own occupational safety and health standards without obtaining the Secretary's approval, and petitioner concedes that § 18(b) would require an approved plan if Illinois wanted to "assume responsibility" for the regulation of occupational safety and health within the State. Petitioner contends, however, that an approved plan is necessary only if the State wishes completely to replace the federal regulations, not merely to supplement them. She argues that the correct interpretation of § 18(b) is that . . . a State may either "oust" the federal standard by submitting a state plan to the Secretary for approval or "add to" the federal standard without seeking the Secretary's approval.

. . . .

Cutting against petitioner's interpretation of § 18(b) is the language of § 18(a), which saves from pre-emption any state law regulating an occupational safety and health issue with respect to which no federal standard is in effect. Although this is a saving clause, not a pre-emption clause, the natural implication of this provision is that state laws regulating the same issue as federal laws are not saved, even if they merely supplement the federal standard. Moreover, if petitioner's reading of § 18(b) were correct, and if a State were free to enact nonconflicting safety and health regulations, then § 18(a) would be superfluous: there is no possibility of conflict where there is no federal regulation. . . . [W]e conclude that § 18(a)'s preservation of state authority in the absence of a federal standard presupposes a background pre-emption of all state occupational safety and health standards whenever a federal standard governing the same issue is in effect.

. . . .

Looking at the provisions of § 18 as a whole, we conclude that the OSH Act precludes any state regulation of an occupational safety or health issue with respect to which a federal standard has been established, unless a state plan has been submitted and approved pursuant to § 18(b). Our review of the Act persuades us that Congress sought to promote occupational safety and health while at the same time avoiding duplicative, and possibly counterproductive, regulation. It thus established a system of uniform federal occupational health and safety standards, but gave States the option of pre-empting federal regulations by developing their own occupational safety and health programs. In addition, Congress offered the States substantial federal grant monies to assist them in developing their own programs. *See* OSH Act § 23, 29 U.S.C. §§ 672(a), (b), and (f) (for three years following enactment, the Secretary may award up to 90% of the costs to a State of developing a state occupational safety and health plan); 29 U.S.C. § 672(g) (States that develop approved plans may receive funding for up to 50% of the costs of operating their occupational health and safety programs). To allow a State selectively to "supplement" certain federal regulations with ostensibly nonconflicting standards would be inconsistent with this federal scheme of establishing uniform federal standards, on the one hand, and encouraging States to assume full responsibility for development and enforcement of their own OSH programs, on the other.

We cannot accept petitioner's argument that the OSH Act does not pre-empt nonconflicting state laws because those laws, like the Act, are designed to promote worker safety. . . . The OSH Act does not foreclose a State from enacting its own laws to advance the goal of worker safety, but it does restrict the ways in which it can do so. If a State wishes to regulate an issue of worker safety for which a federal standard is in effect, its only option is to obtain the prior approval of the Secretary of Labor, as described in § 18 of the Act.

III

Petitioner next argues that, even if Congress intended to pre-empt all nonapproved state occupational safety and health regulations whenever a federal standard is in effect, the OSH Act's pre-emptive effect should not be extended to state laws that address public safety as well as occupational safety concerns. As we explained in Part II, we understand § 18(b) to mean that the OSH Act pre-empts all state "occupational safety and health standards relating to any occupational safety or health issue with respect to which a Federal standard has been promulgated." We now consider whether a dual impact law can be an "occupational safety and health standard" subject to pre-emption under the Act.

The OSH Act defines an "occupational safety and health standard" as "a standard which requires conditions, or the adoption or use of one or more practices, means, methods, operations, or processes, reasonably necessary or appropriate to provide safe or healthful employment and places of employment." 29 U.S.C. § 652(8). Any state law requirement designed to promote health and safety in the workplace falls neatly within the Act's definition of an "occupational safety and health standard." Clearly, under this definition, a state law that expressly declares a legislative purpose of regulating occupational health and safety would, in the absence of an approved state plan, be pre-empted by an OSHA standard regulating the same subject matter. But petitioner asserts that if the state legislature articulates a purpose other than (or in addition to) workplace health and safety, then the OSH Act loses its pre-emptive force. We disagree.

Although "part of the pre-empted field is defined by reference to the purpose of the state law in question, . . . another part of the field is defined by the state law's actual effect." *English v. General Electric Co.,* 496 U.S. 72, 84 (1990). In assessing the impact of a state law on the federal scheme, we have refused to rely solely on the legislature's professed purpose and have looked as well to the effects of the law. . . .

Our precedents leave no doubt that a dual impact state regulation cannot avoid OSH Act pre-emption simply because the regulation serves several objectives rather than one. As the Court of Appeals observed, "it would defeat the purpose of section 18 if a state could enact measures stricter than OSHA's and largely accomplished through regulation of worker health and safety simply by asserting a non-occupational purpose for the legislation." Whatever the purpose or purposes of the state law, pre-emption analysis cannot ignore the effect of the challenged state action on the pre-empted field. The key question is thus at what point the state regulation sufficiently interferes with federal regulation that it should be deemed pre-empted under the Act.

In *English v. General Electric Co., supra,* we held that a state tort claim brought by an employee of a nuclear-fuels production facility against her employer was not pre-empted by a federal whistle-blower provision because the state law did not have a "direct and substantial effect" on the federal scheme. In the decision below, the Court of Appeals relied on *English* to hold that, in the absence of the approval of the Secretary, the OSH Act pre-empts all state law that "constitutes, in a direct, clear and substantial way, regulation of worker health and safety." We agree that this is the appropriate standard for determining OSH Act pre-emption. On the other hand, state laws of general applicability (such as laws regarding traffic safety or fire safety) that do not conflict with OSHA standards and that regulate the conduct of workers and non-workers alike would generally not be pre-empted. Although some laws of general applicability may have a "direct and substantial" effect on worker safety, they cannot fairly be characterized as "occupational" standards, because they regulate workers simply as members of the general public. In this case, we agree with the court below that a law directed at workplace safety is not saved from pre-emption simply because the State can demonstrate some additional effect outside of the workplace.

In sum, a state law requirement that directly, substantially, and specifically regulates occupational safety and health is an occupational safety and health standard within the meaning of the Act. That such a law may also have a nonoccupational impact does not render it any less of an occupational standard for purposes of pre-emption analysis. If the State wishes to enact a dual impact law that regulates an occupational safety or health issue for which a federal standard is in effect, § 18 of the Act requires that the State submit a plan for the approval of the Secretary.

IV

We recognize that "the States have a compelling interest in the practice of professions within their boundaries, and that as part of their power to protect the public health, safety, and other valid interests they have broad power to establish standards for licensing practitioners and regulating the practice of professions." But under the Supremacy Clause, from which our pre-emption doctrine is derived, "any state law, however clearly within a State's acknowledged power, which interferes with or is contrary to federal law, must yield." We therefore reject petitioner's argument that the State's interest in licensing various occupations can save from OSH Act pre-emption those provisions that directly and substantially affect workplace safety.

We also reject petitioner's argument that the Illinois acts do not regulate occupational safety and health at all, but are instead a "pre-condition" to employment. By that reasoning, the OSHA regulations themselves would not be considered occupational standards. SARA, however, makes clear that the training of employees engaged in hazardous waste operations is an occupational safety and health issue, and that certification requirements before an employee may engage in such work are occupational safety and health standards. Because neither of the OSH Act's saving provisions are implicated, and because Illinois does not have an approved state plan under § 18(b), the state licensing acts are pre-empted by the OSH Act to the extent they establish occupational safety and health standards for training those who work with hazardous wastes. Like the Court of Appeals, we do not specifically consider which of the licensing acts' provisions will stand or fall under the pre-emption analysis set forth above.

The judgment of the Court of Appeals is hereby

Affirmed.

3. CRIMINAL PROSECUTIONS OF EMPLOYERS

PEOPLE v. CHICAGO MAGNET WIRE CORP.
Supreme Court of Illinois
534 N.E.2d 962 (1989)

JUSTICE WARD delivered the opinion of the court:

The issue we consider on this appeal is whether the Occupational Safety and Health Act of 1970 (OSHA) preempts the State from prosecuting the defendants, in the absence of approval from OSHA officials, for conduct which is regulated by OSHA occupational health and safety standards.

Indictments returned in the circuit court of Cook County charged the defendants, Chicago Magnet Wire Corporation, and five of its officers and agents, with aggravated battery and reckless conduct. The individual defendants were also charged with conspiracy to commit aggravated battery. In substance, the indictments alleged that the defendants knowingly and recklessly caused the injury of 42 employees by failing to provide for them necessary safety precautions in the workplace to avoid harmful exposure to "poisonous and stupefying substances" used by the company in its manufacturing processes. On the defendants' motion, the trial court dismissed the charges, holding that OSHA has preempted the State from prosecuting the defendants for the conduct alleged in the indictments. The appellate court affirmed and we granted the State's petition for leave to appeal. . . .

Defendant Chicago Magnet Wire Corporation is an Illinois corporation whose principal business is the coating of wire with various substances and chemical compounds. [The individual defendants] are officers or managerial agents of the corporation.

The indictments charged that the defendants unreasonably exposed 42 employees to "poisonous and stupefying substances" in the workplace and prevented the employees from protecting themselves by "failing to provide necessary safety instructions and necessary safety equipment and sundry health monitoring systems." The indictments also alleged that the defendants improperly stored the substances, provided inadequate ventilation and maintained dangerously overheated working conditions. . . .

The circuit court dismissed the indictments, holding that OSHA preempts the States from prosecuting employers for conduct which is governed by Federal occupational health and safety standards, unless the State has received approval from OSHA officials to administer its own occupational safety and health plan. The court stated that because the conduct of the defendants set out in the indictments was governed by OSHA occupational health and safety standards, and the State had not received approval from OSHA officials to administer its own plan, it could not prosecute the defendants for such conduct.

The extent to which State law is preempted by Federal legislation under the supremacy clause of the Constitution of the United States is essentially a question of congressional intendment. Thus, if Congress, when acting within constitutional limits, explicitly mandates the preemption of State law within a stated situation, we need not proceed beyond the statutory language to determine that State law is preempted. Even absent an express command by Congress to preempt State law in a particular area, preemptive intent may be inferred where "the scheme of federal regulation is sufficiently comprehensive to make reasonable the inference that Congress 'left no room' for supplementary state regulation," or where the regulated field is one in which "the federal interest is so dominant that the federal system will be assumed to preclude enforcement of state laws on the same subject." Congressional intent to preempt State law may also be inferred where " 'the object sought to be obtained by the federal law and the character of obligations imposed by it may reveal the same purpose.' "

. . . .

The defendants read section 18(a) of OSHA to mean that under it Congress explicitly provided that the States are preempted from asserting jurisdiction over any occupational health and safety issue that is governed by OSHA occupational health and safety standards unless the State obtains approval from OSHA officials to administer its own occupational health and safety plan under section 18(b). Section 18 provides:

> (a) Nothing in this chapter shall prevent any State agency or court from asserting jurisdiction under State law over any occupational safety or health issue with respect to which no standard is in effect under section 655 of this title.

> (b) Any State which, at any time, desires to assume responsibility for development and enforcement therein of occupational safety and health standards relating to any occupational safety or health issue with respect to which a Federal standard has been promulgated under section 655 of this title shall submit a State plan for the development of such standards and their enforcement.

The defendants state that the conduct alleged in the indictments is governed by OSHA occupational health and safety standards. Specifically, they claim that OSHA standards define permissible exposure limits for the toxic substances which allegedly injured their employees and that OSHA also regulates the conduct that the prosecution says rendered the company's workplace unsafe. The defendants contend that therefore the trial court correctly held that, because the State had not received approval from OSHA officials pursuant to section 18(b) to prosecute the conduct set out in the indictments, the charges must be dismissed. We disagree.

Contrary to this argument, we cannot say that the language of section 18 of OSHA can reasonably be construed as explicitly preempting the enforcement of the criminal law of the States as to conduct governed by OSHA occupational health and safety standards. The language of section 18 refers only to a State's development and enforcement of "occupational health and safety standards." Nowhere in section 18 is there a statement or suggestion that the enforcement of State criminal law as to federally regulated workplace matters is preempted unless approval is obtained from OSHA officials.

The defendants argue, however, that because the charges set out in the indictments are based on conduct related to an alleged failure to maintain a safe work environment for their employees, in practical effect, the State is attempting to enforce occupational health and safety standards. They contend that the primary purpose of punishing conduct under criminal law is to deter conduct that society deems harmful and to secure conformity with acceptable norms of behavior. In that way, the criminal law establishes standards of care in society. When applied to conduct in the workplace, the defendants argue, criminal law serves the same purpose as OSHA, i.e., to compel adherence to a particular standard of safety that will minimize the risk of injury. . . .

We cannot accept the defendants' contention that it must be concluded that Congress intended to preempt the enforcement of State criminal laws in regard to conduct of employers in the workplace because the State criminal laws implicitly enforce occupational health and safety standards.

Although the imposition of sanctions under State penal law may effect a regulation of behavior as OSHA safety standards do, regulation through deterrence, however, is not the sole purpose of criminal law. For example, it also serves to punish as a matter of retributive justice. Too, whereas OSHA standards apply only to specific hazards in the workplace, criminal law reaches to regulate conduct in society in general. In contrast, occupational health and safety standards are promulgated under OSHA primarily as a means of regulating conduct to prevent injuries in the workplace.

It is to be observed also that for the most part OSHA imposes strict liability for violation of its standards, and that the criminal charges here allege that the defendants knowingly or recklessly injured several of their employees by unreasonably exposing them to toxic substances in the workplace. In order to be convicted of the charges, the State must establish that the defendants not only committed acts causing injury but that they also had the charged mental state, i.e., that they recognized the risk of injury and nevertheless willfully failed to take precautions to prevent injury. Thus, the criminal charges here do not set any new or other standards for workplace safety but rather seek to impose an additional sanction for an employer's conduct that, if proved, would certainly violate the duty set out in section 5(a) of OSHA.

There is nothing in the structure of OSHA or its legislative history which indicates that Congress intended to preempt the enforcement of State criminal law prohibiting conduct of employers that is also governed by OSHA safety standards. We would observe that the Supreme Court declared in *Jones v. Rath Packing Co.* (1977), 430 U.S. 519, 525, that "[w]here . . . the field which Congress is said to have pre-empted has been traditionally occupied by the States, . . . 'we start with the assumption that the historic police powers of the States were not to be superseded by the Federal Act unless that was the clear and manifest purpose of Congress.'"

Certainly, the power to prosecute criminal conduct has traditionally been regarded as properly within the scope of State superintendence. The regulation of health and safety has also been considered as "primarily, and historically" a matter of local concern. It cannot be said that it was the "clear and manifest" purpose of Congress to preempt the application of State criminal laws for culpable conduct of employers simply because the same conduct is also governed by OSHA occupational health and safety standards.

Although the provisions of OSHA are comprehensive, that Congress, in section 18, invited the States to administer their own occupational health and safety plans demonstrates that it did not intend to preclude supplementary State regulation. Indeed, section 2 of OSHA provides that the States are "to assume the fullest responsibility for the administration and enforcement of their occupational safety and health laws." It seems clear that the Federal interest in occupational health and safety was not to be exclusive.

Too, considering that until the recently increased interest in environmental safety charges were rarely brought under State law for conduct relating to an employer's failure to maintain a safe workplace, it would be unreasonable to say that Congress considered the preemption of State criminal law when enacting OSHA. Indeed, OSHA provides principally civil sanctions and only a few minor criminal sanctions for violations of its standards. Even for willful violations of OSHA standards which result in an employee's death an employer can be sentenced only to a maximum of six months' imprisonment. There is no penalty provided for conduct which causes serious injury to workers. It seems clear that providing for appropriate criminal sanctions in cases of egregious conduct causing serious or fatal injuries to employees was not considered. Under these circumstances, it is totally unreasonable to conclude that Congress intended that OSHA's penalties would be the only sanctions available for wrongful conduct which threatens or results in serious physical injury or death to workers.

We judge that the purpose underlying section 18 was to ensure that OSHA would create a nationwide floor of effective safety and health standards and provide for the enforcement of those standards. It was not fear that the States would apply more stringent standards or penalties than OSHA that concerned Congress but that the States would apply lesser ones which would not provide the necessary level of safety. . . . While additional sanctions imposed through State criminal law enforcement for conduct also governed by OSHA safety standards may incidentally serve as a regulation for workplace safety, there is nothing in OSHA or its legislative history to indicate that Congress intended to preempt the enforcement of State criminal law simply because of its incidental regulatory effect.

A question with resemblance to the one here was before the Supreme Court in *Silkwood v. Kerr-McGee Corp.*, 464 U.S. 238 (1984). There, the Court addressed the issue of whether State courts are preempted under the Atomic Energy Act from assessing punitive damages against defendants that cause injuries by excessive radiation. . . . [T]he Court had held [previously] that under the Atomic Energy Act the States are precluded from regulating the safety aspects of nuclear energy. The defendant argued that a "State-sanctioned award of punitive damages . . . punishes and deters conduct relating to radiation hazards" and therefore should be preempted by the Atomic Energy Act. The Court upheld the award notwithstanding the fact that it would have an incidental regulatory effect. . . .

We note, too, that Congress expressly stated that OSHA was not intended to preempt two bases of liability that, like criminal law, operate to regulate workplace conduct and implicitly set safety standards — State workers' compensation and tort law. Section 4(b)(4) of OSHA provides:

> Nothing in this chapter shall be construed to supersede or in any manner affect any workmen's compensation law or to enlarge or diminish or affect in any other manner the common law or statutory rights, duties, or liabilities of employers and employees under any law with respect to injuries, diseases, or death of employees arising out of, or in the course of, employment.

There is little if any difference in the regulatory effect of punitive damages in tort and criminal penalties under the criminal law. We see no reason, therefore, why what the Court declared in *Silkwood* should not be applied to the preemptive effect of OSHA. Also, if Congress, in OSHA, explicitly declared it was willing to accept the incidental regulation imposed by compensatory damages awards under State tort law, it cannot plausibly be argued that it also intended to preempt State criminal law because of its incidental regulatory effect on workplace safety.

It is a contention of the defendants that it is irrelevant that the State is invoking criminal law jurisdiction as long as the conduct charged in an indictment or information is conduct subject to regulation by OSHA. The defendants argue that the test of preemption is whether the conduct for which the State seeks to prosecute is in any way regulated by Federal legislation. The defendants assert that because the conduct charged in the indictments is conduct regulated under OSHA, a State prosecution for that conduct is preempted by OSHA. The contention is not convincing.

Simply because the conduct sought to be regulated in a sense under State criminal law is identical to that conduct made subject to Federal regulation does not result in State law being preempted. When there is no intent shown on the part of Congress to preempt the operation of State law, the "inquiry is whether 'there exists an irreconcilable conflict between the federal and state regulatory schemes.'" A conflict arises where "compliance with both federal and state regulations is a physical impossibility," or when State law "stands as an obstacle to the accomplishment and execution of the full purposes and objectives of Congress."

The defendants argue that the prosecutions here would conflict with the purposes of OSHA. They say that Congress intended that under OSHA the Federal government was to have exclusive authority to set occupational health and safety standards. The standards were to be set only after extensive research to assure that the standards would minimize injuries in the workplace but at the same time not be so stringent that compliance would not be economically feasible. The defendants correctly point out that although the States are given the opportunity to enforce their own occupational health and safety standards, the plan submitted must contain assurances that the State will develop and enforce standards "at least as effective" as OSHA's. Even after a State plan is approved, the Occupational Safety and Health Administration retains jurisdiction to enforce its own standards until it determines, based on three years of experience, that the State's administration of the plan is "at least as effective" as OSHA's.

The defendants maintain that Federal supervision over State efforts to enforce their own workplace health and safety programs would be thwarted if a State, without prior approval from OSHA officials, could enforce its criminal laws for workplace conduct of employers which is also subject to OSHA standards. They say that the States would thus be permitted to impose standards so burdensome as to exceed the bounds of feasibility or so vague as not to provide clear guidance to employers.

We believe the concern of the defendants is unfounded. We cannot see that State prosecutions of employers for conduct which is regulated by OSHA standards would conflict with the administration of OSHA or be at odds with its goals or purposes. On the contrary, prosecutions of employers who violate State criminal law by failing to maintain safe working conditions for their employees will surely further OSHA's stated goal of "assur[ing] so far as possible every working man and woman in the Nation safe and healthful working conditions." State criminal law can provide valuable and forceful supplement to insure that workers are more adequately protected and that particularly egregious conduct receives appropriate punishment.

The defendants' statements that the State will now have the ability to enforce more stringent standards than OSHA's does not persuade. As stated, the charges here are based on the defendants' alleged willful failure to remove workplace hazards which create a substantial probability that they will cause injuries to their employees. Thus, employers are not left without guidance as to what standard of care they must meet. Too, in practical terms, if a defendant were in compliance with OSHA standards it is unlikely that the State would bring prosecutive action. Enforcement of State criminal law in the workplace will not "stand as an obstacle to the accomplishment and execution of the full purposes and objectives of Congress."

To adopt the defendants' interpretation of OSHA would, in effect, convert the statute, which was enacted to create a safe work environment for the nation's workers, into a grant of immunity for employers responsible for serious injuries or deaths of employees. We are sure that that would be a consequence unforeseen by Congress.

. . . .

For the reasons given, the judgments of the appellate court and circuit court are reversed and the cause is remanded to the circuit court of Cook County for further proceedings.

NOTES

1. *Criminal Prosecution Under the Occupational Safety and Health Act.* The OSHAct primarily relies on a civil enforcement scheme to assure safe and healthful working conditions. The OSHAct does contain some

provisions establishing criminal penalties, however. The most significant is section 17(e), which provides for criminal liability in the event of a willful violation of a standard, rule, order, or regulation that causes the death of an employee. The maximum fine is $250,000 for an individual and $500,000 for an organization.

The scope of the criminal provisions is limited. Coverage only extends to employer violations that result in a worker's death and that are willful. A willful violation requires deliberate action taken with knowledge of the OSHA standard or with plain indifference to its requirements. Thus an employer who repeatedly violates a standard without meeting the willful test or who commits a violation that only results in a serious permanent injury is not subject to criminal prosecution.

A review of OSHA data from 1982 to 2002 identified 2,197 workplace deaths, which resulted in $106 million in civil OSHA fines and jail sentences totaling less than 30 years, of which 20 years were from the chicken-plant fire that killed 25 workers in North Carolina in 1991. OSHA concluded that 1,242 of the deaths were due to their employer's willful safety violations, but only 7 percent of these cases were referred by OSHA to the Department of Justice (DOJ) for criminal prosecution. David Barstow et al., *U.S. Rarely Seeks Charges for Deaths in Workplace*, N.Y. TIMES, Dec. 22, 2003, at A1. Between fiscal year 2001 and 2005, OSHA referred 38 cases to the DOJ for prosecution. *EEP Cases in FY 2005 Nearly Double Over Previous Year's Tally, OSHA Figures Show*, 35 O.S.H. Rep. (BNA) 1117 (December 8, 2005). The DOJ often declines to pursue cases referred by OSHA for criminal prosecutions, as it did in 92 of the 183 referred cases between 1974 (when referrals began) and 2005. *Id.*

2. *Criminal Prosecutions Under Other Federal Laws.* A partnership between OSHA, other federal agencies, and the Department of Justice to prosecute employers who are the most flagrant violators of workplace safety and other laws began in 2005. The strategy is designed to supplement the limited criminal penalties in the OSHAct with those included in environmental laws, statutes used for racketeering and white-collar crimes, some provision of the Sarbanes-Oxley Act, and other employment laws. David Barstow & Lowell Bergman, *With Little Fanfare, a New Effort to Prosecute Employers That Flout Safety Laws*, N.Y. TIMES, May 2, 2005, at A17. The approach resulted in Atlantic Scates Cast Iron Pipe Co, and four company officials being convicted of 32 counts involving the Clean Water Act, the Clear Air Act, and the OSHAct. *New Jersey Pipe Company Found Guilty Under Environmental, Worker Safety Laws*, 36 O.S.H. Rep. (BNA) 424 (May 4, 2006). Another example involved Kang Yeon Lee, who was sentenced to 30 months in prison and ordered to pay more than $2 million in compensation and penalties after pleading guilty to violating the OSHAct and federal wage and hour laws. *New York Builder Gets 30 Months in Prison, Fines of $2 Million for Safety, Pay Violations*, 36 O.S.H. Rep. (BNA) 567 (June 22, 2006).

3. *Criminal Prosecutions Under State OSHA Plans.* The Secretary of Labor has approved twenty-three state plans that provide for criminal penalties for violations of state health and safety programs. Some of these state plans contain criminal provisions significantly more comprehensive than those included in section 17(e) of the OSHAct. Minnesota has a particularly broad provision that permits fines and/or imprisonment of up to six months for *any* willful or repeated violations of the state plan — not just, as in the OSHAct, those that are willful and result in an employee's death. In California, an employer who commits a safety violation resulting in a worker's death can be fined $1.5 million and sent to prison for up to three years. Additional jurisdictions that have state plans providing criminal penalties for violations beyond those encompassed by section 17(e) of the OSHAct include Alaska, Indiana, and Washington.

4. *Criminal Prosecutions Under General Criminal Laws of the States.* The holding of the Illinois Supreme Court in *People v. Chicago Magnet Wire Corp.*, 534 N.E.2d 962 (Ill. 1989), is probably still valid despite the holding in *Gade v. National Solid Wastes Management Ass'n*, 505 U.S. 88 (1992), because the *Chicago Magnet Wire* prosecutions were based on general criminal laws. In contrast, state criminal penalties explicitly related to violations of occupational safety and health requirements are of doubtful validity. Thus, in the aftermath of the *Gade* decision, the Supreme Judicial Court of Massachusetts held in *Commonwealth v. College Pro Painters (U.S.) Ltd.*, 640 N.E.2d 777 (Mass. 1994), that state regulations, which provided for criminal sanctions for failing to comply with scaffold safety standards for painters, were preempted by OSHA construction industry standards.

5. *The Role of Criminal Prosecutions in Workplace Safety.* Criminal prosecutions, it is clear, will never be a common method of encouraging workplace safety. At most, after more than three decades, a dozen individuals have spent time in jail for violating the OSHAct. Thus, criminal prosecutions are unlikely to have any significant direct effect in encouraging workplace safety. Moreover, substantial resources are needed to prosecute criminal cases, resources that could be used in promulgating standards, inspecting workplaces, or enforcing civil penalties. What then is the appropriate role of criminal prosecutions?

On deterrence, the argument would have to be that criminal prosecutions tend to focus attention on workplace safety, and especially the attention of high-level executives who may not worry much about relatively modest civil fines paid out of corporate coffers, but may well worry about personal criminal consequences. The deterrence argument cannot be limited to the fate of the few who are actually prosecuted, but must also consider the extent to which the prosecutions raise public consciousness about workplace safety issues and about the extent of corporate responsibility for them, especially among corporate executives themselves. *See generally* V.S. Khanna, *Corporate Criminal Liability: What Purpose Does It Serve?*, 109 HARV. L. REV. 1477 (1996).

The criminal law also serves an important expressive function that must be considered in this context. Even if criminal prosecutions have no deterrent effect whatsoever, it may be that criminal prosecutions are justified as a societal statement of its strong disapproval of the types of conduct that result in prosecution. JOEL FEINBERG, DOING & DESERVING: ESSAYS IN THE THEORY OF RESPONSIBILITY 95-118 (1970).

4. TORT SUITS

A violation of an OSHA standard does not create a private right of action against an employer or a third party. Nor does an OSHA violation by itself create an exception to the exclusive remedy doctrine, which makes workers' compensation benefits the sole remedy of an employee against an employer for a work-related injury or disease. (As discussed in Chapter 22, an intentional injury of the employee by the employer may abrogate the exclusive remedy shield, and a violation of the OSHAct may help establish that the injury was intentional.)

The OSHAct does not preempt common law suits by an injured worker against a third party. *See, e.g., Pedraza v. Shell Oil Co.*, 942 F.2d 48 (1st Cir. 1991). Some courts have held that a violation of an OSHA standard can be used to help establish negligence. Thus, violation of an OSHA standard by an employer that resulted in an injury of the employee of a contractor was held to be negligence *per se* under Tennessee law, although the employee still had to prove the violation of the standard was the proximate cause of the worker's injury, as well as the extent of the injury. *Teal v. E.I. DuPont De Nemours & Co.*, 728 F.2d 799 (6th Cir. 1984). Other courts hold that violation of an OSHA standard is only some evidence of negligence. In still other jurisdictions, evidence that an OSHA standard was violated is inadmissible. *See* MARK A. ROTHSTEIN, OCCUPATIONAL SAFETY AND HEALTH LAW § 21:13 (2006).

Chapter 24
RETHINKING THE APPROACHES TO WORKPLACE INJURIES AND DISEASES

> "I am stunned by what people put up with around here," said Lawrie Morello. "You can see and smell the pollution. The noise never stops. People get hurt and killed and flowers won't even grow in the soil. What's a job worth?"
>
> "I'll tell you what it's worth," said [Tony] Miller, settling into the recliner at the liquor store. "It's worth $14.75 an hour."
>
> —Judy Peet, *Danger at a Decent Wage*, STAR-LEDGER (Newark, N.J.), April 10, 2006, at 1.

Part VIII explores two goals: the prevention and the compensation of work-related injuries and diseases. The Introduction to Part VIII introduced four approaches to reach these goals: the labor market, tort suits, workers' compensation, and safety and health laws. These approaches can be evaluated using the criteria of adequacy, equity, and delivery system efficiency. Adequacy requires the approach to provide sufficient resources and incentives to achieve the prevention and compensation goals. Equity requires that various classes of workers and employers be treated fairly under the approach. Delivery system efficiency requires the approach achieve the desired levels of adequacy and efficiency with the least use of delivery system resources. *See* John F. Burton, Jr., *Permanent Partial Disability Benefits, in* WORKPLACE INJURIES AND DISEASES: PREVENTION AND COMPENSATION 69, 95-101 (Karen Roberts et al., eds. 2005).

This chapter returns to these topics. To supplement the material in previous chapters, several selections concerned with the prevention and compensation of workplace injuries and diseases are provided. Each section begins with an excerpt from the 1987 ECONOMIC REPORT OF THE PRESIDENT and ends with a note providing an evaluation of the approach.

A. THE LABOR MARKET

ECONOMIC REPORT OF THE PRESIDENT 195-96 (1987)

Labor Market Safety Incentives

. . . The labor market provides strong incentives for employers to improve safety. In order to make a hazardous job attractive to workers, a firm must offer higher wages than it would have to pay otherwise. Wage premiums are a critical device for controlling job hazards because they provide employers with incentives to reduce hazards in order to reduce wage costs. . . .

In efficient labor markets, wage premiums result in appropriate matching of workers and jobs based on risk and other factors. . . . Imperfect information may militate against fully efficient labor market outcomes, thus providing a rationale for regulation or other government intervention. However, studies have found evidence that job safety information, although not perfect, is generally adequate. Workers have reasonably accurate perceptions of risks, and if they acquire new information suggesting risks greater than they originally had expected, their likelihood of quitting increases.

Workers' knowledge of health risks is probably less accurate than their knowledge of safety risks. . . . Government also has limited knowledge of occupational health hazards, but it can improve the information available to both employees and employers by supporting research on job safety and disseminating the results. Government, however, has no clear advantage over workers, labor unions, and employers in using this information to determine appropriate levels of workplace safety or the best way to reduce hazards.

Pecuniary costs of job injuries are commonly shifted to the general public by income transfers such as social security disability payments, welfare, and food stamps. This reduces firms' incentives to take safety measures, by enabling them to pay lower wage premiums. Even where information is not perfect or pecuniary externalities exist, however, wage premiums serve a useful function in providing safety incentives and in matching workers with jobs.

NOTE

An Evaluation of the Labor Market. How well does the labor market achieve the goals of prevention and compensation? The adequacy criterion would require that wage premiums for dangerous work be fully compensating, so that workers on average receive adequate compensation and employers accordingly receive the proper economic incentives to improve safety and health conditions at the workplace.

As the contrasting views of Rose-Ackerman versus Moore and Viscusi in Chapter 21 suggest, and as the selection from Ehrenberg attests, no clear answer exists as to whether the market is fully compensating workers for risk of injury. A particularly sharp attack on the compensating wage differential evidence was made by Dorman, who argues that most studies have been improperly specified and that, after controlling for industry level factors, the evidence for compensating wage differentials for most workers disappears. PETER DORMAN, MARKETS AND MORTALITY: ECONOMICS, DANGEROUS WORK, AND THE VALUE OF HUMAN LIFE (1996). And even those studies that do provide evidence of compensating differentials rely on a critical assumption:

> Furthermore, all of these results are premised on an assumption of individual rationality. If individuals do not fully understand the risk and respond to risks in a rational manner, then the risk tradeoff that people are actually making may not be those that researchers believe they are making based on objective measures of the risk.

W. Kip Viscusi, *The Value of Risks to Life and Health*, 31 J. ECON. LITERATURE 1912, 1938 (1993).

Since it is impossible to decide whether the wage differentials fully compensate workers for the risks of workplace injuries and diseases, a clear judgment on the adequacy criterion is impossible.

There is little doubt, however, that the labor market approach to prevention and compensation has serious equity problems. The evidence that union workers receive higher risk premiums than nonunion workers in jobs with comparable risks indicates an equity problem prior to the occurrence of any injuries that will, for example, distort the financial incentives for employers to improve workplace safety. Moreover, since injuries are to some extent due to chance, those workers who are injured are likely to experience much greater losses than the amount of the risk premiums they received before their injuries, while uninjured workers in the same facility will receive the risk premiums but experience no losses.

The deficiencies of the labor market as evaluated by the equity criterion are offset to some degree by the virtue of the approach in meeting the delivery system efficiency criterion. Measured by this standard — the minimal use of delivery system resources to achieve adequacy and equity — the labor market excels. Whether the superior record on the efficiency criterion justifies reliance on the labor market in light of the deficiencies on the equity criterion and the uncertainties on the adequacy criterion cannot be resolved "scientifically." Most observers, however, would probably be unwilling to rely solely on the market, which is one reason why we consider the other approaches to prevention and compensation, such as reliance on tort suits.

B. TORT SUITS

ECONOMIC REPORT OF THE PRESIDENT 190-91 (1987)

The Tort System

In addition to self-inflicted injury, harm can result from the actions of others. Tort law, the civil law governing harms other than breach of contract, serves to compensate persons injured by the negligent or wrongful conduct of others, and also to deter such conduct.

Two general rules of liability guide accident law — negligence and strict liability. Negligence is determined by reasonableness of conduct. If the injurer acted unreasonably, that is, failed to exercise due care, then ordinarily the injurer would be required to compensate the victim. Strict liability, on the other hand, focuses on whether a product that caused an injury was defective in such a way as to make it unreasonably dangerous for its intended use. Both standards seek to impose a duty of care; strict liability, however, allows demonstration of the breach of that duty by examination of the product itself.

The product user's degree of care also can affect the risk of accidents. In certain instances, the user can more easily eliminate or reduce the risk of injury than can the manufacturer. The rule of contributory negligence limits the scope of liability so that an injurer is not liable for harm that could have been avoided had the victim not been negligent. Many states have adopted the rule of comparative fault, under which an injurer is liable only for that share of the harm corresponding to the injurer's share of responsibility. Determining the reasonableness of a party's conduct depends in part on the costs of avoiding the accident. When both parties can affect the probability or seriousness of an accidental injury, the rule of negligence (or the rule of strict liability accompanied by the defense of contributory negligence or comparative fault) leads both the potential injurer and potential victim to behave reasonably to avoid accidents.

JOHN F. BURTON, JR. & JAMES R. CHELIUS, WORKPLACE SAFETY AND HEALTH REGULATIONS: RATIONALE AND RESULTS, in GOVERNMENT REGULATION OF THE EMPLOYMENT RELATIONSHIP 253, 272-74 (Bruce E. Kaufman ed., 1997)*

Theoretical stimulus of tort law to safety. When negligence is the legal standard used for tort suits, an injured employee may sue his employer for damages when the employer is at fault. If the employer has not taken proper measures to prevent accidents and thus is at fault, the employer will be liable for all of the consequences of the injury. The standard for the proper prevention measure was developed by Judge Learned Land and restated by Posner as:

> the judge (or jury) should attempt to measure three things in ascertaining negligence: the magnitude of the loss if an accident occurs; the probability of the accident's occurring; and the burden [cost] of taking precautions to prevent it. If the product of the first two terms, the expected benefit, exceeds the burden of precautions, the failure to take those precautions is negligence.

[Richard A. Posner, *A Theory of Negligence*, 1 J. LEGAL STUD. 29, 32 (1972).]

Posner argued that proper application of this standard will result in economically efficient incentives to avoid accidents. As Chelius notes, the added costs of determining liability in a court may appear to be inconsistent with achieving an efficient use of resources, since legal fees are usually a significant percentage of the total award. [JAMES R. CHELIUS, WORKPLACE SAFETY AND HEALTH 34-35 (1977).] The benefits of legal proceedings, however, *may* outweigh their costs if the incentives created by such a system are more accurate than those present under alternative systems.

Evidence on the tort law stimulus to safety. The generally accepted view is that tort suits were largely ineffective as a remedy for workplace injuries in the late 1880s and early 1900s. Not only were workplace injuries and fatalities increasing, but employees were generally unsuccessful in suits, in large part because of legal defenses available to employers, such as the contributory negligence defense that eliminated any recovery if the worker was negligent, even if the employer was negligent to a greater degree. The leading legal treatise on workers' compensation concludes that "the precompensation loss-adjustment system for industrial accidents was a complete failure. . . ."

[ARTHUR LARSON & LEX K. LARSON, LARSON'S WORKERS' COMPENSATION: DESK EDITION § 4.50 (1997).] However, Berkowitz and Berkowitz indicate that workers were beginning to enjoy considerable success with tort suits at the beginning of the workers' compensation era. [Edward D. Berkowitz & Monroe Berkowitz, *Challenges to Workers' Compensation: An Historical Analysis, in* WORKERS' COMPENSATION BENEFITS: ADEQUACY, EQUITY, AND EFFICIENCY 158, 160 (John D. Worrall & David Appel eds., 1985).] Perhaps the tort system if left in place for workplace injuries would have evolved and produced a major stimulus to workplace safety.

There are two types of empirical evidence that indicate skepticism is nonetheless warranted about the stimulus to workplace safety from tort suits. First, as previously discussed, Chelius found that the replacement of the negligence remedy with workers' compensation led to a reduction in workplace fatalities. Second, in other areas of tort law, there is a major controversy among legal scholars about whether the theoretical incentives for safety resulting from tort suits actually work. One school of thought is exemplified by Landes and Posner, who state that "although there has been little systematic study of the deterrent effect of tort law, what empirical evidence there is indicates that tort law . . . deters, even where, notably in the area of automobile accidents, liability insurance is widespread . . . and personal safety might be expected to be of greater concern than the potential financial consequences of an accident." [WILLIAM M. LANDES & RICHARD A. POSNER, THE ECONOMIC STRUCTURE OF TORT LAW 10 (1987).]

An opposing view on the deterrent effects of tort law is provided by Priest, who finds almost no relationship between liability payouts and the accident rate for general aviation, and states that: "This relationship between liability payouts and accidents appears typical of other areas of modern tort law as well, such as medical malpractice and products liability." [George L. Priest, *The Modern Expansion of Tort Liability: Its Sources, Its Effects, and Its Reform*, 5 J. ECON. PERSP. 31, 44 (1991).]

A survey of the deterrent effects of tort laws by Schwartz distinguished between a strong form of deterrence (as postulated by Landes and Posner) and a moderate form of deterrence, in which "tort law provides a significant amount of deterrence, yet considerably less than the economists' formulae tend to predict." [Gary T. Schwartz, *Reality in the Economic Analysis of Tort Law: Does Tort Law Really Deter?*, 42 UCLA L. REV. 377, 378-79 (1994).] Schwartz surveys a variety of areas where tort law is used, including motorist liability, medical malpractice, and product liability, and concludes that sector by sector the evidence undermines the strong form of deterrence but provides adequate support for the deterrence argument in its moderate form. As to workers' injuries, Schwartz . . . concludes "it is unclear whether a tort system or workers' compensation provides better incentives for workplace safety; in an odd way . . . [the studies are consistent] with the general idea that a properly designed set of liability rules can produce beneficial results."

Based on both the ambiguous historical experience of the impact of workers' compensation on workplace safety, and the current controversy over the deterrence effect in other areas of tort law, the law and economics theory concerning tort law does not provide much assistance in designing an optimal policy for workplace safety and health. We will be even more assertive in our assessment of the virtues of tort law as a strategy for improving workplace safety and health: we are sufficiently persuaded of the favorable effects of workers' compensation experience on safety, and sufficiently skeptical of the deterrent effects of tort suits, that we would resist the use of tort suits to deal with work injuries unless much more compelling evidence of the deterrent effect if produced.

NOTES

1. *The Tort System and Latent Diseases.* Would the tort system do a good job in preventing work-related diseases? In an analogous situation — legal actions against manufacturers of products that cause latent diseases — the deterrence effect of the tort system was criticized, Donald G. Gifford, *The Peculiar Challenges Posed by Latent Diseases Resulting From Mass Products*, 64 MD. L. REV. 613 (2005). Gifford identified three factors that frustrate the deterrence impact of liability: (1) the extended period between the time the product was distributed and the imposition of liability, (2) the frequent inability to attribute liability for damages to the activity that caused the harm, and (3) activities of parties other than the manufacturer that were contributing causes to the disease. Gifford argued that the questionable ability of the tort system to fulfill its loss avoidance objective suggests "that compensation for latent diseases should be handled by an administrative no-fault compensation system and that legislative or administrative regulation must play a larger role in preventing such harms."

2. *The Tort System and Insurance.* The deterrence or prevention effect of tort suits may also be muted if the tort-feasor purchases insurance, especially if the insurance contract covers punitive damages. However, insurance companies have incentives to address the deterrence objective through their underwriting and contracting practices. Tom Baker, *The Incidence, Scope, and Purpose of Punitive Damages: Reconsidering Insurance for Punitive Damages*, 1998 WIS. L. REV. 101 (1998).

3. *An Evaluation of Tort Suits.* The failure of most workers to recover damages for their workplace injuries meant that reliance on tort suits provided inadequate financial incentives to employers to prevent injuries as well as inadequate compensation for workers. There were, moreover, serious equity problems: some workers — those who were successful in their suits — may have done well, but other workers experienced significant uncompensated losses. Finally, the tort suits typically required long delays and required workers to pay legal fees from their awards, thus raising serious questions about the delivery system efficiency of the tort suit approach to prevention and compensation. These criticisms were major reasons why the workers' compensation programs began to be adopted by the states around 1910. Whether the modern tort system would do a better job is questionable in light of the recent scholarship on the deterrent effects of the tort system.

C. WORKERS' COMPENSATION

ECONOMIC REPORT OF THE PRESIDENT 197-98 (1987)

Workers' Compensation

. . . Except for the largest firms, which are allowed to self-insure, employers must buy insurance from a private carrier or a State insurance fund to cover their workers' compensation liabilities. . . . Premiums are experience-rated — that is, linked to past loss experience — only for larger firms. . . .

Although the impetus for adoption of workers' compensation was to replace employers' tort liability with a no-fault system, safety incentives were an additional consideration. Workers' compensation was expected to induce employers to provide greater workplace safety because each firm would assume the costs of its workers' injuries more predictably than under tort liability. The costs of industrial injuries thus would be included among other business costs, and employers would be motivated to reduce them by increasing job safety. This expectation of improved safety, however, overlooked factors that would undermine safety: reduced wage premiums in response to lower but more certain recovery of damages, and reduced incentives for employers to increase safety when workers' compensation premiums are not closely related to the injuries suffered by employees.

A growing body of research has found that workers' compensation benefits have unfavorable effects on safety. Higher benefits appear to increase both the frequency of work injuries and the number of compensation claims filed. One explanation for the positive connection is the claim effect. Even if actual injuries remain constant, workers are more likely to file claims when benefits are higher, thereby producing more reported injuries.

Lack of experience rating of workers' compensation premiums reduces an employer's incentive to invest in safety measures. A firm that is not forced to bear the full costs of compensating its workers for their injuries has a diminished incentive to make expenditures that promote safety. . . . Employers' safety incentives could be strengthened by requiring them to make a deductible payment and copayment on each claim. . . .

Workers' compensation has improved the reliability of compensation to injured workers. By replacing lost wages, it also has enabled injured workers to recuperate more fully before returning to work. There is evidence, however, analogous to findings on the effects of unemployment insurance, that higher levels of workers' compensation benefits create work disincentives. Recipients whose benefits are relatively high compared with their previous wages have longer durations of work disability. Work disincentive effects can be important: because benefits are not taxable, the after-tax rate of wage replacement for some workers exceeds 100 percent of their prior wages.

Although one goal of workers' compensation was to reduce the high transactions costs of litigation, many workers' compensation claims are still contested. Workers, moreover, are making liability claims with increasing frequency against suppliers of inputs, commonly in situations where adverse effects on health, such as those related to cancer, may be delayed. Such suits are not barred under the no-fault workers' compensation system.

NOTE

Economists' Logic, or Run That by Me Again, Please. The ECONOMIC REPORT OF THE PRESIDENT recognizes the distinction between two possible consequences of increases in workers' compensation benefits: a "true injury effect," in which the actual level of workplace risk may rise, and a "reporting effect," in which injured workers are more likely to report their injuries and press for higher payments. Which of these two possible explanations for a positive relationship between higher benefits and higher reported injuries should be of primary concern to policymakers? Which of these possible explanations is represented in the first sentence ("A growing body . . .") of the third paragraph in the passage from the ECONOMIC REPORT? Which is represented in the second sentence? The third? The fourth? What difference is there between the implications of the first and fourth sentence for the consequences of higher workers' compensation benefits in achieving the goal of promoting workplace safety? Of some interest is that the explanation in the first sentence appears to dominate the balance of the selection from the ECONOMIC REPORT.

H. ALLAN HUNT, ADEQUACY OF EARNINGS REPLACEMENT, in WORKERS' COMPENSATION PROGRAMS 127-34 (2004) *

A critical objective of workers' compensation programs is to maintain a socially acceptable income stream for disabled workers while they recover from job-related injuries or illnesses. This report addresses a key aspect of workers' compensation systems: to what extent to cash benefits paid to injured workers replace their lost earnings?

In this book, we examine earnings replacement in several ways. First, what are the earnings losses suffered by disabled workers, and to what extent are those losses replaced by the benefits received through workers' compensation programs? . . .

Next, to what extent are these benefits adequate? To answer this question, we must confront the issue of what we mean by "adequate" benefits. . . .

We use several yardsticks for wage replacement adequacy. First, we use the historical yardstick of replacing two-thirds of gross wages as a measure of benefit adequacy. While this may not be the ideal measure, 36 states now use it as their statutory replacement rate for temporary total disability (TTD). We acknowledge that this is a somewhat arbitrary choice, but it has the advantages of historical primacy, widespread acceptance, and analytical simplicity.

Second, we use the Model Workers' Compensation Act (Revised), promulgated by the Council of State Governments in 1974. The Model Act represented an attempt to specify the benefit structure that would constitute "best practice" in workers' compensation, largely through implementing the recommendations of the National Commission on State Workmen's Compensation Laws. While not all members of the panel approve of this measure, we use the standards of the Model Act as another yardstick to evaluate the overall benefit structure of workers' compensation programs.

Finally, we have a social policy interest in preventing workers and their families from becoming destitute because of work injuries. When the National Commission on State Workmen's Compensation Laws issued its report in 1972, maximum weekly benefits in many states were so low that full-time workers who had earned reasonable wages could fall into poverty while receiving workers' compensation benefits. To determine whether this is still occurring, we asked: "Are workers' compensation wage-replacement benefits sufficient to keep injured workers from falling below the official poverty line?" For this assessment we compare statutory benefit levels to the U.S. poverty threshold for a family of four.

Findings

Our historical analysis of statutory workers' compensation benefits found a significant upward trend in statutory benefit levels after the *Report of the National Commission on State Workmen's Compensation Laws* was released in 1972. With regard to the question of social adequacy, the average workers' compensation weekly benefit for TTD rose from about 80 percent of the poverty level for a family of four in 1972 to around 110 percent in 1998. However, substantial interstate variation remains, and average TTD benefits in 16 states still were below the poverty level in 1998.

When statutory workers' compensation benefits are measured against the benefit levels included in the Model Act (Revised) adopted by the Council of State Governments, it appears that TTD benefits have improved steadily relative to the Model Act, rising from an average of 60 percent in 1972 to nearly 90 percent by 1998. Trends in benefit levels for permanent disability claims and fatal claims also improved substantially in the 1970s but have been relatively constant for the past 20 years.

In summary, evidence from the analysis of statutory benefits suggests that TTD benefits rose relative to the poverty threshold and came closer to meeting the levels in the Model Act over time. No similar trend is evident for the more expensive permanent disability benefits.

The [National Academy of Social Insurance] panel believes it is vital to check these findings on statutory benefits with the results of recent empirical wage loss studies. The wage loss studies compare the benefits received by injured workers with estimates of the earnings they lost after the injury. Thus, wage loss studies offer two advantages over statutory benefit measures: 1) the measurement of actual benefits received, and 2) an improved estimate of wage losses due to disability.

. . . .

Most recently, Reville, Boden, *et al.* [ROBERT T. REVILLE ET AL., AN EVALUA-TION OF NEW MEXICO WORKERS' COMPENSATION PERMANENT PARTIAL

DISABILITY AND RETURN TO WORK (2001)] conducted a study of New Mexico PPD workers' compensation benefits. They also brought the results of the other wage loss studies into a common analytical framework to facilitate comparisons among five states. Focusing only on PPD claims, they extrapolated aggregate wage losses and benefits paid for 10 years after the injury. . . . [U]nder identical assumptions, 10-year wage replacement rates ranged from a low of 29 percent in Wisconsin to a high of 46 percent in New Mexico. No state exceeded 50 percent wage replacement for permanent partial disabilities.

Further, . . . aggregate wage losses continue at significant levels (15 to 20 percent) even four to five years after injury. Yet, most workers' compensation payments occur within the first two to three years. These results indicate that replacement rates for PPDs in the aggregate fall short of the yardstick of two-thirds of gross wages, often by a large margin.

MONROE BERKOWITZ & JOHN F. BURTON, JR., PERMANENT DISABILITY BENEFITS, in WORKERS' COMPENSATION 379-82 (1987) *

Efficient Permanent Disability Benefits

The question of efficiency concerns the administrative costs of providing benefits incurred by the participants in the workers' compensation delivery system, including employers, insurance carriers, workers, attorneys, and governmental agencies. The term *efficiency* is used to describe two concepts. . . . One meaning of efficiency, termed *myopic efficiency,* is that administrative costs are at the lowest possible level without regard to the quality of benefits provided. Although this disregard for quality is usually not made explicit, it appears that what some people mean by maximum efficiency is the cheapest delivery system. The other meaning of efficiency, termed *panoramic efficiency,* is that a particular quality of benefits is provided at the least possible administrative costs. Thus, if two delivery systems provide benefits of equal adequacy and equity, the delivery system that does so with lower administrative costs has greater panoramic efficiency.

We do not believe it is meaningful to say that one delivery system has lower administrative costs than another delivery system unless the differences in the quality of the benefits are specified. Only with the latter information can judgments be made about the relevant concept, namely the panoramic efficiency of the delivery systems. . . .

Evaluation using the efficiency criterion is especially difficult. For one thing, data on the expenses of administering the program that are borne by employers and others in the private sector, the amount of attorneys' fees, and the lags in payments of permanent disability benefits after a workers' condition is permanent and stationary, as well as a variety of other types of data relevant to the assessment of the efficiency of the delivery system, are scarce. Another reason the efficiency criterion is hard to apply is that the quality of benefits and the administrative costs must be simultaneously considered in order to evaluate the panoramic efficiency of a state's workers' compensation program. It would be foolish, for example, to prefer one jurisdiction merely because its administrative costs are lower than the costs in a second jurisdiction. The first jurisdiction's administrative costs may result from lower-quality benefits, and thus represent no greater panoramic efficiency. . . .

Application of the Efficiency Test. An important aspect of the efficiency test concerns the types of delivery system used to provide workers' compensation benefits. One model (typified by Wisconsin) relies on an active state agency that makes many decisions itself, closely supervises the operation of employers and private carriers, and limits the role for attorneys. A considerably different model (typified by the federally operated Longshore and Harbor Workers' Compensation Act) relies on the private parties, particularly attorneys, to make most of the decisions about benefit payments. The agency is essentially passive, although it will resolve disputes brought to it by the private parties. An intermediate model (typified by Florida prior to the 1979 reforms and by California) involves a state agency that conducts a minimal review of the decisions made by the private parties and that resolves disputes in a relatively high proportion of the cases, but that nonetheless relies on extensive attorney involvement to make the delivery system operate.

How attorneys are used is an important feature differentiating these three delivery system models. As recounted by many commentators on the history of workers' compensation, the original notion was that the elimination of the fault concept and the prescription of benefits by statute would enable employees to protect their interest without external assistance. From that standpoint, the substantial reliance on lawyers in California and Florida before 1979 suggests at the minimum a lack of myopic efficiency. And yet, the involvement of attorneys can also be viewed as a *prima facie* indictment of the idea that workers' compensation laws can be self-administering; attorneys may be in the system because they help achieve the criteria of adequate and equitable benefits. In other words, their involvement may represent a lack of myopic efficiency but not a lack of panoramic efficiency. Whether, in fact, attorneys help achieve the equity and adequacy of benefits is not clear *a priori*. On one hand, they receive fees that generally are subtracted from the workers' awards, which, in a nominal sense, reduce the adequacy of the benefits. On the other hand, attorneys increase the awards in some cases in which they are involved and probably have an indirect impact on the amount of benefits in other cases in which they are not involved (similar to the "threat" effect that unions have on wages in nonunionized firms). Thus on *a priori* grounds, the impact of attorneys on the adequacy of benefits is unclear. Likewise, the impact of attorneys on the equity of benefits is unclear. They may take cases in which benefits would otherwise be inappropriately low, or alternatively their involvement may be on a basis unrelated to the relative undercompensation of the case, such as the worker's membership in a union.

The data from Wisconsin, Florida, and California shed some light on the question of whether the use of attorneys improves panoramic efficiency. In terms of the ability to deliver benefits without litigation, Wisconsin clearly surpassed California and Florida before 1979. . . . More than 5 out of 6 permanent partial disability cases in Wisconsin were resolved without a contest (including use of compromise and release agreements). By contrast more than 2 out of 3 Florida permanent disability cases were controverted, and only 1 in 10 California permanent disability cases was resolved by use of informal ratings rather than reliance on a more litigious approach, such as use of a compromise and release agreement or a formal hearing before an Administrative Law Judge. A related finding is that legal fees amounted to only about 3 percent of benefits for the workers in our Wisconsin sample, compared to about 12 percent in Florida and about 6 percent in California.

Wisconsin thus appeared to be superior to California and Florida in the handling of permanent partial disability benefits without excessive litigation, thus providing some evidence that it had greater myopic efficiency. Moreover, the Wisconsin benefits for the workers in our samples were more adequate and more equitable than the Florida and California benefits, suggesting that the Wisconsin delivery system also provided greater panoramic efficiency than the delivery systems in the other two states. We believe this conclusion is valid even when consideration is taken of the administrative expenditures in both the public and private sectors, including the expenses of operating the state workers' compensation agencies and state courts as well as the cost of attorneys' fees for claimants, employers, and carriers. The Wisconsin agency has a particularly impressive record in terms of budget and staff compared to the other jurisdictions in our study. . . .

The Florida and California delivery systems are representative of the systems in most of the jurisdictions in our 10-state study. There appears to be a general concern for myopic efficiency in workers' compensation, which manifests itself in inadequate resources for state agencies and undue reliance on litigation. The consequence of this narrow concern appears to be a loss of panoramic efficiency.

JOHN F. BURTON, JR. & JAMES R. CHELIUS, WORKPLACE SAFETY AND HEALTH REGULATIONS: RATIONALE AND RESULTS, in GOVERNMENT REGULATION OF THE EMPLOYMENT RELATIONSHIP 253, 264-67 (Bruce E. Kaufman ed., 1997) [*]

Workers' compensation and experience rating. The workers' compensation program in each state relies on two levels of experience rating to promote safety. Industry-level experience rating establishes an insurance rate for each industry that is largely based on prior benefit payments by the industry. Firm-level experience rating determines the workers' compensation premium for each firm above a minimum size by comparing its prior benefit payments to those of other firms in the industry. . . .

The essence of the "pure" neoclassical economics approach is that the introduction of workers' compensation (1) will lead to reduced incentives for workers to avoid injuries, assuming that they did not purchase private disability insurance plans prior to the introduction of workers' compensation, and (2) will lead to reduced incentives for employers to prevent accidents, if assumptions such as perfect experience rating are dropped.

In contrast, the OIE ["old" institutional economics] approach argues that the introduction of workers' compensation with experience rating should improve safety because the limitations of knowledge and mobility and the unequal bargaining power for employees mean that the risk premiums generated in the labor market are inadequate to provide employers the safety incentives postulated by the pure neoclassical economics approach. Commons . . . a leading figure in the OIE approach . . . asserted that experience rating provides employers economic incentives to get the "safety spirit" that would otherwise be lacking. [JOHN R. COMMONS, INSTITUTIONAL ECONOMICS: ITS PLACE IN POLITICAL ECONOMY 804-05 (1934).] The modified neoclassical economics approach would also accept the idea that experience rating should help improve safety by providing stronger incentives to employers to avoid accidents. . . . Where the OIE theorists would probably disassociate themselves from the modified neoclassical economics theorists would be the latter contingent's emphasis on the moral hazard problem aspect of workers' compensation, which could result in more injuries.

A number of recent studies of the workers' compensation program provide evidence that should help us evaluate the virtues of the pure neoclassical economics, the modified neoclassical economics, and the OIE approaches. However, the evidence is inconclusive. One survey of the literature by Boden concluded that: "research on the safety impacts has not provided a clear answer to whether workers' compensation improves workplace safety." [Leslie I. Boden, *Creating Economic Incentives: Lessons from Workers' Compensation Systems, in* PROCEEDINGS OF THE FORTY-SEVENTH ANNUAL MEETING 282, 285 (Industrial Relations Research Association, 1995).] In contrast, a recent survey by Butler found that, with the exception of the study by Chelius and Smith, most recent studies provide statistically significant evidence that experience rating "has had at least some role in improving workplace safety for large firms." [Richard J. Butler, *Safety Incentives in Workers' Compensation, in* 1995 WORKERS' COMPENSATION YEAR BOOK I-82, I-87 (John F. Burton, Jr. & Timothy P. Schmidle eds., 1994); James R. Chelius & Robert S. Smith, *Experience-Rating and Injury Prevention, in* SAFETY AND THE WORKFORCE 128 (John D. Worrall ed., 1983).] Based on our knowledge of the literature, we believe the Butler conclusion is more reasonable, although additional research is clearly warranted in order to support this finding. Some estimates of the magnitude of the safety effect are substantial: Durbin and Butler suggest that a 10% increase in workers' compensation costs may reduce fatality rates by 4.1% to 15.4%. [David Durbin & Richard J. Butler, *Prevention of Disability from Work-related Source: The Roles of Risk Management, Government Intervention, and Insurance, in* NEW APPROACHES TO DISABILITY IN THE WORKPLACE (Terry Thomason et al. eds., 1998).] This evidence on experience rating is consistent with the positive impact on safety postulated by the OIE approach and the modified neo-classical economists, and inconsistent with the pure neoclassical view that the use of experience rating should be irrelevant or may even lead to reduced incentives for employers to improve workplace safety.

There is also evidence that the presence of workers' compensation benefits leads to changes in worker behavior. Thomason and Burton summarize a number of studies that found the reported frequency and severity of workers' compensation claims increase in response to higher benefits, which suggests that a moral hazard problem exists. [Terry Thomason & John F. Burton, Jr., *Economic Effects of Workers' Compensation in the United States: Private Insurance and the Administration of Compensation Claims*, 11 J. LAB. ECON., (Jan. 1993).] Caution is needed in interpreting these studies, however, since the increased frequency or severity reported in the claims can result from a "true injury effect" (workers take more risks as a result of higher benefits and as a result actually experience more injuries) or from the "reporting effect" (workers report claims that would not have been reported as a result of the higher benefits, and/or extend their period of reported disability because of the higher benefits). Most studies of the relationship between workers' compensation benefits and the frequency and severity of claims have not distinguished between the true injury and reporting effects. Durbin and Butler conclude that the latter effect dominates, which implies that the concerns of modified neoclassical economists that the use of workers' compensation benefits to provide ex post compensation for injured workers will lead to more injuries may be exaggerated.

TERRY THOMASON, ECONOMIC INCENTIVES AND WORKPLACE SAFETY, in WORKPLACE INJURIES AND DISEASES: PREVENTION AND COMPENSATION 9, 26-27 (Karen Roberts et al., eds., 2005) [*]

Out of 14 studies reviewed here, 11 found evidence that experience rating results in an amelioration of workplace health and safety. This evidence was produced by research that is remarkably mixed with respect to both data sources and methodology. And, as indicated, a careful examination reveals that studies failing to detect this relationship were methodologically weaker than those that did. Taken as a whole the evidence is quite compelling: experience rating works.

However, as Hyatt and Thomason point out, the leap from the observation that experience rating is associated with lower injury or claims rates to the conclusion that experience rate enhances firm safety is short, but perilous. Experience rating may lead to increased claims management by employers, who file claims, as well as pro-active staffing practices designed to screen job applicants likely to file a workers' compensation claim. This has the effect of reducing injury reporting, while leaving workplace hazards undisturbed. Two studies show experience rating increases employers claims management activity.

. . . .

Using a survey data set consisting of over 450 Quebec manufacturers, Thomason and Pozzebon (2002) examined the estimated relationship between experience rating and a wide range of firm health and safety and claims management practices. . . . They found that experience-rated firms were both more likely to engage in more aggressive claims management and to make greater effort to increase workplace health and safety. Interestingly, however,

---

[*] Copyright © 2005 by the W.E. Upjohn Institute for Employment Research. Reprinted with permission.

the evidence also suggested that high wage firms are more likely to reduce workers' compensation claim costs by increasing their accident prevention efforts (relative to their claims management efforts) than low wage firms. This result implies that there may be a "high road" and a "low road" response to experience rating.

NOTE

Evaluation of Workers' Compensation. Evaluation of the workers' compensation program by use of the criteria of adequacy, equity, and delivery system efficiency is complicated by the decentralized nature of the program. Each state has its own statute and set of practices and so generalizations are difficult. With that caveat in place, what brief assessment is possible?

The compensation goal for workers' compensation requires that two-thirds of income lost because of work-related injuries or diseases be replaced by workers' compensation benefits in order to meet the adequacy standard established by the National Commission on State Workmen's Compensation Laws. At the time the National Commission submitted its report in 1972, only one state met the commission's essential recommendation that the maximum weekly benefit for temporary total disability in each state be at least 100% of that state's average weekly wage. (Since the typical workers' compensation statute provides that the worker gets the *lesser* of two-thirds of the worker's pre-injury wage or the maximum weekly benefit prescribed by the state statute, a low maximum can limit a worker's recovery.) As of January 2005, thirty-two states plus the District of Columbia had maximum weekly benefits that were at least 100% of the jurisdiction's average weekly wage. Thus — with some notable exceptions — most states now probably provide benefits for temporary disability that are generally adequate.

While temporary total disability benefits are the most common type of worker' compensation cash benefits, permanent partial disability (PPD) benefits are the most expensive type of cash benefits and provide the greatest amount of protection to workers with relatively serious injuries. The recent studies discussed by Allan Hunt indicate that the PPD benefits replaced less than half of lost wages for workers in the five states and there is no reason to assume that most other states would be markedly different. Thus, there appears to be a serious adequacy problem for this component of the workers' compensation program.

Workers' compensation has serious equity problems in meeting the compensation goal. While benefits may be generally adequate nationally, significant interstate differences in liberality of benefits mean that workers with similar earnings losses are treated differently depending on where they receive benefits. Consider this westward journey as of January 2005: the maximum weekly benefit for a worker who was permanently and totally disabled was $588 in Indiana, $1,012 in Illinois, and $1,133 in Iowa.

The equity problem in workers' compensation involves much more than interstate differences in statutory levels of benefits. There are also significant intrastate differences in how workers are treated. This is particularly true for those workers who receive permanent partial disability benefits. As discussed in Monroe Berkowitz & John F. Burton, Jr., Permanent Disability Benefits in Workers' Compensation 373-78 (1987), the approaches used to provide permanent partial disability benefits did a poor job of matching benefits to actual losses of earnings in California, Florida, and Wisconsin. Some workers received more benefits than they experience in lost wages, while other workers had only a small proportion of lost wages replaced by workers' compensation benefits. A recent study confirmed the lack of horizontal equity in the PPD benefits provided in the California workers' compensation program, and found "substantial and systematic variation in proportional earnings losses for impairments to different regions of the body, even though these impairments have very similar ratings [and thus received very similar PPD benefits]." Robert T. Reville et al., An Evaluation of California's Permanent Disability Rating System 89 (2005).

The delivery system efficiency criterion as applied to the compensation goal of workers' compensation is also widely violated, as indicated in the Berkowitz and Burton analysis. The costs of the legal system in California — including attorneys' fees, payments to doctors to prepare reports for litigation purposes and to testify, and the state's expenditures for administrative law judges and support personnel for workers' compensation cases — exceeded $1 billion per year in the early 1990s.

The prevention goal may be better served by workers' compensation, according to the evidence presented by Burton and Chelius and by Thomason in the preceding articles. The workers' compensation approach to prevention may be efficient, since the incentives to safety are produced by the experience rating plans that are relatively easy to administer. However, the approach may not provide adequate incentives for safety because many firms do not qualify for firm-level experience rating and the amounts of PPD benefits are inadequate. Moreover, an equity problem exists with the workers' compensation approach to promoting safety: it is generally small firms that are not eligible for experience rating and thus receive muted economic incentives to improve safety and health conditions in the workplace.

D. THE OCCUPATIONAL SAFETY AND HEALTH ACT

ECONOMIC REPORT OF THE PRESIDENT 182, 198-201 (1987)

Government Management of Risk

Government provides the legal and judicial framework for the market and tort systems, offers insurance against some risks, imposes regulatory standards, and operates programs to control risk directly. . . .

Several circumstances may provide a rationale for government regulation. First, consumers may lack the information or the ability to assess particular risks accurately. Second, individuals or firms fail in some cases to take account of the costs of harm they impose on others. The tort system may not be able to force a person who causes harm to bear these costs if the person's wealth is insufficient to compensate the victim, the cost of using the tort system is too high, or the person who caused the harm cannot be identified. Third, if markets and the tort system cannot adequately control externalities such as those leading to environmental pollution, government regulation may be warranted. . . .

Regulation of Job Safety

. . . Compared with the magnitude of safety incentives provided in the market, OSHA's fines and enforcement activities are small. One estimate of wage premiums generated by job risks is approximately $90 billion per year, which compares with about $9 million in OSHA fines. By comparison, workers' compensation benefits are about $20 billion annually.

A number of studies have found that OSHA's activities have not been effective in promoting workplace safety. . . . Over recent decades, the job fatality rate has declined fairly steadily by more than 2 percent per year. OSHA has not made an identifiable difference in this rate of decline. One recent study, however, has found that OSHA's activities have resulted in a small reduction in work injuries. It is more difficult to assess OSHA's effects on health, because of the time lag between a worker's exposure to a toxic chemical or environmental hazard and the manifestation of disease. This Administration has taken steps to enhance the effectiveness and reduce the burdens of OSHA's inspections. Inspections are now less confrontational and are targeted toward high-risk firms and serious workplace hazards.

OSHA's effects on health and safety may be small because of the type of regulations it has promulgated. Many require specific changes in the physical work environment rather than encouraging safe behavior. For example, OSHA has not required the use of automobile safety belts, although motor vehicle fatalities account for about one-third of total work deaths. . . . Even in manufacturing, motor vehicle deaths are close to 20 percent of work deaths. . . .

Although precise causation of work injuries is difficult to establish, studies show that individual behavior is a major factor in many work accidents. Studies of occupational fatalities have found that 9 to 40 percent are alcohol-related. . . .

A major criticism of OSHA is that many of its regulations have unnecessarily increased costs by preventing employers from using flexible means to meet health and safety goals. In contrast, OSHA's hazard communication rule requires that workers be informed about chemical hazards, but leaves employers leeway in implementation. . . .

Many of OSHA's standards increase costs and reduce productivity and competitiveness. Where OSHA's rules increase capital requirements, they also reduce employment opportunities, by encouraging the substitution of capital for labor. Where OSHA's rules specify characteristics of workplace design, they impose fixed costs that tend to favor larger firms over smaller ones.

The evidence on whether workers' compensation and OSHA have improved safety is mixed at best. Most studies indicate that these programs have failed to reduce job injuries in the aggregate. Although workers' compensation achieved some of its goals, it also may have undermined safety incentives. Both workers' compensation and OSHA have generated costs and indirect effects that have tended to reduce productivity.

NOTE

Overwhelmed by the Market? The ECONOMIC REPORT OF THE PRESIDENT indicates that, "Compared with the magnitude of safety incentives provided in the market, OSHA's fines and enforcement activities are small." How small? The ratio of wage premiums to OSHA fines in the data provided by the REPORT is 10,000 to 1 — $90 *billion* in wage premiums to $9 *million* in OSHA fines.

JOHN F. BURTON, JR. & JAMES R. CHELIUS, WORKPLACE SAFETY AND HEALTH REGULATIONS: RATIONALE AND RESULTS, in GOVERNMENT REGULATION OF THE EMPLOYMENT RELATIONSHIP 253, 276-80 (Bruce E. Kaufman ed., 1997)*

The evidence suggests that the OSHAct has done little to improve workplace safety. The workplace fatality rate declined by 57% between 1970 (the year the OSHAct was enacted) and 1993. However, Kniesner and Leeth point out that the drop in the frequency of workplace fatalities from 1947 to 1970 (the thirteen years prior to OSHA) was 70% larger than the drop in the thirteen years after OSHA, and assert that "OSHA might actually have slowed the downward trend in fatal injuries." Kniesner and Leeth also found "no downward trend in either the total frequency of workplace injuries or the frequency of injuries resulting in at least one lost workday." . . . [Thomas J. Kniesner & John D. Leeth, *Abolishing OSHA*, 18 REGULATION 46, 49.]

Several possible reasons have been offered for the apparent failure of the OSHAct to improve workplace safety. Kniesner and Leeth note that the self-employed account for about 9% of the workforce but about 20% of all workplace fatalities; these workers are not covered by the OSHAct. In addition, [the Bureau of Labor Statistics] found that 40% of recent workplace fatalities were from transportation accidents and about 20% from assaults and other violent acts, and Kniesner and Leeth argue these leading causes of work-place deaths "are unlikely to be reduced much by OSHA inspections." [*Id.*]

OSHA's ineffectiveness in part may be due to the lack of inspection activity . . . . According to Kniesner and Leeth, "the federal government has six times more fish and game inspectors than workplace health and safety inspectors." [*Id.* at 48.] But the evidence also suggests that transferring resources from walleye inspection to wall-to-wall plant inspections may be imprudent. Kniesner and Leeth reviewed the empirical studies of OSHA inspections and concluded "that OSHA has reduced injuries by no more than 4.6%. OSHA's impact, however, may be considerably smaller than 4 to 5%, considering that the majority of studies have found neither an abatement nor a deterrence effect from OSHA inspections." [*Id.* at 50.] Smith provided a more exhaustive review of the studies of OSHA inspections, and reached a similar conclusion:

---

the studies "suggest that inspections reduce injuries by 2 to 15%" although the estimates often are not statistically significant (and thus cannot be confidently distinguished from zero effect). [Robert S. Smith, *Have OSHA and Workers' Compensation Made the Workplace Safer?, in* RESEARCH FRONTIERS IN INDUSTRIAL RELATIONS & HUMAN RESOURCES 557, 566-71 (David Lewin et al. eds., 1992).]

Several recent studies have provided a more favorable assessment of the OSHA inspection process. Weil examined the custom woodworking industry and found that OSHA inspections resulted in improved compliance with a set of OSHA standards particularly relevant for that industry. However, Weil was unable to determine if the improved compliance with OSHA standards resulted in lower injury rates. [David Weil, *If OSHA Is So Bad, Why Is Compliance So Good?*, 27 RAND J. ECON. 618 (1996).] Even more promising results were provided by Gray and Scholz, who examined firms that had been inspected more than once for exceeding OSHA exposure limits for dangerous substances and found that the effect of an inspection leading to a penalty was to reduce the firm's injury rate by 20% over the following three years. [WAYNE B. GRAY & JOHN T. SCHOLZ, DO OSHA INSPECTIONS REDUCE INJURIES? A PANEL ANALYSIS (National Bureau of Economics Research, Working Paper No. 3774, 1991).] However, even Dorman, who supports an aggressive public policy to reduce workplace injuries, provided a qualified interpretation of such evidence: "these new results portray an OSHA with unfulfilled potential for improving working conditions . . . however, even the most optimistic reading indicates that . . . more vigorous enforcement alone cannot close the gap between US safety conditions and those in other OECD countries." [PETER DORMAN, MARKETS AND MORTALITY: ECONOMICS, DANGEROUS WORK, AND THE VALUE OF HUMAN LIFE 196 (1996).]

[Others] are more optimistic about the potential impact of OSHA inspections:

> Analysts who have attempted to isolate OSHA's impact using econometric models have produced inconsistent results. To the abolitionists these equivocal results suggest that OSHA is ineffective. However, a more plausible interpretation is that they demonstrate OSHA's unrealized potential.

[Thomas O. McGarity & Sidney A. Shapiro, *OSHA's Critics and Regulatory Reform*, 31 WAKE FOREST L. REV. 587, 596 (1996).]

OSHA inspections might be more effective if the size of the monetary penalties were increased or if criminal sanctions were utilized more frequently. But some critics of OSHA are skeptical this would help; Kniesner and Leeth argue that "the economic incentives to improve safety by reducing compensating wage differentials and workers' compensation expenses far surpass the safety-enhancing incentives from the relatively small fines currently imposed by OSHA." [Kniesner & Leeth, *supra,* at 55.] Even if OSHA fines were doubled, the amounts would be far surpassed by these other sources of economic incentives.

While the inspection and fines approach to improving safety relied on by OSHA is thus of questionable effectiveness based on the evidence concerning trends in workplace fatalities and injuries, and the studies of the impact of inspections, some critics of OSHA have identified other problems. Kniesner and Leeth argue that the annual compliance costs with OSHA health and safety standards are $11 billion (considering the effect on productivity and the cost of OSHA-mandated capital equipment), while the upper range of the benefits of OSHA in terms of reducing injuries is $3.6 billion a year. [Kniesner & Leeth, *supra,* at 50-51.] This unimpressive cost-benefit ratio is in part a result of the excessive stringency of some of the various safety and health standards that have been promulgated by OSHA. Viscusi examined OSHA standards using an implicit value of life of $5 million as the standard for efficient regulation. [W. Kip Viscusi, *Economic Foundations of the Current Regulatory Reform Efforts*, 10 J. ECON. PERSP., 119, 124-25 (1996).] Four of the five OSHA safety regulations adopted as final rules had costs per life saved of less than $5 million; only the 1987 grain dust standard with $5.3 million per life saved failed the efficiency test proposed by Viscusi. In contrast, only one of the five OSHA health regulations adopted as final rules had costs per life saved of less than $5 million, namely the 1983 Hazard Communication Standard that cost $1.8 million per life saved. The four health standards that failed the efficiency tests had costs that ranged from $17.1 million per life saved (the 1987 benzene standard) to $72,000 million per life saved (the 1987 formaldehyde standard).

The Viscusi analysis has been challenged by Stone, who specifically focuses on the formaldehyde standard. Viscusi confined his analysis of the benefits of the standard to the number of lives saved without considering the other beneficial effects of OSHA standards, such as reductions in the number of injuries and illnesses. Stone indicates that the OSHA regulations typically prevent roughly 5 to 25 injuries for every life saved. However the formaldehyde standard has an extraordinarily high ratio of reduced illnesses to reduced fatalities. According to OSHA's estimates, the standard prevents approximately 17,000 illnesses per year and 0.6 deaths per year, for a ratio of 30,000 avoided illnesses for every life saved. Stone, using an implicit value of a typical avoided illness or injury of $20,000 to $50,000 (which he attributes to Viscusi) calculates that the illness-reduction benefits of the OSHA formaldehyde standard are between $340 million and $850 million annually, with a midpoint of about $600 million. Since OSHA estimates that the annualized cost of the standard is only $64 million, Stone argues that the cost-benefit test of efficiency is clearly met. [Robert F. Stone, *Correspondence on Benefit-Cost Analysis*, 11 J. ECON. PERSP. 187 (1997).]

To be sure, cost-benefit analysis of health standards issued under the OSHAct is not legal, and so those standards that fail the cost-benefit test (considering both lives saved plus injuries and illnesses avoided) do not violate the letter and presumably the purpose of the law. But to the extent that the rationale . . . for regulation of health is that workers lack enough information to make correct decisions and therefore the government is in a better position to make decisions about how to improve workplace health, the evidence on the variability and magnitude of the cost/benefit ratios for OSHA health standards is disquieting. Rather than OSHA standards reflecting interventions in the market place that overcome deficiencies of the market, the explanation of why the stringency of regulation varies so much among industries would appear at best to be a result of technology-based decisions that could well aggravate the alleged misallocation of resources resulting from operation of the market, and at worst could reflect relative political power of the workers and employers in various industries.

NOTES

1. *Evaluation of OSHA.* The goal of the OSHAct is the prevention of workplace injuries and diseases. For the first two decades after the Act was enacted, there was no clear decline in the injury and illness rates. The total number of claims per 100 workers declined from 10.9 in 1972 to 8.9 in 1992, but during the same period, the number of lost workday cases per 100 workers increased from 3.3 in 1972 to 3.9 in 1992. After 1992, however, both measures of workplace injuries and diseases rapidly declined. By 2004, the total number of claims per 100 workers was 4.8 and there were 2.5 lost workday cases per 100 workers, both record low numbers.

Secretary of Labor Elaine Chao celebrated the thirtieth anniversary of the effective date of the OSHAct by stating: "OSHA, its state partners, employers and employees together share the credit for the progress that has been done." *Decreasing Job Fatalities and Injuries Cited During OSHA's 30 Years as Federal Agency*, 31 O.S.H. Rep. (BNA) 414 (May 3, 2001).

But does OSHA deserve credit for achieving a reduction during the last 35 years in the injury and illness rates and thus meet the adequacy criterion for the prevention goal? Some of the improvement is safety is due to the declining importance of manufacturing, which has injury rates higher than in most other sectors of the economy. Most of the studies discussed in the excerpt from Burton and Chelius suggest that OSHA inspections probably do not significantly reduce the injury rate. Moreover, the effectiveness of inspections on reducing injuries appears to be declining. An OSHA inspection imposing a penalty reduced lost-workday injuries by about 19% in 1979 and by about 11% in 1987-1991, but only by a statistically insignificant 1% in 1992-98. Wayne B. Gray & John M. Mendeloff, *The Declining Effects of OSHA Inspections of Manufacturing Injuries, 1979-1998*, 58 IND. & LAB. REV. 571 (2005). The limited contribution to safety from additional inspections is also suggested by an interesting relationship. Between 1972 and 1992, when there was no clear decline in injury rates, the number of OSHA inspections exceeded 42,000 per year in every year but 1972. However, between 1993 and 2005, when injury rates rapidly declined, the number of OSHA inspections was less than 40,000 per year in every year but 1994. Moreover, the total number of violations cited in OSHA inspections was in excess of 100,000 per year in every year between 1972 and 1994 (except 1982), but was less than 100,000 per year in every year between 1995 and 2005

What may have helped OSHA reduce workplace injuries and illnesses is the relatively new emphasis on criminal prosecutions and the policy of megafines, which has raised the consequences for flagrant violations of the Act into the million-dollar range. Annual fines never exceeded $25 million until 1988, but have never been less than $65 million since 1990.

One continuing problem that OSHA faces is the inability to promulgate new standards at a reasonable pace. This problem has been aggravated in recent years by political considerations.

> Since 1994, significantly fewer Occupational Safety and Health Administration regulations have been promulgated than had been in the previous decade. Whether the slowdown can be linked directly to the shift in political philosophy in the Congress, or because of a combination of factors, many OSHA observers agree that job safety and health regulations have slowed to a trickle, particularly those described as "economically significant" with an impact of $100 million or more on the economy.

Dramatic Slowdown of OHSA Regulations Seen Since Republicans Swept Into Congress, 35 O.S.H. Rep. (BNA) 916 (October 13, 2005).

Equity is also a serious problem for OSHA. Most of the current OSHA standards are the "interim standards" that were derived from preexisting federal standards or voluntary organization guidelines. Some industries were affected more than others by this hodgepodge of regulations, and many are seriously out of date. A trade association of crane manufacturers critiqued the existing OSHA standard that was originally an ANSI standard issued in 1968 and was adopted by OSHA in 1971 as an interim standard and never updated. The trade association wrote to OSHA: "It is inconceivable that OSHA regulations reference a standard that does not cover hydraulic cranes when at least 80 percent of the cranes in use today are hydraulic." *Industry Group Asks for Updated Standard; Rule is Not Applicable to Majority of Cranes*, 31 O.S.H. Rep. (BNA) 233 (March 15, 2001). The industry group may take comfort from the recent assurance from OSHA Administrator Edwin Foulke, Jr. that "I've been looking at Cranes and Derricks, because I want to move that along." Josh Cable, *ASSE: Will Foulke's OSHA Set More Standards?*, OCCUPATIONAL HAZARDS (June 13, 2006), *available at* http://www.occupationalhazards.com/articles/15286.

The thirty-five years of promulgation of new standards have not reduced the disparity among industries in the effect of the standards. The new standards promulgated in this period have had varying success in the courts and, again, failure of the generic rulemaking approach has left the permissible exposure levels for some substances vastly out of date, while other substances have more appropriate standards based on our current knowledge of health risks. Economists have used one of their favorite analytical tools — cost-benefit analysis — to point out that the compliance costs per life saved vary considerably among different OSHA standards.

There are also equity problems with OSHA because of the variations among states with their own safety programs — with different degrees of enforcement and stringency of standards — and between the federal OSHA program and the state-run programs. States that administered their own programs are associated with fewer fatalities than states regulated by the national OSHA program, and had all states been in charge of safety, over 14,000 fewer workplace deaths would have occurred over 15 years. John Charles Bradbury, *Regulatory Federalism and Workplace Safety: Evidence from OSHA Enforcement, 1981-1995*, 29 J. REG. ECON. 211 (2006). But do states really have better safety programs? In construction, state inspectors typically impose lower fines per violation and the frequency of injuries is approximately ten percent higher with state enforcement. Alison D. Morantz, *Has Regulatory Devolution Injured American Workers? A Comparison of State and Federal Enforcement of Construction Safety Regulations* (Stanford Law and Econ. Olin Working Paper No. 308, 2005).

The delivery system efficiency of the OSHA approach to prevention is also a problem. The evidence from most studies of OSHA suggests that the payoff from additional inspections is not very high. Moreover, a cynic might argue that the main beneficiaries of the effort to promulgate new standards have been lawyers, who are marshaled to defend or, more likely, attack the proposals. Perhaps greater efficiency will result from the efforts to use the general duty clause to deal with workplace problems. Perhaps the megafine policy and the increased use of criminal indictments will improve efficiency.

2. Imponderable Questions. What is the proper mix of approaches to achieve the goals of prevention of workplace injuries and compensation for those workers who are injured? Should we, for example, rely solely on OSHA to achieve safe and healthy workplaces, and have workers' compensation solely concentrate on providing cash benefits and medical care to injured workers? Or should OSHA be declared a failed experiment and terminated, to permit the marketplace, workers' compensation, and (perhaps) an expanded array of tort suits to serve the goals of prevention and compensation?

Part IX

ENFORCEMENT OF EMPLOYMENT RIGHTS

Chapter 25

COMMON ENFORCEMENT ISSUES

Policymakers must do more than merely establish rights and duties between workers and employers. That problem "is matched, if not surpassed, by the problem of how to provide remedies which will make those rights real." Clyde Summers, *Effective Remedies for Employment Rights: Preliminary Guidelines & Proposals*, 141 U. PA. L. REV. 457, 545 (1992). Yet a quick survey across the procedures and remedies used in employment cases discloses a "jumble" without "any coherent pattern." *Id.* at 529. Some employment rights are enforced by employees themselves, others by government agencies. Sometimes class actions are favored, at other times discouraged. Sometimes damages include fines and punitive damages as deterrents, sometimes not. All of these differences reflect important policy choices. This chapter will consider several issues that must be addressed in enforcing employment laws.

A. WHO ENFORCES?

CHRISTIANSBURG GARMENT CO. v. EEOC
United States Supreme Court
434 U.S. 412 (1978)

MR. JUSTICE STEWART delivered the opinion of the Court.

Section 706(k) of Title VII of the Civil Rights Act of 1964 provides:

"In any action or proceeding under this title the court, in its discretion, may allow the prevailing party . . . a reasonable attorney's fee . . . ."

The question in this case is under what circumstances an attorney's fee should be allowed when the defendant is the prevailing party in a Title VII action — a question about which the federal courts have expressed divergent views.

I

Two years after Rosa Helm had filed a Title VII charge of racial discrimination against the petitioner Christiansburg Garment Co. (company), the Equal Employment Opportunity Commission notified her that its conciliation efforts had failed and that she had the right to sue the company in federal court. She did not do so. Almost two years later, in 1972, Congress enacted amendments to Title VII. Section 14 of these amendments authorized the Commission to sue in its own name to prosecute "charges pending with the Commission" on the effective date of the amendments. Proceeding under this section, the Commission sued the company, alleging that it had engaged in unlawful employment practices in violation of the amended Act. The company moved for summary judgment on the ground, *inter alia*, that the Rosa Helm charge had not been "pending" before the Commission when the 1972 amendments took effect. The District Court agreed, and granted summary judgment in favor of the company. . . .

The company then petitioned for the allowance of attorney's fees against the Commission pursuant to § 706(k) of Title VII. Finding that "the Commission's action in bringing the suit cannot be characterized as unreasonable or meritless," the District Court concluded that "an award of attorney's fees to petitioner is not justified in this case." A divided Court of Appeals affirmed and we granted certiorari to consider an important question of federal law.

II

It is the general rule in the United States that in the absence of legislation providing otherwise, litigants must pay their own attorney's fees. *Alyeska Pipeline Co. v. Wilderness Society*, 421 U.S. 240 (1975). Congress has provided only limited exceptions to this rule "under selected statutes granting or protecting various federal rights." *Id.*, at 260. Some of these statutes make fee awards mandatory for prevailing plaintiffs; others make awards permissive but limit them to certain parties, usually prevailing plaintiffs. But many of the statutes are more flexible, authorizing the award of attorney's fees to either plaintiffs or defendants, and entrusting the effectuation of the statutory policy to the discretion of the district courts. Section 706(k) of Title VII of the Civil Rights Act of 1964 falls into this last category, providing as it does that a district court may in its discretion allow an attorney's fee to the prevailing party.

In *Newman v. Piggie Park Enterprises*, 390 U.S. 400 (1968), the Court considered a substantially identical statute authorizing the award of attorney's fees under Title II of the Civil Rights Act of 1964. In that case the plaintiffs had prevailed, and the Court of Appeals had held that they should be awarded their attorney's fees "only to the extent that the respondents' defenses had been advanced 'for purposes of delay and not in good faith.' " *Id.* at 401. We ruled that this "subjective standard" did not properly effectuate the purposes of the counsel-fee provision of Title II. Relying primarily on the intent of Congress to cast a Title II plaintiff in the role of "a 'private attorney general,' vindicating a policy that Congress considered of the highest priority," we held that a prevailing plaintiff under Title II "should ordinarily recover an attorney's fee unless special circumstances would render such an award unjust." *Id.* at 402. We noted in passing that if the objective of Congress had been to permit the award of attorney's fees only against defendants who had acted in bad faith, "no new statutory provision would have been necessary," since even the American common-law rule allows the award of attorney's fees in those exceptional circumstances. *Id.* at 402 n. 4.

In *Albemarle Paper Co. v. Moody*, 422 U.S. 405 (1975), the Court made clear that the *Piggie Park* standard of awarding attorney's fees to a successful plaintiff is equally applicable in an action under Title VII of the Civil Rights Act. 422 U.S. at 415. It can thus be taken as established, as the parties in this case both acknowledge, that under § 706(k) of Title VII a prevailing *plaintiff* ordinarily is to be awarded attorney's fees in all but special circumstances.

III

The question in the case before us is what standard should inform a district court's discretion in deciding whether to award attorney's fees to a successful *defendant* in a Title VII action. Not surprisingly, the parties in addressing the question in their briefs and oral arguments have taken almost diametrically opposite positions.

The company contends that the *Piggie Park* criterion for a successful plaintiff should apply equally as a guide to the award of attorney's fees to a successful defendant. Its submission, in short, is that every prevailing defendant in a Title VII action should receive an allowance of attorney's fees "unless special circumstances would render such an award unjust." The respondent Commission, by contrast, argues that the prevailing defendant should receive an award of attorney's fees only when it is found that the plaintiff's action was brought in bad faith. We have concluded that neither of these positions is correct.

A

Relying on what it terms "the plain meaning of the statute," the company argues that the language of § 706(k) admits of only one interpretation: "A prevailing defendant is entitled to an award of attorney's fees on the same basis as a prevailing plaintiff." But the permissive and discretionary language of the statute does not even invite, let alone require, such a mechanical construction. The terms of § 706(k) provide no indication whatever of the circumstances under which either a plaintiff *or* a defendant should be entitled to attorney's fees. And a moment's reflection reveals that there are at least two strong equitable considerations counseling an attorney's fee award to a prevailing Title VII plaintiff that are wholly absent in the case of a prevailing Title VII defendant.

First, as emphasized so forcefully in *Piggie Park*, the plaintiff is the chosen instrument of Congress to vindicate "a policy that Congress considered of the highest priority." 390 U.S. at 402. Second, when a district court awards counsel fees to a prevailing plaintiff, it is awarding them against a violator of federal law. As the Court of Appeals clearly perceived, "these policy considerations which support the award of fees to a prevailing plaintiff are not present in the case of a prevailing defendant." A successful defendant seeking counsel fees under § 706(k) must rely on quite different equitable considerations.

But if the company's position is untenable, the Commission's argument also misses the mark. It seems clear, in short, that in enacting § 706(k) Congress did not intend to permit the award of attorney's fees to a prevailing defendant only in a situation where the plaintiff was motivated by bad faith in bringing the action. As pointed out in *Piggie Park*, if that had been the intent of Congress, no statutory provision would have been necessary, for it has long been established that even under the American common-law rule attorney's fees may be awarded against a party who has proceeded in bad faith.[13]

Furthermore, while it was certainly the policy of Congress that Title VII plaintiffs should vindicate "a policy that Congress considered of the highest priority," *Piggie Park*, 390 U.S., at 402, it is equally certain that Congress entrusted the ultimate effectuation of that policy to the adversary judicial process. A fair adversary process presupposes both a vigorous prosecution and a vigorous defense. It cannot be lightly assumed that in enacting § 706(k), Congress intended to distort that process by giving the private plaintiff substantial incentives to sue, while foreclosing to the defendant the possibility of recovering his expenses in resisting even a groundless action unless he can show that it was brought in bad faith.

B

The sparse legislative history of § 706(k) reveals little more than the barest outlines of a proper accommodation of the competing considerations we have discussed. The only specific reference to § 706(k) in the legislative debates indicates that the fee provision was included to "make it easier for a plaintiff of limited means to bring a meritorious suit." During the Senate floor discussions of the almost identical attorney's fee provision of Title II, however, several Senators explained that its allowance of awards to defendants would serve "to deter the bringing of lawsuits without foundation," "to discourage frivolous suits," and "to diminish the likelihood of unjustified suits being brought." If anything can be gleaned from these fragments of legislative history, it is that while Congress wanted to clear the way for suits to be brought under the Act, it also wanted to protect defendants from burdensome litigation having no legal or factual basis. . . .

The first federal appellate court to consider what criteria should govern the award of attorney's fees to a prevailing Title VII defendant was the Court of Appeals for the Third Circuit in *United States Steel Corp. v. United States*, 519 F.2d 359 (1975). There a District Court had denied a fee award to a defendant that had successfully resisted a Commission demand for documents, the court finding that the Commission's action had not been "unfounded, meritless, frivolous or vexatiously brought." *Id.* at 363. The Court of Appeals concluded that the District Court had not abused its discretion in denying the award. *Id.* at 365. A similar standard was adopted by the Court of Appeals for the Second Circuit in *Carrion v. Yeshiva University*, 535 F.2d 722 (1976). In upholding an attorney's fee award to a successful defendant, that court stated that such awards should be permitted "not routinely, not simply because he succeeds, but only where the action brought is found to be unreasonable, frivolous, meritless or vexatious." *Id.* at 727.

To the extent that abstract words can deal with concrete cases, we think that the concept embodied in the language adopted by these two Courts of

---

[13] Had Congress provided for attorney's fee awards only to successful plaintiffs, an argument could have been made that the congressional action had pre-empted the common-law rule, and that, therefore, a successful defendant could not recover attorney's fees even against a plaintiff who had proceeded in bad faith. But there is no indication whatever that the purpose of Congress in enacting § 706(k) in the form that it did was simply to foreclose such an argument.

Appeals is correct. We would qualify their words only by pointing out that the term "meritless" is to be understood as meaning groundless or without foundation, rather than simply that the plaintiff has ultimately lost his case, and that the term "vexatious" in no way implies that the plaintiff's subjective bad faith is a necessary prerequisite to a fee award against him. In sum, a district court may in its discretion award attorney's fees to a prevailing defendant in a Title VII case upon a finding that the plaintiff's action was frivolous, unreasonable, or without foundation, even though not brought in subjective bad faith.

In applying these criteria, it is important that a district court resist the understandable temptation to engage in post hoc reasoning by concluding that, because a plaintiff did not ultimately prevail, his action must have been unreasonable or without foundation. This kind of hindsight logic could discourage all but the most airtight claims, for seldom can a prospective plaintiff be sure of ultimate success. No matter how honest one's belief that he has been the victim of discrimination, no matter how meritorious one's claim may appear at the outset, the course of litigation is rarely predictable. Decisive facts may not emerge until discovery or trial. The law may change or clarify in the midst of litigation. Even when the law or the facts appear questionable or unfavorable at the outset, a party may have an entirely reasonable ground for bringing suit.

That § 706(k) allows fee awards only to prevailing private plaintiffs should assure that this statutory provision will not in itself operate as an incentive to the bringing of claims that have little chance of success. To take the further step of assessing attorney's fees against plaintiffs simply because they do not finally prevail would substantially add to the risks inhering in most litigation and would undercut the efforts of Congress to promote the vigorous enforcement of the provisions of Title VII. Hence, a plaintiff should not be assessed his opponent's attorney's fees unless a court finds that his claim was frivolous, unreasonable, or groundless, or that the plaintiff continued to litigate after it clearly became so. And, needless to say, if a plaintiff is found to have brought or continued such a claim in *bad faith*, there will be an even stronger basis for charging him with the attorney's fees incurred by the defense. . . .

IV

In denying attorney's fees to the company in this case, the District Court focused on the standards we have discussed. The court found that "the Commission's action in bringing the suit cannot be characterized as unreasonable or meritless" because "the basis upon which petitioner prevailed was an issue of first impression requiring judicial resolution" and because the "Commission's statutory interpretation of § 14 of the 1972 amendments was not frivolous." The court thus exercised its discretion squarely within the permissible bounds of § 706(k). Accordingly, the judgment of the Court of Appeals upholding the decision of the District Court is affirmed.

It is so ordered.

NOTES

1. *Alternative Enforcement Schemes.* Congress and other policymakers have a broad array of options available when deciding how to enforce an employment right:

(a) Congress can rely principally on private enforcement and encourage such enforcement with a rule that permits successful plaintiffs (but not successful defendants) to recover their attorneys' fees, while also authorizing government agencies to participate in the enforcement process and to file suit themselves. This, of course, is a short description of the Title VII enforcement structure discussed in *Christiansburg Garment.* The FLSA also follows this model.

(b) Congress can establish an administrative agency with the sole authority to prosecute claims arising under the statute. As under the National Labor Relations Act and the Occupational Safety and Health Act, employees or unions may be permitted to file charges with the agency, but the agency would have the authority to decide which charges to pursue and would be the prosecutor.

(c) Congress can rely on private enforcement alone, authorizing only persons alleging discrimination to sue, and may implement either the American rule (parties bear their own costs) or the British rule (loser pays other side's costs) for allocating the costs of suit, including attorneys' fees.

Consider the pros and cons of these enforcement options on factors such as the types of suits that are likely to be brought, the amounts expended by the parties on attorneys' fees, the incidence of the costs of enforcement, the likely effects on primary behavior (how much discrimination or other "bad" conduct occurs), and the influence of the government on the shape and direction of public policy.

2. *Attorneys Fees Provisions.* Attorneys' fees provisions raise a number of implementation issues, such as:

(a) Who is entitled to recover attorneys' fees? *See Kay v. Ehrler,* 499 U.S. 432 (1991) (attorney representing himself in a case not entitled to attorneys' fees).

(b) What does it mean to be a "prevailing party"? *See Hewitt v. Helms,* 482 U.S. 755 (1987) (plaintiff who establishes violation, but does not obtain any relief or change the defendant's behavior toward him, is not a prevailing party); *Maher v. Gagne,* 448 U.S. 122 (1980) (plaintiff who obtains consent decree but no judicial determination of discrimination was a prevailing party).

(c) How should courts determine the amount of the fees? *See Pennsylvania v. Delaware Valley Citizens' Council,* 478 U.S. 546 (1986) (basing fees on "lodestar" amount, determined by multiplying hours by a reasonable hourly rate, and adjustments based on other relevant factors such as the risk of losing case); *City of Burlington v. Dague*, 505 U.S. 557 (1992) (not permissible to adjust lodestar amount because of contingency-fee arrangement).

B. WHO BENEFITS?

BAHRAMIPOUR v. CITIGROUP GLOBAL MARKETS, INC.
United States District Court, N.D. California
11 Wage & Hour Cas. 2d (BNA) 498 (2006)

WILKEN, J.:

Defendant Citigroup Global Markets, Inc. moves for partial summary judgment of the first cause of action brought by Plaintiff Guita Bahramipour under the California Unfair Competition Law, Bus. & Prof. Code § 17200 *et seq.* (UCL), based upon violations of the Fair Labor Standards Act (FLSA), 29 U.S.C. § 201 *et seq.* Plaintiff seeks to recover restitutionary damages for any of Defendant's wage and hour violations which fell within the UCL's four-year statute of limitations. Plaintiff also indicates that she will move to certify an "opt-out" class pursuant to Rule 23 of the Federal Rules of Civil Procedure. Defendant argues that the four-year statute of limitations and the "opt-out" class certification procedure sought by Plaintiff in her UCL claim are pre-empted by the FLSA and, alternatively, that Plaintiff's UCL remedies should be limited to those available under the FLSA. . . .

On September 16, 2004, Plaintiff, a former securities broker for Defendant, filed a class action suit in State court, alleging that Defendant engaged in various illegal pay practices. Plaintiff's first cause of action alleges that Defendant misclassified securities brokers as "exempt" employees under the FLSA, thereby denying them overtime pay in violation of the FLSA, which constitutes unfair competition under the UCL. On October 20, 2004, alleging federal question jurisdiction under 28 U.S.C. § 1331, Defendant removed the action to federal court pursuant to 28 U.S.C. § 1441. On October 28, 2005, Defendant moved for partial summary judgment. . . .

II. *The UCL and the FLSA*

The UCL prohibits any "unlawful, unfair or fraudulent business act or practice." Cal. Bus. & Prof. Code § 17200. The UCL incorporates other laws and treats violations of those laws as unlawful business practices independently actionable under State law. Violation of almost any federal, State, or local law may serve as the basis for a UCL claim.

In 1938, finding that the existence of labor conditions "detrimental to the maintenance of the minimum standard of living necessary for health, efficiency, and general well-being of workers" burdened interstate commerce, Congress passed the FLSA. 29 U.S.C. § 202(a). Absent an exclusion for "exempt" employees, the FLSA requires employers to pay employees overtime at the rate of one-and-one-half times their normal pay. 29 U.S.C. § 207(a)(1). The original provision had no statute of limitations and courts applied varying statutes of limitation borrowed from the States in which claims were brought.

In 1947, in response to the Supreme Court's decision in *Anderson v. Mount Clemens Pottery Co.*, 328 U.S. 680, 692 (1946) (extending compensable "work" under the FLSA to preliminary activities of the employee, regardless of contrary custom or contract), Congress passed the Portal-to-Portal Act, amending the FLSA. The amendments included a limitation on retroactive relief and a statute of limitations. As amended, the FLSA places a two-year statute of limitations on wage and hour claims, although the period may be increased to three years where there is a finding of "willful" statutory violations. 29 U.S.C. § 255(a). Moreover, as amended, the FLSA prohibits any employee from pursuing an FLSA claim "unless he gives his consent in writing to become such a party and such consent is filed in the court in which such action is brought." 29 U.S.C. § 216(b).

III. *Conflict Preemption*

Defendant does not assert that the FLSA expressly preempts State law, that the FLSA preempts the entire field of wage and hour protections, or that a party could not comply with both State and federal requirements. Instead, Defendant relies on the theory of conflict preemption that the UCL, as applied in Plaintiff's claim, stands as an obstacle to the congressional purposes embodied by the FLSA.

A. *Identification of a Conflict*

Under California law, there is a four-year statute of limitations for UCL claims. Moreover, California law allows a UCL class to be certified as an "opt-out" class.

As noted above, under the FLSA there is a two-year statute of limitations which may be extended to three years only upon a showing of willful statutory violations. Moreover, in FLSA class actions, all individual plaintiffs must affirmatively "opt-in" by providing their written consent to participating in the class. 29 U.S.C. § 216(b); *see also Kinney Shoe Corp. v. Vorhes*, 564 F.2d 859, 862 (9th Cir. 1977) (parties cannot pursue Rule 23 "opt-out" certification for claims falling under section 216(b)), overruled on other grounds by *Hoffmann-La Roche Inc. v. Sperling*, 493 U.S. 165 (1989). Defendant argues that these procedural differences between the FLSA and the UCL result in conflict preemption. However, these differences would result in conflict preemption only if the UCL procedures stand as an obstacle to the "accomplishment and execution of the full purposes and objectives of Congress." *Williamson v. General Dynamics Corp.*, 208 F.3d 1144, 1152 (9th Cir. 2000). . . .

C. *The UCL Procedures In Question Do Not Conflict With Congressional Purpose*

[The] evidence cited by Defendant fails to show that the procedures of the UCL at issue stand as an obstacle to the congressional purpose in enacting the FLSA, as amended by the Portal-to-Portal Act.

1. *Opt-out certification*

Defendant relies primarily on congressional statements in 29 U.S.C. § 251 to argue that the purpose of the Portal-to-Portal Act amendments, which limit FLSA claims to "opt-in" certifications, would be frustrated by Plaintiff's intention to seek an "opt-out" UCL class. However, because congressional concern in enacting the "opt-in" provision was directed towards "windfall payments, including liquidated damages," absent in a UCL action limited to restitution, there is "no reason to believe that Congress considered whether plaintiffs who are limited to restitution [under the UCL] should have to comply with the opt-in requirement of Section 216(b)." *Tomlinson v. Indymac Bank*, 359 F. Supp. 2d 898, 901 (C.D. Cal. 2005) (quoting 29 U.S.C. § 251(a)). More broadly, the Portal-to-Portal Act was "enacted in response to judicial interpretations of the FLSA — not in response to a proliferation of state wage claims." *Barnett v. Washington Mut. Bank*, 2004 WL 2011462, at *6; (N.D. Cal. 2004). . . .

The cases cited by Defendant are inapplicable. In *Leuthold v. Destination Am., Inc*, 224 F.R.D. 462, 469-70 (N.D. Cal. 2004), the court declined to certify an "opt-out" class to pursue claims based on California's fair labor standards and the UCL because it had approved conditional certification of an "opt-in" class under the FLSA and it was concerned that (1) confusion would result in asking potential plaintiffs both to opt in and opt out of the two classes and (2) because the State claims were pendant to the FLSA claim, the court might lack jurisdiction over the State law claims if a large number of plaintiffs in the State law class chose not to prosecute their federal claims. Because there will only be one class in this case, the court's concerns in *Leuthold* are not present here.

In *Rodriguez v. The Texan, Inc.*, 2001 WL 1829490, at *2 (N.D. Ill. 2001), the plaintiff also sought an "opt-in" class under the FLSA and an "opt-out" class for supplemental State labor claims. Although the court was concerned that the policy underlying the Portal-to-Portal Act's "opt-in" requirement would be thwarted if claims for violations of similar State labor laws were allowed to be brought in an "opt-out" class action, the court was also concerned that an "opt-out" class would affect its supplemental jurisdiction over the State claims. As discussed in *Leuthold*, a request for an "opt-in" and an "opt-out" class presents unique concerns which do not apply here. In *La Chapelle v. Owens-Illinois, Inc.*, 513 F.2d 286, 288 (5th Cir. 1975), although the court stated that "opt-out" and "opt-in" classes are mutually exclusive and irreconcilable, it made this statement in determining whether a suit brought under the Age Discrimination in Employment Act (ADEA) may be an "opt-out" class action. Cases in which plaintiffs attempt to circumvent the "opt-in" requirement of 29 U.S.C. § 216(b) for other federal claims, like the ADEA, are inapplicable to State law claims such as the one at issue here. . . .

Plaintiff did not bring an FLSA claim; she brought a State law claim in State court. Therefore, the purpose of the FLSA's "opt-in" requirement, to limit the enormous liability for employers which had been threatened by the thousands of federal wage and hour claims filed in the wake of the *Anderson* decision, is not directly implicated by Plaintiff's claim. Accordingly, the Court finds that the UCL's opt-out procedure does not stand as an obstacle to the congressional purpose in enacting the FLSA, as amended.

2. *Statute of Limitations*

Defendant cites provisions of the FLSA and its legislative history as evidence of congressional intent to limit, through the statute of limitations in the Portal-to-Portal Act, the period of time during which claims can be brought for wage and hour violations under State statutes premised on violations of FLSA. *See* 29 U.S.C. § 251(a) ("the varying and extended periods of time for which, under the laws of the several States, potential retroactive liability may be imposed upon employers, have given and will give rise to great difficulties in the sound and orderly conduct of business and industry"); *see also* 93 Cong. Rec. H2183 (1947) (statement of Rep. Donnell) (discussing unfairness to similarly situated workers and employers created by borrowing statutes of limitations from different State laws for FLSA claims). However, these statements of congressional purpose refer only to the problems engendered by the fact that the absence of a statute of limitations in the original FLSA resulted in non-uniform statutes of limitation for a nation-wide federal law. As noted by the sponsor of the bill in the House of Representatives:

> We believe that the reasons for a uniform statute of limitations are clear. In the administration of a Federal law which applies all over the United States, no difference should exist with respect to the time within which a plaintiff may file suit under that law.

Id. The motivation for the two-year statute of limitations was not simply to protect employers, but to ensure uniformity. In fact, in the interest of uniformity, Congress rejected the suggestion that States utilizing a one-year statute of limitations period for FLSA claims be allowed to retain it.

The UCL is a State law and therefore does not present the problems of uniformity addressed by Congress in administering the FLSA. Moreover, when discussing the federal statute of limitations Congress "expressly state[d] that this limitation does not apply to actions for the recovery of wages brought under state law . . . [and] envisioned not only that state based claims for wages could be asserted, but that they could be governed by separate procedures." *Aragon v. Bravo*, 1993 WL 432402, *6 (D. Ariz. 1993) (citing U.S. Code and Cong. Service, 80th Cong., 1st Session, at 1035 (1947)). In sum, a longer statute of limitations for a State law claim does not stand as an obstacle to congressional purpose.

By allowing "opt-out" class actions and longer statute of limitations for UCL claims, California provides increased protections for its workers, furthering the central purpose of the FLSA. The UCL as invoked in Plaintiff's claim does not stand as an obstacle to the purposes of the FLSA.

Based on the foregoing, Defendant's motion for partial summary judgment is DENIED.

NOTES

1. ***Litigation Strategies.*** Bahramipour was claiming that Citigroup had violated the overtime provisions of the Fair Labor Standards Act. Yet he filed the action only under a state law in state court. The goal was clearly to facilitate a class action and expand the time limit for damages. There was

a trade-off in doing this. He sacrificed the liquidated damages that otherwise would have been available under the FLSA. But his calculation clearly had to be that the advantages of more favorable class action rules and a longer time limit would outweigh that disadvantage. This is reminiscent of the litigation strategy discussed in Chapter 6 where plaintiffs' attorneys attempt to frame contract claims as tort claims to take advantage of more favorable tort remedies.

2. *Statutes of Limitations.* Time limits vary widely in employment law, generally for no apparent reason. In wage-and-hour suits, however, they are particularly important. In the typical case, time limits will usually function not to foreclose the possibility of suit, but rather to define the time period over which damages are calculated. In *Bahramipour*, for example, moving from the FLSA's two-year statute of limitations to the UCL's four-year statute meant that plaintiffs, if successful, would be entitled to damages for a period extending four years back from the time suit was filed, approximately doubling the available damages. Thus, for employees who worked for Citigroup for the full four years, this advantage alone would approximately make up for the liquidated damages disadvantage of the state suit.

3. *Class Actions and Social Change.* Employment laws often pursue broad social change. Title VII would be the classic example and, in those cases, the Supreme Court has recognized that "suits alleging racial or ethnic discrimination are often by their very nature class suits, involving classwide wrongs." *East Texas Motor Freight Sys. v. Rodriquez*, 431 U.S. 395, 405 (1977). Class actions can be an important tool in pursuing such broad social goals.

At the same time, class actions raise a host of problems. Some of those problems are highly practical problems of judicial administration:

> The emergence of the group as the real subject or object of the litigation . . . raises far-reaching new questions: How far can the group be extended and homogenized? To what extent and by what methods will we permit the presentation of views diverging from that of the group representative? When the judgment treads on numerous — perhaps innumerable — absentees, can the traditional doctrines of finality and preclusion hold? And in the absence of a particular client, capable of concretely defining his own interest, can we rely on the assumptions of the adversary system as a guide to the conduct and duty of lawyers?

Abram Chayes, *The Role of the Judge in Public Law Litigation*, 89 HARV. L. REV. 1281, 1291 (1976). *See also* Deborah L. Rhode, *Class Conflicts in Class Actions*, 34 STAN. L. REV. 1183 (1982).

More broadly, however, the issue is the role of the courts in debates about social policy. Class actions expand the ability of courts to influence those debates, which have been raging since at least the time of *Brown v. Board of Education*, 347 U.S. 483 (1954). *See* Susan Poser, *What's a Judge to Do?: Remedying the Remedy in Institutional Reform Litigation*, 102 MICH. L. REV. 1307, 1327 (2004) ("assessing the propriety and success of institutional reform litigation is akin to figuring out if the glass is half empty or half full").

4. *Wage-and-Hour Class Actions.* Wage-and-hour class actions have been a growth industry, especially in California. In 2006 alone, for example, many major companies settled high-stakes wage-and-hour cases, including Pizza Hut for $12.5 million, Electronic Arts for $14.9 million, Sears for $15 million, UBS for $89 million, and Smith Barney for $98 million.

5. *Overlapping Rights and Procedures.* Employees often have overlapping protections. Sometimes the overlap is between federal and state law. Sometimes it is between statutory law (state or federal) and common-law protections. A broad range of issues arises from overlapping protections and those issues are resolved in a variety of ways.

For example, preemption is one issue obviously raised by overlapping protections. *Bahramipour* considers preemption under the Fair Labor Standards Act which specifically does not preempt state laws with more generous standards. FLSA § 218. But if the plaintiffs in the case had been complaining about a failure to pay pensions rather than a failure to pay proper wages, any state cause of action clearly would have been preempted under ERISA's broad preemption provision. ERISA § 514.

Overlap also raises issue and claim preclusion issues. For example, the Supreme Court has held that state administrative proceedings alone do not have preclusive effect in a subsequent case in federal court under Title VII or the ADEA, but could have preclusive effect under sections 1981 and 1983. State *court* decisions, however, can be used to preclude subsequent federal court litigation under all of these statutes. *Kremer v. Chemical Constr. Corp.*, 456 U.S. 461 (1982) (Title VII); *Astoria Fed. Sav. & Loan Ass'n v. Solimino*, 501 U.S. 104 (1991) (ADEA); *University of Tenn. v. Elliott*, 478 U.S. 788 (1986) (Sections 1981 and 1983).

6. *Choice of Laws and the "Race to the Courthouse."* As borders between states have become increasingly fluid for companies and the employees they recruit, conflict of laws has become more significant. One area in which it has had a significant impact is in litigating trade secret and restrictive covenant cases. An employee who has signed a non-compete covenant in one state but then goes to another state, say California, that has a strong public policy against enforcement of non-competes, will have a strong strategic interest in having his case heard in California. Conflict of laws doctrine supplies the principles for deciding which state's laws will apply, taking into account the domicile of the parties' relationship to one another, the locus of the injury, and whether public policy favors application of one state's laws over the other's. A judge deciding a question of conflict of laws may feel tempted to find that the public policy of the state in which the judge sits is most compelling, even when the contract contains a choice of law provision specifying the law of the other state. Meanwhile, it is the practice of federal courts to follow a "first-filed rule." There is a strong presumption in federal law that if two lawsuits involve overlapping issues and parties, the courts must allow the lawsuit filed first to proceed, and will stay the second-filed suit until resolution of the first or even dismiss it. Taken together, the choice of law doctrine and the first-filed rule create incentives for litigants to shop for the courthouse whose law is most favorable to their own interest, and to get there first. Hence, we have the proverbial "race to the courthouse."

A recent case from the 11th Circuit is illustrative. In *Manuel v. Convergys Corp.*, 430 F.3d 1132 (11th Cir. 2005), Manuel, who worked for Convergys in

Ohio, was offered a job with a competitor in Georgia. He had signed a non-compete agreement with Convergys, but consulted an attorney who advised him that the non-compete, although probably enforceable in Ohio, would likely be unenforceable under the stricter Georgia laws. Manuel then accepted the job in Georgia, telling Convergys that he was not going to work for a competitor and that he had not accepted a job with another company. He moved to Georgia and immediately filed for a declaratory judgment in a Georgia district court that the non-compete was invalid. Convergys filed its own lawsuit in Ohio to enjoin Manuel's employment with the competitor. Based on the Ohio lawsuit, Convergys requested that the Georgia district court stay the lawsuit until after the Ohio lawsuit was concluded, but the Georgia district court denied this motion based on the "first-filed" rule. The Georgia district court then decided the case applying Georgia law, and found the non-compete agreement overbroad and invalid. The 11th Circuit affirmed, notwithstanding that Manuel had behaved dishonestly and engaged in strategic forum shopping.

The upshot of this phenomenon of warring declaratory judgments in the early stages of a trade secret or non-compete dispute is that competitive advantage may turn more on having a nimble legal team with strategic finesse than it does on the substantive merits of the dispute.

C. REMEDIES

BALBUENA v. IDR REALTY LLC
Court of Appeals of New York
845 N.E.2d 1246 (2006)

GRAFFEO, J.:

Gorgonio Balbuena is a native of Mexico who entered the United States without the permission of federal immigration authorities. In April 2000, he was employed as a construction worker by third-party defendant Taman Management Corp. on a site owned and managed by defendants IDR Realty LLC and Dora Wechler. According to Balbuena, he fell from a ramp while pushing a wheelbarrow, sustaining severe head trauma and other debilitating injuries that have rendered him incapacitated and unable to work.

Balbuena and his wife sued defendants for common-law negligence and violations of Labor Law §§ 240(1) and 241(6), seeking various categories of damages, including past wages from the time of the accident until a verdict and the future loss of earnings (collectively referred to as lost wages). During discovery, Taman sought documentation from Balbuena demonstrating that he had obtained the necessary authorization to work in the United States as required by federal law. After Balbuena objected to this request and failed to produce such documentation, Taman moved for a court order resolving the immigration and work authorization issues [and for] partial summary judgment dismissing Balbuena's claim for lost wages. . . .

The Supreme Court denied defendants' motion for partial summary judgment, concluding that state law allows an undocumented alien to recover lost wages. . . . The Appellate Division, First Department, modified by granting Taman's motion for partial summary judgment dismissing Balbuena's claim for lost earnings to the extent it sought damages based on wages plaintiff might have earned in the United States. [The] Court determined that Hoffman precludes an alien who has not obtained work authorization from claiming lost wages derived from income earned in the United States, but may seek wages based on income that could be earned in the alien's home country. . . .

The Federal Immigration Reform and Control Act of 1986

[In] 1986 Congress adopted the Immigration Reform and Control Act (IRCA). Both Congress and the President expressed the view that "the principal means of closing the back door, or curtailing future illegal immigration, was through employer sanctions" that were intended to "remove the incentive for illegal immigration by eliminating the job opportunities which draw illegal aliens" into the country. To attain this goal, the most important component of the IRCA scheme was the creation of a new "employment verification system" designed to deter the employment of aliens who are not lawfully present in the United States and those who are lawfully present, but not authorized to work. See 8 U.S.C. § 1324a(b).

Under this system, aliens legally present and approved to work in the United States are issued formal documentation of their eligibility status by federal immigration authorities, usually in the form of a "green card," a registration number or some other document issued by the Bureau of Citizenship and Immigration Services. Before hiring an alien, an employer is required to verify the prospective worker's identity and work eligibility by examining the government-issued documentation. If the required documentation is not presented, the alien cannot be hired. See 8 U.S.C. § 1324a(a)(1). An employer who knowingly violates the employment verification requirements, or who unknowingly hires an illegal alien but subsequently learns that an alien is not authorized to work and does not immediately terminate the employment relationship, is subject to civil or criminal prosecution and penalties. See 8 U.S.C. § 1324a(a)(1), (2), (f)(1).

In addition to the provisions relating to the responsibilities of employers, IRCA also declares that it is a crime for an alien to provide a potential employer with documents falsely acknowledging receipt of governmental approval of the alien's eligibility for employment. See 8 U.S.C. § 1324c(a). [H]owever, IRCA does not penalize an alien for attaining employment without having proper work authorization, unless the alien engages in fraud, such as presenting false documentation to secure the employment. In order to preserve the national uniformity of this verification system and the sanctions imposed for violations, Congress expressly provided that IRCA would "preempt any State or local law imposing civil or criminal sanctions (other than through licensing and similar laws) upon those who employ, or recruit or refer for a fee for employment, unauthorized aliens" 8 U.S.C. § 1324a(h)(2).

The Impact of Hoffman

It was against this federal statutory backdrop that the United States Supreme Court decided *Hoffman Plastic Compounds Inc. v. National Labor*

Relations Bd., 535 U.S. 137 (2002). The issue was whether an illegal alien who, in violation of IRCA, gained employment by presenting false work authorization documents could be awarded back pay by the National Labor Relations Board (NLRB) after the worker was impermissibly terminated for engaging in union-organizing activities. The Supreme Court concluded that such an award was prohibited because it would conflict with the purpose of IRCA. The Court observed that "under the IRCA regime, it is impossible for an undocumented alien to obtain employment in the United States without some party directly contravening explicit congressional policies. Either the undocumented alien tenders fraudulent identification . . . or the employer knowingly hires the undocumented alien in direct contradiction of its IRCA obligations" *Id.* at 148.

The Court emphasized that the salient factor in the case was that "Congress has expressly made it criminally punishable for an alien to obtain employment with false documents" and that the alien had, in fact, committed this crime. *Id.* at 149. Thus, the Court determined that "awarding back pay in a case like this not only trivializes the immigration laws, it also condones and encourages future violations" because the alien would qualify for an NLRB award "only by remaining inside the United States illegally" and could not "mitigate damages . . . without triggering new IRCA violations, either by tendering false documents to employers or by finding employers willing to ignore IRCA and hire illegal workers." *Id.* at 150-51. . . .

The Supremacy Clause and Preemption Principles

The Supremacy Clause, in article VI of the Constitution, "may entail preemption of state law either by express provision, by implication, or by a conflict between federal and state law." *New York State Conference of Blue Cross & Blue Shield Plans v. Travelers Ins. Co.*, 514 U.S. 645, 654 (1995). It is "never assumed lightly that Congress has derogated state regulation, but instead [courts] have addressed claims of preemption with the starting presumption that Congress does not intend to supplant state law." *Id.* The presumption against preemption is especially strong with regard to laws that affect the states' historic police powers over occupational health and safety issues and is overcome only if it "was the clear and manifest purpose of Congress to supplant state law." *Id.* at 655. . . .

Express [and Field] Preemption

. . . IRCA does not contain an express statement by Congress that it intended to preempt state laws regarding the permissible scope of recovery in personal injury actions predicated on state labor laws. As relevant to these cases, Congress expressly preempted only state and local laws that impose "civil or criminal sanctions" on employers of undocumented aliens. 8 U.S.C. § 1324a(h)(2). A sanction is generally considered a "penalty or coercive measure," such as a punishment for a criminal act or a civil fine for a statutory or regulatory violation. The plain language of section 1324a(h)(2) appears directed at laws that impose fines for hiring undocumented aliens, such as the California statute at issue in *DeCanas v. Bica*, 424 U.S. 351 (1976). . . .

In contrast, the primary purpose of civil recovery in a personal injury action premised on state Labor Law provisions is not to punish the tortfeasor but to compensate the worker for injuries proximately caused by negligence or the violation of statutory safety standards. . . .

We are similarly unpersuaded by defendants' field preemption argument. Certainly IRCA and related statutes thoroughly occupy the spectrum of immigration laws. But there is nothing in those provisions indicating that Congress meant to affect state regulation of occupational health and safety, or the types of damages that may be recovered in a civil action arising from those laws. To the contrary, the legislative history of IRCA shows that the Act was not intended "to undermine or diminish in any way labor protections in existing law."

Conflict Preemption

The more difficult issue is whether an award for lost wages to an undocumented immigrant injured as a result of a responsible party's violation of the Labor Law would conflict with or otherwise erode the objectives of IRCA in a manner sufficient to surmount the strong presumption against preemption.

The Supreme Court has recognized that, notwithstanding the federal government's exclusive control over immigration and naturalization, the "States possess broad authority under their police powers to regulate the employment relationship to protect workers within the State," which includes the power to enact "laws regulating occupational health and safety." *DeCanas v Bica*, 424 U.S. at 356 — issues that have been "primarily, and historically, a matter of local concern." *Hillsborough County v. Automated Med. Labs. Inc.*, 471 U.S. 707, 719 (1985). In the Labor Law context, we have noted that "the legislative history of the Labor Law, particularly sections 240 and 241, makes clear the Legislature's intent to achieve the purpose of protecting workers by placing ultimate responsibility for safety practices at building construction jobs where such responsibility actually belongs, on the owner and general contractor, instead of on workers, who 'are scarcely in a position to protect themselves from accident.' " *Zimmer v. Chemung County Performing Arts, Inc.*, 65 N.Y.2d 513, 520 (1985). The Labor Law, therefore, applies to all workers in qualifying employment situations — regardless of immigration status — and nothing in the relevant statutes or our decisions negates the universal applicability of this principle.[6]

Additionally, limiting a lost wages claim by an injured undocumented alien would lessen an employer's incentive to comply with the Labor Law and supply all of its workers the safe workplace that the Legislature demands. Given the clear statement in IRCA's legislative history that the Act was not intended "to undermine or diminish in any way labor protections in existing law," we are unpersuaded that IRCA requires such a diminution in the force and effect of state workplace safety mandates. To the contrary, in order to further the

---

[6] In the related context of workers' compensation statutes, also enacted for the benefit of employees, courts have found such statutes applicable to all persons within the State's borders, even those who are not entitled to be here. *See e.g. Design Kitchen & Baths v. Lagos*, 882 A.2d 817 (Md. 2005); *Farmers Bros. Coffee v. Workers' Compensation Appeals Bd.*, 133 Cal. App. 4th 533 (2005). *But see, Tarango v. State Indus. Ins. Syst.*, 25 P.3d 175, 179 (Nev. 2001).

laudable purposes of IRCA and our Labor Law, "tort deterrence principles provide a compelling reason to allow an award of such damages against a person responsible for an illegal alien's employment when that person knew or should have known of that illegal alien's status." *Rosa v. Partners in Progress, Inc.*, 868 A.2d 994, 1000 (N.H. 2005).

[A] different conclusion would not only diminish the protections afforded by the Labor Law, it would also improvidently reward employers who knowingly disregard the employment verification system in defiance of the primary purposes of federal immigration laws. An absolute bar to recovery of lost wages by an undocumented worker would lessen the unscrupulous employer's potential liability to its alien workers and make it more financially attractive to hire undocumented aliens. This, coupled with the fact that illegal aliens are willing to work in jobs that are more dangerous and undesirable — and for less money — than their legal immigrant and citizen counterparts, would actually increase employment levels of undocumented aliens, not decrease it as Congress sought by its passage of IRCA.

Aside from the compatibility of federal immigration law and our state Labor Law, plaintiffs here — unlike the alien in *Hoffman* — did not commit a criminal act under IRCA. Whereas the undocumented alien in Hoffman criminally provided his employer with fraudulent papers purporting to be proper federal work documentation, there is no allegation in these cases that plaintiffs produced false work documents in violation of IRCA or were even asked by the employers to present the work authorization documents as required by IRCA. Notably, IRCA does not make it a crime to work without documentation. *Hoffman* is dependent on its facts, including the critical point that the alien tendered false documentation that allowed him to work legally in this country. This was a clear violation of IRCA. We see no reason to equate the criminal misconduct of the employee in *Hoffman* to the conduct of the plaintiffs here since, in the context of defendants' motions for partial summary judgment, we must presume that it was the employers who violated IRCA by failing to inquire into plaintiffs' immigration status or employment eligibility.

We recognize, of course, that plaintiffs' presence in this country without authorization is impermissible under federal law. Standing alone, however, this transgression is insufficient to justify denying plaintiffs a portion of the damages to which they are otherwise entitled. Under our precedent, civil recovery is foreclosed "if the plaintiff's conduct constituted a serious violation of the law and the injuries for which he seeks recovery were the direct result of that violation." *Barker v Kallash*, 63 N.Y.2d 19, 24 (1984). Although recoveries have been denied to parties who have engaged in illegal activities, in those cases it was the work being performed that was outlawed, whereas here, the construction work itself was entirely lawful. Moreover, neither IRCA nor any other federal or state statute makes it a crime to be an employed but undocumented alien, unless the alien secured employment through the use of false work authorization documentation. We also find it significant that the records here do not indicate that administrative proceedings or criminal prosecutions have been initiated against plaintiffs based on their presence or employment in this country.

Nor do we believe that the issue of mitigation of damages creates a conflict between state labor law and federal immigration law. Under our common-law doctrine of mitigation of damages, recovery for future lost earnings is subject to reduction by the amount of compensation that the injured party could have earned despite the injuries inflicted by the tortfeasor. Mitigation of damages is not implicated when a worker's injuries are so serious that the worker is physically unable to work. Here, [plaintiff has] alleged serious, permanent injuries that impede [his] ability to be employed, allegations we must presume to be true at this preliminary stage of the litigation. [His situation is] therefore readily distinguishable from the alien worker in *Hoffman*, who was not physically injured and could have sought new employment in violation of IRCA by tendering the same false documents that allowed him to work in the first place.

In any event, any conflict with IRCA's purposes that may arise from permitting an alien's lost wage claim to proceed to trial can be alleviated by permitting a jury to consider immigration status as one factor in its determination of the damages, if any, warranted under the Labor Law. An undocumented alien plaintiff could, for example, introduce proof that he had subsequently received or was in the process of obtaining the authorization documents required by IRCA and, consequently, would likely be authorized to obtain future employment in the United States. Conversely, a defendant in a Labor Law action could, for example, allege that a future wage award is not appropriate because work authorization has not been sought or approval was sought but denied. In other words, a jury's analysis of a future wage claim proffered by an undocumented alien is similar to a claim asserted by any other injured person in that the determination must be based on all of the relevant facts and circumstances presented in the case.

In light of these considerations, defendants have not overridden the presumption against preemption afforded by the Supremacy Clause. In the context of Labor Law claims, a per se preclusion of recovery for lost wages would condone the employers' conduct in contravention of IRCA's requirements and promote unsafe work site practices, all of which encourages the employment of undocumented aliens and undermines the objectives that both IRCA and the state Labor Law were designed to accomplish. Moreover, there is no evidence in the records before us that [the plaintiff] (like the alien worker in *Hoffman*) tendered false documentation in violation of IRCA or that [his] employer satisfied [its] duty to verify plaintiffs' eligibility to work. In addition, plaintiff [has] allegedly suffered physical injuries that have limited [his] ability to be employed, unlike the alien worker in *Hoffman* who suffered no bodily injury whatsoever. We therefore hold, on the records before us in these Labor Law §§ 200, 240(1) and 241(6) cases, and in the absence of proof that plaintiff tendered false work authorization documents to obtain employment, that IRCA does not bar maintenance of a claim for lost wages by an undocumented alien. . . .

NOTES

1. *Compensating Employees vs. Deterring Employers*. Remedies in employment cases are designed both to compensate employees and to deter employers. *Balbuena* is a recent example of a situation in which the two are in tension. On the one hand, a good argument can be made that a plaintiff is being overcompensated if he receives damages for future wage loss when it would be illegal for him to work. On the other hand, failing to compensate the plaintiff would mean that the employer would have weaker incentives to comply with both New York's labor law and federal immigration law.

2. *Optimum Deterrence.* In theory, when employers violate employment laws, they would be optimally deterred if fines and damages were set to be slightly more than the probability of detection times the harm caused by their violation, $F > p(H)$. To illustrate why this is so, assume a) that OSHA can find and fine every violation of safety standards, b) that it has a safety standard for a machine designed to protect the hands of workers, and c) that the full damages for a lost hand are $250,000. Since p is 1.0 by assumption, we only have to compare F and H. If F were set at less than H, employers would have financial incentives to ignore the safety standard and just pay for lost hands when they occur. If F were set a lot higher than H, employers might take too many precautions to avoid the harm (e.g., they might eliminate the machines and the jobs). Thus, for proper deterrence the fine should be set at very slightly more than harm.

But, of course, real life is much more complicated. Consider some problems. First, OSHA is fining for violations of the standard, not for lost hands. But violating the standard may result in only one lost hand per year. Should OSHA fine at a daily rate when it finds violations ($250,000/365 = $685)? Or a yearly rate ($250,000)? Or based on how long the machine has been out of compliance (*e.g.*, $250,000 × 10 years = $2.5 million)? Second, our example assumed perfect detection of violations. The *theory* is clear about what should happen if detection is less than perfect. If there's a 10% chance the violation will be detected, the fine should increase ten-fold; if a 1% chance, one hundred-fold; etc. But would a fine of $25 million for a violation with a 1% chance of detection be optimal? Again, employers may be over-deterred by such large fines. In addition, such large fines impose great harm from legal error and cause inequity between unlucky violating employers who are caught vs. violating employers who avoid detection.

One implication of this type of analysis is that fines or damages that are set equal to harm are almost always too low. Specifically, they are too low in every case except when every violation is detected. It is rare, however, for fines or damages to be set equal to harm. The Fair Labor Standards Act, for example, provides for liquidated damages equal to unpaid wages to account for this problem. FLSA § 216(b). Even a statute like Title VII, which on its face merely compensates plaintiffs for actual harm by providing back pay and reinstatement, generally has an implicit penalty. For example, when an employer has to compensate an employee fired improperly because of sex discrimination, it has to pay that employee back wages even though she performed no work, plus a roughly equal amount to the employee who actually did the work.

3. *Practical Deterrence.* Consider a calculating employer who is contemplating whether to violate the Fair Labor Standard Act's requirement of pay at one-and-one-half times the regular rate for overtime hours. The benefit of noncompliance is obvious: the employer saves one-half the regular rate of pay for every overtime hour worked. The cost side of a decision not to comply includes the calculation suggested by the theory above: probability of being detected times damages (which include liquidated damages and reputational harm). The costs of noncompliance would also include the possibility of increased turnover by disgruntled employees. Since the FLSA is primarily enforced by employees themselves, the employer's calculation of the probability of being detected depends importantly on the *employee's* calculation of whether to bring suit. Employees, in turn, have their own cost-benefit analysis. The benefit, again obviously, would be receipt of an extra one-half times their regular rate of pay for overtime hours worked, including hours worked over the past two or three years which alone could add up to a hefty sum. On the cost side, employees may be fired in retaliation for complaining (which would be illegal, of course, but difficult to prove and an enormous hassle) and they may be offered fewer overtime hours (which may result in lower pay after the suit than before). *See* Ronald G. Ehrenberg & Paul L. Schumann, *Compliance with the Overtime Pay Provisions of the Fair Labor Standards Act*, 25 J. Lab. Econ. 159 (1982).

Thinking about compliance in this way can be useful in assessing how legal changes might affect compliance. For example, the analysis suggests that an increase in the premium for overtime hours from one-and-one half times the regular rate to double the regular rate would have an uncertain effect on compliance, while an increase in the amount of liquidated damages from an amount equal to backpay to an amount double back pay would increase compliance. Do you see why?

Chapter 26
ARBITRATION OF EMPLOYMENT DISPUTES

A. INTRODUCTION

A major current issue is whether the forum for employment dispute resolution should be courts or arbitration. There are two fundamental types of arbitration. First is interest arbitration, in which an arbitrator establishes rights or terms between parties who cannot agree by themselves. Some public-sector collective-bargaining systems use interest arbitration. For example, if a city refuses to pay more than a 2 percent wage increase and the firefighters' union insists on 8 percent (and the union is forbidden from striking, which is how the impasse would be resolved in private-sector collective bargaining), the system may allow an interest arbitrator to resolve the dispute by setting a wage increase. Interest arbitration is highly unusual in the American private sector.

The second, and more common, type is grievance arbitration, also called rights arbitration. Here, a prior statute or collective bargaining agreement, rather than an arbitrator, has set the rights or terms, but the parties cannot agree how they should apply in a particular situation. An impartial arbitrator interprets how the statute or collective bargaining agreement should be applied.

Grievance arbitration has a long history in unionized employment. A typical situation arises when a unionized employee is fired. The union and management have already agreed on a collective bargaining agreement that declares that the employer cannot fire employees without just cause. The collective bargaining agreement also sets forth a grievance arbitration procedure. The parties now disagree, however, about whether this particular firing meets the just-cause standard. If earlier steps of the grievance procedure cannot resolve the dispute, the parties select an arbitrator (by means specified in the collective bargaining agreement) to resolve the dispute.

The basic goal of arbitration is to resolve disputes quickly and cheaply. The arbitrator typically will conduct a hearing to hear evidence from witnesses. Hearings are informal and the rules of evidence are not strictly enforced. The arbitrator renders a decision, often but not always with a written explanation (or opinion). The parties generally share the costs of arbitration. The collective bargaining agreement typically declares that the arbitrator's decision is final and binding.

Sometimes one side to the dispute refuses to submit an issue to arbitration, and the other side goes to court to seek judicial enforcement of the promise to arbitrate. Under the older common law, courts would often refuse to enforce promises to arbitrate, under the theory that arbitration would usurp the court's jurisdiction to resolve disputes. In the famous 1960 Steelworkers Trilogy, the Supreme Court rejected the common-law hostility for grievance arbitration pursuant to collective-bargaining agreements. The Court held that courts were to vigorously enforce agreements to arbitrate, based on the jurisdiction given courts under § 301 of the Labor-Management Relations Act to hear suits alleging breach of collective-bargaining contracts. *See United Steelworkers v. American Manufacturing Co.*, 363 U.S. 564 (1960) (declaring that "[t]he function of the court . . . is confined to ascertaining whether the party seeking arbitration is making a claim which on its face is governed by the contract"); *United Steelworkers v. Warrior & Gulf Navigation Co.*, 363 U.S. 574 (1960) (declaring that "[a]n order to arbitrate the particular grievance should not be denied unless it may be said with positive assurance that the arbitration clause is not susceptible to an interpretation that covers the asserted dispute").

In other situations, a party goes through the arbitration process but refuses to abide by the arbitrator's award. The winning party will then go to court to seek judicial enforcement of the arbitrator's award. The losing party typically challenges the award on various grounds, such as the arbitrator exceeded her authority under the contract or that the arbitrator's award violates public policy. In the unionized context once again, the grounds for not enforcing an arbitrator's award are narrow. *See United Steelworkers v. Enterprise Wheel & Car Corp.*, 363 U.S. 593 (1960) (declaring that courts must enforce the arbitrator's award, even if repugnant to logic and justice, so long as "it draws its essence from the collective bargaining agreement").

While grievance arbitration is well accepted in the unionized sector, it remains controversial in nonunion employment disputes, particularly when employers attempt to force employees to resolve alleged violations of statutory rights through arbitration rather than through the courts. *See generally* Samuel Estreicher, *Predispute Agreements to Arbitrate Statutory Employment Claims*, 72 N.Y.U. L. REV. 1344 (1997); Martin H. Malin, *Privatizing Justice but by How Much? Questions* Gilmer *Did Not Answer*, 16 OHIO ST. J. ON DISP. RESOL. 589 (2001).

GILMER v. INTERSTATE/JOHNSON LANE CORP.
Supreme Court of the United States
500 U.S. 20 (1991)

JUSTICE WHITE delivered the opinion of the Court.

The question presented in this case is whether a claim under the Age Discrimination in Employment Act of 1967 (ADEA) can be subjected to compulsory arbitration pursuant to an arbitration agreement in a securities registration application. The Court of Appeals held that it could, and we affirm.

I.

Respondent Interstate/Johnson Lane Corporation (Interstate) hired petitioner Robert Gilmer as a Manager of Financial Services in May 1981. As required by his employment, Gilmer registered as a securities representative with several stock exchanges, including the New York Stock Exchange (NYSE). His registration application, entitled "Uniform Application for Securities Industry Registration or Transfer," provided, among other things, that

Gilmer "agree[d] to arbitrate any dispute, claim or controversy" arising between him and Interstate "that is required to be arbitrated under the rules, constitutions or by-laws of the organizations with which I register." Of relevance to this case, NYSE Rule 347 provides for arbitration of "[a]ny controversy between a registered representative and any member or member organization arising out of the employment or termination of employment of such registered representative."

Interstate terminated Gilmer's employment in 1987, at which time Gilmer was 62 years of age. After first filing an age discrimination charge with the Equal Employment Opportunity Commission (EEOC), Gilmer subsequently brought suit in the United States District Court for the Western District of North Carolina, alleging that Interstate had discharged him because of his age, in violation of the ADEA. In response to Gilmer's complaint, Interstate filed in the District Court a motion to compel arbitration of the ADEA claim. In its motion, Interstate relied upon the arbitration agreement in Gilmer's registration application, as well as the Federal Arbitration Act (FAA), 9 U.S.C. § 1 *et seq.* The District Court denied Interstate's motion . . . [, but the Court of Appeals reversed.] We granted certiorari to resolve a conflict among the Courts of Appeals regarding the arbitrability of ADEA claims.

II.

The FAA was originally enacted in 1925, and then reenacted and codified in 1947 as Title 9 of the United States Code. Its purpose was to reverse the longstanding judicial hostility to arbitration agreements that had existed at English common law and had been adopted by American courts, and to place arbitration agreements upon the same footing as other contracts. Its primary substantive provision states that "[a] written provision in any maritime transaction or a contract evidencing a transaction involving commerce to settle by arbitration a controversy thereafter arising out of such contract or transaction . . . shall be valid, irrevocable, and enforceable, save upon such grounds as exist at law or in equity for the revocation of any contract." 9 U.S.C. § 2. The FAA also provides for stays of proceedings in federal district courts when an issue in the proceeding is referable to arbitration, § 3, and for orders compelling arbitration when one party has failed, neglected, or refused to comply with an arbitration agreement, § 4. These provisions manifest a "liberal federal policy favoring arbitration agreements." *Moses H. Cone Mem'l Hosp. v. Mercury Constr. Corp.*, 460 U.S. 1, 24 (1983).[2]

It is by now clear that statutory claims may be the subject of an arbitration agreement, enforceable pursuant to the FAA. Indeed, in recent years we have held enforceable arbitration agreements relating to claims arising under the Sherman Act; § 10(b) of the Securities Exchange Act of 1934; the civil

---

[2] Section 1 of the FAA provides that "nothing herein contained shall apply to contracts of employment of seamen, railroad employees, or any other class of workers engaged in foreign or interstate commerce." 9 U.S.C. § 1. Several *amici curiae* in support of Gilmer argue that that section excludes from the coverage of the FAA all "contracts of employment." The arbitration clause at issue is in Gilmer's securities registration application, which is a contract with the securities exchanges, not with Interstate. Consequently, we leave for another day the issue raised by *amici curiae*.

provisions of the Racketeer Influenced and Corrupt Organizations Act (RICO); and § 12(2) of the Securities Act of 1933. *See Mitsubishi Motors Corp. v. Soler Chrysler-Plymouth, Inc.*, 473 U.S. 614 (1985); *Shearson/American Express Inc. v. McMahon*, 482 U.S. 220 (1987); *Rodriguez de Quijas v. Shearson/ American Express, Inc.*, 490 U.S. 477 (1989). In these cases we recognized that "[b]y agreeing to arbitrate a statutory claim, a party does not forgo the substantive rights afforded by the statute; it only submits to their resolution in an arbitral, rather than a judicial, forum." *Mitsubishi*, 473 U.S. at 628.

Although all statutory claims may not be appropriate for arbitration, "[h]aving made the bargain to arbitrate, the party should be held to it unless Congress itself has evinced an intention to preclude a waiver of judicial remedies for the statutory rights at issue." *Ibid.* In this regard, we note that the burden is on Gilmer to show that Congress intended to preclude a waiver of a judicial forum for ADEA claims. If such an intention exists, it will be discoverable in the text of the ADEA, its legislative history, or an "inherent conflict" between arbitration and the ADEA's underlying purposes. *See ibid.* Throughout such an inquiry, it should be kept in mind that "questions of arbitrability must be addressed with a healthy regard for the federal policy favoring arbitration." *Moses H. Cone*, 460 U.S. at 24.

III.

Gilmer concedes that nothing in the text of the ADEA or its legislative history explicitly precludes arbitration. He argues, however, that compulsory arbitration of ADEA claims pursuant to arbitration agreements would be inconsistent with the statutory framework and purposes of the ADEA. Like the Court of Appeals, we disagree.

A.

Congress enacted the ADEA in 1967 "to promote employment of older persons based on their ability rather than age; to prohibit arbitrary age discrimination in employment; [and] to help employers and workers find ways of meeting problems arising from the impact of age on employment." 29 U.S.C. § 621(b). To achieve those goals, the ADEA, among other things, makes it unlawful for an employer "to fail or refuse to hire or to discharge any individual or otherwise discriminate against any individual with respect to his compensation, terms, conditions, of privileges of employment, because of such individual's age." § 623(a)(1). This proscription is enforced both by private suits and by the EEOC. In order for an aggrieved individual to bring suit under the ADEA, he or she must first file a charge with the EEOC and then wait at least 60 days. § 626(d). An individual's right to sue is extinguished, however, if the EEOC institutes an action against the employer. § 626(c)(1). Before the EEOC can bring such an action, though, it must "attempt to eliminate the discriminatory practice or practices alleged, and to effect voluntary compliance with the requirements of this chapter through informal methods of conciliation, conference, and persuasion." § 626(b); *see also* 29 C.F.R. § 1626.15 (1990).

As Gilmer contends, the ADEA is designed not only to address individual grievances, but also to further important social policies. We do not perceive any inherent inconsistency between those policies, however, and enforcing agreements to arbitrate age discrimination claims. It is true that arbitration focuses on specific disputes between the parties involved. The same can be said, however, of judicial resolution of claims. Both of these dispute resolution mechanisms nevertheless also can further broader social purposes. The Sherman Act, the Securities Exchange Act of 1934, RICO, and the Securities Act of 1933 all are designed to advance important public policies, but, as noted above, claims under those statutes are appropriate for arbitration. "[S]o long as the prospective litigant effectively may vindicate [his or her] statutory cause of action in the arbitral forum, the statute will continue to serve both its remedial and deterrent function." *Mitsubishi, supra,* at 637.

We also are unpersuaded by the argument that arbitration will undermine the role of the EEOC in enforcing the ADEA. An individual ADEA claimant subject to an arbitration agreement will still be free to file a charge with the EEOC, even though the claimant is not able to institute a private judicial action. Indeed, Gilmer filed a charge with the EEOC in this case. In any event, the EEOC's role in combating age discrimination is not dependent on the filing of a charge; the agency may receive information concerning alleged violations of the ADEA "from any source," and it has independent authority to investigate age discrimination. *See* 29 C.F.R. §§ 1626.4, 1626.13 (1990). Moreover, nothing in the ADEA indicates that Congress intended that the EEOC be involved in all employment disputes. Such disputes can be settled, for example, without any EEOC involvement.[3]

Finally, the mere involvement of an administrative agency in the enforcement of a statute is not sufficient to preclude arbitration. For example, the Securities Exchange Commission is heavily involved in the enforcement of the Securities Exchange Act of 1934 and the Securities Act of 1933, but we have held that claims under both of those statutes may be subject to compulsory arbitration.

Gilmer also argues that compulsory arbitration is improper because it deprives claimants of the judicial forum provided for by the ADEA. Congress, however, did not explicitly preclude arbitration or other nonjudicial resolution of claims, even in its recent amendments to the ADEA. "[I]f Congress intended the substantive protection afforded [by the ADEA] to include protection against waiver of the right to a judicial forum, that intention will be deducible from text or legislative history." *Mitsubishi,* 473 U.S. at 628. Moreover, Gilmer's argument ignores the ADEA's flexible approach to resolution of claims. The EEOC, for example, is directed to pursue "informal methods of conciliation, conference, and persuasion," 29 U.S.C. § 626(b), which suggests that out-of-court dispute resolution, such as arbitration, is consistent with the statutory scheme established by Congress. In addition, arbitration is consistent with Congress' grant of concurrent jurisdiction over ADEA claims to state and federal courts, *see* 29 U.S.C. § 626(c)(1) (allowing suits to be brought "in any court of competent jurisdiction"), because arbitration agreements, "like the

---

[3] In the recently enacted Older Workers Benefit Protection Act, Congress amended the ADEA to provide that "[a]n individual may not waive any right or claim under this Act unless the waiver is knowing and voluntary." *See* 29 U.S.C. § 626(f)(1). Congress also specified certain conditions that must be met in order for a waiver to be knowing and voluntary.

provision for concurrent jurisdiction, serve to advance the objective of allowing [claimants] a broader right to select the forum for resolving disputes, whether it be judicial or otherwise." *Rodriguez de Quijas, supra,* at 483.

B.

In arguing that arbitration is inconsistent with the ADEA, Gilmer also raises a host of challenges to the adequacy of arbitration procedures. Initially, we note that in our recent arbitration cases we have already rejected most of these arguments as insufficient to preclude arbitration of statutory claims. Such generalized attacks on arbitration "res[t] on suspicion of arbitration as a method of weakening the protections afforded in the substantive law to would-be complainants," and as such, they are "far out of step with our current strong endorsement of the federal statutes favoring this method of resolving disputes." *Rodriguez de Quijas, supra,* at 481. Consequently, we address these arguments only briefly.

Gilmer first speculates that arbitration panels will be biased. However, "[w]e decline to indulge the presumption that the parties and arbitral body conducting a proceeding will be unable or unwilling to retain competent, conscientious and impartial arbitrators." *Mitsubishi, supra,* at 634. In any event, we note that the NYSE arbitration rules, which are applicable to the dispute in this case, provide protections against biased panels. The rules require, for example, that the parties be informed of the employment histories of the arbitrators, and that they be allowed to make further inquiries into the arbitrators' backgrounds. In addition, each party is allowed one peremptory challenge and unlimited challenges for cause. Moreover, the arbitrators are required to disclose "any circumstances which might preclude [them] from rendering an objective and impartial determination." The FAA also protects against bias, by providing that courts may overturn arbitration decisions "[w]here there was evident partiality or corruption in the arbitrators." 9 U.S.C. § 10(b). There has been no showing in this case that those provisions are inadequate to guard against potential bias.

Gilmer also complains that the discovery allowed in arbitration is more limited than in the federal courts, which he contends will make it difficult to prove discrimination. It is unlikely, however, that age discrimination claims require more extensive discovery than other claims that we have found to be arbitrable, such as RICO and antitrust claims. Moreover, there has been no showing in this case that the NYSE discovery provisions, which allow for document production, information requests, depositions, and subpoenas, will prove insufficient to allow ADEA claimants such as Gilmer a fair opportunity to present their claims. Although those procedures might not be as extensive as in the federal courts, by agreeing to arbitrate, a party "trades the procedures and opportunity for review of the courtroom for the simplicity, informality, and expedition of arbitration." *Mitsubishi, supra,* at 628. Indeed, an important counterweight to the reduced discovery in NYSE arbitration is that arbitrators are not bound by the rules of evidence.

A further alleged deficiency of arbitration is that arbitrators often will not issue written opinions, resulting, Gilmer contends, in a lack of public knowledge of employers' discriminatory policies, an inability to obtain effective appellate review, and a stifling of the development of the law. The NYSE rules, however, do require that all arbitration awards be in writing, and that the awards contain the names of the parties, a summary of the issues in controversy, and a description of the award issued. In addition, the award decisions are made available to the public. Furthermore, judicial decisions addressing ADEA claims will continue to be issued because it is unlikely that all or even most ADEA claimants will be subject to arbitration agreements. Finally, Gilmer's concerns apply equally to settlements of ADEA claims, which, as noted above, are clearly allowed.[4]

It is also argued that arbitration procedures cannot adequately further the purposes of the ADEA because they do not provide for broad equitable relief and class actions. As the court below noted, however, arbitrators do have the power to fashion equitable relief. Indeed, the NYSE rules applicable here do not restrict the types of relief an arbitrator may award, but merely refer to "damages and/or other relief." The NYSE rules also provide for collective proceedings. But "even if the arbitration could not go forward as a class action or class relief could not be granted by the arbitrator, the fact that the [ADEA] provides for the possibility of bringing a collective action does not mean that individual attempts at conciliation were intended to be barred." *Nicholson v. CPC Int'l Inc.*, 877 F.2d 221, 241 (3rd Cir. 1989) (Becker, J., dissenting). Finally, it should be remembered that arbitration agreements will not preclude the EEOC from bringing actions seeking class-wide and equitable relief.

C.

An additional reason advanced by Gilmer for refusing to enforce arbitration agreements relating to ADEA claims is his contention that there often will be unequal bargaining power between employers and employees. Mere inequality in bargaining power, however, is not a sufficient reason to hold that arbitration agreements are never enforceable in the employment context. Relationships between securities dealers and investors, for example, may involve unequal bargaining power, but we nevertheless held in *Rodriguez de Quijas* and *McMahon* that agreements to arbitrate in that context are enforceable. As discussed above, the FAA's purpose was to place arbitration agreements on the same footing as other contracts. Thus, arbitration agreements are enforceable "save upon such grounds as exist at law or in equity for the revocation of any contract." 9 U.S.C. § 2. "Of course, courts should remain attuned to well-supported claims that the agreement to arbitrate resulted from the sort of fraud or overwhelming economic power that would provide grounds 'for the revocation of any contract.'" *Mitsubishi*, 473 U.S. at 627. There is no indication in this case, however, that Gilmer, an experienced businessman, was coerced or defrauded into agreeing to the arbitration clause in his registration application. As with the claimed procedural inadequacies discussed above, this claim of unequal bargaining power is best left for resolution in specific cases.

---

[4] Gilmer also contends that judicial review of arbitration decisions is too limited. We have stated, however, that "although judicial scrutiny of arbitration awards necessarily is limited, such review is sufficient to ensure that arbitrators comply with the requirements of the statute" at issue. *Shearson/American Express Inc. v. McMahon*, 482 U.S. 220, 232 (1987).

IV.

In addition to the arguments discussed above, Gilmer vigorously asserts that our decision in *Alexander v. Gardner-Denver Co.*, 415 U.S. 36 (1974), and its progeny — *Barrentine v. Arkansas-Best Freight System, Inc.*, 450 U.S. 728 (1981), and *McDonald v. West Branch*, 466 U.S. 284 (1984) — preclude arbitration of employment discrimination claims. Gilmer's reliance on these cases, however, is misplaced.

In *Gardner-Denver*, the issue was whether a discharged employee whose grievance had been arbitrated pursuant to an arbitration clause in a collective-bargaining agreement was precluded from subsequently bringing a Title VII action based upon the conduct that was the subject of the grievance. In holding that the employee was not foreclosed from bringing the Title VII claim, we stressed that an employee's contractual rights under a collective-bargaining agreement are distinct from the employee's statutory Title VII rights:

> "In submitting his grievance to arbitration, an employee seeks to vindicate his contractual right under a collective-bargaining agreement. By contrast, in filing a lawsuit under Title VII, an employee asserts independent statutory rights accorded by Congress. The distinctly separate nature of these contractual and statutory rights is not vitiated merely because both were violated as a result of the same factual occurrence." 415 U.S. at 49-50.

We also noted that a labor arbitrator has authority only to resolve questions of contractual rights. The arbitrator's "task is to effectuate the intent of the parties" and he or she does not have the "general authority to invoke public laws that conflict with the bargain between the parties." *Id*. at 53. By contrast, "in instituting an action under Title VII, the employee is not seeking review of the arbitrator's decision. Rather, he is asserting a statutory right independent of the arbitration process." *Id*. at 54. We further expressed concern that in collective-bargaining arbitration "the interests of the individual employee may be subordinated to the collective interests of all employees in the bargaining unit." *Id*. at 58, n. 19.[5]

Barrentine and *McDonald* similarly involved the issue whether arbitration under a collective-bargaining agreement precluded a subsequent statutory claim. In holding that the statutory claims there were not precluded, we noted, as in *Gardner-Denver*, the difference between contractual rights under a collective-bargaining agreement and individual statutory rights, the potential disparity in interests between a union and an employee, and the limited authority and power of labor arbitrators.

There are several important distinctions between the *Gardner-Denver* line of cases and the case before us. First, those cases did not involve the issue

---

[5] The Court in *Alexander v. Gardner-Denver Co.*, also expressed the view that arbitration was inferior to the judicial process for resolving statutory claims. That "mistrust of the arbitral process," however, has been undermined by our recent arbitration decisions. *McMahon*, 482 U.S. at 231-232. "[W]e are well past the time when judicial suspicion of the desirability of arbitration and of the competence of arbitral tribunals inhibited the development of arbitration as an alternative means of dispute resolution." *Mitsubishi Motors Corp. v. Soler Chrysler-Plymouth, Inc.*, 473 U.S. 614, 626-627 (1985).

of the enforceability of an agreement to arbitrate statutory claims. Rather, they involved the quite different issue whether arbitration of contract-based claims precluded subsequent judicial resolution of statutory claims. Since the employees there had not agreed to arbitrate their statutory claims, and the labor arbitrators were not authorized to resolve such claims, the arbitration in those cases understandably was held not to preclude subsequent statutory actions. Second, because the arbitration in those cases occurred in the context of a collective-bargaining agreement, the claimants there were represented by their unions in the arbitration proceedings. An important concern therefore was the tension between collective representation and individual statutory rights, a concern not applicable to the present case. Finally, those cases were not decided under the FAA, which, as discussed above, reflects a "liberal federal policy favoring arbitration agreements." *Mitsubishi*, 473 U.S. at 625. Therefore, those cases provide no basis for refusing to enforce Gilmer's agreement to arbitrate his ADEA claim.

V.

We conclude that Gilmer has not met his burden of showing that Congress, in enacting the ADEA, intended to preclude arbitration of claims under that Act. Accordingly, the judgment of the Court of Appeals is

Affirmed.

JUSTICE STEVENS, with whom JUSTICE MARSHALL joins, dissenting.

The Court today, in holding that the FAA compels enforcement of arbitration clauses even when claims of age discrimination are at issue, skirts the antecedent question whether the coverage of the Act even extends to arbitration clauses contained in employment contracts, regardless of the subject matter of the claim at issue. In my opinion, arbitration clauses contained in employment agreements are specifically exempt from coverage of the FAA, and for that reason respondent Interstate/Johnson Lane Corporation cannot, pursuant to the FAA, compel petitioner to submit his claims arising under the Age Discrimination in Employment Act of 1967 to binding arbitration. . . .

When the FAA was passed in 1925, I doubt that any legislator who voted for it expected it to apply to statutory claims, to form contracts between parties of unequal bargaining power, or to the arbitration of disputes arising out of the employment relationship. In recent years, however, the Court "has effectively rewritten the statute," and abandoned its earlier view that statutory claims were not appropriate subjects for arbitration. *See Mitsubishi Motors v. Soler Chrysler-Plymouth, Inc.*, 473 U.S. 614, 646-651 (1985) (STEVENS, J., dissenting). Although I remain persuaded that it erred in doing so, the Court has also put to one side any concern about the inequality of bargaining power between an entire industry, on the one hand, and an individual customer or employee, on the other. Until today, however, the Court has not read § 2 of the FAA as broadly encompassing disputes arising out of the employment relationship. I believe this additional extension of the FAA is erroneous. Accordingly, I respectfully dissent.

NOTES

1. *Circuit City.* Ten years after *Gilmer*, the Supreme Court resolved the question skirted by the majority in footnote two. In *Circuit City Stores, Inc. v. Adams*, 532 U.S. 105 (2001), the Court by a 5-4 vote held that the FAA covers most employment contracts. The majority thus interpreted Section 1 of the FAA narrowly to exempt only employment contracts of seamen, railroad workers, and any other class of workers actually engaged in the movement of goods in interstate commerce in the same way that seamen and railroad workers are.

2. *Older Workers Benefit Protection Act.* In footnote 3, the majority noted that under a recent amendment to the ADEA, the Older Workers Benefit Protection Act of 1990 (OWBPA), 29 U.S.C. § 626(f)(1)(A)-(H), an individual may not waive any right or claim under the ADEA unless the waiver is knowing and voluntary. The OWBPA sets out a number of criteria for satisfying the "knowing and voluntary" requirement, such as that:

(1) the waiver must be in writing and be understandable to an average employee;

(2) the waiver must specifically refer to ADEA rights or claims;

(3) the individual cannot waive rights that arise after the waiver is executed;

(4) the employer must provide additional consideration other than continued employment for the waiver;

(5) the individual must be advised in writing to consult with an attorney;

(6) the individual must be given at least 21 days to consider the waiver and has 7 days after signing the waiver in which he or she may revoke the agreement.

Assuming these requirements are met, however, the OWBPA does not invalidate a pre-dispute contractual agreement to submit resolution of claims to an arbitrator rather than a court.

3. *Contractual Shortening of Statute of Limitations.* Rather than using an arbitration clause to get all workplace disputes out of court, some employers seek a contractual clause in which employees promise to bring all lawsuits within a short period of time after termination. In *Soltani v. Western & Southern Life Insurance*, 258 F.3d 1038 (9th Cir. 2001), the court upheld a clause requiring employees to file suit within six months of termination, effectively waiving any longer statute of limitations. The *Soltani* court refused to enforce as unconscionable, however, a clause requiring employees to give ten-days notice before filing a lawsuit. The ten-day period was too short for the employer to investigate or attempt to settle the claim, reasoned the court, and thus was simply an unnecessary hurdle set up to "maximize employer advantage."

4. *Selecting the Arbitrator.* Arbitration clauses often specify that the arbitrator will be chosen from a neutral source such as the American Arbitration Association or National Academy of Arbitrators. If employers use their own method for choosing an arbitrator, they risk having the agreement to arbitrate invalidated on grounds of unconscionability. For example, in *McMullen v. Meijer, Inc.*, 355 F.3d 485 (6th Cir. 2004), the parties signed an arbitration agreement stating that arbitrators must be selected from a list created exclusively by the employer. The court ruled that an agreement containing this type of arbitrator-selection clause was invalid and unenforceable. "When the process used to select the arbitrator is fundamentally unfair, as in this case, the arbitral forum is not an effective substitute for a judicial forum. . . ." *Id.* at 494.

5. *Vacating Arbitration Awards.* An important feature of arbitration is the narrow grounds on which the decisions of arbitrators may be overturned by a court. Section 10 of the Federal Arbitration Act states the grounds for vacating an award:

> **(a)** In any of the following cases the United States court in and for the district wherein the award was made may make an order vacating the award upon the application of any party to the arbitration —

> **(1)** Where the award was procured by corruption, fraud, or undue means.

> **(2)** Where there was evident partiality or corruption in the arbitrators, or either of them.

> **(3)** Where the arbitrators were guilty of misconduct in refusing to postpone the hearing, upon sufficient cause shown, or in refusing to hear evidence pertinent and material to the controversy; or of any other misbehavior by which the rights of any party have been prejudiced.

> **(4)** Where the arbitrators exceeded their powers, or so imperfectly executed them that a mutual, final, and definite award upon the subject matter submitted was not made.

Even apart from the FAA's grounds, an arbitrator's award may also be overturned for violating public policy. In *State v. AFSCME*, 758 A.2d 387 (Conn. App. Ct. 2000), for example, the court vacated an arbitrator's decision on public policy grounds where the arbitrator reinstated a driver of children for the Department of Children and Families who was convicted for possession of marijuana and cocaine with intent to sell. In contrast, in *Eastern Associated Coal Corp. v. United Mine Workers*, 531 U.S. 57 (2000), the Supreme Court declared that arbitration awards should be overturned only if a contract between employer and employee reaching that result would violate public policy. It held that public policy does not require a court to refuse to enforce an arbitration award that ordered an employer to reinstate an employee truck driver who twice tested positive for marijuana, because it would be lawful for an employer to agree to hire such an employee. *See also Major League Baseball Players Ass'n v. Garvey*, 532 U.S. 504, 509 (2001) (upholding arbitrator's award under section 301, declaring that "the fact that a court is convinced [the arbitrator] committed serious error does not suffice to overturn his decision," and "the arbitrator's improvident, even silly, factfinding does not provide a basis for a reviewing court to refuse to enforce the award.").

6. *Gilmer and Unionized Employees.* Most union contracts have arbitration clauses. The majority in *Gilmer* carefully distinguished its holding from *Alexander v. Gardner-Denver Co.*, in which the Court held that arbitration clauses in union contracts generally have no effect on the ability of plaintiffs to pursue statutory employment claims. In applying this distinction, most lower courts have held that plaintiffs can bypass union grievance and arbitration procedures, even though they would be bound to follow them in a non-union context. As a result, non-union plaintiffs may be bound by a grievance and arbitration procedure even though they may have had limited influence in designing the procedure, while plaintiffs represented by a union can bypass a procedure that was the product of hard bargaining between the company and union.

In *Wright v. Universal Maritime Service Corp.*, 525 U.S. 70 (1998), the Supreme Court acknowledged that "[t]here is obviously some tension" between the *Gardner-Denver* and *Gilmer* lines of cases, but it refused to resolve whether a collective-bargaining contract could waive the rights of individual members to have statutory claims heard in federal court. Wright was a longshoreman injured on the job who received $250,000 in settlement of a workers' compensation claim, as well as social security disability benefits. He then tried to return to work, but the stevedore companies refused to hire him, arguing he was disabled. Rather than following the grievance/arbitration procedure set up by the collective bargaining agreement "to cover all matters affecting wages, hours, and other terms and conditions of employment," the longshoreman filed charges of discrimination in violation of the Americans with Disabilities Act with the EEOC. After receiving a right-to-sue notice, he sued in federal court. The District Court dismissed the claim for failure to pursue the grievance/arbitration procedure, and the Fourth Circuit affirmed. The Supreme Court reversed. The Court declared that, at the very least, *Gardner-Denver* requires that a union-negotiated waiver of employees' statutory right to a federal judicial forum be "clear and unmistakable," a standard not met by the collective bargaining agreement at issue. The Court expressly refused to decide, however, whether a clear and unmistakable waiver would be enforceable.

7. *EEOC Hostility to Mandatory Predispute Arbitration Provisions.* The EEOC has taken the position that "agreements that mandate binding arbitration of discrimination claims as a condition of employment are contrary to the fundamental principles evinced in these laws." Their Policy Statement explains:

> The private arbitral system . . . is structurally biased against applicants and employees. . . . The nature of the arbitral process allows — by design — for minimal, if any, public accountability of arbitrators or arbitral decision-making. Unlike her or his counterparts in the judiciary, the arbitrator answers only to the private parties to the dispute, and not to the public at large. . . . The public plays no role in an arbitrator's selection; s/he is hired by the private parties to a dispute. Similarly, the arbitrator's authority is defined and conferred, not by public law, but by private agreement. . . . Arbitral decisions may not be required to be written or reasoned, and are not

made public without the consent of the parties. Judicial review of arbitral decisions is limited to the narrowest of grounds. As a result, arbitration affords no opportunity to build a jurisprudence through precedent. . . . [I]n the arbitral forum juries are, by definition, unavailable. Discovery is significantly limited compared with that available in court and permitted under the Federal Rules of Civil Procedure. In addition, arbitration systems are not suitable for resolving class or pattern or practice claims of discrimination. They may, in fact, protect systemic discriminators by forcing claims to be adjudicated one at a time, in isolation, without reference to a broader-and more accurate-view of an employer's conduct.

Mandatory arbitration systems include structural biases against discrimination plaintiffs. . . . First, the employer accrues a valuable structural advantage because it is a "repeat player." The employer is a party to arbitration in all disputes with its employees. In contrast, the employee is a "one-shot player"; s/he is a party to arbitration only in her or his own dispute with the employer, who can better keep track of an arbitrator's record. . . . In addition, unlike voluntary post-dispute arbitration — which must be fair enough to be attractive to the employee — the employer imposing mandatory arbitration is free to manipulate the arbitral mechanism to its benefit. The terms of the private agreement defining the arbitrator's authority and the arbitral process are characteristically set by the more powerful party, the very party that the public law seeks to regulate. We are aware of no examples of employees who insist on the mandatory arbitration of future statutory employment disputes as a condition of accepting a job offer — the very suggestion seems far-fetched. Rather, these agreements are imposed by employers because they believe them to be in their interest, and they are made possible by the employer's superior bargaining power. It is thus not surprising that many employer-mandated arbitration systems fall far short of basic concepts of fairness. . . .

The trend to impose mandatory arbitration agreements as a condition of employment also poses a significant threat to the EEOC's statutory responsibility to enforce the federal employment discrimination laws. Effective enforcement by the Commission depends in large part on the initiative of individuals to report instances of discrimination to the commission. Although employers may not lawfully deprive individuals of their statutory right to file employment discrimination charges with the EEOC or otherwise interfere with individuals' protected participation in investigations or proceedings under these laws, employees who are bound by mandatory arbitration agreements may be unaware that they nonetheless may file an EEOC charge. Moreover, individuals are likely to be discouraged from coming to the Commission when they know they will be unable to litigate their claims in court. These chilling effects on charge filing undermine the Commission's enforcement efforts by decreasing channels of information, limiting the agency's awareness of potential violations of law, and impeding its ability to investigate possible unlawful actions and attempt informal resolution. . . .

EEOC Policy Statement on Mandatory Binding Arbitration of Employment Discrimination Disputes as a Condition of Employment, II EEOC COMPLIANCE MANUAL § 603.

Several commentators are equally hostile to mandatory predispute arbitration provisions. For example, Reginald Allene states, "statutory discrimination grievances relegated to . . . arbitration forums are virtually assured employer-favored outcomes," given "the manner of selecting, controlling, and compensating arbitrators, the privacy of the process and how it catalytically arouses an arbitrator's desire to be acceptable to one side." *Statutory Discrimination Claims: Rights 'Waived' and Lost in the Arbitration Forum*, 13 HOFSTRA LAB. L.J. 381, 428 (1996).

Every circuit has rejected the EEOC's position, and the Supreme Court in *Circuit City* seems to go against it as well. For a time, the Ninth Circuit sided with the EEOC. *See Duffield v. Roberson Stevens & Co.*, 144 F.3d 1182 (9th Cir. 1998) (refusal to enforce an agreement to arbitrate a discrimination claim). In 2002, however, the Ninth Circuit overruled *Duffield*, deeming it a "fruitful error." *EEOC v. Luce, Forward, Hamilton & Scripps*, 303 F.3d 994, 1004 (9th Cir. 2002). The court declared that *Circuit City*'s "language and reasoning decimated *Duffield's* conclusion that Congress intended to preclude compulsory arbitration of Title VII Claims."

8. Class Actions and Arbitration. Courts have recently debated whether class actions can be heard in an arbitral forum. Most decisions seem to say yes. An important development was the decision in *Green Tree Financial Corp. v. Bazzle*, 539 U.S. 444 (2003), in which the Supreme Court vacated a decision of the South Carolina Supreme Court that compelled class-wide arbitration of a commercial lending dispute. The parties had agreed to arbitrate disputes, but their agreement was silent on class actions. The Supreme Court held that the question of whether the parties' agreement allowed for class actions was a matter for the arbitrator, not the courts, to decide. Notably, there was nothing in the decision to suggest that an arbitrator would not have the authority to hear and decide a class action. In response to *Bazzle*, some employers have begun to incorporate clauses into arbitration agreements that bar class actions. Challenges to this practice on grounds of unconscionability have met with varied responses in the courts. *Compare Adkins v. Labor Ready, Inc.*, 303 F.3d 496 (4th Cir. 2002) (finding no support in FLSA for the view that class actions are unwaivable, or would defeat the strong congressional preference for an arbitral forum), *with Discover Bank v. Superior Court*, 113 P.3d 1100 (Cal. 2005) (provision in bank-customer arbitration agreement that barred class actions was unconscionable because potential dollar amount of recovery for each customer made individual arbitration impractical).

9. The EEOC's Independent Role in Enforcement. Even if mandatory predispute arbitration agreements are enforceable, it is undisputed that an employee cannot waive the EEOC's right to sue. But can the EEOC recover damages or obtain other relief on behalf of an employee who signed an agreement to arbitrate? The circuit courts were split on this issue. *Compare EEOC v. Frank's Nursery*, 177 F.3d 448 (6th Cir. 1999) (private arbitration agreements cannot limit the scope of an EEOC lawsuit), *with EEOC v. Kidder, Peabody*, 156 F.3d 298 (2d Cir. 1998) (EEOC cannot seek reinstatement, back pay, compensatory damages, or punitive damages on behalf of employee). In *EEOC v. Waffle House Inc.*, 534 U.S. 279 (2002), the Supreme Court ruled that the EEOC could seek all appropriate relief under the statute, including damages and reinstatement for employees who had agreed to arbitrate their disputes.

   10. *Minimum Safeguards in Enforcing Federal Statutes.* An important part of *Gilmer* is Part III, where the Court rejected the argument that Congress, in enacting the ADEA in 1967, impliedly limited the FAA. The Court emphasized that the arbitration procedure at issue contained significant safeguards for workers, and thus the FAA was consistent with the framework and purposes of the ADEA. Numerous courts post-*Gilmer* have tried to delineate basic procedural safeguards required for enforceability of a manda-tory predispute arbitration agreement. An early and influential case was *Cole v. Burns Int'l Security Servs.*, 105 F.3d 1465 (D.C. Cir. 1997), in which the court established five basic safeguards to ensure adequate vindication of individuals' federal statutory rights: 1) a neutral arbitrator, 2) more than minimal discovery, 3) a written award, 4) availability of all remedies that would be available in court, and 5) no requirement for the employee to pay either unreasonable costs or any of the arbitrator's fees or expenses.

   Courts have been especially concerned with the question of whether the costs of arbitration, which might include both fees paid to the arbitrator and fees paid to the arbitration organization that supplies the arbitrator, will inhibit employee access to dispute resolution as compared with the costs of court fees in a civil trial. Most courts have adopted a case-by-case approach following the decision of the Supreme Court in *Green Tree Financial Corp. v. Randolph*, 531 U.S. 79 (2000), a commercial arbitration case that involved a consumer financing agreement requiring arbitration of all disputes. The plaintiff in that case argued that an arbitration agreement that was silent on which party would bear the costs of litigation was unenforceable because it posed the risk of saddling the plaintiff with prohibitive costs. The Court rejected this categorical position, holding that a plaintiff who seeks to invalidate an arbitration agreement on the basis that arbitration would be prohibitively expensive bears the burden of showing the likelihood of incurring such costs.

B. STATE CLAIMS AND THE FAA

LITTLE v. AUTO STIEGLER, INC.
Supreme Court of California
63 P.3d 979 (2003)

Moreno, J.

   In this case, we consider four interlocking questions: (1) Is a provision in a mandatory employment arbitration agreement that permits either party to "appeal" an arbitration award of more than $50,000 to a second arbitrator, unconscionable; (2) if it is unconscionable, then should that unconscionable provision be severed from the rest of the arbitration agreement and the agreement enforced, or is the entire agreement invalid; (3) if the former, then in reviewing the rest of the arbitration agreement, do the minimum require- ments for arbitration of unwaivable statutory claims that we set forth in *Armendariz v. Foundation Health Psychcare Services, Inc.*, 6 P.3d 669 (Cal. 2000), apply also to claims that an employee was terminated in violation of public policy; (4) if yes, then must one of those requirements that the employer imposing mandatory arbitration on the employee must pay all costs unique to arbitration be reconsidered and revised in light of a post-*Armendariz* United States Supreme Court decision on arbitration costsharing, *Green Tree Finan- cial Corp. v. Randolph*, 531 U.S. 79 (2000).

We conclude as follows: (1) the appellate arbitration provision for arbitration awards over $50,000 is unconscionable; (2) that provision should be severed and the rest of the arbitration agreement enforced; (3) a suit claiming wrongful termination in violation of public policy should be subject to the requirements set forth in *Armendariz*; and (4) *Green Tree* does not require that we modify *Armendariz*'s cost requirements. We accordingly partly reverse the Court of Appeal's judgment.

I. *Statement of Facts*

Alexander Little worked for Auto Stiegler, Inc., an automobile dealership. Little eventually rose to become Auto Stiegler's service manager. He alleges that he was demoted, then terminated, for investigating and reporting warranty fraud. He filed an action against defendant for tortious demotion in violation of public policy; tortious termination in violation of public policy; breach of an implied contract of continued employment; and breach of the implied covenant of good faith and fair dealing. . . .

Little signed three nearly identical arbitration agreements while employed by defendant in June 1995, October 1996, and January 1997. The most recent of the three stated as follows:

> I agree that any claim, dispute, or controversy (including, but not limited to, any and all claims of discrimination and harassment) which would otherwise require or allow resort to any court or other govern- mental dispute resolution forum between myself and the Company . . . arising from, related to, or having any relationship or connection whatsoever with my seeking employment with, employment by, or other association with, the Company, whether based on tort, contract, statutory, or equitable law, or otherwise, shall be submitted to and determined exclusively by binding arbitration under the Federal Arbitration Act, in conformity with the procedures of the California Arbitration Act. . . . Awards exceeding $50,000.00 shall include the arbitrator's written reasoned opinion and, at either party's written request within 20 days after issuance of the award, shall be subject to reversal and remand, modification, or reduction following review of the record and arguments of the parties by a second arbitrator who shall, as far as practicable, proceed according to the law and proce- dures applicable to appellate review by the California Court of Appeal

of a civil judgment following court trial. I understand by agreeing to this binding arbitration provision, both I and the Company give up our rights to trial by jury.

[T]he trial court . . . denied defendant's motion to compel arbitration. . . . The Court of Appeal reversed. . . . We granted review.

II. *Discussion*

A. *Unconscionability of Appellate Arbitration Provision*

. . . Little contends [the provision triggering an arbitration appeal following an award greater than $50,000] is unconscionable. We agree.

To briefly recapitulate the principles of unconscionability, the doctrine has "both a procedural and a substantive element, the former focusing on oppression or surprise due to unequal bargaining power, the latter on overly harsh or one-sided results." *Armendariz, supra*, 6 P.3d at 690. The procedural element of an unconscionable contract generally takes the form of a contract of adhesion, "which, imposed and drafted by the party of superior bargaining strength, relegates to the subscribing party only the opportunity to adhere to the contract or reject it. In the case of preemployment arbitration contracts, the economic pressure exerted by employers on all but the most sought-after employees may be particularly acute, for the arbitration agreement stands between the employee and necessary employment, and few employees are in a position to refuse a job because of an arbitration requirement." *Id*. It is clear in the present case that Auto Stiegler imposed on Little an adhesive arbitration agreement.

Substantively unconscionable terms may take various forms, but may generally be described as unfairly one-sided. One such form, as in *Armendariz*, is the arbitration agreement's lack of a "modicum of bilaterality," wherein the employee's claims against the employer, but not the employer's claims against the employee, are subject to arbitration. Another kind of substantively unconscionable provision occurs when the party imposing arbitration mandates a post-arbitration proceeding, either judicial or arbitral, wholly or largely to its benefit at the expense of the party on which the arbitration is imposed. Two Court of Appeal cases have addressed this kind of unconscionability.

In *Beynon v. Garden Grove Medical Group*, 161 Cal. Rptr. 146 (Cal. Ct. App. 1980), the medical group imposed on its patients a mandatory arbitration agreement. Paragraph B of the agreement authorized the medical group, but not the patient, to reject the first arbitration award and submit the dispute to a second arbitration panel. The court held the provision unconscionable. . . .

Saika v. Gold, 56 Cal. Rptr. 2d 922 (Cal. Ct. App. 1996), also arose in the doctor/patient setting. The arbitration agreement in that case had a provision that permitted either party to reject an arbitration award of $25,000 or greater and request a trial de novo in superior court. The Court of Appeal refused to enforce the provision and instead directed the trial court to confirm the $325,000 award in the patient's favor. . . .

Auto Stiegler and its amici curiae make several arguments to distinguish this case from *Benyon* and *Saika*. First, they claim that the arbitration appeal provision applied evenhandedly to both parties and that, unlike the doctor/patient relationship in *Saika*, there is at least the possibility that an employer may be the plaintiff, for example in cases of misappropriation of trade secrets. But if that is the case, they fail to explain adequately the reasons for the $50,000 award threshold. From a plaintiff's perspective, the decision to resort to arbitral appeal would be made not according to the amount of the arbitration award but the potential value of the arbitration claim compared to the costs of the appeal. If the plaintiff and his or her attorney estimate that the potential value of the claim is substantial, and the arbitrator rules that the plaintiff takes nothing because of its erroneous understanding of a point of law, then it is rational for the plaintiff to appeal. Thus, the $50,000 threshold inordinately benefits defendants. Given the fact that Auto Stiegler was the party imposing the arbitration agreement and the $50,000 threshold, it is reasonable to conclude it imposed the threshold with the knowledge or belief that it would generally be the defendant.

Although parties may justify an asymmetrical arbitration agreement when there is a "legitimate commercial need," that need must be "other than the employer's desire to maximize its advantage" in the arbitration process. *Armendariz*. There is no such justification for the $50,000 threshold. The explanation for the threshold offered by amicus curiae Maxie, Rheinheimer, Stephens & Vrevich that an award in which there is less than that amount in controversy would not be worth going through the extra step of appellate arbitral review makes sense only from a defendant's standpoint and cannot withstand scrutiny.

Auto Stiegler also argues that an arbitration appeal is less objectionable than a second arbitration, as in *Benyon*, or a trial de novo, as in *Saika*, because it is not permitting a wholly new proceeding, making the first arbitration illusory, but only permitting limited appellate review of the arbitral award. We fail to perceive a significant difference. Each of these provisions is geared toward giving the arbitral defendant a substantial opportunity to overturn a sizable arbitration awarde. . . .

We therefore conclude that the arbitral appeal provision in this particular agreement is unconscionably one-sided and may not be enforced. We next turn to the question whether this provision may be severed and the rest of the arbitration agreement enforced, or whether the entire agreement should be invalidated.

B. Is the Unconscionable Portion of the Agreement Severable?

In *Armendariz*, we reviewed the principles regarding the severance of illegal terms from an arbitration agreement. As we stated: "Two reasons for severing or restricting illegal terms rather than voiding the entire contract appear implicit in case law. The first is to prevent parties from gaining undeserved benefit or suffering undeserved detriment as a result of voiding the entire agreement particularly when there has been full or partial performance of the contract. Second, more generally, the doctrine of severance attempts to conserve a contractual relationship if to do so would not be condoning an illegal scheme. The overarching inquiry is whether the interests of justice . . . would be furthered by severance. Moreover, courts must have the *capacity* to cure the unlawful contract through severance or restriction of the offending clause, which . . . is not invariably the case." (*Armendariz, supra,* 6 P.3d at 696). Accordingly, "courts are to look to the various purposes of the contract. If the central purpose of the contract is tainted with illegality, then the contract as a whole cannot be enforced. If the illegality is collateral to the main purpose of the contract, and the illegal provision can be extirpated from the contract by means of severance or restriction, then such severance and restriction are appropriate." *Id*.

In *Armendariz*, we found two factors weighed against severance of the unlawful provisions. "First, the arbitration agreement contains more than one unlawful provision; it has both an unlawful damages provision and an unconscionably unilateral arbitration clause. Such multiple defects indicate a systematic effort to impose arbitration on an employee not simply as an alternative to litigation, but as an inferior forum that works to the employer's advantage. . . . Second, in the case of the agreement's lack of mutuality, . . . permeation [by an unlawful purpose] is indicated by the fact that there is no single provision a court can strike or restrict in order to remove the unconscionable taint from the agreement. Rather, the court would have to, in effect, reform the contract, not through severance or restriction, but by augmenting it with additional terms. Civil Code section 1670.5 does not authorize such reformation by augmentation, nor does the arbitration statute. Code of Civil Procedure section 1281.2 authorizes the court to refuse arbitration if grounds for revocation exist, not to reform the agreement to make it lawful. Nor do courts have any such power under their inherent limited authority to reform contracts." *Armendariz, supra,* 6 P.3d at 696-97.

Neither of these factors are operative in the present case. There is only a single provision that is unconscionable, the one-sided arbitration appeal. And no contract reformation is required the offending provision can be severed and the rest of the arbitration agreement left intact. . . .

We therefore conclude that Auto Stiegler's arbitration agreement is valid and enforceable once the unconscionable appellate arbitration provision is deleted. Whether a court should refuse to enforce it on other grounds will be considered below.

C. Is Arbitration of a Tameny Claim Subject to the Minimal Procedural Requirements Set Forth in Armendariz?

In *Tameny v. Atlantic Richfield Co*, 610 P.2d 1330 (Cal. 1980), we recognized that although employers have the power to terminate employees at will, they may not terminate an employee for a reason that is contrary to public policy. Little claims that arbitration of *Tameny* claims are subject to the minimum requirements set forth in *Armendariz*, reviewed below. We agree.

In *Armendariz*, we held that arbitration of claims under the FEHA is subject to certain minimal requirements: (1) the arbitration agreement may not limit the damages normally available under the statute; (2) there must be discovery "sufficient to adequately arbitrate their statutory claim;" (3) there must be a written arbitration decision and judicial review "sufficient to ensure the arbitrators comply with the requirements of the statute;" and (4) the employer must "pay all types of costs that are unique to arbitration."

These requirements were founded on the premise that certain statutory rights are unwaivable. "This unwaivability derives from two statutes that are themselves derived from public policy. First, Civil Code section 1668 states: 'All contracts which have for their object, directly or indirectly, to exempt anyone from responsibility for his own fraud, or willful injury to the person or property of another, or violation of law, whether willful or negligent, are against the policy of the law.' 'Agreements whose object, directly or indirectly, is to exempt [their] parties from violation of the law are against public policy and may not be enforced.' Second, Civil Code section 3513 states, 'Anyone may waive the advantage of a law intended solely for his benefit. But a law established for a public reason cannot be contravened by a private agreement.' " We concluded that the FEHA was enacted for public reasons and the rights it conferred on employees were unwaivable. We then concluded that the above requirements were necessary to enable an employee to vindicate these unwaivable rights in an arbitration forum.

A *Tameny* claim is almost by definition unwaivable. "[The] public policy exception to the at-will employment rule must be based on policies carefully tethered to fundamental policies that are delineated in constitutional or statutory provisions . . . ." *Silo v. CHW Medical Foundation*, 45 P.3d 1162 (Cal. 2002). Moreover, the public policy that is the basis for such a claim must be "'public' in that it affects society at large rather than the individual, must have been articulated at the time of discharge, and must be 'fundamental' and 'substantial.' " *Id*. Thus, a legitimate *Tameny* claim is designed to protect a public interest and therefore "cannot be contravened by a private agreement." *Armendariz, supra,* 6 P.3d at 680. In other words, an employment agreement that required employees to waive claims that they were terminated in violation of public policy would itself be contrary to public policy. Accordingly, because an employer cannot ask the employee to waive *Tameny* claims, it also cannot impose on the arbitration of these claims such burdens or procedural shortcomings as to preclude their vindication. Thus, the *Armendariz* requirements are as appropriate to the arbitration of *Tameny* claims as to unwaivable statutory claims.

Auto Stiegler cites *Brown v. Wheat First Securities, Inc.*, 257 F.3d 821 (D.C. Cir. 2001), which came to a contrary conclusion with respect to a claim for termination in violation of public policy under District of Columbia law. The court held that *Cole v. Burns International Security Services*, 105 F.3d 1465 (D.C. Cir. 1997), a case on which *Armendariz* relied, and which set forth requirements for arbitrating claims under title VII of the Civil Rights Act of 1964 similar to the *Armendariz* requirements, should be limited to federal statutory claims, not state tort claims derived from common law. . . .

The *Brown* court, in rejecting the extension of *Cole* to nonstatutory claims, pointed to language in *Cole* limiting its holding to such claims. The court further stated: "We also see no basis for extending *Cole*. As we have explained, our central rationale respecting congressional intent does not extend beyond the statutory context. Moreover, by enacting the Federal Arbitration Act, Congress manifested a liberal federal policy favoring arbitration agreements. The Act also pre-empted state restrictions on the enforcement of arbitration agreements. *Gilmer*, as we've seen, framed the question as whether dispute resolution under the FAA was consistent with the federal right-creating statute in question. For a common law claim under District of Columbia law, any such inconsistency would be resolved in favor of the only federal law involved, the FAA."

We disagree with the *Brown* court, at least insofar as its decision would be interpreted to preclude extension of the *Armendariz* requirements to *Tameny* claims. First, although *Cole* was a Title VII case properly focused on mandatory arbitration of federal statutory rights, its rationale extends beyond that context generally to unwaivable rights conferred for a public benefit. The statement in *Gilmer* that provides the point of departure in *Cole* "by agreeing to arbitrate a statutory claim, [an employee] does not forgo the substantive rights afforded by the statute; [he] only submits to their resolution in an arbitral, rather than a judicial, forum" would apply equally to nonstatutory public rights.

The *Brown* court's apparent position that only *federal* statutory rights may be subject to *Cole*'s requirements, because any attempt to place conditions on arbitration based on state law would be preempted by the Federal Arbitration Act (FAA), is incorrect. The FAA provides that arbitration agreements are "valid, irrevocable, and enforceable save upon such grounds as exist at law or in equity for the revocation of any contract." Thus, "[a] state-law principle that takes its meaning precisely from the fact that a contract to arbitrate is at issue does not comport with the text of section 2 [of the FAA]." *Doctor's Associates, Inc. v. Casarotto*, 517 U.S. 681, 685 (1996). But under section 2 of the FAA, a state court may refuse to enforce an arbitration agreement based on "generally applicable contract defenses, such as fraud, duress, or unconscionability." One such long-standing ground for refusing to enforce a contractual term is that it would force a party to forgo unwaivable public rights, as reviewed above.

Thus, while we recognize that a party compelled to arbitrate such rights does not waive them, but merely "submits to their resolution in an arbitral, rather than a judicial, forum," *Gilmer*, arbitration cannot be misused to accomplish a de facto waiver of these rights. Accordingly, although the *Armendariz* requirements specifically concern arbitration agreements, they do not do so out of a generalized mistrust of arbitration per se, but from a recognition that *some* arbitration agreements and proceedings may harbor terms, conditions and practices that undermine the vindication of unwaivable rights. The *Armendariz* requirements are therefore applications of general state law contract principles regarding the unwaivability of public rights to the unique context of arbitration, and accordingly are not preempted by the FAA. . . .

[W]ith regard to arbitration costs at issue in this case and in *Brown*, the principle that arbitration costs may prevent arbitration claimants from effectively pursuing their public rights would apply with equal force to *Tameny* claims as to FEHA claims or to federal statutory claims. Nothing in the FAA prevents states from controlling arbitration costs imposed by adhesive contracts so that the remedy of prosecuting state statutory or common law public rights through arbitration is not rendered illusory. The *Armendariz* cost-shifting requirement is unique to arbitration only to the extent that arbitration, alone among contract provisions, may potentially require litigants to expend large sums to pay for the costs of the hearing that will decide his or her statutory other public rights. In other words, it is not the arbitration agreement itself but the imposition of arbitration forum costs that under certain circumstances violate state law.

Moreover, *Armendariz*'s cost rule does not "require a judicial forum for the resolution of claims which the contracting parties agreed to resolve by arbitration." *Southland*, 465 U.S. at 10. Rather, we simply required that employers pay arbitration forum costs under certain circumstances as a condition of arbitration. Nothing in the United States Supreme Court case law leads us to believe that a state requirement shifting arbitration costs in mandatory employment agreements to the employer pursuant to established state law contract doctrine violates the FAA.

Furthermore, Code of Civil Procedure section 1284.2, which provides that each party pay a pro rata share of arbitration costs unless the agreement provides otherwise, does not alter our conclusion. We held in *Armendariz* that this statute does not preclude the judicial imposition of proportionally greater costs on the employer in the case of FEHA claims. We reasoned that "the agreement to arbitrate a statutory claim is implicitly an agreement to abide by the substantive remedial provisions of the statute" and that the FEHA implicitly prohibited large arbitration costs that would stand as an obstacle to successfully pursuing rights conferred on the employee. We similarly conclude that an agreement to arbitrate a claim of wrongful termination contrary to public policy must be interpreted to implicitly include an agreement to proportion costs in a manner that is reasonable for the employee/claimant, in order to prevent the de facto waiver of unwaivable rights. . . .

Therefore, we conclude that a plaintiff/employee seeking to arbitrate a *Tameny* claim should have the benefit of the same minimal protections as for FEHA claims as a means of ensuring that they can effectively prosecute such a claim in the arbitral forum. These include the availability of damages remedies equal to those available in a *Tameny* suit brought in court, including punitive damages; discovery sufficient to adequately arbitrate *Tameny* claim; a written arbitration decision and judicial review sufficient to ensure that arbitrators have complied with the law respecting such claims; and allocation of arbitration costs so that they will not unduly burden the employee.

We have already rejected the contentions that the arbitration agreement in the present case limited Little's remedies or his ability to obtain adequate judicial review. Nor is it evident from the agreement that Little will be unable to obtain adequate discovery. Little argues, however, that there is a risk of burdensome costs being imposed on him, contrary to *Armendariz*. We consider this argument in the next part of our opinion.

D. Cost Sharing and Arbitration of Tameny Claims

Little argues that the arbitration agreement's silence on the issue of costs means that he would be statutorily compelled to share costs under Code of

Civil Procedure section 1284.2, and that the imposition of such costs renders the arbitration agreement unenforceable. *Armendariz* did not conclude that an arbitration agreement silent on costs was unenforceable. On the contrary, we held we would infer from such silence an agreement that "the employer must bear the arbitration forum costs" and that "the absence of specific provisions on arbitration costs would . . . not be grounds for denying the enforcement of an arbitration agreement." *Armendariz*, *supra*, 6 P.3d at 689.

The California Motorcar Dealers Association, amicus curiae on behalf of Auto Stiegler, argues that our holding on costs in *Armendariz* has been supplanted by the United States Supreme Court's holding in *Green Tree*. Because the allocation of arbitration costs will be at issue on remand, we address the relationship between *Armendariz* and *Green Tree*.

In *Green Tree*, the plaintiff, purchaser of a mobile home, sued her lender on various federal statutory grounds, including violation of the Truth in Lending Act, for failing to disclose certain finance charges. The buyer's agreement with the lender contained a binding arbitration clause that included all statutory claims. The agreement was silent on the issue of who would pay the costs of arbitration. The district court granted the lender's motion to compel arbitration but the court of appeals reversed, holding that the agreement posed the risk that the plaintiff's "ability to vindicate her statutory rights would be undone by 'steep' arbitration costs and therefore was unenforceable."

The United States Supreme Court reversed. It first reaffirmed its longstanding position that statutory claims are arbitrable under the FAA absent the expression of congressional intent "to preclude a waiver of judicial remedies for the statutory rights at issue." Finding no such expression in the TILA, the court proceeded to address the borrower's argument that silence on the matter of arbitration costs created an unacceptable risk that she might have to pay prohibitive costs and therefore not be able to vindicate her statutory rights through arbitration. The court stated: "The 'risk' that Randolph will be saddled with prohibitive costs is too speculative to justify the invalidation of an arbitration agreement."

The court further explained: "To invalidate the agreement on that basis would undermine the 'liberal federal policy favoring arbitration agreements.' It would also conflict with our prior holdings that the party resisting arbitration bears the burden of proving that the claims at issue are unsuitable for arbitration. . . . Similarly, we believe that where, as here, a party seeks to invalidate an arbitration agreement on the ground that arbitration would be *prohibitively expensive*, that party bears the burden of showing the likelihood of incurring such costs. Randolph did not meet that burden. How detailed the showing of prohibitive expense must be before the party seeking arbitration must come forward with contrary evidence is a matter we need not discuss; for in this case neither during discovery nor when the case was presented on the merits was there any timely showing at all on the point. The Court of Appeals therefore erred in deciding that the arbitration agreement's silence with respect to costs and fees rendered it unenforceable."

Although *Green Tree* was not an employment case, most courts interpreting it have done so in the employment context. . . .

Armendariz and *Green Tree* agree on two fundamental tenets. First, silence about costs in an arbitration agreement is not grounds for denying a motion to compel arbitration. Second, arbitration costs can present significant barriers to the vindication of statutory rights. Nonetheless, there may be a significant difference between the two cases. Although *Green Tree* did not elaborate on the kinds of costsharing arrangements that would be unenforceable, dicta in that case, and several federal cases cited above interpreting it, suggest that federal law requires only that employers not impose "prohibitively expensive" arbitration costs on the employee, and that determination of whether such costs have been imposed are to be made on a case-by-case basis. *Armendariz*, on the other hand, categorically imposes costs unique to arbitration on employers when unwaivable rights pursuant to a mandatory employment arbitration agreement are at stake. Assuming that *Green Tree* and *Armendariz* pose solutions to the problem of arbitration costs that are in some respects different, we do not agree with amicus curiae that the FAA requires states to comply with federal arbitration costsharing standards.

As reviewed in the previous part of this opinion, Armendariz's cost-shifting requirement is not preempted by the FAA. It is not a barrier to the enforcement of arbitration agreements, nor does it improperly disfavor arbitration in comparison to other contract clauses. Rather, it is derived from state contract law principles regarding the unwaivability of certain public rights in the context of a contract of adhesion. We do not discern from the United States Supreme Court's jurisprudence on FAA preemption a requirement that state law conform precisely with federal law as to the manner in which such public rights are protected. . . .

In short, for reasons stated above, we do not believe that the FAA requires state courts to adopt precisely the same means as federal courts to ensure that the vindication of public rights will not be stymied by burdensome arbitration costs. We continue to believe that *Armendariz* represents the soundest approach to the problem of arbitration costs in the context of mandatory employment arbitration. We therefore conclude that on remand the court compelling arbitration should require the employer to pay in this case "all types of costs that are unique to arbitration."

III. *Disposition*

The judgment of the Court of Appeal is reversed insofar as it (1) permits enforcement of a clause allowing arbitral review only of awards greater than $50,000 and (2) requires arbitration of Little's *Tameny* claim, assuming he has adequately alleged such a claim, without requiring Auto Stiegler to pay arbitration forum costs as set forth in *Armendariz*. The cause is remanded to the Court of Appeal with instructions to direct the superior court to conduct further proceedings consistent with the views expressed in this opinion. In all other respects, the Court of Appeal's judgment is affirmed.

Concurring and Dissenting Opinion By BAXTER, J.

Despite *Green Tree*, the instant majority retain *Armendariz*'s "employer always pays" cost formula. The majority say *Green Tree* does not strictly require us to alter *Armendariz*'s application of California contract law to the issue of arbitration costs. On that technical point, the majority may or may not be correct. . . . *Green Tree* holds in essence that even where the vindication of statutory rights is at stake, when courts interfere with an arbitration agreement by *presuming* undue cost to one party, they exhibit particular "hostility" and suspicion toward contractual arbitration, which the FAA was intended to prevent.

At direct odds with this principle is the current California requirement that the employer must always pay the employee's "forum costs" of arbitrating a statutory claim, regardless of actual need, and contrary to a California law that implies a cost-sharing term in every arbitration contract unless the parties expressly agree otherwise. I believe *Green Tree* warrants reconsideration of the *Armendariz* majority's views on cost allocation. . . .

Under the circumstances, I would overrule *Armendariz*'s arbitrary cost allocation formula. In its place, I would adopt *Green Tree*'s principle that if a party resists mandatory contractual arbitration of a statutory claim on grounds of undue cost, he must make a timely, particularized showing of the expected expense, and must also demonstrate that, in his particular case, this cost would make arbitration prohibitively expensive as compared to court litigation. Evidence on this issue could be presented to the court deciding a motion to compel arbitration. If the party opposing arbitration demonstrated prohibitive expense, the court could grant the motion to compel upon the condition that the proponent of arbitration accept, with the caveat discussed below, a more equitable allocation of costs. . . .

Concurring and Dissenting Opinion By BROWN, J.

Like the majority, I find the appellate arbitration provision in the arbitration agreement unconscionable. I also agree that this "provision should be severed and the rest of the arbitration agreement enforced." . . . Unlike the majority, [however,] I found *Brown v. Wheat First Securities, Inc.*, 257 F.3d 821 (D.C. Cir. 2001), persuasive and would not apply *Armendariz* to *Tameny* claims. . . .

As explained above, we carefully limited the application of *Armendariz* to statutory rights. And our rationale for imposing the . . . *Armendariz* requirements on the arbitration of FEHA claims — respecting legislative intent — does not extend beyond the statutory context.

Indeed, we are precluded from doing so by both Congress and our own Legislature. Congress enacted the FAA " 'to assure those who desired arbitration and whose contracts related to interstate commerce that their expectations would not be undermined . . . by state courts . . . .' " *Southland Corp. v. Keating*, 465 U.S. 1, 13 (1984). Recognizing "the widespread unwillingness of state courts to enforce arbitration agreements", Congress intended the FAA "to be a broad enactment appropriate in scope to meet the large problems Congress was addressing" — i.e., judicial hostility to arbitration — and "unencumbered by state law constraints." As such, the FAA preempts all state laws and rules disfavoring arbitration.

Of course, Congress is free to circumscribe the scope of its enactments. Consistent with this principle, the United States Supreme Court has recognized that the FAA does not govern if "Congress itself has evinced an intention to preclude a waiver of judicial remedies for the statutory rights at issue." *Gilmer v. Interstate/Johnson Lane Corp.*, 500 U.S. 20, 26 (1991). Such an intention may, however, be discerned *only* from "the text [of a federal statute], its legislative history, or an 'inherent conflict' between arbitration and" that statute's underlying purposes. Thus, in the absence of a statute evidencing a clear congressional intent to restrict arbitration, the FAA controls and precludes courts from imposing their own arbitration-specific restrictions.

Similarly, California's arbitration scheme precludes California courts from restricting arbitrations in the absence of an express legislative intent to do so. . . . Absent certain statutorily enumerated grounds not relevant here, courts must enforce an arbitration agreement *as written*. While the Legislature may create exceptions to this strong statutory policy in favor of arbitration and selectively limit arbitrations, we may not.

Nonetheless, the majority does just that. A *Tameny* claim is a common law cause of action created by this court — and not by the Legislature. Thus, *Tameny* claims are a judicial — and not a legislative — construct, and the public policy underlying these claims "is inconsequential as a measure of [the Legislature's] interest in the stated policy." *Brown*, 257 F.3d at 826. As a result, the majority's extension of *Armendariz* violates the FAA and our own statutory arbitration scheme. . . .

. . . The crucial question is whether there is any evidence of a congressional or legislative intent to place restrictions on the arbitration of *Tameny* claims. While the unwaivability of a statutory right established by the statute's text, history, or purpose may evidence such an intent, a judicial finding of unwaivability for public policy reasons cannot. Indeed, the public policy exception the majority adopts subjects most, if not all, tort claims to the . . . *Armendariz* requirements. "All claims not based on contract — including, for example, . . . defamation and tortious interference claims . . . — implement values that society has in one way or another thought deserving." *Brown*, 257 F.3d at 826. Under this public policy rationale, "it is hard to see what falls outside it." (*Ibid.*) . . .

Our extension of *Armendariz* to *Tameny* claims therefore usurps Congress's authority to establish "the supreme law of the land" and the Legislature's "responsibility to declare the public policy of the state" Moreover, by imposing arbitration-specific restrictions that have no congressional or legislative basis, the majority not only undermines the "liberal federal policy favoring arbitration" but also contravenes California's "strong public policy in favor of arbitration as a speedy and relatively inexpensive means of dispute resolution."

NOTES

1. ***Procedural Safeguards in Enforcing State Law Claims.*** In *Gilmer*, the issue was whether the FAA required enforcement of predispute promises to arbitrate federal employment law claims. *Circuit City*, by contrast, involved predispute promises to arbitrate state-law claims. It is perhaps significant that the court in *Circuit City*, in contrast to *Gilmer*, did not discuss the safeguards in the arbitration scheme. In part, this was because state law, unlike

later-enacted federal statutes, can not possibly limit the reach of the federal FAA statute.

Thus, the question arises whether the FAA would preempt any state law attempt to impose safeguards of the type set out in *Cole* on agreements to arbitrate state claims. The California Supreme Court in *Little* says no.

2. *Severability and Incentives.* *Little* allows a court to sever an unconscionable provision and enforce the balance of the agreement. Does this rule serve as an adequate deterrent against the inclusion of oppressive terms in arbitration agreements?

C. IMPLEMENTATION

While the EEOC decries the movement towards arbitration, others see arbitration of employment disputes as a praiseworthy development:

> [M]ediation and arbitration of statutory disputes conducted under proper due process safeguards should be encouraged in order to provide expeditious, accessible, inexpensive and fair private enforcement of statutory employment disputes for the 100,000,000 members of the workforce who might not otherwise have ready, effective access to administrative or judicial relief. [S]uch a system will [also] serve to reduce the delays which now arise out of the huge backlog of cases pending before administrative agencies and courts.

Task Force on Alternative Dispute Resolution in Employment, A DUE PROCESS PROTOCOL FOR MEDIATION AND ARBITRATION OF STATUTORY DISPUTES ARISING OUT OF THE EMPLOYMENT RELATIONSHIP (1995). The Task Force's Protocol provides guidelines on important issues, such as the selection and training of arbitrators, the right of representation during arbitration proceedings, discovery, and judicial review. The protocol has been endorsed by the National Academy of Arbitrators, the ABA Labor and Employment Section, and the National Employment Lawyers Association.

RICHARD A. BALES, COMPULSORY ARBITRATION: THE GRAND EXPERIMENT IN EMPLOYMENT 102-13 (1997) *

Brown & Root was one of the first major companies in the United States to institute an in-house program for the nonjudicial resolution of employment disputes. . . . Brown & Root's dispute resolution program demonstrates that compulsory arbitration and employee fairness are not necessarily mutually exclusive.

Brown & Root is a Houston-based company that employs between 25,000 and 30,000 employees, all of whom are nonunion. Its principal products are construction, maintenance, and engineering services. . . .

The company decided to explore alternatives to litigation after a sexual harassment trial in which the company prevailed cost it $450,000 in outside legal fees. During the five years between the alleged harassment and the trial,

---

the litigation profoundly affected the lives and careers of several employees and former employees, including the plaintiff. The financial and human costs associated with such litigation prompted the company to examine alternatives to the litigation system for resolving employment matters. . . .

Just as the Program compels employees to use the Program in lieu of litigation, it also creates a contractual obligation on the part of the company, explicitly amending the at-will employment relationship for that limited effect. Brown & Root can cancel the Program only after giving ten days' notice to employees, and such cancellation does not effect any dispute arising prior to cancellation. Similarly, Brown & Root can amend the Program and its rules at any time, but no such amendment affects any dispute of which the company had notice on the date of amendment.

The Program covers all types of employment disputes, including tort, contract, and statutory claims, as well as claims for equitable relief. It explicitly lists sex, race, religion, national origin, and disability discrimination; sexual harassment; defamation; intentional infliction of emotional distress; and claims related to employee benefits as types of claims to which the Program applies. The Program excludes claims for workers' compensation benefits or unemployment compensation benefits, but includes claims for workers' compensation retaliation. It makes clear to employees that they are still free to contact the EEOC or their state Human Rights Commission about workplace discrimination if they so desire. . . .

Brown & Root employs a full-time Program Administrator to run the dispute resolution program. Employees are encouraged to call this Administrator with questions or to initiate conferences and other internal dispute resolution processes.

In addition to administration, the Program Administrator has benefited the company by providing "upward feedback" about how company employees are being supervised. The Administrator is in a position to recognize which sections of the company have an unusually large number of employee complaints. This recognition allows the Administrator to recommend proactive action, such as removing or retraining supervisors, addressing concerns important to employees, and helping prevent future disputes from occurring. Brown & Root's Associate General Counsel, William Bedman, notes that this has had the unintended consequence of helping the company avoid union attempts to organize the company's employees by helping to resolve problems before they induce employees to seek assistance from a union. . . .

Brown & Root pays for the employees or former employees to consult with and retain attorneys of their choice, provided that their disputes involve legally protected employee rights. Reimbursements for attorneys' fees are paid like benefits under standard medical plans. The employee pays a deductible of $25.00. After the deductible, the employee pays 10 percent of the balance; Brown & Root reimburses the employee for the remainder, up to a maximum of $2,500 per year. The employee is solely responsible for choosing the attorney. . . .

An employee is not required to take advantage of the company's legal representation reimbursement. An employee may, without jeopardizing reimbursement, consult with or hire an attorney before initiating any part of the dispute resolution program; this would be considered an initial consultation that would be reimbursed by Brown & Root. . . .

[The final step, after an open-door meeting, an in-house conference, and outside mediation,] of Brown & Root's dispute resolution program requires employees who have a legal claim against the company to submit that claim to binding arbitration. . . .

If an employee elects not to bring a lawyer to arbitration, Brown & Root also will agree not to bring a lawyer to arbitration. This does not, however, preclude a Brown & Root attorney from working "behind the scenes" to prepare witnesses for the hearing or to draft briefs supporting Brown & Root's argument. . . .

Prior to the arbitration hearing, and on a schedule determined by the arbitrator, each party must produce, both to the arbitrator and to the other parties, the names and addresses of the witnesses it intends to bring to the hearing and any documents it intends to present. The arbitrator has the discretion to determine the form, amount, and frequency of other prehearing discovery. This discovery may take any form permitted by the Federal Rules of Civil Procedure. . . .

At the hearing, witnesses are required to testify under oath. The arbitrator may subpoena witnesses or documents at the request of a party or on the arbitrator's own initiative. Strict conformity to the federal or state rules of evidence is not required; as with arbitration in the labor and commercial context, the arbitrator is "the sole judge of the relevance, materiality, and admissibility of evidence offered." A witness may testify by affidavit, but such testimony is only given "such weight as the arbitrator deems it is entitled to after consideration of any objection made to its admission." The award must be in writing and signed by the arbitrator. The arbitrator is required to write a summary of the reasons for the decision if so requested by the parties in either the request for arbitration or the answering statement.

The arbitrator's authority is limited to the resolution of legal disputes between the parties. The arbitrator is bound by, and is required to apply, all applicable law, including that related to the allocation of the burdens of proof as well as substantive law. The arbitrator does not have the authority either to abridge or enlarge substantive rights available under existing law. The arbitrator has the authority to order any relief that a party could obtain from court, including injunctive and other equitable relief, and all forms of damages, including punitive damages. However, the arbitrator, at his or her discretion, may allow an employee a reasonable attorneys' fee as part of the award, regardless of the employee's right to request an attorneys' fee under existing law. This award must be reduced by any amounts which have been paid by the Legal Expense Reimbursement Program. There is no provision permitting the arbitrator to award attorneys' fees to Brown & Root under circumstances in which existing law does not give the company the right to request such fees.

[In the first three years, the Brown & Root program] handled approximately 1,529 employment disputes. Nearly half involved the termination of an employee's employment. Of the disputes that did not involve termination, approximately 10 percent concerned wage and benefits issues. Fewer than 10 percent involved an allegation that the employee had been discriminated against or harassed because of his or her membership in a class protected by federal civil rights laws. The remainder involved conflicts with supervisors and coworkers; morale; job assignments; retaliation; health, safety, and injury issues; and complaints about the hiring process.

The median amount of time taken to resolve each dispute is slightly less than three weeks; the mean is a little more than six and one-half weeks. Forty-one percent of the disputes were resolved within one week of the employee's initial complaint; approximately 65 percent were resolved within four weeks. The longest any dispute took was slightly more than two years; only twenty-one took more than one year. This represents a marked contrast to litigation, which easily can take half a decade or more.

Of the 1,529 disputes filed thus far, approximately 45 percent have been resolved by Program staff, approximately 20 percent have been resolved by an Advisor, 2.5 percent have been resolved through in-house mediation, and only approximately 6 percent had to be referred to outside mediation or arbitration (several of these, however, settled before mediation/arbitration). Approximately 8.5 percent have been resolved in some other manner and approximately 7.5 percent remain pending. In the remaining 10.5 percent of disputes, the employee decided not to pursue the matter further.

In the first two years (the only period for which these particular statistics are available), only eighty employees have requested reimbursement for legal expenses. During this time, Brown & Root paid approximately $85,000 in employees' legal fees. The relatively low number of employees requesting reimbursement reflects the fact that employees seldom decided to hire an attorney to represent them in their dispute. Employees elected to proceed without the use of legal counsel in two-thirds of the arbitrations that have occurred. . . .

Not surprisingly, Brown & Root has had far fewer employment lawsuits filed against it than it did prior to implementing the Program. Before implementation, the company averaged approximately fifteen to twenty lawsuits per year; in the first three and one-half years following implementation, Brown & Root was sued in court a total of fifteen times. In twelve of those suits, the employee voluntarily elected to dismiss the suit and to submit the claim to arbitration. . . .

The number of disputes filed by Brown & Root's employees after the program was implemented — approximately five hundred per year — is commensurate with the number of annual complaints that Brown & Root received through its internal channels before implementation of the Program. Similarly, the company's settlement rate and its annual budget for those settlements did not change significantly after implementing the Program. Neither did its budget for paying arbitration/litigation awards. The company's adjudicatory winning percentage has actually decreased slightly since arbitration was substituted for litigation.

What has changed dramatically is the company's legal budget. Over the three years that the Program has been in place, the company's outside legal fees, plus the costs of administering the Program (including arbitrator and mediator fees, the salaries of the Program's three administrators, the reimbursement program for employees' legal expenses, and the company's outside legal fees in arbitrations where the employee is represented by counsel) is less than half — approximately forty-seven percent — of what the company spent on outside legal fees before the Program was put in place. . . .

The fact that the company's settlement rate, settlement budget, and award budget have remained constant would seem to indicate that the Program is at least as fair to employees as litigating the company's employment disputes would be. The increased success rate for employees in arbitration (as compared to litigation) means that more employees are receiving adjudicatory awards, although the awards of victorious employees are likely to be smaller than in litigation. Though empirically unverifiable, this may mean that employees with meritorious claims, who before could not obtain redress because they were unable to hire a lawyer, or because they ran afoul of the convoluted procedural requirements of the federal antidiscrimination statutes, now are obtaining the redress they deserve. The smaller awards indicate a departure from the "jackpot" litigation system. This means that instead of a very few employees receiving very large awards, awards are distributed more equitably among a larger number of aggrieved employees.

TABLE OF CASES

[References are to pages; principal cases appear in capital letters.]

[References are to pages; principal cases appear in capital letters.]

[References are to pages; principal cases appear in capital letters.]

[References are to pages; principal cases appear in capital letters.]

[References are to pages; principal cases appear in capital letters.]

F

[References are to pages; principal cases appear in capital letters.]

[References are to pages; principal cases appear in capital letters.]

[References are to pages; principal cases appear in capital letters.]

[References are to pages; principal cases appear in capital letters.]

[References are to pages; principal cases appear in capital letters.]

[References are to pages; principal cases appear in capital letters.]

[References are to pages; principal cases appear in capital letters.]

[References are to pages; principal cases appear in capital letters.]

[References are to pages; principal cases appear in capital letters.]

U

V

[References are to pages; principal cases appear in capital letters.]

[References are to pages; principal cases appear in capital letters.]

INDEX

[References are to page numbers.]

[References are to page numbers.]

[References are to page numbers.]

[References are to page numbers.]

[References are to page numbers.]

[References are to page numbers.]